Academic American Encyclopedia

Aretê Publishing Company, Inc.

Princeton, New Jersey

Library of Congress Cataloging in Publication Data
Main entry under title:

Academic American encyclopedia.

Includes bibliographies and index.
1. Encyclopedias and dictionaries.
AE5.A23   031   79-27430
ISBN 0-933880-45-6
ISBN 0-933880-63-4 (vol 18)
ISBN 0-933880-67-7 (lib. bdg.)
ISBN 0-933880-85-5 (vol 18)

sneezeweed

Sneezeweed is the common name for plants in two genera of the family Compositae that are suspected of causing hay fever. *Achillea ptarmica* is naturalized in eastern North America from Europe and Asia; species of *Helenium* are native to North and South America. Both genera contain glucosides that are poisonous to cattle.

JANE PHILPOTT

Snefru, King of Egypt   [snef'-roo]

Snefru, fl. *c.*2780 BC, who was probably the last king of the Egyptian 3d dynasty, built the earliest surviving examples of true pyramids. His reign, for part of which extensive records exist, appears to have been a time of prosperity.

Snefru raided Nubia and Libya, and also conquered Sinai. He was responsible for the construction of two pyramids at Dahshur, one of them showing faults that indicate this attempt may have been the first at building such a structure.

ROBIN BUSS

Snell, Willebrord van Roijen

Willebrord van Roijen Snell, b. 1591, d. Oct. 30, 1626, a Dutch professor of mathematics at the University of Leiden, is best known for effectively showing (1621) that the sines of the indices of refraction and incidence always bear the same ratio for a given interface between two media of different densities (Snell's law; see REFRACTION). Snell did not publish his result, and credit initially went to Descartes. Snell was also extremely interested in geodetics, particularly the determination of the length of the meridian (a line of longitude).

CATHERINE WILSON

Snell's law: see REFRACTION.

snipe

The common snipe, C. gallinago, is an inland shore bird that marks its breeding territory with a spectacular dance accompanied by a whistling sound produced by its tail feathers.

Snipes are small game birds belonging to the SANDPIPER family, Scolopacidae. They measure 28 cm (11 in) in length and have long, straight bills. Their mottled brown-and-white plumage blends well with their wetlands cover, and they have a swift, zigzag flight. The common snipe, *Capella gallinago,* of both the Old and New Worlds, is the only species regularly found in North America.

Some similarly long-billed birds also are colloquially called *snipe,* including the American woodcock and the dowitchers, of New World beaches and mudflats.   WILLIAM F. SANFORD

snipefish

Snipefishes, 11 species of marine fishes constituting the family Macrohamphosidae, are related to other tube-mouthed fishes (order Syngnathiformes) such as the sea horses. Usually found at mid-water depths in tropical and subtropical seas, they attain about 30 cm (1 ft) in length and have a deep, sideways-flattened body and a long fin spine on their backs. Snipefishes usually swim in a head-down position.

SNOBOL

SNOBOL is a COMPUTER LANGUAGE for processing text, such as English sentences or mathematical formulas. (The term is an acronym for *str*ing-*o*riented sym*bol*ic language.) Its basic operation is pattern matching, in which the components of a series, or "string," of characters are identified. For example, the pattern for an integer is an optional sign followed by a string of digits; the integer −123 matches that pattern. SNOBOL has been widely used for problems requiring complicated text processing and formula manipulation.

SUSAN OWICKI AND ELLIOTT ORGANICK

Snodgrass, W. D.   [snahd'-gras]

The American poet and translator William DeWitt Snodgrass, b. Wilkinsburg, Pa., Jan. 5, 1926, was awarded the Pulitzer Prize for his first book of poems, *Heart's Needle* (1959). His second volume, *After Experience,* appeared in 1968. Snodgrass's work is characterized by its confessional tone and by the use of traditional poetic elements and forms.

snook   [snuk]

The snook is a long-bodied, shovel-headed fish, *Centropomus undecimalis,* of the snook family, Centropomidae. Its name is derived from the Dutch word for pike, *snoek.* Occurring in coastal waters on both sides of the American tropics and subtropics and also ranging into freshwater, it may reach more than 1.2 m (4 ft) in length and weigh up to 23 kg (50 lb).

Snorri Sturluson   [snor'-ee stur'-loo-sohn]

Snorri Sturluson, b. *c.*1179, d. Sept. 23, 1241, was an Icelandic historian and poet whose works typify the golden age of ICE-LANDIC LITERATURE. He is the author of two major works: *Heimskringla* (*c.*1220–35; trans. 1964), a history of the kings of Norway; and the *Edda* (usually called the *Younger* or *Prose Edda, c.*1222; trans. 1954), a handbook for poets containing a treasury of mythological lore. He is also the probable author of *Egil's Saga* (*c.*1226; trans. 1960), one of the major sagas. Snorri was active in the violent political struggles of his time and served three terms as law speaker of the Icelandic commonwealth. He was killed at the instigation of King Haakon the Old of Norway.   HALLBERG HALLMUNDSSON

Bibliography: Ciklamini, Marlene, *Snorri Sturluson* (1979); Einarsson, Stefan, *A History of Icelandic Literature* (1957); Hallberg, Peter, *The Icelandic Sagas* (1962) and *Old Icelandic Poetry* (1975).

Snow, C. P., Baron Snow

Charles Percy Snow, Lord Snow, English novelist, civil servant, and physicist, b. Oct. 15, 1905, d. July 1, 1980, illustrated with his own success that his proclaimed division of Western society into "two polar cultures"—the sciences and the humanities—need not be absolute. Snow earned a doctorate (1930) in physics at Cambridge, recruited scientific talent for the Ministry of Labour during World War II, and later served (1964–66) as a member of parliament and of the cabinet. Between 1940 and 1970, Snow published an acclaimed 11-volume novel sequence, collectively titled *Strangers and Brothers.* His Rede Lecture (1959) at Cambridge, "The Two Cultures and the Scientific Revolution," which recognized the lack of communication between scientists and humanists and warned of the consequences inaugurated a famous controversy with literary critic F. R. Leavis.

Although Lord Snow has had a distinguished career as a scientist and politician, he is best known as C. P. Snow, author of Strangers and Brothers (1940–1970). This 11-volume work of fiction is a semiautobiographical account of the conflicts, compromises, and moral complexities faced by various members of British society during the mid-20th century.

Snow's novels have been well received. *The Search* (1934) details the life of a scientist and foreshadows themes taken up in the semiautobiographical *Strangers and Brothers* (1940), the first in the series chronicling the career of its narrator, Lewis Eliot, and presenting a portrait of English society from the end of World War I to the 1960s. Other novels in the series—among them *The Masters* (1951), *The New Men* (1954), and *Corridors of Power* (1964)—deal with the pursuit of power, a major theme in the sequence.

Other works by Snow include several plays written with his wife, Pamela Hansford Johnson; *Public Affairs* (1971), essays; *Trollope: His Life and Art* (1975); and *A Coat of Varnish* (1980), a detective novel. Snow was made a life peer in 1964.

RICHARD A. JOHNSON

Bibliography: Davis, Robert G., *C. P. Snow* (1965); Karl, Frederick, *C. P. Snow: The Politics of Conscience* (1963); Ramanathan, Suguna, *The Novels of C. P. Snow* (1978); Schusterman, David, *C. P. Snow* (1975); Thale, Jerome, *C. P. Snow* (1964).

snow and snowflake

Snow is composed of small crystals of frozen water; the crystals form directly by condensation of atmospheric water vapor around solid nuclei at temperatures below 0° C (32° F). As individual crystals of ice (snow crystals) fall through the atmosphere, they cluster together and form snowflakes. The term *snow* is also applied to deposits on the ground that may occasionally cover as much as 23 percent of the Earth's land surface.

Because the quantity and frequency of snowfall vary with the availability of moisture and the prevalence of below-freezing air temperatures, annual rates of snowfall can range from several meters of water-equivalent in places such as the high mountain snow fields of the Pacific Northwest of North America to less than 2 cm (0.8 in) of water-equivalent in the interior of Antarctica.

Formation. Snow crystals forming at temperatures above −40° C (−40° F) generally need foreign particles on which to nucleate. This kind of nucleation is termed *heterogeneous*. The most common types of nuclei are silicate minerals of terrestrial origin (especially clay minerals and micas that probably account for 80 percent of the global atmospheric nuclei) and sea salt. Locally, particles from industrial sources and automobile exhaust may also be important. Nuclei generally range in size from 10^{-5} to 10^{-2} mm. At temperatures below −40° C water can solidify spontaneously, without the need for nuclei, by a process called homogeneous nucleation.

Ice-crystal formation in the atmosphere can be stimulated artificially by injecting silver-iodide particles into a supercooled cloud. Attempts at large-scale seeding of clouds to induce precipitation of snow and rain have been only partially successful.

Snow-Crystal Shape. Photomicrography made possible rapid documenting of the structure of snow crystals. The technique of preparing plastic replicas of freshly precipitated snow crystals is also widely used to examine structural details of the crystals. Photographing snow crystals was first popularized by W. A. Bentley and W. J. Humphreys in their book *Snow Crystals* (1931). This was followed in 1954 by U. Nakaya's *Snow Crystals, Natural and Artificial*. Nakaya was primarily interested in investigating the meteorological factors that control the shape of snow crystals, which occur in an almost endless variety of forms exhibiting sixfold, or hexagonally symmetrical, structure.

Under the widely used systematic classification of crystals that was first proposed (1951) by the Commission of Snow and Ice of the International Association of Hydrology, solid PRECIPITATION is divided into ten separate classes comprising seven types of snow crystals—plates, stellars (stars), columns, needles, spatial dendrites, capped columns, and irregular crystals—as well as graupel, ice pellets, and hail (see HAIL AND HAILSTONES). A more comprehensive classification suggested (1966) by C. Magono and C. Lee that subdivides crystals into 80 separate classes, however, is gaining acceptance.

The shapes of snow crystals depend largely on the temperature of formation and to a lesser extent on the atmospheric humidity. The size of a crystal appears to depend mainly on the moisture content of the air. Because absolute moisture content of the atmosphere increases with increasing temperatures, crystals formed at higher temperatures tend to grow larger than those at lower temperatures.

Relation of Snow-Crystal Shape to Temperature of Formation

Temperature Range °C	°F	Shape
−3 to 0	26.6 to 32.0	Thin hexagonal plates
−5 to −3	23.0 to 26.6	Needles
−8 to −5	17.6 to 23.0	Hollow prismatic columns
−12 to −8	10.4 to 17.6	Hexagonal plates
−16 to −12	3.2 to 10.4	Dendritic crystals
−25 to −16	−13.0 to 3.2	Hexagonal plates
−50 to −25	−58.0 to 13.0	Hollow prisms

Changes in Snow Cover. Because freshly deposited snow is frequently light-textured and fluffy, winds may redistribute it into characteristic surface features such as snow dunes and sastrugi. Further changes in the snow cover, such as rounding of snow grains and significant changes in density, cohesiveness (degree of intergranular bonding), and hardness, occur mainly in response to temperature fluctuations. Snow that has survived at least one year is called firn. In the snow fields of mid-latitude glaciers, refreezing of summer meltwater, together with densification resulting from the weight of the

The vast majority of snow crystals occur in a hexagonal, or six-sided, form as a result of the arrangement of oxygen atoms within the crystals. The exact form is directly related to the temperature formation, and a seemingly limitless variety of shapes can be found.

overlying snow, causes the firn to transform rapidly into glacier ice. On a large polar glacier such as Antarctica, however, where surface air temperatures rarely reach 0° C, the transformation of firn to glacier ice may take hundreds or even thousands of years to accomplish.   ANTHONY J. GOW

Bibliography: Bentley, W. A., and Humphreys, W. J., *Snow Crystals* (1931; repr. 1963); Hobbs, P. V., *Ice Physics* (1974); Kingery, W. D., ed., *Ice and Snow: Properties, Processes and Applications* (1963); Kirk, Ruth, *Snow* (1978).

snowberry

Snowberry, or waxberry, is the common name for 18 species of shrubs in the genus *Symphoricarpos,* family Caprifoliaceae, in particular *S. albus.* This plant, a small, deciduous, berried shrub of North America, produces thin stems that bend under the weight of puffy white- or pink-tinted berries. Snowberries grow to 90 cm (3 ft) and make useful decorations in winter.

Snowdon, Antony Armstrong-Jones, 1st Earl of [snoh'-duhn]

Antony Charles Robert Armstrong-Jones, 1st earl of Snowdon, b. Mar. 7, 1930, is an English photographer, writer, and artistic advisor to the London *Sunday Times.* He is the former husband of Princess Margaret Rose, sister of Great Britain's Queen Elizabeth II. Armstrong-Jones, educated at Eton and Cambridge, designed (1965) Snowdon Aviary in the London Zoo and helped to film many television productions. After 16 stormy years of marriage, he and his wife were separated in 1976 and divorced in 1978, four centuries after the last divorce occurred in the immediate royal family—that of Henry VIII from Anne of Cleves.

Bibliography: Cathcart, Helen, *Lord Snowdon* (1968); Snowdon, Antony Charles, *Snowdon: A Photographic Autobiography* (1979).

snowdrop

The snowdrop, genus *Galanthus,* is any of about 12 species of hardy, bulbous plants belonging to the amaryllis family, Amaryllidaceae. It is native to Europe and Asia. Planted in the fall, the snowdrop produces nodding flower stalks bearing white and green bell-like flowers that appear above the snow in the early spring.   JANE PHILPOTT

snowmobile

Snowmobile is the generic word for a large group of powered vehicles used for transportation and recreation over snow and ice. Until about 1950 there were few in regular use, although patents for powered sleds date back to the late 1800s. Modern snowmobile design can be traced to a Canadian by the name of Joseph Armand-Bombardier. His troop-carrying snow vehicles, built during the 1930s, have many of the same features found in today's snowmobiles: a half-track driven by a gasoline engine in the rear of the vehicle to provide the motive power, and steerable, ski-type runners supporting the front end. Most snowmobiles are designed for sport and are ridden astride like a motorcycle and steered by handlebars. Larger vehicles are available for special purposes. On the Antarctic continent, where falling into hidden crevasses is an ever-present hazard, the overall length of the snowmobile is increased and the tracks and skis are arranged to aid in avoiding crevasses or bridging them successfully. Four-track vehicles are common in the Antarctic. In most cases the snowmobile has replaced the DOGSLED, but the dog team is still important and is often preferred where a long journey must be made over totally uninhabited regions, where any mechanical failure could mean death.

Snowmobiling has become a popular winter sport in North America. The popularity of the sport is in part due to the influence of snowmobiling clubs, which maintain snowmobile trails and organize snowmobile events, such as races in which the snowmobiles may reach speeds in excess of 190 km/h (118 mph).

In 1979 about 3 million snowmobiles were in use in the

Snowmobiles race near Malone, N.Y., during the Eastern Snowmobile Championships. The speed record for these half-tracked, engine-driven vehicles was established in 1977 by the American Don Pitzer, who achieved a speed of 218.71 km/h (135.93 mph).

United States and Canada, and 268,000 had been produced that year in the United States, Canada, and Japan. The soaring number of recreational snowmobiles has given rise to concerns about their potentially damaging effect on wildlife habitats in areas that were previously unreachable by any type of motorized vehicle.   BILL GUNSTON

Bibliography: Malo, John W., *Snowmobiling* (1971); Wimer, Sally, *The Snowmobiler's Companion* (1973).

Snowy Mountains

The north-south trending Snowy Mountains are located in the Australian Alps in New South Wales, Australia. Covered by snow for 6 months of the year, the range has an average elevation of 760 m (2,500 ft). Lying within the Snowy Mountains is Mount KOSCIUSKO, the highest peak of Australia.

The range, first explored in 1840 by Paul Strzelecki, is a site of an irrigation and hydroelectric power project. The Snowy Mountains Hydroelectric Authority diverts water from the Snowy River through the mountains to irrigate the arid interior of the continent.

Snyder, Gary

Best known as a poet, Gary Snyder, b. San Francisco, May 8, 1930, was brought up in poverty on his parents' farm north of Seattle, Wash. He attended Reed College, where he developed sympathies for anarchist ideas and radical politics. Snyder became a seaman, worked for the Forest Service, and did graduate work in linguistics at Indiana University. While

Gary Snyder, an American writer, received the 1975 Pulitzer Prize for poetry. He has combined rugged labor as a forester and sailor with the difficult psychical assimilation of Zen Buddhism. These experiences are manifest in his poetry, which is imbued with images of nature and myth. His association with the Beat Generation is evident in his work.

studying Oriental languages at Berkeley (1953–56), he met Allen Ginsberg, Jack Kerouac, and other members of the BEAT GENERATION. Kerouac later memorialized Snyder as Jaffy Ryder in *The Dharma Bums*.

Snyder spent most of the period between 1956 and 1964 as a lay acolyte learning the strenuous discipline of Zen Buddhism in Daitoku-ji, a monastery in Kyoto, Japan. His poems celebrate communal life and advocate an existence controlled by the rhythms of nature. Snyder won a Pulitzer Prize for poetry in 1975.   JOHN TYTELL

Bibliography: Kherdian, David, *A Biographical Sketch and Descriptive Checklist of Gary Snyder* (1965) and *Six Poets of the San Francisco Renaissance* (1967); Steuding, Bob, *Gary Snyder* (1976).

Snyders, Frans   [sny'-durs]

The Flemish painter Frans Snyders, b. 1579, d. Aug. 19, 1657, is primarily remembered for executing the animal figures in paintings by Peter Paul Rubens. He trained under Pieter Brueghel the Younger and became a master painter in 1602, but it took a dozen years more for him to reach his maturity as an artist. It was then that Rubens asked him to collaborate on the animals in his paintings. Snyders painted the eagle, for example, in Rubens's *Prometheus* (1611–12; Philadelphia Museum of Art). Rubens also supplied Snyders with oil sketches of subjects that Snyders enjoyed using for his own large canvases. Motifs sketched by Rubens continually reappear in his paintings. Snyders painted solidly and with great vigor. His skillful application of unbroken color and his employment of reflected light probably antedate Rubens's use of these techniques. Snyders also painted still-life subjects such as fruits and vegetables, and he may even have executed human figures in some of Rubens's paintings. Late in his career Snyders specialized in violent hunting scenes, which were then very popular. They resemble Rubens's late treatment of this subject.   THOMAS BUSER

Bibliography: Gerson, H., and ter Kuile, E. H., *Art and Architecture in Belgium: 1600–1800* (1960).

Soami   [soh-ah'-mee]

Like his father, Geiami, and his grandfather Noami, the Japanese artist Soami, d. 1525, served the Ashikaga shoguns as art curator, painter, garden designer, and master of the tea ceremony. His soft, mist-filled ink landscapes, as in *Landscapes of the Four Seasons* (Metropolitan Museum, New York City), were influenced primarily by the work of the Sung Chinese painter MU-CH'I. Noami's *Okazari-ki* (Notes on Decorating) and other writings supply much information about the taste of the Muromachi period (1333–1573).

BARBARA BRENNAN FORD

Bibliography: Shimizu, Yoshiaki, and Wheelwright, Carolyn, *Japanese Ink Paintings from American Collections* (1976).

Soane, Sir John   [sohn]

The career of the English architect Sir John Soane, b. Sept. 10, 1753, d. Jan. 20, 1837, spans the period of the classic revival; he was a leader as well as an innovator within this movement, bringing a new taste for the "picturesque" into fashion with his novel interpretations of Greek and Roman architecture.

Soane, the son of a builder, received much of his early training from the architect George Dance, his first employer, who helped shape his style and remained his lifelong friend. He left Dance in 1772 to work for the architect Henry Holland, also attending the newly founded Royal Academy, and winning its Gold Medal in 1776. Thereafter, a traveling scholarship enabled him to spend 2 years in Italy; it was not until 1788, when he was appointed architect to the Bank of England, that his independent architectural career began.

Drawing heavily on his experience with Dance and on his own interpretation of neoclassical ideas, Soane remodeled and greatly enlarged the Bank of England over the next 40 years. His first work there was the Bank Stock Office (1789), where he used pendentives to support the vault with high

side-lit lunettes and a restricted use of architectural ornament. Later, in his Rotunda (1796) for the bank, he carried similar ideas still further. Soane's work at the bank survives only on the exterior.

Soane's interest in the picturesque dates from around 1800. His Dulwich Art Gallery (1811–14) near London is a surviving example. The profile of the building is not tied together into a cumulative entity, as in buildings of the baroque; instead, each element is separated and divided to make a plain, pared-down structure with each part clearly and simply articulated.

In his own large row house (1812–13) at Lincoln's Inn Fields, London, Soane used many ingenious if idiosyncratic architectural devices to break up the monotony of cubic rooms. It is now the Sir John Soane Museum and houses Soane's large art collection.

Soane's last major work was the Stables of the Royal Hospital, Chelsea (1814–17), which are plain and practical in design. He was appointed professor of architecture at the Royal Academy in 1806 and knighted in 1831.   NICHOLAS ADAMS

Bibliography: Bolton, A. T., *The Works of Sir John Soane* (1924); Summerson, John, *Sir John Soane* (1952); Stroud, Dorothy, *The Architecture of Sir John Soane* (1961).

Soap Box Derby

The Soap Box Derby is an annual racing tournament for coasting cars that are designed, built, and driven by 11- to 15-year-olds. The cars may use only gravity to propel them down an incline. Thousands of American youngsters compete for fewer than 200 places in the national finals held each August.

Rules restrict the cost of the cars to $75 or less, and limit size to an overall length of 84 in. (2.1 m), width to 34.75 in. (88 cm), height to 28 in. (71 cm) and a maximum weight, including the driver, of 260 lb (118 kg). Although cars were once made out of wooden soap boxes, fiberglass is now the most common construction material.

The first Derby was held in Dayton, Ohio, in 1934. The following year it moved to Akron, Ohio. In 1936, Derby Downs was built in Akron, and the race has been held there ever since, except for a 4-year interruption during World War II.

soap and detergent

Soap is a natural cleansing agent produced by the reaction of an alkali, such as sodium hydroxide, with animal fat or vegetable oil. Soap classifications include toilet soap, which is manufactured as a cleansing agent for the body, and soaps for household use, such as bars, flakes, and granules.

A detergent is a cleansing preparation synthesized from a number of readily available raw materials—hydrocarbons from crude oil are most frequently used. All detergents contain a surface-active agent (surfactant) or, more often, a combination of surfactants. The surfactant lowers the surface tension of water and is able to dislodge dirt from surfaces, emulsify it, and suspend it in water.

A second important ingredient is a builder, often used in detergents but infrequently used in soap. A builder is incorporated in detergents for such purposes as controlling minerals in hard water, providing alkalinity and buffering so that alkalinity is maintained at an efficient level, suspending soil particles and controlling the redeposition of soil, emulsifying oily soil, and enhancing the surfactant's wetting action. Other detergent ingredients may include antiredeposition agents, brighteners, bleaches, corrosion inhibitors, suds-control agents, perfumes, and colorants. Detergents are formulated for a full range of household, industrial, and institutional uses.

The Cleansing Process. A number of physical and chemical processes occur simultaneously during washing. The basic explanation of how soaps and detergents work is that their surfactant molecules have polar, or hydrophilic, ends, which attract water molecules; and nonpolar, or hydrophobic, ends, which lack attraction to water. As these molecules lower the water's surface tension, they improve the water's ability to penetrate and loosen soil. The opposite attractions of the

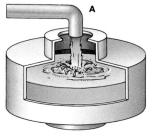

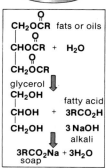

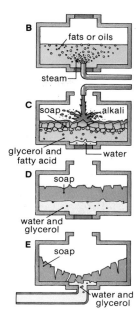

This engraving portrays an 18th-century soap works, showing the mixture of oil and lye (background) and packaging of the finished product (foreground). Until the 19th century, soap manufacturing was limited by imprecise processes and remained a small-scale industry.

Modern processes for continuous soap manufacture (A) begin with rapid hydrolysis, or chemical breakdown, of fats and oils by water at high temperature and pressure (B). The resulting hydrolysis products— fatty acids and glycerol—are treated with alkali (C), which saponifies, or reacts with the fatty acids to produce soap (D). The soap then is separated from the mixture (E), washed, dried, and formed into bars.

molecule loosen the dirt, often aided by hand or machine agitation. The molecules then surround and suspend dirt particles in the water until they are rinsed away.

Soap, however, presents problems in hard water, because the water-seeking portion of the molecule unites with some minerals in water to form an insoluble curd, which leaves visible deposits on clothing, bathtubs ("bathtub ring"), and washing machines. Most detergent surfactants do not form

A detergent confines fatty oils (black dots) as droplets, which then can be easily washed away by water. A detergent molecule has a water-attracting, or hydrophilic, end (blue) and a water-repelling, or hydrophobic, end (white). Fatty oils are also hydrophobic. The fatty oils and the hydrophobic ends of the detergent molecules tend to cluster together not just because they are attracted to each other but because water molecules are strongly attracted to the hydrophilic ends.

curds, and builders in detergents control those properties in the wash water which reduce the surfactant's effectiveness.

History of Soaps and Detergents. Soap has been used for millennia, whereas detergents have been used for only a relatively short time. The earliest literary reference to soap was found on clay tablets dating from the 3d millennium BC in Mesopotamia. They contained a soap recipe calling for a mixture of potash and oil to be used in the manufacture of cloth. Another recipe contained the ingredients of a medicated soap prescription. The first authentic reference to soap as a cleansing agent as well as a medicinal product appears in the writings of Galen, the 2d-century AD Greek physician. Galen also noted that cleanliness helped cure skin diseases.

The ancient Romans spread their knowledge of soapmaking, and in the Middle Ages important centers of soapmaking developed in Spain, France, and England. Manufacturing remained on a crude level, however, until discoveries by Nicolas Leblanc in the 18th century and Michel Eugène Chevreul in the 19th century made it possible to manufacture soap by a formula leading to exact and predictable results. Inventions such as the steam engine and improved equipment and techniques enabled soapmaking to become competitive industry.

The formation of curd when soap is used in hard water provided the principal impetus for the development of detergents. The first light-duty detergents, introduced in the United States in the early 1930s, were unbuilt granules, which performed better than soaps did in hard water but which had limited cleaning ability. The next breakthrough was the intro-

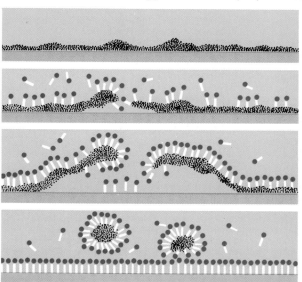

The use of soap has pervaded all cultures since ancient times. This late-19th-century lithograph for Pears soap is representative of the sophisticated advertising campaign that developed when the soap industry became competitive.

duction, after World War II, of the first built synthetic detergent, which provided the benefits of the early detergents when used in hard water as well as all-around cleaning power. A key factor in producing these products was the development of complex phosphates, primarily sodium tripolyphosphate.

Some early detergent surfactants were slow to biodegrade; that is, bacteria could not break them down rapidly. Concentrations occasionally built up to the extent that foaming resulted in some sewage-treatment plants and in streams. In 1965, however, the U.S. detergent industry voluntarily changed to new biodegradable materials that are quickly broken down and eliminated from the environment. Now all household laundry products manufactured for use in the United States are readily biodegradable.

Another detergent ingredient that has been involved in environmental controversy is the phosphate builder, which contains the element phosphorus. Phosphorus is one of many nutrients essential to water plants and algae, and contributes to accelerated eutrophication—the too-rapid growth of aquatic plant life in water bodies. Detergent manufacturers have noted that the contribution of phosphorus from detergents is normally only a small part of the total phosphorus going to bodies of water and does not have an appreciable effect on algal growth. They hold that the effective way to solve the problem is by waste treatment, which removes nutrients from all sources, and by control of nutrient sources from agriculture and from soil erosion. Nevertheless, the industry has reduced its phosphate use and has continued research for developing phosphate substitutes.

MARY ANSBRO

Bibliography: Davidsohn, A., and Milwidsky, B. M., *Synthetic Detergents*, 6th ed. (1978); Poucher, W. A., *Perfumes, Cosmetics, and Soaps*, vols. 2 and 3 (1974); Sittig, Marshall, *Detergent Manufacture* (1976).

soap opera

The term *soap opera* refers to serialized domestic dramas broadcast on a continuing basis and so named because in their early years on radio their principal sponsors were soap companies. From the beginning the so-called soaps have been criticized for sentimentalism. The plots, which often take years to unravel, usually focus on the romantic difficulties of stereotyped upper-middle-class characters.

The first network radio broadcasts of soap operas began in the 1930s after local stations discovered that a large audience existed for daytime radio drama. By the 1940s between 30 and 60 different serials were broadcast each weekday. Following radio's tested formula, television adopted the soap opera in the 1940s. "Search for Tomorrow," the first network television soap, premiered on Sept. 3, 1951, and was followed by "Love of Life" (Sept. 24, 1951) and "The Guiding Light" (1952). All had previously been radio serials. "As the World Turns" (premiere, Apr. 2, 1956) was the top-ranked television soap opera for many years, with ratings rivaling some nighttime shows.

By the 1960s almost all radio soaps had vanished, but by 1978 about 14 daytime soap operas were being produced on television. Some of these, such as "All My Children," "The Young and the Restless," and "Ryan's Hope," have been praised for their willingness to deal with controversial themes, such as abortion, interracial relationships, and drug abuse. Exaggerated soap operas, some of them satirical or exploiting bawdy humor, have had late-night or prime-time success in the 1970s, notably "Mary Hartman, Mary Hartman!" and "Soap." BRIAN ROSE

Bibliography: LaGuardia, Robert, *From Ma Perkins to Mary Hartman* (1977) and *The Wonderful World of TV Soap Operas* (1977); Newcomb, Horace, *TV* (1974); Soares, Manuela, *The Soap Opera Book* (1978); Stedman, Raymond, *The Serials*, 2d ed. (1977).

See also: RADIO AND TELEVISION BROADCASTING.

soapberry

Soapberry, genus *Sapindus*, is the common name for about 13 species of deciduous or evergreen trees in the soapberry family, Sapindaceae. They are native to the New and Old Worlds. The fruit contains a soapy substance called saponin that is used as a cleaning agent in the tropics. The leaves alternate and have 4 to 12 leaflets. The white flowers are small and occur in terminal racemes or panicles. There are 4 to 5 petals. The brown fruit, which succeeds the flowers, has a soft pulp with the saponin. The deciduous tree *S. drummondii* reaches a height of 15 m (50 ft). It is found in the United States from Missouri to Arizona and to Mexico. An evergreen, *S. mukorossi* is planted in Florida for its seeds, which are used for beads. The evergreen soapberry, or false dogwood, *S. saponaria*, and *S. drummondii* are the only soapberries native to the New World. A few soapberries are grown as ornamentals.

soapstone: see TALC.

soapwort   [sohp'-wurt]

Soapwort, genus *Saponaria*, is the common name for about 30 species of hardy annuals and perennials in the pink family, Caryophyllaceae. Their brightly colored flowers are white, pink, or red. The bruised leaves or stems of some plants have been used in soap production, hence the name *soapwort*.

Soares, Mário   [swah'-ruhsh]

A lawyer and cofounder of Portugal's Socialist party, Mário Soares, b. Dec. 7, 1924, was prime minister of Portugal from 1976 to 1978. Soares had organized a movement against the dictatorial regime of António de Oliveira Salazar and was arrested and exiled both in 1968 and again in 1970. Soares returned shortly after the 1974 revolution that ousted Salazar's successor Marcello Caetano and became foreign minister (1974–75) for the new military junta. In 1976, new elections resulted in a strong socialist minority and Soares was selected to form a new government. He later formed (1978) a coalition government that helped to back a program of economic recovery. Soon thereafter, the Social Democratic Center party withdrew from the coalition, and the Soares government fell.

Sobieski, John: see JOHN III, KING OF POLAND.

soccer

Soccer is probably the most popular sport in the world. Two teams of 11 players attempt to kick an inflated ball into goal cages at opposite ends of a grass playing field. Soccer is unique because of its total restriction on the use of the hands; only the goal keeper may use his hands, and then only within a limited area. The other 10 players must advance the ball using primarily their feet, although a proficient soccer player can use almost every part of the body to control and guide the ball, including the head.

The action in soccer is constant as teams attempt to control the ball and score. The fast pace has made soccer a major spectator sport throughout the world, and for the same reason it has attracted millions of players. The name of the game presents some confusion. In countries other than the United States soccer is called football. The word *soccer* is a corruption of the abbreviation for "association football."

The Fédération Internationale de Football Associations (FIFA), the governing body of international soccer, estimates that there are about 22.4 million registered soccer players in the world. This figure does not include the many millions of unregistered players who participate informally. The world's premier soccer players are the top professionals of each country who compete for the World Cup, soccer's most coveted prize. A tournament is organized in which teams of allstar players from over 100 countries meet in elimination rounds until only 16 semifinalists remain. These particular matches are probably the most popular athletic events in the world. The last game of the 1978 World Cup, between Argentina and the Netherlands, is estimated to have had a worldwide television audience of 900 million.

Englishmen compete for control of the ball in a game of association football, an early form of soccer. Since the rules of the game were first codified by various athletic organizations during the late 19th century, soccer has become the world's most popular team sport.

HISTORY

Soccerlike games undoubtedly predate recorded history. Historians of the sport find its ancestry in the wild kicking, running, and throwing games that were a feature of medieval English village life. Not until 1863, when the London Football Association issued its first set of rules, was order brought to the sport. All major innovations in the sport, such as international matches (between England and Scotland, in 1872), the introduction of professionalism (1885), and the first full-time league (1888), all took place in England. It was not long, however, before the sport began to spread to the rest of the world. Soccer was carried to continental Europe, South America, and India by British sailors and settlers, and the sport seemed to gain instant appeal wherever it was demonstrated. In 1908 the sport was made a regular Olympic Games event.

Soccer's international governing body, the FIFA, was formed in 1904. Its main objective was to organize championship matches between professional teams of different nations. England already had professional clubs, but it was not until the 1920s that professionalism arrived in Europe and not for another decade in South America. By 1930 the caliber of play and the interest in the sport were high enough to ensure the success of the first World Cup, in spite of the fact that only 13 countries entered. Soccer arrived in the United States dur-

(Right) The goalie prepares to block a shot as the action nears his net during a soccer match in England. Soccer, a popular spectator sport throughout the world, has an especially enthusiastic following in the British Isles, where the sport originated, and important matches have attracted crowds of nearly 150,000.

(Above) The national teams of Yugoslavia and Scotland compete in a World Cup elimination match at Wald Stadium in Frankfurt, West Germany. Finals of World Cup competition are staged every 4 years and involve teams from 16 nations.

(Left) Pelé, the world's most famous soccer player, led his Santos team of Brazil to three World Cup titles (1958, 1962, 1970). His brief stint (1975–77) with the N.Y. Cosmos of the NASL did much to popularize soccer in the United States.

ing the late 19th century, but it remained a sport limited to immigrants and ethnic groups. Various organizations promoted and regulated the sport, and the National Collegiate Athletic Association (NCAA) recognized (1959) it as an official collegiate sport with a national championship tournament. Soon after the North American Soccer League (NASL) was formed (1967) the sport became one of the fastest-growing games in America at every level from little league to professional.

EQUIPMENT AND RULES

One of the factors in soccer's popularity is the simplicity of its rules and the minimal equipment needed. Players wear shirt, shorts, cleated shoes, and sometimes shin-guards tucked inside their socks. The soccer ball, made of leather or plastic, has a circumference of 27–28 in (66–71 cm) and weighs 14–16 oz (397–454 g). Considerable variation is allowed in the field dimensions; the length should be 100–130 yd (91.4–118.8 m) and the width 50–100 yd (45.7–91.4 m), although the field must always be longer than it is wide.

A line across the middle of the field divides it into two halves, and the midpoint of the line is the center of a circle 20 yd (18.2 m) in diameter. At each end of the field, around each goal, is a penalty area 18 yd (16.5 m) deep and 44 yd (40.2 m) wide; within the penalty areas are goal areas 20 yd (18.2 m) wide and 6 yd (5.5 m) deep. The goals, which are centered on each end line, are net-backed cages 8 ft (2.4 m) high and 8 yd (7.3 m) wide. The game is controlled by a referee on the field who is assisted by two linesmen, one on each sideline. Contact with the ball from the elbows to the hands is forbidden, and the following constitute offenses against the opponent: intentional kicking, charging from behind or in dangerous manner, striking, holding, pushing, tripping. For these the referee will stop play and award a direct free kick, from the point of the infraction, against the offending team. It is possible to score a goal directly with such a kick. If one of the offenses is committed by a player inside the team's own penalty area, then the other team gets a penalty kick; the ball is placed on the penalty spot, 12 yd (11 m) from the goal, and only the unassisted goalkeeper may defend the goal. Other, lesser offenses include obstruction and dangerous play, for which the referee will award an indirect free kick. A goal cannot be scored on such a kick; the kicker must pass the ball to a teammate who then may score a goal. An indirect free kick is also awarded in cases of offside violations. Offside occurs when the ball is passed forward over the midfield line to an attacking player, and that player has only one opponent (usually the goalkeeper) between him and the goal-line; when the attacker is ahead of the ball; or when the attacker is in the opponent's half of the field when the ball is in the other half. The linesman has two main functions: (1) to spot offside infractions; and (2) whenever the ball goes out of play, the linesman will indicate which team has possession (the opponent of the team that touched the ball last is given possession). When a ball goes beyond the sidelines, it is returned to play with an overhead, two-handed throw. When it goes over the goal-line but not into the goal, it is either a corner-kick for the attacking team (in which case the ball is kicked toward the goal), or the goalkeeper kicks the ball for the defending team, clearing the ball downfield. A soccer game is generally 90 minutes long, played in two 45-minute halves, with a 10-minute intermission. In American college soccer, teams play four 22-minute periods, and high school games are usually played in 15-minute quarters.

Substitution has never been an important aspect of soccer, and in international play it is generally limited to one or two players per game. Players that are removed from a game for any reason (injury, ejection, substitution) are not allowed to return. In college and high school soccer in the United States, however, free substitution is permitted, and players may reenter the game.

STRATEGIES

In its infancy, soccer strategy placed great emphasis on the offense and on goal-scoring plays. Teams were loaded with forwards, and the few defenders were assigned the task of defending against overwhelming numbers of attackers. As the

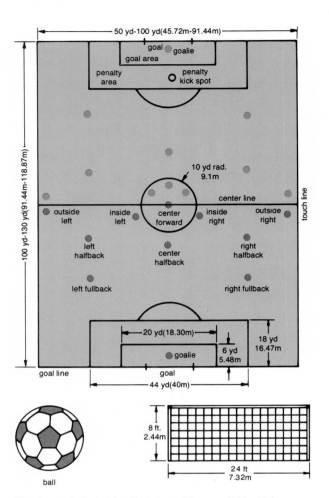

The diagram indicates the dimensions of a soccer field, which vary slightly according to the level and location of play. Also indicated are the dimensions of the goal and positions of the 11 players on a team in one of the many possible defensive alignments.

game grew in international appeal, however, a philosophy of play entailing a more cautious approach prevailed until, in the 1960s, it appeared that the sport was stagnating because of an overly defensive mentality. Since then, soccer has come closer to achieving a reasonable balance between offense and defense, although it becomes increasingly clear that the key to attractive, spectator-oriented soccer lies with the skills of outstanding individual players rather than in the area of rule-changes or tactical formations.

In the United States, the NASL has adopted a system called a "shootout" to resolve the frequent tie games that many American fans find so unsatisfying. Five players from each

WORLD CUP COMPETITION

Year	Countries and Scores	Location
1930	Uruguay 4, Argentina 2	Montevideo, Uruguay
1934	Italy 2, Czechoslovakia 1	Rome
1938	Italy 4, Hungary 2	Paris
1950	Uruguay 2, Brazil 1	Rio de Janeiro
1954	West Germany 3, Hungary 2	Bern, Switzerland
1958	Brazil 5, Sweden 2	Stockholm
1962	Brazil 3, Czechoslovakia 1	Santiago, Chile
1966	England 4, West Germany 2	London
1970	Brazil 4, Italy 1	Mexico City
1974	West Germany 2, Netherlands 1	Munich
1978	Argentina 3, Netherlands 1	Buenos Aires

team take alternate turns kicking the ball at the goal with only the goalkeeper defending. In most cases this breaks the tie.   JAMES GREIFF

Bibliography: Chyzowych, Walter, *The Official Soccer Book of the United States Soccer Federation* (1978); Gardner, Paul, *The Simplest Game* (1976); Gardner, Paul, and Tyler, Martin, eds., *The International Book of Soccer* (1977); Glanville, Brian, *History of the Soccer World Cup* (1973); Hishey, David, and Bodo, Peter, *Pelé's New World* (1977); Rote, Kyle, and Kane, Basil, *The Complete Book of Soccer* (1978); Tyler, Martin, *Soccer: The World Game* (1978); Woosnam, Phil, and Gardner, Paul, *Sports Illustrated Soccer* (1972).

Sochi   [soh'-chee]

Sochi is a city of Krasnodar kray in the Russian Republic of the USSR. The city has a population of 287,000 (1979). Situated on the Black Sea, Sochi is one of the USSR's largest seaside resorts, with a municipal area extending 130 km (80 mi) along the coast. It is served by an airport at nearby Adler. Recreational facilities range from large hotels for foreign tourists to sanatoriums and camping grounds.   THEODORE SHABAD

social anthropology

Social anthropology formulates sociological generalizations derived from the comparative and integrative analysis of such social institutions as marriage and kinship, law, religion, and political and economic organization. It is distinguished from ETHNOGRAPHY and ethnology in its deemphasis of historical and purely descriptive data. It is distinguished from SOCIOLOGY in its emphasis on understanding the community in its entirety and on taking part in the activities of the community under observation; it is further distinguished by its tradition of studying and comparing non-Western cultures. Although many American anthropologists tend to identify social with cultural anthropology, social anthropology is specifically concerned with the functions of social institutions (functionalism) and the functional integration of social structures. These concepts arose mostly in Great Britain and France in the 19th and 20th centuries.

Functionalism and structural-functionalism developed as theoretical alternatives to the evolutionism popular in the late 19th century. Anthropologists objecting to evolutionism charged that its thesis that civilization was reached through successive levels of development encouraged ethnocentric and even racist ideas (see RACISM) and, further, that although evolutionism might describe cultural differences, it failed to explain them.

French sociologist Émile DURKHEIM is regarded as one of the founders of social anthropology, particularly the theoretical framework of structural-functionalism. Among Durkheim's theoretical contributions were (1) the "organismic" view of society, the concept that society functions as an organism, with structures analogous to bodily systems; and (2) the "superorganic" view of society, the concept that social facts have a reality of their own, and must be understood on a different level from individual needs or psychology. The British social anthropologists A. R. RADCLIFFE-BROWN and Bronislaw MALINOWSKI rejected cultural evolutionism and adopted Durkheim's organismic view of society. Radcliffe-Brown's structural-functionalist analysis, however, derived from Durkheim's concept of social solidarity, sought to identify the ways by which institutions maintain the unity of social structure. By contrast, Malinowski's functionalist analysis was directed at the ways in which cultural traits served seven basic biopsychological needs of individuals: nutrition, reproduction, bodily comforts, safety, relaxation, movement, and growth.

Functionalism and structural-functionalism have been criticized for their lack of historical perspective and their tendency to promote conditions as they are. Recently, such social anthropologists as Fred Eggan (b. 1906) and Raymond Firth (b. 1901) have attempted to reintegrate historical (diachronic) perspectives into the field's traditionally present-oriented (synchronic) analytic techniques.   ELAINE J. SCHECHTER

Bibliography: Harris, Marvin, *The Rise of Anthropological Theory: A History of Theories of Culture* (1968); Kaplan, David, and Manners, Robert A., *Culture Theory* (1972); Kardiner, Abram, and Preble, Edward, *They Studied Man* (1963); Mair, Lucy, *An Introduction to Social Anthropology,* 2d ed. (1972).

See also: ANTHROPOLOGY.

social behavior, animal: see ALTRUISM; ANIMAL BEHAVIOR; ANIMAL COMMUNICATION; ANIMAL COURTSHIP AND MATING; SOCIOBIOLOGY.

social class: see CLASS, SOCIAL.

social contract

The social-contract theory concerns the origin of organized society, holding that the state originally was created through a voluntary agreement entered into among individuals living in an anarchical state of nature. This contract defines and regulates the relations among the members of society and between the individual and the governing authority. The social-contract theory challenged the DIVINE RIGHT of kings as the basis for a state's legitimacy and laid the foundation for theories of constitutional government.

The most influential proponents of social-contract theory were the English philosophers Thomas HOBBES and John LOCKE and the French philosopher Jean Jacques ROUSSEAU. According to Hobbes, the individual's natural right to self-government was surrendered by means of the social contract to an absolute ruler. Locke held that the state was brought into being to protect the "natural rights" of the citizen to life, liberty, and property. These rights, however, remain with the individual. According to Locke, citizens are entitled to resist or rebel if the state abrogates the original contract by not protecting these rights. Rousseau extended the concept of rights to encompass all the people and not the narrow propertied class of citizens included by Locke. In Rousseau's state, political authority reflects the "general will" of the people.
                                                            RITA J. IMMERMAN

Bibliography: Barker, Ernest, ed., *Social Contract: Essays by Locke, Hume, and Rousseau* (1947; repr. 1960); Gough, John W., *The Social Contract: A Critical Study of Its Development,* 2d ed. (1957; repr. 1978); Rousseau, Jean Jacques, *The Social Contract,* trans. by Maurice Cranston (1968).

See also: REPRESENTATION; STATE (in political philosophy).

Social Credit party

The Social Credit party is the collective name of political organizations in Canada that have been particularly strong in Alberta (where the party, led originally by William ABERHART, ruled from 1935 to 1971), British Columbia (where the party ruled from 1952 to 1972), and Quebec (where it is known as Ralliement Créditiste). Social Credit, which had its beginnings in the Great Depression, is based on the theories of an Anglo-Scottish engineer, Clifford Hugh Douglas (1878–1952). The party originally hoped to enact a number of radical monetary measures aimed at correcting the lack of purchasing power. The intention was to provide more money to consumers to make up for what it considered deficiencies in the capitalist economic system. Some of the measures, one of which included giving citizens a $25 monthly dividend, were later invalidated by the courts. Today the party is considered more conservative than either of Canada's two major parties.

Bibliography: Irving, John A., and Pinard, Maurice, *The Rise of a Third Party: A Study in Crisis Politics* (1971).

Social Darwinism

Social Darwinism was a late-19th-century sociological theory that was based on the theories of biological evolution and natural selection put forth by biologists Charles DARWIN and Alfred Russel WALLACE and on social philosopher Herbert SPENCER's theory of sociocultural evolution, "survival of the fittest." The school originated with the appearance of Walter BAGEHOT's *Physics and Politics* (1872) and reached its most radical formulation in the works of the Austrian sociologist Ludwig Gumplowicz (1838-1909), notably in his *Der Rassenkampf* (The Racial Struggle, 1883). Bagehot sketched the historical development of social groups into nations by means of intergroup struggles; Gumplowicz formulated a universal law to the effect that all social evolution was a product of group conflict.

Social Darwinists argued that societies—like organisms—evolved by a natural process through which the most fit members survived or were most successful. The theory went hand-in-hand with political conservatism; the most successful social classes were supposedly composed of people who were biologically superior. Social Darwinism was also used to support imperialism—peoples who viewed themselves as culturally superior, being allegedly more fit to rule those that they deemed less advanced. In the United States the foremost publicist of the theory was William Graham SUMNER.

Bibliography: Hofstadter, Richard, *Social Darwinism in American Thought*, rev. ed. (1959); Service, Elman R., *Origins of the State and Civilization: The Process of Cultural Evolution* (1975); Spencer, Herbert, *On Social Evolution: Selected Writings*, ed. by J. D. Y. Peel (1972); Sumner, William G., *Essays of William Graham Sumner*, ed. by Albert Keller and Maurice Davie, 2 vols. (1934; repr. 1969); Wilson, Edward O., *On Human Nature* (1978).

Social Gospel

The Social Gospel movement, led by American Protestants of liberal theological orientation, was an attempt to bring the message and power of faith to bear on the social problems of the day. Most effective in the years 1870 to 1918, it began as a result of the economic and labor crises of the 1870s and in reaction to the economic conservatism of the churches. Pioneer leaders included Jesse Jones and Edward Rogers with their Christian Labor Union and Washington GLADDEN with his book *Working People and Their Employers* (1876). Walter RAUSCHENBUSCH emerged as the most effective spokesman for the movement, interpreting its economic goals in *Christianity and the Social Crisis* (1907) and its theological position in *A Theology for the Social Gospel* (1917). The movement stimulated the founding of the Federal Council of Churches in 1908. The council's Social Creed spelled out some of the practical goals of the movement, including the social and physical protection of workers, higher wages, and the abolition of child labor.   JOHN F. PIPER

Bibliography: Handy, Robert T., ed., *The Social Gospel in America, 1870-1920* (1966); Hopkins, Charles H., *The Rise of the Social Gospel in American Protestantism, 1865-1915* (1940); Hopkins, Charles H., and White, Ronald C., Jr., *The Social Gospel* (1976); Meyer, Donald B., *The Protestant Search for Political Realism: 1919-1941* (1960).

social groups

Human beings are social animals. Their very existence depends on social groups, especially on the family, which must provide the care children need. Although the forms of social groups vary vastly, as long as there are human beings there will be social groups. A social group is generally defined as any set of human beings who interact directly with one another (face to face) and whose behavior is partially patterned, interdependent, and cooperative.

The best possible idea of what social groups are can be obtained by considering how groups differ from closely related sets of human beings that do not compose groups. The first crucial step in human interaction comes at the point of what Jean Paul Sartre calls "the glance." As soon as human beings are in sight of one another so that they actually exchange glances, they enter a minimal relationship. The mere fact of being seen, or potentially being seen, by others is of basic importance to human beings: nothing is more convincing of the fact that humans are social animals. When people are in the presence of each other in this minimal way they constitute a congeries, or aggregation.

The next crucial point comes when human beings in the presence of one another are also indirectly related to each other by the fact that they are all oriented toward something that motivates them. An obvious example is a crowd at a football game. Members of a crowd do not all interact, but they act jointly in patterned ways, such as cheering at the same time when a touchdown is made. Crowds have been very important in history since urbanization brought masses of strangers together. Social scientists analyze crowds in terms of collective behavior as distinct from group behavior.

The simplest kind of group is the dyad, or two-person group. The mother-child dyad is probably the most important of all groups. The addition of a third person to make a triad introduces major new dimensions in human relationships: with a third person the possibility always exists that two group members will be more cooperative with one another than either is with the third, so that conflicts such as those aroused by simple jealousy become more prevalent.

Whereas no absolute number divides the small group from the large, social scientists have consistently found that when a group reaches a size of seven or eight members, it becomes very difficult for all of the individuals to interact directly and the group tends to develop a more complex structure. For instance, six persons constituting a dinner party are far more likely to talk as one group than eight or more persons, who will subdivide into smaller groups for discussions.

In general, the more group members interact with one another in a cooperative way, the more they will tend to feel friendly toward each other, develop common values, and hold together. Research on small groups has shown how this operates: a group of boys formed into a baseball team quickly begins to develop common liking, values, and group identity. Moreover, the more they share a common problem, such as the competitive struggle to beat another team, the more likely they are to cooperate and thus become even more cohesive. Of course, there are limits to such group cohesiveness. Group identities may compete. Attachment to a family puts a limit on a person's attachment to a small business group. The less group work satisfies the motive that led a person to join the group, the less he or she will identify with the group. A baseball team that loses consistently is likely to begin falling apart.

Sociometry, the measurement of groups, has been one important way of studying small groups. Sociometrists commonly try to determine how group members develop a ROLE. Most groups, especially those which include seven or more people, begin to develop role specialists, such as task leaders, who try to get people to do the work of a group, and the best-liked group members, who generally are not the task leaders.

Groups that interact cooperatively over long periods of time and do so with intensity commonly begin to take on a life of their own. That is, the members begin to look at the group as something outside of themselves—as something more than the sum of their own lives. This is the basis for "institutions" and "nationhood." If the Lions baseball team struggles hard against intense competition and overcomes their problems together, they may come to feel that the "Lions" as a group is something special—almost a social institution (then they may shout "Do it for the Lions!"). Many people feel this way about their nations—the nation goes on even when the members die off because new members assume the roles others have vacated. Once group membership and roles are transmitted to new members in that way, the group becomes self-sustaining and can be considered a culture, or a subculture if it is only a small group within a larger one.   JACK D. DOUGLAS

Bibliography: Homans, George, *The Human Group* (1951); Kanter, Rosabeth, and Stein, Barry, eds., *Life in Organizations* (1978); Moreno, Jacob L., *Who Shall Survive?* (1953); Raven, Bertran, and Rubin, Jeffrey, *Social Psychology: People in Groups* (1976); Rowan, John, *The Power of the Group* (1976); Rudé, George, *The Crowd in History* (1964); Shepherd, Clovis R., *Small Groups: Some Sociological Perspectives* (1964); Sherif, Muzafer and Carolyn, *Groups in Harmony and Tension* (1966); Tiger, Lionel, *Men in Groups* (1970).

See also: GROUP DYNAMICS.

social norm: see NORM, SOCIAL.

social psychology

Social psychology is the study of individuals' thoughts, feelings, and behavior as they affect or are affected by other individuals. The discipline gradually developed from its 19th-century, speculative-philosophical stage—heavily influenced by Auguste Comte, Karl Marx, Charles Darwin, and Herbert Spencer—to a more scientific, 20th-century stage in which there is a preoccupation with the empirical testing of hypotheses. Researchers in the broad field of social psychology investigate such varied topics as the effects of childhood experiences on adult personality; the ways in which people influence one another through NONVERBAL COMMUNICATION; the extent to which AGGRESSION in society is traceable to violence on television; the comparative impacts on creativity of working alone and in groups; the effects of racial segregation on intergroup prejudice; and the factors that inhibit people from coming to the aid of a person in distress.

Working Methods of the Social Psychologist. A social psychologist attempts to formulate knowledge about interpersonal processes such as those mentioned above into hypotheses. The hypotheses make it possible to describe, predict, and influence the impact that people have on one another. Social psychology purports to be a science, and therefore its hypotheses about human interactions must have two characteristics. First, the hypotheses must be derived from explicitly stated general principles that constitute theories about the nature of the person and of society. Second, the hypotheses must be testable in situations that provide objective evidence regarding their validity.

Without the broad integrating principles of a theory, social psychological findings would be simply an inventory of isolated relationships, and it would be impossible to generalize from the outcome of a specific investigation. The main theories currently guiding social psychological research are described in the last section of this article. To prevent the theories and the hypotheses derived from them from remaining mere speculations, the concepts involved must be firmly anchored to reality by being defined in terms of observable events. Relations between the concepts must be capable of being tested objectively.

A typical hypothesis in social psychology will state a relationship between two observable social phenomena. For example, a hypothesis might state that a person's liking for a stranger is a curvilinear function of how far away the stranger stands, and so one will like the stranger who stands at an intermediate distance more than one who stands very close or very far away. This hypothesis is derived from a theory regarding people's antithetical desires for privacy and intimacy, and from the social meanings of certain uses of space. The hypothesis can be tested if *liking for stranger* and *distance between stranger and self* are defined in ways that allow objective measurement. Having developed such a hypothesis from a theory, the social psychologist then tests it. He or she sets up conditions in a laboratory or in a natural situation where people will be confronted by a stranger at randomly differing distances and then measures people's liking for the stranger. Descriptive and inferential statistical analyses are then used to determine the extent to which the outcome of the experiment supports the predicted curvilinear relationship. Such support provides confidence in the hypothesis and also in the broader theoretical formulations from which it is derived.

Topics Studied in Social Psychology. One major field is research on socialization practices—investigating how child-rearing practices connected with the age of weaning, adolescent initiation, number of brothers and sisters, and so on, affect adult personality. Findings indicate that differences among individuals and cultural groups in preferred art forms, beliefs about the nature of illness, and the content of dreams are all affected by early social experiences. Socialization theorists also account for some of the adult differences between the sexes and among national groups in terms of differences among the groups in their early socialization experiences.

Other social psychologists study interpersonal COMMUNICA-

TION, investigating such topics as how differences in the structure of the languages spoken in different cultures result in differences in the thought patterns of people in those societies. Sociolinguists study topics such as the role of bilingualism in intergroup conflict and the role of differences in speech patterns in separating the socioeconomic classes. Other research topics in this area include persuasive communication and nonverbal communication.

Another focus in social psychology research is on processes of social influence through suggestion, modeling, and the mass media. Social influence is discussed in more detail in the articles ATTITUDES AND ATTITUDE CHANGE; CONFORMITY; PROPAGANDA; and PUBLIC OPINION.

A wide variety of topics having to do with GROUP DYNAMICS has been studied by social psychologists. Some investigate how communication in groups is affected by status differences among the members or by the length of time they have been together; others study the determinants of leadership and the effects of leadership style on group productivity and morale. Still other group theorists study how the person's creativity and decision-making processes differ when working alone as compared with working in a group.

A less heavily investigated (but far from neglected) topic is that of social perception, which studies such issues as the extent to which an individual's perception of the environment is selective and distorted in the service of his or her motivation and how an individual's hopes and prejudices influence what is remembered.

A particularly popular topic in this area is how people perceive one another—for example, the importance of a person's first impressions and implicit personality theories; how items of information about the other person are put together; and how motivation is attributed to another.

The area of interpersonal hostility has also received considerable attention in social psychology. Research has been done on interpersonal and intergroup hostility, investigating such topics as the effects of televised violence on fear and antisocial behavior in the viewer and the causes of intergroup hostility that lead to racial prejudice and international wars. Social psychologists also investigate how interpersonal conflicts can be resolved; for example, they study the effects of racial integration on ameliorating prejudice.

The opposite topic, interpersonal attraction, has received at least equal attention from social psychologists. A variety of factors contributing to people's liking for one another has been identified, such as similarities of beliefs, length of acquaintanceship, extent to which the one person's goals are facilitated by the other person, and the extent of the one person's liking for the other person. Studies of "good Samaritans" coming to the aid of people in distress have indicated that altruistic helping behavior is encouraged by having witnessed other people showing such behavior and by observing the need for personal action so that there is no possible diffusion of responsibility.

Theories in Social Psychology. Social psychologists choose their topics of investigation and their explanatory concepts from one of several dominant theories about the individual in society. These general orientations often seem to be in contention with one another but can perhaps more appropriately be regarded as complementary. Each emphasizes one of the many aspects that make up the whole person. Some of these social psychological viewpoints are labeled consistency theory, attribution theory, autonomy theory, ego-defensive theory, reinforcement theory, and modeling theory.

Consistency theorists stress the human need to keep beliefs mutually consistent and in harmony with feelings and actions. Attribution theorists stress a person's need to give meaning to his or her life and environment by attributing causes and motives to the events he or she experiences. Autonomy theory stresses the person's need for a feeling of control over his or her own destiny, combined with a feeling of some measure of personal freedom. The ego-defensive theorists emphasize a person's need to maintain self-esteem by interpreting his or her own behavior and that of others in a way that will maintain his or her illusions about the self. Reinforcement theorists stress the person's tendency to behave in ways that in similar circumstances in the past have brought rewards. Modeling theorists stress the person's tendency to look to the behavior of others in order to adopt a gratifying role model for imitation.

The first two theories—consistency and attribution—are derived from cognitive psychology. The second two theories—autonomy and ego-defensive—derive from the ego psychology position of the psychoanalytic school. The final two—reinforcement and modeling theories—stem from behaviorism, or learning theory.   WILLIAM J. MCGUIRE

Bibliography: Lindzey, Gardiner, and Aronson, E., eds., *Handbook of Social Psychology,* 5 vols., 2d ed. (1968); McGuire, William J., "Social Psychology," in *New Horizons in Psychology—Two,* ed. by P. C. Dodwell (1972); Schellenberg, James, *Masters of Social Psychology* (1978); Seidenberg, Bernard, *Social Psychology: An Introduction* (1976); Strickland, Lloyd H., ed., *Social Psychology in Transition* (1976).

social realism

As used in art, the term *social realism* describes both a specific stylistic approach and an overall attitude toward subject matter. Like genre art, social realism aims at the unadorned depiction of the contemporary life; unlike genre, however, social realism's primary goal is not to amuse but to convince the observer of the evils of poverty, immorality, and war.

The intellectual roots of social-realist art lie in the 18th-century Enlightenment. Its artistic forebears include William HOGARTH, who attacked drunkenness, wantonness, and foolish extravagance among both the poor and the well-to-do with his didactic engravings of the 1730s to the '50s; Francisco de GOYA, whose horrifying series of etchings entitled *The Disasters of War* (1808 onward) was published in 1863; and Honoré DAUMIER, whose satirical lithographs of the 1830s and '40s reflect deep social concern. True social-realist art, however, grew out of the atmosphere of the failed Revolution of 1848 in France. Their political hopes crushed by the ensuing reactionary regime, a group of French artists expressed their social concern in realistic depictions of the barren lot of the poor. Gustave COURBET's avowedly socialist aims are clearly seen in his monumental immortalization of an obscure country burial entitled *A Funeral at Ornans* (1849; Louvre, Paris). Courbet's canvases were judged by conservative critics to be as dangerously inflammatory as the noble peasants in François MILLET's *The Gleaners* (1857; Louvre, Paris) and *Man with a Hoe* (1863; private collection)—works whose social-realist content was softened by their markedly sentimental overtones.

Social-realist painting in France declined after the 1860s, at precisely the time it became important in Great Britain. Sir

Ben Shahn's Scotts Run, West Virginia (1937), a succinct commentary on industrialized America, protests the bleakness of workers' lives through their starkly lined faces and the grim setting of boxcars and grubby houses. (Whitney Museum of American Art, New York City.)

Luke FILDES's *Applicants for the Casual Ward* (1874; Royal Holloway College, Egham, Surrey), Frank Holl's (1845–88) *Newgate: Committed for Trial* (1878; Royal Holloway College), and Hubert Herkomer's (1849–1914) *Pressing to the West* (1884; Leipzig Museum, East Germany) depict grimy scenes of urban poverty that British critics found distasteful if not dangerous. In the early 1900s the British social-realist tradition was carried on in the United States by the ASHCAN SCHOOL, whose emphasis was echoed by several major American painters after 1920. In the late 1920s and early '30s, Ben SHAHN showed farmers, laborers, and other victims of the Depression as well as scenes of the Sacco and Vanzetti trial and execution; Ivan ALBRIGHT and Edward HOPPER focused on the loneliness and isolation of the individual in an urbanized society.
                                                                    HOWARD RODEE

Bibliography: Egbert, Donald, *Social Radicalism and the Arts—The French Revolution to 1968* (1968); Finkelstein, Sidney, *Realism in Art* (1954); Nochlin, Linda, *Realism* (1971); Shapiro, David, *Social Realism, Art as a Weapon* (1973); Shikes, Ralph, *The Indignant Eye* (1969).

social science education

Education in the social sciences has as its goal the introduction of students to the systematic study of society. At postsecondary levels it focuses on teaching about society through the study of individual social-science disciplines. At the elementary and secondary levels the term *social studies* is more commonly used and the emphasis is more interdisciplinary, with a focus on citizenship training or studies.

At postsecondary levels the social sciences usually consist of anthropology, economics, geography, political science, psychology, and sociology. Whereas history is not usually considered a part of the social sciences on the college level, it is a major component of social studies in elementary and secondary schools. The study of history has always held an important place in elementary and secondary education; it was formally established in 1916 as a result of the report of the National Education Association. At this time, as well, the term *social studies* came into common usage.

The 1916 report established a pattern for social studies that persisted with little change for many decades. In general, this pattern was based on the theory that children can learn best by understanding first those settings that are close at hand. Accordingly, the typical curriculum based on the 1916 pattern begins with a study of the family and school in the 1st grade, the neighborhood in the 2d grade, cities in the 3d grade, the regions in the 4th grade, and U.S. history in the 5th grade. Geography is usually taught in either the 6th or 7th grade or both, U.S. and state history in the 8th grade; civics in the 9th grade, world history in the 10th, and U.S. history in the 11th grade. The 12th grade presents various options, of which American government and problems of democracy have been the most common. Some states offer, and may require, courses in their own history.

In the late 1960s the 1916 pattern was modified but was not displaced by the so-called new social studies, devised to parallel similar developments in mathematics and natural sciences. The new social studies strongly emphasize the content of the social sciences; more collaboration by college and university professors in curriculum development; more attention to values; the use of inductive methods of learning; the development and use of educational games, simulations, and case studies; use of original documents; and a greater variety of media, including filmstrips, recordings, and artifacts.

The result of the new social studies was the infusion of a number of new ideas about methods and content, resulting in a patchwork on the 1916 pattern rather than a new pattern for the curriculum. Courses in anthropology, economics, political science, psychology, and sociology were added to the curricula of many schools, and subject matter from these disciplines was infused into curriculum materials not labeled by these names. History, however, was not displaced from its dominant role in the curriculum.

Whereas interest in the social studies curriculum as such

declined in the 1970s, interest in a variety of topics related to social problems—including ethnic and minority groups, values, morals, careers, women, death, global perspectives, and the future—increased, and consideration of these topics was usually included in the social studies curriculum.

IRVING MORRISSETT

Bibliography: Bruner, Jerome S., *The Process of Education* (1960); Carr, Edwin R., *The Social Studies* (1965); Chase, Stuart, *The Proper Study of Mankind*, rev. ed. (1963; repr. 1978); Ehrmann, Henry W., *The Teaching of the Social Sciences in the United States* (1954; repr. 1975); Haas, John D., *The Era of the New Social Studies* (1977); Hunkins, Francis P., et al., *Review of Research in Social Sciences Education, 1970-1975* (1977); Lynd, Robert S., *Knowledge for What* (1969).

social security

Social security consists of public programs intended to protect workers and their families from income losses associated with old age, illness, unemployment, or death. The term is sometimes also used to include a broad system of support for all those who, for whatever reason, are unable to maintain themselves (see SOCIAL AND WELFARE SERVICES). In the United States the term has a more specific connotation, referring to a complex of national programs that began to evolve with the passage of the Social Security Act of 1935 and that are now administered by the Social Security Administration. The principal programs are Old Age, Survivors, and Disability Insurance (OASDI)—now officially called Retirement, Survivors, and Disability Insurance—and Hospital Insurance (HI), or MEDICARE. They provide direct payments to maintain the income of retired or disabled workers, their dependents, and their survivors and to defray some of the medical expenses of retirees and their spouses at age 65 and older.

U.S. social security programs are financially self-sustaining in that they are funded on a pay-as-you-go basis through payroll taxes collected in equal amounts from employees and employers during the workers' years of active employment in accordance with the Federal Insurance Contribution Act (FICA). Participation in social security is compulsory and benefits are paid as an "earned right." For these reasons, social security is a form of social insurance and is distinguished in the public mind from social welfare, or direct grants of aid to the indigent, based on need and financed by general tax revenues.

HISTORY OF SOCIAL INSURANCE

In its modern form, the concept of social insurance may be said to have originated during the Industrial Revolution. The transformation of agrarian nations into predominantly urban, industrialized societies where most citizens worked for wages increased the economic insecurity of the individual and added greatly to the problems of the aged and the disabled. These conditions fostered the belief that society as a whole should bear at least some responsibility for the economic protection of its members. Although the degree to which countries have adopted the concepts of the WELFARE STATE varies enormously, the idea that a minimum state social responsibility exists is now almost universally accepted.

In 1883-84, Chancellor Otto von Bismarck of Germany established the first social insurance programs, sickness insurance, and WORKERS COMPENSATION plans supported by the compulsory contributions of workers and employers; in 1889 an old-age insurance program was added, to which the government also contributed.

Although France introduced a voluntary national unemployment insurance plan in 1905, little more was done until 1928 when a vast range of compulsory programs was adopted. The 1920s also saw the development of national social security plans in many other European nations, in some Latin American countries, and in Japan.

Great Britain instituted a national social insurance scheme, establishing a rudimentary unemployment and old-age insurance program in 1911. This program was greatly expanded and liberalized in 1925 and again after World War II when a program of "cradle-to-grave security," advocated by Sir William Henry BEVERIDGE, was adopted. New Zealand, under the pressure of economic hardship, adopted a sweeping social insurance and welfare plan in 1938, and Australia gradually instituted a similar program in the late 1930s and '40s.

Canada introduced a national unemployment insurance program funded by equal contributions from employers and employees in the late 1940s. It also developed an old-age pension program that is financed by general tax revenues and instituted a family allowance plan under which families receive a small monthly payment for each child. In addition, the compulsory Canada Pension Plan is a contributory retirement plan that provides retirement and disability benefits to covered workers. The Guaranteed Income Supplement program ensures a minimum income for persons over age 65.

Countries with Communist governments have tended to model their social insurance plans after the all-embracing social security program adopted by the USSR in 1922.

SOCIAL SECURITY IN THE UNITED STATES

The creation of a national social security system in the United States did not come until the 1930s. The Social Security Act of 1935, passed as part of President Franklin D. Roosevelt's NEW DEAL legislative program, was intended to provide pensions for most retired commercial and industrial workers aged 65 years or more. At the same time it established a joint federal-state system of UNEMPLOYMENT INSURANCE.

Evolution of the U.S. System. Unemployment insurance developed as a joint responsibility of the states and the federal government, with the U.S. Department of Labor administering it at the national level. The OASDI program has been the principal responsibility of the Social Security Administration, which replaced the original Social Security Board in 1946 and became part of the newly created U.S. Department of Health, Education, and Welfare in 1953 (reorganized in 1979 as the Department of Health and Human Services). Headquartered in Baltimore, Md., the administration maintains 10 major regional offices and many district and branch offices throughout the country.

The Social Security Act of 1935 provided retirement benefits only to retired workers themselves. In 1939, however, before any benefits had been paid, the first of numerous extensions to the system provided for survivors and dependents benefits. Later extensions included several classes of workers not covered under the original law. For example, during the 1950s state and local government employees, members of the armed forces, and many farm workers, domestic workers, and self-employed professionals were taken into the system. In 1956 the age at which women become eligible for some benefits was reduced from 65 to 62, and in 1961 men were given the option of retiring at a reduced level of benefits at the age of 62.

The year 1957 saw the introduction of the national Disability Insurance (DI) program, under which a separate fund was established to provide cash benefits to workers over age 50 who become totally and permanently disabled. In 1965 Medicare was introduced, providing medical benefits for those over 65 and creating yet another social security fund to finance them. (In 1965, Congress also established the separate MEDICAID program.) In 1974 the Social Security Administration established the federal Supplemental Security Income (SSI) program, which took over responsibility from state-administered programs for providing aid to the blind, the disabled, and the indigent aged.

The System in its Fifth Decade. Through the years of the system's development, the level of benefits was gradually increased in an effort to keep pace with inflation. By the late 1970s retired workers, their dependents, and their survivors were receiving about $85 billion annually from the Old Age and Survivors Insurance (OASI) portion of the program. Disability Insurance was dispensing about $12 billion to disabled workers and their dependents, and about $20 billion in medical benefits was being provided under the Medicare program, with all of these totals increasing rapidly. The system covered more than 90% of the working population.

Benefits are financed by a payroll tax that has risen from a rate of 1% at the inception of the program to more than 12% in 1980. The taxable wage base, or maximum amount of earnings that can be taxed, is escalating as well. In 1980 the payroll tax amounted to 12.26% of the first $25,900 of wages and the taxable wage base is scheduled to increase to $29,700 in 1981, after which time automatic adjustment provisions will raise the base each year by the same percentage as the growth in average wages. The tax rates are also scheduled to increase.

For most workers, benefit amounts are based on covered earnings averaged over 20 years. Benefits are not related strictly to earnings, however; the benefit formula is weighted heavily in favor of low-income workers, assuring them of a higher percentage of their preretirement earnings than high-wage workers. Workers with dependent spouses also receive additional benefits, regardless of the latter's employment history. The Social Security program thus combines the insurance objective of wage replacement with welfare considerations.

The total of benefits paid out is reduced by the so-called earnings test, which is a limit on the amount of income that beneficiaries may earn from employment while receiving benefits. In 1980 benefits to recipients under the age of 72 were reduced by one dollar for each two dollars earned above a maximum of $5,000 per year. The earnings test is heavily criticized, however, as discriminating against retired persons who want to continue some degree of employment. Congress voted in 1978 to raise the level of exempt earnings to $6,000 in 1982 and to eliminate the test entirely in that year for beneficiaries more than 70 years of age.

Unlike private insurance, the U.S. Social Security program does not provide for the accumulation of large trust fund reserves but functions on a pay-as-you-go basis, with current payroll tax receipts used to finance current benefits. Because the government's power of taxation assures that all future obligations will be met, the trust fund balances may serve simply as a contingency reserve.

Equity versus Adequacy. The 1935 Social Security Act attempted to set up a system under which workers would receive at least as much in benefits as they had contributed. This goal was considered crucial to public acceptance of a compulsory program. In a social insurance plan, however, where universal and compulsory protection is the goal, individual equity may be deemphasized in favor of social adequacy—a standard of living below which it is felt no one should fall. In cases where any individual's contributions do not entitle him or her to the socially desired level of benefits, individual equity and social adequacy conflict.

The 1939 amendments to the Social Security Act resolved the conflict in favor of social adequacy, because the needs of millions of the elderly were not being met by the states' old-age assistance programs. At that time the 1935 principle of a fair rate of return was weakened, and benefits were based on average earnings during a shorter period of coverage than the original base of lifetime contributions.

The Problem of Funding. The conflict between equity and adequacy has given rise to controversy about whether social security benefits should continue to be financed exclusively by the payroll tax or whether some portion of the program should be funded by another source of revenue, such as the personal income tax.

Many consider the payroll tax regressive, that is, excessively burdensome to low-income workers because they contribute a greater share of their income than highly paid people. Substantial increases in the taxable wage base, however, have mitigated the regressivity of the payroll tax.

The choice of whether to rely exclusively on the payroll tax or to introduce other types of financing also involves questions about the role of social security and the effect that a change in financing might have. Some persons fear that the use of general funds would lead to excessive expansion of social security at the expense of other government programs. Others are even more opposed to the change because they believe that the program should be divested of its welfare function and that benefits should be based entirely on the earnings record of each participant.

Important factors in the debate are the growing burden imposed by the payroll tax itself and the serious financial problems expected to confront the social security system after the turn of the century. In the late 1970s there were about 30 beneficiaries per 100 covered, contributing workers. By the year 2025, the number of beneficiaries is expected to grow to more than 50 per 100 workers. Under a pay-as-you-go system, an increase in the ratio of beneficiaries to workers implies an inevitable matching increase in taxes. It has been calculated that combined expenditures for OASDI and Medicare in the year 2025 might require a payroll tax of as much as 26%.

The costs of the U.S. Social Security program for the rest of the century seem to be manageable under the traditional funding system. As the proportion of retirees in the general population grows, however, the country may have to choose between such alternatives as enduring substantially larger payroll taxes, spreading the tax load by relying on general tax funds, or cutting costs, either by reducing benefits or extending the retirement age.   ALICIA H. MUNNELL

Bibliography: Ball, Robert M., *Social Security: Today and Tomorrow* (1978); Boskin, Michael J., ed., *The Crisis in Social Security: Problems and Prospects* (1977); Brown, J. Douglas, *An American Philosophy of Social Security: Evolution and Issues* (1972) and *Essays on Social Security* (1977); Campbell, Rita R., *Social Security: Promise and Reality* (1977); Drucker, Peter F., *The Unseen Revolution: How Pension Fund Socialism Came to America* (1976); Kaplan, Robert S., *Financial Crisis in the Social Security System* (1976); Munnell, Alicia H., *The Future of Social Security* (1977); Turnbull, John G., et al., *Economic and Social Security*, 4th ed. (1973).

social structure and organization

Every human group has structure and organization. Social structure means an orderly, fixed arrangement of parts making up an integral whole: a society, a community, or an institution. Social organization refers to the dynamic efficiency of a structure in relation to concerted action by group members or to their enduring common purposes.

Because the two concepts are closely allied, the terms are sometimes used interchangeably. Concrete planning and task-oriented activities, however, are best considered as social organization. Statements about the structure of a group are normally made in abstract terms, often in the form of models. Such statements refer not to the way members compete and cooperate in particular activities, but to the similarities and differences they perceive among themselves and that provide them with their most important social distinctions. Political, economic, religious, and kinship structures may be described for any human community. In each instance the description will focus on the distinct social roles or offices entailed with the powers, rights, and duties interconnecting them. As soon as the focus shifts to the customary political, economic, religious, or kin-oriented activities of the community, however, the emphasis is on social organization.

SOCIAL STRUCTURE

Social structure may be studied through the development of models to represent typical cases. A model usually incorporates several simplifying assumptions to allow concentration on those components of the structure under study. Two models that refer to different types of society are given below to illustrate the range of problems encountered in moving from folk and tribal societies to the greater complexity of industrialized societies.

Egalitarian Society. It is not hard to imagine a small, isolated, and homogeneous society comprising some few hundreds (or thousands) of families, each with its own domicile, each getting its own food and clothing from nature, and recognizing no chiefs. The rules that generate this type of society are of two sorts: one set governs the structure of the family groups, and the other regulates their interrelationships. Family-group rules will be related to a full cycle of development through one full generation to the establishment of the next. Rules will allocate authority, work, and privilege according to sex, age, and status. In particular, incest will be strongly prohibited. Provision will be made for dissolution or reconstitution of the group when a member dies. The headship may belong to a man or a woman, or it may be shared. Sons, daughters, or both may be obliged to shift residence when they marry.

In accordance with such rules, the internal structure of the domestic unit, its typical composition at each stage of the cycle, and the organization of tasks will be established.

The net effect of these rules is to create a reasonably stable, self-reliant primary group able to meet most of the demands put upon it without turning elsewhere for help. The further set of rules required to generate a viable egalitarian society, however, pertains to just those concerns with which a family on its own cannot be expected to cope. These rules include the regulation of marriage and fosterage, torts and property rights, intergroup hostility, and cooperative alliance. Typical of egalitarian societies is the use of clan membership to help regulate public life: rules of descent determine the clan of each person at birth, and clan rules in turn define property and hunting rights, ceremonial standing, and the choice of partners in marriage. Also important to the morale and good order of any folk community is a ceremonial life that affirms an identity of interest among all the members, even while recognizing divisions.

Many examples of egalitarian societies exist. Such societies are not necessarily agricultural but have subsistence economies, making the family an all-purpose institution. Hunting-gathering people usually have a band structure, combining several families and attached individuals in small, nomadic communities, or communities that follow the seasonal movement of game, suited to survival in a given region. Pastoral people often modify their egalitarian values sufficiently to allow for at least nominal leadership and authority at the clan or subtribal level of organization. This change occurs because pastoralism generally demands the preservation of exchange relationships with far-flung peoples, entailing potentially hostile contacts. Among the best-known examples of egalitarian structure are the Eskimo or Inuit, as hunters; the Pueblo Indians of Arizona and New Mexico, as gardeners; and the Nuer of the Eastern Sudan, as pastoralists. The Navajo, inhabiting a semiarid region near the Pueblo settlements, are another example of an egalitarian people. Navajo success in the present century as sheepherders with a strong tradition of personal dignity and independence stands in contrast to the fate of other peoples who have been unable to maintain effective self-reliance at the domestic level.

Stratified Society. Contemporary urban-industrial societies are sprawling entities so complex as to defy conceptualization as complete units. To overcome problems of scale and the anomalies of urban sprawl, the most satisfactory studies have been of a town or village typical of its region, letting it stand for others. Some useful community studies were made in the United States a few decades ago, particularly in the South, where a town would normally exhibit the two major types of stratification, ethnic and class, clearly juxtaposed. In the North ethnic stratification—for example, prejudicial treatment of Danes in Wisconsin or Irish in Boston early in this century—would flare up as an initial response to immigration but soon die away. In the South the color bar was both more explicit and more durable, being backed by racist doctrines. Owing to the relative stability of most communities, class differences were also pronounced. Class lines are never absolute barriers, but caste is.

For caste the cardinal rule is that individuals of different caste must not be members of the same family. The class barrier entails a contrary rule that, regardless of separate class origins, all members of one family belong to one class. In order to maintain the cardinal rule of caste, offspring of the sexual union of whites and blacks in the South were always deemed to be black; union of a white woman with a black man was deemed particularly pernicious, because her family connection with a black child could hardly be denied. In a similar situation in India, when a Brahman woman becomes pregnant by a man of lower caste she may remain in her household until the live birth, when she is evicted for bringing a stranger into the midst of her family.

The cardinal rule of class has very different implications. Because differences accruing within a family through marriage or adoption across class lines must socially disappear, the class identity of a family must be read from its circumstances, not its history. One significant current condition may be name—that is, family reputation built up over time in a stable community. Even in the conditions of the South, however, where "good family" was always an important claim to status, the main criteria of class were current assets and long-term expectations—wealth and connection to it, education and profession, and the moral qualities associated with solvency.

Class is associated with competitive individualism and social mobility, but caste militates against these qualities of the open society. Because the class principle is more pragmatic, it cannot be absolute in any sense: of two brothers in the same community, by local standards one doing well and the other badly, it cannot be categorically affirmed that they belong to different classes unless they have actually severed connections. The criteria of class standing are multiple. The more open the class system has been to mobility, the less exact the lines that may be drawn—but this observation does not mean that class has disappeared. The greater the competition for class and position, the more steeply stratified a society may become, although nominal class identities may be vague. A generation ago in the South the boundaries of the white upper class were blurring as old families lost their wealth, but the line between middle and lower class among blacks was becoming more and more clearly defined as educated or otherwise successful blacks conscientiously set themselves apart from "common folk" on their side of the color bar.

SOCIAL ORGANIZATION

Any attempt to understand the social structure of an industrial society through community studies must be supplemented by knowledge of the organization of work in small companies and in the economic and governing bureaucracies or by studies of schools and universities, churches, voluntary associations, and political parties and movements. Each of these organizations incorporates structural principles characteristic of the society, but each in turn has its effect upon the general structure. French labor unions are not quite like the French-Canadian, and both differ in essentials from British unions. A labor movement cannot be transplanted from one national context to another without provoking change on both accounts—the union movement must adapt, and the host society in turn will react, whether by radicalization or the opposite. By the same token the recent appearance of powerful multinational industrial organizations has affected—homogenized, to some extent—the structure of the modern capitalist world.

Changes of structure may occur with revolutionary violence or by incremental shifts. No social structures are so brittle that they will not bend and change before breaking under stress; however, all social structures in the short run do resist change. Some structures remain highly stable because they function well both with respect to individuals' needs and the larger context, but repressive institutions may be rigidly maintained in spite of the constraints they impose, and the most satisfactory institutions may be swept away by external forces.

Social structures do not maintain themselves in the face of ideological and ethical revolution. A Victorian family structure could never survive in the moral climate of the modern suburb. Historically, new religions and new social structures have been firmly associated, whether in modern China or ancient Rome. The study of social structure may offer a comprehensive view of a society, including even its ideas and moral beliefs, for all social expression has its structural dimensions. Even the fullest picture, however, of family life in the Hebrides, seen in the special frame of social structure, is not a substitute for meeting such a family. One cannot learn all about a religion by studying its priesthood, or all about love by surveying the customs of courtship in a hundred societies.

The irreducible unit of social structure is the social ROLE, and while much may be learned about a person by studying all the roles that person plays, it does not add up to a comprehensive portrait. By the same token, a knowledge of all the component roles and role-relationships comprising an institution will afford only an abstract or schematic knowledge of it, and the knowledge of all the institutions of a society does not fully define that society's place in history. Thus the study of social structure and organization is bounded on one side by a social psychology sensitive to the play of personality and experience and on the other by history.

GEORGE PARK

Bibliography: Béteille, André, ed., *Inequality among Men* (1977); Blau, Peter M., *Inequality and Heterogeneity: A Primitive Theory of Social Structure* (1977) and, as ed., *Approaches to the Study of Social Structure* (1975); Bottomore, T. B., *Classes in Modern Society* (1965); Dollard, John, *Caste and Class in a Southern Town,* 3d ed. (1957); Firth, Raymond, *Elements of Social Organization* (1963); Freeman, James M., *Untouchable* (1979); Keesing, R. M., *Kin Groups and Social Structure* (1975); Park, George, *The Idea of Social Structure* (1974); Porter, John, *The Vertical Mosaic* (1965); Warner, W. Lloyd, and Lunt, Paul S., *The Social Life of a Modern Community* (1941).

See also: BUREAUCRACY; CASTE; CLASS, SOCIAL; INSTITUTION, SOCIAL; SOCIAL GROUPS; STATUS.

social and welfare services

Public assistance programs—commonly called "welfare"—provide cash benefits for particular categories of the financially needy. Public assistance serves as a safety net after all other systems have failed, and in the United States it consists primarily of these major programs: Aid to Families with Dependent Children; Supplemental Security Income; General Assistance; and Emergency Assistance. Such programs are frequently the focus of concern and debate.

Provision for the needy in the United States remains strongly influenced by its historical development, which was based on the POOR LAWS of England. Poor-law aid was strongly punitive, stigmatized, and had several functions: grudgingly helping the poor, supporting the work ethic, controlling masses of people, depressing wage levels, and providing a pool of workers for low-level tasks. Much of the poor-law tradition continues in contemporary American public assistance programs.

MAIN TYPES OF SERVICES

Aid to Families with Dependent Children. The Aid to Families with Dependent Children Program (AFDC) was intended to cover the minimum costs of providing for the care of dependent children in their own homes or the homes of relatives. Such aid is available for dependent children in need who have lost the support of at least one parent because of death, desertion, or incapacity; and to the parents, relatives, or guardians with whom the children live.

First enacted statewide in Illinois in 1911, legislation providing for pensions to enable widows and deserted women to care for their children was quickly passed in other states. Aid to Dependent Children (ADC) was included in the Social Security Act of 1935 as a joint federal-state assistance program. To qualify for the program today, children must be less than 18 years of age, or less than 21 years of age and attending school; lack parental support; and be financially needy. Twenty-seven states provide benefits when either parent is unemployed (AFDC-UP).

The federal government provides matching grants to all state governments for AFDC, and the states in turn administer the program. Because no minimum benefit level has been federally established, benefits vary extensively from state to state. States establish eligibility criteria and standards for basic needs, although in practice these standards are not always met.

In 1977, for example, the amount actually paid to one needy adult and three children was equal to the state-defined cost of basic needs in only 25 states. In Mississippi the state defined the cost of basic needs for such a family at $227 a month but actually paid only $60. In only one state are AFDC benefits as high as the poverty level defined by the federal government.

Supplemental Security Income. Federal-state programs with grants from the federal government were enacted for old-age assistance and aid to the blind as part of the Social Security Act in 1935. Aid to the Permanently and Totally Disabled (APTD) was enacted in 1951. Supplemental Security Income (SSI) was enacted in 1972 and implemented in 1974 to provide a uniform federal minimum cash income to aged, blind, and disabled people. SSI replaced other state-administered and federally reimbursed programs of aid to the aged, blind, and disabled.

In order to prevent the reduction of cash payments to persons transferred from state to federal programs, states were mandated to make supplemental payments to all people receiving assistance as of December 1973 whose income would have been reduced when they were transferred to the federal SSI program. All states but Texas and New Mexico provide some state supplement to the federal SSI payments.

General Assistance. Those people with emergency needs or who are ineligible for federal categorical programs, or both, are eligible for general assistance. Eligibility is based upon need, the definition of which varies from state to state. All income and assets are considered when a means test is applied. Many states have rules that aid from relatives must first be considered. Many states require registration with the employment service. Benefits range from cash payments to groceries and shelter in emergency situations.

All states but one provide General Assistance. General Assistance is administered by state public assistance agencies through local offices; by local jurisdictions under state public assistance agencies; or by local authorities only. The most common local administrative unit is the county. In some states only state funds are used; in others a combination of state and local funds are used; and local funds alone finance some programs.

Emergency Assistance. Emergency public assistance is provided for needy families with children in order to prevent destitution or to provide support for families without available resources. This aid is limited to 30 days in a 12-month period. Benefits are in cash, in kind, or in voucher form and are given directly to the family. This program is operated in about 60 percent of the states. Grants are made by the federal government to state agencies, which match the federal payment on a formula basis. In August 1977 about 32,000 families were aided with average payments of approximately $150 per family. In 1976 approximately $55 million was spent on this program. In some states adults eligible for or receiving SSI can receive emergency aid.

Additional Programs. In addition to the programs described above, the public assistance system includes the following: housing allowances; MEDICAID; food stamps (see FOOD STAMP PROGRAM); school lunches; the Work Incentive Program (WIN), which provides employment, placement, training, or public service employment for people referred by public assistance programs; the Comprehensive Employment and Training Act (CETA), under which jobs are provided; tax exclusion of public assistance payments, which aids mainly those people who are assisted for only part of the year; and an earned income credit in the form of tax relief and direct cash payments, providing benefits to low-income workers who have dependent children by allowing the workers a tax credit against tax liability on certain amounts of earned income. Social services provided include day care; foster or protective care; family planning; services to the mentally retarded; and drug and alcohol abuse treatment.

RECENT TRENDS AND INCREASED COSTS

The number of families and individuals aided by AFDC has increased sharply in recent years. In 1960 about 800,000 families and 3 million individuals received AFDC assistance. The totals for August 1977 were more than 3.5 million families and almost 11 million individuals, including nearly 8 million children—1 child in every 8 under the age of 18 in the United States.

The total cost of money payments for AFDC alone rose from less than $1 billion in 1960 (total public assistance costs in 1960 were slightly more than $2 billion) to reach more than $10 billion in 1976. This increase sparked criticism of public assistance programs from many quarters. Grants for public assistance reached a total of $26.513 billion in 1976 (the federal share was $13.124 billion and the state and local share $13.389 billion); this included AFDC, medical, emergency, and general assistance programs but did not include SSI payments and food stamps. In a time of restricted budgets, critics of government spending frequently focused on public assistance categories.

Regardless of the total cost of public assistance, AFDC families received in August 1977 an average payment of $241.98, or $78.73 for each recipient. This amounts to just over $2,900 a year for an average AFDC family. In comparison, the median income for all American households in 1976 was $12,686, and the federal government considered that any family of four with an income less than $5,500 was living in poverty.

CRITICISMS AND REFORM

Criticism of public assistance programs is expressed across the political spectrum. Some critics charge that the total cost is excessive, that welfare fraud is widespread, and that welfare undermines the work ethic. Others argue that benefit levels are inadequate, that the system has too many inequities and is inefficient, and that costs are increased through overzealous surveillance and investigations of means.

In regard to criticisms of cost, it is important to recognize that public assistance cannot be separated from larger events in society. The number, types, and locations of jobs; population trends; discrimination; and the state of the economy influence the numbers of recipients. Factors such as education, housing, health care, and tax policy, among others, also contribute to the increase in numbers of recipients. Cost is also influenced by the nature of public assistance regulations themselves, which, in the case of AFDC regulations, encourage family separations, and by the government tactic of deliberately increasing unemployment in order to fight inflation.

Since World War II several factors have contributed to an increase in the number of people on AFDC rolls, including population growth; family breakdown; periods of high unemployment; an increase in the number of one-parent families; a greater proportion of women marrying and bearing at least one child; and the tendency for mothers to form separate households. Despite the greater need for public assistance programs, however, taxpayers resist those programs whose beneficiaries lack political power. Eligibility rules and benefits differ from state to state and even within states. People in similar circumstances receive very different treatment. Regional adjustments are difficult to make, however, and the cost of living may vary more within states than among states. Incentives exist for husbands and wives to separate. The current system discourages single mothers from remarrying. Some people who could work are discouraged from taking jobs. People are discouraged from saving because savings make them ineligible for assistance. When a family receives benefits from one or more programs, increased income can make it ineligible for some of the benefits.

Criticism of social and welfare services quickly raises more basic issues. What proportion of a nation's resources should be spent on the needy? Should the poor be required to work, and if so, can jobs be created? How can fraud and abuse be minimized while protecting individual rights? What importance does society attach to the responsibility of raising children? Essentially, two approaches to reform have been suggested—comprehensive and incremental. It is easier for Congress to accomplish incremental change; Congress can move faster on areas of agreement than debate and resolve complex across-the-board considerations. Recent presidential administrations have made some attempts at comprehensive plans but have ended up with a few incremental changes.

A genuine reform might include the establishment of a federal, and more adequate, minimum of benefits; universal eligibility for all persons and families who qualify on the basis of income and resources, regardless of their categories; consolidation into one cash program of various programs providing income maintenance; exemption from work requirements on the basis of age, disability, or socially productive activities such as providing care for children or for disabled or aged persons; creation of a sufficient number of training positions and job positions for employable recipients; taxing the earnings of recipients at a rate designed to enhance work incentives; liberalizing costs and improving administration of the programs; and assigning to family stability a high priority.

Public assistance is complicated and politically charged; the most basic questions it involves, however, relate to the views that society holds of poor people and the degree to which society will tolerate poverty amid plenty.   RALPH DOLGOFF

Bibliography: Anderson, Martin, *Welfare: The Political Economy of Welfare Reform in the United States* (1978); Esterly, Stanley, *Freedom from Dependence: Welfare Reform as a Solution to Poverty* (1971); Feagin, Joe R., *Subordinating the Poor: Welfare and American Beliefs* (1975); Furniss, Norman, and Tilton, Timothy, *The Case for the Welfare State: From Social Security to Social Equality* (1977); Gilbert, Neil, *Dimensions of Social Welfare Policy* (1974); Grønbjerg, Kirsten A., *Mass Society and the Extension of Welfare, 1960-1970* (1977); Grønbjerg, Kirsten, et al., *Poverty and Social Change* (1978); Levitan, Sar A., et al., *Work and Welfare Go Together* (1974); Piven, Frances F., and Cloward, Richard A., *Regulating the Poor: The Functions of Public Welfare* (1971); Salamon, Lester M., *Welfare, the Elusive Consensus* (1978); Stein, Bruno, *Work and Welfare in Britain and the U.S.A.* (1976); Steiner, Gilbert, *The State of Welfare* (1971).

social work: see SOCIAL AND WELFARE SERVICES.

socialism

The term *socialism* is commonly used to refer both to an ideology—a comprehensive set of beliefs or ideas about the nature of human society and its future desirable state—and to a state of society based on that ideology. Socialists have always claimed to stand above all for the values of equality, social justice, cooperation, progress, and individual freedom and happiness, and they have generally sought to realize these values by the abolition of the private-enterprise economy (see CAPITALISM) and its replacement by "public ownership," a system of social or state control over production and distribution. Methods of transformation advocated by socialists range from popular education through constitutional change (achieving parliamentary majorities, for example) to violent revolution.

ORIGINS OF SOCIALISM

Some scholars believe that the basic principles of socialism derived from the philosophy of Plato, the teachings of the Hebrew prophets, and some parts of the New Testament (the Sermon on the Mount, for example). Modern socialist ideology, however, is essentially a joint product of the 1789 French Revolution and the Industrial Revolution in England—the word *socialist* first occurred in an English journal in 1827. These two great historical events, establishing democratic government in France and the conditions for vast future economic expansion in England, also engendered a state of incipient conflict between the property owners (the bourgeoisie) and the growing class of industrial workers; socialists have since been striving to eliminate or at least mitigate this conflict. The first socialist movement emerged in France after the Revolution and was led by François Noël BABEUF, Filippo Michele Buonarrotti (1761–1837), and Louis Auguste BLANQUI; their insurrection in 1796 ended in failure. Other early socialist thinkers, such as the comte de SAINT-SIMON, Charles FOURIER, and Étienne CABET in France and Robert OWEN and William Thompson (c.1785–1833) in England, believed in the possibility of peaceful and gradual transformation to a socialist society by the founding of small experimental communities; mainly for this reason, later socialist writers dubbed them with the label *utopian* (after the title of a work by Sir Thomas More, which described an ideal state).

THE EMERGENCE OF MARXISM

In the mid-19th century, more elaborate socialist theories were developed, and eventually relatively small but potent socialist movements spread. The German thinkers Karl MARX and Friedrich ENGELS produced at that time what has since been generally regarded as the most sophisticated and influential doctrine of socialism. Marx, who was influenced in his youth by German idealist philosophy and the humanism of Ludwig Andreas FEUERBACH, believed that human beings, and particularly workers, were "alienated" in modern capitalist society; he argued in his early writings that the institution of private property would have to be completely abolished before the individual could be reconciled with society and nature. His mature doctrine, however, worked out in collaboration with Engels and based on the teachings of classical English political economy, struck a harder note, and Marx claimed for it "scientific" status.

The first important document of mature MARXISM, the COMMUNIST MANIFESTO (1848), written with Engels, asserted that all known human history is essentially the history of social classes locked in conflict. There has in the past always been a ruling and an oppressed class. The modern, or bourgeois, epoch, characterized by the capitalist mode of production with manufacturing industry and a free market, would lead according to Marx and Engels to the growing intensity of the struggle between capitalists and workers (the proletariat), the latter being progressively impoverished and as a result assuming an increasingly revolutionary attitude.

Marx further asserted, in his most famous work, Das KAPITAL, that the capitalist employer of labor had, in order to make a profit, to extract "surplus value" from his employees, thereby exploiting them and reducing them to "wage-slavery." The modern state, with its government and law-enforcing agencies, was solely the executive organ of the capitalist class. Religion, philosophy, and most other forms of culture likewise simply fulfilled the "ideological" function of making the working class contented with their subordinate position. Capitalism, however, as Marx claimed, would soon and necessarily grind to a halt: economic factors, such as the diminishing rate of profit, as well as the political factor of increasing proletarian "class consciousness" would result in the forcible overthrow of the existing system and its immediate replacement by the "dictatorship of the proletariat." This dictatorship would soon be superseded by the system of socialism, in which private ownership is abolished and all people are remunerated according to their work, and socialism would lead eventually to COMMUNISM, a society of abundance characterized by the complete disappearance of the state, social classes, law, politics, and all forms of compulsion. Under this ideal condition goods would be distributed according to need, and the unity of all humankind would be assured because of elimination of greed.

VARIETIES OF EUROPEAN SOCIALISM

Marxist ideas made a great impact on European socialist movements. By the second half of the 19th century socialists in Europe were organizing into viable political parties with considerable and growing electoral support; they also forged close links in most countries with trade unions and other working-class associations. Their short-term programs were mainly concerned with increasing the franchise, introducing

Beatrice and Sidney Webb, whose leadership in the Fabian Society did much to shape British socialism, devoted their lives to pioneering historical research and social activism. Their writings and organizational efforts greatly influenced the British Labour party.

state welfare benefits for the needy, gaining the right to strike, and improving working conditions, especially shortening the work day.

Moderate Socialism. Ideas other than those of Marx were at this time also becoming influential. Such ideas included moderate socialist doctrines, for example, those of the FABIAN SOCIETY in England, founded by Sidney WEBB and including among its adherents the writers H. G. Wells and George Bernard Shaw; those of Ferdinand LASSALLE in Germany; and of Louis BLANC in France. These moderates sought to achieve socialism by parliamentary means and by appealing deliberately to the middle class. Fabianism had as one of its intellectual forebears the utilitarian individualism of Jeremy BENTHAM and John Stuart MILL, and it became a doctrine that sought to reconcile the values of liberty, democracy, economic progress, and social justice. The Fabians believed that the cause of socialism would also be aided by the advancement of the social sciences, especially economics and sociology. These doctrines, collectively known as social democracy, did not, like Marxism, look toward the complete abolition of private property and the disappearance of the state but instead envisaged socialism more as a form of society in which full democratic control would be exercised over wealth, and production would be controlled by a group of responsible experts working in the interests of the whole community. The achievement of socialism was seen by social democrats as a long-term goal, the result of an evolutionary process involving the growth of economic efficiency (advanced technology, large-scale organization, planning), education in moral responsibility, and the voluntary acceptance of equal shares in benefits and burdens; socialism would be the triumph of common sense, the inevitable outcome of LIBERALISM, the extension of democracy from politics to industry.

CHRISTIAN SOCIALISM spread from its beginnings in England to France and Germany. Charles KINGSLEY, John Malcolm Forbes Ludlow (1821–1911), and Frederick Denison MAURICE were among its founders. They in the main supported moderate social democracy, emphasizing what they understood as the central message of the church in social ethics, notably the values of cooperation, brotherhood, simplicity of tastes, and the spirit of self-sacrifice. Their ideas proved fertile in both the short and the long runs, although in actual political terms Christian socialism never succeeded in altering the predominantly secular orientation of most socialist movements.

Radical Socialism. On the other hand, many doctrines and movements were decidedly more militant than Marxism. Anarchists (see ANARCHISM), influenced mainly by the ideas of the Frenchman Pierre Joseph PROUDHON and later of the Russian émigrés Mikhail Aleksandrovich BAKUNIN and Pyotr Alekseyevich KROPOTKIN, were intent on immediately overthrowing the capitalist state and replacing it with small independent communities. Unlike the Marxists, whom they

Das Kapital.

Kritik der politischen Oekonomie.

Von

Karl Marx.

Dritter Band, erster Theil.

Buch III:
Der Gesammtprocess der kapitalistischen Produktion.
Kapitel I bis XXVIII.

Herausgegeben von **Friedrich Engels.**

Das Recht der Uebersetzung ist vorbehalten.

Hamburg
Verlag von Otto Meissner.

The first volume of Karl Marx's Das Kapital (1867), published nearly 20 years after his Communist Manifesto (1848), detailed the social and economic theories that rapidly came to dominate socialist thought. Marx's emphasis on the inevitable direction of historical development contrasted with the perspective of the earlier utopian socialists.

bitterly criticized, anarchists were against the formation of socialist parties, and they repudiated parliamentary politics as well as the idea of revolutionary dictatorship. Their followers, never very numerous, were and are found mainly in the Latin countries of Europe and America. SYNDICALISM, an offshoot of anarchism, was a movement of militant working-class trade unionists who endeavored to achieve socialism through industrial action only, notably by using the weapon of the general strike. Their doctrine was similar to Marxism in that they also believed that socialism was to be achieved only by and for the working class, but unlike the Marxists they rejected the notion of a future centralized socialist state. Their most eminent theorist was Georges SOREL. Syndicalist ideas also had intermittent success in the British and American trade union movements, for example, the INDUSTRIAL WORKERS OF THE WORLD, an American-based syndicalist union active around the turn of the century. Guild socialism in England, dominated by George Douglas Howard Cole (1889-1959), the academic economist and historian, represented a modified and milder form of syndicalism.

In Russia, where it was impossible to organize openly a popular socialist movement under the tsarist regime, socialism became mainly the ideology of young militant intellectuals whose favored means of furthering the cause were secret conspiracies and acts of individual terrorism. Debate raged between those who believed in the native socialist ethos of the Russian village community and those who wanted to adopt Western ideas of modernization. The latter party, which eventually emerged victorious, soon came under Marxist influence. Among its adherents was V. I. LENIN, who emerged at the turn of the century as the leader of a small but dedicated group of "professional revolutionaries," the Bolshevik (see BOLSHEVIKS AND MENSHEVIKS) wing of the illegal Russian Social Democratic Workers' party. Lenin was also the theorist who irrevocably gave a markedly elitist and authoritarian twist to Marxism: he worked out the theory of the proletarian vanguard, that is, the Communist party, which is destined to lead the masses toward socialism, irrespective of the masses' present inclinations.

SCHISM AND CONTROVERSY
Throughout the 19th century the socialist movement was beset by a number of ever-deepening conflicts and doctrinal controversies.

The Internationals. The International Workingmen's Association (First International; see INTERNATIONAL, SOCIALIST), founded in 1864, was expected to achieve unity among various socialist and militant trade union organizations, but its

efforts were greatly hindered by, among other things, the conflict between the followers of Bakunin and those of Marx. It came to its demise soon after the suppression of the COMMUNE OF PARIS (1871).

The Second International (1889-1914) assumed for a time at least an outward appearance of unity, in that it represented the high watermark of classical Marxist influence in West European socialism. It was dominated by the largest socialist parties then in existence, the French—led by Jean JAURÈS, Jules Guesde (1845-1922), and Paul Lafargue (1842-1911)—and the German—led by August BEBEL, Karl Johann KAUTSKY, and Wilhelm Liebknecht (see LIEBKNECHT family)—who agreed at least in their broad understanding of the aims and methods of socialism. Their spokesmen emphasized the need to foster international solidarity among the mass of the working class and thus to avert the threat of a major war in Europe. This effort proved singularly unsuccessful: NATIONALISM in 1914 and later proved a much stronger mass emotion than socialism. Apart from a few exceptions, such as Lenin and his Bolshevik group, socialist movements supported the war effort of their respective governments. As a result of the general conflagra-

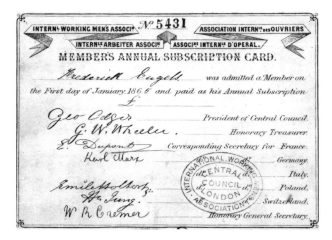

(Above) *Friedrich Engels's membership card for the International Workingmen's Association includes Karl Marx among its signatories. Divided by doctrinal disputes and personality conflicts, the association collapsed (1876) twelve years after its founding.*

Gustave Courbet's Proudhon and his Children *(c.1865) portrays the French writer whose theories formed the basis of anarchist thought. Proudhon's acceptance of gradual social change was later repudiated by the anarchist Mikhail Bakunin. (Musée du Petit Palais, Paris.)*

(Below) *Vladimir Ilich Lenin, revolutionary leader and first head of the Soviet state, influenced Marxist socialism through his theory of a vanguard revolutionary party and his leadership of the Bolsheviks. His theories are now accepted as "orthodox" Marxist doctrine.*

tion in 1914 the Second International disintegrated and therewith also the hopes of socialist unity.

Revisionism. Another important controversy broke out in the 1890s within Marxism, involving the German Social Democratic party. This party was divided then between a militant revolutionary left wing, an orthodox center that held to the classical Marxist doctrine of economic determinism, and a right wing moving rapidly toward a position of open reformism. The right wing had as its most renowned spokesman Eduard BERNSTEIN, a personal friend of Marx and Engels, who was, however, also influenced by English Fabian ideas.

Bernstein repudiated the notion of violent revolution and argued that conditions in civilized countries such as Germany made possible a peaceful, gradual transformation to socialism. He sought to reinterpret Marxist doctrine in the light of fresh advances made in economic science, such as those also embraced in Fabian doctrine, and argued that socialism was compatible with individual economic responsibility. He rejected, furthermore, the idea of "class morality," which judged all actions according to their revolutionary import. Instead he advocated a code of individual morality, derived from Kant's moral philosophy. Consequently, Bernstein asserted the need for socialists to concentrate on immediate tasks instead of ultimate and remote objectives; the movement, he wrote, was everything; the goal, nothing.

This doctrine, henceforward called revisionism, immediately became the subject of bitter attacks by the revolutionary left wing, represented above all by Rosa LUXEMBURG, which on this issue was supported by the orthodox center and its principal theorist, Karl Kautsky. The terms of the debate on revisionism centered on the facts, noted by Bernstein, of considerable improvement in the living standards of the working class, its resultant political integration in the constitutional (republican or monarchical) state, the purely reformist stance of trade unions, and the virtual absence of any desire for a radical change on the part of the great majority of workers.

The opponents of revisionism, while acknowledging these tendencies, argued that material improvements were insufficient and ephemeral. They felt that if the working class and its organizations accepted the constitutional state they were merely postponing indefinitely the change to socialism. According to them, the principal tasks of the socialist leader are to arouse dissatisfaction with existing conditions and to reemphasize constantly the worth of the ultimate goal. The arguments on both sides continue today with only slight changes in the debate between reformist and revolutionary socialists everywhere. In Marxist jargon the term *revisionism* has remained synonymous with *treason*. Ironically—but in a way that pointed toward the subsequent fate of Marxist doctrine—the orthodox center in the German party was soon to be denounced by left-wingers as revisionist. Lenin, too, came

to condemn sharply the German social democrats and the "renegade" Kautsky. The latter, in turn, vehemently denounced Lenin and the Bolsheviks for their adoption of terrorist methods in the consolidation of their revolutionary gains in Russia. Marxist unity, like the Second International, thus also fell victim to World War I and its aftermath: from then on Marxists have tended to be either Marxist-Leninists, that is, communists embracing the elitist doctrine of the vanguard party, or moderate revisionists moving ever closer to the position of reformist social democracy.

MARXIST SOCIALISM TODAY

Modern socialism owes its shape and fortune at least as much to secular events as to the continuing attraction of its various doctrines. The major upheavals caused by two world wars greatly contributed to the success of the Russian (1917) and Chinese (1949) revolutions, and the governments of these two powerful countries have since been endeavoring by diverse means to spread the Marxist revolutionary doctrine further afield, resorting to military methods (as in Eastern Europe), economic pressures, military and economic aid, as well as subversion and propaganda. Indigenous Marxist movements also succeeded in gaining and maintaining power in Yugoslavia (1945) and in Cuba (1959). Marxist socialism in practice has generally meant the dictatorial rule of the Communist party, intensive industrialization, central state direction of the economy, and the collectivization of agriculture. These have been accompanied, particularly during the dictatorship of Joseph STALIN in the USSR, by a reign of terror and the general absence of individual freedom—a far cry from Marx's original vision. Yugoslavia under TITO, however, has introduced a certain amount of decentralization and workers' self-government, and in the 1960s and '70s in most of Eastern Europe a cautious and halting process of liberalization has been detectable, notably in Hungary and Poland. Since the late 1950s, the USSR and China have been pulling apart and now regard each other as irreconcilable enemies, vying for the allegiance of other socialist countries, especially those in the Third World. The Chinese Marxists under MAO TSE-TUNG and his successors have also governed through the party, but the People's Liberation Army and mass mobilization (for example, the CULTURAL REVOLUTION) have played a much greater role than in Soviet-type communist regimes.

EUROPEAN SOCIAL DEMOCRACY

In Western Europe, despite the presence of large Marxist parties (as in Italy and France) and the Marxist influence among intellectuals, socialism is still principally represented by widely based social democratic and labor movements, which generally enjoy the active support of trade unions. This predominance of reformist trends over revolutionary aspirations has undoubtedly been occasioned by economic stability and the deterrent example of Marxist rule in the East. The social democratic parties of Sweden, Great Britain, and West Germany in particular have governed their respective countries for lengthy periods during the postwar era, gaining political power through constitutional means and fully accepting the principles of parliamentary liberal democracy. Their spirit has tended to be pragmatic and tolerant, seeking accommodation rather than confrontation. Their programs repudiate the doctrines of the class war, revolution, and communism. Instead they have relied on the expedients of progressive taxation, deficit financing, selective nationalization, the mixed economy, and vast welfare programs in order to bring about socialism; their political success has depended on considerable middle-class support. On the other hand, in no Western country have socialist parties commanded the allegiance of the whole of the working class.

Social democratic foreign policy is generally pacific and has been mainly concerned with defusing the cold war and accelerating the processes of decolonization and the banning of nuclear weapons. In domestic politics they have refused to cooperate with communist parties and other extremist socialist groups. The Social Democratic party (SPD) in Germany, although at one time the citadel of orthodox Marxism, has since 1959 been a purely reformist party, abandoning its original goals. The British LABOUR PARTY, socialist in its aims (its

Eduard Bernstein, the principal theorist of "revisionist" Marxism, argued that economic and social improvements since the period of Marx's writings precluded the necessity of violent revolution. His theories were vehemently denounced by militant Marxists and have since been the source of much disagreement among socialist parties.

THE HOPE OF THE WORLD

MACDONALD THE PEACEMAKER

A British Labour party campaign poster, dating from Britain's post–World War I economic slump, promises a bright future for the worker. The reformist Labour party gained substantial popular support during the early 1920s and formed its first minority government in 1924.

constitution since 1919 has had reference to "public ownership"), has never had any serious doctrinal or organizational links with Marxism, although its powerful left wing consistently advocates radical policies. The French Socialist party only recently modified its doctrinal position, moving away from its orthodox Marxism. At the same time, however, under the leadership of François MITTERRAND, it entered in the 1960s into an electoral alliance with the Communist party, on several occasions coming close to winning the presidency of the Fifth Republic. Italy since World War II has had two major social democratic parties, one allied to the Communists.

The French Communist party, for a long time subservient to the USSR and known for its rigid Stalinism, has recently become more eclectic in its interpretation of Marxism. The Italian Communist party, the largest and most experienced of any such group in an advanced industrial country, relies on an indigenous Marxist tradition, associated mainly with the teaching of Antonio GRAMSCI, who was a founder of the party and is now widely regarded as one of the most significant European Marxist thinkers in recent times. Gramsci argued that in Western liberal-democratic countries, where relative prosperity has dulled the masses' interest in socialist change, Marxists must fight against the cultural "hegemony" of the bourgeoisie, not merely against its overt political power. Primary importance is therefore attached to the propaganda work of intellectuals. The Italian Communist party has often obtained the largest percentage of the popular vote in Italian parliamentary elections and has continuously governed several municipalities (Bologna is a prime example). Lately the large communist parties of France, Italy, and Spain have embraced a novel doctrine known as Eurocommunism, which signifies a resolution to break not only with Stalinism, but also with some aspects of the Leninist tradition and to move toward the full acceptance of parliamentary democracy and the multiparty system. It remains to be seen how genuinely this resolution will be followed by Communists and whether or not they will, as a result of their moderation, be outflanked on the left by new groups of militant revolutionaries. To the left of mainstream and increasingly moderate communist parties are found today many other revolutionary groups, such as Trotskyites, Maoists, and anarchists, engaged in subversive and terrorist activity.

SOCIALISM IN THE UNITED STATES

In North America, Marxist influence never spread very far. In the United States no socialist movement has ever held a very large following, and although the country has produced renowned socialist authors and popular leaders, they have not been distinguished for their originality or for their impact on the worldwide development of socialism. Socialism has not taken a firmer root in the United States for several reasons, of which the country's cultural traditions and its wealth in natural resources are the most important. Whereas in Europe the distribution of wealth was a pressing problem, facilitating the rise of socialist movements, in the United States the moving "frontier" meant the constant creation of new land and wealth and its accessibility for those endowed with initiative and a spirit of individual enterprise. Thus in the United States even radical thinkers have tended to be "individualists" and "anarchists," rather than socialists. In this development the country's tradition of republican self-government and its ethos of egalitarianism and democracy also played a decisive role: unlike Europe, the United States had no entrenched aristocratic privileges or monarchical absolutism and consequently no need for democratic aspirations to be combined with the socialist demand for economic equality and security. LABOR UNIONS also, for the most part, have concentrated on the achievement of higher earnings and have not been greatly interested in economic and social organization.

Numerous, although small, utopian socialist communities did flourish, however, in the United States, mostly during the early 19th century. Also, a celebrated economist, Henry GEORGE, and writers of repute, such as Edward BELLAMY, advocated socialism, and socialist political leaders, such as Victor L. BERGER, Eugene V. DEBS, Daniel DE LEON, and Norman THOMAS, had at one time considerable popular appeal. The U.S. SOCIALIST PARTY, founded in 1901, reached its greatest strength in the 1912 and 1920 presidential elections, when its candidate, Debs, received more than 900,000 votes. In 1932, Norman Thomas, running on the Socialist ticket, polled more than 800,000 votes. Thereafter the party's strength ebbed. The New Deal in the 1930s, although not socialist in inspiration, also tended to draw votes away from the party. The New Deal's policies of economic redistribution seemed to meet demands of those who previously supported the Socialists.

In the economic boom following World War II and especially in the cold-war era of the 1950s and '60s socialism was at a low ebb. More recently, however, socialist ideas have made considerable, although indirect, impact on various radical (see RADICALISM) and liberal movements. In the United States, however, many people no longer discuss socialism in its conventional political and economic sense, but rather as a remote ethical and social ideal.

SOCIALISM IN THE THIRD WORLD

Socialism has assumed a number of distinct forms in the Third World. Only in Israel has moderate social democracy proved successful for long periods, mainly as a result of the European socialist tradition brought by immigrants. Here the Labor party in various forms has had a large following and

A campaign poster for the U.S. Socialist party promotes the 1904 presidential ticket. Organized during the late 1890s and initially led by Eugene V. Debs, the party did not gain prominence until 1912, when Debs polled 6% of the popular vote for president.

THE SOCIALIST PARTY

EUGENE V. DEBS   BEN HANFORD

Julius Nyerere, first president of Tanzania, initiated (1967) socialist programs that have emphasized rural development through the creation of communal villages. His goals, detailed in his Freedom and Socialism (1968), have focused on the traditions and needs of an African agricultural economy.

governed the country for the longest time since the foundation of the republic. Israel has other socialist parties as well, including a militant Marxist party. At least of equal significance, however, are the cooperative agricultural communes (*kibbutzim*), which have flourished since 1948. Commentators have argued that *kibbutzim* more than anything else show the viability of socialist principles in practice; however, the peculiarities of Israeli conditions (for example, religious tradition and constant war readiness) could not easily be duplicated.

Elsewhere in the Third World, Marxism and various indigenous traditions have been predominant in socialist movements. In developing countries socialism as an ideology generally has been fused with various doctrines of nationalism, also a European cultural import but enriched by diverse motifs drawn from local traditions and cast in the idiom of indigenous cultures. In India, for example, the largest socialist movement has partially adapted the pacifist teaching of Mahatma Gandhi, and distinct native brands of socialism exist in Japan, Burma, and Indonesia. Similarly, in black Africa native traditions have been used in the adaptation of socialist, mainly Marxist, doctrines and political systems based on them. Noteworthy instances are the socialist system of Tanzania and the socialist theories of intellectual leaders such as Kwame NKRUMAH of Ghana, Julius K. NYERERE of Tanzania, Léopold Sédar SENGHOR of Senegal, and Sekou TOURÉ of Guinea. Socialism in these theories is usually understood as a combination of Marxism, anticolonialism, and the updated

Herbert Marcuse, a German-American political philosopher whose Marxian critiques greatly influenced the New Left, called for revolutionary change in Western economic stuctures and social values. His vision of a nonrepressive socialist society combines Freudian and Marxist ideals.

tradition of communal landownership and tribal customs of decision making, trying mainly to bypass Western "individualism" and capitalist economic organization. Arab socialism likewise represents an effort to combine modern European socialist ideology with some Islamic principles. The BAATH PARTY in Iraq and Syria and the Destour party in Tunisia have held power for considerable periods; Algeria also has had a socialist system since its independence. In the Third World, however, socialism is often simply an ideology of anticolonialism and modernization. Overtly Marxist movements, materially helped by either the USSR (and its ally Cuba) or China, have lately been successful in taking power in some African countries, notably Angola, the Congo, Ethiopia, and Mozambique.

THE NEW LEFT

In the West in the 1960s a radical socialist movement, known as the New Left, arose principally out of the disaffection of young people with the way of life of advanced industrial society, and not least with its prosperity and conformism. The movement, which was apolitical in nature, sought to expose the growing "alienation" of the individual in advanced industrial conditions, castigating the values of the "consumer society" and attacking many prevailing social institutions. The beliefs of this movement, particularly strong in France, West Germany, and the United States, sprang from many diverse sources. Most important among these were the ideas found in Marx's early writings; the idea of "alienation," as interpreted by such contemporary socialist philosophers as György LUKÁCS and Herbert MARCUSE; EXISTENTIALISM; romantic and utopian ideas adapted from earlier socialist writers (for example, Fourier); sexual radicalism derived from the teaching of Sigmund Freud; and some aspects of oriental religious cults, such as ZEN BUDDHISM. Despite its initial appeal and short-lived successes, however, the New Left has not so far proved a significant or lasting influence on socialism in its worldwide context or even within advanced industrial societies where conventional varieties still dominate.

It could well be argued that socialism as an alternative system of society and government has failed hitherto to live up to its promises; by and large it is still no more than a dream or at best a set of ideal criteria whereby to judge the shortcomings of existing institutions. Socialist ideology, however, is undoubtedly among the most popular and widely held political beliefs today, and it has deeply penetrated other ideologies, as can be seen, for example, in the acceptance by many conservatives of the WELFARE STATE and planning. The worldwide spread of socialist ideas has also been accompanied by a process of dilution of original principles, as in Western social democracy, and by the degeneration and falsification of its values, as in Marxist states.   R. N. BERKI

Bibliography: Beer, Max, *The General History of Socialism and Social Struggle* (1957); Berki, R. N., *Socialism* (1975); Charney, George, *A Long Journey* (1968); Cole, G. D. H., *A History of Socialist Thought*, 5 vols. (1953–60); Crossman, R. H. S., *The Politics of Socialism* (1965); Fried, Albert, and Sanders, Ronald, eds., *Socialist Thought: A Documentary History* (1964); Hall, Robert L., *The Economic System in a Socialist State* (1937); Harrington, Michael, *Socialism* (1970); Howe, Irving, ed., *Essential Works of Socialism* (1970); Hyams, Edward S., *The Millennium Postponed* (1973); Kilroy-Silk, Robert, *Socialism Since Marx* (1972); Lichtheim, George, *A Short History of Socialism* (1970); Momjan, Kh. N., *Socialism*, trans. by B. Strakhov (1963); Salvadori, Massimo, *Modern Socialism* (1968); Sternberg, Fritz, *Capitalism and Socialism on Trial*, trans. by Edward Fitzgerald (1968); Vetterli, Richard, and Fort, William E., *The Socialist Base of Modern Totalitarianism* (1968).

Socialist International: see INTERNATIONAL, SOCIALIST.

Socialist Labor party

The Socialist Labor party, an outgrowth of a New York City workers' party (1874), became a national U.S. political party by the end of the decade and took the name Socialist Labor party in 1877. In 1880 it allied itself temporarily with the GREENBACK PARTY; in the 1890s it was led by the Marxist Daniel DE LEON, editor of the weekly *The People*; and in 1892 it ran its first presidential ticket. De Leon's syndicalist tendency, however, was opposed by many members, who, led by Morris Hillquit, split off and helped form the Socialist party. The Socialist Labor party then declined, and its continuing influence has been minimal.

Bibliography: Kuhn, Henry, and Johnson, O. M., *Socialist Labor Party* (1931).

socialist law

Socialist law is a term used to describe the legal systems of the USSR and other Communist countries. According to the official ideology of these countries, their legal systems reflect in practice the ideas of leading communist figures—Karl Marx, Friedrich Engels, and Vladimir Lenin. The basic elements of socialist law were developed under Lenin in the 1920s and under Joseph Stalin in the 1930s. After World War II socialist law was adopted in those countries of Europe and Asia which came under Communist rule.

Certain features are common to all Communist legal systems. These include control of all governmental organizations by a self-perpetuating Communist party leadership; government ownership of the major means of industrial production and government planning of industrial production; government control of the press, radio, and television; legal guarantees of full employment, social security benefits, free medical care, and education; and constitutional guarantees of equal rights regardless of race or sex.

The socialist law of property and contracts plays two roles, one affecting private citizens and the other, government units. Private citizens are paid in accordance with their work and may freely spend their income to buy houses, cars, and consumer goods. Such transactions are regulated by traditional property and contract law. The more important function of property and contract law, however, is that of providing a legal structure for the regulation of relations among the government agricultural and industrial corporations.

Criminal law and procedure function differently in nonpolitical and political cases. According to socialist law, persons accused of ordinary crimes, such as murder or robbery, are generally guaranteed the right to have a lawyer and the other rights necessary for a fair trial. On the other hand, persons disseminating political or religious views regarded as dangerous are often subjected to legal penalties with little regard for fundamental human rights.

Particular features of socialist labor law include the control of both union and management by the Communist party, which means that strikes and lockouts never happen. Job security is guaranteed by legal procedures weighted so heavily in the workers' favor that it is extremely difficult for management to fire inefficient workers.

Housing law reflects the fact that in most urban areas a majority of the apartments belong to the government and are rented at a rate so low that demand far exceeds supply. To control this demand, an elaborate system of housing allocation and rationing has been introduced, and movement from rural to urban areas is restricted by police regulations.

Broad differences exist among socialist legal systems in the agricultural areas. In all Communist countries a certain amount of private farming is allowed as an exception to the general rule of public ownership. In the USSR the major part of farmland is controlled or owned by the government. In some other Communist legal systems, however, most agriculture is still in private hands.   PETER B. MAGGS

Bibliography: Barry, D. D., et al., *Soviet Law after Stalin*, 3 vols. (1977–79); Butler, W. E., et al., *The Soviet Legal System*, 2 vols. (1977–78); Johnson, E. L., *An Introduction to the Soviet Legal System* (1969).

Socialist party

During the Progressive Era (early 20th century), the American Socialist party presented the only significant political challenge to U.S. capitalism. Formed in 1901 by Victor L. BERGER, Job Harriman, and Morris Hillquit of the Socialist Labor party and Eugene V. DEBS of the American Railway Union, the party

faced two serious handicaps. At the 1894 convention of the American Federation of Labor (AFL), which represented skilled craftworkers, federation leader Samuel GOMPERS had skillfully maneuvered to prevent AFL endorsement of socialism; thus the party never won the skilled-trade-union support that bolstered its European counterparts. In addition, the INDUSTRIAL WORKERS OF THE WORLD (IWW) failed in its goal of building a permanent organization of unskilled migrant workers and immigrants; therefore, the Socialists also lacked a base among nonskilled-industrial-union members. Because of these and other problems, the party collapsed after a decade of promise.

The Socialist party reached its apex in 1910–12 with about 118,000 dues-paying members—70 percent of them native born. One thousand Socialists were elected to state and local public office. In 1910, Berger became the first Socialist elected to Congress; Debs won 6 percent of the presidential vote in 1912. Among the party's hundreds of publications were the *Appeal to Reason, Jewish Daily Forward, Masses,* and *International Socialist Review.*

The party was torn, however, between the reformist, AFL-oriented, center-right of Hillquit and Berger, who controlled the organization, and leftist advocates of revolution, such as William HAYWOOD and Debs, who hoped to achieve their aims by organizing and educating workers in industrial unions. The removal of Haywood—the head of the IWW—from the executive committee in 1913 cost the party its cutting edge on the left. Its decline was furthered by a reformist drift toward the progressive Democrat Woodrow Wilson and by the departure of intellectuals disturbed by the party's pacifism during World War I.

Drastically reduced by government repression and Bolshevik defections, the party joined (1924) the PROGRESSIVE PARTY coalition behind the independent presidential candidacy of Robert La Follette. After 1926, Norman THOMAS attempted to re-create a leftist coalition, but during the Depression of the 1930s the garment workers' unions defected to the New Deal, depleting the Socialists' financial base. Increasingly fragmented, the Socialists abandoned even presidential campaigns after 1948.   FRED GREENBAUM

Bibliography: Bell, Daniel, *Marxian Socialism in the United States* (1967); Kipnis, Ira, *The Socialist Movement, 1897–1912* (1952; repr. 1972); Miller, Sally M., *Victor Berger and the Promise of Constructive Socialism, 1910–1920* (1973); Nash, Howard, *Third Parties in American Politics* (1959); Shannon, David A., *The Socialist Party of America* (1955); Weinstein, James, *The Decline of Socialism in America, 1912–1925* (1967).

socialist realism

Socialist realism has been the Soviet Union's official doctrine on literature since it was first formulated by the Communist party in 1932 and then articulated by Maksim GORKY at the First Congress of the Union of Soviet Writers in 1934. According to this doctrine, all literature must serve the higher purposes of Soviet society by educating the working masses in the principles and practices of socialism; literature must be realistic and comprehensible, not experimental or negative, as it is in bourgeois societies.

Typical of socialist realism is the "positive hero" or "new Soviet man," usually a worker who strives heroically and optimistically for the future perfection of socialism. Examples of such fiction include *The Nineteen* (1927; Eng. trans., 1929) by Aleksandr Aleksandrovich FADEYEV; *How the Steel Was Tempered* (1932–34; Eng. trans., 1937) by Nikolai Alekseyevich Ostrovsky; and *The Virgin Soil Upturned* (1932–33 and 1960; Eng. trans., 1935 and 1960) by Mikhail Aleksandrovich SHOLOKHOV. The doctrine has also influenced the plastic arts in the Soviet Union and has been adopted by other Eastern-bloc countries.

Bibliography: James, C. Vaughan, *Soviet Socialist Realism* (1973); Mathewson, Rufus W., *The Positive Hero in Russian Literature* (1975); Struve, G., *Russian Literature under Lenin and Stalin, 1917–1953* (1971).

Socialist Workers' party

The Socialist Workers' party, headquartered in New York City, was founded Dec. 31, 1937, as a successor to the Communist

League of America by James P. Cannon and a group of American followers of Leon Trotsky, then living in exile in Mexico. Its goal was to overthrow the capitalist state and found a workers' state governed by the proletariat. From its inception the party has been active within the Fourth Socialist International. The Young Socialist Alliance, its youth wing, was founded in 1957. The party participates in local and national elections; in the 1976 presidential election, its candidate, Peter Camejo, received 91,314 votes. From 1945 to about 1963 the FBI conducted electronic surveillance of party members.

Bibliography: Cannon, James P., *History of American Trotskyism*, rev. ed. (1972).

socialization

Socialization is a term used by sociologists and other social scientists for the means by which the members of one generation in a society acquire knowledge, behavior, and ideals from older generations. The process of socialization, which starts in infancy, includes learning acquired from the family, from playmates, and through formal education. It involves learning the informal and formal rules of one's society by imitation, by rewards and discipline, and from conscious indoctrination as well as unconscious approval or disapproval. Socialization ensures the continuation of society. Some anthropologists use the term *enculturation* to refer to the process of socialization.   CHARLES WAGLEY

Bibliography: Brim, Orville G., and Wheeler, Stanton, *Socialization after Childhood* (1966; repr. 1976); Elkin, Frederick, and Handel, Gerald, *The Child and Society*, 3d ed. (1978); Roberts, Joan I., and Akinsanya, Sherrie K., eds., *Schooling in the Cultural Context* (1976); Rose, Peter I., ed., *Socialization and the Life Cycle* (1979).

Society Islands

The Society Islands, part of FRENCH POLYNESIA, consist of two island groups—the Leeward Islands and the Windward Islands. They have a total land area of about 1,680 km² (650 mi²) and a population of 117,700 (1977 est.). The main islands are TAHITI and Moorea in the Windwards and BORA-BORA and Raiatea in the Leewards. The capital, PAPEETE, lies on Tahiti. Volcanic in origin, the islands rise to 2,241 m (17,352 ft) in Mount Orohena on Tahiti. Crops include copra, fruits, sugarcane, and vanilla. Some phosphate is mined, but the main source of income is tourism.

The first Europeans to visit the islands were probably the Portuguese in 1607. The islands were named by James Cook, who visited them in 1769. A French protectorate since 1843, they were grouped into a single colony in 1880 and became an overseas territory of France in 1958.

Society for the Prevention of Cruelty to Animals

The Society for the Prevention of Cruelty to Animals (SPCA) is the umbrella name for about 600 separate organizations throughout the United States that seek to assure humane treatment of animals through education of the public, the maintenance of animal shelters, and enforcement of the laws relating to animal care.

The first such society, the American Society for the Prevention of Cruelty to Animals (ASPCA), was chartered in the state of New York in 1866. In New York, ASPCA agents are empowered to act as officers of the peace. They may carry firearms, may sue an owner for mistreatment of an animal, and may, with court permission, remove an animal from the possession of its owner. The ASPCA is the principal provider of shelters for abandoned animals.

SPCA organizations in other states have modeled their programs on New York's, although legal powers and the services offered vary from state to state.

Bibliography: Niven, Charles G., *History of the Humane Movement* (1967).

Socinianism [soh-sin'-ee-uhn-izm]

Socinianism is the name given to the specific form of antitrinitarianism or UNITARIANISM stated by the Italian theologian Socinus (Fausto Paolo Sozzini, 1539–1604) and developed during the early 17th century, particularly in Poland. Socinus grew up in Italy under the influence of his uncle Laelius Socinus. When he raised doubts about the divinity of Christ, he came into conflict with the teachings of both Roman Catholicism and the Reformation. After a short period in Transylvania, Socinus took refuge in Poland, where he spent the rest of his life in leadership of the antitrinitarian movement there. In 1598 he was forced to flee from Kraków, and he spent the rest of his life in Luclawice.

Socinus prepared drafts for the Racovian Catechism, the first formal statement of Socinian beliefs, which was published at Raków, in southern Poland, in 1605. It set forth a moderate form of unitarianism that stated that Christ was a man who received divine power as a result of his blameless life and miraculous resurrection. The movement was suppressed in Poland after 1658, but Socinian groups survived in Transylvania, England, and elsewhere. John BIDDLE, the founder of English unitarianism, was influenced by Socinianism.   FREDERICK A. NORWOOD

Bibliography: Kot, Stanislau, *Socinianism in Poland*, trans. by E. M. Wilbur (1957); Wilbur, E. M., *A History of Unitarianism: Socinianism and Its Antecedents* (1945); Williams, George H., *The Radical Reformation* (1962).

Socinus, Laelius [soh-sy'-nuhs, lee'-lee-uhs]

Laelius Socinus (Lelio Francesco Maria Sozini), b. Mar. 25, 1525, d. May 14, 1562, was an Italian theologian whose ideas influenced the later antitrinitarian and unitarian movements. A member of a long line of wealthy jurists and canonists, his formal education was in law at Bologna, but he early developed an interest in biblical and theological studies and was led to doubts about Catholicism. From 1545 he traveled widely in Europe, establishing close contacts with such Reformation leaders as John Calvin, Heinrich Bullinger, and Philipp Melanchthon, often serving as their messenger. Although personable and generally well liked, his uninhibited questioning of such doctrines as the Trinity and the Incarnation ultimately gave rise to suspicions on the part of some of the reformers. He died at the age of 37, shortly after the sequestration of his property by the Inquisition. Although few of his writings are preserved, his work probably influenced his nephew, Fausto, the father of Socinianism.   T. TACKETT

Bibliography: Tedeschi, John A., ed., *Italian Reformation Studies* (1965).

sociobiology

Sociobiology, or the study of animal and human social behavior in terms of evolutionary biology, holds that the theory of evolution by natural selection applies to behavior in the same way that it applies to structure and physiology. Accordingly it relies upon the principle that genes are able to influence behavior and will be selected if the behaviors they encourage contribute ultimately to the reproductive success of the individuals carrying those genes. The "fitness" of an organism or a gene is a measure of the ability of that organism or gene to project copies of itself into future generations. Because natural selection would influence genetically controlled behaviors, sociobiologists believe that individuals will tend to behave in ways that maximize their fitness.

In the 1960s, population geneticist W. D. Hamilton developed the concept of kin selection, which emphasized evolution from the gene's point of view. This concept was first applied to understand altruism among animals, a behavior in which social animals such as ants care for young other than their own. At about the same time, biologists were also becoming increasingly aware of the role of selection acting upon individuals, rather than species or groups, in generating adaptive traits. This information, along with that resulting from extensive studies of wild animals, behavior genetics, and evolutionary ecology, provided theoretical bases for the development of sociobiology. Models of evolution also were applied to behavior such as territorial defense, mate selection, reciprocal altruism, parental investment, and parent-offspring conflict. Mathematical game theory was also used to analyze the interaction of two individuals. Harvard zoologist Edward O. Wilson combined a massive amount of theory and data in an encyclopedic volume titled *Sociobiology: The New Synthesis* (1975), which defined the field and attracted wide attention.

Sociobiology is very new and still very controversial. Supporters claim that it provides a valuable perspective on social behavior, one that promises to unify the social sciences under a biological theme. Detractors claim that sociobiology's theorizing has gone far beyond its data and that there is not enough clear evidence for the influence of genes upon complex behaviors. Sociobiology has been most successful in understanding animal behavior, especially altruism among the social insects and animal reproductive and foraging strategies. The field is most controversial in the area of human behavior, where its value is suggested but unproved. The idea that individuals behave in a manner that maximizes their fitness is likely to be extended and tested, nonetheless, in many specific behaviors such as aggressiveness, male-female differences, dominance hierarchies, mate selection, care of offspring, territoriality, division of labor, foraging, and predator avoidance.   DAVID P. BARASH

Bibliography: Barash, David, *Sociobiology and Behavior* (1977) and *The Whisperings Within* (1979); Caplan, Arthur L., *The Sociobiology Debate* (1978); Dawkins, Richard, *The Selfish Gene* (1976); Gregory, Michael, et al., eds., *Sociobiology and Human Nature* (1978); Wilson, Edward O., *Sociobiology: The New Synthesis* (1975) and *On Human Nature* (1979).

sociolinguistics

Sociolinguistics is the study of all facets of the relation between language and social organization. Although it is a relatively new science—it developed during the early 1960s as an interdisciplinary field combining aspects of ANTHROPOLOGY, LINGUISTICS, social and educational PSYCHOLOGY, and sociology—sociolinguistics has already developed three prominent subdisciplines: sociolinguistic variation, involving the evolution and description of languages; the ethnography of speaking, which examines the social conventions governing linguistic interaction; and the sociology of language, which focuses on how a society's structure affects its choice of a language. All three subdisciplines view language as a social rather than a personal or individual phenomenon, and all share the assumption that language both reflects and contributes to the organization of individuals in societies.

SOCIOLINGUISTIC VARIATION

Late-19th-century dialectologists had already formulated the key concept of sociolinguistic variation—that speakers have available to them different ways of saying the same thing—and went on to note such explanatory factors as geographical area (see GEOGRAPHICAL LINGUISTICS), socioeconomic class, and age. Although the dialectologists took as their data the results of linguistic change, they did not believe that the processes of change could be discerned.

During the first half of the 20th century attention centered on developing new techniques for describing languages—the response of linguists to the growing number and diversity of languages available for study. In 1954, Uriel Weinreich called for greater mutual influence between dialectology and descriptive studies. Nine years later William Labov, the leading developer of current sociolinguistic methodology, demonstrated in a paper, on the spread of two sound changes on Martha's Vineyard, that linguistic change could actually be observed in progress.

Methods of Data Collection. In subsequent studies of English in New York City, first in the Lower East Side (1964) and then in the predominantly black community of south central Harlem (1968), Labov and his coworkers built upon and revised the methods of data collection of American dialectology.

They adapted from sociology more precise methods for measuring social categories as well as the survey techniques of random sampling to ensure that a relatively small population fairly represents a much larger one; they also developed tape-recorded interviewing techniques to maximize the output of the speakers sampled.

Whereas European dialectologists had used only rural and so-called lower-class speakers in their samples, as early as 1933 the American dialectologist Hans Kurath distinguished between lower- and middle-class speakers. Labov's subsequent use of more precise sociological categories succeeded in providing a more detailed view of the social basis of linguistic variation. Labov demonstrated that in the colloquial speech of New York City, the lower-middle class had advanced the pronunciation of /æ/—the vowel-sound of *bad*—toward that of the vowel-sound heard in *beard* to a greater degree than had any other class, including the lower, upper-middle, and upper. (All classes continued to believe that the standard pronunciation of *bad* uses the vowel-sound of *bat*, a word unaffected by the sound change.)

Bilingualism, Pidgins, and Creoles. In 1967, Roger Shuy and Walt Wolfram adapted Labov's methods to investigate social correlates, including class, age, sex, and race, of linguistic variation in Detroit. The next year Joshua Fishman and associates applied sociolinguistic methodology to their study of Spanish and English in a bilingual Puerto Rican community in Jersey City, N.J.

During the 1970s sociolinguists turned their attention to pidgin and creole languages. Never spoken as a first language, a PIDGIN develops exclusively among bilinguals or multilinguals. A CREOLE evolves from a pidgin when the children of pidgin speakers acquire the pidgin as their first language. Using the methodology devised for analyzing variation in speech, Gillian Sankoff studied (1971) the process of creolization of Tok Pisin, a New Guinea pidgin; Derek Bickerton did the same (1977) for the Hawaiian English spoken by first- and second-generation Japanese and Filipino immigrants.

Variation within Languages. In 1958 sociologist Charles Ferguson, citing French and Haitian Creole in Haiti and vernacular and standard Arabic, described a situation in which two varieties of the same language were known throughout the community but used on different occasions. During the same year anthropologist John Fischer examined the distribution in English of the -*in'* and -*ing* variants of such words as *talking* and *nothing*. Although most speakers classified -*ing* as the standard form and -*in'* as a colloquial variant, Fischer found that everyone used both forms on all occasions, with only the proportions changing in different situations. For instance, pupils used -*in'* more often outside of school than in the classroom.

Labov, beginning in the early 1960s, discussed such irreducible variation and developed the concept of the sociolinguistic variable—a linguistic unit always presenting more than one variant but sensitive to social and linguistic context. In a crucial example, he showed (1968) that English speakers variably omit the last consonant of word-final clusters, such as the *t* in *mist* so that it sounds like *miss*. The variable deletion of *t* follows a social pattern of conditioning—speakers omit it more often under some social circumstances (as when addressing a familiar) than under others (as when addressing a stranger). In addition, linguistic factors, such as the phonetic shape of the following word, affect the variation: omission usually precedes a consonant, making *firs' base* (for *first base*) more common than *firs' out*. Also important is the grammatical status of the *t*. The formative element -*ed*, meaning past tense and pronounced *t* in such words as *missed*, is deleted less often than the nonmeaningful *t* of *mist*.

Rules of Variation. Influenced by the rule-writing conventions being developed during the 1960s by Noam CHOMSKY, Morris Halle, and others to explicate phonology and syntax, Labov and his coworkers devised a model for rules of linguistic variation of the type exemplified by the nonarbitrary deletion of final *t* from English consonant clusters. In the early 1970s David Sankoff and Henrietta Cedergren revised the earlier variable-rule model and designed a computer program,

VARBRUL, to test correlations between linguistic and social variants.

Sociologists committed to developing such models or programs are sometimes called variationists. Others see only a limited linguistic application for variable-rule analysis. The Argentinian sociolinguist Beatriz Lavandera has found a correlation in Buenos Aires Spanish between the sex of the speaker and his or her use of the subjunctive and indicative in if-clauses. She questions, however, whether the two variants of the if-clause mean the same thing and suggests that women's preference for the subjunctive reflects only their particular communicative style.

THE ETHNOGRAPHY OF SPEAKING

A second subdiscipline of sociolinguistics, the ethnography of speaking, so-named by Dell Hymes in 1962, deals with aspects of language traditionally of more concern to anthropologists than to linguists. Another term of Hymes's, *communicative competence*, points up the need for linguists to go beyond Chomsky's goal of understanding an individual's ability to create and apprehend sentences and to analyze such extra-sentence-processing abilities as knowing when to speak and when not to speak, knowing the kind of speech appropriate to different occasions, and knowing how to construct and recognize discourses connecting many sentences, such as extended jokes or directions.

ETHNOGRAPHY—the description and classification of cultures—comes to the fore when sociolinguists examine linguistic interaction between small groups or individuals representing different cultures. During the early 1970s, John Gumperz and associates analyzed the verbal communication between white teachers and black students in Oakland, Calif. Labov's 1968 study of the rules for the exchange of ritual insults among black American adolescents, which identified differences in language customs that may lead to gross misinterpretation across cultural boundaries, has already become a classic. Unknowledgeable outsiders often misconstrue this verbal contest as a serious confrontation rather than as a game performed for the entertainment of the players' peers.

THE SOCIOLOGY OF LANGUAGE

The sociology of language explores the social correlates of multilingualism. Joshua Fishman, pursuing questions that crystalized during the early 1960s, has analyzed the conditions that have led some populations to abandon one language in favor of another, while other populations have remained multilingual. The subdiscipline remains distinct from that of sociolinguistic variation in that it always works at the macro-level (involving large groups or societies) and studies the effect of social structure on language choice rather than on linguistic structure.

BENJAMIN WALD

Bibliography: Bailey, Charles-James, and Shuy, Roger, eds., *New Ways of Analyzing Variation in English* (1973); Bauman, Richard, and Scherzer, Joel, eds., *Explorations in the Ethnography of Speaking* (1974); Fishman, Joshua, *The Sociology of Language: An Interdisciplinary Approach to Language in Society* (1972); Giglioli, Pier, ed., *Language and Social Context* (1972); Gumperz, John, and Hymes, Dell, eds., *Directions in Sociolinguistics* (1972); Hall, William, and Freedle, Roy, *Culture and Language: The Black American Experience* (1975); Hymes, Dell, *Foundations in Sociolinguistics: An Ethnographic Approach* (1974); Labov, William, *Language in the Inner City: Studies in the Black English Vernacular* (1972) and *Sociolinguistic Patterns* (1972); Shuy, Roger, ed., *Sociolinguistics: A Crossdisciplinary Perspective* (1971); Trudgill, Peter, *Sociolinguistics: An Introduction* (1974); Whiteley, W. H., ed., *Language Use and Social Change* (1971); Wolfram, Walt, and Fasold, Ralph, *The Study of Social Dialects of American English* (1974).

sociology

Sociology is often described as the study of human social relations or group life or as the science of society. Such descriptions convey very little, for other disciplines within the social sciences—including economics, political science, and much of anthropology and even of history—are also concerned with social life, and the focus of each also falls within the scope of human society. Unlike sociology, however, these other disciplines are each unmistakably linked to a particular aspect of human activity; economics, for example, is concerned with buying and selling; political science, with gov-

ernment; and anthropology, largely with early humankind and with present-day preliterate peoples. The field of sociology, on the other hand, seems to lay claim almost to the whole of human life beyond the biological level because virtually all human activities possess a social aspect—that is, they are engaged in or at least influenced by people together. Thus sociology is perhaps best viewed as a broad perspective on human activities that differs from the particular viewpoints from which such activities are perceived by direct participants or by students of other social scientific disciplines.

THE SOCIOLOGICAL PERSPECTIVE

In analyzing and theorizing about the social aspects of human activity, sociologists have developed a number of important concepts. The most comprehensive of these concepts are the sociological definitions of society and CULTURE. Sociologists use the term *society* to refer to all the social relations and groups formed by human beings; *a society*, as a singular unit, refers to members of a particular population occupying a particular territory.

The term *culture* refers to all ways of thinking, feeling, and acting that people learn from others as members of society (not only to so-called higher aesthetic activities). Culture includes nonsocial skills, such as how to plant crops, drive a car, play the violin, and so on. Apart from the social relationships in which they are taught and learned, such activities are not of primary concern to the sociologist; they are instead studied by the cultural anthropologist, who may take the entire culture of a society, from marriage customs to magic, as a field of inquiry (see ANTHROPOLOGY).

Major Concepts. Social interaction, or the mutual responses of two or more individuals, is perhaps the most basic sociological concept, for such interaction is the elementary component of all the relationships and groups constituting human society. Sociologists who concentrate on the details of particular interactions as they manifest themselves in everyday life are sometimes called micro-sociologists, whereas those concerned with the broader pattern of relations among large organizations, such as those composing the state and the economy, and even among entire societies, are called macro-sociologists. Thus some sociologists study how people avoid bumping into each other on the street or how they open and close telephone conversations, whereas other sociologists study world-systems, or the entire range of economic, political, and other interdependencies among all peoples on Earth (except for a few remaining isolated tribal groups). Most sociologists, however, study social phenomena falling somewhere between these two extremes.

Human interaction both creates and is governed by social NORMS—rules or imagined models of conduct present in people's consciousness that guide and control their interactions. Social norms are the part of culture learned by members of a society that is of special concern to sociologists. The laws enforced by the state are one kind of social norm but by no means the only kind; FOLKWAYS, etiquette, rituals, and fashion

Auguste Comte, considered a founder of sociology, believed that the scientific study of social organization would make possible a reconstitution of the social order based on principles of moral progress. His social philosophy, positivism, cast sociology in the role of a secular, humanistic religion.

The French sociologist Émile Durkheim demonstrated a correlation between cultural values and the quality of individual lives. In his seminal work Suicide (1897), Durkheim identified materialism and mechanization as threats to social and personal stability.

The German social theorist Max Weber made important contributions to political sociology and to the sociology of religion. Weber investigated the relationship between belief systems and economic development in his influential book The Protestant Ethic and the Spirit of Capitalism (1904-05).

are also social norms, although not embodied in legal statutes. Not all norms apply to every member of society, for individuals differ in the parts they play in interaction with others. When these different parts become expectations to which people feel an obligation to conform, they are called social ROLES—clusters of norms and expectations that apply to different classes of persons. Examples of social roles in various societies include those of son, wife, priest, beggar, aristocrat, sales clerk, old man, and warrior.

A SOCIAL GROUP is a plurality of individuals in recurring interaction, their interactions controlled by common norms and differentiated roles. The members of a group are at least partially aware of their membership and perceive the group as a coherent, fairly permanent entity. Groups may vary in size from two or three friends who lunch together to thousands of people, not all of whom are personally acquainted. Any recurring pattern of interaction among individuals playing different roles may be said to possess or to constitute a SOCIAL STRUCTURE. One may therefore speak of the social structure of the American middle-class family, of a nonliterate tribe, of General Motors or Harvard University, of a juvenile gang, or even of American society as a whole. The study of such structures of interlinked roles and groups differentiates sociology proper from SOCIAL PSYCHOLOGY, the study of the impact of norms, roles, and groups on the individual personality.

Sociological concepts range from universal concepts applicable to all societies, such as those just described, to more historically specific concepts, relevant only to some societies in particular times and places, such as the city, bureaucracy, or social class. The sociological perspective brings both kinds of concepts to bear on human activities. The concepts reviewed here amount to a minimum standard vocabulary shared by sociologists. The discipline has expanded in so many different directions, however, creating specialties and subfields employing such a variety of research methods and theoretical approaches, that heterogeneity rather than a single coherent point of view has become its outstanding characteristic.

Subfields. Many of the major subfields of sociology involve the naming of a recognized area of human activity preceded by the phrase "the sociology of." Established fields of teaching and research include sociologies of politics, law, religion, education, industry, art, language (called SOCIOLINGUISTICS), science, medicine, and the city (called urban sociology). The sociologies of some of these areas have been more highly developed than others; some have yet to achieve full recognition as subfields with courses, textbooks, readers, and sometimes journals specifically devoted to them.

Sociologists also study some social phenomena that are not the subjects of any other scholarly discipline; these include MARRIAGE and the FAMILY; CRIME and DEVIANCE; social inequality and stratification; ethnic and racial relations; population growth and its determinants; social gerontology; and the sociology of sex, or gender, differences. Several of these subfields

have a history older than sociology itself. Criminology and DEMOGRAPHY have both become virtually autonomous specialties within sociology, especially in the United States. Criminology has been penetrated by more-general sociological concerns and has tended to become part of the broader study of all kinds of deviant behavior, including those not involving violations of the law. In demography the study of fertility and of migration has been greatly influenced by sociological ideas, but the analysis of mortality and the application of mathematical models to population growth and change are more closely tied to other disciplines.

Sociologists are also active in some subfields that are fully interdisciplinary. The oldest and most important of these subfields is social psychology, which is virtually a separate discipline in its own right, drawing practitioners from both sociology and psychology. Sociological social psychologists have pioneered in the study of interaction in small informal groups (GROUP DYNAMICS); the distribution of beliefs and attitudes in a population, often called PUBLIC OPINION; and how individual personality is shaped through the experience of SOCIALIZATION, or the formation of character and outlook under the influence of the family, the school, the peer group, and other socializing agencies. Psychoanalytic ideas derived from Sigmund Freud and later psychoanalysts have been particularly influential in this last field of social psychology.

A newer interdisciplinary subfield is SOCIOBIOLOGY, which investigates the causal relations between the human genetic constitution and social behavior. Named by the Harvard University entomologist Edward O. Wilson (1929–), sociobiology has attracted a small but vigorous number of sociologists, although it has been assailed by others as a revival of post-Darwinian biological determinism, the rejection of which played a major role in the development of early-20th-century Anglo-American sociology.

Methods. Sociologists make use of nearly all the methods used in the other social sciences and the humanities, from advanced mathematical statistics to the interpretation of texts. Quantitative methods, increasingly refined and adapted to computer technology, continue to play a central role in the discipline, tending to predominate, at least in the United States, in the research reported in sociology journals. Quantitative research draws data from a variety of sources: official statistics, such as those contained in censuses and in reports on crime or unemployment made by government agencies; opinion and attitude surveys based on questionnaires submitted to large samples of people; and computer simulations of social processes.

Qualitative methods range from ethnographic fieldwork to documentary historical research. Such methods, especially direct social observation at the level of everyday life and the interpretative (or hermeneutical) understanding of the meaning of any and all human productions, have been preferred by sociological followers of various newly influential philosophies of human action, including phenomenology, existen-

The school of thought founded by the American sociologist Talcott Parsons seeks to analyze interaction and equilibrium between the component parts of large-scale social systems. Parsons expounded his approach, known as structural-functionalism, in a series of works written during his professorship (1931–74) at Harvard University.

tialism, neo-Hegelian Marxism, post-Wittgensteinian linguistic analysis, and structuralism. These approaches, except perhaps the last, have given priority to the methods of everyday experience and of ordinary language over the quantitative measurement of human conduct and the elaboration of highly abstract conceptual schemes still favored by many sociologists.

HISTORY OF SOCIOLOGY

Origins in Europe. The concept of "civil society" as a realm distinct from the state—as expressed in the writings of Thomas Hobbes, John Locke, and later political thinkers of the Enlightenment—anticipated the subsequent focus of sociology, as did the philosophies of history of the Italian Giambattista Vico and the German G. W. F. Hegel with regard to the study of social change. The first definition of sociology was put forth by the French philosopher Auguste COMTE. In 1838, Comte coined the term *sociology* to describe his vision of a new science that would discover laws of human society resembling the laws of nature by applying the methods of strictly factual investigation that had proved so successful in the physical sciences. The philosopher Herbert SPENCER in England soon took up both Comte's term and his mission.

Several near-contemporaries of Comte and Spencer who never called themselves sociologists are today also counted as founding fathers of the discipline. Karl MARX is the most important among them, but their number also includes Henri de SAINT-SIMON, Alexis de TOCQUEVILLE, and to some extent John Stuart MILL. These men were largely speculative thinkers, although a quite different tradition of empirical, chiefly quantitative reporting of social facts also developed in the 19th century and later became incorporated into academic sociology.

Not until the 1880s and '90s did sociology begin to be recognized as an academic subject. In France, Émile DURKHEIM, the intellectual heir of Comte, taught sociology at the universities of Bordeaux and Paris and founded the first real school of sociological thought. In Germany, not until the first decade of the 20th century was sociology recognized as an academic discipline, largely owing to the efforts of Max WEBER. German sociology, in contrast to the attempt to model the field after the physical sciences dominant in France and the English-speaking countries, was in large part an outgrowth of far-ranging historical scholarship; of a dialogue with Marxism; and of the human-centered focus of German philosophical idealism. The first two emphases were central to Weber's work, and the last predominated in the efforts of Georg SIMMEL to define sociology as a distinctive discipline.

Emergence in the United States. It was in North America that sociology embedded its deepest roots, originally under the influence of Herbert Spencer's efforts to apply the Darwinian idea of evolution to human society. One of the key American Spencerians was William Graham SUMNER, who is believed to have taught the first course in sociology at Yale University as early as 1875. The first sociology professorship on the Eastern seaboard was held (1906) by Lester Ward (1841–1913), a more

critical Spencerian, at Brown University, although the first department of sociology had earlier been established (1893) at the University of Chicago. Following the emergence of a coherent Chicago school after World War I, that city remained the center of American sociology until the 1940s.

Despite its European origins, sociology during the first half of the 20th century became primarily an American subject. After the decline of broad evolutionist theories in the Comtean and Spencerian mode, American sociology grew heavily empirical, quantitative, and oriented to the study of particular social problems, such as crime, marital discord, and the acculturation of immigrants. An exception was the influence at Chicago of George Herbert MEAD, a pragmatist philosopher who had studied in Germany and whose stress on the roots of mind, self, and society in linguistic communication gave rise to an approach named *symbolic interactionism* by the sociologist Herbert Blumer (1900–), one of Mead's students. This approach was largely social psychological and micro-sociological in emphasis. The most eminent sociologist influenced by it today is Erving GOFFMAN, although his individual style and choice of subject defy identification with any school.

In the 1930s, Talcott PARSONS of Harvard University introduced the ideas of the European sociologists Durkheim, Weber, and Vilfredo PARETO in a major work (*The Structure of Social Action*, 1937) that singlehandedly overcame the parochialism of American sociology. Leadership in sociology under the stewardship of such theorists as Parsons and Russian-born Pitirim A. SOROKIN for a time passed to Harvard and on to Columbia University. There a student of Parsons's, Robert K. MERTON, attempted to unite theory, or at least what he called "middle-range theory," with empirical research. He was aided in this effort by the quantitatively skilled Austrian-born sociologist Paul F. Lazarsfeld (1901–76). Another Columbia sociologist, C. Wright MILLS, brought the ideas of Weber and European Marxism to bear on his overall historical analysis of American society. At Harvard, Parsons constructed an elaborate theoretical system that attempted to account for virtually everything in human society. In the 1960s he was assailed by Mills and others, including a new generation of academic Marxists, for his allegedly conservative bias reflected in his relative neglect of group conflict, social change, and the role of power in society.

Recent Developments. In the 1970s the currents of theoretical influence began once again to flow in a westward direction out of Europe. Jürgen Habermas (1929–), the heir of Germany's Frankfurt school of neo-Marxism, emerged as a master synthesizer, the role Parsons had played in the first postwar decades. French neo-Marxist structuralism also became an influence. In addition, a number of highly sophisticated younger British sociologists, of whom Anthony Giddens (1937–) and Steven Lukes (1941–) are among the best known, combined British analytic philosophy with the themes of both European and American micro- and macro-sociology. New versions of symbolic interactionism, systems theory (formerly called structural-functionalism), and phenomenology (especially a school originating in California called ethnomethodology) also flourished on both sides of the Atlantic. At the level of theory as well as of method and subject matter, sociology has become a house of many mansions with no single school of thought, nation, university, or topic holding clear ascendancy.   DENNIS H. WRONG

Bibliography: Berger, P. L., *Invitation to Sociology* (1963); Bottomore, Tom, and Nisbet, Robert, eds., *History of Sociological Analysis* (1978); Coser, L. A., *Masters of Sociological Thought,* 2d ed. (1977); Giddens, Anthony, *Studies in Social and Political Theory* (1977); Goudsblom, Johan, *Sociology in the Balance* (1977); Mills, C. Wright, *The Sociological Imagination* (1959); Parkin, Frank, *Class Inequality and Political Order* (1974); Sykes, Gresham M., *Criminology* (1978); Wrong, D. H., *Population and Society,* 4th ed. (1977); Wrong, D. H., and Gracey, H. L., eds., *Readings in Introductory Sociology,* 3d ed. (1977).

Socotra [suh-koh'-truh]

Socotra, which became a part of Yemen (Aden) in 1967, is a 3,580-km² (1,382-mi²) island in the Indian Ocean, south of Arabia, at the mouth of the Gulf of Aden, 225 km (140 mi)

east of Somalia. The population is 15,000 (1976 est.), and the capital and largest town is Tamrida. Except for narrow coastal plains, Socotra is occupied by the Haggier Mountains. Economic activities include tobacco and date cultivation, the extraction of myrrh and frankincense, fishing, pearl diving, and livestock raising. Known since biblical times, Socotra was held by the Portuguese (1507–11). The inhabitants converted from Christianity to Islam during the 16th and 17th centuries. Socotra became part of Britain's Aden Protectorate in 1886.

Socrates   [sahk'-ruh-teez]

Socrates, the great philosopher of classical Athens, reportedly spent his life in conversation with Athenian citizens, seeking true knowledge and exposing the errors of those who claimed to have wisdom. His persistent questioning so antagonized the city fathers that he was accused of heresy and of corrupting the youth; Socrates was sentenced to death by poisoning in 399 BC.

The life of the Greek philosopher Socrates (469–399 BC) marks such a critical point in Western thought that standard histories divide Greek philosophy into pre-Socratic and post-Socratic periods. Socrates left no writings of his own, and his work has inspired almost as many different interpretations as there have been interpreters. He remains one of the most important and one of the most enigmatic figures in Western philosophy.

As a young man Socrates became fascinated with the new scientific ideas that Anaxagoras and the latter's associate Archelaus had introduced to Athens. He seems for a time to have been the leader of an Athenian research circle—which would explain why the first appearance of Socrates in literature is as a villainous, atheistic scientist in *The Clouds* of Aristophanes. Young Socrates also knew the SOPHISTS and listened to their debates and ceremonial orations.
Socrates and the Sophists. Neither science nor Sophistry, however, could answer a new philosophic question that struck him. The earlier Greek thinkers had been concerned almost wholly with physics and cosmology until the Sophists suggested that what should be done instead was to teach young men skills to satisfy their natural self-interest. Instead, Socrates wondered: "What is a 'self'?" Although "Know Thyself!" was one of three sayings carved on the Temple of Apollo at Delphi, the directive proved difficult to carry out.

The so-called scientific views of the time, particularly that of atomism, defined the self as a physical organ that responded to environmental pressure. Socrates felt, however, that the Sophists, for all their talk of self-interest, had little curiosity about the status of a self; they assumed that it was merely an isolated center constantly greedy for more pleasure, prestige, and power. The Sophists further thought that the values that people advocated were all conventional, varying from one culture to another, and that no one would ever act against his or her own interest, regardless of how many people talked as though they would. This complex of ideas offered little to explain human nature and excellence.
Socrates' Later Life and Thought. Socrates, setting about his search for the self, was convinced of the importance of his

quest. Until educators and teachers knew what human excellence was, he thought, they were engaging in false pretenses by claiming that they knew how to improve students or societies. Socrates believed that objective patterns, or "forms," exist that define human excellence, that these are neither culturally relative nor subjective, and that philosophic inquiry could discover them.

In the period after Athenian defeat in the Peloponnesian War, however, the political leaders did not want to be awakened; uncritical patriotism seemed to them what they and Athens needed. In an attempt to frighten Socrates away, they threatened to bring him to trial for "impiety and corrupting the youth of Athens." Socrates stayed and stood trial. In his APOLOGY, PLATO reconstructs his speech to the jury in defense of his beliefs. He was convicted and executed in 399 BC.
Evaluation. Different observers saw, and still see, Socrates from different perspectives. Plato viewed him as a great philosopher; to the comic poet Aristophanes, he was an irreligious scientist; his friend Xenophon saw him as a tough retired soldier. Each of four later philosophic Socratic schools caught one facet of Socrates and made that their ideal of philosophy.

In modern times Socrates has been admired by Søren Kierkegaard, among others. Martin Heidegger, a major figure in contemporary existential thought, believed that Socrates' search for the self showed that Socrates had indeed discovered and lived the definition of human nature—that "man is the being whose nature is to ask what is his nature."

ROBERT S. BRUMBAUGH

Bibliography: Guthrie, W. K. C., *Socrates* (1971); Levin, Richard, ed., *The Question of Socrates* (1961); Plato, *The Last Days of Socrates,* trans. by Hugh Tredennick (1954; repr. 1961); Spiegelberg, Herbert, and Morgan, B. Q., *The Socratic Enigma* (1964); Strauss, Leo, *Xenophon's Socrates* (1972); Taylor, A. E., *Socrates: The Man and His Thought* (1933); Vlastos, Gregory, ed., *The Philosophy of Socrates* (1971); Xenophon, *Recollections of Socrates,* trans. by Anna S. Benjamin (1965).

Socrates Scholasticus   [skoh-las'-ti-kuhs]

The Greek historian Socrates "Scholasticus," *c.*380–*c.*450, is best known for his church history, designed as a continuation of EUSEBIUS OF CAESAREA's *Historia ecclesiastica.* The work is arranged in seven books, each of which covers the life of one of the Roman emperors from 305 to 439.

soda

Soda is the collective name for several forms of sodium carbonate; the most commercially important form is the dehydrated product soda ash (Na_2CO_3). The decahydrate ($Na_2CO_3 \cdot 10H_2O$) is also known as washing soda or sal soda. Soda ash is so called because it was once extracted from plant ashes; now almost all is manufactured by the Solvay or ammonia-soda process (see SOLVAY PROCESS). The primary users of soda are the glass and chemical industries. Sodium carbonate occurs in nature in combination with the bicarbonate as trona and is recovered from evaporated lakes in California.

See also: SODIUM.

soda niter: see NITRATE MINERALS.

sodalite

Sodalite is a comparatively rare chlorine-containing aluminum-sodium silicate. It is usually found as granular or nodular masses in volcanic and intrusive rocks. Commonly blue in color, it may be white, gray, green, or red, and often it is used in ornaments.

Sodalite ($Na_4Al_3Si_3O_{12}Cl$), a relatively rare sodium aluminosilicate, is one of the FELDSPATHOID minerals. (Lazulite, a blue variety containing sulfur, is the principal component of LAPIS LAZULI.) Sodalite forms dodecahedral crystals (isometric system), embedded grains, and concentric nodules. Gray, greenish, yellowish, or white in color, it has a hardness of 5½ to 6, a vitreous luster, and a specific gravity of 2.3 to 2.5. Sodalite occurs with other feldspathoids in igneous rocks that have crystallized from sodium-rich magma.

Soddy, Frederick [sahd'-ee]

The British physicist Frederick Soddy, b. Sept. 2, 1877, d. Sept. 22, 1956, received (1921) the Nobel Prize for chemistry for the conception of isotopes and the displacement law of radioactive change. With Ernest RUTHERFORD he developed the disintegration theory of radioactivity, which explained radioactivity as the decay of atoms to form other elements. Soddy proposed the isotope concept—that atoms could have the same chemical identity but different atomic weights. His displacement law of radioactive change suggests that an element emitting an alpha particle becomes a new element with a lower atomic number, whereas emission of a beta particle raises the element's atomic number.   ROBERT J. PARADOWSKI

Bibliography: Howarth, Muriel, *Pioneer Research on the Atom* (1958).

Söderberg, Hjalmar [sur'-dur-bairg, hee-ahl'-mahr]

The Swedish writer Hjalmar Erik Fredrik Söderberg, b. July 2, 1869, d. Oct. 14, 1941, was an opponent of both Christianity and Nazism. His first novel, the pessimistic *Martin Birck's Youth* (1901; Eng. trans., 1930), draws on autobiographical materials; it was followed by the controversial *Doctor Glas* (1905; Eng. trans., 1963), which explores the events leading up to a murder. Söderberg's economical style is apparent throughout his four volumes of short stories.

Söderblom, Nathan [sur'-dur-blohm]

A Swedish Lutheran theologian, Nathan Söderblom, b. Jan. 15, 1866, d. July 12, 1931, promoted the "Life and Work" movement, a branch of the ecumenical movement. He taught at universities in Uppsala and Leipzig before his appointment (1914) as archbishop of Uppsala. Söderblom was a leading organizer of the Universal Christian Conference on Life and Work at Stockholm in 1925, an effort to promote Christian influence on political, social, and economic life. In 1930 he was awarded the Nobel Peace Prize.

Bibliography: Sundkler, Bengt, *Nathan Söderblom* (1968).

Södergran, Edith [sur'-dur-grahn]

Now credited with introducing modernism to Finland, the Swedish-language poet Edith Irene Södergran, b. Apr. 4, 1892, d. June 24, 1923, went virtually unrecognized during her lifetime. The extreme individualism and visionary aestheticism characteristic of her poetry reveal the influence of Nietzsche and Walt Whitman. *Landet som icke är* (The Land That Is Not, 1925) contains some of her best work. She had little contact with other writers, but generations of Swedish and Finnish poets subsequently learned from her, and her fame has continued to grow.

sodium

The chemical element sodium is a soft, silver-colored metal, waxlike at room temperature but becoming brittle as the temperature falls. Its symbol is Na; atomic weight, 22.9898; and atomic number, 11. Sodium is a member of the ALKALI METALS, a family that includes lithium, potassium, rubidium, cesium, and francium.

HISTORY

Compounds of sodium were known and used extensively during ancient times, but the highly reactive nature of the element prevented its preparation as a pure substance until 1807. Until recently the Natron valley near Cairo, Egypt, because it is below sea level, annually formed lakes upon inundation by the floodwaters of the Nile. These lakes become nearly dry during summer, leaving a deposit of a white, salt-like substance that came to be called "natron." For thousands of years it has been used for embalming, in ceramic pastes, as a detergent, and, when mixed with sand, in the production of glass. We now know that natron, or natrum, is principally sodium carbonate containing smaller quantities of sodium bicarbonate, sodium sulfate, and sodium chloride.

As chemistry evolved from alchemy, natron, niter, and soda (sodium carbonate) were recognized as identities, although it was many years before potassium carbonate was differentiated from the sodium salt. Although differences were recognized, both were known as ALKALI. Sodium was called mineral alkali, or soda, and the potassium carbonate was known as vegetable alkali, or potash.

In 1807, Humphry Davy, director of the laboratory of the Royal Institution and one of the earliest electrochemists, electrolytically produced a heretofore unknown element from molten potash. Because of its source, he called it POTASSIUM. Within days Davy repeated the experiment using molten soda, and after increasing the voltage of his electrical source, produced another elemental metal, which he named sodium.

OCCURRENCE

Because of its extreme reactivity, sodium is not found free in nature, nor can it be used in its elemental state except by using methods that exclude oxygen from the process. The seventh most prevalent element, sodium composes 2.83% of the Earth's crust, and the annual world consumption of sodium and sodium compounds is more than 100,000,000 tons, ranking sodium usage in the same range as iron. The seas are large reservoirs of sodium as common salt, sodium chloride (NaCl); tremendous subterranean deposits of salt are common throughout the world, as exemplified by the still-worked beds discovered in Poland in 1251 and by similar beds in Kansas, Oklahoma, Texas, Louisiana, Ohio, Michigan, and New York. Sodium is present in basalt, lava, feldspar, and as sodium silicate in the various sands and silicate rocks of the Earth. Although the element is not essential to plant life, it is normally found in plants, principally as sodium chloride. Sodium is essential to all animal life.

PROPERTIES

Sodium is a soft metal, easily cut with a knife or pressed into wire. Its melting point is 97.81° C, and it boils at 882.9° C. Its density is 0.97, slightly less than that of water. Sodium has only one stable isotope, mass number 23.

Sodium reacts readily with a large variety of elements and compounds by acting as a reducing agent; that is, it reacts by giving up (losing) an electron. The tendency to do so is so strong that sodium can replace hydrogen from water: $2Na + 2H_2O \rightarrow 2NaOH + H_2$. The reaction is very vigorous, often generating enough heat to ignite the hydrogen gas and cause an explosion. Sodium forms compounds in which its valence is +1. Some of its typical reactions with inorganic materials are:

$2Na + F_2 \rightarrow 2NaF$ (sodium fluoride; reactions with all halogens are similar)
$4Na + O_2 \rightarrow 2Na_2O$ (sodium oxide)
$2Na + O_2 \rightarrow Na_2O_2$ (sodium peroxide)
$2Na + S \rightarrow Na_2S$ (sodium sulfide)
$6Na + N_2 \rightarrow 2Na_3N$ (sodium azide)
$3Na + P \rightarrow Na_3P$ (sodium phosphide)
$2Na + H_2 \rightarrow 2NaH$ (sodium hydride)
$2Na + 2H^+ \rightarrow 2Na^+ + H_2$ (sodium ion)
$2Na + 2NH_3 \xrightarrow{\text{catalyst}} 2NaNH_2 + H_2$ (sodamide)

A typical reaction with organic compounds is:
$2Na + 2ROH \rightarrow 2NaOR + H_2$ (an alkoxide, where R is either an alkyl or aryl compound)

PRODUCTION

Elemental sodium is prepared by the electrolysis of molten sodium chloride, whether laboratory or commercial quantities are desired. Large quantities are readily produced using the Downs cell (see CHLORINE). The sale of the chlorine by-product produced by this method helps reduce the cost of the sodium.

Although sodium can now be purchased in any quantity and with prompt shipment, small quantities can be made in the laboratory by the earliest of practical methods, the reduction of sodium carbonate by carbon: $Na_2CO_3 + 2C \rightarrow 2Na + 3CO$. Purification of the metal is commonly accomplished by distillation in a dry atmosphere.

USES

Both its high reactivity and its cost prevent the use of large quantities of elemental sodium. Sizable quantities are, however, used in the production of sodium vapor lamps for inexpensive highway lighting and as the coolant in liquid-metal fast-breeder reactors (LMFBR) under study in the United States, Great Britain, Germany, and France. The Soviet Union's reactor of this type began operation in 1972. Using sodium chloride rather than pure metal, the United States developed a molten-salt reactor (MSR) that operated almost flawlessly for 4 years before being shut down in 1969 for the design study that precedes scale-up to a larger unit. Significant amounts of the metal are used in such metallurgical processes as removing antimony from lead and oxygen from silver. Sodium amalgams (solutions in mercury) of various sodium concentrations are useful and manageable reducing agents, even in contact with water. When dispersed on carbon supports it is used as a catalyst for various organic reactions, such as the production of 4-methyl-1-pentene from its monomer, propene.

Sodium Hydroxide. In contrast to the free element, compounds of sodium have industrial uses that require millions of tons annually. Perhaps the most important of these compounds is sodium chloride (NaCl), from which over 10 million tons of sodium hydroxide (NaOH) were made in 1970. Sodium hydroxide, also called caustic soda, is essential to the production of soap, detergents, cleaning compounds, dyes, cosmetics, and pharmaceuticals. It is also necessary in the manufacture of rayon, cellophane, phenol, naphthol, resorcinol, and oxalic acid. Such industrial processes as boiler-water softening, food processing, engraving, printing, pulp and paper production, petroleum refining, metallurgy, and household-bleach preparation all depend on it.

Although historically sodium hydroxide has been made from sodium carbonate (Na_2CO_3) and is still so made to a small extent in the pulp and paper industry, nearly all is now produced electrolytically in either the diaphragm or Downs cell or by the mercury-cell process. In the latter process the cathode is a flowing film of mercury in which the free sodium amalgamates (dissolves) as rapidly as it is formed and is thus removed from the reaction vessel. The second step destroys this amalgam by the addition of water, which causes it to decompose into hydrogen gas, sodium hydroxide, and mercury, the last then being recycled back into the process. Unfortunately, the recycling is not quite complete, and mercury is lost to the environment at the rate of 2 kg (4½ lb) per day, even in the better operations.

Sodium Carbonate. Though widely used in the chemical industry, sodium carbonate (Na_2CO_3), soda ash, is principally consumed by the glass industry, in which nearly 7 million tons are needed annually. Large quantities are used as well in sewage treatment and in water softening for municipalities and industry. Sodium carbonate is also used in the production of the sodium acetate used in textile dyeing and leather tanning and for making sodium arsenate as well.

Other important compounds manufactured from sodium carbonate are sodium bisulfite, sodium sulfite, sodium carboxymethyl cellulose, sodium perborate, sodium linoleate, sodium thiosulfate, and sodium hydrosulfide.

Sodium arsenate and sodium arsensite are pesticides and bacteriocides. Sodium sulfite and bisulfite are used in photographic products and in the pulp-and-paper and textile industries. In cleaning compounds, sodium carboxymethyl cellulose prevents the redeposition of soils loosened by detergents. Sodium perborate is used in dentifrices, deodorants, and cold-wave neutralizers. Sodium linoleate is used as a drier in paints. Sodium thiosulfate is an antioxidant used in cosmetics

and an image fixer in photography. Sodium hydrosulfide removes hair in the tanning of leather. Natural sodium carbonate is obtained in the United States principally from brines of the dry lakes in southern California and from deep deposits in Wyoming. Sodium hypochlorite (NaOCl), sodium chlorite ($NaClO_2$), and sodium chlorate ($NaClO_3$) find use in ore preparation, defoliants, explosives, rocket fuels, and herbicides, although they are best known for their bleaching and sanitation uses (see CHLORINE).

Sodium Silicate. Although often written as Na_2SiO_3, sodium silicate is a complex mixture of Na_2O and SiO_2. Since the proportion of silicon dioxide may vary, a more correct notation of its formula might be $Na_2O \cdot xSiO_2$. It is commercially called water glass and is produced by fusing high-purity sand (SiO_2) and sodium carbonate.

Variation in the Na_2O/SiO_2 ratio produces properties that allow its use as builders in soaps and detergents, as lubricants in petroleum recovery, as catalysts, as desiccants, and as adhesives. Large quantities of sodium silicate adhesives are used in making fiberboard boxes, because the quick setting permits low-cost, continuous, high-speed manufacture of corrugated boxes.

In the form of silica gel, sodium silicate has a high surface area and therefore a great capacity for moisture absorption. It is used in catalytic processes, as a drying agent, as fillers, and as pigments. When very finely ground it can be used as a pigment in the production of colored rubbers. It is an effective coagulant in removing suspended solids from water and wastewater, and it is also used as a corrosion inhibitor.

The construction industry uses sodium silicates to stabilize soils and to seal against moisture seepage. It fireproofs flammable insulations and makes concrete acid-resistant. Surface coating with sodium silicate waterproofs concrete, increases its hardness, and increases its stain resistance. Metal producers use these silicates as deflocculants in ore floation and in the production of cores and molds.

Other Sodium Compounds. Sodium metasilicate is used in heavy-duty cleaning operations, such as industrial floors and walls, bottling equipment, and dairy clean-up. Sodium acid pyrophosphate controls the carbon dioxide produced in baking to improve production scheduling. It also sequesters iron to prevent food discoloration. Disodium phosphate is used as an emulsifier in the production of processed food spreads, in preparing instant pudding mixes and quick-cooking cereals, and in meat-curing solutions. Sodium metaphosphate is a water softener and is used in dentifrices with sodium fluorophosphate.

The first of the modern synthetic detergents, Tide, was introduced in 1947 by Proctor and Gamble. This combination of a syndet (synthetic detergent), sodium alkylbenzene, with sodium tripolyphosphate leaves no residue and improves cleaning action.

In the form of a naturally occurring sodium mineral known as cryolite, sodium aluminum fluoride is used in tremendous quantities in the production of aluminum metal. The demand is so great that more than 200 million pounds of synthetic sodium aluminum fluoride are produced each year to augment the natural supply.   CHARLES HOWARD

Bibliography: Alexander, W. O., and Street, A. C., *Metals in The Service of Man* (1972); Cotton, F. A., and Wilkinson, Geoffrey, *Basic Inorganic Chemistry* (1976); Hart, W. A., et al., *The Chemistry of Lithium, Sodium, Potassium, Rubidium, Cesium, and Francium* (1975); Pauling, Linus, *General Chemistry*, 3d ed. (1970).

sodium pentothal

Sodium pentothal is an extremely fast-acting barbiturate whose generic name is thiopental sodium. It is a central-nervous-system depressant that, when injected into the bloodstream, rapidly produces deep sleep from which arousal also occurs rapidly. Sodium pentothal is used most commonly to put patients to sleep for surgical operations or dental work. It has also been used, however, to produce a kind of chemical trance during which suppressed memories may be recalled or psychotherapeutic suggestions reinforced—hence its popular, inaccurate name, "truth serum."   RICHARD H. RUNSER

sodium pump: see BIOPOTENTIAL.

Sodom and Gomorrah

According to Genesis 19, Sodom and Gomorrah were two "cities of the Plain" that God destroyed with a rain of "brimstone and fire" as punishment for their evil ways. Before the destruction God warned LOT to leave Sodom and not to look back; Lot's wife, who looked back on the burning city, was turned into a pillar of salt. The cities were probably located at the southern end of the Dead Sea and devastated by an earthquake c.1900 BC.

Sodoma, Il   [soh'-doh-mah]

The paintings of Il Sodoma, b. Giovanni Antonio Bazzi, 1477, d. Feb. 14 or 15, 1549, demonstrate the degree to which individual Renaissance styles were based on the work of such great masters as Leonardo da Vinci and Raphael. Sodoma's early Milanese pictures, not surprisingly, reflect Leonardo's style. By 1501, when he had moved to Siena, Sodoma's frescoes showed the influence of such Central Italian painters as Pintoricchio, Luca Signorelli, and Perugino, as seen in his *Life of Saint Benedict* (1505-08; Mont'Oliveto Maggiore, Chiusure, Siena). Having visited Rome in 1508 and 1516-17, Sodoma came under the influence of Raphael and Baldassare Peruzzi, as seen in his *Marriage of Alexander and Roxanne* (1516-17; Villa Farnesina, Rome).   WILLIAM HOOD

Bibliography: Cust, Robert H. H., *Giovanni Antonio Bazzi* (1906); Freedberg, Sydney J., *Painting in Italy 1500-1600* (1970).

sodomy

Sodomy has been defined as carnal copulation against the order of nature and is considered a crime at common law. The name is derived from the ancient biblical town of Sodom, destroyed by heavenly fire for its wickedness. Acts of sodomy include "unnatural," or "deviant" (noncoital, usually referring to anal), sexual intercourse between persons of the same sex or of different sexes. Sodomy was made a felony in England during the early 16th century and carried a severe punishment.

Objections have been raised in recent years to statutes that punish "deviant" sexual activity between consenting adults in private. It is argued that persons should not be interfered with so long as their activities are not injurious to the public welfare or seriously harmful to others. This argument relies on the "right of privacy" (see PRIVACY, INVASION OF) decisions of the U.S. Supreme Court. In the 1969 case of *Stanley* v. *Georgia*, for example, the Court held that a statute penalizing the mere personal possession of pornographic material was an unconstitutional interference with the right of privacy and 1st Amendment freedoms. There was, said the Court, "a right to be free, except in very limited circumstances, from governmental intrusions into one's privacy."

Other students of this problem contend that parents' interest in protecting their children against sexual practices that they consider wrong justifies action by the state. They approve statutes punishing acts of sodomy by forcible compulsion or with children or intoxicated or mentally ill persons. In 1975 a federal district court upheld the constitutionality of Virginia's sodomy laws, a decision the Supreme Court affirmed (1976). State legislatures, however, have begun to remove or to decrease criminal penalties for such "deviant" activity.

Bibliography: Barnett, Walter E., *Sexual Freedom and the Constitution* (1973).

Sofala   [soh-fah'-lah]

Sofala (formerly Beira), a port in east central Mozambique and the second largest city of the country, lies on the Mozambique Channel of the Indian Ocean and has a population of 130,000 (1970 est.). Food processing and cement factories, cotton mills, and railroad and ship repair shops are the main industrial plants. The port has been severely affected by the civil war in Zimbabwe, which led to a British blockade in 1965 and the closure of rail links across the Zimbabwe-Mozambique border in 1976. Sofala was founded in 1891 by the Mozambique Company of Portugal on the site of an Arab settlement dating back to the 10th century.

Sofia   [soh-fee'-uh]

Sofia is the capital and largest city of Bulgaria. The political, cultural, industrial, and commercial center of the nation, Sofia is located in the western part of Bulgaria on a plateau surrounded by the Balkan Mountains. Sofia's population (1977 est., 1,020,700), representing about 12% of the national total, is composed mainly of native Bulgarians. Annual precipitation is about 635 mm (25 in), and the average annual temperature is 11° C (51° F).

Contemporary City. Sofia is a modern city of wide boulevards and streets arranged in a grid pattern. Soviet-style architecture characterizes the majority of the post–World War II buildings, and new communities of apartment houses ring the city. Parks and gardens, mineral springs, and the surrounding mountains attract tourists.

Sofia's most important industries produce metal goods, heavy machinery, textiles, processed foods, rubber, leather goods, paper products, and chemicals. The city is also the major market center for Bulgaria's agricultural products and a transportation hub with connections to the rest of the country. The international airport provides service to 50 foreign countries, and the international railroad line of the famous Orient Express passes through Sofia.

The region surrounding Sofia is mostly agricultural but contains workable deposits of anthracite and lignite (at the nearby town of Dimitrovo), lead, zinc, and iron ores.

The University of Sofia (1888) is the major institution of higher education. The city is the site of the National Art Gallery, the Cyril and Methodius National Library, and the National Theater. Among its notable buildings are the Alexander Nevsky Cathedral (consecrated 1924), the churches of Saint George (4th century) and Saint Sofia (6th century), a 16th-century mosque, and the mausoleum of Georgi M. Dimitrov, the founder of the People's Republic of Bulgaria.

Two famous structures symbolize Sofia's diverse cultural heritage—the Buyuk Dzhamiya (foreground), a 16th-century Turkish mosque, and Alexander Nevsky Cathedral (center, background), dedicated to Russian troops killed in the war of Bulgarian liberation (1876–78).

Administratively, Sofia is divided into seven municipal districts. In recent years the Bulgarian government has deliberately slowed the growth rate of the city.

History. Sofia was founded in AD 29 on the site of an 8th-century-BC Thracian settlement by the Romans, who named it Ulpia Serdica. The city was destroyed by Attila the Hun in 447 but was rebuilt in the 6th century by the Byzantines, who renamed it Triaditsa. It was the capital of the first and second Bulgarian empires (809–1018, 1186–1396) and after 1396 was ruled by Turks. In 1879, Sofia became the capital of independent Bulgaria.

IVAN VOLGYES

soft-coated Wheaten terrier

The soft-coated Wheaten terrier is a medium-sized working terrier with a soft, shaggy coat. Native to Ireland and related to the Irish and Kerry blue terriers, it has been used as a farm and hunting dog. The breed was introduced into the United States in 1946.

The soft-coated Wheaten terrier has long been used as a drover, a home and stable guard, and a vermin dog in its native Ireland, but it has received official recognition only recently. The Irish Kennel Club recognized the breed in 1937, the English Kennel Club in 1943, and the American Kennel Club in 1973. A male Wheaten terrier stands 46 to 48 cm (18 to 19 in) at the withers and weighs 16 to 20 kg (35 to 45 lb). Wheaten terriers have small, drop ears and short, docked tails. The Wheaten-colored, medium-sized coat is profuse and soft, covering the entire animal in large, wavy or curled locks. The breed is less aggressive toward other dogs than is common with most terriers.

JOHN MANDEVILLE

Bibliography: Braund, Kathryn, *The Uncommon Dog Breeds* (1975); Marvin, John T., *Book of All Terriers*, 2d ed. (1976).

softball

Softball is a sport similar to BASEBALL, played in the localities where baseball is also popular. The game is played with a larger ball—11.8–12.1 in. (30.1–30.7 cm) in circumference—on a smaller field, and with the same basic equipment as that used in baseball. More than 27 million adults and children of both sexes played some form of competitive or recreational softball in the United States in 1978, making it one of the largest team sports in the country.

Softball is a popular alternative to baseball for women at both the high school and college levels. During the 1970s men's and women's professional leagues were formed—the North American Professional Slo-Pitch League for men and the Women's Professional Fast-Pitch League.

Before the formation of professional leagues, softball was played primarily on a regional basis with national tournaments. Joan Joyce, who is credited with pitching more than 130 no-hitters, earned fame while leading Connecticut and California teams to amateur championships. Eddie Feigner

A young girl awaits her pitch as opponents look on during a softball game. Because it requires less equipment and offers less potential for serious injuries than does conventional baseball, softball is widely accepted as an athletic activity for school-age children.

traveled widely with a four-man team known as "The King and His Court," combining softball skills with slapstick comedy. Feigner is reported to have pitched more than 750 no-hit games and 200 perfect games (no runs, no hits, no walks).

Fast pitch and slow pitch are the two most popular styles of softball. Softball games customarily last seven innings. The ball is pitched underhand in all versions. Fast pitch is played with teams of 9 players, slow pitch with 10 players per side. Approximately 85 percent of the registered amateur teams in the U.S. in 1978 played the slow-pitch game. The ball is pitched slowly in a high arc, making it an easy target for hitters. Thus the emphasis in the slow-pitch game is on hitting and on defensive abilities. Slow pitch is usually a high-scoring game. Fast-pitch games are more often low-scoring games and are usually dominated by pitchers.

In fast-pitch softball, bases are 60 ft (18.3 m) apart, and the pitcher's mound is 46 ft (14 m) from home plate, although women sometimes play on a smaller field. The standard 12-in. (30.5-cm) ball is used, and bats are generally lighter and shorter than those used in regular baseball.

Slow-pitch softball is played on a field of the same size, but the pitcher is required to lob the ball in such a way that its flight has no less than a 3-ft (0.91-m) arc, with the ball crossing the plate on its downward flight. Slow-pitch teams use either the standard 12-in. ball or larger ones up to 16 in. (40.6 cm) in circumference. Bunting is not allowed, and base runners are not allowed to leave the bases until the ball is hit. Base stealing is not allowed. The 10th player is used either as a short fielder, roving the area between the infield and outfield, or as a fourth outfielder. Hollow metal-alloy bats are widely used in softball.

Softball originated in Chicago in 1887 as a form of indoor baseball, played with a 16-in. ball. The forerunner of the present-day game was developed in Minneapolis, Minn., by Lewis Rober. Softball went through a series of changes, and each region had its own rules until a rules committee standardized (1923) the game.

The Amateur Softball Association, founded in 1933, is the largest softball governing body in the United States, with more than 100,000 registered teams, in both fast- and slow-pitch leagues, in 1978. The United States Slo-Pitch Softball Association (USSSA) was founded in 1969 and registered approximately 7,500 teams in 1978.

CURT SYLVESTER

Bibliography: Clickener, Robert, *Official's Manual: Softball* (1979); Joyce, Joan, and Anquillare, John, *Winning Softball* (1975); Walsh, Loren, *Contemporary Softball* (1978).

software, computer

Software is a general term for computer programs, in contrast to hardware, which is physical computer equipment (see PRO-

GRAMMING, COMPUTER). Although software includes all programs, the term is most commonly applied to programs that are intended to be useful in a variety of applications or to a variety of users of a particular type of computer. Examples are compilers, general-purpose subroutines, and programs used for producing and editing documents. Software is often the most significant part of a computer system.

SUSAN OWICKI AND ELLIOTT ORGANICK

soil

The term *soil* generally refers to the loose surface of the Earth, as distinguished from solid rock. To the farmer or agronomist, soil is the natural medium for growth of all land plants; civil engineers consider soil an easily disaggregated earth material that supports most foundations, roads, runways, and other constructed works and from which earth dams, embankments, and other earth structures are built.

SOILS AND FARMING

The term *soil* as used in agricultural contexts can be more specifically defined as a thin layer of loose earth materials composed of weathered minerals and decaying organic matter. It provides physical support and nutrients as well as sufficient quantities of air and water for plant growth. Specialists who study and manage soils as a medium for plant growth are called agronomists, or soil scientists.

Soil Profile. All mature soils are made up of a sequence of distinct layers, called horizons, that roughly parallel the Earth's surface. These horizons commonly range from a few centimeters to a few meters in thickness, and each horizon in the sequence differs markedly from the other horizons in chemical, physical, and biological properties. A section cut downward from the surface through the various soil horizons forms the soil profile. From the surface downward, the major soil horizons are designated A, B, and C, respectively. In some cases these layers are further divided into subhorizons designated A1, A2, B1, and so forth. The A horizon (topsoil) is characterized by high biotic activity and an accumulation of organic matter. Water percolating through the A horizon commonly carries fine-grained materials (principally clay particles and colloidal organic matter) downward and deposits them in a zone of accumulation called the B horizon. Thus a principal distinguishing characteristic of the B horizon is a high clay content. The A and B horizons together make up the solum, or true soil. The C horizon is composed of relatively unaltered materials underlying the B horizon.

The soil profile is dynamic because it changes with time. Four states of profile development are commonly recognized in the life cycle of a soil: parent material, immature soil, mature soil, and old-age soil. Soils begin their development with parent materials—loose earth materials laid down by wind, water, or glacial ice, or materials weathered in place from rocks. Exposure of the parent material to the weather in most climates results in the establishment of plants. The plants die and leave organic residues on which animals, bacteria, and fungi feed, breaking the residues down to more elementary chemical forms. The breakdown sets nutrients free, making the parent material more fertile for another cycle of plant growth. As more and more organic matter is worked into the parent material, the upper layer assumes a darker color, and an A horizon develops. Such a soil has only A and C horizons and is in the immature stage. This amount of profile development commonly takes less than 100 years.

Continued weathering, which is usually accelerated by the actions of plant growth, releases additional nutrients into the soil. This action leads to greater plant growth and more demanding species. Weathering also breaks the soil particles down to finer sizes, the smallest of which may be carried downward by percolating water to an underlying soil layer. These finer particles accumulate in the underlying layer,

The color of a soil indicates the climatic conditions under which it formed and its composition. The dark soils (1) of cold tundra regions are derived from humus, or partially decomposed vegetation. Light-colored desert soils (2) have little vegetation and humus. The humus-rich earth of semiarid grasslands varies from chestnut-brown (3) to the black of chernozem (4) as rainfall increases. Iron-containing red latosol soils (5) are found in tropical grasslands. Acid podzol soils form in cool humid climates. They include brown deciduous forest soil (6), red yellow pine-forest soil (7), gray brown deciduous forest podzol (8), and gray white mixed pine- and deciduous-forest soils (9).

Soil profiles, or cross sections, may be divided into four layers, or horizons. Humus (A$_0$) forms the uppermost portion of the topsoil horizon (A), which covers a mixed organic-inorganic subsoil layer (B) that lies above a partially weathered rock zone (C). Unchanged bedrock (D) forms the bottom layer. Soil types vary with climate. Acid brown earth on sandy rock (1) and cultivated brown earth (2) are seen in temperate climates. Leached peat pedzol (3) is found in cold, wet climates. Iron-rich brown oxisol (4) is seen in warm, humid areas.

A$_0$

A

B

C

D

1	2	3	4

	A	leached acid horizon
	A	organomineral horizon
	A	plowed or cultivated
	A$_0$	fresh litter and humus
	B	enriched in oxidized iron
	B	enriched in mineral humus
	C	weathered rock zone

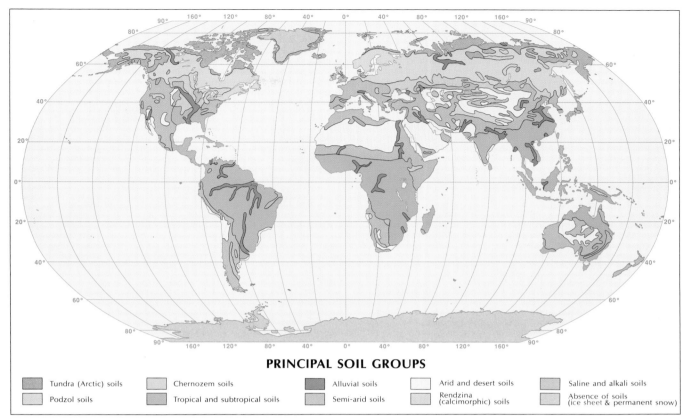

PRINCIPAL SOIL GROUPS

- Tundra (Arctic) soils
- Podzol soils
- Chernozem soils
- Tropical and subtropical soils
- Alluvial soils
- Semi-arid soils
- Arid and desert soils
- Rendzina (calcimorphic) soils
- Saline and alkali soils
- Absence of soils (ice sheet & permanent snow)

forming the B horizon. Soils having all three (A, B, and C) layers are termed *mature*.

With continued weathering, nearly all of the mineral nutrients may be released and removed from the soil by plant growth and water percolation. This stage is in many cases accompanied by the development of deleterious acidic by-products. When soil nutrients have been removed or deleterious by-products have accumulated to an extent that retards plant growth, the soil is said to have reached old age. Fortunately, such processes as erosion, flooding, dust storms, and volcanic eruptions expose or provide new, unweathered parent material to begin a new soil life cycle.

Physical and Chemical Composition. The physical and chemical compositions of soil horizons also differ according to the various conditions under which soils develop. These differences form the basis for categorizing soils into different soil groups and types. The five major factors that control the kinds of soil that develop are climate, particularly temperature and precipitation; living organisms, especially the types of native vegetation; the nature of the parent material (chemical and mineralogical composition as well as particle size); topography (ground slope and elevation); and time.

Climate is the most influential of the factors controlling soil development. Part of this influence, however, comes from the control it has on other factors, such as the types of plants that can grow in a given climate. Temperature and precipitation control the rates and types of chemical and physical processes that are active in weathering parent materials. Weathering in turn controls the rate of nutrient release and the profile development. For instance, in arid regions, where the weathering process is slow, soil profiles are much shallower and generally less well developed than in humid regions. Soils in cold regions tend to be shallower than soils in warm regions, and the mineral and organic matter in cold-region soils tends to be less decomposed.

Perhaps the second most important factor controlling soil development is living organisms. The rate of organic matter accumulation and, to some extent, of weathering is dependent on plant growth. Chemical composition is in part dependent on the types of plants growing on the soil. For example, the soils that develop under grasslands are chemically different from soils that develop under forests. Even within forested areas different soil profiles develop under conifer trees than under deciduous trees. In places where organic matter is produced faster than it can be decomposed and reused by new plant growth, an organic-rich horizon, or O horizon, develops on top of the soil profile. Such soils are called peats and normally form in marshy or boggy areas.

The type of parent material has a great influence on the texture (particle sizes and shapes) and chemistry of the soil matrix. These factors in turn directly influence soil-profile development. For example, the rate of downward movement of water is controlled in part by the texture of the soil. Also, chemical and mineralogical composition affects rates of weathering; for instance, olivine minerals weather much faster than do quartz minerals. Chemical composition has some influence on the species of plants that grow in the soil; for example, only salt-resistant plants will grow in saline soils. The influence of parent material on soil characteristics is much more pronounced in younger than in older soils.

Topography affects soil development largely by influencing drainage and erosion. Excess water is removed much more slowly over smooth, flat terrain than over rolling terrain. Water may accumulate in some lowlands and depressions to form swamps, marshes, and bogs (see SWAMP, MARSH, AND BOG). Erosion is more active on sloping ground than on flat ground. Each of these factors has an important influence on the depth and character of the soil profile.

Finally, soils evolve with time; soils on relatively new surfaces, such as an eroded area or an area covered by glacial debris from the most recent ice age, may be very different from nearby soils that appear to be in similar settings but have developed on an older landscape surface.

The physical properties of a soil have much to do with its

suitability as a medium for plant growth, a fact that has been recognized by farmers from the beginnings of modern civilization. Thus an understanding of basic soil properties, combined with the use of procedures developed by modern technology for managing and improving soils, has led to revolutionary advances in crop production. These advances are necessary to provide food and fiber for a growing world population.

SOILS AND ENGINEERING

To the engineer, the materials making up the Earth's crust are divided into the categories of soil and rock. Soil is a natural aggregate of mineral grains often containing some organic particles that can be separated into individual aggregates by such gentle mechanical actions as agitation in water. In contrast, rock is a natural aggregate of mineral grains held together by strong and permanent cohesive bonds; these bonds resist rupture even when subjected to vigorous mechanical actions such as striking the rock with a hammer. What the agronomist terms *soil* extends downward only to about the depth of root penetration, which is seldom more than a few feet. What the engineer terms *soil* extends from the ground surface down to its contact with a layer of hard rock, which in many localities is hundreds of feet below the surface. Engineers who deal with soils are a specialized group of civil engineers known as geotechnical engineers, and the branch of physical science dealing with the mechanical behavior of soils is called soil mechanics.

Engineers use their understanding of soils to design and construct buildings, tanks, roads, and runways and to construct embankments for dams, dikes, and highway grades. Strength, compressibility, and permeability of the soil are the properties of particular importance to geotechnical engineers. These properties in turn depend on many factors, including grain size and shape, density, mineral types, amount of water in the voids, and forces that have previously acted on the soil body. Because of the complexity of soil behavior and the many parameters that influence that behavior, specialized knowledge and skill is needed in using soil in engineered structures. Recent developments in this knowledge have enabled geotechnical engineers to design and construct many innovative foundations and earth structures.   T. LESLIE YOUD

Bibliography: Alexander, Martin, *Introduction to Soil Microbiology*, 2d ed. (1977); Buckman, H. O., and Brady, N. C., *The Nature and Properties of Soils*, 7th ed. (1979); Helfman, Elizabeth S., *Our Fragile Earth* (1972); Kellogg, Charles E., *The Soils That Support Us* (1941); Kuhnelt, Wilhelm, *Soil Biology*, rev. ed. (1976); Mitchell, J. K., *Fundamentals of Soil Behavior* (1976); Millar, C. E., et al., *Fundamentals of Soil Science*, 4th ed. (1965).

See also: AGRICULTURE AND THE FOOD SUPPLY; FARMS AND FARMING.

soil mechanics

All buildings, embankments, pavements, and other constructed works eventually transmit their loads to the Earth. The response of the ground under their applied loads is of fundamental importance to the safe and satisfactory performance of these works. The branch of physical science that deals with the response of the ground or soil bodies within the ground to applied loads is called soil mechanics. The application of soil-mechanics principles to engineering problems is performed by specialists in a branch of civil engineering called geotechnical engineering.

Although human use of soil as a building material dates back to the beginning of modern civilization, only in recent years has the use of soils as a construction material or as a base for structures been treated scientifically. In large part, this change was brought about by the publication in 1925 of the book *Erdbaumechanik* (Earth-building Mechanics) by Karl Terzaghi. Prior to this publication, only a few scattered theories existed relating to the behavior of soils, and most engineering design in soils was based on local experience and rules of thumb. Terzaghi's work introduced scientific methods for predicting the behavior of soils and developed a basis for rational engineering design.

The primary reason for the delay in applying scientific analyses to soil is the more complex behavior of soils compared to other construction materials such as concrete and steel. Whereas a few relatively easily measured properties are adequate to define the behavior of steel or concrete under almost any loading condition, numerous properties are required to similarly define the behavior of a soil under load. This behavior usually varies with the amount of load applied, the length of time over which it is applied, the past loading history, the amount of water in the void spaces, and many other factors. In addition, natural soils are usually nonhomogeneous; soil properties may thus vary greatly from layer to layer and from point to point within a layer. Some properties also vary directionally within the same soil element. Permeability, for example, is usually greater in a horizontal direction than in a vertical direction. Consequently, soil properties to be used in engineering calculations usually can be only approximately defined. As a result, less precise calculations can be made for soils than for manufactured materials such as steel. The following two design applications illustrate typical uses of soil-mechanics principles.

Foundations. The first application might be exemplified by a large building to be built on several unconnected slab footings, with one footing beneath each column in the building (see FOUNDATION, BUILDING). Two possible modes of failure must be considered in formulating the design. In the first mode, the soil beneath the footings could shear and allow the footings to punch into the ground. To prevent this type of failure the footing must be designed to provide adequate bearing capacity. The determination of the bearing capacity involves the engineer's investigation of the subsurface soils with the aid of borings and soundings, the measurement of the strength and density of test specimens using laboratory and field tests, the estimation of the in-place soil strength from this information, and then the calculation of the amount of load that can be placed on the footing as a function of footing size. The engineer then selects the size and type of footing required to bear the column load.

The other possible mode of failure results from ground settlement caused by compression of soil layers beneath the building. This compression occurs as a result of the additional load applied to the soil by the building. Such compression and settlements commonly continue to occur at a decreasing rate over a period of years. If the settlement is large and uneven, the building will be distorted and may eventually fail. To determine the amount of settlement beneath the building, the engineer determines the configuration of soil layers beneath the building with the aid of subsurface borings. Using laboratory tests, the amount and rate of compression is determined from test specimens taken from the soil layers. Appropriate field or design values are then estimated for these parameters, and finally the amount of settlement to be expected and the period of time over which it will occur is calculated. If the settlements are too large, the design of the foundation must be altered; for example, a pile foundation might be recommended rather than footings.

Dams. For the second typical application, consider an earth DAM to be constructed to empound a large reservoir. The weight of the embankment, the force of the water pressing against the dam, and the pressures in the water seeping through the dam all contribute forces that tend to cause the embankment to slump and fail. The strengths of the soils in the embankment provide forces resisting failure. To design a safe dam, the engineer calculates the forces in the dam that tend to cause failure; this can be done from analyses of the weight and geometry of the dam, the depth of water in the reservoir, and an analysis of the rate and distribution of water seeping through various segments of the dam. These forces are then summed and compared with the forces tending to resist failure. The geometry of the dam, soil types used in various segments of the dam, and configurations of drains built into the structure are then adjusted to provide an economical and safe design.

Other applications of soil mechanics include embankments, pavements and roadways, and tunnels.   T. LESLIE YOUD

Bibliography: Das, Braja, *Introduction to Soil Mechanics* (1979); McCarthy, David F., *Essentials of Soil Mechanics and Foundations* (1977);

Mitchell, James K., *Fundamentals of Soil Behavior* (1976); Pritchett, William L., *Properties and Management of Forest Soils* (1979); Scott, C. R., *Introduction to Soil Mechanics and Foundations*, 2d ed. (1974); Sowers, George B. and George F., *Introductory Soil Mechanics and Foundations*, 3d ed. (1970).

soil organisms

A large and diverse population of organisms resides in the soil and is responsible for such important activities as making nutrients available to plants, weathering soil minerals, decomposing organic waste materials, and detoxifying many environmental toxins that reach the soil. The importance of the soil biota is particularly evident in their extensive involvement in the geochemical cycles of carbon, nitrogen, sulfur, and other elements (see CARBON CYCLE and NITROGEN CYCLE). Their participation in these processes is important for soil fertility and plant growth. Not all soil organisms are beneficial, and some may cause plant disease, produce plant toxins, or compete with plants for soil nutrients.

Soil organisms may best be classified on the basis of size into the microbiota (such as algae, protozoa, fungi, and bacteria), the mesobiota (such as nematodes and small arthropods), and the macrobiota (such as earthworms, mollusks, burrowing rodents, reptiles, amphibia, and the roots of higher plants). Most of the vertebrates and insects that inhabit the soil do not remain below the ground all the time, or for their entire life cycles. Although the activity of the soil fauna (mesobiota and macrobiota) is important, particularly in the forest ecosystems, the soil microbiota (bacteria and fungi) are generally considered of greater significance in nutrient cycling, mineral weathering, and other biological activities.

The types and number of organisms present in soil differ somewhat from soil to soil because of differences in the chemical and physical characteristics of each soil. Generally, the highest populations and the greatest diversity of population of the microbiota and mesobiota are found in the litter and the top 5 cm (2 in) of a forest soil or in the top 15 cm (6 in) of grassland and agricultural soils. It is here that a more nearly optimum environment occurs, because of a greater amount of available carbon and other nutrients, better aeration, and a better moisture content in the soil.

The region close to the plant root growing in soil is called the rhizosphere. The soil of the rhizosphere has a higher population of soil microorganisms than does soil away from the plant root because of the availability of many organic compounds leaking from the root or from dead root cells. Consequently, microbial activity goes on at a much more rapid rate in this region. Some fungi in the rhizosphere are able to penetrate the defense mechanisms of plants, forming specialized symbiotic associations with the roots of higher plants called mycorrhizae (literally, "fungus root").

Modern agriculture uses large quantities of organic PESTICIDES to control weeds, insects, fungi, nematodes, and so on.

Research has shown that some pesticides may adversely affect certain segments of the soil biota. Insecticides generally result in the greatest change by killing substantial numbers of soil invertebrates. The soil microbiota may also be affected in numerous ways by pesticides, but neither absolute numbers, biomass, nor particular functions or activities are seriously altered.

ROBERT H. MILLER

Bibliography: Alexander, Martin, *Introduction to Soil Microbiology*, 2d ed. (1977); Burges, Alan, and Raw, F., eds., *Soil Biology* (1967); Gray, T. R., and Williams, S. T., *Soil Microorganisms* (1971); Tsutomu Hattori, *Microbial Life in the Soil: An Introduction* (1973).

Soka-gakkai   [soh'-kah-gahk'-ky]

The Soka-gakkai ("Value Creation Society") is perhaps the most vigorous and successful of the Japanese "new religions." Founded in 1930 by Tsunesaburo Makiguchi and revitalized after World War II by Josei Toda, it continues to gain new members not only in Japan but in the United States and throughout the world. In the early 1970s it claimed over 10 million adherents. Claiming to be simply a lay organization of the NICHIREN sect of Buddhism, Soka-gakkai has distinguished itself by its active involvement in social and political affairs (its affiliated political party, the Komeito, or Clean Government party, is one of the largest in Japan); by its special doctrine of "value origination" (so-ka); by its emphasis on world peace; and, early in its history, by its use of the method of "forceful conversion" (shakufuku).

JOSEPH M. KITAGAWA AND JOHN S. STRONG

Bibliography: Brannen, Noah S., *Soka Gakkai: Japan's Militant Buddhists* (1968); Murata, Kiyoaki, *Japan's New Buddhism* (1969); White, James W., *The Sokagakkai and Mass Society* (1970).

Sokolow, Anna   [soh'-kuh-lawv]

The works of the American modern-dance choreographer and teacher Anna Sokolow, b. Hartford, Conn., February 1912, are in the repertories of more than a score of dance companies around the world (see MODERN DANCE). Sokolow, raised in New York City's lower east side, danced with Martha Graham's company from 1930 to 1939 and presented her own work as early as 1932. Her dances prior to 1954 were on themes of social injustice and have not survived. In that year Sokolow created *Lyric Suite*, to the music of Alban Berg; this dance was the first of several recognized masterpieces. Beginning with this work, Sokolow devised dances on emotional themes, in which images of alienation, despair, and mental agony are presented within a virtually abstract framework.

ROBERT J. PIERCE

Bibliography: McDonagh, Don, *The Complete Guide to Modern Dance* (1976).

Sokotra: see SOCOTRA.

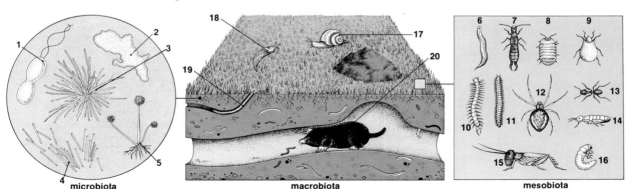

Soil organisms are essential in breaking down organic matter, converting nutrients into forms that can be utilized by plants, and maintaining aeration of the soil. Microbiota, which are generally less than 100 microns in length, include bacteria (1), protozoa (2), algae (3), viruses (4), and fungi (5). Common mesobiota include eelworms (6), earwigs (7), wood lice (8), mites (9), centipedes (10), millipedes (11), spiders (12), ants (13), springtails (14), crickets (15), and the larvae (16) of various insects. Largest of all soil organisms are the macrobiota, which include snails (17), slugs (18), larger earthworms (19), and such small animals as moles (20).

Sol

An ancient god of Mesopotamian origin, Sol was introduced into Roman religion in the 3d century AD as the Roman equivalent of the Greek sun god HELIOS. He was worshiped by the Roman emperors as their principal protector.

sol

A sol is a colloidal system consisting of a solid dispersed in a liquid (see COLLOIDAL STATE). If the dispersing medium is water, it may be called a hydrosol. If the interaction between the solid and liquid components gives a stable system, the sol is said to be lyophilic; if the solid is more stable in bulk form and eventually aggregates to that state, the sol is called hydrophobic. Lyophilic sols that contain large linear molecules, such as gelatin, have a much greater viscosity than the solvent and may on cooling form a semisolid colloid called a GEL. On the other hand, the viscosity of hydrophobic sols is typically about the same as that of the solvent.

GEORGE GORIN

solar apex

The solar apex is the point in the sky toward which the Sun and the entire solar system are moving at a velocity of about 20 km/sec (12 mi/sec) relative to the nearby stars. The apex is approximately located at a right ascension of 18 hours and a declination of 30° north in the constellation of Hercules near the bright star Vega.

ARTHUR F. CACELLA

solar cell

Solar, or photovoltaic, cells are devices that directly convert sunlight into electricity. A photon of light energy striking a solar cell can release an electron for power production if its energy exceeds the gap energy of the electron. The excess energy of the photon, together with that of all low-energy photons, is dissipated as heat. The efficiency of solar cells, therefore, is inherently low—about 20% for the best silicon cells. Solar cells were first developed by the Bell Laboratories

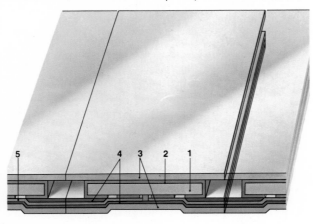

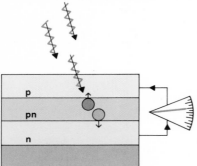

(Above) *In this solar cell, an n-type (1) and p-type (2) semiconductor are enclosed by plastic layers (3). Cells are linked by interconnectors (4) separated by an insulator (5).*
(Left) *When light enters, it causes electrons and holes to migrate from the pn junction; when the semiconductors are linked, current flows.*

in the 1950s for space applications. Recently they have also been used for remote terrestrial applications—buoys, oil-drilling platforms, and mountaintop microwave repeaters—for which long-distance power lines would be more expensive.

A solar cell consists of two layers of material, one of which is doped with an impurity such as boron to make it negative (n-type), and the other of which is similarly doped to make it positive (p-type; see SEMICONDUCTOR). Because sunlight must penetrate to the junction of the two layers (the p-n junction), one layer must be extremely thin. For silicon cells, this thin layer has been obtained at high cost by slicing an expensive silicon ingot; much of the silicon is lost in saw cuts. Other, more recent methods of producing silicon cells, such as growing the crystal in ribbon form or using tiny silicon pellets, promise great reductions in cost. Other substances, such as cadmium sulfide and gallium arsenide, are also being used to make solar cells. Cadmium sulfide, although relatively cheap, has a low efficiency because of its high gap energy; gallium arsenide is very efficient but also very costly.

In recent years the cost of solar cells has fallen from about $50 per peak watt (full sunlight) to between $7 and $10 per peak watt in 1980, and the cost continues to fall. When the price falls below $1 per peak watt, solar electricity could be competitive, at least in sunny areas, with conventional power production.

Bibliography: Backus, Charles E., ed., *Solar Cells* (1976); Pulfrey, David L., ed., *Photovoltaic Power Generation* (1978).

solar collectors

Solar collectors are devices that absorb solar energy and produce heat. They are becoming important for space heating and cooling and for heating water for buildings and industry.

One common type of collector, the flat-plate type, is made of a copper, aluminum, or steel heat-absorber plate, the surface of which is blackened to make the plate more efficient in absorbing solar energy. Tubes are often soldered or clamped to the plate to allow a heat-transfer liquid (usually a water-and-antifreeze solution) or air to circulate through and remove heat from the plate; alternatively, passageways for liquid or air may be integrally incorporated into the plate, or the heat-transfer medium may simply flow across the surface of the absorber. The heat may be stored in a water tank (liquid, or hydronic; system) or a bed of gravel (air system).

Two layers of glass or transparent plastic, separated by an air space, are placed above the plate (for low-temperature applications, such as swimming-pool heating, one or even no layers may be used). The air space minimizes convective and conductive heat losses to the atmosphere. The cover plates also minimize reradiation from the collector. To further reduce heat losses, the back and sides of the collector are heavily insulated, as are all pipes or ducts leading to and from the heat-storage area. The plate is mounted in such a direction that the glass surface is at the same angle as the sun's winter path across the sky. Efficiencies of flat-plate collectors may be as high as 70% when operating at close to the ambient (surrounding) temperature. When a collector is operated at 100° C (212° F), however, its efficiency may drop to less than 30%.

A high-quality flat-plate collector system may cost $100–$200 per m² ($10–$20 per ft²) of surface area, including heat storage and delivery components. The average home may require 60–100 m² (600–1,000 ft²) of collector area for space heating or about 10 m² (100 ft²) for heating domestic hot water only. Much cheaper collectors are available, but they may be expensive to maintain or may tend to deteriorate more rapidly. When collector panels are mass-produced, costs are expected to be reduced significantly.

A recent development, the evacuated-tube collector, consists of two glass tubes, one within the other, with a vacuum between the tubes to minimize heat loss. Because the tubes are round and backed with reflecting material, this type can absorb more sunlight and has a significantly higher overall efficiency than the flat-plate collector.

Concentrating solar collectors focus the Sun's rays on a

tube (trough-type collector) or a point (dish-type) to provide higher temperatures for special purposes, such as absorption-chiller air conditioning and industrial process heat. Such collectors must track the Sun through the sky on one or two axes. Fresnel lenses can also be used to focus sunlight.

JESSE S. DOOLITTLE

Bibliography: Anderson, Bruce, *Solar Energy: Fundamentals in Building Design* (1977); McPhillips, Martin, ed., *Solar Age Resource Book* (1979).

See also: SOLAR ENERGY.

solar constant

The solar constant is the total flux of solar energy per unit area and unit time measured above the Earth's atmosphere. Scientists in many fields wish to know whether the Sun's output is truly constant. The best measurements obtained in the past ten years from RADIOMETERS carried on rockets and balloons yield a value of $S = (1.373 \pm 0.008) \times 10^6$ erg/sec cm². The longest set of daily continuous observations made from ground level between 1923 and 1952 indicate that any variation of the solar constant must be at the level of 0.2% or less over a 30-year period.

PETER FOUKAL

solar cycle

The solar cycle is a recurrent pattern of magnetic activity in the SUN. It was first identified in 1843 by the German observer Samuel Heinrich Schwabe from the approximately 11-year cycle in the number of SUNSPOTS seen on the solar disk. Sunspots are only one observable feature of localized magnetic disturbances in the magnetically active solar atmosphere. The 11-year cycle of sunspots corresponds to similar 11-year cycles of other observable features in these active regions, such as the number of FACULAE, the rate of incidence of SOLAR FLARES, and the intensity of coronal X-ray and radio-frequency emissions. Two consecutive 11-year cycles in the number of sunspots complete a 22-year solar magnetic cycle, in which both the number and the magnetic polarities of the bipolar spot groups return to their initial values. Although the solar cycle has been relatively regular over the past century, historical records extending to the 17th century show that its amplitude may vary dramatically over longer time scales.

PETER FOUKAL

solar energy

Solar energy is a term that encompasses a broad range of energy forms. The Sun's energy profoundly affects the world's wind patterns, causes ocean water to evaporate as part of the hydrologic cycle, and is essential for plant growth. The winds may be used to turn windmills (see WINDMILLS and WIND-POWER); the hydrologic cycle makes HYDROELECTRIC POWER possible; and vegetation, which grows in the presence of sunlight, may be burned directly—for instance, as wood in a stove or fireplace—or processed into fuels, such as the fermentation of grain to produce ethyl alcohol, which can be used alone or mixed with gasoline (see GASOHOL) to power an internal-combustion engine. Solar energy also makes it possible to harness OCEAN THERMAL ENERGY, which uses the temperature difference between Sun-warmed surface water and cold water from the ocean depths to produce power.

Although all these indirect means of using energy from the Sun are considered solar technologies, the term *solar energy* most commonly refers to direct use of the Sun's energy: by means of photovoltaic SOLAR CELLS, which convert sunlight into electricity (see PHOTOELECTRIC EFFECT), and by the use of various devices and techniques to convert solar radiation to heat that may be used for heating and cooling buildings; providing hot water for homes, businesses, and industry; and generating electricity by thermal means.

POWER GENERATION

Besides the direct conversion of sunlight into electricity by means of photovoltaic cells, sunlight may be used to generate steam, which can then be used to power a turbine for producing electricity. One solar-thermal design, called a power tower, consists of a field of movable mirrors that surround a tower, at the top of which is a boiler. The mirrors, called heliostats, track the Sun so as to constantly focus its light on the boiler. At the bottom of the tower is a building that houses a turbine-generator. A prototype 10-megawatt power tower will be constructed in Barstow, Calif., as part of a federal program to develop the concept.

Some scientists have suggested building huge photovoltaic arrays in Earth orbit for producing large amounts of power. Such arrays, called solar space power satellites (SSPSs), would beam collected energy to Earth by way of microwaves.

INDUSTRIAL APPLICATIONS

About 40% of the energy consumed by U.S. industry is used to provide temperatures of less than 315° C (600° F); such temperatures can be attained by using concentrating solar collectors that focus sunlight onto a pipe (parabolic-trough collector), onto a single point (parabolic-dish collector), or through a Fresnel lens. Such collectors must track the Sun as it moves across the sky in order to maintain proper focus of the light. Solar furnaces use large arrays of mirrors to achieve temperatures high enough (thousands of degrees) for metallurgical work; sunlight, unlike fuels, does not introduce impurities into the crucible in which a metal is formed. Solar energy is also being used in agriculture to power irrigation systems and to produce the heat needed to dry crops.

RESIDENTIAL APPLICATIONS

The greatest public interest in solar energy has been directed toward its use in heating and cooling buildings. Residential and commercial solar applications may be divided into two types: active systems, which rely on SOLAR COLLECTOR panels; and passive design, by which a building is designed, situated, and oriented so as to receive and store heat from the Sun during the winter, but also to keep sunlight out—and thereby keep the interior cool—during the summer.

Active Systems. Active solar heating systems commonly consist of several hundred square feet of solar collector panels, plus a storage medium to hold the heat collected during the day, and a set of automatic controls that monitor and regulate both heat collection and delivery between the storage medium and the living space. Active systems use either a liquid (of which the most popular is a mixture of water and an antifreeze, such as propylene glycol) or air as the heat-transfer medium. Insulated pipes or ducts carry the heat-transfer medium, called the working fluid, to the collector panels—where the fluid absorbs heat—and then back to the storage, which in liquid-based (hydronic) systems is an insulated tank or in air systems is an insulated bin of fist-sized rocks. (Alternatively, phase-change materials may be used to store heat.) The absorbed heat is transferred to the storage medium, and the cooled working fluid is then returned to the collectors to pick up more heat. Heat is removed from storage and delivered to the living space as needed. Most types of active systems require an auxiliary heating system to provide extra heat during extended periods of cloudiness or extreme cold. A typical active heating system might cost (1980) between $2,000 and $5,000 per thousand square feet of living space in the northeastern United States—depending on the type of system, its efficiency, and so forth.

A large portion of a building's annual domestic hot water (DHW) needs can be supplied by a relatively inexpensive (between $2,000 and $2,500 in 1980) active hydronic system using about 9 m² (100 ft²) of collectors for a typical residence. A heat exchanger, usually in the hot-water tank, keeps the working fluid separate from the potable water supply. Such systems, although they require a backup energy source, can often pay for themselves in energy savings in less than 10 years.

High-temperature solar collector panels may be used to power absorption-chiller AIR CONDITIONING. Such systems are relatively expensive but may be cost-effective in climates where plentiful sunshine and a substantial need for air conditioning exist. Also, HEAT PUMPS may be used in conjunction with solar panels; solar heat boosts the heat pump's source during the winter, and during the summer the heat pump can discharge heat to the outdoors at night through the collectors.

An increasing number of houses, such as this one, are being designed and built to make use of solar energy for heating. Flat-plate solar collectors cover the south-facing roof, set at an angle that catches the winter sun most efficiently. As fossil-fuel costs mount, the arguments for solar energy as a practical alternative become more persuasive.

The thermal envelope house, conceived by California architect Lee Porter Butler, is actually a house within a house—it has two south walls, two roofs, and two north walls. The south side of the house incorporates a greenhouse area between the two walls; as the Sun warms the air in the greenhouse, that air rises into the double roof area, while the coolness of the north wall causes air to fall from there into an insulated basement or crawl space that contains a thermal mass (rocks or dirt). Heat produced in the greenhouse is carried over the house and deposited in the thermal mass; spaces between the greenhouse's floorboards allow the air to rise again into the greenhouse to maintain a convective loop. At night the cool greenhouse glass causes a loop to operate in the reverse direction, and heat from the thermal mass warms the space between the building's two skins, both of which are insulated. During the summer, windows at the top of the greenhouse are opened, and a 30-m (100-ft) culvert pipe buried beneath the frost line is opened to the basement or crawl space. Warmed air in the greenhouse rises and flows

Since the 1950s, France has been putting solar energy to novel use at a facility near Mount Louis in the French Pyrenees. Reflectors there collect the Sun's rays to achieve sustained high temperatures. The photograph (right) shows some of the 63 separate mirrors that individually track the Sun by means of photoelectric equipment. They reflect the light onto a parabolic mirror, 40 m (132 ft) high by 54 m (178 ft) wide, at the focus of which is a high-temperature laboratory (left). A temperature of 3,000° C (5,430° F) is available about 1,200 hours a year.

Passive Solar. Many architects are now designing new houses and retrofitting older houses to passively use the Sun and other environmental factors to reduce energy costs. Passive systems are characterized by having few or no moving parts; usually, the south side of the building has extensive areas of insulating glass (or even a greenhouse); the east and west sides, less glass; and the north side, which receives no sun and is exposed to winter winds, little or no glass. (The orientation is reversed in the Southern Hemisphere.) Roof overhangs jut out over the south-facing glass; their function is to admit sunlight to the building in the winter, when the Sun is low in the sky and heating loads are high, and to keep sunlight out of the building's interior in the summer, when the Sun's path is higher. Effective insulation is considered an essential element of passive design.

Aside from passive adaptations of more-or-less conventional houses, two other passive approaches have received considerable attention: the underground house and the thermal-envelope house. Underground houses make use of the fact that below the frost line—typically a foot or two below the ground's surface—the Earth's temperature remains nearly constant (usually about 13.3° C/56° F) throughout the year. The walls and roof are insulated and waterproofed, and the roof is covered with soil and vegetation, which provide additional insulation. Usually, an underground house will follow conventional passive-design practice in the incorporation of south-facing glass and roof overhangs. Such houses require only small amounts of auxiliary heating and cooling because the constant temperature of the earth is close to the desired interior temperature.

out the windows, and replacement air is sucked through the culvert, where it is cooled, and into the envelope. East and west windows, as well as windows and doors opening into the greenhouse, may be opened or closed to provide temperature adjustments at any time of the year. The thermal envelope house requires little auxiliary energy, and its cost is comparable to that of a nonsolar house.

HISTORY
Humanity's use of the Sun's energy extends far back into prehistory. The Indian pueblos of the American Southwest, for example, seem to have been designed to use solar energy. Many ancient and primitive cultures have exhibited a sophisticated knowledge of how to use solar energy to maintain comfortable temperatures inside dwellings. Adaptive architecture probably played an important role in the survival and success of human groups in prehistoric times. Coupled with the use of fire, solar shelter orientation probably made it possible for some human communities to remain in one place year-round rather than migrating with the changing of the seasons.

The ancient Greeks were also aware of how to build and orient structures so as to take advantage of the Sun's heat in the winter and to keep sunlight out—and living spaces cool—in the summer. XENOPHON wrote (c.400 BC) of how the Sun should penetrate and warm south porticoes in the winter but would be overhead in the summer, leaving the roofed porticoes in shade and relatively cool and comfortable. He also wrote that the south side of a house should be tall, to let more sunlight in, and the north side lower, to keep out the winter winds. The Roman architect VITRUVIUS wrote in detail

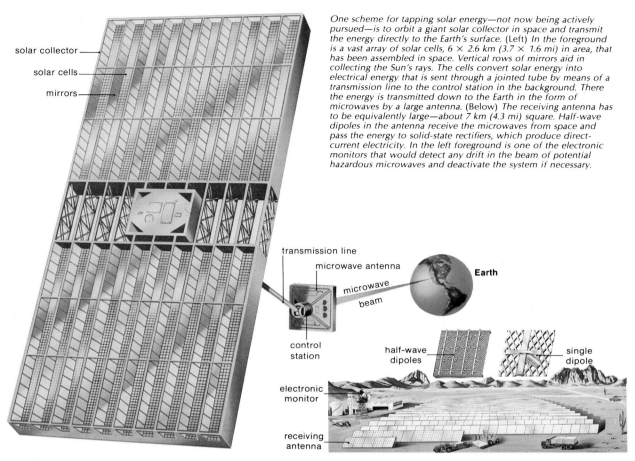

solar collector

solar cells

mirrors

One scheme for tapping solar energy—not now being actively pursued—is to orbit a giant solar collector in space and transmit the energy directly to the Earth's surface. (Left) In the foreground is a vast array of solar cells, 6 × 2.6 km (3.7 × 1.6 mi) in area, that has been assembled in space. Vertical rows of mirrors aid in collecting the Sun's rays. The cells convert solar energy into electrical energy that is sent through a jointed tube by means of a transmission line to the control station in the background. There the energy is transmitted down to the Earth in the form of microwaves by a large antenna. (Below) The receiving antenna has to be equivalently large—about 7 km (4.3 mi) square. Half-wave dipoles in the antenna receive the microwaves from space and pass the energy to solid-state rectifiers, which produce direct-current electricity. In the left foreground is one of the electronic monitors that would detect any drift in the beam of potential hazardous microwaves and deactivate the system if necessary.

transmission line

microwave antenna

Earth

microwave beam

control station

half-wave dipoles

single dipole

electronic monitor

receiving antenna

about solar-oriented architecture in *Ten Books on Architecture* (before 30 BC). The ancient Inca city of MACHU PICCHU, the ruins of which lie 2,340 m (7,675 ft) above sea level in the Andes, appears to have been built so that solar energy was used to maintain comfortable indoor temperatures day and night. Thick rock walls were built facing east, to be sun-warmed in the morning, when heat would be needed most. The rock retained the heat all day and into the night. The city itself was built on an east-facing hillside, and the west sides of the buildings were therefore backed with earth, which held additional heat from the daytime into the night and reduced the rate of heat loss from the buildings' interiors.

As the use of fire became more technologically advanced, however, adaptive architecture became less and less necessary until, with the rather large heat-to-weight ratios of coal and oil, architecture became freed from the constraints of energy-efficient design. Energy became so cheap during the 20th century that it became customary to maintain constant temperatures of 22° C (72° F) indoors year-round by artificial means: heating in the winter and air conditioning in the summer. Although civilization by this time had grown accustomed to the "comfort zone" of building temperatures, and styles of dress had changed accordingly (no more heavy woolens for indoor winter comfort), vast quantities of "cheap" energy—derived, mostly, from fossil fuels (coal, oil, and natural gas)—were being used for space conditioning. Also, by the middle of the 20th century, industries and electricity-generating plants throughout the developed world were consuming massive amounts of these same fossil fuels.

A few individuals in recent history experimented with the use of solar energy to provide mechanical power. Among them were the Frenchman Augustin Mouchot (1825–1911), who built several solar-powered steam engines, one of which operated a printing press in Paris in 1882; the Swedish-Ameri-

can inventor John ERICSSON, who built efficient solar-powered hot-air engines, which were later converted to run on coal and gas because the apparatus required for collecting the solar energy was costly; and Dr. Charles Greeley Abbot (1872–1973), an American, who investigated solar energy and many of its possible uses from the late 19th century until his death. Dr. Abbot is considered by many to have been the father of modern solar-energy use. One of his friends and fellow scientists, Robert GODDARD, also did a great deal of pioneering work in solar power during the 1920s.

During the 1970s solar energy emerged from relative obscurity and became a promising alternative energy source. At the beginning of that decade the industrialized world was still enjoying the age of cheap and plentiful petroleum. In 1973, however, the Organization of Petroleum Exporting Countries (OPEC) declared an oil embargo against the industrialized world in a bid for sharp price increases. The increases were soon won, and the price of petroleum subsequently continued to rise to match its true value to a world that had become heavily dependent on oil and gas for advanced economic development and activity. At the same time, it became apparent that world petroleum reserves would not be sufficient to continue to meet such high demand for much more than another 50 to 100 years, if that long. By the law of supply and demand, the average price of oil on the world market rose from $2 per barrel in 1970 to more than $30 per barrel in 1980. Solar energy, which previously had been considered far too expensive to be of practical use, became more economically feasible.

During the same decade public demands for a cleaner environment further increased the cost of using fossil fuels (oil, gas, and coal) and nuclear energy, and environmental hazards, widely spoken about, were the impetus for the public's cautious attitude toward these energy sources. Solar energy, on the other hand, was perceived by many to be a clean and safe energy source, besides being one that could not suddenly be cut off or made more costly. The U.S. government responded to public and private interest in solar energy by passing legislation and providing increased funding to encourage rapid development of this resource. In 1978 federal income tax credits went into effect, allowing homeowners to subtract as much as $2,200 from their income tax payment if they installed solar equipment on a residence. The federal budget for solar-energy research and development went from less than $4 million in 1973 to more than $800 million in fiscal year 1980.   GEORGE ELLIS

Bibliography: Anderson, Bruce, and Riordan, Michael, *The Solar Home Book* (1976); Clark, Wilson, *Energy for Survival* (1974); Duffie, John A., and Beckman, William A., *Solar Energy Thermal Processes* (1974); Mazria, Edward, *The Passive Solar Energy Book* (1979); McCullagh, James, ed., *The Solar Greenhouse Book* (1978); Olgyay, V. V., *Design with Climate* (1963); Watson, Donald, *Designing and Building a Solar House* (1977); Williams, J. Richard, *Solar Energy: Technology and Applications*, rev. ed. (1977); Yanda, Bill, and Fisher, Rick, *The Food and Heat Producing Solar Greenhouse* (1976).

solar flare

Solar flares are powerful and rapid eruptions that occur in the atmosphere of the SUN, in magnetically active regions. These eruptions are closely associated with SUNSPOTS and FACULAE. Observations of stellar light variations indicate that similar eruptions take place on other stars. Solar flares typically exhibit a rapid increase—within tens of seconds—of X-ray and ultraviolet emissions to 10–100 times the normal level. A slower but closely correlated relative increase is also seen in centimeter radio waves. Some flares also produce powerful bursts of meter-wave radio emission. The rapid initial rise is then followed by a slow decay phase that may last as long as several hours.

A large flare may cover a billion km² (386,000,000 mi²) of the Sun's surface as observed in chromospheric radiations. The total energy involved in radiation, relativistic particles, and thermal plasma accelerated from a large flare can reach 10^{32} ergs. The mechanism responsible for such rapid and powerful eruptions is not yet understood.   PETER FOUKAL

Bibliography: Baxter, W. M., *The Sun and the Amateur Astronomer*, rev. ed. (1973); Menzel, Donald H., *Our Sun*, rev. ed. (1959); Moore, Patrick, *The Sun* (1968).

solar radiation

Solar radiation, the electromagnetic radiation emitted by the Sun, is the direct source of all energy and life on Earth. It drives the atmospheric and oceanic currents, evaporates the water that later falls as rain and snow, and induces the plant photosynthesis that provides food, fiber, and fuel.

Only about one two-millionth of all the energy emitted by the Sun is received by the Earth, 150 million km (93 million mi) distant. The solar constant, the average energy from the Sun received at this average distance, is uncertain; recent measurements taken from high-flying aircraft, rockets, and satellites vary from 1.92 langleys (ly) per minute (a langley being one gram-calorie per square centimeter), or 1,340 to 1,361 W/m² (124 to 126 W/ft²). The present adopted value is 1.940 ± 0.03 ly/min, or $1,354 \pm 21$ W/m² (126 ± 2.0 W/ft²).

When solar radiation enters the Earth's atmosphere, it is partially absorbed and partially reflected, largely by cloud, snowfields, and deserts. The fraction reflected, called the ALBEDO, is variously estimated at 28 to 35 percent for the Earth as a whole. Absorption is by ozone in the stratosphere (see OZONE LAYER), by carbon dioxide, water vapor, clouds, and dust in the troposphere, and by the Earth's surface. Thus, solar radiation is absorbed primarily by water—in the atmosphere, on the surface, and in plants—and nearly half of its energy (a quarter of the total reaching the uppermost level of the atmosphere) goes to evaporate water.

Radiation leaving the Sun is from about 0.2 to 10 μ; such wavelengths are fairly close to those of the radiation emitted by a black body at a temperature of 6,000 K. The ozone layer absorbs radiation in the ultraviolet region, and water vapor

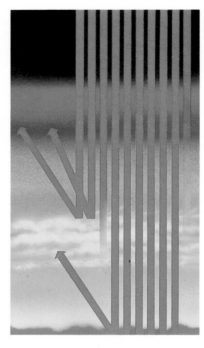

Less than half of the solar energy passing through the Earth's atmosphere reaches the surface. For each 100 units of entering radiation (red bars), about 20 units—consisting mainly of ultraviolet and infrared rays—are absorbed by the ozone layer, water vapor, carbon dioxide, and clouds. About 35 units of visible and infrared radiation are reflected (red arrows) from clouds and from the Earth's surface. The average amount of radiation absorbed by the surface is about 45 units.

absorbs radiation in the infrared region and at several parts of the visible region.   ARNOLD COURT

Bibliography: Coulson, Kinsell L., *Solar and Terrestrial Radiation* (1975); Henderson, S. T., *Daylight and Its Spectrum*, 2d ed. (1977); Paltridge, G. W., and Platt, C. M. R., *Radiative Processes in Meteorology and Climatology* (1976).

solar system

The solar system is the group of celestial bodies, including the Earth, orbiting around and gravitationally bound by the star known as the SUN, one of at least a hundred billion stars in our galaxy. The Sun's retinue includes nine PLANETS, at least 34 SATELLITES, more than 1,000 observed COMETS, and thousands of lesser bodies known as minor planets (ASTEROIDS) and meteoroids (see METEOR AND METEORITE). All of these bodies are immersed in a tenuous sea of fragile and rocky interplanetary dust particles, perhaps ejected from comets at the time of their passage through the inner solar system or resulting from minor planet collisions. The Sun is the only star known through direct observation to be accompanied by such an extensive planetary swarm, although it has frequently been speculated that many other stars in the galaxy may be accompanied by planetary systems, some of which may also have given rise to technological civilizations.

HISTORY OF SOLAR SYSTEM STUDIES

Since primitive times humanity has been aware that certain of the stars in the sky are not fixed, but wander slowly across the heavens. The Greeks gave these moving stars the name *planets,* or "wanderers." They were the first to predict with accuracy the positions of the planets in the sky, and they devised elaborate theoretical models in which the planets moved around combinations of circles that in turn circled the Earth. The Greek mathematician Claudius Ptolemy systematized an elaborate geocentric scheme of this kind in the 2d century AD, which passed with minor changes through the Middle Ages and on to the Polish astronomer Nicolaus Copernicus (see ASTRONOMY, HISTORY OF). In his work of 1543, Copernicus proposed that planetary motions centered on the Sun rather than on the Earth, but he retained the description of planetary motions as being a series of superimposed circular motions, mathematically equivalent to the Ptolemaic theory. In the same year Copernicus died. During the 17th century a German mathematician by the name of Johannes Kepler abandoned the concept of circular motion in favor of

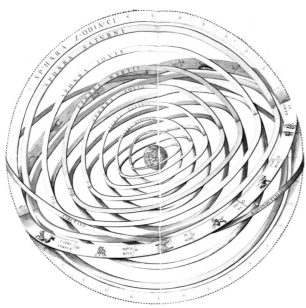

an elliptical scheme, in which the motions of the planets describe a simple series of ellipses in which the Sun is at one of the foci. Basing his work on the observations of Tycho Brahe, his former employer and a renowned astronomer, Kepler found (1609, 1619) three important empirical relationships, concerning the motion of the planetary bodies, now known as KEPLER'S LAWS. Kepler's labors laid the groundwork for Sir Isaac Newton's law of GRAVITATION (1687), from which it became possible for astronomers to predict with great accuracy the movements and positions of the planets.

Only the planets Mercury, Venus, Mars, Jupiter, and Saturn were known to the ancients. The English astronomer William Herschel accidentally discovered Uranus in 1781 as the result of telescopic observations. Discrepancies between the observed positions of Uranus and those predicted led John Couch Adams and Urbain Jean Joseph Leverrier to propose (1846) that another large planet was exerting a gravitational force on Uranus. In the same year the planet Neptune was found close to its predicted position. In the 20th century smaller residual discrepancies in the apparent positions of Uranus and Neptune led to predictions of the presence of still another planet, and in 1930, Clyde Tombaugh discovered the planet Pluto close to one of the areas of prediction. Pluto's mass, however, is so small that the discovery is now considered to have been an accident resulting from intense scrutiny of that part of the sky to which the predictions had called attention. Yet another planet may remain to be discovered.

Galileo was in 1609 the first to use the telescope for astronomical purposes, and it has since become an essential tool in planetary studies. In the 19th century planetary astronomy flourished, thanks to the construction of large telescopes and their systematic use for planetary observations. Two new tools, the spectroscope and the photographic plate, were also developed in the 19th century and gave rise to the new science of astrophysics. For the first time it became possible to determine not only the orbits and masses of objects in the solar system, but also their temperatures, compositions, and structures (see ASTRONOMY AND ASTROPHYSICS). During the early years of the 20th century great advancements took place in the understanding of the physics and chemistry of the planets in the solar system, and during the middle years of the century important further advances were derived from RADIO ASTRONOMY and RADAR ASTRONOMY.

Although most astronomers gradually turned their attention away from the solar system to the study of stars and galaxies, the launch (1957) of the first artificial satellite ushered in an

(Above) *A geometrical model of the Ptolemaic concept of the universe is pictured in this 17th-century engraving. The stars, planets, Sun, and Moon were thought to circle the Earth in 24 hours.*

(Left) *This diagram of the solar system was published by Nicolaus Copernicus in 1543. It depicts a heliocentric universe in which the known planets, including Earth, are circling the Sun.*

(Left) *The looping paths of the major planets with respect to the stars over a 17-year period are simulated in this planetarium photograph.*

(Below) *These diagrams reveal the complex motions (1-5) of the planets as seen from Earth. A loop (6) results when a planet P appears from Earth E to reverse its motion with respect to the stars S_1 and S_2.*

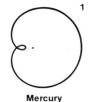

1

Mercury

2

Venus

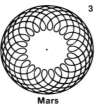

3

Mars

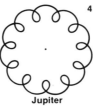

4

Jupiter

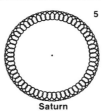

5

Saturn

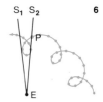

S_1 S_2

6

P

E

CHARACTERISTICS OF THE PLANETS

| Planet | Mean Distance | | | Length of Year (Earth days and years) | Length of Day (Earth days, hours, minutes, and seconds) | Inclination of Axis | Inclination of Orbit to Ecliptic, Degrees | Eccentricity of Orbit | Equatorial Diameter | | Mass (compared to Earth) | Density (g/cm³) |
	Astronomical Units	Millions of km	Millions of mi						km	mi		
Mercury	0.387	57.9	36.0	88 d	58.6 d	7°	7.00	0.2056	4,880	3,030	0.054	5.4
Venus	0.723	108.2	67.0	224.7 d	243 d (retrograde)	3° 24'	3.39	0.0068	12,104	7,517	0.815	5.2
Earth	1	149.6	93.0	365.26 d	23 hr 56 min 4 sec	23° 27'	———	0.0167	12,756	7,921	1	5.51
Mars	1.524	227.9	141.6	687 d	24 hr 37 min 23 sec	23° 59'	1.85	0.0934	6,787	4,210	0.107	3.9
Jupiter	5.203	778.3	483.3	11.86 yr	9 hr 50 min 30 sec	3° 05'	1.30	0.0485	143,000	88,800	317.9	1.32
Saturn	9.539	1,427.0	886.4	29.46 yr	10 hr 14 min	26° 44'	2.49	0.0556	120,000	74,500	95.2	0.7
Uranus	19.18	2,869.6	1,783.0	84.01 yr	23 hr (retrograde)	97° 54'	0.77	0.0472	51,800	32,200	14.6	1.2
Neptune	30.06	4,496.6	2,794.0	164.8 yr	22 hr	28° 48'	1.77	0.0086	49,500	30,750	17.2	1.67
Pluto	39.44	5,900.0	3,660.0	248.4 yr	6 d 9 hr	> 50°	17.2	0.249	3,000	1,860	0.0026	~1

age that transformed solar-system studies. During the 1960s and 1970s spacecraft accomplished flyby, orbiting, and landing missions on many of the planets. At the present time the reconnaissance of the planets in the solar system has been accomplished for Mercury through Saturn. The U.S. MARINER spacecraft have provided a good model of the atmosphere of Venus, and the Soviet VENERA spacecraft have returned pictures from the surface of that planet. Mariner and VIKING (U.S.) spacecraft have extensively photographed Mars from orbit, and the Viking landers have carried out important initial measurements of surface properties. The investigation of the Moon has progressed through the stages of flybys, orbiters, and landers both of the manned variety (U.S. Apollo) and the unmanned variety (U.S. RANGER, SURVEYOR, and LUNAR ORBITER, and Soviet LUNA). The success achieved in bringing to the Earth samples from several different lunar landing sites has made possible a continuing series of laboratory investigations and further intensive study of Earth's satellite (see SPACE EXPLORATION).

THE SUN

The Sun is the only star whose surface can be studied in detail from the Earth. This surface presents a scene of churning, turbulent activity, largely dominated by strong magnetic fields. Magnetic lines of force emerging from the solar surface appear as sunspots. Arches of the magnetic lines of force extending across the surface give rise to bright, shining solar prominences. Wave motions generated below the surface of the Sun flicker across the surface and mount into the atmosphere. Brilliant flares appear in the vicinity of sunspots, generating bursts of ultraviolet and X-ray emissions from the Sun and accelerating ions and electrons to create the high-energy particles known as cosmic rays.

The upper levels of the Sun's atmosphere are of very low density, but the solar activity heats the gases there to very high temperatures. Here the electrons are stripped from atoms to form ions, and the two types of particles together form a plasma. The gravitational field of the Sun is unable to retain this superhot plasma, and it streams outward into space as the solar wind. Measurements of the properties of the solar wind are routinely carried out by U.S. spacecraft at many different locations within the solar system.

Most of the mass (99.86 percent) of the solar system is concentrated in the Sun, which thus exerts the gravitational force that holds the scattered members of the system together. There is a remarkable degree of orderliness in the motions of the members of the solar system under the influence of the Sun's gravity. With the exception of the comets and some of the asteroids, the motions of the bodies in the solar system are confined to approximately the same plane, called the plane of the ecliptic. There is a striking similarity in the way in which these bodies revolve and rotate. The planets all revolve around the Sun in the same direction, and the Sun rotates in this direction as well. With only two exceptions, Venus and Uranus, the planets also rotate in this common direction. Many of the planets, particularly the outer solar system, are accompanied by swarms of satellites, and again, with a few exceptions, these also tend to revolve in a plane close to the plane of the ecliptic and with the same sense of motion. All of these tendencies can be summarized by saying that the angular momentum vectors of the bodies in the solar system are for the most part aligned.

THE PLANETS

The nine planets of the solar system may be divided into two groups: the inner, or terrestrial, planets, and the outer, or Jovian, planets. This division is based not only on distance from the Sun, but also on the physical properties of the planets.

The Inner Planets. The inner planets are all comparable in size, density, and other characteristics to the Earth and so are generally referred to as the terrestrial, or Earth-like, planets. Included are Mercury, Venus, Earth, and Mars.

The Earth is the largest of the terrestrial planets. By far the most massive constituents of the Earth are the iron core and the rocky mantle and crust. The water in the oceans and the gases in the air form only a thin veneer of volatile materials surrounding the rock of the planet proper. The Sun provides the heat and light that make the Earth habitable for life as we know it. The oceans and atmosphere of the Earth absorb and redistribute the heat in a complex fashion. Various types of geological evidence indicate that the Earth has passed through ice ages in the past, but it is not known whether some unknown variability in the Sun has been responsible for these, or whether the source lies in the great complexity of the atmospheric weather system. The early years of the Earth were apparently rather violent, as no geological record is preserved of the first half-billion years of its existence.

The Earth-Moon system is often referred to as a "double planet" system, because the Moon is more nearly comparable in size to the Earth than the other satellites are to their primaries (except for Pluto and its moon). The Earth's MOON is 81 times less in mass than the Earth but only 4 times less in mass than the planet Mercury. It is one of a group of the six largest satellites in the solar system that have approximately comparable mass, and the only such large one in the inner solar system. Compared to the mass of its primary, the Earth, the Moon is abnormally massive. The return of samples from several lunar sites during the Apollo program, and the establishment of stations to measure seismic activity and other physical quantities at these sites, has provided more knowledge about the Moon than currently exists for any other body in the solar system except the Earth. If the Moon has a central iron core, it is unexpectedly small, compared to that of the Earth, and of surprisingly little mass; the bulk of the Moon is mantle and crust that has had an extensive history of melting and chemical differentiation. The Moon contains no atmosphere, and its surface is heavily cratered. Its topmost soil is a very fine-grained substance with little chips of rock sprinkled throughout. This is called the lunar regolith. The Moon is heavily depleted in the more volatile elements and compounds as compared to the Earth.

The next inner planet toward the Sun is VENUS, long considered a mystery planet because it is shrouded in clouds that hide the details of its underlying surface. Venus is nearly as large and as massive as the Earth, contains relatively little water, and has nothing resembling the oceans of the Earth. Instead, carbon dioxide in an amount comparable to that in the carbonate rocks of the Earth fills the Venusian atmosphere, producing a pressure at the surface about 100 times higher than that at the surface of the Earth and a temperature far too high to support life of any kind as we know it. Venus has a slow retrograde rotation, so that it rotates in a direction opposite to that of most of the other objects in the solar system.

The next planet outward from the Earth away from the Sun

(Above) *A diagram of the solar system (A) reveals that the four inner planets (spheres) are concentrated in nearly circular orbits (white curves) close to the Sun (red), whereas the five outer planets are spread over larger distances. Of all the planets, the orbit of Pluto—the farthest known planet—is the most eccentric and the most highly inclined to the ecliptic, or the plane of the Earth's orbit about the Sun. Pluto's orbit periodically falls inside that of the planet Neptune. Most of the asteroids lie within a belt (dotted band) between the inner and the outer planets. Some of the asteroids (blue curves) and most of the comets (red curves) have highly inclined and eccentric orbits. In a diagram (B) of the Sun (1) and the planets drawn to the same scale, the Sun's size is indicated by comparing a solar prominence, or jet of glowing gases (2), with the inner planets Mercury (3), Venus (4), Earth (5) with its Moon (6), and Mars (7) with its tiny moons Phobos (8) and Deimos (9). The asteroid belt (10) is found between Mars and the outer planet Jupiter (11) with its four largest, or Galilean, satellites, Io (12), Europa (13), Ganymede (14), and Callisto (15). The other outer planets are Saturn (16), which is shown with its rings and its satellites, the largest of which is Titan (17); Uranus (18), with its five small satellites; Neptune (19), with Triton (20), the largest of its two moons; and Pluto (21).*

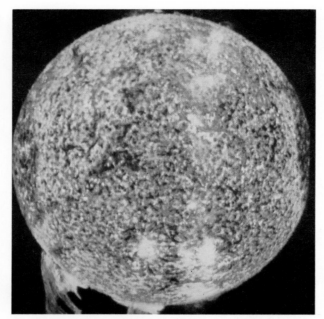

(Left) *This view of the Sun was photographed in the ultraviolet radiation of ionized helium by the astronauts in Skylab on Dec. 19, 1973. The colors were added during processing to reveal areas of similar brightness. Portions of a solar prominence, or jet of burning gas, can be seen (lower left).*

The Outer Planets. The terrestrial planets just described have in common a rocky composition whose major constituents have high boiling points and are therefore described as refractory. It is believed that the entire solar system, including the Sun, was formed from the gravitational contraction of a large cloud of gas and dust composed mainly of hydrogen and helium and only a small percentage of heavier atoms such as oxygen, silicon, and iron. The Sun's composition, which is about three-quarters hydrogen and nearly one-quarter helium, with less than two percent heavy elements, is believed to be essentially the same as that of the original nebula. The inner planets lost most of their lighter, volatile elements early as a result of their proximity to the hot Sun, whereas the more distant, cold, outer planets were able to retain their light gases. The result is that the outer planets became far more massive than the terrestrial planets and were able to hold very extensive atmospheres of light gases such as hydrogen, as well as light, icy substances such as water (H_2O), ammonia (NH_3), and methane (CH_4).

The most massive planet in the solar system, with about one-thousandth the mass of the Sun and more than 300 times the mass of the Earth, is JUPITER. Composed primarily of hy-

(Above, left to right) *A photomosaic of Mercury was made from photographs taken by Mariner 10 in March 1974 at a distance of less than 234,000 km (145,000 mi). It reveals a heavily cratered terrain and long bright rays much like those of the Moon. An image of the cloud cover of Venus, photographed in ultraviolet light by Mariner 10 in 1974, shows a banded cloud structure and swirling features at different levels. Strong, rapidly moving winds and sulfuric-acid droplets were found in the upper layers. Parts of Europe and Asia and most of Africa can be seen in a photograph of the Earth taken by the Apollo 11 astronauts in July 1969 from a distance of 182,000 km (113,000 mi).*

is MARS, which is only about one-tenth of the mass of the Earth. Its tenuous atmosphere is composed principally of carbon dioxide, with a pressure at the surface more than 100 times smaller (0.7 percent) than that at the surface of the Earth. The surface of Mars can be considered to be roughly divided into two hemispheres, one a surface of ancient, heavily cratered terrain and the other a geologically younger terrain having a much lower density of cratering. Mars has long been suspected to be a possible abode for other forms of life within the solar system, and apparent seasonal differences in its appearance were attributed to the presence of life. Experiments performed by the Viking spacecraft landers, however, found no evidence for the presence of Martian life forms, however, and it has been found that the Martian surface apparently contains oxidizing agents highly incompatible with any form of organic life.

The planet closest to the Sun is MERCURY, a planet whose mass is half as great as that of Mars and that has no detectable atmosphere. Mercury's surface is heavily cratered. The planet possesses an interesting resonance with its orbital motion, presenting first one face and then the other during its closest approaches to the Sun.

drogen and helium, Jupiter may have an interior composed of ice (and other frozen volatiles) and rocks, or both, exceeding several times one Earth mass of rocky material and three Earth masses of the ices. The total amount of material heavier than hydrogen and helium is unknown but is probably in the range of 10–20 Earth masses. Jupiter rotates rapidly on its axis, so that its figure is significantly flattened toward its equatorial plane, and the gases in its surface show a banded structure along lines of latitude. Infrared measurements from high-flying aircraft on the Earth and from flyby spacecraft have determined that Jupiter radiates into space about twice as much energy as it absorbs from the Sun; the additional heat emerges from the interior of the planet. Spacecraft also revealed that Jupiter is ringed.

The next planet outward from Jupiter is the strikingly ringed SATURN, another gas giant also thought to be composed predominantly of hydrogen and helium. Its mass is slightly less than a third that of Jupiter, but it also appears to have something approaching 20 Earth masses of heavier materials in the form, presumably, of icy or rocky materials. Saturn also rotates rapidly, is highly flattened toward its equatorial plane, and exhibits a banded structure along latitude lines.

Beyond Saturn are URANUS and NEPTUNE, two giant planets similar to each other. Each of these is slightly less than 20 times the mass of the Earth; unlike Jupiter and Saturn, hydrogen and helium may make up less than half the mass of these planets. Because hydrogen and helium predominate at the surface, the precise character of the underlying composition is not known, but it is again presumed to be some combination of ices and rocky materials. If these materials should be present in approximate proportions that are the same as in solar composition, then Uranus and Neptune would have roughly three Earth masses each of rocky materials and nine Earth masses of icy materials. The rotation periods of the two planets are uncertain, but they appear to be about one Earth day in each case. Uranus is distinguished by being tilted on its rotation axis by about 98 degrees with respect to the plane of the ecliptic, so that the rotation of the planet is retrograde. It is also distinguished by at least five, and perhaps eight, rings that encircle it, a discovery made in 1977.

PLUTO is a planet whose characteristics were largely unknown until the discovery of its moon in 1978. This discovery suggested a value for Pluto's diameter of about 3,000 km (1,900 mi), and for its moon of about 1,200 km (750 mi). The density of the planet is about the same as that of water, so that it may be composed of an ice-rock mixture. Pluto has a rather elliptical orbit that at times takes the planet closer to the Sun than Neptune. Until 1999, Pluto will be within Neptune's orbit. This would ordinarily be a rather unstable state of affairs, but perturbations of the Pluto orbit caused by Neptune occur in such a way that a collision between the two planets cannot occur.

THE SATELLITES

Of the 34 known satellites in the solar system, only three circle the inner planets. Earth has its abnormally massive Moon, and Mars has two tiny satellites, DEIMOS and PHOBOS. Very dark and heavily cratered, the Martian satellites may resemble the chondritic meteorites (fragile, low-density, stony-type meteorites that contain large amounts of carbon, water, and other volatile substances).

Most of the outer planets have large swarms of satellites attending them. In many cases the satellites are arranged in regular orbits that are suggestive of miniature solar systems. Jupiter has four giant satellites, each comparable in mass to Earth's Moon, called the Galilean satellites for their discoverer. The internal densities of these satellites are now reasonably well known as the result of measurements made by the flyby Pioneer spacecraft. The innermost two Galilean satellites, Io and EUROPA, are largely rocky in composition. On the other hand, the outer two giant satellites, GANYMEDE and CALLISTO, are of a lower density, suggestive of a much higher ice content. Closer to Jupiter than these Galilean satellites is a much smaller one, Amalthea. These five satellites lie in the plane of Jupiter's equator and have very nearly circular orbits. Because of this ordered arrangement, they are called the regular satellites.

Orbiting far from these regular satellites are the irregular satellites, in two swarms of much smaller bodies, each only a

(Above, left to right) *An image of the planet Mars that was obtained by the Viking 2 spacecraft on Aug. 5, 1976 at a distance of 419,000 km (260,000 mi) discloses water-ice clouds (upper right) near the large volcano Ascreasus Mons and the enormous Valles Marineris canyon (center). The Great Red Spot and the characteristic multihued banded structure of Jupiter's outer cloud layers are seen in Voyager 1 photograph taken on Feb. 5,1979 Io, which is the innermost of the Galilean moons, and its shadow on the planet's cloudtops are also visible. A view of Saturn and its rings from an angle that cannot be seen from Earth, was taken by Pioneer 11 in August 1979. Because the rings were sunlit from behind, the normally dark inner C ring appears bright, whereas the usually very bright middle B ring appears as a wide, dark band. The outer light band is the A ring, and the small dot is Titan. (Below, left to right) Uranus and its five satellites are visible in a picture taken through an Earth based telescope. Uranus is so distant that it appears as only a greenish blur. Neptune and its inner satellite Triton (arrow) are revealed in a photograph taken from Earth. Triton, which is larger than the Moon, is one of the largest satellites in the solar system. Neptune's tiny second moon, Nereid, can only be seen through very large telescopes. Two photographs taken in January 1930, resulted in the discovery of Pluto (arrow), the farthest known planet, by Clyde Tombaugh.*

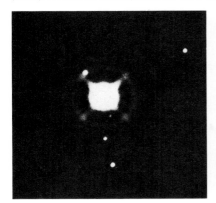 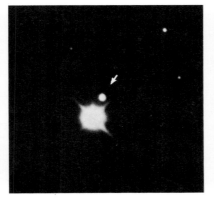 

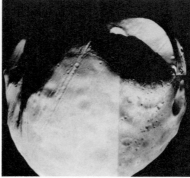

(Left) *Phobos, the largest and innermost of Mars's two tiny satellites, was revealed by the Mariner 9 spacecraft in 1971 to be full of craters, suggesting that it is extremely old. Craters as small as 30 m (100 ft) in diameter can be seen in this photograph. Phobos's longest axis, which measures only 27 km (17 mi), always points toward Mars.*

(Left) *Callisto, the second largest moon of Jupiter, was found by the Voyager 2 space probe in 1979 to be the most heavily cratered body in the solar system. Its surface of mixed dirt and water ice is darker and older than the other Galilean satellites. Bright rays like those on Earth's moon extend from many craters.*

(Above) *The side of the Moon that always faces Earth is characterized by numerous large maria, or craters flooded with dark lava during their formation. Innumerable smaller craters pockmark the entire lunar surface. Bright ray features extend from the younger craters. Several mountain ranges, valleys, and domes also cover the surface.*

few kilometers in radius. Eight of these bodies are so far known to exist, and there are indications of additional members. The orbits of these satellites are inclined at substantial angles with respect to the plane of Jupiter's equator, and the orbits themselves are quite elliptical. Some of these small satellites rotate in a direct (west to east) sense, but the others rotate in a retrograde (east to west) sense.

Saturn also has a system of regular satellites. One of these, TITAN, has a mass slightly greater than that of Earth's Moon. Because of its low density, however, Titan is large—larger than the planet Mercury. Titan is unique among the satellites in the solar system in that it has a substantial atmosphere, in which frozen methane appears to be a major constituent. The other regular satellites of the Saturnian system are smaller in radius than Titan by factors of as much as ten, and smaller in mass by factors of as much as one thousand. Saturn also possesses irregular satellites, for a total of 11 or 12.

The five satellites of Uranus are closely clustered in the plane of the Uranian equator, so that the plane of their orbits is also rotated 98 degrees to the plane of the ecliptic. These satellites are relatively small, comparable in size to the lesser regular satellites of Saturn.

The unusual system of Neptune contains one major satellite, TRITON—whose mass is not exactly known but may be comparable to that of the Moon—which moves in a circular but inclined retrograde orbit. Neptune also has a smaller, direct-rotating satellite.

A single moon of Pluto was discovered on June 22, 1978, and named Charon. It appears to have about 5–10 percent of the mass of Pluto, meaning that it is the solar system's largest moon compared to its planet.

ASTEROIDS AND METEOROIDS

The major planets in the solar system are greatly outnumbered by the swarms of smaller bodies called minor planets, or asteroids, and by the even more numerous and smaller bodies known as meteoroids. Most of the asteroids exist within the relatively large gap lying between the orbits of Mars and Jupiter, whereas meteoroids are randomly distributed. A few large asteroids have radii of a few hundred kilometers, but most are much smaller. The smaller meteoroids produce meteor trails when they enter the Earth's atmo-

sphere, and the larger ones form meteorite craters. A large number of the asteroids appear similar to the carbonaceous chondritic meteorites and are probably of relatively lower density than ordinary rocks. Nearly 2,000 of the asteroids have accurately determined orbits and have been given names. It is generally believed that the smaller asteroidal bodies have been created in collisions involving larger ones, so that there probably exist many small bodies that have not been detected by photographic surveys.

Many asteroids have orbits that cross the orbit of Mars; some cross the orbit of the Earth or go even further into the inner solar system. These are called the Apollo asteroids. It has been suggested that many of the meteorites that strike the Earth are chips of the Apollo asteroids caused by collisions. These asteroids can collide with the Earth or one of the other terrestrial planets, and some of the major craters that exist on these planets have probably been caused by such collisions.

Other asteroidal bodies, called Trojan asteroids, have been observed both 60 degrees ahead of Jupiter in its orbit and 60 degrees behind. These positions of special orbital stability are called Lagrangian points.

It is possible that swarms of dust particles are concentrated in the Moon's orbit, both 60 degrees ahead of the motion of the Moon and 60 degrees behind it. These are sometimes called the L4 and L5 Lagrangian points. Although there has not been clear confirmation of the presence of these dust swarms, they may exist in a manner similar to that of the Trojan asteroids with respect to Jupiter. There have been suggestions that future human colonies in space might be established at one of these Lagrangian points.

Until recently it was believed that minor planets were confined to the inner solar system. Recently, however, an object has been discovered called CHIRON, a body some hundreds of kilometers in radius that orbits between Saturn and Uranus.

COMETS

Comets are sometimes spectacular objects from the outer regions of the solar system, as far away as a substantial fraction of the distance to the nearest star. They appear to be typically a few kilometers in radius and are composed largely of icy substances. Their chemistry is, however, clearly complex. As a

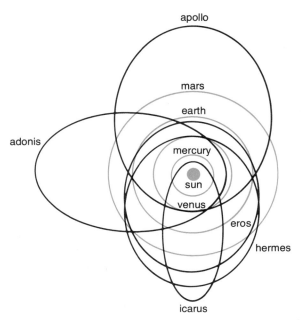

Although most of the minor planets, or asteroids, move in a belt between Mars and Jupiter, several asteroids have highly elliptical orbits that take them inside Earth's path. Icarus, which comes within only a few million kilometers of Earth, passes closer to the Sun than any other asteroid and travels within Mercury's orbit.

A large meteorite formed Meteor Crater, Ariz., 22,000 years ago. Such cratering of Earth-type planets was common in the early solar system, and on a smaller scale it still goes on. Erosive processes on Earth, however, tend to eradicate or obscure such craters relatively quickly.

comet enters the inner solar system, it emits large amounts of volatile materials that are transformed by the energy of sunlight and of the solar wind into a variety of individual atoms, molecules, and ions, mostly of the common materials carbon, nitrogen, oxygen, and hydrogen, and combinations that include these. Many complex molecules have been detected by spectroscopic analysis of comet tails. Comets also emit a large number of tiny dust particles. Occasionally a comet is seen to break into two or more pieces while it passes through the inner solar system.

The Dutch astronomer Jan H. Oort recognized (about 1950) that most of the apparently fresh comets coming into the inner solar system started from initial distances beyond 50,000 astronomical units (the distance from the Earth to the Sun is defined as one astronomical unit). Furthermore, he recognized that the ease with which planetary perturbations can change the orbits of the comets meant that typical comets were unlikely to endure many orbital passages through the inner solar system. Because several comets are observed each year, this means that there must be a very large reservoir of them in the outer solar system. Oort suggested that this reservoir lies principally between 50,000 and 100,000 astronomical units, in a thick shell surrounding the solar system. Oort

showed that the passage of stars relatively near to the Sun would greatly change the orbital parameters of comets within the Oort cloud, such that some of them could plunge deep into the inner solar system and be observed.

ORIGIN OF THE SOLAR SYSTEM

For more than 300 years there has been serious scientific discussion of the processes and events that led to the formation of the solar system. For most of this time lack of knowledge about the physical conditions in the solar system prevented a rigorous approach to the problem. Explanations were especially sought for the regularity in the directions of rotation and orbit of objects in the solar system, the slow rotation of the Sun, and the Titius-Bode law, which states that the radii of the planetary orbits increase in a regular fashion throughout the solar system. In a similar fashion, the radii of the orbits of the regular satellites of Jupiter, Saturn, and Uranus increase in a regular manner. In modern times the slow rotation of the Sun has been explained as resulting from the deceleration of its angular motion through its magnetic interaction with the outflowing solar wind, so that this feature should not have been considered a constraint on theories of the origin of the solar system.

The many theories concerning the origin of the solar system that have been advanced during the last three centuries can be classified as either dualistic or monistic. A common feature of dualistic theories is that another star once passed close to the Sun, and tidal perturbations between the two stars drew out filaments of gas from which the planets condensed. Theories of this type encounter enormous difficulties

This sequence of photographs of Halley's comet was taken during its most recent return, in 1910. From left to right the pictures show the typical formation and disappearance of a comet's tail during its solar orbit. The tail usually appears when the comet is about 1.5 to 2 AU from the Sun, grows rapidly in length, and reaches a maximum near the Sun. It then contracts as it recedes and finally disappears.

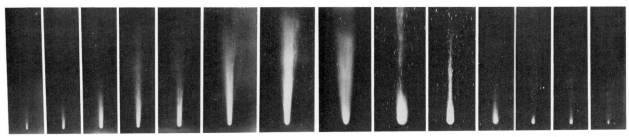

April 26 April 27 April 30 May 2 May 3 May 4 May 6 May 15 May 23 May 28 June 3 June 6 June 9 June 11

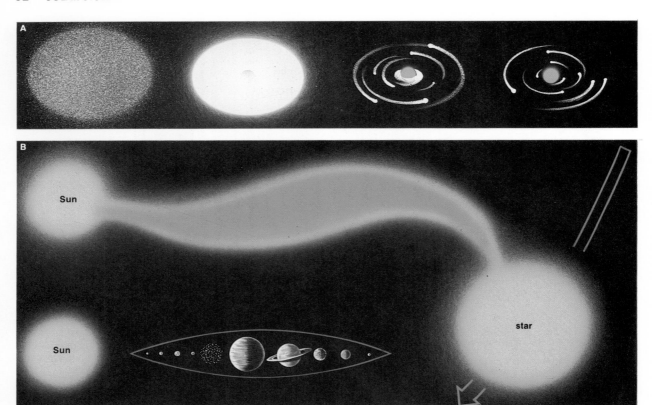

Current nebular theories of the origin of the solar system assume that the Sun and planets were formed at the same time from the gravitational collapse of a huge cloud of interstellar gas and dust. An older, now rejected, variant (A) of the nebular hypothesis suggested that the Sun was formed first from a swirling cloud of gas and dust. The newly formed Sun was then postulated to have rotated so rapidly that it threw off material that moved outward, cooled, and condensed to form the planets. In the tidal theory (B), also rejected, James Jeans proposed that a passing star drew a long, cigar-shaped filament of material from the Sun that condensed into planets.

in trying to account for modern information about the solar system, and they have generally been discarded. By contrast, monistic theories envisage a disk of gas and dust, called the primitive solar nebula, that formed around the Sun. Many of these theories speculate that the Sun and the planets formed together from the primeval solar nebula. This type of theory has dominated thinking about the origin of the solar system since World War II, but there has also been a great variety of hypotheses within this general framework.

The large amount of activity that has taken place in the last 20 years in the renewed exploration of the solar system has also provided a great impetus for renewed studies of the origin of the system. One important component of this research has been the detailed studies of the properties of meteorites that has been made possible by modern laboratory instrumentation. The distribution and abundance of the elements within different meteoritic mineral phases has provided much information on the physical conditions present at the time the solar system began to form. Recent discoveries of anomalies in the isotopic compositions of the elements in certain mineral phases promise to give information about the local galactic interstellar environment that led to the formation of the solar system. Investigations of the properties of other planets has led to the new science of comparative planetology, in which the differences observed among the planets not only lead to a better understanding of the planets, but also pose precise new questions concerning the mechanisms by which the planets may have been formed.

Studies of the stars within our galaxy have shown that the age of our galaxy is much greater than the age of the solar system. Therefore, processes observed in the formation of stars within our galaxy today are likely to be found relevant to the formation of our solar system. Stars appear to form in

groups or associations, as a result of the gravitational collapse of clouds of gas and dust in the interstellar medium. Modern monistic theories envisage the gas and dust in the primitive solar nebula to be the collapsed remnant of a fragment of an interstellar cloud.

There has been much discussion of how the planets might have formed from the primeval solar nebula. In recent years attention has focused on the possibility that gravitational instabilities might have played an important role in this process. Such gravitational instabilities may be of two types. One of these is a gravitational instability in the gas of the primitive solar nebula, from which there would be formed a giant gaseous protoplanet. From the evolution of such protoplanets there could arise, in the outer solar system, the giant planets that are observed today. In the inner solar system, the possibility exists that giant gaseous protoplanets formed rocky cores at their centers, which survived the stripping away of the gaseous envelopes caused by gravitational and thermal forces from the growing Sun.

The other form of gravitational instability involves the condensed materials in the solar nebula. Small dust particles that may have been present in the gas of the solar nebula could be expected to settle toward the midplane of the nebula if the gas were not subject to extensive turbulent churning. Gravitational instabilities acting on a thin dust layer might have formed bodies ranging from tens to hundreds of kilometers in radius. Collisions among these bodies may have played a major role in accumulations of material to form the planets.

It must be stressed that all theories of the origin of the solar system currently being formulated respond to and are limited by the rapid accumulation of facts about planetary bodies within the solar system. Because of the rapid rate of progress in such studies, it is generally recognized that such theories are preliminary and simplified, so that ideas and theories in this area of research can be expected to continue to evolve rapidly.   A. G. W. CAMERON

Bibliography: Abell, George O., *Exploration of the Universe* (1975); Berman, Louis, and Evans, J. C., *Exploring the Cosmos* (1977); Burnham, Robert, *Burnham's Celestial Handbook*, 2 vols. (1978); Butler, S. T., and Raymond, Robert, *The Family of the Sun* (1975); Gardner, Martin, *Space Puzzles: Curious Questions about the Solar System* (1971); Hartmann, William K., *Astronomy: The Cosmic Journey* (1978); Kopal, Zdanek, *The Solar System* (1973); Kuiper, G. P., ed., *The Solar System*, 4 vols. (1953-63); Page, Thornton and Lou, eds., *The Origin of the Solar System* (1966); Scientific American Editors, *The Solar System* (1975); Wood, John, *The Solar System* (1979).

solar wind

The solar wind is a continuous outward flow of ionized gas (plasma) from the corona of the SUN, which extends beyond the Earth's orbit and into interstellar space. Measurements from space probes since 1962—the date of the solar wind's first direct detection—have shown that its velocity at the Earth's orbit varies between 300 and 700 km/sec (185 and 435 mi/sec). The highest speeds occur in recurrent wind streams that sweep past the Earth, like a searchlight beam, as the Sun rotates on its axis every 27 days.

The charged particles of the solar wind consist mainly of protons and electrons, with 5% by number of helium nuclei. Their total densities range between 1 and 10 particles/cm³. The magnetic field carried with the wind has a mean intensity at the Earth's orbit of about 5×10^{-5} gauss compared with a maximum magnetic field for the Earth of 0.3 gauss. Probe studies in the ecliptic plane (the line of sight from the Earth to the Sun) show that the mean outflow velocity increases with distance, at least to approximately the Earth's orbit. Relatively little is known about the wind velocity, density, and time dependence out of the ecliptic plane except indirectly from study of its influence on comet tails. This fact makes it difficult to derive an accurate figure for the rate of total mass loss from the Sun, although the loss is estimated at approximately 10^{-13} solar masses per year. This rate is very low compared to that measured in stellar winds of some hot young stars, where loss rates of 10^{-6} solar masses per year have been inferred from observations.

(For interactions of the solar wind with the Earth's magnetic field, see EARTH, GEOMAGNETIC FIELD OF; MAGNETOSPHERE.)
                                                    PETER FOUKAL

Bibliography: Brandt, John C., *Introduction to the Solar Wind* (1970); King, J. W., and Newman, W. S., *The Solar Wind* (1966).

soldering: see WELDING AND SOLDERING.

sole

Soles are about 117 species of flatfishes constituting the family Soleidae in the order Pleuronectiformes (formerly called Heterosomata). They exhibit the unique FLATFISH pattern of development, with one eye migrating to the other side of the flattened body of the mature sole. They are found mainly in shallow, temperate or tropical, marine waters, but some species, such as the American hogchoker, *Trinectes maculatus*, are common to freshwater. Most species are less than 30 cm

The European sole, S. solea, is a warm-water flatfish that is found in the Mediterranean and the eastern Atlantic.

(12 in) long, but the common European sole, *Solea solea*—the original Dover sole—grows to about 50 cm (20 in) long. The term *fillet of sole* initially pertained to this fish but is now applied to any flatfish fillet. The lemon sole, *Microstomus kitt*, is a member of the right-eyed flounder family, Pleuronectidae.

solenodon   [soh-lee'-nuh-dahn]

The Haitian solenodon, S. paradoxus, is a small nocturnal mammal native to the forests of the island of Hispaniola. Shrewlike in appearance, it uses its long snout to forage in the ground for food.

Solenodons are primitive mammals of the family Solenodontidae in the order Insectivora. Only two species still survive, the Haitian solenodon, *Solenodon paradoxus*, and the Cuban solenodon, *S. cubanus*. Solenodons resemble big-footed, rat-sized shrews, reaching about 25 cm (10 in) in length, plus a tail almost equally long, and 1 kg (2 lb) in weight. Like some shrews, solenodons have poisonous saliva. Both species are rare and in danger of extinction, particularly the Cuban species.

solenoid   [soh'-luh-noyd]

A solenoid is an electromechanical device consisting of a coil of wire, usually wound in the form of a long, narrow cylinder, and a core, or plunger, made of a magnetic material such as iron placed partly within the coil. When an electric current passes through the coil of wire, the coil becomes an electromagnet, and a magnetic field is created within it. This field exerts a force on the core that tends to pull it further into the coil. The motion of the core can, in turn, be used to actuate some other device such as a switch or relay.

Soler, Antonio   [soh-layr']

Antonio Soler, b. November or December 1729, d. Dec. 20, 1783, was a Spanish priest and composer important in the development of the keyboard sonata. He was ordained in 1752 at El Escorial, where he became organist and choirmaster, and shortly afterward studied harpsichord with Domenico Scarlatti. He wrote much church music and some songs, but his best works are his keyboard fugues, fandangos, and especially sonatas, which show Scarlatti's Italian influence while retaining Spanish rhythms. Soler's six concertos for two organs remain popular among organists.   WILLIAM HAYS

Bibliography: Newman, W. S., *The Sonata in the Classic Era* (1963).

Soleri, Paolo   [soh-lay'-ree]

Paolo Soleri, b. Turin, Italy, June 21, 1919, is a visionary designer whose utopian "arcology" "demands a transfiguration of the earth without defiling or disfiguring its own cosmic aspects" by housing human society in a few highly compact megastructures. After emigrating to the United States in 1947 and studying with Frank Lloyd Wright at Taliesin West, Soleri made his home at Cosanti, 113 km (70 mi) north of Scottsdale, Ariz. There, students attracted by his theories pay to help build Arcosanti, a model of the global arcology that Soleri believes to be the only alternative to the destruction of "sclerotic, asphyxiated" human society.   J. MEREDITH NEIL

Bibliography: Soleri, Paolo, *Arcology* (1969), *The Bridge between Matter and Spirit Is Matter Becoming Spirit* (1973), and *The Sketchbooks* (1971); Wall, Donald, *Visionary Cities* (1971).

solicitation

Solicitation, as a criminal offense, is the act of enticing or urging another person to commit a felony or a misdemeanor considered harmful to the public welfare. If the solicited person agrees to join the solicitor in an offense, a conspiracy may be established, superseding the solicitation offense. In some cities, the public solicitation of business by prostitutes is treated as a public nuisance and punished as a misdemeanor.

solicitor: see BARRISTER.

solicitor general: see JUSTICE, U.S. DEPARTMENT OF.

solid solution

A solid solution, or diadochy, is the random substitution of IONS (charged atoms) of one element for ions of a different element in the structure of a crystalline solid. Such substitution, which may be negligible to extensive, results in compositional variations of a given mineral.

Factors Affecting Extent of Substitution. Ion size is the most important factor influencing the extent to which substitution can take place. Ions of two elements can readily substitute for each other if their radii differ by less than 15%. If the ionic radii differ by 15% to 30%, substitution is limited; if the difference is greater than 30%, substitution is rare.

Temperature of crystallization also influences the extent of solid solution. As the temperature increases, the crystal lattice becomes more open and the space requirements become less rigorous, allowing more ionic substitution to occur. For example, the FELDSPAR sanidine, the high-temperature form of $KAlSi_3O_8$, contains appreciable amounts of sodium ion (Na^+; ionic radius, 0.97 Å) substituting for potassium ion (K^+; ionic radius, 1.33 Å); whereas only small amounts of sodium ions can be tolerated in the low-temperature form, microcline.

Maintenance of electrical neutrality in the crystal structure is a third factor in ionic substitution. When, as in the above example, Na^+ substitutes for K^+, no electrical imbalance results. If Ca^{2+} substitutes for Na^+, however, as in the plagioclase feldspars, other substitutions must take place to preserve electrical neutrality.

Types of Substitution. Most solid solution is the result of one or the other of two basic types of substitution, simple and coupled. Simple substitution takes place when ions (cations or anions) of one element substitute for ions of another element of the same valence. For example, small amounts of K^+ take the place of Na^+ in the sodium chloride (NaCl) structure. Because of the difference in ionic radii, however, only limited solid solution is present. One ion substituting for another ion of like valence and similar size gives rise to complete solid solution series, such as are common in the rock-forming minerals. For example, OLIVINE [$(Mg,Fe)_2SiO_4$] is a solid-solution series between the pure end members forsterite (Mg_2SiO_4) and fayalite (Fe_2SiO_4); Fe^{2+} substitutes for Mg^{2+} in all proportions. An example of simple substitution of atoms, rather than ions, is given by gold and silver. A complete solid-solution series exists between the two metals because their atoms are the same size.

In coupled substitution, an ion substitutes for another of different valence, requiring another substitution elsewhere in the structure to maintain electrical neutrality. The plagioclase feldspars with end members albite ($NaAlSi_3O_8$) and anorthite ($CaAl_2Si_2O_8$) offer an illustration of such a mechanism. For each Ca^{2+} that replaces Na^+, one Al^{3+} takes the place of Si^{4+} in the structure.

In some crystals interstices exist between the ions or ionic groups of the crystal structure. The housing of atoms, ions, or molecules in these structural voids is called interstitial solid solution.   CORNELIUS S. HURLBUT, JR.

Bibliography: Collins, E. W., and Gegal, H. L., eds., *Physics of Solid Solution Strengthening* (1975); Hurlbut, Cornelius S., and Klein; Cornelis, *Manual of Mineralogy, After J. D. Dana*, 19th ed. (1977); Krauskopf, Konrad Bates, *Introduction to Geochemistry* (1967); Saxena, S. K., *Thermodynamics of Rock-Forming Crystalline Solutions* (1973).

solid-state physics

Solid-state physics emerged as a separate branch of physics after World War II. Virtually any observable property of solid materials comes under the umbrella of solid-state physics, but research has concentrated on such questions as the magnetic properties, transport properties (electrical and thermal conductivity), superconductivity, Fermi surfaces, atomic arrangement, and electron structure of materials.

Even though there are only 80 elements in sufficient abundance to be used in preparing solid compounds and alloys, there appears to be an unlimited number of ways to combine them and produce materials with unusual properties. Physicists engaged in theoretical solid-state research are unable to predict accurately the properties of pure elements, compounds, and alloys, because these fundamental properties arise from the complexity of their electronic structure. Thus new materials are generally discovered from the empirical effort of mixing elements under varying conditions of heat, pressure, and so on.

At the present time there are perhaps 20,000 to 30,000 solid-state physicists in the world holding doctorates, and Nobel prizes in this field have become commonplace. The transistor is probably the outstanding product of solid-state physics.

General Properties. Typical data determined by solid-state physicists on a material are its crystal structure, density, electrical conductivity, thermal conductivity, magnetic structure, compressibility, coefficient of expansion, and specific heat. The identification of these measurable properties and their variation with temperature has been a major concern to solid-state physicists. Because measurable properties evidence similarities in various materials, solid-state physics has been traditionally but not rigidly subdivided into groups concerning themselves principally with metals, insulators, or semiconductors. There is a vast group of solids, however, such as plastics, organic materials (wood and bone), and rocks, that has received less attention because these solids have much more complex atomic arrangements and are therefore more difficult to understand. It is implicit that the solid-state physicist is dedicated to developing the relationship between measurable properties of solids (and even liquids) and their electronic structure.

Metals. As an example, a single atom of lithium has only three electrons, and atomic physicists are able to calculate with a high degree of accuracy the energies and arrangements of these electrons and the effect of magnetic, electric, and electromagnetic fields on these arrangements. When these lithium atoms join together to form lithium metal, however, the electrons of each atom are affected by the electrostatic repulsion of the electrons on all the surrounding atoms and the electrostatic attraction of the surrounding nuclei. It subsequently becomes very difficult to calculate with accuracy any of the known properties of lithium metal such as atomic positions, electron arrangement and velocities, electrical and thermal conductivity (and how it varies with temperature, pressure, and magnetic field), melting temperature, atomic vibrations, specific heat, compressibility, color, absorption and scattering of light of different wavelengths, the cohesive energy (the energy required to evaporate the metals), changes in atomic position with temperature and pressure, and the work function (how much photon energy is required to eject an electron from its surface). As the atomic number increases (hence the number of electrons per atom), the theory becomes even more complex.

At the present time, solid-state physicists have measured and tabulated numerous properties of elements, alloys, compounds, and other substances and have observed certain systematic variations in these properties; for example, the electrical conductivity of a metal decreases with increasing temperature, whereas the reverse holds for a semiconductor such as silicon or germanium. To a great extent, intuition based on this vast accumulation of existing measurements—with some help from simplified theoretical calculations—seems to be the best guide for predicting the behavior of new alloys or compounds. Intuition is unreliable, however, in predicting new discoveries of material behavior, and such new discoveries are reported almost annually.

Methods. The principal experimental techniques employed in solid-state physics are photon and neutron scattering and absorption to examine atomic positions, magnetic properties, atomic vibrations, electron positions, electron velocities, and electron energies; application of electric and magnetic fields and heat (or removal of heat), accompanied by measurements of their effects on the electrons and nuclei in the solid; and application of pressures to see how the atoms and electrons change their behavior.

Magnetism. A major problem that has challenged solid-state physicists is magnetism. It is not known why only four of all the naturally occurring elements in the periodic table are ferromagnetic: iron, cobalt, nickel, and gadolinium. Even in the case of iron, only the commonly stable arrangement (α iron) is ferromagnetic. There are two other crystalline forms of iron metal that are not—one achieved under high pressure (123,000 atmospheres) and the other by raising the temperature to 910° C. Even though these forms have been studied extensively, the theoretical physicist is unable to calculate these differences. On the other hand, cobalt metal has two crystal forms that both have ferromagnetic strength identical to within one percent.

From a variety of measurements and limited theoretical understanding, the following is known about ferromagnetism: every electron is an individual magnet, but in most of the elements the electrons pair off with their north and south poles oppositely aligned. For example, in aluminum or copper any experimental technique that can find the magnetic field on one individual electron, such as neutron scattering, reveals that the electrons pair off so well that their magnetic fields cancel exactly. Even in α iron, 24 of the 26 electrons on each atom pair off, but two of them do just the opposite and maintain their north poles rigidly fixed in the same direction. This orientation is maintained up to the boiling point of 3,000° C. The magnetic strength of each electron is thousands of times too weak to account for such a strong adherence to this arrangement. Additionally, this pair of electrons on one atom is rigidly fixed to the pairs on all other atoms. It is the total magnetic field from all these pairs that enables a magnet to lift a piece of iron. Even the force that keeps these pairs all pointing in the same direction cannot be overcome until a temperature of 776° C is attained, again thousands of times more than the magnetic forces between the pairs can produce.

The Fermi-Dirac Principle. The answer to the origin of magnetism lies in the mysteries of the Fermi-Dirac principle, which states that only pairs of electrons, each with north pole opposite, can occupy the same energy level in atomic systems. This is a powerful force and accounts for the different quantized energy levels on atoms. On each atom in α iron, the magnetic pair of electrons is actually in different energy levels; otherwise their magnetic north poles would have to be opposite. The reason they can exist in these two particular different energy levels is that the electrons are relatively far from each other on the atom; this separation reduces the electrostatic repulsion between like charges. Thus the Fermi-Dirac principle and electrostatic forces, which are thousands of times stronger than the magnetic forces, combine to produce magnetism. Only in a few elements are the conditions just right to take advantage of these forces and produce ferromagnetism.

To complicate matters even further, in 1950, Clifford Shull and James Smart discovered antiferromagnetism in manganese oxide, MnO. Of the 25 electrons on each manganese atom, 20 pair off, but 5 remain rigidly fixed with their north poles in the same direction. The electrons of alternate manganese atoms in MnO, however, are reversely aligned; so the sample is not attracted by a magnet. There are literally thousands of compounds such as MnO.   RICHARD J. WEISS

Bibliography: Blackmore, John S., *Solid State Physics,* 2d ed. (1974); Clark, Hylton, *Solid State Physics: An Introduction to Its Theory* (1968); Coleman, B. V., ed., *Solid State Physics* (1974); Cracknell, A. P., *Group Theory in Solid-State Physics* (1975); Dekker, Adrianus J., *Solid State*

Physics (1957); Kittel, Charles, *Introduction to Solid State Physics,* 5th ed. (1976); Omar, M. Ali, *Elementary Solid State Physics: Principles and Applications* (1974); Peierls, R. E., *Quantum Theory of Solids* (1955); Sachs, Mendel, *Solid State Theory* (1974); Weller, Paul F., ed., *Solid State Chemistry and Physics: An Introduction,* 2 vols. (1973–74).

See also: CONDUCTION, ELECTRIC; CRYOGENICS; MAGNETISM; METAL; SEMICONDUCTOR; SUPERCONDUCTIVITY; TRANSISTOR.

solid waste pollution: see POLLUTION, ENVIRONMENTAL.

Solingen   [zoh'-ling-en]

Solingen is a city in northwestern West Germany in the state of North Rhine–Westphalia with a population of 169,600 (1976 est.). Located 19 km (12 mi) southeast of Düsseldorf, it has been famous for ironworking, especially cutlery, since the 13th century. Other manufactures include medical equipment, chemicals, leather, bicycles, textiles, and candy. Solingen was settled in 1067 and developed into an administrative center for the region. It became part of Prussia in 1815.

solipsism   [soh'-luhp-sizm]

Solipsism is the philosophical view that only the self exists or can be known to exist. In its most extreme form, solipsism holds that all perceived objects and events are merely the products of personal consciousness and that this consciousness alone is genuinely real. Most forms of solipsism, however, are derived from SKEPTICISM and argue that the only things of which genuine knowledge is possible are the mind and its contents; hence these alone may justifiably be said to exist. A variant of this form argues that only in the first person case is knowledge of the mind possible. The problem of the minds of others has received considerable discussion in contemporary Anglo-American philosophy.

Bibliography: Buford, F. O., *Essays on Other Minds* (1970); Unger, Peter, *Ignorance: A Case for Skepticism* (1975); Wisdom, A. J. T. D., *Other Minds* (1953).

solitaire   (bird)

Solitaire is the common name for about nine species of robinlike songbirds of the thrush family, Turdidae. Native to the New World, solitaires are found mostly in the tropics, but Townsend's solitaire, *Myadestes townsendi,* occurs west of the Rocky Mountains, wintering from northern Mexico into southern Canada and breeding as far north as southern Alaska. Smaller and slimmer than the closely related American robin, it is gray, with a buff wing patch, white eye ring, and white outer tail feathers. Two Caribbean islands species, the Cuban solitaire, *M. elisabeth,* and the rufous-throated solitaire, *M. genibarbis,* are considered endangered species. Solitaire is also the name for two species of extinct DODO BIRDS.

WILLIAM F. SANDFORD

Townsend's solitaire, Myadestes townsendi, *a small perching songbird that resembles a mockingbird, is found in coniferous forests and brushlands west of the Rockies, from Alaska to Mexico.*

solitaire   (card game)

Solitaire, or patience, card games, of which there are many varieties, are intended primarily for one player; simultaneous games between two or more persons in competition are also played. In the most popular solitaire game, klondike, the player uses a standard 52-card deck, and the cards are normally ranked with ace low. Play begins by dealing one card face up and six cards face down in a row from left to right. Next, one card is dealt face up on top of the card just to the right of the original face-up card, then the deal continues along the row with the placement of five cards face down. The deal proceeds in this manner, one card fewer being dealt in each round until 28 cards are in the seven stacks, or piles. These seven piles, called the tableau, show seven cards face up. The remaining 24 cards form the stock.

The object of klondike is to build sequences of cards in each suit. Any time an ace becomes available, either from the stock or the tableau, it is placed directly above the tableau to form a foundation, and the player then attempts to build up from the ace to the king in that suit. Sequences are also built down on the tableau, alternating red and black cards with no regard for suit. Tableau sequences may be moved from one pile to another as a unit. After such a move, a newly exposed face-down card on the pile is turned up and is available for play. At any time during play when the last card of a pile is moved, the vacancy may be filled only by a king or by a sequence with a king as its base. The final element of play involves the 24 stock cards. These 24 cards are turned up either one at a time or at intervals of every third card and are placed on a waste pile. As these cards are placed face up on the waste pile, the top card is available for play; if it is used, then the card beneath it can also be played.

A player goes out when all 52 cards are transferred to the foundations above the tableau. In casino play, the player is charged $52, or points, by the house for one game, and the player is credited for each card on the foundation. The odds against recouping the initial charge are 4 to 1.

Bibliography: Gibson, Walter B., *How to Play Winning Solitaire* (1976); Morehead, Albert H., *The Complete Book of Solitaire and Patience Games* (1973).

Sollers, Philippe   [soh-lairs']

Philippe Sollers, b. Nov. 28, 1936, is the foremost exponent of an offshoot of the French new novel known as the "new novel" (*nouveau nouveau roman*). Founder (1960) of the influential journal *Tel Quel,* he has attempted, in such works as *Drame* (Drama, 1965) and *Nombres* (Numbers, 1968), to lay the groundwork for a novel of the future, which would transcend current categories of meaning and generate a revolutionary culture.

Solo man

In 1931–33 a team of Dutch paleontologists working in eastern Java, Indonesia, recovered prehistoric human skeletal remains of 11 individuals, popularly known as Solo man, from a bank of the Solo River near the village of Ngandong. Once regarded as contemporaries of the European NEANDERTHALERS (*Homo sapiens neanderthalensis*), these hominids are now recognized as advanced members of the species HOMO ERECTUS. This conclusion is based on detailed comparisons of the Solo specimens with *Homo erectus* fossils from sites in Asia and Africa. Based on an analysis of animal bones found with the human fossils, the Solo specimens are estimated to date from 200,000 years ago. Stone tools were also found in the deposits, but their association with the hominids has been questioned. As with many *Homo erectus* fossil finds, the Solo skeletons are incomplete; few bones are present, and the skulls are badly damaged. Some observers have suggested that these early humans may have been the victims of cannibalistic activities by their contemporaries.

ALAN MANN AND NANCY MINUGH

Bibliography: Howells, W. W., *Evolution of the Genus Homo* (1973).

See also: PREHISTORIC HUMANS.

Sologub, Fyodor   [suh-luh-goop']

A novelist of genius and a poet of high distinction, Fyodor Sologub, b. Fyodor Kuzmich Teternikov, Mar. 1 (N.S.), 1863, d. Dec. 5, 1927, was a major figure of Russian symbolism. A high school teacher and administrator until 1907, he possessed a sensitive but perverse intellect. His masterpiece, *The Little Demon* (1907; Eng. trans., 1916), concerns an evil schoolteacher. His trilogy, *The Created Legend* (1908–12; Eng. trans., 1916), is strikingly original in its mixture of realism and fantasy. A prolific writer and great stylist, Sologub expresses a belief that the only escape from the ugliness and cruelty of life is through the transforming power of art—and, ultimately, death.

Solomon, King of Israel

The son and successor of King DAVID, Solomon was the third king of Israel, reigning from about 972 BC until his death in 922. David's son by BATHSHEBA, Solomon was unexpectedly elevated to the throne after his half brother Adonijah had attempted unsuccessfully to seize the kingship. The young Solomon quickly mastered the situation, ruthlessly eliminating all the potential threats to his rule. His reign was marked by foreign alliances, especially with Egypt and the Phoenicians, and by military strength, and was thus untroubled by major wars or internal revolts, leaving him free to pursue other interests. Solomon fully exploited the economic possibilities of his empire and used the resulting wealth to support vast building projects, the most famous being the Temple in Jerusalem. He was also an author and a patron of literature, although many of the writings attributed to him—for example, the Book of Proverbs, Ecclesiastes, and the Song of Solomon—were not his work. Solomon's success in so many spheres contributed to his legendary reputation for wisdom, but his reign ended with simmering resentment over heavy taxes and the religious syncretism fostered by his marriages.

J. J. M. ROBERTS

Bibliography: Bright, John, *A History of Israel* (1972); Maly, Eugene H., *World of David and Solomon* (1966).

Solomon Islands

The Solomon Islands are a chain of seven large and many small islands trending northwest-southeast for 1,500 km (930 mi) in the western Pacific Ocean. Except for the northernmost islands, which are part of PAPUA NEW GUINEA, the archipelago is politically constituted as an independent state within the British Commonwealth. The capital is Honiara (1976 pop., 14,942) on GUADALCANAL. Most of the islands are volcanic, mountainous, and heavily forested. Rainfall exceeds 2,500 mm (100 in) annually; temperatures, averaging 27° C (80° F), vary little during the year.

The Solomons' population is predominantly MELANESIAN. Their literacy rate of 60% should increase under a program to provide 6 years of primary education for all. The Honiara Technical Institute for advanced studies was opened in 1969. Health clinics are under construction to provide basic care.

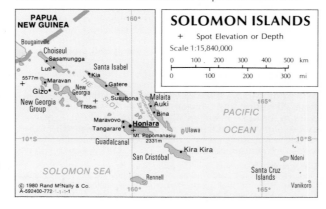

SOLOMON ISLANDS

Official Name: Solomon Islands
Capital and Largest City: Honiara (1976 pop., 14,942)
Area: 29,785 km² (11,500 mi²)
Elevation: *Highest*—Mount Popomanasiu, 2,331 m
  (7,648 ft); *lowest*—sea level
Population: 219,000 (1979 est.). *Distribution*—9% urban,
  91% rural; *density,* 7 persons per km² (19 per mi²);
  annual rate of increase (1970-77), 2.8%
Principal Languages: English, Pidgin English
Principal Religions: Anglicanism, Roman Catholicism
Principal Products: *Agriculture*—copra, cocoa, chillies,
  spices. *Manufacturing and industry*—fishing, forestry,
  food products, jute, rattan, asbestos fabrics, leather
  goods; gold panning
Railroads: None
Roads: 241 km/150 mi (1978 paved)
Currency: 1 Solomon Islands dollar = 100 cents

Tuberculosis and leprosy remain major health problems. Life expectancy is 51 years.

Agriculture supports 90% of the population. Bananas, coconuts, cacao, and rice are grown, and livestock is raised. Fish, timber, copra, and palm oil are exported. No major commercial mining has taken place, but large deposits of bauxite, copper, phosphates, and nickel are known to exist.

The Solomons were discovered by a Spaniard, Álvaro de Mendaña de Neyra, in 1568. The name is derived from Mendaña's belief that the islands were the source of King Solomon's gold for the Temple in Jerusalem. Periodic sightings were made of the islands, but the hostility of the indigenous population prevented European settlement. A British protectorate was established over the Southern Solomons in 1893, and the high commissioner for the Western Pacific assumed control in 1877. By 1900 the present political composition of the Solomon Islands had been established.

Following World War II, a period of opposition to British rule set in under the Marching Rule movement. Self-government was achieved in 1976. Full independence was granted in 1978, with the British monarch as head of state and a prime minister elected from the National Parliament as head of government. Peter Kenilorea became the nation's first prime minister.   MICHAEL MCINTYRE

Bibliography: Kent, Janet, *The Solomon Islands* (1972); Lord, Walter, *Lonely Vigil* (1977); Oliver, D. L., *A Solomon Island Society* (1955).

Solomon's seal

Solomon's seal, genus *Polygonatum,* is any of about 30 species of wild flowers belonging to the lily family, Liliaceae. The plant has a tall, slender stem and alternate leaves, and bears bell-shaped flowers and red or blue-black berries. Its young shoots and rootstock are edible. Solomon's seal is common to woodlands throughout North America and Europe.

Solomos, Dionysios   [sawl-aw-mohs']

The prominent Greek romantic poet Dionysios Solomos, b. Apr. 8, 1798, d. 1857, was educated in Italy and wrote his early verse in Italian. He was later persuaded to use the demotic language of Greece and was the first modern Greek poet to do so. His *Ymnos eis tin eleftherian* (Hymn to Liberty, 1823), which became the Greek national anthem, shows his enthusiasm for national liberation. His mature poetry, published posthumously and mostly in fragments, reflects a vision of spiritual liberation.

Bibliography: Raizis, M. B., *Dionysios Solomos* (1972).

Solon   [soh'-luhn]

Solon, *c.*639–*c.*559 BC, an Athenian statesman, archon in 594 BC, was granted absolute authority to remedy grave ills afflicting Athens. A serious economic crisis had forced many Athenians into debt; many had been sold as slaves into foreign lands. The monopoly of the aristocracy excluded many well-to-do people from participating in government. To stave off revolution or tyranny, Solon canceled all debts and forbade debt-slavery. He made wealth, not birth, the criterion for public office by establishing four income classes and according political rights to members of each of the top three classes on a graduated scale. Solon also passed sumptuary legislation, and he modified the Athenian system of weights and measures, perhaps causing inflation. He may also have established an Athenian council or senate consisting of 400 members of the propertied classes; its purpose was to prepare proposals that were later voted on by the people sitting in assembly (the *ekklesia*).

After completing his reforms, Solon left Athens as much to escape controversy as to satisfy his curiosity about foreign lands. Accounts of his visit to the court of Croesus, king of Lydia, are doubtful on chronological grounds. Returning to Athens, Solon died shortly after Peisistratus became tyrant. His life, in part, is known from his poetry.
                    CHARLES W. FORNARA

Bibliography: Freeman, Kathleen, *The Work and Life of Solon* (1926; repr. 1976); Linforth, I. M., *Solon the Athenian* (1919); Woodhouse, William J., *Solon the Liberator* (1938; repr. 1965).

Soloviev, Vladimir Sergeyevich   [suh-luhv-yawf']

A Russian philosopher, poet, and publicist, Vladimir Sergeyevich Soloviev, b. Jan. 28 (N.S.), 1853, d. Aug. 13 (N.S.), 1900, intellectually dominated the Russian religious revival at the beginning of the 20th century. As a student at Moscow University (1868-74), he underwent a religious crisis primarily under the influence of Arthur Schopenhauer, F. W. J. Schelling, and G. W. F. Hegel. After travels in Europe he began to teach at the University of Saint Petersburg, where in 1877 he delivered his famous lectures *"On Godmanhood."* In these he presented an elaborate cosmological and theological system, criticizing Eastern Orthodoxy for forgetting man and Western Christianity for neglecting God. During these years, he had a decisive influence on Fyodor M. Dostoyevsky.

In his later years Soloviev moved toward the mystical and gnostic doctrine of Sophia ("Wisdom"), a substantial reality uniting God and creation. This conception led him to advocate a synthesis of Eastern and Western Christianity in *Russia and the Universal Church* (1889; Eng. trans., 1948). His picture of the Antichrist in *Three Conversations on War, Progress, and the End of Universal History* (1899; Eng. trans., 1915) was seen by many in Russia as a prophecy of things to come. Soloviev was also noted for his mystical poetry, literary criticism, and political writings.   JOHN MEYENDORFF

Bibliography: Allen, P. M., *Vladimir Soloviev: Russian Mystic* (1973); Frank, S. L., ed., *A Solovyev Anthology* (1950); Munzer, Egbert, *Solovyev: Prophet of Russian-Western Unity* (1956); Zernov, Nicholas, *Three Russian Prophets: Khomiakov, Dostoevsky, Soloviev,* 3d ed. (1974).

solstice: see EARTH, MOTIONS OF.

Solti, Sir Georg   [shohl'-tee, gay'-ohrg]

Sir Georg Solti, b. Oct. 21, 1912, made his conducting debut (1933) in his native Hungary with the Budapest Opera. During

World War II he lived in Switzerland, performing as a pianist. After the war he conducted the Munich State Opera (1947–51) and the Frankfurt Opera (1951–61) and became music director (1961–71) at Covent Garden, London.

The high point of Solti's career came with his directorship (1969–79) of the Chicago Symphony Orchestra, which under his leadership regained the success it had previously enjoyed under Fritz Reiner and became internationally known as one of the world's greatest orchestras. He also served (1971–75) as music director of L'Orchestre de Paris. In 1979 he became the principal conductor of the London Philharmonic. Solti established himself as a leading interpreter of the music of Richard Wagner when, in the late 1950s and the 1960s, he led the first complete recording of *The Ring of the Nibelung,* for London/Decca Records. KAREN MONSON

Bibliography: Furlong, William B., *Season with Solti* (1974).

Discography: Beethoven, L. v., *Missa Solemnis and Symphonies Nos. 1–9;* Bruckner, A., *Symphonies Nos. 7 and 8;* Mahler, G., *Symphonies Nos. 5–8;* Wagner, R., *Die Meistersinger, Parsifal, The Ring of the Nibelung,* and *Tristan and Isolde.*

solubility

The solubility of a substance is the amount of substance required to form a saturated solution with a solvent. For example, the solubility of salt (NaCl) in water is 37 grams of NaCl per 100 grams of water at room temperature. The solubility is therefore a property of a pair of substances and is, in general, temperature dependent.

Solution theory is not advanced enough to be able to predict solubilities. General structural chemistry can be applied, however, to predict relative solubilities of materials in a given solvent. When discussing liquids, the statement that "like dissolves like" is a useful general rule. "Like" in this sense means "structurally similar." An example is ethyl alcohol (C_2H_5OH), which is miscible with water (HOH). These two molecules each have the structurally similar OH group. For other alcohols, as the length of the carbon chain increases the alcohol becomes more and more unlike water and, therefore, progressively less soluble in water. The principle thus provides a satisfactory general qualitative means of predicting relative solubilities of substances. GERALD C. ROPER

solution

In chemistry, a solution is a homogeneous mixture of two or more substances. It may be gaseous, as air; liquid, as seawater; or solid, as a nickel coin. In each case, one substance is uniformly dispersed throughout another; its particles are molecular in size.

The relative amounts of the substances (see CONCENTRATION) in the solution may be varied, usually between limits. The solute is the material present in the smaller proportion; the solvent is the material present in the larger proportion. Some substances are able to form solutions in all proportions, and these substances are said to be miscible; ethyl alcohol and water are two substances completely miscible in each other.

Most solutions reach a SATURATION point at which no more solute will dissolve and further addition of solute causes the formation of a second phase. This saturation point depends on the temperature, because some materials are more soluble at higher temperatures, whereas others are more soluble at lower temperatures. GERALD C. ROPER

See also: PHASE EQUILIBRIUM.

Solutrean   [suh-loo'-tree-uhn]

The Solutrean, in archaeology, is a short-lived but spectacular tool industry of the PALEOLITHIC PERIOD that was geographically limited to central and western France and northeastern Spain. Named for the site of Solutré near Macon, France, the Solutrean first appeared about 20,000 years ago in southwestern France with few tool forms to suggest its typological ancestry. Cultural deposits indicate that the industry underwent numerous changes for approximately 3,000 years and then died out.

Although widely separated temporally from the Mousterian tool industry, the initial Solutrean assemblages contain numerous side scrapers and disks reminiscent of the MOUSTERIAN or ACHEULEAN tradition.

Solutrean assemblages are generally characterized by an abundance of side scrapers; fewer, but still numerous, borers and gravers; and relatively few burins. The most characteristic implement is the so-called laurel leaf, a finely worked lanceolate point of variable length. The Solutrean laurel leaf initially appeared as a unifacially worked point; later examples are bifacially retouched. DAVID S. BROSE AND ROY LARICK

Bibliography: Bordes, François, *The Old Stone Age,* trans. by J. E. Anderson (1968).

Solvay, Ernest   [sohl-vay']

Ernest Solvay, b. Apr. 16, 1838, d. May 26, 1922, a Belgian chemical manufacturer, member of the senate, and minister of state, achieved fame and fortune with his process of soda (sodium carbonate) production. Solvay learned much about industrial chemistry from his father's salt-making business and from a gasworks managed by an uncle. Despite previous failures by other chemists to develop the soda-production process commercially, Solvay pursued the reaction on a practical level. He established a small pilot plant in Brussels in 1861, patented his process, and sold licenses to other soda manufacturers. Later he built plants in most industrial countries of the world and established the Solvay Institutes of Chemistry, Physics, and Sociology.

Solvay process

The Solvay process is a simple method of making sodium carbonate beginning with common salt. It was developed (1861) by a Belgian, Ernest Solvay; his first commercial plant using the process, at Couillet, Belgium, began production in 1865. The first U.S. plant using the process was built at Syracuse, N.Y., in 1882. The development of this process not only made the manufacture of soap and glass less expensive but also led to the establishment of the chlorine and chloralkali industries.

By this process, common salt (sodium chloride) in a strong brine solution is treated with ammonia and carbon dioxide to yield sodium bicarbonate and ammonium chloride. Sodium bicarbonate is heated, yielding the carbonate, and the ammonium chloride is treated with lime to yield calcium chloride and ammonia (the latter being fed back into the first step of the process). Calcium chloride, often mixed with salt, is widely used as a snow removal and dust abatement chemical on highways and streets.

The Solvay process replaced an earlier method, the Leblanc process, developed in 1775, and was itself replaced by the development of electrochemical processes. About 70 Solvay process plants are still in operation, but no new plants using it are being built.

E. N. BRANDT

solvent

A solvent is a liquid chemical compound used for dissolving other compounds. Solvents are also used for the EXTRACTION of materials from other media, for the purification of solid substances by recrystallization, or as media in which to conduct chemical reactions. Water is one of the most important of all solvents, because it can dissolve many inorganic compounds and some organic substances.

The principal qualification a liquid must possess in order to function as a good solvent is that it be capable of dissolving another substance without reacting with it. A second important characteristic of a solvent is its volatility, as judged by its boiling point. Solvents that have reasonably low boiling points can be removed readily from a reaction mixture or a recrystallization operation by distillation or evaporation. The recent development of aprotic solvents (polar solvents of moderately high dielectric constant) such as dimethyl sulfoxide, N,N-dimethylformamide, and hexamethylphosphoric tri-

COMMON SOLVENTS

Hydrocarbons	Boiling Point	Alcohols	Boiling Point
Pentane	36° C	Methanol	65° C
Hexane	69	Ethanol	78
Benzene	80		
		Ethers	
Chlorocarbons		Diethylether	35
Methylene		Tetrahydrofuran	66
chloride	40		
Chloroform	61	**Others**	
Carbon		Acetone	56
tetrachloride	77	Ethylacetate	77

amide has made commercially available a range of high-boiling solvents to function as reaction media at elevated temperatures.   HERMAN E. ZIEGER

Bibliography: Durrans, T. H., *Solvents*, 8th ed. (1971); Tess, Roy W., ed., *Solvents: Theory and Practice* (1973); Zingaro, Ralph A., *Nonaqueous Solvents* (1968).

Solzhenitsyn, Aleksandr   [sohl-zhuh-neet'-sin]

Aleksandr Solzhenitsyn became a powerful symbol of Russian dissidence when he exposed the Soviet Union's system of labor camps in three novels and a heavily documented study. For his literary indiscretions and political activism, Solzhenitsyn was exiled in 1974 and has since settled in the United States.

One of the leading Russian writers of the 20th century, Aleksandr Isayevich Solzhenitsyn, b. Rostov-on-Don, Dec. 11 (N.S.), 1918, received the Nobel Prize for literature in 1970 "for the ethical force with which he has pursued the indispensable traditions of Russian literature." Solzhenitsyn's novels are autobiographical, presenting a vivid account of a man maintaining his freedom against the vicious repressions of an authoritarian regime. Clearly a novelist in the 19th-century tradition, he is often considered Russia's greatest 20th-century novelist.

Solzhenitsyn studied mathematics and physics at the University of Rostov-on-Don, graduating at the beginning of World War II. He served for 4 years in the Soviet army and attained the rank of captain in the artillery. His difficulties with the authorities began on Feb. 8, 1945, when he was arrested for having written critical remarks about Stalin in a letter to a friend that was intercepted by the censors. Sentenced without a trial to 8 years of hard labor, he remained until 1953 in a number of labor camps, one of which was a research institute (the setting for *The First Circle*), where he worked (1953) as a mathematician. In 1952 he contracted cancer of the skin, and was treated (1953) in a hospital in Tashkent (the setting for *Cancer Ward*). Pronounced cured, he completed his sentence a year later and, although still in exile, was able to teach mathematics and to begin writing.

During the period of de-Stalinization, he was called "rehabilitated" and in 1956 was allowed to return to European Russia. He settled in a town southeast of Moscow, taught high school mathematics and physics, and worked on his stories and novels. The short novel ONE DAY IN THE LIFE OF IVAN DEN-

ISOVICH (1962; film, 1971) was the first of Solzhenitsyn's works to be published in the Soviet Union. It created an instant sensation because its subject is Stalin's forced labor camps, and it brought Solzhenitsyn immediate recognition. Although the novel was praised initially, it became the basis for further action against him and, after 1963, his work was not published in the Soviet Union.

Open conflict erupted with Solzhenitsyn's May 1967 letter to the Fourth National Congress of Soviet Writers, in which he demanded the abolition of censorship, the "rehabilitation" of many writers killed during the purges, and the restoration of his personal papers, confiscated by the KGB (secret police) in 1965. The confrontation grew more intense after the publication abroad of *The First Circle* (1968)—the title of which refers to the first circle of Dante's hell—and *The Cancer Ward* (1968–69), and after his winning the Nobel Prize in 1970. Further public statements by Solzhenitsyn, as well as the publication of the first volume of *August 1914* (1971) and the first volume of the GULAG ARCHIPELAGO (1973), led the Soviet authorities to exile him to the West in February 1974. Having settled first in Zurich, Solzhenitsyn and his family later moved to the United States, where they took up residence in a small Vermont town. While in the West, Solzhenitsyn completed the *Gulag Archipelago* (three parts, 1974–78); *Bodalsya telënok s dubom* (The Calf Butted the Oak Tree, 1975), the memoir of his last 10 years in the Soviet Union; and excerpts from his projected volumes on the Russian Revolution (*Lenin in Zürich*, 1975).   LASZLO M. TIKOS

Bibliography: Bjorkegren, Hans, *Aleksandr Solzhenitsyn: A Biography*, trans. by Kaarina Eneberg (1972); Dunlop, John B., et al., eds., *Aleksandr Solzhenitsyn: Critical Essays and Documentary Materials* (1974); Grazzini, Giovanni, *Solzhenitsyn* (1973); Kodjak, Andrej, *Alexander Solzhenitsyn* (1978); Labedz, Leopold, ed., *Solzhenitsyn: A Documentary Record* (1973); Lukacs, Georg, *Solzhenitsyn*, trans. by William D. Graf (1970); Rothberg, Abraham, *Aleksandr Solzhenitsyn: The Major Novels* (1971).

Somali   [soh-mahl'-ee]

The Somali are a people of northeast Africa who live in Somalia and in parts of neighboring nations. They speak an Afroasiatic language as well as Arabic, and they numbered an estimated 5.5 million in 1980. Among the earliest converts to Islam, the Somali are thought to have arrived in their present homeland from southern Ethiopia by the 12th century. About 80 percent of the population belongs to the Somal or Samaale group in the north; the rest belong to the Sab, or southern Somali. All trace their descent from a common male ancestor and his two sons, Somali and Sab, a familial closeness that leads to both alliances and blood feuds.

The Sab live in permanent settlements near rivers and have a mixed economy, but the Somali are principally nomadic camel herders. Independent family communities are united into a larger social and political unit called a *rer,* each with its own elected chief. Wealth is important, and slaves traditionally formed a separate social class. Marriages to multiple wives and a dowry system are mainly secular contracts but also follow Islamic patterns. Some Somali choose to become warriors, but others follow an Islamic religious life. Ancestor worship still plays a central role in the Somali religious system.   JAMES W. HERRICK

Bibliography: Lewis, I. M., *The Modern History of Somaliland from Nation to State* (1965), *A Pastoral Democracy* (1961), and *Peoples of the Horn of Africa: Somali, Afar and Saho* (1969).

Somali Democratic Republic: see SOMALIA.

Somalia   [soh-mahl'-ee-uh]

The Somali Democratic Republic is located on the Horn of Africa, the easternmost extension of the African continent. It is bordered by Djibouti, Ethiopia, Kenya, the Gulf of Aden (see ADEN, GULF OF), and the Indian Ocean. Livestock herding is the most important economic activity. Once under both Italian and British colonial rule, Somalia became independent in 1960.

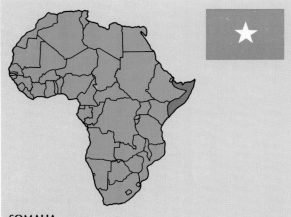

SOMALIA

Official Name: Somali Democratic Republic
Capital and Largest City: Mogadishu (1973 est. pop., 400,000)
Area: 637,657 km² (246,200 mi²)
Elevation: *Highest*—Surud Ad, 2,408 m (7,900 ft); *lowest*—sea level, along the Gulf of Aden and the Indian Ocean
Population: 3,469,000 (1979 est.). *Distribution*—9% urban, 91% rural; *density*, 5 persons per km² (14 per mi²); *annual rate of increase* (1970-77), 2.7%
Principal Languages: Somali and Arabic (official), Italian, English
Principal Religion: Islam
Principal Products: *Agriculture*—bananas, sugarcane; livestock, meat. *Manufacturing and industry*—leather goods, hides and skins
Railroads: None
Roads: 1,900 km/1,180 mi (1979 paved)
Currency: 1 Somali schilling = 100 centesimi

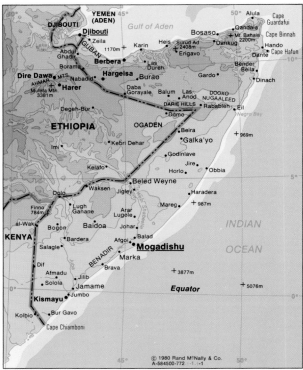

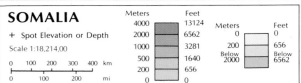

SOMALIA

+ Spot Elevation or Depth
Scale 1:18,214,00

Meters	Feet
4000	13124
2000	6562
1000	3281
500	1640
200	656
0	0

Meters	Feet
0	0
200	656
Below 2000	Below 6562

0 100 200 300 400 km
0   100   200 mi

© 1980 Rand McNally & Co.
A-584500-772 -1 -1

LAND, PEOPLE, AND ECONOMY

The country is geographically divided into northern desert and southern coastal plains and plateaus. The northern "burned" zone of desert plains rises through a series of hills to the Ogo and Migiurtinia mountains, which reach 2,408 m (7,900 ft) at Surud Ad. The Ogo Plateau extends south from the mountains into the grazing land of the Haud Plateau. In the south the sandy and arid coastal plains lead to the Shebeli-Juba lowlands and plateau with their more temperate climate. The plateau consists mainly of gneisses and schists, whereas the plains and maritime margins between the coast and the plateau are of limestone.

The average annual rainfall totals 76 mm (3 in) in the north and about 300-500 mm (12-20 in) in the south. During the summer the northeast coast is brutally hot, with average temperatures of 35° to 38° C (95° to 100° F). In the south the mean annual temperature is about 28° C (82° F), and the humidity is high.

All Somalia's major rivers flow into the Indian Ocean. The main river system is composed of the Juba and Webi Shabeelle rivers, which descend from Ethiopia and flow through the south. The two largest northern streams are the Daror and the Nugaaleed (formerly Nogal); both are ephemeral. Only 13% of the land is arable. Evidence suggests the presence of untapped deposits of uranium, thorium, iron ore, and rare earth minerals.

Ethnic homogeneity is a marked feature of Somali society. SOMALIS, who constitute 98% of the country's population, are divided into two groups—the Somal (79%) and the Sab, residing in the north and south, respectively. The other inhabitants are Arabs, Europeans, and Asians. Nomads travel with their cattle herds through Somalia, Kenya, and Ethiopia.

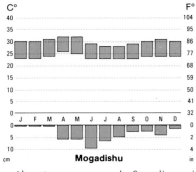

Bars indicate monthly ranges of temperatures (red) and precipitation (blue) of Mogadishu, the capital of Somalia. Located in the arid nation's coastal lowland, Mogadishu has a steppe climate.

Mogadishu

Almost everyone speaks Somali, a written form of which was introduced in 1976. Arabic is also widely used. Nearly all Somalis are devout Sunni Muslims. After MOGADISHU (Somali: Muqdisho), the capital and principal city, the most populous town is Hargeisa.

Educational facilities are meager, and 75% of the population is illiterate. Health services are provided by 179 doctors in 75 hospitals.

Life expectancy is 41 years, and the infant mortality rate is 177 per thousand live births.

The nomads' livestock and livestock products are major exports. Bananas are Somalia's biggest agricultural crop. Sugar and cotton are also grown. Leather tanneries, shoe factories, and textile mills make up the small manufacturing sector. Imports of textiles, cereals, manufactured goods, and petroleum products create a large trade deficit. Somalia's major trade partners are the Arab countries and Italy.

Mogadishu, Somalia's capital, largest city, and Indian Ocean port, was established during the 10th century as one of the first of many settlements founded by Arab seafaring traders on the African continent. Some of the city's mosques date from the 13th century.

GOVERNMENT AND HISTORY

The head of state and government is President Muhammad Siad Barré, who took office in a 1969 military coup. The Somali Revolutionary Socialist party, created in 1976, forms the executive branch of government. The party has a 74-member central committee and a 5-member politburo headed by President Siad. Somalia is a member of the Arab League.

In the 7th century Arabs and Persians developed a series of trading posts along the Gulf of Aden and the Indian Ocean. In the 10th century the area was peopled by Somali nomads and pastoral GALLA from southwest Ethiopia. For the next 900 years Somalis spread throughout the Horn of Africa. Britain and Italy occupied different parts of the territory in the 1880s, and until World War II, Somalia remained under colonial control. In 1941, Britain occupied Italian Somaliland and in 1948 gave the Ogaden region to Ethiopia, although it was populated largely by Somalis. By 1950 the United Nations had voted to grant independence to Somalia, and in 1960 the two former colonies were united to form the Somali Republic.

The civilian government that ruled until 1969 did not immediately attempt to regain what it considered lost Somali territories, including Djibouti, the Ogaden, and northeast Kenya. The military government, however, succeeded in regaining almost the entire Ogaden region by 1978. Somalia was closely allied to the USSR until 1977, when Soviet forces were expelled for their support of Ethiopia. In 1978, 11,000 Cuban troops and thousands of Ethiopian soldiers defeated the Somali army inside Ethiopia and drove out the Somali troops. The conflict created a serious refugee problem, with as many as 500,000 people from Ethiopia now in Somalia.

PETER SCHWAB

Bibliography: Bayne, E. A., *Four Ways of Politics: State and Nation in Italy, Somalia, Israel, Iran* (1965); Burton, Richard F., *First Footsteps in East Africa,* ed. by Gordon Waterfield, rev. ed. (1966); Hess, R. L., *Italian Colonialism in Somalia* (1966); Kaplan, Irving, et al., *Area Handbook for Somalia* (1969); Legum, Colin, et al., *Horn of Africa in Continuing Crisis* (1979); Lewis, I. M., *The Modern History of Somalia, from Nation to State* (1965); Noor, Muhammad N. A., *The Development of the Constitution of the Somali Republic* (1966); Touval, Saadia, *Somali Nationalism* (1963); Travis, William, *The Voice of the Turtle* (1967).

somatotrophin: see GROWTH; GROWTH HORMONE; HORMONES; PITUITARY GLAND.

Somerset   [suhm'-ur-set]

Somerset is a county in southwestern England with an area of 3,458 km² (1,335 mi²) and a population of 411,400 (1977 est.). Bordering on the Bristol Channel in the north, Somerset consists of central lowlands and hilly areas in the west and east.

The county town is Taunton. Dairying is the principal economic activity; the Cheddar district is world famous for its cheese. Livestock raising, tourism, fruit growing, the manufacture of woolens and leather goods, and coal and limestone mining complement the economy. Occupied by the Romans in the 1st century AD, the region became part of the Anglo-Saxon kingdom of Wessex in the 7th century. During the English Civil War, Somerset was a Royalist stronghold.

Somerset, Edward Seymour, 1st Duke of

Known as Protector Somerset, Edward Seymour, c.1506–1552, was the virtual ruler of England from 1547 to 1549. Seymour became prominent at court as a result of Henry VIII's marriage to his sister, Jane SEYMOUR, in 1536. Jane died in 1537 after giving birth to Henry's only legitimate son, who succeeded to the throne as EDWARD VI in 1547. Henry's will provided that England should be governed by a group of 16 regents during Edward's minority, but Somerset set this provision aside and assumed sole authority as protector. He fell from power in 1549, primarily because of his inability to suppress Kett's Rebellion, a protest against the enclosure of common land for sheep grazing. After a brief period of incarceration, Somerset was pardoned, but he was finally beheaded at Tower Hill on Jan. 22, 1552. Somerset favored Protestantism—the first Book of Common Prayer was published during his supremacy—and although he governed in an autocratic manner, he is usually thought of as a liberal in social policy.

STANFORD E. LEHMBERG

Bibliography: Bush, Michael L., *The Government Policy of Protector Somerset* (1975); Jordan, W. K., *Edward VI: The Young King: The Protectorship of the Duke of Somerset* (1968).

Somerville   [suhm'-ur-vil]

Somerville is a city in Middlesex County, eastern Massachusetts, on the Mystic River. A suburb of Boston, it has a population of 75,300 (1979 est.). The city's industries produce auto bodies, meat products, tools, dies, and paper products. Settled in 1630 as part of Charlestown, Somerville was incorporated in 1842. The first ship built in Massachusetts was launched there in 1631. The first American flag with 13 stripes was flown by General Israel Putnam at Somerville (Jan. 1, 1776). Development of a canal (1803) and rail connections (1835) spurred the growth of industry.

Somme, Battles of the   [suhm]

The Battles of the Somme were two encounters fought along the Somme River in northwestern France during World War I. **The First Battle of the Somme (June 24–Nov. 13, 1916).** The Allies' long-standing plans to attack the Central Powers were delayed when the Germans launched (Feb. 21, 1916) an offensive at Verdun (see VERDUN, BATTLE OF) in an attempt to breach the French line. On July 1, following a week-long artillery barrage, the Allies finally began their attack on the highly fortified German line along the Somme; they now had the secondary purpose of relieving the pressure on Verdun. The British, under Field Marshal Sir Douglas HAIG, played the leading role, with a smaller French force to their right. Only small gains were made on the first day of battle, and the British suffered 60,000 casualties, including 19,000 dead; it was the greatest one-day loss in the history of the British army.

Throughout the summer and autumn, the British continued a series of limited attacks, including the last large-scale use of horse cavalry in Western Europe. The British also used tanks for the first time in battle, although not very effectively. The battle ended in a deadlock. Little land had changed hands; the campaign had succeeded only in the objective of relieving Verdun. The cost was enormous: the British lost 420,000 men; the French lost 195,000; German casualties were about 600,000.

The Second Battle of the Somme (Mar. 21–Apr. 5, 1918). In early 1918, German general Erich LUDENDORFF opened the Second Battle of the Somme, also known as the Somme Offensive. His purpose was to breach the Allied line before American reinforcements could arrive. German shock troops struck along a 92-km (60-mi) front and succeeded in rolling back the Allies as much as 64 km (40 mi). It was the Germans' first major breakthrough since the early days of the war. Haig failed to get support from the French forces under General Henri PÉTAIN, who was occupied with the defense of Paris, and the Allies assigned General Ferdinand FOCH the task of coordinating the Allied efforts. Foch immediately sent French reserves to the Somme, and the German drive lost momentum. Like the First Battle of the Somme, the second was fought at enormous cost: the British suffered 163,000 casualties and the French, 77,000; German losses were almost as high as those of the Allies.   COL. T. N. DUPUY

Bibliography: Keegan, John, *The Face of Battle* (1976); Matloff, Maurice, *World War I: A Concise Military History* (1978).

Somme River

The Somme River, a 240-km-long (150-mi) stream in northern France, rises northeast of Saint Quentin and flows west to Amiens, and then northwest to the English Channel. The river is paralleled by canals for 72 km (45 mi). The surrounding valley was the scene of heavy fighting in World War I in 1916 as well as World War II.

Sommerfeld, Arnold   [zoh'-mur-felt]

The German theoretical physicist Arnold Sommerfeld, b. Dec. 5, 1868, d. Apr. 26, 1951, is known for his contributions to QUANTUM MECHANICS. Sommerfeld earned his doctorate in 1891 at the University of Königsberg, where he studied mathematics with David HILBERT. In 1906 he accepted the chair of theoretical physics at the University of Munich, where he later established an important physical institute. He worked out a major extension of the early quantum theory in 1916, with the development of his quantization rules. In 1919 he published the first edition of his *Atombau und Spektrallinien* (Atomic Structure and Spectral Lines), which, through successive editions, became widely used as the authoritative text on atomic physics until the introduction of quantum mechanics. His later work involved the calculation of energies and rates of atomic processes and of the macroscopic properties of matter resulting from them.   JOHN G. MAY

Somnus   [sahm'-nuhs]

In Roman mythology, Somnus was the god of sleep and was identified with the Greek Hypnos. Somnus was the father of Morpheus, the god who shaped men's dreams, the son of Nox (Night), and the brother of Mors (Death).

Somoza   (family)   [soh-moh'-sah]

Anastasio Somoza Garcia, b. Feb. 1, 1896, d. Sept. 29, 1956, was the founder of the Nicaraguan political dynasty that came to an end in July 1979 after a bloody revolution. A commander of the National Guard (1933), he led (1936) a rightist coup, which deposed his uncle, Juan Sacasa. He served as president from 1937 to 1947 and became president again in 1950. He was assassinated in 1956.

The older son of Somoza Garcia, **Luis Somoza Debayle**, b. 1922, d. Apr. 13, 1967, succeeded his father in 1957. Educated in the United States, he implemented limited social and economic reforms. Forbidden by a law—which he supported—that prevented succession by himself or a close relative, he selected an interim successor who held the presidency until 1967, when his brother, Anastasio, was elected.

General **Anastasio Somoza Debayle**, b. Dec. 5, 1925, was educated at the U.S. Military Academy at West Point and took over as head of the National Guard at the age of 21. Somoza Debayle was president until 1972, when he yielded power to a three-man junta, through whom he ruled until he could be reelected in 1974. He came under increasing attack in the late 1970s for his autocratic rule and his anti–civil rights practices toward dissenters. In 1979 he was overthrown by a revolution uniting a wide spectrum of his opponents and headed by the Sandinista guerrillas—named after Augusto César Sandino, a revolutionary executed in 1934 by Somoza Garcia. After his overthrow Anastasio Somoza settled in the United States.

Bibliography: Millett, Richard, *Guardians of the Dynasty* (1977); Reyes, Manuel Cordero, *Nicaragua under Somoza* (1944).

sonar

Sonar (an acronym for *so*und *na*vigation *a*nd *r*anging) is a system for underwater detection and location of objects by acoustical echo. The first sonars, invented during World War I by British, American, and French scientists, were used to locate submarines and icebergs and were called *asdics* (for *a*nti-*s*ubmarine *d*etection *i*nvestigation *c*ommittee) in Britain. *Sonar* is an American term dating from World War II. Most of the advances made in sonar technology since World War II are shrouded in military secrecy. It is known, however, that the system is used to hunt submarines, to control antisubmarine weapons, to direct homing torpedoes, and to locate mines. Civilian sonar systems called echo sounders are used by both commercial and sport fishermen. Marine seismologists employ a sonar that generates sound by means of a small explosion.

Sonar operates by transmitting regular pulses of sound energy that travel through the water and are reflected by a target; the echo is received, amplified, and then displayed. The time that elapses between transmission and reception indicates the distance from the sonar to its target. The display mechanism transforms the received sound waves into electrical impulses that normally cause a stylus to mark a strip of paper that is moving on rollers. The display has a time base. The ability of a sonar to show resolution (detail) improves as the transmitted pulse is made shorter. If the sound beams are narrowed, the angular resolution (the capability for distinguishing two targets at different angles) improves.

The range and effectiveness of sonar are affected by many factors. The water surface and bottom are natural limits to propagation. In some cases the water may refract the acoustic waves, deflecting a horizontal sound beam toward the bottom, where it is reflected upward to the surface, down again, and so on, rendering the sonar useless. Turbulent areas of water may scatter the beam, causing the signal strength to fluctuate and distorting the results. The water may also absorb the sound energy, transforming it into heat; this effect rapidly increases as frequency rises. The velocity of the sound wave (and hence the accuracy of distance measurements) is affected by the temperature, depth pressure, and salinity of the water. Generally, velocity rises as these parameters do. Acoustic noise limits the range of sonar, because it blots out the reflected signal. Such noise may be caused by wave action, aquatic animals, or boats.

Bibliography: Cox, Albert W., *Sonar and Underwater Sound* (1975); Kock, Winton E., *Radar, Sonar and Holography: An Introduction* (1973); Tucker, D. G., *Underwater Observation Using Sonar* (1966).

Gen. Anastasio Somoza Debayle ruled Nicaragua from 1967 until his overthrow by the Sandinista movement in 1979. The Somoza family had dominated the country both politically and economically since the 1930s.

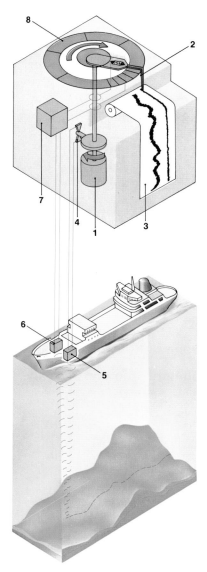

Sonar is an underwater sound-ranging system used for locating objects substantial and extensive enough to return an echo. The same technique is used by porpoises when they emit sounds to echolocate schools of fish. A typical sonar device has a motor (1) that drives a recording arm (2) and—through a system of gears, not shown—a recording chart (3). A rotating contact (4) causes a transmitter (5) to emit a sound impulse once every revolution. No further impulse is sent until an echo arrives at the receiver (6) from the seafloor or from some intervening object. The echo is passed through an amplifier (7) and then activates the recording arm; a pen at the tip of the arm marks on the chart the time taken for the impulse to return. This time is given in terms of depth by a calibrated scale (8). A series of such readings is seen at the center of the chart; the steadier line at the right is the echo picked up almost immediately at the surface as the signal is transmitted.

sonata

Along with the SYMPHONY, CONCERTO, and STRING QUARTET, the sonata ranks as one of the grandest forms of instrumental music. Among them it can boast the longest and most consistent history, dating back more than four centuries to the earliest uses of sonata as a musical title. Since the latter part of the 17th century, most sonatas have been divided into two, three, or four movements, and since the late 1700s most have been scored for piano alone, or with one other instrument. Most sonatas have been conceived as nondescriptive music; that is, they have been composed for the sheer pleasure of playing and hearing them, without a specific function or occasion in mind.

The term *sonata* is used in three distinct ways. First, it may mean a complete work, or cycle of movements. Second, it may be the overall, generic term for any instrumental cycle, whatever its scoring, that is primarily abstract rather than functional. In that sense the term applies to all three form types mentioned at the outset—the symphony for full orchestra, the concerto for one or more soloists and orchestra, or the string quartet for two violins, viola, and cello. Finally, *sonata* is used in the term *sonata form* to mean a design found mainly after 1750 in the first movement of a sonata cycle.

SONATA FORM

Sonata form is divided into three main sections. (1) An exposition presents in succession two or more ideas, or themes, that contrast in style and often in mood. (2) The development explores the potential meanings of any or all of these ideas by variously dissecting, expanding, combining, or interchanging them. (3) The recapitulation restates the exposition much as the exposition had gone before, except for those fuller meanings the themes now evoke.

When prepared by a slow introduction, capped by a coda, or framed by both, sonata form achieves greater extension. Its three main sections describe a grand A-B-A design. The two A sections, however, differ in their tonal directions and tensions; that is, the exposition creates tension by modulating (moving away) from the home key, whereas the recapitulation relaxes that tension by returning to and remaining in the home key. In between, the development creates further tensions by modulating more continuously and into more remote keys.

SONATA CYCLE

Within the sonata cycle, sonata form is identified especially with the first movement and therefore is often called sonata-allegro form, because that movement typically is marked allegro (spirited, fast). The second movement is usually the slowest, anywhere from very slow (adagio) to moderate (andante), and is characteristically lyrical and melodious.

When there are four movements, the third is normally a dancelike piece in triple meter (three beats per measure), especially a *minuet* at a moderate tempo or a faster scherzo. A-B-A design prevails in this movement, too, with a B section, or trio, that typically provides the lightest movements in the whole cycle. The last movement, or finale, is generally more rapid, lively, and brilliant than the previous movements. Frequently it is a light rondo, alternating a tuneful refrain (A) with various episodes, as in the design A-B-A-C-A-B-A coda.

HISTORY

The sonata first took hold as a musical form in the baroque era (about 1600 to 1750). In its most popular baroque scoring it became known as a trio sonata, with two high, intertwining parts for violins over a bass part for cello. Usually an organist or harpsichordist reinforced such a bass while filling in the harmony indicated by symbols supplied with the bass (see FIGURED BASS). The violins were often replaced by flutes or oboes, and the cello by a bassoon. Along with trio sonatas, solo sonatas for violin and figured bass abounded in the middle and late baroque era, composed by such masters as Arcangelo CORELLI, Johann Sebastian BACH, George Frideric HANDEL, Giuseppe TARTINI, and Jean Marie Leclair.

The sonata is viewed by many as having reached its period of highest achievement in the classical era (about 1750 to 1825), above all in the masterworks of Franz Josef HAYDN, Wolfgang Amadeus MOZART, and Ludwig van BEETHOVEN. By 1790 the early fortepiano largely replaced the clavichord and harpsichord, becoming a main vehicle of the sonata. When the violin or other instrument joined in, it was merely as an accompaniment at first, only later becoming a true partner.

Most composers of the romantic era tended to treat the sonata academically. Some of the greatest romantics, however—including Franz SCHUBERT, Frédéric CHOPIN, Robert SCHUMANN, and Franz LISZT—wrote large-scale, highly emotional examples. In the 20th century the sonata has retained its importance at least among the first two or three generations of composers. Thus among the leading composers until about 1950, Béla BARTÓK, Paul HINDEMITH, Sergei PROKOFIEV, and Aleksandr SCRIABIN gave some of their best efforts to the solo and duo sonata.

WILLIAM S. NEWMAN

Bibliography: Newman, William S., *The Sonata in the Baroque Era*, 3d ed. (1972), *The Sonata in the Classic Era*, 2d ed. (1972), and *The Sonata since Beethoven*, 2d ed. (1972); Rosen, Charles, *Sonata Form* (1979).

Sondheim, Stephen [sahnd'-hym]

A highly successful Broadway composer and lyricist, Stephen Sondheim, b. New York City, Mar. 2, 1930, won recognition with his lyrics for *West Side Story* (1957), with music by Leonard Bernstein. Sondheim has subsequently written both lyrics and music for a number of musicals, including *A Funny Thing Happened on the Way to the Forum* (1962), *A Little Night Music* (1973), and *Sweeney Todd* (1979).

Bibliography: Wilk, Max, *They're Playing Our Song* (1973); Zadan, Craig, *Sondheim & Company* (1974).

song

Song is the heightened personal vocal utterance, transcending the limits of speech, that is employed for social, religious, and artistic expression. In Western cultures, song comprises three broad kinds: folk song, popular song, and art song.

The subject matter of folk song is timeless and often deals with the woes and joys of ethnic, regional, or local groups rather than the personal griefs or pleasures of individuals. The text, music, meaning, and sometimes the function of a folk song change gradually as they pass from one generation to the next by oral transmission. Lacking the stability of musical notation, folk song gains richness of content through its gradual modification, continuing to reflect its past as it becomes assimilated into a changing world.

Popular vocal music is topical; its style changes frequently to reflect current public taste and fashions. Since the advent of radio, recordings and television, popular music has taken a rapidly changing succession of forms. Of all varieties of vocal music, popular song reaches the widest audience.

Art song, more complex than the simply rhymed, often strophic, folk song or the topical popular song, began in the Middle Ages with the troubadours and trouvères who wedded poetry to melody (see MINSTRELS, MINNESINGERS, AND TROUBADOURS). With them developed the first fixed forms in music: the lai, virelai, rondeau, and ballade. Some songs were associated with a function, such as songs of service, long epic poems (*chansons de geste*), and dawn songs (*albas*). Medieval songs often alternated between soloist and chorus and were probably accompanied by heterogeneous instrumental groups that duplicated the voice part and provided rhythmic vitality.

In the 15th and 16th centuries song accompaniments emerged in which instruments played parts separate from the vocal line. English lute songs and ayres, French *airs de cour*, Italian *frottole*, and Spanish *villancicos* are representative of this idiom. As singers replaced the instrumental parts, polyphonic songs and part-songs became popular.

The recitative-aria combination gained wide favor in the 17th century, invading opera, oratorio, and cantata as an orchestrally accompanied solo song. After the mid-18th century, J. A. Hiller, J. F. Reichardt, and C. F. Zelter cultivated the solo German song, paving the way for the developments by Haydn, Mozart, and Beethoven. German song, or *Lied*, reached its height in the romantic period when the music of Johannes BRAHMS, Franz SCHUBERT, Robert SCHUMANN, Richard STRAUSS, and Hugo WOLF was united with the verse of leading poets. In addition to solo songs, the Germans and Austrians wrote song cycles, sets of songs with words from groups of related poems.

Solo song in France rose to prominence with Henri DUPARC and Gabriel FAURÉ, continuing to be composed by Claude Debussy, Maurice Ravel, and Francis Poulenc. In England the finest songwriters were John DOWLAND and Henry PURCELL until the 20th century, when numerous composers came to the fore, among them Benjamin Britten, Frederick Delius, and Ralph Vaughan Williams, all of whom acknowledged a debt to English folk song.

American composers of songs have reflected a variety of tastes and used a number of styles. The popularity of Stephen Foster may be attributed to his superb gift for melody that compensated for his lack of variety and finesse. In popular song, Irving BERLIN, George GERSHWIN, Jerome KERN, and Cole PORTER were among those who made lasting marks. Charles Ives, Samuel Barber, Aaron Copland, and Ned Rorem contributed to the large body of American art songs.

All European countries have produced a wealth of song. Only the limitations of language have kept much of the literature of song from international acceptance, for song is so wedded to poetry that translation loses an essential part of the union between text and music.   ELWYN A. WIENANDT

Bibliography: Hall, James H., *The Art Song* (1974); Ivey, Donald, *Song: Anatomy, Imagery and Styles* (1970); Meister, Barbara, *An Introduction to the Art Song* (1980); Stevens, Denis W., ed., *A History of Song*, rev. ed. (1970).

Song of Hiawatha, The

The Song of Hiawatha (1855), a narrative of an Ojibwa Indian's life in an era of peace and prosperity, was Henry Wadsworth LONGFELLOW's attempt to create an American epic. Longfellow employed a poetic meter based on that of the Finnish epic *Kalevala*, but his experiment was not wholly successful. The meter so dominates the reader's attention that frequently it is all that is remembered of the poem.   CHARLOTTE D. SOLOMON

Song of Myself

A poem in free verse that first appeared untitled in *Leaves of Grass* (1855), *Song of Myself* is generally considered Walt WHITMAN's best poem. It has inspired successive generations of American poets. The poem, which comprises 1,336 lines and 52 sections, gives expression to the poet's belief that his "self" is identical to all selves on earth. His body achieves union with his soul, and the world becomes alive to all his senses. Perceiving death as merely the separation of the self from one of its identities, Whitman suggests, "If you want me look for me under your bootsoles."   JAMES K. ROBINSON

Song of Roland: see CHANSON DE ROLAND.

Song of Solomon

A book in the Old Testament of the BIBLE, the Song of Solomon, also known as the Song of Songs or the Canticles, is a collection of lyric poetry celebrating human love. The tradition of Solomonic authorship does not stand scrutiny. The milieu of the poetry is heavily northern Israelite and the imagery rural, although it may have been among sophisticated urbanites. A reasonable hypothesis is that love lyrics from the period 950–750 BC were collected and supplemented in postexilic times and accepted among religious Jews as an allegory of the relationship of God and Israel. The early Christian church accepted this explanation, with the allegory becoming that of Christ and his church. Other scholars interpret the song as a collection of hymns to true love, sanctified by union. The poetry describes nature and the male and female bodies with an ardent and unjaded eroticism.   NORMAN K. GOTTWALD

Bibliography: Gordis, Robert, *The Song of Songs and Lamentations: A Study, Modern Translation, and Commentary* (1974); White, John B., *A Study of the Language of Love in the Song of Songs* (1978).

songbirds

Songbirds, with about 4,000 species, comprise nearly half of all birds. Their most basic characteristic is the structure of the syrinx, or vocal organ. Commonly called "oscines," they are represented by about 42 families in the suborder Oscines, order Passeriformes. General disagreement exists as to the sequence of families from most to least advanced, and it has also been found difficult to arrange families in groups by common origin. Songbirds include such forms as the BIRD OF PARADISE, CROW, FINCH, JAY, LARK, ORIOLE, SHRIKE, SWALLOW, WARBLER, and WREN.

Songbirds range in length from 7.5 to 110 cm (3 to 43 in) and in weight from 5 to 1,350 g (up to 3 lb). The syrinx is located at the junction of the trachea and bronchi and includes muscles involved in vocalization, as well as modified supporting rings and membranes and air passages. The mechanisms of the syrinx are poorly understood, but structurally the syrinx of the oscines, which possesses four pairs of intrinsic muscles, is more complex than that found in other passeriform suborders (suboscines).

The name *songbird* implies a high degree of vocal capability, and in most cases the vocalizations are acoustically complex and often attractive to humans, as in the songs of the CANARY and the NIGHTINGALE. Vocalizations of many songbirds, however, such as crows and jays, hardly merit the name "song." Several songbirds do not sing, even poorly. The singing behavior that is so characteristic of many songbirds during breeding season functions in territorial advertising and in attracting a mate. In this way, singing operates in species recognition as a reproductive isolating mechanism.

The songs of closely related species are different, and, even within a given species, different local populations may show distinct dialects in their songs that act to reduce interbreeding. Along with the conspicuous and distinctive plumages worn by many species, especially by males in breeding season, these vocalizations have played a role in the evolution of many species.

For most songbirds, insects are the staple diet, but in many groups other feeding specializations have developed. Some, such as the TANAGERS of the family Thraupidae, feed on fruit in addition to insects. Finches and sparrows of various types eat seeds. They have short, heavy, conical bills and powerful jaw muscles for cracking seed coats. Several groups have independently evolved specializations for taking nectar from flowers. They often have tubular tongues, sometimes brush-tipped, that apparently act like soda straws. A wide variety of bill types and foraging strategies is used in association with these and other feeding specializations. ROBERT J. RAIKOW

Bibliography: Risdon, D. H., *Color Treasury of Songbirds* (1974); Terres, John, *Songbirds in Your Garden*, rev. ed. (1977); Time-Life Books Editors, *Song Birds* (1978); Welty, Joel Carl, *The Life of Birds* (1963).

Songhai (empire) [sahng'-gy]

Songhai (or Songhay) is the name applied to the imperial state that ruled much of the West African grasslands area from 1464 to 1591. From its capital at Gao, and major trading cities at TIMBUKTU and Jenne—all located along the great bend of the Niger River—merchants and soldiers developed and protected a lucrative trading enterprise that extended both south toward the forests and north across the Sahara Desert. Songhai was governed by gifted leaders, including its founder, Sunni Ali (r. *c*,1464-92), and the illustrious king Askia Muhammed Toure (r. 1493-1528). The Songhai rulers were able to sustain a strong Islamic culture in the towns and trading centers while presiding as "traditional" kings over the mass of the non-Muslim population. Timbuktu in particular achieved fame as a center of Islamic scholarship. The Songhai empire fell in 1591 after invasion by a Moroccan army. ROBERT R. GRIFFETH

Bibliography: Bovill, E. W., *Golden Trade of the Moors* (1958); Davidson, Basil, *The Lost Cities of Africa* (1959); Miner, Horace, *The Primitive City of Timbuctoo*, rev. ed. (1965).

Songhai (people)

The Songhai (Songhay) are an African people living principally in Mali, Niger, and Upper Volta. Their population, estimated at over 850,000 in 1980, is ethnically and racially mixed, including not only Negroid subgroups but also Caucasoid subgroups of TUAREG, BERBER, and Arabic descent. Songhai has been tentatively classified as one of the Sudanic languages (see AFROASIATIC LANGUAGES). The Songhai farm grains and other crops and keep livestock, but trade is also vital to their subsistence, especially for those groups living in desert areas. Hereditary guilds work in smithing, leatherwork, weaving, canoe building, and other crafts. The Songhai religion is Islam, with residual pagan elements. The stratification of their class society reflects the tradition of empire from which the Songhai are descended. PHOEBE MILLER

Bibliography: Trimingham, J. S., *Islam in West Africa* (1959).

Songs of Innocence and of Experience

The best-known work of the English poet and artist William BLAKE, *Songs of Innocence and of Experience* employs the mediums of poetry and colored engraving in a series of visionary poems "shewing the two contrary states of the human soul." *Songs of Innocence* (1789) was followed by *Songs of Experience* (1794), and the two were then combined. Written in simple lyrical form, as if they were children's songs, the poems contrast an innocent view of life with a more experienced and, in some instances, jaded one. Each poem is illustrated, and Blake occasionally pairs poems in the two groups by giving them the same title. HAZARD ADAMS

Bibliography: Gillham, D. G., *Blake's Contrary States: The Songs of Innocence and Experience as Dramatic Poems* (1966); Gleckner, Robert F., *The Piper and the Bard* (1959); Hirsch, E. D., *Innocence and Experience: An Introduction to Blake* (1964; repr. 1975).

Sonneborn, Tracy Morton [suhn'-bohrn]

The geneticist Tracy Morton Sonneborn, b. Baltimore, Md., Oct. 19, 1905, demonstrated that factors in the cell cytoplasm play a role in transmitted hereditary characteristics. He did this after successfully developing methods of crossbreeding paramecia—thus providing geneticists with an important research tool.

sonnet

Derived from the Italian *sonetto*, meaning "little song," the sonnet is a poem of 14 iambic pentameter lines. Sonnets have been written in various rhyme schemes, but the most durable pattern has been the Italian, or Petrarchan, sonnet. It consists of an octave (8 lines) rhyming *abbaabba* and a sestet (6 lines) using two or three rhymes in various combinations. The most famous practitioner of the Italian sonnet was PETRARCH; a variation of the form entered English poetry in the 16th century through translations of his sonnets. Although the original topic of the sonnet was love of a mistress (as in Petrarch), the form has since been used for a variety of subjects. WILLIAM McCARTHY

Bibliography: Fuller, John, *The Sonnet* (1972); Lever, J. W., *The Elizabethan Love Sonnet* (1956).

See also: VERSIFICATION.

Sonnets from the Portuguese

Written by Elizabeth Barrett BROWNING before her marriage (1846) to the poet Robert Browning, *Sonnets from the Portuguese* (1850) is a sequence of 44 passionate sonnets that charts the progress of the couple's love for each other and reveals the poet's struggle with her own feelings of inferiority and unworthiness. She comes to accept the knowledge that she will escape from the death that had once seemed so imminent and rejoices in the sudden unexpected fulfillment of her life. JANET M. TODD

Sonnets of Shakespeare

Originally published in 1609, William SHAKESPEARE's sonnets are 154 poems that scholars believe were written in the 1590s. Conjecture continues on several points—the sequence of composition, whether the sonnets have a chronological and thematic order, and the identity of the people addressed. Many of the first 126 sonnets were apparently written to a young man, and some of those numbered 125-154 are addressed to a mysterious "dark lady." Shakespeare, or his publisher, dedicated the volume to a "Mr. W. H.," whose identity has never been established.

Unlike the Italian, or Petrarchan, SONNET, Shakespeare's sonnets—also called Elizabethan or English sonnets—consist of three quatrains and a rhyming   uplet, with a rhyme scheme of *abab cdcd efef gg* (see VERSIFICATION). They cover a variety of philosophical themes such as time and death, love, friendship, and the immortality of poetry.

Bibliography: Booth, Stephen, *An Essay on Shakespeare's Sonnets* (1972); Hubler, Edward, *The Riddle of Shakespeare's Sonnets* (1962) and *The Sense of Shakespeare's Sonnets*, rev. ed. (1954); Leishman, J. B., *Themes and Variations in Shakespeare's Sonnets* (1961); Rowse, A. L., *Shakespeare's Sonnets* (1973).

Sonnino, Sidney, Barone [sohn-nee'-noh]

As foreign minister of Italy in 1914–19, Giorgio Sidney, Barone Sonnino, b. Mar. 11, 1847, d. Nov. 24, 1922, brought his country into World War I on the Allied side after the Central Powers had failed to meet his demands. Sonnino entered Parliament in 1880 and later served both as finance minister (1893–94) and as prime minister (1906, 1909–10). When the Allies refused to grant hoped-for portions of Austria-Hungary to Italy at the Versailles peace settlement, Sonnino retired; he was, however, appointed a senator in 1920.

Sonora [soh-noh'-rah]

Sonora, a mountainous state in northwestern Mexico on the Gulf of California, borders the United States. It has an area of 184,934 km² (71,403 mi²) and a population of 1,558,500 (1978 est.). It is the country's second largest state in area but the least densely populated (8 inhabitants per km²; 20 inhabitants per mi²). The capital is HERMOSILLO. Sonora has been important for its silver, gold, and lead mining since the colonial times. Crops include wheat, corn, cotton, and rice. Home to the YAQUI and Seri Indians, the region was first explored by the Spanish in the 16th century and became a state of independent Mexico in 1830.   LEON YACHER

Sonora Pass

The Sonora Pass, lying 2,934 m (9,625 ft) above sea level, is a passage in the SIERRA NEVADA range in eastern California north of Yosemite National Park. It was used by prospectors following the discovery of gold in California in 1848.

Sons of Liberty

The Sons of Liberty was a secret American intercolonial organization founded in November 1765 to oppose the STAMP ACT. The term *sons of liberty* was traditionally used to designate those dedicated to the defense of civil liberties, but it took on special meaning when a group led by John Lamb and Isaac Sears formed the Sons of Liberty in New York City. Chapters soon appeared throughout the colonies, mainly in cities and larger towns. Although representing a cross section of society, the Sons of Liberty were mostly tradesmen, laborers, and shopkeepers. Besides transmitting intelligence to other chapters, local members resisted implementation of the stamp tax by persuasion, pressure, or violence. In some places, notably New York and Connecticut, the group also functioned as a paramilitary association. The organization disbanded after repeal of the Stamp Act in March 1766; thereafter *sons of liberty* became a generic term applied to persons or groups who supported the independence movement.
                                                                LARRY R. GERLACH

Bibliography: Maier, Pauline, *From Resistance to Revolution: Colonial Radicals and the Development of American Opposition to Britain, 1765–1776* (1972); Walsh, Richard, *Charleston's Sons of Liberty: A Study of the Artisans* (1959).

Sons and Lovers

An autobiographical novel by D. H. LAWRENCE, *Sons and Lovers* (1913) is considered one of the most significant works of its time, particularly for its treatment of the Oedipal relationship between mother and son and for its realistic depiction of family life in an enervating industrial environment. The novel concerns the relationships between Paul Morel, who is an artist in the making, and the three women who influence his development—his mother and his two lovers, Miriam and Clara.   R. M. FORD

Bibliography: Farr, Judith, ed., *Twentieth-Century Interpretations of "Sons and Lovers"* (1970).

Sontag, Susan [sahn'-tag]

An American essayist and novelist, Susan Sontag, b. New York City, Jan. 16, 1933, is best known for her iconoclastic essays on aesthetics in *Against Interpretation* (1966), especially

Susan Sontag, a critic, author, and film director, is best known for the polemical essays contained in Against Interpretation *(1966) and* Styles of Radical Will *(1969). In the former she rebuts traditional criticism, which interprets art as a metaphor of reality, preferring to approach art through sensory rather than intellectual experience.*

"Notes on Camp," which discusses the vulgar and mass-produced as a source of pleasure. Aversion to the traditional critical practice of extracting moral meanings from art is reflected in her novels *The Benefactor* (1963) and the Kafka-like *Death Kit* (1967). *Styles of Radical Will* (1969) contains the essays "The Aesthetics of Silence" and "The Pornographic Imagination." Sontag has also written and directed two films, *Duet for Cannibals* (1969) and *Brother Carl* (1974). Her most recent works include *On Photography* (1977), *Illness as Metaphor* (1978), and the experimental short stories in *I, Etcetera* (1978).

Soochow (Suzhou) [soo-chow]

Soochow is a city of 600,000 inhabitants (1979 est.) in southern Kiangsu province, China. It lies on the GRAND CANAL, about 85 km (50 mi) west of Shanghai, with which it is linked by a railroad. The city's silk industry, established in the 12th century, dominates the economy. Founded in the 6th century BC, Soochow has always been noted for its beauty. Because of a maze of waterways and canals and numerous scenic gardens with temples, it is sometimes called the Venice of China and City of Gardens.   JAMES CHAN

Soong (family) [sung]

The politically prominent Soong family holds a unique place in the early history of Nationalist China. The three Soong sisters were married to key revolutionary leaders: **Soong Ai-ling**, b. 1888, to H. H. Kung, who briefly served (1938) as president of the Nationalist government; **Soong Ching-ling**, b. 1892, to SUN YAT-SEN; and **Soong Mei-ling**, b. c.1897, to CHIANG KAI-SHEK. Their father, **Charles Jones Soong**, d. c.1927, a Methodist missionary and Shanghai merchant, was a financial supporter of Sun Yat-sen. Their brother, **T. V. Soong**, 1894–1971, headed Nationalist banks and served as the first Nationalist minister of finance. Madame Sun Yat-sen broke with the Nationalists after Chiang Kai-shek became president and joined the Chinese Communists under Mao Tse-tung. Madame Chiang Kai-shek, whose U.S. speaking tours brought worldwide celebrity, fled with the Nationalist government from the mainland to Taiwan in 1949.

Bibliography: Hahn, Emily, *The Soong Sisters* (1941; repr. 1970); Spencer, Cornelia, *Three Sisters: The Story of the Soong Family of China* (1939).

Sophia [soh-fy'-uh]

Sophia Alekseyevna, b. Sept. 27 (N.S.), 1657, d. July 14 (N.S.), 1704, served as regent of Russia for her brother, Ivan V, and her half brother, PETER I, from 1682 until 1689. The daughter of Tsar ALEXIS and his first wife, Maria Miloslavsky, Sophia was also the sister of Fyodor III, who succeeded to the throne in 1676. An adept intriguer, Sophia outmaneuvered her stepmother, Natalia Naryshkin, and gained the regency when Fyodor died in 1682. Sophia's attempt (1689) to seize the Russian throne for herself was repulsed by Peter, who confined her to the Novo-Devichy convent in Moscow. An uprising in her name by the guards regiments in 1698 impelled Peter to have her shorn as a nun and put under heavy guard. She died at the convent.   DONALD L. LAYTON

Bibliography: Bergamini, John, *The Tragic Dynasty: A History of the Romanovs* (1969).

Sophists

The Greek Sophists (from the Greek *sophos*, "wise") were professional educators and lecturers who first appeared in the 5th century BC. Although not a school as such, the members of this group had several new ideas in common. They turned their attention from science and philosophy to more practical studies, principally rhetoric, politics, and law—the skills young Greeks needed to become successful. Part of their educational ideal still survives in the modern notion of "sophistication." They also encouraged some acquaintance with arts and crafts.

The older Sophists tended to be agnostics in religion, relativists in ethics, and power theorists in politics, but they did not go out of their way to shock people with these ideas. PLATO, in his attempts to demonstrate that SOCRATES was not a Sophist, created imaginary conversations portraying the leading figures of this group. These include Gorgias, the master of rhetoric; Protagoras, expert lawyer; Hippias, a kind of animate encyclopedia who professed to know everything; and Prodicus, one of the first Greek students of language and grammar. The younger Sophists of the next generation were much more outspoken, and therefore unpopular.

From the outset the Sophists believed that an opposition existed between "nature" (*phusis*) and "custom" or "convention" (*nomos*). They treated legal codes, ethical ideals, and social systems as merely conventional. They argued, for example, that by nature the weak have no rights against the strong and that the gods were invented by rulers to intimidate their subjects.   ROBERT S. BRUMBAUGH

Bibliography: Guthrie, W. K. C., *Sophists* (1971); Plato, *Dialogues*, trans. by Benjamin Jowett, 2 vols. (1937); Untersteiner, Mario, *The Sophists,* trans. by Kathleen Freeman (1954).

Sophocles   [sahf'-uh-kleez]

The career of Sophocles, *c.*497–406 BC, one of the three great tragic dramatists of ancient Greece, spanned the period of

Sophocles, often regarded as the finest tragic dramatist of ancient Greece, was also a distinguished statesman and soldier. Aristotle credited Sophocles with several theatrical innovations, including the introduction of a third actor, which greatly increased dramatic complexity.

greatest political and cultural achievement in Athens. According to tradition, Sophocles wrote 123 plays and won 24 victories in the city's annual dramatic contests. Of these, only 7 tragedies are preserved in full, but they are sufficient to reveal the playwright's genius. Sophocles' tragedies are usually regarded as the high point of Attic drama.

Born of a wealthy family, Sophocles enjoyed the friendship of such leading political and intellectual figures as Pericles and Herodotus. He was active in public life, in 443–442 serving as a treasurer concerned with regulating the tribute of the subject allies of Athens, and in 441–440 serving jointly with Pericles as general during the Samian revolt. Tradition reports that he owed his election to the success of *Antigone* the preceding year. He may also have served as general during the Peloponnesian War, and in 413–411 he was one of the ten commissioners who governed Athens after the disastrous Sicilian expedition.

The author of a critical essay, *On the Chorus,* Sophocles divided his work into three periods. The first, which *Ajax* may exemplify, reflects the stylistic influence of his older contemporary Aeschylus. The second, represented by *Antigone,* is marked by "a harsh and contrived" style. The third period, his maturity, to which the other plays belong, encompassed the development of a method "most suited to depicting character."

Ajax (*c.*465–450?), Sophocles' earliest extant play, dramatizes the uncompromising nobility, but also the rigidity, of the old heroic ideal. *Antigone* (442–441), which turns on the heroine's devotion to her dead brother Polyneices, portrays the conflict between a woman's emotional and religious values and the masculine, secular rationalism of King Creon of Thebes. Hegel's interpretation of the play as a clash between the state and the individual has some truth but oversimplifies the issues. OEDIPUS REX (*c.*429–425) is one of the most influential plays ever written. Powerful in its conjunction of character and destiny, its relentless recognition of hidden truth, and its paradoxes of human knowledge and ignorance, it provided Aristotle in the POETICS with his model tragic plot and Sigmund Freud in *The Interpretation of Dreams* (1900) with a mythic prototype for the Oedipus complex, a central feature of modern psychoanalytic theory.

The Trachinian Women (*c.*430–420) is Sophocles' only surviving play to deal with the violence of sexual passion. ELECTRA (*c.*420–410), like the *Oresteia* of Aeschylus, concerns justice and vengeance in the House of Atreus but focuses on the sensitively drawn character of Electra. Its relation to Euripides' *Electra* (*c.*420–413) is still uncertain. *Philoctetes* (409) and *Oedipus at Colonus* (performed posthumously in 401) both deal with exiled, embittered heroes who are ultimately reconciled with society and the gods.

Sophocles' technical innovations made possible the further development of the drama along more realistic lines. According to Aristotle, Sophocles added a third actor, introduced scene painting, and increased the chorus from 12 to 15 members. The third actor allowed for more complex characterizations and a wider range of personal encounters. Aristotle praises Sophocles for his close integration of the chorus into the action.

Presenting a tragic situation in a single play rather than in an Aeschylean connected trilogy, Sophocles poses the questions of divine justice in terms of human character rather than in terms of the cosmic order. In his focus upon a single powerful hero, he originated the form of tragedy that Western literature has most cultivated. His heroes and heroines are towering figures of violent passions, unyielding in their commitment to their ideals, harsh in their judgment of themselves and others. To be a hero in Sophocles is to be the bearer of a destiny that is mysteriously bound up with the divine will, but one that nevertheless must be worked out in the individual's life. The hero's task is to discover and realize that destiny, often at the price of suffering or death, and to remain faithful to the innate nobility of his great nature.

Sophocles' famed "piety" is not synonymous with complacency. His gods, like Apollo in *Oedipus Rex,* are remote and ambiguous, and their justice often seems unclear or even cruel. Unlike the gods of Aeschylus and Euripides, they rarely intervene directly but are present indirectly through oracles and omens. They embody the ultimate, inexorable realities that man must struggle to understand.

Sophocles' plots stress the strong, clear lines of character in a harmonious and economical structure. The style is solemn and lofty, richly poetical in the choral odes, but also graceful and supple, with a wide range of tones. Less exuberant than Aeschylus, Sophocles is grand without being ponderous, dense without seeming rhetorical or artificial.

Sophocles' great dramatic achievement was to reinterpret the ancient myths through a fuller development of individual character and to endow surface detail with deeper symbolic significance. Recent scholarship has stressed Sophocles' mythic imagination and the darker side of his celebrated "classic serenity." These strengths amply explain the powerful effect his plays continue to exert over modern audiences.

CHARLES SEGAL

Bibliography: Bowra, C. M., *Sophoclean Tragedy* (1944); Grene, David, *Reality and the Heroic Pattern: Last Plays of Ibsen, Shakespeare and Sophocles* (1967); Kitto, H. D. F., *Sophocles, Dramatist and Philosopher* (1958); Knox, Bernard M. W., *The Heroic Temper: Studies in Sophoclean Tragedy* (1965); Melchinger, Siegfried, *Sophocles,* trans. by David A. Scrase (1974); Segal, Charles, *Tragedy and Civilization: An Interpretation of Sophocles* (1981); Waldock, A. J. A., *Sophocles the Dramatist* (1966); Whitman, Cedric H., *Sophocles: A Study of Heroic Humanism* (1951); Winnington-Ingram, R. P., *Sophocles* (1979).

Sophonisba [soh-fuh-niz'-buh]

Sophonisba, d. 203 BC, was the daughter of the Carthaginian general Hasdrubal (d. c.202). She married the Numidian Syphax, who then fought for Carthage in the Second PUNIC WAR and was defeated (203 BC) by MASINISSA and the Romans. To avoid capture by the Romans, she took poison, perhaps sent by Masinissa, who had fallen in love with her.

soprano

The term *soprano* encompasses all the high voice ranges of women upward from middle C for two octaves or more. The coloratura is the highest, lightest, and most flexible; the dramatic and lyric sopranos are slightly darker and heavier. The mezzo-soprano lies midway between the soprano and contralto ranges, and the soprano voice between the dramatic and lyric is called spinto. Composers do not consistently designate the type of soprano required but expect the range and character of the written part to serve as guides for the selection of voices. The voices of young boys also lie in the soprano range.

ELWYN A. WIENANDT

Sopwith Camel [sahp'-with]

Acclaimed as the most successful fighter plane of World War I, the single-seat Camel biplane, with an 8.4-m (28-ft) wingspan and a characteristic short nose, achieved more combat victories (1,294 enemy aircraft) than any other individual type of airplane. Most Sopwith Camels were equipped with the

The Sopwith F.1 Camel biplane was England's most successful World War I fighter, credited with shooting down 1,294 enemy aircraft. It was highly maneuverable, carried two machine guns, and had a top speed of 196 km/h (122 mph) and a ceiling of 7,315 m (24,000 ft).

130-hp Clerget rotary engine, but some received the 110-hp le Rhône engine. Twin Vickers machine guns were installed on the coaming in front of the pilot. Other important features of the Camel were its outstanding degree of maneuverability and its ability to carry four 11-kg (25-lb) bombs in a rack beneath the fuselage. On the western front the Camel—of which 5,490 were built—joined squadrons of both the Royal Flying Corps and the Royal Naval Air Service during mid-1917. Home-defense Camels fought zeppelins and Gotha bombers attacking the United Kingdom, and the 2F.1 variant was evolved specifically for use at sea. PETER M. H. LEWIS

Bibliography: Munson, Kenneth, *Fighters: Attack and Training Aircraft, 1914-1919* (1968).

Soqotra: see SOCOTRA.

Sorbonne: see PARIS, UNIVERSITIES OF.

Sorby, Henry Clifton

The English chemist and geologist Henry Clifton Sorby, b. May 10, 1826, d. Mar. 9, 1908, founded (1849) the science of PETROGRAPHY, the description and classification of rocks based on microscopic study of their components. The technique of using the microscope to examine thin, transparent slices of bones, teeth, wood, and shells had been in use for several decades. Sorby recognized the great potential for such use of microscopy in earth science and developed a technique for preparing slides from thin sections of rocks. His first paper (1850) presented a microscopic study of limestone, in which he distinguished shell debris from coral, measured particle sizes, and determined the relative abundances of the constituents. He then investigated the origin of slaty cleavage (1853), observing the parallel arrangement of mica flakes. He concluded that this alignment occurred during deformation of the rock, thus providing natural planes of weakness along which cleavage could develop. Sorby speculated on the igneous versus solution-deposition origins of granite (1858) based on his microscopic observation of numerous tiny fluid inclusions in quartz crystals.

The importance of Sorby's work was recognized in 1876 when he was elected President of the Geological Society, named a fellow of the Royal Society, and awarded an honorary doctorate from Cambridge. Sorby then turned his attention to meteorites and made (1877) an important discovery: he recognized the textural similarity between terrestrial igneous rocks and chondrules (the enigmatic spherical objects in chondrites) and suggested that chondrules were crystallized droplets of molten rock. PETER B. LEAVENS

Sorel, Georges [sohr-el']

The French social philosopher Georges Sorel, b. Nov. 2, 1847, d. Aug. 30, 1922, is best known for his *Reflections on Violence* (1908; Eng. trans., 1912), which advances his socialist theory of revolutionary SYNDICALISM. Sorel espoused various forms of violent action in order to achieve the ends of social revolution, including the action of a general strike—which, according to syndicalist ideas, could occur if an inert working class were to be galvanized into mass unanimous action by a militant minority. Sorel considered creative "violence" to be the proletariat's heroic means of opposing and overturning the existing bourgeois "force." Mussolini later interpreted Sorel's "violence" as a justification for brutality. Although Sorel supported different aspects of socialism at different times, he always defended both liberty and order, bold social action and moral discipline.

Bibliography: Horowitz, Irving L., *Radicalism and the Revolt against Reason* (1961); Humphrey, Richard, *Georges Sorel, Prophet without Honor* (1951; repr. 1971); Vernon, Richard, *Commitment and Change: Georges Sorel and the Idea of Revolution* (1978).

Sørensen, Søren Peter Lauritz [sur-uhn-suhn']

The Danish biochemist Søren Peter Lauritz Sørensen, b. Jan. 9, 1868, d. Feb. 12, 1939, invented the term PH to describe the acidity of a solution. The term simplified many mathematical expressions of relationships in chemistry and biochemistry. Known also for his work on amino acids and enzymes, Sørensen, who was director (1901–39) of chemistry of the Carlsberg Laboratory in Copenhagen, did important research on the physical properties of proteins, devised analytical methods for their determination, and, with his wife, was the first to crystallize the protein egg albumin.

sorghum   [sohr'-guhm]

The sorghum Sorghum bicolor, *is an annual, coarse grass that is grown worldwide as a commercial crop and is used as livestock feed. Other sorghum species produce a sweet, edible syrup.*

Sorghum, a member of the grass family, is of great agricultural importance in dry and arid lands. Its hundreds of varieties and many hybrids are generally classified into four groups: the grain sorghums, used mainly for stock and poultry feed; the grass sorghums, used for hay and pasture; the sweet sorghums, which provide molasses and syrup as well as hay and silage; and broomcorn, whose fibers are used to make brooms. All sorghums have extensive branching root systems that provide exceptionally good resistance to drought. The plants are also able to withstand hotter climates than other grain crops are.

Sorghum has been a major crop in Africa since prehistoric times. In 1979 the world production of sorghum was estimated at 68,819,000 metric tons. The largest producers were the United States with 20,746,000 metric tons, China with 11,515,000 metric tons, India with 10,500,000 metric tons, and Argentina with 6,300,000 metric tons.

Methods of cultivating, harvesting, and handling sorghum are similar to those used for other cereal crops. A self-pollinated annual planted in the spring, sorghum can reach heights of 5 m (16 ft). Seed color ranges from white to dark reddish brown.

Milo and *grain sorghum* are popular terms used to refer to sorghum, and the term *cane* is sometimes used for the sweet sorghum crop. Sorghum improvement research is conducted worldwide.

In industrial countries sorghum is almost entirely a feed grain. It is ground and used with other grains for formula feeds. The fermentation industries use sorghum for brewing, distilling, and making industrial alcohol. Industrial uses of sorghum involve some wet and dry milling operations for starch and by-products. Sorghum makes excellent pasture for livestock as well as high-quality silage. For human food, the kernels can be parched, popped, or whole-boiled. Ground or cracked grain is made into flat, unleavened bread, porridge, or paste.

Bibliography: Delorit, Richard J., et al., *Crop Production,* 4th ed. (1973); Wall, J. S., and Ross, W. M., *Sorghum Production and Utilization* (1970).

Sorokin, Pitirim A.   [soh-roh'-kin, pit-ir-eem']

Pitirim Alexandrovitch Sorokin, b. Russia, Jan. 21 (N.S.), 1889, d. Feb. 10, 1968, was a major 20th-century sociologist and social philosopher. He was educated at the University of Saint Petersburg and became its first professor of sociology in 1919. Expelled from Russia because of his anti-Bolshevik opinions, Sorokin came to the United States in 1922. He joined (1924) the faculty of the University of Minnesota, where he made important contributions to the field of rural sociology. In 1930 he moved to Harvard and founded that university's sociology department.

Sorokin, who was especially interested in the study of social change, distinguished three basic types of sociocultural systems, based on three different ways of perceiving reality: the sensate, oriented toward what can be perceived with the senses (modern Western society belongs to this category); the ideational, which emphasizes faith in supersensory means of knowledge; and the idealistic, which tries to balance the first two. Sorokin's basic philosophy, which he called integralism, posits reality as a combination of the sensate, intellectual, and intuitive perspectives. His works include *Social Mobility* (1927), *Social and Cultural Dynamics* (1937–41), *Society, Culture, and Personality* (1947), and *Altruistic Love* (1950).

JOHN ROBINSON

Bibliography: Matter, Joseph A., *Love, Altruism and World Crisis: The Challenge of Pitirim Sorokin* (1974); Zimmerman, Carle C., *Sociological Theories of Pitirim A. Sorokin* (1973).

sororities: see FRATERNITIES AND SORORITIES.

sorrel   [sohr'-ul]

Sorrel is the name used for various edible plants that have a sour juice. Most belong to the genus *Rumex* of the buckwheat family. Several *Rumex* species are perennials whose fleshy, spearhead-shaped leaves are used in soups and salads, such as *R. patientia,* also called spinach-dock; *R. acetosa,* known as garden sorrel; and *R. scutatus,* called French sorrel.

Garden sorrel, R. acetosa, *is an herb that has spikes of flowers, which can be used in dried floral arrangements. Its leaves add a sour flavor to sauces, omelets, and soups and may be used as salad greens.*

Sorrel is especially popular in Europe; some U.S. cultivation occurs in California and the southern states. Sheep sorrel, *R. acetosella,* a widespread weed, was introduced into the United States from Europe. Wood sorrel is the name of several plants in the genus *Oxalis.*

Sorrows of Young Werther, The

An epistolary novel with autobiographical elements, *The Sorrows of Young Werther* (1774; Eng. trans., 1779–80) earned its author, Johann Wolfgang von GOETHE, an international reputation and proved influential in the development of the romantic movement. The novel concerns the frustrated passion and sense of social alienation of the hero, Werther, who eventually commits suicide. Expressing the tragic incompatibility between a rich inner life and the practical life required by society, it glorifies the emotions and places its primary emphasis on individual fulfillment.   R. M. FORD

Sotatsu   [soh'-taht-soo]

The Japanese painter Tawaraya Sotatsu (1576–1643) is credited with founding the school of decorative ink painting known as *Rimpa.* His highly influential style combined classical motifs with fluid brushstrokes and flat masses of color. In collaboration (c.1606–20) with the artist KOETSU, to whom he was related through marriage, he produced beautifully decorated literary texts as well as scrolls in which Koetsu wrote classic poetry over Sotatsu's designs of birds, flowers, or deer rendered in gold and silver. After 1620, Sotatsu worked independently, transforming motifs taken from illustrated narratives of the 12th and 13th centuries into decorative designs on gold-leafed screens and sliding doors. The screen painting *Waves at Matsushima* (Freer Gallery, Washington, D.C.) epitomizes his fluid brush style and masterly sense of design and color.
BARBARA BRENNAN FORD

Bibliography: Burling, Judith and Arthur Hart, *Sotatsu* (1962); Tanaka, Ichimatsu, ed., *Tawaraya Sotatsu,* trans. by Elise Grilli (1956).

Sothern, Edward H.   [suhth'-urn]

The son of a famous English actor, Edward Hugh Sothern, b. New Orleans, La., Dec. 6, 1859, d. Oct. 28, 1933, was noted for his Shakespearean and romantic comedy roles, many of which he played opposite his second wife, Julia MARLOWE. Famous in the title role of *The Prisoner of Zenda* (1895), Sothern was also outstanding in *Hamlet* (1919 and 1923) and in *Romeo and Juliet* (1923).

Sotho   [soh'-toh]

The Sotho (Basotho) are a people who now live in the constitutional monarchy of Lesotho, the former British Protectorate of Basutoland; they numbered about 1 million in the late 1970s. The term *Sotho* is also frequently used to refer to that group of African peoples inhabiting Lesotho, Botswana, and parts of South Africa who speak a subdivision of BANTU languages known as SeSotho. In this subdivision would be included the TSWANA, Pedi, Sotho, and several other peoples among the approximately 4 million (1974 est.) speakers of the SeSotho language. Sotho can thus be regarded as a major linguistic group in southern Africa differing markedly from NGUNI. Broad cultural differences also exist between Sotho and Nguni peoples. For example, the Nguni are shocked to learn that many Sotho traditionally marry their cousins, because in the Nguni kinship system this relationship is considered incestuous. The Nguni have a ritually ordained aversion to eating fish, which the Sotho do not. Also, the status of women is relatively higher among Sotho peoples.

Sotho political history is complex, involving battles with Nguni tribes as well as conflicts with the British and the Boers (see AFRIKANERS). The integrity of the Basotho nation, in spite of a period of British colonial rule, was inspired by the remarkable statesmanship of MOSHESHWE in his negotiations with black and white foreigners during the 19th century. His greatest achievement, however, was his success in bringing rival Sotho tribes under his central authority.

After achieving independence from Britain in 1966, the landlocked nation of Lesotho was obliged to continue strong economic ties with South Africa for trading purposes. South Africa is thought to employ more than half of Lesotho's able-bodied men and women as migrant laborers; in 1976, 90,000 Sotho miners were reportedly working in South Africa. Political relations between the two countries are strained, notably regarding South Africa's policies of APARTHEID.
PETER CARSTENS

Bibliography: Ashton, E. Hugh, *The Basuto: A Study of Traditional and Modern Lesotho,* 2d ed. (1967); Lagden, Sir Geoffrey Y., *The Basutos* (1969); Wilson, Monica, and Thompson, Leonard, eds., *The Oxford History of South Africa,* 2 vols. (1969–71).

Soufflot, Jacques Germain   [soo-floh']

Jacques Germain Soufflot, b. July 22, 1713, d. Aug. 29, 1780, was the greatest French exponent of neoclassical architecture (see NEOCLASSICISM, art). His style owes much to the fact that he trained in Rome (1731–38). Thus his earliest buildings—the Hôtel Dieu (1741–49) and the Exchange (1747–50), both in Lyons—are derived from the 17th-century monuments of the Roman classical baroque and depart from French tradition by emphasizing cubic monumentality at the expense of pavilions and decorative sculpture. With his theater in Lyons (designed in 1753), Soufflot brought to France the innovation of the horseshoe-shaped auditorium. The extraordinary Church of Sainte Geneviève (1757–90), in Paris, which combined the height and transparency of the Gothic with the structural principles and decor of the antique, perfectly embodied the concepts of contemporaneous architectural theory. Unfortunately, its conversion (1791) into the Panthéon required the loss of both its original space-defining flood of light and the festive gaiety of its religious reliefs.   ROBERT M. NEUMAN

Bibliography: Kalnein, Wend Graf, and Levey, Michael, *Art and Architecture of the Eighteenth Century in France* (1972).

soul

Soul is a term rarely used with precise definition in philosophy, religion, or common life. It is generally regarded as descriptive of an entity related to but distinguishable from the body—the spiritual part of human beings that animates their physical existence and survives death.

Primitive religions tend to associate the soul with the vital force in humans and often identify it with particular parts or functions of the body (the heart or kidneys, the breath or pulse). Other religions show traces of such animistic ideas. In Hinduism, the Atman (originally meaning "breath") is the individual factor that is indestructible and that after death is reborn in another existence. But Atman is identified with Brahman, the Source of all things to which the soul ultimately returns when it ceases to have a separate existence. (Buddhism, on the other hand, repudiates the notion of Atman, positing the theory of Anatta, nonself.) Early Jewish thought did not conceive the soul as existing apart from the body except in the shadowy realm of departed spirits (*Sheol*). Greek and especially Platonic thought divided humans into two parts: body and soul. The soul, often referred to as the *psyche,* was considered both preexistent and immortal.

The early Christian church lived under the influence of Greek ideas about the body and soul, although biblical teachings about RESURRECTION were superimposed on them. Throughout the history of the Christian church, there has been no clearly defined and universally accepted metaphysical conception of the soul. Nevertheless, Christian theology and worship have adhered firmly to the conviction of personal survival after death rooted in belief in the love of God and the resurrection of Jesus Christ from the dead.

Philosophy has long been preoccupied with speculation about the existence and nature of the soul and its relationship to the body. In the 20th century many philosophers have argued, following William JAMES, that the concept of the soul is neither verifiable nor necessary to an understanding of humankind's mode of existence in the world.
CHARLES W. RANSON

Bibliography: Cullmann, Oscar, *Immortality of the Soul or Resurrection of the Dead?* (1958); Kenny, Anthony J. P., *The Anatomy of the Soul: Historical Essays in the Philosophy of Mind* (1973); Laird, John, *The Idea of Soul* (1970); Rank, Otto, *Psychology and the Soul* (1961).

Soul on Ice

Written by Eldridge CLEAVER during a term at Folsom Prison, *Soul on Ice* (1968) is a collection of letters and essays that was smuggled out of prison for publication. The book discusses a wide variety of subjects including the forces that shaped Cleaver's life and religion, the Watts riots, and the Vietnam War. In the book, Cleaver criticizes black political leaders and the work of such black writers as Richard WRIGHT and James BALDWIN. Cleaver's opinions had significant political influence on the civil rights movement as well as on the antiwar movement of the late 1960s.

CHARLOTTE D. SOLOMON

soul music

Aretha Franklin, known as Lady Soul, was the leading soul singer of the 1960s and early '70s. Trained as a gospel singer, Franklin expanded her powerful, emotional style to include elements of popular music and rhythm and blues. "Respect," "Chain of Fools," and "Natural Woman," all released in 1967, are among her most successful records.

A successful popular music style, soul music is derived from black GOSPEL MUSIC, with its highly decorated, emotional singing style, fervent backup choruses, and rhythmic instrumental backing. In the late 1940s and early 1950s, BLUES singers such as Bobby Bland, and vocal groups like the Ravens, used a gospel-tinged sound. Church singers and groups began to record popular music in the 1950s, among them The Dominoes, led by Clyde McPhatter, and Sam Cooke, who was well known as a gospel singer before he "crossed over" to popular music. The most important names in 1950s soul music, however, were James BROWN, whose 1956 "Please, Please, Please" had all the raw urgency of black preaching, and Ray CHARLES, whose 1959 "What'd I Say?" took the new sound to a wide audience.

The soul style was greatly popularized in the 1960s by the success of the MOTOWN group of record labels, and by Aretha FRANKLIN, the daughter of a well-known Detroit preacher, whose recordings—especially the 1967 "Respect"—became national hits. Other important soul singers of the 1960s included Otis REDDING and Wilson Pickett. Throughout the 1960s the soul style was smoothed and softened to make it more acceptable to mass audiences. This tendency continued during the 1970s, when "soul music" became an accepted element of American popular music, growing increasingly sophisticated, but retaining its basic church elements: decoration, drive and verve.

Bibliography: Shaw, Arnold, *The World of Soul* (1970).

Soulages, Pierre   [soo-lahzh']

Pierre Soulages, b. Dec. 24, 1919, is one of France's best-known contemporary artists. He fought with the French army in 1940 and, once the war was over, began exhibiting his paintings. His works relied heavily on large strokes of black paint laid over a lighter ground. Soulages's technique has been compared to the subconscious calligraphy of American abstract expressionists like Franz Kline; there is occasional violence in the rough and angry edges of the forms. Soulages is also known for his stage and ballet sets.

PHIL PATTON

Bibliography: Sweeney, James J., *Soulages* (1973).

Soult, Nicolas Jean de Dieu   [soolt]

Nicolas Jean de Dieu Soult, b. Mar. 29, 1769, d. Nov. 26, 1851, was a French soldier and politician. He served in the FRENCH REVOLUTIONARY WARS, rising to the rank of general after the Battle of Fleurus (1794). Promoted (1804) to marshal by Napoleon I, he further distinguished himself at Ulm and Austerlitz (1805) and at Jena (1806) and was created duc de Dalmatie in 1808. He commanded ably in the Peninsular War (1808–14; see NAPOLEONIC WARS) but was defeated by the future duke of Wellington. Although Soult turned royalist during the First Restoration (1814), he rejoined Napoleon as chief of staff at Waterloo. Returning (1819) from exile, he served in three ministries (1832–34, 1839–40, 1840–47) but again became a republican after the Revolutions of 1848.

sound and acoustics

The science, engineering, and art of the generation, propagation, and reception of sound waves constitute the subject of acoustics. Although the Greek origin of the term refers to sounds that can be heard, the subject of acoustics embraces all mechanical waves, from the very slow vibrations of the Earth and its atmosphere to the very rapid vibrations of atoms in solids. The impact of the study of acoustics is extremely widespread. Acoustics is important, for example, in the fields of speech and hearing, the production of music, the design of theaters, the control of unwanted vibrations and noise in the environment, and medical diagnosis and therapy.

DEVELOPMENT OF ACOUSTICS

In the 4th century BC, Aristotle understood that sound is propagated by some motion of the air. Two centuries earlier Pythagoras is said to have observed that when sound is emitted from two vibrating strings, the shorter string provides the higher pitch. Much earlier civilizations, such as the Egyptian, Persian, and Chinese, had developed musical instruments, and the fact that a solid body emits a sound when it is struck must have been known to our earliest ancestors. In early civilizations, and indeed up to modern times, music has provided much of the impetus for the study of acoustics.

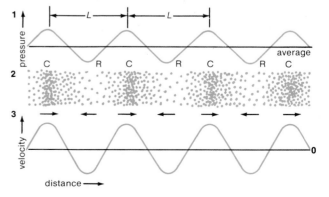

The transmission of sound through air involves alternate regions (2) of increased (C) and decreased (R) pressure. At increasing distances from a source of sound with a wavelength L, the changing pressures and velocities of air molecules moving back and forth (arrows) within these regions can be represented mathematically by sine curves (1, 3).

Galileo's discussion of vibration and sound in his *Dialogues Concerning Two New Sciences* (1638) announced the reemergence of the study of acoustics following the Middle Ages. During the ensuing two and a half centuries, experiments were performed and the mathematics was developed that led to the present understanding of the fundamentals of acoustics. The end of the 19th century marked the beginning of the modern study of acoustics. The British scientist J. W. Strutt, Lord Rayleigh, published *The Theory of Sound* (1877), in which he gathered together, clarified, and extended the current knowledge of acoustics and thereby laid the foundation for future studies in the science.

PROPAGATION

Sound needs an elastic medium—solid, liquid, or gas—through which to propagate. Unlike light and other electromagnetic waves, sound cannot exist in a vacuum. When a small region of the elastic medium is compressed, it exerts a tug on its neighboring regions, and they in turn pull on their neighbors. If the region is expanded, it will push on its neighbors, and that push will also propagate through the medium. If the compressions and expansions are alternated in a regular way, regions of alternating high and low density will propagate throughout the medium; the result is a sound wave. As the wave goes by, each particle in the medium oscillates. Neighboring particles do not oscillate in unison, but are slightly out of phase, alternately coming closer together and farther apart, thus creating the density changes. Sound waves are longitudinal, because the motion of the particles is parallel to the direction of propagation of the wave.

CHARACTERISTICS OF SOUND WAVES

The pitch of the sound is determined by its frequency—the rate at which the vibrations occur. The units of frequency are called Hertz (Hz); 1 Hz is equal to 1 vibration per second. The human ear is sensitive to frequencies between about 20 Hz and 20,000 Hz. Frequencies lower than 20 Hz are called infrasonic; those higher than 20,000 Hz are called ultrasonic.

The magnitude of the changes associated with a sound wave are remarkably small. For example, a tone of middle C (261 Hz) played in air as loudly as the ear can tolerate results in density changes about 0.02% above and below the density of quiet air; the maximum displacement of air molecules is less than one-tenth of a millimeter (0.004 in).

The wavelength of sound is the distance between two adjacent compressions. For a tone of middle C in air, the wavelength is about 1.2 m (4 ft); for an ultrasonic wave with a frequency of 75,000 Hz in water, the wavelength is 2 cm (0.9 in). The frequency, the wavelength, and the speed of sound have this relationship: speed equals frequency times wavelength.

Speed of Sound. The speed of sound is characteristic only of the medium through which it propagates and does not depend on the frequency of the sound wave. The fact that the speed is independent of the frequency is clear to anyone who listens to a band concert from a long distance. The sounds from all the instruments, from the bass drum to the piccolo, arrive at the same time.

The properties of the medium that determine the sound speed are its compressibility and density. The more difficult it is to change the volume of the medium by squeezing it, the greater the sound velocity; the greater the density, the slower the velocity. Although air has a low density, the speed is, in fact, quite small because air is so easily compressed. Solids, on the other hand, are generally difficult to compress and thus have high sound speeds.

TABLE 1: SPEED OF SOUND IN SELECTED MEDIA

Medium	Sound Velocity	
	m/sec	ft/sec
Air (20° C)	343	1,125
Water	1,498	4,915
Seawater	1,531	5,023
Lucite plastic	2,680	8,793
Steel	5,060	16,600
Aluminum	5,100	16,700
Pyrex glass	5,640	18,500

Wave Properties of Sound. DIFFRACTION is the bending of waves around obstacles. This book can serve as a barrier to light but not to sound. Both light and sound are waves and are diffracted around the barrier, but the light wavelength is so small that the bending is not noticeable. The sound wavelength, on the other hand, is larger than the size of the barrier; therefore there is very little acoustic shadow.

REFRACTION is the bending of a wave when it goes from a region of one propagation velocity to that of another. The wave bends toward the low-velocity region. Optical lenses are an example of the refraction of light waves. Refraction of sound waves is not something noticeable in everyday experience, but it is important for the study of sound propagation in the ocean. The sound velocity is not uniform throughout the ocean; with increasing depth, the pressure increases and the temperature decreases, and both of these affect the sound velocity. The resultant velocity profiles indicate how a sound wave bends as it propagates through the ocean. Shadow zones (regions that the sound from a particular source cannot reach) and sound channels (layers in which the sound is confined) are commonly found.

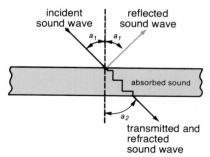

A sound wave traveling in one medium may be in part reflected, absorbed, and transmitted when it strikes another medium. The wave is reflected at the same angle (a_1) at which it strikes. The transmitted part's angle of refraction (a_2) depends on the second medium.

REFLECTION of sound is easily observed in any enclosed space. In fact, reflections are so prevalent that in order to study the behavior of audio equipment or of people in their absence, it is necessary to use a specially designed room with 100 percent sound-absorbing walls called an anechoic chamber. The eerie feeling experienced by an individual in such a chamber is ample evidence of the ubiquity of acoustic reflections. On the other hand, the acoustic design of a room for clarity and brightness of spoken or musical sounds must strike a proper balance of reflections and absorption. Reflections are needed to provide a full, diffuse, and uniform

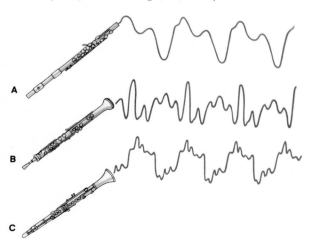

Complicated waveshapes are obtained for the sounds produced by the periodic vibrations of a column of air in a flute (A), an oboe (B), and a clarinet (C). The waveforms are distinctive for each instrument and depend on the relative strengths of a series of different sound frequencies generated simultaneously within the vibrating air column.

sound, but absorption must limit the reverberations to avoid confusion. This balance is characterized by the reverberation time, which for large concert halls is between one and two seconds.

SOURCES OF SOUND

Any vibrating object, such as a taut string, a solid plate, or a column of air, is a source of sound. In addition, air rushing past an obstacle fast enough to cause turbulence generates sound waves; an example of this is a whistle. A drum or cymbal is an example of a vibrating plate directly generating sound. In a flute or an organ pipe, rushing air sets the column of air in the tube in motion; the vibration of the air at the end of the tube radiates into the atmosphere. In brass and reed instruments and in the human voice, a vibrating plate (lips and reed, and vocal cords, respectively) sets an air column into vibration. In a piano, violin, or guitar some sound is radiated directly by the vibrating strings, but it is augmented by the sounding board, which is a vibrating plate (see MUSIC, ACOUSTICS OF).

Electronically produced or amplified sound is a common—some might even say dominant—component of the modern acoustic environment. The loudspeaker, the end of the electronic chain, is simply a vibrating diaphragm that is electrically driven. An alternating electric current in a coil moves a magnet that is attached to the diaphragm, causing it to vibrate.

The field of ULTRASONICS was made accessible by the discovery (1880) by Jacques and Pierre Curie of the phenomenon of PIEZOELECTRICITY. Certain crystals, such as quartz, will expand and contract slightly when they are placed in an alternating electric field. Furthermore, their response is rapid; they can be driven at microwave frequencies—as high as a billion vibrations per second. The reverse effect also occurs (and, in fact, is the effect discovered by the Curies); that is, when squeezed, for example, by a sound wave, a piezoelectric crystal creates an electric potential (voltage). Piezoelectric crystals can therefore be used as both receivers and sources of sound waves, from audible to ultrasonic frequencies.

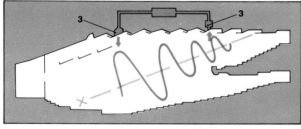

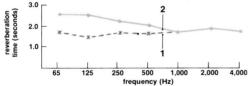

After the Royal Festival Concert Hall in London was built, it was found that the reverberation time, or the time required for a sound to die out, was too short (1) for the lower frequencies. A full, rich sound was provided in the hall by increasing (2) the reverberation time of low frequencies with electronic resonators (3) in the ceiling.

RECEIVERS OF SOUND

The most important, and technically the most impressive, of all sound receivers is the ear. The ear is capable of detecting sound for which the fluctuations of density of the air are less than one ten-millionth of 1 percent. This figure corresponds to a particle displacement of less than one atomic diameter. Because the range of acoustic amplitudes that the ear can detect is so large, it has been convenient to define a compressed scale to describe acoustic intensities. In this decibel scale, a 10-decibel (dB) difference between two sounds is perceived as a loudness difference of a factor of two.

TABLE 2: RELATIVE SOUND LEVELS

Decibels (dB)	Acoustic Condition
0	Threshold of hearing
30	Bedroom at night
60	Conversation at one meter
90	Subway train
110	Rock band
140	Threshold of pain
200	Saturn rocket at close range

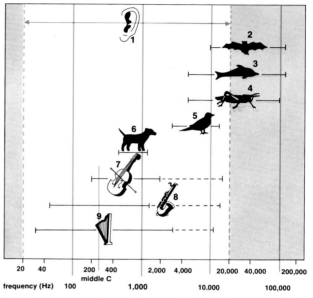

The frequency range of sounds that can be heard by human ears (1) extends from about 20 to 20,000 Hz. Bats (2), porpoises (3), and grasshoppers (4) can generate ultrasonic frequencies to about 100,000 Hz. Birds (5) and dogs (6) produce much lower frequency sounds, all within the range of human hearing. Musical instruments, such as violins (7), saxophones (8), and harps (9), produce a range both of fundamental frequencies (solid lines) and of overtones (dashed lines) that give the different instruments their distinctive tonal qualities.

Regular exposure to sounds of about 90 dB will eventually cause hearing loss, and sounds of 130 dB can cause immediate and permanent hearing loss.

A MICROPHONE is a device that detects the existence of a sound wave and converts the acoustic signal into an electric signal. The electric signal can then be transmitted over large distances, amplified and reemitted, or stored (see SOUND RECORDING AND REPRODUCTION). A simple microphone, such as that used in a telephone receiver, works on the principle that a lump of carbon granules changes its electrical resistance when it is squeezed.

ULTRASONICS

Sound waves with frequencies above the range of human hearing, especially when operated at high intensities, have found widespread industrial uses. Ultrasonic waves can be used for cleaning small parts, for welding plastics and metal, for driving piles, and for drilling holes in glass. In most of these high-power applications the action is caused not by the direct agitation of the sound wave, but by the secondary effects of (a) heating, caused by the absorption of the sound; (b) streaming, the steady flow induced in a liquid by the sound; or (c) cavitation, the formation and collapse of bubbles in a liquid.

Medical ultrasonics is a rapidly growing field. Focused ultrasound can be used to destroy unwanted tissues. Lower-intensity sound can be used much like X rays to visualize the body's interior structure. Heartbeat and blood flow can be monitored using an ultrasonic Doppler shift.

STEPHEN V. LETCHER

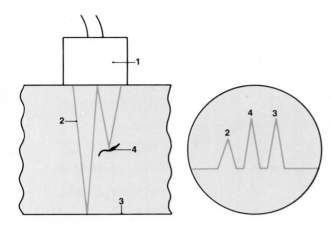

The ultrasonic pulse-echo technique of finding cracks and other flaws in various materials makes use of the reflection properties of sound waves. A probe (1) transmits a pulsed beam (2) of ultrasound waves with frequencies above 20,000 Hz into the material. The transmitted and reflected waves from the bottom surface (3) and from flaws (4) are converted into electrical signals and displayed on an oscilloscope.

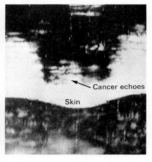

The ultrasonic pulse-echo technique was first used by doctors in 1950 to detect tumors in a human body. A woman's breast was scanned with a beam of ultrasound, and the sound reflections from different regions were displayed on a cathode-ray tube. The scan of a normal breast (left) was found to differ from that of a tumorous breast (right).

Bibliography: Backus, John, *The Acoustical Foundations of Music* (1969); Chedd, Graham, *Sound: From Communication to Noise Pollution* (1970); Hunt, Frederick V., *Origins of Acoustics: The Science of Sound from Antiquity to the Age of Newton* (1978); Kinsler, Lawrence E., and Frey, Austin R., *Fundamentals of Acoustics*, 2d ed. (1962); Kock, Winton E., *Seeing Sound* (1971); Lindsay, R. B., ed., *Acoustics: Historical and Philosophical Development* (1973); Tannenbaum, Beulah, and Stillman, Myra, *Understanding Sound* (1973); White, Frederic A., *Our Acoustic Environment* (1975).

See also: DOPPLER EFFECT; MACH NUMBER; SOUND BARRIER; WAVES AND WAVE MOTION.

sound barrier

An airplane or any vehicle is said to be crossing the sound barrier when its speed exceeds the speed of sound (see MACH NUMBER). Many attempts were made by normal aircraft in the 1940s to break the sound barrier, but they caused the planes to disintegrate because the transition from subsonic to supersonic speeds causes strong nose-heavy changes of trim and sets up structural vibrations that can tear a plane apart. The sound barrier was finally breached on Oct. 14, 1947, by U.S. Air Force captain Charles E. Yeager in a *Bell X-1* research plane. Proper airplane design has since made supersonic flight routine. Design improvements include streamlining, adjustable stabilizers, adjustable incidence tailplanes, and hydraulic-ram positioners for control surfaces.

Sound and the Fury, The

A four-part novel by William FAULKNER, *The Sound and the Fury* (1929) dramatizes the disintegration of the Compson family from four points of view. The first section is told from the viewpoint of a 33-year-old idiot, the second by a neurotic on the day of his suicide, the third by a paranoid on the day that his worst fantasies become real, and the fourth by the omniscient author. This STREAM OF CONSCIOUSNESS novel explores past and present to reveal the lovelessness of the Compson brothers. The title is from Shakespeare's metaphorical description of life in *Macbeth* (act 5, scene 3)—"a tale/ Told by an idiot, full of sound and fury,/Signifying nothing."

Bibliography: Meriwether, James B., *Studies in "The Sound and the Fury"* (1970).

sound recording and reproduction

Sound recording and reproduction involves the translation of sound into a permanent physical medium by mechanical, electrical, or optical means in order that the sound subsequently may be reproduced. The majority of sound recordings are made on PHONOGRAPH records, magnetic tapes, and motion-picture sound tracks. All practical recording processes involve the use of an electrical analog—that is, an electric current varied in frequency and amplitude in correspondence to the original sound. The electric current is modulated by the sound by means of a MICROPHONE or other TRANSDUCER. An artificial analog also may be created by synthesis, as in the electronic organ. This modulation, or signal, is then amplified, by means of an AMPLIFIER, to a value sufficient to actuate the recording mechanism.

In reproduction, the recorded medium actuates the reproduce transducer, which in turn creates a facsimile of the original signal. Amplification is applied to the signal thus recovered so that it can actuate headphones or loudspeakers and thereby reproduce the original sound.

MAGNETIC RECORDING

A magnetic recording can be made and played back using a TAPE RECORDER. The electrical signal is fed to an iron-core ELECTROMAGNET called the recording head, while a magnetically coated plastic tape is being drawn past the head. The head induces a varying magnetic field (flux), which is imparted to the moving tape. The recording can be reproduced at a later time by drawing the magnetized tape past the same head (or one similar), which is connected to an amplifier. The magnetized, moving tape imparts a magnetic flux to the head, which generates a small electrical signal (the analog). The signal is amplified and fed to LOUDSPEAKERS to reproduce the original sound.

As many as 32 separate sound signals may be recorded on the same tape in longitudinal parallel paths called tracks. Any single-track recording is monophonic, whereas two tracks are used to record a stereophonic signal. At least 95 percent of all recordings are first made on tape, because it can be erased and rerecorded many times. Editing is simple; any recording is easily added to or treated with special effects when made on multiple tracks. Finally, in normal use tape-recording quality is unsurpassed by any other medium.

DISC RECORDING

Phonograph records can be played back on an ordinary phonograph (gramophone), or record player. They are generally produced commercially on special equipment. The recording mechanism in disc recording is a specialized electric motor (transducer) called a cutting head. It has a cutting stylus attached that is suspended above a rotating table that holds a platter of lacquer-coated aluminum. The stylus contacts the lacquer, cutting a continuous, closely spaced spiral groove that reproduces the undulations induced by the cutting head. The undulations, called modulation, are an analog of the original electrical signal. The number of undulations corresponds to the frequency of the signal, and the lateral distance corresponds to its amplitude. When no modulation is present, as in the spacer grooves between bands of a long-playing record, no lateral or depth change in the groove occurs.

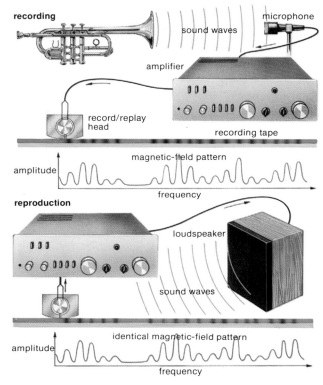

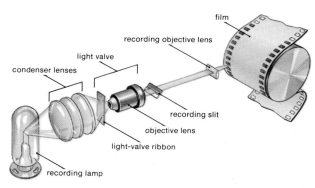

In optical recording, light passed through condenser lenses enters a light valve containing overlapping metal ribbons that move apart in a magnetic field and let light through. The amount of light transmitted depends on the magnetic field, which varies in accordance with the sound. The transmitted beam is focused and then recorded on film.

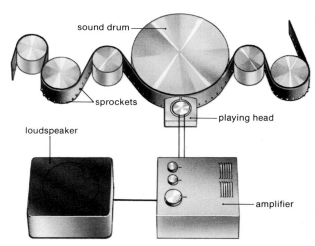

In tape recording and reproduction of sound, the sound to be recorded is first picked up by a microphone and converted to electrical signals of corresponding frequency and amplitude. The amplified signals are fed to a recording head that induces a varying magnetic field in accordance with the signals. The magnetic-field pattern is transferred to iron-oxide particles coated on a tape strip that is drawn past the head. By reversing the process, the head can reproduce the electrical signals and feed them to a loudspeaker for reproduction of the sound.

Film that has a magnetic stripe for a tape-recorded sound track provides sound reproduction of higher quality than does the optical system above. Sprockets guide the film around a sound drum, where a magnetic playing head converts the stored information to electrical signals. The amplified signals are sent to one or more loudspeakers, depending on how many tracks of sound were on the recording tape.

The groove modulation is reproduced with a specialized transducer called a phonograph pickup. The stylus, or needle, within the pickup vibrates as the grooved record rotates. A transducer converts these vibrations back into the original electrical signal, which is then amplified and fed to loudspeakers to re-create the original sound. Lateral motion in the groove creates only a monophonic signal; a combination of lateral and vertical motion creates a stereophonic signal. In both the stereo cutting head and stereo phonography cartridge, there is a cross-coupled pair of transducers that operate on planes 90° apart. Monaural, stereophonic, or specially processed quadraphonic signals may all be recorded and reproduced by this system.

OPTICAL RECORDING
Primarily used in CINEMATOGRAPHY (motion pictures), optical recording is a photographic process for recording sound on film. The recording mechanism, called a light valve, is magnetically actuated by the (analog) signal, causing varying amounts of light to fall upon, and thus variably expose, the moving film. The changing densities thus obtained correspond in frequency and amplitude to the original sound. In reproduction, a light source is focused on a PHOTOELECTRIC CELL, and the optical sound track is drawn between the source and the cell, producing a fluctuating signal, which is converted into sound.

Optical recording does not compare in fidelity with other available techniques because of inherent mechanical limitations in the process. Accordingly, magnetic recording tracks have been incorporated into some motion-picture films for improved sound reproduction.

GENERAL CONSIDERATIONS AND LIMITATIONS.
All sound recording and reproduction equipment has various limitations. Because the human ear can differentiate among sounds that range in intensity from 1 part to more than 1 trillion parts (by sound-pressure measurement), the system designer is presented with the problem of accurately duplicating original sound with minimal distortion, minimal excess noise, and minimal insufficiencies of frequency response and dynamic response. Distortion factors can be introduced, for example, when the power-handling capability of any device is exceeded, as in the case of an overloaded cutting head. These distortions are discernible as extraneous sound in the desired reproduction, or as undesirable change in the physical parameters of the groove. This limitation applies in principle to all recording processes.

Noise in a recording system is produced by the system's own operation, as in the case of disc recording. For example, the friction produced by the stylus tracking the groove creates a background noise in reproduction, and amplifiers produce a background noise because of thermionic processes.

Frequency response may be defined as the ability of a system to reproduce all frequencies of interest at their original respective amplitudes. Frequency response in the home high-fidelity system, for example, may be adjusted with tone controls.

The dynamic response problem may be illustrated as follows. If a record groove has been alternately cut with no signal and then with maximum signal applied to the cutting head, a measurement can be made during reproduction of the signals generated in the modulated and nonmodulated portions of the groove. The maximum useful dynamic range is about 1 part to 2 million parts (in electrical power) in the best equipment currently available. Measurement of maximum signal above noise provides a quality factor of system performance known as signal-to-noise ratio (S/N). The S/N ratio of the human ear is 500,000 times greater than that of the best disc-recording process. The best analog tape-recording systems with noise reduction have perhaps 10 to 15 times greater S/N than an analog disc.

A number of analog tape noise-reduction systems similar in function are currently in widespread use. In the recording process, signal dynamics are compressed in an exact mathematical relationship so that low-level signals, which would otherwise be masked by tape noise, are boosted. This encoded signal is stored on magnetic tape in the same manner as analog signals. In reproduction, the system decodes the signal by expansion action in an exact reciprocal relationship. The expansion-compression functions therefore reduce noise by artificially increasing the S/N ratio of the tape.

DIGITAL RECORDING TECHNIQUES
A new departure in recording technique realized during the late 1970s, known as pulse code modulation (PCM), or digital recording, has afforded a significant improvement in recording quality. The PCM technique converts the basic form of recorded information so that it is rendered immune to or no longer relates to the characteristic noise and distortion inherent in the recorded medium. In the record mode, the PCM device graphically analyzes the instantaneous values of an analog signal many thousands of times per second and generates chains of pulses, each related to a specific portion of the information in the analog signal. In the reproduce mode the PCM device converts the pulses back to the instantaneous signal values originally sampled, then processes them through a special filter to form analog curves, thus re-creating the original signal. This process is conceptually similar to plotting points on a graph and connecting them to form a curve depicting a mathematical relationship. If noise or distortion is present at the beginning of the PCM process, it will by defini-

tion be preserved by the process and be reproduced at the end of it.

Currently, several digital-tape systems are in use; analog tape units are not suitable for use because of insufficient frequency response. In addition, a system known as the digital laser disc is currently being developed. It has recording and reproduce transducers that have no physical contact with the modulated medium. PCM is inscribed on the disc in a "dot-and-dash" pattern by the laser cutting beam in a spiral path similar to that on the phonograph disc. Reproduction is achieved by means of a reproduce laser, which tracks the "dot-and-dash" modulation; the reflected beam of the reproduce laser is refracted by the modulated groove. The modulated beam is converted by a special photoelectric cell to a facsimile of the original PCM signal, which is decoded to analog form and reproduced in a conventional fashion.

COMMERCIAL RECORDING PRACTICE
In a commercial recording session, a variety of microphones and audio pickups is strategically placed in the performance environment to favor selected aspects of the performance. The various signals that are obtained are routed through a multichannel control console that adjusts such factors as amplification, tonal values, and dynamic content and sends the processed signals to a multitrack tape recorder, which records the signals on a multitrack master tape having 2, 4, 8, 12, 16, 24, or 32 tracks. In the process, these tracks may be encoded for digital or noise-reduced modes.

In the remixing phase the encoded multitrack tape is reproduced, decoded from digital or noise-reduced modes, and routed to the mixing console, where the individual signals are again processed and electrically mixed in their final form (monaural, stereo, or quadraphonic signals). All of these processes are continuously monitored by means of amplifiers and loudspeakers. At this stage most of the special-effects processing occurs: equalization (tonal change), compression or limiting (dynamic alteration), phasing (electronic or tape delay), artificial reverberation or echo, sound synthesis, and stereo panning ("ping-pong" effect). This final mix is recorded on tape again in 1-, 2-, or 4-track format to produce the final tape production master. In the mastering process the master tape is used to make a disc master by disc recording methods or a tape duplication master by tape-to-tape copy.

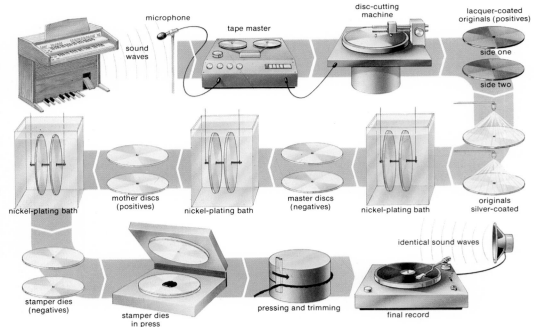

To make a phonograph record, a tape master of the sound is fed into a machine that cuts discs of lacquer-coated metal. These discs—one for each side of the final record—are sprayed with silver and then coated electrochemically to produce master discs of nickel. The masters are called negatives because they have ridges corresponding to the grooves of the originals, or positives. They are used in turn to make another pair of positives, the mother discs. From these are made the stamper dies that press out the final record, which is trimmed and packaged.

microphone

sound waves

tape master

disc-cutting machine

lacquer-coated originals (positives)

side one

side two

nickel-plating bath

mother discs (positives)

nickel-plating bath

master discs (negatives)

nickel-plating bath

originals silver-coated

stamper dies (negatives)

stamper dies in press

pressing and trimming

identical sound waves

final record

Mass production of tapes and discs is the final step in the process. The disc master, or lacquer, is manufactured, by a series of electrochemical processes, into a special stamping die, which forms the finished plastic record by means of heat and pressure. The tape duplication master is played on a high-speed tape reproducer called the master; this high-speed signal is then sent to many high-speed recorders called slaves. The slaves produce the final product, which is inserted into the appropriate package—cassette, cartridge, or open reel.

KENNETH C. ROBERTSON

Bibliography: Aldred, John, *Manual of Sound Recording*, 3d ed. (1978); Bernstein, Julian L., *Audio Systems* (1966; repr. 1978); Borwick, John, ed., *Sound Recording Practice: A Handbook Compiled by the Association of Professional Recording Studios* (1976); Crawford, Doug, *Tape Recording from A to Z* (1975); Overman, Michael, *Understanding Sound, Video, and Film Recording* (1978).

sounding rocket

Sounding rockets are research rockets that carry data-gathering equipment into the atmosphere at altitudes that are too low for the operation of SATELLITES and too high for BALLOONS. These altitudes usually range from about 32 km (20 mi) to 160 km (100 mi), although sounding rockets may occasionally ascend to altitudes of hundreds of kilometers. The data gathered by the rockets' equipment may be telemetered to Earth in the form of electronic signals, or the entire apparatus may be designed for recovery. Sounding rockets have been used since the mid-1940s, when captured German V-2s were used by the United States. The U.S. Navy used V-2 technology to develop the Viking rocket; the more recent AEROBEE is still used today in advanced versions. Many types of sounding rockets have since been developed by many countries.

Meteorological research requires rockets that can ascend to altitudes of 16 to 80 km (10 to 50 mi) to measure pressure, temperature, air density, and winds. Rockets in this category are the U.S. Loki-Dart, the British Skua, the Japanese MT-135P, and the Soviet M-100-B. Larger, mid-range sounding rockets ascend into the upper atmosphere, where physical properties are often highly variable because of such factors as sunspots and solar flares. Typical areas of study involving mid-range rockets are the electron and ion content of the atmosphere, the Earth's magnetic field, and the aurora. Research rockets serving these needs include the U.S. Aerobee 200, the British Skylark, Canada's Black Brant 5B, France's Dragon 3, and Japan's K-9M.

High-altitude research rockets, which may ascend to hundreds of kilometers, gather and return data on cosmic rays, the Van Allen radiation belts, ultraviolet rays, X rays, solar

A sounding rocket is a rocket that can make measurements within the atmosphere. The 6-sec second-stage burn of this Nike-Apache sounding rocket, developed from the Nike antiaircraft missile, can take a 34-kg (75-lb) scientific payload to a height of 210 km (130 mi).

flares, micrometeoroids, and many other phenomena. Examples of high-altitude rockets are the U.S. Astrobee 1500, the Japanese L-3H, and the Soviet Vertikal. Vertikal 6, launched from Kapustin Yar in October 1977, projected its payload to an altitude of 1,500 km (932 mi). The equipment aboard gathered data on the Earth's upper atmosphere and ionosphere and the interaction of the Sun's shortwave radiation with the atmosphere. A stabilized recoverable instrument capsule, which separated from the Vertikal rocket at a height of 173 km (107 mi), soared to its zenith and then descended by parachute.

Sounding rockets have also been used to test scientific instruments and equipment intended for use in satellites. Rockets also carry cameras, returned by parachute, for Earth-resources multispectral photography. Space-factory experiments have been flown in Black Brant and Skylark rockets to test the processing of samples of materials under short periods of microgravity, in preparation for more extensive experiments to be performed later in orbiting manned laboratories.

KENNETH GATLAND

Bibliography: Gatland, Kenneth, *Missiles and Rockets* (1975).

See also: ROCKETS AND MISSILES.

Souphanouvong   [soo-fah'-noo-vahng]

Prince Souphanouvong, b. 1902, has served as head of the Lao People's Democratic Republic since December 1975. Souphanouvong studied engineering in France, and after World War II fought against the French. He joined the communist insurgent (Pathet Lao) forces and became their leader, representing them at the Geneva Conference (1961-62). He was included (1974) in a coalition government under the premiership of his half brother Prince SOUVANNA PHOUMA, whom he ousted in 1975.

sourwood

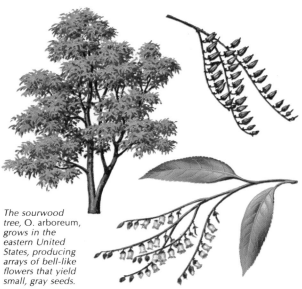

The sourwood tree, O. arboreum, grows in the eastern United States, producing arrays of bell-like flowers that yield small, gray seeds.

Sourwood *Oxydendrum arboreum*, also known as sorrel tree, is native to the southeastern United States. About 15 m (50 ft) in height, it produces small white flowers in branching clusters during the summer. Its large, sour-tasting leaves are chewed by hikers to relieve thirst. Sourwood honey is a product of the southern Appalachian region.

Sousa, John Philip   [soo'-zuh]

America's greatest composer of MARCH music was John Philip Sousa, b. Washington, D.C., Nov. 6, 1854, d. Mar. 6, 1932. The popularity of his 136 marches—headed by "The Stars and Stripes Forever" (1896)—gained him the title The March King, but he also composed 15 operettas, 70 songs, 27 fantasies, more than 300 arrangements, and wrote 132 articles and 7 books, including his autobiography *Marching Along* (1928) and 3 novels.

At the age of 13, Sousa enlisted as an apprentice in the U.S. Marine Band. He left the Marines when he was 18 years of age and played violin in theater and symphonic orchestras, gaining valuable experience also as a conductor. He reenlisted in the Marine Band in 1880—this time as leader—and began composing; his first hit march was "The Gladiator" (1886), and his "Washington Post March" (1889) became a ballroom rage associated with a new dance, the two-step.

He left the Marines in 1892 to form his own band, which quickly became the most successful in the nation; tours through Europe in 1900, 1901, 1903, and 1905 and a global circuit in 1910–11 brought him worldwide celebrity. With the entry of the United States into World War I, Sousa again enlisted, this time to lead the Navy Band, and he continued an active musical life until his retirement in 1931.

EDWARD A. BERLIN

Bibliography: Berger, Kenneth, *The March King and His Band* (1957); Bierly, Paul D., *John Philip Sousa* (1973); Goldman, R. F., "John Philip Sousa," *HiFi Stereo Review*, July 1967.

South, University of the

Established in 1858 and affiliated with the Protestant Episcopal Church, the University of the South (enrollment: 1,030; library: 310,000 volumes) is a 4-year private coeducational institution in Sewanee, Tenn. It has a school of theology. The university publishes *The Sewanee Review* (1892), the oldest literary quarterly in the United States.

South Africa

The Republic of South Africa, formerly the Union of South Africa, occupies the southern extremity of the African continent, stretching from the Limpopo River in the north to Cape AGULHAS in the south. The Indian Ocean lies to the east and the Atlantic Ocean to the west. The strategic sea route around the Cape of GOOD HOPE has long made South Africa important in world commerce.

South Africa shares boundaries, from west to east, with Namibia (formerly Southwest Africa), Botswana, Zimbabwe (Rhodesia), Mozambique, Swaziland, and Lesotho, the latter being an independent enclave in the eastern part of the country. The country consists of four provinces—CAPE PROVINCE and NATAL (former British colonies) and the TRANSVAAL and ORANGE FREE STATE (former Boer republics)—as well as the former Bantu "homelands" of TRANSKEI, BOPHUTHATSWANA, and Venda, which have been granted complete independence, recognized only by South Africa. South Africa has an area of 1,221,040 km² (471,446 mi²), excluding WALVIS BAY—administered by Namibia—but including Transkei, Bophuthatswana, and Venda. The population of 28,055,000 (1979) includes Transkei, Bophuthatswana, and Venda. South Africa has three capitals: Cape Town (legislative), Pretoria (administrative), and Bloemfontein (judicial).

The South African economy is the most diversified and developed in Africa, but vast differences exist between the economies of white South Africans and "South Africans of Colour," as they are known, who outnumber whites by almost five to one. This tremendous disparity prevails because development—economic, political, and social—takes place within an APARTHEID ("apartness" in Afrikaans) framework that is prescribed and enforced by the ruling white minority; the government seeks to retain control of the country's abundant resources and industries to ensure white, particularly Afrikaner, supremacy.

LAND AND RESOURCES

South Africa is a country with a great diversity of natural landscapes. The 2,955-km (1,836-mi) coastline (including Transkei) has few natural harbors and is rimmed by a narrow, sometimes mountainous, coastal lowland that gives way to a

vast interior plateau covering most of the Transvaal, Orange Free State, and Cape Province. The central portion is called the Highveld. Elevations range between 1,200 m and 1,850 m (4,000 ft and 6,000 ft), and the terrain consists of an undulating prairie sometimes broken by isolated hills and low mountain ranges. The principal range is the gold-bearing WITWATERSRAND, an east-west–trending ridge in the southern Transvaal. In the northwest the plateau gives way to the KALAHARI DESERT.

Along the eastern and southern edges of the plateau, the Great Escarpment—a series of mountain chains and outward-facing escarpments—separates the plateau from the strip of coastal lowland. The most prominent range is the DRAKENSBERG, which extends parallel to the Indian Ocean coast from the eastern Transvaal to the Cape Province. The country's highest peak, Injasuti (3,408 m/11,181 ft), is located in the Drakensberg where the Great Escarpment stands almost 2,000 m (6,550 ft) above the lowlands of Natal to the east. Farther south the escarpment declines and swings inland through the Stormberg and Sneeuwberg ranges.

In the southern tip of the country the plateau gives way to a broad, semiarid basin of mesas and buttes known as the

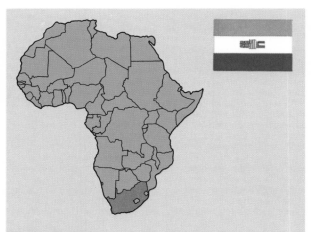

SOUTH AFRICA

Official Name: Republic of South Africa
Administrative Capital: Pretoria (1970 pop., 545,450)
Largest City: Johannesburg (1970 pop., 654,232)
Area: 1,221,040 km² (471,446 mi²; excluding Walvis Bay)
Elevation: *Highest*—Injasuti, 3,408 m (11,181 ft); *lowest*—sea level, along the Indian and South Atlantic oceans
Population: 28,055,000 (1979 est.). *Distribution*—48% urban, 52% rural; *density*, 23 persons per km² (60 per mi²); *annual rate of increase* (1975–76), 2.5%
Principal Languages: English and Afrikaans (both official), Xhosa, Zulu, Sesotho
Principal Religions: Traditional African religions, Dutch Reformed church, Anglicanism, Roman Catholicism, Hinduism
Principal Products: *Agriculture*—sugarcane, corn, wheat, sorghum, cotton, potatoes, grapes, citrus fruit, apples, fishing, forestry, cattle, sheep. *Manufacturing and industry*—processed food, beverages, automobiles, iron and steel, metalworking, chemicals, machinery, mineral products, textiles, paper products, tobacco products. *Mining*—gold, diamonds, coal, copper, iron ore, asbestos, manganese, nickel, chrome ore, limestone, vanadium, phosphate, tin, zinc, granite, antimony, silver, platinum
Railroads: 21,759 km/13,520 mi (1977)
Roads: 57,434 km/35,688 mi (late 1970s paved)
Currency: 1 rand = 100 cents

Great Karroo and, farther south, the Little Karroo. Elevations rise again in the Cape Ranges located parallel to the southern coast between Cape Town and Port Elizabeth.

Drainage. None of the rivers in South Africa are navigable, primarily because of the inadequate rainfall and broken terrain. Most of the interior plateau is drained by the ORANGE RIVER and its two major tributaries, the Vaal and the Caledon. Some of the waters of the Orange are being diverted for industrial, urban, and agricultural uses around Bloemfontein and Kimberley and south to the Cape coast. This undertaking is part of the Orange River Project (scheduled for completion c.2000), designed to provide both irrigation and hydroelectric power. The LIMPOPO RIVER runs along a portion of South Africa's northern boundary and drains much of the Transvaal. Many smaller rivers such as the Tugela and Great Fish rise in the Drakensberg and cut valleys across the foothills and coastal lowlands of Natal, Transkei, and the eastern Cape.

Climate. South Africa has great climatic variety influenced primarily by elevation and latitude. A Mediterranean climate prevails in the southwest around Cape Town, whereas a humid subtropical climate occurs along the Natal coast. Climate conditions associated with highland savanna and steppe characterize much of the Highveld, and semidesert and desert climates are found in the Cape interior and the northwest. The mean annual temperature ranges from 23° C (73° F) in the north to 12° C (54° F) in the southern and eastern sections of the Great Escarpment.

The highest precipitation (more than 1,000 mm/40 in) occurs in the Drakensberg and coastal Natal, and the lowest (less than 200 mm/8 in) along the northwestern coast. About 65% of the country receives less than 500 mm (20 in) annually, the minimum amount required for dry-grain farming.

Soils. Most South African soils are low in humus content and not especially fertile. Unleached alkaline soils characterize the arid regions, thin immature soils are found in the winter-

Johannesburg, South Africa's largest city, is a relatively young metropolis, having been founded during the gold rush into Transvaal province during the 1880s. Although mining remains important, the city has also developed into a major industrial and financial center.

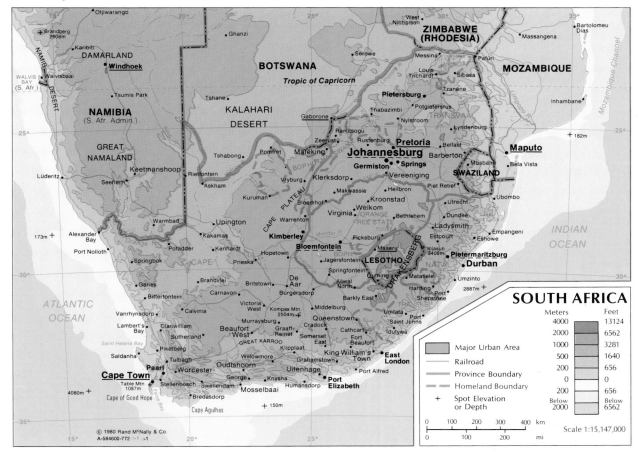

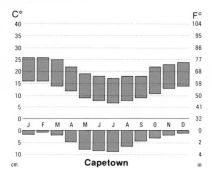

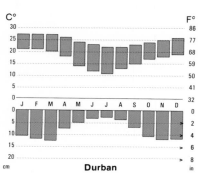

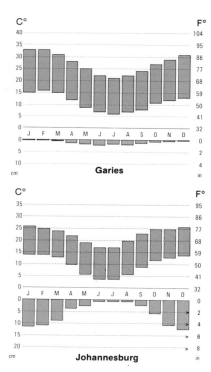

Annual climate charts for four cities in South Africa illustrate distinct climate zones in that country. Bars indicate the monthly ranges of temperatures (red) and precipitation (blue). (Left) Cape Town, situated on the Cape of Good Hope at the southeastern extreme of Africa, has a Mediterranean climate. (Right) Garies, a small settlement in the Namib, a coastal desert that extends along much of South Africa's Atlantic coast, has a desert climate.

(Left) The port and resort city of Durban, located along the east coast of South Africa, has a subtropical humid climate. (Right) Johannesburg, which lies at the heart of the Witwatersrand, a gold-mining district in the northeastern portion of the nation, has a steppe climate.

rainfall regions, and more fertile podzolic soils cover the summer-rainfall region with moderate temperatures; red lateritic soils predominate in the lowlands of Natal and the Transvaal.
Vegetation and Wildlife. A natural deficiency of timber has always existed in South Africa, and only 0.2% of the land is naturally forested. Savanna occurs in the northern Transvaal and eastern lowlands, and grasslands cover the Highveld and dry southwest. Afforestation projects have been undertaken along the Great Escarpment.

The wildlife of South Africa is extremely rich and diverse. Elephants, rhinoceroses, giraffes, zebras, and antelope are protected in game reserves such as KRUGER NATIONAL PARK, Hluhluwe, and Mkuze. Bird life is varied, and more than 100 species of snakes exist.
People. Four major ethnic groups make up South Africa's multiracial society: black South Africans; whites, or Europeans (consisting of two groups, the AFRIKANERS, or Boers, of Dutch descent, and the English-speaking group); COLOUREDS (of mixed black, Malayan, and white origins); and Asians (mostly descendants of early indentured laborers brought from India). Black South Africans constitute 71% of the population; the white minority represents 17% of the population; Coloureds 9%; and Asians 3%. The Khoisan-speaking peoples—SAN (called Bushmen by whites) and KHOIKHOI (Hottentots), survivors of the country's earliest-known inhabitants—number only a few thousand and pursue their traditional way of life in the Kalahari Desert.

The whites, who dominate South Africa's political and economic institutions, are descendants of the 17th-century Dutch settlers in the Cape, refugee Huguenots from France, British settlers dating back to 1820, and more recent immigrants from Europe and excolonial Africa. About 60% are Afrikaners (of Dutch descent) and one-third are English-speaking.
Language and Religion. The Bantu-speaking South Africans comprise four major ethnolinguistic groups. The largest group is composed of the NDEBELE, NGUNI, SWAZI, XHOSA, and ZULU, who together constitute 60% of all BANTUS. The remainder fall into the SOTHO, THONGA, and Venda groups. These languages are not mutually intelligible, however, and a lingua franca, known as Fanakalo, has been developed by black mine workers (see AFRICAN LANGUAGES).

Afrikaans and English are the official languages. Afrikaans, spoken by 60% of the white population, is derived from the Dutch of the original 17th-century settlers. The Coloured population, long in close association with the Afrikaners, is mostly Afrikaans-speaking; the Asians for the most part speak English.

The politically influential Dutch Reformed church, a fundamentalist type of Calvinist Protestantism, is the church of 55% of the white population, mostly Afrikaners and Coloureds. About 10% of whites belong to the Anglican church. Most Africans follow traditional religious practices. Most Asians are Hindu.
Ethnic Distribution. Bantu peoples first reached the Limpopo River about 1,000 years ago and by the mid-17th century had

Conical thatched roofs and earthen walls are characteristic of residences built by Bantu peoples of the eastern portion of South Africa. Almost half of the nation's nonwhite population are required to live on reserves known as Bantustans, or homelands.

Capetown, a provincial capital and the seat of the South African Parliament, is the nation's leading Atlantic port. Capetown, the oldest European settlement in South Africa, was founded in 1652 as a supply base for ships of the Dutch East India Company.

penetrated as far south as the Orange and Great Fish rivers. The highest concentrations today are along the east coast (Natal and Transkei) in Bophuthatswana and Venda, and in the Lebowa homeland. Many live in segregated black townships in and around the urban centers of white South Africa. Fewer than half live within the prescribed homelands. Under the apartheid policy with its pass laws, blacks may legally leave their homeland only after receiving permission from the government. Often men with jobs in cities and mines are granted passes, whereas their families are not, leading to long separations. Black rural-urban migration increases despite severe government influx control measures.

Almost 87% of the whites are urban dwellers. In general, the white rural population is composed of Afrikaners. The whites in Orange Free State are Afrikaans-speaking for the most part, and those in Natal are mostly English-speaking. The Coloured population lives mostly in Cape Province and forms the largest racial component in Cape Town. Three-fourths are urban dwellers. The Asians live in Natal, primarily in the city of Durban. Some are market gardeners, but most work in the cities in commerce, manufacturing, and finance. They are forbidden to live in Orange Free State. A Jewish minority constitutes 5% of the white population. Small Chinese communities exist in Johannesburg and Port Elizabeth.

Demography. JOHANNESBURG is the country's largest city. DURBAN is the principal port. CAPE TOWN is the second largest port, the legislative capital, and a major educational center. Other large cities include BLOEMFONTEIN, EAST LONDON, GERMISTON, KIMBERLEY, PIETERMARITZBURG, PORT ELIZABETH, and PRETORIA. All cities are racially segregated. Approximately one million blacks live in Soweto, near Johannesburg.

South Africa's population had grown 2.5% annually since the 1950s, one of the highest growth rates in the world. The highest rate is among Coloureds and the lowest among whites. Encouragement of white immigration is an official government policy, and in 1975, South Africa admitted 50,312 immigrants, mainly from Great Britain, Zimbabwe (Rhodesia), and West Germany.

Health and Education. South Africa has about 14,000 medical practitioners (1976), and 117,411 hospital beds are available (1975). Wide disparities exist between races in health indicators, however. Life expectancy at birth is 55 years for blacks; 53 years for Coloureds; 60 years for Asians; and 69 years for whites. The crude death rate per 1,000 inhabitants is 14 for blacks, 12.8 for Coloureds, 6.8 for Asians, and 8.4 for whites. The average infant mortality rate is about 110 per 1,000 live births.

Education at all private and state schools is racially segregated. Schooling is compulsory for all white and most Coloured children between the ages of 7 and 16, for Asians between the ages of 7 and 14, and for blacks between the ages of 7 and 11. About 75% of all school-age children attend. Ten residential universities are available for whites—five conducting lectures in Afrikaans, four in English, and one (in Port Elizabeth) in both languages. The University of South Africa, a correspondence university, is open to all races. One university is primarily for Coloureds, one for Asians, and four for blacks.

The Arts. Each population group has contributed to South Africa's rich and diversified artistic heritage. African art, dance, and literature have gained international acclaim and popularity, and Chief Albert LUTHULI, author of Let My People Go (1962), is South Africa's only Nobel laureate (for peace, 1960). (See AFRICAN ART; AFRICAN LITERATURE; AFRICAN MUSIC.) Contemporary white authors who write in English and enjoy international reputations include Nadine GORDIMER, Alan PATON, and Laurens van der Post. Dennis Brutus and Adam Small also write in English; André Brink and Uys Krige write in Afrikaans. Six professional orchestras are located in the country, and opera and ballet are performed each year in the major cities. The Africana Museum in Johannesburg houses the most comprehensive collection of art, handicrafts, ceramics, and silver in South Africa.

ECONOMIC ACTIVITY

The discovery of diamonds near Kimberley (1867) and gold on the Witwatersrand (1886) accounts for the transformation of South Africa from a land of subsistence farming—for both Afrikaners and blacks—into a modern urban-industrial nation controlled by the white minority but reliant on labor by blacks, who compose more than half of the work force.

The discovery of minerals provided the stimulus for railroad expansion from the coast to the interior. The mines brought Africans into the wage economy for the first time, and they created demands for explosives, machinery, energy, and many other goods and services.

The South African government has sought to move toward self-sufficiency in many sectors of the economy by relying on indigenous resources and encouraging local industry. The economy depends, however, on private investment from Britain, Europe, and the United States, which together account for 20% of the total value of all private investment.

These Afrikaners are descendants of the Dutch, Germans, and French Huguenots, the first Europeans to settle in South Africa. The Afrikaners, who speak the West Germanic language Afrikaans, make up nearly 60% of the nation's white minority.

(Below) *The mining of gold and diamonds has helped South Africa to maintain a favorable balance of trade.*

(Above) *The Ndeble people, who inhabit portions of the Transvaal near Pretoria, adorn their homes and enclosure walls of their villages with boldly colored geometric designs.*

Agriculture and Fishing. About 53% of the labor force is engaged in farming. Despite the limited supply of arable land (about 12%), South Africa is virtually self-sufficient in foodstuffs, and agriculture contributes 9% of the gross domestic product (GDP). Principal crops are sugarcane, corn, wheat, citrus fruit, sorghum, and cotton. Cattle and sheep are important. South Africa is among the 10 leading fishing nations in the world.

Mining. Minerals account for almost all of the country's foreign exchange, and the mining industry contributes 15% to the GDP. South Africa leads the world in the production of gold, gem diamonds, antimony, and vanadium and is among the leading producers of asbestos, chrome, copper, manganese, platinum, and uranium. Petroleum and bauxite are the only major industrial resources that have not been found in commercial amounts. About 10% of the petroleum requirements are met by an oil-from-coal plant at Sasolburg, and much greater reliance on coal gasification-liquefaction is planned. The largest coal reserves are found in Natal and the Transvaal (South Africa possesses 60% of all African coal resources). Coal mined domestically provides more than 70% of the country's energy needs. Mining is heavily dependent on cheap black migrant labor recruited from the homelands and neighboring countries.

Industry. Factories in the southern Transvaal (Witwatersrand) account for about 45% of the country's GDP, and the region is the most diversified industrial zone in Africa. A further 25% is derived from the four primary port cities—Cape Town, Durban, Port Elizabeth, and East London. Two new ports and multifaceted industrial complexes are under construction at Richards Bay in Natal and Saldanha Bay northwest of Cape Town.

Most South African manufactured goods are marketed domestically, and manufacturing is the leading contributor to the annual GDP, amounting to 22% in 1977, although it employs only about 8% of the labor force. Principal industries include the manufacture of foodstuffs, chemical products, metal products other than machinery, iron and steel, motor vehicles and accessories, beverages, and textiles.

Trade. South Africa's major trading partners are the United Kingdom, United States, West Germany, and Japan, the main exports being gold and gold coins, diamonds, foodstuffs, including beverages, spirits, and tobacco; and mineral ores. Because of gold exports South Africa usually has a trade surplus. In 1978, with a GDP of $460 billion (about $1,450 per capita), South Africa had exports (excluding gold) of $9.1 billion and imports of $10.2 billion. Gold output was $4.4 billion. The Southern African Customs Union is composed of South Africa, Namibia, Botswana, Lesotho, and Swaziland.

GOVERNMENT

The legislative power of the republic is vested in a Parliament that consists of a state president (a largely ceremonial post), the Senate, and House of Assembly. The legislature in actuality is controlled by the powerful executive council (cabinet). The prime minister leads the government and is chosen by the majority party in the House of Assembly, and this choice is approved by the state president. The president is elected for a 7-year term by the Senate and Assembly. The Senate consists of 61 members, of whom 43 are elected and 18 are nominated by the state president. The House of Assembly is composed of 165 members. Elections must be held at least once every 5 years. Only whites are eligible to vote. In the 1977 elections the National party, which has been in power since 1948, won 134 seats; the Progressive Federal party, 17; the New Republic party, 10; and the South African party, 3. In 1978, B. Johannes Vorster resigned as prime minister and was replaced by Pieter Botha.

Africans, Coloureds, and Asians are not represented in the Parliament. The Coloured Persons' Representative Council and the South African Indian Council are primarily advisory in nature and have limited legislative powers. In 1979 new legislation called for the establishment of separate national parliaments for Asians and Coloureds. Africans are represented solely by their respective homeland governments regardless of their place of residence.

HISTORY

The first-known inhabitants of present-day South Africa were San and Khoikhoi hunters and gatherers; they were followed southward by Bantu-speaking peoples between AD 1000 and 1500. In 1488, Portuguese mariners led by Bartolomeu Dias rounded the Cape of Good Hope. The Dutchman Jan van Riebeeck established the first permanent European settlement at Table Bay (present-day Cape Town) in 1652 as a way station for the Dutch East India Company. Dutch pioneers spread eastward, and in 1779 war broke out between the Xhosas migrating south and the Dutch near the Great Fish River.

Britain controlled the Cape sporadically during the Napoleonic Wars, and in 1820, Britain formally received the territory, according to provisions made by the Congress of Vienna. Soon large-scale British settlement began. To preserve their Calvinist way of life and the practice of slavery, abolished by the British, the Dutch farmers (Boers) began (1836) to move into the interior, the so-called Great Trek. In 1838 approximately 70 of the Voortrekkers were massacred by Zulus. Seeking vengeance, Andries Pretorius led the Dutch against the Zulus, defeating them in the Battle of Blood River. The Voortrekkers eventually established independent republics, including the Orange Free State (1854) and the South African Republic—later the Transvaal—(1852).

The discovery of diamonds and gold in the Witwatersrand region drew British immigrant entrepreneurs (Uitlanders, or "foreigners") into the interior, and conflict over ownership ensued. Paul KRUGER (Oom Paul), leader of the Transvaal, resisted British attempts to claim the area, including those by Cecil RHODES, prime minister of British-controlled Cape Colony, who encouraged the Uitlanders to take over the Transvaal. The unsuccessful Jameson Raid, engineered by the British and intended to aid the Uitlanders in an uprising, added to the mounting tension (see JAMESON, SIR LEANDER STARR). Eventually, the SOUTH AFRICAN WAR (1899–1902) erupted between the British and the Afrikaners, with the British the victors. In 1910 leaders such as Jan SMUTS helped create the Union of South Africa, with dominion status, out of the former British colonies and the two defeated Boer republics. Louis BOTHA, a moderate Afrikaner advocating close cooperation between British and Afrikaners, became the first prime minister.

Between the two world wars (in both of which South Africa fought on the side of the Allies), mining and manufacturing expanded. The Depression of the 1930s, however, forced black Africans and white farmers alike into the cities to compete for unskilled jobs. As a result, both African and Afrikaner nationalisms emerged. At the same time a segregationist policy was adopted by James Barry HERTZOG's government (1924–39) to preserve South Africa as a white country in which Africans would be restricted as far as possible to reserves defined in 1913. The constitution was amended to deny franchise rights to the Coloured population, a right that had been protected by an entrenched clause in the 1910 constitution.

In 1948, Dr. Daniel MALAN's National party was elected to office, which was to mark a new phase in South African development. Black, Asian, and Coloured South Africans were to be more and more severely repressed under the policy of apartheid—"separate development." The policy (known more recently as "plural democracy"), already in existence unofficially, became official. In 1959, during the premiership of Hendrik VERWOERD, Parliament adopted the Promotion of Bantu Self-Government Act, which created the legal machinery by which ten African homelands, defined in cultural-linguistic terms, would eventually receive self-government and independence. The Transkei achieved self-government in 1963 and full independence (recognized only by South Africa) in 1976. Bophuthatswana gained its independence a year later, despite its severe geographic fragmentation and economic backwardness, and Venda followed in 1979. The ten African homelands constitute 13% of the total land area.

African opposition to apartheid intensified in the 1950s, spearheaded by the African National Congress and Pan African Congress, which were banned in 1960 following the Sharpeville massacre near Johannesburg in which 69 Africans, demonstrating against the pass laws, were killed by police. In 1961, the Union of South Africa withdrew from the Commonwealth of Nations due to opposition among the body to apartheid policies, and the republic was declared. Opposition at home continued, and after Sharpeville, organized urban violence replaced passive resistance, and rioting broke out in 1976 in several cities including Soweto, a black township of Johannesburg. The government retaliated by detaining its critics, including Stephen Biko, a young black activist who died from head wounds sustained in police custody in 1977. The government also banned some newspapers and civil-rights organizations. In November 1977 the United Nations imposed a 1-year mandatory embargo on arms sales to South Africa, and many multinational corporations have been pressured to withdraw from the republic. The country, hoping to improve its image abroad, created a Department of Information, which was dissolved in 1978 after investigations showed it had been involved in illegal activities. Under Prime Minister Pieter Botha (who succeeded John Vorster in 1978) the South African government began to amend some apartheid laws (the word *apartheid* was banned), while reaffirming the sub-

stance of separate development for whites and blacks. South Africa was scheduled by the United Nations to relinquish its control of Namibia in 1979, but it had not done so by 1980.

ALAN C. G. BEST

Bibliography:

GENERAL: DeKiewiet, Cornelius W., *A Socioeconomic Profile of South Africa* (1973); Kaplan, Irving, et al., *Area Handbook for the Republic of South Africa* (1971); *Republic of South Africa* (Official Yearbook of the Republic of South Africa, annual); Thompson, Leonard, and Butler, Jeffrey, eds., *Change in Contemporary South Africa* (1975).

GEOGRAPHY: Pollock, Norman, and Agnew, Swanzie, *An Historical Geography of South Africa* (1963); Wellington, John, *Southern Africa: A Geographical Study* (1955).

HISTORY: Davenport, T. R., *South Africa: A Modern History* (1977); Inskeep, R. R., *The Peopling of Southern Africa* (1979); Keppel-Jones, Arthur, *South Africa: A Short History*, 5th ed. (1975); Marquard, Leopold, *A Short History of South Africa* (1968); Wilson, Monica, and Thompson, Leonard, eds., *The Oxford History of South Africa*, 2 vols. (1969, 1971).

POLITICS AND GOVERNMENT: Brotz, Howard, *The Politics of South Africa* (1977); Butler, Jeffrey, et al., *The Black Homelands of South Africa* (1977); Gerhart, Gail M., *Black Power in South Africa: The Evolution of an Ideology* (1978); Kotzé, D. A., *African Policies in South Africa: Parties and Issues* (1975); Sachs, Albie, *Justice in South Africa* (1973); Van Den Berghe, Pierre L., ed., *The Liberal Dilemma in South Africa* (1979).

PEOPLE AND SOCIAL CONDITIONS: Biko, Steve, *I Write What I Like: A Selection of His Writings*, ed. by Aelred Stubbs (1979); Frye, William R., *In Whitest Africa: The Dynamics of Apartheid* (1968); Macmillan, William M., *Bantu, Boer and Briton: The Making of the South African Native Problem* (1963; repr. 1979); Millin, Sarah G., *The People of South Africa* (1954; repr. 1976); Peterson, Robert W., *South Africa and Apartheid*, rev. ed. (1975).

South African War

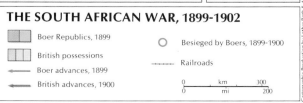

THE SOUTH AFRICAN WAR, 1899-1902

Boer Republics, 1899

British possessions

⟵ Boer advances, 1899

⟶ British advances, 1900

○ Besieged by Boers, 1899-1900

⊷⊷⊷ Railroads

0   km   300
0   mi   200

The South African War (1899–1902), also known as the Boer War, was a conflict between Great Britain and the two Afrikaner (Boer) governments of the South African Republic (the Transvaal) and the Orange Free State. The European settlers in both areas were mainly of Dutch ancestry and were known as Boers, or AFRIKANERS. In response to Boer pressures Britain had awarded independence to the Orange Free State in 1854. A brief revolt in 1881 (sometimes called the First South African War) had restored to the Transvaal the independence it had lost to Britain in 1877. Both republics remained under British suzerainty, however.

The discovery (1886) of gold at the Witwatersrand in the Transvaal attracted a large number of European immigrants—mainly British—who built up the country's mining industry and came to control the major part of its wealth. President Paul KRUGER welcomed the economic enterprise of these Uitlanders (foreigners) but at the same time feared the threat that they posed to the Boers' agricultural and noncommercial way of life; he refused to make any major political concessions to the newcomers. Anglo-Boer relations worsened because of disputes over the franchise and a variety of economic issues and especially after an illegal and unsuccessful raid carried out in 1895 by British administrator Sir Leander Starr JAMESON against the Transvaal in support of the Uitlanders. The Transvaal strengthened its armed forces, concluded an alliance with the Orange Free State, and presented the British with an ultimatum protesting the reinforcement of the British garrison in South Africa.

The Afrikaners called the ensuing war the Second War of Freedom. During the first phase of the war (1899–1900), the Boer forces gained some immediate victories. They laid siege to Mafeking, Kimberley, and Ladysmith, but all were eventually relieved by British troops under Lord KITCHENER and Frederick Sleigh ROBERTS. In the second phase of the war (1900) the British defeated the main Boer armies and occupied Pretoria, the Transvaal capital. In the last phase (1900–02) the Boers took to guerrilla warfare, and the British retaliated by subjecting the Boer population to harsh treatment, including detention in concentration camps. The Boers were finally forced to conclude peace at Vereeniging in 1902. The two Boer republics were reduced to British colonies, but they were able to exact some important concessions from the British.

The South African War was the largest military conflict waged in sub-Saharan Africa. The British mobilized nearly 450,000 soldiers—as opposed to a maximum of about 80,000 Boers. The conflict was both a war of imperial supremacy and a civil war among whites; about 53,000 white, mainly English-speaking, South Africans fought in the British ranks. The black Africans stood aloof. In Britain the excesses of the war aroused the first significant outpouring of antiimperialist sentiment. In South Africa the war led to a rebirth of Afrikaner nationalism and to the unification of South Africa through the formation of the Union of South Africa (1910), in which the Afrikaners ultimately gained political supremacy.

L. H. GANN

Bibliography: Belfield, Eversley, *The Boer War* (1976); Farwell, Byron, *The Great Anglo-Boer War* (1976); Holt, Edgar, *The Boer War* (1958); Kruger, Rayne, *Good-Bye Dolly Gray: The Story of the Boer War* (1960); Lehmann, Joseph H., *The First Boer War* (1972); LeMay, Godfrey Hugh Lancelot, *British Supremacy in South Africa, 1899–1907* (1965); Maurice, John F., *History of the War in South Africa, 1899–1902*, 4 vols. (1906–10); Pakenham, Thomas, *The Boer War* (1979).

South America

The continent of South America stretches for about 7,400 km (4,600 mi) from north to south and about 5,150 km (3,200 mi) from east to west, covering more than 17.8 million km² (6.8 million mi²). It is bounded by the Atlantic Ocean on the east and the Pacific Ocean on the west. Central America and the Caribbean Sea are found to the north. The Drake Passage separates South America from Antarctica to the south. The westernmost coast is situated at about the same longitude as Miami, Fla. South America is the world's fourth largest continent—it is smaller than North America but larger than Antarc-

SOUTH AMERICA

Area: 17,804,526 km² (6,874,600 mi²); 12% of the world's land area
Population: 237,588,000 (1978 est.); 5.4% of the total world population; *density,* 13.3 persons per km² (34.6 per mi²); *annual rate of increase* (1970–75), 2.6%
Coastline: 31,951 km (19,854 mi)
Elevation: *Highest*—Mount Aconcagua, 6,959 m (22,831 ft); *lowest*—Salinas Grandes, Valdés Peninsula, Argentina, 40 m (131 ft) below sea level
Principal Rivers: Amazon, Paraná-Paraguay-Plata, Orinoco, Magdalena, São Francisco
Principal Lakes: Titicaca, Maracaibo
Principal Mountain Range: Andes
Principal Deserts: Atacama, Patagonia
Political Divisions: 12 independent countries, 1 French overseas department, and 1 colony
Largest City: São Paulo, 7,198,600 (1975 est.)
Busiest General Cargo Port: Rio de Janeiro
Most Populous Country: Brazil, 124,428,000 (1979 est.)

tica. Offshore areas considered part of South America include EASTER ISLAND, the FALKLAND ISLANDS (or Malvinas), the GALÁPAGOS ISLANDS, and TIERRA DEL FUEGO.

South America has a number of outstanding features. The ANDES, which parallel the western side of the continent, form the longest mountain chain in the world. The AMAZON RIVER surpasses all others in volume of flow, and the Amazon Basin is the world's largest area of tropical rain forest. The continent is part of Latin America, so named because most of its settlers during the colonial period came from the Iberian Peninsula. The cultural characteristics brought with these immigrants included the Spanish and Portuguese languages, the Roman Catholic religion, a two-class social system, and a belief that large landholdings impart great prestige to the owner. The latter two cultural characteristics have only recently begun to disappear.

The first European explorer to sight the coast of South America was Christopher COLUMBUS while on his third voyage to the New World in 1498. The first explorer to recognize the Western Hemisphere as separate from Asia was the Italian Amerigo VESPUCCI, for whom the Americas are named. The 1494 Treaty of TORDESILLAS divided the continent into an eastern sector, in which the Portuguese could settle, and a western sector, for the Spaniards. Perhaps the most outstanding of the CONQUISTADORS was Francisco PIZARRO, who overthrew the INCA empire in 1532. Argentina was the first of South America's colonies to gain independence (1810). In recent years industrialization, social upheaval, and political ferment have characterized many of South America's nations. Dictatorial regimes govern most of them. South America is divided

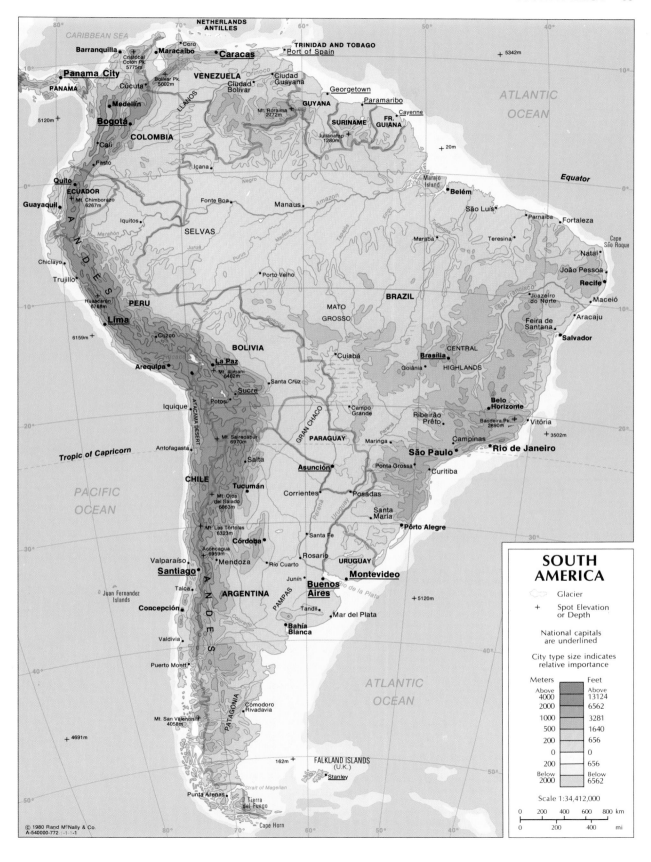

CARIBBEAN SEA

NETHERLANDS
ANTILLES

Barranquilla • • Coro
Cristóbal
Colón Pk.
5775m • **Maracaibo**

TRINIDAD AND TOBAGO
Port of Spain

+ 5342m

Panama City
PANAMA
Cúcuta
Bolívar Pk.
5002m

Caracas

VENEZUELA
Ciudad
Bolívar

Ciudad
Guayana

Georgetown

Paramaribo

Cayenne

GUYANA

SURINAME

FR.
GUIANA

Medellín

LLANOS

Mt. Roraima
2772m

5120m +

Bogotá

COLOMBIA

Julianatop
1280m

• Cali

ATLANTIC

OCEAN

+ 20m

• Pasto

Içana

Quito

ECUADOR

Mt. Chimborazo
6267m

Fonte Boa

Manaus •

Marajó
Island

• Belém

Equator

Guayaquil

Iquitos

Marañón

SELVAS

São Luís •

Parnaíba •

Fortaleza

Negro

Amazon

Cape
São Roque

Chiclayo

A

Madeira

Juruá

Purús

Teresina •

Natal •

João Pessoa •

Trujillo

N

D

Porto Velho •

BRAZIL

Recife

Huascarán
6768m

E

PERU

MATO

GROSSO

São Francisco

Juàzeiro
do Norte •

• Maceió

Lima

S

6159m +

Cuzco •

Aracaju

BOLIVIA

Feira de
Santana •

Salvador

Arequipa

La Paz
Mt. Illimani
6462m

Sucre

Santa Cruz

Cuiabá •

Brasília

Goiânia •

CENTRAL

HIGHLANDS

Potosí

Campo
Grande •

Ribeirão
Prêto •

Belo
Horizonte

Iquique

ATACAMA DESERT

Mt. Sairecabur
6970m

GRAN CHACO

PARAGUAY

Paraná

Bandeira Pk.
2890m

• Vitória

+ 3502m

Antofagasta •

• Salta

Maringá •

Campinas •

São Paulo

Rio de Janeiro

Tropic of Capricorn

Mt. Ojos
del Salado
6663m

CHILE

Tucumán

Corrientes •

Ponta Grossa •

• Curitiba

PACIFIC

OCEAN

Mt. Las Tórtolas
6323m

Aconcagua
6959m

Córdoba

Santa Fe •

Asunción

Paraná

Posadas •

Uruguay

Santa
María •

Pôrto Alegre

Valparaíso •

Mendoza •

Río Cuarto •

Rosario •

URUGUAY

Río de la Plata

Santiago

Talca •

Junín •

**Buenos
Aires**

Montevideo

• Juan Fernández
Islands

Concepción

ARGENTINA

PAMPAS

Tandíl •

+ 5120m

• Mar del Plata

Valdivia •

Colorado

**Bahía
Blanca**

Puerto Montt •

PATAGONIA

Comodoro
Rivadavia •

ATLANTIC

OCEAN

Mt. San Valentín
4058m

+ 4691m

162m +

FALKLAND ISLANDS
(U.K.)

• Stanley

Punta Arenas •

Tierra
del Fuego

Strait of Magellan

Cape Horn

© 1980 Rand McNally & Co.
A-540000-772

SOUTH
AMERICA

Glacier

+ Spot Elevation
or Depth

National capitals
are underlined

City type size indicates
relative importance

Meters	Feet
Above 4000	Above 13124
2000	6562
1000	3281
500	1640
200	656
0	0
200	656
Below 2000	Below 6562

Scale 1:34,412,000

0   200   400   600   800 km

0   200   400 mi

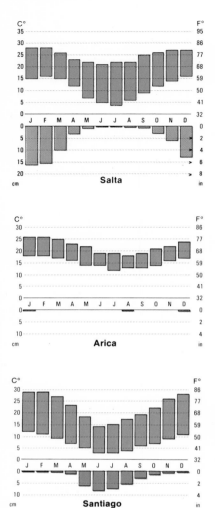

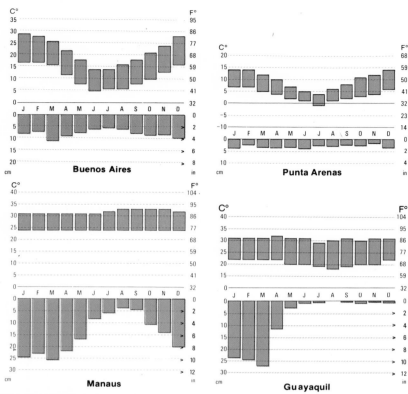

Salta

Buenos Aires

Punta Arenas

Arica

Manaus

Guayaquil

Santiago

Annual climate charts for seven localities in South America illustrate the diverse climate zones of the continent. Bars indicate monthly ranges of temperatures (red) and precipitation (blue). Salta, a commercial city of north central Argentina, has the steppe climate characteristic of the Andean foothills. Buenos Aires, the capital of Argentina, is situated on the Río de la Plata near the Atlantic coast and has a subtropical humid climate. Punta Arenas, Chile, on the Strait of Magellan, has a marine west-coast pattern of low temperatures and moderate precipitation, whereas Arica, a mining city in Chile's sun-baked northern region, has a desert climate. Manaus, Brazil, is located in the heart of the Amazon region and has the high temperatures and harsh precipitation of a tropical wet climate. Ecuador's principal port, Guayaquil, has a tropical wet-dry pattern of high temperatures and seasonal precipitation. Santiago, the capital of Chile, has the Mediterranean climate typical of Chile's central valley.

politically into 12 independent countries, 1 French overseas department, and 1 colony.

LAND AND RESOURCES

South America may be divided into eight major geomorphological provinces. Outstanding among these regions is that of the Andes, which extend for more than 6,440 km (4,000 mi) along the Pacific coast. These high, rugged mountains form a barrier to east-west travel. More than 60 peaks are higher than any found within the conterminous states of the United States. The highest peak in the Andes is Mount ACONCAGUA on the Chile-Argentina border, which reaches an elevation of 6,960 m (22,834 ft). The Andes serve as a drainage divide for the continent's rivers and, as part of the "Pacific Ring of Fire," they are subject to a great deal of volcanic activity and frequent earthquakes. The chain of mountains is seldom more than about 320 km wide (200 mi), except in Colombia where it splits into three distinct ranges and in Bolivia where it widens to about 645 km (400 mi) to accommodate the Bolivian Altiplano—a large intermontane basin lying more than 3,650 m (about 12,000 ft) above sea level. Many of the mountains are snowcapped all year, and in southern Chile the effects of glaciation are evident in the U-shaped valleys and fjords. The rocks that make up the mountains are largely hard and crystalline and contain several types of mineral ores such as copper and tin and precious gems, including emeralds.

Another of South America's physiographic regions is the Brazilian Shield. It is comprised of Precambrian crystalline rocks overlain with erosional sediments. The more resistant

The snow-capped cone of Cotopaxi, the highest active volcano in Ecuador, towers to a height of 5,897 m (19,347 ft) above sea level in the Andes. Located only 56 km (35 mi) south of Quito, it is considered to be South America's most dangerous volcano.

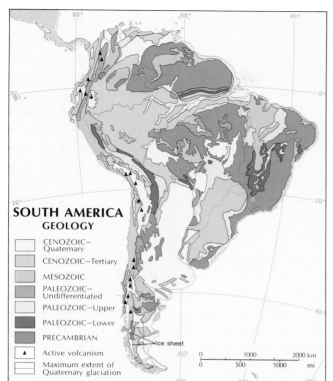

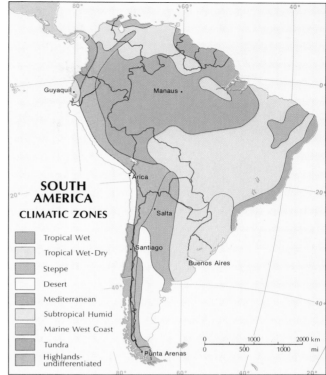

sandstone has been exposed to form buttes and mesas. Elsewhere, resistant diabase is associated with the presence of cuestas—elevated landforms with one side steeply scarped—over which flow a number of rivers, producing spectacular waterfalls. The Guiana Shield, located in the northern part of the continent, is essentially similar in origin, development, and character to the Brazilian Shield. The major difference between the two is that the mesas in the Guiana Shield are higher in elevation. ANGEL FALL, the highest cataract in the world, lies within the Guiana Shield.

Two South American landform regions can be classified as either highland or lowland. One of these is the Paraná Plateau, often considered part of the Brazilian Shield. It is named for the river that slices through it. Made up of one of the world's single largest accumulations of lava, the Paraná Plateau resulted from a long series of lava flows. The second marginal region is the low Patagonian Plateau (or high Patagonian Plain). PATAGONIA has a rough surface. An ancient massif, it was first covered by sediments and then eroded by streams flowing eastward from the Andes. The steep-walled valleys through which many of these streams flow make north-south travel very difficult.

Insofar as lowlands are concerned, South America has narrow coastal plains, but the Amazon Basin is the largest of the continent's landform provinces, covering about 7 million km² (2.7 million mi²). Composed of very thick sedimentary deposits, it is flat to gently rolling. The Amazon Basin is widest near the Andes and narrowest near the mouth of the Amazon River.

The Orinoco Plain is separated from the Amazon Basin by a low interfluve. Like the Amazon Basin, it is named for and is a product of the major river that flows across it. The last of the lowlands is the Paraná-Paraguay-Plata Plain, where an ancient rocky surface has been covered by alluvium. Only a few peaks of the original surface protrude through the alluvium, much like the tips of icebergs. Those lowland areas in which the layers of sedimentary rocks are relatively undisturbed are frequently associated with sizable deposits of petroleum. Laterization in tropical regions frequently results in the formation of iron and aluminum ore.

South America has few good harbors. The best is probably that of RIO DE JANEIRO. Although others may have protected anchorages, their harbors are often shallow and must be continually dredged to permit access for oceangoing vessels.

Climate. Eight factors affect the climate of South America. Latitude is the most significant of these. Tropicality is the dominant feature of South America's climate, and much of the continent remains frost-free throughout the year. Altitude is a second factor, for the most part moderating the hot, tropical temperatures. The ocean's proximity—in combination with prevailing winds—affects the amounts and distribution of rainfall. Several coastal areas receive in excess of 2,540 mm (100 in) of rainfall annually; these are the southeast coast of Brazil, the region from Guyana to the mouth of the Amazon, the Pacific coast of Colombia, and southern Chile. The Amazon Basin also receives abundant precipitation, where most rainfall is convectional in origin. In contrast no rainfall has ever been recorded at Calama, Chile, in the ATACAMA DESERT. This aridity results from latitudinal position and a stable temperature inversion consisting of cold air brought by the Humboldt current underlying warmer upper air. The invasion of air masses and the frequent passage of cyclonic storms account for both the precipitation and the variability of weather in the southern part of the continent. Finally, human habitation has altered the climate, especially in urban regions where air pollution has increased temperatures and the density of particulates.

Seven major climate types are found in South America. Most of the Amazon Basin and coastal regions where onshore winds blow for much of the year have a tropical rainy climate. Rainfall there is not only heavy but evenly distributed throughout the year. Daytime temperatures typically reach 29° C (85° F). Arid and semiarid climates dominate the coast of Peru and northern Chile. Aridity also characterizes a small area in northeast Brazil and a diagonal strip crossing Argentina from northwest to southeast. Wide temperature extremes, low rainfall, and unreliable precipitation typify these dry regions. The principal characteristic of the tropical wet and dry climate covering most of Brazil and the Orinoco River basin is an alternating precipitation regime. Six months

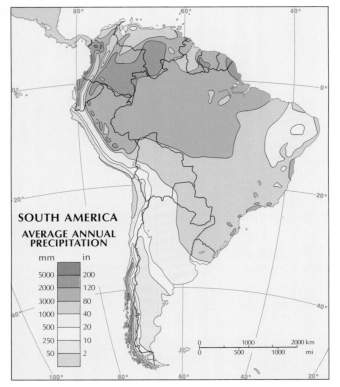

SOUTH AMERICA

AVERAGE ANNUAL PRECIPITATION

mm	in
5000	200
2000	120
3000	80
1000	40
500	20
250	10
50	2

of summer rain followed by six months of winter drought is a consequence of the seasonal shifting of wind, pressure, and precipitation belts.

The Mediterranean climate of central Chile also experiences alternating periods of rain and drought—but there the rainfall comes during the wintertime. In contrast, the temperate marine climate of southern Chile is cool, rainy, and windy throughout the year. The humid subtropical climate of southern Brazil, Uruguay, Paraguay, and northeastern Argentina is similar to that of the U.S. state of Georgia. Finally, South America's mountain regions experience considerable variation in rainfall and temperature conditions over very short distances, with elevation and exposure the major determinants.

Drainage. South America's longest river is the Amazon. Originating in the Peruvian Andes, the Amazon flows approxi-

mately 6,450 km (4,000 mi) to its mouth in the Atlantic—it is the world's second longest river. No other river approaches its volume of flow, which exceeds that of the world's 10 next largest rivers combined. Oceangoing ships can navigate almost 1,600 km (1,000 mi) upstream, whereas vessels with drafts of 4 m (13 ft) or less can travel about 3,700 km (2,300 mi) upriver.

Next largest in South America is that of the Paraná, Paraguay, and Uruguay rivers, the waters from which empty into the Plata estuary. The PARANÁ RIVER is navigable for oceangoing vessels as far upstream as Rosario, Argentina. Boats regularly travel upstream on the PARAGUAY RIVER to Corumbá, Brazil. A large combined bridge and dam currently under construction at Salto Grande marks the head of navigation on the URUGUAY RIVER.

Other navigable rivers in South America include the MAGDALENA RIVER in Colombia, the ORINOCO RIVER in Venezuela, and the SÃO FRANCISCO RIVER in eastern Brazil. Of these the Magdalena carries the largest amount of general cargo traffic. Massive quantities of iron ore are shipped from the mouth of the Orinoco. The São Francisco is more significant for its hydroelectric potential than for its navigability.

South America has few sizable lakes. Lake TITICACA—although not the largest—is the highest navigable body of water in the world. The elevation of its surface is 3,810 m (12,500 ft) above sea level. Lake Titicaca is shared by the countries of Peru and Bolivia, and regular hydrofoil service is available between them. Lake MARACAIBO, in Venezuela, the largest body of water in South America, is connected to the Caribbean Sea by a narrow inlet. Maracaibo is mostly freshwater, shallow, and punctuated frequently by petroleum derricks. Rather more picturesque is the Andean Lake District of Argentina and Chile, a recreational zone reminiscent of Switzerland.

Soils. Two major categories of soil may be found in the continent. Azonal soils, poorly developed and immature, may be subdivided into the thin, stony lithosol or mountain soil and the thick, rich regosol or alluvial soil, recently deposited on river floodplains.

Well-stratified zonal soils are much more widespread and important than azonal soils. Red-colored lateritic soils are perhaps the most infertile because most of their nutrients have been washed away by abundant rainfall. Much of their humus content has been destroyed by the rapidity of bacterial action associated with continuously hot temperatures in the wet tropics. Most of the rainy tropical and subtropical lowland regions of South America have lateritic soils, often underlain with a hardpan layer.

Dark-colored grassland soils, also zonal in nature, are among the most fertile known. Favorable temperatures and adequate rainfall, along with the best possible source of hu-

(Above) *Uru Indians live on a "floating island" constructed of reeds in Lake Titicaca, along the Peruvian-Bolivian border.* (Left) *The dark water of the Rio Negro, colored by acid formed by decomposing organic matter, is still visible against the lighter Amazon some distance from the two rivers' junction.*

mus—grass, provide optimal conditions for fertile soil development. Argentina and Uruguay are fortunate in that each contains broad areas of these rich grassland soils. Desert soils, developed in response to arid climates, can be agriculturally productive if irrigated and if their mineral salt content is low.

Vegetation. Natural vegetation is often referred to as the "mirror of climate" because specific plant types are usually found in association with particular climates. The most humid parts of tropical South America are covered with tropical rain forest, or selva.

Three "tiers" of vegetation can be distinguished in the rain forest, the tallest of which comprise the tropical trees. Many hardwoods have such high specific gravities that they do not float. These trees experience no dormant period and therefore lack annual growth rings. Root growth extends far below the surface to absorb any available moisture, and support for the tree is provided by buttress roots. Their interlocking crowns form a canopy that blocks most sunlight. Jungle results where sunlight reaches the forest floor.

In southern Brazil and in central and southern Chile, mid-latitude forests with mixed stands of trees are common. South America as a whole is seriously short of softwood lumber, which many countries are forced to import.

Tropical scrub woodlands cover large areas in northeastern Brazil, western Paraguay, and northern Argentina. Dense tangles of thorny bushes are common in the interior of northeast Brazil. The quebracho (literally, "break-ax") of Paraguay and Argentina is a source of tannin for leather processing. Regions with a summer rainy season are normally associated with savanna vegetation. Such areas are generally used for cattle ranching. In the PAMPAS and other parts of northeastern Argentina, in Uruguay, and in the far south of Brazil, prairie grasslands that have been extensively modified by human action predominate.

Desert shrub vegetation is related to arid climates, whereas in the mountains plants are arranged into zones based on elevation. In sequence from low to higher elevations, these zones are known as the *tierra caliente* (or zone of tropical crops), *tierra templada* (zone of coffee), *tierra fría* (zone of grains), the zone of uncleared forest, and the zone of alpine meadows.

Fauna. Despite extensive areas of tropical grassland, South America has no large game animals such as are associated with the plains of Africa. Nevertheless, the continent offers a tremendous variety of wildlife, and—as in Africa—some spe-

SOUTH AMERICA

NATURAL VEGETATION

- Tropical rain forest
- Subtropical evergreen forest
- Temperate deciduous forest
- Chapparal or Mediterranean scrub
- Tropical grassland and savanna
- Temperate grassland (prairie, steppe, pampa)
- Semidesert
- Desert
- Tundra
- Alpine tundra
- Ice sheet

cies are endangered. In the rain forest, monkeys (which, unlike their Old World relatives, have prehensile tails) and parrots are declining as they fall prey to hunters. The chinchilla is native to the continent. The electric eel and the flesh-eating piranha can be found in South American waters.

One of the most distinctive animals of the South American tropical forest and grassland is the tapir, a hoglike creature standing higher than 1 m (40 in) at the shoulders. Equally distinctive is the rhea, a relative of the ostrich, which inhabits the mid-latitude grasslands of Argentina. An endangered spe-

An aerial photograph surveys a portion of Moon Valley, a boulder-strewn waste in the Atacama Desert. In some sections of this desert, a vegetationless region running parallel with the Pacific coast in northern Chile, no measurable precipitation has ever been recorded.

The Iguaçu Falls are located on the border between Argentina and Brazil a short distance upstream from the confluence of the Iguaçu and Paraná rivers. The region surrounding the falls is maintained as two national parks by the Brazilian and Argentinian governments.

SOUTH AMERICA
AGRICULTURE AND MINERALS

	Commercial plantation agriculture
	Grain crops
	Mixed farming, livestock
	Livestock ranching
	Mediterranean agriculture
	Irrigated agriculture
	Tropical forests; shifting agriculture
	Rudimentary agriculture, herding
	Non-agricultural

Al	Aluminum (Bauxite)
Sb	Antimony
A	Asbestos
Cr	Chromium
+	Coal
Cu	Copper
◇	Diamonds
Au	Gold
Fe	Iron Ore
Pb	Lead
Mn	Manganese
Hg	Mercury
Mo	Molybdenum
O	Natural Gas
Ni	Nickel
⌂	Oil
Pt	Platinum
•	Salt
□	Saltpeter
Ag	Silver
S	Sulphur
Sn	Tin
Ti	Titanium
U	Uranium
V	Vanadium
Zn	Zinc

| 0 | 500 | 1000 | 1500 km |
| 0 | | 500 | mi |

The Catavi tin mine in west central Bolivia is one of the largest tin mines in the world. Bolivia ranks third among all nations in the production of tin—trailing only Malaysia and the USSR—and the mineral has traditionally been Bolivia's most valuable export.

cies is the condor, which nests along the Pacific coast. In the Andes Mountains, Indians have domesticated llamas for use as beasts of burden and guinea pigs for food. Other animals found only in South America are the anaconda, the capybara, the giant otter, and the spectacled bear.

On the Galápagos Islands, about 965 km (600 mi) west of Ecuador, are many animals found nowhere else on Earth. The naturalist Charles Darwin visited the islands in 1835, studying such life forms as the flightless cormorant, the giant land tortoise, and the marine iguana.

Mineral Resources. South America's mineral resources have often been described as superlative but poorly matched. For example, Brazil and Chile both have massive deposits of iron ore but lack the good-quality coking coal needed to convert it to steel. Recent discoveries of iron ore may eventually give Brazil the world's second largest proven reserves, after the USSR. Venezuela has the second largest production of iron ore on the continent; it is followed by Peru and Chile.

Brazil also has sizable deposits of manganese and bauxite,

Thousands of tourists crowd the beaches of Ipanema, a coastal suburb of Rio de Janeiro. Although it has experienced less commercial development than its famous neighboring community, Copacabana, Ipanema is an important contributor to Brazil's tourist-related income.

but Suriname is South America's leading bauxite miner. Bolivia's tin exports are exceeded only by those of Malaysia. Although Chile is only third among world nations in copper production, its reserves of this metal are surpassed by no other nation. Peru is South America's second most important producer of copper.

Energy resources have gained increased attention in recent years. In this regard Venezuela reigns supreme because of its petroleum deposits. Argentina, Brazil, Colombia, Ecuador, Peru, and Bolivia also have petroleum but only in moderate amounts.

Other significant minerals and the countries known for their export are as follows: lead, zinc, silver, and mercury (Peru); gold and emeralds (Colombia); sulfur, iodine, and nitrates (Chile); phosphates (Brazil, Peru, and Venezuela).

Arable Land. The amount of a nation's arable land is not only a function of its size but of such other factors as topography, climate, and soil fertility. Another important consideration is land quality, in part a function of the preceding factors.

Brazil has the largest amount of arable land of any South American nation—more than 300,000 km² (115,830 mi²). This figure represents almost 40% of the continent's total. Argentina ranks second, with about 214,400 km² (82,800 mi²). Although no other countries in South America have as much arable land, both of these nations suffer from handicaps. Much of the soil in the tropical parts of Brazil is low in fertility, whereas a great deal of Argentina is arid or semiarid. Both conditions limit crop yields.

PEOPLE

South America's racial heritage stems from three basic sources: Caucasian, African, and Indian. The Indians, who arrived perhaps 11,000 to 14,000 years ago, were at first hunters and gatherers. Many groups took up agriculture about 5,000 years ago. Three major groups settled in and around the Andes: the CHIBCHA in the north; the Indians subjugated by the Incas in the area of present-day Peru; and the ARAUCANIANS to the south. Other groups settled along the shores of the Caribbean, in the tropical rain forests, and on the eastern margins of the continent. All these Indians together are thought to have numbered about 14 million in the year 1500, approximately one-third of whom lived in the Inca empire.

The Europeans arrived in the 1500s, enslaved the Indians, and forced them to work in mines and on plantations. At the same time, European missionaries were converting the Indians to Christianity. The distribution of Indians influenced the direction of the Spanish colonial effort more than any other factor. Although large numbers of Indians died of mistreatment or exposure to European diseases against which they had no immunity, more than 9 million of their descendants survive. Indian women intermarried with the European conquerors, and from these unions a new racial type was born—the mestizo or *mameluco* (the word used in Brazil).

Because of labor shortages in several areas, the Europeans imported thousands of black slaves from Africa, the largest number brought to Brazil and Colombia. They also intermarried with their masters, creating a new racial type known as the mulatto. The first pronouncement against slavery on the continent was British Guiana's Emancipation Act of 1833. The process was completed with Brazil's abolition of slavery in 1888.

South America's ethnic composition has been further modified by the arrival of large numbers of Europeans who have immigrated since 1850, coming from such nations as Spain, Portugal, Italy, Germany, and Poland. The Japanese are among the more recent arrivals.

Hundreds of skiers convene on the Andean slopes for competition in a meet at Portillo, a winter resort situated at an elevation of 2,880 m (9,450 ft) in east central Chile. The downhill course of Portillo was once regarded among the fastest in the world.

Cartagena, an important Caribbean port in northern Colombia, is the capital of Bolívar department. Founded and fortified by conquistadores during the 16th century, Cartagena contains some of the most extensive surviving examples of Spanish architecture in the Western Hemisphere.

Today the continent's racial geography can be summarized as follows: Indians are concentrated in the Andean Highlands (especially in Peru, Bolivia, and Ecuador) and in the wet tropical lowlands. Argentina, Uruguay, and southern Brazil are inhabited primarily by pure Caucasians. Blacks and mulattos are dominant in several parts of Brazil and Colombia; elsewhere, mestizos are in the majority.

Spanish is the official language of nine countries in South America. In Brazil, Portuguese is spoken. English and Dutch are used in Guyana and Suriname, respectively. French is the language of French Guiana.

Many Indians are monolingual, speaking only their aboriginal languages. As many as 82 different Indian language groups have been identified.

Roman Catholicism is found throughout South America; only Guyana and Suriname are predominantly Protestant. Argentina has the largest Jewish population, estimated at about 500,000, some of whom live in agricultural colonies.

Education and Health. Argentina, Chile, and Uruguay are doing the most effective job of educating their citizens; each has a literacy rate of 90% or greater. At the other end of the scale is Bolivia, where 67.6% of the population were able to read and write in 1979. The percentage of literate women is generally less than that of literate men. Rural areas have a greater percentage of illiterates than urban areas.

Bolivia, Ecuador, Peru, Guyana, and Colombia fail to supply their people with adequate diets in terms of caloric and protein intakes. The leading causes of death by country are dysentery (especially in Colombia), tuberculosis (Peru), whooping cough (Bolivia, Ecuador, and Peru), and measles (Ecuador, Bolivia, and Colombia). Leading causes of morbidity among reportable diseases are syphilis and typhoid fever; Colombia had the highest incidence of both for any country in Latin America in 1970.

Infant mortality is exceptionally high in the less-developed South American nations. Argentina, with good sanitation and 1 physician for every 500 people, has a low infant mortality rate. Life expectancy in 1975 ranged from 69.8 years in Uruguay to 46.8 years in Bolivia.

Demography. The population is increasing more rapidly in South America than anywhere else in the world. The continent's rate of natural increase exceeds 2.9% a year, higher than that of any other major region except Mexico and Central America. Average annual growth rates for 1970–76 ranged from lows of 0.6% for Uruguay, 1.3% for Argentina, and 1.9% for Chile to highs of 3.0% for Peru, 3.1% for Venezuela, and 3.4% for Paraguay. The substantial growth rates result from recently lowered death rates in concert with continuing high

The Teatro Colón of Buenos Aires, an internationally famous opera house, is one of the most sophisticated cultural facilities in South America. The theater houses the Argentinian National Symphony Orchestra as well as its own ballet and opera companies.

The Cordillera Darwin, a lesser range of the Andes mountain system, dominates the landscape of Chilean (western) Tierra del Fuego. Tierra del Fuego, an archipelago separated from the mainland by the Strait of Magellan, is the southernmost extension of South America.

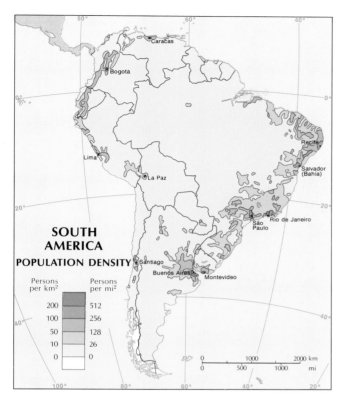

SOUTH AMERICA
POPULATION DENSITY

Persons per km²	Persons per mi²
200	512
100	256
50	128
10	26
0	0

Caracas

Bogota

Lima

La Paz

Recife

Salvador (Bahia)

Rio de Janeiro

São Paulo

Santiago

Buenos Aires

Montevideo

0   1000   2000 km
0   500   1000   mi

SOUTH AMERICA: LANGUAGES

INDO-EUROPEAN

MALAYO-POLYNESIAN

AMERICAN INDIAN

Unclassified aboriginal

Chibcha · Chocó · Arawa · Otomac · English and Indian · Dutch and Indonesian · French · Spanish · Chibcha · Tucano · Yanoáma · Karaib · Karaib · Tupi · Spanish · Macú · Portuguese · Galápagos Is. · Spanish · Quechua · Catuquína · Arawa · Mundúrucan (Tupi) · Gamela · Spanish · Pano · Pano · Chapacura · Gê (Zé) · Portuguese · Quechua · Tacana · Nambicuára · Tupí · Gê (Zé) · Tupí · Portuguese · Spanish · Aymará · Bororo · Gê (Zé) · Portuguese · Humahuaca · Zamuco · Gê (Zé) · Portuguese · Mataco · Yyabuti · Spanish · Portuguese · Spanish · Portuguese · Spanish · Spanish · Huarpe · Spanish · Spanish · Falkland Is. · English · Spanish

0   1000   2000 km
0   500   1000   mi

birthrates. Approximately 45% of South America's population is under 15 years of age, and the size of the population is expected to double in approximately 28 years.

The population is unevenly distributed in South America. Most of the people live in clusters around the periphery of the continent—a reflection of its early role as a supplier of raw materials to the European nations. This uneven population distribution lessens the value of population density figures. South America's most densely populated country is Ecuador, with 28 persons per km² (72 per mi²).

Urbanization has brought about a significant redistribution of people and has resulted in the rapid growth of South

American cities in the past several decades. Uruguay is now 83% urban, Argentina 80%, and Chile 79%. Brazil's cities are growing at an annual rate of 4.8%. If the current trend continues, SÃO PAULO, Brazil, will become the world's largest city before the end of the century.

ECONOMIC DEVELOPMENT AND COMMERCE
South America has not fully entered the age of industrialization. Venezuela was South America's leader in per-capita gross national product in 1978 at $2,807. However, much of Venezuela's wealth comes from its petroleum exports; income in the country is in fact very unevenly distributed. Argentina, ranking second with $1,877, has a much more bal-

The twin towers of the Simón Bolívar Center, which house government offices and a major shopping center, rise above Caracas, the Venezuelan capital. The complex is named for South America's "liberator," Simón Bolívar, who was born in this city.

Camanito Street in La Boca, site of the original Spanish settlement at Buenos Aires, is maintained by the city government as an example of prefabricated architecture of the late 19th and early 20th centuries. La Boca, a waterfront barrio, is famous as an artist's community.

(Left) *A worker tends pineapple plants on a hillside plantation in Risaralda, a department in west central Colombia. Cultivated alongside the pineapples is coffee, of which Colombia is the world's second largest producer.*

(Below) *A gaucho ropes a calf near Tornquist, a town on the pampas, or plains, of Argentina. Argentina's economy traditionally has been dominated by the export of meat, hides, and various animal by-products.*

anced economy. Using the measure of value added by manufacturing, in 1975, Brazil ranked highest with a figure of $19 billion and Argentina next with a total of $13 billion. All other countries in South America combined have less than 20% of Argentina's total using this measure, although the less-developed nations are expanding their manufacturing sectors at faster rates. In terms of total GNP, Brazil ranks first, with $187 billion in 1978. Argentina again is second, with $51 billion. Guyana is last, with only $418 million.

Agriculture. South American countries have been known for the agricultural commodities they export. The income derived from the sale of foodstuffs is used to purchase food and manufactured goods. Brazil has long been the world's leading exporter of coffee, despite recent production declines resulting from severe frosts. Brazil is first in the world in sugarcane production and the fourth leading exporter of cacao in the world. Bananas are the principal crop of Ecuador; that country exports 16% of the world's total.

Argentina and Brazil are widely known for their beef cattle. About 99.5 million head roam the pastures of Brazil, whereas Argentine pastures support close to 56.8 million head (1978 ests.). Although Uruguay ranks second behind Argentina in numbers of sheep, it has 6.68 sheep per person—the highest ratio in the world. Pigs are raised throughout South America.

The most important grain crops are maize, rice, and wheat. South Americans supplement these foods with root crops such as cassava and potatoes. Cassava production in 1977 exceeded in volume that of any other grain or root crop.

South American farmers have been successful in their struggle to keep ahead of the baby boom. Per-capita food harvests have increased over those of the last decade in every country except Uruguay and Guyana.

Forestry and Fishing. Although short of softwood lumber, South America's forests are the source of innumerable by-products. Among these are quinine (from the bark of the cinchona tree), eucalyptol (a cough-drop ingredient taken from the eucalyptus tree), rubber, chicle (chewing-gum base), coconuts, tannin (for leather curing), and palm oil (squeezed from the tree's nuts and used to make soap and cosmetics). Brazil is the leading exporter of forest products.

Peru is exploiting one of South America's major biological resources just off its coast: the anchovy. Peruvian fishermen caught enough anchovies during the 1960s to propel their country into first place in the world for volume of fish caught. The anchovies are ground into fish meal, which is exported primarily to Europe for use in chicken feed and in fertilizer. Catches declined during the 1970s, perhaps because of overfishing. Tuna are also caught off the Pacific coast.

Transportation. The most industrialized countries have the most highly developed land transportation facilities. Argentina, Brazil, and Chile have by far the longest rail networks. These same three countries also have more lengthy paved and gravel road systems than any other nation in South America. Brazil, Argentina, Venezuela, and Colombia are able to supplement their railroads and highways with important inland waterways. The airplane is particularly important in maintaining communications in the rugged Andean countries.

Trade. The nations of South America have joined with some of their neighboring countries to the north to form the LATIN AMERICAN FREE TRADE ASSOCIATION (LAFTA). The purposes of LAFTA are to encourage intraregional trade and at the same time to create a common tariff wall for imports from other regions.

Exports have diversified somewhat in recent decades, but petroleum still accounted for about a fourth of the regional exports in 1965. Other commodities, in order of the volume exported, are coffee, 15%; copper, 5.3%; cotton, 5.2%; meat, 4.2%; wheat, 3.6%; iron ore, 3.4%; sugar, 2.8%; and bananas, 2.0%. The United States is the leading trade partner for both imports and exports for every country in South America. The balance of trade during most years of the 1970s was unfavorable to South America as a whole. Those countries with deficits use loans, capital investment, and tourism to balance their budgets. Argentina has been especially successful in attracting tourists. That nation's receipts from tourism remain consistently higher than those for Colombia, Peru, and Venezuela—the next most successful countries.

Indian women display handicrafts and manufactured goods at the open-air market of Cuenca, in south central Ecuador. This city, the capital of Azuay province, is one of the most important inland commercial centers in the southern portion of the nation.

Energy. Petroleum is one of South America's principal sources of power. As of 1975 the only countries with a surplus were Venezuela, Ecuador, Bolivia, and Colombia. Brazil had the greatest deficit.

South America is estimated to have 17.3% of the world's potential water power. Of this amount Brazil and Colombia have the largest shares, with 6.6% and 2.8%, respectively. South America lags behind North America, Europe, and the USSR, however, in tapping this potential, with only 7.1% of the world's developed water power. Brazil ranks first on the continent in hydroelectric production, generating 5.1% of the world total. Brazil is constructing the largest hydroelectric installation in the world at the Itaipú damsite.

JAMES N. SNADEN

Bibliography:

GENERAL: Brooks, John, ed., *The South American Handbook* (1979); Goodman, E. J., *The Explorers of South America* (1972); Gunther, John, *Inside South America* (1967); James, Preston, *Latin America*, 4th ed. (1969); Pendle, George, *South America*, 2d ed. (1970); UCLA Latin American Center, *Statistical Abstract of Latin America* (annual).

GEOGRAPHY: Butland, Gilbert J., *Latin America: A Regional Geography*, 2d ed. (1966); Carlson, Fred A., *Geography of Latin America*, 3d ed. (1952); Cole, J. P., *Latin America: An Economic and Social Geography* (1965); Webb, K. E., *The Geography of Latin America* (1972); Whitbeck, Ray H., and Williams, Frank E., *Economic Geography of South America*, 3d ed. (1971).

NATURAL HISTORY: Bates, Marston, *The Land and Wildlife of South America* (1964); Dorst, Jean, *South America and Central America* (1967); Fittkau, E. J., et al., eds., *Biogeography and Ecology in South America*, 2 vols. (1968–69); Jenks, William F., ed., *Handbook of South American Geology* (1956); Meyer de Schauensee, Rodolphe, *A Guide to the Birds of South America* (1970).

PEOPLE: Mörner, Magnus, *Race Mixture in the History of Latin America* (1967); Steward, Julian H., ed., *Handbook of South American Indians*, 7 vols. (1946–59); Steward, Julian H., and Faron, Louis C., *Native Peoples of South America* (1959).

ECONOMICS AND POLITICS: Anderson, Charles W., *Politics and Economic Change in Latin America* (1966); Barclay, Glen, *Struggle for a Continent: The Diplomatic History of South America, 1917–1945* (1972); Beyer, Glenn H., ed., *The Urban Explosion in Latin America* (1967); Burnett, Ben G., and Johnson, Kenneth F., eds., *Political Forces in Latin America*, 2d ed. (1970); Inter-American Development Bank, *Economic and Social Progress in Latin America* (annual); Stokes, C. J., *Transportation and Economic Development in Latin America* (1968).

See also: LATIN AMERICA, HISTORY OF; individual countries, major cities, and regions of South America.

South Asian universities

Universities in South Asia constitute a large and diverse system of higher education. The largest nation in the region, India, boasts the third largest university system in the world, after the United States and the Soviet Union, with more than 3 million students in about 100 universities and more than 3,000 colleges. The other countries of the region, Afghanistan, Pakistan, Sri Lanka (Ceylon), and Bangladesh, pattern their universities on those in India, which in turn were patterned on British universities. South Asian countries are among the poorest in the world, with literacy rates of only 40 percent or less. Their universities therefore exist in societies facing major social and economic problems. The contrast between the modern universities and the traditional surrounding society is a sharp one and is also the cause of considerable social pressure. The universities have contributed to the development of nationalist movements in the past and to social and political activism in recent years. They have also contributed to technological development by training the skilled personnel required for industry, agriculture, and administration.

Many South Asian universities were founded by the British, were modeled on the British university system, and were intended to assist the British colonial establishment rather than to contribute to national development. The heritage of colonialism, including the continued use of English, along with the language of the region, as a language of instruction at the higher levels of the academic system, remains strong in South Asia. The earliest universities were established in 1857 at Bombay, Calcutta, and Madras. They were founded mainly as

SOUTH ASIAN UNIVERSITIES

University and Location	Date Founded	Enrollment
Afghanistan		
Kabul University	1947	9,900
Bangladesh		
Bangladesh Agricultural University, Mymensingh	1961	2,500
Bangladesh University of Engineering and Technology, Dacca	1961	1,800
University of Chittagong	1966	23,000
University of Dacca	1921	68,100
Jahangirnagar University, Dacca	1970	950
University of Rajshahi	1953	41,300
India		
Banaras Hindu University	1915	17,500
Bangalore University	1964	54,000
University of Bombay	1857	156,500
University of Calcutta	1857	293,500
University of Delhi	1922	132,300
University of Madras	1857	168,000
University of Mysore	1916	99,200
University of Poona	1948	92,100
Shivaji University	1962	78,200
Pakistan		
University of Baluchistan, Quetta	1970	1,300
University of Islamabad	1965	910
University of Karachi	1951	15,000
University of Peshawar	1950	8,000
University of the Punjab, Lahore	1882	50,000
University of Sind, Hyderabad	1947	11,150
University of Agriculture, Lyallpur	1961	3,100
University of Engineering and Technology, Lahore	1923	3,000
Allama Iqbal Open University, Islamabad	1974	34,000
Sri Lanka		
University of Sri Lanka		
Colombo Campus	1967	4,200
Jaffna Campus	1974	1,000
Katubedda Campus	1972	2,700
Peradeniya Campus	1972	5,000
Vidyalankara Campus, Kelaniya	1959	2,500
Vidyodaya Campus, Gangodawila	1959	2,500

examining institutions, not offering instruction until 1904, controlling the awarding of degrees at a large number of semiindependent colleges affiliated with them. A university was established as early as the late 19th century in what is now Pakistan and in Sri Lanka (Ceylon). Higher education in Afghanistan lagged far behind; Kabul University was founded in 1947, although it had been established in 1932 as a faculty of medicine.

South Asian universities now offer a full range of undergraduate and graduate programs, with several institutions in India operating at the highest international levels of quality. Such universities as Jawaharlal Nehru University, the University of Delhi, the University of Bombay, and the five Indian Institutions of Technology offer high-level advanced training. Most of the students in South Asia come from urban, relatively affluent backgrounds (in countries where the urban population is less than 20 percent of the total). Although considerable unemployment exists among graduates (especially in the liberal arts), a university degree is a virtual prerequisite for most white-collar jobs and thus is highly prized.

PHILIP G. ALTBACH

Bibliography: Haggerty, William J., *Higher and Professional Education in India* (1970); Huq, Muhammad Shamsul, *Education and Developmental Strategies in South and Southeast Asia* (1965); Singh, Amrik, and Altbach, Philip G., *The Higher Learning in India* (1974).

South Australia

The state of South Australia, located in the south central part of Australia, covers 984,381 km² (380,070 mi²). It occupies about one-eighth of the continent and has a population of 1,291,000 (1978 est.). The capital is ADELAIDE.

Underlain by a crystalline shield in the west and sedimentary basins elsewhere, South Australia's topography is low and mostly flat; more than 80% of the land is less than 300 m (1,000 ft) in elevation. About 75% of the terrain receives less than 250 mm (10 in) of rainfall per year. The remainder, mostly in the southeast, receives about 635 mm (25 in). Temperatures average 13° C (55° F) in winter and 24° C (75° F) in summer. The northeast is part of the Great Artesian Basin, the world's largest region of natural springs.

South Australia's population is predominantly of British ancestry. The largest religious denomination is the Anglican church, followed by the Roman Catholic and Methodist churches. South Australia grew faster than Australia as a whole until the mid-1960s, when rising unemployment reversed the trend. Almost 85% of the population lives in cities, primarily Adelaide.

About 10% of the labor force is engaged in primary production, including mining and quarrying. The state's Middleback Range is a major producer of iron ore, and South Australia is a major world source of opals. Large natural gas fields supply much of Australia's energy requirements. The automotive industry employs about 30% of the labor force. Other industries manufacture metal products, chemicals, and textiles. The two major sources of export revenue are sheep and wheat; of secondary importance are fruits and vegetables, which are produced from irrigated farms and vineyards.

Matthew Flinders explored the South Australian coast in 1802, but permanent settlement did not begin until 1836. Unlike other parts of the continent, South Australia was never a penal colony. The population increased rapidly during the mid-1800s as disappointed gold miners from Victoria and New South Wales migrated to South Australia to raise sheep and grow wheat. South Australia became a state in 1901. Recurring droughts have led to periodic economic depressions in inland areas.

CALVIN WILVERT

South Bend

South Bend (1979 est. pop., 109,300), the seat of Saint Joseph County, lies on the Saint Joseph River in northern Indiana, about 130 km (80 mi) east of Chicago. Surrounded by farmlands, South Bend is a processing and shipping center; it also manufactures farm and electrical machinery, transportation equipment, paints, and plastic products. A treaty with the Miami and Illinois Indians was negotiated on the site by Robert Cavalier, Sieur de LA SALLE, in 1681. The city was settled in the 1820s.

South Carolina

South Carolina, the Palmetto State, was one of the original 13 U.S. states. Located on the Atlantic coast, it is bounded by North Carolina on the north and Georgia on the southwest. Its 80,429 km² (31,055 mi²) were inhabited in 1979 by approximately 2,930,300 people, ranking it 25th among the states in population. The capital is Columbia, located in the geographic center of the state. The state's name is derived from Charles II of England, who granted "Carolina" in 1663 to lords proprietors. The first permanent European settlement was at Charles Town—renamed Charleston in 1783—in April 1670. South Carolina assumed a position of political and social leadership during the colonial, revolutionary, and antebellum periods. The post–Civil War era and the early 20th century witnessed a severe social and economic decline in the state, but the rise of the New South in the last few decades has renewed the state's vitality.

LAND AND RESOURCES

South Carolina can be divided into three physiographic regions. The Coastal Plain, the largest and geologically youngest region, extends from the Sea Islands inland to the Sand Hills. The topography is flat near the coast but more rolling in the interior, where elevations reach 92 m (302 ft). Sandy barrier islands, many of which are being eroded, and salt marshes, covered by salt-marsh grass and black needle rush, constitute the common coastal environment. Old beach ridges are covered with maritime forests of palmetto (the state tree), live oak, loblolly pine, and wax myrtle. In the outer Coastal Plain, especially along rivers, numerous swamps support bald cypress, swamp tupelo, water oak, and willow trees. A physiographic feature unique to the plain are the many Carolina Bays, whose origin is still unknown. These elliptical bogs or lakes have a northwest-southeast axis and are bordered, predominantly on the eastern quadrant, by a sand rim. Characteristic vegetation includes sweet and red bay (for which the feature is named), cypress, loblolly pine, and sweet gum. The Coastal Plain culminates in the Sand Hills, which extend from Aiken northeastward through Columbia to Cheraw. The sandy soils of these hills support scrub oak, blackjack oak, and longleaf pine.

The PIEDMONT rises from the FALL LINE, which marks the boundary with the Coastal Plain, to an elevation of about 427 m (1,401 ft). Streams have cut deeply into the surface and left a rolling-to-hilly topography. Severe-to-moderate erosion, which followed extensive agricultural clearing, removed much of the topsoil and left the heavy red-clay subsoil now characteristic of the region. Native vegetation is basically hardwood: black, white, and red oak; pignut hickory; and dogwood. Shortleaf pine also grows in the Piedmont. Along

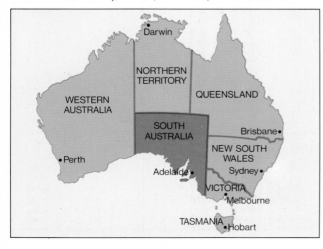

streams cottonwood, yellow poplar, willow, sycamore, and sweet gum are common. The loblolly pine, which is not native to the Piedmont, has been widely planted for pulpwood.

The BLUE RIDGE MOUNTAINS occupy a small portion of the northwest corner of the state. Elevations vary from 427 m (1,401 ft) to 1,085 m (3,560 ft) at Sassafras Mountain, the highest point in South Carolina. The thin, well-drained soils of the steep slopes are clayey to loamy.

Drainage. Cutting across the physiographic provinces, which rise in elevation northwestward from the coast, are the southeastward-flowing river systems, including the Savannah, Black, Edisto, Pee Dee, and Santee. The most extensive drainage basin is that of the Santee and its tributaries. The state's largest

SOUTH CAROLINA

Capital and Largest City: Columbia (1979 est. pop., 109,600)

Population: 2,930,300 (1979 est.). *Distribution*—47.6% urban, 52.4% rural; *density*, 36 persons per km² (94 per mi²); *increase* (1970–79), 13%; *population rank*, 25th

Area: 80,429 km² (31,055 mi²), including 2,150 km² (830 mi²) of inland water; *area rank*, 40th

Elevation: *Highest*—Sassafras Mountain, 1,085 m (3,560 ft); *lowest*—sea level, along the Atlantic Ocean

Principal Products: *Manufacturing and industry*—textiles, chemicals, nonelectrical machinery, clothing, paper and wood products, electrical equipment, food products, metals. *Agriculture*—tobacco, soybeans, cotton, maize, vegetables, peaches, cattle, pigs, poultry, and dairy products. *Mining*—cement, kaolin, clay, stone, sand, vermiculite, feldspar

Government: *State legislature*—46 senators, 124 representatives. *Representation in Congress*—2 U.S. senators, 6 U.S. representatives

Number of Counties: 46

Statehood: May 23, 1788; the 8th state

State Nickname: The Palmetto State

State Bird: Carolina wren

State Flower: Yellow jessamine

State Tree: Palmetto

State Mottoes: *Animusque Opibusque Parati* ("Prepared in mind and resources"); and *Dum Spiro Spero* ("While I breathe, I hope")

lakes are Clark Hill and Hartwell reservoirs, and Lakes Marion, Moultrie, and Murray.

Climate. Average temperatures in January vary from 11° C (51° F) in Charleston to 7° C (44° F) in Greenville-Spartanburg. July averages are 26° C (79° F) in Greenville-Spartanburg and 28° C (82° F) in Charleston. The mean annual precipitation throughout the state totals 1,295 mm (51 in). Adequate rainfall complements a growing season of 290 days on the southern coast and more than 200 days in the northwest. Hurricanes infrequently threaten the coast.

Animal Life. The abundance of white-tailed deer permits a long hunting season. Fox, mink, muskrat, opossum, otter, rabbit, raccoon, skunk, and squirrel are protected species in South Carolina. Duck, geese, quail, and wild turkey attract hunters, and a wide variety of freshwater and saltwater fishes is found in South Carolina's waters.

Resources. Forests cover more than 60% of South Carolina. Metallic minerals, including gold, were once mined, but major resources today are limestone, sand, and gravel in the Coastal Plain, kaolin or china clay mined principally in Aiken County, granite in the Piedmont, and various clays for brick and tile mined in many areas. Other minerals include vermiculite, kyanite, and sericite. Petroleum deposits may lie off the South Carolina coast. Many rivers provide hydroelectric power.

PEOPLE

About 32% of South Carolina's population is nonwhite—one of the highest percentages in the nation. Most of the state's nonwhites are black. Almost 45% of the population lives in the areas of CHARLESTON, GREENVILLE, SPARTANBURG, and COLUMBIA. Major growth continues in those areas and along the northeastern coast.

South Carolina's growth rate through the 20th century has lagged behind that of the United States as a whole. This resulted from net out-migration, which characterized the state

(Left) *Table Rock State Park is located in the Blue Ridge Mountains in the northwestern corner of South Carolina. The peak for which the park is named reaches 962 m (3,157 ft). To the southeast in South Carolina's Piedmont region is Columbia (below), the state's largest city. The site was chosen as the state capital in 1786 because of its location between the coastal lowlands and the mountains.*

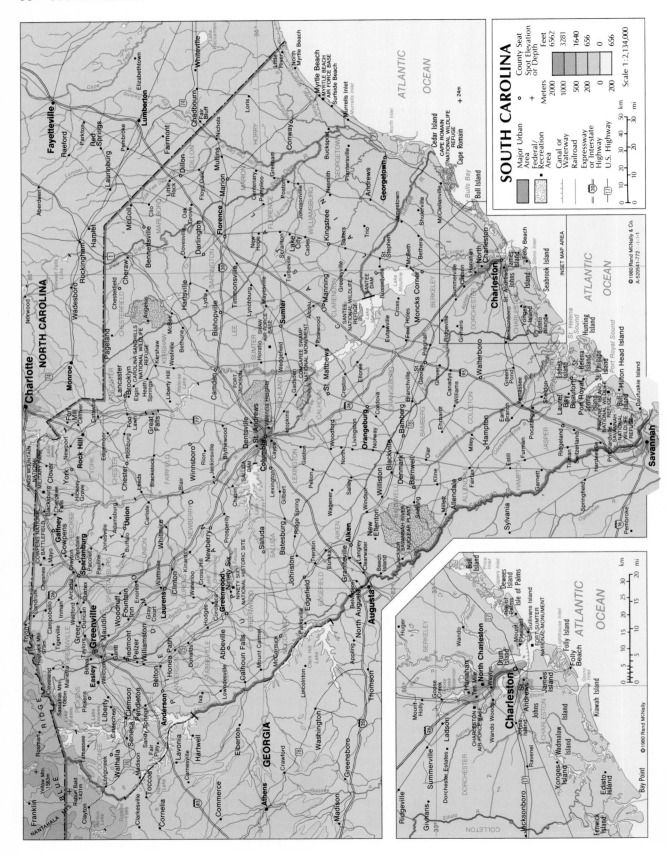

SOUTH CAROLINA

	County Seat			Feet
○	County Seat			6562
+	Spot Elevation or Depth			3281
				1640
	Meters			656
	2000			0
	1000			656
	500			
	200			
	0			
	200			

Scale 1:2,134,000

Major Urban Area
Federal/Recreation Area
Canal or Waterway
Railroad
Expressway or Interstate Highway
U.S. Highway

© 1980 Rand McNally & Co.
A-520541-772 -1-1-1

INSET MAP AREA

(Left) *Charleston, a major seaport and the seat of Charleston County, is on a peninsula near the estuaries of the Ashley and Cooper rivers. The site of the first permanent European settlement in the Carolinas, Charleston was a colonial and then a state capital from 1670 until 1790.*

(Below) *The pentagonal design of Fort Sumter is clearly defined in an aerial photograph taken above Charleston Harbor. The fort was shelled by Confederate artillery in April 1861 in the earliest fighting of the Civil War.*

until the 1970s. Between 1960 and 1970, the out-migration was 153,000. About 44,000 whites moved into South Carolina, but 197,000 blacks left. Between 1970 and 1975 the total net in-migration was 98,000. South Carolina's population increased 13% between 1970 and 1979, almost twice the national rate of 7%, and the number of blacks leaving the state appears to be declining. The largest religious group is the Southern Baptists. Methodists and Presbyterians form the other major denominations in the state.

Education. Antebellum education was provided by private academies. Despite the 1868 constitution's commitment to free education for all children, public education did not begin in South Carolina until ratification of the 1895 constitution. It provided for the allocation of school funds and establishment of a state board of education. In 1978 per-pupil expenditures totaled $1,340, or 77% of the national average; South Carolina ranked 39th among the states in per-pupil expenditures. Public school enrollment totaled 612,000 in 1977. Private school enrollment, more than 50,000 in 1976, experienced marked growth during the 1960s and early '70s but has stabilized. South Carolina's 47 public and private colleges and universities, including FURMAN UNIVERSITY, enrolled 124,000 students in 1977 (see SOUTH CAROLINA, STATE UNIVERSITIES AND COLLEGES OF). The state's technical education program, begun in 1969, provides job training for high school graduates to meet the needs of new industries moving into the state. The 17 technical education centers enrolled 142,058 students in 1977-78.

Cultural and Historical Sites. Major museums in South Carolina include Gibbes Art Gallery in Charleston, the Columbia Museum of Art and Science, and the religious art collection at Bob Jones University in Greenville. The Charleston Museum (established 1773) is the oldest public museum in the United States. County and regional museums complement these. Many antebellum homes, plantations, and gardens are open to the public. National and state historical parks include FORT SUMTER, where the Civil War began, and Kings Mountain National Military Park. A total of 39 state parks have been established in South Carolina. Popular resorts are located along the Atlantic coast, especially on the section known as the Grand Strand (near Myrtle Beach), on the offshore Sea Islands, and in the mountains.

Communications. South Carolina is served by 20 daily and 52 weekly newspapers and has 11 television and 164 radio stations. The South Carolina Educational Radio Network has won national broadcasting awards.

ECONOMIC ACTIVITY

South Carolina's economy traditionally has been based on agriculture, principally rice and cotton. Recently, however,

manufacturing has been increasing in importance. Before the Civil War, industry in South Carolina was limited to a few cotton spindles, but in the late 1880s textile mills began locating in the Piedmont. By the early 20th century, the state had become a leading cotton manufacturer, and in 1940 about 75% of the state's industrial workers were employed in the textile industry. Imaginative tax legislation, the work of the State Development Board, and the passage of a right-to-work law in 1954 have created an amenable environment for industry.

Manufacturing. In 1978 manufacturing employed 371,000 in the state and had a value-added figure of $7.2 billion. Although textiles retained their leadership in the 1970s (40% of the manufacturing employment), the diversified industrial base also included food processing, metallurgy, and the manufacture of apparel, pulp and paper, and chemicals. Between 1972 and 1977 annual industrial investment for new and expanded plants averaged $785 million.

Agriculture. Cash receipts from agriculture in 1977 totaled $762.4 million, $277.2 million of which was derived from livestock. The major commodities, in order of cash receipts, are: tobacco, soybeans, poultry, corn, hogs, dairying, beef cattle, cotton, and peaches. Commercial fishing has been valued at $9.5 million (1977). Forest products were valued at $269 million in 1977.

Mining. South Carolina has a small mining industry, accounting for only 0.18% of U.S. output value. In 1977, the value of mining was $146.6 million. South Carolina ranks second in the United States in production of both vermiculite and kaolin.

(Left) *Vacationers and oceanfront buildings crowd the shore of Myrtle Beach, South Carolina's largest seaside resort. The city lies near the center of the Grand Strand, an 80-km (50-mi) stretch of beach extending along the Atlantic Ocean to the North Carolina border.*

(Below) *The Blue Ridge Mountains, which form a segment of the Appalachian Mountains of eastern North America, occupy the northwestern corner of South Carolina. Some of the area is suitable for pasture or commercial logging.*

Other minerals produced are cement, stone, sand, and clays.
Energy. The total installed electrical generating capacity in 1976 was 11.5 million kW. The largest hydroelectric installation is the Santee-Cooper project, producing about 133,000 kW, followed by the Lake Murray dam, which produces 130,000 kW. A large nuclear reprocessing and storage plant is located on the Savannah River. The Keowee-Toxaway complex in northwestern South Carolina has three nuclear reactors.

Tourism. About 39.6 million travelers through the state spent $1.4 billion in 1977. Of these, 14 million had destinations in South Carolina: the Myrtle Beach area (33%), Charleston (18%), and Columbia (10%); 45% of their expenditures were in Myrtle Beach, attesting to the Grand Strand's reputation as a summer resort.

Transportation. In 1975, about 4,830 km (3,000 mi) of railroad crossed the state. A total of 61,628 km (38,295 mi) of highway, 1,093 km (679 mi) of which is in the interstate system, had been constructed by 1977. Charleston, South Carolina's major port, handled foreign cargo valued at $2.161 billion, making the city a leading South Atlantic port. International airports are at Charleston and Greenville-Spartanburg.

GOVERNMENT

South Carolina state government, based on the 1895 constitution, has three branches. Legislative authority rests with the general assembly, composed of the house of representatives and the senate. The 124 representatives serve 2-year terms and are elected from districts based on population. The 46 senators serve staggered 4-year terms and are elected from districts based on population distribution and county boundaries. The executive branch includes the governor, the lieutenant governor, and eight constitutional officers; each serves a 4-year term. Judicial authority is vested in the supreme court, composed of the chief justice and four associate justices. The justices, elected by the legislature, serve staggered 10-year terms. The legislative branch wields the greatest power, controlling appropriations, finances, and appointments to the state courts and to boards, commissions, and agencies. The governor is a virtual figurehead, who can do no more than persuade the legislature. The state is represented in the U.S. Congress by six representatives and two senators. The county is the unit of local government, supplemented by special districts such as school and fire districts.

For many decades following RECONSTRUCTION, South Carolina was staunchly Democratic. In return, the Democrats did not interfere with the state's racial status quo. During the Truman presidency, however, Republicans began to challenge

Democratic strength, and in 1964, 1968, and 1972 the state, rejecting the growing liberalism of the national Democratic party, voted Republican. Divisiveness in the Democratic party facilitated the election of Republican James B. Edwards as governor in 1974, but Republican strength ebbed in later local and state elections. In 1976, South Carolina supported Democrat Jimmy Carter with 56.3% of the popular vote. In 1978, Democrat Dick Riley was elected governor.

HISTORY

About 25 or 30 distinct native tribes lived in South Carolina at the time of first European contact. The major groups were the CHEROKEE, the CATAWBA, and the YAMASEE. By 1800 virtually all had been driven from the state.

Francisco Gordillo was the first European to visit South Carolina in 1521. The Spanish attempted the first European settlement near present-day Georgetown in 1526, but it failed after 9 months. In 1663, King Charles II of England granted the territory that now comprises both North and South Carolina to eight lords proprietors, one of whom was Anthony Ashley Cooper, later 1st earl of Shaftesbury. The first permanent settlement, at Charles Town (Charleston) on the Ashley River, was established by the English in 1670. (It was moved in 1680 to the peninsula between the Cooper and Ashley rivers.) At first the new colony of Carolina was economically dependent on furs and skins from the Indian trade and on forest products such as lumber, resin, and turpentine. By the end of the 17th century, experiments with rice cultivation proved

A couple stroll past a terraced lawn in the Middleton Place Gardens near Charleston. These landscaped gardens, among the oldest in the United States, were laid out in 1741 on the estate of Henry Middleton, president (1774-75) of the Continental Congress.

successful, and it became the leading crop of colonial Carolina—complemented after 1744 by indigo. The wealth derived from these crops supported the colony's cultural and intellectual efflorescence. Settlement spread from Charles Town south toward BEAUFORT (founded 1710), north toward Georgetown (1735), and inland along the rivers.

By the 1750s, Germans and Scottish-Irish from Pennsylvania and Virginia were settling the Piedmont on small, subsistence farms in contrast to the coastal plantations. The pre-Revolutionary period (1725-75) was a prosperous one based on pelts and the rapidly expanding rice and indigo crops. The Southern Indian trade and agricultural exporting centered on Charleston, which became an increasingly rich and important port. The colony became more and more independent as the British did little to exercise control.

South Carolina was early in resisting British rule. In 1693 the colony won the right to initiate legislation in the British House of Commons. In 1704 an act that would have required members of the colonial assembly to adhere to the rites of the Church of England was defeated. The church was, however, made official in 1706 and remained so until 1778. In 1719 the populace rebelled against the British proprietors and their reactionary policies, expelling them and electing James Moore as governor. As a result the British crown assumed (1729) jurisdiction, and North and South Carolina were constituted as separate colonies. A survey of the boundary between the two, begun in 1735, was not completed until 1815.

The Revolutionary War, after the British repulse at Charleston in 1776, temporarily bypassed South Carolina. Then the British captured Charleston on May 12, 1780. The numerous battles and skirmishes fought in the state after 1780 included important American victories at Kings Mountain and Cowpens (see COWPENS, BATTLE OF).

South Carolina was the eighth state to ratify the federal Constitution, on May 23, 1788. To mollify Piedmont settlers, who demanded increased representation, the General Assembly agreed in 1786 to move the capital. Columbia was established as the new seat of government. In the first federal census of 1790, South Carolina's population of 249,073 ranked 7th. Nonwhites accounted for 43.7% of the total and were concentrated in the low country around Charleston.

Of major economic importance was the adoption at the end of the 18th century of short-staple, green-seed cotton. It was grown increasingly in the interior, and the cotton gin, greater European demand, and improved transportation (the canal system and river improvements began in 1795) made it a viable economic staple. Its success turned many Piedmont farmers into slave-holding planters and unified the state economically, socially, and politically.

During the 1820s and '30s cotton prices collapsed, and the state's economy and population growth stagnated. Blaming these problems on the national tariff policies, South Carolina—led by Vice-President John C. CALHOUN—asserted its right to nullify federal legislation. In 1832 a special state convention nullified the Tariff Act of that year. President Andrew Jackson responded to this action with a Force Act. The NULLIFICATION crisis was resolved by compromise, but STATE RIGHTS sentiment continued to grow in South Carolina.

Dissatisfaction culminated in the convention that, on Dec. 20, 1860, voted to remove South Carolina from the Union, the first Southern state to secede. The Civil War began on Apr. 12, 1861, with the firing on Fort Sumter in Charleston Harbor. Beaufort and Port Royal fell to Union forces on Nov. 7, 1861, but not until Sherman's invasion of the state at the beginning of 1865 was the impact of war felt. Severity of property loss, however, paled before the mortality figures for South Carolina: about 25% of the 63,000 who served were killed.

Reconstruction was hard on South Carolina, and corrupt officials left the state with heavy debts. The election of Wade HAMPTON (1818-1902) as governor in 1876 and removal of federal troops by President Rutherford Hayes ended congressional Reconstruction.

Poor cotton prices and severe soil erosion after 1880 stymied economic improvement, and agricultural distress led to political success for the farmers' movement. Its leader, Benjamin Ryan TILLMAN, was elected to the governor's post (1890-94) and the U.S. Senate (1895-1918). A state constitutional convention in 1895 largely disenfranchised blacks. Strong populist leanings characterized South Carolina's politics for decades.

By 1910 rice production had virtually disappeared, although cotton remained the state's leading crop into the 1950s. During the late 19th century the tenant system developed, and in 1930 it characterized 65% of the state's farms. During the early 20th century urban concentrations developed around Piedmont textile centers such as Greenville and Spartanburg, and the out-migration of blacks reduced their percentage of the population.

World War I temporarily revived agricultural fortunes, but an economic depression, which lasted for two decades, and infestation by the boll weevil, which destroyed half the cotton crop, began in 1921. World War II was a watershed in South Carolina's history, enormously increasing emphasis on industrialization. By the early 1950s the state was actively seeking industry to complement the textile mills that had virtually monopolized the nonagricultural sector of its economy. This, complemented by a diversifying agricultural base, underpinned an expanding economy.

Despite the 1954 Supreme Court decision (see BROWN V. BOARD OF EDUCATION OF TOPEKA, KANSAS), South Carolina initially resisted racial integration. In the 1960s, however, under the leadership of moderate governors, school integration was realized with minor difficulty.   JOHN J. WINBERRY

Bibliography: Ashley, Franklin, ed., *Faces of South Carolina* (1974); Federal Writers' Project, *South Carolina, A Guide to the Palmetto State* (1941; repr. 1971); Guess, William, *South Carolina* (1960); Lander, Ernest M., *A History of South Carolina, 1865-1960,* 2d ed. (1970); McCrady, Edward, *The History of South Carolina in the Revolution,* 2 vols. (1901-02); Simkins, F. B., and Woody, R. H., *South Carolina during Reconstruction* (1932; repr. 1966); Su, T. T., *The South Carolina Economy* (1970); Williams, G. C., *A Social Interpretation of South Carolina* (1946); Wright, Louis B., *South Carolina* (1976).

South Carolina, state universities and colleges of

All the state colleges and universities of South Carolina are coeducational, and nearly all grant both undergraduate and graduate degrees. The **University of South Carolina** (1801; enrollment: 20,300; library: 1,500,000 volumes), at Columbia, offers a liberal arts program and has a law school. Its library contains the papers of John C. Calhoun. **South Carolina State College** (1896; enrollment: 5,300; library: 200,000 volumes), a land-grant school at Orangeburg, grants bachelor's and master's degrees.

The state's other schools are **Clemson University** (1889; enrollment: 11,280; library: 741,000 volumes), at Clemson, a land-grant institution; the **College of Charleston** (1770; enrollment: 5,050; library: 185,000 volumes), at Charleston; **Francis Marion College** (1970; enrollment: 7,660; library: 180,000 volumes), at Florence; **Winthrop College** (1886; enrollment: 4,500; library: 350,500 volumes), at Rock Hill; and **Lander College** (1872; enrollment: 1,670; library: 100,000 volumes), an undergraduate school at Greenwood. **The Citadel, the Military College of South Carolina** (1842; enrollment: 3,360; library: 265,000 volumes), at Charleston, has liberal arts and military curricula.

South China Sea:　See CHINA SEA, SOUTH.

South Dakota

South Dakota is located in the center of the North American continent, bounded on the north by North Dakota, on the east by Minnesota and Iowa, on the south by Nebraska, and on the west by Wyoming and Montana. Its area of 199,544 km² (77,047 mi²) ranks 16th in size. The population is 695,500 (1979 est.), ranking 44th among the U.S. states. The capital is Pierre (pronounced *pier*), with 12,100 inhabitants (1979 est.).

Dakota is a Sioux word meaning "alliance of friends." The state's nicknames include the "Sunshine State" and the "Coyote State." The territory was explored by the French in the mid-18th century, and settlement began in 1857. On Nov. 2, 1889, South Dakota became the 40th state in the Union. South Dakota has traditionally been an agricultural state, but recently it has become a major tourist center and has also experienced commercial and industrial growth.

LAND AND RESOURCES
The state is divided in half by the north-south–flowing Missouri River, which was formed when glaciers to the east blocked the flow of western rivers, forcing them southward. It runs through a channel about 90 to 150 m (300 to 500 ft) below the surface of the surrounding plain. The state's elevation averages 670 m (2,200 ft).

Dense forest covers much of Spearfish Canyon, situated in the Black Hills of southwestern South Dakota. Within this region, from which considerable mineral wealth is extracted, lies the Homestead Mine, the greatest gold-producing mine in the Western Hemisphere.

Glaciated eastern South Dakota is known as Prairie Country. The melted ice left the land covered with glacial debris, resulting in low rolling hills, marshy areas and small lakes, and shallow river valleys. The eastern part of the state is covered with rich chernozem prairie soils.

Unglaciated western South Dakota is part of the GREAT PLAINS. It is composed of smooth hills, isolated buttes, and flat dissected plateaus. Fertile chestnut brown soils cover the drier plains. The beautiful, castellated BADLANDS follow the White River, in the southern part of the state.

The BLACK HILLS form a third topographic region in the southwest corner of South Dakota. They are a domed mountain region composed of an ancient crystalline core with deep valleys, surrounded by ridges of sedimentary strata. The state's highest point, Harney Peak (2,207 m/7,242 ft), is located in the Black Hills. Thin, infertile grey wooded soils are found there.

SOUTH DAKOTA

Capital: Pierre (1979 est. pop., 12,100)
Largest City: Sioux Falls (1979 est. pop., 76,100)
Population: 695,500 (1979 est.). *Distribution*—44.6% urban, 55.4% rural; *density,* 3.5 persons per km² (9.0 per mi²); *increase* (1970-77), 3.4%; *population rank,* 44th
Area: 199,544 km² (77,047 mi²), including 2,828 km² (1,092 mi²) of inland water; *area rank,* 16th
Elevation: *Highest*—Harney Peak, 2,207 m (7,242 ft); *lowest*—Big Stone Lake, 293 m (965 ft)
Principal Products: *Manufacturing and industry*—food products, nonelectrical machinery, printing and publishing, wood products, electronics. *Agriculture*—wheat, corn, soybeans, oats, flaxseed, barley, rye; cattle, pigs, sheep; dairy products; bees. *Mining*—gold, silver, gypsum, sand and gravel, limestone; quartzite, feldspar, bentonite, mica, tin, manganese, coal; petroleum, uranium
Government: *State legislature*—35 senators, 70 representatives. *Representation in Congress*—2 U.S. senators, 2 U.S. representatives
Statehood: Nov. 2, 1889; the 40th state
Number of Counties: 66
State Nicknames: Sunshine State; Coyote State
State Bird: Ring-necked pheasant
State Flower: American pasque flower
State Tree: Black Hills spruce
State Motto: Under God the People Rule

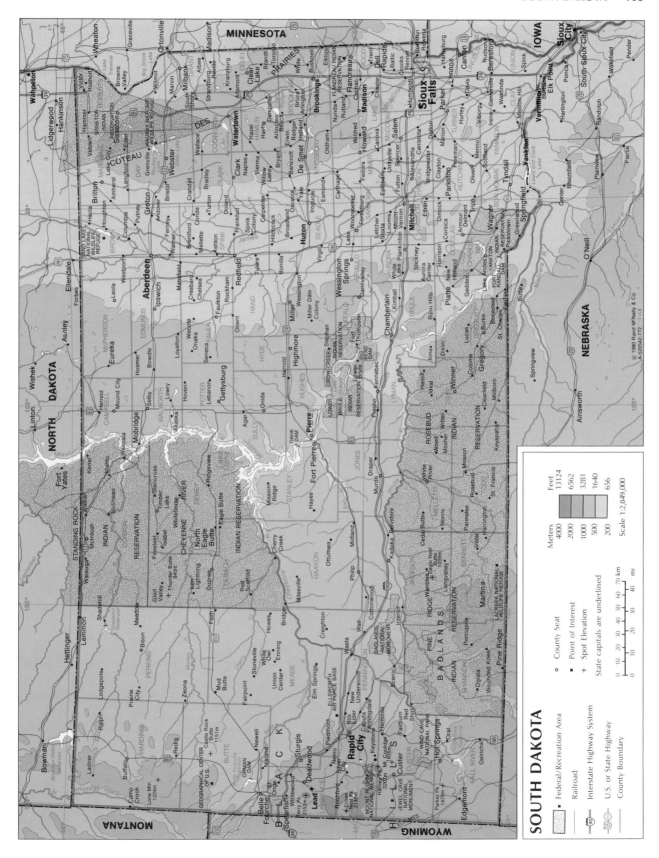

SOUTH DAKOTA

- **Federal/Recreation Area**
- **Railroad**
- **Interstate Highway System**
- **U.S. or State Highway**
- **County Boundary**

○ County Seat
■ Point of Interest
+ Spot Elevation
State capitals are underlined

Meters	Feet
4000	13124
2000	6562
1000	3281
500	1640
200	656

Scale 1:2,849,000

0 10 20 30 40 50 60 70 km
0   10   20   30   40 mi

© 1980 Rand McNally & Co.
A-520542-772   -1-1

(Left) *The features of four American presidents—Washington, Jefferson, Roosevelt, and Lincoln—were carved into the granite face of Mount Rushmore by Gutzon Borglum over a period of 14 years. The sculpture, in southwestern South Dakota, is a national monument.*

(Below) *A solitary truck travels past the eroded landscape of the Badlands in southwestern South Dakota. Much of the Badlands lies within large Indian reservations, but a portion of this arid region is maintained as a national park.*

Climate and Drainage. The climate is continental with distinct seasons. Great extremes in diurnal and yearly temperatures can occur, modified by low humidity, moderate winds, and low precipitation. In January temperatures average from −12° to −7° C (10° to 20° F) in the north and between −7° and −4° C (20° and 24° F) in the south. In July temperatures range from 18° to 21° C (65° to 70° F) in the north, and between 21° and 24° C (70° and 75° F) in the south. Precipitation varies from 660 mm (26 in) in the southeast to 330 mm (13 in) in the northwest. Over two-thirds of the precipitation falls during the 130-day average growing season. The state can experience blizzards during winter and severe thunderstorms and tornadoes in spring and summer.

The MISSOURI RIVER, which flows into the Mississippi River and then to the Gulf of Mexico, receives drainage from all regions but northeastern South Dakota, which drains into the Hudson Bay. Principal eastern streams are the Big Sioux, Vermillion, and James rivers. The major western streams are the Grand, Moreau, Cheyenne, Bad, White, and Keya Paha rivers. The two largest natural lakes are Big Stone and Traverse, both in the northeast; the many large artificial lakes include Lake Oahe.

Vegetation, Animal Life, and Resources. Vegetation ranges from tall prairie grasses in the east to short steppe grasses in the west. Coniferous forests cover the Black Hills, and some deciduous trees such as elm, oak, box elder, and cottonwood occur along streams and in eastern shelterbelts. Animal life varies from pheasant, jackrabbit, and coyotes to antelope and bison.

South Dakota's resources include fertile farmlands, rich grazing areas, and forests. Minerals include gold, copper, silver, lead, iron, uranium, lignite, and petroleum. Reservoirs on the Missouri River impound surface water. The state has great concern for the environment, with citizens increasingly involved in environmental decisions.

PEOPLE

South Dakota has a population of 695,500 (1979 est.), giving it a density of 3.5 persons per km² (9 per mi²). In recent years the state has experienced heavy out-migration due to a lack of jobs. The population is 44.6% urban; RAPID CITY and SIOUX FALLS are the two principal cities; ABERDEEN and PIERRE are also important.

The population is predominantly white, with only 5% Indian and 0.3% black. Many settlers came from New England and New York, and the major European immigrants were German, Norwegian, Swedish, and Danish. The major religious groups are Lutheran, Roman Catholic, and Methodist.

Education, Culture, and Communications. Public school districts were organized in 1865 but were reorganized in 1968 to

place a greater emphasis on regional schools. Their enrollment in 1977 was 143,531 students in 195 districts. About 13,114 students (1977) attended 159 private schools in the state. South Dakota has 7 state institutions of higher education (see SOUTH DAKOTA, STATE UNIVERSITIES AND COLLEGES OF). Augustana College (1860) in Sioux Falls is the largest of several private colleges in the state. More than 125 libraries serve South Dakota.

Cultural development began with opera houses that were set up in mining camps. Excellent museums include art museums at Brookings and Vermillion; Indian and geological museums at Rapid City; the Adams Museum at Deadwood, with historical exhibits; and the Pettigrew Museum in Sioux Falls, with Indian, historical, and natural history exhibits. Theater is popular, with many programs centered on the college campuses. South Dakota has 12 daily and 110 weekly newspapers. It is served by 51 radio stations and 11 television stations.

Tourism and Recreation. Historic sites include DEADWOOD, an old mining town that included figures like Calamity Jane and Wild Bill Hickok among its residents; Yankton, the state's first white settlement; Fort Pierre, the site of the earliest trading post; and the WOUNDED KNEE Battlefield, located near Pine Ridge in the Oglala Sioux Indian reservation. Mount RUSHMORE is a national memorial in the Black Hills. National parks include Badlands and Wind Cave (limestone caverns located in the Black Hills). Recreational activities—hunting, fishing, camping, boating, skiing, and skating—take place in South Dakota's 4 national parks and 33 major state recreation areas.

ECONOMIC ACTIVITY

South Dakota is still a predominantly agricultural state, but both tourism and manufacturing have increased in importance since World War II, and mining is a vital part of the state economy.

Manufacturing and Energy. Manufacturing is growing rapidly, with meat packing the largest single industry in the state. Other major industries are food products, lumber, electrical equipment, stone products, and medical products. The 1976 value added by manufacturing was $494 million. All food processing was valued at $116.9 million.

The four federal dams on the Missouri River, smaller hydroelectric plants, and coal-burning plants furnish residents with excellent access to electrical power. In 1977, South Dakota produced 8 billion KW h of electricity—5.3 billion KW h from hydroelectric sources and 2.7 billion KW h from mineral sources. Natural gas supplies are limited to extreme eastern and western cities.

Agriculture and Forestry. Agriculture is the most important segment of the economy. Livestock production accounted for about 70% of the agricultural income of $1.6 billion in 1977. South Dakota's 43,000 farms in 1978 averaged more than 420 ha (1,050 acres) in size. The principal crops are wheat, hay, corn, and small grains; South Dakota is the leading U.S. producer of rye, second in flax, and third in durum wheat. The state's 60 forest-product firms in the Black Hills utilize the ponderosa pine as the principal source of timber.

Mining and Transportation. The Homestake Mine in Lead is the nation's largest gold mine. Other major minerals are sand, gravel, and stone. Uranium was discovered in 1951 and petroleum in 1953. Mining was valued at $102 million in 1976.

About 132,600 km (82,400 mi) of highways are located in South Dakota, including 1,110 km (690 mi) of interstate highway. Railroad service is declining; less than 5,300 km (3,300 mi) of track remains, and no passenger service is provided. Four airlines serve nine cities.

GOVERNMENT AND POLITICS

The state constitution was adopted in 1889. It provides for a 35-member senate and a 70-member house of representatives, with members of both houses serving 2-year terms. Both legislative bodies are reapportioned every 10 years. The executive branch is composed of a governor, lieutenant governor, and 6 administrative officials elected to 4-year terms. The judiciary is composed of a supreme court with 5 judges who serve 8-year terms, and 36 circuit court judges who also serve for 8 years. All judges are elected on a nonpartisan ballot. The state is divided into more than 3,500 units of local government.

South Dakota has usually been a staunchly Republican state. A notable exception occurred during the drought and depression of the 1890s, when South Dakota supported the Populist party; the state elected a Populist governor and voted overwhelmingly for Democratic and Populist candidate William Jennings Bryan in the 1896 presidential election. The state returned to the Republican cause, however, with the return of prosperity and has continued to vote for Republican candidates, except for Theodore Roosevelt on the Progressive ticket in 1912, for Franklin D. Roosevelt in 1932 and 1936, and for Lyndon B. Johnson in 1964.

HISTORY

Evidence indicates the presence of hunters in South Dakota as early as 7,000 years ago. About AD 500 the MOUND BUILDERS appeared along the Big Sioux River. By 1250 settlers who may have been the forebears of the ARIKARA tribe arrived, constructing fortresses with a capacity to contain up to 5,000 people, along the Missouri River. By the 16th century, the Arikara inhabited the area. Their fortified villages served as centers for agriculture, horse trading, military, and tribal organization.

The territory was explored (1742–43) by the brothers François and Louis Joseph La Vérendrye, who claimed the land for France. In 1762, France ceded the area (which was part of the huge territory called Louisiana) to Spain, and thereafter both the SIOUX Indians and European fur traders began filtering into the territory. The Sioux, changing from a sedentary to a hunting existence, pushed the Arikara westward. This conflict, as well as susceptibility to European diseases, caused the downfall of the Arikara.

In 1803 the United States acquired the area as part of the Louisiana Purchase. Trading posts such as Fort Pierre (established 1817) prospered from the fur trade. The first permanent European settlement was at Yankton in 1859, following a treaty with the Yankton Sioux. In 1862, Yankton became the capital of the newly established Dakota Territory. In the next decade settlements were established along the Missouri River and its tributaries, and the number of settlements increased rapidly with the coming of the railroad in the 1870s.

In 1874, Gen. George CUSTER led an exploratory expedition into the Black Hills, discovering gold. With the resultant influx of settlers, new towns such as Deadwood were established. With new settlers, conflicts with the Sioux intensified, as much of the land had previously been granted to the Sioux

(Left) *Combines harvest wheat on a farm situated along the Missouri River Valley, which traverses South Dakota along a north-southeast axis. South Dakota harvested 1,220,533 ha (3,016,000 acres) of wheat in 1977, and the crop ranked second in value in the state behind hay.*

(Below) *A herd of Hereford cattle are watered at a small pond. South Dakota's farm economy is dominated by livestock and related products. In 1978 almost 4 million head of cattle were being raised on its ranches, found mostly in the eastern portion of the state.*

Indians, attempting to preserve their unique cultural heritage, reenact a ceremonial dance, wearing garb similar to that worn by their ancestors. Eight Indian reservations are in South Dakota, and more than 1 million ha (2.47 million acres) of the state are tribally owned.

by treaty. Although General Custer and his troops were defeated (1876) at the Battle of the LITTLE BIGHORN, Indian resistance was finally crushed (1890) with the massacre at Wounded Knee (1890). Since then, the Indian population has primarily resided on the seven reservations in South Dakota. Their population has grown to an estimated 35,000 persons today.

With the opening of land to homesteading, the population increased to 281,000 by 1890; the lands east of the Missouri were settled mostly by northern Europeans. Pressure for statehood ensued, but the movement was delayed by the Democrats in Washington who were reluctant to add another predominantly Republican state. North and South Dakota finally became states simultaneously on Nov. 2, 1889.

Under the governorship of Peter Norbeck (1917–21) constitutional amendments sponsored by the Progressive wing of the Republican party enabled the state government to become involved in various commercial enterprises such as railroad rates regulation, coal mining, insurance, and credit. With the exception of the state cement plant, these failed dismally and left South Dakota deeply in debt by the mid-1920s. These failures combined with the Depression and the Dust Bowl droughts of 1933 and 1934 to put the state into a financial crisis that was not resolved until 1946. By 1933 one farm in every ten was lost by foreclosure or tax sale. After World War II, however, this rate changed to one in every 1,000.

Since World War II the state has progressed rapidly, building a strong agricultural base on which to develop expanding tourism, industry, and commerce. By 1950 tenancy and mortgage indebtedness were at record lows. Road construction has boomed. Tourism has increased rapidly, and industrialization is on the rise. The discovery of oil in 1953 and the potential wealth of undeveloped minerals augers well for the future.   EDWARD P. HOGAN

Bibliography: Federal Writers' Project, *South Dakota: A Guide to the State,* 2d ed. (1952); Hogan, E. P., *Geography of South Dakota* (1976); Hogan E. P., et al., *Atlas of South Dakota* (1970); Jennewein, John L., and Boorman, Jane, eds., *Dakota Panorama* (1961; repr. 1973); Karolevitz, Robert F., *Challenge: The South Dakota Story,* 2d ed. (1979); Milton, John R., *South Dakota* (1977); Schell, Herbert S., *A History of South Dakota,* 3d ed. (1975), and *South Dakota: A Students' Guide to Localized History* (1971).

South Dakota, state universities and colleges of

All of South Dakota's state universities are coeducational and offer undergraduate and graduate programs. **The University of**

South Dakota (1862; enrollment: 6,000; library: 410,000 volumes), at Vermillion, is coeducational, as are South Dakota's public universities and colleges. It offers undergraduate and graduate degrees and has schools of business, law, nursing, medicine, and education. A 4-year campus is at Springfield (1881; enrollment: 827; library: 86,000 volumes).

South Dakota State University (1881; enrollment: 6,420; library: 310,000 volumes) in Brookings is a land-grant school offering courses in liberal arts and emphasizing those in sciences and technology. State colleges are **Black Hills State** (1883; enrollment: 1,900; library: 97,000 volumes), at Spearfish; **Dakota State** (1881; enrollment 1,000; library 69,000 volumes), at Madison; and **Northern State** (1901; enrollment: 1,700; library: 175,000 volumes), at Aberdeen. The **South Dakota School of Mines and Technology** (1885; enrollment: 1,800; library: 170,000 volumes), at Rapid City, grants bachelor's and master's degrees in many fields of science and doctorates in some.

South India, Church of

The Church of South India is the result of the union of churches of varying traditions—Anglican, Methodist, Congregational, Presbyterian, and Reformed—in that area. It was inaugurated in September 1947, after protracted negotiation among the churches concerned.

Organized into 16 dioceses, each under the spiritual supervision of a bishop, the church as a whole is governed by a synod, which elects a moderator (presiding bishop) every 2 years. Episcopacy is thus combined with synodical government, and the church explicitly recognizes that episcopal, presbyterial, and congregational elements are all necessary for the church's life. The Scriptures are the ultimate standard of faith and practice. The historic creeds are accepted as interpreting the biblical faith, and the sacraments of baptism and the Lord's Supper are recognized as of binding obligation.

The Church of South India represents the first successful attempt since the Reformation to unite episcopal and nonepiscopal communions and for this reason is regarded as an ecumenical landmark. It has a membership (1980) of about 1.25 million.   CHARLES W. RANSON

Bibliography: Hollis, Michael, *The Significance of South India* (1966); Sundkler, Bengt, *Church of South India,* rev. ed. (1965).

South Moluccans: see AMBONESE.

South Pole

The South Pole is that location marking the southern end of the Earth's axis of rotation. The pole is located on the continent of Antarctica, at 90° south latitude, and, along with the North Pole, is one of two locations on Earth that receive 6 months of continuous daylight and 6 months of continuous darkness each year. The South Pole has an altitude of 2,800 m (9,186 ft). It was first reached by Roald AMUNDSEN in 1911.
                                                                                 ROBERT S. WEINER

South Sea Bubble

The South Sea Bubble is the name given to a speculative boom in England that collapsed in 1720. The financial disaster was caused by the South Sea Company, founded for trade in 1711. Stock in the company sold well, and by 1718 investors were receiving 100 percent interest. In 1720 the company proposed—and Parliament accepted—that it take over much of the national debt. This move created a wave of speculation in the company's stock, which rose from £128½ in January to £1,000 in August. In September the bubble burst. Stocks plummeted, banks failed, and investors were ruined. Robert WALPOLE, however, was able to restore the company's credit and save the Whig government.

Bibliography: Carswell, John, *The South Sea Bubble* (1960); Cowles, Virginia, *The Great Swindle* (1960).

South Sea Islands: see OCEANIA.

South West Africa: see NAMIBIA.

Southampton [sowth-amp'-tuhn]

Southampton is a port city of 212,200 (1977 est.) in southern Hampshire, England, where the rivers Test and Itchen combine to form the estuary of Southampton Water. The Isle of Wight shelters the approaches to the harbor. Southampton's principal industry is the building and repairing of ships. Extensive docks, some built as early as 1831, include a deepwater quay 2.4 km (1.5 mi) long and a dry dock capable of accommodating the largest ocean liners. Southampton is also a leading port dealing with miscellaneous goods, particularly imported foodstuffs. It is also the site of the University of Southampton (1952).

Romans and Saxons settled on the site, and after the Norman Conquest (1066), Southampton served as England's chief military base and port. In the 18th century Southampton was a fashionable resort, becoming an important port once again after the arrival of the railroad from London (1840) and the construction of modern docks. It was heavily bombed during World War II.

Southampton Island

Southampton Island, at the entrance to Hudson Bay, in Canada's Northwest Territories, has an area of about 40,660 km² (15,700 mi²). Sighted in 1613 by Thomas Button, it was used as a whaler's base from 1860 to 1920.

Southeast Asia

Southeast Asia, a term used since World War II, usually refers to the region south of China and east of India and includes Thailand, Laos, Vietnam, Kampuchea (Cambodia), Burma, Indonesia, Malaysia, the Philippines, and Singapore. Europeans began to penetrate the area during the 16th century and gradually colonized it, with the exception of Thailand. Since World War II most of the area has achieved independence; the remaining colonies are British Brunei and Portuguese Timor. Strategically significant, Southeast Asia was the locus of heavy fighting during World War II, when most of the area was overrun by the Japanese. Repeated conflicts have also occurred in the postwar period—wars of independence, communist insurgencies, and the prolonged Vietnam War.

Bibliography: Steinberg, David, et al., *In Search of Southeast Asia* (1971); Williams, Lea E., *Southeast Asia: A History* (1976).

Southeast Asia Treaty Organization

A treaty signed in Manila in 1954 by Australia, France, Great Britain, New Zealand, Pakistan, the Philippines, Thailand, and the United States created the Southeast Asia Treaty Organization (SEATO), a defensive alliance. Its protective umbrella was meant to shelter the Asian signatories in addition to Cambodia, Laos, and South Vietnam under a special protocol. The signatories pledged collective action in case of external aggression or internal subversion against any one of them, as well as economic cooperation, but the priority was always on anticommunist and military measures. SEATO's creation had been urged by U.S. Secretary of State John Foster Dulles in the wake of the French defeat (1954) in Indochina by communist forces.

Unlike NATO, SEATO never secured long-term military commitments from its members, and SEATO members were reluctant to support U.S. involvement in the Vietnam War. In 1972, following the Indo-Pakistani War, Pakistan withdrew from SEATO; and in 1977, the organization, which had maintained headquarters in Bangkok, was dissolved.

Southeast Asian art and architecture

Southeast Asian art and architecture comprises the artistic traditions of the southeastern Asian mainland and a vast arc of islands extending from Sumatra in the west to Sulawesi (Celebes) in the east. The present-day countries in this area include Burma, Thailand, Laos, Vietnam, Kampuchea (Cambodia), Malaysia, and Indonesia. The Philippines, although in many ways similar to the other countries of Southeast Asia, never shared in the main cultural influence that united the rest—the spread of Indian culture, which took place gradually from about AD 20 to about 1200. During this era first traders and then colonists from India settled along the coasts and principal rivers and roads of Southeast Asia, establishing dynasties that came to rule the surrounding territory and compete for the great wealth of the region. In the wake of Indian merchants and settlers came the two major Indian religions, Hinduism and Buddhism, which provided the inspiration for most Southeast Asian monumental art. Lastly, the travels of Buddhist monks and pilgrims were a significant factor in the cultural evolution of this vast and disparate region.

Indigenous Folk Traditions. Prior to the impact of Indian culture, Southeast Asia seems to have been a part of the great web of animist culture and religion that still extends out through New Guinea and the Melanesian, Micronesian, and Polynesian islands of the Pacific (see OCEANIC ART). Vestiges of animist culture can still be found today in Southeast Asia, permeating, in modified forms, the superimposed layers of "higher" civilization.

The indigenous tribal cultures upon which Indianization was imposed flourished in cleared villages set in densely forested terrain. With the aid of stone tools, tribal artisans used wood, especially the omnipresent bamboo, to build houses and shrines and to carve artistic objects such as funereal effigies. The houses seem to have followed a fairly consistent pattern throughout the region: even today, a close generic similarity appears in the dwellings made by such geographically dispersed peoples as the BATAK of northern Sumatra, the highland tribes of Laos, the BALINESE islanders, the DAYAK of Borneo, and the Toradja of central Sulawesi. Common elements include floors raised on piles; strong center and corner posts; woven or plank walls; and vast, towering gable roofs masking complex inner structures and usually covered with palm fronds or thatch. Some of the most important structures are painted in brilliant colors.

The stylized designs of these structures refer to spirit beings and to ceremonials, especially buffalo sacrifice. According to animist beliefs, the spirits of the dead are to be pacified and worshiped if they are ancestors, enslaved if they are enemies; therefore, the cult worship of the skull as a recepta-

A Toradja house in Sulawesi (Celebes), Indonesia, is decorated with the brilliantly painted abstract motifs typical of indigenous folk art. Architectural designs such as these are associated with the traditional animistic religious beliefs of the Indonesian peoples.

cle of a dead person's spirit traditionally has pervaded the whole area. Many tribes made (and still make) *korvars* (wooden figures in which the skulls of ancestors are incorporated); most villages have skull shrines; and the original designs of the predyed and woven ceremonial textiles called ikat appear to represent early references to the dead, to skulls, and to spirit beings. A sense that the countryside teems with spirits, good and bad, even today informs the culture of the entire region. The presence of the spiritual is expressed particularly in ornamental forms: among the many objects still looked on with religious awe as repositories of spiritual power are large and small stones, bronze drums, and finely ornamented swords called kris or keris.

Prehistoric stone tools were made of a variety of stones, including semiprecious jasper, agate, and chalcedony. The more sophisticated tools were produced in two principal forms: the adze, or ax, of rectangular section, which seems to have been distributed southeastward from Malaysia into the Indonesian islands; and the pickadze, triangular or five sided in section, with a top rib. Ancient examples of these implements are still treasured as powerful communal AMULETS.

Ancient Megalithic and Dong-son Cultures. By about 1000 BC, the people known as the MON of Thailand and southern Burma apparently were making large stone funerary monuments that were ornamented with figures. These monuments may have been connected with a megalithic culture extending westward beyond India and southern Arabia through Malaysia and Indonesia. On some of the Indonesian islands, notably Sumatra, evidence suggests that such megalithic monuments were made until relatively recently. Sizable stone coffins finely carved in the round have been found at Lake Toba on Sumatra, and ornamented menhirs (freestanding stones) appear on various islands.

About 700 BC an important bronze-using culture appeared on the Tonkin plain, in present-day northern Vietnam. Called Dong-son, after one of its principal sites, this culture seems to have spread by sea along the mainland coast and down into the main islands of Indonesia. Along with the first really extensive use of bronze, the Dong-son disseminated throughout the region a decorative style related to that of the late Chou period (770–221 BC) in China. The chief characteristic of the Dong-son style is the frequent use of heavy, slightly square spirals in relief; other motifs include key patterns and rows of dots. Although Dong-son artists decorated lamps, weapons, bowls, huge ceremonial jars shaped like axes, and in-the-round human and animal figures, their most important works were large bronze drums, or drum-shaped gongs, that perhaps were used in rain ceremonials. Of the many such drums dating from the period 500–100 BC, as well as the later imitations that survive, the largest, known as the Moon of Bali, stands 1.8 m (6 ft) high and is still revered in the temple at Pedjeng, Bali. In Thailand, these drums apparently were looked on as sacred symbols of power and royalty. On some Indonesian islands, small versions cast in stone molds are still

used in the traditional payment of BRIDE-PRICE. After the Dong-son homeland was occupied (111 BC) by the Han Chinese, Dong-son culture waned throughout the region, eclipsed by Chinese and, later, Indian influence.

CAMBODIA AND VIETNAM

Artistically as well as politically, the most important of the Indianized cultures of ancient Southeast Asia was that of Cambodia. Cambodia probably was first colonized from India in the 1st century AD, when a kingdom known to the Chinese as Funan was established on the lower Mekong River. The Funan state was succeeded in the 5th century by another kingdom, known as Chen-la, centered upriver in what is now Laos. A vast number of Funan and Chen-la sites remain to be excavated. Among artworks that have already been recovered is a remarkable series of powerfully sculpted stone images of Buddhist and Hindu deities, along with a few remaining wooden Buddha figures. Such works probably stood in brick shrines, where they provided a cultural and ceremonial focus at first for the colonies of Indian settlers and then for the entire local population. Although these early Cambodian works echo the sensuousness and concern for anatomical detail characteristic of Indian sculpture, they also display an architectonic and monumentalized quality foreign to Indian art.

The full flowering of Cambodian culture took place under the KHMER EMPIRE, which ruled much of what is present-day Cambodia and Laos from the 7th to the 15th century. Firmly based in Indian culture and artistic motifs, Khmer art gradually assumed a distinct identity characterized by grandiose and monumental forms, particularly in architecture and architectural decoration. An increasingly important emphasis on the exalted status of god-kings led successive Khmer monarchs to build increasingly elaborate religious edifices, from the isolated brick towers of the 7th century to the vast com-

(Above) *The delicate bas-reliefs that ornament the gallery walls of Angkor Wat depict mythological and legendary scenes, especially the events associated with Vishnu, the Hindu deity to whom the shrine is dedicated. This elegant relief sculpture, covering almost every open space of gallery wall, was originally painted and gilded. The city of Angkor was the capital of the Khmer empire from AD 880 until the 13th century.*

(Left) *Angkor Wat, the greatest temple of the sacred city of Angkor, Kampuchea, remains one of the most impressive examples of temple architecture. Constructed during the early 12th century, the elaborate architectural design of Angkor Wat is derived from the stupa form and represents the golden age of Khmer art. The compound at Angkor Wat covers an area of 1,500 by 1,300 m (4,920 by 4,265 ft) and is surrounded by a 180-m-wide (590-ft) moat.*

plex built (9th–13th century) at ANGKOR. At Angkor, the larg-est integrated complex of architecture and sculpture ever built, a net of huge reservoirs and canals encloses the great temple mountains of successive kings—the monumental stone structures at which they maintained spiritual contact with their Hindu patron deities. Comprising assemblages of shrines linked by cloisters, corridors, and stairways, these structures grew in size as each king strove to outdo his predecessors in the glory of his own building. Culminating in the colossal (1,500-by-1,300-m/4,920-by-4,265-ft) Angkor Wat built by Suryavarman II (r. 1113–50), all the temple mountains of Angkor were filled with three-dimensional images and miles of relief sculpture that covered every inch of available wall space. After Angkor Wat was sacked (1177) by the Cham, Jayavarman VII (r. 1181–c.1218) constructed the biggest shrine of all, called the Bayon, inside his own city, Angkor Thom. The 15th-century conquest of the Khmer kingdom by the Thais resulted (1431) in the final abandonment of Angkor.

Until the ascendancy of the Thais, Khmer dominance of much of Southeast Asia was contested only by the Champa kingdom, an Indianized, largely Hindu state that flourished in central and southern Vietnam. The Cham people, whose his-tory reflects a long (1st–15th century) struggle for existence pressed between the Chinese and the Khmer, built a series of small but elaborately ornamented Hindu tower shrines, first (4th–11th century) at Mi Son in the north, then (11th–15th century) at Binh Dinh in the south. A characteristic feature of Cham temple architecture is the multilobed arches above porticoes and windows, decorated with carved foliage spring-ing from the mouth of a monster. Cham sculpture is notable for its powerfully modeled forms. Most other art of ancient Vietnam, known to us only in fragments, can be described as provincial versions of Chinese models.

THAILAND
The first great dynastic state of present-day Thailand was the Dvaravati kingdom established (6th century) by the Eastern Mon people. Between the 6th and 11th century, the largely Buddhist Mon produced a significant body of STUPA (Buddhist temple mounds) architecture, of which only fragments remain at Nakhon Pathom, Ku Bua, U Thong, and elsewhere. The most important examples of Mon–Dvaravati art to survive are Buddhist sculptures of the 6th–8th century, executed in bronze or stone, that reflect the influence of contemporary northern Indian sculpture but display typically Mon faces, with delicate, turned-out lips and almond-shaped eyes. Mon-Dvaravati art also was strongly affected by that of a powerful but thus far enigmatic Sumatran kingdom called Shrivijaya. The famous, elegant *Bodhisattva Torso* (8th century; National Museum, Bangkok) from Chaiya may be a Shrivijaya work. In the 11th century, southern Dvaravati became part of the Khmer Empire, and Khmer styles of architecture and sculpture were imposed, notably at Phimai and Lopburi.

The eclipse of the Dvaravati kingdom was followed by infil-tration into northern Thailand of the ethnic THAI, an animist

This 14th-century bronze Buddha with his right hand resting in the traditional position of calling the earth to witness (bhumisparsa) belongs to the high Classic period of Sukhodaya art. Artisans at Sukhothai, a Buddhist city of central Thailand, worked prolifically in bronze, abandoning the elaborate designs of Khmer art to produce pieces noted for their simplicity and fluidity. Buddhist art in Thailand, most fully developed in sculpture, was greatly influenced by the art of Ceylon (Sri Lanka).

people who adopted the Theravada Buddhism of Ceylon and whose northern capital was at Chiengmai. After the Khmer downfall in the 13th century, another Thai branch established a kingdom (fl. 1350–1767) in the southern and central areas of the country, with its capital at AYUTHIA (Ayuthaya). Control over the great Buddhist city of Sukhothai, a city that main-tained special links with Ceylon, was continually disputed be-tween the northern and southern Thais. The principal Thai ar-chitectural form was a tall, tapering, bell-shaped, ornamented stupa set amid associated monastic structures. Large-scale sculpture, the principal art of Sukhothai and Ayuthia, was de-voted to sacred, highly spiritualized bronze Buddha icons. During the 14th century, Sukhothai produced a basic set of Buddha types whose smooth and sinuously curved surfaces, looped linear features, and tightly curled hair crowned by a flame or lotus-bud headdress are well represented in the so-called *Walking Buddha* (14th century; Monastery of the Fifth King, Bangkok). Two other sculptural styles, the northern Chieng Sen type (15th–16th century) and the southern U Tong type (14th–16th century), evolved later. Close versions of these three types, both large scale and small scale, are still made today. Paintings in styles related to Thai sculpture adorned the interiors of shrines and halls which in later cen-turies reflected Burmese influence. Fine ceramics, versions of Chinese originals, were made in Thailand from the 14th cen-tury on, notably at Sawankhalok, Sukhothai, and Chiengmai.

BURMA
Burmese art also was predominantly Buddhist. During the earliest phase, between the 6th and 11th centuries, present-day Burma was divided into two distinct zones. In the north flourished the kingdom of the Pyu people, which was known to the Chinese for its large and wealthy cities. Still extant at Hmawza, the Pyu capital, are three huge brick stupas whose cylindrical structures and bell-shaped domes set the pattern for all later Burmese stupas. Southern Burma was ruled by the Western Mon, who were confederated with, and shared the art styles of, the Dvaravati culture. During the 10th century the north was infiltrated by the ethnic Burmese, an animist people who introduced a set of spirit beings called the 36 *nats*, which are still being portrayed in Burmese sculpture. When they were converted to Theravada Buddhism, the Bur-mese included the Buddha as the 37th *nat*.

In the 11th century, the Burmese king Anawrahta united the entire country and carried off Mon monks and craftsmen to his northern capital, PAGAN, which was continually embel-lished and expanded until the Mongol conquest of 1287. Pa-gan still stands today, the largest surviving example of the great medieval complexes of brick and plaster that once were widespread in Southeast Asia. Its temples are centrally planned complexes in which four axially disposed, roofed ap-proaches converge on a stupalike tower that rises from the

The celestial dancer (10th century), a sandstone architectural decoration from one of the Hindu tower shrines at the holy city of Mi Son, Vietnam, reflects the powerful sculptural rendering peculiar to Cham art. The kingdom of Champa, whose culture was strongly influenced by Indian religious and artistic concepts, flourished in Vietnam from the 2d to the 17th century. (Museé Henri Parmentier, Da Nang.)

(Right) *The Shwesandaw cetiya (1047), a Burmese architectural innovation combining the attributes of stupa and shrine, stands in the ruins of Pagan, the capital of Burma until the late 13th century. Within this cetiya, which consists of 5 square, receding terraces resting on an octagonal base, are contained Buddhist relics.* (Below) *The structure of the Buddhist monument (800) at Borobudur, Java, designed with 8 diminishing terraces connected by stairways, symbolically re-creates the Buddha's path toward spiritual enlightenment. A pilgrim ascends along the corridors (1) of the square lower terraces (2), representing this world, and then rounds 3 terraces of the world of God (3), rising in concentric rings of 72 stupas. Passageways (4) rise at each cardinal point from the first terrace to the summit. The top of the shrine is surmounted by the Great Stupa (5), goal of the pilgrimage and symbol of Eternal Truth.*

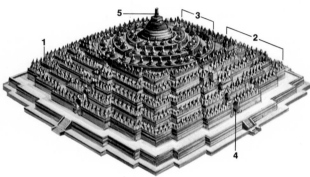

floor through to the sky. Inside are Buddha icons of brick. Narrative paintings and modest terra-cotta reliefs survive in some temples. Libraries and monastery halls, originally royal palace-pavilions, later were dedicated to religious uses.

In Southern Burma, notably at Rangoon and Mandalay, Buddhist followers built vast monastery complexes whose buildings have been continually torn down and refurbished with plaster cladding and gilt ornament. Right up to the present day, flaring porches, elaborately ornamented doors and finials, as well as whole halls have been added on, augmenting ancient building patterns by use of an aesthetic of glittering and expansive grace.

INDONESIA

Indian traders and settlers first reached the Indonesian islands in the 1st century AD, bringing with them both Buddhism and Hinduism. From the 3d to the 6th century, Buddhist monasteries apparently were built in the Sumatran kingdom of Shrivijaya and in Sulawesi, where a fine early bronze Buddha has been found. The Hindu dynasty that ruled central Java in the 7th century was replaced (8th–9th century) by the Buddhist Shailendra princes, who were devotees of Mahayana Buddhism. The oldest Javanese monuments, all undated, are Hindu shrines erected on volcanic mountain plateaus; they were dedicated to the god Shiva, who was identified thereafter with cosmic subterranean energy. The huge Buddhist stupa mountain of BOROBUDUR, built about 800 in stone and profusely decorated throughout with ornate sculpture, is the largest structural MANDALA (cosmic diagram) in the world. Its iconography summarizes Buddhist doctrine concerning both the cosmos and spiritual enlightenment. Other 9th-century Shailendra temples, such as those at Kalasar (8th century) and at Mendut and Sari (both 9th century), incorporate similar but more condensed doctrinal summaries.

The largest Javanese religious complex is the Hindu shrine of Lara Jonggrang, built about 900 at PRAMBANAN. Originally 232 separate temples were incorporated into the Prambanan complex; the fact that its temple towers are adorned with rows of small Buddhist stupas illustrates how the two great Eastern religions intermingled in ancient Indonesia. Superb figure sculpture depicting Hindu epics runs around the balconies in a manner similar to the Buddhist work at Borobudur.

An eastern Java dynasty that arose in the 10th century built temples in the form of open courts with small stone shrines; the chief examples are located at volcanic springs—notably Belahan, where royal tomb chambers were cut into low cliffs. Beginning in the 11th century, relief sculpture developed toward the deeply incised and caricatured forms of what is now known as the Wayang puppet style, although splendid three-dimensional icons of Hindu and Buddhist deities were still executed. Particularly fine reliefs are the 14th-century terra-cotta panels that once adorned the walls of the capital city of Majapahit with elaborate landscape images as well as figures of deities and spirits.

In the 15th century, Islam largely supplanted Indian culture throughout Indonesia, except in Bali, where a modified but fascinating form of East Javanese religion survives today. The colorful ceremonies still performed in terraced courts of Balinese shrines give some idea of what life around older shrines must have been like in their heyday.

PHILIP S. RAWSON

Bibliography: Bernet Kempers, A. J., *Ancient Indonesian Art* (1959); Griswold, A. B., and Kim Ch'ewon Pott, P. H., *The Art of Burma, Korea, Tibet* (1964); Groslier, B. P., *The Art of Indochina including Thailand, Vietnam, Laos, and Cambodia* (1966) and *Indochina, Melting Pot of Races,* trans. by George Lawrence (1964); Rawson, P. S., *The Art of Southeast Asia* (1967) and *The Making of Indian Asia* (1977); Rowland, Benjamin, *The Art and Architecture of India,* 3d rev. ed. (1967; repr. 1977); Swaan, Wim, *Lost Cities of Asia* (1966); Wagner, F. A., *Indonesia, the Art of an Island Group* (1959); Zimmer, Heinrich R., *The Art of Indian Asia* (1955).

Southeast Asian languages

Approximately 1,000 mutually unintelligible languages are spoken in Southeast Asia, of which only the major national and regional languages have writing systems and literary traditions. From the standpoint of genetic relationship, the languages can be divided into nine separate stocks: Sinitic, or Chinese, Tibeto-Burman, Karen, Miao-Yao, Tai, Malayo-Polynesian, Mon-Khmer, Viet-Muong, and Papuan.

The first five stocks have traditionally been classed as Sino-Tibetan. It has also been proposed that Miao-Yao, Tai, and Malayo-Polynesian are related in an Austro-Thai stock. Most authorities agree that Viet-Muong is related to Mon-Khmer in an Austroasiatic stock, but the further affiliation of Austroasiatic with Malayo-Polynesian in an Austric superstock is more speculative. Some scholars suggest that all nine stocks are related in an Indo-Pacific family, but none of these larger groupings has been conclusively demonstrated.

Sinitic languages—particularly Cantonese, Hokkien, Hakka,

and Mandarin—are spoken by large Chinese communities in the major cities of Southeast Asia, such as Singapore, Bangkok, and Manila. Among the Tibeto-Burman languages are Burmese, the national language of Burma, and hundreds of related languages such as Chin and Kachin in Burma, Akha and Lisu in Thailand, and Lolo in Laos and Vietnam. Karen languages, spoken by small minorities on both sides of the Thai-Burmese border, are probably related to Tibeto-Burman. The Miao-Yao languages, also called Meo and Man, are found in northern Thailand, Laos, and Vietnam and are spoken by small numbers of relatively recent immigrants from southern China. The Tai family comprises Thai, or Siamese, and Lao—the national languages of Thailand and Laos—and such minority languages as Shan in the Shan states of Burma, and Black Tai, Nung, and Tho in northern Vietnam.

The Malayo-Polynesian family, also called Austronesian, stretches a third of the way around the globe, from Madagascar to Taiwan, and includes such national languages as Malay in Malaysia, Bahasa Indonesia in Indonesia, and Tagalog in the Philippines, as well as hundreds of regional and minority languages in these three countries and in the South Pacific.

The major representative of the Mon-Khmer family is Khmer, spoken in Kampuchea, formerly Cambodia, and in adjacent areas of Thailand and Vietnam. Other Mon-Khmer languages are found among approximately 100 minority groups, such as the Mon and Palaung in Burma, the Lawa and Kuy in Thailand, the So in Laos, the Bahnar, Stieng, and Bru in Vietnam, and the Semang and Senoi in Malaysia.

Viet-Muong includes Vietnamese plus several closely related Muong languages spoken in northern Vietnam. The Papuan languages are found among indigenous groups in eastern Indonesia, especially in West Irian; it has been suggested that these languages are related to those spoken in the Andaman Islands of India and to the languages of the Australian aborigines (see OCEANIC LANGUAGES).

Typologically, the Southeast Asian languages fall into two groups. The Sinitic, Tibeto-Burman, Karen, Miao-Yao, Tai and Viet-Muong tend to be monosyllabic and tonal, relying heavily on word order for their meaning. The Malayo-Polynesian, Mon-Khmer, and Papuan languages, on the other hand, are typically disyllabic and nontonal and make use of a certain number of grammatical affixes. Southeast Asian languages as a whole are characterized by complex systems of status-related personal pronouns, a high degree of semantic specialization in the verb, and the use of classifiers, or counters, in numerical noun phrases.   FRANKLIN E. HUFFMAN

Bibliography: LeBar, Frank M., Hickey, Gerald C., and Musgrave, John K., eds., *Ethnic Groups of Mainland Southeast Asia* (1964); LeBar, Frank M., ed., *Ethnic Groups of Insular Southeast Asia*, 2 vols. (1972-75); Zide, Norman H., *Studies in Comparative Austroasiatic Linguistics* (1966).

Southeast Asian universities

Southeast Asian universities are rapidly assuming a major independent role in national and regional development. This role reflects the various histories, educational traditions, and political goals of Dutch, English, French, Spanish, American, and, most recently, Communist rulers.

In colonial periods national development was not considered the university's primary goal. Colonial powers tried to suppress education—except to train people to run the country—as they thought it not in the countries' best interests. The first universities were established in Southeast Asia either to train native priests (as in the Roman Catholic institutions of the Philippines) or to educate and westernize a small, native elite in professional fields such as engineering, law, and medicine (as in the early colleges of the University of Indonesia). But in spite of such narrow purposes, small enrollments, and strict controls, these universities eventually became centers of rebellion and revolution and, after their countries' independence, graduated many of the leaders who consolidated national unity and planned the first development policies.

Providing such leadership after independence was achieved has required major changes in the size, organization, and

scope of Southeast Asian universities. With the help of foreign assistance programs (particularly from former colonial powers) and steadily increasing government budgets, new facilities have been built and thousands of lecturers have received further education. Older institutions have become truly national universities as enrollments and the number of programs have increased and new teaching methods have been introduced. New universities have begun to play greater roles in national development. Many institutions of the region have built their own graduate programs in economics, agriculture, and education and have begun to cooperate in Southeast Asian research and training programs.

SOUTHEAST ASIAN UNIVERSITIES

University and Location	Date Founded	Enrollment
Burma		
Arts and Science University, Rangoon	1920	7,200
Arts and Science University, Mandalay	1958	7,000
Cambodia		
University of Fine Arts, Phnom Penh	1965	*
University of Phnom Penh	1960	*
Indonesia		
Airlangga University, Surabaya	1954	5,000
Andalas University, Padang, West Sumatra	1956	4,000
Brawijaya University, Malang, East Java	1963	5,000
Diponegoro University, Semarang	1960	6,500
Gadjah Mada University, Yogjakarta	1949	15,600
University of Indonesia, Jakarta	1950	10,600
Pajajaran State University, Bandung, Java	1952	10,500
Laos		
University of Sisavangvong, Vientiane	1958	2,000
Malaysia		
University of Agriculture, Serdang	1971	3,100
University of Malaya, Kuala Lumpur	1962	8,600
National University of Malaysia, Selangor	1970	3,900
University of Science, Penang	1969	3,500
University of Technology, Kuala Lumpur	1972	2,900
Philippines		
Adamson University, Manila	1932	18,500
Bicol University, Legaspi City	1969	12,600
Central Escolar University, San Miguel	1907	10,400
University of the East, Manila	1946	66,000
Far Eastern University, Manila	1928	66,000
Feati University, Manila	1946	35,500
University of Manila, Manila	1913	10,700
University of Mindanao, Davao City	1946	20,600
University of Pangasian, Dagupan City	1925	11,000
Philippines Women's University, Manila	1919	8,500
University of the Philippines, Quezon City	1908	22,000
Manuel L. Quezon University, Manila	1947	14,500
University of Santo Tomas, Manila	1611	42,900
University of the Visayas, Cebu City	1919	20,000
Singapore		
Nanyang University, Singapore	1953	2,400
University of Singapore	1962	6,600
Thailand		
Chiang Mai University, Chiang Mai	1964	7,800
Chulalongkorn University, Bangkok	1917	15,900
Kasetsart University, Bangkok	1943	6,800
Sri Nakharinwirot University, Bangkok	1954	22,000
Thammasat University, Bangkok	1933	10,800
Vietnam		
University of Cantho	1966	4,550
University of Cao-Dai, Ho Chi Minh City	1971	650
University of Dalat	1957	3,500
University of Hanoi	1964	1,500
University of Hue	1957	6,500
University of Ho Chi Minh City, Ho Chi Minh City	1917	25,000
Van Hanh University, Ho Chi Minh City	1964	4,560

* Latest figures unavailable.

These impressive developments, however, have not re-solved several persistent problems in Southeast Asian higher education. As the importance of a university education has grown and the number of applicants to colleges and universities has increased, Southeast Asian governments have been forced to decide between expanding university enrollments and increasing educational quality. Indonesia, by refusing to build new universities, is focusing its resources on its 41 government institutions and nearly 300 private universities and teacher-training institutes. State universities have competitive entrance examinations. Educators have recommended that the number of universities be held steady in order to maintain high quality in education. Universities and colleges in the Philippines have a fairly general policy of open enrollment. As a result, the availability of education to the poor and the unemployed is increasing. The cost of an education at a private institution is often less than at a public institution. Malaysia, by not permitting private schools, is putting all of its resources into its 5 government universities; it plans to consolidate the public institutions in order to improve the quality of education. Whereas such policies have generally maintained and even improved the quality of the region's higher education, they have also restricted this education to less than 5 percent of the population. Because of high fees and few scholarship opportunities, few of the students come from lower-income or rural backgrounds.

An even greater dilemma facing Southeast Asian universities concerns their role in political and economic development. In the region's non-Communist countries they have become centers of antigovernment activity. Students criticize national development policies and the universities' role in training technocrats more interested in economic growth than in equality. They also criticize the elite character of the universities and the tendency of graduates to enter private enterprise rather than public service. Thus, although governments of Southeast Asia are putting their faith—and their resources—into universities so that they can play an even larger role in national development, many of these institutions, based on long traditions of academic questioning and political dissent, are challenging the purposes and programs of the development process.   SHELDON F. SHAEFFER

Bibliography: Nguyen-dinh-Hoa, *Higher Education in the Republic of Vietnam* (1965); Sinco, Vicente G., *Reflections on Education in the Philippines* (1970); Tapingkae, Amnuay, *The Growth of Southeast Asian Universities: Expansion versus Consolidation* (1974); Thomas, Robert Murray, *A Chronicle of Indonesian Higher Education* (1973); Yip, Yat Hoong, *Development of Higher Education in Southeast Asia: Problems and Issues* (1973).

Southern, Terry

An American novelist, humorist, and screenwriter, Terry Southern, b. Alvarado, Tex., May 1, 1924, mingles black humor, parody, and satire in outrageous proportions. His fiction includes *The Magic Christian* (1960; film, 1971); *Candy* (1964; film, 1968), his parody of an erotic novel; and *Red-Dirt Marijuana and Other Tastes* (1967), short stories. Southern also collaborated on the screenplays for *Dr. Strangelove* (1963), *The Loved One* (1964), and *Easy Rider* (1969).

Southern Christian Leadership Conference

The Southern Christian Leadership Conference (SCLC) is a U.S. civil-rights organization founded (1957) in Atlanta, Ga., under the leadership of Dr. Martin Luther KING, Jr. The SCLC reflected Dr. King's philosophy of assertive nonviolence and was intended to broaden the civil-rights effort through peaceful but potent demonstrations. In 1963 the SCLC campaigned for desegregation of restaurants, hotels, and department stores in Birmingham, Ala. It organized the 1963 March on Washington, where some 250,000 Americans gathered in support of civil-rights legislation. The organization also conducted voter-registration drives in the South, including one in 1965 that focused national attention on Selma, Ala., when the local police attempted to stop the drive. By the mid-1960s, however, the SCLC's policy of non-violence was being chal-lenged by more militant civil-rights groups, and after Dr. King's death in 1968, the organization began to lose its central role in the civil-rights movement.

See also: BLACK AMERICANS; CIVIL RIGHTS.

Southern Cross: see CRUX.

Southern Rhodesia: see ZIMBABWE   (Rhodesia).

southern white cedar

The southern white cedar, *Chamaecyparis thyoides*, is the common name for a swamp or bog tree in the cypress or cedar family, Cupressaceae. Native to freshwater swamps and bogs in eastern North America, this tree reaches 24 to 26 m (80 to 85 ft) in height. The crown is small and narrowly cone-shaped, composed of slender limbs and compressed, irregularly arranged branchlets. Its wood is light, soft, and fragrant and is used for boats, shingles, posts, and cabinetwork.

Southern Yemen: see YEMEN   (Aden).

Southey, Robert   [suhth'-ee]

Although poet laureate of England, Robert Southey, b. Bristol, Aug. 12, 1774, d. Mar. 21, 1843, is best remembered as an associate of Samuel Taylor Coleridge and William Wordsworth. Southey's epics, *Joan of Arc* (1796), *Thalaba* (1801), *Madoc* (1805), and *The Curse of Kehama* (1810), achieved some contemporary success but are now read only for their historical significance. His *Life of Nelson* (1813), *History of Brazil* (1810–19), and *History of the Peninsular War* (1823–32) established him as one of the outstanding prose stylists of his time. *The Doctor* (1834–47), a work of fiction, contains his rendition of the children's tale "The Three Bears."

After leaving Oxford without a degree in 1794, Southey joined Coleridge in planning "Pantisocracy," a utopian colony of farmer-philosophers on the Susquehanna River in Pennsylvania, but the project fell through. In 1795, Southey married Edith Fricker and commenced his lifelong career as a poet, journalist, reviewer, and political writer. He moved to Keswick in 1803 to renew his friendship with Coleridge and initiate a friendship with Wordsworth. The three poets were grouped and criticized by reviewers as the "Lake school" of poets, although this grouping was justified by little besides their Cumberland location. Southey was made poet laureate in 1813. His wife died in 1837 after several years of mental illness, an illness to which Southey himself succumbed in his later years. He remarried in 1839.

Southey's present reputation as a poet is negligible, but recent appraisals emphasize the continuing worth of his prose and the merit of his collected letters.   E. B. MURRAY

Bibliography: Carnall, Geoffrey, *Robert Southey and His Age* (1960); Curry, Kenneth, *Southey* (1975); Simmons, Jack, *Southey* (1945).

Southwell, Saint Robert   [sowth'-wel]

Robert Southwell, b. c.1561, d. Mar. 4, 1595, was an English Jesuit poet and martyr of the Elizabethan period. After studies in France and Rome he was ordained (1584) a priest and returned (1586) to London to serve as missionary to the oppressed Roman Catholics. Captured in 1592, he was arrested, tortured, and finally executed. Southwell's religious poetry prefigures that of George Herbert and Richard Crashaw. Southwell was canonized in 1970 as one of the Forty Martyrs of England and Wales. Feast day: Oct. 25.

Bibliography: Devlin, Christopher, *The Life of Robert Southwell*, 2d ed. (1967); Scallon, Joseph, *The Poetry of Robert Southwell* (1968).

Southworth, Albert Sands, and Hawes, Josiah Johnson

Pioneers of the booming American trade in portrait daguerreotypes in the 1840s, Albert Sands Southworth, b. West Fairlee, Vt., Mar. 12, 1811, d. 1894, and Josiah Johnson Hawes, b. East

Sudbury, Mass., Feb. 20, 1808, d. Aug. 7, 1901, are remembered for their rare ability to reveal character in an accurate likeness. Opening a studio together in Boston in 1843, they specialized in portraiture but also made fine landscapes. Among the many celebrities who sat for them were John Quincy Adams, Emerson, Oliver Wendell Holmes, Longfellow, and Daniel Webster. In spite of the long exposure required for daguerreotypes, the portraits by Southworth and Hawes are lively and expressive and mark a departure from the stiff poses favored by conventional photographers of the period.

Bibliography: Sobieszek, Robert A., and Appel, Odette M., *The Spirit of Fact: The Daguerreotypes of Southworth and Hawes* (1976).

Soutine, Chaim   [soo-teen', ky'-im]

The Head Valet, painted in 1928 by Russian emigrant to Paris, Chaim Soutine, is a brutal portrait of a servant in a changing modern world using flat shapes and violent brushwork to suggest psychological content. Soutine's expressionistically painted portrayals of anxious subjects are an important contribution to School of Paris painting. (Walter Guillaume Collection, Paris.)

A Russian-born painter of the school of Paris, Chaim Soutine, b. 1893, d. Aug. 9, 1943, produced works characterized by a violent expressionism. Having grown up in an orthodox Jewish family that was not only extremely poor but also strongly opposed to his artistic bent, Soutine moved to Paris in 1913. There, he became a friend of the painter Amedeo Modigliani, who—through his dealer Leopold Zborowski—helped him to achieve artistic notice and the financial security that came with the patronage of the American collector Dr. Albert C. Barnes. In Soutine's work, his unhappy memories seem to surface in the disturbed faces of the people he painted, the tumbled landscapes, and the famous still lifes with dead fowl or carcasses of beef. He generally smeared his canvases with a thick impasto of blood reds and gloomy grays and used savagely distorted proportions, as in *The Old Mill* (c.1922; Museum of Modern Art, New York City).   IRMA B. JAFFE

Bibliography: Tuchman, Maurice, *Chaim Soutine* (1968); Werner, Alfred, *Chaim Soutine* (1977).

Souvanna Phouma   [soo-vah'-nah foo'-mah]

The Laotian neutralist politician Prince Souvanna Phouma, b. Oct. 7, 1901, was prime minister (1951–54, 1956–58, 1960, 1962–75) of Laos. Educated as an engineer in France, he worked in Laos with the Public Works Service of Indochina from 1931 to 1950. He formed a coalition government with the communist Pathet Lao forces in 1974 and was ousted by the Pathet Lao under his half brother SOUPHANOUVONG in December 1975.

Bibliography: Dommen, Arthur J., *Conflict in Laos*, rev. ed. (1971); Fall, Bernard B., *Anatomy of a Crisis: The Laotian Crisis of 1960–1961*, ed. by Roger Smith (1969).

sovereignty

Sovereignty refers both to the powers exercised by an autonomous state in relation to other countries and to the su-

preme powers exercised by a state over its own members (see STATE, in political philosophy). In the context of international law, a sovereign state is independent and free from all external control; enjoys full legal equality with other states; governs its own territory; selects its own political, economic and social systems; and has the power to enter into agreements with other nations, to exchange ambassadors, and to decide on war or peace. A protectorate, because it has ceded some of its powers to another state, is not sovereign. Although a sovereign state theoretically enjoys absolute freedom, its freedom is, in fact, often abridged by the need to coexist with other countries, as well as by treaties, international laws, and the strength of its military power. Sovereign power, which is the power to make and enforce the law and to control the nation's finances and military establishment, may be vested in one person (a monarchy, for example), in a small group of people (an oligarchy), or in all the people, either directly or through representatives (a democracy). It may be limited by natural or divine law, constitutions, or customs.

Bibliography: Brierly, J. L., *The Law of Nations*, 6th ed. (1963); Hinsley, F. H., *Sovereignty* (1966); Jouvenal, Bertrand de, *Sovereignty: An Inquiry into the Political Good,* trans. by J. H. Huntington (1957).

soviet

The soviet, from the Russian word for "council," is the principal legislative and administrative unit in the USSR's formal power structure. Soviets operate at every level from villages to cities up to the Supreme Soviet, constitutionally the nation's highest legislative body. At lower levels they supervise local enterprises and cultural affairs; at higher levels they are usually legislative in nature. All deputies, or members of a soviet, carry out their duties in addition to holding full-time jobs.

Originally revolutionary workers' councils, soviets first emerged during the Revolution of 1905 and reappeared in the 1917 Revolution when the Petrograd (Leningrad) Soviet, led by Leon Trotsky, became an organ for the Bolsheviks' victory under the slogan "All Power to the Soviets."

Before the Stalin Constitution of 1936, lower soviets elected higher ones, but since then, according to that constitution, all soviets of every level are elected directly, with candidates screened by the party. The latest constitution (the Brezhnev Constitution) retains these features. In actuality, the soviets are the Communist party's instruments for implementing party policy.

Soviet education

At the time of the Revolution of October 1917 as much as 80% of the population of Russia was illiterate. Educational provision was totally inadequate as a result of many decades of neglect. A declaration was issued on October 29, 1917, within a week after the Bolsheviks assumed power, that there were to be free compulsory schools, teacher training, a unitary system of secular education for all, equal access by all to the highest level of education possible, a battle against illiteracy, and allocation of the necessary funds for education. In 1918 coeducation was decreed, a unitary work-school was proposed, and instruction in the mother tongue was allowed to the different national groups. Atheistic materialism was to be the basis of education. Famine, civil war, and the wars of intervention, however, aborted these plans. Political and religious conflicts generated by the policies of the proletariat dictatorship and by antireligious propaganda alienated many groups. All forms of punishment, homework, and examinations were abolished, and pupil councils were made responsible for organizing the work of the schools. Lenin decreed that the priority was the elimination of illiteracy. A chaotic regime dominated the schools—teachers were powerless, the theories and methods of instruction were inappropriate, and the economic, political, and social support systems were almost nonexistent. In 1931 a decree reforming the system removed the worst excesses of the revolutionary innovations. By 1934 the plan recognized three categories of compulsory education: elementary education for 4 years, beginning at age

8 (after 1943, from age 7); incomplete secondary education for 7 years; and complete secondary education for 10 years. Complete progress in implementing these plans throughout the Soviet Union was held back by the drive for collectivization and industrialization during the 1930s, by the preparation for and waging of war during the 1940s, and by reconstruction during the 1950s and '60s. The 1939 census showed that 87.4% of the population between the ages of 9 and 49 was literate; in 1959, virtually everyone in that age group was literate. At present, compulsory 10-year education is available throughout the Soviet Union.

The distinguishing and unique features of Soviet education are its attempt to realize Marx's view that education should be closely related to practical activity, that is, work; and that it should be based on science and on dialectical philosophy, involving militant atheism. These constitute twin educational and socialization problems with which the Soviets are continually confronted. Lenin's concept that education must be "socialist in content and nationalist in form" has been realized at the elementary school and sociocultural levels by emphasis on the mother tongue and native culture. The acceptance of science and technology as the basis of education, industrialization, and collectivization is reflected in the curricula at all levels. The periodic reviews of education and science attest to the Communist party's continuing concern for the integration of education and politics, of partisanship and the commitment to atheism, and of dialectics and Marxism. Other features of the educational system are disciplinary controls by student organizations—the Octobrists (ages 7-10), Young Pioneers (ages 10-15), and the Komsomol (ages 15-27); the close involvement of parental, social, and trade-union groups in the affairs of the school; the universal and centralized structure of the system; and the unitary character of the curriculum in the school system with all students studying the required subjects: Russian, one's native language, all branches of science, mathematics, literature, history, and, in the senior classes, logic, psychology, and politics. Teaching methods are very formal and cognitively oriented. Outstanding pupils receive gold, silver, or bronze medals on graduation. Correspondence schools and institutes provide instruction at all levels. Extracurricular activities such as sports, cultural activities, and hobbies are given in Pioneer Palaces and Children's Palaces. Boarding schools (which used to be available mainly to orphans and to children from large or poor families, and which are generally found in rural areas, where farms and schools are far apart), special schools for gifted children, and schools for handicapped children exist in the Soviet Union. Nursery schools and kindergartens are neither compulsory nor free of charge; fees are based on the parents' ability to pay. These schools are not available to all children. The right to elementary education for all citizens is guaranteed: it is compulsory for 10 years and free of charge at all levels. Stipends are paid to students who distinguish themselves. In spite of massive expenditures on education, resources are still in short supply. Students attend on a two-shift system, and many of the city schools are very old and unsuitable in accommodation. There is, however, a remarkable enthusiasm for education, although some hooliganism and vandalism are found in Soviet schools. In 1978, with more than 5 million students graduating from the 8-grade primary-school system, 6.1 million students were enrolled in general secondary schools (grades 9-10), 3.1 million in one-to-three-year vocational-technical schools, 4.8 million in schools for working and rural youth (part time), and 4.7 million in specialized secondary schools (for technicians, nurses, and elementary school teachers). Five million students were enrolled in universities and higher educational institutes (medical, engineering, agricultural, and pedagogical institutes), of which 45% were part-time students. The Soviet education budget was 22.5 billion rubles, or 9.3% of the total budget. The median number of years of schooling completed by the population 16 years of age and older was 8.7 in 1972.

Bibliography: Ablin, Fred, ed., *Contemporary Soviet Education* (1969) and *Education in the USSR*, 2 vols. (1963); Grant, Nigel, *Soviet Education*, 3d ed. (1979); Jacoby, Susan, *Inside Soviet Schools* (1974); John-son, William H., *Russia's Educational Heritage* (1950; repr. 1969); Kuzin, N. P., et al., *Education in the U.S.S.R.* (1972); Pennar, Jaan, et al., *Modernization and Diversity in Soviet Education* (1971); Tomiak, J. J., *Education in the Soviet Union* (1972).

Soviet labor camps: see GULAG.

Soviet literature: see RUSSIAN LITERATURE.

Soviet music: see RUSSIAN MUSIC.

Soviet Union: see UNION OF SOVIET SOCIALIST REPUBLICS; RUSSIA/UNION OF SOVIET SOCIALIST REPUBLICS, HISTORY OF.

Soya, Carl Erik Martin   [soh'-yah]

A controversial Danish playwright and novelist, Carl Soya, b. Oct. 30, 1896, shocked Scandinavian audiences of the 1930s and '40s with crude language, Freudian themes, and merciless satire of middle-class values. Soya also has written short stories, aphorisms, and verse. His most popular work is the semi-autobiographical novel *Grandmother's House* (1943), a treatment of a turn-of-the-century middle-class household from the point of view of a five-year-old.   RAYMOND JARVI

soybean

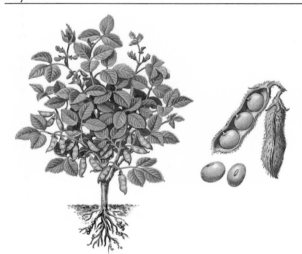

The soybean, G. max, one of the most important agricultural crops in the world, has ovate leaflets in groups of three, pink or purple flowers, and pods that contain one to three beans. A major source of protein, the beans are eaten fresh, made into meal, or processed into oil.

The soybean, *Glycine max*, is a leguminous crop grown in many parts of the world and is of great economic significance as a source of edible oil and of high-protein foods and stockfeed. It is a cultigen (a species created through cultivation) and is not known in the wild. Its wild ancestor is believed to be *Glycine ussuriensis*, a rambling vine native to northeastern Asia. Other relatives are found in parts of Asia and in Australia and Africa. Like many leguminous crops, the soybean has lost the winding and climbing growth pattern of its wild relatives. It is an erect, bushy herb growing to a height of 30-90 cm (1-3 feet) and developing a profusion of roots that may reach up to a meter or more (3-4 feet) in loose soils.

History. The cultivation of soybeans in China predates recorded history and spread from there to other countries in eastern Asia before the modern period. So essential was the soybean to Chinese civilization that it was considered one of the five sacred grains (the others being rice, barley, wheat, and millet). The popularity of soybeans in the Orient was due to their wide use as a food.

In the late 19th century the soybean plant attracted the attention of the U.S. Department of Agriculture (USDA), which began introducing a number of varieties into the United States. The vegetable oil industry became interested in the plant's potential. Starting in the 1930s, a large cooperative program involving both U.S. and Canadian researchers began to develop improved soybean varieties through selective breeding. This program led to the introduction of varieties that differed markedly from the original Asian plants. The new varieties had higher yields and oil content. With these new varieties, the United States became the world's leading producer of soybeans. The rapid increase in production in a period of little more than 30 years is one of the most striking developments in U.S. agricultural history.

From American strains, soybean cultivation has recently spread to numerous countries in Asia, Africa, and Latin America. Genetic improvement, which aims at higher yields as well as improved protein composition, began late in the United States. As a result, American soybeans represent a narrow range of genetic variation.

Cultivation and Characteristics. Soybeans do not tolerate frost and are photoperiod-sensitive, which means that flowering cannot begin until summer nights grow longer. Plants require abundant moisture and, in the absence of irrigation, do not do well in areas of winter precipitation such as Europe and Pacific America. Soybeans can be grown in nearly all types of soil but do best in fertile loams. Depending on the variety, soybean plants mature in 75 to 200 days. When used as a green manure, the plants are plowed under while still green. When used as hay, the soybeans are cut before they are completely ripe. After the leaves fall and the pods and stems dry naturally, the seeds are harvested with combines. Soybean seeds are hard, generally yellow, and pea-shaped. Like other leguminous plants, the soybean can associate with nitrogen-fixing bacteria in the soil.

Uses. Soybeans are an important human food because they are unusually complete in proteins: of the eight essential amino acids, soybeans contain seven in sufficient quantity and are deficient only in methionine, which can be supplied from wheat or corn. Soybeans are eaten in numerous ways—as a green or dried bean and as the constituent of soy milk, curds, cheese, and various sauces—and are a major source of vegetable oil. Soybean protein is increasingly used as a meat imitation, or meat substitute. Soybean products are also important in animal feeds, and the green crop is used for hay, forage, and as a fertilizer. In addition, a number of industrial uses have been developed: the manufacture of glycerin, paints, soaps, linoleum, rubber substitutes, plastics, and printing ink.

In the United States, almost half of the soybean oil produced is used in margarine and shortening, and another 20% is used to make other food products. Almost all of the soybean meal, the high-protein residue from the processing of soybean oil, is used to feed poultry and livestock.

Principal Areas of Cultivation. The world's three major national producers of soybeans are the United States (mainly the corn belt and the South), which produces 55%–60% of the world crop, and China and Brazil, which together account for more than a third of the world's production. The three countries contribute more than 90% of the world's production, which is in the range of 55–80 million metric tons annually. Minor producing countries, where soybeans are of some consequence, include Argentina, North and South Korea, Indonesia, the USSR (in its Far East region), and Canada. In Japan, production has dwindled in recent years. In 1978 the world production of soybeans was 80,232,000 metric tons, of which the United States produced 50,149,000, China 15,257,000, and Brazil 9,800,000.

Bibliography: American Soybean Association, *The Soybean Blue Book* (annual); Caldwell, B. E., ed., *Soybeans: Improvement, Production and Uses* (1973); Houck, James P., et al., *Soybeans and Their Products* (1972); Norman, Geoffrey A., *The Soybean* (1969) and *Soybean Physiology, Agronomy, and Utilization* (1978); Scott, Walter O., and Aldrich, Samuel R., *Modern Soybean Production* (1970); Smith, Allan K., and Circle, Sydney, *Soybeans: Chemistry and Technology*, rev. ed. (1978).

Soyer brothers [soy'-ur]

The twins Raphael and Moses Soyer, b. Borisoglebsk, Russia, Dec. 25 (N.S.), 1899, rank among the most important American figurative painters of the 20th century. The Soyer family settled in New York City in 1913, and from a very early age the brothers were encouraged to paint and draw. They attended art classes at Cooper Union and, later, at the National Academy of Design, along with Ben Shahn, Paul Cadmus, and the future art historian Meyer Schapiro. Always painting what they knew best, the brothers produced numerous portraits of themselves and their friends as well as scenes of the city life around them. Noted for sympathetic honesty, they never painted types but always presented the individual. Moses Soyer died on Sept. 2, 1974.   HARRY RAND

Bibliography: Goodrich, Lloyd, *Raphael Soyer* (1967); Smith, Bernard, *Moses Soyer* (1944); Soyer, Raphael, *Paintings and Drawings*, text by Walter K. Gutman (1960) and *Self-Revealment* (1969); Werner, Alfred, *Moses Soyer* (1970).

Soyinka, Wole [soh-ying'-kuh]

Wole Soyinka, a Nigerian dramatist, staged several productions of his works in London before being commissioned to compose a play in honor of Nigerian independence. That work, A Dance of the Forests (1962), draws heavily on Yoruba mythology in its exploration of the role of the artist in society.

Wole Soyinka, b. Isata, Nigeria, July 13, 1934, is one of the foremost poets and novelists and the most famous playwright in Africa. *The Invention* was produced at the Royal Court Theatre in London in 1955. In 1962 he published five other plays, including *A Dance of the Forests,* which was commissioned by the Nigerian government to celebrate independence. In 1973–74 he published two volumes of collected plays.

Soyinka experiments with language and form, and his novels, especially *The Interpreters* (1965), are reminiscent of the works of James Joyce. Soyinka's first collection of verse, *Idanre and Other Poems* (1967), demonstrates his remarkable ability to write, in English, poetry that effectively synthesizes British and Yoruba traditions.

After attending the University of Ibadan, Soyinka matriculated at Leeds University in England, where he received a B.A. in 1959. He returned to Nigeria in 1960 but subsequently was held in detention during the Biafran war. After a self-imposed exile in Ghana and England during the early 1970s, he returned to Nigeria, where he is chairman of the dramatic arts department at the University of Ife.   RICHARD K. PRIEBE

Bibliography: Jones, Eldred, *Wole Soyinka* (1973); Moore, Gerald, *Wole Soyinka* (1971).

Soyuz [soh-yoos']

The Soviet manned spacecraft Soyuz, in service since 1967, has been used in a wide variety of missions.

Missions. Western observers believe that the first manned Soyuz mission (Apr. 23, 1967) was to have involved a spectacular linkup between two spacecraft launched separately, fol-

SOYUZ PROGRAM FLIGHTS

Name	Launch Date	Touchdown or Decay Date	Days in Orbit	Crew at Launch	Mission
Cosmos 133	Nov. 28, 1966	Nov. 30, 1966	2		Unmanned test flight
Cosmos 140	Feb. 7, 1967	Feb. 9, 1967	2		Unmanned test flight
Soyuz 1	Apr. 23, 1967	Apr. 24, 1967	1	Komarov	First manned flight of Soyuz craft; Komarov killed during reentry after the shroud lines of the main recovery parachute became twisted
Cosmos 186	Oct. 27, 1967	Oct. 31, 1967	4		Docked with *Cosmos 188;* first automatic docking
Cosmos 188	Oct. 30, 1967	Nov. 2, 1967	3		Target vehicle for docking with *Cosmos 186;* 5 hours of linked flight
Cosmos 212	Apr. 14, 1968	Apr. 19, 1968	5		Docked with *Cosmos 213*
Cosmos 213	Apr. 15, 1968	Apr. 20, 1968	5		Target vehicle for docking with *Cosmos 212;* 3 hr 50 min of linked flight
Cosmos 238	Aug. 28, 1968	Sept. 1, 1968	4		Target vehicle; no linkup attempted
Soyuz 2	Oct. 25, 1968	Oct. 28, 1968	3		Target vehicle for *Soyuz 3*
Soyuz 3	Oct. 26, 1968	Oct. 30, 1968	4	Beregovoi	Maneuvered to within 200 m (650 ft) of *Soyuz 2*
Soyuz 4	Jan. 14, 1969	Jan. 17, 1969	3	Shatalov	Shatalov performed manual docking with *Soyuz 5;* first linkup of two manned vehicles
Soyuz 5	Jan. 15, 1969	Jan. 18, 1969	3	Khrunov Volynov Yeliseyev	Khrunov and Yeliseyev performed 1 hr of extravehicular activity while transferring to *Soyuz 4;* Volynov landed alone
Soyuz 6	Oct. 11, 1969	Oct. 16, 1969	5	Kubasov Shonin	Began world's first triple launch of manned ships; cosmonauts performed welding experiments
Soyuz 7	Oct. 12, 1969	Oct. 17, 1969	5	Filipchenko Gorbatko Volkov	Cosmonauts performed experiments in Earth photography, tested new scientific equipment, and experimented with equipment designed for future space station
Soyuz 8	Oct. 13, 1969	Oct. 18, 1969	5	Shatalov Yeliseyev	Cosmonauts conducted rendezvous maneuvers with *Soyuz 7,* but no docking or approach within 1.6 km (1 mi) was attempted
Soyuz 9	June 1, 1970	June 19, 1970	18	Nikolayev Sevastianov	Set new space-endurance record
Soyuz 10	Apr. 23, 1971	Apr. 25, 1971	2	Rukavishnikov Shatalov Yeliseyev	Docked with *Salyut 1* space station, but did not enter
Soyuz 11	June 6, 1971	June 30, 1971	24	Dobrovolsky Patsayev Volkov	Docked with and entered *Salyut 1;* cosmonauts died during reentry when a pressure-equalization valve in the hull of the command module was jarred open
Cosmos 496	June 26, 1972	July 2, 1972	6		Unmanned retest of Soyuz spacecraft
Cosmos 573	June 15, 1973	June 17, 1973	2		Unmanned test flight
Soyuz 12	Sept. 27, 1973	Sept. 29, 1973	2	Lazerev Makarov	First manned flight of new model of Soyuz ferry spacecraft
Cosmos 613	Nov. 30, 1973	Jan. 29, 1974	60		Long-duration test flight
Soyuz 13	Dec. 18, 1973	Dec. 26, 1973	8	Klimuk Lebedev	Tested Salyut scientific equipment; performed astronomical research
Cosmos 638	Apr. 3, 1974	Apr. 13, 1974	10		Apollo-Soyuz Test Project (ASTP) test flight
Cosmos 656	May 27, 1974	May 29, 1974	2		Test flight
Soyuz 14	July 3, 1974	July 19, 1974	16	Artyukhin Popovich	Docked with *Salyut 3;* crew spent 15 days in space station
Cosmos 672	Aug. 12, 1974	Aug. 18, 1974	6		ASTP test flight
Soyuz 15	Aug. 26, 1974	Aug. 28, 1974	2	Demin Sarafanov	Automatic docking system failed, preventing linkup with *Salyut 3*

Name	Launch Date	Touchdown or Decay Date	Days in Orbit	Crew at Launch	Mission
Soyuz 16	Dec. 2, 1974	Dec. 8, 1974	6	Filipchenko Rukavishnikov	Manned ASTP test flight
Soyuz 17	Jan. 10, 1975	Feb. 9, 1975	30	Grechko Gubarev	Docked with *Salyut 4;* crew spent 28 days in space station
Soyuz 18A	Apr. 5, 1975	Apr. 5, 1975	0	Lazerev Makarov	Failed to reach orbit when stages of launch vehicle did not separate
Soyuz 18	May 24, 1975	July 26, 1975	63	Klimuk Sevastyanov	Docked with *Salyut 4;* crew spent 62 days in space station
Soyuz 19	July 15, 1975	July 21, 1975	6	Kubasov Leonev	ASTP mission; docked with U.S. Apollo spacecraft
Soyuz 20	Nov. 17, 1975	Feb. 16, 1976	91		Unmanned craft; docked with *Salyut 4;* test for later Progress resupply missions
Soyuz 21	July 6, 1976	Aug. 24, 1976	49	Volynov Zholobov	Docked with *Salyut 5;* crew spent 48 days in space station
Soyuz 22	Sept. 15, 1976	Sept. 23, 1976	8	Aksenov Bykovsky	Cosmonauts conducted program of Earth photography
Soyuz 23	Oct. 14, 1976	Oct. 16, 1976	2	Rozhdestvensky Zudov	Malfunction in the rendezvous-and-approach electronics aboard *Soyuz 23* prevented planned docking with *Salyut 5*
Soyuz 24	Feb. 7, 1977	Feb. 25, 1977	18	Glazko Gorbatko	Docked with *Salyut 5;* crew spent 17 days in space station
Soyuz 25	Oct. 9, 1977	Oct. 11, 1977	2	Kovalenok Ryumin	Unspecified malfunction prevented docking with *Salyut 6*
Soyuz 26	Dec. 10, 1977	Jan. 16, 1978	38	Grechko Romanenko	Docked with *Salyut 6;* crew spent 95 days in space station and returned to Earth aboard *Soyuz 27* craft; Grechko undertook EVA on December 19
Soyuz 27	Jan. 10, 1978	Mar. 16, 1978	65	Dzhanibekov Makarov	Docked with *Salyut 6;* crew spent 5 days in space station and returned to Earth aboard *Soyuz 26* craft
Progress 1	Jan. 20, 1978	Feb. 8, 1978	19		Unmanned resupply ship; docked with *Salyut 6*
Soyuz 28	Mar. 2, 1978	Mar. 10, 1978	8	Gubarev Remek	Docked with *Salyut 6;* crew spent 7 days in space station; Remek, a Czech, became first non-Soviet cosmonaut to fly in space
Soyuz 29	June 15, 1978	Sept. 3, 1978	81	Ivanchenkov Kovalenok	Docked with *Salyut 6;* crew spent 138 days in space station and returned to Earth aboard *Soyuz 31* craft; both cosmonauts undertook EVA on July 29
Soyuz 30	June 27, 1978	July 5, 1978	8	Hermaszewski Klimuk	Docked with *Salyut 6;* crew spent 7 days in space
Progress 2	July 7, 1978	Aug. 4, 1978	28		Unmanned resupply ship; docked with *Salyut 6*
Progress 3	Aug. 7, 1978	Aug. 24, 1978	17		Unmanned resupply ship; docked with *Salyut 6*
Soyuz 31	Aug. 26, 1978	Nov. 2, 1978	68	Bykovsky Jähn	Docked with *Salyut 6;* crew spent 7 days in space station and returned to Earth aboard *Soyuz 29* craft
Progress 4	Oct. 3, 1978	Oct. 26, 1978	23		Unmanned resupply ship; docked with *Salyut 6*
Soyuz 32	Feb. 23, 1979	June 13, 1979	108	Lyakhov Ryumin	Docked with *Salyut 6;* crew spent 174 days in space station and returned to Earth aboard *Soyuz 34* craft
Progress 5	Mar. 5, 1979	Apr. 5, 1979	31		Unmanned resupply ship; docked with *Salyut 6*
Soyuz 33	Apr. 10, 1979	Apr. 12, 1979	2	Ivanov Rukavishnikov	Propulsion system failure on *Soyuz 33* prevented docking with *Salyut 6*
Progress 6	May 13, 1979	June 9, 1979	28		Unmanned resupply ship; docked with *Salyut 6*
Soyuz 34	June 8, 1979	Aug. 19, 1979	72		Unmanned craft used by Lyakhov and Ryumin to return to Earth
Progress 7	June 28, 1979	July 20, 1979	22		Unmanned resupply ship; docked with *Salyut 6*

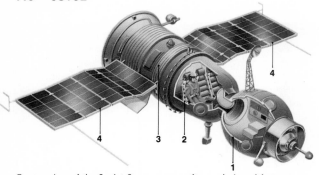

One version of the Soviet Soyuz spacecraft was designed for cosmonauts to live and work in Earth orbit. It contains a working and living orbital module (1), a command module (2) for crew during launching and landing, an equipment module (3), and solar panels (4).

lowed by a space walk of two cosmonauts from one craft to the other. Instead, *Soyuz 1* was called back to Earth because of some malfunction, and its pilot, Vladimir Komarov, was killed in a landing mishap. After two years of unmanned and manned test flights, the two-craft docking and spacewalk eventually succeeded in January 1969, when *Soyuz 4* linked up with *Soyuz 5* and two cosmonauts from the latter transferred via a spacewalk to *Soyuz 4.* In response to the *Apollo 11* Moon-landing success, Soviet space engineers launched *Soyuz 6, 7,* and *8* on Oct. 11, 12, and 13, 1969, carrying out a series of maneuvering experiments of uncertain success. For the APOLLO-SOYUZ TEST PROJECT, *Soyuz 16* (1974) was a dress rehearsal and *Soyuz 19* (1975) was the actual linkup with American astronauts.

Along with the Earth-orbital missions, modified unmanned Soyuz capsules were launched (under the ZOND program) around the Moon in September and November 1968, and plans evidently were made to send a cosmonaut around the Moon early in 1969. These plans were canceled after the unexpectedly rapid progress of the Apollo program overtook the Soviet space schedule.

The Soyuz spacecraft has also been used to ferry crews and supplies between the Earth and the SALYUT space stations. Numerous difficulties have been encountered, including the deaths of the *Soyuz 11* cosmonauts on their way back from *Salyut 1* in 1971, the failure to rendezvous by *Soyuz 15* (1974), *Soyuz 23* (1976), and *Soyuz 25* (1977), the launch failure of *Soyuz 18A* (1975), and the propulsion-system failure of *Soyuz 33* (1979). Soyuz ships have also made special-purpose flights: *Soyuz 9* (1970) conducted medical experiments; *Soyuz 13* (1973) made astronomical observations; and *Soyuz 22* (1976) carried out a program of Earth photography. A modified version of the Soyuz ship, called Progress, with cosmonaut equipment replaced by fuel and cargo, has been introduced to resupply Salyut space stations.

The Spacecraft. The 7-ton Soyuz consists of three primary sections: a conical command module, in which the crew rides during launch and landing; a cylindrical equipment module, attached aft of the command module, which contains electrical power equipment, and rocket engines; and a spherical so-called orbital module, attached forward of the command module, which provides additional working space. Soyuz ships that are to link up with Salyut space stations have docking equipment on the front of the orbital module and are powered by batteries; Soyuz ships intended for independent flight are powered by solar panels. The Soyuz spacecraft was flown initially by as many as three cosmonauts, but the deaths of the *Soyuz 11* crew led to the introduction of new safety equipment that squeezed out room for a third crew member. A much-improved Soyuz, introduced in late 1979, heralded a return to a larger crew size.

Launch occurs from the Baikonur Cosmodrome on a standard Soviet booster called the A-2, an improved version of a similarly designed vehicle that launched the Sputnik satellites and the earlier Vostok manned spacecraft. In the event of booster malfunction, a solid-fuel launch escape tower pulls the Soyuz away from the rocket. On the return to Earth, the command module is slowed by a large parachute and by a small soft-landing engine that fires just prior to touchdown in Soviet Central Asia.
JAMES E. OBERG

Bibliography: Clark, Phillip S., "Soyuz Missions to Salyut Stations," *Spaceflight*, June 1979; Hooper, Gordon R., "Missions to Salyut 4," *Spaceflight*, June 1975, January 1976, and February 1977, "Missions to Salyut 5," *Spaceflight*, April and July-August 1977, and "Missions to Salyut 6," *Spaceflight*, March, June, November, and December 1978 and March, May, July, and August-September 1979; Oberg, James, "Russia Meant to Win the 'Moon Race,' " *Spaceflight*, May 1975, "The Hidden History of the Soyuz Project," *Spaceflight*, August-September 1975, and "Soyuz 1 Ten Years After: New Conclusions," *Spaceflight*, May 1977; Riabchikov, Evgeny, *Russians in Space*, trans. by Guy Daniels (1971); Smolders, Peter, *Soviets in Space*, trans. by Marian Powell (1974); *Space World*, May 1977 (special issue on Soyuz).

Spaak, Paul Henri   [spahk]

Paul Henri Spaak, a former Belgian premier, was an ardent advocate of European unification. He was instrumental in founding the Benelux customs union, an economic confederation linking Belgium, the Netherlands, and Luxembourg. In 1957, Spaak represented Belgium at the Rome conference that established the European Common Market.

The Belgian statesman Paul Henri Spaak, b. Jan. 25, 1899, d. July 31, 1972, was a founder of Benelux—an economic union of Belgium, the Netherlands, and Luxembourg—and a leader of numerous international organizations; in 1946 he was the first president of the United Nations General Assembly. A Socialist, he was elected to the Belgian Chamber of Deputies in 1932 and retained his seat almost continuously—except for his term as secretary general of NATO (1957-61)—until 1966. He served repeatedly as prime minister (1938-39, 1946, 1947-49) and foreign minister (1936-39, 1946-49, 1954-57, 1961-66) both at home and as a member of the government-in-exile during World War II.

After the war, Spaak's strong nationalism gave way to advocacy of European unity in the face of Soviet pressure. He was chairman of the European Economic Community (1948-50) and the European Coal and Steel Community (1952-54), earning the nickname "Mr. Europe."
HERBERT H. ROWEN

Bibliography: Huizinga, J. H., *Mr. Europe, a Political Biography of Paul Henri Spaak* (1961); Spaak, P. H., *Continuing Battle, Memoirs of a European, 1936-1966*, trans. by Henry Fox (1971).

space exploration

The exploration of space by instrumented and manned spacecraft is one of the most exciting and rewarding accomplishments of modern times. New and valuable data pertaining to the Earth, the Sun, the solar system, and the entire universe have led to a better understanding of many natural processes and phenomena that affect daily life. Space exploration has directly benefited the fields of communications, weather forecasting, crop-yield prediction, and navigation of ships and aircraft.

Astronomy was one of the most ancient sciences, but for many centuries the only means of exploring space was by using instruments on the Earth's surface. BALLOONS were eventually used to carry instruments to very high altitudes and to observe ultraviolet rays, X rays, and cosmic rays without the attenuation of most of the Earth's atmosphere. These were followed by a variety of SOUNDING ROCKETS, which carried instruments high above the atmosphere on short ballistic flights.

After the development of the nuclear bomb, the need for an efficient delivery system led to an intense competition among nations to develop powerful strategic missiles. As a consequence, rocket propulsion systems became available that were powerful enough to put satellites into orbit around the Earth and to send space probes into flight beyond the reaches of the Earth's gravity (see ROCKETS AND MISSILES).

The space age dawned with the launching of SPUTNIK 1 on Oct. 4, 1957. Since that event, more than 2,000 operating spacecraft have been placed into orbit by various countries. Furthermore, 69 have been launched on lunar missions, 40 have been sent to the planets, and 6 have been sent into solar orbit or on nonplanetary missions. The majority have been by the United States and the USSR, with the Soviets accounting for 56% of all successful launches.

DEVELOPMENT OF NATIONAL SPACE PROGRAMS

Since the early 1950s scientists and engineers in both the USSR and the United States had been planning for the flight of an artificial SATELLITE (see SATELLITE) in connection with the International Geophysical Year (IGY). The IGY was designated as an 18-month period, from July 1, 1957, to Dec. 31, 1958, during which an intensive and coordinated effort was made throughout the world to obtain data on a great variety of natural phenomena, leading to a better understanding of meteorology, seismology, oceanography, and the Earth's gravity and magnetism. On July 29, 1955, President Dwight D. Eisenhower approved the launching of a small Earth-circling satellite as part of the United States' participation in the IGY. Four days later the Soviets made a similar announcement in the Moscow press.

In actuality, the IGY represented a suitable occasion for the United States and the USSR to launch artificial satellites. Both countries were already vigorously pursuing missile programs that created the requisite technology. At the time of the Eisenhower approval, the Army, the Navy, and the Air Force in the United States each had a current proposal for putting up the first artificial satellite. The Naval Research Laboratory's VANGUARD proposal was approved. It involved upgrading two existing sounding rockets—the Viking and the Aerobee—and construction of a new solid-propellant rocket, creating a three-stage launch vehicle.

The First Satellites. During the early morning of Oct. 5, 1957 (the late evening of October 4 in the eastern United States), the Soviets launched *Sputnik 1,* an aluminum sphere 58 cm (23 in) in diameter and weighing 84 kg (184 lb). Not only did this achievement thrust a scientific challenge on the United States, it also brought great political pressure to bear. After three successful development flights of the first stage of Vanguard, an attempt to launch the complete system was made 2 months after *Sputnik 1* was launched. Less than one second

(Above, left to right) *James Pickering, James Van Allen, and Wernher von Braun hold aloft a replica of Explorer 1, shortly after the Earth-orbiting satellite, America's first, had been successfully placed in orbit by a modified Jupiter C rocket on Jan. 31, 1958. A Geiger counter in the 14-kg (31-lb) satellite revealed the existence of the Van Allen belts of electrically charged particles surrounding the Earth.*

(Left) *The first attempt by the United States to place a satellite in Earth orbit ended in an explosion of the Vanguard rocket booster on the launch pad on Dec. 6, 1957.*

after lift-off, the first-stage engine lost thrust. The vehicle settled back on the launch pad and exploded. The small-diameter (15-cm/6-in) satellite continued to transmit signals as it lay on the pad.

In the meantime, on Nov. 3, 1957, the Soviets had launched *Sputnik 2,* a much larger satellite than *Sputnik 1,* weighing 508 kg (1,121 lb). Most important, *Sputnik 2* carried a live dog named LAIKA. Although the life-support materials aboard were only enough to keep the dog alive for a week, the flight proved that animals could exist in a condition of weightlessness for an extended period of time. The flight was also a clear indication that the USSR was embarking on a space program that would include manned flight.

The contrast between the Vanguard failure and the Soviet successes generated even greater domestic pressure for a strong U.S. space program. On November 8 the Army Ballistic Missile Agency (ABMA) in Huntsville, Ala., was asked to provide a backup to the Vanguard for launching an American satellite. The group, led by Wernher von Braun, had already converted the Redstone missile into the Jupiter launcher (see JUPITER, rocket) for reentry tests and now proceeded to modify the Jupiter C to a satellite launcher by adding a spinning cluster of solid-propellant rockets arranged as three upper stages. On Jan. 31, 1958, the modified Jupiter C, renamed JUNO 1, put the first American satellite into orbit. The payload, called EXPLORER 1, weighed 13.6 kg (30 lb) and carried instruments designed to measure cosmic rays, temperature, and possible collisions with micrometeorites. This first Ameri-

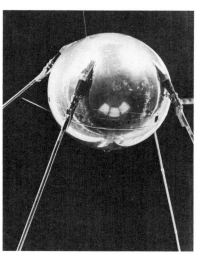

Sputnik 1, *the world's first artificial moon, was placed in Earth orbit by the Soviets on Oct. 4, 1957. The satellite, an aluminum sphere 58 cm (23 in) in diameter, had 4 antennas attached to it and weighed 84 kg (184 lb). It contained a radio transmitter and equipment that was used to monitor its internal temperature, to detect punctures by micrometeoroids, and to study the Earth's ionosphere. After 92 days in orbit, Sputnik 1 reentered Earth's atmosphere and burned up completely.*

(Left) *The Thor Able launch vehicle, used in early U.S. space efforts, was one of several multistage boosters making use of the Thor missile.*

(Right) *Films of a Soviet·Vostok spacecraft launch, released several years later, revealed a five-rocket booster using parallel staging.*

(Right) *The Saturn V launch vehicle, shown lifting* Apollo 11 *into space in 1969 for the first manned landing on the Moon, used 11 rocket engines in a series of 3 stages. It is likely to remain the largest booster to be developed by the U.S. space program in the 20th century.*

can satellite detected an unexpectedly high density of charged particles, trapped in the Earth's magnetic field, that make up what are now known as the Van Allen radiation belts. Not until March 1958 did the U.S. Navy's Vanguard fulfill its mission by launching a 1.8-kg (4-lb) satellite during the IGY.

Formation of NASA. The significance of the Sputnik launches was not lost on American political leaders. These launches confirmed an earlier claim by the USSR that it possessed the ability to build intercontinental ballistic missiles, and they demonstrated substantial Soviet competence in science and technology. Furthermore, the implied threat to U.S. national security and the fact that the USSR was the first country to achieve space flight detracted from the international image of the United States as the leader in advanced technology.

The United States did not then possess an integrated national space program, and the president and congressional leaders became involved in creating a new organization for space activity. One of the leading issues concerned whether the program should be of a military nature. On Mar. 5, 1958, President Eisenhower approved the recommendations, made by his Advisory Committee on Government Organization, that would create a civilian space agency from the already existing National Advisory Committee for Aeronautics (NACA), which had at that time about 8,000 civilian employees and an annual budget of $100 million. The NACA had a reputation of being a competent research organization that worked closely with the Department of Defense. Although primarily concerned with flight within the atmosphere, NACA felt that about half its research could be classified as space related. It had its own rocket launch station at Wallops Island, Va., and had provided the technical leadership for the X series of research aircraft, which had been primarily funded by the military. The rocket-powered X-15 (see X-15), the current project

in the series at the time, was in reality part spacecraft because it would fly ballistically above the atmosphere for several minutes.

With congressional approval of the National Aeronautics and Space Act, signed by President Eisenhower on July 29, 1958, the NACA was transformed into the NATIONAL AERONAUTICS AND SPACE ADMINISTRATION (NASA) on Oct. 1, 1958.

In addition to NACA, the Vanguard project team and other employees from the Naval Research Laboratory (NRL) were transferred to NASA. The NRL group became the nucleus of the Goddard Space Flight Center. Later in the year the jurisdiction of the Jet Propulsion Laboratory was transferred from the U.S. Army to NASA. Finally, on July 1, 1960, the Development Operations Division (the part of ABMA supervised by Dr. Wernher von Braun) was transferred to NASA, becoming the Marshall Space Flight Center. Since its formation, NASA has led the United States on a broad program of space exploration.

Worldwide Activities in Space Exploration. Although the USSR and the United States have been the countries most active in space science, many other nations now have space programs. In November 1965 the French became the third nation with an independent space capability when they placed their first satellite, named *A-1*, in orbit from an Algerian launch site. In April 1967 an Italian team placed their *San Marco* satellite into orbit using an American Scout launch vehicle sent up from a shallow-water platform off the coast of Kenya, representing the first equatorial launch.

In 1970, Japan and Red China became the fourth and fifth nations to possess independent launch capability. *Osumi* and *China 1* were launched from within these two countries, respectively. Great Britain became the sixth nation to join the club when it successfully launched the *Prospero* satellite from Woomera, Australia, using a Black Arrow launch vehicle.

The French, who have moved their launch operations to Kourou, Guiana, have also obtained launch services from both the Americans and the Russians. Many other countries have orbited satellites using launch services from other countries. American launch vehicles have been used by Australia, Canada, France, West Germany, Great Britain, Netherlands, Spain, and Italy. The Russians have launched satellites for France and India. In addition, many other countries have flown experiments on foreign satellites or otherwise participated in space programs by such activities as providing tracking sites and launching sounding rockets or balloons for corollary observations with various geophysical programs.

Space missions are so costly that a number of European countries have formed a consortium called the EUROPEAN SPACE AGENCY (ESA) to share the cost of programs of mutual benefit and as a means by which some of the smaller countries may participate in space programs. ESA has launched a number of satellites using American launch vehicles. It is also planning a number of launches from Kourou, Guiana, with the new ARIANE launch vehicle.

DEVELOPMENT OF SPACE HARDWARE

During its period of organization, NASA, together with the Army and Air Force, was busy creating a versatile stable of launch vehicles. In addition, preliminary plans for the design of both manned and unmanned spacecraft were drawn up.

Launch Vehicles. In general, launch vehicles were created from ballistic missiles by the addition of upper stages. The THOR-Able, THOR-AGENA, THOR-DELTA, ATLAS-Agena, and Atlas-CENTAUR were derived from Air Force missiles. The Juno vehicle was derived from the Army's Jupiter missile. In July 1958, several months before NASA was officially constituted, Dr. Hugh Dryden, the director of NACA, authorized the development of the SCOUT, the first vehicle totally developed by NASA. In subsequent years NASA and the U.S. Air Force developed the SATURN and TITAN vehicles to provide extra-heavy lift capability.

Launch vehicles are characterized by several significant components. Fundamentally, a launch vehicle consists of rocket propulsion systems, propellant tanks, and electromechanical and electronic GUIDANCE AND CONTROL SYSTEMS. There must also be sufficient structure to hold the rocket together and to provide for the attachment of payloads and additional stages. A rocket propulsion system must not only reach an escape velocity of 7,600 m/sec (25,000 ft/sec) to achieve a minimum orbit, but it must also lift the payload to an altitude of at least 160 km (100 mi) and overcome the drag of the air during ascent. Consequently, by the time orbit is achieved, the total effort required by the vehicle is equivalent to accelerating the payload to about 9,100 m/sec (30,000 ft/sec). Vehicles using high-performance PROPELLANTS such as liquid oxygen and liquid hydrogen can launch payloads equal to about 4% of their weight into low-altitude orbits. The Scout, which employs only solid-propellant stages, injects less than 1% of its initial weight into orbit. Solid-propellant rockets, however, tend to be less costly and more reliable than liquid-propellant rockets. It has proved economical to use powerful low-cost solid-propellant rockets for the first stage and the more costly high-performance liquid-propellant combinations for upper stages.

The propellant tanks are usually an integral part of the structure. In order to minimize weight, the tanks and other structural elements are designed to have a minimum, but safe, margin over predicted flight loads. The result is an extremely flexible vehicle that would probably come apart if the control system were to give steering commands that would resonate the rocket structure.

The launch vehicle is steered by moving the direction of thrust of the gimballed rockets to produce the corrective steering moment. Further aggravating the control process are the aerodynamic forces encountered during launch. These considerations have resulted in the development of highly sophisticated guidance and control systems that suppress structural vibratory modes and alleviate loads associated with wind shears, yet which steer the vehicle along a path that optimizes the use of the propulsive energy. Although expensive, such systems are cost-effective, particularly for larger vehicles, where a heavy (and costly) payload is at stake.

Spacecraft and Spacecraft Systems. The design of spacecraft and their systems must take into account the unique environment of space. Probably the most severe aspect of this environment is thermal, because an object in space does not benefit from the moderating effects of the atmosphere. Shaded from the Sun and nearby planets, an object will radiate heat in proportion to the fourth power of its surface temperature. A warm object would cool quite rapidly at first and then more gradually as its temperature approached the background temperature of space, which is virtually absolute zero. On the other hand, a surface facing the Sun will reach a condition of equilibrium, which may range in temperature from near freezing to well above boiling, depending on whether the surface is painted white or black.

For unmanned spacecraft, a rather wide range of operating temperatures is acceptable, and simple patterns of black and white paint are usually adequate for thermal control. Manned spacecraft present a much more challenging problem. Comfort requirements dictate a rather small range of acceptable

(Above) *This Ranger craft, shown being tested by technicians, was one of a series of probes that televised pictures of the lunar surface back to Earth before crashing into the Moon. Of the 9 Rangers launched, the last 3 succeeded in returning a total of 12,954 photographs.*

(Left) *Because the Lunar Module of the Apollo spacecraft was designed to function under lunar gravity while taking crews to and from the surface of the Moon, testing of the LM required an elaborate system that could simulate those conditions. Astronaut trainees made use of it in learning how to cope with emergencies.*

temperature and humidity. The temperature of the cabin walls and equipment must be maintained above the dew point to prevent water condensation. Active thermal control systems, which may employ electric heaters, radiators, and evaporative cooling, are required.

In addition to temperature considerations, the hazard to men and equipment posed by the radiation environment of space was a great concern during the early years of space exploration. Although ultraviolet rays, X rays, gamma rays, cosmic rays, and electrons and protons streaming from the Sun surround the Earth, almost all spacecraft equipment has been able to function well with only minor design considerations for protection against radiation damage. Experience has demonstrated that the Earth's magnetic field provides an excellent shield against charged particles by trapping them in the Van Allen radiation belts. Such protection is limited, however, to flights at altitudes below a few hundred kilometers. At higher altitudes the belts themselves become a hazard and must be avoided. The danger from micrometeoroids has proved slight; no spacecraft is known to have been seriously damaged by these particles.

Another aspect of the spacecraft environment is the effect of a vacuum on materials, for instance, the molecular cohesion phenomenon whereby two flat, highly polished surfaces become stuck or frozen together. In practice simple techniques such as sealing and proper selection of materials and lubricants have eliminated this concern. Similarly, electrical arcing and corona discharge associated with vacuum conditions can be avoided by proper design.

Complex spacecraft are characterized by a variety of supporting systems, including communications, guidance and navigation, attitude control, and (for manned missions) LIFE-SUPPORT SYSTEMS. Two-way radio transmission is usually required between ground stations and a spacecraft. Information is telemetered to the ground, and commands are transmitted to the spacecraft to control its mission. Early spaceflights were tracked by high-powered radar stations located around the world. Later, however, the up-link and down-link communications carriers were used for this function. A coded subcarrier transmitted from the ground and then turned around for retransmission by the spacecraft provides distance and Doppler-velocity measurements. The extreme precision of such a system is sufficient for accurate studies of the Earth's gravitational anomalies, which cause minor perturbations in a satellite's orbit.

For flights to the Moon and beyond, NASA operates TRACKING STATIONS in California, Spain, and Australia. They are so located as to provide continuous radio contact with distant spacecraft as the Earth rotates. Tracking data, when used for navigation, is fed into a computer for determination of deviations from the intended position and velocity. During the Apollo missions, position errors as small as 9 m (30 ft) were detectable. High-powered data-processing techniques were employed that could detect velocity to an approximate accuracy of 1 mm/sec (0.04 in/sec).

The procedure for guiding a spacecraft to the Moon or a planet is straightforward. The spacecraft is first launched into a parking orbit that will pass through the unique location from which the departure maneuver must be made. A high-velocity maneuver then injects the spacecraft into its departure path. Once the craft is on its way, tracking commences. After an accurate calculation of the injection error is made, the spacecraft's maneuvering propulsion system is commanded to make a corrective maneuver. After this maneuver, small errors may still exist. Continued tracking will reveal these as they propagate to larger values and necessitate further corrective maneuvers (see ASTRONAUTICS).

When making velocity-change maneuvers in space, both the amount and direction of velocity to be added must be controlled. Systems for doing this may be quite simple, or they may be highly sophisticated, depending on the desired accuracy. Simple systems may employ gyroscopic stabilization of the entire satellite by spinning it about its longitudinal axis. The desired velocity change can then be obtained by igniting a solid-propellant rocket of the proper size.

The most sophisticated attitude-control systems employ GYROSCOPES, star trackers, and computers to control attitude. Very precise ACCELEROMETERS measure velocity changes. The gyros may be directly mounted to a firm structure or to a gimballed platform. In either case, the computer continuously determines the attitude of the spacecraft based on measurements of the gyro's motion or the motion of the platform gimbals. The star trackers detect the position of bright stars whose locations are cataloged in the memory of the computer. The computer uses the apparent position error of the stars to correct for errors accumulated from gyro drift between star sightings. The position of at least two stars (preferably about 90° apart) must be measured to provide accurate alignment about all three axes of rotation.

Life-support systems for manned spaceflight supply a breathable atmosphere, food, water, controlled temperature and humidity, and a waste disposal system. These systems add greatly to a spacecraft's weight. By far the most common source of the power required for these spacecraft systems is the Sun. Arrays of photovoltaic cells, which convert the Sun's energy into electricity, provide long-lasting, highly reliable power with only a few drawbacks. A charging system and storage batteries may be required if the spacecraft's orbit carries it into darkness. For missions to the outer planets, solar power is inadequate, and thermoelectric devices, which convert heat from the radioactive decay of plutonium-238 into electric power, are used instead. Radioisotope-powered electric generators also provided power for five of the six experi-

NASA's mission-control room at what is now called the Johnson Space Center, near Houston, Tex., served as the central communications link between Earth and spacecraft for all the U.S. manned space missions. Data from tracking stations around the world were fed into this room.

In order to train for actual space flights, astronauts underwent testing in as many simulations of the space environment as could be achieved on Earth. Here Edwin Aldrin, who became the second man to walk on the Moon, experiences near weightlessness in an underwater chamber; his body's reactions are being monitored.

ment stations that were left operating on the Moon.

UNMANNED SPACE MISSIONS

Unmanned spacecraft have been employed for a great variety of missions. They have gathered data from regions well within the orbit of Mercury and far beyond that of Jupiter. They have studied the radiation belts, the magnetosphere, and the ionosphere of the Earth, as well as its atmosphere, its oceans, its ice caps, and its landmasses. The Moon, Mercury, Venus, Mars, Jupiter, and Saturn have all been visited by instrumented spacecraft. Landings have been made on the Moon, Mars, and Venus.

Earth Satellites. Satellites in orbit around the Earth may provide information about astronomical objects (see ASTRONOMY AND ASTROPHYSICS), or they may be scientific or applications satellites oriented toward studying the Earth and its environment. One of the most important astronomical objects is the Sun. Besides those spacecraft that measure the particles and fields of the Sun in interplanetary space, NASA has successfully launched eight Orbiting Solar Observatory (see OSO) spacecraft whose scanners and telescopes are able to observe the activity of the Sun over the entire spectrum without the obstruction of the Earth's atmosphere. NASA has also launched three observatories to study regions beyond the confines of the solar system. Two Orbiting Astronomical Observatories (see OAO) were placed into long-duration orbits. Each OAO carries a variety of telescopes. In 1977 the first HIGH ENERGY ASTRONOMY OBSERVATORY (HEAO) went into operation. The HEAO carries equipment designed to map the X-ray and gamma-ray sources throughout the celestial sphere and to investigate such exciting new phenomena as black holes, pulsars, and quasars.

Both the United States and the USSR have used Earth-oriented satellites for reconnaissance since the early 1960s. Satellites have also been extensively used as navigational aids to ships and aircraft. Several TRANSIT satellites were placed into orbit by the U.S. Navy. Geodetic surveys and accurate navigational data may be obtained from precise tracking of the position of these satellites. NAVSTAR is the most recent navigation satellite. Ships and aircraft can use a network of these satellites for precise navigation.

The most accurate geodetic data are obtained from pulsed laser beams. The *Laser Geodynamic Satellite,* placed into orbit in 1976, allows measurements of the movement of the Earth's crust to an accuracy of 2 cm (0.8 in), thereby providing information vital to earthquake prediction research. A geostationary or geosynchronous orbit, in which a satellite matches the Earth's rotation period and remains fixed over the same point on Earth, provides special advantages for Earth applications satellites. The most popular use for these orbits is COMMUNICATIONS SATELLITES, which act as relay stations between two points on the Earth's surface. NASA's experimental communications satellites heralded the growing importance of this space application when the 1964 Olympics were telecast live from Japan to American and European audiences via SYNCOM

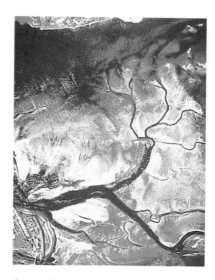

Infrared photographs of Earth from space by means of such satellites as Landsat have provided vast amounts of new information on resources, land use, and pollution hazards. Surfaces can be given color values according to how they absorb infrared light. Thus, in this photo, water appears deep blue and vegetation bright red. Patterns of land use or misuse and signs of encroaching pollution and resource waste over large areas are revealed in this way.

3 over the Pacific and RELAY *1* over the Atlantic. On June 28, 1965, the Communications Satellite Corporation (Comsat), acting as the U.S. participant in the International Telecommunications Satellite Organization (INTELSAT), began commercial satellite communications across the Atlantic with EARLY BIRD. In 1979, Intelsat began using communications satellites with 50 times the telephone-circuit capacity of Early Bird. Now more than four dozen relay satellites, operated by several nations and organizations, are in synchronous orbit.

Because synchronous orbit provides a stationary vantage for continuous viewing of a large portion of the Earth, it is ideal for use in environmental monitoring and meteorology. The SYNCHRONOUS METEOROLOGICAL SATELLITES, GOES, and GEOS are all providing valuable service of this type.

Earth-viewing satellites designed to cover the entire Earth's surface are placed in a near-polar orbit; as the Earth rotates under such an orbit, its entire surface becomes exposed daily. Observation of the Earth's surface is greatly improved if it is always illuminated at nearly the same Sun angle when viewed from the satellite. Precession of the orbit caused by the equatorial bulge is sufficient to provide proper synchronization with the Earth's orbit around the Sun, when the plane of the satellite's orbit is displaced about 10° from a true polar orbit. Most weather, Earth resources, and reconnaissance satellites are in these Sun-synchronous orbits, including NIMBUS, TIROS, LANDSAT, and GEOS. Most navigation and geodetic-survey satellites are in nearly perfect polar orbits.

Lunar Probes. The most interesting use of unmanned spacecraft has been in the exploration of the Moon, the planets, and other regions of the solar system by probes that travel

(Left) *Seven Nimbus experimental research and development weather satellites were orbited by the United States between 1964 and 1978. The solar-powered craft have been used to develop new microwave, infrared, and visible-light remote-sensing devices. Nimbus 7 is the first to monitor atmospheric pollutants.*

Early Bird was the world's first commercial communications satellite. The outer cylindrical surface was covered with 6,000 solar cells that converted sunlight energy into electrical energy to power the satellite's 240 two-way voice circuits. It was launched on Apr. 6, 1965, into a geosynchronous orbit—remaining stationary over one Earth location—at an altitude of about 36,000 km (22,400 mi).

The first Moon probe, Luna 1, was launched by the Soviets on Jan. 2, 1959. The 362-kg (797-lb) sphere was equipped with two Geiger counters and other instruments that provided information on magnetic fields, interplanetary gases, solar wind particles, and cosmic rays at great distances from Earth. Luna 1 missed the Moon by 6,000 km (3,700 mi) and went into orbit about the Sun. It was then renamed Mechta and listed as an interplanetary probe.

beyond the Earth's orbit. The first target for extraterrestrial exploration was the Moon. Initially, spacecraft were aimed to crash into or fly by the Moon, with the objective of obtaining rudimentary information such as magnetic-field detection and measurement of background radiation emanating from the Moon. The success ratio of these early probes was very low. Launch-vehicle failures ruined five of the six U.S. PIONEER lunar missions. The fourth launch attempt in 1959 sent a spacecraft within 59,000 km (37,000 mi) of the Moon. In the meantime, the Soviet LUNA 1 had flown within 7,400 km (4,600 mi) of the Moon 2 months earlier. Later that same year, Luna 2, carrying the Soviet flag, impacted on the Moon, and Luna 3 transmitted the first photos of the Moon's far side.

(Above) Ranger 9, the last of the series of picture-taking U.S. probes sent crashing into the Moon, targets in on the floor of the crater Alphonsus, about 113 km (70 mi) wide, on Mar. 21, 1965. The small circle shows the point of impact. (Left) This Surveyor spacecraft was one of seven launched from 1966 to 1968 to soft-land on the Moon, following the Ranger series. Five of them succeeded, returning data on the nature of the lunar surface.

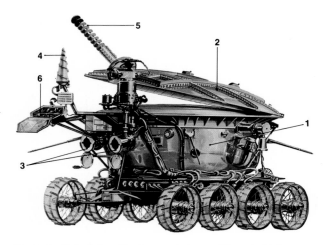

The Soviet Union's Lunokhod, somewhat resembling a bathtub on wheels, was sent to roam the lunar surface under remote control from Earth, providing television images and analyzing rocks and soil. Two such vehicles reached the Moon, in 1970 and 1973, carried by Luna 17 and Luna 21. The body, or "bathtub" (1), a pressurized compartment for instruments, was covered by a hinged solar array (2), which could be raised. The Lunokhod had two television cameras (3), an omnidirectional antenna (4), a narrow-beam directional antenna (5), and a laser reflector (6) for determining the Moon's distance.

After six failures, the last three RANGERS provided excellent close-up pictures of the Moon. This was an important milestone in the manned lunar-landing program, because the best resolution of lunar surface detail from earthbound astronomical telescopes had been no better than one kilometer (about half a mile). Meanwhile, the Soviets were also having problems. After Luna 3, the next five officially announced Luna attempts either missed the Moon or crashed into it while trying to make a soft landing. Luna 9 made a successful landing on Feb. 3, 1966, and transmitted to Earth the first pictures of the lunar landscape taken from the Moon's surface.

NASA instituted two other programs to support the upcoming APOLLO manned lunar-landing program. SURVEYOR was a soft-lander that provided valuable data on terrain roughness and the mechanical properties of the soil. The LUNAR ORBITERS transmitted high-resolution pictures of potential landing sites and pictures of sufficient quality to produce the maps required for navigation. All five Lunar Orbiters were successful. As a result, landing sites that were both operationally suitable and of high scientific interest were selected for each Apollo mission. During the period of Apollo lunar exploration Luna 16 landed on the Moon, removed a sample of the soil, and successfully returned to Earth. Less than 2 months later, Luna 17 landed on the Moon carrying LUNOKHOD, an eight-wheeled, bathtub-shaped vehicle that could be driven across the lunar terrain under the control of a crew on Earth.

Interplanetary Probes. A spacecraft embarking on an interplanetary mission must first achieve escape velocity from the Earth's gravitational field. The spacecraft then becomes a satellite of the Sun and will usually arrive at the target planet after having traveled halfway around the Sun. In order for the planet to be at the proper location for the encounter with the spacecraft, launch must take place during a "launch window." These occur at particular intervals (equal to the synodic period) for each of the planets. Launch windows for Mars and Venus occur approximately every 26 and 19 months, respectively. For Jupiter, which takes nearly 12 years to orbit the Sun, the launch window occurs approximately every 13 months. Mercury, with an orbital period of only 88 days, overtakes the Earth more than three times a year, so that launch windows occur every 116 days.

Although the Soviets made the first attempt at a Venus encounter with VENERA 1 in February 1961, NASA's MARINER 2 was the first successful Venus probe, passing within 34,800 km (21,600 mi) of Venus in December 1962. It found that Venus had neither a magnetic field nor radiation belts. Surface temperatures and cloud structure were measured with microwave and infrared radiometers. The USSR successfully launched eight more Venera spacecraft and one ZOND spacecraft on missions to Venus. *Venera 3* crashed on Venus on Mar. 1, 1966, becoming the first artificial object to reach that planet. *Veneras 4* through *7* successfully landed on Venus. Built as a spherical spacecraft to withstand the crushing pressure of the Venusian atmosphere, and equipped with thermal insulation and a stored refrigerant to cool the spacecraft, *Venera 7* sent back information indicating a surface atmospheric pressure 90 times greater than that on Earth and a surface temperature for the carbon-dioxide atmosphere of 470° C (800° F). *Veneras 9* and *10* each separated into an orbiter and a lander. In October 1975 both lander spacecraft transmitted panoramic pictures of the Venusian landscape, using the orbiters as relay stations. The U.S. *Mariner 10* spacecraft flew by Venus in February 1974 and returned photographs revealing a complex cloud structure. Then, using the gravitational attraction of Venus to alter its orbit around the Sun, *Mariner 10* flew by Mercury three times. The pictures transmitted from the Mercury encounters, the only close-ups that have been obtained of that planet, revealed a highly cratered surface not unlike the Moon's.

The first successful Mars probe was *Mariner 4,* which flew by that planet during July 1965 and transmitted pictures revealing that portions of the Martian surface are covered with craters similar to those on the Moon. *Mariner 4* also discovered that Mars has essentially no magnetic field. In 1969, *Mariners 6* and *7* returned more pictures during flyby. In 1971 two Soviet and two U.S. spacecraft were launched toward Mars. *Mariner 9,* whose primary mission was to map the Martian surface, arrived first on November 13, maneuvered into an orbit, and revealed a huge dust storm that obscured al-

Technicians work on a Venera probe in a Soviet laboratory. By 1978, 12 such probes had been sent toward Venus to explore that shrouded planet, 9 with notable success. In December 1970, Venera 7 became the first probe to transmit data from the surface of another planet.

most the entire surface of the planet. In February, after the dust storm cleared, *Mariner 9* mapped almost the entire surface of Mars, transmitting more than 7,000 high-resolution images back to Earth. Although the Soviet *Mars 3* landed safely and activated its panoramic television system, television signals were received for only 20 seconds and revealed no detail.

The U.S. VIKING program was the most ambitious, best-equipped, and most successful expedition to Mars. *Viking 1* and *2,* launched in the late summer of 1975, each consisted of an orbiter and a lander. A number of experiments aboard the lander were designed especially to search for indications of life on Mars. Both Vikings arrived safely and successfully maneuvered into orbit. For more than 4 weeks photographs of the Martian surface were studied before the *Viking 1* lander was commanded to descend to a large Martian desert on July 20, 1976. Once on the surface, all of the equipment and experiments performed almost perfectly. Photographs showed a barren, reddish desert strewn with a few rocks. After the success of *Viking 1,* a rougher terrain was selected for the *Viking 2* lander. It landed about 7,200 km (4,500 mi) from *Viking 1* on a plain in a cratered region. Its experiments and equipment also performed well. No conclusive indication of life was

(Left) *The U.S. spacecraft* Mariner 6, *launched on Feb. 24, 1969, to photograph Mars during a flyby, showed conclusively that no "canals" exist there.* (Below) Mariner 10, *sent into space on Nov. 3, 1973, photographed the banded cloud cover of Venus and then flew on to Mercury — shown here — to reveal that the planet has a cratered, Moon-like surface.*

A July 1976 view of the Martian surface at the Viking Lander 1 site discloses a red plain strewn with angular rocks. The extendable sampler scoop dug trenches near the spacecraft to obtain samples for instrumental detection of possible life forms.

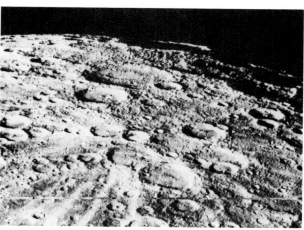

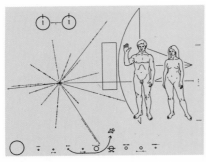

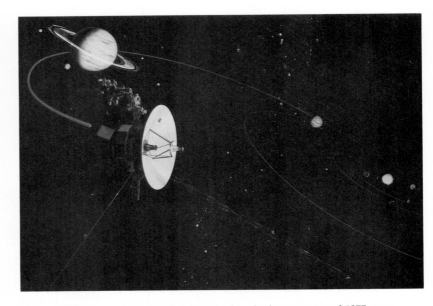

(Above) *This plaque is aboard* Pioneers 10 *and* 11, *both headed out of the solar system. If alien life forms intercept a probe and, using the encoded scientific data, decipher this plaque, they will learn the location of the Earth in the solar system and of the Sun in our galaxy, as well as the appearance and the size of humans.* (Right) *The two Voyager probes, also outward bound, carry records encoded with images of Earth, human voices, and musical selections ranging from Bach to Chuck Berry.*

found, and the probability of ever finding evidence of life on Mars is now considered remote.

NASA launched two Pioneers to Jupiter in March 1972 and April 1973. Both spacecraft were completely successful. They were the first to pass through the asteroid belt and the first to fly by an outer planet, and they surpassed previous distance records for transmission of commands and data. *Pioneer 10* returned more than 300 pictures of Jupiter and its satellites before Jupiter's tremendous mass boosted the probe's speed to greater than escape velocity from the Sun; *Pioneer 10* will thus depart from the solar system and drift through the Galaxy forever. *Pioneer 11* was maneuvered into a pass that sent it 160 million km (100 million mi) above the orbital plane of the solar system. *Pioneer 11's* solar plasma analyzer was then able to map the solar wind in the northern magnetic hemisphere of the Sun; the probe then proceeded toward an encounter with the planet SATURN in September 1979 that revealed new data about that planet and its many moons.

NASA sent two more spacecraft to the outer planets. VOY-

Jupiter's Great Red Spot is viewed by Voyager 1. *This object, long a puzzle, turns out to be a hurricanelike disturbance of the atmosphere of Jupiter, one large and stable enough to have endured for centuries.*

AGERS 1 and 2, launched in the late summer of 1977, were about three times as heavy as the Jupiter Pioneers. They had much more powerful transmitters permitting a data transmission rate that enabled real-time video transmissions from Jupiter. *Voyager 1* relayed spectacular pictures of Jupiter in March 1979, and *Voyager 2* was similarly successful in July. *Voyager 1* was maneuvered so as to take advantage of Jupiter's gravity to send the probe toward a rendezvous with Saturn in November 1980. If this encounter is successful, *Voyager 2*, after a similar Saturn encounter, will be directed toward a Jan. 30, 1986, encounter with Uranus at a point almost 3.2 billion km (2 billion mi) from the Sun.

Interplanetary space has also been the object of extensive study. Scientific experiments are directed at the space environment and at Sun-dominated phenomena, including the Sun's magnetic field, the solar wind, solar plasma changes associated with levels of solar activity, and interactions of the Sun and the Earth (the only inner planet with a magnetic field of its own). Other investigations are aimed at the origin and nature of cosmic rays and interplanetary dust. The United States has launched a series of IMP (see IMP) and EXPLORER spacecraft into highly eccentric orbits about the Earth and Moon for these investigations. Five Pioneers have also been placed into eccentric orbit about the Sun to serve as deep-space probes. Using the powerful Titan-Centaur rocket, the Germans launched two Helios solar probes that were placed into highly eccentric solar orbits with perihelions well inside Mercury's orbit. *Helios 2* passes within 43 million km (27 million mi) of the Sun every six months.

MANNED SPACE MISSIONS

The most challenging and exciting aspect of space exploration has been manned spaceflight. Not only has this required venturing into an alien environment, but it also required machines that could fly safely at speeds far greater than the capability of current aircraft. The X-15 high-altitude aircraft, which was considered a bold assault on the fringes of outer space, had been under construction for more than 2 years when *Sputnik 1* abruptly made orbiting the Earth the next urgent goal for manned flight. The X-15's design speed of 6,500 km/h (4,000 mph) seemed almost trivial compared to the 27,000 km/h (17,000 mph) required to achieve orbit. A completely new type of vehicle would be required.

Early Programs. In October 1958 the U.S. MERCURY PROGRAM was begun. The Mercury spacecraft was designed to be launched into orbit using a modified Atlas missile. At the inception of the program it was estimated that the Atlas could not lift much more than 900 kg (2,000 lb) into orbit. The challenge was to design a spacecraft that could carry an ASTRONAUT safely to orbit and back within that weight constraint.

On May 5, 1961, Alan B. Shepard, Jr., became the first American to be launched into outer space. The Freedom 7 Mercury capsule in which he rode was boosted into a 188-km-high (117-mi) ballistic trajectory that landed in the ocean 486 km (302 mi) from the launching site. The flight, which lasted 15 minutes, demonstrated that humans could function well under weightless conditions and that the capsule could be used safely in space.

which the retro-rockets were fired determined the area of splashdown in the ocean. Control of the mission was carried out on the ground. Communications with the spacecraft and the acquisition of tracking data were performed through a network of stations around the world. It was on the basis of this processed tracking data that the proper firing time for the retro-rockets was determined. The location for splashdown was selected to accommodate tracking after the retro-maneuver, thereby improving predictions of recovery location.

Alan SHEPARD made a suborbital flight on May 5, 1961, only 2½ years after Project Mercury commenced. Shepard was not the first person in space, however; Soviet cosmonaut Yuri GAGARIN had made a one-orbit flight in a VOSTOK spacecraft less than a month earlier, on April 12. During the next 2 years five more Mercury flights were successfully flown. On May 25, 1961, President Kennedy declared that an American should land on the Moon by the end of the decade, thereby committing the United States and its aerospace industry to the APOLLO PROGRAM, one of the most difficult ventures ever attempted. Two new spacecraft were needed, the LUNAR EXCURSION MODULE and the Command and Service Module, with a combined weight of about 47,000 kg (100,000 lb). To propel these modules into a translunar trajectory, a huge new launch vehicle, the Saturn (see SATURN, rocket), was required.

The increase in mission difficulty between Mercury and

Yuri Gagarin, a Soviet cosmonaut, was the first human to orbit the Earth. The 27-year-old Russian was launched into space on Apr. 12, 1961, aboard a 4,725-kg (10,417-lb) Vostok spacecraft to a maximum altitude of 327 km (203 mi). After making one complete orbit about the Earth, the spacecraft reentered the atmosphere and soft-landed on Russian soil with the aid of parachutes. The entire flight lasted about 1 hr 48 min.

John Glenn's 295-minute flight in his Friendship 7 Mercury capsule on Feb. 20, 1962, made him the first American and third man to orbit the Earth. He soon left the space program and later became a senator.

The cosmonaut Valentina Tereshkova, the first woman in space, made a 49-orbit flight in Vostok 6 in June 1963. Five months later she again drew world attention by marrying the cosmonaut Andrian Nikolayev.

There were a number of problems and unknowns. Statistically, the Atlas was expected to fail 20% of the time. Once in orbit, the space capsule would have to be tracked and monitored and then returned to the desired recovery area. To do this it would have to survive safely the severe heating of aerodynamic deceleration and then land safely.

The compact Mercury capsule, with its escape rocket, high-drag ballistic entry, and water landing by parachute, achieved the desired results. It imposed special demands on the crew, however. The ballistic entry resulted in a sustained period of deceleration peaking at 8 times normal Earth gravity. Other potential hazards in the realm of SPACE MEDICINE included disorientation and the physiological and psychological reactions to weightlessness.

The scheme for flight control of Mercury was as simple as was the concept of the spacecraft itself. The capsule was inserted into a low Earth orbit using the launch vehicle's guidance system. Once the capsule was in orbit, no further velocity change maneuvers were required until it came time for descent. Return to Earth was accomplished by maneuvering the spacecraft to the proper attitude and then firing a cluster of three solid rockets. This deflected the flight path to one that entered the Earth's atmosphere. Because the spacecraft was designed to produce no lift, it followed a highly predictable ballistic reentry trajectory. Consequently, the time at

Apollo has been crudely compared to that between the flight of the Wright brothers and Lindbergh's crossing of the Atlantic. The intervening GEMINI PROGRAM provided an intermediate step. The objectives of this program were to gain operational experience with extravehicular astronautics, control of maneuvering spacecraft, rendezvous between two spacecraft, and active on-board flight-path control during reentry. Gemini also provided excellent training for both the astronauts and the mission-control crews. Most of the flight and control procedures later used in the Apollo missions were developed during the Gemini program. Ten manned Gemini were flown.

The mission sequence for the Apollo flights to the Moon consisted of a great number of separate maneuvers. Most of these maneuvers required significant velocity changes and great precision. The Saturn launch vehicle, using an inertial guidance system, first carried the Apollo spacecraft into a low-altitude parking orbit above the Earth. After verification of proper orbit insertion from tracking data, the third stage of the Saturn was restarted at the proper time, propelling the Apollo spacecraft into its translunar trajectory. This trajectory, which was modified as necessary by midcourse correction maneuvers, carried Apollo to the far side of the moon, where both tracking and communications with Apollo were blocked. At this position the Apollo spacecraft made a deceleration maneuver that inserted it into a lunar orbit that would carry it over the landing site.

The landing was made by two astronauts in the Lunar Module while the third crewman stayed in the Command Module. The landing maneuver was similar to a launch maneuver in reverse, ending with the Lunar Module hovering over the landing area at a few hundred feet of altitude. Enough propellant was on board to accommodate one to two minutes of hover time, allowing the crew to select a suitable spot for

The astronaut David Scott begins a space walk from the Command Module of Apollo 9 as James McDivitt and Russell Schweickert look on from the Lunar Module (LM). Apollo 9 was an Earth-orbit test flight of the LM that took place 4 months before the historic Moonlanding mission of Apollo 11 in July 1979. Apollo 10, with John Young, Thomas Stafford, and Eugene Cernan, later tested the LM in a lunar orbit.

(Left) *On June 3, 1965, Edward H. White became the first American to move outside an orbiting spacecraft. He was tethered to the Gemini 4 capsule as he maneuvered about for 20 minutes.*

(Below) *A photograph of Gemini 7 was taken from Gemini 6 at an altitude of about 260 km (160 mi) on Dec. 15, 1965, during the first rendezvous by U.S. spacecraft.*

landing and to perform the landing maneuver.

When ready to return, the astronauts launched the Lunar Module into an orbit that was properly synchronized to overtake and rendezvous with the orbiting Command and Service Module. After rendezvous the two spacecraft docked together, and the astronauts in the Lunar Module transferred themselves and the materials they were bringing back to the Command Module, subsequently discarding the Lunar Module. Departure from lunar orbit also had to be performed on the other side of the Moon without tracking assistance from the Earth. Midcourse correction maneuvers were made as needed on the return trip to Earth. Just prior to reentry, the Service Module was discarded, leaving only the Command Module to survive reentry heating. Reentry into the Earth's atmosphere was made at a shallow, grazing angle.

With the words "Houston, Tranquility Base here. The Eagle has landed," on July 20, 1969, Neil ARMSTRONG and Edwin AL-

The crew of Apollo 10 took this picture of the rising Earth while circling the Moon in May 1969. During the lunar orbit the crew separated the LM from the Apollo Command Module and took it to within 14.5 km (9 mi) of the Moon's surface before docking again with the Command Module and returning to Earth. Astronauts, seeing Earth from this new perspective, spoke repeatedly of the need of humans to see their planet as a whole—as a fragile spaceship that needed careful treatment to survive.

(Below) *The first Lunar Rover was taken to the Moon by the Apollo 15 astronauts and driven 28 km (17.4 mi) during their search for rock samples. James B. Irwin, working beside the Rover near Hadley Rille, is picking up rocks with a lunar scoop.*

(Above) *Neil Armstrong, the first man on the Moon, took this picture of Edwin Aldrin, Jr., on the lunar surface on July 20, 1969. Reflected images of Armstrong and the Apollo 11 lunar module are visible in Aldrin's helmet visor.*

DRIN became the first men to land on another world. Michael COLLINS, the third astronaut of the *Apollo 11* crew, remained in lunar orbit in the Command Module. Altogether, 12 Americans walked on the Moon during six Apollo flights. These astronauts carried out numerous scientific experiments and exploration tasks. At each landing site a science station was set up and continued to transmit data from a number of experiments. The astronauts returned numerous samples of lunar material for study by scientists throughout the world.

While the Americans were progressing from Mercury to Gemini to Apollo, the Soviets progressed from Vostok to VOSHKOD to SOYUZ. During this period the Soviets made notable achievements, including the first "spacewalk" (Aleksei LEONOV), the first multiperson spacecraft (Voshkod), and the first transfer of crews after docking (*Soyuz 4* and *5*).

What had begun as a Soviet-American space race ended with a display of cooperation. Both countries agreed that space rescue operations would be greatly facilitated if common systems for rendezvous and docking were jointly developed and then used in all future spacecraft. An Apollo and a Soyuz spacecraft were then modified accordingly. To prove the hardware and the joint-operation procedures, the APOLLO-SOYUZ TEST PROJECT (ASTP) was initiated in an agreement signed by President Nixon and Premier Kosygin in Moscow in May 1972. On July 15, 1975, a Soyuz spacecraft lifted off from the BAIKONUR COSMODROME, followed 7½ hours later by an Apollo spacecraft launched from the KENNEDY SPACE CENTER. Two days later the astronauts and cosmonauts were shaking hands in orbit. The two spaceships stayed joined for another 2 days and then separated and returned to Earth after several days of conducting experiments.

Both the American and Soviet programs experienced not only triumph but also tragedy. Virgil GRISSOM, Edward WHITE, and Roger CHAFFEE died when their Apollo spacecraft suddenly caught fire while undergoing a simulated launch test on Jan. 27, 1967. Vladimir KOMAROV was killed Apr. 24, 1967, when the landing parachute on *Soyuz 1* fouled during deployment after an 18-orbit mission. Georgy DOBROVOLSKY, Vladislav VOLKOV, and Viktor PATSAYEV became the first crew to operate a space station when they occupied *Salyut 1* after docking their *Soyuz 11* with it on June 7, 1971. They returned

to their spacecraft after a record-setting time in space of 23 days. They were killed, however, when their Soyuz craft became depressurized during descent from orbit on June 30, 1971.

Space Stations. On May 14, 1973, using the first two stages of a Saturn V rocket, NASA launched SKYLAB, an 85-ton space station equipped with science experiments. The core of *Skylab* was a Saturn third-stage tank converted into a living area and equipped with a solar power system, an airlock, and a battery of solar telescopes. During launch, one of *Skylab's* large arrays of solar cells was torn away and the other jammed in a partially open condition. After a delay of 10 days

The Soviet Soyuz 19 spacecraft was photographed from the U.S. Apollo capsule with which it docked during the cooperative Apollo-Soyuz Test Project in July 1975. During the two days the spacecraft were linked in orbit, the two crews conducted joint experiments.

This photograph of the U.S. Skylab was taken on Feb. 8, 1974, as the last crew of astronauts returned to Earth. Clearly visible are the two superimposed makeshift aluminum-covered fabric shields that were set up in space to protect the orbital workshop from the Sun's heat.

to construct and load specially designed repair equipment, three astronauts in an Apollo spacecraft rendezvoused with Skylab, deployed the damaged array of solar cells, and erected a sunshade over the skin where insulation had been lost. They stayed aloft for 28 days, setting a new record. The next crew further extended this record to 59 days, and the final crew stayed aloft 84 days. These long periods in space were of great significance to space medicine. The astronauts showed only minor physiological effects, from which they fully recovered. They quickly adapted to the weightless environment and demonstrated that normal everyday tasks could be performed there with little or no difficulty.

Starting with the launch of SALYUT 1 in 1971, the USSR has also pursued a vigorous space-station program. Although the Soyuz 11 crew, the first to occupy a Salyut, was killed during their return to Earth, four successful missions were subsequently accomplished between 1974 and 1977. Salyut 6, launched on Sept. 29, 1977, was improved to accommodate the docking of two Soyuz craft at the same time. Both Soyuz

26 and Soyuz 27 docked with Salyut 6 in December 1977; the station was resupplied in January 1978 by Progress 1, an unmanned spacecraft capable of automated rendezvous. A stripped-down version of the Soyuz spacecraft, Progress 1 carried more than a ton of propellant, food, water, clothing, and scientific materials. The crew of Soyuz 27 departed in Soyuz 26, and the original Salyut crew—which had arrived aboard Soyuz 26 in early December—was visited once again, this time by Soyuz 28, which carried the first non-Soviet cosmonaut, Vladimir REMEK, a Czechoslovakian citizen. Soyuz 28 returned after only one week, and on Mar. 16, 1978, after 96 days in space, the original crew of the Salyut returned to Earth safely after setting a new record for time in space.

Salyut 6 was reactivated 3 months later by the crew of Soyuz 29, who were visited by the crew of Soyuz 30 and resupplied by Progress 2. The Soyuz 30 crew included Mirosław HERMASZEWSKI, a citizen of Poland. The Soviets are training a number of cosmonauts from other Soviet-bloc countries, including Romania, Bulgaria, East Germany, Mongolia, and Cuba.

Space Shuttle. In 1972, NASA initiated the construction of the SPACE SHUTTLE, a versatile, winged vehicle that is launched by a rocket and glides back to Earth to land on a runway. The shuttle greatly improves accessibility to space and thereby facilitates many opportunities for space applications that would otherwise not be possible. Through lowered cost and improved operational capability and flexibility, the shuttle can participate in a wide variety of missions and activities in space. It can fly sortie missions lasting from one to several weeks and involving one or more of the SPACELAB modules developed by the European Space Agency. These sortie missions consist of a variety of experiments and observations that require considerable participation on the part of the crew. The shuttle can also be used as an orbiting launch platform, whereby a spacecraft is carried in the cargo bay and launched by one or more solid rocket stages attached to the spacecraft. Most of these missions will involve launching of satellites into geosynchronous orbit, but there will also be planetary exploration missions launched by the shuttle from Earth orbit. Finally, the shuttle will deploy satellites directly into orbit. In subsequent flights the shuttle may retrieve or service these satellites, thereby adding a new dimension of utility. In some cases the satellites will be equipped with modest propulsion capability, allowing them to move into and out of an orbit somewhat higher than the operating altitude of the shuttle. Most shuttle missions will probably combine several objectives in order to utilize cargo capacity more fully.

A total of four or five shuttles is planned, with launch facilities at both Kennedy Space Center on the East Coast and

A Soyuz spacecraft (upper left) carrying cosmonauts begins its docking approach to a Salyut space station (lower right). Some USSR space stations have been used for scientific research, whereas others have been devoted to military reconnaissance and Earth observation.

On Aug. 12, 1977, the space shuttle Enterprise successfully completed its first free-flight test. After being carried to an altitude of 6,700 m (22,000 ft) by a modified jumbojet, the shuttle was released. It glided without power to a safe landing in the Mojave Desert.

In this artist's conception a space shuttle approaches a large solar-power satellite under construction in orbit high above the Earth's surface. Such satellites would convert sunlight into electricity, which would then be beamed to Earth in the form of microwaves and reconverted to electricity.

Vandenberg Air Force Base on the West Coast. The shuttle fleet should be able to carry out 50 missions a year, and it is expected to replace most of the expendable launch vehicles when it becomes fully operational. The USSR may also be developing a space shuttle.

THE FUTURE OF SPACE EXPLORATION
With a cargo capacity in excess of 30 tons and with great versatility of operation, the shuttle will facilitate the further exploration of space. Improved Earth-oriented satellites will be flown for a variety of purposes. These satellites will undertake long-range and large-scale weather forecasting, water-availability and crop-production forecasting, atmospheric-pollution and water-quality monitoring, earthquake prediction,

and timber, rangeland, and geological resources inventory. The weightless environment in space will be exploited for commercial and research activity. Inorganic and biological materials research and applications will be explored, as well as basic physics and chemistry and the production of new or improved materials that cannot be produced in the presence of gravity. The shuttle's cargo capacity is great enough to carry special machinery for fabricating large, lightweight structures in space. Because engineers do not have to contend with gravity or wind loads, the size of the structures that can be built is virtually limitless. Large antenna arrays for communications satellites will soon be needed to prevent overcrowding in synchronous orbit.

To send a probe to a distant heavenly object, such as a star or galaxy, engineers would have to design a rocket that could provide a relatively slow acceleration over a long period of time, rather than the short-lived high acceleration provided by current rockets. In the hypothetical photon rocket, such an acceleration would be produced by the ejection of a beam of light particles, or photons, created by the annihilation of matter and antimatter in the rocket engines. The practical difficulties of producing and storing sufficient antimatter greatly hinder the development of this means of propulsion.

A much bolder application for large structures is the proposal to locate huge solar energy collectors in geostationary orbit. The solar energy would first be converted by photovoltaic cells to electricity, and then to a microwave beam that would carry the power to antenna arrays on Earth, where the energy in the beam would be reconverted to electricity for use in the commercial power grid. Power obtained by this means would consume no fuel and produce no waste products. It would also make none of the demands currently placed on the Earth's dwindling supply of water for the disposal of waste heat and the processing of fuel. Electric power from space, if it becomes commercially feasible, may ultimately become one of the most significant benefits of space exploration.　　MAXIME FAGET

Bibliography: Bono, Philip, and Gatland, Kenneth, *Frontiers of Space*, rev. ed. (1976); Calder, Nigel, *Spaceships of the Mind* (1978); Clarke, Arthur C., *The Promise of Space* (1968); Freedman, Russell, *2000 Years of Space Travel* (1963); Gatland, Kenneth, *Missiles and Rockets* (1975) and *Robot Explorers* (1972); Heppelheimer, T. A., *Toward Distant Suns* (1979); Lewis, Richard S., *Appointment on the Moon* (1969); Ley, Willy, *Rockets, Missiles and Men in Space* (1968); Moore, Patrick, *The Next Fifty Years in Space* (1976); Nicolson, Iain, *The Road to the Stars* (1978); Shelton, William, *American Space Exploration: The First Decade* (1967); Smolders, P. L., *Soviets in Space*, trans. by Marian Powell (1974); Strong, James, *Search the Solar System: The Role of Unmanned Interplanetary Probes* (1973); von Braun, Wernher, and Ordway, Frederick I., *The History of Rocketry and Space Travel*, rev. ed. (1969); Wilding-White, T. M., *Jane's Pocket Book of Space Exploration* (1976).

space law

Space law is a field of INTERNATIONAL LAW concerned with the law applicable to humans' exploration and use of outer space. With the launching of the first satellites in the 1950s, questions arose over the problem of sovereignty in space.

Numerous resolutions of the UN General Assembly and five major international treaties took up these problems. Perhaps the most important treaty was the 1967 Outer Space Treaty. It stated that the Moon and all other celestial bodies were to be free for exploration and use by all states and that international law would apply to the settlement of disputes. Signatories pledged not to place weapons of mass destruction, including nuclear weapons, in space or to establish military bases there. (The 1963 Nuclear Test Ban Treaty had already prohibited nuclear testing in outer space.)

The treaties referred to astronauts as "envoys of mankind" and require all states to assist them if they land outside their national borders. Each nation is responsible for the activities of its nationals in space and is liable for damages to persons and property of another state resulting from its space activities.

The 1968 Treaty on the Rescue and Return of Astronauts, the 1972 Treaty on Outer Space Liability for Damage Caused by Space Objects, the 1974 Treaty on Registration of Space Objects with the United Nations, and a 1979 Moon Treaty, including use of its natural resources, added to the growing body of space law.

During the 1970s and '80s the UN Committee on Peaceful Uses of Outer Space discussed resolutions that might lead to further treaties: one dealt with direct-broadcast satellites; another defined the boundaries of outer space. Some proposals are: a point where Earth's gravitational pull is offset by other forces; atmospheric composition criteria; or a realistic variable, for instance, the point where aerodynamic lift is lost—between 100 and 110 km (62 and 68 mi).

The launching and stationing of communications satellites presented practical legal problems. The United States, involved in one way or another in many of these launchings, made bilateral arrangements with other countries for tracking, data acquisition, communications testing, and transmission of meteorological information; and it made provisions to launch satellites for other countries.

Advances in space technology, especially with the U.S. Space Shuttle, may require further legal development. Space stations, for example, designed to enable humans to work in space for long periods of time, could lead to space manufacturing, space transportation, and new activities in communications, navigation, and meteorology. Space law will be needed to regulate all these activities and their by-products (space "junk").　　EDWARD R. FINCH, JR.

Bibliography: Bhatt, S., *Legal Control of Outer Space* (1974) and *Studies in Aerospace Law, from Competition to Cooperation* (1974); U.S. Senate Committee on Aeronautical and Space Sciences, *Space Law—Selected Documents* (1976); White, Irvin L., *Decision-Making for Space* (1970).

space medicine

Space medicine, or bioastronautics, is the branch of medicine involved in protecting humans from the environment of space and, at the same time, in determining their reactions to that environment. Those involved must review the entire operation of a space flight—from the conception of the vehicle through selection of the crew and conduct of the actual flight. Space medicine is a logical extension of aviation medicine, and the term *aerospace medicine* has evolved to encompass activity in both areas. Clearly one of the preventive-medicine disciplines, aerospace medicine has been a certified subspecialty of the American Board of Preventive Medicine since 1953. Approximately 400 U.S. physicians are currently certified as specialists in aerospace medicine. Also involved in such work are engineers, veterinarians, dentists, nurses, physiologists, psychologists, bacteriologists, toxicologists, and biochemists.

EARLY HISTORY

The early history of spaceflight was marked by a deep concern on the part of many scientists that humans would not be able to withstand the rigors of the space environment. A large group felt that animals should be used to explore the possible hazards of the space environment; the United States therefore flew a number of monkeys aboard captured German V-2 rockets between 1948 and 1952. Between 1949 and 1956 the Soviets flew 15 experiments with dogs, reaching an altitude of 213 km (132 mi). Finally, the dog LAIKA ("Barker") orbited in *Sputnik 2* (launched Nov. 3, 1957) and survived for a period of 7 days before the spacecraft's oxygen supply was exhausted. The United States flew monkeys in suborbital and orbital missions between 1958 and 1961. These flights showed that pulse and respiration rates, blood pressure, and performance of the specific trained tasks were basically unaffected.

On Apr. 12, 1961, the cosmonaut Yuri GAGARIN from the USSR demonstrated that humans could successfully orbit the Earth; his success confirmed a U.S. decision to use humans rather than animals to obtain most of the necessary data on space flights. A decision was also made in the U.S. program to progress cautiously by doubling the exposure time of humans in space at each step of the program and observing the effects carefully.

ENVIRONMENTAL AND LIFE-SUPPORT FACTORS

The atmosphere of spacecraft interiors has been carefully tested prior to flight for possible offgassing products from the

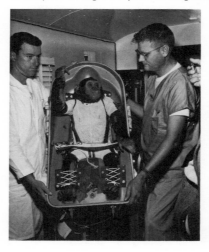

Ham, a 17-kg (37-lb) chimpanzee, is strapped into his seat before takeoff in a Mercury capsule on Jan. 31, 1961. Human beings were sent into space only after monkeys, dogs, and other animals proved capable of surviving in space without sustaining permanent physiological damage.

various carefully selected materials used. Cabin and suit temperatures have been maintained in the comfort range by adding life-support equipment. Radiation levels have been minimal—the average skin radiation dose received on the Apollo missions ranged from 0.16 to 1.14 rads, less than that received with some diagnostic X-ray procedures. (The maximum dose on the 84-day *Skylab 4* mission was 17.85 rads to the skin and 7.29 rads to the blood-forming organs, still a minimal dose.) Circadian (24-hour-period) body rhythms have been maintained in U.S. programs by keeping crews on Kennedy Space Center or Houston time frames or by shifting their cycles to meet the demands of reentry timing.

To deal with the increased acceleration, or g (gravity) loading, that occurs during launch and reentry, crews in U.S. and USSR spacecraft have all been placed so that they take the increased g loads in the chest-to-back position, because the human body can withstand a much higher g loading in this position. These loads have varied from 3 to 8.2 g and have raised no problems. In the U.S. Space Shuttle the crew will take the reentry accelerative force in a feet-first orientation, thus pushing the blood toward the feet rather from the chest to the back. The load will be only 1.5 g, but it will occur after 7 days of weightless flight. In addition, the crew will be provided with anti-g suits that will produce pressure on the lower portion of the body and prevent blood pooling in these areas.

PHYSIOLOGICAL AND PSYCHOLOGICAL FACTORS

In order to determine the effects of the space environment, sensors that interfere as little as possible with the comfort and functions of a crew have been developed. The physiological functions monitored are voice, heart action, respiration, body temperature, and blood pressure. The Skylab experiment program also provided detailed and sophisticated data on brain waves, exercise capacity, and the effect of lower-body negative pressure on heart and blood-vessel function, as well as samples of urine and blood.

The approximately 70,000 man hours of activity already conducted in the weightless environment of space have provided a great deal of knowledge about the capability of humans in this environment. During flights of short and long duration up to 84 days, crew members (except for some individual variability) have always been able to perform their inflight tasks and have suffered no permanent postflight physiological changes, but rather only time-limited readaptational changes, provided they have been supplied with an acceptable atmosphere, adequate food and hygiene facilities, exercise, a balance between work and rest, and enough time to acclimatize.

Weightless State. Case histories of astronauts and cosmonauts have revealed a general sense of enjoyment and well-being in the weightless state (see WEIGHTLESSNESS). Crew members have experienced sensations of fullness in the head, however, and occasional motion-sickness symptoms associated with the

The freedom of weightlessness is experienced by American astronauts Charles "Pete" Conrad, Jr. (left), and Paul J. Weitz during the first manned Skylab *flight in 1973. After a period of adjustment, astronauts lived comfortably in conditions of zero gravity for up to 84 days.*

freedom of movement and ease of activity in the weightless environment.

Heart and Blood Vessels. The cardiovascular system (heart and blood vessels) was the first system to show physiological change during spaceflight. Noted early was a pooling of blood in the legs when crew members stood in the immediate postflight state. Decreased postflight exercise capacity on the bicycle ergometer, coupled with a marked decrease in the amount of blood the heart could move in a minute, became understandable when related to this phenomenon. In postflight studies on the 84-day *Skylab 4* mission, echocardiography coupled with lower-body negative pressure demonstrated that changes in blood volume, rather than any malfunction of the heart muscle, were being observed. None of the cardiac electrical activity, measured in detail by vectorcardiography, was significantly altered. Episodes of cardiac arrhythmia (irregular beats) occurring with the slowing of heart rate were minimal.

Blood. In the hematology (blood) area, a loss of red-blood-cell mass during spaceflight has been observed. The mean losses as observed postflight were 9.4%, with means of 15%, 8.5%, and 5.9% respectively for the 28-, 59-, and 84-day *Skylab* missions. Apparently a suppression of red-cell production occurs but is governed in some way, limiting this suppressive effect so that it does not tend to increase with increasing flight duration. In addition, a replacement curve apparently develops by which the red-cell mass tends to return toward the normal level.

Nervous System. In the nervous system, the most important positive finding involved the development of motion sickness early in flight by a number of Apollo astronauts and USSR cosmonauts. These afflictions responded, however, to oral medication, and adaptation eventually occurred—within 7 to 10 days *Skylab* crew members were able to develop a marked increase in their tolerance to head movements and rotation in a power chair, as compared to their preflight baseline. Upon return to Earth the crew members had some obvious inner-ear (vestibular) disturbance that was evidenced by abnormal gait and a sensation of vertigo (dizziness) lasting for several days after reentry. The threshold tolerance to head movements with rotation also gradually decreased to the preflight baseline.

Muscles and Skeleton. Moderate losses of calcium, phosphorous, and nitrogen in the muscles and skeleton occur throughout the duration of a flight. Detailed mineral-balance studies indicate that these losses are comparable to those observed when normal persons are confined to bed rest for the same time periods and that the trend continues with increased duration. The rate of loss is about 6 g (0.2 oz) of calcium per month, or roughly 0.5% of the total body calcium per month. A relatively low but measurable mineral loss from the bone of the heel also occurs. This loss appears to be predictable based on initial bone mineral content and hydroxyproline levels.

Body Fluids and Electrolytes. The observed changes in hormones and in electrolytes (sodium and potassium) in *Skylab* crews are consistent in many ways with the hypothesis that blood volume increases in the upper half of the body in the weightless state. This apparent expansion of blood volume produces a loss of water and electrolytes, particularly sodium. A reduction of blood volume follows (mostly of plasma), and increased secretion of certain hormones leads to establishment of a new fluid and electrolyte balance appropriate to the zero-g situation. These changes in biochemical fluid and electrolyte balance have been well tolerated for the flight durations thus far undertaken.

Psychological Responses. Clearly, no dire psychological effects on performance have resulted from such problems as isolation, separation from the Earth, and boredom. The crews were originally selected as persons with strong psyches, good self-images, and both great achievement needs and great prior accomplishments. Several Apollo astronauts who visited the Moon, however, subsequently did exhibit various activities that appeared to be out of context with the public's perception of these individuals prior to flight. In one instance, a reactive depression occurred, related to demands for public appearances and to the individual's perception that the public subsequently reacted only in a minor way to an accomplishment he had felt to be of great magnitude. In other well-known instances, certain individuals have concentrated their postflight lives on religious pursuits, while another has devoted himself to the study of psychic phenomena and parapsychology; in all instances, however, these individuals had these interests prior to flight.

USSR Results. None of the body-system findings from USSR long-direction space missions differs significantly from those noted for the 84-day U.S. *Skylab 4* flight. The cosmonauts used a lower-body negative-pressure device (to decrease the pressure about the legs and lower abdomen and thereby suck the blood into this area) every day for 5 days prior to reentry, to prevent the deconditioning of the heart and blood vessels; this action, however, resulted in the pooling of blood in the lower legs and feet when standing up after the flight. Salt-water loading of each crew member was also used as a protective measure.

THE FUTURE

As longer-duration flights are conducted, effective countermeasures to prevent detrimental body-system changes will have to be used. To prevent the pooling of blood in the legs on return to Earth, a "crutch"—a garment putting pressure on the legs to return the blood toward the heart—has been used. More-effective countermeasures might be the use of a lower-body negative pressure device daily for several days before return to Earth and perhaps the increase of blood volume in the body with a salt solution or plasma.

The motion sickness encountered in space has been treated with medication, primarily with a combination of dexedrine and scopolamine. To date, the selection and training procedures for crews have not worked as countermeasures, but research must continue to try to develop effective methods.

Better methods of exercise in a reasonable in-flight time period are needed to maintain muscles. The only promising countermeasure for the loss of calcium from the skeleton is an oral phosphorous and calcium combination, but further research is required. The loss of red blood cells, however, appears to be self-limiting, and the biochemical changes appear to be adaptive.

At any rate, the future of space medicine is assured, as is that of spaceflight, because humanity has embarked on the ocean of space and will most likely continue the exploration of the universe.   CHARLES A. BERRY

Bibliography: Benedict, E. T., ed., *Weightlessness: Physical Phenomena and Biological Effects* (1960); Busby, D. E., *Space Clinical Medicine* (1968); Calvin, Melvin, and Gazenko, Oleg G., eds., *Foundations of Space Biology and Medicine,* vols. 1–3 (NASA SP-374; 1975); Gagarin, Yuri, and Lebedev, Vladimir, *Psychology and Space,* 2d ed. (1971); Graybiel, Ashton, ed., *Basic Environmental Problems of Man in Space* (1973); Henry, James P., *Biomedical Aspects of Space Flight* (1966); Johnson, R., and Dietlein, L., eds., *Bioastronautics Data Book* (NASA SP-30006; 1973) and *Biomedical Results of Skylab* (NASA SP-377; 1976); Link, Mae Mills, *Space Medicine in Project Mercury* (NASA SP-4003; 1965); Parker, J. F., and West, V., eds. *Biomedical Results of Apollo* (NASA SP-368; 1975); Schaefer, Karl E., ed., *Bioastronautics* (1964); Slager, Ursula T., *Space Medicine* (1962).

Space Shuttle

The space shuttle is a reusable vehicle capable of operating both in the Earth's atmosphere and in orbit; it will transport passengers and cargo into orbit and return them to the Earth's surface.

Although the USSR is believed to be developing such a vehicle, the most advanced version is the U.S. Space Shuttle,

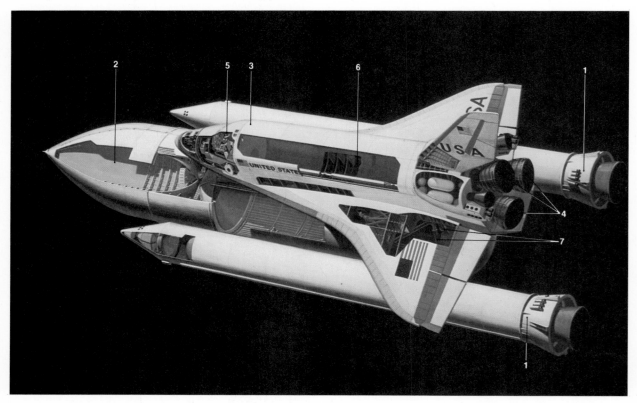

The NASA space shuttle is designed to orbit the Earth at speeds of up to 27,400 km/h (17,000 mph). Two solid-rocket boosters (1) and an external fuel tank (2) contribute to initial propulsion. The orbiter (3), a craft about the size of a DC-9 airplane, enters Earth orbit powered by its own engines (4), with the crew members in its cabin (5) breathing a pressurized mixture of nitrogen and oxygen. Equipment for astronomical observations, satellite repair, and scientific experiments is carried in the cargo bay (6), an area 18.3 m (60 ft) long that can accommodate payloads of 29,500 kg (65,000 lb). Fuel cells (7) using liquid hydrogen and oxygen supply electric power for the orbiter.

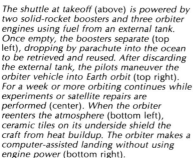

The shuttle at takeoff (above) is powered by two solid-rocket boosters and three orbiter engines using fuel from an external tank. Once empty, the boosters separate (top left), dropping by parachute into the ocean to be retrieved and reused. After discarding the external tank, the pilots maneuver the orbiter vehicle into Earth orbit (top right). For a week or more orbiting continues while experiments or satellite repairs are performed (center). When the orbiter reenters the atmosphere (bottom left), ceramic tiles on its underside shield the craft from heat buildup. The orbiter makes a computer-assisted landing without using engine power (bottom right).

which will become part of the U.S. Space Transportation System in the early 1980s. This system will consist of at least four (and possibly five) space shuttles, ground support facilities at two launch and landing sites, and upper stages for boosting satellites into higher orbits.

Components. The space shuttle consists of the orbiter, the external tank, and two solid rocket boosters. The orbiter, with a length of 37.3 m (122.4 ft) and a wingspan of 23.79 m (78 ft), carries the cargo and crew and is the only component that actually reaches orbit. The forward part of the orbiter will consist of an upper flight deck containing the displays and contents that will be used to pilot, monitor, and control the vehicle, and a lower cabin, containing the living quarters of the astronauts. The lower cabin will be connected by an airlock to the payload, or cargo, bay, 18.3 m (60.0 ft) long and 4.6 m (15.0 ft) in diameter, which will take up the middle and greatest part of the fuselage. The tail section of the orbiter will contain the three main engines and the propellant lines bringing liquid oxygen and liquid hydrogen from the external tank.

The solid-fuel rocket boosters, each 45.5 m (149.2 ft) long, will function for only two minutes before they are separated from the craft and return to the Atlantic Ocean. The external tank, 47 m (155 ft) long and 8.38 m (27.5 ft) in diameter, will provide propellants to the orbiter's three engines, and the total liftoff weight with fuel is almost 2 million kg (4.5 million lb). The overall length of the shuttle system on the launch pad is 56.1 m (184.0 ft), compared to 110.7 m (363 ft) for the Saturn V.

Testing. Piloted by astronauts Fred HAISE and Gordon Fuller-

ton, the first approach and landing tests of the shuttle began on Aug. 12, 1977, when the orbiter separated from a specially equipped Boeing 747 carrier aircraft at an altitude of 6,800 m (22,300 ft) over a dry lake bed in California. Dropping at a rate of 3,800 m/min (12,500 ft/min), the shuttle descended to the desert in 5 min 21 sec. A total of five such approach and landing tests were completed by Oct. 26, 1977. The first three were flown with a streamlined tailcone added to the orbiter to enhance its flight characteristics. The last two were flown with the tailcone off and simulated main rocket engines mounted in place; with this configuration the descent took only 2 to 2½ min.

Crew and Programs. On Jan. 16, 1978, the administrator of NASA announced the selection of 35 men and women as new ASTRONAUT candidates for the Space Shuttle program. This group reported to the Johnson Space Center in Houston, Tex., on July 1, 1978, to begin a 2-year training program. Each shuttle crew will consist of at least three full-time NASA astronauts. The commander and pilot will operate the orbiter; the mission specialist will have the overall responsibility for orbital operations in the areas of crew activity planning, use of consumables, and other space-shuttle activities affecting experiment operations in orbit. In addition, the orbiter can carry one to four payload specialists, drawn from various academic, government, and industrial research facilities, who will be responsible for specific experimental modules or other payload equipment they may have helped develop. The mission and payload specialists will not have to pass as demanding a physical as that required of the commander and pilot.

The space shuttle can place as much as 29,500 kg

(65,000 lb) into low Earth orbit. Among the most important early missions will be the orbiting (within the shuttle) of SPACELAB, designed by the European Space Agency, and the insertion into orbit of a variety of satellites and space probes. The shuttle, which in an emergency can carry as many as ten people, can be used to rescue other crews in orbit with only 24 hours' notice.

Typical Mission. Liftoff begins with the ignition of all five shuttle rocket engines. Two minutes into the flight the boosters burn out and are separated from the rest of the vehicle. They then parachute into the Atlantic Ocean and are recovered for reuse. The three main rocket motors continue to burn until a point just short of orbital insertion. The external tank is then separated and the orbiter continues into orbit through the use of two small rocket motors. The external tank reenters the atmosphere and is largely burned up. Any remaining pieces or chunks fall into the Indian or South Pacific Oceans. Once in orbit, to carry out its mission, the shuttle will remain there as many as 7 days, although flights lasting 30 days can be achieved by trading payload weight for consumables. Reentry will be accomplished with the same two small engines that injected the vehicle into orbit. Shuttles will land at the same sites from which they were launched—the Kennedy Space Center in Florida and, for missions requiring high-inclination orbits, the Vandenberg Air Force Base in California. The orbiter will land on a special 4,600-m (15,000-ft) runway. It will then begin the recycling process to prepare it for its next launch two weeks later.

From 1980 through its projected life into the early 1990s the Space Transportation System will fly more than 500 missions. As the year 2000 approaches, larger future shuttles will most likely be used to construct larger and larger structures in orbit, possibly even for the colonization of space.

MARSHALL KAPLAN

Bibliography: Baker, David, *Space Shuttle* (1979); Beatty, J. Kelly, "Space Shuttle: Problems and Progress," *Sky and Telescope,* June 1979; Grey, Jerry, *Enterprise* (1979); Kaplan, Marshall, *Space Shuttle: America's Wings to the Future* (1978); Powers, Robert M., *Shuttle: The World's First Spaceship* (1979); Stine, Harry G., *Shuttle into Space* (1978).

See also: SPACE EXPLORATION.

space station

A space station is any vehicle that provides a platform for humans and instruments in outer space. The term is rarely defined so broadly; it usually denotes a permanent inhabited base in Earth or planetary orbit. Space stations have been envisioned as science-research bases to study the Earth, the Sun, and the heavens; as facilities for manufacturing; and as locales for large colonies of inhabitants. Serious proposals for such stations emerged in the 1920s with the advent of modern rocket experiments. Hermann OBERTH, the father of modern astronautics, was the first to explore the problems of building a space station. In 1929, Hermann Noordung (a pseudonym for a Captain Potocnik of the Imperial Austrian Army) authored *The Problems of Space Flight,* in which he described a toroidal station that would rotate to provide artificial gravity through the centrifugal effect. The wheel-shaped station was popularized in 1951 by Wernher von Braun and others in *Across the Space Frontier.*

In the 1950s, Krafft EHRICKE, one of von Braun's associates, proposed placing an Atlas rocket into Earth orbit and outfitting its interior as a small space station. This idea was later proposed by Douglas Aircraft Corp. for its Manned Orbiting Laboratory (MOL) concept, which would have used the S-IV second stage of the Saturn I rocket.

Although the MOL concept was never realized, a similar concept was the Apollo Applications Program. Its wet orbital workshop would have used the S-IVB stage of the Saturn IB rocket. "Wet" meant that the stage would have been filled with propellants at launch and outfitted in orbit by astronauts. But budgetary problems and doubts about an astronaut's ability to do such work in a weightless environment later prompted program officials to approve a dry orbital workshop with a telescope mount attached instead of launched separately. SKYLAB, as it came to be called, was launched (1973) by a two-stage Saturn V rocket. Crews were orbited separately aboard an Apollo command/service module launched by a Saturn IB rocket. The project was highly successful and was manned (1973–74) for a total of nearly 172 days by three 3-man crews. Ironically, launch damage to *Skylab* had to be repaired by the first crew, thus eliminating earlier doubts about the ability of astronauts to work in a weightless environment.

Plans were made for a larger station—10 m (33 ft) wide versus the 6.7-m (22-ft) width of *Skylab*—also to be launched by

A wheel-shaped space station housing a colony of workers could feasibly be constructed within the next few decades, according to recent studies by NASA. The rim of the wheel would provide a pollution-free habitat for a population of 10,000, complete with schools, shops, and hospitals and have a photosynthetic agricultural system designed to recycle all biological wastes. Adults would work in nearby space factories, processing construction materials from lunar ore and producing electric power for the Earth from solar energy. Light and heat inside the habitat would be regulated to achieve artificial days, nights, and seasons.

a two-stage Saturn. But studies showed that such a project was impractical without a reusable space transportation system to supply it. Priority was thus switched to the Space Shuttle program, and further space-station studies have involved modules orbited by the shuttle or a station outfitted inside the shuttle's throwaway external tank.

The Soviet Union has launched several space stations—the first preceded *Skylab* by 2 years—in its SALYUT series. Cosmonauts aboard them have conducted Earth observations, astronomy, space manufacturing, physiology, and military reconnaissance work. Drawings and photographs indicate that Salyut is also based on a rocket-stage structure.

Since 1969, Princeton University physicist Gerard K. O'Neill has proposed design concepts for large space colonies—space stations capable of housing thousands of inhabitants in an Earthlike environment. Space colonies might be built from materials mined either on the Moon or from asteroids, and the inhabitants employed to construct giant solar satellite power stations that would beam solar energy to Earth. O'Neill's concept would cost billions of dollars, but it has been studied by NASA. DAVID DOOLING

Bibliography: Brand, Steward, ed., *Space Colonies* (1977); Cooper, Henry S. F., *A House in Space* (1976); Golden, Frederic, *Colonies in Space: The Next Giant Step* (1977); Heppenheimer, T. A., *Colonies in Space* (1977) and *Toward Distant Suns* (1979); Johnson, Richard D., and Holbrow, Charles, *Space Settlements: A Design Study* (NASA SP-413; 1977); Kidger, Neville, "The Salyut 6 Space Station," *Spaceflight*, April 1979; O'Neill, Gerard K., *The High Frontier* (1977).

space suit: see LIFE-SUPPORT SYSTEMS.

Space Telescope

The goal of NASA's Space Telescope program is to place into orbit a large telescope that will permit scientists to see 7 to 10 times farther into the universe than they can with earthbound instruments. The satellite is scheduled to be placed in orbit by the space shuttle in 1983 at an altitude of 520 km (320 mi).

Designed to be maintained in orbit by astronauts, the Space Telescope can also be brought back to Earth every 4 to 7 years for major repairs and overhaul. It will be housed within an aluminum cylinder 4.3 m (14 ft) in diameter and 13 m (43 ft) long. The entire spacecraft will weigh about 9,100 kg (20,000 lb). Two panels covered with solar cells will be able to supply 4.9 kW of electric power to the satellite.

The telescope will have a Ritchey-Chrétien optical system with a primary mirror 2.4 m (8 ft) in diameter. The secondary mirror, positioned at the prime focus of the primary, reflects light to five instruments located at the principal focus. Each instrument will be housed within a separate but identical module, thus permitting later substitution of other or more-advanced instruments. The faint-object camera, to be provided by the European Space Agency, will examine the ultraviolet, visible, and near-infrared regions of the spectrum and has a small field of view. The wide-field camera will have a field about 40 times greater but with degraded resolution. The high-resolution and faint-object spectrographs will have a wide range of spectral resolutions that would be impossible to realize with a single instrument. A single-channel photometer will measure the brightness of stars and the galactic background and will perform high-speed photometry, among other tasks. Other instruments planned for use in the Space Telescope include a planetary camera for observing bright objects at high magnification, an infrared photometer, and an astrometer that will be able to measure the proper motions of stars ten times more accurately than at present.

The primary mirror of the Space Telescope is capable of being corrected during operation to minimize variations from its original accuracy. A system of bright star sensors and precision gyroscopes will point the telescope to an accuracy of 0.01 arc sec, an angle only slightly greater than that made by a dime viewed at a distance of 370 km (230 mi). The system will also allow the telescope to stay on a target for extended periods of time within 0.007 arc sec. The resolving power of two point images is about 0.1 arc sec. Because exposures of

Orbiting above the Earth's atmosphere, the Space Telescope, scheduled for deployment by the space shuttle in 1983, will enable astronomers to obtain sharper images of celestial objects at all wavelengths and to make unhindered ultraviolet and infrared observations.

instruments to objects for as long as 10 hours are anticipated, such a system is a necessity. The Space Telescope, unlike earthbound instruments, will be able to operate in daylight and will have the capability of detecting objects 50 times fainter than those observable from Earth. MITCHELL R. SHARPE

Bibliography: Field, George, "The Space Telescope," *Astronomy*, November 1976; Lindop, Geoffrey Hugh, "The Space Telescope," *Spaceflight*, September-October 1978; *The Space Telescope* (NASA SP-392; 1976).

space-time continuum

The space-time continuum is a concept associated with the theory of RELATIVITY, in which time is treated as a fourth dimension. It replaced the Newtonian concept of space and a separate, absolute time. In Newtonian mechanics, any event (a flash of light or the decay of a radioactive atom, for example) can be associated with a location in space described by three coordinates, usually x, y, and z, and a moment in time described by one coordinate (t). Although the coordinates chosen are completely arbitrary, there are two quantities that are independent of that choice: the spatial distance between two events, $\Delta l = \sqrt{\Delta x^2 + \Delta y^2 + \Delta z^2}$ and the difference in time Δt. This is true in Newtonian mechanics because time is an absolute quantity.

With the advent of relativity, it became clear that time depended on velocity and that Δl and Δt are no longer separately invariant, suffering the FITZGERALD-LORENTZ CONTRACTION and time dilation, respectively. Instead, a new quantity Δs is invariant and is known as the "line element" or "invariant interval," given by $\Delta s^2 = -c^2\Delta t^2 + \Delta x^2 + \Delta y^2 + \Delta z^2$. The quantity Δs is now the invariant measure of intervals between events, and for this reason the term *metric* (from the Greek word for measure) often refers to the quadratic expression for Δs^2. Herman Minkowski developed (1908) the idea that a "space-time continuum" having a metric of the form given above was the underlying "geometry" of special relativity and the Lorentz transformations; hence that geometry is often referred to as "Minkowski space-time." In general relativity the space-time metric is more complicated than that given above and corresponds to curved space-time. CLIFFORD M. WILL

Bibliography: Graves, John C., *Conceptual Foundations of Contemporary Relativity Theory* (1977); Mermin, N. D., *Space and Time in Special Relativity* (1968); Sklar, Lawrence, *Space, Time, and Spacetime* (1977); Taylor, E. F., and Wheeler, J. A., *Spacetime Physics* (1966).

See also: CLOCK PARADOX; WORLD LINE.

Spacelab

Spacelab is a combination workshop and laboratory built by ten European nations for a variety of missions in Earth orbit aboard the U.S. SPACE SHUTTLE. Spacelab began officially in March 1973 when the European Space Research Organization (ESRO; now incorporated into the EUROPEAN SPACE AGENCY) asked interested nations to sign an arrangement for a Space Laboratory Program. Signatories now include nine ESA members—Belgium, Denmark, West Germany, France, Italy, the Netherlands, Spain, Switzerland, and the United Kingdom—and one nonmember, Austria.

A memorandum of understanding was signed between ESRO and the U.S. National Aeronautics and Space Administration (NASA) in September of that year, specifying that ESRO would design, fabricate, pay for, test, and deliver a Spacelab flight unit and would have the capability to produce additional ones; NASA would be responsible for Spacelab operations after delivery.

Scheduled to begin service during the early 1980s, Spacelab will consist basically of two modules: a pressurized laboratory section providing a shirtsleeve environment for researchers and an open pallet whose equipment and materials will be exposed directly to space. Extension modules of each type can be added to adapt Spacelab for different mission configurations, in such fields as astronomy, biomedicine, physics, materials testing, and manufacturing.

Spacelab will remain within the cargo bay of the space shuttle during typical missions lasting from 7 to 30 days. Its personnel, known as payload specialists, will ride in the crew compartment of the shuttle, entering the Spacelab's pressurized work section through a tunnel from the shuttle cabin. After a day's work in Spacelab they will return to the shuttle cabin for sleeping, eating, and other life-support functions. On some missions only the unpressurized pallet modules will be used, powered from a small, unmanned, pressurized housing dubbed an "iglo." Like the shuttle itself, each Spacelab will be reusable, designed to endure as many as 50 missions.

The first mission will carry out at least 75 separate investigations utilizing 40 different instruments. The proposed studies will be conducted in orbit by the payload specialists in communication with the selected researchers on the ground. The Spacelab payload specialists will be healthy men and women of any nation, nominated for flight by whatever organizations are sponsoring the payloads of a given mission; they will not have to meet the stringent selection criteria of regular U.S. astronauts.　　　　　　　　　JONATHAN EBERHART

Bibliography: Baker, David, "Spacelab: Europe Prepares for Manned Flight," *Spaceflight,* November 1975; Buedeler, Werner, and Karaman-dis, Stratis, *Spacelab: Europe's Space Laboratory* (1976); Powers, Robert M., *Shuttle: The World's First Spaceship* (1979); "Europe's Space Laboratory," *Spaceflight,* October 1974.

SPAD

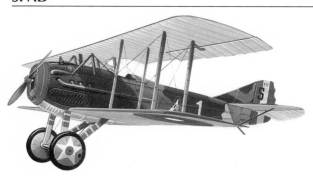

The 1917 Spad XIII one-seater biplane was considered to be the best French fighter of World War I. The plane had a top speed of 222 km/h (138 mph) and two forward-firing machine guns. The Spad XIII was used by all leading French and American pilots, including the American ace Capt. Eddie Rickenbacker.

The SPAD XIII was one of the most successful of the French World War I single-seat fighters. It first flew in April 1917. A biplane, the SPAD had an 8.1-m (26.5-ft) wingspan and was designed by a team under the direction of Louis Béchereau. In its final form the SPAD XIII was powered by a supercharged 220 hp Hispano-Suiza 8 Be engine and armed with two fuselage-mounted 7.65-mm (0.3-in) Vickers machine guns. Apart from its extensive service with 81 French fighter squadrons, the SPAD XIII was also used by British, Italian, Belgian, and American units.　　　　　　PETER M. H. LEWIS

spadefish

The spadefish comprises several species of deep-bodied, laterally compressed fishes in the family Ephippidae. Schools are usually found in the tropical and temperate marine waters of the Americas and West Africa. The American Atlantic spadefish, *Chaetodipterus faber,* a commercially important species in the tropics, ranges from Cape Cod to Brazil. It may reach a length of 3 m (10 ft) and a weight of 9 k (20 lb).

ALFRED PERLMUTTER

Spahn, Warren

Warren Edward Spahn, b. Buffalo, N.Y., Apr. 23, 1921, an American professional baseball player, was the most-successful pitcher in history, with 363 victories. His major league career began in 1942 when he joined the Boston Braves. After the Braves moved to Milwaukee, Wis., in 1953, Spahn enjoyed his best seasons. During his career he won 20 or more games in a season 13 times, made 750 pitching appearances, and led the National League in completed games 9 times. In 1963, two years before he retired at the relatively advanced age of 42, Spahn won 23 games. In 1973 he was voted into the Baseball Hall of Fame.

Spain

Spain, Europe's third largest nation, occupies most of the IBERIAN PENINSULA at the western edge of the continent. Integral parts of the nation are mainland Spain, containing about 98% of the national territory; the BALEARIC ISLANDS, in the Mediterranean Sea; the CANARY ISLANDS, 1,046 km (650 mi) southwest of the mainland off the coast of Africa; the cities of CEUTA and MELILLA, Spanish enclaves on the northern coast of Morocco; and small offshore islands. Mainland Spain shares borders with Portugal on the west, France and Andorra on the north, and GIBRALTAR, held by the British since 1704, on the south. Spain was united under the Catholic "kings" FERDINAND II of Aragon and ISABELLA I of Castile in the 15th century

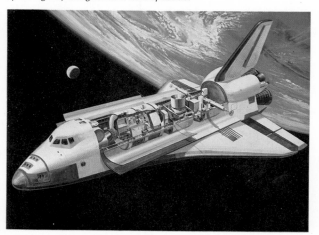

Spacelab, designed to fit in the cargo bay of NASA's space shuttle, will allow scientists to conduct experiments in physics, biology, chemistry, and astronomy under weightless and airless conditions. The European Space Agency designed and built Spacelab.

and reached a "golden age" in the 16th and 17th centuries based on gold and silver derived from colonies in the New World. Briefly a republic in 1873–74, Spain became one again in 1931. The leftist republican regime was overthrown in the SPANISH CIVIL WAR (1936–39), however, and for 36 years Spain was ruled by the right-wing dictator Generalissimo Francisco FRANCO. Following Franco's death in 1975, Spain began the transition to a constitutional monarchy under JUAN CARLOS I. A new constitution was adopted in 1978. In 1980 regional autonomy was granted to the BASQUES and to CATALONIA. Spain's name is derived from its Latin name, Hispania, used by the Romans, and may have come from the Phoenician *i-sch-phannim*, meaning "rabbits' coast."

LAND AND RESOURCES

The second highest country in Europe (after Switzerland), Spain has an average elevation of 660 m (2,165 ft), with 25% of the surface over 1,000 m (3,280 ft) and only 11% less than 200 m (656 ft). Mulhacén, which rises to 3,478 m (11,411 ft) in the SIERRA NEVADA of southern Spain, is the highest point on the mainland; Pico de Teide, rising to 3,718 m (12,195 ft) on the island of Tenerife in the Canaries, is the highest point in Spain.

The dominant landform on the mainland is the Meseta (or Tableland), a broad plateau that occupies the central 40% of the nation. It has an average elevation of 700–800 m (2,300–2,600 ft) in Old CASTILE and 600–700 m (1,968–2,300 ft) farther south in New Castile. It is crossed by the Cordillera Central north of Madrid that rises to more than 2,500 m (8,200 ft) in the Sierra de Gredos and by the Toledo Mountains south of Toledo that rise to 1,419 m (4,656 ft). The Can-

tabrian Mountains form the northern edge of the Meseta and reach a high point of 2,648 m (8,689 ft) in the Picos de Europa. To the northwest rise the hills and mountains of LEÓN and GALICIA, and to the west rise the broken uplands of Estremadura that separate Spain from Portugal. The southern edge is formed by the Sierra Morena, which rises to only 1,323 m (4,339 ft). To the east, beginning about 25 km (15 mi) east of Burgos, are the northwest-southeast trending Iberian Mountains, which exceed 2,100 m (7,000 ft) in elevation.

To the north of the Meseta and its mountain rim are the Basque region and the PYRENEES, which mark the border with France and reach 3,404 m (11,168 ft) in Aneto Peak. To the south are the snowcapped Sierra Nevada and other ranges of the Betic Cordillera that stretch from Gibraltar to near Alicante and reappear offshore in the Balearic Islands. The two principal lowlands are the Ebro Basin, a structural depression between the Pyrenees, Iberian Mountains, and Catalan Mountains along the coast between Valencia and Barcelona; and the Guadalquivir (or Andalusian) Basin, between the Sierra Morena and Betic Cordillera in the south.

Soils. Spain's most fertile soils are of alluvial origin and occur along the major river valleys and on small coastal plains in Andalusia, Murcia, and Valencia. Infertile, shallow soils (rankers) predominate on the siliceous rocks (granites, slates, and quartzites) underlying the western Meseta, with some podzolized, brown soils in humid areas and brown forest soils in drier regions. Red Mediterranean soils, suitable for cultivation, occur in Badajoz, Salamanca, Ciudad Real, Toledo, and Jaén. Calcareous rocks weather into moderately fertile brown forest soils in humid areas and to rendzinas and easily eroded red Mediterranean soils in drier regions.

Climate. Spain has three temperate types of climate. Mild, humid conditions, typical of the northwest European type of climate, prevail in the northwest, north, Pyrenees, and Central Mountains. A Mediterranean type of climate, with mild temperatures and summer drought lasting from two to five months, prevails along the Mediterranean littoral, in Andalusia, and in the Balearic Islands. A continental variant of the Mediterranean climate, with sporadic rainfall, cold winters, and hot summers, occurs in the northern Meseta, Ebro Basin, and other inland areas. Except in the north and in the mountains, rainfall is everywhere scanty; annual amounts decrease from between 600 and 1,000 mm (24 and 40 in) along the

SPAIN

Official Name: Spanish State
Capital and Largest City: Madrid (1978 est. pop., 3,994,000)
Area: 504,782 km² (194,897 mi²)
Elevation: *Highest*—Pico de Teide, 3,718 m (12,195 ft); *lowest*—sea level, along the Mediterranean Sea and Atlantic Ocean
Population: 37,551,000 (1979 est.). *Distribution*—74% urban, 26% rural; *density*, 74 persons per km² (193 per mi²); *annual rate of increase* (1970–77), 1.1%
Principal Languages: Castilian Spanish, Catalan, Galician, Basque
Principal Religion: Roman Catholicism (official)
Principal Products: *Agriculture*—citrus fruits, vegetables, olives, grapes, corn, wheat, barley, maize; sheep, pigs, cattle, fish. *Manufacturing and industry*—iron and steel, motor vehicles, ships, plastics, pharmaceuticals, rubber, processed foods, textiles, footwear. *Mining*—mercury, coal, sulfur, iron, copper, lead, manganese, magnesite, tin, uranium, wolframite, zinc, bauxite, petroleum, natural gas, salt, potash, gypsum
Railroads: 15,758 km/9,792 mi (1977)
Roads: 146,410 km/90,977 mi (1977)
Currency: 1 Spanish peseta = 100 céntimos

The Castillo de Santa Barbara, located on the site of an ancient Roman fortress, overlooks the Mediterranean resort city and port of Alicante in southeastern Spain. A provincial capital, the city is a major tourist center of Spain's Costa Blanca along the Mediterranean Sea.

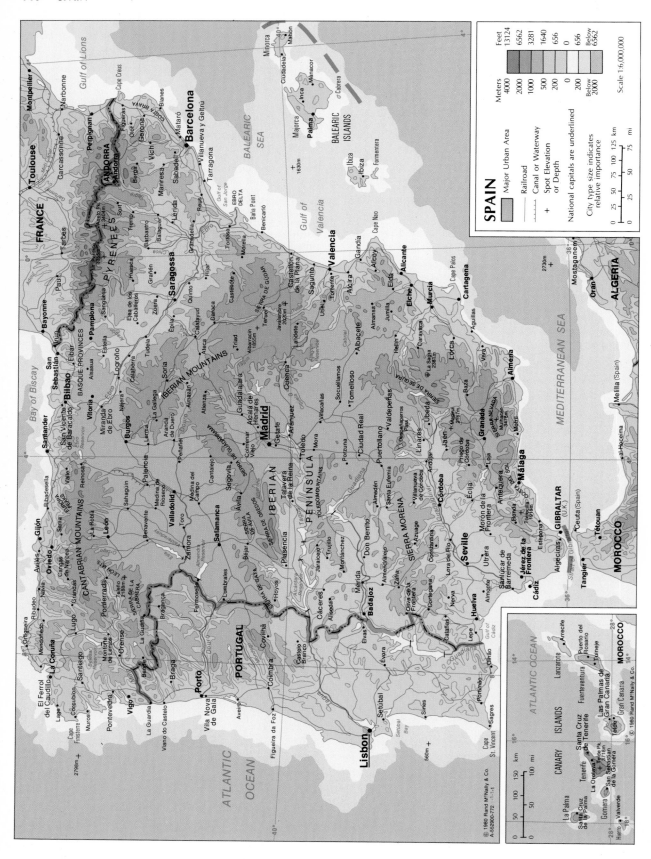

SPAIN

Major Urban Area
Railroad
Canal or Waterway
+ Spot Elevation or Depth

National capitals are underlined

City type size indicates relative importance

Feet	Meters
13124	4000
6562	2000
3281	1000
1640	500
656	200
0	0
656	200
Below 6562	Below 2000

Scale 1:6,000,000

0 25 50 75 100 125 km
0 25 50 75 mi

FRANCE

Gulf of Lions

Bay of Biscay

ATLANTIC OCEAN

PYRENEES

BASQUE PROVINCES

CANTABRIAN MOUNTAINS

IBERIAN MOUNTAINS

IBERIAN PENINSULA

TOLEDO MOUNTAINS

SIERRA MORENA

SIERRA DE SEGURA

SIERRA NEVADA

PORTUGAL

BALEARIC SEA

BALEARIC ISLANDS

Gulf of Valencia

MEDITERRANEAN SEA

Gulf of Cadiz

ALGERIA

MOROCCO

Montpellier
Narbonne
Toulouse
Carcassonne
Bayonne
Perpignan
ANDORRA Andorra
Figueras
Olot
Gerona
Blanes
Cape Creus
COSTA BRAVA
Barcelona
Mataró
Vich
Berga
Manresa
Sabadell
Villanueva y Geltrú
Tarragona
Reus
Lérida
Balaguer
Tremp
Sort
Huesca
Barbastro
Grañén
Tortosa
Morella
Benicarló
Baña Point
EBRO DELTA
Gulf of San Jorge
Minorca
Mahón
Ciudadela
Inca
Manacor
Majorca
Palma
Ibiza
Formentera
Cabrera
Pamplona
Estella
San Sebastián
Vitoria
Logroño
Calahorra
Tudela
Soria
Calatayud
Ateca
Daroca
Teruel
Albarracín
Castellón de la Plana
Sagunto
Valencia
Gandía
Cape Nao
Alcira
Alcoy
Alicante
Elda
Elche
Murcia
Cartagena
Cape Palos
Saragossa
Bilbao
Santander
San Vicente de la Barquera
Burgos
Madrid
Getafe
Aranjuez
Toledo
Guadalajara
Alcalá de Henares
Cuenca
Albacete
Almansa
Jumilla
Hellín
Caravaca
Lorca
Vera
Almería
Motril
Granada
Málaga
Córdoba
Seville
Huelva
Cádiz
Jerez de la Frontera
Algeciras
GIBRALTAR (U.K.)
Ceuta (Spain)
Tangier
Tétouan
al-Hoceima
Melilla (Spain)
Oran
Mostaganem
Gijón
Oviedo
La Coruña
Santiago
Vigo
Pontevedra
Orense
León
Ponferrada
Valladolid
Salamanca
Zamora
Ávila
Segovia
Cáceres
Mérida
Badajoz
Porto
Coimbra
Lisbon

CANARY ISLANDS
Santa Cruz de Tenerife
Las Palmas de Gran Canaria
Gran Canaria
Tenerife
Teide
La Palma
Gomera
Hierro
Lanzarote
Fuerteventura
Arrecife
Puerto del Rosario
MOROCCO
ATLANTIC OCEAN

© 1980 Rand McNally & Co.

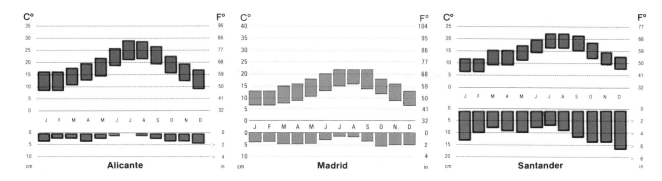

Annual climate charts for three cities in Spain indicate climate zones of the nation. Bars indicate monthly ranges of temperatures (red) and precipitation (blue). Santander, located north of the Cantabrian Mountains on the Bay of Biscay, has a marine west coast climate of moderate temperatures and high precipitation. Madrid, the capital, has the steppe climate that characterizes much of Spain's central plateau. Located in an arid belt on the Mediterranean, Alicante has a steppe climate of moderate temperatures and low precipitation.

Cantabrian and Galician coasts to less than 600 mm (24 in) in the southern Meseta, Andalusia, and Mediterranean coastal regions and as little as 350 mm (14 in) in some inland areas.

Drainage. The longest rivers are the TAGUS RIVER, which crosses the Meseta to enter the Atlantic Ocean in Portugal, and the EBRO RIVER, which flows into the Mediterranean. Other major rivers draining to the Atlantic are the DOURO (Duero), GUADALQUIVIR, Guadiana, and Miño. Extensive marshes occur on the Ebro Delta and at the mouth of the Guadalquivir below Seville.

Vegetation and Animal Life. Slightly more than 20% of Spain is forested, and the remainder—where not cultivated—supports a variety of scrub vegetation used for low-grade pasture. The principal trees in the north are beech, oak, chestnut, eucalyptus, and some pine and fir. A more open, evergreen type of forest with groves of holm oaks and cork oaks predominates in drier regions. Wild animals include Hispanic goats, boars, chamois, wolves, foxes, deer, fallow deer, rabbits, and hares. Partridges and quail are common game birds, and storks, eagles, and vultures are sometimes seen.

Resources. About 35% of the land is cultivated; 7% is planted with permanent crops such as olives, wine grapes, and citrus; and 27% is used for pasture and meadow. Irrigation is practiced extensively, making water a major resource in drier regions. Fuel resources are inadequate, despite some deposits of bituminous coal, anthracite, lignite, petroleum, and natural gas. Large deposits of sulfur, mercury, gypsum, nickel, copper, phosphates, potassium, lead, zinc, and uranium occur, but most deposits lie in folded and faulted areas surrounding the edges of the Meseta and are difficult to extract. Hydroelectric power is important, but costly dams are required to regulate the seasonal flow of most rivers.

(Right) The highland valley of Aran, located near the French border in the central Pyrenees, contains such small agricultural villages as Salardú and Viella. The glaciated peaks of the Maladeta region, including some of the highest in the range, tower in the distance.

(Below) The Alhambra, located on a ridge overlooking the Andalusian city of Granada in southeastern Spain, was begun in 1238 when Granada became the capital of the last Moorish kingdom in Spain. This fortified palace became the center of Moorish arts and learning.

PEOPLE

Most Spaniards are more conscious of regional differences based on cultural and historical factors than of minor racial differences. The three principal regional minority groups are the Basques, who make up about 2% of the total population and are concentrated in the three northern provinces of Vizcaya, Guipúzcoa, and Álava and also in Navarre; the Catalans, who make up about 19% of the total population and live mainly on the east coast; and the Gallegos (Galicians), who constitute about 7% of the total population and are concentrated in the northwest.

Language. Spain's official language is Castilian Spanish, but Catalan, Basque, and Galician are important regional languages with their own literature. Catalan includes Valencian and Balearic as subtypes and is related to Provençal French. The BASQUE LANGUAGE is of unknown affinity. Galician is related to Portuguese. Distinctive regional accents include that spoken by Asturians (called "bable") in the north and that spoken by Andalusians in the south, although neither group encounters major difficulties in being understood in other parts of Spain.

Religion. Roman Catholicism is the official religion, and about 99% of the people are baptized as members of that church. Less than 1% belong to Protestant groups and small communities of Jews and Muslims located in the larger cities.

Demography. Approximately 70% of the total population lived in urban areas of more than 10,000 inhabitants in 1975, compared with only 53% in 1950. The two largest cities, each with more than 1 million inhabitants, are MADRID and BARCELONA. Other large cities are VALENCIA, SEVILLE, Saragossa, BILBAO, MÁLAGA, and LAS PALMAS. Rural-to-urban migration accelerated during the 1960s and 1970s, the urbanization occurring at a faster rate and more recent date than in most of the rest of Europe. Nuclear settlements have long existed in Spain because of the population's need for access to water.

In 1976, Spain's crude birthrate was 18.2 per 1,000 inhabitants and the death rate 8 per 1,000, resulting in an annual rate of natural increase of about 1.1%. Population densities are generally lower than in most other parts of Europe and range from regional highs of 508 per km² (1,316 per mi²) in Barcelona and 474 per km² (1,228 per mi²) in Madrid to regional lows of 12 per km² (31 per mi²) in sparsely populated Guadalajara and 5 per km² (13 per mi²) in barren Teruel.

Education and Health. The present educational system is based on laws adopted in 1970. The system provides for optional preschool education and 8 years of compulsory general basic education beginning at age 6. Education is free in state-run schools, which offer a primary program lasting 5 years and a 3-year program of secondary education. Students thereafter may enter the 3-year *Bachiller* (B.U.P.) program, after which a 1-year college orientation program (C.O.U.) is required for entrance to a university. Higher education is pursued by about 1% of the population and is structured in three cycles: the first cycle lasts 3 years, and the second and third cycles 2 years each. Major universities are located in Madrid and Barcelona, and there are regional universities in most larger cities. Despite these educational provisions, an estimated 10% of all school-age children do not attend school and about 8% of the total population of 10 years of age or more is illiterate.

A compulsory health insurance program under the National Social Security Institute covers about 85% of the population. In addition, more than 7 million persons supplement their medical benefits by paying into private health insurance programs. Altogether, in 1974 there were 1,348 civil hospitals, with more than 185,000 beds, 64,597 physicians, 3,703 dentists, 19,253 pharmacists, and 4,356 midwives. The infant mortality rate is 10.7 per 1,000 live births.

The Arts. Cultural institutions are overseen by the Ministry of Culture, and official culture centers are located in each of the provincial capitals. Additional cultural centers, both official and private, are concentrated in Madrid, Barcelona, and other large urban centers. Of special importance in Madrid are the Centro de Cooperación, Iberoamericana, the Ateneo, the Villa de Madrid cultural center; several private foundations such as the March, Mediterránea, Universitaria Española; and the Club Siglo XXI. For further discussion of the arts in Spain see SPANISH ART AND ARCHITECTURE, SPANISH LITERATURE, and SPANISH MUSIC.

ECONOMIC ACTIVITIES

Slow to industrialize in the 18th and 19th centuries, Spain remained predominantly agricultural until 1950. During Franco's rule, the state-run INI (National Industrial Institute) attempted to lessen imports and make Spain industrially self-sufficient by rapidly expanding petroleum refining, shipbuilding, automobile assembly, aeronautics, and the production of chemicals, fertilizers, petrochemicals, and electricity. With the 1959 stabilization program, private industry and foreign investment were again encouraged, and Spain grew rapidly under the economic development plans covering the years 1964–67, 1968–71, and 1972–75. In 1975 a new economic stage began as efforts were made to correct some of the imbalance resulting from earlier growth and to reduce dependence on imported petroleum as an energy source. In 1977, Spain had a gross national product of $116 billion, or $3,190 per capita.

Manufacturing and Mining. About 37% of the labor force is employed in manufacturing and construction, with the greatest concentrations of industry in the areas of Bilbao-Santan-

The Plaza de la Cibeles in central Madrid is lined with the banks and business establishments of the capital city's principal commercial district. A leading manufacturing city and the center of Spanish government, Madrid has become Spain's most populous city.

Fishing boats and bathers share the beach of a small village on the Costa Brava, or "wild coast," of Spain's northern Mediterranean shore. Although fishing was traditionally the principal source of income, tourism is now more important to the area's economy.

Picturesque windmills, traditionally used to process wheat, rise above a city in Spain's arid central plateau. Despite its low rainfall, the plateau, called Meseta, is primarily an agricultural region and produces substantial harvests of wheat and other grains.

der-Oviedo and in Catalonia; a smaller concentration occurs around Madrid. The iron and steel industry, centered in the north, is the leading metal-processing industry, with steel production reaching 11.1 million metric tons (12.2 million U.S. tons) in 1977. The cement industry grew rapidly in the 1960s and 1970s, as did the shipbuilding, chemical, rubber, machinery, and electronics industries. Production of consumer goods is growing in volume. Spain is an important producer of textiles, shoes and leather goods, toys, and furniture.

The most valuable mineral mined is mercury, followed by anthracite, bituminous coal, lignite, iron ore, sulfur, potassium chloride, fluorspar, lead, and zinc. Major natural gas fields were discovered in the 1970s in the Pyrenees and off the east coast, and small deposits of petroleum have been found in the vicinity of Burgos and off the east coast near the Ebro delta.

Power. In 1975, 68% of all Spain's energy requirements were met by imported petroleum and its derivatives; 17% was supplied by coal, and 12% by hydroelectricity. In 1978, Spain produced 100 billion kW h of electricity; 24% was from hydroelectricity, approximately 4% of nuclear origin, and the remainder from thermal plants fired by coal and petroleum. In 1979 a 10-year energy plan covering the years 1977–87 was adopted that calls for the construction of nuclear plants, the doubling of coal output to 16 million metric tons (17,640,000 U.S. tons), and increased use of natural gas—to lessen petroleum imports.

Agriculture. About 19% of the labor force is employed in agriculture—a significant drop from the 55% so employed in 1950. Cereals occupy more than 60% of the cultivated area, with wheat and barley the main crops. In general, rainfall in inland and southern regions is not sufficient for diversified farming, and the lands are either dry-farmed or irrigated. Unirrigated areas are traditionally planted to wheat one year and left fallow the next, although this low-yielding method of cultivation is being replaced by a triennial rotation based on cereals the first year, a soil-enriching leguminous crop the second year, and a fallow third year. Olive trees and vineyards cover large areas, Spain being the world's largest producer of olives and the world's fourth largest producer of wines. Irrigated agriculture is important in the Ebro Basin, Douro Valley, Guadalquivir Basin, and lowlands along the Mediterranean; high yields of citrus and other fruits, vegetables, sugar beets, cotton, and tobacco are obtained. Some beef and dairy cattle are raised but are greatly outnumbered by sheep and pigs.

Forestry and Fishing. Lumber, cork, and resin are the leading forest products. The 1976 fish catch of approximately 1.5 million metric tons (1.6 million U.S. tons) has since declined as seafloors close to Spain approached exhaustion and territorial claims by nations bordering the Atlantic Ocean were extended. The fish catch consists primarily of sardines, mackerel, whiting, and anchovies.

Transportation. Almost half of all roads are suitably surfaced for modern traffic, but only 1,091 km (678 mi) are superhighways. The railroads are operated by Spanish National Railways (RENFE), but—unlike the rest of Europe—wide-gauge tracks are used. Only 4,783 km (2,972 mi) of track are electrified, and only 2,162 km (1,351 mi) are double track. The rail network is less dense than in other European countries, but a major upgrading program is under way. Air transportation is dominated by nationally owned Iberia and Aviaco airlines. The main airports are in Madrid, Palma de Mallorca, Barcelona, Las Palmas, Málaga, Santa Cruz de Tenerife, and Alicante. The busiest ports are Bilbao, Santa Cruz de Tenerife, Cartagena, La Coruña, Santander, and Málaga.

Trade. In most years Spain has an unfavorable balance of trade, with earnings from tourism significantly reducing the deficit. The main exports are iron and steel products, machinery, appliances, motor vehicles, shoes and leather items, ships, electrical goods, and refined petroleum products. Agricultural products now constitute only 29% of all exports, with citrus fruit, canned fish and vegetables, wines, olive oil, and fresh vegetables the most important. The principal imports are petroleum, iron and steel products, basic chemicals, machinery and equipment, and food products (mainly meat, coffee, and tea). More than 50% of all exports go to member countries of the European Economic Community (EEC) and to the United States. Most imports are derived from these same areas and most petroleum from Saudi Arabia. Spain has applied for membership in the EEC.

GOVERNMENT

According to the 1978 constitution, Spain is a hereditary, constitutional monarchy with a parliamentary form of government. The head of state is King Juan Carlos I, who came to power in 1975. The head of government is Prime Minister Adolfo Suárez, who was appointed to office in 1977. Executive power rests with the king, the prime minister, and the council of ministers. Legislative power is invested in the Cortes, a bicameral legislature consisting of a 350-member Congress of Deputies and a Senate with 208 elected senators. Elections for each house are held every four years.

Spain is divided into 50 provinces, each with an appointed governor and a local council. Four provinces in Catalonia and three in the Basque country were granted autonomous status in 1980.

AURORA GARCÍA BALLESTEROS

Bibliography:

CIVILIZATION: Burckhardt, Titus, *Moorish Culture in Spain*, trans. by Alisa Jaffa (1972); Bradford, Saxton E., *Spain in the World* (1962); Pritchett, Victor S., *The Spanish Temper* (1954; repr. 1976).

LAND AND PEOPLE: Fisher, William B., and Bowen-Jones, Howard, *Spain: An Introductory Geography* (1966); Houston, James McIntosh, *The Western Mediterranean World: An Introduction to Its Regional Landscapes* (1964); Loder, Dorothy, *The Land and People of Spain* (1972); Lowe, Alfonso, *The Spanish* (1975).

ECONOMICS: Baklanoff, Eric N., *The Economic Transformation of Spain and Portugal* (1978); Salisbury, William T., and Theberge, James D., eds., *Spain in the 1970s: Economics, Social Structure, Foreign Policy* (1976); Roman, Manuel, *The Limits of Economic Growth in Spain* (1971); Wright, Alison, *The Spanish Economy, 1959–1976* (1977).

GOVERNMENT AND POLITICS: Amodia, José, *Franco's Political Legacy: From Dictatorship to Facade Democracy* (1977); Coverdale, John F., *The Political Transformation of Spain after Franco* (1979); Payne, Stanley G., *Politics and the Military in Modern Spain* (1967); Robinson, Richard A. H., *The Origins of Franco's Spain* (1970; repr. 1971).

Spain, history of

Because of its geographical location on the Iberian Peninsula, Spain has a history that is in many ways unique. Isolated by seas and mountains from many of the main currents of European culture, subject to conquest from Africa, and possessing ready access to the Atlantic Ocean and the wealth that lay beyond it, the Spanish have a rich and varied national experience that highlights and yet diverges from many of the important developments in European history.

TO THE MUSLIM CONQUEST

Spain has been inhabited for probably half a million years. At TORRALBA AND AMBRONA (in Soria, to the northeast of Madrid) lie the bones of elephants trapped by bands of the early human species *Homo erectus*. More recent peoples have left bones and tools at many Spanish sites. Of all the remains of Stone Age peoples, none is more impressive than the polychrome paintings of bison, horses, and other animals painted on the ceilings of the caves at ALTAMIRA (in Santander, on the Bay of Biscay) by *Homo sapiens* artists about 15,000 years ago.

An agricultural revolution came to Spain about 3000 BC. Farming and herding brought a population boom. In the south of Spain many dolmens and megalithic tombs have survived, attesting to the vitality of this culture, called the Almería. About 1000 BC waves of migrants began to bring in new cultural influences. CELTS, people speaking an Indo-European language, entered from the north, and settlers from more advanced civilizations founded towns on the Mediterranean coast: Phoenicians at Cádiz, Greeks at Málaga and Ampurias, and Carthaginians at Cartagena.

Roman Conquest. During the 3d century BC the Carthaginians expanded from their base in North Africa into much of the Iberian Peninsula. Spanish resources were vital to Carthage in its ongoing conflict with Rome. In 218 BC, at the beginning of the Second PUNIC WAR, the Romans invaded Iberia; they defeated (201) the Carthaginians but had to overcome fierce resistance from the Spanish, especially in the north. Roman control of the Iberian Peninsula was not complete until 19 BC. The peninsula became one of the empire's most valuable provinces as Spanish gold, silver, copper, iron, tin, and lead enriched Rome. Most Iberians learned Latin and acquired Roman citizenship. Of the many structures built by Roman engineers, the aqueduct of Segovia, the theater of Mérida, and the bridge of Córdoba are still standing.

Visigothic Spain. Early in the 5th century the Roman Empire was invaded by Germanic barbarians. Among those who settled in Spain were VANDALS (who gave their name to Andalusia) and Visigoths (see GOTHS). The latter, migrating from France and numbering fewer than 250,000, were able to dominate 6 or 7 million Hispano-Romans. The Visigoths intervened in Spain as early as 415, but it was not until the reign of King Leovigild (r. 568-86) that they moved their capital from France to Toledo. Leovigild conquered the Suevi and Basques and allowed intermarriage between Visigoths, who were Arian Christians (see ARIANISM), and Hispano-Romans. King Reccared (r. 586-601) converted the Visigoths to Catholicism, thus further encouraging assimilation.

The Visigothic kings built churches and ruled with the help of bishops and nobles. King Reccesvinth (r. c.649-72) promulgated a legal code that was based largely on Roman precedents, although traces of Germanic traditions remained. The Visigothic monarchy, however, was generally weak; because their position was elective, the kings were continually subject to the intrigues of their nobles. In 711 the family of the late King Witiza (r. 701-c.710) asked the Muslims of Morocco to help them overthrow King Roderick (r. 710-11). The Muslim general Tariq ibn Ziyad (fl. 711) crossed over to Gibraltar, defeated Roderick, and—taking advantage of divisions among the Visigoths—began the conquest of Spain.

MUSLIM SPAIN AND THE RECONQUEST

The Muslims easily defeated the Visigoths and by 718 were masters of almost the entire peninsula. Many Christians converted to Islam, and Muslims of different nationalities—Arabs, Syrians, Berbers—settled in Spain, although their numbers were never great. The rich lands of southern Spain, which they called al-Andalus, were especially attractive in comparison with the deserts of North Africa. Despite many successful military expeditions, few Muslims—or Moors, as the Christians called them—chose to settle on the barren highlands of Castile.

Al-Andalus. The UMAYYAD dynasty ruled al-Andalus from 756 to 1031. ABD AL-RAHMAN I, survivor of a family of caliphs of the Arab empire, fled from Syria in 750, gathered tribal followers around him in Spain, and, through constant warfare, ruled al-Andalus until 788. Abd al-Rahman III (891-961) ended a period of disorder, reunited Moorish Spain, and declared himself caliph of Córdoba. Relying on an imperial guard of

(Below) *A miniature from the 13th-century* Cántigas de Santa María *portrays the fighting between the Christian Visigoths and the Muslims who overran most of Spain beginning in AD 711. (Escorial, Madrid.)*

(Left) *A Roman mosaic (early 4th century) found near Barcelona portrays a Roman circus. The Roman conquest of Spain was completed by the 1st century AD. (Museo Arqueologico, Barcelona.)*

European slaves, he reduced the power of the Arab aristocracy. His reign (929-61) marks the apogee of Muslim Spain, a time of economic and cultural splendor.

Al-Andalus contrasted sharply in many respects with Christian Europe. At a time when Europe had become rural and impoverished, al-Andalus was a region of prosperous cities and intense trade. Its goods—including glass, paper, leather, metalwork, and silk—were renowned as far away as India. The Muslim rulers generally tolerated Christians and Jews and encouraged cultural diversity. Science, medicine, and philosophy flourished, especially in the capital, Córdoba. Spanish Islamic scholars such as AVERROËS (1126-98) studied the works of Aristotle and other Greeks, which were translated into Latin and eventually spread to the rest of Europe.

After the death in 1002 of the dictator al-MANSUR, al-Andalus broke up into small quarreling taifas, or factional states. It was briefly reunited by North African Muslim invaders, the ALMORAVIDS (1086-1147) and the ALMOHADS (1147-1212), who sought to instill a more fanatic brand of Islam in the native Moors. Despite temporary successes, however, Muslim Spain was already on the defensive.

Rise of the Christian Kingdoms. The few Christian enclaves that the Muslims allowed to survive in the mountainous regions of the north had meanwhile grown into powerful kingdoms. In ASTURIAS, on the Bay of Biscay, a group of Visigoth nobles elected Pelayo (r. c.718-37) their king. Leading a band of mountaineers, Pelayo even defeated (c.722) a Muslim army—a victory that was later hailed as the beginning of the Reconquest of Spain. Alfonso I (c.693-757, r. 739-57) added Galicia to the Asturian domains. His successors pushed south into León and beyond, and the discovery (c.815) of the alleged tomb of Saint James at SANTIAGO de Compostela enhanced Asturian prestige.

In the northeast of the peninsula, Frankish warriors under CHARLEMAGNE established the Spanish March, embryo of a future Catalonia, with strong links to France and a Mediterranean focus. Between this region and Asturias the kingdom of NAVARRE rapidly rose to prominence in the 10th century. Enriched by contacts with France and the passage of pilgrims to Santiago de Compostela, King SANCHO III, the Great, of Navarre briefly ruled (1000-35) all Christian Spain, although his empire was later divided among his four sons. Under Sancho European influences—such as the Cluniac monastic reform and feudalism—were able to permeate Spanish society.

Most significant in laying the foundations of modern Spain were Aragon and Castile. Aragon became an independent kingdom when Ramiro I (r. 1035-63) received it from his father, Sancho the Great. Temporarily united (1076-1134) with Navarre, Aragon expanded its territory at the expense of the Moors, and in 1137 marriage added mercantile Catalonia. Thereafter, while the two regions remained distinct, they were linked under the crown of Aragon. The Aragonese kings carried out an aggressive foreign policy, extending their rule to the Balearic Islands (1230-86), Valencia (1238), and, at different periods, to Sardinia, Sicily, and Naples.

Aragon eventually adopted the Mediterranean orientation of Barcelona (Catalonia), but Castile, situated on the La Mancha tableland in the center of the peninsula, provided the central driving force for the Christian Reconquest. Originally an autonomous county subject to the kingdom of León, Castile lay on the frontier with Islam, where a warlike, dynamic society developed in which warriors, such as EL CID Campeador, could achieve great power and wealth. After the death of Sancho the Great, Castile was united (1037-65, 1072-1157) with León in a subordinate relationship, but by 1188, King Alfonso VIII (1155-1214, r. 1158-1214) had asserted Castilian superiority. At that time Castile had already pushed the frontier far to the south and was identified in the rest of Europe as Spain; foreigners called its language Spanish. The Castilians adopted an intense Christianity. When added to the fanaticism of the Almoravid enemy, this devotion transformed the Reconquest, once fought for the Visigothic ideal of peninsular unity, into a religious crusade. Taking advantage of Moorish divisions, Castile, supported by Aragon and Navarre, decisively defeated (1212) the Almohads at Navas de Tolosa. More

The Castilian warrior known as El Cid Campeador, "the lord conqueror," served both Castilian and Moorish rulers before conquering (1094) Valencia and establishing himself as a ruler. His exploits have been greatly romanticized in Spanish literature.

victories followed, and by 1248 only Granada was in Muslim hands.

Although the Muslim kingdom of Granada was weak and paid tribute to Castile, Muslim invasions from North Africa continued to threaten Christian Spain until the Reconquest was completed with the taking of Granada in 1492. During the 14th and 15th centuries, Aragon and Castile became more involved in European affairs, including the Hundred Years' War, and fought against each other and Portugal, a separate kingdom since 1112, and Navarre. The Castilian monarchy was internally weakened by its nobles, who sought to gain perpetual feudal privileges for themselves. In this struggle the crown could usually depend on the support of the towns, which had representatives sitting in the parliament (Cortes) and military associations (hermandades) policing the countryside. Ultimately, however, the monarchy was able to subject the clergy, towns, and even the great nobility to its will.

SPAIN DURING THE SIXTEENTH CENTURY

Spanish unity, although it would continue to be threatened by regionalist sentiment, was dynastically if not administratively settled before 1500.

The Reign of the "Catholic Kings." By a chance of dynastic fortune—the accession of ISABELLA I to the throne of Castile in 1474 and of her husband FERDINAND II to that of Aragon in 1479—the two most important kingdoms of Spain were joined. The "Catholic kings," as they are known, were exceptionally gifted, Isabella in internal politics and Ferdinand in foreign policy.

Isabella sought to centralize power in her hands, using the church as her instrument. In 1480 the Spanish INQUISITION began interrogating suspected heretics and converted Jews, whose financial activities had made them unpopular; in 1492 all Jews were expelled from Spain. The Inquisition thus helped identify Spain with orthodox Catholicism, contributing to the growth of national feeling. Also in 1492, Granada was conquered, ending the Reconquest, and Christopher COLUMBUS discovered America.

Ferdinand, meanwhile, had turned his attention to the conquest of Naples and to disputes with France over the control of Italy. In addition, he added Navarre and territories on the French border to the family's domains. Upon his death in 1516—Isabella had died in 1504—both of their crowns went to their grandson Charles I.

The Habsburg Monarchs. Hardly had Charles set foot in his new kingdoms when he was elected Holy Roman Emperor CHARLES V and departed for Germany. For the next two centuries the fate of Spain was tied to that of the HABSBURG dynasty. Charles spent most of his life defending his scattered domains against French, Turkish, and Protestant enemies. At the beginning of his reign, his foreignness—in terms of his

(Above) The "Catholic kings," Ferdinand II of Aragon and Isabella I of Castile, enter Granada after the final defeat (1492) of the Moors. (Royal Chapel, Granada, Spain.)

(Right) This world map (1502) shows newly discovered lands as divided between Spanish and Portuguese influence by the Treaty of Tordesillas (1494). The line of demarcation was intended to end conflict between the two expanding powers. (British Museum, London.)

upbringing, advisors, and interests—made him unpopular in Spain. Later, however, Charles was able to win the loyalty of his subjects despite his long absences from Spain. He also adopted his grandparents' ideals of Catholic unity and imperial conquest, financed by wealth from the New World. He was backed in these goals by the JESUITS, founded in 1540 by Saint IGNATIUS LOYOLA.

Columbus's discoveries were followed by Hernán CORTÉS's conquest of Mexico (1519–21) and Francisco PIZARRO's of Peru (1531–33). The resulting influx of gold and silver from America, however, tended to undermine Spain's domestic industry, encouraging not only inflation but also a spirit that valued bravery and piety over hard work. Taxation and warfare also contributed to the Castilian economy. Charles realized this situation when he abdicated in 1555–56, leaving Spain to his son, Philip II, and his German dominions to his brother, later Holy Roman Emperor Ferdinand I. Nonetheless, the wealth of

the New World was sufficient to make Spain the greatest European power of the age.

Philip II, though hated by Spain's enemies, was enormously popular among his people. Although brilliant, he often confused the interests of Spain with the defense of Catholic purity, and his intransigence entangled Spain in ruinous wars in the Netherlands (see DUTCH REVOLT). In 1580, Philip acquired Portugal with all its possessions. This union, far from strengthening the empire, only brought upon the Portuguese colonies and sea routes the attacks of Spain's Dutch and English enemies and increased Portuguese hostility toward the king. Philip's reign was marked by two crucial naval encounters. After a century of advances, the Ottoman Empire was stopped in 1571 at the Battle of LEPANTO by JOHN OF AUSTRIA, Philip's half brother. The victory temporarily crippled Turkish sea power and greatly boosted the morale of Christian Europe. In 1588, in retaliation for English interference in the

(Left) The Moorish (Muslim) principalities in Spain, established after the rapid conquest of the peninsula during the 8th century, were largely united during the 10th century under the Umayyad Emirate (later Caliphate) of Córdoba. (Center) Fragmentation of this state aided the reconquest by the Christian kingdoms of northern Spain. (Right) Despite resurgences under the Almoravid and Almohad dynasties, Muslim power was reduced by sporadic victories from the Battle of Las Navas de Tolosa (1212) to the fall of Granada (1492).

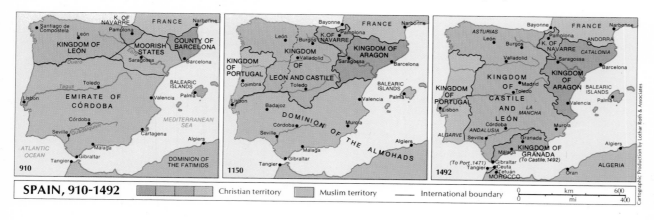

SPAIN, 910-1492   Christian territory   Muslim territory   —— International boundary

Philip II, heir to the Spanish domains of Charles V, sought to consolidate a Catholic empire through suppression of revolts in the Netherlands (1576) and Granada (1568-71) and by use of the Inquisition. Although power was centralized under his absolute rule, Philip's military expenditures and the defeat (1588) of the Armada by the English considerably weakened the Spanish empire.

Netherlands, Philip attempted to invade England with his "invincible" SPANISH ARMADA, which was destroyed by storms and English ships.

SPAIN 1598-1814

When the 17th century began, Spain was at the peak of its cultural splendor, epitomized by Miguel de CERVANTES and Lope de VEGA in literature and EL GRECO and Diego VELÁZQUEZ in art. Spanish military power and diplomacy were still feared and respected. By the end of the century, however, the country's economic and political power had declined drastically, and the cultural leadership of Europe had passed to France.

Decline of Spanish Glory. Spain's downfall was due in part to a succession of unfit kings whose favorites brought mismanagement and corruption into government. PHILIP III (r. 1598-1621) was pious but lazy and left the work of government to his favorite, the duque de Lerma (1553-1625). The productive MORISCOS (converted Muslims) were expelled, many people entered religious orders, and others went off to war or to America. On the other hand, a truce (1609) with the Netherlands and peace with England (1604) were achieved. Lerma's successors, however, dragged Spain into the THIRTY YEARS' WAR (1618-48). Under PHILIP IV (r. 1621-65), a notable patron of the arts, the brilliant but tactless conde-duque de OLIVARES prosecuted the war strenuously. The Spanish won spectacular victories early in the war, but after the Battle of Rocroi (1643), French arms confirmed Spain's military decline. Meanwhile, Olivares's centralizing efforts led to rebellions in 1640 in Portugal and Catalonia. Portugal regained its independence, and Catalonia came under French control until 1652. Habsburg rule ended in Spain with the infirm CHARLES II, whose reign (1665-1700) was marked by domestic and foreign intrigue and economic collapse. In order to preserve what remained of his empire, Charles named as his heir the grandson of the French king, Louis XIV.

The Spanish Bourbons. The 18th century opened with the War of the SPANISH SUCCESSION (1701-13), by which Louis acquired some Spanish territory and put his grandson, who became PHILIP V, on the throne against English and Dutch opposition. The early Bourbons—Philip (r. 1700-46), FERDINAND VI (r. 1746-59), and CHARLES III (r. 1759-88)—were more capable than their recent Habsburg predecessors and more discriminating in choosing their chief ministers. Government administration became more rationalized and centralized, and greater attention was given to fostering economic development. By midcentury Spain had experienced considerable population increase and relative prosperity. The Bourbons also quickly achieved what Olivares had long pursued: the destruction of the special privileges enjoyed by Catalonia, Aragon, and Valencia. Spain had become a union of provinces instead of a collection of kingdoms.

With the introduction of ENLIGHTENMENT ideas—particularly under Charles III—came anticlericalism and pressures for secularization. In 1767 the Jesuits were expelled from the em-

pire. At the same time the powers of the Inquisition were reduced.

The importance of French intellectual and cultural influences did not, however, imply Spanish subservience to French foreign policy. Philip's marriage to an Italian, Elizabeth FARNESE, soon led to territorial ambitions in Italy, almost constant warfare, and the departure of French advisors. Ferdinand, in contrast, brought peace by remaining neutral in Anglo-French conflicts, appointing Spanish advisors, and devoting his administration to the task of economic recovery. Charles, a prime example of an enlightened despot, paid considerable attention to the American empire, even establishing imperial free trade in 1778. He was convinced, though, that England was the major threat to Spanish America and formed a family compact with France, thus involving his country in the SEVEN YEARS' WAR (1756-63) and the AMERICAN REVOLUTION (1776-83). These wars brought negligible territorial results, but the latter conflict set a dangerous example for Spain's own colonial subjects.

The French Revolutionary and Napoleonic Period. CHARLES IV (r. 1788-1808), a weak and unintelligent man, was dominated by Manuel de GODOY, his wife's lover and his prime minister after 1792. When the French Revolution started in 1789 the frightened government tried to seal Spain off from revolutionary ideas and stopped all reform plans. In 1793, Spain, having joined the aristocratic crusade against France, was crushed and made an alliance with the French. By 1796 it was essentially a French satellite. Besides subsidizing costly French wars, Spain suffered from English attacks on its empire and shipping, and a Franco-Spanish fleet was destroyed by the British at the Battle of TRAFALGAR in 1805. NAPOLEON I persuaded Godoy in 1807 to allow French troops to cross Spain in order to conquer Portugal.

Aristocratic and popular resentment turned against Godoy and Charles. In March 1808 a riot, stirred up by Charles's son, forced the king to abdicate in favor of this son, who took the throne as FERDINAND VII. In May, Napoleon induced Charles and Ferdinand to meet him in France, forced them both to give up their claims to the throne, and then installed his brother Joseph Bonaparte as king of Spain (see BONAPARTE family). The Spanish people rose up against France's occupying army, helping to set off the Peninsular War (see NAPOLEONIC WARS). The French suffered some defeats at the hands of Spaniards and the British but under Napoleon's personal direction reconquered the peninsula, except Portugal and Cádiz, by 1810. Continued guerrilla warfare, however, weakened the French, while British general Arthur Wellesley (later duke of WELLINGTON) advanced from the west and pushed the

Francisco de Goya's The Executions of May 3, 1808 *(1814) depicts savage French reprisåls against the popular uprising in Madrid. The French invasion of Spain, perpetrated as a strategic maneuver against Portugal, led to the 6-year Peninsular War. (Prado, Madrid.)*

French back into Aragon. Opposition to the French also forced the Spanish people to adopt their own governmental forms in the absence of the king and a large part of the nobility. Dominated by the bourgeoisie, the Cortes of Cádiz proclaimed a democratic constitution in 1812. After Wellington's great victory at Vitoria in 1813 forced the French to evacuate Spain, however, Ferdinand returned (1814) to the Spanish throne.

SPAIN 1814 TO THE PRESENT
The Spain that Ferdinand VII found was ravaged by war and impoverished by its loss of strength in America; it was reduced to the status of a minor underdeveloped nation on the periphery of a fast-industrializing Europe. Economic recovery was retarded for decades by the lack of a capitalist bourgeoisie and by political turmoil.

Period of Turmoil: 1814–75. Ferdinand proved to be a vindictive reactionary whose brutality led to a liberal revolutionary interlude (1820–23), which was ended only by French intervention. Ferdinand took severe reprisals against the liberals. When he died the First Carlist War (1833–39) broke out between the liberal supporters of his daughter ISABELLA II (r. 1833–68) and the CARLISTS, the reactionary followers of his brother Don Carlos. The victorious liberals nationalized and sold church lands, creating new landowners who supported the conservative political group known as the Moderates. When Isabella's mother, the regent María Cristina (1806–78), tried to overturn the constitution of 1837, the army drove her into exile (1840) and in 1843 declared the 13-year-old Isabella of age. During the Moderate era (1843–68) many military men became prominent in party leadership positions and three more constitutions were adopted; the first signs of interest in socialist ideas and in peasant anarchism also appeared. Meanwhile Isabella continued in her attempts to impose despotic rule on Spain, thus encouraging the growth of the first significant Spanish republican movement.

In 1868 a military uprising under generals Juan PRIM and Francisco Serrano (1810–85) forced Isabella into exile, triggered sharper conflicts at home, and even resulted in repercussions outside Spain. As the government changed from monarchy to republic to monarchy in 6 years, revolts of Federalists, Carlists, and Cubans threatened to break Spain into pieces.

The Bourbons Restored. The government that the conservative statesman Antonio Cánovas del Castillo (1828–97) created for the restored Bourbon ALFONSO XII (r. 1874–85) rested on popular exhaustion, fear of revolution, and electoral manipulation. In 1876 a conservative constitution replaced the liberal charter of 1869. For about 20 years Cánovas's party alternated in power with the Liberals in orderly—but artificial—fashion. Peace combined with free trade brought some economic development, benefiting mainly the Catalan and Basque bourgeoisie, who began giving stronger support to regional autonomy movements. At the same time the labor movement developed rapidly along socialist and anarchist lines. By the 1890s republicanism was again a growing force.

A contemporary cartoon portrays the United States and Spain grappling over Cuba, the principal issue of the Spanish-American War (1898). The war cost Spain its last colonies—the Philippines, Guam, Puerto Rico, and Cuba.

The peaceful era of Cánovas ended when he was assassinated in 1897. The following year Spain lost its last remaining colonies—Cuba, Puerto Rico, and the Philippines—in the SPANISH-AMERICAN WAR. This disaster caused much soul-searching by José ORTEGA Y GASSET, Miguel de UNAMUNO, and other intellectuals of the "Generation of 1898" who began a reinterpretation of Spanish history. An attempt to regain prestige through imperialism led only to a long, bitter war in northern Morocco (1909–25). A general strike in Barcelona in 1909 gave the army an excuse to conduct a reign of terror against its critics. European opinion was outraged, but even well-intentioned politicians such as Antonio Maura (1853–1925) and José Canalejas (1854–1912) could not strengthen the government and were helpless against the meddling of King ALFONSO XIII, who had come of age in 1902, after a regency of his mother. In 1917 a wave of strikes and terrorism exploded in Barcelona, army officers formed military unions, and no governing cabinet lasted long enough to impose order. Meanwhile the Moroccan War situation deteriorated. In 1921 a Spanish army was routed by Moroccans, and the king was blamed.

Alfonso XIII was rescued by a military uprising, and in September 1923, Gen. Miguel PRIMO DE RIVERA became dictator.

RULERS OF SPAIN

Castile and León

Ferdinand I (León 1037-1065)	1035-65	Henry I (Castile only)	1214-17
Sancho II (Castile only)	1065-72	Ferdinand III (León 1230-1252)	1217-52
Alfonso VI (León 1065-1109)	1072-1109	Alfonso X	1252-84
Urraca	1109-26	Sancho IV	1284-95
Alfonso VII	1126-57	Ferdinand IV	1295-1312
Sancho III (Castile only)	1157-58	Alfonso XI	1312-50
Ferdinand II (León only)	1157-88	Peter the Cruel	1350-69
		Henry II of Trastamara	1369-79
Alfonso VIII (Castile only)	1158-1214	John I	1379-90
		Henry III	1390-1406
Alfonso IX (León only)	1188-1230	John II	1406-54
		Henry IV	1454-74
		Isabella	1474-1504

Aragon

Ramiro I	1035-63	Alfonso III	1285-91
Sancho Ramirez	1063-94	James II	1291-1327
Peter I	1094-1104	Alfonso IV	1327-36
Alfonso I	1104-34	Peter IV	1336-87
Ramiro II	1134-37	John I	1387-95
Petronilla	1137-62	Martin I	1395-1410
Alfonso II	1162-96	Ferdinand I	1412-16
Peter II	1196-1213	Alfonso V	1416-58
James I	1213-76	John II	1458-79
Peter III	1276-85	Ferdinand II	1479-1516

UNIFIED KINGDOM

Habsburg Dynasty		Bourbon Dynasty	
Joanna the Mad	1504-06	Philip V	1700-24
Philip I	1506	Louis I	1724
Charles I	1516-56	Philip V	1724-46
Philip II	1556-98	Ferdinand VI	1746-59
Philip III	1598-1621	Charles III	1759-88
Philip IV	1621-65	Charles IV	1788-1808
Charles II	1665-1700	Ferdinand VII	1808

Since 1808

Joseph Bonaparte (king)	1808-13	Alfonso XIII (Bourbon king)	1886-1931
Ferdinand VII (Bourbon king)	1814-33	Niceto Alcala Zamora y Torres (president, Second Republic)	1931-36
Isabella II (Bourbon queen)	1833-68	Manuel Azaña (president, Second Republic)	1936-39
Francisco Serrano (regent)	1869-70		
Amadeus (elected king)	1870-73	Francisco Franco (general and dictator)	1939-75
First Republic	1873-74		
Alfonso XII (Bourbon king)	1874-85	Juan Carlos I (Bourbon king)	1975-

ropean than ever before. After Franco's death in 1975, King JUAN CARLOS I and Premier Adolfo SUÁREZ GONZÁLEZ helped Spain move toward liberal democracy.   DANIEL R. HEADRICK

Bibliography: Brenan, Gerald, *The Spanish Labyrinth* (1960); Carr, Raymond, *Spain, 1808-1939* (1966); Carr, Raymond, and Fusi, Juan Pablo, *Spain: Dictatorship to Democracy* (1979); Castro, Americo, *The Spaniards: An Introduction to Their History* (1971); Davies, R. Trevor, *The Golden Century of Spain, 1501-1621*, rev. ed. (1954); Elliott, John, *Imperial Spain 1469-1716* (1963); Gallo, Max, *Spain Under Franco* (1974); Herr, Richard, *An Historical Essay on Modern Spain* (1971); Jackson, Gabriel, *The Making of Medieval Spain* (1972) and *The Spanish Republic and the Civil War 1931-1939* (1965); Livermore, Harold, *A History of Spain* (1966); Lomax, Derek W., *The Reconquest of Spain* (1978); Lynch, John, *Spain Under the Habsburgs*, 2 vols. (1964-69); MacKay, Angus, *Spain in the Middle Ages* (1977); Madariaga, Salvador de, *Spain: A Modern History* (1958); Merriman, R. B., *The Rise of Spanish Empire*, 4 vols. (1918-36; repr. 1962); Rowdon, Maurice, *The Spanish Terror: Spanish Imperialism in the Sixteenth Century* (1974); Thomas, Hugh, *The Spanish Civil War* (1961).

Spallanzani, Lazzaro   [spahl-lahn-tsah'-nee, laht-sah'-roh]

The Italian naturalist Lazzaro Spallanzani, b. Jan. 12, 1729, d. Feb. 11, 1799, was one of the founders of experimental biology. Through numerous studies, including microscopic studies of minute airborne organisms and experiments that involved killing microorganisms by boiling, Spallanzani helped to discount the theory of the spontaneous generation of life. He also studied the role of oxygen and carbon dioxide in respiration and investigated gastric secretions.

Spangenberg, Augustus Gottlieb   [spahng'-en-bairk]

Augustus Gottlieb Spangenberg, b. Prussia, July 15, 1704, d. Sept. 18, 1792, a bishop of the MORAVIAN CHURCH (1744-90) and its leader from 1762, founded the first Moravian settlements in North America. Sent from his native Germany, Spangenberg conducted missionary work in Georgia (1735), worked in Pennsylvania (1736-39), establishing a communal society at Bethlehem, and directed mission work in North Carolina in the 1750s. In 1762, Spangenberg returned to Germany to lead the denomination following the death of his predecessor, Graf von ZINZENDORF.   JAMES D. NELSON

Spanish-American War

The Spanish-American War (1898) marked the emergence of the United States as a great power and the advent of American overseas imperialism.

During the 19th century, American exponents of MANIFEST DESTINY likened Cuba, a Spanish colony, to a ripening fruit destined ultimately to fall into outstretched American hands. The expansionists' hunger intensified after 1895, when Cuban nationalists began a bloody insurrection against the Spanish colonial government. Spain's ruthless Gen. Valeriano Weyler herded Cuban farmers into squalid concentration camps. Many men, women, and children died, and Weyler was dubbed "butcher" by William Randolph Hearst's sensationalist New York *Journal*. This and other "yellow" journals (see YELLOW JOURNALISM) fanned American public opinion and editorialized for humanitarian intervention and the annexation of Cuba by the United States. On Feb. 9, 1898, Hearst published a purloined private letter in which the Spanish minister to the United States sharply criticized President William McKINLEY; on February 15, the American battleship MAINE exploded in Havana harbor. McKinley had resisted the surging pressure for intervention as long as resistance was politically expedient, but the drift toward war soon became inexorable despite accelerated Spanish attempts to withdraw from Cuba without losing face. On April 11, McKinley in effect requested a declaration of war, which Congress passed on April 25.

The Fighting. Combat lasted only 10 weeks, but it proved one-sided and decisive. In the Pacific, Commodore George DEWEY steamed swiftly from Hong Kong aboard his flagship *Olympia*, one of the modern steel cruisers of the "new navy"

Generals Francisco Franco (left center) and Emilio Mola (right center), leaders of the military uprising (1936) that precipitated the Spanish Civil War, appear in this 1936 photo. Franco's 1939 victory initiated his 36-year period of rightist, strongman rule.

Initially popular, he defeated the Moroccans—with French aid—in 1925, but his attacks on intellectuals, his government's financial mismanagement, and severe economic depression forced him to leave Spain in 1930. A year later the king followed him into exile.

Republican Spain and the Rule of Francisco Franco. The Second Spanish Republic (1931-39) was notable for the intense participation in politics that it generated among people of all classes. This participation, however, was not conciliatory but divisive as Spain became polarized into two opposing blocs. On the right were the church, the army, the landowners, and many small farmers. Aligned against them were workers, landless peasants, intellectuals, and most Catalans and Basques. Despite social, regional, and anticlerical violence, many reforms were initiated during the first two years of the republic. From 1933 to 1936, however, a conservative government undid its predecessor's reforms and mercilessly crushed workers' uprisings. After February 1936 a leftist coalition threatened to bring about a social revolution. A conspiracy of conservatives and officers turned to rebellion in July 1936 but failed to seize the major cities.

In the resulting SPANISH CIVIL WAR (1936-39), the Nationalist army under Gen. Francisco FRANCO received considerable German and Italian aid and quickly conquered the western half of Spain. The Republicans—divided into Socialists, Anarchists, and Communists—often fought among themselves. Despite heroic resistance, some Soviet aid, and the participation of sympathizers from all over the world, the republic crumbled before the slow advance of Franco's army into the populous industrial provinces of the east. It is estimated that the Nationalist victory may have cost Spain up to a million people, including emigrés as well as those killed during the conflict.

Franco proved to be a harsh but flexible ruler. His regime began as a repressive totalitarian system supported by the army, the church, and the Falange (the official state party). He resisted pressure to set up a thoroughgoing fascist state on the German and Italian models (see FASCISM), and his regime survived World War II by remaining neutral. In 1947, Spain was declared a monarchy, with a king to be named to succeed Franco. After years of international isolation, Spain signed (1953) a concordat with the Vatican and an agreement granting the United States the use of military bases in Spain in return for economic and military aid. In 1955, Spain became a member of the United Nations.

After the severe economic distress of the 1940s and '50s, Franco agreed to substantial economic liberalization in the '60s. Spain is now far more industrialized, prosperous, and Eu-

The explosion of the U.S. battleship Maine in Havana harbor on Feb. 15, 1898, helped precipitate the Spanish-American War. Although Spain denied responsibility for the explosion, the American public, encouraged by sensationalist newspapers, urged U.S. intervention to avenge the deaths of 266 seamen and expel the Spanish from Cuba.

fashioned in the 1880s and '90s. Dewey's squadron slipped into Manila harbor and on May 1 destroyed the obsolete Spanish fleet lying at anchor. Reinforced by the army in June, Dewey besieged the Spanish garrison in Manila, capturing the city on August 13. In July—to support these combined operations—the U.S. Navy had seized Spanish Guam and previously unclaimed Wake Island, and Congress by joint resolution had annexed Hawaii.

In the Caribbean, Spanish ships under Adm. Pasqual Cervera sailed safely into the harbor of Santiago de Cuba. By the end of May, however, they were blockaded there by U.S. naval forces. U.S. troops under Gen. William R. SHAFTER landed in Cuba in late June and pressed toward Santiago. These ground forces included the regular army as well as special volunteer regiments, the most famous of which were the ROUGH RIDERS, led by Theodore ROOSEVELT and Leonard WOOD. The Americans were victorious at the battles of El Caney and San Juan Hill on July 1. Determined to maintain Spain's honor, Cervera made a dash for the open sea on July 3, although the imbalance between his outdated Spanish vessels and the modern American ships off Cuba was almost as great as the disparity between the fleets in the Philippines.

The Battle of San Juan Hill was fought on July 1, 1898, on the outskirts of Santiago de Cuba. Among the U.S. forces charging the Spanish positions was the volunteer "Rough Riders" regiment, led by Theodore Roosevelt. Santiago surrendered 17 days later, after a sea battle.

The guns of the new battleships and cruisers commanded by Rear Admiral William T. SAMPSON and Commodore Winfield Scott SCHLEY sank most of the Spanish ships in less than 4 hours. Spain suffered 474 casualties to only 2 for the United States. On July 17, Santiago and Cuba's 24,000 Spanish troops surrendered. Madrid sued for peace 9 days later.

The Treaty of Paris. During the peace negotiations the United States did not seek annexation of Cuba because the Teller Amendment to the declaration of war forbade American acquisition of the island. However, McKinley demanded Spanish cession of Puerto Rico, Guam, and the Philippine Islands. In the Treaty of Paris, concluded on December 10, a humiliated Spain yielded to American imperialism.

The imperialistic grab was not universally popular in the United States, and the Senate fight over the treaty was intense. Among those opposed to annexation of the Philippines were Mark Twain, Andrew Carnegie, several senior Republican senators, and many Democrats. They argued that acquisition of noncontiguous areas populated by peoples allegedly unsuited for assimilation into American society was contrary to the principles of American democracy. The imperialists stressed the role of the United States as an agent of civilization and the importance of possessing a threshold to the trade with China, on which the Americans and British were atttempting to impose the so-called Open Door Policy. The imperialists carried the day, in large measure because William Jennings BRYAN, an avowed antiimperialist and the probable Democratic candidate for president in 1900, urged Democratic senators to vote for the Treaty of Paris in order to terminate the state of war. By the narrow margin of 57 to 27 (only 2 votes more than the number needed for ratification) the Senate approved the pact on Feb. 6, 1899. Bryan, who intended to relinquish the Philippines if elected president, lost the election of 1900 to McKinley, and the United States retained the islands.

The "splendid little war" established the United States as a major power in the Far East and the dominant power in the Caribbean. Although Filipino nationalists fought a bitter 4-year struggle for immediate independence, the United States clung to the archipelago because it seemed a portal to the China market. Puerto Rico became an American colony and the site of an American naval base, and nominally independent Cuba ceded territory for naval stations to the United States under the terms of a constitution—with the so-called PLATT AMENDMENT appended to it—imposed by the American Congress and Secretary of War Elihu ROOT. These two islands were strategically significant to the defense of the Panama Canal, which was begun in 1904.   KENNETH J. HAGAN

Bibliography: Chadwick, French E., The Relations of the United States and Spain: The Spanish-American War, 2 vols. (1911; repr. 1968); Chidsey, Donald B., Spanish American War (1971); Foner, Philip S., The Spanish-Cuban-American War and the Birth of American Imperialism, 1895-1902, 2 vols. (1972); Freidel, Frank, The Splendid Little War (1958); Millis, Walter, The Martial Spirit (1931); Pratt, Julius W., Expansionists of 1898: The Acquisition of Hawaii and the Spanish Islands (1936; repr. 1959).

Spanish Armada

The Armada was a great Spanish fleet assembled in 1588 as part of the attempt by PHILIP II to invade England. Philip had come to believe that only conquest could halt English aid to the rebels against Spain in the Low Countries or stop the English depredations in the New World. The plan was to send a fleet of 130 ships commanded by the duque de Medina Sidonia (1550-1619) to cover an invasion force from Flanders under Alessandro FARNESE. This plan proved strategically unsound and beyond Spain's logistical capabilities.

When the outgunned and inadequately provisioned Armada appeared off Plymouth on July 30, it was met by an English fleet of equal or superior strength. In spite of the efforts of Francis DRAKE, Martin FROBISHER, John HAWKINS, and other English captains, the Spanish maintained their order of battle and lost only two ships before arriving at Calais. The rendezvous with Farnese failed, however. Lacking adequate ships of his own and blockaded by Dutch rebels whose shallow-draft flyboats easily eluded the Spanish galleons, Farnese could not embark his troops. Then, on August 8, English fire ships drove the Armada out of its Calais anchorage. The Spanish regrouped and fought another action off Gravelines, but they were now out of ammunition. Realizing that the situation was lost, Medina Sidonia sailed north around Scotland and Ireland and returned to Spain. He suffered heavy losses because of disease and shipwreck.

The defeat of the Armada did not affect the naval balance of power: England had been a major sea power before 1588, and the Spanish fleet was quickly rebuilt afterward. It did demonstrate that Spain lacked the power to impose religious unity on Europe.
WILLIAM S. MALTBY

Bibliography: Graham, Winston, *The Spanish Armada* (1972); Mattingly, Garrett, *The Armada* (1959).

Spanish art and architecture

The art of Spain has, throughout its history, been marked by a rich diversity stemming from the geographical position of the Iberian Peninsula. As both the western boundary of the Mediterranean Sea and the link between Africa and Europe, Spain has been repeatedly invaded and colonized from the north, east, and south since prehistoric times; Iberians, Basques, Celts, Romans, Visigoths, and Moors have all contributed to Spanish painting, sculpture, and architecture.

PREHISTORIC AND PRE-ROMAN ART

For a period of several thousand years during the later Paleolithic Period, cave dwellers in northern Spain and southern France painted animals on the walls of caves and scratched drawings on bones. These examples of PREHISTORIC ART culminated in works of the middle Magdalenian period (c.12,000 BC) at ALTAMIRA, where astonishingly lifelike bison, horses, deer, and other animals cover the low cave ceilings. The Neolithic Period (c.2000 BC) saw the development of geometrically decorated pottery and megalithic dolmens—primitive stone structures that preceded the well-constructed dwellings and towers of the Bronze Age (c.1500 BC).

Spain is rich in archaeological remains dating from the first millennium before Christ. An abundance of sculpture, pottery, and jewelry has been found in the coastal areas colonized by the Phoenicians, Carthaginians, and Greeks. Surviving masterworks are the great bronze bulls' heads (6th century BC; Museo Arqueológico Nacional, Madrid) excavated at Costitx on the island of Mallorca, and the Phoenician-influenced polychrome stone bust of the regal *Dama de Elche* (c.400 BC; Prado, Madrid).

(Left) *The map traces the route taken by the Spanish Armada, a powerful naval force dispatched in 1588 by King Philip II to support an invasion of England by Spanish forces from the Netherlands. Outmaneuvered by the English and Dutch in the Channel, the Armada was forced to sail north around Scotland and Ireland to return to Spain.*

THE SPANISH ARMADA

— Route of Armada

▧ Area of Netherlands controlled by Spain

(Below) *Warships of the Spanish Armada clash with English and Dutch vessels in this painting by Aert van Antum. During this engagement in August 1588, the Spanish fleet was driven out of its anchorage at Calais and lost a major battle off the coast of Gravelines, France.*

ROMAN AND EARLY CHRISTIAN ART

Rome colonized Spain beginning in the 3d century BC, and cities such as Barcelona and Tarragona still retain Roman structures. Modern Lugo is surrounded by Roman walls, Alcántara is approached by a Roman bridge (AD 106), Segovia is served by a magnificent Roman aqueduct, and Mérida is a veritable Roman museum. At Italica, near Seville, a Roman town has been excavated, revealing fine mosaics.

The spread of Christian and Byzantine influence in Spain from the 4th to 7th centuries is reflected principally in surviving mosaics and sarcophagi; the Early Christian basilicas have largely vanished. From the early 6th century the Visigoths dominated Spain; their few surviving churches display primitive, vigorous stonework and carved capitals and lintels. After the Moorish invasion (711) the Christians in the far north began a slow reconquest and by the mid-9th century held much of northwest Spain. Dating from this period are several churches and the diminutive Naranco Palace (c.850) near the Christian capital of Oviedo, in the Asturias.

THE MIDDLE AGES

Moorish Art. After overrunning Spain in the first half of the 8th century, the Moors established a brilliant court at Córdoba, from which they ruled an ever-shrinking portion of the country until their expulsion (1492) from Granada. Moorish rule in Spain may be divided into three periods: that of the Arab emirate and caliphate (759–1031), that of the Almoravids and Almohads (1086–1212), and that of the Nasrid Dynasty in the south (1230–1492). Each period produced one outstanding monument. The Cathedral of Córdoba (786–999), one of the world's greatest mosques, is highlighted by a staggering array of double-tiered, polylobed arches. Just as the Córdoba mosque reflects the brilliance of the early Moorish court, the minaret of Seville, or the Giralda (completed 1198; now the cathedral bell tower), embodies the strength of the ascetic Almohads in its combination of monumental proportions and restrained decoration. The last phase of Moorish rule left the most lavishly decorated of Moorish palaces, the ALHAMBRA (1238–1391) of Granada.

The influence of Moorish art in Spain spread well beyond the areas actually held by the Moors. The Christians who lived under or fled the Moors created a unique artistic style,

(Above) *The massive Great Mosque (now Cathedral) of Córdoba was begun in the 8th century by Emir Abd al-Rahman I and enlarged by subsequent Muslim rulers. The hundred of columns, of Roman origin, support double horseshoe arches of alternating brick and stone that raise the ceiling to an appropriate height.*

both in architecture and in manuscript illumination, that flourished from the 9th to the early 11th century. In this so-called Mozarabic art, Visigothic or Northern antecedents merged with Moorish and Eastern influences to form a composite style that consists of elements particularly evident in a scattering of isolated, highly individualistic churches with horseshoe arches and occasional carved elements. Also indicative of Mozarabic art are a group of colorful, vigorously stylized Beatus manuscripts (commentaries on the Apocalypse) from northern monasteries (see ILLUMINATED MANUSCRIPTS). As the Christians extended their reconquest, they employed

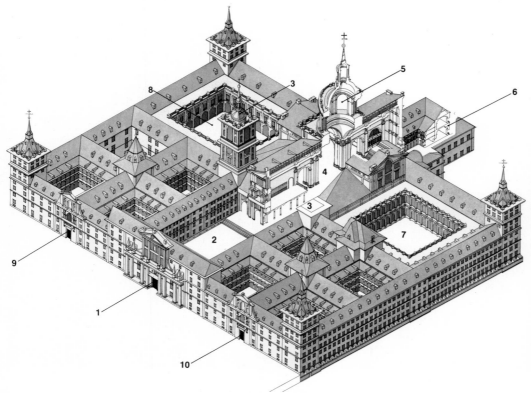

(Left) *The Escorial, built (1562–92) for King Philip II of Spain, is a huge complex of granite structures in the mountains near Madrid. The grand entrance in the center of the west facade (1) opens into the Courtyard of the Kings (2). Twin towers (3) dominate the approach to the austere church, seen here in a cutaway view (4). The dome (5) of the church soars 98 m (320 ft) above the crossing, beneath which is the octagonal royal mausoleum. Behind the church are the state apartments (6). To the south is the Courtyard of the Evangelists (7); to the north is the Great Court of the Palace (8). Flanking the grand entrance are the College (9) and the Monastery of Saint Lawrence (10).*

Moorish workmen who introduced into Christian architecture Moorish building and decorative techniques and developed a style called Mudejar, which persisted even after the withdrawal of the Moors.

Romanesque Art. Northern Spain embraced the artistic revival that spread throughout Europe after the year 1000 known as ROMANESQUE ART AND ARCHITECTURE. In Catalonia a very early group of Romanesque churches—the largest being Santa Maria in Ripoll (1020–32)—shows Italian Lombard influence; many of these churches were decorated subsequently with imaginatively stylized frescoes and altar frontals. By the late 11th century French Romanesque influences had begun to spread along the pilgrimage road that led across the Pyrenees to the shrine of Saint James at Santiago de Compostela (begun 1077). Romanesque architecture in Spain persisted into the 13th century, producing many notable monuments in regionally varied styles.

The Impact of Gothic Art. The solid walls and dark interiors of the Romanesque suited the Spanish climate and temperament; French GOTHIC ART AND ARCHITECTURE came to Spain relatively late and as a borrowed style. From the 13th through the 15th century, however, Gothic formulations took root and developed a typically Spanish aspect that flowered throughout the country in a number of magnificent cathedrals. In the northern capital of Léon the elegant mid-13th-century cathedral represents the purest example of French Gothic in Spain. Also begun in the 13th century, in the French tradition but with later exotic accents, are the cathedrals of Burgos and Toledo (completed 1227). Into the 15th century, structures increasingly exhibited variety in forms and a new vigor that reflected the emerging Spanish national spirit. The development of the dwarfed clerestory led to such lofty nave arcades as that of Barcelona Cathedral (begun 1298); audacious engineering resulted in the extraordinary vaulting spans of Gerona Cathedral (before 1312); civic pride led to building on a gigantic scale that culminated in Seville Cathedral (1402–1506), one of the largest in Europe.

The final phase (c.1450–1520) of Spanish Gothic art witnessed extensive construction, both religious and secular, accompanied by an exuberant architectural sculpture characteristic of the Isabelline style, named for Queen Isabella of Castile. Great *retablos*—multipaneled frames containing sculpture in low or high relief (see RETABLE)—were erected behind the main altars of churches. Similar compositions began to cover the entire central facades of a variety of structures, including the Colegio di San Gregorio (1492) in Vallodolid.

THE FLOWERING OF SPANISH ART

The Renaissance. Throughout much of its history Spanish architecture has favored geometric forms. The Moorish, Mudejar, Isabelline, and Early Renaissance styles added to this basic structural aesthetic a rich embellishment of ornament. During the first half of the 16th century the transition from the Gothic decoration of the Isabelline style to the Italian Renaissance motifs of the so-called Plateresque—from *platero*, "silversmith"—was gradual and often delightfully whimsical.

Architecture corresponding structurally to the Italian High Renaissance style—based not merely on surface ornament but on classical proportion and spatial order—came to Spain sporadically, appearing first in Charles V's unfinished palace in Granada (begun c.1526). Only after the middle of the 16th century did an austere, typically Spanish Renaissance style develop, epitomized in the works of Juan de HERRERA, the principal architect of Philip II's massive monastery-palace, the Escorial (1563–84). The severe Herreran manner represented in the Escorial remained influential well into the following century.

In painting and sculpture a number of important artists emerged during the 15th century. Although some were influenced by Northern styles, and others by Italian masters, almost all display a distinctly Spanish stamp of realism and expressive intensity. In Catalonia, a vigorous school of painting culminated in the dark, brooding *Pietá* (1490; Barcelona Cathedral) of Bartolomé Bermejo (fl. 1474–95). The early-16th-century sculpture and architecture of Diego de SILOE show a

graceful Renaissance style, whereas the sweeping Mannerist carving of Alonso BERRUGUETE foreshadows the drama of El Greco's paintings.

The Baroque—Spain's Golden Age. In the 1570s, with the arrival of the Cretan-born and Venetian-trained painter Domenico Theotocopoulos, called EL GRECO, Spain entered upon a century in which painting led the arts. El Greco's Mannerist painting, with its powerful marshaling of form and color to expressive ends, reflects a personality in harmony with his time and place—the period of the Counter-Reformation in Toledo, the religious capital of Spain. Francisco de ZURBARÁN's stark portrayals of saints, on the other hand, belong to the Spanish monastic world of the 17th century, whereas Esteban MURILLO's gracious yet earthy paintings reflect the warmth of Andalusia. José RIBERA settled in Naples, which was then un-

(Above) Prince Baltasar Carlos (c.1635) is one of many equestrian portraits of the royal family of Spain by Diego Velázquez, who usually set them in the Sierra de Guadarrama, the royal hunting preserve; the prince was 5 years old. (Prado, Madrid.)

(Left) *Francisco de Zurbarán's Adoration of the Magi (1638–39) one of four paintings originally intended for an altar at the Charterhouse of Jérez de la Frontera, near Seville, is characteristic of the Spanish master's mature style. (Musée des Beaux-Arts, Grenoble, France.)

(Left) The Nude Maja (c.1800), by Francisco de Goya, is considered one of the most frankly pleasing nudes ever painted. The subject is the Duchess of Alba, Goya's close friend and patroness; he also painted her as The Clothed Maja in the same pose. (Prado, Madrid.)

(Left) Christ Carrying the Cross (1590-95) by El Greco conveys the anguish of Christ's Passion through deliberate distortion of the face and hand, elongation of the neck, dramatic lighting, and strong color contrasts. (Brooklyn Museum, New York.)

(Right) The baroque retablo (1693-96) behind the high altar of Salamanca's Church of San Esteban was designed by José Benito de Churriguera, one of the family of architects for whom the Spanish rococo style—the Churrigueresque—was named.

der Spanish rule, and developed a strongly modeled realism influenced by Caravaggio yet typically Spanish. The art of Spain's Golden Age reached its height in the baroque paintings of Diego VELÁZQUEZ, who served for many years as court painter to Philip IV.

Seventeenth-century Spanish architecture, continuing under the influence of Herrera and the Escorial, slowly entered the mainstream of the international baroque. Late in the century, however, a long-dormant taste for elaborate decoration reasserted itself in the works of José de Churriguera. Although the term Churrigueresque sometimes is applied broadly to late Spanish baroque architecture, strictly speaking it covers only the work of the CHURRIGUERA family. The ornate form of Churrigueresque appears in José's main altar (1693-96) of San Esteban in Salamanca; a more restrained example occurs in Alberto de Churriguera's Plaza Mayor in Salamanca (begun 1728).

Outside the Churrigueresque circle, Spanish architects of the early 18th century manifested delightful imagination in works ranging from the soaring facade (1650-1750) of the Cathedral of Santiago de Compostela to Narciso Tomé's (fl. 1715-42) astonishing Transparente (1721-32) in the Cathedral of Toledo.

Goya. Architecture was Spain's liveliest art in the first part of the 18th century, until the restraining effects of a new wave of classicism gripped all of the Spanish arts in the late 1700s. Only the irrepressible talent of the painter Francisco de GOYA

y Lucientes enlivened the arts in this era. Goya's intensely personal vision emerged in his mature works and ultimately became the chief mark of his genius in the human comedies, tragedies, dreams, and nightmares that he recorded on canvas and in prints.

THE MODERN ERA

The sterile neoclassicism of much of 18th- and 19th-century Spanish art was shattered first in architecture. The idea that a modern age demanded a new art—the underlying premise of ART NOUVEAU in France and the Modernista movement in Barcelona—fired the imagination of Antonio GAUDÍ, who en-

(Above) In Salvador Dalí's Discovery of America by Christopher Columbus (1959) the Spanish surrealist has portrayed his wife, Gala, as the Virgin Mary on the banner held by an incongruously young Columbus; the banner is echoed by repeated verticals. (Salvador Dalí Museum, Cleveland, Ohio.)

(Above) The retablo behind the high altar of the Cathedral of Toledo, carved between 1498 and 1504, is a monumental example of Late Gothic woodcarving. Its wealth of polychrome and gold detail incorporates elements of French, German, and Flemish Gothic style that fuse into a distinctly Spanish style.

(Below) Casa Milà, an apartment house built (1905–10) in Barcelona by Antonio Gaudí in his idiosyncratic Art Nouveau style, is made of hand-cut stone, with elaborate wrought-iron balconies. The abstract sculptural forms on the roof conceal chimneys, vents, and stairwells.

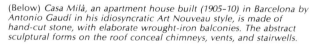

(Right) Pablo Picasso developed an entirely new classical style following his first visit to Rome in 1917; Three Women at the Spring (1921), with its solid, statuesque figures bathed in sunlight, is an exemplar of it. (Museum of Modern Art, New York City.)

dowed Barcelona with structures of novel form and fantastic ornament. His most impressive work is the ambitious, still-incomplete sanctuary of the Church of the Sagrada Familia (Holy Family; begun 1882).

Spanish artists played key roles in the revolutionary outburst of modern art that occurred in Paris during the early 20th century. Foremost among them was the inexhaustibly fertile Pablo PICASSO, brutal and tender by turns, the most influential painter of the 20th century. Other distinguished Spaniards of the modern era include the Cubist painter Juan GRIS, the sculptor Julio GONZÁLEZ, and two very different surrealists—Joan MIRÓ, the creator of bold, lyrical fantasies, and the master surrealist showman Salvador DALÍ.

Emerging during the 1950s and 1960s was a vigorous generation of Spanish artists of international impact, associated with Madrid and Barcelona rather than with Paris. Modern activity is widespread and varied, ranging from social commentary and neorealism to pop art. DAVID W. SCOTT

Bibliography: Alcolea, Santiago, *Spanish Sculpture* (1969); Bevan, Bernard, *History of Spanish Architecture* (1939); Dyches, William, *Contemporary Spanish Art* (1975); Gudiol y Ricart, José, *The Arts of Spain* (1964); Kubler, George, and Soria, Martin, *Art and Architecture in Spain and Portugal and Their American Dominions, 1500–1800* (1959); Lassaigne, Jacques, *Spanish Painting*, 2 vols. (1952); McKendrick, P. L., *The Iberian Stones Speak* (1969); Smart, Alistair, *The Renaissance and Mannerism in Northern Europe and Spain* (1972); Smith, Bradley, *Spain, A History in Art* (1966).

Spanish bayonet: see YUCCA.

Spanish Civil War

The Spanish Civil War was an internal struggle in Spain that began with the military uprising of July 17–18, 1936, and ended with the defeat of the Spanish republic on Mar. 28, 1939. Many parties and groups were involved in the hostilities. Besides the military, the Nationalist side included conservatives from many parties and extreme rightists such as the CARLISTS and members of the Falange. On the Republican or Loyalist side were republicans, Socialists, Communists, the anarchist CNT (Confederación Nacional del Trabajo), and the revolutionary Marxist POUM (Partido Obrero de Unificación Marxista), the dissident faction of the Spanish Communist party.

The story of the Spanish republic before 1936 was one of increasing polarization: from 1931 to 1934 a mildly reformist government alienated landowners, officers, and clergy; from 1934 to 1936 a conservative government reversed the reforms of its predecessor and repressed workers' rebellions; and in

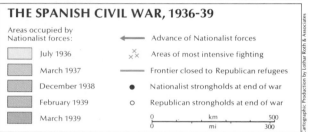

THE SPANISH CIVIL WAR, 1936-39

Areas occupied by Nationalist forces:

July 1936	Advance of Nationalist forces
March 1937	×× Areas of most intensive fighting
December 1938	Frontier closed to Republican refugees
February 1939	● Nationalist strongholds at end of war
March 1939	○ Republican strongholds at end of war

0 — km — 500
0 — mi — 300

Cartographic Production by Lothar Roth & Associates

The map shows the areas of intensive fighting and the extension of Nationalist control during the Spanish Civil War. Although the Republicans fought stubbornly, the Italo-German-aided Nationalists effectively ended the war with the capture (March 1939) of Madrid.

1936 a leftist Popular Front government threatened to bring about a social revolution.

The war began with a military uprising in Spanish Morocco, led by Gen. Francisco FRANCO, that rapidly spread to garrisons in Spain. The insurgents seized control of the agrarian provinces of western Spain but failed in the more urban industrial regions of Catalonia, Aragon, the Basque provinces, the Levant, and Madrid. By the end of July 1936, Spain was split in two. From the north, the army of Gen. Emilio Mola pushed toward Madrid; Franco's forces did likewise from Andalusia; and the leftist parties and labor unions prepared to defend Madrid. The defense was successful, but the Loyalists could not push the Nationalists back, and the fighting turned into a stalemate during the winter of 1936–37.

During its first months, the war acquired international political and ideological significance. Within less than a year from the conflict's onset, Fascist Italy sent about 70,000 ground troops to aid the Nationalists, and Nazi Germany provided planes, pilots, arms, and technicians. The USSR sent weapons and advisors to the Republicans; the Comintern organized thousands of liberals and leftists from 53 foreign countries—particularly from France—into volunteer International Brigades formed to fight fascism.

The conflict in Spain represented in microcosm the polarization of much of the Western world into extreme left and right camps. Under these ideologically charged circumstances, both sides engaged in mass arrests and executions in the name of anticommunism or antifascism. Serving as a battleground for conflicting nations and as a proving ground for new weapons, the Civil War later became known as a dress rehearsal for World War II. Missing, however, were the West-

This poster issued by the Spanish anarchists during the Spanish Civil War (1936–39) reads "Tomorrow the world, today Spain," warning of the threat of fascism to Europe as a whole. The anarchists were one of the disparate groups within the Republican, or Loyalist, camp, which battled in vain to prevent the takeover of Spain by the Nationalists under Francisco Franco.

ern democracies. The United States embargoed arms shipments to both sides, and Britain and France also pursued a policy of nonintervention. These actions represented a great blow to the Loyalists, who as representatives of Spain's legal government had hoped for aid from the Western powers.

In 1937 the Nationalists scored some gains, taking Malaga in February and the Basque provinces and Asturias by October. Madrid, however, held out. Meanwhile, the Loyalists, unlike their well-disciplined opponents under Franco's dictatorial rule, were beset by internal strife. In May 1937 anarchists and radical Marxists staged an abortive revolution in Barcelona that was opposed by the Socialists and Communists. The Communists, who as the conduit for Soviet aid became increasingly influential on the Loyalist side, led a drive to repress the ultraleftist elements.

Soviet supply shipments declined in 1938, giving the Nationalists a substantial military edge. In December 1937 the Loyalists captured Teruel in a counteroffensive, but in February 1938 the Nationalists recaptured the town and drove from there to the Mediterranean, dividing the Loyalist forces in two. After an unsuccessful drive into Valencia during the summer, Franco moved on Catalonia in the winter of 1938–39, and Barcelona was captured on Jan. 26, 1939. Isolated in Madrid and Valencia, the Loyalists were sharply divided over whether to continue fighting. When Madrid fell to Franco's forces on Mar. 28, 1939, the Civil War was over.

DANIEL R. HEADRICK

Bibliography: Broué, Pierre, and Temime, Emile, *The Revolution and the Civil War in Spain*, trans. by Tony White (1973); Fraser, Ronald, *Blood of Spain: An Oral History of the Spanish War* (1979); Jackson, Gabriel, *The Spanish Republic and the Civil War* (1965); Kurzman, Dan, *Miracle of November* (1980); Orwell, George, *Homage to Catalonia* (1938); Thomas, Hugh, *The Spanish Civil War*, rev. ed. (1977).

Spanish colonial architecture: see LATIN AMERICAN ART AND ARCHITECTURE.

Spanish Guinea: see EQUATORIAL GUINEA.

Spanish language: see ROMANCE LANGUAGES.

Spanish literature

Spanish literature enjoyed one tremendous burst of energy during its Golden Age, roughly from the mid-16th to the late-17th century, when virtually all forms of literature practiced by Spanish writers, but particularly the drama, reached the apex of their development. Although no straight line of development characterizes Spanish literature, the continuing strength of certain themes, qualities, and genres can be discerned. The heroic motifs, the soaring lyricism of its poetry, the tension between idealism and a cynical realism, the satirical, self-critical bent shared by writers of intense patriotism, the ingenious mixing of the traditional with the new—all make their appearance in every century. The novel as it was developed by Spanish writers during the 16th century endowed European literature with a major contribution to a then emerging form.

The first Spanish literature consists of 40 or 50 love lyrics in the Mozarab dialect, known as *jarchas*, that were appended to Hebrew and Arabic poems produced in Moorish Spain during the 11th century. They are considered Europe's earliest Romance-language poetry. Shortly thereafter, the *cantar de gesta*, or epic poem, made its appearance in Spain. The first substantial work in this genre, *The Poem of the Cid* (*c.*1140; Eng. trans., 1959), portrays Spain's national hero, Rodrigo Díaz de Vivar. Realistic and well-grounded historically, the composition largely avoids the fantastic elements found in the epic poems of other countries. It relates the unjust exile of EL CID from Castile, his pardon, the marriage and betrayal of his daughters by the arrogant Leonese, and the Cid's revenge.

THE MEDIEVAL PERIOD

The two principal poetic forms used in medieval Spain were the *mester de juglaría*, or minstrel's mode, employed in epic

poems, and the *mester de clerecía*, the cleric's mode. The clerics preferred rhymed quatrains to the minstrel's assonated lines. Most of the lyrics produced between the 12th and early 15th centuries were written in Galician-Portuguese and modeled on the poems of the troubadours (see PROVENÇAL LITERATURE). These satirical songs and amorous laments were replaced by the ballads, probably purple passages from epic poems transmitted orally from one generation to the next, which flourished especially in the 16th century and have remained popular to this day.

Alfonso the Wise, king of Castile (r. 1252–84), the first to use Spanish as a cultural language, encouraged translations of the Old Testament and studies in all branches of learning. He wrote important historical and scientific treatises and, in *Las siete partidas* (The Seven Parts, 1256–65), produced the first modern code of laws. His most evocative personal work, *Las cantigas de Santa María* (The Canticles of Saint Mary), is probably the best Marian poetry of the Middle Ages.

The greatest prose writer of the period was Alfonso's nephew, Prince Juan Manuel (1282–1349), who wrote 50 apologues, or allegorical narratives, under the title of *Count Lucanor* (1328–35; Eng. trans., 1868). Appearing 13 years before Boccaccio's *Decameron* (1349–53), the stories concern a young count who constantly seeks advice from his counselor, Patronio. From Patronio's tales, such as "The Emperor's New Clothes," the Count draws obvious moral lessons. The first full-length Spanish novel, *El Caballero Cifar* (*c.*1300–50)—an anonymous work filled with magical and religious elements —was also the first novel of chivalry. In the character of Squire Ribaldo can be seen a prototype of the *pícaro*, or antihero, of later picaresque fiction.

One of the monuments of Spanish literature, *The Book of Good Love* (1330; Eng. trans., 1972)—known as the "human comedy of the Middle Ages"—was written by the archpriest of Hita, Juan Ruiz (*c.*1283–1350). Ruiz used a variety of poetic meters in his ironic, sensual, sometimes delicate, sometimes coarse treatment of love. In addition to fables and scandalous parodies, Ruiz includes moving poems to the Virgin Mary. As an ambivalent actor in his panoramic 14th-century poem, he succumbs to human temptations and never quite resolves the conflict between carnal love and divine love.

The influence of Italian poetry began to make itself felt in the 15th century. Even so, the aristocratic Íñigo López de Mendoza, the marquis of Santillana (1398–1458), won greater fame for his simple *serranillas*—popular songs concerning rustic encounters between refined knights and simple shepherdesses—than for his elegiac, allegorical Italianate verse. Juan de Mena (1411–56), Spain's first professional man of letters, wrote Latin-influenced poetry and an allegorical masterpiece, *El laberinto de Fortuna* (The Labyrinth of Fortune, 1444). Jorge Manrique (1440–79) created what became the single best-known poem in the Spanish language, *Coplas*, translated by Longfellow in 1833 as *On the Death of His Father*. In its 40 stanzas Manrique meditates on the transitory nature of worldly possessions and portrays this life as merely a preparation for the one after death.

THE SPANISH RENAISSANCE

In Spain the term *Renaissance* generally refers to the 16th century, and *Baroque* to the 17th. The humanistic Renaissance enjoyed by Italy and France never fully triumphed in Spain because of the grip of the Spanish church and the tenacity of medieval tradition. Yet scholastic and human truth achieved an uneasy coexistence as Spain entered the period of its greatest expansion and quickly emerged as the preeminent power on the Continent.

One of the greatest expressions of Spanish literary genius at the turn of the new century, *The Tragicomedy of Calisto and Melibea* (1499–1502; trans. 1959, and as *The Spanish Bawd*, 1631)—commonly called CELESTINA for its central character— melded medieval and Renaissance motifs. A novel written in dialogue form and divided into 21 acts, it features both humor and tragedy as it contrasts the erotic exaltation of the aristocratic Melibea and noble Calisto with the sordid transactions of the go-between Celestina and her greedy servants. The author, Fernando de Rojas (1465–1541), a Jewish convert

Miguel de Cervantes Saavedra's masterpiece, Don Quixote *(2 vols.; 1605, 1615), a richly imaginative and inventive satire on the chivalric romance, is considered one of the world's greatest novels. Cervantes, also a noted dramatist, created the first Spanish short stories in* Exemplary Novels *(1613), a collection of 12 moral tales whose form was derived from Italian literary tradition.*

to Catholicism, here preaches the theme of moral retribution.

Known as the "faultless" poet of the 16th century, GARCILASO DE LA VEGA fused Italian forms with Spanish tradition in his poetry to create a world of the imagination that exalted love and beauty. Even more important than his pastoral themes are the musicality and harmony of his sophisticated and elegant eclogues. More exuberant and sonorous in style, Fernando de Herrera (1534–97), the leader of the southern school of poetry, patriotically praised the triumph of Don Juan of Austria over the Turks at Lepanto in his *Canción . . . por la vitoria del Señor Don Juan* (Song in Thanks for the Victory of Don Juan, 1572). Luis de Léon (1527–91), the leader of the northern school of poetry based in Salamanca, and perhaps Spain's finest poet, also wrote prose works of note. A kind of Christian Horace, he represented a perfect amalgam of the Christian and Platonic ideals.

Spanish mystics of the 16th century relied on a highly original use of metaphor and a complicated yet popular language to create their powerful blend of realism and idealism. Saint TERESA OF AVILA, writing familiarly but passionately of her mystical experiences in her masterpiece, *The Interior Castle* (1588; Eng. trans., 1852, 1972)—also known as *The Mansions of the Soul*—had great literary impact. Saint JOHN OF THE CROSS, Spain's other preeminent mystic, wrote abstract, metaphysical poetry about his attempts at union with God and his struggles to illuminate the "dark night of the soul."

The Novel. In addition to novels of chivalry such as *Amadis of Gaul* (1508; Eng. trans., 1803)—based on an early 14th-century romance—whose hero overcomes incredible odds to win his lady, 16th-century Spanish prose forms included pastoral romances, sentimental allegorical novels about love, and Moorish novels filled with impossibly gallant protagonists. The most significant contribution of the period, however, was the anonymous, satirical *Life of Lazarillo de Tormes and of his Fortunes and Adversities* (1554; Eng. trans., 1586), Spain's first important PICARESQUE NOVEL. Later notable examples of the genre—which was to exert an immense influence on the development of the novel in France and England in the 18th century—include the often moralistic *The Rogue, or the Life of Guzmán de Alfarache* (2 vols., 1599 and 1604; Eng. trans., 1621) by Mateo ALEMÁN and *The History of the Life of the Squire Marcos of Obregon* (1618; Eng. trans., 1816) by Vicente Martínez ESPINEL.

The culmination of the Spanish novel in the Golden Age was reached in Miguel de CERVANTES SAAVEDRA's masterpiece, *El ingenioso hidalgo Don Quixote de la Mancha* (2 vols.; 1605, 1615)—considered one of the world's greatest novels. More than a parody of the novel of chivalry, DON QUIXOTE (first translated into English, 1612–20) combines the real and the ideal with a quest for truth and the meaning of good and evil. The protagonist, "crazed" through his exposure to too many novels of chivalry, tries to apply his idealistic beliefs to real situations. Inevitably he fails, but the lesson of his goodness and kindness remains as a legacy for his down-to-earth

companion, Sancho Panza. Possibly Spain's greatest literary figure, Cervantes also wrote a pastoral novel (1585), dramas, one-act farces, and 12 *Exemplary Novels* (1613; Eng. trans., 1640), which were prototypes of the Spanish short story.

The Drama. Spanish dramatists of the late 16th century were important for developing the themes and dramatic techniques that a theater going beyond the *autos sacramentales*—or religiously inspired one-act plays performed at Corpus Christi—would need. Among the leading figures who prepared the way for Spain's great dramatic achievements in the Golden Age are Juan del ENCINA, known as the father of Spanish drama; Bartolomé de Torres Naharro (1485–1524), who elaborated the rules governing dramatic composition and who brought a new realism to the stage; Juan de la CUEVA, the first to use national themes and to mix tragedy and comedy; and Lope de RUEDA, the inventor of the *paso*, or brief comic interlude, based on real life and filled with popular, witty dialogue.

LITERATURE OF THE GOLDEN AGE

The four greatest figures of Spanish 17th-century theater are undoubtedly Lope de VEGA, TIRSO DE MOLINA, Juan RUIZ DE ALARCÓN Y MENDOZA, and Pedro CALDERÓN DE LA BARCA. Lope, a lyrical genius who also wrote didactic poetry, novels, and short stories, virtually revolutionized theatrical practice with the 1,500 or so plays attributed to him. Rejecting classical precepts for the complicated intrigues that became the hallmark of the so-called comedies of cloak and sword, Lope extolled love, defended the monarchy and the Catholic faith, and evoked patriotism and honor in works that dealt with dramatic conflicts and ingeniously combined tragic and comic elements. Among his best works are *Fuenteovejuna* (c.1613), concerning the revolt of a village against a corrupt nobleman; *Peribáñez y el Comendador de Ocaña* (c.1610), a play on the theme of honor; and *The Knight from Olmedo* (c.1620–25; Eng. trans., 1961), an artistic tragedy involving love rivalries, witchcraft, and death.

One of Lope's disciples, Guillén de CASTRO Y BELLVÍS, is notable as the author of *Las Mocedades del Cid* (The Youth of the Cid, 1618), the first drama about Spain's national hero and the inspiration for Pierre Corneille's great tragedy on the same subject (1636). Another, Tirso, in the theologically loaded *The Trickster of Seville* (1630; Eng. trans., 1959), presented the first DON JUAN, a figure that continued to haunt the European imagaination. Ruiz de Alarcón keenly observed social vices in his stylized comedies of manners. Calderón's beautiful, allegorical, religious, and philosophical dramas, which rank among the greatest ever written, show the work of a careful craftsman, in contrast to that of the spontaneous Lope. In his rustic masterpiece, *The Mayor of Zalamea* (1643; Eng. trans., 1959), Calderón stresses the honor code, whereas in his ornamented *Life Is a Dream* (1635; Eng. trans., 1968) he meditates on free will and human destiny.

In the 17th century, baroque literary forms involved the artificial exaggeration of language and abstract thought. The

Pedro Calderón de la Barca was the last great dramatist of Spain's Golden Age of literature. Calderón's autos sacramentales, produced in connection with the annual celebration of the feast of Corpus Christi, remain his most highly acclaimed works, although his comedias *and history plays are also highly regarded, exhibiting the same philosophic and linguistic complexity as his religious works.*

most famous exponent of the distortion of language for beauty's sake, Luis de GÓNGORA Y ARGOTE—who gave his name to the style known as GONGORISM—wrote a number of celebrated works but is primarily known for his highly ornate, pastoral poetic vision, *Solitudes* (1613; Eng. trans., 1921). Francisco Gómez de QUEVEDO Y VILLEGAS wrote ascetic, philosophical, moral, and satirical works in which he exposed the decadence of his country. In addition to more than 1,000 poems and his ferocious picaresque novel, *The Life and Adventures of Buscon* (1626; Eng. trans., 1657), Quevedo penned *Visions* (1627; Eng. trans., 1640), a collection of fantasies on hell and salvation in which he condemns the hypocrisy of Spanish life. Baltasar Gracián y Morales (1601-58), for his part, in his allegorical novel *The Critick* (1651-57; Eng. trans., 1681), contrasts natural and instinctive man with civilized and cultured man, showing the importance of experience as a source of prudence.

In reaction against the previous century, 18th-century Spanish neoclassicists turned to French and Italian models. The period marked a decline from the originality and self-confidence that had once characterized Spanish literature. Among the few who stood out were Ramón de la Cruz (1731-94), the author of colorful and popular one-act farces; Leandro Fernández de Moratín (1760-1828), who wrote modern thesis plays; and the essayist Benito Jerónimo Feijóo y Montenegro (1676-1764), who brought European culture to Spain.

ROMANTICISM AND REALISM

Spain shared in the tendencies and movements that shaped poetry, drama, and the novel throughout Europe in the 19th century. Representing romanticism, Ángel de Saavedra (1791-1865), the duke of Rivas, published important narrative poetry and ballads and, with *Don Álvaro* (1835), produced the most exaggerated romantic drama of the century, on which Verdi based his opera *La Forza del destino*. Fusing all poetic tendencies in his experimental verse forms, José de Espronceda (1808-42) wrote of happiness as an illusion for which only death provides a solution. José ZORRILLA Y MORAL more affirmatively represented the spirit of Spanish romanticism in his poetry and plays, the most famous of which is *Don Juan Tenorio* (1844; Eng. trans., 1846). Ramón de CAMPOAMOR wrote short, ironic poems exemplifying eternal truths. Gustavo Adolfo BÉCQUER, the greatest lyric poet of the 19th century, composed suggestive, musical verse to express the impalpable quality of frustrated love.

Turning away from the picaresque and the allegorical, Spanish novelists embraced realism as a forum for the expression of their social views. Cecilia Böhl von Faber, who adopted the pen name Fernán CABALLERO, published the first well-known regional novel, *The Sea-Gull* (1849; Eng. trans., 1867), and in so doing transferred the essayistic mode known as *costumbrismo* to fiction. The best-known realistic novels, however, were concentrated in the last quarter of the 19th century: *The Three-Cornered Hat* (1874; Eng. trans., 1918, 1935), by Pedro Antonio de ALARCÓN; *Pepita Jiménez* (1874; Eng. trans., 1891), by the ironic and urbane Juan VALERA Y ALCALÁ GALIANO; and *Peñas Arriba* (Up the Mountain, 1894), which praised the virtues of tradition and country life, by José Mariá de Pereda (1833-1906). Benito PÉREZ GALDÓS, a Spaniard as prolific and protean as Balzac, wrote almost 80 novels dealing with every aspect of Spanish history and society, in which he stressed Christian love and spiritual and ethical values. Among the best were *Doña Perfecta* (1876; Eng. trans., 1894), an exposure of religious bigotry, and *Fortunata and Jacinta* (1886-87; Eng. trans., 1973), a panoramic portrayal of 19th-century Madrid.

Toward the end of the century realism ceded to naturalism in the novels of Emilia PARDO BAZÁN, Leopoldo ALAS (better known as Clarín), and Vicente BLASCO IBÁÑEZ. Clarín, in *La Regenta* (The Judge's Wife, 1884-85), examined the sexual, political, and religious mores of a provincial town and, with his protagonist, Ana Ozores, created one of the great feminine figures of Spanish literature. Of the numerous novels by Blasco Ibáñez, *The Four Horsemen of the Apocalypse* (1916; Eng. trans., 1918), dealing with the pain and violence of World War I, became best known internationally.

THE 20TH CENTURY

The "Generation of '98" demonstrated a love of countryside, nostalgia for past virtues, and passionate interest in the historical debate over the modernization of Spain: they were dedicated to the regeneration of their country through will and action. Miguel de UNAMUNO, the most cultured member of the group, tried his hand at all genres. His long poem, *The Christ of Velázquez* (1920; Eng. trans., 1951), and his best-known essay, *The Tragic Sense of Life* (1912; Eng. trans., 1921), as well as his dramas and novels, all reflect the spiritual anguish of modern individuals confronted by their mortality and the failure to reconcile reason with natural human needs. José Martínez RUIZ (also known as Azorín), sensitive to history and classical literature, evoked the timelessness of the Castilian countryside in his descriptive essays. Even more influential abroad than in his homeland, José ORTEGA Y GASSET brought erudition to his discussions of the human condition, art, and the shape of the future in long philosophical essays such as *The Revolt of the Masses* (1930; Eng. trans., 1932) and *The Dehumanization of Art* (1925; Eng. trans., 1948).

Modernism, a literary renovation of form, promoted an evasive aestheticism, but 20th-century poets soon found their own styles. Antonio MACHADO represents the eternal verities of the Castilian landscape in his *Campos de Castila* (1912), which became the spiritual and poetic breviary of the Generation of '98. Juan Ramón JIMÉNEZ stressed beauty and pantheism, as opposed to Machado's metaphysical anguish, in his delicate, abstract poems, which in 1956 won him the Nobel Prize. His *Platero and I* (1917; Eng. trans., 1957) remains a classic of poetic prose. León Felipe Camino y Galicia (1884-1968) employed epic and biblical tones to convey the tragedy of modern humanity and of the Spanish Civil War.

A leader of the Generation of 1927, which opened poetry to new influences, Federico GARCÍA LORCA combined popular poetry with odd sensory combinations and magic metaphors in his celebrated *Gypsy Ballads* (1928; Eng. trans., 1953). As one of the purest lyric voices of the 20th century, García Lorca continues to exert an influence far beyond the confines of the Spanish-speaking world. A surrealist poet, Vicente ALEIXANDRE concentrated in his early poetry on death and erotic fusion with the cosmos; later he discovers man as a social being. In 1977 he won the Nobel Prize for literature. Rafael ALBERTI, in exile in Argentina from the Civil War to 1977, seeks values in an absurd, distintegrating world. Many of the poets of the Generation of 1927 experimented with poetry in the tradition of Góngora. The next generation returned to Garcilaso's graceful rhythms.

In the 20th century Jacinto BENAVENTE Y MARTÍNEZ freed Spanish drama from the melodramatic dictates of José ECHEGARAY Y EIZAGUIRRE, subtly satirizing Spanish society with irony and elegance in such dramas as *The Bonds of Interest* (1907; Eng. trans., 1936). The author of 172 plays, he was honored by the Nobel Prize (1922) midway in his career. Ramón del VALLE INCLÁN, author of lyrical erotic novels, in the 1920s

Federico García Lorca was one of the most compelling figures of 20th-century Spanish literature. A superb lyric poet and a gifted dramatist, García Lorca evoked the beauty and violence of Spain in his work. Among his most acclaimed verse works are Gypsy Ballads *(1928) and* Lament for Ignacio Sánchez Mejías *(1935), considered by many the finest and most powerful elegy in Spanish literature.*

developed the *esperpento*, an expressionistic type of theater that grotesquely distorted reality through the deformation of language and the use of puppetlike characters in order to express his mordant view of Spanish civilization. García Lorca concentrated on elementary passions and concepts such as virginity and motherhood in his powerful dramatic trilogy made up of *Blood Wedding* (1933; Eng. trans., 1939), *Yerma* (1934; Eng. trans., 1941), and *The House of Bernarda Alba* (1936; Eng. trans., 1947). Alejandro Casona (1903–65) wrote about the need to face life bravely in his special fusion of fantasy and realism. Antonio Buero VALLEJO, in fantastic, philosophical, psychological, and historical tragedies of hope, dramatizes human dignity and responsibility. In a more pessimistic vein, Alfonso SASTRE, Spain's best-known contemporary playwright, deals with the social and existential dilemmas of people tortured and trapped by their own weaknesses.

Pío BAROJA Y NESSI used the cynicism of the picaresque vagabonds and men of action he portrays in his novels to attack the hypocrisies of modern civilization. Ramón Pérez de Ayala (1880–1962) extols the merits of tolerance and justice in his ironic, intellectual novels. The symbolic works of Ramón Sender (b. 1902) express an ultimate faith in humanity, but this faith is not shared by Camilo José CELA in his violent, starkly realistic *The Family of Pascual Duarte* (1942; Eng. trans., 1953). Among younger writers such as José María Gironella (b. 1917), Miguel Delibes (b. 1920), Juan Benet (b. 1927), and Juan GOYTISOLO (b. 1931), Goytisolo enjoys the greatest reputation nationally and internationally. Beginning in 1954 with *The Young Assassins* (Eng. trans., 1959), which dissected an aimless postwar generation, he has continued to hold Spanish society up to a harsh light.   KESSEL SCHWARTZ

Bibliography: Brenan, Gerald, *The Literature of the Spanish People from Roman Times to the Present Day*, 2d ed. (1953); Chandler, Richard E., and Schwartz, Kessel, *A New History of Spanish Literature* (1961); Cobb, Carl W., *Contemporary Spanish Poetry, 1898–1963* (1976); Crawford, James P., *Spanish Drama before Lope de Vega* (1937; repr. 1975); Eoff, Sherman H., *The Modern Spanish Novel* (1961); Green, Otis H., *The Literary Mind of Medieval and Renaissance Spain* (1970) and *Spain and the Western Tradition*, 4 vols., (1963–66); Ilie, Paul, *The Surrealist Mode in Spanish Literature* (1968); McClellan, I. L., *Origins of the Romantic Movement in Spain*, 2d ed. (1975); Monteser, Frederick, *The Picaresque Element in Western Literature* (1975); Peers, Edgar A., *A History of the Romantic Movement in Spain*, 2 vols. (1940; repr. 1976); Post, Chandler R., *Medieval Spanish Allegory* (1915; repr. 1974); Shaw, Donald Leslie, *The Generation of Eighteen Ninety-Eight in Spain* (1975); Shergold, N. D., *A History of the Spanish Stage* (1967); Wellwarth, George E., *Spanish Underground Drama* (1972); Wilson, Margaret, *Spanish Drama of the Golden Age* (1969); Young, Howard T., *The Victorious Expression:A Study of Four Contemporary Spanish Poets: Unamuno, Machado, Jimenez, and Lorca* (1964).

Spanish missions

The history of Spain's missions in the American South and Southwest reveals much about Spain's strategy, contributions, and failures in these regions. The expeditions of Francisco Vázquez de CORONADO (1540–42) and Juan de OÑATE (1598) convinced Spanish authorities that no wealthy Indian empires like that of the Aztecs were to be found north of Mexico. Consequently the Spanish came to view the northern frontier of their empire as a defensive barrier and as a place where pagan souls might be saved. In what are now the states of Florida, Texas, New Mexico, Arizona, and California missions were founded to propagate Roman Catholicism. To protect these missions as well as the mines and ranches of Mexico from attack from the north, the Spanish established presidios—fortified garrisons of troops.

Franciscan priests founded a series of missions in Florida after 1573, mainly along the Atlantic and Gulf coasts. The first missions in New Mexico were established by friars accompanying the Oñate expedition of 1598; during the next 100 years Franciscan priests founded more than 40 additional missions, most of them along the Rio Grande. Especially influential was Father Alonso de Benavides, who directed the founding of 10 missions between 1625 and 1629 and thereafter promoted them ably in Spain. By 1680 missions had been established among most of the New Mexican Indians.

A French landing led by Robert Cavelier, sieur de LA SALLE, on the Texas coast in 1684 spurred the Spanish to build missions in that area. The first of these, founded (1690) near what is now Weches, Tex., failed because of the Indians' hostility, but others were founded in east Texas after 1716, and some of them prospered. San Antonio became the home of several missions, including San Antonio de Valero (the ALAMO). The Franciscan mission of Nuestra Senora del Espíritu Santo de Zúñiga, built at Matagorda Bay in 1722 to help protect the coast from the French, was later moved inland.

Between 1687 and 1711 the missionary and explorer Father Eusebio KINO established many missions in northern Mexico and Baja California as well as some in southern Arizona, the

Two of the finest Spanish missions in the American southwest are the mission of San José y San Miguel de Aguayo (1720–31; restored 1933) (left) in San Antonio, Tex., and the mission of San Xavier del Bac (1700; rebuilt 1783–97) (above) near Tucson, Ariz. Used for religious education and training in European agriculture, the mission compounds included such structures as the chapel, friars' quarters, storehouses, and work areas. Some compounds, such as the Alamo, were later used for military purposes.

most notable of which was Mission San Xavier del Bac. When the Spanish began to settle in California, Father Junípero SERRA accompanied the expedition of José de Gálvez in 1769 and founded the Mission San Diego de Alcalá at San Diego, the first of 21 Franciscan missions in California. The last was San Francisco Solano (1823), located in the Sonoma Valley.

Missions varied enormously in their economic and religious success. Some could not support themselves; others developed fertile fields and vineyards and huge herds of cattle. Virtually all successful religious conversion was among sedentary Indians who were easier to control and more adaptable to agriculture and herding. The few attempts to convert such warlike nomads as the Apaches and Comanches failed dismally.

In seeking to introduce both Catholicism and European methods of agriculture, the missions encouraged the Indians to establish their settlements close by, where the priests could give them religious instruction and supervise their labor. Unfortunately this arrangement exposed the Indians to the Europeans' diseases, against which they had little immunity. An epidemic in New Mexico, for instance, killed 3,000 Indians in 1640. Critics charged also that the mission system destroyed much of the Indians' native culture and turned them into an exploited and degraded labor force. Indeed, there were sporadic rebellions; the most spectacular was led by an Indian named POPÉ in 1680; almost 400 Spaniards were killed, and the rest were temporarily driven from Santa Fe and northern New Mexico. After 1834 the Mexican government secularized most surviving missions, converting them for non-religious use.

In design the missions reflected Gothic, Moorish, and Romanesque architectural styles—the various cultural influences brought by the Spanish. Paintings on interior walls sometimes depicted the Southwestern landscape and the artistic traditions of the Indians. Among the best surviving examples are Missions San José y San Miguel de Aguayo in San Antonio, Tex.; San Juan Capistrano, in the California town of the same name; and San Xavier del Bac near Tucson, Ariz.

ELLIOTT WEST

Bibliography: Bannon, John Francis, *The Spanish Borderlands Frontier, 1513-1821* (1971); Berger, John A., *The Franciscan Missions of California* (1947); Burke, James Wakefield, *Missions of Old Texas* (1971); Dominguez, Francisco A., *The Missions of New Mexico, 1776,* ed. by E. B. Adams and Angelico Chavez (1956; repr. 1975); Kelly, Henry W., *Franciscan Missions of New Mexico, 1740-1760* (1941); Kocher, Paul H., *California's Old Missions: The Story of the Founding of the 21 Franciscan Missions in Spanish Alta California, 1769-1823* (1976); Parsons, Francis, *Early 17th Century Missions of the Old Southwest* (1975).

See also: LATIN AMERICAN ART AND ARCHITECTURE.

Spanish moss

Spanish moss, or graybeard, *Tillandsia usneoides*, is an epiphytic herb belonging to the pineapple family, Bromeliaceae. This moss, whose individual stems bear threadlike leaves and green or blue inconspicuous flowers, hangs from tree branches in strands up to 6.1 m (20 ft) long. It ranges from the southeastern United States to Argentina. Besides being considered a graceful ornamental plant, Spanish moss is used as packing material and as upholstery stuffing.

Spanish music

Spain comprises many regions with their own historical and cultural characteristics, including a variety of languages (Castilian, Catalan, Basque, Galician), and this regional diversity is strongly reflected in its music. Also an important influence on the music of Spain was the invasion by the Arabs and Moors and the long occupation that followed (711-1492). It was particularly significant in the southern region of Andalusia and is reflected in the style called *cante jondo* ("deep song"), with its florid melodies and exotic scales. Moorish musicians were also active at the court of Alfonso the Wise (1221-84), who ruled the united kingdom of Castile and Léon and who compiled a famous collection of religious songs with instrumental accompaniment in praise of the Virgin Mary, the *Cantigas de Santa María*.

(Left) *Enrique Granados is best known for his two-part piano suite* Goyescas, *which was inspired by the paintings and tapestries of the Spanish master Francisco de Goya.*

(Below) *Manuel de Falla's ballet* The Three-Cornered Hat, *produced in London by Serge Diaghilev in 1919, had sets and costumes designed by Pablo Picasso.*

By 1492, Spain had achieved some degree of political unity under the rule of Ferdinand and Isabella, and music and the arts flourished. Secular vocal music began with ballads that recounted heroic exploits, tragic events, and tales of love. These ballads were part of the folklore of the common people, but they also appeared in arrangements by court composers for three or four voices, or for solo voice with guitar or *vihuela* (a combination of lute and guitar).

The ballad was called *romance* in Spanish, and its rustic counterpart was the *villancico*, originally a song of the peasants or villagers. The *villancico* became popular during the Renaissance, in the form of part-songs arranged by the leading composers of that period, such as Juan del ENCINA. The most important collection of *villancicos* is the so-called *Cancionero de Palacio* (Palace Songbook), containing nearly 500 songs.

During the 16th and 17th centuries, many composers published collections of instrumental and vocal music, at first for the *vihuela* and later the guitar. Among the best-known were Luis de Milán's *El Maestro* (The Master; 1535), Enríquez de Valderábano's *Silva de Sirenas* (Songs of the Sirens; 1547), Miguel de Fuenllana's *Orphénica Lyra* (Orpheus' Lyre; 1554), and Esteban Daza's *El Parnaso* (The Poetry Collection; 1576). These compositions were all written for the six-string guitar, which in the 17th century was replaced by the guitar with five strings, known as the Spanish guitar—the characteristic instrument of Spain.

Spain could boast of having some of the greatest composers of church music in this period, notably Cristóbal de Morales (c.1500-53), Francisco Guerrero (1527-99), and above all Tomás Luis de VICTORIA, whose masterpiece is his magnificent *Requiem Mass* (1605).

The Spanish lyric drama began its development in the 17th century with an opera titled *La Selva sin Amor* (The Loveless Forest). Its text was written by Lope de Vega, but the composer is unknown. Juan Hidalgo (c.1600-85) wrote the music for several opera librettos by Calderón de la Barca. The most popular form of musical theater in Spain, however, was the ZARZUELA, which combined singing and spoken dialogue and generally had a comic or entertaining plot. It originated in the 18th century but had its greatest vogue during the 19th, when hundreds of *zarzuelas* were produced. The greatest master of this form was Francisco Asenjo Barbieri (1823-94), famous for his *Pan y Toros* (Bread and Bulls; 1864) and *El Barberillo de Lavapiés* (The Barber of Lavapiés; 1874).

As the 20th century approached, Spain produced three of the best-known composers of modern times: Isaac ALBÉNIZ, Enrique GRANADOS, and Manuel de FALLA. All were influenced by the scholar Felipe Pedrell (1841-1922), who advocated the creation of a Spanish "national" expression based on Spain's rich heritage of folk music. Albéniz's greatest contribution was *Iberia* (1909), a suite of 12 pieces for piano brilliantly evoking the regions and cities of Spain. Granados did the same, in a more lyrical manner, with his *Spanish Dances* and the suite *Goyescas* (1912-14), both works written for piano. The themes and scenes of the latter, based on tapestry designs by the painter Goya, were also used by Granados in an opera of the same title, produced in 1916.

Manuel de Falla achieved worldwide fame with his ballets *El Amor Brujo* (Love the Sorcerer, 1915) and *The Three Cornered Hat* (1919), the former humorous, the latter dramatic, and both imbued with the folklore and dances of Spain. He evoked the legendary spirit of Andalusia in *Nights in the Gardens of Spain* (1909-15), composed for piano and orchestra.   GILBERT CHASE

Bibliography: Chase, Gilbert, *The Music of Spain* (1959); Schindler, Kurt, *Folk Music of Spain and Portugal* (1941); Stevenson, Robert, *Spanish Music in the Age of Columbus* (1960) and *Spanish Cathedral Music in the Golden Age* (1961), Trend, John B., *Manuel de Falla and Spanish Music* (1934).

Spanish Sahara: see WESTERN SAHARA.

Spanish Succession, War of the

The War of the Spanish Succession (1701-14)—the last, longest, and bloodiest of the wars of French King LOUIS XIV—was fought over the vast Spanish Empire, which had been left without an uncontested heir in 1700, when the last Spanish Habsburg king, CHARLES II, died childless. Hoping to preserve the European balance of power, Louis and Britain's King WILLIAM III had drawn up treaties (1698, 1700) dividing the inheritance of the sickly Charles between the leading claimants, the French Bourbons and the Austrian Habsburgs. However, the dying king bequeathed all his territories to Philippe, duc d'Anjou, grandson of Louis XIV; if Philippe declined the inheritance, it would go to the Austrian archduke Charles (later Emperor CHARLES VI), second son of Holy Roman Emperor LEOPOLD I.

Louis accepted the inheritance for his grandson, who became PHILIP V of Spain, breaking the partition agreement. By subsequently coordinating the military, commercial, and political policies of Spain and France, Louis upset the European power balance. As a result, an anti-French alliance was formed. Ultimately, France, Spain, and Bavaria faced a Grand Alliance of the Austrian Habsburgs, most German princes, the United Provinces, Britain, and, after 1703, former French allies Portugal and Savoy.

French victories by the duc de VILLARS in southwest Germany at Friedlingen (1702) and Höchstädt (1703) were offset by Britain's seizure of Gibraltar and by the allied conquest of Bavaria following the brilliant victory (1704) at Blenheim (see BLENHEIM, BATTLE OF) by the duke of MARLBOROUGH and the Austrian commander EUGENE OF SAVOY. France lost the Spanish Netherlands through Marlborough's decisive maneuvering (1706) at Ramillies, although the transfer of the French commander, the duc de VENDÔME, from Italy stopped the British

The War of the Spanish Succession (1701-14) erupted when Bourbon inheritance of the Spanish dominions shifted the European balance of power heavily in favor of France. A settlement left Bourbons on the thrones of both France and Spain but as separate dynasties.

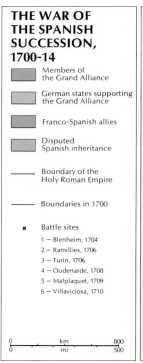

advance short of French soil. Meanwhile, Vendôme's successors lost Turin and all of Italy to Eugene, and Vendôme's mismanagement (1708) of the Battle of Oudenarde left France open to northern invasion. Franco-Spanish success was limited to Spain, where the duke of BERWICK saved Philip V's cause by routing (1707) the allied forces at Almanza. Louis XIV, faced with defeats, a financial crisis, a crippling winter, and the revolt of the CAMISARDS, offered to renounce the Spanish inheritance but fought on when Anglo-Dutch diplomats insisted that he drive his grandson from Spain. Villars's last-ditch stand (1709) against Marlborough at Malplaquet, although a French defeat, crippled the allies, who suffered 20,000 casualties, whereas the French lost only 11,000. Vendôme's victory (1710) at Villaviciosa demonstrated that Philip V could not be dislodged by military force.

Political events broke the military impasse. In Britain, Marlborough's Whig party was replaced by the propeace Tories. The Dutch ceased hostilities with British assurance of a Dutch-controlled "barrier" of fortresses against France. The deaths of all but two direct descendants of Louis XIV (Philip V of Spain and the future LOUIS XV of France) and of Emperor Leopold and his first son (leaving Emperor Charles VI as sole Austrian Habsburg) forced a compromise settlement of the Spanish succession.

The Peace of Utrecht (1713–14; see UTRECHT, PEACE OF) awarded Spain and its colonies to Bourbon Philip V, keeping France separate but without significant territorial losses. Britain emerged as the great colonial, commercial, and naval power in the world, gaining Gibraltar, Minorca, Hudson Bay, Nova Scotia, Newfoundland, Saint Kitt's, and the sole right to the slave trade with Spain's American colonies. Austria acquired the Spanish Netherlands, Naples, Milan, and Sardinia; the declining United Provinces gained their promised barrier; and Savoy received Sicily. This new balance of power remained until the War of the Austrian Succession (1740–48).

A. LLOYD MOOTE

Bibliography: Francis, David, *The First Peninsular War, 1702–1713* (1975); Geikie, Roderick, et al., *Dutch Barrier, 1705–1719* (1930; repr. 1969); Kamen, Henry, *The War of Succession in Spain, 1700–15* (1969); Wolf, J. B., *The Emergence of the Great Powers, 1685–1715* (1951).

Spark, Muriel

Proficient in many genres, the English writer Muriel Sarah Spark, b. Feb. 1, 1918, is best known for her novel *The Prime of Miss Jean Brodie* (1961; play, 1964; film, 1969), which tells the story of an Edinburgh school mistress who is eventually punished because of her penchant for self-dramatization. Although Spark's fiction is witty and detached on the surface, her Catholicism imparts depth and occasional horror to her satires of human folly and sin. Her other novels include *Memento Mori* (1959; play, 1964), *The Mandelbaum Gate* (1965), *The Public Image* (1968), *The Driver's Seat* (1970; film, 1974), *The Takeover* (1976), and *Territorial Rights* (1979). Spark has also written poetry, short stories, plays, biography, and criticism.

Bibliography: Kemp, Peter, *Muriel Spark* (1975); Malkoff, Karl, *Muriel Spark* (1968).

spark chamber

The spark chamber is one of several experimental devices used by physicists to observe the tracks of high-energy charged particles produced in an accelerator. It is distinguished from a CLOUD CHAMBER by its geometry. In its most common form the spark chamber consists of an array of parallel thin metal plates spaced about 10 mm (0.375 in) apart, like the plates of a capacitor, in an atmosphere of helium and argon. The plates are usually made of aluminum foil 0.025–0.050 mm (0.001–0.002 in) thick. For high-energy gamma rays, lead may be used. When a high-voltage pulse is applied across the plates in step with the accelerator pulse, a spark discharge is produced that follows the paths of the ionized particles. To record the events, stereo cameras are used with lenses that "see" into the narrow gaps. Any number of tracks can be seen simultaneously when observing complex events.

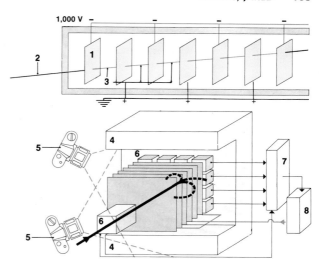

A spark chamber is used to observe the path of high-energy charged particles. It consists of a series of closely spaced metal plates (1) connected to a high-voltage source and enclosed in a helium-argon or helium-neon atmosphere. When a charged particle (2) enters the chamber, sparks (3) occur between the plates along the path of ions produced by collisions of the particle with gas atoms. If the chamber is placed between the poles (4) of a magnet, the path's curvature—which is photographed by stereo cameras (5)—reveals the particle's energy and mass. Particle detectors (6) connected to a computer (7) switch on the high-voltage power supply (8) to initiate sparking.

Data may be read out in digitized form by observing the x,y coordinates of discrete points on the track.

In narrow-gap chambers—up to 20 mm (¾ in)—the discharge is usually perpendicular to the plates. Fewer plates are used in wide-gap chambers, and they are easier to "see into." The spark discharge may be up to an angle of 50° or parallel to the plates. The intrinsic accuracy of track location in the spark chamber approaches that of a BUBBLE CHAMBER. If the initiating pulse is made short and intense, a streamer discharge grows parallel to the plates and, when viewed from the end, appears as bright dots. When strong magnetic fields are applied, the tracks become curved, and magnetic moments or spin characteristics of charged particles can be determined.

FRANK J. OLIVER

Bibliography: Allkofer, Otto C., *Spark Chambers* (1969); Shutt, R. P., *Bubble and Spark Chambers*, 2 vols. (1967).

Sparkman, John J.

John Jackson Sparkman, b. Hartselle, Ala., Dec. 20, 1899, served as Democratic U.S. senator from Alabama (1946–79) and was an unsuccessful candidate for vice-president in 1952. Educated at the University of Alabama, he practiced law privately until 1936, when he was elected to the U.S. House of Representatives. He served as chairman of the Banking, Housing, and Urban Affairs Committee (1967–75) and of the Foreign Relations Committee (1975–79).

Sparks, Jared

An American historian and McLean Professor of History at Harvard University (1839–49), Jared Sparks, b. May 10, 1789, d. Mar. 14, 1866, aroused interest in American history through his biographies and compilations of original manuscripts. His writings include *The Life of John Ledyard* (1828) and *The Life of Gouverneur Morris*, 3 vols. (1832). Sparks edited several multiple-volume works—*The Writings of George Washington* (1834–38), *The Works of Benjamin Franklin* (1836–40), *The Diplomatic Correspondence of the American Revolution* (1829–30), and *The Library of American Biography* (1834–47). He sometimes altered documents to present national heroes in a more favorable light.

The male house sparrow, P. domesticus (top left), has a black throat; the female (bottom) is brown and gray. Both the male and female chipping sparrow, Spizella passerina (center), are similarly colored, as are the male and female song sparrow, M. melodia (right).

sparrow

Sparrows are perching birds that are typically 8 to 24 cm (3 to 9.4 in) long, are generally dull colored—brown, gray, white, or pale yellow—and have cone-shaped bills. Although omnivorous, they mostly eat seeds and feed on or near the ground.

Old and New World sparrows are not considered to be closely related in taxonomy; the former belong to the family of Old World sparrow-weavers, Ploceidae, and the latter to either the bunting family, Emberizidae, or the finch family, Fringillidae, depending on the classification used.

The sparrow-weavers, native to Eurasia and Africa, include about 35 species, the most widely familiar being the house sparrow, *Passer domesticus*. This species commonly lives close to human habitats. Originally restricted to Eurasia, house sparrows were introduced after 1850 in parts of North America, South America, southern Africa, Australia, New Zealand, and Hawaii. Old World sparrow-weavers generally build domed nests. Both sexes care for the eggs and later the young.

Many of the 55 New World species occur in North America. These sparrows often seek food by scratching away the ground litter with both feet simultaneously during a backward jump. They generally build cup-shaped nests. The song sparrow, *Melospiza melodia*, is one of the most widely known of the native North American sparrows.

GEORGE A. CLARK, JR.

Bibliography: Banks, Richard C., *Geographic Variation in the White-Crowned Sparrow* (1964); Bent, Arthur C., et al., *Life Histories of North American Cardinals, Grosbeaks, Buntings, Towhees, Finches, Sparrows, and Allies*, 3 vols. (1968); Summers-Smith, James Denis, *The House Sparrow* (1963).

Sparta

Dorian Sparta grew out of four villages settled in and after the 11th century BC. The eventual fusion of these separate villages into a *polis*, or city-state, may explain Sparta's double kingship. The Spartans gradually conquered Laconia, the lower southeastern quarter of the Peloponnesus. Pre-Dorian Amyclae, the last holdout, was absorbed into Sparta by the 8th century. Many of the conquered pre-Dorians became helots, or serfs; members of various neighboring groups in Laconia were granted the semiautonomous status of *perioikoi*, but they were required to serve in the Spartan army. The Spartans acquired the western portion of the lower Peloponnesus by conquering MESSENIA in the First Messenian War (late 8th century). The Messenians, who were also Dorians, rebelled and were suppressed in the Second Messenian War (mid-7th

century). TYRTAEUS was active in the war and described it in his poetry.

The relation of these events to Sparta's amazing social and military reorganization is obscure. Some elements of the "new" Sparta seem primitive survivals paralleled elsewhere, notably in Crete. Others connect with its need to control its subject population. Sparta's agrarian and stagnant economy also played its part. In any case, Sparta was transformed into a collectivist warrior society. Seven-year-old boys of the ruling class were removed from their families to be trained for war. Educated by the state, the young grew up in barracks; they learned discipline and austerity. Spartans became the best warriors in Greece; the word *Spartan* has since become a byword for endurance and rugged simplicity.

By the mid-6th century Sparta had taken possession of Argive territory along the southeastern Peloponnesian coast, in a battle for supremacy that soon left ARGOS a second-class power. By the end of the century Sparta headed a confederation of all major Peloponnesian cities except Argos—the Peloponnesian League, which in 480–479 became the bulwark

This bronze statue of a Spartan hoplite, or heavily armed infantryman, celebrates the martial spirit so valued in Sparta. Although Spartan society cultivated the arts before 600 BC, later generations neglected them entirely in favor of military pursuits.

of the Greek defense against Persia in the PERSIAN WARS. Athens, which headed a similar alliance of Ionian states, the Delian League, arose to challenge Sparta. Spartan supremacy was also threatened in 464 by a revolt of helots and *perioikoi*, the Third Messenian War, which was suppressed with difficulty. After an initial confrontation (446–445) with Athens terminated indecisively, the PELOPONNESIAN WAR broke out in 431; it ended in 404 with Sparta's conquest of Athens. Sparta resumed leadership of all of Greece.

Spartan predominance did not last. The campaign of King AGESILAUS II against the Persians in Anatolia was disappointing, and he was recalled when the Corinthian War broke out in 395. Sparta retained control of Greece in 386 with Persian assistance, but, in 371, Sparta's army and reputation were shattered by THEBES at Leuctra, and Messenia was liberated shortly thereafter. Weakened and suffering from a decline in manpower, the Spartans were helpless before PHILIP II of Macedonia.

In the 3d century they were confronted by the superior power of the Achaean League. Agis IV (r. 244–241) tried to revitalize Sparta in 242 but was killed in the attempt. CLEOMENES III instituted several reforms, overthrowing the main governmental body, the EPHORS, and widely extending citizenship. He fell from power in 222, defeated by the Achaean League and the Macedonians at Sellasia.

After 195, Sparta joined the Achaean League, which was destroyed by the Romans in 146. Under the Romans, Sparta thereafter enjoyed prosperity and a certain vogue. In AD 395, Goths under Alaric I destroyed Sparta. The sparse ruins of the ancient city-state lie outside the modern Greek city of Spárti.

CHARLES W. FORNARA

Bibliography: Barrow, Robin, *Sparta* (1975); Forrest, W. G., *A History of Sparta, 950–192 B.C.* (1968); Huxley, G. L., *Early Sparta* (1962; repr. 1970); Jones, A. H. M., *Sparta* (1967); Michell, Humfrey, *Sparta* (1952; repr. 1964).

See also: DORIANS; GREECE, ANCIENT.

Spartacus

Spartacus, d. 71 BC, was a gladiator of Thracian origin who led an uprising of Italian fugitive slaves in 73 BC. His force—eventually 90,000 strong—defeated the Romans seven times and advanced through southern Italy, laying waste to the land. The rebellion was crushed when Spartacus was killed in battle against Marcus Licinius CRASSUS at Lucania, and Crassus and POMPEY had 6,000 of the rebel slaves crucified along the road from Capua to Rome. When the fighting ended, 3,000 Roman prisoners were found unharmed in Spartacus's camp.

Spartanburg

Spartanburg is a city in the foothills of the Blue Ridge Mountains of northwestern South Carolina. The seat of Spartanburg County, it has a population of 47,000 (1979 est.). Fertile soil and a temperate climate support a basic agricultural economy producing peaches, cotton, and livestock. Diversified industries manufacture machinery, textiles, furniture, and food products. A statue in the town square commemorates the Revolutionary Battle of Cowpens, fought (1781) nearby. Founded in 1785, the city was named for the Spartan Rifles, a local Revolutionary War unit.

Spassky, Boris [spahs'-kee]

Boris Vasilyevich Spassky, b. Jan. 30, 1937, became an international Soviet chess grand master and was world champion from 1969 to 1972. He learned to play chess at the Kirov region children's home, to which he had been evacuated from Leningrad during World War II. He attained grand master standing in 1955, was world junior champion in 1955–57, and became Soviet champion in 1961. In 1965 he won the Candidates' Tournament, earning the right to challenge for the world championship. It was not until 1969, however, that he won the crown. Spassky held the title for three years before losing it to Bobby Fischer of the United States.

Bibliography: Soltis, A., *The Best Chess Games of Boris Spassky* (1972).

SPCA: see SOCIETY FOR THE PREVENTION OF CRUELTY TO ANIMALS.

Speaker, Tris

Tris Speaker, a professional baseball player, spent 22 seasons in the major leagues, dividing most of his career between the Boston Red Sox and the Cleveland Indians. Despite Speaker's lofty lifetime batting average of .344, he won only a single batting championship.

Tristram Speaker, b. Hubbard, Tex., Apr. 4, 1888, d. Dec. 8, 1958, was an American professional baseball player whose 22-year major-league career was a model of consistent hitting and flawless fielding. Playing for four teams from 1907 until 1928, Speaker compiled a .344 career batting average in addition to establishing several fielding records. He is the holder of the record for unassisted double plays by an outfielder, with 4, and has the most putouts in a career. Speaker's hitting prowess was equally impressive: he has more career doubles than any American League player; he led the league in doubles 8 times and ranks fourth in total hits in a career with 3,515.

In 1919, while still an active player, he became the coach of the Cleveland Indians. In the course of achieving a 616-520 won-lost record, Speaker led the team to victory in the 1920 World Series. In 1937 he was elected to the Baseball Hall of Fame.

Speare, Elizabeth [speer]

An American writer of children's literature, Elizabeth Speare, b. Melrose, Mass., Nov. 21, 1908, is one of only two writers who have won the Newbery Medal twice. She received the awards for *The Witch of Blackbird Pond* (1958) and *The Bronze Bow* (1961). These moving and suspenseful novels are set, respectively, in colonial New England and Roman-occupied Palestine, and each gives authentic life to its historical setting. Speare has also written *Calico Captive* (1957), *Life in Colonial America* (1963), *Ice Glen* (1967), and *Prospering* (1967).

spearfish

The spearfishes are two species of billfishes in the family Istiophoridae. Certain marlins are usually classified with the spearfishes in the genus *Tetrapturus*. The shortbill spearfish, *T. angustirostris*, is found in the central and western Pacific. The longbill spearfish, *T. pfluegeri*, is a longer-billed species of the Atlantic Ocean. Both spearfishes rarely exceed 1.8 m (6 ft) in length and 27 kg (60 lb) in weight.

spearmint

Spearmint is the common name for a perennial herb, *Mentha spicata*, of the family Labiatae. Native to Europe, this popular garden mint has become naturalized in North America. Spearmint sprigs are used to flavor drinks such as mint julep; meats, particularly lamb; and, in Moslem countries, teas. Oil

Spearmint, M. spicata, has the strongest taste of all mints, and its leaves are used to flavor drinks, sauces, jellies, toothpastes, and chewing gum. New spearmint plants spring up from an old plant's root system and can rapidly overrun a garden.

from the leaves is used for flavoring chewing gums and medicines.　　　　　ARTHUR O. TUCKER

Special Astrophysical Observatory

The world's largest optical and radio telescopes are part of the Special Astrophysical Observatory of the USSR Academy of Sciences. The observatory is located east of the Black Sea near the village of Zelenchukskaya along the northern slope of the Caucasus Mountains in southwestern Russia.

The 6-m (236-in) optical reflector, located atop the 2,100-m-high (6,900-ft) Mount Semirodniki, was completed in 1976. It is noted for a novel computer-controlled altazimuth mounting; a conventional equatorial mounting would have been too large and inaccurate. The BTA (Russian equivalent of Big Telescope-Altazimuth) has a mirror ground out of pyrexlike borosilicate glass; its optical surface is well (but not perfectly) corrected to focus light. In the 1980s a replacement, made of vitreous ceramic, may be completed. Optically, BTA can be used at f/4 from the prime focus or at f/30 from either side of the altitude axis. Extremely heavy auxiliary instruments can be mounted on platforms there, enabling studies not possible with smaller telescopes.

The RATAN-600 instrument—an acronym for Radio Astronomy Telescope of the Academy of Sciences (Nauk) and the approximate diameter (actual: 576 m/1,889 ft) of the ring-shaped primary reflector—is located 20 km (12 mi) northeast of the BTA. The instrument's wide spectral range, broad-band reception, and high angular resolution enable it to be used for study of radio galaxies, extragalactic nebulae, and separate clouds of neutral and ionized hydrogen and hydroxyl; in particular, it can investigate fluctuations in galactic background radio emissions with emphasis on items of small angular diameter. The RATAN-600 can also be used to radiolocate and communicate with Soviet space probes in remote parts of the solar system.　　　　　NORMAN SPERLING

Bibliography: Gatland, Kenneth W., and Lawton, Anthony T., "Opening the Far Frontier," *Spaceflight*, February 1975; Ioannisiani, Bagrat K., "The Soviet 6-meter Altazimuth Reflector," *Sky and Telescope*, November 1977; Korolkov, D. V., and Pariiskii, Yu. N., "The Soviet RATAN-600 Radio Telescope," *Sky and Telescope*, April 1979; Philip, A. G. Davis, "A Visit to the Soviet Union's 6-meter Reflector," *Sky and Telescope*, May 1974.

special drawing rights:　see INTERNATIONAL MONETARY FUND.

special education

Special education provides unconventional instructional services to individuals who would not receive maximum benefit from conventional educational practices. These individuals include those with physical handicaps, sensory disabilities (blindness and deafness), differences in intellectual capacity (giftedness and mental retardation), speech disorders, behavioral disorders (emotional disturbance), and academic learning disabilities. Special instructional services include special teaching techniques, materials, equipment, facilities, and adjunctive services.

The history of special education can be traced at least as far back as Plato's recommendation that gifted children should be provided special leadership training, but special education did not grow extensively until schooling became common. During the late 18th and early 19th centuries special educational procedures for teaching some school skills to sensorially handicapped pupils were devised. For example, deaf individuals were taught meanings for printed words by repeated simultaneous presentations of a printed word and a picture of what the word represented. Shortly thereafter attempts to educate retarded and disturbed individuals increased in number and success. During the 19th century many severely handicapped children and youth were taught self-help skills. More recently, medical advances, which help keep more exceptional individuals alive, and the enactment and implementation of compulsory education laws, which put or kept more students in schools who otherwise would not be there, have led to an increasing need for special education services.

Special equipment, one part of special education services, is used more extensively with sensorially and physically handicapped individuals. Such equipment usually makes it possible for people with handicaps to benefit from otherwise conventional instruction. Machines to magnify printed material, convert it into tactile representations, or to record it on audio tape are used in educating visually handicapped individuals. Special desks, chairs, writing devices, and school buses may be used with physically handicapped individuals. Hearing aids make it possible for many hearing-handicapped individuals to study in regular classrooms. Special materials such as books printed in large type or braille may be used for the blind or visually impaired. Special facilities including ramps and doors wide enough for wheelchair access, swimming pools for physical education, and schoolrooms strung with wire for transmitting sounds to special hearing aids worn by the deaf are part of special education. Special adjunctive services are provided to exceptional individuals in addition to regular and special education. These services include speech training for students who have difficulties related to speaking, physical and occupational therapies for students with physical handicaps, counseling for students who manifest behavioral disorders, and vocational training for the mentally retarded.

By far the most common element of special education is the adoption of specialized instructional techniques. Often teachers of hearing-impaired individuals will use sign language as a part of instruction. Programmed instruction procedures that are designed to present educational content in small, easily acquired steps are often used with exceptional individuals. Behavior modification techniques such as reinforcement and token economies may be adopted in order to help teach students to complete assignments, work more neatly, not disrupt other students, and so forth. Techniques that provide experiences with concrete rather than abstract representations of concepts are common in special education.

Most special education takes place in regular public schools, but some is provided in special public or private day or residential schools, public or private hospitals, and, in some cases, the homes of exceptional individuals. Usually it is not necessary to provide an entire program of services that are different from conventional instruction, but rather to modify only those aspects of the educational program that must be changed in order to meet the unique needs of the exceptional individual. In general, the smaller the degree of deviation from normal, the fewer special education services are required, and the more likely it is that these services will be provided in normal settings.

In general, children with minimal handicaps from low-income families are more likely to be found in special education programs than are similarly handicapped children from middle- and upper-income families. When children are considered able to benefit from participation with other children, they are usually taught in the normal school program. This concept, called *mainstreaming*, is widely advocated and is becoming prevalent in the United States.

Within a regular public school, special education services may be provided in a number of ways. In many cases where the handicaps of individuals are minor, a special education teacher may work with the students' regular classroom teacher to develop appropriate services. For example, the special and regular education teachers may develop and use special worksheets to help an individual learn a particularly difficult reading skill. This approach is usually called a consulting or itinerant teacher model. For individuals with slightly greater handicaps, special education may be provided in a separate classroom for a part of the school day. For example, students who have difficulty only with reading skills and not in other areas may attend a special class for reading instruction but receive all other instruction in regular classes. This approach is often called a resource-room model. When a student's learning and behavioral problems are more severe and pervasive, he or she may be assigned on a full-time basis to a special education room. This approach is often called a self-contained class model. In resource-room and self-contained class models, the number of students working with a teacher at any one time is typically much lower than that working with a teacher in a regular classroom. In hospital and home settings, services are provided to more severely handicapped individuals, and instruction may involve only one teacher and one student at a time.

The goals toward which instruction is directed in special education are sometimes different from those which are sought in regular education. Whereas special education for mildly handicapped individuals often is focused on academic and cognitive skills, as is regular education for nonhandicapped individuals, special education for severely handicapped students is often aimed at teaching basic self-help and self-care skills. Individuals who are severely emotionally disturbed and mentally retarded are taught skills as basic as sitting, chewing, toileting, dressing, and responding when their names are called. When academic and cognitive skills are taught to severely handicapped individuals, the breadth of instruction may be limited. For example, reading for moderately retarded students may be restricted to words that are essential to daily living, such as *men, women, walk, wait, exit,* and so forth. Special education for some other exceptional students may, however, be aimed at teaching them skills that will allow them to benefit from otherwise conventional education. For example, when blind individuals have available to them and can read braille materials, they are able to participate in many regular education programs. Similarly, when physically handicapped individuals are not impeded from participation by architectural barriers, that is, when there is adequate wheelchair access, and when those who require it have special equipment that allows them to express their answers, many can receive the bulk of their education in regular school programs.

Special education for gifted individuals is designed to take advantage of that which makes the students exceptional, whereas special education for other exceptional individuals is usually focused on remedying, circumventing, or compensating for handicapping conditions. In spite of this difference special education for the gifted still has as its goal provision of services that meet the unique needs of individuals and make it possible for them to develop to their maximum. Although there are no unanimously accepted methods, education for gifted students has included enrichment through special activities beyond the regular curriculum, acceleration by allowing gifted students to progress through conventional education at a faster-than-normal pace, and special programming in which gifted students are taught in homogenous groups and provided with opportunities to do such things as conduct extensive experiments, produce artworks, and study special topics with older students.

Legislative action (The Education of All Handicapped Children's Act of 1975) requires that all exceptional (excluding the gifted) students have available to them a free and appropriate public educational opportunity that takes place in an educational environment as nearly regular as an individual's handicap permits, and that no individuals may be denied services because of their handicaps. In practice this usually means that more mildly handicapped individuals, that is, those whose handicaps require fewer special education services, are provided those services in consultative or itinerant and resource-room models.   JOHN LLOYD

Bibliography: Abramo, Barbara A., et al., *Teaching the Retarded Child* (1975); Bradley, R. C., *The Education of Exceptional Children* (1970); Brown, Jean W., *A Humanistic Approach to Special Education* (1973); Das, J. P., and Baine, David, *Mental Retardation for Special Educators* (1978); Dunn, Lloyd M., ed., *Exceptional Children in the Schools: Special Education in Transition,* 2d ed. (1973); Egg, Maria, *Educating the Child Who Is Different* (1968); Gearheart, Bill R., *Learning Disabilities: Educational Strategies,* 2d ed. (1977) and *Teaching the Learning Disabled: A Combined Task and Process Approach* (1976); Guilliford, Ronald, *Special Educational Needs* (1971); Hallahan, Daniel, and Kauffman, James M., *Exceptional Children: Introduction to Special Education* (1978); Haring, Norris G., and Brown, Louis J., eds., *Teaching the Severely Handicapped* (1976); Kirk, Samuel A., and Gallagher, James, *Educating Exceptional Children,* 3d ed. (1979); Kneedler, Rebecca D., and Tarver, Sara G., *Changing Perspectives in Special Education* (1977); Siegel, Ernest, *Special Education in the Regular Classroom* (1969); Stevens, Mildred, *The Educational and Social Needs of Children with Severe Handicaps,* 2d ed. (1976); Van Osdol, Bob M., and Perryman, Patricia, eds., *Special Education: A New Look* (1974).

special-interest groups

Special-interest groups—also called pressure groups or lobbies—are collections of individuals who join together to pursue common interests through agreed-upon activities. The term generally refers to groups that attempt to influence public policy.

Special-interest groups have been part of the American political process since its beginning and have been viewed ambivalently for more than 200 years. As early as 1787, James Madison warned about the "mischiefs of 'factions,'" his term for such groups. The U.S. Congress has periodically, through the 19th and 20th centuries, set up committees to investigate alleged corruption and scandal in interest-group activities. In recent years, groups such as the American Milk Producers and International Telephone and Telegraph Company have been embroiled in political and legal controversy related to their lobbying activities. In 1979, President Jimmy Carter blamed the oil lobby for blocking his energy program in the Congress.

Special-interest groups have also been viewed as an integral and beneficial part of the American political process, legitimized in the U.S. Constitution by the 1st Amendment guarantees of freedom of speech and the right to "petition the Government for a redress of grievances." Political observers generally acknowledge that instances of outright corruption and bribery involving groups are rare.

Governmental officials frequently praise the involvement of special-interest groups as a necessary component of governmental decision making, providing important information on public opinion and on the substantive impact of policy proposals.

The Range of Activities. No definitive tally of special-interest groups exists; in the United States alone, however, they number in the thousands. Comparable numbers exist in other large industrialized nations. Groups may be classified in a variety of ways. Some of the broader categories are business, banking, labor, education, farm, health, energy, environment, professional associations, foreign political and economic interests, senior citizens, consumers, ideology-oriented, women, the "public," the poor, and religion. Many individuals and groups overlap in categories and in group membership.

Groups may act individually or through broader "umbrella" organizations. Business groups, for example, include individual corporations (such as Mobil Oil or U.S. Steel); trade associations (such as the American Petroleum Institute, representing oil producers and refiners, including Mobil); and broader organizations, including the NATIONAL ASSOCIATION OF MANU-FACTURERS. Labor groups include individual unions, such as the TEAMSTERS and the UNITED MINE WORKERS, and labor federations, the most prominent of which is the AMERICAN FEDERATION OF LABOR AND CONGRESS OF INDUSTRIAL ORGANIZATIONS (AFL-CIO).

Various education interest groups represent teachers, students, parents, school administrators, universities, professors, professional schools, vocational and adult educational institutions, and libraries. In addition, there is an umbrella "Committee for Full Funding of Education Programs," which includes 90 separate interest groups in education, labor, and civil rights.

Farm groups, outside of individual agricultural producers and processors, include associations such as the Associated Milk Producers and the National Cotton Association of America. Broad farm organizations include the AMERICAN FARM BUREAU FEDERATION and the NATIONAL FARMERS UNION.

Examples of environmental groups include the SIERRA CLUB and the Environmental Action Coalition. Ideological groups include AMERICANS FOR DEMOCRATIC ACTION, a liberal group, and Americans for Constitutional Action, a conservative group. Public-interest or citizens groups include Public Citizen (one of the Ralph NADER groups), COMMON CAUSE, and the LEAGUE OF WOMEN VOTERS. Consumers are represented by such groups as the Consumers Union and the Consumer Federation of America, and women by the NATIONAL ORGANIZATION FOR WOMEN.

How the Groups Operate. A large number of special-interest groups engage in extensive activity in both national and state capitals and at the local level, attempting to influence government policy decisions. Many groups have permanent Washington offices; some retain law firms or other groups to act as LOBBYISTS. At the national level, special-interest groups may attempt to exert influence on the Congress, the regulatory agencies, executive departments, and the White House. Their goals may range from passing, blocking, or amending legislation to achieving a favorable regulatory ruling, receiving a government contract, or obtaining a favorable presidential decision. Generally, the same tactics are used at state and local levels.

When dealing with the Congress, interest groups focus most of their operations on the committees of the House and Senate, which are the key units for considering legislation. Groups monitor committee and subcommittee activities to keep abreast of possible political and legislative developments that might affect them; they will frequently testify at committee hearings to put their views on the official record. Many groups rely also on "grass-roots" activity—generating letters and telegrams to political leaders from their constituents around the country—to demonstrate their political clout. Occasionally mass demonstrations and picketing are used in order to demonstrate a group's mass appeal.

Groups use a variety of resources to gain access to legislators and other government officials. These resources include money for campaigns, substantive expertise, and political and leadership skills. In 1976, special-interest groups gave nearly $23 million in campaign contributions to candidates for the U.S. Congress. Millions more were spent on state and local campaigns. Many groups are represented in Washington by former members of the Congress, former congressional or White House staff members, or former Cabinet officers; these people presumably are able to provide both political skills and substantive knowledge of the workings of the government.

Regulating Special-Interest Groups. Groups' activities in the Unites States are regulated by the Federal Regulation of Lobbying Act of 1946. It requires paid lobbyists to register with the Congress and to file quarterly reports with the clerk of the House of Representatives. The law has many loopholes, however, and is generally considered to be ineffective; registrations are incomplete, and the law does not tightly regulate interest-group activity. A Foreign Agent Registration Act was adopted in 1938 to regulate lobbying on the part of foreign nations and companies. It has many of the same limitations as the domestic law. Efforts to strengthen both acts have for the most part been unsuccessful.   NORMAN J. ORNSTEIN

Bibliography: Banfield, Edward C., *Political Influence* (1961); Congressional Quarterly, *The Washington Lobby* (1974); Deakin, James, *The Lobbyists* (1966); Greenwald, Carol, *Group Power: Lobbying and Public Policy* (1977); Kimber, Richard, and Richardson, J. J., *Pressure Groups in Britain* (1974); Milbraith, Lester, *The Washington Lobbyists* (1963; repr. 1976); Sinclair, John, *Interest Groups in America* (1976); Truman, David B., *The Governmental Process: Political Interests and Public Opinion* (1971); Ziegler, Harmon, *Interest Groups in American Society*, 2d ed. (1972).

Special Olympics

The Special Olympics is organized athletic competition at the local, national, and international levels for retarded children and adults. In order to compete boys and girls must be 8 years of age or older, and most entrants usually have IQ scores of 80 or lower. They are encouraged, nevertheless, to go on to interscholastic and intramural sports programs. Since its creation in 1968, using funds from the Joseph P. Kennedy, Jr., Foundation, the Special Olympics has grown to include more than 1 million participants in the United States and in 35 foreign countries. The program culminates in August of the year before the regular Olympic Games and includes the following events: basketball, bowling, diving, floor hockey, frisbee throwing, gymnastics, ice skating, poly hockey, soccer, softball, track and field, volleyball, and wheelchair events. There may also be demonstration events in badminton, cross-country running, dance, equestrian events, field hockey, golf, and rhythmic exercises. A recent addition is winter sports, which about 30 states in the United States have adopted. The First International Winter Special Olympics, held in 1977, attracted over 500 participants for skiing and skating events. Local games take place in more than 10,000 communities around the world.

specific gravity

Specific gravity is the ratio of the density of a given substance to the density of a standard of reference at standard temperature and pressure. The density of water is the standard of reference for solids and liquids; the density of air is the standard of reference for gases.   KENNETH W. KILMER

specific heat: see HEAT CAPACITY.

spectroheliograph

A spectroheliograph is an instrument for producing monochromatic photographs of the Sun. George Ellery HALE designed the first spectroheliograph in 1891, in which square prisms were rotated in front of a first slit and behind a second. The image of the Sun falls on the first slit and the second isolates the selected wavelength. The monochromatic image of the Sun develops on a plate behind the second slit. Modern instruments use SPECTROSCOPES in place of prisms. Usually, only a segment of the Sun is photographed by a spectroheliograph; a complete picture of the Sun may be made by taking a series of pictures and combining them or by coordinating oscillating slits. Any wavelength may be chosen, but interest centered first on the K line of ionized calcium (393.3 nm), and later on the H-alpha line of hydrogen (656.3 nm). In this way spectroheliograms were produced that showed the distribution of calcium and helium on the Sun's surface. During solar emissions, images can be taken of the disturbed areas.

spectrophotometer

A spectrophotometer is an optical instrument for comparing the composition and intensity of light with light from another source. When a substance is burned in a flame, the light emitted contains wavelengths of light that are specific for the elements of the substance. A flame spectrophotometer can be used to analyze this light and identify and quantitate the ele-

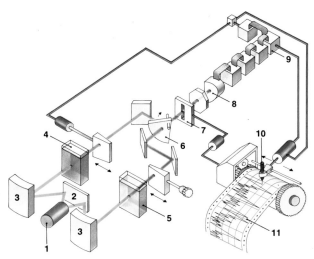

Spectrophotometers are used to determine the nature and amounts of a substance in a sample by measuring its absorption of electromagnetic radiation of a specific wavelength. In a double-beam automatic recording instrument, light from a source (1) is split in half by a combination of a plane mirror (2) and two concave mirrors (3). One beam is led through the test sample (4), and the other through a known reference sample (5). A sector mirror (6) rotates to switch the light paths from one sample to the other. Light of one wavelength, selected from the emerging beam by a monochromator (7), reaches a detector (8) that produces an electrical signal. The signal is amplified (9) and used to drive a spectrum recorder pen (10) on a chart (11).

ments. The absorbance spectrophotometer is widely used in all analytical laboratories to identify and quantitate substances in solutions. In routine chemical analysis, only one substance is analyzed at a time by a beam of monochromatic (single-wavelength) light directed through the sample. The wavelength is selected to be one that the solute absorbs strongly but that other components in the solution do not absorb. The concentration of the solute is calculated from the absorbance of the light by comparing it to the absorbance of a standard solution. For example, the color of paint can be exactly defined using a reflective spectrophotometer that measures the bands of colors in the spectrum of light reflected from a painted surface.

LESLIE W. LEE

See also: ABSORPTION, LIGHT; COLORIMETER; SPECTROSCOPY.

spectroscope

The spectroscope is a visual optical instrument that separates a beam of radiation into its component wavelengths. The early, fundamental spectroscopes of Augustin Fresnel and Joseph Fraunhofer (early 1800s) stemmed from Isaac Newton's experiment of 1669 in which he demonstrated that white light is a mixture of all the colors of the rainbow. Since then the spectroscope has been greatly improved, and it has spawned a score or more of technically related research and analytical instruments, all members of what might be termed a *spectro* family.

Spectro Instruments. The term *scope* in the word *spectroscope* adequately describes an instrument for visually viewing a spectrum; if a meter is added to substitute for a manually performed reading procedure the instrument becomes a spectrometer. If the apparatus includes a recording device the word *spectrograph* is appropriate, although *recording spectrometer* would be equally descriptive. A spectroscope is generally assumed to operate in the range of visible light unless other regions of the electromagnetic spectrum are specified. Specialized spectrometers analyze infrared, ultraviolet, and gamma radiation and magnetic resonance phenomena.

Spectro analyzers measure either the absorption or the emission of certain wavelengths of radiation. When the energy level of a sample must be raised before it can be analyzed, the name of the instrument suggests the activation

process—for example, the optical emission spectrometer or the flame photometer.

The Spectroscope. The fundamental spectroscope—which includes both the early instruments and the simpler teaching instruments of the present—is comprised of a slit to admit light, a collimator for rendering the light from the slit parallel before it enters the prism, one or more dispersing prisms, and a telescope for forming images of the slit in the various wavelengths. A camera may be used in place of the telescope eyepiece and the prism replaced with a DIFFRACTION GRATING to improve the optical performance of the instrument.

In 1856, George Bunsen and others shifted the emphasis of the spectroscope from research on the properties of light and the effects of light on various materials to use for chemical analysis. By heating materials in the tip of a Bunsen burner at temperatures of up to nearly 1,800° C, vaporization was achieved, making it possible to determine the light radiation characteristics of the vaporized material and thus to establish spectral lines for the chemical elements. Once reliable spectra were created from the use of pure materials, it was a comparatively easy next step to compare unknown samples against established spectra. In addition to flames of various types (Bunsen, oxyhydrogen, for example), electric current (arcs, brush discharges, sparks) is used to activate samples. This technology is called emission spectrometry.

Automated Spectroscopy. Fully automatic analysis equipment is particularly useful where there are many similar samples to be analyzed, such as samples of steel from large numbers of furnaces or serum from many patients. Instruments have been developed for the quantitative determination of specific components of a process stream, as for example the analysis for a specific gas in mixed-gas stream. The first such analyzers operated on samples brought to the control laboratory but later were fully automated and close-coupled to the actual process so that signals generated by the instrument are used to actuate process controls.

DOUGLAS M. CONSIDINE

Bibliography: Cutting, Thomas A., *Manual of Spectroscopy* (1949); Davison, Joan and P. S., *An Introduction to Spectrometry* (1967);

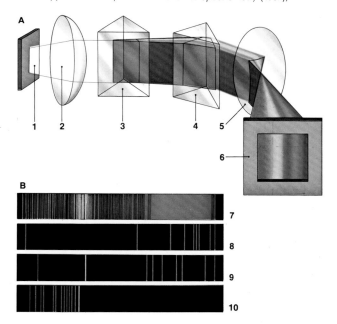

A spectroscope (A) produces a spectrum by separating the component wavelengths in radiant energy. Light rays emitted by a substance are passed through a narrow slit (1), made parallel by a collimating lens (2), then refracted by a prism (3). The resulting spectrum is enlarged by a second prism (4), then focused through a lens (5) onto a screen or photographic plate (6) to be analyzed. Elements can be identified by their characteristic spectra (B). Seen here are the spectra of molecular hydrogen (7), atomic hydrogen (8), helium (9), and neon (10).

Drago, Russell S., *Physical Methods in Chemistry* (1977); Tarasov, K. I., *The Spectroscope,* trans., by J. H. Dixon (1974); Vanasse, George A., ed., *Spectrometric Techniques* (1977); Whiffen, D. H., *Spectroscopy* (1966); Williams, Dudley, ed., *Spectroscopy,* 2 vols. (1976).

spectroscopy

Spectroscopic methods are currently the most important methods of research and analysis in chemistry and are of particular value to other sciences, especially astronomy. The most frequently used techniques are infrared (IR) spectroscopy, ultraviolet (UV) spectroscopy, and, recently, nuclear magnetic resonance (NMR) spectroscopy. All spectroscopic methods are based on the exposure of the sample substance to radiation. Different materials absorb radiation to different extents, depending on their electronic structures. It is often possible to determine the chemical structure of an unknown substance by studying its spectrum. Spectroscopy, in conjunction with the related MASS SPECTROMETRY, has almost completely replaced classical chemical analysis in the investigation of the structure of compounds.

SPECTRUM AND MOLECULAR STRUCTURE

The spectrum of a compound gives direct information about its structure. Toward the end of the 19th century physicists began a systematic investigation of the structure of the ATOM. Atomic spectroscopy was the most important aid to the evolution of the modern theories of atomic structure—the ability to explain mathematically an observed spectrum of an atom or to predict and subsequently discover new spectral lines was the strongest evidence that the theories used were correct (see HYDROGEN SPECTRUM). It was only later that molecular spectra were studied. Infrared spectroscopy, which was developed shortly after World War II, was the greatest step in this direction. Spectra originating from the absorption of shorter wavelengths (UV and visible light) correspond to transitions of electrons in atoms from one energy level to another; the IR spectrum corresponds to the vibrational transitions of atoms with respect to each other, the most important being the mutual vibrations of two atoms bonded to each other. The vibrations of larger fragments of the molecule are less important for obtaining direct information.

In IR spectroscopy the two vibrating atoms are regarded as two point masses connected by a spring (representing the bond between the two atoms). The frequency of the vibration corresponds to the frequency of the absorbed radiation, and it depends on the masses of the atoms and the bond strength. This frequency is characteristic of the two atoms and is practically independent of the rest of the molecule. For example, the IR spectrum of an organic compound will immediately reveal whether the molecule contains a carbonyl group (C=O). Many such groups can be immediately recognized from an IR spectrum, superseding the need to carry out complicated or time-consuming chemical analyses.

After the war the investigation of small-energy transitions (which occur in many molecules in a magnetic field) began. This study led to the development of NMR spectroscopy, a technique that is now the most important method of analysis in the chemical laboratory.

INFRARED SPECTROSCOPY

The vibrations in molecules that consist of many atoms are very complex. In the simple water molecule (H_2O) three different modes of vibration occur; in a fairly complicated molecule such as acetone (CH_3COCH_3) with ten atoms, not fewer than 24 modes of vibration are possible, where, in principle, all atoms oscillate with respect to a common center of gravity. Fortunately, not all vibrational modes are important. The most distinct vibration in the acetone molecule is that of the carbonyl group (C=O), and the remainder of the molecule can be regarded as being partially fixed. The absorption frequency of the carbonyl group is not strongly influenced by the remainder of the molecule, so that most compounds that contain this group exhibit a similar absorption of IR frequencies between 5.0 and 5.6 10^{13} Hz. It is more common to express these frequencies in terms of the wave number (the number of waves per centimeter), which is found by dividing the frequency by c (the speed of light, 3×10^{10} cm/sec).

It is because of the existence of group frequencies that IR spectroscopy has developed into such a common, routine technique. The most important group frequencies are those in which the light hydrogen atoms (H) vibrate with respect to the remainder of the molecule, and those that originate from the vibrations of double bonds.

When the region of a spectrum in which the group frequencies occur is examined, it is easy to find strong indications of the presence of certain groups of atoms. Together with other chemical evidence, this information may suffice to determine the chemical structure of the substance. Outside the region of the group frequencies is the so-called fingerprint region, which corresponds to complicated vibrations of the molecule as a whole. It is not possible to draw rapid conclusions concerning the structure of the molecule from this region. Each compound, however, has a unique fingerprint pattern, and it is easy to determine whether an unknown compound is identical to a known compound by comparing their respective spectra. It is also possible to detect certain peculiarities in the behavior of molecules, such as the presence of hydrogen bonds.

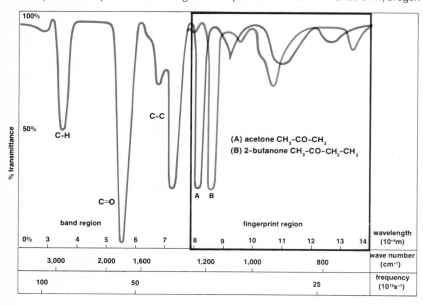

Infrared (IR) absorption spectra are used by chemists to identify organic compounds and are obtained by measuring a substance's absorption of IR radiation at different frequencies. The frequencies absorbed are the same as the frequency with which the atoms within the molecules vibrate relative to one another, and depend on the atomic masses and on the atomic-bond strengths. Absorptions of about 3-7 microns (10^{-6} m) are associated with certain functional groups, such as C−H, C=O, and C−C. The presence of specific absorption peaks can thus be used to indicate the presence of such groups in a molecule. Other vibrational frequencies in the 7- to 14-micron region are characteristic of the entire molecule. This region is called the fingerprint region because it can be used to differentiate between molecules with the same functional groups. Acetone (CH_3COCH_3) and 2-butanone ($CH_3COCH_2CH_3$) are two chemically related compounds that have essentially the same spectra in the band region (left). In the fingerprint region (right), however, the spectra differ enough to allow identification of acetone (blue) and of 2-butanone (red).

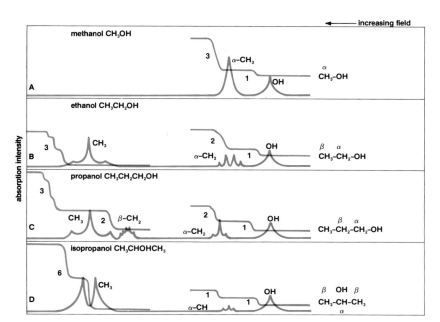

← increasing field

Nuclear-magnetic-resonance (NMR) spectroscopy, which is used to determine molecular structures, is based on the magnetic properties of atomic nuclei. It involves placing a compound in a varying magnetic field and determining the field strength at which a nucleus will absorb radio waves of fixed frequency. Protons, or hydrogen nuclei, attached to different elements absorb the radio waves at different field strengths. Thus the NMR spectrum (blue) of methanol (A) shows that the absorption peak for a proton attached to oxygen, O, occurs at a lower field strength than for a proton on carbon, C. The area under each peak indicates the total number of hydrogen atoms, H, present and is recorded in a separate curve (blue) that indicates three hydrogens attached to carbon and one to oxygen. Protons on neighboring carbon atoms in ethanol (B) interact with each other as a result of so-called spin-spin coupling and cause splitting of each single peak into multiple peaks. The spectra for propanol (C) and for isopropanol (D) are more complex but follow a trend similar to that for ethanol.

Microwave Spectra. A molecule can also undergo rotations as well as vibrations. The difference in energy between two rotational states is very small, and the absorbed radiation lies in the far infrared region or even in the microwave region. The instrumentation for microwave spectroscopy is very complicated; both the construction and adjustment of the emitter (source of radiation) and the receiver (detector) require special techniques. The apparatus is unsuitable for routine analysis, and the interpretation of patterns is difficult. It is possible to calculate, however, the moment of inertia of not-too-complicated molecules by means of microwave spectra. Bond angles and bond distances can be derived from this data.

ULTRAVIOLET SPECTROSCOPY
Ultraviolet spectroscopy also includes spectroscopy with visible light, as the atomic processes by which the absorptions take place (electron transitions) are similar in both regions. Because many more compounds absorb in the UV region (colorless compounds) than in the visible region (colored compounds), it is more practical to talk, in general, of UV spectroscopy. The light source usually has a spectral range of $2-8 \times 10^{-7}$m (2000–8000 Å), which is normally achieved by the use of two separate sources: an incandescent lamp for the visible region, and a hydrogen lamp for the UV region. Glass lenses and cells cannot be used for UV measurements, because glass itself strongly absorbs in the UV region. Quartz is generally used, but for wavelengths shorter than 2000 Å fluorite is used. The conclusions that can be drawn from UV spectroscopy give less information on the structure of compounds than those from IR spectroscopy. Therefore, UV spectroscopy is not a standard technique for this purpose.

A major use of UV spectroscopy—so common that a spectrometer or colorimeter is considered an essential instrument in any laboratory—is to measure concentrations of solutions. The principle at work is Beer-Lambert's law, which states that the amount of light absorbed by a substance in solution is proportional to its concentration (see ABSORPTION, LIGHT). A series of solutions is prepared containing known amounts of the substance to be measured. The light absorbance (optical density) of the unknown solution is compared to the absorbance of the standard solutions, and from this the unknown concentration is determined.

It is not necessary to examine a complete spectrum of any solution. In practice, the absorbance at a single wavelength is measured, typically in the region of the spectrum where absorbance is the strongest. Another use for UV spectroscopy is in chemical kinetics, in which the course of a chemical reaction is followed by observing the change in absorbance as a function of time.

NUCLEAR MAGNETIC RESONANCE SPECTROSCOPY
A relatively recent development, NMR spectroscopy has now become the best method for obtaining information on the structure of complicated organic compounds, notwithstanding the high cost of the NMR apparatus. Since the introduction of NMR spectroscopy in the 1960s, infrared spectroscopy has declined somewhat in importance.

Protons and neutrons in the atomic nucleus behave as tiny magnets. In some nuclei their magnetism cancels out, but in others a residual magnetism remains. This is called nuclear spin. Nuclei common in organic chemistry that have no net nuclear spin are carbon-12 and oxygen-16. The nuclei hydrogen-1, hydrogen-2 (deuterium), carbon-13, nitrogen-14, oxygen-17, and fluorine-19, however, show magnetic properties and may be studied by NMR. When magnetic nuclei are placed in a magnetic field, an interaction takes place. In the simplest case the nuclear magnet can be either aligned with the magnetic field or opposed to it. These two states have different energies, and the system can convert from one to the other by an absorption or release of energy. These energy differences are very small, even at high magnetic field strengths, and the absorption of energy takes place at radiations of relatively low frequencies (compared to other forms of spectroscopy). The frequencies used are 40–360 MHz (megahertz), the same range as used in television and FM broadcasts. These frequencies are generated by the same type of electronic generator and are received by antennas. In practice, the frequency is kept constant and the magnetic field is varied (field sweep), although the results are presented as though the field were constant and the frequency varied (frequency sweep).

For different nuclei with different frequency responses, a completely different range of magnetic field strength is used. Thus, a scan for protons shows only the effects caused by the presence of protons. The point at which the absorption occurs is called the *resonance frequency.*

From the resonance frequency alone, nothing can be deduced about the molecular structure. An isolated hydrogen nucleus (proton, or H⁺ ion) has a resonance frequency of 60

Some Important Organic Group Frequencies (cm⁻¹)

—OH	3580–3670	C≡N	2000–2500
—NH₂	3300–3500	C≡C—	2000–2500
=C—H	3010–3030	C≡CS	1620–1680
≡C—H	3300	C=O	1650–1850
—CH in CH₃	2950–2975	C—O—C	1100–1250
—CH in CH₂	2915–2940	aromatics	1450–1625

In ultraviolet (UV) spectrophotometry of a substance the extinction coefficient, or the extent of UV absorption, and the wavelength at which absorption occurs depend among other things on the types of double bonds present. According to molecular orbital theory, the absorption of UV light raises a molecule's outer, or valence, electrons from the lowest energy states in π and n orbitals to higher π^* states. Thus, the UV curve (blue) of butene exhibits a strong absorption peak that is attributed to excitation of electrons in the C=C group. A ketone, such as butanone (green), has two peaks that result from the transitions of different C=O electrons. When combined in a compound such as 3=buten=2=one (red), the two double-bond groups interact and shift the peaks to longer wavelengths.

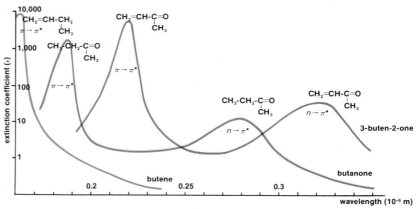

MHz at a magnetic field strength of 14,092 gauss. A proton in a molecule, however, is shielded to some extent by the electrons that surround it and thus does not experience the full field strength. This decreases the resonance frequency. The more electrons that are present, the greater the screening effect and vice versa. Most of the atoms that frequently occur in organic compounds have the tendency to draw electrons away from the hydrogen atom. Thus the resonance frequency of any particular hydrogen atom depends on what it is bonded to. The differences in resonance frequency are called *chemical shifts* (the shifting of the absorption spectrum by the chemical bond).

In the ethyl alcohol molecule, $CH_3—CH_2—OH$, there are three kinds of hydrogen atoms (protons): those of the CH^3 group, those of the CH^2 group, and those of the OH group. These three kinds of proton have different resonance frequencies and therefore a tracing of the NMR spectrum of ethyl alcohol will show three separate peaks. In NMR spectroscopy, all protons give signals of the same strength; by comparing the size of the peaks, the number of protons of each group can be determined.

If the resolution of the instrument is sufficiently high, each peak can be seen to consist of a number of closely spaced finer peaks. This effect is called *spin-splitting*, or *spin-coupling*, and results from the shielding effect on protons by the field of neighboring protons. Spin-splitting is not direct but is caused by neighboring protons through the various chemical bonds. This fine structure in the NMR spectrum provides information as to how groups are arranged within the molecule.

In addition to the resonance frequencies of hydrogen protons, the frequencies of other nuclei are also studied, for which the same considerations are used. By means of these data and others, such as formula and molecular weight (readily available from mass spectrometry), one can often discover the molecular structure of the compound.   MARK S. VOGEL

Bibliography: Brittain, E. F. H., *Introduction to Molecular Spectroscopy* (1970); Chang, Raymond, *Basic Principles of Spectroscopy* (1971); Engelson, Morris, and Telewski, Fred, *Spectrum Analyzer Theory and Application* (1974); King, G. W., *Spectroscopy and Molecular Structure* (1964); Meloan, Clifton E., *Elementary Infrared Spectroscopy* (1963); Rao, C. N., and Ferraro, J. P., *Spectroscopy in Inorganic Chemistry*, 2 vols. (1970–71); Straugham, B. P., and Walker, S., eds., *Spectroscopy, 3 vols.*, 2d ed. (1976); Van der Maas, J. H., *Basic Infrared Spectroscopy* (1969); Whiffen, D. H., *Spectroscopy* (1966); Williams, Dudley, ed., *Spectroscopy*, 2 vols. (1976).

spectrum

A spectrum, in general, is the dispersion or display of LIGHT, RADIATION, or ENERGY into its components. White light is a continuous spectrum; all wavelengths (or frequencies) of visible light are present. The separation of white light is effected by a PRISM or DIFFRACTION GRATING to create a spectrum of colors; the RAINBOW is a natural example of this spectrum. Some spectra comprise only a few wavelengths, whereas others contain all except a handful that are conspicuously absent. As recorded on spectrograph film, the former appear as bright

lines on a dark background and the latter as dark lines on a continuous spectrum.

Atomic Spectra. If a glass tube is filled with some atomic or molecular gas—say, neon—and if a sufficient voltage is applied across it, the gas would glow with a (seemingly) single color. Allowing this light to then pass through a spectrograph (a series of prisms) creates a bright-line spectrum. The light would separate into differently colored light beams moving at different angles, each then falling at a different place on a spectrograph film.

The radiation spectrum emitted from atoms and molecules consists of several discrete sets of frequencies. Between any two neighboring spectral lines there are no other lines from this set. The radiation spectrum of hydrogen is unique to hydrogen; similarly, the spectrum of each atomic and molecular species is unique to that species. Scientists have been able to use this feature of the emitted radiation of the atoms of matter to identify unknown elements of radiating gases, even in distant stars, by comparing the emitted spectrum with the appropriate superposition of spectra of known elements.

The Electromagnetic Spectrum. It was discovered in the 19th

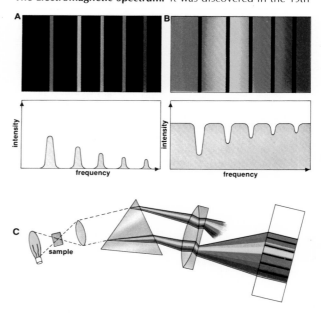

Line spectra are of two fundamental types. An emission spectrum (A) is the result of light emitted by an atom when its electrons return to their original low-energy states from higher energy levels. An absorption spectrum (B) is a series of dark lines obtained as atoms absorb selective wavelengths of incident light. The lines of each spectrum occur in the same positions. An absorption spectrum is observed (C) by passing white light through a sample and then a spectrograph; the absorbed wavelengths appear as black lines.

and 20th centuries that a wide variety of physical phenomena—light, gamma rays, and so on—were merely separate or overlapping regions of the same spectrum. Thus, all of these phenomena were conceptually unified in terms of one physical explanation—the electromagnetic spectrum (see ELECTROMAGNETIC RADIATION; MAXWELL'S EQUATIONS). The wavelength of electromagnetic radiation is pertinent to the size ranges of matter that absorbs it, so different wavelengths of radiation are useful as experimental tools to probe the properties of matter in different size ranges. For example, gamma rays are absorbed by atomic nuclei, so they are used in the study of nuclear physics; X rays are absorbed by the individual atoms of a gas or a solid, so they are used to study atomic and solid-state phenomena; and wavelengths of the order of 10^{-4} cm (ultraviolet) are appropriate for studying viruses.

Energy Level Spectrum. The explanation for the discreteness, or sharp lines, of radiation spectra is that the energy of the electrons of "excited" atoms also forms a discrete spectrum. If an atom is given excess energy (say, by applying a voltage across it), it would then proceed to "de-excite" itself, dropping to lower energy levels. Only discrete amounts of energy can be lost, corresponding to the energy values of the emitted radiation. The latter is called "quantized" radiation. (For a more complete explanation, see QUANTUM MECHANICS.)

Similarly, the possible energy values of nuclei, which give rise to gamma rays, also lie in a discrete energy spectrum. A major problem of contemporary nuclear physics is to explain the details of these energy spectra for the different nuclei as a consequence of the features of nuclear forces.

MENDEL SACHS

Bibliography: Bellamy, L. J., *The Infra-red Spectra of Complex Molecules*, 3d ed. (1975); Hershenson, Herbert M., *Infrared Absorption Spectra*, 2 vols. (1959) and *Ultraviolet and Visible Absorption Spectra*, 3 vols. (1956); Herzberg, Gerhard, *Molecular Spectra and Molecular Structure*, 3 vols. (1945–66); Little, L. H., *Infrared Spectra of Absorbed Species* (1967).

spectrum-luminosity diagram: see
HERTZSPRUNG-RUSSELL DIAGRAM.

speech

Human speech makes possible the expression and communication of thoughts, needs, and emotions through vocalization in the form of words. It is a process whose specialized adaptations differentiate it from the mere making of sounds—a capacity humans share with most animals. In addition to the capacity for laryngeal production of sound (which some animals also possess), speech requires a resonance system for modulation and amplification of that sound and an articulation process for the shaping of that sound into the communally established word-symbols of meaning that constitute the language of a given culture. The use of language is made possible by certain cerebral functions: the formation of thoughts; the comprehension, storage, and recall of words; and the selection of words to express the thoughts and the arrangements of these words in a sequence or organization that constitutes (or attempts to constitute) intelligible communication.

Communication exists in all animal species, either in the form of sound utterance or in a large repertory of soundless codes formed and stereotyped by the respective genetic potentials. Some of the higher animal forms possess voices of various types and inflections and may even be trained to imitate the sound of simple words. The vocalizations made, however—for example, by monkeys and chimpanzees—appear to be primarily under the control of centers in the limbic system, or "emotional brain," rather than the cortex. Electrical stimulation of the limbic system can produce all the vocal responses that monkeys are capable of making. Destruction of the cortical speech centers in humans, however, either destroys speech or affects it critically, whereas destruction of similar areas of the cortex in monkeys does not affect their vocalization (see ANIMAL COMMUNICATION). Thus the human brain appears to be uniquely adapted for speech. Only

in humans have the centers of speech been transferred from instinctive or reflex centers to the cortex, making possible a highly voluntary control of speech and language.

When and how this transfer occurred and what made it occur are matters of theory, and the theories are related to the orientations of the investigators. According to behaviorists (for example, psychologist B. F. Skinner), all verbal behavior is learned. According to linguist Noam Chomsky, the central nervous system and the cortex are biologically programmed not only for the physiological aspects of speech but also for the organization of language itself; these areas "map," or translate, mental experience into sequential organization, or "grammar"; the capacity for organizing words into relationships of words to each other is inherent. Psychologist Julian Jaynes claims that speech and language arose as a survival response to new and more complex environmental conditions and social organizations at the end of the last Ice Age. The general consensus, however, is that both speech and language arose more than 1 million years ago, under conditions that have not yet been definitively identified. Whatever its origins, speech is now more than a mode of oral expression and communication. Speech and language together serve to consolidate personal and communal experience; they involve not only physiological mechanisms and their brain control areas, but also psychological, cultural, and emotional functions.

PHYSIOLOGY OF SPEECH
The speech process involves the speech centers of the brain, the respiratory center in the brain stem, the respiratory system, the chest cavity, the structures of the larynx, the pharynx, the nose and nasal cavities, and the structures and parts of the mouth and related facial muscles.

Speech Centers of the Brain. There are three identified speech areas. The supplementary motor cortex, on the very top of the left frontal lobe, involves the process of vocalization itself. Broca's area, lower down at the back of the left frontal lobe, appears to involve functions of articulation, vocabulary, inflection, and word sequence. Wernicke's area is mainly the posterior part of the left temporal lobe, with parts of the parietal area; any large destruction of this area results in the loss of the capacity for meaningful speech but not the loss of sound production.

The mechanisms of vocalization perform four major functions: breathing, phonation, resonance, and articulation.

Breathing. The speech process starts with an expiration of air, produced by the respiratory mechanisms of lung expansion and contraction: the downward and upward movements of the diaphragm to lengthen or shorten the chest cavity, and the elevation and depression of the ribs to increase or decrease the diameter of the chest cavity. These movements depend on the functions of the upper abdominal muscles. Overall, the muscles that elevate the chest cage are muscles of inspiration (inhalation), and those that depress the chest are muscles of expiration (exhalation). If forceful expiration is required, relative to body or speech needs, all abdominal muscles combined can serve as muscles of expiration. Expiration can then be passive or it can be forcefully active, depressing the cage and starting a current of air upward from the lungs. The driving energy for speech production, generated by the mechanisms of expiration, varies with individual physiology, breathing habits, and training for correction where needed.

Phonation. In the process of phonation the current of air is vibrated in the larynx by the vocal cords, which are folds along the lateral walls of the larynx that are stretched laterally between two sets of cartilages. Air pressure from below first pushes the vocal cords apart. This creates a partial vacuum between the cords that may pull them together again, thus continuing a vibrating pattern. The elasticity of the folds, however, probably accounts for their returning to their original position.

The coordination, size, elasticity, and health of the complex structures of the larynx, vocal cords, and intrinsic and extrinsic laryngeal muscles acting on the current of air—in combination with the shaping and positioning of the vocal cords—

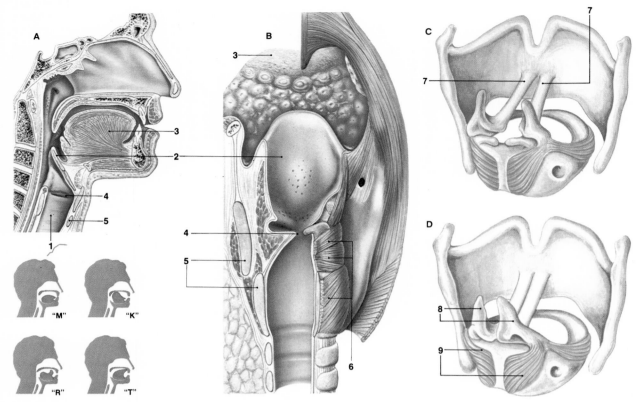

The principal speech organs, seen here in a side view (A) and back view (B), include the larynx (1), epiglottis (2), tongue (3), mouth, and lips. Air expired from the lungs and forced through the larynx causes the vocal cords (4) to vibrate, producing a continuous tone—the voice. The pitch of the voice is regulated by the arrangement of the various cartilages (5) in the larynx, which are controlled by muscle (6) action. During breathing (C), the vocal cords (7) are held apart, forming a V-shaped opening. The voice is produced (D) when the moving cartilages (8) are drawn together by the muscles (9), forming a linear gap between the vocal cords. The cartilages tilt to regulate vocal-cord tension. Greater tension produces a higher pitch, and less tension produces a lower pitch. Loudness depends on how fast the air travels; the faster the air is forced through the gap, the louder the voice. When the voice is further modified by altering the position and shape of the other organs, speech can occur. Different vowels are produced by varying the shape of the mouth cavity. Consonants, which depend on the relative positions of the lips and tongue (lower left), are produced when the air is expired suddenly or stopped sharply.

not only produce sound but also account for the individuality of that sound. The immediate result of vocal-cord vibration is the fundamental tone, or pitch, of the voice. In physical terms, the frequency of vibration (fast, slow, or intermediate) as the primary vocal attribute corresponds to the number of air puffs per second. This frequency, resulting in voice pitch, is determined by both stable and variable factors. Stable factors relate to the laryngeal dimensions, as determined by sex, age, and body type. Within these fixed elements, variables include the tension of the cords, the force of glottis closure, and the expiratory air pressure. Tension of the external laryngeal muscles increases the voice pitch or depresses it. For example, a frequency of 100 vibrations per second produces the low chest sound of the male voice, whereas 1,000 vibrations per second represents the high C of a trained female soprano. An average vocal range normally encompasses 100 to 400 vibrations per second. Thus the fundamentally recognizable tone of the voice, determined primarily by the frequency of the vibration, is a function of the larynx. These functions are determined by inborn characteristics and learned behavior.

Resonance. The resonance process, which is fundamentally the amplification of sound on its way to utterance, involves the pharynx, the mouth, the nose, the nasal sinuses, and the chest cavity. The quality of that resonance, which may range from stridency to virtual inaudibility, also depends on both fixed and variable factors, with regard to physical conditions and learned behaviors, and relates to the intent of the individual and his or her personality as well as his or her speech behaviors. It also relates to the force of the expiration of air and the dimensions of the chest cavity. Through all the var-

ious effects and usage of these parts of the resonance mechanisms, certain types of speech mannerisms are exhibited— such as nasality, which represents overreliance on the nasal cavities for resonance; or good sound projection, which utilizes the chest cavity as well as the other organs.

Articulation. The process of articulation constitutes the formation of the amplified sound into words, through movements of the lips, tongue, and soft palate of the mouth, and of the related facial muscles. Moreover, the qualities of a given language may require different forms of articulation because the linguodental zone (between the tip of the tongue and the teeth) may be used differently in one language than the way it is in another. Universally, however, speech sounds in articulation are grouped as oral sounds or nasal sounds, and both relate to structural conditions and speech behaviors as well as to related disciplines of LINGUISTICS, SPEECH DEVELOPMENT, and pronunciation.

SPEECH DISORDERS

The existence of pathology, either functional or organic, is the basic distinction between true speech disorders and those faulty speech habits which arise from a complex of environmental, cultural, local-regional, educational, and socioeconomic factors. Another distinction, at the behavioral level, is whether the speech disorder is assessed as a handicap.

Prevalence. Speech disorders, both functional and organic, at the handicap level, affect about 22 million persons in the United States, according to U.S. Public Health Service estimates. Approximately 40% are due to hearing loss, approximately 10% to neurological disease, and approximately 50% to a range of other causes. The highest incidence of speech disorders occurs developmentally among children and youth; functional disorders in articulation are the leading cause, stuttering is the second, and hearing impairment with speech defect is the third.

Functional Disorders. Voice disorders, or dysphonias, consist of two main types: those arising from faulty speech habits, and psychogenic types arising from emotional disturbance. Both types represent either overactive (hyperkinetic) muscular activity, creating harsh, grating speech, or underactive (hypokinetic) activity, creating subdued or sluggish speech.

Speech impediments include the following three types. Cluttering (tachyphonia) is an erratic, jerky speech. Lisping, or immature speech (dyslalia), may relate to abnormality of the external speech organs, for example, in tongue-teeth relationships. STUTTERING (dysphemia) is considered to be psychogenic in origin.

Language disorders may lie between the functional and the organic, depending on the diagnostic assessment of the underlying cause. For example, if schizophrenia is viewed as an organic disorder, then its bizarre language (dysphrenia) is organically related. Similarly, the disturbed speech of mental retardates (dyslogia) may be an organic behavior if the retardation can be attributed organically, or it may be a learning disability arising from the intellectual impairment. Other functional disorders include those caused by sensory deficits in the family setting, such as the presence of deaf parents; delayed maturation of motor or brain function; emotional trauma due to parental neglect or abuse; and institutional deprivations or adverse socioeconomic factors, which result in learning disabilities related to the development of speech or such disabilities as the improper formation of word sequences (dysgrammatism).

ORGANIC SPEECH DISORDERS
Genetic defects and hereditary diseases include structural abnormalities of any of the organs related to vocalization and are frequently exemplified by cleft lip or cleft palate; hereditary diseases of the muscular system, such as muscular dystrophy, or of the nervous system, such as ataxia; chromosome aberrations, such as Down's syndrome (mongolism), which are associated with mental retardation; organic brain injury (genetic or birth defects); and hearing and related sensory losses. Developmental disabilities represent a large and serious group of organic diseases and disorders that affect the development of speech, either directly or through learning disabilities that affect, physically or intellectually, the normal maturation of speech. Major disorders in this area are cerebral palsy and the associated speech disorder (dysarthria); epilepsy and the related convulsive seizures; damage, by injury or disease, to any of the parts involved in articulation (dysglossia); the learning impairments of organic mental retardation; sensory losses, auditory and visual; and other types of brain damage due to injury or disease.

Speech center trauma in the brain occurs in two categories: damage to the speech centers and related sensory aspects of speech function (sensory aphasia); and damage to the motor control functions of the speech centers (motor aphasia). The basic aspect of aphasia—whether due to stroke, paralysis, head injury, or disease—is the loss of the capacity for the meaning of language or its comprehensible organization into words or word sequences (Wernicke's aphasia). In other cases the intellectual functions appear to be retained, whereas the vocalization system cannot be utilized to emit words but rather only sounds (Broca's aphasia).

MILDRED NAVARETTA

Bibliography: Chomsky, Noam, *Language and Mind* (1972); Denes, Peter B., and Pinson, Elliott N., *The Speech Chain: The Physics and Biology of Spoken Language* (1973); Dickson, David R., and Maue, Wilma M., *Human Vocal Anatomy* (1977); Fry, D. B., *The Physics of Speech* (1979); Greene, Margaret C., *The Voice and Its Disorders*, 3d ed. (1972); Jaynes, Julian, *The Origin of Consciousness in the Breakdown of the Bicameral Mind* (1976); Kaplan, H. M., *Anatomy and Physiology of Speech*, 2d ed. (1971); Luchswanger, R., and Arnold, G., *Voice, Speech, Language* (1965); Penfield, Wilder, and Roberts, Lamor, *Speech and Brain Mechanisms* (1959); Travis, L. E., ed., *Handbook of Speech Pathology* (1957).

See also: SPEECH THERAPY.

speech development

Speech development is a "robust" process that goes smoothly for most children and on that account does not constitute an obvious problem for science. It is robust, however, not because it is simple, but because it is so vital that both biological and cultural evolution have operated to safeguard its operation. In fact, its complexity is such that it poses some of the most difficult theoretical problems in natural science, and because even speech development sometimes goes badly, there are human problems that advances in theoretical understanding may help to solve.

By two weeks of age, an infant can distinguish the human voice from other sounds, and by about one month, it can discriminate vowel-consonant segments such as "ba" and "pa." The speech that many children first hear is special enough to have been given a name: the "parental register." This is a set of adjustments of approximately 100 aspects of pitch, articulation, loudness, sentence complexity, and vocabulary. It may be that the parental register facilitates language learning, but that has never been shown. The adult is best advised not to attempt any deliberate tinkering in talking with a child, but to focus on communication; the adjustments will follow naturally.

Many people believe that comprehension of speech precedes production, and that when the first words are produced, they carry the meanings of whole sentences. These impressions are, however, largely based on home observation where the general setting is often such as to make any speech at all superfluous. Careful research does not uniformly support the generalization that comprehension comes before production.

At the age of about 18 months, many children begin to make combinations of two or three words that are heard as sentences. The average length of these sentences increases gradually at rates that vary widely among individuals. There is no evidence whatever that this variation in rate predicts adult intelligence. The first sentences are always composed primarily of nouns and verbs, and everywhere in the world the most frequent forms in the language—words like articles and prepositions, and word-parts like inflections for plural number and past tense—are omitted. Early child sentences have a "telegraphic" quality. They also share a very limited subject matter. They name people, foods, toys, pets, and body parts, and remark on their disappearance and reappearance as well as their usual locations and the simple actions in which these objects take part.

As the preschool years pass, the rules grow in complexity, and the child can soon do more than string out simple sentences; he or she can embed or nest them, one in another. At about the same point or a little later, the child learns that some sentences can be knocked together into a more compact structure by deleting shared portions and joining the rest with a conjunction.

By the time the child is of school age, he or she can state no grammatical rules at all, but may be extremely articulate. In grade school years, the child adds a few grammatical rules of special complexity, but is primarily occupied with larger expository structures of which sentences are now the atomic units.

Some aspects of language must be memorized; this is true of words, and because adults may recognize several hundred thousand words, it may be assumed that human memory is prodigious in capacity. It is not, however, prodigious enough to accommodate all possible sentences. Another process is involved, and it surfaces when a child makes mistakes: e.g., "He hurt hisself"; "Why the car won't go?" These are good errors suggested by analogy with correct forms. The errors show what the child's brain is doing; it is extracting a set of rules that will make it possible to create an infinite variety of sentences. This is the central phenomenon of speech development. It sets the major theoretical problems, including that of distinguishing between innate and learned knowledge.

Extreme theoretical positions on the development of speech have long been championed by the psychologist B. F.

SKINNER and the linguist Noam CHOMSKY. Skinner contends that "verbal behavior" is learned in accordance with general principles of positive and negative reinforcement, which he believes account for all learning in all animal species. Chomsky holds that the "competence" to produce an infinite variety of sentences, the routine outcome of language development in the preschool years, can never be explained by any learning theory or set of data-processing procedures. It is necessary, in Chomsky's view, to postulate innate knowledge (corresponding to linguistic universals) of the types of linguistic rules that are possible and the types that are impossible. A language-specific "acquisition device," which Chomsky does not hesitate to call a "mental organ," might then sample linguistic input and hit upon the correct rules underlying that input.

The developmental psychologist Jean PIAGET concerned himself with *Language and Thought of the Child* (1923; Eng. trans., 1926) long before the discipline of PSYCHOLINGUISTICS came into existence, but has never taken a position on the complex problems of grammar-acquisition. Several developmental psycholinguists who are persuaded of the general applicability of Piaget's theories to all aspects of development, however, have done research on grammar-acquisition within a Piagetian framework.

None of the three theorists—Skinner, Chomsky, or Piaget—has actively engaged in empirical work on speech development as it is conceived by contemporary psycholinguistics, and none of the three has attempted to explain the massive body of general information deriving from empirical studies. All three theories have served to inspire empirical research, but Chomsky's ideas have been far more influential than the others. The most important feature of Chomsky's theory is its emphasis on possible universals of linguistic development. Partially as a consequence of this emphasis, developmental psycholinguistics is one of the few fields of psychology that is not an exclusively European enterprise. It conceptualizes its problems with close attention to human behavior and has collected data from an impressive sample of the "exotic" languages of the world. As yet, it cannot be said that the results clearly support any of the three general theories. A majority of specialists in this very active field would probably now agree that results of research on speech development in the human species are only likely to be explained by a new theory that is explicitly guided by the discoveries of recent years.

ROGER BROWN

Bibliography: Brown, Roger, *Words and Things* (1958) and *A First Language* (1973); Dale, P., *Child Language Acquisition* (1972); deVilliers, Peter and Jill, *Early Language* (1979); Ferguson, Charles A., and Slobin, Dan Isaac, *Studies in Child Language and Development* (1973); Hopper, Robert, and Naremore, Rita J., *Children's Speech: A Practical Introduction to Communication Development*, 2d ed. (1978); Leitch, Susan M., *A Child Learns to Speak: A Guide for Parents and Teachers on Preschool Children* (1977); Piaget, Jean, *Language and Thought of the Child*, 3d ed. (1962); Potts, Marion, et al., *Structure and Development in Child Language: The Preschool Years* (1979).

speech therapy

Speech therapy is the process by which impairments of normal speech, such as STUTTERING, stammering, and APHASIA, are treated in an effort to permit normal voice communication by the individual. The conduct of speech therapy is one of the functions of the profession now known as speech/language pathology. In addition to treating speech and language problems, the speech/language pathologist also diagnoses the nature of communicative disorders and determines their causes. Specialists in this field also provide counseling to individuals with speech and language disorders and engage in research relating to communicative disorders and their possible causes and treatment.

Speech pathology first emerged as a specialty during and immediately after World War I. By 1925 a national association of people engaged in the field had been organized, now known as the American Speech and Hearing Association.

Presently, it is estimated that about 40,000 speech/language pathologists are practicing in the United States. Of this number approximately one-half are employed in elementary and secondary schools. The remainder fulfill a wide variety of roles in government, in medical settings, or in research.

EDMUND J. McTERNAN

Bibliography: Boone, Daniel R., *The Voice and Voice Therapy*, 2d ed. (1977); Sheehan, Joseph, *Stuttering: Research and Therapy* (1970); Van Riper, Charles, *Speech Correction: Principles and Methods*, 6th ed. (1972).

See also: SPEECH.

speed

Speed is the distance an object moves during a unit of time. Common units of speed are meters per second (m/s) and miles per hour (mph). Speed refers only to the rate of motion without specifying any direction of motion. It therefore differs from VELOCITY in a technical sense, because velocity is a vector quantity and specifies a direction.   GARY S. SETTLES

See also: MOTION, PLANAR.

speedball

Speedball is a unique sport combining aspects of soccer, football, and basketball. Popular in colleges, it was invented by Elmer D. Mitchell of the University of Michigan in 1921 and remains largely an amateur sport.

Teams of 11 compete on a regulation football field using a soccer ball. Play begins with a kickoff, as in football, and continues for four 10-minute periods. The game progresses by means of the players throwing, punting, or drop-kicking the ball and taking only one step while holding the ball. As in soccer, however, once the ball touches the ground, it can be advanced only with the feet or the body until it is again caught on the fly.

Although there are some differences in scoring the men's and women's versions of the game, there are five ways to score: a field goal, worth 3 points, is scored by kicking or using the body to send the ball between the goal posts but under the goal crossbar; a touchdown, worth 2 points, is scored by catching a forward pass in the opponent's end zone; a dropkick, worth 2 points, is scored by catching the ball in flight and drop-kicking the ball over the crossbar; and an end kick (kicking the ball across the end line from within the end zone) and a penalty kick (a free kick allowed after a foul), each worth 1 point.

speedwell

Speedwell, genus *Veronica*, is the common name for about 250 species of herbaceous plants belonging to the Scrophulariaceae family. Most species produce showy, blue or mauve flowers in loose clusters and have opposite leaves; all are rich in vitamin C. The leaves of water speedwell, *V. americana*, which grows in freshwater ponds and springs, have been eaten to prevent scurvy.

Speer, Albert   [shpayr]

Nazi leader Albert Speer, b. Mar. 19, 1905, was a German architect who designed (1934) the Nuremberg stadium and directed Germany's armament production and road construction, using slave labor, during World War II. Speer joined the National Socialist party in 1931, became minister of arms and munitions in 1942, and expanded his planning responsibilities during the following year. In 1946 he was sentenced to 20 years in Spandau prison by the Nuremberg war crimes tribunal. After serving his sentence, he published the autobiographical *Inside the Third Reich* (1970) and *Spandau: The Secret Diaries* (1976).

Bibliography: Fest, Joachim C., *Face of the Third Reich* (1970); Hamsher, William, *Albert Speer—Victim of Nuremberg?* (1970).

Speke, John Hanning   [speek]

English explorer John Hanning Speke, b. May 3, 1827, d. 1864, was the first European to reach the source of the Nile River. He joined Sir Richard BURTON late in 1856; after exploring East Africa with him, Speke continued alone and on July 30, 1858, discovered Victoria Nyanza (see VICTORIA, LAKE), which he identified as a source of the White Nile. In 1861–63, Speke led a further expedition, locating another source of the great river, but Burton disputed his claims of discovery. On Sept. 18, 1864, the day that they were to meet in public debate, Speke accidentally shot and killed himself.   ROBIN BUSS

Bibliography: Maitland, Alexander, *Speke* (1971); Moorhead, Alan, *The White Nile,* rev. ed. (1971).

speleology   [spee-lee-ahl'-uh-jee]

Speleology is the study of CAVES. It encompasses their geology, geography, biology, and history. Thus, studies of karst (limestone) topography and groundwater hydrology (flow of water through caves) are included as parts of speleology. One of the newest of sciences, speleology has had an extraordinary expansion since 1950 and has produced unifying principles leading to wide-ranging conclusions about the origin of caves, their environment, their actual measurements, their age, and the life cycles of cave animals. Speleological research has led to the economic utilization of caves as sources of water and as storage areas, the mining of cave-related minerals, and the gathering of data about early human cultures.
BROTHER G. NICHOLAS, F.S.C.

Bibliography: Ford, T. D., *The Science of Speleology* (1976); Moore, George, and Brother G. Nicholas, *Speleology, the Study of Caves* (1978).

Spellman, Francis Joseph

Cardinal Francis Joseph Spellman, b. Whitman, Mass., May 4, 1889, d. Dec. 2, 1967, was one of the most influential church figures in American history. During his years as archbishop of New York (1939–67) he was close to five American presidents, especially Franklin D. Roosevelt. He was also deeply involved in the delicate diplomatic maneuvering during World War II, when the shape of the postwar world became the primary consideration of the world's leaders, including Pope Pius XII, with whom Spellman was in regular contact. Spellman, created a cardinal in 1946, was a staunch anticommunist and identified closely with the soldiers of the U.S. armed forces. He served as military vicar—chief shepherd of all Catholics in the military—and each Christmas for many years visited troops stationed abroad.

Bibliography: Gannon, Robert J., *The Cardinal Spellman Story (1962);* Steibel, Warren, *Cardinal Spellman, the Man* (1966).

Spelman College

Established in 1881, Spelman College (enrollment: 1,290; library: 45,000 volumes) is a private Baptist liberal arts school in Atlanta, Ga. It is America's oldest college for black women and one of the six schools of the Atlanta University Center.

spelunking   [spuh-luhng'-king]

Spelunking is the amateur pursuit of speleology, the exploration and study of caves as a hobby or sport. It is a popular recreation among both adults and children in parts of the world where there are caves. Spelunkers vary from casual explorers out for a day's adventure to highly sophisticated sportsmen using specialized equipment. Most cave exploration, however, is still conducted by professional scientists.

Prehistoric humans used caves for burial places, and they remained objects of mystery for thousands of years. North American caves were explored by curious adventurers in the 19th century, although European caves were examined much earlier. Spelunking is largely a 20th-century phenomenon.

Spelunkers explore caves as much for the beauty of the cave interiors as for the excitement of the sport. In many cases spelunkers must be accomplished climbers in order to descend into deep pits, boatsmen to navigate underground rivers and lakes, and divers to examine water-filled caves.

Bibliography: Halliday, William R., *American Caves and Caving: Techniques, Pleasures, and Safeguards of Modern Cave Exploration* (1974); McClurg, D. R., *The Amateur's Guide to Caves and Caving* (1973).

Spemann, Hans   [shpay'-mahn]

Hans Spemann, b. June 27, 1869, d. Sept. 12, 1941, a German zoologist, discovered the organizer effect in embryonic development, winning the 1935 Nobel Prize for physiology or medicine for his work. Using frog and newt embryos, Spemann found that development is determined by interactions between various parts of the embryo, with special areas serving as organizers for the development of nearby related tissues.

Spence, Sir Basil

An influential British architect, Sir Basil Spence, b. Aug. 13, 1907, d. Nov. 18, 1978, worked in a popular modern vein. Before World War II, he specialized mainly in Scottish country houses. In 1951, however, he directed the design of the Festival of Britain Exhibition and won the architectural competition for a new cathedral at Coventry. COVENTRY CATHEDRAL, consecrated in 1962, incorporates as a forecourt the walls and tower of the bombed Gothic church it replaced; it employs sawtooth walls, a faceted roof, and angular accents to create a "medievalizing" composition.

Spence did extensive work at several British universities and designed the Knightsbridge Barracks (1970) in London as well as the British embassy (1971) in Rome.
ANN VAN ZANTEN

Bibliography: Spence, Basil, *Phoenix at Coventry; the Building of a Cathedral* (1962); Yarwood, Doreen, *The Architecture of England* (1963).

Spencer, Anna Garlin

Educator and lecturer Anna Garlin Spencer, b. Attleboro, Mass., Apr. 17, 1851, d. Feb. 12, 1931, was known for her work in the women's suffrage and peace movements. Her career expanded from public school teacher to ordained Unitarian minister, lecturer, and public service executive. From 1903 to 1909 she was Associate Director of the New York Society for Ethical Culture.   MILDRED NAVARETTA

Spencer, Herbert

Herbert Spencer, b. Apr. 27, 1820, d. Dec. 8, 1903, was the major Victorian English philosopher of biological and social evolution. Although he received no formal education and was derided by the academic establishment of his time, he won a large popular following for his optimistic view that evolution is synonymous with progress. His work significantly influenced 19th-century developments in biology, psychology, sociology, and anthropology. Spencer's book *The Principles of Biology* (1864–67) was used as a text at Oxford University; his *The Principles of Psychology* (1855) became a text at Harvard University; and at Yale University, his *Study of Sociology* (1873) was the textbook for the first course offered in the United States on sociology.

Spencer's significance to these diverse disciplines is that he was one of the first to affirm that human society may be studied scientifically and that he did so from an evolutionary point of view based on the assumption that human behavior is socially determined. His evolutionary theories were conceived before those of Charles DARWIN, and Spencer is thought to have coined the phrase "survival of the fittest." In his later 3-volume work, *Principles of Sociology* (1876–96), Spencer clarified his belief that social structures arise out of social functions. Spencer's *Autobiography* was published in 1904.   MILDRED NAVARETTA

Bibliography: Duncan, David, *The Life and Letters of Herbert Spencer* (1908); Elliot, Hugh S., *Herbert Spencer* (1917; repr. 1970); Peel, J. D., *Herbert Spencer: The Evolution of a Sociologist* (1971); Wiltshire, David, *The Social and Political Thought of Herbert Spencer* (1978).

Spender, Stephen

The British poet Stephen Spender, b. Feb. 28, 1909, became associated at Oxford University with W. H. Auden, C. Day Lewis, and Louis MacNeice. These writers, although not really

Stephen Spender, a British poet who became prominent during the 1930s, expressed his reactions to such events as the depression, Hitlerism, and the Spanish Civil War in deeply personal, lyrical verse. Also a critic, novelist, and dramatist, Spender later edited Encounter *and* Horizon *magazines.*

an organized group, were greatly affected by the political events of the 1930s—the Depression, the rise of Nazism, the Stalinist purges, the Spanish Civil War, and the events leading to World War II. In response, Spender, like the others, adopted a form of Marxist political belief. These events are reflected in his poetry as the causes of his carefully described personal feelings. Spender is more personal and compassionate than Auden, Day Lewis, or MacNeice, and his poetry has retained a directness and authenticity of feeling. Spender's autobiography, *World within World* (1951), is a valuable record of the intellectual enthusiasms of the 1930s and '40s; *The Struggle of the Modern* (1963) describes the transitions of literary taste that have taken place since the publication of the early poems of T. S. Eliot and Ezra Pound.

Since the modest *Selected Poems* appeared in 1965, he has written relatively little verse but continues to be a notable public figure. He was coeditor from 1939 to 1941 of *Horizon,* an important magazine, and of *Encounter* from 1953 to 1967. When he discovered that *Encounter* was secretly financed by the U.S. Central Intelligence Agency, he resigned.

Bibliography: Spender, Stephen, *World within World: The Autobiography of Stephen Spender* (1977); Weatherhead, A. K., *Stephen Spender and the Thirties* (1975).

Spener, Philipp Jakob   [shpay'-nur]

German Lutheran theologian Philipp Jakob Spener, b. Jan. 23, 1635, d. Feb. 5, 1705, is called the father of PIETISM. While senior minister of Frankfurt am Main, he produced his pietist manifesto, *Pious Desires* (1675; Eng. trans., 1964), outlining a program of church reform. Deploring ceremonialism, government domination, and theological hairsplitting, Spener proposed group study of the Bible, the priesthood of all Christians, the resolution of controversy by prayer and example, and a ministry trained in devotion and spiritual preaching. In 1686 he became chief pastor at the Saxon court, but he came into conflict with the theologians of Leipzig and moved (1691) to Saint Nicholas's Church in Berlin, where he headed the Pietist party and influenced church appointments in Prussia. Spener also organized the faculty of theology at the University of Halle, which was the center of pietism in Europe.

JAMES D. NELSON

Bibliography: Stoeffler, F. Ernest, *The Rise of Evangelical Pietism* (1965).

Spengler, Oswald   [shpeng'-glur]

Oswald Spengler, b. May 29, 1880, d. May 8, 1936, a German historian and philosopher, developed a pessimistic philosophy of history that earned him considerable renown. A student at the universities of Munich, Berlin, and Halle, Spengler read widely in literature, history, and philosophy although he was trained in mathematics and the natural sciences.

In 1918 the publication of the first volume of his *The Decline of the West* (2 vols., 1918–22; Eng. trans., 1932) brought him fame. Spengler held that history followed definite laws of growth and decay that are observable in the careers of all

cultures. Tracing the unfolding of these laws in his own era, he predicted that Western culture, already well into its twilight, would experience further decline as a future of rationalism, mass manipulation, and material expression succeeded the profound art, religion, and philosophy of the past. In later nationalistic political tracts Spengler contended that Germany, with its Prussian authoritarian tradition, could dominate this future.

PETE A. Y. GUNTER

Bibliography: Hughes, H. Stuart, *Oswald Spengler: A Critical Estimate* (1952; repr. 1975); Sorokin, Pitirim A., *Modern Historical and Social Philosophies* (1963).

Spenser, Edmund

Edmund Spenser, b. London, c.1552, d. Jan. 13, 1599, was the greatest of Elizabethan nondramatic poets. Although he was acclaimed after his death as "Prince of poets," during his lifetime he did not enjoy the unstinting favor of the queen, who may have found his poetry too subtle and equivocal to be used as propaganda.

Nevertheless, from his first major work, the anonymously published *The Shepheardes Calendar* (1579), Spenser was recognized as a major poet who could adapt the new continental poetry to a native English setting. His long allegorical epic, The FAERIE QUEENE, unfinished at his death, attempted to provide Elizabethan England with a poem comparable to Vergil's *Aeneid.* Although it has disappointed readers looking for either the unified plot of classical epic or the unambiguous moral lessons of allegory, it has been admired by others who recognize it as a triumph of art. Modern critics have likened Spenser's profound sense of the possibilities of language to that of such modern writers as James Joyce.

Education. Spenser's education at Merchant Taylors' School under the classical scholar Richard Mulcaster and at Cambridge, where he met the learned Gabriel Harvey, exposed him to both ancient and modern literatures. In 1569, the year he entered Cambridge, he published translations from Du Bellay and from Marot's version of Petrarch for a book of emblems compiled by Jan van der Noodt. *The Shepheardes Calendar* was a book of pastoral eclogues, printed with introduction and notes by an unidentified "E. K.," possibly Edward Kirke, a friend of Spenser's, or the poet himself. Signing himself *Immerito,* "Without Merit," and dedicating the volume to Sir Philip Sidney, Spenser invited (and received) comparison with the eclogues of Vergil. In later pastoral works, Spenser used the name of the lovesick shepherd of this volume, Colin Clout, as his pseudonym.

Ireland. After a brief period in the service of the earl of Leicester, Spenser became secretary to Arthur Lord Grey, Elizabeth's Lord Deputy to Ireland, in 1580 and was to serve in Ireland in various capacities for most of the remainder of his life. Upon publication (1590) of the first three books of *The Faerie Queene,* he received an annual pension of £50 from the queen; he was not fortunate as a courtier, however, and saw more than his share of the dark side of Elizabeth's

Edmund Spenser was the most acclaimed poet of Elizabethan England. His Faerie Queene *brilliantly combines the literary traditions of the classical epic, moral allegory, medieval verse narrative, and courtly romance. The Spenserian stanza, invented for The* Faerie Queene, *is a nine-line verse form composed of eight lines of iambic pentameter completed by one line of iambic hexameter.*

Irish policy, although he tried to justify it in his *Vewe of the Present State of Ireland* (publ. 1633).

Frustration and disappointment are reflected in Spenser's later writings: *Complaints* (1591), *Daphnaida* (1591), *Colin Clouts Come Home Againe* (1595), *Prothalamion* (1596), and Books 4-6 of *The Faerie Queene* (1596). An exception may be *Amoretti and Epithalamion* (1595), which celebrates his courtship and marriage. Spenser died shortly after returning to England and was buried in Westminster Abbey. Poets attended his hearse and threw poems and pens into his grave.

DONALD CHENEY

Bibliography: Berger, Harry, ed., *Spenser: A Collection of Essays* (1968); Ellrodt, Robert, *Neoplatonism in the Poetry of Spenser* (1960); Hamilton, A. C., ed., *Essential Articles for the Study of Edmund Spenser* (1972); Lewis, C. S., *Spenser's Image of Life* (1967); Nelson, William, *The Poetry of Spenser* (1963); Spenser, Edmund, *Works: A Variorum Edition*, 10 vols. (1932-49).

Speransky, Mikhail Mikhailovich   [spir-ahn'-skee]

The Russian statesman Mikhail Mikhailovich Speransky, b. Jan. 12 (N.S.), 1772, d. Feb. 23 (N.S.), 1839, was one of the most gifted civil administrators of his time. The son of a priest in Vladimir province, he advanced rapidly in the government civil service and in 1808 became vice minister of justice. As virtual prime minister to Emperor ALEXANDER I, Speransky drafted several reform projects—including a constitution—for Russia. The cold and austere Speransky was never popular at court, however, and his enemies had him exiled in disgrace in 1812. He reentered the civil service in 1816 and returned to Saint Petersburg in 1821. After the accession (1825) of Emperor NICHOLAS I, Speransky worked until 1833 codifying the empire's laws.   FORRESTT A. MILLER

Bibliography: Raeff, Marc, *Michael Speranksy: Statesman of Imperial Russia, 1772-1839*, 2d ed. (1968).

sperm

Sperm, or spermatozoon, is a broadly used term for the diverse types of male gametes (sex or reproductive cells) found in all animals and lower plants. Each sperm contains the paternal genetic information to be contributed through FERTILIZATION to the resulting individual. Its secondary function is to initiate EGG development. Commonly, the spermatozoon has a head with a nucleus but little cytoplasm, and a tail, or flagellum, used for locomotion. The cell, excluding the tail, may be only 50 to 60 µm; thus the sperm is about 1/195,000 the size of an egg. A wide range of shapes and sizes, however, exists. Each cell can swim in an aqueous medium to reach an egg. In higher animals, sperm cells are produced (spermatogenesis) by germ cells in the male testes and conveyed to the outside in a viscous fluid called semen. Mammalian sperm may be stored for long periods of time through freezing. Banks of human sperm are maintained for ARTIFICIAL INSEMINATION, where sperm from one male may fertilize many females. Successful fertilization of an egg in vitro (test tube) has been performed.

Bibliography: Baccetti, Baccio, *The Biology of the Sperm Cell* (1976); Duckett, J. G., and Racey, P. A., eds., *The Biology of the Male Gamete* (1975); Hafez, E. S. E., *The Human Semen and Fertility Regulation in Man* (1976).

See also: REPRODUCTION.

sperm oil

Sperm oil is the oily substance taken from the head and sometimes the fat and bones of the sperm whale. The head, comprising one-third of the whale's total length, may contain up to 50 barrels of the oil, which has been valued for centuries as a fuel for lamps, a lubricant for precision instruments, an ingredient of soaps, detergents, and cosmetics, and a softener and preserver of leather. Sperm oil is classed chemically as a liquid wax. It contains another waxy substance, spermaceti—so called because it was thought to be the coagulated semen of the whale—which is removed from the oil by chilling. Spermaceti is used in making ointments, pomades, face creams, and candles. Whale oil, which is taken from baleen whales such as the blue and the humpback, is a genuine fat. It is edible and, in addition to being used like sperm oil, is a principal ingredient in margarines made in Europe.

See also: WHALING.

spermatophyte   [spur-mat'-uh-fyt]

Spermatophyte, or, literally, a seed plant, is a term used to refer to those plants which bear true seeds; the term encompasses all flowering plants (angiosperms), such as roses and palm trees, and all "nonflowering" plants with true seeds (gymnosperms), such as pine trees and the ginkgo. In older classifications the spermatophytes were also called phanerogams (*phanero*, "visible"; *gam*, "sexuality") because the sexual structures (stamens and pistils) of these plants were plainly evident. The phanerogams were contrasted to the cryptogams (*crypto*, "hidden"), such as the algae, mosses, and ferns, which lacked these sexual structures.

In one of the latest classifications, each of the major groups within the plant kingdom is placed in a division (equal to a phylum in the animal kingdom) of its own, such as the Pinophyta (gymnosperms), Lycophyta (club mosses), and Magnoliophyta (angiosperms). The term *spermatophyte* is not used in this classification.

Sperry, Elmer Ambrose

The work of the inventor and engineer Elmer Ambrose Sperry, b. Cortland, N.Y., Oct. 21, 1860, d. June 16, 1930, marks the transition in the history of American technology from the heroic age of invention to the era of corporate research and development. Sperry received more than 350 patents in such diverse fields as electric light and power, mining machinery, the automobile, aviation, industrial chemistry, gyrocompasses, and gyrostabilizers; most of these patents relate to automatic control systems. After receiving (1880) his first patent on a dynamo-electric machine, Sperry embarked on a career as a professional, independent inventor. He established invention, development, and manufacturing companies and hired university-trained engineers and scientists to institutionalize inventive activity. The most important phase of Sperry's career began (1907) when he became interested in applications for GYROSCOPES. He developed the Sperry gyrostabilizer, a gyrocompass for ships, and established (1910) the Sperry Gyroscope Company, the progenitor of the Sperry Rand Corporation.   DAVID A. HOUNSHELL

Bibliography: Hughes, Thomas Parke, *Elmer Sperry: Inventor and Engineer* (1971); Hunsaker, J. C., *Biographical Memoir of Elmer Ambrose Sperry, 1860-1930* (1955).

spessartine: see GARNET.

Spessivtseva, Olga Aleksandrovna   [spes-eeft'-se-vah]

Olga Aleksandrovna Spessivtseva (also known as Olga Spessiva), b. Rostov-on-Don, Russia, July 18 (N.S.), 1895, is classed among the supreme classical ballerinas of the 20th century because of her extraordinary technique and the remarkable spiritual beauty of her dancing. A graduate (1913) of the Imperial Ballet School in Saint Petersburg (now Leningrad), she danced with the Imperial (now Kirov) Ballet, where she was named prima ballerina in 1918; the BALLETS RUSSES DE SERGE DIAGHILEV, creating the lead in his revival of Marius Petipa's *Sleeping Beauty* in 1921 and in Balanchine's *La Chatte* in 1927; the Paris Opéra Ballet; and other companies. In 1939, Spessivtseva came to the United States. In 1943, suffering a nervous breakdown, she was confined to a mental hospital but was released in 1963. A few film clips survive showing her as Giselle, her most famous role; although technically deficient, the films confirm unmistakably her greatness as a dancer.   DALE HARRIS

Bibliography: Dolin, Anton, *The Sleeping Ballerina* (1966).

sphalerite [sfal'-ur-yt]

Sphalerite (ZnS), a common and widely distributed zinc SUL-FIDE MINERAL, is the major ore of zinc. Found in a variety of crystal forms (isometric system) as well as in cleavable, granular, or foliated masses, it ranges from colorless to brown and black in color, darkening as the amount of iron impurities increases. Hardness is $3\frac{1}{2}$ to 4, streak is brownish, luster is resinous to adamantine, and specific gravity is 3.9 to 4.1. Sphalerite, usually in association with the lead sulfide galena, occurs in contact metamorphic deposits, in replacement deposits within limestone and dolomite, and in veins.

sphene

Sphene [CaTiSiO$_4$ (O,OH,F)], also called titanite, is a titanium and calcium SILICATE MINERAL. When transparent and of good color, it is faceted to produce a brilliant, multicolored GEM. Sphene forms wedge-shaped crystals (monoclinic system) of various forms and granular masses that range in color from brown to black through gray and green to yellow and red. Hardness is 5 to $5\frac{1}{2}$, luster is adamantine to resinous, and specific gravity is 3.4 to 3.6. Sphene occurs as an accessory mineral in igneous rocks, notably nepheline syenites, and in gneisses, schists, and marbles.

sphere

A sphere is the set of all points in space that are equidistant from a fixed point called the center. Any line segment drawn from the center to the surface of the sphere is called a radius; the length of this segment is also called the radius. A chord is any line segment that has both endpoints on the sphere. A diameter is a chord that passes through the center. If the radius is r, then all points less than r units from the center constitute the interior of the sphere, whereas the exterior is the set of all points that are more than r units from the center.

A sphere may be generated by rotating a circle about any one of its diameters. For example, a coin will trace out the surface of a sphere when it is given a spin. The sphere with center at point (a,b,c) and radius r has the equation $(x-a)^2+(y-b)^2+(z-c)^2=r^2$. If the center is at the origin of the coordinate system, the equation reduces to $x^2+y^2+z^2=r^2$. A sphere of radius r has volume $V=\frac{4}{3}\pi r^3$, and surface area $A=4\pi r^2$.   JOE K. SMITH

Bibliography: Newman, James R., ed., *The World of Mathematics*, 4 vols. (1956–1960); Schaaf, William L., *Basic Concepts of Elementary Mathematics*, 3d ed. (1969); Thomas, George B., and Finney, Ross L., *Calculus and Analytic Geometry*, 5th ed. (1979).

spherical aberration: see ABERRATION, SPHERICAL.

spherical coordinates: see COORDINATE SYSTEMS (mathematics).

spherical trigonometry

Spherical trigonometry is concerned with the study of triangles on the surface of a sphere (spherical triangles). It should be distinguished from the ordinary TRIGONOMETRY of plane figures. It involves the concept of a spherical triangle as part of a spherical surface, and the arc of a great circle as the side of a spherical triangle. A great circle on the surface of a sphere is the intersection with the surface made by a plane that passes through the center of the sphere. The shortest distance between two points on a spherical surface is an arc of a great circle. Although the Earth is not exactly a sphere, as an approximation it may be assumed spherical. With such an approximation, arcs of a great circle, called geodesics, may be drawn on the surface of the (spherical) Earth. Navigation by sea or air involves choosing routes that are geodesics.

A spherical triangle is part of a spherical surface bounded by arcs of three great circles. The size of the spherical angle between two great circles is that of the dihedral angle between the planes of the great circles. The distance along the arc of a great circle between two points can be represented by the angle subtended by the arc at the center of the sphere. This angle, the dihedral angle and the spherical angle, measured in degrees, should be distinguished from what is referred to as a spherical degree. A spherical degree is the amount of area on the surface of a sphere equal to 1/720 of the whole spherical surface. It is defined by the spherical triangle known as a birectangular spherical triangle, whose angles are two right angles and a third angle of one ordinary degree.

The position of a point in space can be described by spherical or by polar coordinates (see COORDINATE SYSTEMS). A point P in space can be described in terms of its distance from a fixed point O, the angle ϕ between terminal line OP and initial line OZ, and the dihedral angle θ between the initial plane through OZ and the plane containing OP and OZ. The point O is called the *pole*; r is the length of OP (the *radius vector*); OZ is the polar axis; θ is the longitude (azimuth); and ϕ is the colatitude of the system. The coordinates of P are written (r, θ, ϕ). The spherical (polar) coordinates are related to the Cartesian (rectangular) coordinates by associating the pole with the origin and the polar axis with the z-axis. The initial plane coincides with the zx-plane, and θ is the angle between the positive direction of the x-axis and the projection of OP on the xy-plane. The rectangular and spherical coordinates of P are related in the following way:

$$x = r \sin\phi \cos\theta \qquad r = (x^2 + y^2 + z^2)^{1/2}$$
$$y = r \sin\phi \sin\theta \qquad \tan\theta = y/x$$
$$z = r \cos\theta \qquad \tan\phi = (x^2 + y^2)^{1/2}/z$$

The above relations hold for any point P in space. When r, the radius vector, is constant while θ varies from 0° to 360° and ϕ varies from 0° to 180°, the point P generates a spherical surface; when θ is constant and r and ϕ vary, P generates a half-plane containing the polar axis and radius vector, making a dihedral angle θ with the initial plane; this angle is the longitude (azimuth) of P. When ϕ is constant and r and θ vary, P generates the surface of a cone, ϕ being the colatitude of P. For a particular sphere, the intersection of the plane (θ-constant) and the surface of the sphere is a *meridian*. A circle of *latitude* is the intersection of the cone (ϕ-constant) and the surface of the sphere.   ALARIC MILLINGTON

Bibliography: Brink, Raymond W., *Spherical Trigonometry* (1942).

sphinx

A mythical creature that originated in ancient Egypt, the sphinx combined a beast's body (usually a lion's) with the human face of the ruling pharaoh. Large-scale examples carved in stone often served to guard sanctuaries in ancient Egypt. Although usually depicted in a recumbent position, some sphinxes were shown trampling Egypt's foes. The sphinx image also appeared in various forms among other ancient cultures of Western Asia and the Mediterranean, notably in Mesopotamia, Greece, and Etruria. Wings were often added to the leonine body, and female sphinxes were also created, especially in Greece (8th–6th century BC). The most famous sphinx lies near the pyramid (see PYRAMIDS) of KHAFRE at Giza, 10 km (6 mi) from Cairo. Originally built to guard the pyramid, this sphinx was later worshiped as the god Rahorakhty, "Ra of the Two Horizons." Unfortunately, its nose, used by soldiers of a later era for target practice, is now missing.

                    ROBERT S. BIANCHI

Bibliography: Ivimy, John, *The Sphinx and the Megaliths* (1974); Stewart, Desmond, *The Pyramids and Sphinx* (1971).

Spice Islands: see MOLUCCAS.

spice trade

Since ancient times the aromatic spices of the Far East have been in demand by peoples of the East and West, and control of the lucrative trade in these spices has been highly coveted. Because the primary source of aromatic spices has been concentrated in the MOLUCCAS (or Spice Islands) in the East Indies, control has tended to be monopolistic.

The overland transport of spices to China and Arabia began long before the Christian era, but the large-volume, primarily seaborne, trade developed later. The first major monopoly arose in the 9th century among Indian traders operating from Java. In the 12th century other Indians—Muslim traders cooperating with Arab and Persian sailors—began encroaching on the trade, gaining control of the port of MELAKA around 1450 and of all Java by 1528.

Many Europeans in the age of discovery were, like Christopher COLUMBUS, spurred in part by a desire to reach the source of the much-valued spices. The Portuguese, after rounding Africa and reaching India, captured Melaka in 1512 and dominated the trade for the rest of the century. Dutch and British fleets drove Portugal from Asian waters after 1600, but the Dutch seized Melaka in 1641 and denied the British access to the Moluccas. They established the profitable Dutch EAST INDIA COMPANY and—except for some intervals of British domination—controlled the spice trade into the 20th century.

JOHN F. CADY

Bibliography: Anderson, John, *English Intercourse with Siam in the Seventeenth Century* (1890; repr. 1976); Marshall, Peter James, *Problems of Empire: Britain and India 1757–1813* (1968).

spicebush

The common spicebush, *Lindera benzoin*, grows in wooded bottomlands of eastern North America. It bears clusters of small, yellow flowers in early spring and small, bright, red berries in summer. The leaves, twigs, and bark of this spicy-scented shrub have been used to make tea. Dried and powdered spicebush berries are known as a substitute for allspice.

spicule [spik'-yool]

Spicules are jets of gaseous material from the SUN's low chromosphere that move into the corona along very strong magnetic field lines. They are about 1,000 km (620 mi) across, ten times that in height, move at about 20 km/sec (12 mi/sec), and last only 5 to 10 minutes.

spider

Spiders comprise a large, widespread group of carnivorous arthropods. They have eight legs, can produce silk, and most have poison glands associated with fangs. More than 30,000 species of spiders are found on every continent except Antarctica in almost every kind of terrestrial habitat and a few aquatic ones as well. Spiders range in body size from about 0.5 mm (0.02 in) to 9 cm (3.6 in). The term *spider* is derived from the Old English *spinnan* ("to spin") referring to the group's use of silk. Spiders make up the order Araneae in the class Arachnida, which takes its name from the mythological character Arachne, a peasant girl who challenged the weaving skill of the goddess Athena. Arachne equalled Athena's skill in a contest, and in response to Athena's anger she hanged herself. In belated remorse, Athena changed the body of

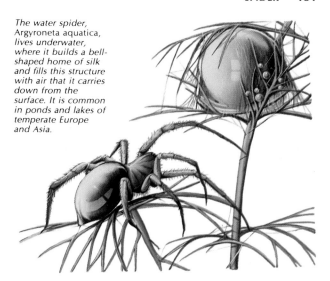

The water spider, Argyroneta aquatica, lives underwater, where it builds a bell-shaped home of silk and fills this structure with air that it carries down from the surface. It is common in ponds and lakes of temperate Europe and Asia.

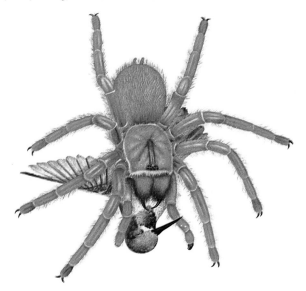

(Below) This bird-eating spider, genus Sericopelma, is one of several large tarantulas known to kill small birds. It measures about 6 cm (2.4 in) in length and is found in Panama.

An orb weaver spider begins its web by spinning a single thread, the bridge line, that is carried by wind until it attaches to a twig or other object. The spider then lays down other foundation lines (1). Radial threads (2) are connected between the foundation lines and an attachment zone near the center of the web. Next, the spider lays down a nonsticky scaffolding spiral (3) that holds the radials in place. Finally, the spider spins a spiral of viscid, or sticky, threads (4) and removes the temporary scaffolding.

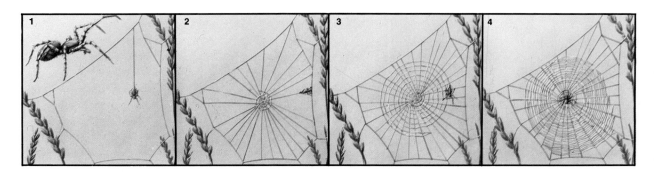

The anatomy of a spider, with labels:
cephalothorax, sucking stomach, eyes, brain, abdomen, intestine, heart, carapace, poison gland, ovary, silk glands, anus, pedipalp, patella, tibia, digestive tube, book lung, lung slit, trachea, spinnerets, femur, mouth, fang, chelicera, epigynum, legs, metatarsus, tarsus, claw

The anatomy of a spider, an arachnid, includes four pairs of legs and a body divided into two regions, the cephalothorax and the abdomen. The spider produces silk from spinnerets located in its abdomen and uses the silk to spin webs, to line its burrow, to wrap its eggs in cocoons, and to lower itself by a single strand to the ground. Its scientific class, Arachnida, is named for the Greek tapestry weaver Arachne, who was turned into a spider by the goddess Athena.

Arachne into a spider and allowed her to retain her weaving skill.

Classification. The order Araneae is usually divided into two suborders with classification determined primarily by the structure of the chelicerae (anterior appendages below the eyes). The suborder Orthognatha, or mygalomorph spiders, comprises about 12 families and includes the trap-door spiders of the family Ctenizidae and the large tarantulas of the family Theraphosidae, often kept as pets. The suborder Labidognatha, or araneomorphs, with about 60 families, have chelicerae with fangs that open sideways and work against one another. These are the true spiders and include most of the familiar ones. Among the major families are those that capture prey in webs—Araneidae, or orb weavers; Theridiidae, which include the notorious black widow; and Agelenidae, which capture prey that lands on their sheet webs—and those that hunt—Lycosidae, or wolf spiders, mostly nocturnal; Salticidae, or jumping spiders, diurnal with excellent eyesight; and Thomisidae, or crab spiders.

Structure and Function. Spiders have two major body parts, the cephalothorax and the abdomen, which are connected by a thin pedicel. The cephalothorax bears six pairs of appendages. A pair of chelicerae with fangs associated with food capture is followed by a pair of leglike pedipalps, which are modified in adult males as intromittent organs for the transfer of sperm to the female. The pedipalps are followed by four pairs of walking legs. Pedipalps and legs often have many sensory hairs. The legs have seven segments and usually bear two or three claws, which may be obscured by the hairs, at their apex. The top of the cephalothorax is covered by a carapace with usually four pairs of simple eyes on the anterior end. Some spiders have fewer eyes, and certain cave species have lost their eyes entirely. The abdomen is usually unsegmented, and its ventral surface has the genital openings.

The hemolymph (blood) of the circulatory system is used for both the distribution of food and oxygen (some spiders having the bluish oxygen-carrying pigment, hemocyanin) and the hydraulic system by which the legs are extended by blood pressure. Much of the nervous system is condensed as a complex brain (group of ganglia) in the prosoma.

Spiders use two systems for respiration: thin tubes, or trachea, that ramify from abdominal openings (spiracles) and book lungs, which are groups of thin-walled invaginations that open on either side of the genital region at the anterior end of the abdomen. Most true spiders have both trachea and a pair of book lungs, but some of the smallest have lost their book lungs, and some have two pairs of book lungs and no trachea.

The spinnerets are fingerlike appendages usually located at the spider's posterior end and supplied with liquid protein silk by several silk glands within the abdomen. The protein polymerizes into dry silk as it is pulled out of the thousands

The black widow, L. mactans, is a common inhabitant of warm areas of the world. The female, about 1.2 cm (0.5 in) long, is black with a red hourglass figure on the underside of her globe-shaped abdomen; the male is smaller and more conspicuously marked.

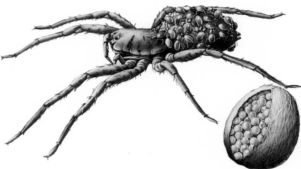

A female wolf spider (family Lycosidae) carries newly hatched young on her back for about a week. Spiders of most families, however, take little care of their offspring. Spiderlings, which resemble adults in form, must undergo several molts to reach adult size.

of tiny spigots covering the four to eight spinnerets. Various types of silk are spun by spiders and are used for trap building, lining tubes and cavities, wrapping eggs, wrapping prey, as safety lines, and, in small spiders, as a way to "balloon," or to be carried by the wind.

All spiders have moveable fangs at the ends of their chelicerae and most have poison glands that open at the tips of the fangs. The poison is effective on arthropods, and a few spiders have poisons toxic to vertebrates, including humans. In the United States, the black widow, *Latrodectus mactans,* has a potent neurotoxin, and the brown recluse, *Loxosceles reclusa,* possesses an ulcer-producing poison. Most spiders, however, are quite harmless to humans.

Spiders are predaceous animals that feed primarily on other insects. They usually kill their prey with poison injected through their bite. Because spiders can swallow only liquids, digestive juices are pumped out onto the prey, where digestion occurs externally. The spider then swallows the resulting nutritive soup.

Spiders use several strategies to capture prey: active hunting, waiting in ambush, and making and using traps of silk. The most distinctive strategy is the use of a silk orb web. This aerial net uses a minimum of silk threads to "strain" the air for insect prey of the proper size. Most orb webs are made up of strong support threads for the frame and radii, which radiate from the hub, and a spiral sticky thread that makes up the catching surface. The spider often sits at the hub with each of its legs on a different radiating thread. When a prey is caught, the spider can feel its vibrations; it runs rapidly to the prey and quickly bites it or wraps it in silk. Each species of orb weavers makes a distinctive form of web.

Reproduction. Reproduction is sexual, with the male often displaying complex courtship behavior. The male makes a simple sperm web and deposits a drop of sperm on it from his genital pore. The sperm is then taken up by the copulatory organs at the ends of his pedipalps. The male finds a female, courts her, and then mates—inserting the pedipalps into special openings on the venter of the female's abdomen, where the sperm is stored. Within days the female will construct a silken egg case; the eggs are fertilized as they are laid into the egg case. A single egg sac may have from a few to 3,000 eggs. Development begins in the egg sac, and the first molt usually takes place there. After emerging, the spiderlings (miniature adults) begin to grow, and they undergo from 5 to 12 molts—15 in large species—in direct development to the mature form. In some spiders the mother protects her young for a few days after emergence. Female wolf spiders carry their spiderlings on their back for approximately a week. A few species exhibit colonial and subsocial systems atypical of most spiders. Most spiders live about a year, although some (including the tarantula) have life spans of up to 20 years.

Importance. Spiders play an important role in natural ecosystems. As one of the major groups of predators, they keep the number of insects in check. They are beneficial in agricultural systems as aids in controlling insect pests. In turn, they are preyed upon by other animals, especially wasps. Spider silk is used commercially in the preparation of cross hairs in optical instruments.

Spiders are used to test certain drugs, because studies have shown that drugs given to spiders can affect their web building. Orb weaver spiders have been observed building normal webs in the total weightlessness of a space station.

JONATHAN REISKIND

Bibliography: Bristowe, W. S., *The World of Spiders* (1976); Gertsch, W. J., *American Spiders* (1979); Kaston, B. J., *How to Know the Spiders,* 3d ed. (1978); Levi, H. W. and L. R., *Spiders and Their Kin* (1967).

spiderflower

The spiderflower, *Cleome hasslerana,* is a tall, tropical, annual plant in the caper family, Capparidaceae. Native from southeastern Brazil to Argentina, it has become a popular garden plant despite its strong scent. The flowers are dark pink to white with stamens almost 8 cm (3 in) long. The name *spiderflower* is derived from the appearance of the long, clawed petals of each flower.

spiderwort [spy'-dur-wurt]

Spiderwort is the common name for the more than 20 species of perennial herbs in the plant genus *Tradescantia,* in the spiderwort family, Commelinaceae. They are so called because of the hairy flower stalks enclosed by sheathing leaves at the base. Several species are common house and greenhouse plants, including purple selections of *Tradescantia fluminensis* (WANDERING JEW) and *Tradescantia virginiana.*

Spieghel, Henric Laurenszoon [spee'-kul]

Henric Laurenszoon Spieghel, b. Mar. 11, 1549, d. Jan. 4, 1612, was a Dutch poet, playwright, and humanist whose work blends medieval and Renaissance traditions. His unfinished masterpiece, *Hertspiegel* (1614), an ethical poem written in alexandrines, exemplifies the faith, patriotism, and scholarship of its author. Spieghel also wrote books on language, including the first Dutch grammar (1584), which helped to popularize the national language.

spikenard [spyk'-nahrd]

Spikenard is the common name for a Himalayan plant, *Nardostachys jatamansii,* of the valerian family, Valerianaceae. An essential oil used in ointments and in perfumery is obtained by distillation of the aromatic root; spikenard ointment is mentioned several times in the Bible. The American spikenard, *Aralia racemosa,* of the ginseng family, Araliaceae, is a plant native to the eastern United States. A decoction of the root was used by Indians for backache, rheumatoid arthritis, and coughing. Another plant of eastern North America, *Smilacina racemosa,* of the lily family, Liliaceae, is sometimes known as wild spikenard.

KENNETH R. ROBERTSON

Spillane, Mickey [spil-ayn']

An American mystery writer, Mickey Spillane, (pen name of Frank Morrison), b. Brooklyn, N.Y., Mar. 9, 1918, created the private eye Mike Hammer and became a best-selling author. The formula for the Hammer novels was established in the first, *I, the Jury* (1947; film, 1953). Like nearly all of Spillane's books, it relies on violence and sex and on Hammer's remorseless desire to punish wrongdoers who manage to escape an impotent judicial system. In the tradition of the hard-boiled private detective, Hammer usually walks a fine line between the law and the underworld. Seven of Spillane's novels have been filmed; in *The Girl Hunters* (1962; film, 1963), Spillane himself played Hammer. Later works include *The Death Dealers* (1965) and *Survival: Zero* (1970).

Spina [spee'-nah]

Spina, an ancient port on the Po delta at the head of the Adriatic, between Ravenna and Venice, Italy, was founded by Greeks at the end of the 6th century BC. It flourished as a commercial center from the 5th century until the Gallic invasion (4th century BC). A classical version of Venice, the site covered 300 ha (740 acres) surrounded by palisades and earthen ramparts, its streets divided by canals that were connected to the sea by a harbor canal 15 m (50 ft) wide. Houses were built on wooden platforms set on pilings. Only the cemeteries of Spina have been systematically excavated, yielding more than 4,000 graves (6th to 3d centuries BC) that were found to contain great numbers of fine Attic vases, Etruscan bronzes, and pieces of gold jewelry. The grave finds, now housed in the Archaeological Museum in Ferrara, include vases by the early Greek masters Polygnotus and the Berlin, Penthesilea, and Niobid painters, as well as by native Italic artists.

JEAN MacINTOSH TURFA

Bibliography: Alfieri, N., and Arias, P. E., *Spina* (1958); Scullard, H. H., *The Etruscan Cities and Rome* (1967).

spinach

Spinach is an annual herb, *Spinacia oleracea,* which is grown for its nutritious green leaves. Believed to have originated in

Spinach, S. oleracea, must be planted in early spring or fall because it goes to seed quickly in hot weather. Both wrinkled and smooth-leaved varieties grow in broad rosettes.

southwestern Asia, it was introduced into Europe during the Middle Ages and is now widely cultivated throughout the world. The United States, the Netherlands, and the Scandinavian countries are the major producers. Within the United States, California is the leading state for growing commercially processed spinach, and Texas is the major producer of fresh-market spinach. Spinach thrives in relatively cool weather. Generally, spinach plants have either male flowers or female flowers. Female forms are slower to bolt, a characteristic that led to the development of warm-weather varieties in which the plants are primarily female. Under good growing conditions, spinach is ready for harvest about 40 days after seeding. Picking may begin after five leaves have developed and can continue until the seedstalks develop.

O. A. LORENZ

spinal cord

The spinal cord, a tube about 1 cm (0.4 in) thick with a small central canal, is present within the vertebral column of all vertebrate animals, where it runs from the brain stem, at the level of the first cervical (neck) vertebra, to the tail. A cerebrospinal fluid flows through the central canal and around the spinal cord. The cord is encased in three layers of membranes: the dura mater, the pia mater, and the arachnoid. Together with the BRAIN, the spinal cord constitutes the central NERVOUS SYSTEM.

In cross section, the spinal cord has a centrally positioned butterfly-shaped gray area surrounded by white matter. The gray color comes from unmyelinated cell bodies of nerve cells (neurons), the white from the myelinated axonal fibers.

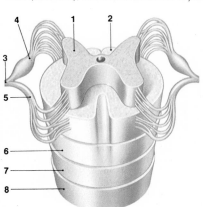

As seen in cross section, the spinal cord consists of gray matter (1) surrounded by white matter (2). Each spinal nerve (3) divides into a dorsal sensory root (4) and a ventral motor root (5). Both the brain and spinal cord are enclosed by three protective membranes, or meninges: the pia mater (6) and the arachnoid (7)—which enclose the cerebrospinal fluid— are surrounded by the dura mater (8).

A cell body contains the nucleus of the nerve cell, and it sends out a single axon and numerous fibrous extensions known as dendrites—short, branchlike processes. In the spinal cord, dendrites receive stimuli from the axons of other neurons whose cell bodies are located either elsewhere in the central nervous system or in the peripheral nervous system. The latter consists of all nerve cells whose axons lie outside of the brain or spinal cord (see NEUROPHYSIOLOGY).

Thirty-one pairs of spinal nerves are present in humans, and each pair has two roots. The ventral roots, located at the front side of the spinal cord, stem from ventral or lateral horns and carry the initial segment of motor neuron axons. The dorsal roots, located at the back side of the cord, carry the terminal segments of sensory neurons, whose terminal branches lie within the dorsal horn of the spinal cord. The cell bodies of the sensory neurons are located within a spinal ganglion adjacent to the cord, and their dendrites are located in the skin, the belly of muscles, the tissues of soft organs (viscera), and blood vessels.

The dorsal horns are located on the back side of the spinal cord, where the incoming sensory neurons form synapses with dendrites of neurons carrying information to the brain, or with motor neurons, to form a REFLEX arc. Ventral horns, which are located at the belly side of the spinal cord, contain the cell bodies of motor neurons. These carry impulses from the spinal cord to the body. Lateral horns, present only in the thoracolumbar region, are situated between the dorsal and ventral horns; they protrude laterally and contain cell bodies of neurons from the autonomic nervous system. The axons of these neurons are carried, together with the axons of motor neurons, in the ventral roots. Immediately outside of the spinal cord, just before leaving the vertebral column, the ventral and dorsal roots unite into a spinal nerve on each side of the body.

Bibliography: Austin, George, ed., *The Spinal Cord: Basic Aspects and Surgical Considerations,* 2d ed. (1972); Crock, Henry V., *The Blood Supply of the Vertebral Column and Spinal Cord in Man* (1977); Eccles, John C., and Schade, J. P., *Physiology of Spinal Neurons* (1964); Kostyuk, P. G., *Stucture and Function of Descending Systems of the Spinal Cord* (1978).

spinal fluid: see SPINAL CORD; SPINE.

spinal nerve: see SPINAL CORD.

spindle tree

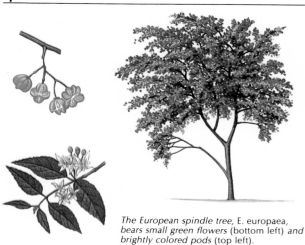

The European spindle tree, E. europaea, bears small green flowers (bottom left) and brightly colored pods (top left).

Spindle tree, genus *Euonymus,* is the common name for about 170 species of deciduous and evergreen trees, shrubs, and woody creepers in the staff-tree family, Celastraceae. Most are native to Asia. The name was originally applied to *E. europaea,* because its hard wood was used to make spindles. The stems are four-angled, the flowers are small and are greenish or purplish, the fruits are 3- to 5-valved capsules, and the seeds are enclosed in a reddish cover. A number of species are cultivated, including the winged spindle tree, or burning-bush, *E. alatus,* native to temperate eastern Asia; the strawberry-bush, or wahoo, *E. americanus,* of the eastern United States; the wintercreeper, *E. fortunei,* originally from China; and the Japanese spindle tree, *E. japonicus,* from Japan.

KENNETH R. ROBERTSON

spine

The spine, or spinal column, consists of bone and forms the primary support of the skeleton in vertebrates. The functions of the spine are the protection of the SPINAL CORD and the roots of the spinal nerves and the provision of attachment points for the skull, ribs, pelvis, muscles, and ligaments.

The flexible portion of the spine, or backbone, in humans consists of 24 individual vertebrae: 7 in the neck (cervical vertebrae), 12 in the thorax (thoracic vertebrae), and 5 in the lower back (lumbar vertebrae). The sacrum, located below the lumbar vertebrae and joined to the pelvis, consists of 5 fused vertebrae. The coccyx, or tailbone, is located below the sacrum and consists of 3 to 5 fused, rudimentary vertebrae in humans.

In general, the major part of a vertebra, the body, is a short, solid, cylindrical structure called the centrum. The remaining part is called the vertebral arch, or neural arch. The spinal cord passes through the large hole, or foramen, in the center of each vertebral arch of the spinal column. The foramen is continuous and protects the spinal cord; spinal fluid circu-lates within it. Spinal nerves pass from the cord through notches in the vertebral arch. A spiny projection extends from each side of the vertebral arch; a third projection in the middle of the vertebral arch may be seen or felt through the skin. Thoracic vertebrae have articulating surfaces for attachment of ribs. The bodies of the vertebrae are separated from each other by cartilagenous pads called intervertebral disks. The vertebrae are held together by strong ligaments, but the general design of the spinal column allows considerable flexibility. The spine is subject to injury, curvature, arthritis, infections, and slipped disks.

PETER L. PETRAKIS

Bibliography: Chaffee, Ellen E., and Greisheimer, Esther M., *Basic Physiology and Anatomy*, 3d ed. (1974); Rothman, R. H., and Simeone, F. A., eds., *The Spine*, 2 vols. (1975).

spinel [spuh-nel']

Spinel is a hard, vitreous magnesium and aluminum oxide mineral that has long been valued as a gemstone. It may be found as eight-sided crystals in loose or massive form, or in coarse-grained mixtures with calcite, corundum, and other minerals. A transparent to opaque substance, it occurs in all colors, especially red, blue, green, brown, or black. The red form is often mistaken for ruby, which it greatly resembles.

The magnesium aluminate mineral spinel ($MgAl_2O_4$) is used as a GEM when transparent and finely colored. Ruby spinel has been confused with RUBY, the Black Prince's Ruby in the British Imperial State Crown being a famous example. The different colors of the mineral, caused by impurities, include various reds, yellow, blue, green, brown, and black. Hardness is 8, luster is vitreous, and specific gravity is 3.5 to 4.1. Gem spinels occur as crystals and pebbles in placer deposits, where they accumulate because they resist weathering. Common spinel occurs in metamorphic rocks and as an accessory mineral of some basic igneous rocks.

spinet [spin'-et]

The spinet, along with the VIRGINAL, was one of a group of smaller KEYBOARD INSTRUMENTS that was contemporary with the HARPSICHORD. They all have the same action; the strings are plucked by means of a quill or plectrum mounted in a jack. The spinet and virginal have about the same relationship to the harpsichord as the upright piano has to the grand. As is the case with the term *virginal*, *spinet* may refer to several different instruments.

In Italy the word *spinetta* was applied to all small instruments, whether they were rectangular or polygonal. In the Low Countries *spinet* was the name applied to a rectangular version with the keyboard left of center, and *muselar* described the same instrument with the keyboard right of center; they were also known as *virginals*. In France *épinette* was used for all small keyboard instruments.

In all countries these instruments are smaller and have a different tone quality than the harpsichord. They should not be considered an important group of instruments but rather as domestic keyboard varieties that were available to those who could not afford the larger harpsichord. The best-known model of spinet was developed in England, where the wing-shaped form was popularly known as "leg of mutton."

RICHARD REPHANN

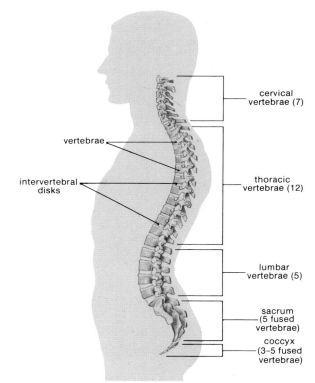

thoracic vertebra

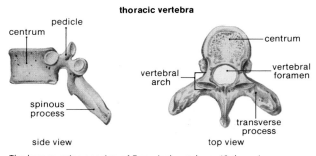

The human spine consists of 7 cervical vertebrae, 12 thoracic vertebrae, and 5 lumbar vertebrae—separated by disks—plus the sacrum and coccyx, each formed from fused vertebrae. The major parts of each vertebra are the centrum and vertebral arch.

spinning

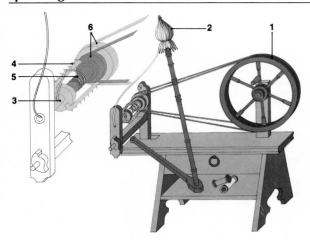

This 15th-century spinning wheel streamlined older methods of spinning by simultaneously spinning and winding the yarn. While the right hand turns the driving wheel (1), the left hand draws the mass of loose yarn (roving) from the distaff (2) through a small opening on the spindle shaft (3). The fiber is then caught over one of a series of hooks on the flyer (4) and wound onto the spool (5). The flyer, revolving more rapidly than the spool because of the difference in the diameters of their pulleys (6), winds the roving into yarn as it whirls. The yarn is periodically shifted to another hook to ensure even winding. The yarn is then ready to be woven into cloth on a loom.

Spinning is the process by which cotton, wool, flax, and other short fibers are twisted together to produce a yarn or thread suitable for weaving into cloth, winding into rope or cable, or used in sewing. (Long, continuous fibers, such as silk, are not spun. To achieve strength and the appropriate thickness, they are thrown, or twisted, together.) In hand spinning, the fibers are first cleaned and disentangled and then carded. In hand carding, the fibers are placed between two boards covered with leather, through which protrude fine wire hooks that catch the fibers as one board is pulled gently across the other. When sufficiently loosened, the fibers are pulled off in a roll, or sliver. The fibers can now be drawn out and, with sufficient twist, will be locked together so firmly that they can no longer slide past each other, thus forming a strong yarn.

Until about 1300 yarn was spun on the spindle and whorl. A spindle is a rounded stick with tapered ends to which the fibers are attached and twisted; a whorl is a weight attached to the spindle that acts as a flywheel to keep the spindle rotating. The fibers were pulled by hand from a bundle of carded fibers tied to a stick called a distaff. The spindle, which hung from the fibers, twisted the fibers as it rotated downward, and spun a length of yarn as it was pulled away from the fiber bundle. When the spindle reached the bottom of its descent, the spun yarn was unhitched from its tip and wound around the spindle body, and the spinning of an additional yarn length was begun.

The Spinning Wheel. The spinning wheel made its European appearance during the 14th century. It consisted of a horizontally mounted spindle that was connected to a large, hand-driven wheel by a circular band. The spinner's left hand fed the fibers into the spindle from a distaff that was sometimes mounted on the frame of the wheel, and the right hand turned the wheel. When a length of fiber had been spun, the process stopped while the yarn coils on the tip of the spindle were cleared by reversing the spindle's rotation.

About 150 years after the introduction of the spinning wheel, a mechanical improvement, the Saxon wheel, was introduced. The Saxon wheel was operated by a foot pedal that left both hands free to manipulate the fibers. The yarn passed through a hole in the end of the spindle. Fixed to the spindle was a U-shaped flyer, one arm of which guided the spun yarn to the side of the spindle and onto a spool, or bobbin. As it

circled the spindle, the flyer twisted the yarn, then wound it evenly around the bobbin. Spinning and winding-on were continuous. Sometimes two sets of bobbins, spindles, and flyers were mounted on the wheel to spin two yarns at once.

Spinning Mechanization. The first of several developments during the 18th century, the invention (1733) of the flying shuttle by John KAY increased LOOM production to such an extent that it created a yarn shortage, and three new spinning machines were shortly introduced. In 1766, James HARGREAVES perfected his spinning jenny. Based on the spinning wheel, the jenny featured a series of spindles set in a row, enabling one operator to produce large quantities of yarn. The yarn, however, was soft and lightly twisted and suitable only for coarse-weave fabrics. In 1769, Richard ARKWRIGHT patented the spinning frame, a machine that used a series of rotating rollers to draw out the fibers. His 1771 water frame could open, card, draw, rove, and spin cotton and became the prototype for the spinning machines used in the early stages of English textile industrialization. The third machine was Samuel CROMPTON's mule (1779), which could spin any type of yarn, from fine to coarse, in one continuous operation and in great quantity. Much more efficient and productive than either the Hargreaves or Arkwright machines, the mule, eventually powered by steam, was used for more than 100 years, and later models were huge machines, working 1,200 spindles in a frame 37 m (120 ft) long.

The ring frame, invented (1828) by the American John Thorp, was based on Arkwright's spinning frame. Ring spinning allowed for high spindle speeds and became the most widely used spinning method.

Many natural fibers are now spun by the open-end system, where the fibers are drawn by air into a rapidly rotating cup and pulled out on the other side as a finished yarn.

RICHARD HILLS

Bibliography: Blake, W. A., et al., eds., *Spinning* (1968); Crockett, Candace, *The Complete Spinning Book* (1977); Dyson, Eric, ed., *Rotor Spinning: Technical and Economic Aspects* (1975); French, Gilbert J., *Life and Times of Samuel Crompton* (1970); Morton, William Ernest, *An Introduction to the Study of Spinning*, 2d ed. (1949); Nield, Roy, *Open-end Spinning* (1975); Van Wagenen, Jared, *The Golden Age of Homespun* (1963).

See also: TEXTILE INDUSTRY; WEAVING.

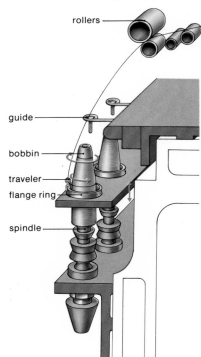

rollers

guide

bobbin

traveler

flange ring

spindle

The ring frame, invented (1828) by John Thorp and based on Richard Arkwright's spinning frame, is used to spin cotton. The fibers are drawn through a series of rollers and a guide down to the traveler on the flange ring. The traveler, replacing the flyer, spins around the flange ring and guides the thread onto the bobbin, which is positioned on the spindle. The traveler and flange ring are located on a movable plate that rises and falls with each revolution of the spindle, distributing the thread evenly on the bobbin. The ring spinning method is today the most common.

Spinoza, Baruch   [spin-oh'-zuh, bah-rook']

An early advocate of intellectual freedom, the 17th-century Dutch metaphysician Baruch Spinoza was formally expelled for heresy by the traditionalist Jewish community of Amsterdam in 1656. Thereafter, he supported his lifelong rationalist inquiries by working as a lens grinder, refusing any compromising scholarly patronage.

Baruch (or Benedict) Spinoza, b. Amsterdam, Nov. 24, 1632, d. Feb. 21, 1677, was one of the most important philosophers of the European tradition of RATIONALISM.

Life. Spinoza was born into a family of Portuguese Jews who were refugees to Holland at the end of the 16th century. His early education was in Hebrew, the Bible, the Talmud, and the Kabbalah. Later he studied such Jewish thinkers as Maimonides, Gersonides, and Crescas. After 1651 he read some Renaissance Neoplatonism and stoicism as well as the work of certain Dutch Calvinist scholastics. He also studied Latin, mathematics, and Cartesian philosophy. Not yet 24 years old, Spinoza rejected traditional interpretations of Scripture and thus deviated from Jewish orthodoxy. In 1656 he was expelled from the synagogue at Amsterdam.

Supporting himself by grinding lenses for optical instruments, Spinoza stayed for a period of time in the vicinity of Amsterdam, where he gave private lessons and carried on a wide correspondence. In 1660 he went to Rijnsburg, near Leiden, where he began his correspondence with Henry Oldenburg, secretary of the Royal Society in London. In 1664 he settled in Voorsburg near The Hague, where he vainly sought solitude and tranquillity, but in 1671 he moved to The Hague itself. In order not to compromise his freedom of thought and speech, he refused a chair at the University of Heidelberg 2 years later. By now he was famous and, among others, even Gottfried Wilhelm von Leibniz came to visit him. He died of tuberculosis, a disease made worse by the dust from his lens grinding.

Works. During his lifetime Spinoza published only one work under his own name: a geometry-style exposition of René DESCARTES's *Principia philosophiae* (Principles of Philosophy), with Spinoza's own *Cogitata metaphysica* (Metaphysical Thoughts) appended (1663). His *Tractatus theologico-politicus* (Theological-Political Treatise) was published anonymously in 1670. Spinoza's *Opera posthuma* (Posthumous Works) appeared shortly after his death in 1677 and included his *Tractatus de emendatione intellectus* (Treatise on the Improvement of Understanding) as well as his definitive work *Ethica ordine geometrico demonstrata* (Ethics Demonstrated in Geometrical Order), which he had completed in draft form by 1665 and had subsequently revised. Translations of these writings include *The Chief Works of Spinoza*, translated by R. H. M. Elwes (2 vols., 1955–56).

Philosophy. Although opinions vary about Spinoza's sources (at his death only 161 volumes were found in his small library), no one can deny the considerable influence of Descartes. Spinoza uses much of Descartes's philosophical vocabulary and definitions, and he often organizes his own thoughts in response to Cartesian problems. He owes to Descartes the idea of a mathematical method that distinguishes his main work, the *Ethics*.

Spinoza's *Ethics* is divided into five parts: "On God," "On the Nature and Origin of the Mind," "On the Nature and Origin of the Emotions," "On Human Bondage," and "On Human Liberty."

Each part follows a rigorous geometrical method, passing through definitions, axioms, and postulates to propositions, demonstrations, corollaries, scholia (biblical exigeses), and lemmata (intermediate theorems). Spinoza had earlier employed the same method in discussing Descartes's *Principles*. The overall aim of the work is to lay out a program for "the perfection of human nature."

In part 1, Spinoza defines God as the only true cause and the unique substance, outside of which "no other substance can be given or even conceived." Although this one Divine Substance has an infinite number of attributes, humans can know only two: thought and extension. Entailed in each attribute (like the way properties are entailed in the essence of a triangle) is an infinity of particular things, or modes. Again, humans can know only those modes emanating from the attributes of thought and extension. Concretely, this concept means that although ideas and bodies appear to be separate things in human experience, they are in fact only aspects of the one Divine Substance.

A basic axiom in the whole unfolding of Spinoza's system states the strict parallelism between the two lines of thought and extension: "The order and connection of ideas is the same as the order and connection of things." As this parallelism develops, a universal necessity is attached to it. Neither in the Divine Substance nor in its attributes or modes is there any room for contingency. What is termed Divine Freedom is simply the absence of external constraint. This determinism emerges in human nature as well; it is nothing more than ignorance of the true causes of an individual's action.

In part 2 human existence is reduced to modes of thought and extension. Descartes's dualism of mind and body is reflected here. Spinoza still sees a dualism, but it is at the level of modes rather than of substance. The mind is a mode of thought and as such it is "a part of the infinite intellect of God." The body is a mode of the Divine extension. In virtue of the parallelism of attributes and their modes, a natural correspondence exists between mind and body in humankind. At the same time, however, no real interaction exists between them. Mind and body are but two aspects, or expressions, of one underlying Divine Substance.

In part 3, Spinoza defines an *affect* as a modification by which the body's power to act is increased or diminished. Affects involve both thought and extension. Human beings are the "adequate cause" (even though ultimately God alone is a cause) of those affects which are actions and the inadequate cause of those which are passions.

In part 4 of the *Ethics*, Spinoza discusses the concept of "human bondage." A natural tendency exists for an individual's passive feelings, or passions, to take control of life and make that individual a slave. The only remedy is to convert passions into actions.

In part 5, Spinoza explains how action is achieved. To the extent that humans understand how everything, including their passion, is a necessary mode of a Divine attribute, they can gain an "adequate idea" of it. As they "clearly and distinctly" understand their passions, they gain power and become a more adequate cause of the passions. The latter become actions, and humans overcome their bondage.

The last stage of human liberation is seeing that "all bodily affections are referred to God." At this stage all passion is transformed into an action that is "the intellectual love of God." This process is the very perfection of human nature, in which humans intuit their oneness with God. It not only liberates and beatifies but also confers upon them a kind of immortality.

During his lifetime Spinoza was a controversial figure, largely because his philosophical pantheism was not widely appreciated in either Jewish or Christian religious circles. His influence then and immediately after his death is not always easy to pinpoint. Although he left no school of disciples, his works were read by Leibniz and others. His popularity increased in the 18th and 19th centuries when he influenced such diverse persons as the French Encyclopedists, Goethe, Coleridge, and even Hegel. Today the depth and rigor of his thought is widely recognized.   JOHN P. DOYLE

Bibliography: Allison, H. E., *Benedict de Spinoza* (1975); Curley, E. M., *Spinoza's Metaphysics* (1969); Freeman, Eugene, and Mandelbaum, Maurice, eds., *Spinoza: Essays in Interpretation* (1973); Grene, M., ed., *Spinoza: A Collection of Critical Essays* (1973); Hampshire, Stuart, *Spinoza* (1951); Kashap, S. P., ed., *Studies in Spinoza* (1972); Kennington, Richard, ed., *The Philosophy of Baruch Spinoza* (1980); Levin, Dan, *Spinoza* (1970); Roth, Leon, *Spinoza* (1954); Wolfson, H. A., *The Philosophy of Spinoza*, 2 vols. (1934; repr. 1969).

spiny anteater

The New Guinean long-nosed spiny anteater, Z. bruijni, *is a primitive mamma with many reptilelike features.*

Spiny anteaters, or echidnas, are egg-laying mammals making up the family Tachyglossidae in the order Monotremata. They have compact, muscular bodies, short limbs with broad feet and large claws, small ears, a stubby tail, and a long, toothless snout. The short-nosed echidna, *Tachyglossus*, considered as one or two species, ranges from Tasmania and Australia proper into New Guinea. It reaches about 50 cm (19.5 in) in length, plus its short tail, and 6.5 kg (14 lb) in weight. The long-nosed echidna, *Zaglossus*, considered as one or three species, is confined to New Guinea. It attains 66 cm (26 in) in length, plus the short tail, and 10 kg (22 lb) in weight. The echidna's body is covered with coarse hair and barbless spines; males, and some females, have a gland-connected spur on each hind leg, but the function of these spurs is unknown. The echidnas use their powerful claws for digging and are believed to feed largely on termites, ants, and worms. A single, leathery egg is laid in a temporary pouch formed on the female's abdomen. The egg of the short-nosed echidna hatches in about 10 days, and the female's milk oozes onto tufts of hair.

spiny eel

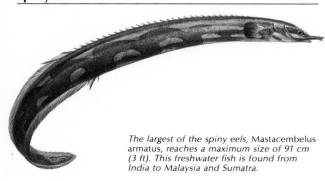

The largest of the spiny eels, Mastacembelus armatus, *reaches a maximum size of 91 cm (3 ft). This freshwater fish is found from India to Malaysia and Sumatra.*

Spiny eels comprise about 50 species of fresh- and brackish-water eellike fishes living throughout the southern half of Africa and Asia. Not related to the true eels, they are placed in the family Mastacembelidae, order Mastacembeliformes. The elongate, compressed fishes reach 80 cm (32 in) in length and bear 17 to 40 isolated spines down the middle of the back, hence their name. A soft dorsal, soft anal, and caudal fin are present. Spiny eels are adept at burying themselves in soft substrates and are popular aquarium fishes. All spiny-eel spe-

cies are in the genus *Mastacembelus* except for the elephant trunk fish, *Macrognathus aculeatus*, whose fleshy trunklike projection, or snout, is somewhat longer than in other spiny eels. Members of a little-known group of deep-sea fish in the family Notocanthidae, order Notocanthiformes, are also called spiny eels.   CAMM SWIFT

spiny-headed worm

Spiny-headed worms are unsegmented parasites that live as larvae in the hemocoels (blood spaces) of insects or crustaceans and as adults in the intestines of vertebrate animals, such as fishes, birds, or mammals. Their cylindrical body has a retractable proboscis ("head") armed with stiff hooks, which gives these parasites the name of their phylum, Acanthocephala. The hooks serve to attach the worms to their hosts. The estimated number of acanthocephalan species varies between 300 and 800, most of which rarely exceed 2.5 cm (1 in) in length; a few kinds may grow to about 50 cm (20 in) long.

spiral

A spiral is a plane curve. It is generated by the endpoint of a radius vector—a vector from a point of origin to the end point—as the radius vector increases (or decreases) in length while rotating about the origin. Many different spirals exist, depending on the exact relation between the length r of the radius vector and the angle θ that it makes with the positive x-axis. If the length is proportional to the angle, the equation in polar coordinates is $r = a\theta$, and the spiral is called an Archimedean spiral for its discoverer.

The logarithmic spiral ($r = e^{a\theta}$) is a shape that occurs in nature in the septa of the nautilus, in the seed pattern of the sunflower, and in pine cones. The logarithmic spiral was discovered by Descartes in 1638. Other important types of spirals are the parabolic spiral ($r^2 = a^2\theta$) and the hyperbolic spirals ($r = a/\theta$).

A helix is a space curve that is the locus of a point moving on the surface of a cylinder or cone so that it makes a constant angle with cross sections of the cylinder, like, for example, the thread of a bolt. Apollonius of Perga was aware of the helix as early as about 200 BC. A spiral staircase would more properly be called a helical staircase.   JOE K. SMITH

Bibliography: Lawrence, J. D., *A Catalog of Special Plane Curves* (1972); Yates, Robert C., *Curves and Their Properties*, rev. ed. (1952; repr. 1974).

spirea   [spy-ree'-uh]

Spireas are about 100 species of deciduous flowering shrubs of the genus *Spiraea* in the rose family, Rosaceae, and are native to the Northern Hemisphere. Their small, white or reddish flowers are typically borne in showy, flat-topped clusters. *S. vanhouttei*, a hybrid of *S. cantoniensis* and *S. trilobata* commonly sold as "bridal wreath," has smooth, arching stems covered with white flowers in late spring.

Spirit of the Laws, The

A major work in political theory, *The Spirit of the Laws* (1748; Eng. trans., 1896–97) by Charles, Baron de MONTESQUIEU is a comparative investigation of the relationship between the legal and political institutions of a given society and the physical and social environmental conditions—geography, climate, demography, economy, religion, mores—in which they are rooted. Of the three categories into which he classified governments—monarchies, republics, and despotisms—Montesquieu himself favored a constitutional monarchy, whose workings in Great Britain, particularly the separation of governmental powers into executive, legislative, and judicial branches, he especially admired. Highly influential in pre-Revolutionary France, *The Spirit of the Laws* exerted an even greater influence on the framing of the American Constitution.

Spirit of St. Louis: see LINDBERGH, CHARLES A.

spiritualism

The belief that after death the human spirit exists and can communicate with the living through mediums or psychics is known as spiritualism. The movement is generally regarded as originating in the United States at Rochester, N.Y., in the 1840s, through the activity of Margaret Fox and her two sisters. Similar manifestations were known, however, in Salem, Mass., during the witchcraft excitement in 1692, as well as in Europe during the French Revolution. Attempts to evoke the spirits of the dead are recorded in ancient Near Eastern and Egyptian sources, and spiritualistic practices have a long history in India, where they are regarded as *bhuta* worship, or worship of the dead. In the early centuries AD the Neoplatonists wrote of the dangers and deceptions involved in attempts to communicate with spirits.

Spiritualistic phenomena include telepathy, clairvoyance, speaking during a trance, supposed communication with disembodied human spirits through seances, materialization of forms, and apparitions. Such physical manifestations as levitation, automatic writing, and poltergeist and ectoplasmic activities also come under the rubric of spiritualism. The aura, which supposedly envelops each living individual, is a colored emanation by which the medium, in observing variations in its hue, can describe the person's needs and personality structure. Among followers of spiritualism have been scientists such as A. R. Wallace, Sir William Crookes, Camille Flammarion, and Robert Dale Owen. Other prominent believers were Arthur Conan Doyle and Stewart Edward White. The phenomena of spiritualism are sometimes regarded as a limited aspect of the more inclusive science of occultism—not widely understood—whose laws explain spiritualistic phenomena.

W. Stainton Moses, a leading 19th-century proponent of spiritualism, admitted that its chief weakness is that "Spiritualists start with a fallacy, viz: that all phenomena are caused by the action of departed human spirits." An understanding of modern spiritualism would probably require an intensive study ranging from the mystical philosophies of the past to modern THEOSOPHY, which, while affirming the genuineness of much of the phenomena, warns of the dangers of psychic infection and offers explanations not accepted by the spiritualists. (See also PARAPSYCHOLOGY.)   JOSEPH R. POPE

Bibliography: Braden, C. S., *These Also Believe* (1949); Hudson, Thompson J., *Law of Psychic Phenomena* (1970); Lawton, George, *The Drama of Life After Death: A Study of the Spiritualist Religion* (1932); Mackintosh, W. H., *The Essence of Spiritualism* (1973).

spirituals

Religious songs of American blacks, especially those songs first brought to public attention in the 19th century, are called spirituals. Inseparable from most aspects of southern black life, they were associated with work, recreation, and religious gatherings. The mixture of African tribal heritage and European folk tradition is not yet clearly understood, but the call-and-response pattern with unison singing clearly points to tribal sources. Pentatonic scales and flatted (or lowered) seventh scale-steps—the characteristic "blue" notes of black music—may be found in the "white spirituals" of the rural South; this suggests that the influence may have been primarily from the blacks to the whites. However, some text references in black spirituals, as well as borrowed tune-fragments, show an assimilation of Anglo-European musical ideas.

Part of the repertory of spirituals is made up of modified tunes that blacks learned at revivals and camp meetings, where they were enthusiastic, but segregated, participants. Early spirituals had in common the repetitions of text, the leader-and-chorus concept that made possible the creation of new songs without rehearsal or prior planning, unison singing, and strong rhythms. Among pieces that became widely known were "Roll, Jordan, Roll," "Go Down, Moses," and "Steal Away to Jesus."

With the establishment of schools for blacks after the Civil War, music instruction brought about the beginning of organized, rehearsed music-making in a style comparable to that of urban whites. The Fisk University Jubilee Singers and groups from Hampton Institute and Tuskegee Institute first brought spirituals to audiences outside the South. The harmonized arrangements they presented lost much of the unique character of the original pieces, but they popularized the idiom, which began to make its way into the repertories of white choral groups and into hymnals.

The spiritual has been generally replaced as a vital, growing expression by a type of GOSPEL MUSIC unique to blacks.
                                            ELWYN A. WIENANDT

Bibliography: Chambers, H. A., ed., *Treasury of Negro Spirituals* (1963); Jackson, G. P., *Spiritual Folk Songs of Early America* (1937) and *White and Negro Spirituals* (1943); Odum, H. W., and Johnson, G. B., *The Negro and His Songs* (1925; repr. 1964); Southern, Eileen, *The Music of Black America: A History* (1971).

Spiro Mound [spy'-roh]

Spiro Mound, near the town of Spiro in eastern Oklahoma, is the site of a series of earthen burial mounds associated with the Mississippian tradition of the MOUND BUILDERS, an ancient North American cultural complex that flourished between 1000 and 1500. The largest mound at Spiro, the Great Temple Mound, measures roughly 55 m (180 ft) in diameter and 24 m (80 ft) in height. Although the site had been extensively looted, formal excavations (1936–38) yielded wooden masks, textiles, stone effigy pipes, engraved copper and shell items, and a monolithic greenstone axe. Many of these objects have come to be identified with the Southern Cult, an assemblage of artifacts that spread rapidly about 1300 among the indigenous peoples of the southeastern United States. Debate continues as to whether this cult was an indigenous development or stimulated by contact with Mesoamerican peoples of northeastern Mexico.

Bibliography: Broun, James, and Hamilton, Henry, *Spiro and Mississippean Antiquities from the McDannald Collection*, The Museum of Fine Arts, Houston (1965).

spirochete [spy'-ruh-keet]

Spirochete, the common name for BACTERIA belonging to the order Spirochaetales, includes species that cause a number of severe diseases in humans and lower animals, such as hemorrhagic JAUNDICE, RELAPSING FEVER, SYPHILIS, and YAWS. Spirochetes are slender, spiral-shaped organisms that differ from eubacteria in that they do not possess rigid cell walls and are therefore flexible. These unicellular organisms vary in length from 2 to 500 microns. They propel themselves usually by spinning around the longitudinal axis of the body. A bundle of very fine fibrils, spirally wound around the organism, has been observed in several types of spirochetes; it appears that propulsion may be aided by contractions of this bundle. Spirochetes are ubiquitous, occurring in soil, in water, in decayed organic matter, and in and on the bodies of animals and plants.

Bibliography: Frobisher, Martin, *Microbiology in Health and Disease*, 13th ed. (1973); Johnson, Russell C., ed., *The Biology of Parasitic Spirochetes* (1976).

Spirogyra [spy-roh-jy'-ruh]

The freshwater species of green ALGAE known as *Spirogyra*, or pond scum, commonly occurs as a floating, light-green mass on the surface of still lakes and ponds. It consists of unbranched filaments having cells that are joined together and form an extensive coil; each cell contains a nucleus and a spiral-shaped chloroplast. *Spirogyra* can reproduce asexually by means of fragmentation and can reproduce sexually by a process of conjugation. During conjugation two adjacent filaments form swellings on the sides of the cells in contact. These swellings enlarge and fuse to form a tubular connection known as a conjugation tube; one cell then migrates in amoeboid fashion through the tube and fuses with another cell, forming a zygote. The zygote forms a thick wall and, after a dormant period, may germinate and develop a new filament.

spirometry: see PULMONARY FUNCTION TEST.

Spirostomum   [spy-rahs'-tuh-muhm]

Spirostomum is a genus of ciliated protozoa in the family Spiromastidea, order Heterotrichida. The largest protozoa common to fresh-water, they are also found in marine environments. *Spirostomum* species are highly contractile, capable of shrinking to one-quarter of normal body length. Member species have a groove (peristome) leading to the mouth (cytostome) and a uniformly ciliated body. *Spirostomum* is distinguished from other heterotrichs by its long cylindrical body.

Spitfire

Designed by Reginald Mitchell, the single-seat, low-wing Spitfire monoplane became the best-known fighter ever built. The first all-metal British fighter, it entered Royal Air Force service in 1938 and was the companion of the Hawker HURRI-CANE in the Battle of Britain (1940). Initially, in the Mk. IA model, the Rolls-Royce Merlin engine was used, having power ratings from 1,030 hp upward, and the elliptical wings (spanning 11.33 m/36 ft 10 in) were armed with eight .303 Browning machine guns. Improvements on the Spitfire design culminated in the Mk. 24 model (1946), and the Seafire, which was developed for use from aircraft carriers of the Fleet Air Arm. The Spitfire was also used to pioneer unarmed photographic reconnaissance.   PETER M. H. LEWIS

Bibliography: Price, Alfred, *Spitfire: A Documentary History* (1979) and *Spitfire at War* (1977); Robertson, Bruce, *Spitfire: The Story of a Famous Fighter* (1960).

The British Spitfire, flown by the RAF in many versions, was the only Allied fighter in continuous production throughout World War II. The combat effectiveness of the Spitfire was a major factor in thwarting German air attacks during the Battle of Britain (1940).

Spitsbergen: see SVALBARD.

Spitteler, Carl   [shpit'-el-ur]

A Swiss writer of epic poetry, stories, novels, dramas, and essays, Carl Georg Friedrich Spitteler, b. Apr. 24, 1845, d. Dec. 29, 1924, won the Nobel Prize for literature in 1919. He is best known for two long epics. The first, *Prometheus and Epimetheus* (1881; Eng. trans., 1931), reflecting the pessimism of Schopenhauer and the romanticism of Nietzsche, reformulates the Prometheus myth in free rhythmic prose. His greatest work, *Olympischer Frühling* (Olympian Spring, 1900–05, 2d version, 1910), presents an even darker picture of the cosmos. His psychoanalytical novel, *Imago* (1906), was highly regarded by Freud. Spitteler's criticism of German nationalism greatly influenced opinions in his homeland during World War I.   MARILYN SIBLEY FRIES

Bibliography: Natan, Alex, ed., *German Men of Letters*, vol. 5 (1969); Seferis, Giorgos, *Mikhail Sholokhov, Henryk Sienkiewicz, and Carl Spitteler* (1971).

spittlebug

Spittlebugs, family Cercipodae, are not true bugs; they are so named because they live as nymphs in a frothy, spittlelike mass that they secrete. They leave this spittle upon achieving adulthood and are active jumping insects called froghoppers

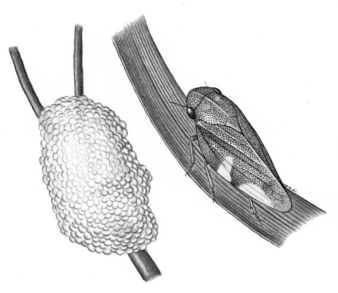

The European spittlebug, Aphrophora alvi, *encloses itself in a frothy mass of spittle* (left) *as protection from enemies and the hot summer sun. An adult spittlebug is known as a froghopper.*

because of their vague resemblance to tiny frogs. Most adults are 5–10 mm (0.2–0.4 in) in length. Spittlebugs feed by sucking the sap from plants, and one species, *Philaenus spumarius*, often does considerable damage to such field crops as clovers.   DONALD J. BORROR

spitz   [spits]

The spitzes are a group of dogs characterized by a dense coat, a wedge-shaped head, erect ears, and a bushy tail carried curled over the back. They range in size from breeds such as the little pomeranian through medium-sized forms such as the Norwegian elkhound to large varieties such as the Japanese akita; the Belgian schipperke, which has a relatively short coat and is often tailless, is sometimes regarded as a modified spitz. Only a few of the spitz group are actually called spitzes: these include the German wolf spitz, the Finnish spitz, and the American spitz; the last, now more correctly known as the American eskimo, was once a well-known breed or type in North America. Broadly, the spitz group includes the northern sled dogs, such as the Alaskan malamute, as well as the more typical spitzes, such as the Dutch keeshond. Some authorities separate the northern dogs from the others on the basis of physiological and behavior differences, including the northern dogs' greater tolerance to cold and their tendency not to bark.   EDWIN E. ROSENBLUM

Bibliography: Hart, Ernest H., *How to Raise and Train a Spitz* (1969).

Spitz, Mark

Mark Andrew Spitz, b. Modesto, Calif., Feb. 10, 1950, is the American swimmer who won a record seven gold medals at the 1972 Olympic Games. No athlete in any event had ever dominated a single Olympics as did Spitz. He gave no indication of greatness in the 1968 Olympics when he won a silver and a bronze medal. In 1972, however, he won the 100- and 200-m (109.4- and 218.7-yd) freestyle and butterfly events, and was a member of the winning 4 × 100- and 4 × 200-m freestyle relay teams and the 4 × 100-m medley relay team. Spitz set 32 world and 38 U.S. swimming records during his career. He retired in 1972 to become a sports commentator.

Bibliography: Olsen, James, *Mark Spitz* (1974); Stambler, Irwin, *Speed Kings* (1973).

Spitzer, Lyman, Jr.   [spit'-sur]

The American astronomer Lyman Spitzer, Jr., b. Toledo, Ohio, June 26, 1914, is especially known for his early work on the feasibility of controlled fusion energy. A graduate of Yale (1935) and Princeton (1938) universities, Spitzer served as professor at Yale and headed the department of astrophysical sciences at Princeton (1947–79). His interest in the physics of plasmas existing in space led him to suggest that such highly ionized gases might be artificially confined by a magnetic field in the laboratory and raised to temperatures and densities high enough to yield fusion power, one of the chief methods still pursued. Spitzer also pioneered the use of artificial satellites for astronomical research.   STEVEN J. DICK

spleen

The spleen, the largest organ of the lymphatic system, is closely associated with the circulatory system. It is located below the diaphragm, behind and to the left of the stomach. The spleen is a richly vascular organ and has a great number of lymphocytes and reticuloendothelial cells, necessary for filtration of cell waste products and worn-out red blood cells as well as for the manufacture of antibodies and certain blood cells. It varies in size and weight according to the amount of blood it contains in storage and its immune functions.

The organ comprises white pulp, red pulp, and marginal zones. The white pulp consists of periarterial lymphatic sheaths and lymph follicles. The lymphatic sheaths, loose meshes of tissue surrounding a central artery, are composed predominantly of small lymphocytes. Red pulp, which is rich in erythrocytes and granulocytes from the blood as well as lymphocytes and macrophages, consists of thin-walled sinuses and splenic cords (cords of Bilroth). Marginal zones receive terminal branches of central arteries and contain blood cells from the arterial vessels, macrophages, and lymphocytes. All animals, except for humans, have smooth muscle surrounding the spleen, which contracts and expels blood from the reservoir during periods of blood loss.

The spleen has trabeculae that extend inward from its surrounding capsule and form an extensive network. Blood vessels, nerves, and lymphatic vessels enter the spleen at the hilum, an indented area on the surface, and course along the trabeculae. The blood vessels end in capillaries and open into the red pulp, and the blood then is collected by veins either slowly through splenic cords and sinuses and subsequently into larger veins or by way of more direct vascular shunts. Splenic nerves, part of the sympathetic nervous system,

course through the spleen in association with blood vessels. Lymphatic vessels are restricted to the capsule and trabeculae and do not extend farther into the parenchyma.

In adult humans the spleen functions as an immunologically active organ and as a filter for white and red blood cells. Lymphocytes as well as plasma cells are manufactured in the white pulp, and circulating antigens can be stored. Antibodies are also produced in the white pulp in response to antigens. The filtration system of the marginal zone and the red pulp allows macrophages to ingest cellular waste transported into the spleen by the blood. When the worn-out red blood cells are destroyed by the spleen, the iron is recycled to make new hemoglobin, and other products are converted into bilirubin, a pigment transported to the liver and later incorporated into bile.

The red pulp is a reservoir for newly mature erythrocytes and blood platelets and, to a lesser extent, for lymphocytes and monocytes. In a developing fetus, the spleen is a major organ of blood production, but this function normally does not continue after birth.   ROBERT A. JOYCE

Bibliography: Battisto, Jack R., and Streilein, Wayne, *Immuno-Aspects of the Spleen* (1976); Enriquez, Pablo, and Neiman, Richard S., *The Pathology of the Spleen* (1976); Lennert, Karl, ed., *Spleen: Structure, Function, Pathology, Clinical Aspects, Therapy* (1970); Macpherson, A. I. S., et al., *The Spleen* (1973).

splenomegaly [splen-oh-meg'-uh-lee]

Splenomegaly is abnormal enlargement of the spleen, an organ lying in the left upper abdomen that functions as a filter for damaged and aged blood cells. If diseases increase the number of abnormal cells in the blood the spleen enlarges, as in various inherited red cell disorders such as sickle-cell anemia, thalassemia, or hereditary spherocytosis. Splenic blood drains into the liver through the hepatic portal vein. Therefore, cirrhosis and other diseases of the liver, in which resistance to blood flow is increased, may also result in splenomegaly. Chronic infections, such as malaria or tuberculosis, may also cause the spleen to enlarge. Other causes are malignancies directly involving the spleen—leukemia and lymphoma—or cancer arising in other organs and spreading to the spleen.   DONALD L. RUCKNAGEL

Split

Split is the main city of Dalmatia, the western region in the Croatian republic of Yugoslavia, and the second largest port of the country. Located on the Adriatic Sea about 260 km (162 mi) south of Zagreb, the city has a population of 151,875 (1971).

The well-preserved old town grew around DIOCLETIAN'S PALACE, where the Roman emperor retired in 305 and died in 313. The palace is one of the finest examples of Roman architecture. The modern Split spreads out around the palace and along the Adriatic shore. The city's two harbors, rebuilt after their destruction in World War II, have deep, well-sheltered berths. The economy is based on shipping, shipbuilding, and the manufacturing of cement, plastics, and chemicals. Split is also a popular tourist resort. It has three universities, an oceanographic institute, and several museums.

Colonized by the Romans in the 1st century AD, the site was settled by Croats in about 639. During the 9th century Split was a major Byzantine city. It was later ruled by Venice (1420–1797). Except for a period of French control (1808–13), Split was dominated by Austria from 1797 until it became part of Yugoslavia in 1918.

split personality: see SCHIZOPHRENIA.

Spock, Benjamin

Dr. Benjamin McLane Spock, b. New Haven, Conn., May 2, 1903, was the first person to complete professional training both as a pediatrician and as a psychiatrist. Dr. Spock is famous both for his book on child care and for his leadership in the peace movement. *The Commonsense Book of Baby*

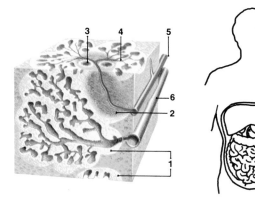

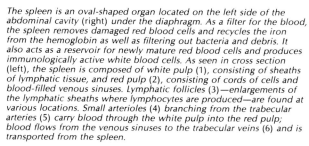

The spleen is an oval-shaped organ located on the left side of the abdominal cavity (right) under the diaphragm. As a filter for the blood, the spleen removes damaged red blood cells and recycles the iron from the hemoglobin as well as filtering out bacteria and debris. It also acts as a reservoir for newly mature red blood cells and produces immunologically active white blood cells. As seen in cross section (left), the spleen is composed of white pulp (1), consisting of sheaths of lymphatic tissue, and red pulp (2), consisting of cords of cells and blood-filled venous sinuses. Lymphatic follicles (3)—enlargements of the lymphatic sheaths where lymphocytes are produced—are found at various locations. Small arterioles (4) branching from the trabecular arteries (5) carry blood through the white pulp into the red pulp; blood flows from the venous sinuses to the trabecular veins (6) and is transported from the spleen.

Benjamin Spock greatly influenced post–World War II child-rearing practices with The Commonsense Book of Baby and Child Care (1946). Spock's controversial association with antinuclear and antiwar movements during the 1960s culminated with his arrest and conviction (1968; overturned, 1969) for violating selective service laws by encouraging drafted men to resist conscription.

and Child Care (1946) was a dramatic contrast to earlier child-care books that had favored rigid feeding schedules and had warned against showing a child too much affection. Spock's book was reassuring in its support of maternal tenderness. It also answered practical questions not even addressed by earlier works. Because his emphasis on flexibility was misinterpreted by some as permitting children to do as they please, in later editions he indicated the limits of permissiveness. More copies (more than 30 million) of the book have been sold than of any other book except the Bible.

Spock had no strong interest in politics until President Kennedy's 1962 announcement that the United States had to resume nuclear testing to stay ahead of the USSR. Concluding that neither power would stop testing if it were behind, Spock foresaw a nuclear buildup leading to an accident or war. He joined the National Committee for a Sane Nuclear Policy (SANE), launching his membership with an ad that warned of radioactive contamination of milk and its effects on children. After campaigning for Lyndon Johnson, Spock felt betrayed by the escalation of the Vietnam War. Spock began to lead peace demonstrations and ran for the presidency in 1972 as a candidate of the People's party.

Bibliography: Bloom, Lynn Z., *Doctor Spock: Biography of a Conservative Radical* (1972); Michalek, Irene R., *When Mercy Seasons Justice: The Spock Trial* (1972).

spodumene: see PYROXENE.

Spohr, Louis [shpohr]

The German composer, violinist, and conductor Louis (or Ludwig) Spohr, b. Apr. 5, 1784, d. Oct. 22, 1859, was one of the leading musical figures of his time. He toured widely throughout Europe—frequently visiting London—as a violinist and conductor, being one of the earliest, if not the first, to use a baton. Although conservative as a composer, he was an early champion of the operas of Richard Wagner. From 1822 to 1857 he was music director at the court of Kassel. He composed much music in a mellifluous romantic style. His greatest success was the opera *Jessondra* (1823), which was performed until the end of the 19th century. His other works include violin concertos, symphonies, oratorios, sacred music, and many chamber music pieces.

spoils system: see PATRONAGE.

Spokan [spoh-kan']

The Spokan are a North American Indian tribe of Interior Salish linguistic stock that traditionally occupied territory along the lower part of the Spokane River and its tributaries. Linguistically and culturally they differed little from neighbors such as the FLATHEAD and the OKANOGAN, and although they differed in language from the Sahaptin-speaking Wanapam and Palouse to their south, they were culturally similar to those tribes also. All these groups relied heavily for subsistence on salmon of several species that annually ascended the Columbia River and its tributaries in vast numbers. Spokan bands residing on smaller streams near headwaters of river systems hunted land game more than their downstream kin. In the 1970s the Spokan numbered over 1,400 members, of whom about 600 were living on a reservation in Washington State.   PHILIP DRUCKER

Bibliography: Manring, B. F., *The Conquest of the Coeur d'Alenes, Spokanes and Palouses* (1912; repr. 1975); Ruby, Robert H., *The Spokane Indians: Children of the Sun* (1970); Wynecoop, David C., *Children of the Sun: A History of the Spokane Indians* (1969).

Spokane [spoh-kan']

Spokane is a city on the Spokane River in eastern Washington. The seat of Spokane County, the city has a population of 176,900 (1979 est.). Located on a falls of the river, Spokane is the industrial, commercial, and transportation hub of the surrounding agricultural and mining region. Nearby are GRAND COULEE DAM and gold, silver, uranium, and copper fields. Industries that have developed in the city are lumber, aluminum, and electrical equipment manufacturing and grain processing. The city is the seat of Gonzaga University (1887) and Whitworth College (1890).

A trading post of the North West Company was built on Spokane's site in 1810, and a settlement was established in 1871. The community called Spokane Falls was laid out in 1878 and was incorporated with the coming of the Northern Pacific Railway (1881). A fire in 1889 destroyed most of the city, but it was quickly rebuilt and renamed Spokane in 1891.

Spoleto Festival [spoh-let'-oh]

The Spoleto Festival of the Two Worlds was begun in 1958 by the composer Gian Carlo Menotti, who resigned as artistic director in 1968 but remains the festival's guiding spirit. Menotti has given various accounts of his aims; from the outset, however, he has sought to draw to the small Italian town both aspiring and seasoned practitioners of all the arts and to provide conditions favorable to their efforts. The first festival, lasting 3 weeks, offered performances of Verdi's *Macbeth*, conducted by Thomas Schippers and directed by Luchino Visconti, and O'Neill's *A Moon for the Misbegotten*, directed by José Quintero. Noteworthy events in later years include readings (1965–67) by Ezra Pound, productions of plays by Edward Albee, Eugene Ionesco, Tennessee Williams, Leroi Jones, and Harold Pinter, and Saul Bellow, a 1965 performance of Mozart's *Don Giovanni* with sets and costumes by Henry Moore, and visits from John Cranko's Stuttgart Ballet and Maurice Bejart's Ballet of the Twentieth Century. Midday chamber concerts, underwritten by Alice Tully and directed by Charles Wadsworth, are a regular feature of the festival. Many of Menotti's own works also have been heard.

Since 1977 the festival has been literally "of two worlds" because of the establishment of the Spoleto Festival, U.S.A. in Charleston, S.C.   LAWRENCE FUCHSBERG

Bibliography: Gruen, John, *Menotti* (1978); Vitiello, Gregory, *Spoleto Viva* (1977).

spondee: see VERSIFICATION.

spondylitis [spahn-duh-ly'-tis]

Spondylitis, a progressive disease of the spine, exists in two forms, ankylosing and tuberculous spondylitis. Ankylosing spondylitis is a disease of unknown cause, but with evidence of genetic transmission, occurring nine times more frequently in males than in females. It is a progressive form of arthritis and begins in the lower back—a common cause of pain in men in their twenties and thirties. The disease is characterized by degeneration of vertebral joints, calcium and bone deposition in associated ligaments, and inflammation of surrounding tissues. Vertebrae tend to fuse as a result of bone deposition between them (ankylosis). Associated compression of spinal nerves causes pain to radiate to other areas. As the disease spreads up the spine, substantial stiffening and deformity can develop over a period of 10 years or more. Patients are treated with anti-inflammatory drugs for the symptoms and exercise programs for maintenance of correct posture.

Tuberculous spondylitis, or Pott's disease, is caused by tuberculosis in a vertebra, where the infection can destroy intervertebral discs and spread to adjacent vertebrae. Infectious agents other than tuberculosis can produce similar effects. Treatment consists of antibiotic therapy and sometimes surgical drainage of abscesses and fusion of affected vertebrae.

PETER L. PETRAKIS

sponge

Sponges comprise about 10,000 known species of aquatic, multicellular animals placed in four classes in the invertebrate phylum Porifera. Species of sponges, an ancient and flourishing group, occur worldwide at all depths of marine water; there are only about 20 species of freshwater sponges. Sponges live in colonies attached to the ocean floor or to other objects. The bath, or commercial, sponges were once commercially valuable, but they have for the most part been replaced by synthetic sponges. Sponges show striking powers of regeneration. Dissociated cells can quickly reaggregate to form a new, perfectly functional sponge.

Apparently, very early in their evolution sponges chanced upon a combination of activities and organization very different from those used by any other group of multicellular animals. Their entire organization is devoted to filtering microorganisms and dissolved organic matter from the water, but they do this without forming discrete tissues and organs. Instead, the whole mass of the sponge is penetrated by innumerable tubes and chambers (the aquiferous system) through which water flows as a result of the actions of groups of specialized cells, the choanocytes. These cells each bear a single flagellum surrounded by a tall collar of fine cytoplasmic projections (microvilli). The beating of the flagella of groups of

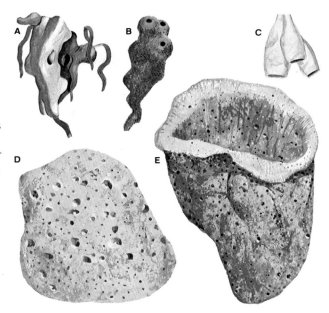

A sponge is classified according to the chemical component that constitutes its skeleton. A breadcrumb sponge, Halichondria panica (A), has a skeleton (B) of rigid, supportive silicon spicules, which keep the water canals open and enable the sponge to grow to a relatively large size. A purse sponge, Grantia compressa (C), is a calcareous sponge, whose skeleton comprises calcium carbonate spicules. Two advanced and commercially important sponges, Hippospongia equina (D) and Euspongia officinalis (E), have skeletons that contain a network of spongin, which is an elastic protein fiber.

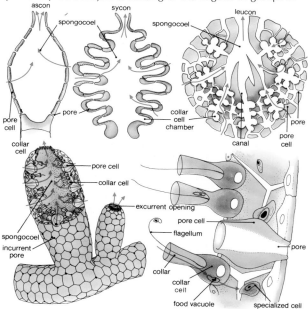

Sponges range in body structure from simple to highly complex. Their anatomy permits water (blue arrows) to flow through, into, and out of the body. The most primitive type of sponge, an ascon, has smooth walls and no canals. A sycon's body is furrowed into simple canals, where water first passes before entering the spongocoel, or body cavity. A leucon, or advanced sponge, has numerous canals and cavities and performs more specialized functions than the simpler sponges. (Lower left) Water enters through pores and passes through collar cells, where microorganisms are trapped. (Detail, lower right) A food vacuole digests the microscopic animals before transporting nutrients to a specialized cell, which supplies the body with energy.

choanocytes raises the water pressure inside the chambers whose walls are formed of choanocytes. Because of the geometry of the openings in the chamber walls and of the ducts connected to these openings, the pumping pressure of the chambers draws water in one direction through the sponge.

Water enters the aquiferous system through minute, incurrent pores (ostia) between the flattened cells (pinacocyte) forming the sponge's outer surface, passes through chambers and branching ducts of decreasing diameter, and enters the choanocyte chambers. Here small particles and large molecules are trapped on the tubular "grids" of the collar microvilli and engulfed by the choanocytes, which ingest food particles and absorb oxygen.

The filtered water passes out of the chambers via anastamosing ducts and cavities to one or a few large exhalant openings—the oscula—from which it is ejected with considerable velocity.

The sponges show a great variation in size and form, from sheets or irregular mats of tubes to arborescent, vase, and barrel shapes. They range in length from a few centimeters to several meters. These varied forms can be understood largely in terms of their need to eject water a safe distance so it will not be inhaled again, because the expelled water is depleted of food and oxygen and contains waste products. A liter volume of sponge tissue can filter between 36 and 125 liters of water per hour.

Between the cavities and tubes of the aquiferous system lie cells of several forms and functions surrounded by their products. Among the cell types of the mesoglea (middle zone of cells) are the amebocytes, which store food from the choanocytes and carry it to other cells. Digestion occurs within the food vacuoles of the amebocytes. Pigmented granules in the amebocytes of some sponges give them a brilliant color. Archaeocytes, another cell type, are capable of dividing and of transforming into any of the other cell types, including the scleroblasts that form the supporting mineral skeleton of most sponges.

All sponges have an organic skeleton in the form of strands of a special protein, spongin, which is similar to the collagen of other multicellular animals. However, the great majority of sponges also possess a mineral skeleton in the form of spicules of calcium carbonate (calcite) or silica. The spicules vary greatly in length and are laid down inside single scleroblasts or between groups of scleroblasts. The spicules are woven together, with a "cement" of spongin, to form elaborate three-dimensional bracing structures. Their enormous range of size and form and pattern of integration is relied upon greatly for the classification and identification of sponges.

Members of the class Calcarea, a minority of sponges, have calcite spicules. Nearly all of the remaining majority of sponges have silica spicules, either basically six-rayed (class Hexactinellida or Triaxonida) or basically four-rayed and single-rayed (class Demospongea). A very small number of species (class Sclerospongea) have both calcite and silica components in their skeletons.

Although adult sponges are always immobile, encrusting or boring into rocks, rooted in silt, or borne high on stalks, most have motile, minute larvae that escape from the parent and swim or creep freely by the beating of their outer layer of cilia. They do not feed during this solely dispersal stage. Most sponges are hermaphroditic, eggs and sperm arising primarily from amebocytes. Sperm enter sponges with the water current, are carried to the eggs in the mesoglea by amebocytes or choanocytes, and fertilization occurs *in situ*. Resting gemmules and swimming larvae, however, are also produced by asexual reproduction.   WILLIAM G. FRY

Bibliography: Berquist, Patricia R., *Sponges* (1978); Harrison, Frederick, and Cowden, Ronald R., eds., *Aspects of Sponge Biology* (1976); Jacobson, Morris, and Pang, Rosemary, *Wonders of Sponges* (1976).

spontaneous combustion

Spontaneous combustion, the self-ignition of certain substances, is initiated by slow oxidation. If the heat of the oxidation reaction cannot be dissipated, the temperature of the substance rises until it reaches its kindling point and bursts into flame. The chemical element phosphorus, for example, ignites in air so readily that it must be stored under water. Coal is also subject to spontaneous combustion and is generally stored in shallow piles to dissipate the heat.

Spontaneous combustion represents a safety hazard in the home and business. Rags impregnated with volatile substances such as oil, paint, or furniture polish are one such hazard unless destroyed, washed, or kept in a metal container with a tight-fitting metal lid. Hay stored in a barn also should be thoroughly dry, because heat is generated in moist hay by the oxidizing action of microorganisms. As the temperature rises, air takes over the oxidation process, increasing the temperature until ignition occurs.   STEPHEN FLEISHMAN

See also: COMBUSTION.

spontaneous generation

Spontaneous generation is the name of the theory that life develops spontaneously from nonliving matter. The belief arose in ancient times as a way of explaining why certain living creatures are commonly found in association with certain inanimate materials—for example, maggots on decaying meat, mice in garbage, and insects in damp hay. Scientific observation, particularly by Francesco Redi, had practically demolished the theory by the 18th century; bacteria, however, were still thought to arise spontaneously from the media in which they were found. This idea was finally disproved in the 1860s, when Louis PASTEUR demonstrated that bacteria would not appear in a nutrient solution if it were sterilized by boiling and if air subsequently entering the flask containing the solution were filtered to remove airborne bacteria.

Although it is now known that all present life on Earth is the result of the reproduction of preexisting life, many scientists accept a modified theory of spontaneous generation to explain the origin of life itself. The theory holds that billions of years ago LIFE originated in the oceans as the result of

spontaneous aggregations of dissolved organic molecules, which in turn arose from inorganic chemical reactions energized by ultraviolet light, electrical discharges, and heat.
                    PETER L. PETRAKIS

Bibliography: Conant, James B., ed., *Pasteur and Tyndall's Study of Spontaneous Generation* (1953); Farley, John, *The Spontaneous Generation Controversy from Descartes to Oparin* (1977).

Spontini, Gaspare   [spohn-tee′-nee]

Gaspare Luigi Pacifico Spontini, b. Nov. 14, 1774, d. Jan. 4, 1851, was the leading composer of French opera in the flamboyant and often melodramatic style dominant in Paris during the time of the Revolution and First Empire; he was Napoleon's favorite composer. Spontini was trained in Naples and wrote his first opera for Rome in 1796. In 1803 he went to Paris to compose opera buffa for the Italian theater there. Soon, however, he was encouraged to follow the grand French style of Cherubini, Lesueur, and Méhul. In 1807 he produced his acknowledged masterpiece, *La Vestale*, an immediate triumph and one of the few operas of the type still in the repertoire today. Although none of Spontini's later operas had such lasting success, they were eminent in their day and enabled Spontini to obtain important positions, including court composer (1814–19) for Louis XVIII and (1820–41) for King Friedrich Wilhelm III.   JOHN WALTER HILL

Bibliography: Dent, E., *The Rise of Romantic Opera*, ed. by W. Dean (1976); Grout, D., *A Short History of Opera*, 2d ed. (1965).

Spoon River Anthology

A collection of poems by Edgar Lee MASTERS, the *Spoon River Anthology* (1915) sensitively reveals the secret feelings and conflicts that have characterized the lives of the inhabitants of Spoon River, a small midwestern town. Masters tells these secrets through epitaphs that often contrast strikingly with the actual epitaphs on the townspeople's graves. Many of the epitaphs are interrelated, thus providing the histories of several families and revealing Spoon River's social structure.

Bibliography: Blout, Harry L., *Spoon River Legacy* (1969); Flanagan, John Theodore, *Edgar Lee Masters* (1974).

spoonbill

The roseate spoonbill, A. ajaja, a strikingly colored long-legged water bird, uses its broad bill to catch fish and shrimp in shallow waters. Once nearly exterminated by those hunting it for its fancy plumage, it is now protected by U.S. law, and its numbers have increased.

Spoonbills are any of several large wading birds, family Threskiornithidae, named for their broadly flattened bills. The colorful roseate spoonbill, *Ajaia ajaja,* is about 80 cm (32 in) long and ranges from Argentina to the U.S. Gulf Coast. The adult roseate is mostly pink, with traces of crimson on the shoulders and white on the neck and back. The spoonbill breeds in colonies, and the female lays two to three eggs. The white spoonbill, *Platalea leucorodia,* of the Old World acquires a bushy, ocher crest during the breeding season. Other species are found in Asia, Africa, and Australia.   WILLIAM F. SANDFORD

spoonworm

A spoonworm is an unsegmented invertebrate that lives in a U-shaped tube made in mud or sand along seacoasts. The body is sausage-shaped, and a soft, often spoon-shaped (hence the name), proboscis (snout) extends for feeding on microscopic organic matter: it contracts when the animal is disturbed. Mostly sedentary, spoonworms range from only a few millimeters to almost 60 cm (24 in) in length. Nearly 60 species of spoonworms comprise the family Echiuroidea, often termed Echiura.   LORUS J. AND MARGERY MILNE

spore

Spores are nondividing cells, produced by many plants and some protozoans, that are either modified asexual reproductive cells or cells characteristically resistant to adverse environmental conditions. The reproductive spores of ferns or fungi, for example, are produced by vegetatively growing cells and serve the reproductive function by their dispersability. These spores may be wind-blown or may be carried by insects and, under the proper conditions, can germinate and give rise to another generation of growing and dividing cells.

Many types of microorganisms form spores modified to survive a harsh environment. Many genera of bacteria form spores, and some have been intensively studied. The genera *Bacillus* and *Clostridium* form an endospore that is one of the most resistant forms of life known; many can withstand boiling or freezing for long periods of time, desiccation and indefinite storage, various types of radiation, toxic chemicals, and physical disruption. The endospores are formed by healthy cells whose growth has been limited by nutritional circumstances through a complex reorganization of the cell's structure.

The mechanisms by which the spore so dramatically survives are not completely clear but are probably related to the lowered water content of the cell. Spores' resistance to such a variety of harsh environmental conditions creates an important practical problem in industrial situations where the continued sterility of a product is necessary. The food industry, for example, has long been concerned with such spore-forming organisms as *Clostridium botulinum,* the organism that produces the deadly botulism toxin.   MARTIN DWORKIN

Bibliography: Gould, G. W., and Hurst, A., eds., *The Bacterial Spore* (1969); Sussman, Alfred S., and Halvorson, Harlyn O., *Spores, Their Dormancy and Germination* (1966); Weber, Darrell J., and Hess, W. M., *The Fungal Spore: Form and Function* (1976).

Sporozoa   [spohr-uh-zoh'-uh]

The Sporozoa are a large subphylum of microscopic, one-celled animals (see PROTOZOA) that live as parasites inside various animals. Its members reproduce asexually by spores, hence the name *Sporozoa.* Sporozoa are immotile and feed by absorbing nutrients from the parasitized host. Many sporozoans are relatively harmless, but some cause serious diseases and are thus of great medical importance. Members of the genus *Plasmodium* are agents of MALARIA. Other sporozoans cause diseases in poultry, quail, sheep, foxes, mink, and other animals.

Sporozoans have a complicated life cycle, usually alternating between sexual and asexual stages of reproduction. All types of animals have sporozoan parasites, and each species is usually restricted to one or two host animals in which different stages of its life cycle may occur. If the sporozoans are not transferred from one type of host to the next, their life cycle cannot continue. Usually, in the asexual phase sporozo-

ans can live only inside a specific vertebrate animal, whereas in the sexual phase they can live only in an invertebrate. In the case of *Plasmodium* the vertebrate host is a human, where the organisms live in the bloodstream, attacking the red blood cells. The invertebrate host is the *Anopheles* mosquito, which picks up the male and female gametocytes by biting an infected person. In the mosquito's body, gametocytes mature into gametes that fuse to form a zygote. Sexual division occurs, and the resulting cells, called sporozoites (spore stage), migrate to the mosquito's salivary glands. When the mosquito bites a human, the sporozoites are injected into the new host's bloodstream, and the cycle begins again.

Bibliography: Barnes, Robert D., *Invertebrate Zoology,* 3d ed. (1974); Brock, Thomas D., *The Biology of Microorganisms,* 3d ed. (1979); Grell, K. G., *Protozoology,* 2d ed. (1973); Kudo, Richard, *Protozoology,* 5th ed. (1977).

sports, history of

An ancient Roman sculpture of two wrestlers suggests the antiquity of the sport. Early references to various holds used in wrestling appear in Egyptian tomb art dating from c.2530 BC. Wrestling was a major event of olympiads in ancient Greece. (Uffizi, Florence.)

Sports, which can be broadly defined as physical exertion for recreation or in competition, date so far back that modern historians cannot determine with certainty what the first sport or sports were. A reasonable assumption is that sports began the first time a person used physical energy under recreational conditions. Such sport could well have been fishing or hunting for pleasure or merely engaging in a playful demonstration of physical prowess.

Modern sports, however, are often thoroughly organized, with complicated sets of rules; sophisticated equipment; precise timing, measuring, and scoring devices; spectators; and extensive coverage by various media. Much of the development in sports, no matter how old such physical pastimes are, has taken place in the past 2 centuries, and the preponderance of this growth in sports has occurred in the last 50 years.

Evidence obtained from archaeological excavations indicates that the Sumerians practiced WRESTLING as a sport about 5,000 years ago. Wrestling was essentially a survival skill that required practice in order to perfect various holds and grips. That it became a sport was almost inevitable. The same may be said for fishing or hunting: these were activities that acquired the status of a sport the first time they were undertaken for fun rather than for self-preservation.

From a historical standpoint the ancient Olympic Games, first recorded in 776 BC, could be called the birth of organized sports. Although the ancient Olympic Games were recorded in writing and statues in honor of the winners were erected at the Olympic site, serving as an additional historical record, even those games have an undetermined origin that historians believe may antedate 776 BC by at least 2 centuries.

When the Olympic Games were revived in AD 1896 (they had been abolished in AD 394), Olympic accomplishments were precisely recorded using tape measures, stop watches, photographs, and newspaper reports. In 1896 sports were on the verge of a true golden age, far surpassing anything in the approximately 49 centuries since the Sumerians were believed to have wrestled for fun. Sports in the 20th century eventually became a lucrative business, often involving highly professional athletes playing at an increasingly competitive level. With industrial progress giving people more and more free time, sports came to be an important diversion for greater numbers of people.

The development of sports from the end of the ancient Olympics to the mass sports events of the 20th century was a slow process, however. The conquest of Greece by Rome almost brought to an end the early golden age of sports. The Romans, although initially scornful of sports, placated the Greeks by allowing them to continue their Olympic Games with the religious connotations of the games left intact. The Romans, in fact, later popularized sports of their own, such as gladiatorial battles and chariot racing, and built coliseums in which to stage the contests.

(Left) *Two female athletes demonstrate gymnastic techniques in this Roman mosaic. It is likely that early forms of gymnastics were practiced more for entertainment than as competitive events. (Piazza Amerina, Florence.)*

(Below) *Chariot racing, which developed as a military art, became one of the most popular sports in ancient Rome.*

Interest in sports dwindled under the Christian dogmatism of the Middle Ages. By AD 1200, however, sports for entertainment and diversion reemerged on a small scale in some countries. The French, for instance, had a hockeylike game called *la soule* in which teams used sticks to knock a ball across an opponent's goal line. Like many rough games of that era, *la soule* was suppressed (1369) by authorities. The interest such early sports generated led to other sports that used a ball, such as TENNIS, which rose to popularity in the 1400s.

The rise of sports in general in England merely whetted people's appetites for more sports. Records show that an unorganized track-and-field competition was held in England in 1510. Mary, Queen of Scots, because of her own interest in GOLF, popularized the game during her reign (1542–67). Her son, James I (r. 1603–25) of England, lifted the ban on football (the ancestor of modern soccer) in 1603 and openly endorsed other organized sporting activities. Queen Anne (r. 1702–14) of England introduced the first sweepstakes in horse racing in 1714. Continental Europe also fostered many sports during this postmedieval era that led to the surge of sports in the 1800s.

What differentiated pre-19th-century sports from those that followed was organization. For example, James Figg

(1695–1734) of England claimed the world title in boxing in 1719, although he did not win it in official competition because there was none. During the 19th century many sports that were invented or had evolved from existing sports became highly organized. The first modern track-and-field meet was held in England in 1825. Oxford and Cambridge universities participated in the first intercollegiate athletic competition when they held a rowing match in 1829. Ten years later Cambridge students popularized an accidentally invented sport they called Rugby's game, the forerunner of other similar games. In the United States RUGBY evolved into a unique sport, American FOOTBALL, which was first played on an intercollegiate level in 1869 in a match between Rutgers and Princeton universities.

BASEBALL, which ultimately became a pastime in many countries, was first regularly played in the United States in 1845 (professionally in 1869); BASKETBALL, another sport with international appeal, was invented in Springfield, Mass., in

(Left) *A "striker" playing a game of rounders assumes a position similar to a contemporary baseball batting stance in an engraving from a book of games published in 1864. Baseball, the most widely viewed professional team sport in the United States, is believed to be a variation of the earlier English game of rounders.*

(Above) *The chaotic action in this 19th-century football game suggests the lack of formal rules governing the sport during its developmental era. American football evolved slowly, borrowing elements of soccer and rugby.*

(Left) *Lawn tennis, which was popularized during the late 19th century, was one of the first athletic events in which British and American women were allowed to participate.*

(Left) *This advertisement offering the basic equipment of basketball appeared in a rule book published in 1893, only 2 years after the sport's invention by Dr. James Naismith.*

(Below) *Spectators crowd around the circular ring of a 19th-century boxing match in this painting by George A. Hayes. The last bareknuckle bout in which the heavyweight title was at stake occurred in 1889. (National Gallery of Art, Washington, D.C.)*

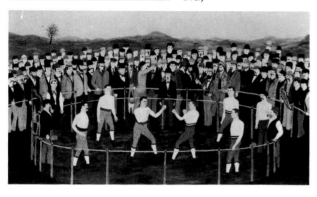

1891. Golf, tennis, and many other sports were organized for local, national, and even international competition. In 1892 the first championship BOXING match in which gloves were used was held between John L. SULLIVAN and James CORBETT in New Orleans.

Boxing and, later, American intercollegiate football and professional baseball attracted large crowds of people; the phenomenon of the spectator became an especially prominent feature of sports before World War II.

With the growth of sports organization and interest, governing bodies were established for sports ranging from the international Olympic Games down to local softball and bowling leagues. With increased coverage of sports events by newspapers and then radio and television, sports began to consume a larger percentage of people's free time than it had prior to the 20th century. Sports stars such as Muhammad ALI (boxing), Paavo NURMI (track), Babe RUTH (baseball), and Jim THORPE (track and field, football) became internationally recognized figures, renowned not only as great athletes but as personalities that inspired other athletes as well as the average person.   JIM BENAGH

Bibliography: Arlott, John, and Daley, Arthur, *Pageantry of Sport, from the Age of Chivalry to the Age of Victoria* (1968); Brasch, Rudolph, *How Did Sports Begin? A Look Into the Origins of Man at Play* (1969); Henderson, Robert W., *Early American Sport*, 3d ed. (1976); Manchester, Herbert, *Four Centuries of Sport in America, 1490–1890* (1931; repr. 1968); Spears, Betty, and Swanson, Richard A., *History of Sport and Physical Activity in the United States* (1978); Yee, Min S., ed., *The Sports Book* (1975); Zeigler, Earle F., ed., *History of Physical Education and Sport* (1979).

sports medicine

Sports medicine is that branch of medical science that deals with the treatment and prevention of injuries incurred while participating in sports. The field also concerns the methodology of scientific research to determine the causes of sports injuries. In recent years physicians who specialize in treating one specific part of the anatomy—such as the knee, back, foot, or elbow—have compiled and exchanged information on their specialty and have also formed associations to promote the study of injury-prone parts of the body. With the growth of professional sports, team physicians and specialists in sports medicine have received wide publicity for their treatment of injuries to star athletes.

The athlete's entire body is subject to countless varieties of sports injuries. The nature of the injuries is attributable to the individual characteristics of the athlete as well as the demands of the particular sport. A clear understanding of how these two factors interrelate is essential for prevention and treatment of sports injuries.

CLASSIFICATIONS OF SPORTS

Sports can be classified according to the physical and mental demands imposed on the participants. There are also environmental demands such as playing conditions, equipment used, and the rigorousness of practice.

Sports can also be categorized according to the kinds of movement that an athlete must perform. There are six basic motions in sports: stance, walk, run, jump, kick, and throw. These basic motions have all been rigidly defined for scientific study. A sport may involve one, a combination, or all of these motions. Baseball, for example, is obviously a sport that uses the throwing motion a great deal, but so are basketball, swimming, and tennis. Although these sports may seem dissimilar, they each require that the athlete make a repetitive throwing motion. These sports will place heavy demands on the upper body of an athlete, demands that may overtax a particular part of the musculoskeletal system and lead to such problems as "pitcher's elbow," "tennis elbow," "basketball finger," or "swimmer's shoulder." The lower extremities and spine are also involved in the throwing motion. This is why a painful toe injury altered Dizzy Dean's pitching motion enough to produce the arm pain that prematurely ended his brilliant career.

BODY TYPES OF ATHLETES

To fully understand the nature of a particular sports injury, one must be able to study the athlete as well. The musculoskeletal system is a complex system of muscle segments, each of which is intimately related to the function of other bones and muscles. Pathological states of the musculoskeletal system are reflected in weaknesses in key muscle segments that may be distant from the site of pathology, or trauma.

The musculoskeletal system of an athlete is analyzed in terms of two main variables: strength and flexibility. Each of these factors plays a major role in the causes, and therefore the prevention, of sports injuries.

The hyperflexible, loose-jointed athlete is more prone to ligament injuries and SPRAINS, as well as partial dislocation of the kneecap and shoulders, and elbow hyperextension. These athletes require strengthening programs to compensate for and protect their joint laxity.

In contrast, the tight-jointed athlete is faced with the opposite problem. There is a greater tendency for muscle pulls and strains. Tight hamstrings are often a factor in lower back problems, and tight Achilles tendons may be a prelude to TENDONITIS, as well as knee and foot problems. The very tight athlete is not able to achieve the range of motion of more flexible athletes. To decrease the incidence of injuries, the tight-jointed individual must stay on a daily stretching program. Adherence to the program must be rigorous, because unlike strengthening, the gains achieved by stretching are not carried over from day to day.

TYPES OF SPORTS INJURIES

With an athlete categorized as either loose- or tight-jointed, it is much easier to understand the nature of many common sports injuries. Whereas doctors once recommended rest and inactivity as a cure for an injury, today many athletes continue to train and compete while undergoing corrective rehabilitation.

Tennis Elbow. Tennis elbow is an inflammation of the structures in and around the lateral epicondyle, the bony knob on the outer side of the elbow. In its typical form tennis elbow is caused by repetitive microtrauma to this area resulting from poor shock absorption on the serve and backhand stroke. This can be caused by improper equipment or poor technique but may also be associated with relative weakness of the extensors of the wrist and fingers that attach in the vicinity of the epicondyle. In fact, a person need not be a tennis player to suffer from tennis elbow. The injury may also arise from job-related activities like hammering or repetitive lifting. Attempts to treat tennis elbow include technique and equipment changes to alter stress points, elastic bands and splints to change the tension in the extensor origins, and even progressive resistance exercises to strengthen the finger extensors.

Shoulder Injuries. Shoulder problems are common in the so-called throwing sports of tennis, baseball, and swimming. Practicing the overhand motion of the Australian crawl for four hours a day can be devastating to a shoulder with a tendency toward partial dislocation. Chronic shoulder ailments are developing at increasingly earlier ages in young swimmers and in tennis players practicing their serves.

Back Injuries. Lumbosacral spine, or lower back, problems are common in sports with a great deal of bending, such as ice hockey, and even more prevalent in heavily muscled, tight-jointed, weight lifters. The keys to prevention of injuries are flexibility in the spine and posterior thigh muscles and strength in the abdominals and anterior thigh muscles. This balance of strength and flexibility acts to functionally unload the spine. Cervical spine, or neck, injuries are seen most frequently in such high-velocity contact sports as football and ice hockey. Prevention is largely a function of good equipment with strict enforcement of safety rules.

Knee Injuries. The most widely publicized lower body injuries are those involving the knee. Football, in particular, has done much to further knowledge of the complexities of the human knee's functioning in health and disease. Proper equipment and playing conditions are crucial but are overshadowed in importance by the precompetition physical examination. Severe knee instability is potentially dangerous; the joint must be properly braced, and a program of strengthening exercises to overcome characteristic weaknesses must be undertaken prior to competition in order to minimize the possibility of a debilitating injury.

Participants in jumping sports, such as basketball and volleyball, are vulnerable to knee problems without violent contact. These problems usually appear in the patellofemoral (kneecap and thigh bone) articulation and are manifested predominantly as inferior pole patella (area just below the kneecap) tendonitis, or jumper's knee. Treatment may involve a program of exercises to strengthen supporting muscles, or if the knee is acutely injured, immobilization or surgery may be required.

The recent advances in sports medicine have enabled athletes, who only a few years ago may have had to abandon sports altogether because of injuries, to participate longer and at higher levels of performance. Sports medicine will continue to be a rapidly growing field as new medical technologies are applied, as understanding of how injuries occur becomes more sharply defined, and as rehabilitation becomes an important aspect of the general health-care field.

ALAN MARC STRIZAK, M.D.

Bibliography: Hirata, Isao, *The Doctor and the Athlete*, 2d ed. (1974); Mirkin, Gave, and Hoffman, Marshall, *The Sports Medicine Book* (1978); Muckle, David S., *Sports Injuries*, rev. ed. (1978); Ryan, Allan J., and Allman, Fred L., *Sports Medicine* (1974); Taylor, Albert W., ed., *The Application of Science and Medicine to Sport* (1975).

spot

A popular game fish, the spot, or drum, *Leiostomus xanthurus*, of the family Sciaenidae, is one of the most common croakers—fishes that make a rumbling noise—found in estuaries from Cape Cod to Texas. It is characterized by a spot just above the base of the pectoral fin. The spot inhabits water bottomed by sand, mud, or grass flats and reaches 30 to 33 cm (12 to 13 in) in length and 0.68 kg (1.5 lb) in weight. It breeds in winter or early spring, and the young appear in the upper estuaries. Adult spot feed primarily on small inverte-

brates that they root out of the bottom with their small, ventral mouths.

CAMM SWIFT

Spotswood, Alexander

The British colonial administrator Alexander Spotswood, b. Tangier, Morocco, 1676, d. June 7, 1740, served as royal governor of Virginia from June 23, 1710, until 1722. He secured passage of an act requiring the inspection of all tobacco for export; although this was an important reform in Virginia's economic system, it was opposed by many influential provincial leaders and was later repealed. Spotswood, one of the first royal governors to recognize the value of the American frontier, facilitated the establishment of settlements in the West and encouraged trade with the Indians. A staunch Tory and firm defender of his own prerogatives, he was often accused of high-handedness by members of both his governor's council and the House of Burgesses, but his term as governor was generally a successful and stable one.

RICHARD R. BEEMAN

Bibliography: Dodson, Leonidas, *Alexander Spotswood, Governor of Colonial Virginia, 1710-1722* (1939; repr. 1969); Havighurst, Walter, *Alexander Spotswood* (1967).

Spotted Tail

Spotted Tail, or *Sinte Gleska*, 1826?-1881, a leader of the Brule SIOUX of the Teton Dakota, vigorously defended the territory, rights, and customs of his people. After 1863 he led his band against the westward-moving white settlers, foreseeing the destruction of the Sioux economy's mainstay, the bison. In 1866, Spotted Tail attended talks at Fort Laramie, which led to the Laramie Treaty two years later. Despite his efforts, the Sioux lost extensive territory.

After gold was discovered (1873) in the Black Hills of present-day South Dakota, Spotted Tail went to the area at the request of the Dakota. During negotiations with treaty commissioners he strenuously opposed the removal of the Dakota to INDIAN TERRITORY, but he nevertheless signed the treaty, which opened the Black Hills and provided for mining and white occupancy. The government named him head chief of the Brule band and gave him the title and pay of a lieutenant in the U.S. Army. In 1877, Spotted Tail and his people settled on Rosebud Reservation in South Dakota.

BEATRICE MEDICINE

Bibliography: Dockstader, Frederick J., *Great North American Indians* (1977); Edwards, R. M., *American Indians of Yesterday* (1948).

Sprague, Frank Julian   [sprayg]

The American engineer Frank Julian Sprague, b. Milford, Conn., July 25, 1857, d. Oct. 25, 1934, was a prolific U.S. inventor. A U.S. Naval Academy graduate (1878), he started his career in the U.S. Navy testing early electrical equipment. For a time (1883–84) he assisted Thomas Edison. In 1884 he formed the Sprague Electric Railway and Motor Company, the first manufacturer to produce industrial electric motors. In 1887, Sprague equipped the first modern trolley in the United States, at Richmond, Va., and thereafter helped construct more than 100 such railways in the United States and Europe. Other inventions included high-speed, automatic electric elevators; a system for operating two elevators on the same rails in a common shaft; and the AC induction smelting furnace. He made numerous innovations in the field of electric railway control, such as automatic signaling and braking devices.

sprain

A sprain is an injury to a joint or its surrounding tissues caused by external forces moving the joint beyond its normal limits or moving it in an unnatural direction. In order of frequency, the most common sites of a sprain are the ankle, knee, wrist, elbow, and spine. The abnormalities commonly seen in a sprain are torn ligaments, tendons, muscles, or synovial membranes in the vicinity of the joint and detached cartilage inside the joint. In some sprains inflammatory fluid collects within the joint. These conditions cause pain, swelling, and restricted movement. Sprains are usually treated by bandaging the area to limit movement while healing takes place. In some cases it is necessary to use a syringe to withdraw fluid that has accumulated inside the joint.

PETER L. PETRAKIS

Spranger, Bartholomäus   [shprahng'-ur]

The Flemish Mannerist painter Bartholomäus Spranger, b. Mar. 21, 1546, d. August 1611, a pupil of Jan Mandyn, worked in Paris about 1565 and also in Rome, where he assisted (1567–75) Federico Zuccaro. In Vienna he worked (1575) for the Emperor Maximilian II and in Prague for Rudolph II. His paintings, characteristically filled with contorted nude figures, were popularized in engravings by Hendrik Goltzius

CHARLES I. MINOTT

sprat

Sprat, *Sprattus sprattus,* are silvery, herringlike fishes in the family Clupeidae. They occur in large schools inshore during the winter in the North, Baltic, Mediterranean, and Black Seas. Each of these areas has its own distinctive population of sprat. They move offshore and spawn in both fall and spring months. At any given time, larger fishes occur farther offshore than smaller ones. By the third summer of life, at a length of 10 to 12 cm (4 to 5 in), sprat begin to spawn. The eggs are pelagic. Sprat reach a maximum of 17 cm (7 in) in length in 4 to 5 years in the North Sea, where they live up to 6 years and attain their largest size. Throughout their range many sprat are canned, smoked, and salted for human consumption.

CAMM SWIFT

Spree River   [shpray]

The Spree River, 398 km (247 mi) long, rises in the Lusatian Mountains in southeastern East Germany and flows north to Cottbus, where it swings west through the marshy Spree Forest and then northward to join the Havel River at Spandau in West Berlin. The Spree is navigable for 180 km (112 mi) and is linked to the Oder by the Oder-Spree Canal.

spring   (device):   see SUSPENSION SYSTEM.

spring   (water)

A spring is any natural surface discharge of groundwater. Springs are of fundamental importance in supplying water to sustain farms, cities, and natural wetlands. They are supplied by groundwater, which in turn is replenished by rainwater and melted snow, and some can go dry during periods of drought. The location of most springs is controlled by a combination of surface topography and rock structure. In horizontal strata with a perched water table, springs will occur where a valley wall exposes the aquiclude. In folded and faulted strata where an aquiclude overlies an aquifer, artesian springs may occur (see ARTESIAN WELL). Many of the world's largest springs emerge in valleys that have been eroded downward to intersect water-filled caverns in limestone.

Spring discharge varies from a few drops per minute to thousands of liters per second. The world's largest reported spring is Ras-el-Ain in Syria, with an average yield of 38,700 l (10,200 gal) per second. The largest spring in the United States is Silver Springs in Florida, which averages 23,000 l (6,100 gal) per second. Spring-water temperatures vary from about the mean annual air temperature in the region of the spring to the boiling point of water (100° C/212° F). Most hot (geothermal) springs are heated by nearby volcanic activity, although some are heated by circulation of water to great depths.

The chemical quality of spring water ranges from almost pure water to brine (saturated with salt). Springs having water containing more than about 2 g of dissolved solids per liter (0.267 oz/gal) are called mineral springs. Gases may be dissolved in the water; carbon dioxide can produce a natural soda water, and hydrogen sulfide gives spring water a characteristic sulfurous odor.

STANLEY N. DAVIS

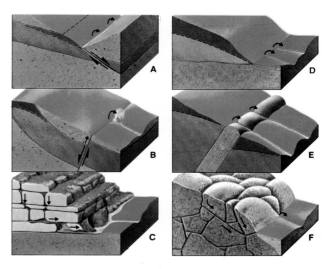

A spring is formed whenever a fault brings an aquifer, or water-bearing rock layer, to the surface (A). Artesian springs are found where an inclined aquifer, sealed between two impermeable rock layers, flows upward under its own pressure through cracks in the layer above it (B). In hilly limestone areas water seeps down through fissures to an impermeable layer and then flows out horizontally (C). Springs also form when an aquifer emerges at the foot of a slope (D). An impermeable intrusive rock that cuts across an aquifer leads to formation of a spring along the top of the intrusion (E). Water may flow through cracks in granite until it finds a surface opening (F).

Bibliography: Davis, S. N., and DeWiest, R. J. M., *Hydrogeology* (1966); Heller, Steven, and Schwartz, Steven, *The Book of Waters* (1979); Todd, D. K., *Ground Water Hydrology* (1959).

spring beauty

Spring beauty is any of 15 to 20 species of spring-flowering perennial herbs of the genus *Claytonia,* in the purslane family, Portulacaceae. Most of them are native to western North America, South America, and the Old World. Carolina spring beauty, *C. caroliniana,* native to eastern North America, produces small, delicate, white to pink flowers in early spring, with broad leaves, unlike other spring beauties.

springbok

The springbok, A. marsupialis, is a high-jumping antelope native to South Africa. Once found in herds of 1 million or more, its numbers are now depleted, and it is found mainly in zoos and parks.

The springbok, or springbuck, *Antidorcas marsupialis,* in the family Bovidae, is a gazellelike antelope noted for its ability to jump as high as 3.5 m (11 ft) when startled, hence its name. It is about 135 cm (5 ft) long, stands nearly 86.4 cm (34 in) at the shoulder, and weighs about 35 kg (78 lb). Both sexes have black, ringed horns. Found in South Africa, where it has been largely exterminated, the springbok is protected in national parks.

EVERETT SENTMAN

springer spaniel: see WELSH SPRINGER SPANIEL.

Springfield (Illinois)

Springfield, the capital of Illinois and seat of Sangamon County, is located in the central part of the state on the Sangamon River. It has a population of 85,700 (1979 est.). The city is a progressive industrial and business community in the midst of a rich agricultural and coal region.

A graceful and historic city, Springfield was the home of Abraham Lincoln from 1837 to 1861, and every year thousands of tourists visit the many original and restored sites associated with his career. The Lincoln Tomb State Memorial is the burial place of Lincoln, his wife, and three of their four sons. The Lincoln Home National Historic Site is a restoration of the house where Lincoln lived from 1844 to 1861. Lincoln made his first "House Divided" speech at the Old State Capitol there, and the state historical library has an outstanding collection of Lincolniana. The city was also the home of the poet Vachel Lindsay. Springfield is the host city of the annual Illinois State Fair, one of the largest state fairs in the United States.

Settled in 1818 by Elisha Kelly and laid out in 1822, the city was named for Spring Creek and developed as a farm distribution center. In 1837, Lincoln was instrumental in having the capital moved there from Vandalia.

Springfield (Massachusetts)

Springfield, the seat of Hampden County in southwestern Massachusetts, lies along the Connecticut River just north of the Connecticut border. With a population of 167,500 (1979 est.), Springfield produces machinery, appliances, tools, printed matter, and the famous Springfield and Garand firearms. Cultural institutions include several museums, a symphony orchestra, and four colleges. The Naismith Basketball Hall of Fame commemorates basketball's origin there in 1891.

Settled in 1636 by William Pynchon, the city was incorporated in 1641 and named for Springfield, England. It was burned during King Philip's War in 1675 but was soon rebuilt. The scene of Shays's Rebellion (1786-87) and home of the U.S. Armory (1794-1968), the city was also a part of the Underground Railroad before the abolition of slavery. The abolitionist John Brown had his wool business in Springfield, and the Duryea brothers started the first U.S. automobile company there in 1895.

Springfield (Missouri)

Springfield, a city in southwestern Missouri at the northern edge of the Ozark Mountains, is the seat of Greene County. Located in a poultry and dairy region, it has a population of 134,000 (1979 est.). The economy is based on agriculture and is supplemented by the manufacture of iron and steel products, clothing, lumber products, and furniture. Springfield is the site of three colleges.

Settled about 1829, the city benefited from its location on several routes used for westward migration. Confederate forces held Springfield after the Battle of Wilson's Creek in August 1861, but Union troops recaptured it in February 1862.

Springfield (Ohio)

Springfield (1979 est. pop., 71,200), the seat of Clark County, is a city in west central Ohio about 40 km (25 mi) northeast of Dayton. The center of a hog-farming and winter-wheat belt, the city manufactures agricultural tools, electrical prod-

ucts, automobile parts, and trucks. Wittenberg University (1845) is located there. Settled in 1799, Springfield grew when it became the terminus of the NATIONAL ROAD in 1838.

springhare

The springhare P. capensis *is a small nocturnal rodent native to eastern and southern Africa that resembles a scaled-down kangaroo. The springhare can jump as far as 3 m (10 ft) when frightened.*

The springhare, or Cape jumping hare, of the genus *Pedetes* is a large rodent, not a true hare, and is the sole member of the family Pedetidae. It has short front legs and long, powerful hind legs and, when frightened, jumps as a kangaroo. The springhare has a bushy tail as long as its body, which measures about 40 cm (16 in) in length. The rodent weighs about 3.5 kg (8 lb). Its coat is soft and tawny to reddish brown with white underparts. It digs burrows in sandy soil and, usually eating at night, consumes plants and insects. Springhares live in eastern and southern Africa.

EVERETT SENTMAN

springtail

The springtail Bourletiella *has a forked appendage, or furcula (A), that enables it to leap up to 10 cm (4 in).*

Springtails (order Collembola) are minute, wingless, primitive insects about 5 to 6 mm (0.20 to 0.24 in) in length that jump with a taillike structure (furcula), which is folded forward under the abdomen when not in use. Although common and abundant, they are seldom noticed because of their secretive habits, living mainly under bark, in leaf litter, or in the soil. Coloration is varied, and some are patterned or mottled. A tubelike structure, the collophore, is believed to aid in water uptake.

DONALD J. BORROR

spruce

The white spruce, P. glauca, *a North American conifer, has bluish green leaves and brown cones that grow to 5 cm (2 in).*

Spruces, genus *Picea,* comprise about 50 species of evergreen conifers in the pine family, Pinaceae. They are widely distributed in the coniferous forests of the cooler north temperate and subarctic regions, particularly in China. Spruces extend as far south as the high mountains of northern Mexico, southern Europe, Anatolia, the Himalayas, and Taiwan. Seven species are found in the United States and are important in forestry.

Spruce trees are characterized by their pyramidal form. The four-angled needles last for up to 10 years and are borne on peglike stalks, which remain on older twigs. Egg-shaped cones are produced mainly in the upper crown of the tree, where they remain attached for a long period of time. Many spruces reach heights of 61 m (200 ft).

The black spruce, *P. mariana,* is an abundant conifer of North America. One of the most important European timber trees is *P. abies,* the Norway spruce, a tall tree identified by its dark green, drooping foliage. Spruce wood is strong and is used in the construction industry, but its primary use is for the manufacture of pulp and paper.

Bibliography: Crockett, James, *Evergreens* (1971).

sprue

Sprue, or malabsorption syndrome, is a collective term for a group of nutritional deficiency diseases characterized by impaired absorption of nutrients, especially fats, glucose, and vitamins, from the small intestine. Celiac disease and nontropical sprue are caused by sensitivity to gliadin, which is a component of gluten, a mixture of proteins found in the seeds of cereals. Tropical sprue is apparently caused by deficiency of the vitamin folic acid.   PETER L. PETRAKIS

spurge

The broad-leaved spurge, E. platyphylla, *has single female flowers surrounded by male flowers enclosed in a leaflike cyathium.*

Spurge is the common name for the more than 1,500 species of the plant genus *Euphorbia* of the spurge family, Euphorbiaceae. These plants are characterized by their milky sap and by the arrangement of the flowers: one female flower and several surrounding male flowers, grouped together in a cuplike structure. Spurges occur in tropical and warm-temperate regions and include annual and perennial herbs, shrubs, trees, and succulents. Among them are CROWN OF THORNS, *E. splendens,* native to Madagascar; IPECAC spurge, *E. ipecacuanhae,* of the eastern United States; POINSETTIA, *E. pulcherrima,* of Mexico; scarlet-plume, *E. fulgens,* of Mexico; and snow-on-the-mountain, *E. marginata,* of the midwestern United States. Allegheny spurge, *Pachysandra procumbens,* and Japanese

spurge, *P. terminalis,* belong to the boxwood family, Buxaceae.   KENNETH R. ROBERTSON

Sputnik

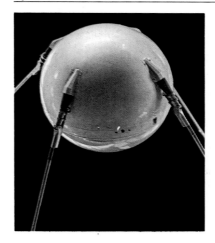

Sputnik 1, *the first artificial Earth satellite, was launched by the USSR on Oct. 4, 1957. An 84-kg (184-lb) sphere with a diameter of 58 cm (23 in), it had four antennae that ranged from 2.4 to 2.9 m (7.9 to 9.5 ft) in length. Sputnik 1 orbited the Earth once every 96 minutes in an elliptical trajectory between 227 km (141 mi) and 945 km (587 mi) in altitude until early in 1958.*

Sputnik was the project name for three artificial satellites (*sputnik* means "traveling companion" in Russian) launched by the USSR in 1957 and 1958. They weighed, in order, 84, 519, and 1,351 kg (184, 1,140, and 2,980 lb). Their scientific purpose was primarily to investigate outer space and to discover if living organisms could survive space conditions. Additionally, they marked the opening of the "space race" between the United States and the Soviet Union.

The Sputniks came as a tremendous shock to the West, which had up to then tended to downgrade Soviet technical capability. In hindsight, the Sputniks should not have been such a surprise, because Moscow had been releasing several explicit communiques about Soviet intentions, announcements that were dismissed as propaganda in the West. Reactions in the United States and Europe, which in some cases bordered on hysteria, initiated the American drive to send astronauts to the Moon.

Sputnik 1 was launched from the BAIKONUR COSMODROME on Oct. 4, 1957. It was simply a test payload containing a radio beacon and a thermometer, and had been referred to by its designers as the "ES" (elementary satellite). A month later, on November 3, a half-ton payload carrying a dog was put into orbit by the same type of rocket. The dog, called Laika, was kept alive for 10 days, proving that life could survive prolonged weightlessness and other unknown conditions of space. *Sputnik 3,* launched on May 15, 1958, weighed almost a ton and a half. A wide array of scientific apparatus was reportedly on board to measure space radiation.

Seven other spacecraft were given Sputnik designations; they functioned either as prototypes for the VOSTOK manned spacecraft (*Sputniks 4, 5, 6, 9,* and *10*) or as platforms from which probes to the planet Venus were launched (*Sputniks 1* and *8*; see VENERA).   JAMES OBERG

Bibliography: Aleksandrov, S. G., and Federov, R. Y., *Soviet Satellites and Cosmic Rockets* (1960); Killian, James R., *Sputnik, Scientists, and Eisenhower* (1977); Krieger, Firmin J., *Behind the Sputniks: A Survey of Soviet Space Science* (1958); Shelton, William, *Soviet Space Exploration: The First Decade* (1968); Smolders, Peter L., *Soviets in Space,* trans. by Marian Powell (1974).

See also: SPACE EXPLORATION.

squall and squall line

Gusty surface winds and heavy precipitation characterize a squall, an isolated, severe, local thunderstorm. In certain regions a number of such storms occasionally become aligned in narrow bands, or squall lines, that may extend for several hundred kilometers perpendicular to their direction of motion. A squall line can form only when the mean wind perpendicular to the line increases rapidly with height. The line tends to move with the speed of the wind in the mid-troposphere and thus faster than the wind near the ground.

Heavy precipitation produced in the thunderstorm cells that comprise a squall line creates a downdraft of cold, dense air that flows out in advance of the squall line at the surface. This gust front lifts the moist air ahead of the squall line and feeds it into the thunderstorm cells, continuously regenerating the line as it propagates along.   JAMES R. HOLTON

Squanto   [skwahn'-toh]

Squanto, c.1580–1622, a Pawtuxet Indian later associated with the WAMPANOAG after his tribe was decimated by plague, was seized (1614) by a ship's captain and taken to Spain as a slave. He went from there to England and finally back (1619) to North America, where he was employed by the governor of Newfoundland. Squanto was later brought to Plymouth, where he taught the colonists to improve their crops by using fish fertilizer, but it has been questioned whether this was an Indian method or something Squanto had learned abroad. He served as interpreter at the 1621 treaty between the colonists and MASSASOIT. Soon after, he died of a disease that he had contracted while guiding Gov. William BRADFORD's expedition across Cape Cod.   JAMES A. CLIFTON

Bibliography: Dockstader, Frederick J., *Great North American Indians* (1977).

Squarcione, Francesco   [skwahr-choh'-nay]

An Italian artist of the early Renaissance, Francesco Squarcione, c.1397–1468, was important primarily as the teacher of several leading painters, including Andrea Mantegna, who came to study with Squarcione in Padua. Unfortunately, only two works known to be by Squarcione exist today: his *Madonna and Child* (c.1455; Staatliche Museen, Berlin) and an altarpiece (1449–52; Museo Civico) at Padua. These display a harsh, linear style and an interest in lively movement.

Bibliography: Lipton, Deborah, *Francesco Squarcione* (1974).

square

In geometry, a square is a four-sided plane figure (a QUADRILATERAL) that has four equal sides of length *l* (making it a *rhombus*) as well as four equal (right) angles (making it also a RECTANGLE). Its area is $A = l^2$. In algebra, the square of a quantity is the second power of that quantity. For example, the square of 4 is $4 \times 4 = 4^2 = 16$, and $(a + b)^2 = (a + b)(a + b) = a^2 + 2ab + b^2$.

square dance

Any American FOLK DANCE that requires the participation of many couples is called a square dance, whether those couples are arranged in a square (square set or quadrille), in two facing lines (longway set or contra dance), or in a circle (running set). A single couple fulfills the requirements of a round dance, such as the waltz or polka. Square dancing also identifies the only folk dance whose form is determined neither by tradition nor by the dancers themselves, but by a caller, a nondancer who names each dance's figures extemporaneously, combining established patterns (chains, stars, cloverleafs) with the caller's own inventions. Dancing for informal recreation, colonial settlers tailored English folk dances to fit any space and any number of untrained participants, and relied on a fiddle, fife, and drum, or regular handclapping, called "ratting," for music, usually in 2/4 or 6/8 time. Many regional variations and preferences developed, but only the square set traveled west with the pioneers. During the 1930s, public interest brought square-dance exhibitions into American cities. Urban and rural folk-dance organizations now teach and preserve the original forms.   BARBARA NEWMAN

Bibliography: Casey, Betty, *The Complete Book of Square Dancing (and Round Dancing)* (1976); Nevell, Richard, *A Time to Dance: American Country Dancing from Hornpipes to Hot Hash* (1977).

square root

The square root of any number is the number whose product with itself is the original number. For example, the square root of 9 is 3, the square root of 16 is 4, and the square root of 121 is 11. Because it is also true that $(-3) \times (-3) = 9$, $(-4) \times (-4) = 16$, and $(-11) \times (-11) = 121$, every positive number has both a positive square root (called the principal square root or just the square root) and a negative square root. The square root of a number can be denoted either by using a fractional exponent, such as $9^{\frac{1}{2}}$, or by using the symbol $\sqrt{\ }$, called a RADICAL sign. Thus, $9^{\frac{1}{2}} = \sqrt{9} = 3$.

The square roots of most positive numbers are IRRATIONAL NUMBERS, because in most cases they cannot be represented exactly by a fraction or a decimal. They can, however, be approximated to whatever accuracy is desired. The number zero has only one square root—itself. The square root of any negative number is not a real number and is said to be imaginary (see COMPLEX NUMBER).

Many methods exist for computing the square root of a number. If that number has a rational square root, then one method of computing it is to first express the number as a product of prime factors, and then for every two times a factor appears under the radical, one such factor can be brought out of the radical. When there are no factors remaining under the radical, the product of the numbers outside is the square root of the original number. For example, $\sqrt{324} = \sqrt{2 \times 2 \times 3 \times 3 \times 3 \times 3} = 2 \times 3 \times 3 = 18$.

When the square root of a number is irrational, a decimal approximation can be obtained from tables, a slide rule, or a calculator, as well as by any of several longhand methods of computation.   JOHN M. PETERSON

See also: ROOT (mathematics).

squash   (game)

Squash, or squash racquets, is an indoor racquet-and-ball game that is similar to handball. Two players, or four players in doubles, use racquets with small, round heads and thin necks to take alternate turns hitting a small, black, rubber ball against the front wall of a special court. Squash tennis is a variant of the basic game; it is played on the same court but uses a livelier ball and a heavier racquet.

The singles court is 32 ft (9.8 m) long and 18.5 ft (5.6 m) wide; the doubles court is 45 ft (13.7 m) long and 25 ft (7.6 m) wide. The front wall has a 16-ft-high (4.9-m) play line across the width and a 20-ft-high (6-m) play line for doubles. The court is divided in half by a line that runs from the front wall to the back wall. The service-court line, beyond which all legal serves must go, is 18 ft (5.5 m) from the front wall. The service line runs the width of the front wall, 6.5 ft (2 m) above the floor. At the two side walls, two service areas in the shape of quarter circles with radii of 4.5 ft (1.4 m) are behind the service-court line. The hollow ball is 1.75 in (4.4 cm) in diameter and weighs about 1 oz (28 g).

To play, the server puts the ball in play while having one foot in the service area. The serve must hit above the service line on the front wall and rebound so that it hits the floor beyond the service-court line in the opposite half of the court. The server scores points until the service is lost. Service is lost when the server fails to hit the ball before it bounces twice, when the ball hits the "telltale" (a metal strip 17 in/43.2 cm high at the bottom of the front wall), or when the server sends the ball above the play line. A game ends at 15 points; if the score is tied at 13 or 14, play may be extended to 16 or 18 points. The player with the best three games out of five wins the match.

Squash began at Harrow School, England, sometime before 1850. It was introduced in the United States at Saint Paul's School in Concord, N.H., in 1882, and it soon spread to other schools, colleges, athletic clubs, and YMCAs.

Bibliography: Francis, Austin, *Smart Squash—Using Your Head to Win* (1977); Rowland, Jim, *Squash Basics* (1976); Torbet, Laura, *Squash: How to Play, How to Win* (1978); Truby, John, *The Science and Strategy of Squash* (1975).

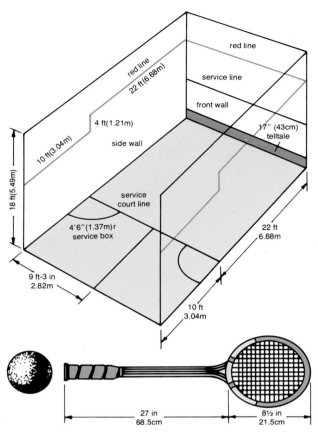

Squash, a sport that originated at Harrow School in England about 1850, is played on an indoor court (top) with a long, narrow racket (bottom right) and a hard rubber ball (bottom left) slightly larger than a golf ball. Squash may be played by 2 or 4 people.

squash (vegetable)

Squash is any of several species of annual plants of the genus *Cucurbita* in the gourd family. The name is derived from an American Indian word. The plants are believed to have originated in South America, but their cultivation had spread throughout the Americas by the time the first Europeans arrived. Squashes are categorized as either summer or winter varieties. Most summer varieties are classified as *C. pepo* and bear relatively small fruits that are eaten while immature. The

Crookneck squash, C. pepo, is a yellow summer variety that is eaten in casseroles and as a side dish.

fruits can sometimes be picked within 50 days of seed planting. Popular varieties of summer squash are zucchini, yellow crookneck, and white bush scallop. Winter varieties of squash generally fall into the *C. maxima* classification and tend to be more nutritious than the summer varieties. Because the winter squashes are eaten when mature, their growing season usually requires 100 or more days. The mature fruit of the winter squash has a tough outer skin and can be stored at moderate temperatures (12°-15° C/54°-59° F) for several months. Hubbard, butternut, and acorn are varieties of winter squash. All squashes are intolerant of frost and are grown throughout the world where weather conditions permit. In the United States production is centered in the New England and mid-Atlantic states and in Florida. O. A. LORENZ

squatter

A squatter, in U.S. law, is a person who occupies land, particularly public land, without holding a legal title to that land. Following the War of 1812, during the period of Western expansion, settlers occupying public lands that the federal government had not yet surveyed or opened to sale contended that their building of homes and clearing of land entitled them to buy these sites at minimum prices. Pressured by Western congressmen, Congress passed the PREEMPTION ACT of 1841, allowing squatters to file claims for a maximum of 160 acres, improve the land, and pay $1.25 an acre in installments. In 19th-century Australia a large-scale sheepfarmer, or a "tenant of the crown," was referred to as a squatter.

squatter sovereignty: see POPULAR SOVEREIGNTY.

squid

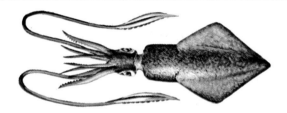

The squid, a marine mollusk related to the octopus, moves by shooting water from its body, propelling itself backward. It can hide from an enemy by squirting an inky, water-clouding fluid.

Squid is the common name for a group of carnivorous marine MOLLUSKS in the class Cephalopoda, phylum Mollusca. Other members of the class include the octopus, cuttlefish, and chambered nautilus. The common squid is often found in shoals, off the eastern coast of the United States.

Squids have elongated, slender bodies with triangular caudal fins. The head-foot region is modified into five pairs of arms, or tentacles, with rows of suckers. The tentacles extend outward from, and surround, the mouth. Four pairs of tentacles are of about equal length and are used to steer in swimming. One pair is somewhat longer and retractile and is used to capture prey. The head of the squid possesses a funnel from which exhalant water-jets from the mantle cavity are shot, thus providing a means of rapid locomotion. The characteristic molluscan shell has been reduced to a horny plate buried under the mantle.

Squids have internal cartilaginous support that is analogous to a vertebrate skeleton, and a cartilaginous brain case that is analogous to a skull. Their nervous system is well developed, and the animals (along with their close relatives, the octopuses) possess large, image-forming eyes that are quite similar to vertebrate eyes. Large single nerve fibers in the squid have been the source of many discoveries on the basic activity of individual nerve cells in animals. The squid breathes through gills. Squids are blue-blooded animals because their respiratory system pigment is a copper compound rather than the red iron found in mammals.

Squids are able to change color rapidly by contracting and expanding pigment granules, called chromatophores, in the integument. Each chromatophore is a fluid-filled sac controlled by 20 to 30 muscles and innervated by nerves from the mantle region. Squids also contain an ink sac, the contents of which can be released to hide the animals' retreat when irritated or challenged.

Although most squids are small, usually less than 30 cm (1 ft) in length, they can attain great size. In the North Atlantic, giant squids of the genus *Architeuthis* can reach up to 15.2 m (50 ft) in length, including tentacles, and weigh two tons. Squid is a popular food in the Orient and the Mediterranean region. Tons of squid are used in the United States for fish bait.   STEPHEN C. REINGOLD

Bibliography: Cousteau, Jacques-Yves, and Diolé, Philippe, *Octopus and Squid* (1973); Vevers, G., *Octopus, Cuttlefish and Squid* (1978).

squill

Squill is the common name for any of about 100 Eurasian plant species of the genus *Scilla* in the lily family, Liliaceae. Common species are the Siberian squill, *S. siberica;* the Spanish bluebell, *S. hispanica;* and the English bluebell, *S. non-*

The Siberian squill, S. siberica, is an easy-to-grow herb of the lily family. It is a favorite rock-garden plant and bears umbrella-shaped flowers.

scripta. Squills are early-spring-flowering bulbs, small in size (usually 15 cm/6 in. in height), with bluish flowers.
                                KENNETH R. ROBERTSON

squinch

A squinch is an architectural element that, placed in the upper corners of a square substructure, helps support a dome, tower, or polygonal superstructure. The typical masonry squinch consists of a sequence of progressively larger arches built out from two adjoining walls; in effect, it rounds off the corner and distributes the weight above it to the two walls. This arrangement probably originated in Islamic architecture; it eventually led to the development of the PENDENTIVE.

squirrel

A squirrel is any member of the rodent family Sciuridae—with the exception of the marmots, *Marmota;* prairie dogs, *Cynomys;* and chipmunks, *Eutamias* and *Tamias*—and typically has a slender body and a long, bushy tail. The name is more commonly used to refer to those forms which live in trees, although it is equally suited to terrestrial types. It is also used for arboreal African rodents of the family Anomaluridae, which are known as scaly-tailed squirrels.

The family Sciuridae contains two subfamilies, the Sciurinae (the tree and ground squirrels), with about 225 species, and the Petauristinae (the FLYING SQUIRRELS), with about 35 species. Squirrels are distributed throughout the world except for the Australian region, Madagascar, southern South America, and certain desert regions, such as the northern Sahara and Arabia.

Squirrels vary in size from such tiny tropical forms as the pygmy squirrels, *Myosciurus,* of Africa, which are about 130 mm (5 in) in length including the tail, to the giant squirrels, *Ratufa,* of Asia, which may attain 91 cm (36 in). The tree and ground squirrels are typically diurnal, and the flying squirrels, nocturnal. Squirrels primarily eat green vegetation, seeds, nuts, berries, fruits, and insects.

The American eastern gray squirrel, *Sciurus carolinensis,* typical of the tree squirrels, is native to the forests of the eastern half of the United States. Introduced into the United Kingdom, it has displaced the smaller native red squirrel, *S. vulgaris,* in many regions. Gray squirrels have many color variations. Nesting is normally in tree hollows; gray squirrels also may construct leaf nests, which are used mainly as feeding shelters. Gray squirrels may breed in midwinter and again in

northern flying squirrel

ground squirrel   **eastern gray squirrel**   **eastern red squirrel**

The northern flying squirrel, Glaucomys sabrinus, glides from tree to tree, storing its food supply in many different locations. The 13-lined ground squirrel, Spermophilus tridecemlineatus, lives in burrows and characteristically sits or stands on its hind legs to look around. The American, or eastern, gray squirrel, Sciurus carolinensis, is a familiar inhabitant of city parks, suburban areas, and woodlands. The eastern red squirrel, Tamiasciurus hudsonicus, one of the most vocal of all squirrels, stores large caches of pine and spruce cones for its winter food supply.

late spring. Gestation is about 44 days, with usually two to four young per litter.

Ground squirrels are similar in appearance to tree squirrels but tend to have shorter and less bushy tails. They typically inhabit open or brushy regions, with some species occurring in tundra or desert. Most are burrowers, and those living in colder climates hibernate, whereas others, in hot, dry areas, may estivate.   CHARLES A. MCLAUGHLIN

Bibliography: Barkalow, Frederick S., *The World of the Gray Squirrel* (1973); MacClintock, Dorcas, *Squirrels of North America* (1970).

squirrelfish

The squirrelfish, Ostichthys japonicus, *is named for the supposed resemblance of its eyes to those of squirrels.*

Squirrelfishes, family Holocentridae, are 9 genera and about 70 species of spiny-rayed (percomorph) teleosts, or bony fish, usually found in tropical marine waters. Most are brightly colored, usually red, and the largest species reaches about 0.6 m (2 ft). Squirrelfishes typically have large eyes, rough, sharp scales, and spines on the opercular bones. They are nocturnal and are usually found on and around reefs in relatively shallow water. Some genera are fished for food.   CAMM SWIFT

Sri Lanka   [sree lahng'-kah]

Sri Lanka is an island republic of Asia, lying in the Indian Ocean off the southern tip of India, from which it is separated by the Gulf of Mannar and Palk Strait. Sri Lanka is an underdeveloped and politically unstable country whose major export is tea. Formerly named Ceylon, it gained its independence from Britain in 1948 and was renamed Sri Lanka (meaning "beautiful island") in 1972.

LAND AND PEOPLE

A mountain mass reaching a height of 2,524 m (8,281 ft) at Mount Pidurutalagala marks the south central region of Sri Lanka. More than 80% of the country lies at elevations below 300 m (1,000 ft), and in all but the southwestern region the extensive coastal lowlands are dotted with lagoons. Numerous small rivers flow from the central heights. The longest is the Mahaweli-ganga, which flows north into the Bay of Bengal.

Sri Lanka lies just north of the equator, in the monsoon belt of the Indian Ocean. Rainfall varies with topography. About 1,016 mm (40 in) of rain falls in the northern lowlands, whereas the precipitation that occurs in the west and in the highlands reaches 5,080 mm (200 in) annually. Temperatures average 28° C (82° F) in the lowlands, with virtually no change throughout the year.

Vegetation ranges from the evergreen forests of the wet highlands to scrub and cactuslike growth in the drier areas. Wildlife includes elephants, leopards, and bears, as well as many species of monkeys and snakes.

Sri Lanka is not rich in minerals, although it does have some iron ore, graphite, and gems such as sapphires and rubies. The extensive timberlands do not satisfy domestic needs. Fish are abundant offshore, and the considerable hydroelectric potential is still unharnessed.

Except for a very small number of aboriginal Vedda, almost all Sri Lankans are the descendants of migrants from India. The two major groups of Indian immigrants differ ethnically,

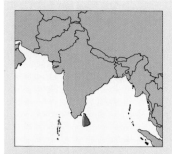

SRI LANKA

Official Name: Democratic Socialist Republic of Sri Lanka
Capital and Largest City: Colombo (1977 est. pop., 616,000)
Area: 65,607 km² (25,332 mi²)
Elevation: *Highest*—Mount Pidurutalagala 2,524 m (8,281 ft); *lowest*—sea level, along the Indian Ocean
Population: 14,502,000 (1979 est.). *Distribution*—22.4% urban, 77.6% rural; *density*, 221 persons per km² (572 per mi²); *annual rate of increase* (1970–77), 1.6%
Principal Languages: Sinhalese (official), Tamil, English
Principal Religions: Buddhism, Hinduism
Principal Products: *Agriculture*—tea, coconuts, rice; rubber. *Manufacturing and industry*—fishing, paper, glassware, ceramics. *Mining*—graphite, precious stones
Railroads: 1,734 km/1,077 mi (1978)
Roads: 24,300 km/15,100 mi (1977 paved)
Currency: 1 Sri Lanka rupee = 100 cents

linguistically, and in religion. The SINHALESE, 71% of the population, speak Sinhalese and are Buddhists. The TAMIL (21%) speak their own language and are Hindus. Smaller numbers of Tamil-speaking Muslims or Moors (6%), Burghers of Dutch descent, Eurasians, Malays, and Europeans make up the remainder. The Sinhalese and the Tamils observe CASTE distinctions, which are often important in politics. Sinhalese is the official language, although Tamil is also listed as a national language. English, commonly used in government, is spoken by about 10% of the population.

Less than 25% of the population is urban, and aside from COLOMBO, the capital, KANDY and Jaffna are the most important cities. A declining death rate, a comparatively high—but slowly decreasing—birthrate, and a large number of young people create a potential for rapid population growth. Government health and welfare services have contributed to a

Colombo, the capital of Sri Lanka, possesses one of the largest manmade harbors in the world. Increased transoceanic commerce coming from the opening (1869) of the Suez Canal transformed Colombo into one of the busiest ports on the Indian Ocean.

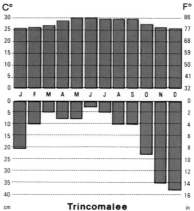

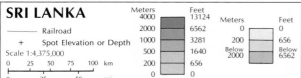

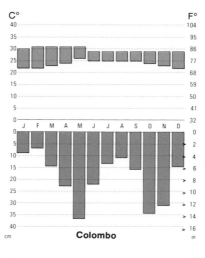

Annual climate charts for two localities in Sri Lanka illustrate the major climate zones of the Asian island nation. Bars indicate monthly ranges of temperatures (red) and precipitation (blue). Colombo, the capital and major port on the Indian ocean, has a monsoon climate. Trincomalee, on the Bay of Bengal, has a tropical wet-dry climate.

Colombo

Trincomalee

SRI LANKA

——— Railroad
+ Spot Elevation or Depth

Scale 1:4,375,000

Meters	Feet
4000	13124
2000	6562
1000	3281
500	1640
200	656
0	0

Meters	Feet
0	0
200	656
Below 2000	Below 6562

© 1980 Rand McNally & Co.
A-560600-772 -1

longer life expectancy of 66 years, but serious health problems such as malaria persist.

Universal, free education has resulted in an 82% literacy rate. University education (see SOUTH ASIAN UNIVERSITIES) has been primarily academic rather than technical, an emphasis that has prompted criticism in light of the nation's high unemployment problem.

ECONOMIC ACTIVITY
The early migrants from India brought with them their practice of irrigated rice farming, which was the basis of the island's economy until the British started plantations. Tea, rubber, and coconuts have since then been by far the most important crops. These products earn about 70% of Sri Lanka's foreign exchange—tea alone more than 50%. Concentration on export crops has contributed to a deficit in food production, resulting in importation of about one-third of the country's food needs. Efforts have been made, with foreign assistance, to improve rice yields and to enlarge fisheries. The annual fish catch is now about 140,000 metric tons (154,000 U.S. tons). Pearling, formerly an important source of income, has recently been revived.

Manufacturing, which with mining employs 15% of the labor force, is based on the processing of agricultural products and on producing some light consumer goods. Sri Lanka's export trade is chiefly with the United Kingdom, the United States, and Pakistan. Imports of crude petroleum from Saudi Arabia and Iran create a large trade deficit. Tourism is grow-

Women harvest tea leaves on this hillside plantation in Sri Lanka. The crop is cultivated primarily in the highlands of the south central portion of the country, an area receiving abundant rainfall; tea has become Sri Lanka's most valuable export commodity.

ing in economic importance. In 1977, Sri Lanka had a gross national product of $3.5 billion ($253 per capita).

GOVERNMENT AND HISTORY
Since promulgation of a new constitution in September 1978, Sri Lanka has had a strong presidential system of government under J. R. Jayawardene, who was elected to a 6-year term. The cabinet is reponsible to the elected parliament. The court system is extensive, and Sri Lankan law is based on a complex mixture of English, Roman-Dutch, Muslim, and customary law. The 9 provinces and 22 districts are further subdivided into towns and villages.

Sri Lanka was known to the ancient Greeks and Romans

and has a recorded history dating to the 5th century BC. Buddhism was brought from India during the 3d century BC. During its early history, the island was seldom united under a single ruler, and for a period during the 15th century it was tributary to China.

The Portuguese arrived in 1505 and found seven indigenous kingdoms. The Dutch defeated the Portuguese in the mid-1600s and controlled most of the island until the British ousted them in 1796. The country became an independent member of the Commonwealth in 1948. Successive governments have faced problems of rapid population growth, food deficits, dependence on foreign markets, and hostilities among the country's ethnic groups. Prime minister Solomon W. R. D. BANDARANAIKE dominated Sri Lankan politics until his assassination on Sept. 25, 1959. His wife, Sirimavo BANDARANAIKE, succeeded him, but her radical socialist policies created opposition and she lost the 1965 elections. Reelected in 1970, she ruled until defeated in the 1977 elections by the conservative United Nationals party, led by J. R. Jayawardene.

JOHN E. MACDONALD

Bibliography:

DESCRIPTION AND TRAVEL: Hall, Basil, *Travels in India, Ceylon, and Borneo* (1931; repr. 1976); Uchiyama, Akira, *Sri Lanka* (1973); Wirz, Paul, *Katargama: The Holiest Place in Ceylon,* 2d ed. (1975).
ECONOMY: Jacob, L. M., *Sri Lanka: From Dominion to Republic* (1974); Karunatilake, H. N., *Central Banking and Monetary Policy in Sri Lanka* (1975); Snodgrass, Donald R., *Ceylon: An Export Economy in Transition* (1975).
HISTORY: Mendis, Garrett C., *The Early History of Ceylon and Its Relations with India and Other Foreign Countries* (1932; repr. 1975); Mills, Lenox A., *Ceylon Under British Rule* (1964); Winius, George D., *Fatal History of Portuguese Ceylon* (1971).
POLITICS AND GOVERNMENT: Jupp, James, *Sri Lanka: Third World Democracy?* (1978); Kearney, Robert N., *The Politics of Ceylon* (1973); Wilson, A. J., *Politics in Sri Lanka: 1945-1973* (1974).
SOCIAL LIFE AND CUSTOMS: Gombrich, Richard F., *Precept and Practice: Traditional Buddhism in the Rural Highlands of Ceylon* (1971); Marby, Heidrun, *Tea in Ceylon* (1972); Phadnis, Urmila, *Religion and Politics in Sri Lanka* (1976).

Sri Lanka universities: see SOUTH ASIAN
UNIVERSITIES.

Srinagar   [sri-nuh'-guhr]

Srinagar, the summer capital of the state of Jammu and Kashmir in northern India and headquarters of the Srinagar district, is situated in the Vale of Kashmir on the Jhelum River at an elevation of 1,593 m (5,227 ft). The city's population of 403,413 (1971) is more than 85% Muslim. Srinagar is located on the edge of picturesque Dal Lake, noted for its houseboats and floating gardens. In addition to being a flourishing trade and tourist center, the city serves a large agricultural area. Its industries produce carpets, silks, metal goods, and wood carvings.

Landmarks include the Jama Masjid (completed 1402), the largest mosque in Kashmir; Mogul Emperor Akbar's 16th-century fort on a hill overlooking the city; the 17th-century Pathar Mosque; and the three Mogul Gardens of Shalimar (1619), Nishat (1620s), and Chashma Shahi (1642). Raja Pravarasen founded the city in the 6th century.   ASHOK K. DUTT

Srivijaya Empire   [sree-vee-jah'-yah]

The Srivijaya Empire, a maritime kingdom centered at Palembang in southern Sumatra, dominated trade between South and East Asia from the 7th to the 13th century by virtue of its control of the Straits of Malacca. Settled before AD 600 by Hindus from southern India, Palembang took on a strong Buddhist coloration in the 7th century after trading vessels began arriving from strongly Buddhist Bengal. By the late 7th century it was a center of Mahayana Buddhist learning, visited by Chinese pilgrims. At Srivijaya's peak of power, after c.800, it controlled the Straits of Malacca, the coastlines of northern Sumatra and the Malay Peninsula, much of western Java, and many island trading centers north toward the Chinese coast. About 1025 the Hindu Chola dynasty of southern India took over most of Java. Muslim traders—including Arabs and those from the Persian Gulf as well as Islamized Bengalis—arrived in the 14th century and took over the growing spice trade. By the late 15th century the Muslim trading center at Melaka had gained dominance over the traditional Srivijayan domain and virtually all of the Indonesian island empire.   JOHN F. CADY

Bibliography: Wolters, O. W., *Early Indonesian Commerce; a Study of the Origins of Srivijaya* (1967) and *The Fall of Srivijaya in Malay History* (1970).

SST: see SUPERSONIC TRANSPORT.

Ssu-ma Ch'ien   (Sima Qian)   [suh-mah chee-en]

Ssu-ma Ch'ien, c.145-c.87 BC, was the official court historian of Emperor Wu Ti of the HAN dynasty in ancient China. He wrote the *Shih Chi* (Records of the Historian), the first general history of China from its earliest times. The work records 2,000 years of history and consists of 130 chapters, 100 of which are biographical. It is written in a lively but terse style and has influenced the historical writing and literary tastes of China, Japan, and Korea to the present time.

Bibliography: Watson, Burton, *The Records of the Grand Historian of China,* 2 vols. (1961) and *Ssu-ma Ch'ien, Grand Historian of China* (1958).

Ssu-ma Kuang   (Sima Guang)   [suh-mah kwahng]

Ssu-ma Kuang, 1019-86, was a Chinese scholar and statesman of the SUNG dynasty. He compiled the *Tzu-chih t'ung-chien* (Comprehensive Mirror for Aid in Government), a mammoth chronicle of Chinese history from 403 BC to AD 959 written from the viewpoint of Confucian moral precepts. The work is still admired in China for its high standards of scholarship.

Bibliography: Beasley, W. G., and Pulleyblank, E. G., eds., *Historians of China and Japan* (1961).

Stabat Mater   [stah'-baht mah'-tur]

The *Stabat Mater dolorosa,* depicting the weeping Mother at the Cross, is the sequence (see SEQUENCE, music) for the Feast of the Seven Dolours (September 15). It was probably written in the 13th century by Jacopone da Todi, but did not become a part of the Roman Catholic liturgy until 1727. Unlike the *Dies irae* sequence, it is the text alone and not the plainsong melody that has received attention in concert settings. It has been popular with composers since the Renaissance settings of Josquin des Prez, Palestrina, and Roland de Lassus. Later composers who have set the *Stabat Mater* include Pergolesi, Haydn, Rossini, Schubert, Verdi, Dvořák, Poulenc, and Virgil Thomson.   ELWYN A. WIENANDT

stabile   [stay'-beel]

A stabile is a stationary abstract sculpture or construction, often on a monumental scale. The artist Jean Arp coined the term *stabile* to describe such works by Alexander CALDER, thereby opposing them to Calder's other MOBILE, or suspended moving, sculptures. Calder first exhibited his stabiles at the Galerie Percier in Paris in spring 1931. His *Whale* (1937; Museum of Modern Art, New York City) is a typical example. A number of other sculptors, such as Anthony CARO, George RICKEY, and David SMITH, developed their own versions of the stabile.   HARRY RAND

Stabler, Ken

Kenneth Michael Stabler, b. Foley, Ala., Dec. 25, 1945, one of the National Football League's (NFL) few left-handed passers, was a star quarterback at Foley High School and the University of Alabama, leading the Crimson Tide to three postseason bowl games. Drafted by the Oakland Raiders in 1968, Stabler did not become a starter until 1973, when he led the American Football Conference (AFC) in passing. In 1976 he led the entire NFL in passing, completing 66.7 percent of his passes for 27 touchdowns and 2,737 yd (2,502.7 m), taking the Raiders to victory in the Super Bowl. Twice (1974, 1976) he was named AFC Player of the Year.   HOWARD LISS

Stacy, Hollis

Hollis Stacy, b. Savannah, Ga., Mar. 16, 1954, is one of the premier female golfers in the United States. Among her victories are the United States Golfers Association (USGA) Junior Girls Championships for 3 consecutive years (1969–71), the 1977 Lady Tara Classic, the U.S. Open twice (1977, 1978), and the 1977 Rail Charity Classic at Springfield, Ill. In 1977, with a 271, she broke Kathy Whitworth's 11-year record for the lowest 72-hole score. Stacy won the mixed team Pepsi-Cola Championship with Jerry Pate in 1977.   HOWARD LISS

stadium

A stadium is a structure specifically designed for sporting contests and other spectator events. The history of the stadium is directly connected to the history of the Olympic Games, perhaps the oldest organized sports event. The name comes from the latinized Greek word *stade*, a unit of measurement equivalent to about 184.7 m (606 ft), which was the length of the footrace in the ancient Olympics and the overall length of the ancient Greek stadia. Construction of the stadium at Olympia, where the quadrennial Olympic Games were held, was begun in the 8th century BC.

The Greeks also built hippodromes for their chariot races. These were wider than the horseshoe-shaped stadia used for athletic contests and could accommodate several chariots pulled by four-horse teams. Chariot races appear to have become part of many Greek athletic competitions as early as the 7th century BC.

The Roman circus was an adaptation of the Greek hippodrome. The Circus Maximus in Rome, which was reconstructed several times, was the finest example of this type of structure. The most important version was built in the 1st century BC and may have held 250,000 spectators, who looked down from three sides on a track 610 m (2,000 ft) long and 183 m (600 ft) wide. The Circus Maximus was destroyed in the Christian era.

The Romans built another type of stadium, called an amphitheater, that appears in those parts of Western Europe where Roman civilization established itself. The best preserved amphitheater is a structure in Arles, France.

The COLOSSEUM in Rome, built AD c.75–80, was used for gladiator fights, uneven encounters between Christians and hungry beasts, and the various other savageries the Romans called games. The size of the arena, the playing area, was not standardized in the amphitheaters and was less important than providing an unobstructed view from each of the approximately 50,000 seats. Today, the Colosseum is a fragile ruin, and the Italian government has banned traffic from the road around it. Amphitheaters fell into disuse after the 5th century and most became ruins.

In the 19th century, when organized sports once again began to attract widespread interest, the stadium reemerged as a significant architectural form. The first modern Olympic Games, held in 1896, gave impetus to modern stadium building. The Athens stadium, which has a capacity of 66,000, was actually constructed using a 2d-century stadium as the base.

The first third of the 20th century saw the construction of more than 100 modern stadia in the United States alone and many more throughout the world. What made this surge of building activity possible was the development of reinforced concrete. Almost all of these stadia were designed for a specific sport, although many of them could accommodate other sports with varying degrees of success. Most of those outside the United States were used primarily for soccer. Most stadia in the United States were built for college football, and many are still in use. The most charming and intimate American stadia from this time, however, were those designed for baseball, with irregular shapes that followed the city streets around them. Forbes Field in Pittsburgh, Pa., built in 1909, and Crosley Field in Cincinnati, Ohio, built 1912, have been destroyed. Fenway Park in Boston, built in 1912, and Wrigley Field in Chicago, built in 1922, are still in use, however.

The requirements of different sports dictated different kinds of stadia. For American football the U-shaped stadium (Harvard Stadium, Cambridge, Mass., 1912), the ellipse (Yale Bowl, New Haven, Conn., 1914), and facing crescent stands (Northwestern University, Evanston, Ill., 1926) proved best. For the Olympic Games the favored shape is a rectangular configuration with the small ends rounded. The original Yankee Stadium in New York, built in 1923, added the innovation of three tiers of seats protected by a roof. Dodger Stadium in Los Angeles, built in 1962, was the first tiered stadium without columns, affording every seat an unobstructed view.

In the late 1960s and early 1970s a trend developed toward more practical and economical bowl-shaped multipurpose stadia. These structures featured seats that could be emplaced or removed depending on the sport played. Movable seating was first introduced in Shea Stadium in New York in 1964. The most notable examples of this kind of stadium include Riverfront Stadium in Cincinnati (1970) and Three Rivers Stadium in Pittsburgh (1970).

The most startling innovation of recent years, however, is the domed stadium with internal climate control and artificial

The Roman Colosseum is a vast, 4-story, elliptical amphitheater that accommodated about 50,000 spectators in seats on concrete tiers arranged around an oval arena. The open-air stadium was the site of gladiatorial events, wild-animal fights, and even mock sea battles.

Seating 66,000 spectators, the plastic-domed Houston Astrodome (1965) is one of the world's largest indoor stadiums, covering an area of 3.8 ha (9.5 acres). The complex is used for many types of sporting events, including baseball, football, basketball, and boxing.

turf. With its 66,000 seats, the Astrodome in Houston, Tex., (1965) dwarfed other indoor arenas such as New York's first Madison Square Garden (1890), Chicago Stadium (1928), and the Palazzetto dell Sport (1960) in Rome. Other recent domed stadia are the Kingdome (1976) in Seattle, Wash., and the Superdome (1975) in New Orleans, La.

The largest stadium in the world is Strahov Stadium in Prague, which was built for gymnastics in 1934 with a capacity of 240,000. Maracaña Stadium in Rio de Janeiro holds 200,000 spectators for soccer. Hamden Park in Glasgow, Scotland, seats 149,500; Wembley in North London, 126,000; Melbourne Cricket Ground in Melbourne, Australia, 116,000; Soldier Field in Chicago, 110,000; John F. Kennedy Memorial Stadium in Philadelphia, 105,000; Lenin Stadium in Moscow, 103,000; Odsal Stadium in Bradford, England, 102,500; the Los Angeles Coliseum, Los Angeles, 102,000; the Rose Bowl in Pasadena, Calif., 101,000; the University of Michigan Stadium in Ann Arbor, Mich., 101,000; Olympic Stadium in Rome, 100,000; and Aztec Stadium in Mexico City, 100,000.

NICHOLAS ACOCELLA

Bibliography: Cichy, Bodo, *The Great Ages of Architecture: From Ancient Greece to the Present Day* (1964); Shannon, Bill, and Kalinsky, George, *The Ball Parks* (1975).

Staël, Madame de   [stahl]

A Swiss-French writer famous for her literary criticism, novels, and flamboyant life, Madame de Staël, originally Anne Louise Germaine Necker, b. Apr. 22, 1766, d. July 14, 1817, was one of the most important intellectuals of a changing Europe. The daughter of the politician Jacques Necker, she married the Swedish ambassador Baron de Staël-Holstein in 1786. She had numerous affairs, the most famous being with the novelist Benjamin Constant. Having grown up in the intellectual milieu of her mother's salon, she quickly established her own and made it a center of progressive discussion. Banned from Paris by Napoleon in 1803, she established a new salon at Coppet on Lake Geneva.

Madame de Staël wrote voluminously. *De la littérature considérée dans ses rapports avec les institutions sociales* (The Influence of Literature upon Society) was published in 1800 and established her reputation. Her two novels, *Delphine* (1802) and *Corinne* (1807), depict lonely and gifted women caught in a clash of cultures and codes. In 1810 she issued *De l'Allemagne* (On Germany), a major work that investigates German romantic literature and philosophy. Its praise of things German so incensed Napoleon, long her persecutor, that he destroyed the first edition and exiled its author. Madame de Staël played a primary role in the development of French romanticism and modern literary criticism. Her other literary works include a memoir of her father (1804), reflections on Rousseau (1788), and a discussion of the Revolution (1818).

JANET M. TODD

Bibliography: Andrews, Wayne, *Germaine: A Portrait of Madame de Staël* (1964); Herold, J. C., *Mistress to an Age* (1958; repr. 1975); Levaillant, Maurice, *The Passionate Exiles: Madame de Staël and Madame Recamier*, trans. by Malcolm Barnes (1958).

Staël, Nicolas de

Nicolas de Staël, b. Mar. 16, 1914, d. Feb. 16, 1955, was a leading contributor to modernist painting in Europe. After his early education in Brussels, de Staël studied painting with various masters, including Fernand Léger. During World War II he served with the French Foreign Legion in Tunisia. After the war he traveled in Europe and Great Britain, finally settling in France. By the mid-1940s he had developed a vigorous, individual style of painting in which heavily textured areas of color hover between suggestions of landscape and total abstraction. De Staël exhibited his works in many places in Europe and the United States until his death by suicide in 1955.

CARTER RATCLIFF

Bibliography: Cooper, Douglas, *Nicolas de Staël* (1961); Demur, Guy, *Nicolas de Staël*, trans. by Fintan O'Connell (1976); Duhuit, Georges, *Nicolas de Staël* (1950).

staff

The musical staff, or stave, is a series of parallel horizontal lines that, in conjunction with a CLEF, provides a convenient means of notating pitch. The positioning of notes on or between the lines of the staff, which in case of need can be extended upward and downward through the use of ledger lines, allows quick visual apprehension of the contours of a melody or part. (The visible graph only approximates the musical shape because pitch is indicated by key signature and accidentals as well as by location on the staff.) The five-line staff standard at present is found in some 13th-century manuscripts. Staffs of fewer lines appear earlier—the four-line staff has endured for the notation of plainsong—and staffs of six lines, later. The staff is among the innovations credited to GUIDO D'AREZZO (d. 1050).

Pitches may be represented without a staff; systems of staffless notation include solmization (also ascribed to Guido d'Arezzo) and the TABLATURES familiar to lutenists and guitarists.

LAWRENCE FUCHSBERG

Stafford, Jean

An American novelist and short story writer, Jean Stafford, b. Corina, Calif., July 1, 1915, d. Mar. 17, 1979, specialized in fiction that explored the effects of isolation on children and adults. The young foreign-born heroine of her first novel, *Boston Adventure* (1944), established Stafford's primary theme, and *The Mountain Lion* (1947), which deals perceptively with a brother and sister's difficult transition from childhood to adolescence, has become a minor classic. Stafford's short stories are collected in *Children Are Bored on Sunday* (1953), *Bad Characters* (1964), which contains "A Winter's Tale," and the 1970 Pulitzer Prize-winning *Collected Stories* (1969), in which her 1955 O. Henry Prize story, "In the Zoo," appears.

Bibliography: Auchincloss, Louis, *Pioneers and Caretakers: A Study of Nine American Women Novelists* (1965).

Stafford, Thomas P.

The American astronaut Thomas Patten Stafford, b. Weatherford, Okla., Sept. 17, 1930, commanded the last test mission before the first manned landing on the Moon. He graduated from the U.S. Naval Academy in 1952, transferred to the Air Force, and was selected as an astronaut in 1962. On *Gemini 6-A* (Dec. 15–16, 1965), Stafford (as pilot) and commander Walter M. Schirra rendezvoused with *Gemini 7*, the first meeting in space of two manned spacecraft. As commander of *Gemini 9-A* (June 3–6, 1966), Stafford and pilot Eugene Cernan performed extensive rendezvous and docking tests (see GEMINI PROGRAM).

Apollo 10 (May 18–26, 1969) was a full-scale test of the Apollo spacecraft for the lunar landing. Stafford (commander) and Cernan (lunar module pilot) flew the lunar module within 14.9 km (9.26 mi) of the lunar surface (see APOLLO PROGRAM). On his last mission in space, Stafford commanded the U.S. part in the APOLLO-SOYUZ TEST PROJECT (July 15–24, 1975), the first international manned space mission. Stafford returned (1975) to Air Force duty and was named (1978) Air Force deputy chief of staff for research and development. He retired (1979) from the Air Force with the rank of lieutenant general.

DAVID DOOLING

Bibliography: Cunningham, Walter, *The All-American Boys* (1977); Lewis, Richard S., *Appointment on the Moon*, rev. ed. (1969); *The Voyage of Apollo* (1974), and *From Vinland to Mars: A Thousand Years of Exploration* (1976); NASA, *Mission Report/Apollo 10* (NASA EP. 70; 1969).

Staffordshire   [staf'-urd-shir]

Staffordshire is a county in the West Midlands of England, with a population of 994,000 (1977 est.). Its area of 2,716 km² (1,049 mi²) is mostly hilly, with limestone moorlands in the north and a central farming region. The area is drained by the River Trent. Stafford (1971 est. pop., 54,900) is the county town. Other important cities are STOKE-ON-TRENT and Burton-on-Trent. Coal mining, dairy farming, brewing, and the manufacture of iron and steel products, shoes, pottery, glass, textiles, and chemicals are mainstays of the economy. Staffordshire was formed from lands once part of the Anglo-Saxon kingdom of Mercia.

Staffordshire bull terrier

The forebears of the Staffordshire bull terrier were the old bulldog and one or more types of British terriers. The old bulldog was used in bullbaiting until this sport was finally outlawed in Britain in 1835. Many of its advocates then turned to dogfighting but found the larger bulldogs too slow, so they crossed the bulldogs with one or more terrier types to obtain the faster and lighter bull-and-terrier. In the 1860s the bull-and-terriers were used to develop the dogs now known as bull terriers; the original bull-and-terriers, popular with the workers in Staffordshire, were then called Staffordshire bull terriers.

The English Kennel Club recognized the Staffordshire bull terrier in 1935, the American Kennel Club, in 1974. The dog has a short, deep body, a broad, deep head, a short muzzle, and very pronounced and powerful cheek muscles. It carries its small ears partly erect. It ranges from 35.5 to 40.5 cm (14 to 16 in) high at the shoulders and from 11 to 17 kg (24 to 38 lb) in weight.   EDWIN E. ROSENBLUM

The Staffordshire bull terrier is a compact, muscular dog developed in England during the mid-1800s. Breeders sought a fighting dog both smaller and faster than those used for bullbaiting and bearbaiting. A mixture of bulldog and native terrier stock—probably including the black and tan terrier—resulted in this agile and aggressive fighter.

Bibliography: Gordon, John F., *Staffordshire Bull Terriers* (1976); Marvin, John T., *Book of All Terriers,* 2d ed. (1976).

Staffordshire terrier: see AMERICAN STAFFORDSHIRE TERRIER.

Staffordshire ware

Staffordshire ware, which includes pottery tableware and figurines, takes its name from the county of Staffordshire, England, where it has been produced at many factories—including Wedgwood, Minton, and Spode—since the 17th century. This area around Stoke-on-Trent, known as the Potteries, was chosen because of the local availability of both clay and coal. Generally the products are earthenware or stoneware made in relatively unsophisticated but charming designs. Staffordshire figurines depict many subjects including dogs, cottages, and even portraits.

Bibliography: Pugh, P. D. Gordon, *Staffordshire Portrait Figures (and Allied Subjects of the Victorian Era)* (1970); Rackham, Bernard, *Early Staffordshire Pottery* (1951); Sekers, David, *Popular Staffordshire Pottery* (1978); Turner, H. A., *Collector's Guide to Staffordshire Pottery Figures* (1971).

stage

A stage is a stratigraphic unit that records sediment deposition during a specific interval of geologic time. It is used by field geologists in problems of local and regional correlation of stratigraphic units. Stages are commonly defined by one or several biostratigraphic zones, although they may also be established by lithologic criteria, radiometric age determinations, stable-isotope distributions, or structural relationships.

stage lighting

Until the Renaissance, most dramatic performances occurred in open-air theaters lit by the sun. When performances moved indoors, the stage was illuminated by candles and, later, by oil and gas lamps. The flames of each of these inevitably produced flickering and variations in color and intensity, although gas could be controlled to some extent. Thus the auditorium and the stage remained lit during performances. This changed in 1876, when Richard Wagner darkened the auditorium of the Bayreuth Festspielhaus.

The general theory and practice of lighting was developed during the 16th and 17th centuries by Sebastiano SERLIO, Leone di Somi (1527–92), Nicola Sabbattini (1574–1654), and Angelo Ingegnari (c.1550–c.1613) in Italy, and by Josef Furttenbach (1591–1667) in Germany. They developed a symmetrical system of stage lighting and experimented with the use of color. Advances since then have focused on increased control and intensity and on adapting lighting to changes in stage architecture and design.

After gas lighting became feasible, Philadelphia's Chestnut Street Theater in 1816 became the first in the world to light the stage with gas. Gas provided unprecedented brightness and control, but also unwanted heat, odor, and fires. The limelight, a light with a lime filament that was the prototype of the spotlight, was invented in 1816 by Thomas DRUMMOND. It produced a brilliant yet mellow white light. The carbon-arc light, first demonstrated in 1808, did not become practical until the introduction of electricity.

Electricity—in the form of the Jablochkoff candle, an electric-arc light—was first used in stage lighting at the Paris Hippodrome in 1878; London's Savoy Theater in 1881 became the first to use INCANDESCENT LAMPS. Electric light allowed more variety and control than ever before and was the perfect complement to naturalistic staging, which developed at the same time. Pioneers in the field included Sir Henry IRVING, André ANTOINE, David BELASCO, and Konstantin STANISLAVSKY.

Much of modern lighting practice is derived from the theories of the Swiss designer Adolphe APPIA, who believed that light should be the unifying element of the theater. His designs typically depended on the strong use of light and shadow to create both atmosphere and an impression of three-dimensionality. The "sky-dome," or cyclorama, invented by Mariano Fortuny (1871–1949), helped illuminate the stage by reflected light.

Since World War I, technology and theory have remained basically unchanged. Most stage lighting today is provided by spotlights, consisting of electric lamps in metal housing with reflectors and lenses to direct and focus the light. Efforts over the past half century have gone into developing higher-wattage instruments and more sophisticated control equipment. The tungsten-halogen lamp has been used increasingly since the 1960s for more efficient lighting. Major innovations, largely in the area of projections, have come from Erwin PISCATOR, Josef SVOBODA, Adolf Linnebach (1876–1963), and Emil F. Burian (1904–59).   ARNOLD ARONSON

Bibliography: Bentham, Frederick, *The Art of Stage Lighting* (1970; rev. ed., 1976); Bergman, Gösta M., *Lighting in the Theatre* (1977); McCandless, Stanley, *A Method of Lighting the Stage* (1932; rev. ed., 1942).

stagecoach

The stagecoach was a public transport vehicle drawn by a team of four or six horses from one station, or stage, to another on a regular schedule. Long-distance stagecoach lines began operating between some major English cities in the late 17th century, but weather and highwaymen often made a sham of their schedules. American stagecoach lines were begun before the Revolution. Many of the routes they followed are still called post roads because, in addition to passengers and baggage, the coaches carried mail. As in England, inns known as coach houses were established at layover stops between major destinations. Additional horse-changing stations were often established between them. Six-passenger stagecoaches carried drivers and shotgun-holding guards on the outside upper front seat and passengers or two more guards

The stagecoach became the most widely accepted mode of long-distance transportation throughout the American West before the building of the railroads during the late 1800s. Used to convey passengers, mail, or goods, the stagecoach was typically drawn by a team of four or six horses. The vehicles' name was derived from their practice of stopping at resupply points, or stages, along the route.

on an outside rear seat. Passengers often had to contend with Indians, robbers, and difficult terrain and weather. The arrival of the railroads ended the stagecoach era, and by the late 19th century, they had disappeared.

Bibliography: Dunlop, Richard, *Wheels West* (1977); Moody, Ralph, *Stagecoach West* (1967).

stagflation

Stagflation is a condition of economic stagnation, or RECESSION, combined with serious INFLATION. Prior to the 1970s inflation was experienced in times of prosperity when demand for goods pushed up prices. In economic slowdowns, unemployment and the consequent drop in consumer spending had a stabilizing effect on prices. That price increases accelerated during the recessions of the 1970s has been attributed at least in part to the economic dislocations caused by large Vietnam War deficits and sharply higher energy costs. Another partial explanation given for stagflation is decreased productivity because of higher costs of production—caused by increased government regulation—and decreased competition (see MONOPOLY AND COMPETITION) in the marketplace—allowing large business firms to reduce output rather than prices. Stagflation makes economic policymaking difficult because the use of FISCAL POLICY and MONETARY POLICY, for example, to stimulate the economy out of a recession may increase inflationary pressures, and measures to decrease inflation may lead to slower economic growth.

Stagg, Amos Alonzo

Amos Alonzo Stagg, b. West Orange, N.J., Aug. 16, 1862, d. Mar. 17, 1965, was an American college football player and the most successful coach in the history of that sport with 314 career victories. He played end at Yale University and in 1892 began the first of 41 years as coach at the University of Chicago. Stagg produced six Big Ten Conference titles (plus a tie for a seventh) while compiling a 268-141 won-lost record. He retired at the age of 70 but soon became coach at the College of the Pacific. He retired again after 14 years only to work 3 more years as an assistant at Susquehanna College. Stagg is credited with inventing numerous offensive strategies—around-the-end plays, the flea flicker, hidden-ball plays—and the tackling dummy. He was honored by the National Football Hall of Fame.

Bibliography: Lucia, Ellis, *Mr. Football: Amos Alonzo Stagg* (1970).

Stagnelius, Erik Johan   [stahg-nay'-lee-uhs]

Regarded as Sweden's most purely romantic poet, Erik Johan Stagnelius, b. Oct. 14, 1793, d. Apr. 3, 1823, worked as a civil servant after his university studies (1811-14) in Lund and Uppsala. He published four anonymous collections of poems during his lifetime: *Wladimir den Store* (Wladimir the Great, 1817), *Liljor i Saron* (Lilies of Sharon, 1821), *Martyrerna* (The Martyrs, 1821), and *Bacchanterna* (The Bacchants, 1822). The remainder of his work, much of it in fragments, appeared posthumously.

Bibliography: Benson, Adolph, B., *The Old Norse Element in Swedish Romanticism* (1914); Gustafson, Alrik, *A History of Swedish Literature* (1961).

Stahl, Georg Ernst   [shtahl]

Georg Ernst Stahl, b. Oct. 21, 1660, d. May 14, 1734, was a German physician and chemist who developed the ideas of Johannes R. Becher into the PHLOGISTON THEORY. This theory conceived of fire as a material substance. It related such diverse processes as rusting and combustion and served as a unifying principle of chemistry until Antoine Lavoisier developed the oxygen theory in the late 18th century. Stahl taught courses as second professor of medicine at the University of Halle from 1694 until 1716, when he became personal physician to Frederick I of Prussia. A prolific author in both medicine and chemistry, he insisted that truth can be fully demonstrated only by experiment.   RALPH GABLE

Bibliography: Partington, J., *A History of Chemistry*, vol. 2 (1961); Stillman, J., *The Story of Alchemy and Early Chemistry* (1960).

stained glass

Stained glass is a term used to describe windows composed of colored glass set in designs. In the West the earliest extant stained glass dates from the 11th century, but the finest stained-glass windows were produced in conjunction with GOTHIC ART AND ARCHITECTURE from about 1130 to 1330. In Islamic countries colored glass, set in wooden or stucco frames in foliate designs, is known to have been used beginning in the 12th century.

History. The earliest surviving Western examples are five windows (early 12th century) depicting Old Testament prophets (Augsburg Cathedral, West Germany). Extensive use of stained glass, however, first occurred in Abbot Suger's rebuilding (1137-44) of the Royal Abbey of Saint-Denis near Paris, which provided enormous new windows (now destroyed or heavily restored), particularly in the ambulatory. They were the direct inspiration for the three great lancet windows (*c.*1150) in the west facade of CHARTRES CATHEDRAL, noted for the famed Chartres blue. They survived the disastrous fire of 1194 and were incorporated in the magnificent new cathedral begun in the same year. Most of the 173 huge windows produced in the next 30 years for Chartres Cathedral remain intact; the church's pictorial program was followed in the windows of Gothic cathedrals and churches throughout

The Virgin and Child, a detail from the 12th-century lancet window known as La Belle Verrière at Chartres Cathedral, forms a luminous mosaic of red and blue panes. The well-preserved windows of Chartres are exceptional for their deep colors and masterly designs.

France and England. The SAINTE-CHAPELLE in Paris, built 1243–48, contains 15 enormous windows with 1,134 narrative scenes that form walls of glass and mark the apogee of Gothic stained glass.

Gothic stained glass owes much of its beauty to the deliberately flat, two-dimensional design perfectly suited to the medium. By the late 14th century, perspective had been introduced in stained-glass design in imitation of painting, which led to a debasement of the art that reached its lowest point in the 18th century. The 19th-century GOTHIC REVIVAL in architecture led to a rebirth of stained glass for both religious and secular buildings. William Morris and Sir Edward Burne-Jones spurred the revival in England, which then spread to the United States, where its most successful practitioners were John LA FARGE and Louis Comfort TIFFANY. A resurgence of the art and a return to two-dimensional design and the use of pure color occurred following World War II. The abstract secular designs of the German Ludwig Schaffrath and the windows by Henri Matisse for the Dominican Chapel of the Rosary (1951) in Vence, France, are the most notable works of modern times. In the United States two remarkable churches have employed stained glass on a large scale: Wallace K. Harrison's First Presbyterian Church (1959) in Stamford, Conn., has stained-glass walls and ceilings supported by concrete ribs; Skidmore, Owings, and Merrill's Air Force Academy Chapel, Colorado Springs, Colo. (1959), is almost entirely of stained glass suspended in aluminum frames, recalling Sainte-Chapelle's walls of glass.

Technique. Stained-glass technique has changed little since its development in the 11th century. Pieces of glass of various colors are placed together on a full-size model or drawing of the window. They are joined with lead strips that are soldered in place. The assembled panels are then suspended in the window frame or the stone tracery on iron bars called ar-

(Above) *Louis Comfort Tiffany's Oyster Bay window (c.1905), a landscape viewed through a wisteria trellis, exhibits the curving natural forms typical of Tiffany's Art Nouveau creations. Tiffany used both translucent and transparent glass in the windows and decorative objects that brought him early recognition. (Morse Gallery of Art, Winter Park, Fla.)*

(Left) *The window of Saint Matthew, one of a series designed by William Morris, reflects Morris's emphasis on medieval principles of design in its traditional subject matter, its two-dimensional style, and its inclusion of the lead framework in the composition. Morris's influential decorative-arts firm produced stained-glass windows for both ecclesiastical and domestic architecture. (Christ Church, Southgate, London.)*

matures; these were straight in 12th-century windows, but by the early 13th century they were shaped into circles, lozenges, quatrefoils, and combinations of these. The colors were achieved by mixing metal oxides with the molten glass during smelting; the Chartres blue was obtained from cobalt mined in Bohemia; the mines were exhausted by the 14th century, and this azure blue could not be reproduced until the 20th century. Red was obtained from oxidized copper, green from bioxide of copper, purple from manganese mixed with cobalt, and yellow from manganese and ferrous oxide. Facial features, decorations, and lettering were painted in GRISAILLE, a gray-brown enamel baked on the glass. The glass was formed either in cylinders that were split and flattened, called muff glass, or spun centrifugally into a disk thicker in the center than at the rim, called crown glass. Bubbles, flaws, and other irregularities diffuse the light and make the glass sparkle. Stained glass, once believed to be impervious to the effects of time, has proved fatally susceptible to air pollution; this vulnerability has spurred conservation efforts throughout the Western world.   EDWARD T. McCLELLAN

Bibliography: Armitage, E. L., Stained Glass: History, Technology and Practice (1959); Beyer, Victor, Stained Glass Windows (1965); Cowen, Painton, Rose Windows (1979); Day, Lewis F., Windows: A Book about Stained and Painted Glass, 3d ed. (1909); Johnson, James Rosser, The Radiance of Chartres (1964); Lee, Lawrence, The Appreciation of Stained Glass (1977); Lee, Lawrence, et al., Stained Glass (1976); Sowers, Robert, Stained Glass: An Architectural Art (1965).

stainless steel

Stainless steels are iron-based alloys that have a very high resistance to rusting and corrosion because of their chromium content, which is greater than that found in other types of steel. Nickel, molybdenum, and other elements are also used, in addition to chromium, to produce stainless steels with a great range of properties. The most widely manufactured stainless steel is the alloy known as "18-8," containing 18% chromium, 8% nickel, and 0.15% carbon. This alloy can be formed into precisely detailed, complicated shapes and is commonly used for making flatware, cooking utensils, and plumbing fixtures and for a variety of processing and manufacturing machinery and equipment.

The method of hardening the alloy provides a major distinction between stainless steel formulations. The chromium steels that are classed as ferritic alloys are not hardenable by heat but are strengthened as they are formed, or worked. The chromium alloys called martensitic, however—which in general have higher proportions of carbon than do ferritic alloys—achieve great strength through heat-hardening. The austenitic group of stainless steels—chromium-nickel alloys such as "18-8"—is hardened by cold-working.

Stainless steels are melted almost exclusively in the electric-arc furnace and are semifinished in slab, rod, or tube form. Finished steels are available in many different forms—plate, sheet, strip, bar, wire, or tubing. Many stainless steel products are produced by casting.

Because of their extraordinary rust and corrosion resistance, stainless steels do not require protective coatings, and the polish produced by a final finishing is extremely durable.

Bibliography: Peckner, Donald, and Bernstein, I. M., Handbook of Stainless Steels, rev. ed. (1977).

See also: IRON AND STEEL INDUSTRY.

stalactite and stalagmite

Stalactites and stalagmites are formations found on the ceiling and floor, respectively, of a cave. Groundwater seeping into a cave chamber contains carbon dioxide (CO_2) absorbed from the atmosphere or the soil. The carbon dioxide may unite with limestone ($CaCO_3$) to form calcium bicarbonate ($CaHCO_3$), which also may be dissolved and carried in the water percolating through the cave. When the water carrying the calcium bicarbonate evaporates, it releases the carbon dioxide, and the remaining molecules are normally deposited as crystals of calcium carbonate (calcite or aragonite).

If the crystals remain in contact with the ceiling they build

This spectacular formation of stalactites (top) and stalagmites (bottom), in the Cave of Clamouse in southern France, was formed from minerals deposited by dripping water. The room is known as The Cemetery because the stalagmites resemble rows of gravestones.

up as a stalactite, a small, circular, hollow tube. The water continues to flow down the center until the stalactite may be 1 m (3 ft) in length, or longer, although stalactites are rarely more than 5 mm (0.2 in) in diameter. The presence of some minerals such as copper or iron results in a colored stalactite.

Stalagmites are produced when water drops directly to the cave floor. The impact of the water striking the floor causes it to break into droplets or into a film, releasing the excess carbon dioxide, and the crystals begin to grow upward. If a stalactite and a stalagmite meet, they form a column. Stalagmites are usually larger in diameter than stalactites, have rounded tops, and possess no central canal. Some stalagmites are 10 m (33 ft) tall, and they can range up to 10 m in diameter.

The rate of growth of stalactites and stalagmites is not constant because it depends on water percolation from the surface. The average rate of growth is approximately 2 mm (0.08 in) per year, but so many variable factors are involved that their age cannot be determined in this way.

                                    BROTHER G. NICHOLAS, F.S.C.

Bibliography: Matthews, P., ed., Speleo Handbook (1968); Moore, George W., and Brother G. Nicholas, Speleology, the Study of Caves (1978).

Stalin, Joseph   [stah'-lin]

Joseph Stalin, became the preeminent Soviet leader after the death of Vladimir I. LENIN in 1924. From 1929 until his own death in 1953, Stalin held absolute authority. Outwardly modest and unassuming and intellectually unimpressive, he applied a shrewd, practical intelligence to political organization and manipulation. Because he rarely appeared to be what he was, Stalin was consistently underestimated by his opponents, who usually became his victims. He brought his country to world power status but imposed upon it one of the most ruthless regimes in history.

Early Life and Career. Stalin was born Joseph Vissarionovich Djugashvili on Dec. 21 (N.S.), 1879, in the Georgian hill town of Gori. His father, a poor, unsuccessful shoemaker, was an alcoholic who beat his son unmercifully and who died in a

Joseph Stalin, dictator of the USSR after the death of Lenin, forced Russia's rapid change from an agrarian nation to a major industrial power and led his country to victory in World War II. Stalin's achievements, however, must be measured against his brutal methods, constituting a reign of terror that was condemned by the 20th Party Congress, 3 years after Stalin's death.

brawl when the boy was 11 years old. Stalin's mother, Ekaterina, was a washerwoman, hopeful that her sole surviving child would be a priest. According to Robert Tucker, a recent biographer, her attentiveness encouraged Stalin toward self-idealization, while the deprivations of his childhood may have made a compensatory fantasy life psychologically indispensable. In any event, young Stalin was given to identifying with hero-figures. His early nickname, Koba, was that of a fictional mountain bandit and rebel; if his family's squalor gave him ambition and an acute class consciousness, his Georgian background also taught him brutality and vengeance.

At the age of 14, Stalin entered the Tiflis Theological Seminary. By his own testimony, the discipline there was another impetus toward revolutionary activism. In 1898 he became involved in radical political activity. The next year he left the seminary without graduating and became a full-time revolutionary organizer. A member of the Georgian branch of the Social Democratic party by 1901, Stalin roamed the Caucasus, agitating among workers, helping with strikes, and spreading socialist literature. He had no oratorical skills or charisma but showed great talent at practical organizational activity. His dull, pockmarked appearance also concealed a genuine intelligence and a particularly acute memory.

When the Social Democrats split (1903) into two groups, the BOLSHEVIKS AND MENSHEVIKS, Stalin supported the more radical Bolsheviks and their leader, V. I. Lenin. Lenin appreciated Stalin's familiarity with Russian nationality problems and his intense personal loyalty. Between 1902 and 1913, Stalin was arrested many times but escaped repeatedly to continue working as a Bolshevik organizer. During these years he also staged robberies to obtain funds for the Bolsheviks.

The Road to Absolute Power. In 1912, Lenin rewarded Stalin by coopting him to the Bolshevik Central Committee. From there, Stalin rapidly gained influence and power among the Bolsheviks and served as the first editor of *Pravda*, the party newspaper. He also began to use the name *Stalin*, meaning "man of steel." Exiled (1913–17) to Siberia by the tsarist government, he returned after the March Revolution had overthrown the monarchy (see RUSSIAN REVOLUTIONS OF 1917). Stalin played an important organizational role in the party after the first unsuccessful Bolshevik attempt to seize power (the "July days") when the Bolshevik Leon TROTSKY was arrested and Lenin was forced into hiding. Following the successful November Revolution, Stalin was appointed to seemingly mundane administrative posts such as commissar of nationalities (1917–23) and commissar of workers' and peasants' inspection (1919–23), but in 1922, without fanfare, Stalin became general secretary of the party's Central Committee.

He now controlled appointments, set agendas, and could transfer thousands of party officials from post to post at will. He was also nourishing a hatred of intellectuals, a disdain for educated "specialists," and an insatiable thirst for power.

After Lenin's death in 1924, Stalin used his control of the party apparatus to crush his opponents. For his deemphasis on world revolution under the slogan "socialism in one country" and his moderate economic policies, the general secretary was attacked by Trotsky, who was belatedly joined by Lev KAMENEV and Grigory ZINOVIEV. By 1928, Stalin had driven this leftist opposition from its party posts. Then, whether for political or economic reasons, he adopted such leftist programs as agricultural collectivization and rapid industrialization and smashed the party's right, which was led by Nikolai BUKHARIN, for opposing measures that he himself had recently attacked. By the end of 1929, Stalin was the undisputed master of the USSR.

Collectivization and Industrialization. Stalin's program of farm collectivization began late in 1928 when he suddenly ordered the expropriation of the lands of the middle-class farmers, or KULAKS. The party managed to seize total control of the harvest, deport about 5 million kulaks as "bourgeois residue" from the countryside, and secure enough capital (through the export of the forcibly seized grain) to finance a massive industrialization drive. Brutally suppressing peasant resistance, Stalin refused to slacken the pace despite a famine in 1932 and mounting opposition within his own party. Disaffection with Stalin was manifest at the 17th Party Congress in January–February 1934, when Leningrad party leader Sergei Kirov, a favorite of moderate delegates, received an ovation equal to Stalin's. Peasant resistance was quashed, however, and collectivization proved a success in terms of facilitating rapid industrial growth. Soviet industrialization was achieved by means of three 5-year plans, lasting from 1928 until World War II interrupted the last one in 1941.

The Great Purges. Having mastered the economic front, Stalin felt free to turn on all those who appeared to have doubted his wisdom and ability. In December 1934, Kirov was assassinated, probably at the behest of Stalin, who used the murder as the pretext for arresting—within the year—virtually all major party figures as saboteurs. From 1936 to 1938 he staged the Moscow show trials, at which prominent old Bolsheviks and army officers were convicted of implausibly monstrous crimes. By 1937, Stalin's blood purge extended through every party cell in the country. By 1939 a total of 98 of the 139 central committee members elected in 1934 had been shot and 1,108 of the 1,966 delegates to the 17th Congress arrested. The secret-police reign of terror annihilated a large portion of every profession and reached down into the general population. Deaths have been estimated in the millions, including those who perished in concentration camps. At the same time, Stalin began promoting a cult of adulation that proclaimed him a genius in every field of human endeavor. By the time the terror eased in 1938, Stalin's dictatorship had become entirely personal, unrestrained by the party or any other institution.

World War II Leadership. In world affairs, Stalin began to fear the growing power of Nazi Germany. After abortive attempts to reach an accord with the Western democracies, he concluded (1939) a nonaggression treaty (see NAZI-SOVIET PACT) with Hitler. After Germany invaded Poland at the start of World War II, Stalin acted to expand Soviet influence in Europe by occupying eastern Poland and attacking Finland (see RUSSO-FINNISH WAR). The nonaggression pact with Germany, however, proved short-lived when German troops invaded the Soviet Union in June 1941.

Taking personal control of the armed forces, Stalin expended troops as easily as he had executed kulaks, but the USSR's industrial plant produced enormous quantities of sophisticated armament and weaponry. Much more so than the other principal Allied leaders, U.S. president Franklin D. ROOSEVELT or British prime minister Winston CHURCHILL, Stalin also commanded his army directly on a day-to-day basis, impressing foreign observers tremendously with his grasp of detail. He proved a skillful negotiator at the major Allied conferences (see TEHRAN CONFERENCE; YALTA CONFERENCE; POTSDAM CONFERENCE).

Last Years. In 1945, Stalin was at the height of his power and prestige, regarded as his country's savior by millions of his subjects. The period between 1945 and his death in 1953, however, saw a new wave of repression and some of Stalin's worst excesses. Returned prisoners of war were incarcerated in concentration camps. New duties on peasants reduced many to the status of serfs, and his imposition of Communist regimes on Eastern European nations helped create a perilous cold-war climate. Stalin turned now on many of his closest associates. In early 1953 he announced that he had uncovered a plot among the Kremlin's corps of doctors; new arrests seemed imminent, and many feared another great purge. Stalin died suddenly on Mar. 5, 1953, however.

Stalin's reputation declined in the USSR after Nikita KHRUSHCHEV revealed many of Stalin's crimes in 1956. But Khrushchev's successors have downplayed anti-Stalinist rhetoric, and in China and much of the Third World he is regarded as a strong revolutionary leader who modernized his nation's economy. Several of his writings have been published in English translation. WILLIAM G. ROSENBERG

Bibliography: Conquest, Robert, *The Great Terror: Stalin's Purge of the Thirties*, rev. ed. (1973); Daniels, Robert V., ed., *The Stalin Revolution* (1965); Deutscher, Isaac, *Stalin: A Political Biography*, 2d ed. (1967); McCagg, William O., Jr., *Stalin Embattled: 1943-1948* (1978); Medvedev, R. A., *Let History Judge: The Origins and Consequences of Stalinism* (1971); Richards, Michael, *Stalin* (1979); Rigby, T. H., ed., *Stalin* (1966); Smith, E. E., *The Young Stalin* (1967); Trotsky, Leon, *Stalin: An Appraisal of the Man and His Influence*, ed. and trans. by Charles Malamuth, 2d ed. (1967); Tucker, R. C., *Stalin as Revolutionary, 1879-1929* (1973); Ulam, A. B., *Stalin* (1973); Warth, R. D., *Joseph Stalin* (1969).

Stalingrad, Battle of   [stah'-lin-grahd]

Stalingrad, now VOLGOGRAD, in the USSR, was the site of a critical WORLD WAR II Soviet victory that reversed Germany's advance to the East. The first phase of the battle lasted from July 17 to Nov. 18, 1942, when the German 6th Army under Friedrich von Paulus closed in on the heart of the city, which was tenaciously defended by Gen. Vasily Chuikov's 62d Army. On November 19, Soviet forces under Gen. Georgy Zhukov attacked north and south of the city, encircling the Germans, who finally surrendered on Feb. 2, 1943. Soviet losses were 750,000 troops, whereas Germany and its allies lost 850,000.

Bibliography: Chuikov, Vasilii Ivanovich, *The Battle for Stalingrad*, intro. by Hanson W. Baldwin (1964); Craig, William, *Enemy at the Gates: The Battle for Stalingrad* (1974); Kerr, Walter, *The Secret of Stalingrad* (1978); Zhukov, George K., *Marshal Zhukov's Greatest Battles*, ed. by Harrison Salisbury, trans. by Theodore Shabad (1969).

Stamboliski, Aleksandr   [stahm-boh-lee'-skee]

Aleksandr Stamboliski, b. Mar. 1, 1879, d. June 14, 1923, was a Bulgarian prime minister (1919–23) and Agrarian party leader. He was jailed (1915–18) for opposing Tsar Ferdinand I's pro-German policy in World War I but became prime minister under Ferdinand's son BORIS III. The authoritarian Stamboliski effected land reforms and tried to establish a peasant-based alliance, the Green International. He was overthrown and executed, however, by reactionaries who opposed his closer ties to Yugoslavia. K. M. SMOGORZEWSKI

Stambolov, Stefan   [stahm-boh-lawf']

Stefan Stambolov, b. Jan. 31, 1854, d. July 18, 1895, was a Bulgarian patriot and prime minister (1887–94). He fought against Turkish rule in 1875–76 and 1877–78. After Prince Alexander abdicated (1886) under Russian pressure, Stambolov headed a regency council and blocked intervention by Russia. Prime minister under Prince Ferdinand, he ruled harshly and stamped out pro-Russian plots. As domestic opposition to Stambolov increased, Ferdinand, seeking closer ties with Russia, forced his resignation. Stambolov died after a street assault by political enemies. K. M. SMOGORZEWSKI

Stamford   [stam'-furd]

Stamford, a city in southwestern Connecticut, about 50 km (30 mi) northeast of New York City, has a population of 103,300 (1979 est.). Settled in 1641, Stamford became known in the 19th century for its inventions and industries. There Simon Ingersoll invented the friction clutch and the spring scale, and Linus Yale, Jr., invented the cylinder lock in 1848.

The maps indicate the progression of the World War II battle for Stalingrad (1942), a Soviet city (now Volgograd) on the Volga River that was a focus of communications in the southern USSR. Although the city was almost completely destroyed by the German offensive, the Soviet armies mounted a heroic defense and subsequently launched a counteroffensive that entrapped the German forces.

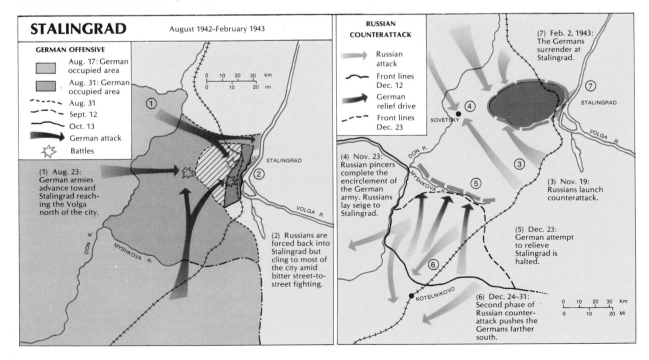

After World War II the city underwent rapid growth and became a center for major corporate headquarters. The city's industries produce machinery, hardware, computers, plastics, and ships. Suburban and semirural areas occupy the hills and ridges north of the city. Stamford is a residential community for many commuters to New York City. Of interest are the Stamford Museum and Nature Center, with its planetarium, and the fish-shaped First Presbyterian Church (1958).

Stamitz (family) [shtah'-mits]

The Bohemian composer and violinist **Johann Wenzel Anton Stamitz**, b. June 19, 1717, d. Mar. 27, 1757, was an important preclassical symphonist and founder of the MANNHEIM SCHOOL. His virtuoso performances on the violin and other stringed instruments led to his engagement by the Mannheim court in 1741. By 1745 he was concertmaster and director of the orchestra, which became famous for its precision, control of dynamics, and brilliant ensemble playing. He remained in Mannheim, except for a triumphant year (1754–55) in Paris, where his symphonies were performed and published. About 70 of Stamitz's symphonies, numerous concertos, and chamber works survive. His symphonies are notable for their incipient sonata form, symmetrical phrase patterns, and distinctive treatment of wind instruments—all features adopted into the classical style. Johann's son **Carl Philipp Stamitz**, b. May 7, 1745, d. Nov. 9, 1801, played in the Mannheim orchestra from 1762 to 1770, later traveling throughout Europe as a violin virtuoso. He composed about 80 symphonies and other instrumental music. His brother **Anton Johann Baptista Stamitz**, b. Nov. 24, 1754, d. between 1796 and 1801, also played (1764–70) in the Mannheim orchestra; he then toured with Carl for several years before settling in Paris as a violinist, composer, and teacher.   EDWARD A. BERLIN

Bibliography: Newman, William S., *The Sonata in the Classic Era,* 2d ed. (1972).

stammering: see STUTTERING.

Stamos, Theodoros [stam'-ohs]

A painter associated with New York City's abstract expressionist school of the 1960s, Theodoros Stamos, b. New York City, Dec. 31, 1922, often works with forms suggested by various living things—such as plants. His surfaces are bright, hazy sheets of color that swathe the forms in mystery. He attended the American Artists School in New York and had his first show in 1943. Initially influenced by Milton Avery, he later turned to abstraction.   PHIL PATTON

Bibliography: Pomeroy, Ralph, *Stamos* (1974); Sawyer, Kenneth, *Stamos* (1960).

Stamp Act

The Stamp Act (Mar. 22, 1765), sponsored by George GRENVILLE, was the first direct tax imposed by Britain on its American colonies. To help cover the cost of maintaining troops in the colonies, Parliament levied a tax on legal and commercial documents as well as printed material such as newspapers and pamphlets, all of which had to carry a special stamp. The act took effect in November 1765. Americans, who did not elect members of Parliament, opposed the act not only because of their inability to pay the tax, but also because it violated the newly enunciated principle of "No taxation without representation."

Resistance to the statute took the form of petitions to the king and Parliament, a boycott of British goods, the refusal of lawyers or printers to use stamps or stamped paper, and violence sparked by the SONS OF LIBERTY. The Massachusetts legislature spearheaded the formation of the first general intercolonial conference, the Stamp Act Congress, which met (October 1765) in New York City and issued a declaration of American rights and grievances. Parliament rescinded the statute on Mar. 18, 1766, but it coupled repeal with passage of the Declaratory Act, which asserted Britain's supremacy over America "in all cases whatsoever." The constitutional

principles and protest tactics established during the Stamp Act crisis laid the groundwork for the American Revolution.
                                                    LARRY R. GERLACH

Bibliography: Morgan, Edmund S. and Helen M., *The Stamp Act Crisis: Prologue to Revolution,* rev. ed. (1963); Thomas, P. D., *British Politics and the Stamp Act Crisis* (1975).

stamp collecting: see PHILATELY.

standard deviation

The standard deviation is the most widely used statistical measure of the spread or dispersion of a set of data. It is the positive square root of the variance (see VARIANCE AND COVARIANCE). If the data points of some set of measurement are denoted by x and their mean by $\bar{x}$, the standard deviation s is found from the formula $s = \sqrt{\sum (x - \bar{x})^2/(n-1)}$, where n is the number of observations.

The standard deviation, like the variance, measures dispersion about the mean as center. But the standard deviation has the same units of measurement as the observations, whereas the units of the variance are the square of the units of the observations. The standard deviation is always greater than or equal to zero. It is zero when all observations have the same value; this value is thus the mean, and so the dispersion is zero. The standard deviation increases as the dispersion increases. The standard deviation of a population is denoted by σ to distinguish it from the standard deviation s of a set of observations.   DAVID S. MOORE

Bibliography: Mosteller, F. R., et al., *Probability with Statistical Applications,* 2d ed. (1970).

Standardbred

The Standardbred is a breed of horse used primarily in harness racing, both trotting and pacing. The breed is part of the social history of Canada and the United States, where it was developed from Thoroughbreds, Norfolks, Morgans, and Arabians in the 19th century. The smart-stepping and almost universally driven light-harness horse that pulled buggies and fancier vehicles in the years before the automobile, the Standardbred was admired by all for its gait and style.

The Standardbred resembles the Thoroughbred but is smaller, with heavier bones, a longer body, shorter legs, a more robust build, and greater endurance. The weight is about 400 to 520 kg (900 to 1,150 lb), and the height at the withers (shoulders) is about 15 hands (1.5 m/60 in). The most common color is bay, but brown, black, chestnut, and gray are also found.

The name *Standardbred* originated when horses were required to meet certain standards of speed in order to be registered in the official studbook, which was begun in 1871.

The Standardbred, a breed of horse used mainly for harness racing, was developed in the United States during the 19th century. The name refers to speed standards met by these trotters to gain official registry.

Stable and long-lived, the Standardbred is one of the most durable horses developed by American breeders. It has been exported worldwide for racing and utility purposes.

EVERETT SENTMAN

Bibliography: Berry, Barbara J., *The Standardbreds* (1979); Harrison, James C., et al., *Care and Training of the Trotter and Pacer* (1968); Hervey, John L., *The American Trotter* (1947).

standing wave

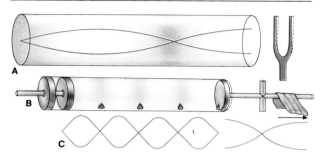

(A) *Standing acoustical waves can be generated by holding a vibrating tuning fork of the appropriate frequency in front of a column closed at one end. The standing wave is caused by reflection, and the air resonates at the frequency of the tuning fork. Only a node can form at the closed end and an antinode at the open end. (B) The standing-wave nodes in a closed column can be located by the accumulation of fine sand at the nodes. (C) Compressing the air in the column increases the speed of sound and thus reduces the wavelength.*

Standing waves, or stationary waves, are waves that appear not to travel. They are formed by the superposition of waves traveling in opposite directions and combining in such a way that wave energy is not transmitted in either direction. They occur, for example, in radio-transmitting antennas, in microwave waveguides, in glass coatings of optical instruments, and in violin strings, organ pipes, and most other musical instruments. To picture a standing wave, the transverse (side-to-side) motion of a stretched string that is fixed at both ends may be considered. Waves propagate down the string and are reflected at each end. For particular wavelengths there are points of the string that do not move at all, called nodes, and the parts of the string between two nodes oscillate in unison. In this case the wave energy does not propagate; these are standing waves.

Standing waves can occur in any extended space in which a wave of some sort can propagate and that is bounded so that the waves are reflected. In an organ pipe or a flute, for example, sound waves propagate in the air in the tube and are reflected from the ends. Two-dimensional standing waves exist in a drumhead or a rigid metal plate, as was first shown by the German scientist Ernst Chladni (1756-1827). He demonstrated the standing-wave modes of a metal plate by sprinkling light sand over the surface and exciting the waves by drawing a violin bow along the edge. The sand was agitated away from the vibrating portions and collected at the quiet nodes, forming symmetrical geometric patterns.

Because of the wave nature of the atomic and subatomic world (see QUANTUM MECHANICS), standing waves are important to an understanding of phenomena at this level. For example, the electron that circles the nucleus of an atom can travel only in orbits for which the electron wave forms a standing wave; thus, no energy is radiated away.

STEPHEN V. LETCHER

Bibliography: Elmore, W. C., and Heald, M. A., *Physics of Waves* (1969); Holden, Alan, *Stationary States* (1971).

Standish, Myles

Myles Standish, b. *c.*1584, d. Oct. 3, 1656, an English-born professional soldier, was hired by the PILGRIMS as military advisor for their PLYMOUTH COLONY in America; eventually he became a full member as well as a valued leader of the community.

Arriving on the *Mayflower* with the first settlers, he initially concentrated on colonial defense and Indian relations. Later, Standish represented (1625-26) Plymouth in England; he also served for many years as one of the governor's assistants and as the colony's treasurer (1644-49). Standish was one of the founders (1632) of the town of Duxbury, Mass.

OSCAR ZEICHNER

Bibliography: Bradford, William, *Of Plymouth Plantation,* ed. by S. E. Morison (1952); Langdon, G. D., Jr., *Pilgrim Colony: A History of New Plymouth, 1620-1691* (1966).

Stanfield, Robert Lorne

The Canadian political leader, Robert Lorne Stanfield, b. Truro, Nova Scotia, Apr. 11, 1914, served as premier of Nova Scotia from 1956 to 1967, when he resigned to become a member of Canada's House of Commons and leader of the opposition Progressive Conservative party. In 1974, Stanfield's party was defeated by the Liberal party under Pierre Elliott Trudeau; Stanfield resigned as party leader. Stanfield graduated from Dalhousie University (1936) and Harvard Law School (1939) and practiced law (1945-56).

Stanford, Sir Charles Villiers

Sir Charles Villiers Stanford, b. Sept. 30, 1852, d. Mar. 29, 1924, was an Irish composer known particularly for his nationalistic music, expressive of both Ireland and England. He was organist at Trinity College (1873-92) and taught at the Royal College of Music (1883-1924) and Cambridge University (1887-1924). He also conducted at the Leeds Festivals (1901-10) and made guest appearances throughout Europe, presenting his own music.

Stanford's work includes six operas, seven symphonies, concertos, chamber music, hundreds of songs, and nine volumes of Irish folk song arrangements.

Bibliography: Fuller-Maitland, J. A., *The Music of Parry and Stanford* (1935).

Stanford, Leland

The American railroad magnate and politician Leland Stanford, b. Watervliet, N.Y., Mar. 9, 1824, d. June 21, 1893, served as Republican governor (1861-63) of California and U.S. senator (1885-93) from California. After being admitted to the bar in 1848, Stanford practiced law in Wisconsin until 1852, when he joined his five brothers in California and became a merchant. As governor he helped keep that state in the Union in the early part of the Civil War. In 1861, with Collis P. Huntington, Stanford started the Central Pacific Railroad Company, and in 1870 he founded the Southern Pacific Railroad Company. In 1885, Stanford founded Stanford University with a grant of $20 million.

Bibliography: Bancroft, Hubert H., *Life of Leland Stanford* (1956; repr. 1976); Tutorow, Norman E., *Leland Stanford, Man of Many Careers* (1971).

Stanford Achievement Test: see EDUCATIONAL MEASUREMENT.

Stanford-Binet test   [stan'-furd-bee-nay']

The Stanford-Binet test is a measure of intelligence administered individually to children. Originated by the French psychologist Alfred BINET in 1905, it was modified at Stanford University by Lewis TERMAN in 1916, revised in 1937 and again— by Terman and Lewis Merrill—in 1960. Performance on the original Binet test was expressed in terms of an age scale, a basal age being established at the age level at which the individual under examination passed all tests; additional months of credit were applied for tests passed above the basal age level. The result was a designation of "mental age."

In the ensuing work at Stanford it was considered necessary to have an index relating the mental age level to the typical performance of the individual's age group. For this purpose, the intelligence quotient, or IQ, was adopted in the modified Stanford-Binet test. A ratio of the mental age factor (MA) to the chronological age factor (CA) provides an index of relative performance.

The Stanford-Binet test is based on a standardization of average performances by age label, having a value of approximately 100 with variations consistently in the range of about 16 above or below 100. Results of the Stanford-Binet test have been shown to be fairly consistent with individual performance over a period of years; this stability has resulted in a widespread application of the Stanford-Binet test as a measure of intelligence. The test does not account, however, as more recent ones do, for developmental and environmental factors in intelligence levels. Criticism of intelligence testing in general is contained in the article INTELLIGENCE.

MILDRED NAVARETTA

See also: PSYCHOLOGICAL MEASUREMENT.

Stanford Linear Accelerator Center

The Stanford Linear Accelerator Center, operated by Stanford University and funded by the U.S. Department of Energy, is a facility for research in high-energy physics. It was founded in 1962 and is located near San Francisco. The research facilities include the world's highest-energy electron linear accelerator, which has a capacity of 30 GeV and a storage ring, called SPEAR, within which 4 GeV electron and positron beams can be collided. A higher energy (18 GeV per beam) electron-positron storage ring, called PEP, was completed in 1980 in collaboration with the Lawrence Berkeley Laboratory.

BRIAN SOUTHWORTH

Bibliography: Neal, R. B., ed., *The Stanford Two-Mile Accelerator* (1968).

Stanford University

Established in 1885, Stanford University (enrollment: 11,700; library: 4,400,000 volumes) is a private coeducational institution in Stanford, Calif. Officially named Leland Stanford Junior University, for the son of Leland STANFORD, it offers undergraduate and graduate degress in its schools of sciences, earth sciences, humanities, engineering, law, medicine, education, and business. The university has a medical center, a marine station at Pacific Grove, a food research institute, and the Hoover Institution on War, Revolution and Peace. The university has eight overseas study centers.

Stanislaus, Saint   [stan'-is-laws]

Saint Stanislaus (Stanisław), b. July 26, 1030, d. Apr. 11, 1079, is the patron saint of Poland. Bishop of Kraków from 1072, he was murdered by King Bolesław II after he excommunicated the king for his scandalous conduct. Stanislaus was the first Pole to be canonized (1253). Feast day: Apr. 11 (formerly May 7; May 8 at Kraków).

Stanislavsky, Konstantin   [stuhn-is-lahf'-skee]

In establishing his "method" for teaching actors to realize a greater degree of verisimilitude on the stage, the Russian actor and producer Konstantin Stanislavsky (whose original name was Alekseyev), b. Jan. 17 (N.S.), 1863, d. Aug. 7, 1938, launched the age of the great director in modern theater. In his early career he was associated with the semiprofessional Society for Art and Literature, both as an actor of classic roles and as an innovative producer.

In 1897, together with Vladimir NEMIROVICH-DANCHENKO, Stanislavsky founded the MOSCOW ART THEATER, dedicated to bringing art to a larger public and to the more realistic (or truthful) presentation of new plays. Opening with a historically accurate production of Count Aleksei Tolstoi's play about Ivan the Terrible, the new group achieved its first notable success with Anton Chekhov's *The Seagull* (1898), a contemporary play perfectly suited to realizing the untheatrical reality that had previously been lacking from the stage. The absence of dramatic gesture, rhetorical declamation, and pur-

The Russian producer, director, and actor Konstantin Stanislavsky brought world fame to the Moscow Art Theater with his realistic stagings of the plays of Chekhov and of other modern dramatists. Stanislavsky appears here as Satin in Maksim Gorky's The Lower Depths (1902).

poseful plot in Chekhov's plays—including also *Uncle Vanya* (1899), *The Three Sisters* (1901), and *The Cherry Orchard* (1904), all produced by the Moscow Art Theater—demanded new acting techniques, which Stanislavsky believed must be discovered by the actor in the "indirect action" and "subtext" of the dialogue. By putting himself or herself in the character's place, the actor was to experience the character's internal emotions (see METHOD ACTING). Stanislavsky often used a tick or idiosyncratic gesture to convey the essence of a character. As director he used sounds or background music to create atmosphere.

Other important plays directed by Stanislavsky included Ostrovsky's *Snow Maiden* (1900), Ibsen's *An Enemy of the People* (1900–01), Gorky's *The Lower Depths* (1902), and, following the Bolshevik revolution, later Soviet plays as well. He also invited the collaboration of such artists as Gordon CRAIG, who designed the theater's 1911 production of *Hamlet*, and Aleksandr BENOIS, who directed Molière's *Imaginary Invalid* (1913).

Stanislavsky sponsored three successive studios at the Art Theater, nurturing the talents of Vsevolod MEYERHOLD and Eugene VAKHTANGOV, who were to make their own contributions to modern theater, and he headed the Opera Studio. Stanislavsky's theories are contained in *My Life in Art* (1924), written in English while touring the United States, and *An Actor Prepares* (1926; Eng. trans., 1948).

MARJORIE L. HOOVER

Bibliography: Edwards, Christine, *The Stanislavsky Heritage: Its Contribution to the Russian and American Theatre* (1965); Gorchakov, Nikolai M., *Stanislavsky Directs*, trans. by Miriam Goldina (1954); Stanislavski, Constantin, *Creating a Role*, trans. by Elizabeth Reynolds Hapgood (1949).

See also: ACTORS STUDIO; GROUP THEATRE, THE; STRASBERG, LEE.

Stanisław I, King of Poland   [stan'-is-luhv]

Stanisław I Leszczyński, b. Oct. 20, 1677, d. Feb. 23, 1766, twice king of Poland (1704–09, 1733–34), was ousted first by Russia, then by Russia and Austria. He was initially elected and crowned king with the support of Charles XII of Sweden, who was fighting Peter I of Russia and his ally AUGUSTUS II of Poland in the Great NORTHERN WAR. Stanisław lost his throne when Peter defeated (1709) Charles at Poltava. His chances of regaining the crown revived with the marriage (1725) of his daughter, Maria, to Louis XV of France and the death (1733) of Augustus II. In the ensuing War of the POLISH SUCCESSION (1733–35) he was elected king with the support of Polish nobles and of Louis XV. A year later, however, he was deposed by Russian forces, and the Austro-Russian candidate AUGUSTUS III was installed on the throne. Stanisław, who fled the country, was given Lorraine and Bar for life by the Treaty of Vienna (1738). He became a writer and a patron of the arts.

ANNA M. CIENCIALA

Stanisław II, King of Poland

Stanisław II, b. Jan. 17, 1732, d. Feb. 12, 1798, last king of Poland (1764–95), an enlightened monarch and great patron of the arts, struggled vainly against the Partitions of Poland (see POLAND, PARTITIONS OF) by Russia, Austria, and Prussia. He wanted to reform and modernize Poland and hoped for Russian support, believing that Russian interest required a strong Polish ally against Austria and Prussia. However, Russian empress CATHERINE II had put Stanisław, her former lover, on the Polish throne to have an obedient satellite, and she obstructed reforms that would strengthen Poland. After the first partition (1772), Stanisław guided educational and economic reforms and helped draft the Polish constitution of 1791, which established a constitutional monarchy and was the first written constitution in Europe. After the second partition (1793), he continued to work to preserve a Polish state. He abdicated just prior to the third partition (1795).

ANNA M. CIENCIALA

Bibliography: Bain, A. N., *The Last King of Poland and His Contemporaries* (1909); Stone, Daniel, *Polish Politics and National Reform, 1775–1788* (1976).

Stankiewicz, Richard   [stang'-kee-e-vich]

Richard Stankiewicz, b. Philadelphia, Oct. 18, 1922, became, in the 1950s, one of the first American sculptors to use discarded objects, such as pipes, nuts, bolts, wheels, and other machine parts, in his work. His early sculptures were humorous parodies of animal and human figures; in the 1960s his work became nonobjective. He studied painting with both Hans Hofmann (1948–49) and Fernand Léger (1950–51) and sculpture with Ossip Zadkine (1950–51).

DIANA KURZ

Bibliography: Calas, Nicolas, and Calas, Elena, eds., *Icons and Images of the Sixties* (1971); Hunter, Sam, ed., *New Art Around the World: Painting and Sculpture* (1966).

Stanley, Sir Henry Morton

Sir Henry Morton Stanley, b. Jan. 28, 1841, d. May 10, 1904, was a British-American journalist and explorer who achieved fame in 1871, when he found the Scottish missionary and explorer David LIVINGSTONE. Born as John Rowlands in Wales, he grew up in a workhouse. At the age of 16 he sailed for New Orleans as a cabin boy. There in 1859 he was adopted by a cotton broker named Stanley. During the Civil War he served first in the Confederate Army, but in 1862 he switched to the Union side. He later sailed on merchant ships and tried to make his living in the American West.

In 1867, Stanley obtained his first regular journalistic position as a reporter for the St. Louis *Weekly Missouri Democrat.*

The journalist and explorer Sir Henry Stanley headed expeditions into Central Africa that opened that part of the continent to European interests. On his first venture Stanley located the Scottish missionary David Livingstone. He subsequently followed the Congo River from its source to the Atlantic, and, under auspices of Leopold II of the Belgians, he surveyed and helped to develop the Congo Free State.

In 1868 he persuaded the New York *Herald* to let him cover Britain's attack on Ethiopia. For the next 2 years he wrote about the Middle East and Europe. His moment of glory arrived when the *Herald* sent him to find David Livingstone, who was "lost" in the heart of Africa.

In 1871, Stanley located Livingstone in Ujiji, in what is now Tanzania (and greeted him with the famous words, "Dr. Livingstone, I presume?"). Three years later he returned to Africa and between 1874 and 1877 circumnavigated Lakes Tanganyika and Victoria, traced the unexplored Congo River to its mouth, and began an era when explorers sought imperial goals. In 1880, on a second trip to the Congo, Stanley secured the south bank of the river for Leopold II, king of the Belgians. From 1887 to 1889, Stanley sought to "save" EMIN PASHA, governor of Egypt's Equatorial Province, supposedly marooned in the Upper Sudan. With great loss of life, Stanley led his large expedition to the Indian Ocean and in the process established the basis of British East Africa.

In retirement Stanley sat in the British Parliament (1895–1900). He was knighted in 1899.

ROBERT I. ROTBERG

Bibliography: Farwell, Byron, *The Man Who Presumed* (1957; repr. 1974); Hall, Richard S., *Stanley: An Adventurer Explored* (1974); Stanley, Henry M., *The Autobiography of Henry M. Stanley*, ed. by Dorothy Stanley (1909; repr. 1969); Symons, A. J. A., *H. M. Stanley* (1933).

Stanley, Wendell Meredith

The American biochemist Wendell Meredith Stanley, b. Ridgeville, Ind., Aug. 16, 1904, d. June 15, 1971, was the first to crystallize (1935) a VIRUS. The work, done at the Rockefeller Institute for Medical Research, in Princeton, N.J., showed that viruses, which were known to reproduce themselves as living organisms, were crystalline chemical compounds, proteinaceous in nature. This finding opened the way for the discovery of DNA and the establishment of the field of molecular biology. Stanley devoted the rest of his life to research on viruses, isolating nucleic acid from crystallized virus in 1936 and helping develop influenza vaccines during World War II. In 1947 he set up the Virus Research Laboratory at the University of California at Berkeley. Stanley won the American Cancer Society Award in 1959 and shared the Nobel Prize for chemistry with James B. Sumner and John Howard Northrop in 1946.

HENRY M. LEICESTER

Bibliography: Corner, George W., *A History of the Rockefeller Institute, 1901–1953: Origins and Growth* (1964).

Stanley, William

The American electrical engineer and inventor William Stanley, b. Brooklyn, N.Y., Nov. 22, 1858, d. May 14, 1916, successfully developed a system for long-distance light and power transmission by alternating current. While working as an engineer for Westinghouse Electric Company, Stanley devised (1886) a multiple system of alternating current distribution, which he installed in his hometown when Westinghouse refused to finance his invention. He later formed his own firm and constructed (1894) a generating plant that supplied alternating current to industrial users. Stanley also invented condensers, two-phase electric motors, generators, and an alternating-current watt-hour meter.

Bibliography: Hawkins, Laurence A., *William Stanley (1858–1916)—His Life and Work* (1951).

Stanley Cup: see ICE HOCKEY.

Stanleyville: see KISANGANI.

Stanovoi Range   [stuh-nuh-voy']

The mineral-rich Stanovoi Range of the USSR lies in eastern Siberia north of Manchuria. The east-west-trending range, which is 725 km (450 mi) long, reaches its maximum elevation at Golets Skalistiy (2,482 m/8,143 ft), located in the eastermost section. The mountains form part of the watershed between the Pacific and Arctic Oceans. Needle-leaf forests cover the lower slopes. The Amur-Yakutsk Highway crosses the range in the west.

Stanton, Edwin M.

Edwin McMasters Stanton, b. Steubenville, Ohio, Dec. 19, 1814, d. Dec. 24, 1869, served as U.S. attorney general (1860–61) and secretary of war (1862–68) in the U.S. Civil War and Reconstruction era. Stanton was a moderately active Democratic party worker and a successful lawyer before President James Buchanan appointed him attorney general in December 1860. Although Stanton had been allied with the pro-Southern wing of the Democratic party before the secession crisis (November–December 1860), he worked secretly with Republicans and cooperated with firm opponents of secession in the cabinet, helping to force the resignations of members of the cabinet's Southern bloc—and to prevent Buchanan's capitulation in the crisis. Resigning when Republican President Abraham Lincoln took office in March 1861, Stanton remained close to both Democratic and Republican leaders.

In January 1862, Lincoln named Stanton secretary of war. In that position, he earned a reputation for energy and administrative ability as well as for abrasiveness. He became Lincoln's chief cabinet advisor and a major cabinet link to Republican congressional leaders, who urged more vigorous prosecution of the war and stronger measures against slavery.

Stanton retained his post under President Andrew JOHNSON. As the differences between Johnson and most Republican leaders grew over Reconstruction policy, Stanton attempted to bridge the gap. The struggle between Johnson and Republican leaders in Congress intensified, however, and Stanton's position became more anomalous. After March 1867, when Congress put the army in charge of Reconstruction, Stanton used his post to prevent Johnson from subverting congressional policy. Johnson suspended him from office in August 1867, but under the terms of a new law—the TENURE OF OFFICE ACT, which was designed to limit the presidential power of removal—Stanton was restored (January 1868) when the Senate refused to concur in the president's action. Johnson's attempt to fire Stanton on Feb. 21, 1868, in defiance of the law, led to the president's impeachment and trial. Stanton relinquished control of his office in May 1868, after the Senate acquitted Johnson.

Johnson's Republican successor, President Ulysses S. Grant, nominated Stanton to the U.S. Supreme Court in December 1869. Confirmed by the Senate, Stanton died before he could take his seat on the bench.   MICHAEL LES BENEDICT

Bibliography: Pratt, Fletcher, *Stanton: Lincoln's Secretary of War* (1953; repr. 1970); Thomas, Benjamin P., and Hyman, Harold M., *Stanton: The Life and Times of Lincoln's Secretary of War* (1962).

Edwin M. Stanton, U.S. secretary of war during the Civil War and Reconstruction, was at the center of the struggle between President Andrew Johnson and the Radical Republicans. Johnson's suspension of Stanton from his post—in violation of the Tenure of Office Act—led to the president's impeachment.

Stanton, Elizabeth Cady

Elizabeth Cady Stanton organized the first U.S. women's rights convention in 1848 and was a leader in the struggle to win voting and property rights for women. Together with Susan B. Anthony she edited a newspaper, the Revolution. *She was also coauthor of a six-volume work,* History of Woman Suffrage.

The American reformer Elizabeth Cady Stanton, b. Johnstown, N.Y., Nov. 12, 1815, d. Oct. 26, 1902, was a founder of the organized WOMEN'S RIGHTS MOVEMENT in the United States. She was active in the antislavery and temperance movements but gave a growing share of her time to women's issues. Marrying abolitionist Henry B. Stanton in 1840, she insisted on the omission of "obey" from the marriage vows. She and Lucretia MOTT organized the SENECA FALLS CONVENTION (July 19–20, 1848), the first women's rights assembly in America. There, Stanton drafted a Declaration of Sentiments that paralleled the wording of the Declaration of Independence and insisted, over some objections, on adoption of a women's suffrage resolution (see SUFFRAGE, WOMEN'S). She was also an advocate of more liberal divorce laws, less restrictive clothing for women, coeducation, and the right of married women to control their property. From 1851, Stanton and Susan B. ANTHONY worked together at the forefront of the women's rights movement. Stanton was the first president of both the National Woman Suffrage Association (1869–90) and the National American Woman Suffrage Association (1890–92). She coedited the feminist journal *Revolution* (1868–70) and wrote prolifically. Her works include *Eighty Years and More* (1898).
          LORETTA ELLEN ZIMMERMAN

Bibliography: Lutz, Alma, *Created Equal: A Biography of Elizabeth Cady Stanton* (1940; repr. 1973); Oakley, Mary A., *Elizabeth Cady Stanton*, 2d ed. (1972).

Staphylococcus   [staf-i-luh-kahk'-uhs]

Staphylococcus is a genus of spherical bacteria, some species of which are normal inhabitants of the skin and others of which cause disease. The most common pathogen, *Staphylococcus aureus*, is frequently responsible for boils, carbuncles, abscesses, osteomyelitis, and, sometimes, meningitis and pneumonia, and is the most common cause of bacterial food poisoning and hospital infections.

star

A star is a large ball of hot gas, thousands to millions of kilometers in diameter, emitting large amounts of radiant energy from nuclear reactions in its interior. Stars differ fundamentally from planets in that they are self-luminous, whereas planets shine by reflected sunlight. Except for the SUN, which is the nearest star, stars appear only as points of light, even in the largest telescopes, because of their distance.

The brightest stars have long been given names. Most of the familiar names originated with the ancient Greeks or with later Arab astronomers; an entirely different system was used

The Pleiades, the most famous of the open clusters, is visible in the constellation of Taurus, high in the southern sky during winter evenings. Although a telescope reveals several hundred stars in the cluster, only the six brightest are normally visible to the unaided eye. The Pleiades is also the best-known example of a reflection nebula, in which a cloud of dust surrounding the hot stars reflects each star's light toward Earth. The circles and spikes about the stars are caused by the diffraction of light around the mounting of the secondary mirror.

by the Chinese, starting hundreds of years earlier, about 1000 BC. Polaris, the North Star, has a Greek name; Betelgeuse, a bright red star, has an Arabic name. Modern astronomers designate the bright stars according to the CONSTELLATIONS they are in. Thus, the brightest star in the Big Dipper (part of the constellation Ursa Major) is called alpha (α) Ursa Majoris. Polaris, in the Little Dipper (Ursa Minor), is γ Ursa Minoris, and Betelgeuse, in Orion, is γ Orionis. VARIABLE STARS (those which periodically change in brightness) have lettered names, such as RR Lyrae in the constellation Lyra. Fainter stars are known by their numbers in a catalog; HD 12938 is the 12,938th star in the *Henry Draper Catalogue of Stellar Spectra.*

CHARACTERISTICS OF STARS

Each star in the universe has its own position, motion, size, mass, chemical composition, and temperature. Some stars are grouped into clusters, and stars and star clusters are collected in the larger groupings called galaxies. Our own galaxy, the Milky Way, contains more than 100 billion stars. Because tens of millions of other galaxies are known to exist, the total number of stars in the universe exceeds a billion billion.

Positions, Motions, and Distances. Stars are seen in the same relative positions, night after night, year after year. They provided early astronomers with a reference system for measuring the motions of planets ("wandering stars"), the Moon, and the Sun. The westward rotation of the celestial sphere simply reflects the daily eastward rotation of the Earth, and the Sun's apparent motion among the stars reflects the Earth's annual orbit around the Sun.

As the construction of larger telescopes during the 19th century improved the accuracy of determining stellar positions, it was found that some stars are not precisely "fixed." They move at various speeds, measured as changes of direction in fractions of a second of arc per year, where one second of arc is the angular size of a pinhead 183 m (200 yd) away. Most of the faint stars are truly fixed as viewed from Earth and are used as a reference frame for the minute motions of nearby stars, known as PROPER MOTION.

PARALLAX is another apparent motion of nearby stars. It is caused by the Earth's orbit around the Sun: the star seems to shift, first one way, then the other, as the Earth moves from 150 million km (93 million mi) on one side of the Sun to 150 million km on the other side. Stellar parallax can be used to determine astronomical DISTANCE. If the shift is 1 second of arc each way, the star is about 32 million million km (20 million million mi) from an observer. This distance is called the parsec and is equal to 3.26 light-years. The parallaxes of several thousand stars have been measured during the past several decades. The nearest star is Proxima Centauri, at about 1 parsec (3.3 light-years). Most of the measured distances are greater than 20 parsecs (65 light-years), which shows why the average star in the sky is so much fainter than the nearby Sun.

Brightness and Luminosity. Star brightness was first estimated by eye, and the brightest stars in the sky were described as "stars of the first magnitude." Later, the magnitude scale was defined more accurately: 6th magnitude stars are just 1/100 as bright as 1st magnitude stars; 11th magnitude stars are 1/100 as bright as 6th magnitude, and so on. The magnitude scale is logarithmic; that is, each magnitude corresponds to a factor of 1/2.54, because $(1/2.54)^5 = 1/100$ (see MAGNITUDE).

Photographs are also used to measure star brightness from the size and blackness of images on a photographic plate exposed in a telescope-camera. With the photographic emulsions available in the early 1900s, a blue star that appeared to the eye to have the same brightness as a red star photographed much brighter. This discrepancy occurred because emulsions at that time were much more sensitive to blue light than to red. Because of this variation, two magnitude scales came into use: visual magnitude (m_v) and photographic magnitude (m_p). The difference for any one star, $m_p - m_v$, measures the color of that star—positive for red stars, negative for blue (see COLOR INDEX). By using filters and special emulsions, astronomers soon had several other magnitude scales, including ultraviolet and infrared. When photoelectric detectors were introduced, the brightnesses of stars were measured with a photoelectric photometer at the focus of a telescope. Standard colors (wavelengths) of light were adopted, and the symbols m_v and m_p were changed to V and

B, with U for the ultraviolet scale, and several other letters for infrared scales.

Measuring the brightness of a star on any of these scales is complicated by factors related to the Earth's atmosphere, which absorbs more light when a star is near the horizon than when it is overhead. The atmosphere also absorbs different amounts of the different colors and can change during the night because of changing dust or moisture in the air. Nevertheless, by comparing a star with a standard at the same height above the horizon, astronomers using photoelectric photometers can measure U, B, and V magnitudes with an accuracy of 0.01 magnitude (see PHOTOMETRY, ASTRONOMICAL).

Such photometry has provided a great deal of information regarding the temperatures and energy output of stars, but it does not give the total energy output. Each measurement (U, B, V) gives only a fraction of the star's light reaching the Earth; even if the measurements are combined, they give only the part that is not absorbed as it passes through the Earth's atmosphere. The atmosphere absorbs all light of short wavelengths below ultraviolet and many of the long wavelengths above red. A theoretical correction can be made, based on the star's temperature, to give a "bolometric" magnitude, m_b, adding the energy absorbed by the atmosphere. True bolometric magnitudes, however, can be measured only from rockets and spacecraft outside the Earth's atmosphere. Before 1975 the astronomical satellites OAO-2 and Copernicus, the Apollo missions, and Skylab provided many new measurements of stars. The SPACELAB and SPACE TELESCOPE, to be launched in the 1980s, will provide many more.

From parallax-distance measurements it is possible to calculate the absolute bolometric magnitude, or luminosity, of a star, which is a measure of its brightness relative to the Sun if it were at the Sun's distance from an observer on Earth. During the 1920s it was found that some stars (giants) are 100,000 times as luminous as the Sun; others (white dwarfs) are 1,000 times less luminous.

Composition. During ancient times and the Middle Ages stars were thought to be made of an ethereal element different from matter on Earth. Their actual composition did not become known until the invention of the SPECTROSCOPE in the 19th century. Through the refraction of light by a prism (see PRISM, physics) or through its diffraction by a DIFFRACTION GRATING, the light from a source is spread out into its different visual wavelengths, from red to blue; this is known as its SPECTRUM. The spectra of the Sun and stars exhibited bright and dark lines, which were shown to be caused by elements emitting or absorbing light at specific wavelengths. Because each element emits or absorbs light only at specific wavelengths, the chemical composition of stars can be determined. In this way the spectroscope demonstrated that the gases in the Sun and stars are those of common elements such as hydrogen, helium, iron, and calcium at temperatures

of several thousand degrees. It was found that the average star's atmosphere consists mostly of hydrogen (87%) and helium (10%), an element discovered from spectra of the Sun, with all 90 other elements at about 3%.

At first, visual estimates of the strengths of spectral lines were used to estimate the amounts of the elements present in the Sun and a few stars, based on an analysis of the lines produced by a laboratory light source. When photographic emulsions came into use, the spectroscope became the spectrograph, with a photographic film or plate replacing the human eye. During the first half of the 20th century, spectrographs were used on telescopes to observe thousands of stars. On the spectrogram, the intensities of the lines are measured from the blackness of the film or plate. Most recently, photoelectric detectors are used to scan the spectrum in a spectrophotometer. Stellar spectra can also be measured by INTERFEROMETER techniques.

Although the ultraviolet, visual, and infrared parts of a star's spectrum can be measured in this way, other techniques must be used, above the atmosphere, to measure the shorter wavelength spectra of X-ray stars and gamma-ray stars. Instead of gratings and prisms, various combinations of filters and detectors are used to measure portions of the X-ray and gamma-ray spectra. At the other extreme (long wavelengths), radio spectra of stars and other radio sources are measured by "tuning" a radio telescope to different frequencies. A radio telescope—the largest is more than 305 m (1,000 ft) across—is like a giant optical reflector with a radio amplifier at the focus. Radio spectra are much more accurate than optical spectra. Pairs of radio telescopes, thousands of kilometers apart, can determine the position of a radio-emitting star as accurately as an optical telescope can, to better than 0.1 second of arc.

Spectral Type and Surface Temperature. During the early decades of the 20th century, Annie J. Cannon at Harvard University examined thousands of stellar spectra. Without concern for the actual atmospheric gases or temperatures, Cannon classified each spectrum as A, B, C, . . .S, depending on the number of absorption lines. Class A has few strong lines, class F has more, and classes M to S have bands, which are many lines close together, produced by molecules (see HARVARD CLASSIFICATION OF STARS). Later studies showed that Cannon's classes are a measure of surface temperature (T_s) in the sequence O, B, A, F, G, K, M, R, N, S. This measurement is based partly on physicist Max Planck's formula, which gives the relative emissions of various colors from a hot body. A cool star emits most of its light in the red; a hot star emits most of its light in the blue. A measurement of the ratio of blue to red light coming from a star (its color index) determines its temperature. O stars are hot ($T_s = 30,000$ K); A stars have $T_s = 10,000$ K; G stars, such as the Sun, have $T_s = 6,000$ K; and M stars have $T_s = 3,000$ K. Other spectrographic measure-

Astronomers believe that stars are continuously forming, evolving, and dying out. A large rotating cloud (1) of gas and dust is thought to contract (2) as a result of mutual gravitational attractive forces to form a nuclear-reacting star (3) and perhaps a number of cold orbiting planets. Eventually, a star like the Sun will undergo a new series of internal reactions that will cause it to expand (4) into a red giant (5). When most of the nuclear fuel is consumed, the star will pulsate (6) and finally contract to a cooling white dwarf (7).

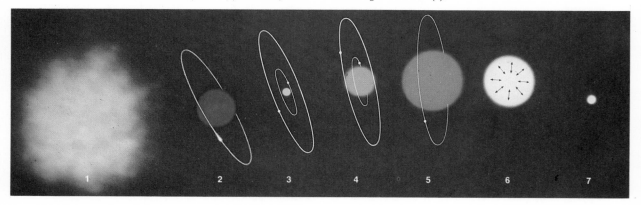

spectral type and typical spectrum	atoms producing main lines of spectrum	color of main radiation	temperatures at surfaces of stars	specimen stars	absolute magnitudes
O	ionized helium, neutral hydrogen, and helium		35,000°–40,000° C	λ Cephei	-6.5
B	neutral helium; ionized silicon, magnesium, oxygen, and nitrogen; neutral hydrogen		11,000°–35,000° C	η Orionis / Alkaid	-5 / -1.5
A	metals (especially calcium) giving weak lines; hydrogen giving very strong lines		7,500°–11,000° C	Sirius / Vega	-1.3 / -0.5
F	metals (especially calcium) giving strong lines; hydrogen giving fairly weak lines		6,000°–7,500° C	Procyon / Canopus	3 / -3.1
G	ionized calcium giving a strong line; neutral metals (fairly strong lines); hydrogen (weak lines)		5,100°–6,000° C	Sun / Capella	-5 / -0.5
K	neutral metals giving strong lines; hydrogen (very weak lines)		3,600°–5,100° C	Arcturus / 61 Cygni	8
M	molecules of titanium oxide (strong bands); neutral metals		2,000°–3,600° C	Betelgeuse / Antares / many others	-5.6 / -5.1 / 12 or 13

Element labels on spectra (right side): hydrogen; sodium; helium; iron; magnesium; titanium oxide; hydrogen; ionized helium; ionized oxygen; strontium; ionized silicon; indium; ionized magnesium; helium; iron; hydrogen; carbon and iron; ionized carbon; chromium; calcium; ionized strontium; potassium; magnesium

When light from the Sun or from a star is passed into a spectrograph, an absorption-line spectrum is obtained. The spectrum consists of a continuous band of colors and a series of superimposed dark lines. The dark lines occur because atoms in the cooler atmospheric layers of the star absorb, and thus remove, specific wavelengths of visible light from the continuous spectrum of radiation emitted by the hot lower layers. The number and positions of the various lines, which are characteristic for each element, depend primarily on the temperature of the star's atmosphere and not on differences in the amounts and types of elements present, as was once thought. The atmospheres of most stars are similar and consist mainly of hydrogen, several percent of helium, and about one percent of the remaining elements. The majority of stars fit into one of seven major classes, labeled O, B, A, F, G, K, and M in the Henry Draper, or Harvard, system of classification. These classes are arranged in order of decreasing temperature, the atmosphere of type-O stars being the hottest and those of type-M stars the coolest. In addition, a continuous change in color exists—from blue for the hottest stars to red for the coolest. The effects of temperature on the nature of the spectra are related to the degree of ionization and excitation of the electrons in each atom in a star's atmosphere. Type-M stars are relatively cool, and molecules can exist in them; strong bands of titanium oxide and strong lines of neutral metals occur in the spectra. With increasing star temperature the neutral metal lines, which are strongest in type-K stars, decrease in strength and finally disappear in type-B stars. Lines of ionized metals, particularly calcium, are strongest in types G and F. Hydrogen lines increase to maximum strength in type-A stars and then decrease rapidly at higher temperatures. Neutral helium lines predominate in type-B stars. Type-O stars are so hot that all atoms are highly ionized, and relatively few lines occur in the visible region, except for those of helium.

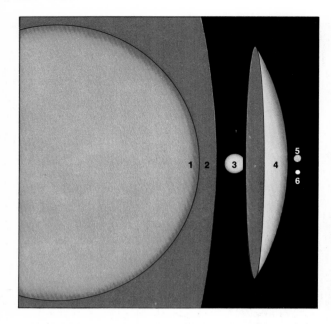

Stars range greatly in size, depending on mass, temperature, state of matter within the star, and stage of evolution. The Sun (3) is a fairly typical star, greatly exceeded in size by a giant star (1) and a red supergiant (2) such as Betelgeuse. If a segment of the Sun (4) is expanded, it can be compared to the size of the Earth (5) and to a white dwarf (6). Neutron stars, greatly condensed, are much smaller.

ments of absorption lines and emission lines help to confirm or modify this so-called color temperature.

From 1911 to 1913, Einar Hertzsprung and H. N. Russell first plotted the luminosity (L) versus the surface temperature (T_s) of stars, using as a measure of temperature the spectral types determined by Cannon. The HERTZSPRUNG-RUSSELL DIAGRAM first showed that highly luminous stars are mostly of classes O and B, with helium lines and $T_s = 25,000$ K, whereas low-luminosity stars are mostly of class M and $T_s = 3,000$ K.

Size. Once the temperature and the bolometric luminosity of a star are known, its size can easily be calculated. Planck's formula gives the total emission of radiant energy per unit area of a hot body's surface at each temperature. From the bolometric luminosity, the total energy emitted is known; from the temperature, the radiant energy emitted per square centimeter is known. The ratio gives the number of square centimeters, from which the radius of the star can be calculated. This rough calculation shows that the radii of stars vary from 1/100 of that of the Sun for WHITE DWARFS to 400 times that of the Sun for SUPERGIANTS. The radius of a nearby star can also be measured directly with an interferometer on a telescope.

Mass. More than half of all stars are BINARY STARS—two or more stars that orbit one another. About 100 orbits have been measured accurately. These measurements provide perhaps the most important characteristic of a star: its mass. From Newton's Laws of gravitation and motion, it is known that two highly massive stars must orbit (one around the other) faster than two stars of lesser mass at the same distance apart; thus the masses can be calculated from the orbit size and the period of the orbit. If the binary stars eclipse each other, this situation also gives estimates of each star's diameter. Orbits of the planets show that the Sun's mass is 2×10^{33} g (2 billion billion billion tons, or about 333,000 times the Earth's mass). Orbits of binary stars show that some stars (giants) are 40 times the mass of the Sun, and others (dwarfs) only 1/10 the mass of the Sun.

The mass of a star is also related to its luminosity; a high-mass star has high luminosity, and a low-mass star has low luminosity. The MASS-LUMINOSITY RELATION states that the lumi-

nosity is approximately proportional to (mass)$^{3.5}$. A star twice the mass of the Sun will have luminosity $2^{3.5}$, or 11.3 times the Sun's. This fact, together with the temperatures and compositions of stars, is closely related to theories of stellar structure.

In addition to luminosity and binary-star orbits, two systematic features in the motions of stars relate to their masses. In many groups and clusters of stars, the stars have similar motions and similar Doppler shifts in the lines of their spectra (see RED SHIFT); these similarities are easy to pick out from the random motions of single stars. The smaller motions of stars within a cluster show the cluster's total mass—the sum of the masses of all the stars bound together in it by their gravitation. These internal motions can also be used statistically to determine the distance from Earth to the cluster.

More dramatic are the general motions of all the stars in the Sun's vicinity, showing a circulation around the center of the Milky Way Galaxy. Again, Newton's laws apply, and from the average orbits of stars around the center, the mass of this GALAXY is found to be 100 billion times the Sun's mass. Because the orbital motions are faster near the center and slower farther away, individual motions can also be used to determine the distances to individual stars. Since interstellar dust obscures more than half of the stars in the Milky Way Galaxy, mass measurements give the only reliable estimate of the total number of stars in the Galaxy, 100 billion, each with a mass between 10^{32}g and 2×10^{35}g.

STRUCTURE OF STARS

The structure of a typical star was worked out by astrophysicists after 1920, largely based on observations of the Sun. The photosphere is the visible surface of a star and is the layer to which the surface temperature and radius apply. Above the photosphere is an atmosphere, mostly transparent, where gases absorb characteristic lines in the spectrum and reveal the chemical composition of the star.

The temperature of the stellar atmosphere is lower than the temperature of the photosphere. Above the atmosphere is a transparent CORONA of diffuse gas at high temperature. For reasons as yet uncertain, outgoing energy from the Sun or star heats the corona to temperatures over 1,000,000 K (1,800,-000° F), so that it emits X rays of much shorter wavelength than visible light. The solar corona also has emission lines in visible light which give it the greenish glow visible during a total solar eclipse. In the atmosphere and corona of a star, explosions known as flares occur in regions several thousand kilometers across, shooting out high-speed protons and electrons and causing plumes of higher temperature in the corona. At a fairly constant rate, high-speed protons and electrons are also shot out in all directions to form the solar or stellar wind. The SOLAR WIND has been measured from spacecraft as far as the planet Jupiter, and stellar winds probably extend to similar distances, larger for giant stars.

The knowledge of a star's internal structure is almost entirely theoretical, based on laboratory measurements of gases. Beneath the photosphere are several layers, some where the hot, ionized gas is turbulent, and some where it is almost at rest. Calculations of structure are based on two principles: convective equilibrium, in which turbulence brings the energy outward, and radiative equilibrium, in which radiation brings the energy outward. The temperature and density are calculated for each depth, using the characteristics of the mix of gases (hydrogen, helium, and heavier elements) derived from the spectrum of the atmosphere. The pressure is calculated from the weight of the gases overhead.

Eventually, deep in the interior the temperature and density are high enough (10,000,000 K and 30 g/cm^3) for a nuclear reaction to occur, converting four hydrogen atoms (4 ^{1}H) to one helium atom (^{4}He), with a 0.7% loss of mass. Because the conversion of this mass (m) to energy (E) follows Einstein's equation $E = mc^2$ (where c is the velocity of light), such a reaction releases 6.4×10^{18} ergs of energy per gram of hydrogen, 60 million times more than chemical reactions such as the burning of hydrogen in oxygen. It is this enormous energy source that makes long-lasting, self-luminous stars possible.

In an attempt to determine the precise mechanism provid-

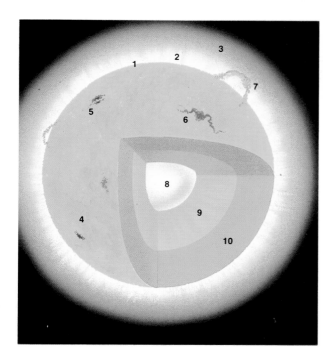

The Sun, a typical star, is a great sphere of burning gases. The photosphere (1) is the surface that is normally visible. The chromosphere (2) and the corona (3) are transparent, upper atmospheric layers of low density. Constantly changing photospheric features include bright, grainlike patches, or granulations (4), sunspots (5), and dark, threadlike filaments (6) of exploding gases that appear as prominences (7) when seen on the solar limb. The energy emitted by the Sun comes from thermonuclear reactions within the core (8). The energy from the core flows out to the surface by radiation through a radiation zone (9) and by convection through a convection zone (10).

THE NEAREST STARS

Name	Distance (light-years)	Apparent Brightness (magnitude)
Sun	—	−26.8
α Centauri A	4.3	−0.01
α Centauri B	4.3	1.33
α Centauri C	4.3	11.05
Barnard's Star	5.9	9.54
Wolf 359	7.6	13.53
Lalande 21185	8.1	7.50
Sirius A	8.6	−1.47
Sirius B	8.6	8.68
Luyten 726–8A	8.9	12.45
Luyten 726–8B	8.9	12.95
Ross 154	9.4	10.6
Ross 248	10.3	12.29
ε Eridani	10.7	3.73
Luyten 789–6	10.8	12.18
Ross 128	10.8	11.10
61 Cygni A	11.2	5.22
61 Cygni B	11.2	6.03
ε Indi	11.2	4.68
Procyon A	11.4	0.37
Procyon B	11.4	10.7

SOURCE: Adapted from a table compiled by Alan H. Batten in *The Observer's Handbook 1976* of the Royal Astronomical Society of Canada and a table in *Drama of the Universe* (1978) by George O. Abell (reprinted by permission of Holt, Rinehart and Winston).

16 times faster than at 10,000,000 K. Lithium (^{7}Li) and beryllium (^{7}Be) are probably also involved. The neutrino is a very-low-mass particle that can penetrate the full radius of the Sun or a star and may be detectable on Earth. One of the great mysteries of modern astrophysics is the failure of experiments to detect the neutrinos expected from nuclear reactions in the Sun.

Whether by the Bethe cycle or by the proton-proton reaction, the Sun and other stars are converting hydrogen to helium in their cores at a considerable rate (600,000,000 tons/sec in the Sun). Because helium has different characteristics, this conversion changes the structure of the star. During the process there is a central core composed entirely of helium, a spherical shell around it in which hydrogen is being converted to helium, and the rest of the star, composed mostly of hydrogen. When a large core of helium has been created, the core may collapse, and new nuclear reactions may start as the temperature and density jump to very high values. When the temperature exceeds 100,000,000 K, helium is converted to carbon by the triple-alpha (ionized helium) process:

$$^4\text{He} + {}^4\text{He} \rightarrow {}^8\text{Be}$$
$$^4\text{He} + {}^8\text{Be} \rightarrow {}^{12}\text{C} + \text{photon}$$

Astrophysicists make use of the Hertzsprung-Russell diagram and large computers to calculate how stars evolve in this way. They find that stars of different masses evolve in different

ing the energy for stars, physicists in the early 1930s measured the rates of several nuclear reactions in the laboratory. In 1938, Hans Bethe showed that the carbon-nitrogen cycle could account for a star's long-lasting luminosity (see CARBON CYCLE, astronomy). In Bethe's theory, carbon (^{12}C) acts as a catalyst in the conversion of hydrogen to helium. That is, a small amount of carbon is necessary for the reactions to occur, but carbon is converted to nitrogen (^{14}N), then converted back to carbon to be used again. The Bethe reactions are

$$^{12}\text{C} + {}^1\text{H} \rightarrow {}^{13}\text{C} + e^+ + \text{photon} + \text{neutrino}$$
$$^{13}\text{C} + {}^1\text{H} \rightarrow {}^{14}\text{N} + \text{photon}$$
$$^{14}\text{N} + {}^1\text{H} \rightarrow {}^{15}\text{N} + \text{photon} + \text{neutrino}$$
$$^{15}\text{N} + {}^1\text{H} \rightarrow {}^{12}\text{C} + {}^4\text{He} + \text{photon}$$

where e^+ is a positron (positive electron), the photons are short-wavelength gamma rays, and the negative electrons are ignored because the atoms H, C, and N are fully ionized (all electrons removed). The reaction rates at the temperature and density in the core of the Sun are fast enough to produce 10^{33} ergs/sec, the luminosity of the Sun.

Later it was shown that the PROTON-PROTON REACTION could also produce the Sun's luminosity, and more recent studies show that in the Sun and smaller stars, where temperature and density in the core are smaller than in larger stars, the proton-proton reaction beats out the Bethe cycle and can occur with no ^{12}C or ^{14}N present, if the temperature is about 10,000,000 K. Equations for the proton-proton reaction are

$$^1\text{H} + {}^1\text{H} \rightarrow {}^2\text{H} + e^+ + \text{neutrino}$$
$$^2\text{H} + {}^1\text{H} \rightarrow {}^3\text{He} + \text{photon}$$
$$^3\text{He} + {}^3\text{He} \rightarrow {}^4\text{He} + {}^1\text{H} + {}^1\text{H}$$

where the rates increase with the fourth power of the temperature, so that at a temperature of 20,000,000 K the rate is

THE BRIGHTEST STARS

Name	Constellation	Apparent Brightness (magnitude)	Distance (light-years)
Sun	—	−26.8	—
Sirius A	Canis Major	−1.47	8.7
Canopus	Carina	−0.72	98
Arcturus	Boötes	−0.06	36
α Centauri	Centaurus	−0.01	4.3
Vega	Lyra	0.04	26.5
Capella	Auriga	0.05	45
Rigel	Orion	0.14	900
Procyon A	Canis Minor	0.37	11.3
Betelgeuse	Orion	0.41	520
Achernar	Eridanus	0.51	118
β Centauri	Centaurus	0.63	490
Altair	Aquila	0.77	16.5
α Crucis	Crux	0.87	400
Aldebaran	Taurus	0.86	68
Spica	Virgo	0.91	220
Antares	Scorpius	0.92	520
Fomalhaut	Piscis Austrinus	1.15	22.6
Pollux	Gemini	1.16	35
Deneb	Cygnus	1.26	1,600
β Crucis	Crux	1.28	490

SOURCE: Adapted from a table compiled by Donald A. MacRae in *The Observer's Handbook 1976* of the Royal Astronomical Society of Canada and a table in *Contemporary Astronomy*, 2d ed., by Jay M. Pasachoff, Holt/Saunders, 1980.

ways and at different rates. The most massive stars (ten times the Sun's mass) rapidly change from blue giants to RED GIANTS and may become unstable and pulsate as variable stars during this stage. Stars of lesser mass, such as the Sun, spend a large fraction of their lives on the main sequence of the Hertzsprung-Russell diagram while they convert hydrogen to helium. After several billion years, these stars become white dwarfs. Depending on mass and other circumstances, a star may evolve to a NOVA or SUPERNOVA, PULSAR, NEUTRON STAR, or BLACK HOLE (see STELLAR EVOLUTION).   THORNTON PAGE

Bibliography: Abell, G., *Exploration of the Universe* (1969); Baade, Walter, *Evolution of Stars and Galaxies* (1975); Kruse, W., and Dieckvoss, W., *The Stars* (1957); Kyselka, Will, and Lanterman, Ray, *North Star to Southern Cross* (1976); Meadows, A. J., *Stellar Evolution* (1978); Merrill, Paul W., *Space Chemistry* (1963); Moore, Patrick, *The New Guide to the Stars* (1976); Page, Thornton, and Page, L. W., *Starlight* (1967) and *Stars and Clouds of the Milky Way* (1968); Shklovskii, Iosif S., *Stars: Their Birth, Life and Death*, trans. by Richard Rodman (1978).

star-of-Bethlehem

Star-of-Bethlehem is the common name for any of several species of the plant genus *Ornithogalum* of the lily family, Liliaceae. Native to Europe, *O. umbellatum* is bulbous, its numerous linear leaves reaching 30 cm (1 ft) in length. The flower stalks are topped with up to 20 starlike flowers, predominantly white.   KENNETH R. ROBERTSON

Star Carr

Star Carr, the first adequately recorded MESOLITHIC site found in Great Britain, is located 8 km (5 mi) south of Scarborough, in Yorkshire, England. Radiocarbon dating indicates that the site was occupied during the mid-8th millennium BC, a period during which Britain was still connected to the continental landmass. This fact would account for the site's affinities with other Maglemosian assemblages of northern Europe. Excavations carried out (1949–51) by Grahame CLARK revealed the birch brushwood foundations of three or four family units occupied by hunter-gatherers; the seasonal occupation evidently was limited to winter and early spring. The basically meat diet of the inhabitants included red deer, elk, and aurochs, as well as some roe deer, pig, and beaver. Along with pollen and allied data, a wealth of artifacts found at Star Carr—notably barbed points of bone and antler—has provided the basis for an informed reconstruction of the economy and environment of the area in Mesolithic times.
          D. W. HARDING

Bibliography: Clark, J. G. D., *Excavations at Star Carr* (1954).

Star Chamber

Star Chamber, an English court of law active in the Tudor and early Stuart periods, was abolished by the LONG PARLIAMENT in 1641. An outgrowth of the royal council, it was made up of privy councilors as well as judges and supplemented the activities of the common-law and equity courts in both civil and criminal matters. Initially well regarded because of its speed and flexibility, Star Chamber became unpopular as the Stuart kings used it with increasing arbitrariness to enforce the royal prerogative. Its name thus became synonymous with secret, irresponsible court proceedings.

Star of David

The six-pointed Star of David, called in Hebrew *Magen David* ("shield of David"), is the accepted symbol of Judaism. It is incorporated in the center of a white background to form the flag of the modern state of Israel. The Red Magen David is used in Israel to designate the equivalent of the Red Cross. Nazi Germany revived the medieval European practice of requiring Jews to wear a yellow star on their clothing.

Star-Spangled Banner, The

The music of "The Star-Spangled Banner" was composed in 1777 by John Stafford Smith, an Englishman, as a setting for the poem "To Anacreon in Heaven," to be sung by members of a convivial social club in London called the Anacreontic Society. The original song celebrates the joys of music, love, and wine. The melody quickly became known in the United States and was used with alternate words, the earliest-known version being written by Francis Hopkinson in about 1790; by 1820 there were 84 different poems being sung to the Anacreontic melody.

The words of "The Star-Spangled Banner" were written by Francis Scott KEY on Sept. 14, 1814, inspired by the sight of the U.S. flag at FORT MCHENRY withstanding a nightlong bombardment from an offshore British warship. He indicated that the words were to be sung to the Anacreontic song, a melody he had used 9 years earlier for another poem. "The Star-Spangled Banner" attained popularity quickly but was no more prominent as a patriotic air than "Yankee Doodle" or "Hail Columbia." During the Civil War it was adopted informally as an anthem by the Union Army, and it was adopted officially by the U.S. Army during World War I. It did not become the U.S. national anthem, however, until signed into law by President Herbert Hoover on Mar. 3, 1931.   EDWARD A. BERLIN

Bibliography: Weybright, Victor, *The Star-Spangled Banner* (1935).

starch

Starch is manufactured by green plants through photosynthesis to serve as a metabolic reserve. It is therefore classified as a nutrient polysaccharide, in contrast to similar CARBOHYDRATE structures that are used for support. Starch occurs in the form of grains in many parts of the plant, principally in embryonic tissues such as seeds, fruit, roots, and tubers. The grains differ in size and shape and may be microscopically examined to identify their source.

When completely hydrolyzed by enzymes or acid, starch yields only *D*-glucose as the product. Nevertheless, nearly all starch is a mixture of two different kinds of carbohydrate, termed *amylose* and *amylopectin*. Amylose gives a deep blue color when tested with iodine. Its structure is a linear chain of glucose units. Amylose from potatoes has a molecular weight of 4,000 to 150,000, although seeds may contain components weighing up to 400,000. Amylopectin gives a red to purple color with iodine. It is a bush-shaped structure made up of branched chains of glucose units, with about 25 to 30 units per branch. The molecular weight of amylopectin from rice starch is about 500,000, and other sources yield particles with molecular weights up to 6 million. Amylopectin is closely related in structure to glycogen, or animal starch, which gives a brown color with iodine.

The most important starch manufactured in the United States is corn starch, which can be hydrolyzed for the manufacture of *D*-glucose and corn syrup. About one-third of the total corn starch and 95% of the corn syrup produced is sold for food purposes. For industrial purposes, the properties of most starches are changed by chemical treatment or enzyme action. Modified starches are used in adhesives; for textile, paper, and leather sizing; and as binders in sand molding.
          STEPHEN FLEISHMAN

Bibliography: Brautlecht, Charles A., *Starch: Its Sources, Production and Uses* (1953); Guthrie, R. D., and Honeyman, J., *An Introduction to the Chemistry of Carbohydrates* (1964); Radley, J. A., *Starch and Its Derivatives*, 4th ed. (1968).

starfish

Familiar seashore animals, starfish, or sea stars (class Asteroidea), are the best-known members of the invertebrate phylum Echinodermata. Usually 5, but up to 20 or more short or long rays, or arms, radiate from a central disk. Starfish exhibit radial symmetry. Each ray is an extension of the body cavity and the vital organs. The group has a worldwide distribution and ranges from along the shore down to depths of 6 km (3.7 mi). Most starfish are 10–30 cm (4–12 in) in diameter, but some species are as small as 1 cm (0.4 in), and the largest known species, *Midgardia xandaros*, exceeds 1 m (3.3 ft) in diameter.

The starfish body is sheathed in a flexible armor of skeletal

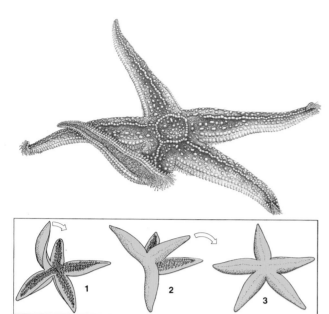

A common starfish, Asterias rubens, *can right itself if it is on its back* (bottom, left to right). *First, it twists one arm* (1), *moving the arm until the body folds over* (2), *then turns right side up* (3).

pieces, or ossicles. From the central mouth on the underside of the body (oral surface), channels with two or four rows of tube feet (suction cups present or absent) radiate outward along the arms. If present, the central anus is found on the upper surface, where a circular sieve plate, or madreporite, opens into the water vascular system, a hydraulic system that moves the tube feet. Each arm has a sensory tentacle that responds to various stimuli, and a red photosensitive eyespot located at the tip of the arm. Starfish vary greatly in color. Bilaterally symmetrical, swimming larvae result from external fertilization. The larvae metamorphose into free-living adult forms.

Most starfish are carnivorous predators or scavengers, feeding on a variety of plant or animal material. Predatory forms favor bivalve mollusks; they can open them slightly by the pulling action of the sucking tube feet and then digest the soft parts externally. They frequently devastate oyster and clam beds, and some cause extensive damage to coral reefs.

DAVID L. PAWSON

Bibliography: Clark, Ailsa M., *Starfishes* (1977); Hyman, L. H., *The Invertebrates: Echinodermata* (1955).

stargazer

Stargazers, family Uranoscopidae, comprise about 25 species of sluggish fish that lie in the sand of ocean bottoms waiting for prey. Small eyes near the front of their heads point upward. Fleshy flaps keep sand from their large mouths. These fish may also resemble worms or other food and thus attract prey, which is then engulfed. Well equipped for defense, stargazers produce electric charges as strong as 50 V from modified optic nerves, and above their pectoral fins they have two poison spines, each with a venom gland at the base. The fishes average about 20 cm (8 in) in length.　C. P. IDYLL

Stark, Johannes

The German physicist Johannes Stark, b. Apr. 15, 1874, d. June 21, 1957, won the 1919 Nobel Prize for physics for his experiments on the positively charged particle stream in electrical discharge tubes. In 1905 he detected a Doppler shift from the light emitted by these "canal" rays, and in 1913 he split their spectral lines with strong electric fields (the Stark effect), thus discovering the electrical counterpart to the magnetic Zeeman effect. In Nazi Germany Stark, an outspoken anti-Semite,

held high positions in scientific institutions, and he is remembered as often for his strong negative influence on German science as for his early contributions to physics.

RICHARD HIRSH

Bibliography: Beyerchen, Alan D., *Scientists under Hitler: Politics and the Physics Community in the Third Reich* (1977).

Stark, John

John Stark, b. Londonderry, N.H., Aug. 28, 1728, d. May 8, 1822, commanded American troops in the American Revolution. During the French and Indian War he served with Rogers's Rangers. As colonel of a New Hampshire regiment, Stark fought in the battles of Bunker Hill (1775), Trenton (1776), and Princeton (1777). Promoted to brigadier general, he gained fame by defeating units of Gen. John BURGOYNE's army near Bennington, Vt., on Aug. 16, 1777. Two months later Stark became a brigadier general in the Continental Army.

Bibliography: Fast, H. M., *The Crossing* (1971); Moore, Howard P., *A Life of General John Stark of New Hampshire* (1949).

starling

Starlings, members of the bird family Sturnidae, are perching birds that number more than 111 species, including the MYNAH. Ranging from 18 to 43 cm (7 to 17 in) in length, they are highly sociable, and many are good mimics. The most common color is black, and the plumage is often glossy. Those in temperate areas migrate part of the winter, often in huge flocks, which can be quite noisy. Although they are tree birds, starlings readily seek food on the ground. The clutch size is 3 to 6 eggs, and the eggs are laid in tree and wall holes. The common starling, *Sturnus vulgaris,* native to Eurasia, has become widely established and has reached nuisance abundance in some areas, often driving out other birds. Starlings, however, are of some value in destroying insect pests and parasites.　WILLIAM F. SANDFORD

The starling S. vulgaris *has white speckles in winter* (foreground) *and a yellow bill in summer* (background).

Starling, Ernest Henry

The English physiologist Ernest Henry Starling, b. Apr. 17, 1866, d. May 2, 1927, contributed to knowledge of heart function, lymph flow, and the role of hormones in the body. With Sir William BAYLISS he isolated (1902) the hormone secreting from the small intestine and determined that chemical secretions, as well as the nervous system, control body functions.

Starr, Bart

Bryan Bartlett Starr, b. Montgomery, Ala., Jan. 9, 1934, was an American professional football player who helped turn a floundering team, the Green Bay Packers, into one of the greatest clubs in league history. After playing as a quarterback at the University of Alabama, he joined the Green Bay Packers of the National Football League (NFL). During his 16-year career he guided the Packers to 6 division, 5 league, and 2 Super Bowl championships. Starr played in the NFL Pro Bowl 4 times (1960-62, 1966) and was named the Most Valuable Player in both Super Bowl appearances. After retiring he became an assistant coach (1972) for the Packers, and in 1975 he became head coach of that organization. Starr was inducted into the Pro Football Hall of Fame in 1977.

Bibliography: Maule, Tex, *Bart Starr: Professional Quarterback* (1973); Starr, Bart, and Cox, Mark, *Quarterbacking* (1967).

Starr, Belle

Belle Starr, originally Myra Belle Shirley, b. Carthage, Mo., 1848, was an American outlaw. During the U.S. Civil War she provided Confederate guerrillas with information about the movements of federal troops. She later joined the outlaw gang headed by William C. QUANTRILL. In 1880 she married Sam Starr, who was of Cherokee and Irish extraction. Their home in Indian Territory in Oklahoma became notorious as an outlaw retreat. Belle Starr was shot and killed on Feb. 3, 1889, by an unknown assailant.

Bibliography: Breiham, C. W., and Rosamond, C. A., *The Bandit Belle* (1970); Hicks, Edwin P., *Belle Starr and Her Pearl* (1963).

Starr, Ringo: see BEATLES, THE.

starvation

Starvation is a syndrome, or abnormal state, that results from a quantitatively inadequate food intake or from a failure to properly metabolize food energy. In contrast, malnutrition is generally due to poor diet and results from deficiencies of particular nutrients (for example, iron deficiency leading to anemia and vitamin A deficiency leading to xerophthalmia). Starvation manifests itself first by weight loss and body wasting, and if unrelieved may progress to emaciation, diarrhea that is difficult to treat, secondary infections, and eventually death by heart failure. Humans may die of cold in a few hours, or of thirst in a few days, but they usually die of hunger only after weeks of starvation.

Starvation may have several causes. Starvation among large groups of persons most commonly results from FAMINE. Starvation in individuals may be secondary to certain diseases, most notably those which affect consumption, absorption, or proper metabolism of food and its nutrients. It may also result from food deprivation, such as during incarceration or when an abusive parent starves a child. Another form of starvation occurs in those who suffer from the disease ANOREXIA NERVOSA.

Starvation leads first to the wasting away of the fat deposits of the body, both those beneath the skin and the deeper deposits. A normal human weighing 68 kg (150 lb) may have 16 kg (35 lb) of fat. After most of the fat reserves have been burned up, there may be progressive wasting of muscles and reduction in size of body organs, including the liver. The physiological response to starvation is to conserve energy by reducing activity. As starvation progresses, changes in the intestines lead to poor absorption of nutrients and diarrhea. Blood pressure falls and the pulse slows. Eventually edema may occur. In women menstruation may cease, and in pregnant individuals spontaneous abortion or miscarriage may result. Psychological changes such as apathy or irritability are common. In young children nutritional MARASMUS or KWASHIORKOR may develop.

The treatment of starvation depends on the severity of the condition. In moderate cases (loss of less than 20% of body weight) and where there is no diarrhea, any available and acceptable food is suitable for treatment. It is recommended that treatment begin with relatively bland foods of high nutritive value. Intake of 4,000 or more calories per day with weight gains of 2 kg (4 lb) per week may occur. If the patient is enfeebled, and especially if diarrhea is severe, extreme caution is necessary in treatment. Injudicious feeding of unsuit-able foods may result in death. Intravenous or intragastric (tube) feeding and the introduction of frequent small feedings of nutritious, easily digestible foods are needed until such time as the patient's digestive tract has had a chance to recover. In all cases appropriate treatment for any infectious disease needs to be a part of treatment. If starvation is secondary to some other disease—for example, malabsorption, tuberculosis, cancer, or anorexia nervosa—then specific treatment appropriate for those conditions is needed.

MICHAEL G. LATHAM

Bibliography: Datta, S. P., and Ottaway, J. H., *Biochemistry*, 3d ed. (1976); Keys, Ancel, et al., *Biology of Human Starvation*, 2 vols. (1950).

Stas, Jean Servais   [stahs]

The Belgian chemist Jean Servais Stas, b. Aug. 21, 1813, d. Dec. 13, 1891, played a major role in accurately determining atomic weights. Working as a student of Jean Baptiste Dumas, he established the atomic weight of carbon as 12, rather than 6 as had been believed. The accuracy of his measurements discredited the hypothesis that the atomic weights of all elements were multiples of the atomic weight of hydrogen and established the use, at that time, of oxygen = 16 as a universal atomic weight standard. Stas also did important research on nicotine, carbonic gas, phlorizin, and vegetable alkaloids.

Stassen, Harold E.   [stas'-en]

When only 31, Republican Harold Edward Stassen, b. W. Saint Paul, Minn., Apr. 13, 1907, became (1938) the governor of Minnesota and held that office until 1943, when he resigned to join the navy for service in World War II. In 1948 he was narrowly defeated by Thomas E. Dewey in a campaign to win the Republican nomination for president. Since then, Stassen has campaigned unsuccessfully for the presidential nomination many times. He has practiced law privately, served (1949–53) as president of the University of Pennsylvania, and held several top appointive posts in the federal government.

Bibliography: Stuhler, Barbara, *Ten Men of Minnesota and American Foreign Policy, 1898-1968* (1973).

state   (political unit)

The state is a political unit that possesses a territory, a population, a GOVERNMENT, and SOVEREIGNTY (or independence). In political theory, the *state*, a term probably first used by Nicolò Machiavelli, is the most fundamental political unit. It is the supreme institution that has recognized legal authority to regulate and control all other institutions within a country. All officers and organs of government—legislative, executive, judicial, and administrative—are creations of the state.

The term *state* is used in another sense in a federal system such as the United States—to refer to one of the 50 semiautonomous political entities that coexist with the federal (or national) government. In the United States some powers belong exclusively to the national government, some belong to the states, and others are shared by both. The 10th Amendment to the U.S. Constitution reserves all powers to the states that are not given by the Constitution to the federal government, nor denied by it to the states.   MARTIN TORODASH

state   (in political philosophy)

The state is frequently defined as the highest or most comprehensive political association having a recognized claim to primacy—first allegiance or ultimate authority. According to another common definition, statehood is the stable possession of preponderant power by a single authority within a delimited territory. Two impediments, however, stand in the way of any simple definition of the state. The first is that the term has been used quite loosely, to designate any sort of political rule at any period in history ("the Byzantine state," "the Papal states"); and at the same time quite restrictively, to designate the kind of political structure mainly characteristic of post-Renaissance Western societies. The second impediment is that notions about what the state is vary systematically with the various political philosophies: a Lockean liberal who advocates a minimalist state that merely enforces natural law and protects natural rights will never be able to agree with a Hegelian that the state is the concrete actualization of rational freedom on earth, or with a Marxian that the state is a mere committee for the management of the interests of the social class owning the means of economic production. Defining the state is not easy unless one is prepared to declare dogmatically that a particular theory of statehood is correct, to the exclusion of all others. The same difficulty afflicts any effort to say what the state's purpose is. A Benthamite utilitarian will urge that the end of the state is the greatest happiness of the greatest number, and that the pursuit of this end gives the state legitimate authority. A Kantian will suggest that the state exists to provide a legal context within which good will and respect for persons is more nearly possible.

Nor is the tracing of the origin of the state free of this same difficulty: some have traced the foundation of the state to a desire for security and peace (Thomas HOBBES); some have insisted on natural sociability as creating states, believing that the stateless human is either a beast or a god (ARISTOTLE); some have put forward economic motives such as a desire for the division of labor and an economy of scale, which can be obtained only by centralizing power and authoritatively allocating work (Edmund BURKE); still others have stressed human depravity in a fallen world creating the need for the state (Saint AUGUSTINE). In trying, then, to say what the state is, what its purposes are, and where its origin is, the problem always exists that the state is itself not simply a fact but a conceptual artifact. The most reasonable and candid way to treat the state, therefore, is to offer a history of theories about it.

Characteristics of the State. The word *state* is ultimately traceable to the Roman legal idea of *status civilis*, or "the civil condition"; at the greatest level of generality *state* does indeed mean "condition" or "way of being" ("the state of one's health"). The use of the English term *state* in its specifically political sense first became current around the 16th century—in England rather later than on the Continent, where the French *état* and Italian *stato* were in use soon after 1500 (by Nicolò MACHIAVELLI, for instance). The modern term *state* was usually accompanied by the notion of SOVEREIGNTY. The ideas of state and sovereignty are intimately related; they arose together historically and still make most sense when juxtaposed. Most—although not all—political philosophies would concur that sovereignty is the hallmark of the state.

In a general attempt to identify state characteristics that would be recognized by a substantial number of political philosophies, one can say that the state is separated conceptually and historically from other kinds of political rule by (1) its extreme centralization or concentration of power internally, coupled with its rejection of so-called supranational power externally; (2) its secularism, or at least its nonreligious basis, necessitating, at a minimum, toleration of religious diversity; (3) its emphasis on the legal rights of its citizens rather than on the direct participation of all in day-to-day decision making; (4) its reliance on the authority of LAWS that it makes, interprets, and enforces itself through its own agents; (5) its operation—once law is in effect—through a bureaucracy, or civil service, that exists mainly to perform services for the public; and (6) its refusal to leave decisive portions of power with any private or voluntary association, such as a church or a corporation.

The theory of state sovereignty explains and defends—opponents would say rationalizes—the historical process that is thought to have taken place in early modern European history: the removal of power from subnational groups and from supranational institutions. State sovereignty can be contrasted with tribal rule, theocratic rule, patriarchal rule, rule by plain violence, or nonrule by spontaneous consensus (ANARCHISM), as well as with FEUDALISM.

Early Development of the Concept of the State. Whether the Greek polis or CITY-STATE, as theorized by PLATO and Aristotle in the 4th century BC, was really the forerunner of the modern state, is a subject of endless dispute. Some political phi-

losophers, stressing the notion that the polis was an ethical community for the attainment of virtue or goodness, have insisted that the polis was as much a church as a state. Others have insisted on the idea that Aristotle first successfully distinguished politics—defined as the art of ruling and being ruled in turn—from other social activities such as parenthood, slavemastery, and household management (economy). They have argued that Aristotle invented the idea of the state as a public, secular, and legal order. (Aristotle does say that the "most general and inclusive association . . . directed to the most general of all goods . . . is the polis . . . or the political association.") Here, then, it is very much a question of how one interprets Aristotle. Comparatively few, however, view Plato, with his notion of a highly personal rule by the philosophic few who have a vision of the Good, as having as much connection with modernity as Aristotle. Plato's connection with the modern state is distant, even if one grants that in the *Laws* Plato countenances the rule of law applied by a "nocturnal council" and abandons the concept of philosopher kings.

The Aristotelian polis, on the other hand, would be a city with a large middle class which would promote stability and balance the conflicting claims of the poor and the rich. The city's constitution would combine elements of democracy with elements of aristocracy (again, to balance opposing claims); the distribution of scarce and valuable goods would be in proportion to contribution to the good of the polis; the citizens would rule and be ruled in turn, insofar as the mixed social system allowed. The rule of law would prevail, moderated by equity in meeting individual claims. Above everything else, a spirit of moderation would prevail. Some of this theory resembles modern ideas about the state: like Hobbes and Immanuel KANT, Aristotle insists on the centrality of the rule of law. Like G. W. F. HEGEL, he insists that a substantial middle class will help produce a moderate, stable polity; like Machiavelli, he draws distinctions between what is ideal and what is best in a given set of circumstances. Even so, Aristotle's notion that "any polis which is truly so called . . . must devote itself to the end of encouraging goodness," that a true city must not be a mere alliance or covenant that guarantees "men's rights against one another," separates him from much of modern state theory.

The State in Roman Thought and Practice. The theoretical attributes of a state—extreme centralization, secularism, legal rights rather than participation, the rule of law, bureaucracy, the divesting of lower associations of their power—were first to be found in a fairly full form in Roman theory and practice. A great deal of the structure of the state as well as theory of sovereignty itself is of substantially Roman origin.

(Left) *A relief depicts the ancient Roman symbol of political authority, the fasces, a bundle of wooden rods bound with a double-headed ax by a red cord.*

(Below) *This early Roman coin shows the fasces borne by lictors, or guards, marching behind Lucius Junius Brutus, traditional founder of the Roman Republic. (British Museum, London.)*

Rome exemplified many characteristics of the state. Its internal power, particularly within Italy, was highly centralized, and its external power was all but unshakable for centuries. It was not truly a secular power, but its toleration of dozens of sects promoted considerable harmony. Its emphasis on the legal rights of its citizens was of great importance—the size of the empire made personal participation in a polis life impossible, but a citizen could at least hope for a certain security of legal expectations. Rome's maintenance of services (courts, roads, water supplies, a postal system) administered by a trained bureaucracy pointed the way to the modern state. Finally, a genuine political rule prevailed—at least before the ultimately fatal militarization of the empire. Rome did not leave vast power to groups within society.

Rome's reliance on the rule of law, uncharacteristic of many ancient systems, gave great importance to courts, to lawyers, to precedent, and to process; moreover, Rome made, interpreted, and enforced its own laws through its own agents. The Romans virtually invented legal philosophy (see LAW, HISTORY OF) or jurisprudence. The distinction between the *ius naturale* (NATURAL LAW), the *ius civilis* (CIVIL LAW), and the *ius gentium* ("law of nations") is largely a Roman invention. To be sure, the content of those notions changed over time: to the Romans, *ius naturale* meant what was reasonable or customary; whereas to a Christian such as Saint Thomas AQUINAS natural law was that part of the divine law which is known by human reason alone, unsupplemented by divine revelation. But either notion of naturalness can be—and has been—used in saying what the state ought to do. The expression of sovereignty through law—very much a Roman idea—is decisive for many later theories of state sovereignty.

The State in Medieval Thought and Practice. The fall of the Roman Empire led, in most views, to the fairly rapid atrophy of the state method of governance and finally to feudal fragmentation. To be sure, the church, which long claimed that the Emperor Constantine (r. 306–37) had donated the Western Empire to the papacy, inherited Rome's universalist pretensions. But these pretensions animated the activities of the Byzantine Empire and the Holy Roman Empire as well, and three authorities could not be universal at the same time. In any case the church rarely tried to pass for a state, given its view that temporal power is lower than spiritual power. In *De Monarchia* (On Monarchy, 1308) Dante Alighieri put forth the doctrine that the *Respublica Christiana* ("Republic of Christendom") is jointly governed by a temporal Holy Roman emperor deriving his authority in unbroken descent from the Roman emperor Augustus and by a spiritual pope deriving his authority in unbroken descent from Saint Peter, and that both authorities should operate harmoniously (within distinct spheres) to produce peace and concord. It was an exceptional, theoretical effort to recover both Romes—the Roman church and the Roman state. More reflective, perhaps, of the realities of medieval fragmentation and of the devaluation of politics generally is Saint Augustine. His *Civitate Dei* (The CITY OF GOD, 413–26) argues that the Roman state, for all its glory, owed its unity to slaughter and to bloodshed, and that in such a state even a well-meaning judge will sometimes, out of ignorance, torture the innocent in his sincere effort to produce justice. For Saint Augustine, necessity required that the misery of this mortal state be restricted by a legal order that makes feeble stabs at justice; but it is only in the Heavenly City that wretchedness will end.

It is usually thought, although on widely differing grounds, that the notions of internal and external state sovereignty began to revive a little in the later Middle Ages, at the beginning of the 14th century. The French monarchy had long claimed its temporal independence from the Holy Roman Empire, which was often supported by the papacy. In political philosophy the rediscovery of Aristotle's doctrines did much to enhance the prestige of temporal government and to weaken the Augustinian view that politics, as a consequence of the Fall, ought to give way to the earthly agents of the Heavenly City.

Aristotle as a political writer was fully resuscitated by MARSILIUS OF PADUA's *Defender of Peace* (1324; Eng. trans., 1535),

Saint Augustine articulated his Christian philosophy of history and political theory in The City of God (413–26). He interpreted human history as a conflict between two mystical cities, the City of God (those destined for salvation) and the Earthly City (the damned). The function of the state (the Christian empire) is to provide the stable conditions in which people may work toward their ultimate salvation.

which quotes Aristotle's *Politics* approvingly at every turn and treats political secularism, or civil government, as wholly respectable. By the 14th century, in any event, the conditions for the theory and practice of state sovereignty were coming back into existence.

The doctrine and the exercise of sovereign power by states can be seen not only as the recovery of antiquity and as an escape from the papacy and the Holy Roman Empire, but also as a liberation of individuals as well as of whole nations from the increasingly outdated prerogatives and private laws (*privileges*) that had come to intervene between individuals and civil authority in the Middle Ages. The destruction of the Western Empire and the subsequent insecurity of about 800 years saw a number of nonpolitical public authorities develop between individuals and the shadowy central authorities of the Middle Ages. Anyone who could manage both to pacify and to control a sizable piece of territory thereby became a landlord. By defending the inhabitants on his lands and by swearing feudal allegiance to a higher authority, he would enjoy political control of those individuals under his protection.

Thus, the private prerogatives of the landlord were extended to public authority. At every level the church, which had replaced the defunct Roman state in all matters touching public morality, preservation of culture, and education, exercised enormous public authority. And on top of the secular and ecclesiastical hierarchies within any particular country were the "universal" authorities, the emperor and the pope. There was a fantastic variety of medieval political forms—feudal monarchies, baronies, earldoms, free cities, ecclesiastical principalities—that contributed to the fragmentation of politics in the Middle Ages; but all these forms could be conceived as part of a vast hierarchy culminating in the empire and the papacy.

The doctrine of the sovereign state could act as a liberating agent by destroying the system of private rights acting as public laws. The development of a theory of supreme political power (as contrasted with paternal authority, or theocratic authority, or power based on land control) was a happy way to get out from under the various prerogatives of feudal nobles, prelates, guilds, and corporations. After the Reformation the doctrine of state sovereignty became particularly attractive as a secular rallying point for those who were looking for a new, nonreligious principle of social unity to end religious civil wars.

By the 16th century doctrines of internal sovereignty had gradually begun to triumph. By then the doctrine of external, or international, sovereignty was perhaps even more advanced. The idea of universal authorities was no longer plausible. The Reformation definitively ended the universal authority of the pope, but it also dealt a crippling blow to the vestiges of the emperor's universal credit.

Nicolò Machiavelli considered the first modern political thinker, is best known for the theories of government expressed in The Prince (1513) and in Discourses on the First Ten Books of Livy (1513–21). Both works—the former treating the ways in which a ruler may achieve and maintain absolute power and the latter exploring a republican political system—while dissimiliar in emphasis, are notable for their advocacy of expedient policies in government. (Palazzo Vecchio, Florence.)

The Modern State. Nicolò Machiavelli (1469–1527) is commonly treated as the first modern political thinker, and sometimes as the first political scientist. Whether he was also the first modern theorist of state sovereignty is problematic. He did indeed argue that politics has laws of its own. He also argued that the universal authorities (above all, the papacy) are contemptible and weak; that a modern government such as France's is stronger than the Ottoman Empire, for all the apparent strength of Oriental despotism. But his notion of rule was highly personalistic. Machiavelli concerned himself with the charismatic personalities of Romulus and Cesare Borgia rather than with law, bureaucracy, or centralization. Machiavelli advanced the notions of secularism and antiuniversalism that are attributes of the modern state, but that is perhaps all. In fact, his notion of the creative use of personal talent seems closer to the Florentine Renaissance than to the sobrieties of Hobbes or Hegel. A true statist like Hegel, for example, argues that an adequate ruler need not have extraordinary personal qualities at all because a rational state governed by law and bureaucracy is self-sufficient.

The first generally recognized theorist of state sovereignty was the French writer Jean BODIN. Bodin defined the state as an authoritative power that can "give laws unto all and every one of its subjects and receive none from them": the state is supreme, not merely one among other lawgiving public authorities. Although Bodin's sovereign was to be above the positive or civil law because he was the law's creator, he was still subject to divine and natural law; the sovereign was also to respect the fundamental constitutional laws of his realm, as well as his subjects' property rights. In short he was—although the highest and the final authority—a lawgiving authority, not an arbitrary or capricious one; the distinction between absolutism and arbitrariness was essential to Bodin, and he would never have countenanced Louis XIV's personalistic "L'état c'est moi" ("The state, it is I"). Bodin was the first to conceive an absolute political power in this sense; although he allowed medieval corporate bodies to remain in his theory of the state, he reduced them to dependence on the sovereign will, thus ensuring that private prerogative would no longer pass for public law.

Bodin not only developed the concept of internal sovereignty; he also denied the existence of a *Respublica Christiana*, declaring that "since the Roman Emperors were never lords of as much as a thirtieth part of the world, and since the Holy Roman Empire does not form a tenth part of the territories of . . . Rome," there was no universal political authority. States, for Bodin, are as independent externally as they are supreme internally. He further rejected the notion that the inherited Roman *ius gentium* could be the basis of international relations, and he went on to formulate a theory of international dealings by treaties between sovereign states.

Thomas Hobbes, after experiencing the ruinous English Civ-

il War (1642–48), took the doctrines of internal and external state sovereignty to their limits. The Hobbesian sovereign (what he called the "Leviathan"), who absorbed by virtue of the SOCIAL CONTRACT all the natural rights of his subjects save self-defense, was an absolute lawgiver in the strictest sense. For Hobbes neither morality nor any kind of law exists before it is willed by a sovereign to whom subjects are obligated by a contract of obedience. The Hobbesian sovereign, then, is the creator not only of positive law but of standards of right and wrong, of a civil religious doctrine, and even in part of public opinion. Moreover, if, as Hobbes asserted, the state creates morality and law and humans must submit to it for their self-preservation, then all justice will exist only within closed single-state systems, and the relations between those states, existing in a moral and legal void, will be like the relations between humans before the social contract. The very creation of a supreme state, then, implies the possibility of its hostility to other similar states if medieval natural law and the Roman *ius gentium* are discarded. For Hobbesians, the doctrine of internal sovereignty, which places states in a "state of nature" while it puts humans under true (positive) law, gives rise by logical necessity to external sovereignty. States, then, being perfectly independent, can be bound only through their own wills, that is, in the same way that individuals are bound to a particular state, through contract or treaty. At this point modern ideas of international relations—inconceivable within a *Pax Romana* ("Roman Peace," 31 BC–AD c.80) or a *Respublica Christiana*—begin. Henceforth the recognized, political unit is the state, and relations between these states take the form of treaty relations.

The rise of state sovereignty had permanent effects on European political thought. It slowly drove out ecclesiastical and private law and prerogative. This gave rise to a progressively more vehement antimedievalism culminating in the French Revolution, at which time most of the corporate bodies intervening between the individual and the state were either abolished or made subject to positive law. This process was reflected in Kant's declaration (1797) that the only natural political relation was that between single individuals and states. By this time the medieval notion of a society made up of smaller societies had been generally discredited.

The greatest "statist" after Hobbes was G. W. F. Hegel. For Hegel the modern state was "mind on earth," the "great hieroglyph of reason," the concrete realization of rational freedom. The Hegelian state is not a mere monolith: the Hegelian state is a monarchy moderated by the law-drafting functions

The title page from Thomas Hobbes's Leviathan (1651) portrays the sovereign as the absolute ruler of his subjects. In this famous work Hobbes showed how the political power of the state could be rationalized, and defended the existence of an absolute government that protects its individual subjects, who are obligated to their sovereign by a contract of obedience. Hobbes's concepts of internal and external sovereignty led to the development of new theories in international relations.

Georg Wilhelm Friedrich Hegel, one of the primary figures of modern philosophical thought, was a major theorist of the modern state. Hegel conceived of the state as the culmination of rational consciousness, a system marked by the progressive development of the individual who sublimates subjective interests to the objective interests and unity of the state.

of disinterested civil servants and moderated above all by the Hegelian notion that individuals must be able to find subjective satisfaction in their being willing members of a rational, free institution that secures the pursuit of absolute values inherent in philosophy, art, and religion. Even in Hegel—usually seen as the theorist of the modern state par excellence—sovereignty and concentrated power is not all that matters; the state must be instrumental in the pursuit of philosophy, art, and religion.

The Limited State.

A formidable concentration of sovereign power was never, in fact, the sole (although it remained the primary) attribute of statehood. If even statists could imagine limiting the state—Bodin through natural law, Hobbes through natural rights, Hegel through subjective satisfaction—others were able and willing to conceive much stronger limitations. Hobbes's greatest immediate English successor, John LOCKE, carefully refrained from using the terms *state* and *sovereignty* at all. Because he saw government as the rule of an impartial judge, set up by voluntary agreement, who simply enforces God-given natural law and defends natural property rights earned by mixing one's labor with the world, Locke's idea of the state was extremely limited. The already slender Lockean state is further limited by the fact that the legislative branch is representative—and hence amenable to popular control (see REPRESENTATION)—and by the Lockean right of revolution, which can be used by the people to bring down a government that fails to preserve natural law and rights. In Locke, then, there is a balance between the state and what can be comprehensively called society; this balance is usually styled the liberal notion of the state.

The most celebrated advocate of a state-society balance is Baron Charles de MONTESQUIEU. Montesquieu argued that if states are to be moderate and avoid Oriental despotism, central power must flow through, and sometimes be checked by, such intermediate bodies as parliaments, the regional nobility, and the church. Where the executive, legislative, and judicial powers are separately constituted and substantially independent, according to Montesquieu, power can be a check to power, and checks and balances can take the place of a civic virtue that largely vanished with the republics of ancient times.

If Locke wished to limit the state in order to protect natural law and rights, and Montesquieu to preserve moderation and liberty, a utilitarian like Jeremy BENTHAM had different reasons for limiting the scope of state power. According to Bentham, the operation of the state must be at least somewhat painful, because the state's general measures do not and cannot maximize the particular pleasure (utility) of each actual individual. This was sufficient reason for Bentham to limit the state, which he thought should confine itself principally to controlling those pains which are more hurtful—murder and robbery, for example—than the activity of the state itself. Some

of Bentham's contemporaries limited the state still further, on very different grounds. They believed that the operation of economic laws, such as supply and demand, could govern society semiautomatically as if by an invisible hand. Adam SMITH and some of the French PHYSIOCRATS were not far from such a view, in which the state nearly evaporates.

Still different reasons for state limitation were adduced by 19th-century liberals such as Alexis de TOQUEVILLE and John Stuart MILL, who agreed that the democratization of politics and the state following the French Revolution and the Industrial Revolution, coupled with the new influence of public opinion, could lead to a possible "tyranny of the majority." This tyranny would be worse than earlier tyrannies, because (in Mill's words) there are "fewer means of escape" where "society is itself the tyrant." Both de Tocqueville and Mill were led to advocate a new kind of aristocracy—not feudal aristocracy, but the leadership of those who, according to Mill, "stand on the higher eminences of thought." According to this view, public power had to be limited because the new democratic public had become potentially dangerous.

The State Eliminated: Marxism, Pluralism, Political Science.

For the much more radical 19th-century theorists the notion of limiting the state was only self-deception: what the state needed, they felt, was not limitation but elimination. Karl MARX, for example, believed that the state was no more than a holding company for the bourgeoisie. The mechanism of the state, according to Marx, arose not to realize freedom or to protect natural law and rights but to facilitate the destruction of the old, feudal modes of production and so hasten the advent of a new, urbanized proletariat that could, by being forced to live on subsistence wages, create profits for the capitalists. Marx viewed the state as an "epiphenomenon," or "reflection," of a given all-important economic substructure of society. For Marx, then, the state should and will "wither away"—not merely be limited or reformed.

One need not, of course, be a Marxist to be hostile to the idea of the state. For Ernst CASSIRER, a Kantian liberal, the "myth" of the state had led to the worship of concentrated power, culminating in FASCISM; without holding Machiavelli, Hobbes, and Hegel strictly accountable for this, Cassirer suggested that state-sovereignty doctrines are fatally easy to pervert. A modern pluralist such as John N. Figgis (1866–1919) insists that the notion of state sovereignty is no more than a venerable superstition, a vestigial relic of Tudor pretensions, and that social life is a "series of groups," all of which have some life of their own not merely granted by the state. Arthur Bentley (1870–1957), an immensely influential modern political scientist, argued that whereas the idea of the state has

Adolf Hitler addresses members of the National Socialist party at a rally in Nuremberg, Germany. National Socialism, or nazism, a fascist ideology that dominated German politics and society from 1933 to 1945, made Germany an example of the extreme totalitarian state.

been "very prominent . . . among the intellectual amusements of the past," it is not really true that the state is a kind of "crystalization" of authoritative power; politics for Bentley is a matter of self-interested groups attempting to determine the behavior of other people and other groups. Even if a group seizes the governing apparatus, what still matters is the group and its interests. For H. L. A. Hart (1907–), perhaps the most eminent post–World War II legal theorist, it is unreasonable to begin political thinking with the state: it is at least as valid to start with voluntary associations or with the international community and then to ask what is left for the state.

Much of recent political science, concerned with groups, interests, and processes, has tended to further erode the importance of the concepts of state and sovereignty. In systems theory, for instance, what matters is the whole interactive political system: its "inputs," its "outputs," and its "transactions." The state, then, is today no longer the central concern of political study. Even when dealing with a modern social scientist who is largely sympathetic to the state—for example, Max WEBER—one still finds a tendency to reduce the state to rational bureaucracy alone. Moreover, for Weber in particular, the concept of the state is an ideal construct that political reality only distantly approximates; statehood, in this formulation, loses much of its concreteness.

The great age of confident, bold state theories, therefore—unclouded by the reservations of pluralists, group theorists, systems analysts, Marxians, anarchists, and liberals—was the period stretching from Hobbes to Hegel. Today it is a great deal less clear than in Hobbes's or Hegel's day whether people should agree with the once-eminent legal theorist Johann K. Bluntschli (1808–81) that political inquiry is "the science that is concerned with the state," or whether they should side with Bertrand de Jouvenel (1903–) in his assertion that it is quite wrong to reduce politics to dangerous "absolute, infinite, perpetual" state power. The main support of modern states lies in the indubitable fact that most modern humans share a view of the state's necessity that roughly approximates Frederick Watkins's (1910–72) elegant formulation that the "whole structure of modern civilization would inevitably collapse in the absence of those conditions of ordered peace that have been ensured through the integrating activities of the sovereign state."

This does not, however, settle what modern civilization and the sovereign state are worth—whether they have a value equal to the cost (in every sense) of realizing them. This uncertainty reinforces, therefore, the idea that states—especially with respect to their purpose—are in part only artifacts of political visions.   PATRICK RILEY

Bibliography: Avineri, Shlomo, *Hegel's Theory of the Modern State* (1972); Bluntschli, Johann Kaspar, *The Theory of the State*, 2d ed. (1971); Cassirer, Ernst, *The Myth of the State* (1946); d'Entrèves, A. P., *The Notion of the State: An Introduction to Political Theory* (1967); Fleisher, Martin, ed., *Machiavelli and the Nature of Political Thought* (1972); Harmon, Mont J., *Political Thought: From Plato to the Present* (1964); Hinsley, F. H., *Power and the Pursuit of Peace* (1964); Jouvenel, Bertrand de, *Sovereignty* (1957); Kelly, George Armstrong, *Hegel's Retreat from Eleusis* (1978); Lindsay, A. D., *The Modern Democratic State* (1947); Meinecke, Friedrich, *Cosmopolitanism and the National State* (1970); Nisbet, Robert, *The Twilight of Authority* (1975); Pitkin, Hanna F., *The Concept of Representation* (1967); Poggi, Gianfranco, *The Development of the Modern State* (1978); Rowe, Constance, *Voltaire and the State* (1968); Sabine, G. H., *A History of Political Theory*, 4th ed. (1973); Service, Elman R., *Origins of the State and Civilization* (1975); Skinner, Quentin, *The Foundations of Modern Political Thought* (1978); Spencer, Herbert, *The Man versus the State*, ed. by Donald MacRae (1969).

State, County, and Municipal Employees:

see AMERICAN FEDERATION OF STATE, COUNTY, AND MUNICIPAL EMPLOYEES.

State, U.S. Department of

The oldest federal department in the United States, the Department of State is responsible under the president's direc-
tion for the conduct of FOREIGN POLICY. The secretary of state is the senior cabinet official. The department negotiates treaties, represents the United States in foreign countries and in international organizations, and recommends and implements policy.

Created by Congress as the Department of Foreign Affairs on July 27, 1789, and given its present name on Sept. 15, 1789, the department, under its first head, Thomas Jefferson, was given various domestic responsibilities in addition to the conduct of foreign policy. The domestic tasks were eventually shifted to other departments. Numerous reforms and reorganizations were made throughout the 19th and early 20th centuries.

During and after World War II both the department's domestic and foreign staffs were greatly increased, and the department was given new functions fitting the U.S. position of world leadership. From 1945 to 1950 the continually expanding department added the Policy Planning Staff, the Bureau of International Organization Affairs, and the Bureau of Economic Affairs. By 1980 the department had 281 embassies and consulates abroad, a staff of 16,300, and a budget of $709 million.

From the inception of the Department of State, outstanding men have served as secretary of state, including John Marshall, James Monroe, John Quincy Adams, Henry Clay, Daniel Webster, William Jennings Bryan, Charles Evans Hughes, Cordell Hull, George Marshall, Dean Acheson, John Foster Dulles, and Henry Kissinger. Cyrus R. Vance has held the office since 1977.

Bibliography: Chittick, William O., *State Department, Press, and Pressure Groups: A Role Analysis* (1970); Esterline, John H., *Inside Foreign Policy* (1975); Estes, Thomas S., and Lightner, E. Allen, *The Department of State* (1976); Simpson, Smith, *Anatomy of the State Department* (1967).

See also: FOREIGN SERVICE; NATIONAL SECURITY COUNCIL.

state attorney: see PROSECUTING ATTORNEY.

state rights

The term *state rights,* or *states rights,* is used to describe the actual or assumed privileges granted to individual states under the U.S. Constitution. The 10TH AMENDMENT (part of the Bill of Rights), ratified in response to protests that the main body of the Constitution did not adequately protect the rights of the states, reflected both the traditions of colonial self-rule and the experiences of the American Revolution, which bred distrust of a centralized authority unfamiliar with local needs and problems. The amendment specifies that those "powers not delegated to the United States by the Constitution, nor prohibited by it to the States, are reserved to the States respectively, or to the people." Even with the addition of the amendment, however, the Constitution defines the boundary between federal power and state rights only in very broad, general terms. A more precise definition has thus been a perennial constitutional issue. Advocates of state rights have traditionally advocated Thomas Jefferson's strict constructionist interpretation, which allows the federal government only those powers explicitly enumerated in the Constitution. Proponents of a more active and centralized federal government have followed Alexander Hamilton's loose constructionist interpretation of the Constitution, which grants to the central government broader implied powers.

Prior to the Civil War the Democratic-Republican party and the Jacksonian Democrats generally called for strict respect of state rights, and the Federalist, National Republican, and Whig parties advocated a more active role for the federal government. The southern states, fearful of federal interference with slavery, were the most dogmatic in their use of state rights doctrine. In the late 19th century, however, the state rights precept was embraced by business interests as a means of resisting federal regulation, and liberal political movements abandoned strict constructionism in favor of government intervention to protect farmers, laborers, and minority groups. The state rights doctrine was also invoked in the 1950s and '60s by opponents of federal civil rights legislation.

ALFRED A. CAVE

Bibliography: Mason, A. T., *The States Rights Debate*, 2d ed. (1972); Murphy, William, *The Triumph of Nationalism* (1968); Owsley, F. L., *State Rights in the Confederacy* (1925; repr. 1961); Warren, Charles, *The Supreme Court and Sovereign States* (1924; repr. 1972).

See also: KENTUCKY AND VIRGINIA RESOLUTIONS; NULLIFICATION.

Staten Island   [sta'-ten]

Staten Island, coextensive with Richmond Borough and Richmond County, is a part of New York City. About 23 km (14 mi) long and 11 km (7 mi) wide, it has an area of 150 km² (58 mi²). The population is 337,000 (1979 est.). Located in New York Bay, 8 km (5 mi) south of Manhattan, Staten Island is linked to Manhattan by ferry, with Brooklyn by the VERRA-ZANO-NARROWS BRIDGE, and with New Jersey by three bridges. The highest point is Todt Hill (125 m/409 ft). Manufacturing, shipbuilding, petroleum refining, and metalworking make the island an important industrial center. Richmond town, a 17th-19th-century village, has been re-created there. Algonquin Indians lived on Staten Island when the Dutch arrived in 1661. It was incorporated into New York City in 1898.

States-General

The States-General, or Estates-General, was a national elective assembly representing the social "estates," or orders, in France and the Netherlands from the 14th to the 18th century. In France the first estate was the clergy; the second estate, the nobility; and the third estate, the middle-class commoners. The French assembly, commonly called the Estates-General, met occasionally between 1302 and 1789 whenever the monarchy needed a broad base of support to overcome fiscal or political crises, but it never advanced from advisory status to control royal taxes or policy on a regular basis. Famous meetings included sessions (1355-57) that briefly controlled France's government after the English victory at Poitiers; the Estates of 1484 after the tyrannical Louis XI's death; several gatherings between 1560 and 1593 during the Wars of Religion; and the assembly of 1614, which disbanded in 1615 amid quarrels between the commoners and the first two estates. It was not summoned thereafter until the FRENCH REVOLUTION, when the financially bankrupt LOUIS XVI called an assembly in 1789; its third-estate delegates forced the alteration of traditional voting by order to "vote by head," thereby transforming that last French Estates-General into a modern, democratic legislature.

The States-General of the Netherlands met regularly after 1464 to approve the taxation and foreign policies of the ruling Burgundian and Spanish dynasties. The revolt of the northern Netherlands made the States-General the Dutch Republic's governing body from 1579 to 1795, while it disappeared from the southern Spanish Netherlands (modern Belgium). The term survives today as the name for the modern Dutch bicameral legislature.

A. LLOYD MOOTE

Bibliography: Major, J. R., *Representative Institutions in Renaissance France, 1422-1559* (1960); Myers, A. R., *Parliaments and Estates in Europe to 1789* (1975).

static

Static is the collective term applied to the various forms of audible interference that are commonly superimposed over the communications heard through telephone and radio receivers. The sounds range from random crackling and popping to hissing, rushing, and humming.

Static may be caused by both natural and technological processes, and its sound often provides helpful clues as to its origin. Lightning produces the most noticeable and dramatic form of static. A nearby electrical storm can block the reception of an AM radio receiver with a series of loud crackles, pops, and crashes. Distant electrical storms and the natural discharges of static electricity in the atmosphere produce a variety of background noises and rushing sounds that some-

times resemble the sound of the surf at a beach. Electromagnetic signals emitted by the Sun can also produce static disturbances in a receiver.

Static from nonnatural sources is generally a by-product of an electrical spark. A sparking contact produces a wide range of electromagnetic frequencies that are heard on AM receivers as popping or crackling sounds. Defective light switches and thermostats are common sources of such static. Certain kinds of direct-current electrical motors produce static with a whirring or whining sound. The static is caused by the spark discharge between the motor's brushes and commutator and can be transmitted to a radio or television through the air or over power lines. The high-voltage discharge at the spark plugs of an internal combustion engine of an automobile or other vehicle is another cause of static.   FORREST T. M. MIMS III

Bibliography: Amos, S. W., ed., *Radio, TV and Audio Technical Reference Book* (1977).

See also: NOISE.

static electricity

Static electricity is electricity at rest—an accumulation of electric CHARGE, as contrasted to the movement of electric charge known as an electric current. The oldest known form of electricity clearly identifiable as such, static electricity is most simply generated by rubbing together certain dissimilar materials such as ebonite and animal fur, or amber and silk. The latter two materials were used by the Greek Thales of Miletus in 600 BC, and the word *electricity* is derived from the Greek word *elektron*, meaning "amber." Most static electricity is generated unintentionally and is considered a nuisance. A familiar example is the buildup of charge on fabrics on a clear, dry day. Vehicles carrying inflammable materials have to provide for the safe discharge of static electricity, and buildings must be protected against the violent discharge of static electricity known as lightning.

Static electricity may be produced purposely by devices ranging from the simple LEYDEN JAR to the powerful VAN DE GRAAFF GENERATOR. The study of static electricity is part of the field of physics called ELECTROSTATICS.

Bibliography: Cheston, Warren B., *Elementary Theory of Electric and Magnetic Fields* (1964); Loeb, Leonard B., *Static Electrification* (1958); Scott, W. T., *The Physics of Electricity and Magnetism*, 2d ed. (1966); Smythe, William R., *Static and Dynamic Electricity*, 3d ed. (1968).

statics

Statics is the study of the interactions of force and matter under equilibrium conditions, for which no acceleration occurs. Statics and dynamics (the study of force, mass, and motion) combine to form the field of mechanics, which is the oldest branch of physical science. The principles of statics apply to all matter, whether it be solid, liquid, or gaseous.

Statics presupposes the condition of equilibrium, which means that all forces and torques on a body are balanced by equal and opposite forces and torques. Under such conditions, accelerations—both linear and rotary—are impossible according to Newton's LAWS OF MOTION. The establishment of equilibrium therefore requires that the object under study be either at rest or in a state of uniform linear motion.

Various stability criteria may be applied to the equilibrium condition. For example, a ball resting inside a round bowl is in stable equilibrium, for it returns to its original position when displaced. If the bowl is inverted, however, and the ball placed on top, it is now in unstable equilibrium, because the slightest disturbance will cause it to roll away. Intermediate to these two criteria is neutral equilibrium, represented by a ball resting on a flat surface.

The same approach is used to solve all problems in statics; all of the forces and torques acting on a system are summed, and the total must equal zero. An unknown quantity may be calculated if the values of the other quantities are known. A simple case is that of an object hanging on a rope. The only forces involved are F, the downward pull of the Earth, equal to the object's weight, and $-F$, the upward pull of the rope.

F and $-F$ are equal in magnitude and opposite in direction; their sum is zero.

If an object is supported by two ropes attached to different supports (as, for example, a hammock), the problem is more complex because the forces do not act in a line. Each rope pulls at an angle. To find the tension in each rope, the force must be treated as a vector quantity and divided by the rules of VECTOR ANALYSIS into horizontal and vertical components. The sum of the horizontal components (one to the left and one to the right) is zero, and the sum of the ropes' vertical components (upward) plus the weight (downward) is zero. From these data can be found all the forces that act on the system.

The same method is used to solve problems of navigation involving the effects of wind and current on the paths of airplanes and ships.

Forces may generate a torque, or turning movement. In many situations, counteracting a torque is desired to prevent twisting, and this process can be done only with another equal and opposite torque. A torque is also called a moment of force and is defined as the product of the force times the perpendicular distance to the axis of rotation. A positive sign is customarily assigned to torques acting to cause counterclockwise rotation, and a negative sign to clockwise torques. A torque may be increased either by applying more force or by lengthening the distance between the axis and point of application.

A typical statics problem might be the determination of the forces in the beams constituting a bridge structure. Because the bridge is motionless, these forces are necessarily in equilibrium. The force vectors are resolved into their rectangular components, which are then summed in each of the three Cartesian coordinate directions and set equal to zero. Moments of force are also summed in a similar fashion. If the weight of the structure is known, the resulting set of algebraic equations can be solved to give the force in each beam. This application of the principles of statics is important in the design and analysis of all structures. Statics will not, however, tell the designer how much a beam will deflect under load or whether or not it will fail. Such considerations are taken up in the related field of materials.

The statics of fluids employs the same mathematical and physical principles as does solid statics. Typical problems in fluid statics include the determination of pressures, atmospheric forces, and forces on lighter-than-air craft.

GARY S. SETTLES

Bibliography: Ginsberg, Jerry H., and Genin, Joseph, *Statics* (1977); Stevens, Karl K., *Statics and Strength of Materials* (1979); White, Harvey E., *Modern College Physics* (1972).

stations of the cross

The stations of the cross are a series of 14 representations that depict the events surrounding Christ's crucifixion. Used primarily by Roman Catholics as visual aids for meditating on the passion, they are mounted at intervals on church walls or placed in outdoor shrines. The idea of the stations emerged during the Middle Ages, when they developed as a devotional substitute for actually following the Via Dolorosa, the route in Jerusalem that Christ followed to Calvary. The events depicted are: (1) the condemnation of Jesus by Pilate; (2) Jesus' acceptance of the cross; (3) his first fall; (4) the encounter with his mother; (5) Simon of Cyrene helping Jesus; (6) Veronica wiping Jesus' face; (7) his second fall; (8) the encounter with the women of Jerusalem; (9) his third fall; (10) Jesus being stripped of his garments; (11) the crucifixion; (12) Jesus' death; (13) Jesus' removal from the cross; and (14) the burial of Jesus.

statistical thermodynamics

Statistical thermodynamics is a subfield of statistical mechanics, a branch of physics that connects the atomic nature of matter on a microscopic level with the observed behavior of materials on the macroscopic level. Statistical thermodynamics is concerned with those macroscopic processes which are independent of time. Time-dependent processes in statistical mechanics are treated in the field of kinetic theory.

On a *macroscopic* level, the "state" of a material is determined by certain thermodynamic variables (see THERMODYNAMICS). As a simple example, consider a glass of water. By definition, two glasses of water in the same thermodynamic state have the same temperature and pressure and share the same physical properties. They must, for example, have the same energy per unit volume. A number of thermodynamic variables can be found for a given physical system, but only a few are independent. In the example above only two of the variables (say pressure and temperature) are independent. All other variables, such as energy, can be expressed in terms of the selected independent variables. There is, therefore, a definite relationship between the energy (the dependent thermodynamic variable) and the pressure and temperature. The equation relating these state variables is called an equation of state. In classical thermodynamics these equations of state are determined experimentally by fixing two state variables and then measuring the value of the other variables. This equation of state yields a great deal of useful information about a system: for example, the most efficient methods for heat transfer in a fluid can be determined.

Statistical thermodynamics goes beyond classical thermodynamics by determining the equation of state of a system from the underlying microscopic properties of the system. Thus, the intent is to compute the equation of state for a macroscopic material in terms of the properties of the atoms and molecules from which the material is constructed.

The microscopic state of a fluid is specified by giving the location and velocities of each particle. Because there are on the order of 10^{23} atoms constituting a macroscopic system, it is hopeless to try to keep track of the positions and velocities of all the particles. Instead, the average or statistical properties of the system are considered. Therefore the probability that a system will be in a particular microscopic state must be determined. The average of some quantity such as the total energy of the system can be computed by multiplying the energy of a particular microscopic state by the probability that the system is in that state. The sum of all possible microscopic states is the average total energy.

Statistical thermodynamics is interested in systems in thermal equilibrium. Systems in thermal equilibrium are characterized by probability distributions for microscopic states that are time-independent and proportional to $exp - (E/k_B T)$, where E is the energy of a particular microscopic arrangement of atoms, k_B is Boltzmann's constant, and T is the temperature measured on the absolute, or Kelvin, scale. This equilibrium distribution is known as the Boltzmann distribution and plays a central role in all statistical thermodynamic calculations.

GENE F. MAZENKO

Bibliography: Fermi, Enrico, *Notes on Thermodynamics and Statistics* (1966); Hayman, H. G., *Statistical Thermodynamics* (1967); Lee, John F., et al., *Statistical Thermodynamics* (1974).

statistics

Statistics is the science of collecting and analyzing data. It is being used more and more in various applications. In government many people are involved in collecting data from censuses and surveys and monitoring trends in economic and financial indices. Such data are often referred to as "official statistics." They are used to evaluate and improve current policies. On a smaller scale, statistics is used in medicine, for example, to assess which of two treatments is better or to aid in the diagnosis of a patient. By comparing data taken from a patient with data from people known to be suffering from two different diseases, the satistician can make some judgment as to which disease is afflicting the patient.

There are many other examples. Statisticians are involved in agriculture, with the comparison of different fertilizers; in geology, with the estimation of oil resources; in the analysis of psychological experiments; in the actuarial profession, with the establishment of suitable premiums; in market research, to discover and interpret trends and frequencies; and in industry, in the optimization of production and the formulation of advertising policies.

Although the science of statistics as a branch of applied mathematics has been developing since the beginning of the 20th century, its major impact has come in the past 3 decades, largely as a result of the revolutionary impact of electronic COMPUTERS, which make it possible to deal with large amounts of data rapidly and efficiently.

Chance and Probability. Statistical procedures can vary from the drawing and assessment of a few simple GRAPHS to carrying out very complex mathematical analysis with the use of powerful computers; in any application, however, there is the essential underlying influence of "chance." Whether some natural phenomenon is being observed or a scientific experiment is being carried out, the analysis will be statistical if it is impossible to predict the data exactly with certainty. On a trivial level, consider the tossing of a coin. If it is double-headed, then the experiment is deterministic, or nonrandom, because it can be predicted confidently that the coin will land "heads" up. If it is a regular coin, however, the experiment is a random, or chance-influenced, phenomenon; the coin may land "heads" or "tails." Statistics can be more precisely defined as the collection and analysis of data from random experiments or phenomena (see RANDOM VARIABLE).

There is clearly an inevitable link between statistics and PROBABILITY, which provides the mathematical basis for setting up models to describe random phenomena. Many statistical techniques, particularly in the field of INFERENCE, are designed to use data to identify or assess the underlying probability model. The influence of probability is strong in physics and chemistry, where the term *statistics* is used in a slightly different sense. Statistical mechanics arose out of the kinetic theory of gases, in which the large-scale (macroscopic) properties of a gas are considered as the "averages" of the phenomena of microscopic collisions of many gas molecules moving in different directions and speeds. In genetics, Mendel's laws of heredity require for their statement the use of probability theory. Although probability was developed in the 17th century in the context of games of chance, the science of statistics is much more recent.

Statistical Procedures. Ideally, the statistician should be involved in any project from the start. First, the underlying population being investigated must be described, as implied in "the incomes of U.S. residents" or "all people suffering from hypertension." The statistician must make sure that the data are collected in a manner that allows them to answer the exact question posed. Sometimes it is not possible to sample this target population. Then the question must be changed slightly. It may involve setting up a SAMPLING procedure to select a small number of individuals from the population, as in opinion polls; or it may involve the allocation of different treatments to different patients. In the latter case, it is important that neither the patients nor the doctors know what the allocation is. Otherwise, their behavior or treatment might be systematically influenced. Usually the allocation will be achieved by a randomization procedure.

Once the data have been obtained, they must be examined, collated, and analyzed. In some cases, all that is needed is the display or publication of the numbers, as in the census results. Even here, however, considerable skill is required to draw up tables, to judge the correct level of detail to report so that a full but comprehensible picture is provided, and to develop and use effective graphical displays.

Before a specific analysis is made, important preliminary procedures such as tabulation, checking, summarization, and plotting of the data are needed. As an example, consider a study of the height of U.S. residents, using a representative sample of 2,000 heights as the data. One possibility is to write down all 2,000 observations; a more sensible approach, however, would be to count the data in various height groups and display the data as a HISTOGRAM. It should be possible to spot gross errors: observations of 51 cm (20 in) or 305 cm (120 in), for example, should be checked for correctness. There are various ways in which the data might be summarized. An idea of the "central value" for the distribution can be con-

veyed by using the average value of the observations, the middle one (with the data written in increasing order), or the value where the histogram is tallest. These values from the data represent, respectively, the MEAN, the MEDIAN, and the MODE of the distribution. Another important feature of the distribution of the data is the variability or spread. A commonly used measure of this for a population is the variance (see VARIANCE AND COVARIANCE), which is the average squared difference between the members of the population and the mean. From the data a sensible estimate of the variance can be computed. Its square root estimates the STANDARD DEVIATION, which is a useful measure of spread in the same units as the observations.

It is often useful to describe a probability distribution by a mathematical formula, which will contain a few unknown quantities called parameters; parametric statistical methods use the data to come to some judgment about these parameters. The commonest formula for data like height is that of the NORMAL DISTRIBUTION, which depends on two parameters, the mean (μ) and the variance (σ^2).

Hypothesis Testing and Estimation. For data from such a distribution, the statisical analysis concentrates on questions about the parameters. For example: (1) Is the mean height greater than 173 cm (68 in)? (2) Is the present variance in

$$\frac{1}{\sqrt{2\pi}\,\sigma} \exp -\frac{1}{2}\frac{(x-\mu)^2}{\sigma^2}$$

height greater than it was 50 years ago? (3) Is there a fairly reliable method of specifying an interval that contains the mean height? The first two questions involve the technique of hypothesis testing. The usual approach is first to set up a NULL HYPOTHESIS that the mean height is 173 cm (68 in) and then to assess the data on this basis. If the data suggest that the null hypothesis is implausible, then the hypothesis is rejected, and the answer to the question is taken as "yes." In the example, this would happen if the average height from the data is much greater than 173 cm (68 in). How much greater depends on the statistical SIGNIFICANCE that is required. This is the probability of wrongly rejecting the null hypothesis, and its value is not fixed, but may be chosen; often the value 0.05 or 0.01 is taken.

The other principal activity in inference is estimation. As has been suggested, the average of the datum values is a reasonable value of a point estimate of the mean in the population. It is therefore natural to construct interval estimates with this value as the center. One rationale is to have a method of constructing intervals that on average contain the true mean on a certain percentage of the occasions. These intervals are called confidence intervals, and the degree of confidence that is required will determine their width.

Procedures for hypothesis testing and estimation methods depend critically on the model. It is important to check the validity of the model, for example, the assumption that the height data satisfy a normal distribution. This can be done visually from the histogram, which gives an approximate picture of the distribution; or by using some other probability plot; or, more formally, by using a goodness-of-fit test (see STATISTICS, NONPARAMETRIC).

Sometimes the result of a statistical analysis has to be more definite, in the form of the selection of a policy—perhaps the choice of the best of several treatments for a disease. In such a case, the natural methodology to adopt is DECISION THEORY, in which the costs of wrong decisions are quantified and the effects of making different choices are compared.

Data Relationships. There are many other specific types of data, with related models, problems, and techniques of analysis. Data may be qualitative, for example, the colors red, yellow, or blue; discrete, for example, numbers of cars; or continuous, for example, ages. Each observation may consist of a single value, as in the example about height, or many values, if several tests are carried out on each individual (multivariate analysis). Important questions may arise if there are two such tests. Suppose age and blood pressure are measured on a sample of patients. It is of interest to determine whether older people tend to have higher blood pressure. In statistical terms, the question is whether or not there is a positive correlation (see CORRELATION AND REGRESSION) between age and blood pressure. (It should be emphasized that even if the answer, from a test of significance, turns out to be "yes," this does not prove any causal relationship between the two factors.) Some more specific relationship might be investigated, such as linear regression. This can be assessed graphically by plotting the points on a scatter diagram, a procedure that can be supported by calculations of the line of best fit, often by the LEAST-SQUARES METHOD. Examples of more complicated methods of analysis are time-series analysis—for example, the search for a trend, or regular fluctuation, in rainfall or economic indices—and FACTOR ANALYSIS—the search for a few common factors governing the variation among many other variables.

Data are often displayed in a 2×2 table. Consider an experiment on disease treatment in which some patients are treated and some are not. The numbers of patients having mild and severe attacks of the disease will be arranged as follows:

	Mild	Severe	Totals
Treated	a	b	$a + b$
Untreated	c	d	$c + d$
Totals	$a + c$	$b + d$	$n = a + b + c + d$

The obvious question is: Does the chance of a severe attack decrease when the patient is treated? One would be inclined to answer "yes," if $b/(a + b)$ is much smaller than $d/(c + d)$. However, two difficulties arise: (1) What is meant by "much smaller"? and (2) Could this difference be caused by the allocation of healthier patients to the group being treated?

The second question can be dealt with by allocating patients to the two groups in a completely random manner. There is then no possibility of overt or unconscious manipulation of the data. If some patients are in fact sicker than others, they will be allotted to the two groups, on the average, in proportion to the total number of patients in each group. Thus the same expected proportions of severe cases will occur in the two groups.

The treatment of 2×2 tables can be extended to contingency tables of r rows and c columns, where r and c are greater than 2. Such tables can be used to test whether several qualitative factors are associated; in the example above, the factors are the presence (or absence) of treatment and the severity of the disease.

There are many situations in which the measurements cannot be relied upon and yet the researcher does not wish to reduce the data down to contingency tables. For example, suppose that x and y are the examination scores of a student in chemistry and physics courses. One would expect them to be positively related. But one might not want to compute a correlation, because other teachers might grade the examinations differently. If, however, it were thought that different teachers would rank the students in the same order, a correlation of the ranks would be useful. Each individual would have a pair of ranks—his or her order in the group for chemistry and order in the group for physics. The rank correlation is frequently used in the social sciences.

The general idea of replacing observations by ranks leads to statistical methods that depend far less on assumptions, especially assumptions regarding the distribution of the data. This part of the subject is, therefore, called distribution-free or nonparametric statistics.   BERNARD SILVERMAN

Bibliography: Bickel, P. J., and Doksum, K. A., *Mathematical Statistics: Basic Ideas and Selected Topics* (1977); Book, Stephen A., *Statistics: Basic Techniques for Solving Applied Problems* (1977); Brunk, Hugh D., *Introduction to Mathematical Statistics*, 3d ed. (1975); Hodges, J. L., and Lehmann, E. L., *Basic Concepts of Probability and Statistics*, 2d ed. (1970); Hogg, Robert V., and Craig, Allen T., *Introduction to Mathe-matical Statistics*, 4th ed. (1978); Lindgren, Bernard, *Statistical Theory*, 3d ed. (1976); Mood, Alexander M., et al., *Introduction to the Theory of Statistics*, 3d ed. (1974); Mosteller, Frederick, et al., *Probability with Statistical Applications*, 2d ed. (1976); Wilks, Samuel S., *Mathematical Statistics*, 2d ed. (1962); Wolf, Frank L., *Elements of Probability and Statistics*, 2d ed. (1974).

statistics, nonparametric

In the science of statistics, populations or distributions are often assumed to be described by formulas containing parameters. For example, the NORMAL DISTRIBUTION with its two parameters, the mean and variance, is often used. A comparison of such populations is then a comparison of their parameters. One cannot always assume, however, a particular parametric formula for a distribution; in such cases, populations cannot be compared parametrically, and nonparametric methods must be used. Because such methods do not require knowledge of the distribution, they are also known as distribution-free methods. For example, the heights of school children of two countries might be compared by drawing the HISTOGRAMS of sample heights. The histograms are nonparametric estimators of the height distributions in the two countries.

Sometimes more than a visual comparison is wanted. A decision may be desired as to whether a new medical treatment is better than the old one, or whether variety A of corn produces more than variety B. In the latter case, an experiment could be laid out by dividing a field into blocks of land and each block into two plots. In each block, a plot is chosen randomly for variety A; in the other, variety B is planted. At the end of the season, all plots are harvested and the produce weighed. A nonparametric analysis of these data may be based on the observations that (1) if the varieties are of equal merit, the probability of A producing more than B in a block is equal to one-half, and (2) the results for blocks are independent. This will be so even if the fertility differs greatly from block to block. Hence, the fraction of blocks in which A outperforms B would vary in such experiments, like the proportion of heads in a set of tosses of a fair coin. By using the BINOMIAL DISTRIBUTION, a test of the statistical SIGNIFICANCE may be derived. This test (the sign test) does not assume that plot yields have any specific distribution. It is therefore a nonparametric, or distribution-free, test.

The ideas that led to the sign test above suggest many other procedures. Suppose that to compare two medical treatments, patients have been randomly allotted to treatments and a measurement made on each patient at the end of the trial. The mean $\bar{x}$ of the measurements from patients receiving treatment A could be compared with the mean of treatment-B patients. If the measurements are assumed to have a normal distribution, this leads to the T-TEST. Alternatively, it could be argued that, if the two treatments have the same effect, then the A and B labels on patients have simply been put there at random. A computer could be programmed to put these labels on the observations at random and then to calculate the difference between the two means. If this were done many times and the distribution of results tabulated, the actual observed difference could be appraised. If it were less than or greater than 95% of the computer-generated differences, then it can be said that treatment A is significantly different from treatment B, at the 5% level of significance. This kind of nonparametric test is often called a randomization test.

To avoid or reduce the computing, the same argument may be applied when the original observations are replaced by numbers that reflect their relative sizes. For example, if all the observations are arranged in increasing size and the largest ranked 1, the next largest ranked 2, and so forth, these ranks may be used in the above calculations instead of the original observations. Tests that use ranks clearly do not depend on specific assumptions concerning the distributions. Most nonparametric procedures are, in fact, rank tests.

In the last example above, it was suggested that a difference of arithmetic means be used as the indicator of treatment differences. Once the nonparametric route is taken, this is seen to be arbitrary, and many alternatives have been suggested. It would seem that these efforts to obtain robust procedures by assuming very little, replacing actual data by integers, and so forth, would lead to insensitive procedures. Rather surprisingly, if one proceeds cleverly, very little efficiency is lost.

Naturally, nonparametric procedures are used more frequently in fields where less is known about the mechanisms generating the observations—for example, in psychology. Even when theory suggests that a specific type of distribution applies, it is usually desirable to check the theory by testing that the data do indeed seem to come from such a distribution. Most simply, a histogram of the sample frequencies is compared to the theoretical curve by using the chi-square test (see CHI-SQUARE DISTRIBUTION). This test is extremely adaptable and handles most goodness-of-fit questions (how well the data fit the curve). Another method using goodness-of-fit tests was devised by Andrei N. Kolmogorov and Nikolai V. Smirnov.   GEOFFREY S. WATSON

Bibliography: Hollander, Myles, and Wolfe, Douglas, *Nonparametric Statistical Methods* (1973); Lehmann, E. L., *Nonparametrics: Statistical Methods Based on Ranks* (1975).

Statius   [stay'-shuhs]

The Roman poet Publius Papinius Statius, AD *c*.40–*c*.96, under the patronage of Emperor Domitian, wrote epics on the youth of Achilles (*The Achilleid*) and on the legendary war between the Theban brothers Eteocles and Polynices (*The Thebaid*). These epics and occasional verses, *Silvae* (Forests) were popular in his own day and medieval times.

Statler, Ellsworth Milton   [stat'-lur]

Ellsworth Milton Statler, b. Somerset County, Pa., Oct. 26, 1863, d. Apr. 16, 1928, founded the chain of U.S. luxury hotels that bears his name. Statler's restaurant in Buffalo, N.Y. (1896), and a hotel that he built and operated there at the Pan-American Exposition of 1901 were his first enterprises. At the peak of his career he owned and operated hotels in Boston, Cleveland, Detroit, New York City, and St. Louis, in addition to the Buffalo facility. He was a prominent member of hotel trade groups. In 1954, Conrad Hilton bought the Statler chain of hotels.

Bibliography: Jarman, Rufus, *A Bed for the Night: The Story of the Wheeling Bellboy, E. M. Statler, and His Remarkable Hotels* (1952); Miller, Floyd, *Statler, America's Extraordinary Hotelman* (1968).

stator

A stator is the stationary member of an electric MOTOR, GENERATOR, or alternator (an alternating-current, or AC, generator) in or about which a ROTOR revolves. In alternators and in AC motors without a commutator, the stator includes the main-current-carrying conductors and is a stationary ARMATURE.

The power source (for a motor) or load (for a generator or alternator) is connected to the terminal leads, which are the ends of the stator windings. A stator is usually constructed of a laminated soft-iron ring having wire coils wound into slots around the ring. In an alternator the revolving magnetic field surrounding the rotor cuts through the stator windings and induces a voltage in them.   DONALD L. ANGLIN

Statue of Liberty

The Statue of Liberty, 46 m (150.9 ft) high, was originally called *Liberty Enlightening the World*; it was conceived as a gift from the French to the American people to honor the 1876 centennial celebration. The exterior copper shell, in the form of a classical, draped female figure carrying a torch aloft, was designed (1870–75) by the French sculptor Frédéric Auguste BARTHOLDI; the wrought-iron pylon inside was the work of Gustave EIFFEL, designer of the Eiffel Tower in Paris; and the stone-and-concrete pedestal was planned by the American architect Richard Morris HUNT. The statue was completed in Paris in 1884 and unveiled in New York Harbor on Oct. 26, 1886, in the presence of the sculptor. The funds for the statue

The Statue of Liberty, a massive sculpture weighing 205 metric tons, is located in New York Harbor a short distance southwest of Manhattan. A gift from the citizens of France, the statue was dedicated in 1886 and established as a national monument in 1924.

were donated by the French people and those for the base were raised in the United States. The Statue of Liberty is probably the best-known symbolic image of America.
          MARIAN BURLEIGH-MOTLEY

Bibliography: Handlin, Oscar, *Statue of Liberty* (1971); Pauli, Hertha, and Ashton, E. B., *I Lift My Lamp* (1948; repr. 1969); Trachtenberg, Marvin, *The Statue of Liberty* (1976).

status

Status refers to a person's position within an institutional or organizational framework. Thus, being middle class is a general status position within the system of social stratification. Status is the positional element in a structure or organization; role refers to the behavior associated with status. Both status and role can be reduced to the characterizations and behavioral expectations that constitute the foundation of all social life. Sociologist Talcott Parsons, for example, made what he called the "status role bundle" his basic analytical unit.

The most pointed and significant applications of status have been in the analysis of stratification, or systems of inequality. The distinctions developed by the German sociologist Max Weber have been particularly influential. Weber made "status group" and "status situation" central categories in his political sociology. Whereas "class," following Karl Marx, refers to those aspects of life's chances determined by economic situation (skills, wealth, knowledge, and so on), Weber's "status situation" means "every typical component of the life fate of men that is determined by a specific, positive or negative, social estimation of *honor*." Status situations may or may not be related closely to class; status groups may include the propertied and unpropertied, the moderately well-off as well as the rich. Nevertheless, status groups tend toward exclusiveness through such mechanisms as preferred or enforced intragroup marriage and special systems of education. In Weber's scheme, castes and ethnic groups are major types of status groups.

The concept of status group (or "social class," a virtual synonym) has been of great importance for sociological studies of communities. Early studies, such as those of W. Lloyd Warner and Paul S. Lunt, regarded the status systems of the American community as fundamental aspects of their structure. Warner suggested the model of a community as a kind of layer cake of status groups (or social classes), based on his study of Newburyport, Mass.; a whole generation of community sociologists employed his model.

Status systems are typically loaded with rituals and ceremonies designed to reinforce and maintain the systems, and even have been defined in terms of such stereotyped expectations and behavior. Thus, although an employer may use the first name of his employees in an easy pseudofamiliarity, he expects to be addressed as "mister." Status conflicts, which include such phenomena as religious and interethnic struggles, tend to be intense because recognition of the superiority of a group's way of life—or even the group's survival—is often at stake.

Status systems are almost inconceivable without status symbols. Status symbols represent the group, in the sense of condensing the meanings central to the life of the group. Thus the six-inch-long fingernails of the classical Chinese mandarin symbolized his independence from any need to perform manual labor. Possession of virtually any kind of material object may become a symbol of one's status, a phenomenon systematically analyzed by Thorstein VEBLEN in the early 1900s; Veblen coined the terms *conspicuous waste* and *conspicuous consumption.*

The seeming universality of status systems in all societies, families, complex organizations, peer work groups, children's play groups, athletic teams, and so on has sometimes been used to suggest and defend the inevitability of inequality. Critics of such claims, however, point out that they cannot be demonstrated scientifically.   DAVID WESTBY

Bibliography: Parsons, Talcott, *The Social System* (1951); Veblen, Thorstein, *The Theory of the Leisure Class* (1899; repr. 1973); Warner, W. Lloyd, and Lunt, Paul S., *The Status System of a Modern Community* (1942; repr. 1973) and *The Social Life of a Modern Community* (1941; repr. 1973); Weber, Max, *From Max Weber: Essays in Sociology*, trans. by Hans H. Gerth and C. Wright Mills (1946).

See also: CLASS, SOCIAL; NORM, SOCIAL; ROLE; SOCIAL STRUCTURE AND ORGANIZATION.

statute of limitations

The law specifying time limits during which legal action may be taken in certain cases is called the statute of limitations. In a civil case, it is a statute of repose, in that it sets a maximum period of time before the expiration of which a suit must be started. In a criminal case it is an act of grace; it specifies the length of time following commission of a crime after which the state must surrender its right to prosecute. Further, the statute of limitations protects an individual from lawsuits in which evidence may not be obtainable due to the passage of time.

This statute figured in the historic EX PARTE MILLIGAN case. Following Milligan's release from prison on Apr. 10, 1866, he sued General Hovey, on Mar. 13, 1868, for unlawful imprisonment. A federal circuit court jury decided in favor of Milligan but awarded him only 5 dollars because the 2-year statute of limitations allowed him damages only for his incarceration from Mar. 13 to Apr. 10, 1866. The varying statute of limitations in different countries has been of some significance in recent years in the prosecution of war criminals.

Bibliography: Cushman, Robert F., *Leading Constitutional Decisions,* 15th ed. (1977); Ross, Martin J., *Handbook of Everyday Law* (1975).

Staubach, Roger   [staw'-bak]

Roger Thomas Staubach, b. Cincinnati, Ohio, Feb. 5, 1942, was an American professional football player who, as quarterback for the Dallas Cowboys of the National Football League (NFL), earned distinction for his passing and running skills and leadership qualities. Although he won (1963) the Heisman Trophy as the outstanding college player in his junior year at the United States Naval Academy, his military obligation delayed his professional career until 1969. After joining

the Cowboys he led the NFL in passing in 1971 and 1973, and until his retirement in 1980 he had piloted the Cowboys to 7 divisional, 4 league, and 2 Super Bowl championships. In 1977, Staubach had his best year, completing 210 out of 361 passes for 2,620 yd (2,396 m), with 18 touchdowns and only 9 interceptions.

Bibliography: Clary, Jack, *Captains* (1978); Sullivan, George, *Roger Staubach: A Special Kind of Quarterback* (1974).

Staudinger, Hermann   [shtow'-ding-ur]

The German organic chemist Hermann Staudinger, b. Mar. 23, 1881, d. Sept. 8, 1965, made fundamental contributions to the study of high-molecular-weight compounds (macromolecules), for which he was awarded the 1953 Nobel Prize for chemistry.

Staudinger was an early advocate of the view that high polymers are giant molecules held together by ordinary chemical bonds. His theory opposed the then-common theory that polymers are aggregates of small molecules (monomers), loosely bound by partial valences. Staudinger disproved the aggregate theory by discovering reactions that could change a polymer chemically while leaving its molecular weight unchanged.   ROBERT J. PARADOWSKI

staurolite   [stohr'-uh-lyt]

The iron and magnesium aluminum SILICATE MINERAL staurolite forms well-developed, brown, prismatic crystals (orthorhombic system). Twinned, cruciform pairs, in which one crystal penetrates another, are called fairy crosses and are worn as charms. The crystals often have a rough surface and subvitreous to resinous luster. Hardness is 7 to 7½, and specific gravity is 3.6 to 3.8.

Staurolite is typical of regional metamorphism, but less so of contact metamorphism. It is often associated with garnet and kyanite in crystalline schists and other altered clay-rich sediments.

Stavanger   [stah-vahng'-ur]

Stavanger is a port city in southwestern Norway on the Bokn Fjord, about 300 km (185 mi) southwest of Oslo. The population is 87,400 (1977 est.). The city's harbor is ice-free year-round. Stavanger's industries include fish processing, shipbuilding, and—since the early 1970s—the refining of North Sea petroleum. The strategically important Sola airfield is located nearby. Points of interest include the Cathedral of Saint Swithin (begun 11th century), an archaeological museum, and an art gallery. Founded in the 8th century, Stavanger served as a bishopric from about 1125 to 1628 and again after 1924.

Stavisky affair   [stah-vee-skee']

The Stavisky affair, a French financial scandal of 1933–34, shook the Third Republic of a France already buffeted by depression and extremist political turmoil and threatened by an aggressive Nazi Germany. In December 1933 it was discovered that financier Serge Alexandre Stavisky had issued large quantities of worthless bonds for the municipal pawnshop at Bayonne. The next month he was found dead, an apparent suicide. Rightist groups such as the fascist-oriented Action Française charged that he had been killed to conceal high-level government protection for his fraudulent activities. Government efforts to play down the matter gave credence to this charge. The resulting riots outside the Chamber of Deputies on Feb. 6, 1934, brought down the existing ministry, but the republic survived.   DONALD J. HARVEY

Bibliography: Brogan, Denis W., *France Under the Republic, 1870-1939* (1940; repr. 1974); Shirer, William L., *The Collapse of the Third Republic* (1969).

Stead, Christina   [steed]

The Australian novelist Christina Stead, b. July 17, 1902, is best known for her novels—*The Man Who Loved Children* (1940) and *For Love Alone* (1944)—containing detailed accounts of family situations, particularly as they affect women. Her fiction also expresses a concern about the pressures of modern-day city life. *The Beauties and the Furies* (1936) and *A House of All Nations* (1938) have London and Paris as their backgrounds, and *A Little Tea, A Little Chat* (1948) is set in New York. She continues this theme in a recent novel, *Miss Herbert (The Suburban Wife)* (1976).

Stead left (1928) Australia and lived in Europe and the United States for 40 years before she returned to her home country to take up a fellowship in creative arts at the Australian National University, Canberra.   LEON CANTRELL

Bibliography: Geering, R. G., *Christina Stead* (1969).

steady-state theory

A cosmological theory proposed by Thomas Gold, Herman Bondi, and Fred Hoyle in 1948, the steady-state theory is based on the "perfect cosmological principle," namely, that the universe is homogeneous in space and time. According to its proposers, HUBBLE'S CONSTANT does not change with time; the density of galaxies in the universe also remains unchanged. Instead, the expansion of the universe is ascribed to a repulsive force. New matter supposedly is being created continuously, forming new galaxies, so that the density of galaxies remains the same despite their mutual recession. Within an average volume equivalent to that within which a galaxy is found, according to the theory, a new galaxy is created once every 12 billion years. This corresponds roughly to a rate of creation of matter of one hydrogen atom per cubic kilometer per year. This rate of "continuous creation" is too small to be observed directly.

The steady-state theory was an important milestone in the development of modern cosmology but has been discarded by most cosmologists because it cannot reasonably account for the 2.7 K microwave background radiation discovered by Arno A. Penzias and Robert W. Wilson in 1965.

HONG-YEE CHIU

See also: BIG BANG THEORY; COSMOLOGY (astronomy).

steam engine

The steam engine, one of the prime movers of the Industrial Revolution, has been used extensively to run factories and to power marine and land vehicles. The first practical steam engines were built by Thomas SAVERY (1698) and Thomas NEWCOMEN (1705); a greatly improved design was later developed by James WATT, also in England.

Steam engines work on the principle that water, when boiled, vaporizes into steam and expands to at least 1,600 times its original volume if unconfined. If steam is generated in a confined space, tremendous pressure, which can be harnessed as power, is formed.

Reciprocating Steam Engines. In single-acting reciprocating steam engines the steam pushes against one side of a piston. In double-acting reciprocating steam engines steam pressure is applied to both sides of a piston, forcing the piston to move back and forth. In either case, the force acting on the piston is transmitted by the piston rod. One end of this rod is attached to the head of the piston. The rod passes through a stuffing box (to prevent steam leakage) and is attached at its other end to a crosshead (a sliding connecting block). The reciprocating motion of the piston and crosshead is translated into rotary motion by means of a connecting rod that links the crosshead to a crankshaft.

Reciprocating steam engines must be equipped with a flywheel, the heavy rim of which compensates for variations in force between downward strokes of the piston. During part of its revolution the flywheel, attached to the crankshaft, absorbs power from the steam's force on the piston; during the other part the flywheel imparts power to keep the crankshaft turning smoothly.

The reciprocating steam engine employs a valve arrangement that allows steam to enter and leave the cylinder at the beginning and end, respectively, of the piston stroke. Most arrangements are activated by an eccentric, or cam. When the crankshaft makes half a revolution, the valve moves a distance equal to the throw of the eccentric. More efficient

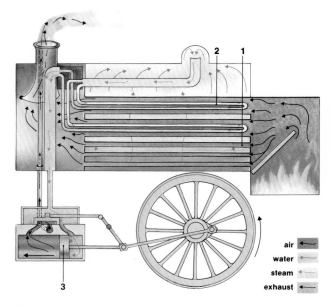

The locomotive is a self-propelled double-acting steam engine. The hot combustion gases leave the firebox where fuel is burned, pass through tubes (1) immersed in water, and are exhausted out the smokestack to the atmosphere. This arrangement is called a fire tube boiler. The heat boils the water and steam collects at the top of the boiler in a "dome." The steam is further heated by passing through superheater tubes (2) in contact with the combustion gases. The superheated steam is capable of doing more work because it does not condense in the cylinder before exhausting from the cylinder. Valves alternately admit and exhaust steam from both sides of the double-acting piston (3). The drive wheels serve also as flywheels. Steam locomotives require frequent stops to replenish their water supply. Because both combustion gases and steam are exhausted from the engine while still at high temperature, much of the available energy is lost and the engine is inefficient.

steam engines have two eccentrics per cylinder—one for the intake valve, one for the exhaust valve. The speed of the engine is controlled by adjusting a separate metering that feeds steam to the intake valve. Reciprocating steam engines range in efficiency from 8.5% to 24%, depending on valve system and steam pressure. Many years ago engines exceeding 5,000 hp were developed, but their vibration, appetite for fuel, slow speed, tremendous weight, large size, and low efficiency rendered them impractical.

Steam Turbines. Growing industrial demands required an engine that would run more smoothly, be capable of higher speeds, develop more horsepower, occupy less space, and, most of all, be more efficient. The steam TURBINE was therefore developed. In this engine, high-pressure steam is piped to nozzles, through which it escapes at high velocity. This jet of steam is made to strike a series of cupped vanes, or blades, attached to a rotor. The rotor is thus made to turn at extremely high speeds. Such turbines are called impulse turbines. In reaction turbines the steam is jetted from the rotor blades onto a set of fixed blades. These blades redirect the flow of the expanding steam so that it strikes and turns a second set of movable blades; this arrangement may be repeated through several stages having longer blades through which to pass the increasing volume of steam.

The steam turbine has become a prime mover of great importance to modern technology. Turbine-powered generating plants produce more than 80 percent of the electricity used in the United States; they are also used to power modern oceangoing vessels.

Steam Generation. All steam engines require a steam generator. The steam generator uses heat created by the burning of fuel or by nuclear fission to make steam. Early steam generators, called BOILERS, were essentially large enclosed kettles filled with water and heated at the bottom; they were not ef-

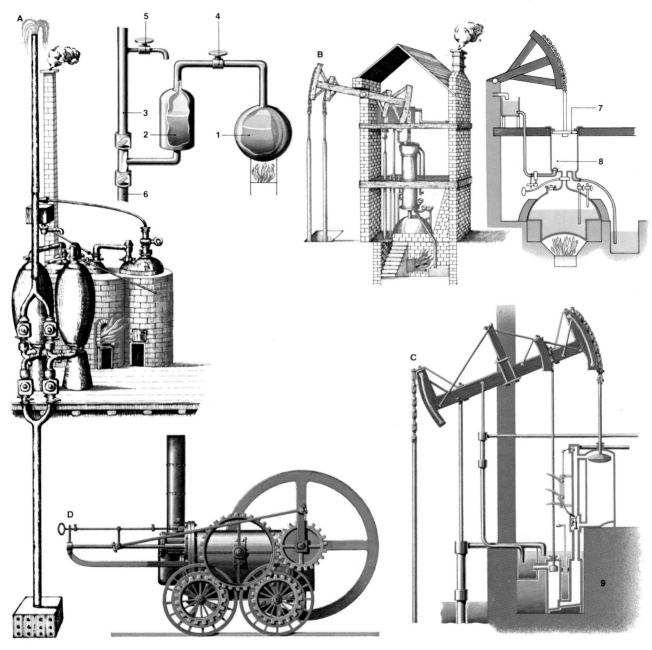

The steam engine converts heat into mechanical energy. The first practical version was invented in 1698, when Thomas Savery developed a model for pumping water. In Savery's engine (A), water in a boiler (1) was heated to produce steam. The steam entered a working chamber (2), forcing the water in the chamber through a valve (3) in a suction pump. The steam cock (4) was then closed and cold water (5) applied to the chamber, condensing the steam. The vacuum thus created drew more water up the suction pump (6) to restart the cycle. Thomas Newcomen's later steam engine (B) was designed to pump water out of mines. The steam produced in the boiler forced a piston (7) upward through a cylinder; then a spray of cold water (8) condensed the steam and created the vacuum necessary to draw the piston down again. The piston's action powered a crossbeam that worked the main pump. A much-needed improvement in fuel efficiency was introduced in 1784 by James Watt, whose double-acting engine (C) condensed the steam outside the cylinder (9) and admitted it to both sides of the piston. Watt's was the first steam engine capable of powering heavy machinery. Richard Trevithick, a Cornish mine engineer, adapted the engine for use by locomotives (D) in 1804. He used high-pressure steam, omitted the condenser, and preheated the boiler with steam from an exhaust pipe.

ficient. Greater efficiency was achieved by the design of fire-tube and water-tube boilers. These boilers, in which tubes pass through the boiler (fire-tube) or the combustion area (water-tube), increase the surface area exposed to heat. The highly efficient water-tube boilers used today may burn a variety of fuels, including coal, gas, and oil. Modern steam generators are capable of producing steam pressures of 1,450 to 5,000 lb/in² (psi) at temperatures in excess of 650° C (1,200° F).

JOSEPH W. DUFFY

Bibliography: Dickinson, Henry W., *Short History of the Steam Engine*, 2d ed. (1963); Pursell, C. W., *Early Stationary Steam Engines in America* (1969); Storer, J. D., *Simple History of the Steam Engine* (1969); Thurston, Robert H., *History of the Growth of the Steam Engine* (1939; repr. 1971).

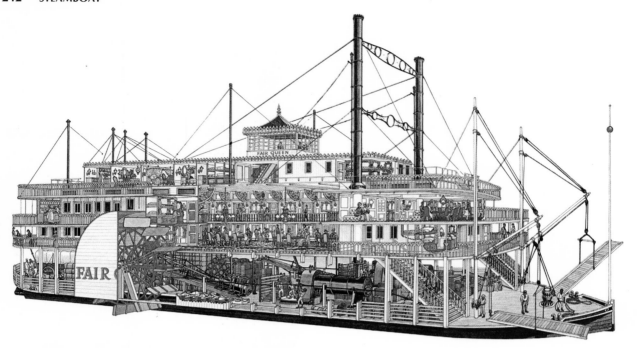

The Mississippi riverboat, which developed from simpler steamships of the early 1800s, became the Mississippi's dominant form of passenger and commercial transport by the mid-19th century. Designed to hazard sandbars and shallows, the flat-bottomed, shallow-hulled craft supported a light but lofty wooden superstructure. Its steam engines burned either coal or wood, powering two large, lateral flywheels. The elegant passenger quarters of the upper decks were crowned by a small pilothouse, from which the captain could survey the river.

steamboat

The term *steamboat* usually refers to a small, shallow-draft vessel operating on inland waters, as distinguished from the large seagoing steamship. As early as 1685, French physicist Denis Papin proposed that steam could be used to propel a ship by means of a paddle wheel. James Watt's improvement of the steam engine in 1769 was followed by the first steamboat, navigated on the Saône River in France in 1783 by Claude Jouffroy d'Abbans.

The first steamboat to find practical application was a paddle-propelled vessel demonstrated in 1787 on the Delaware River at Philadelphia by John FITCH. In 1790, Fitch established the world's first steamboat passenger service, between Philadelphia and Trenton; it was a technical success but a commercial failure.

European experiments continued—notably William Symington's *Charlotte Dundas,* built in 1801 to tow boats on the Forth and Clyde Canal and equipped with a crankshaft connection between piston and paddle wheel. The immensely greater need for steam navigation in America, however, inspired the major developments. In 1802, John Stevens (see STEVENS family) of New York built the *Polacca,* the first steamboat with a screw propeller. Robert FULTON navigated an experimental steamboat on the Seine in Paris in 1803. In 1807, Fulton built the *North River Steamboat* (later renamed the CLERMONT), a long, low, flat-bottomed, box-shaped vessel powered by an imported Watt engine. Although its only innovative feature was the shape of its hull, the vessel's extraordinary commercial success was a historic turning point. Two years later John Stevens's son Robert Stevens sailed their ship *Phoenix* from New York to Philadelphia. It was the first steamboat to navigate the open sea.

By 1811, Fulton's *New Orleans* became the first steamboat on the Mississippi, but its low-pressure engine was a handicap. In 1815 the *Enterprise,* with a high-pressure engine of the type invented by Oliver EVANS, inaugurated a profitable commercial service.

By 1830 nearly 200 steamboats operated on the Mississippi, and the river steamboat had developed its characteristic con-

figuration: a straight-sided, flat-bottomed, and shallow draft that led skippers to boast that they could navigate on a "heavy dew." The intense speed rivalry of Mississippi boats was memorialized in the famous race between the *Robert E. Lee* and the *Natchez* in 1870; the boats went from New Orleans to Saint Louis in 3 days. FRANCES GIES

Bibliography: Deeson, A. F., *An Illustrated History of Steamships* (1977); Flexner, James T., *Steamboats Come True* (1944; repr. 1978); Georgano, G. N., *A History of Transport* (1972); Hunter, Louis C., *Steamboats on the Western Rivers* (1969).

stearin [stee'-rin]

Stearin, a combination of one glycerol and three stearic acid molecules, is a major component of various types of animal fats and vegetable oils. It is made into a variety of commercial products, including candles, margarine, and soap. In soap-making, stearin and an alkali are heated, and the glycerol becomes a by-product. When purified, this by-product has many uses, ranging from explosives to a colloidal base for medicines.

Like many triglycerides, stearin has the unusual quality of having two melting points. It liquefies at 55° C (131° F), solidifies at a higher temperature, and melts again at 72° C (162° F).

See also: FAT; FATS AND OILS; SAPONIFICATION.

steatite: see TALC.

steatopygia [stee-uht-uh-pij'-ee-uh]

Steatopygia is a pronounced, localized accumulation of fat or fatty-fibrous tissue on the upper part of the buttocks, a condition common among Khoikhoi (Hottentot) and San (Bushman) women of southwestern Africa. Rarely manifest prior to puberty, the accumulation enlarges gradually and is a normal physical characteristic in women who otherwise may not be obese.

Rock paintings indicate that ancient populations in southern Africa exhibited this condition, suggesting a selective advantage in its survival, but its physiological significance has not been demonstrated.   RONALD SINGER

Stedman, Edmund Clarence   [sted'-muhn]

An American poet, critic, and successful Wall Street broker, Edmund Clarence Stedman, b. Hartford, Conn., Oct. 8, 1833, d. Jan. 18, 1908, has been little read in the 20th century because of the mannered and imitative nature of his poetry. More effective as a critic, he was editor of *The Poets of America* (1885) and *An American Anthology, 1787-1900* (1900), volumes that succeeded in calling attention to the existence of an American literature.

steel: see IRON AND STEEL INDUSTRY.

Steel, David Martin Scott

A member of Parliament from Scotland since 1964, David Martin Scott Steel, b. Mar. 31, 1938, became a leader of the British Liberal party in 1976, succeeding Jeremy Thorpe. Educated in Nairobi, Kenya, and at Edinburgh University, Steel began his political career as the youngest member of Parliament.
In 1977 he negotiated a Liberal-Labour pact that helped Prime Minister James Callaghan remain in office until 1979.

Steele, Sir Richard

An essayist, dramatist, and political writer of the English AUGUSTAN AGE, Sir Richard Steele, b. Dublin, Mar. 12, 1672, d. Sept. 1, 1729, is remembered mainly for his collaboration with Joseph ADDISON in the two great series of periodical essays, the *Tatler* (1709-11) and the *Spectator* (1711-12).
Having left Oxford for the army in 1692, Steele launched his writing career with publication of his first poem, "The Procession," in 1695. He later turned to stage comedy, producing *The Funeral* (1701), *The Lying Lover* (1703), and *The Tender Husband* (1705).
After serving (1713-22) as a Whig member of Parliament and holding minor government posts, he reverted to the stage with *The Conscious Lovers* (1722). The success of this play began a vogue of "weeping" comedies in which a virtuous hero and heroine come to happiness through adversity. This work, however, was Steele's last; his health had been poor since 1720, and in 1726 he suffered a crippling stroke.
Steele was a zealous crusader for morality and published a manual of religious devotion, *The Christian Hero* (1701). The *Tatler*, written mainly by Steele under the pseudonym of Isaac Bickerstaff, employed the popular periodical essay form to accomplish a new purpose: to refine the manners of its readers. The essays are discussions of current events, literature, and gossip in a deftly ironic style that teases readers into laughing at their own pettiness and folly. The style and purpose of the *Tatler* were continued in the *Spectator*, the writing of which was shared about equally by Addison and Steele.
                                                                    WILLIAM MCCARTHY

Bibliography: Connely, Willard, *Sir Richard Steele* (1934; repr. 1973); Loftis, John, *Steele at Drury Lane* (1952; repr. 1973); Winton, Calhoun, *Captain Steele: The Early Career of Richard Steele* (1964) and *Sir Richard Steele, M.P.: The Later Career* (1970).

Steelworkers of America, United: see UNITED STEELWORKERS OF AMERICA.

Steen, Jan   [stayn]

The works of the Dutch painter Jan Steen, c.1626-1679, represent the climax of the Haarlem school of genre painting. Steen studied in Haarlem under Adriaen van Ostade and in The Hague with Jan van Goyen. His prodigious output of paintings reflects not only an awareness of the Haarlem low-genre tradition but also a familiarity with the clear lighting and hermetic interior scenes of Jan Vermeer and Pieter de

In Woman Undressing *(1663), 17th-century Dutch genre painter Jan Steen illustrates both his skill and his sense of humor. Through an open window flanked by columns-as-frame is seen a smiling woman seated on a bed casually undressing herself. (Private collection.)*

Hooch as well as the smooth surfaces and precise details of the so-called fine painters of Leiden.
As a Roman Catholic in a country dominated by Protestants, Steen executed his many religious paintings with an urgency uncommon in 17th-century Dutch art. He is best known, however, for his genre scenes depicting lower-class life in taverns and brothels. As the owner of a tavern, he had firsthand knowledge of such places that enabled him to present their bawdy drunkenness and vulgarity, as well as their occasional cruelty, without sentimentality and with a saving sense of humor. An exceptional draftsman and a keen observer of contemporary life, he was adept at compressing entire narratives into a single scene populated with vividly rendered characters, as can be seen in his delightful *Feast of Saint Nicholas* (c.1660-65; Rijksmuseum, Amsterdam).
                                                            FRANKLIN W. ROBINSON

Bibliography: De Vries, Lyckle, *Jan Steen* (1976); Kirschenbaum, Baruch, *The Religious and Historical Paintings of Jan Steen* (1977).

steeplechase

A steeplechase is a race for people or horses, over a prescribed course that includes such obstacles as timber rails, stone walls, brush fences, and water hazards. The race takes its name from the early contests in which a local church with a tall steeple was used as a landmark. Steeplechase races using horses can be traced back to 18th-century fox hunting in England and Ireland.
The first organized steeplechase, the Grand National, was held at Aintree, England, in 1839. This race is still considered the most prestigious in the world. Steeplechase racing was first introduced into the United States from Canada in 1865 at Paterson, N.J. Steeplechasing is a favorite sport for amateur riders, and steeplechase events are usually organized by local hunt clubs.
The track and field steeplechase event challenges the skills

The Grand National, England's most prestigious steeplechase, covers a hazardous course of approximately 7,220 m (7,896 yd) that includes 30 varied obstacles. One of the oldest horse races in the world, the event has been held annually at Aintree, England, since 1839.

required for middle-distance running, for hurdling, and for overall balance. At present, the standard steeplechase is run over a 3,000-m (3,281-yd) course, with 35 obstacles. Hurdles are 3 ft (.91 m) high; water obstacles occur after every fifth hurdle, are 12 ft (3.7 m) square, 2 ft 3.5 in (.70 m) deep immediately after the hurdle, and then slope up to the level of the track. The first steeplechase was run in 1850 in Oxford, England, and has been an Olympic Games event since 1900.

GORDON STANG

Bibliography: Francis, Dick, *Sport of Queens* (1969); Pearn, Tony, *The Secret of Successful Steeplechasing* (1973); Smith, Vian, *The Grand National: A History of the World's Greatest Steeplechase Race* (1969).

steering system

The steering system of a vehicle allows its driver to control the vehicle's direction. Rotation of the steering wheel is translated into an angular deflection of the vehicle's front wheels by a steering column that connects the steering wheel to the steering gear.

Modern steering systems are characterized by their type of steering gear: rack and pinion or recirculating ball. With a rack-and-pinion system the steering column ends in the pinion—a helical gear that mates with the rack, which is essentially a geared wheel opened up and laid flat. As the steering wheel is turned, rotation of the pinion causes the rack to move left or right. This lateral movement is carried through track rods to steering arms at the wheels.

The recirculating-ball system is derived from worm-and-nut steering gear in which a threaded portion, the worm, at the end of the steering column engages a nut whose up and down motion is translated into angular motion of the drop arm. The far end of the drop arm is connected to the track rod on one side of the vehicle and to a link transferring the motion to the track rod on the other side of the vehicle by way of an idler, or slave arm.

In the recirculating-ball system, the nut is replaced by a housing containing ball bearings that recirculate through grooves formed by the worm gear. The recirculating balls lessen friction in the steering gear and improve its road feel.

Many modern vehicles have power-assisted steering. A hydraulic pump is used to lessen the effort required to steer. This is especially helpful during parking and other low-speed maneuvers. Some systems reduce hydraulic assistance at higher speeds, where such assistance is undesirable.

The relationship of the front wheels to the road, as measured by camber, caster, and toe-in, is important. Camber is the angle that the wheels make with the vertical, as viewed from the car's front or rear. Camber influences a vehicle's response to side forces in turning. Caster is the angle that the steering axis makes with the vertical, as viewed from the side. Rearward inclination of this axis induces an inherent self-centering that improves vehicular stability. Toe-in is the angular deflection inward of each front wheel, as viewed from above; toe-out is the opposite, with the front wheels slightly closer at their rearmost edges. Toe-in or toe-out is used to compen-

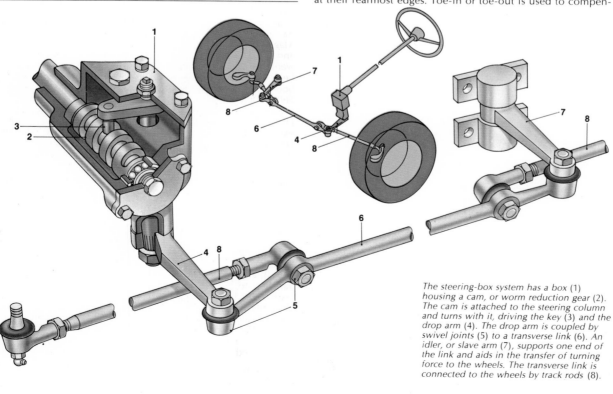

The steering-box system has a box (1) housing a cam, or worm reduction gear (2). The cam is attached to the steering column and turns with it, driving the key (3) and the drop arm (4). The drop arm is coupled by swivel joints (5) to a transverse link (6). An idler, or slave arm (7), supports one end of the link and aids in the transfer of turning force to the wheels. The transverse link is connected to the wheels by track rods (8).

Rack and pinion is the most widely used of the automotive steering systems. The steering column (1) ends in a toothed pinion (2), which engages a transverse rack (3) that is connected at each end (by means of ball joints) to a track rod (4). The joints are enclosed in grease-packed dust boots (5). The steering arm (6), pivoting about the swivel pin (7), turns the linear motion of the track rod into the turning motion of the road wheel (8).

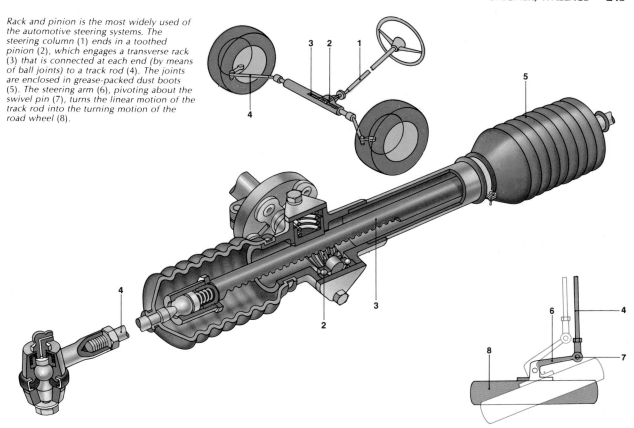

sate for the tendency of the front wheels to deviate from the parallel when subjected to the forces of a moving vehicle.

A front-end alignment measures these three steering system characteristics to ensure that they are within the specifications set by the vehicle manufacturer. A misaligned front end will cause unnecessary tire wear and less-than-optimal handling.   DENNIS SIMANAITIS

Bibliography: Dey, John, *The Bosch Book of the Motor Car* (1976); Dwiggins, B. H., *Automotive Steering Systems* (1968); Ellinger, Herbert E., and Hathaway, Richard B., *Automotive Suspension, Steering and Brakes* (1980).

Stefan, Josef   [shtef'-ahn]

The Austrian physicist Josef Stefan, b. Mar. 24, 1835, d. Jan. 7, 1893, deduced (1879) that total radiation from a blackbody is proportional to the fourth power of its absolute temperature. After his student, Ludwig Boltzmann, showed (1884) that this law could be demonstrated mathematically (the Stefan–Boltzmann law), Stefan applied it to determine the approximate temperature of the surface of the Sun. Stefan also did important work on the kinetic theory of heat and heat conduction in fluids.   RICHARD HIRSH

See also: BLACKBODY RADIATION.

Stefansson, Vilhjalmur   [stef'-uhn-suhn, vil'-heeowl-mur]

Vilhjalmur Stefansson, b. Arnes, Manitoba, Nov. 3, 1879, d. Aug. 26, 1962, was an ethnologist and explorer. By adopting the Eskimo way of life during Arctic expeditions (1908–12, 1913–16), he showed that the culture was adapted to the environment; he also discovered previously unknown tribes and territory. The author of many books, Stefansson was affiliated with Dartmouth College from 1947 until his death.

Bibliography: Diubaldo, Richard J., *Stefansson and the Canadian Arctic* (1978); Stefansson, Vilhjalmur, *The Autobiography of Vilhjalmur Stefansson* (1964).

Steffens, Lincoln   [stef'-uhnz]

One of the most eminent American reformers and journalists around the turn of the 20th century, Joseph Lincoln Steffens, b. San Francisco, Apr. 6, 1866, d. Aug. 9, 1936, was a leader of the MUCKRAKERS. As managing editor (1901–06) of *McClure's Magazine,* he wrote a series of articles that documented graft and corruption in American cities, asserting that some cities were run by political bosses who remained in power with the help of powerful businessmen. These articles appeared in book form as *The Shame of the Cities* (1904), *The Struggle for Self-Government* (1906), and *Upbuilders* (1909).

Steffens joined with other muckrakers in the development (1906) of *American Magazine* and later continued to question existing social processes. After visiting the USSR and meeting Lenin in 1919, he wrote: "I have seen the future and it works." Steffens's *Autobiography* was published in 1931.   ERNEST C. HYNDS

Bibliography: Kaplan, Justin, *Lincoln Steffens* (1974); Palermo, Patrick F., *Lincoln Steffens* (1978).

Stegner, Wallace   [steg'-nur]

Wallace Stegner, b. Lake Mills, Iowa, Feb. 18, 1909, one of the most talented regional writers of the mid-20th century, is the author of twelve novels, many of them about life in the American West. Best known is *The Big Rock Candy Mountain* (1943), a sprawling work describing a Norwegian-American family's struggle to establish a home in the West during the early 1900s. Other major titles by Stegner include *The Preacher and the Slave,* a fictionalized account of labor leader Joe Hill, and *Angle of Repose* (1971), a reconstruction of the life of Western novelist Mary Hallock Foote. Stegner taught (1950–76) creative writing at Stanford University, and in 1971 he received a Pulitzer Prize.   WARREN FRENCH

Bibliography: Robinson, Forrest G. and Margaret G., *Wallace Stegner* (1977).

Stegosaurus [steg'-uh-sohr-uhs]

Stegosaurus is one of the plated dinosaurs, suborder Stegosauria, order Ornithischia; it grew to about 6 m (20 ft) long, 2.5 m (8 ft) high at the hips, and about 4 tons in weight. Its fossil remains have been collected from a number of sites in the late Jurassic Morrison Formation of western North America, dating back about 150 million years. Related forms have been found in similar-aged rocks in Europe and Africa, but stegosaurs apparently were never very abundant or diverse.

Stegosaurus had a blimplike body, long hind legs, short front legs, a short, stocky neck, and a small head. Its long, heavy tail carried several pairs of long, bony spikes, presumably used as defensive weapons against predators. The midline of the back bore two rows of unpaired, alternating, triangular, bony plates that were probably attached by ligaments to the spine and stood upright like fins. The small head and the mouth, with up to about 25 tiny teeth on each side of the upper and lower jaws, seem ill-designed to have fed such a ponderous body. *Stegosaurus* is famed for having a brain no larger than a walnut.

The alternating bony plates along the back have always been interpreted as defensive armor against predators, such as *Allosaurus* and *Ceratosaurus*. Recent studies, however, have shown them to be highly vascularized, presumably to carry an extensive network of blood vessels. This has led to the hypothesis that these plates were cooling devices, carrying heated blood close to the surface and enabling *Stegosaurus* to shed excess heat. JOHN H. OSTROM

Bibliography: Colbert, Edwin H., *Dinosaurs: Their Discovery and Their World* (1961); Desmond, Adrian, *The Hot-blooded Dinosaurs* (1976); Swinton, W. E., *The Dinosaurs*, 5th ed. (1975).

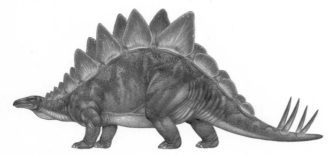

The Stegosaurus *was a dinosaur that became extinct about 140 million years ago. It had a plated, corpulent body, a walnut-sized brain, and long spikes on its tail, which it used for defense.*

Steichen, Edward [sty'-ken]

A major force among 20th-century photographers, Edward Steichen, b. Luxembourg, Mar. 27, 1879, d. Mar. 25, 1973, was a leader in the movement to gain acceptance of photography as a fine art. Steichen was raised in Hancock, Mich. He studied painting in Paris, where his experiments in photographic portraiture led to his recognition early in the century as a photographer of remarkable sensitivity and individuality. Together with Alfred STIEGLITZ, Clarence H. White, and others, he helped found (1902) the PHOTO-SECESSION group in New York; thereafter he served as Stieglitz's lieutenant on the journal *Camera Work* (1903–17) and in mounting exhibitions of the work both of Photo-Secession members and of major French artists not yet known in America.

Until 1914, Steichen specialized in soft-focused photographic images evocative of the paintings of the postimpressionists and symbolists. During World War I he contributed to the development of aerial photography, an experience that led him after 1919 to a different photographic approach, characterized by clearer, more sharply focused images, and experiments with a variety of light settings, as in his close-up studies of plant life and natural, abstract forms. From 1923, when he renounced painting and burned his canvases, to

Edward Steichen's The Flatiron Building—Evening, *photographed in New York City in 1905, is a classic study of shadow and atmosphere. Steichen experimented constantly with new techniques and materials in his quest to have photography accepted as a creative art.*

1938, Steichen practiced commercial photography in New York, where he was chief photographer for *Vogue* and *Vanity Fair* magazines. In charge of the U.S. Navy's combat photography unit during World War II, Steichen later directed (1947–62) the Museum of Modern Art's photography department, under whose auspices he organized (1955) the celebrated Family of Man exhibition that later toured 37 countries. Steichen's last notable work was the experimental color filming (1965) of the seasonal moods of a shadblow tree located on his Connecticut estate. His autobiography, *A Life in Photography*, appeared in 1963. ELIZABETH POLLOCK

Bibliography: Doty, Robert, *Photo-Secession* (1960); Homer, William I., *Alfred Stieglitz and the American Avant-Garde* (1977); Longwell, Dennis, *Steichen: The Master Prints, 1895–1914: The Symbolist Period* (1978); Sandburg, Carl, et al., *Steichen the Photographer* (1961).

Steiger, Rod [sty'-gur]

A graduate of the Actors Studio, Rod Steiger, b. Westhampton, N.Y., Apr. 14, 1925, has had a distinguished career as a leading character actor in films since 1951. His most notable roles have been in *On the Waterfront* (1954), *The Pawnbroker* (1964), *In the Heat of the Night* (1967), for which he won an Academy Award, *The Sergeant* (1968), and, as Napoleon, in *Waterloo* (1970).

Stein, Sir Aurel [styn]

Sir Aurel Stein, b. Nov. 26, 1862, d. Oct. 26, 1943, was a British archaeologist and geographer noted for his pioneering exploration of central Asia. After serving (1888–89) as principal of the Oriental College in Lahore, Pakistan, he set out (1900) on the first of several expeditions along ancient caravan routes in central Asia. At TUN-HUANG, Stein discovered (1906–08) an important cache of Buddhist art and manuscripts. While superintendent of the Indian Archaeological Survey (1910–29), he located eastern battle stations of Alexander the Great. Stein was knighted in 1912.

Stein, Gertrude

Gertrude Stein, an American writer, is seen in a portrait (c.1906) by Pablo Picasso, one of many artists she influenced. Stein abandoned conventional narrative and meaning to experiment with linguistic rhythms and impressions. The expatriate writers Stein called the "lost generation" met in her Paris salon. (Metropolitan Museum of Art, New York City.)

Best known for her innovative prose style, Gertrude Stein, b. Allegheny, Pa., Feb. 3, 1874, exercised a major influence on American writers of the post–World War I generation, which she was the first to describe as "lost." Raised in California, she graduated from Radcliffe College in 1897, then attended Johns Hopkins Medical School for 4 years without taking a degree. Having inherited a sufficient income to live independently, Stein settled in Paris in 1903, first sharing an apartment with her brother Leo and thereafter with her lifelong companion, Alice Toklas. Known both for her avant-garde compositions and for her friendships, she wrote more than 40 books over the next 4 decades and at the same time assembled an extraordinary collection of modern paintings.

Stein's first book, *Quod Erat Demonstrandum,* written in 1903 and published in 1950 under the title *Things as They Are,* was a conventional novel influenced by Henry James. The direction of her work changed in *Three Lives* (1905–06; publ. 1909), where, in the central story, "Melanctha," Stein began to develop her characteristically abstract style. In her massive *The Making of Americans* (1906–08; publ. 1925), an attempt to render the essence of characters and their interrelationships led her to jettison traditional narrative structure and syntax in favor of slow-moving, repetitive images of the continuously evolving present.

From then on, the relationship between Stein's work and painting became quite explicit. She began to write short, nonrepresentational "portraits" of individuals and situations as literary equivalents of the painting of Picasso, Matisse, and others. Her most notoriously difficult work, *Tender Buttons* (1941), were poems that formed a series of "cubist" still lifes.

Stein had difficulty publishing her early writing and did not achieve genuine fame until the mid-1920s, when her literary friendships with Sherwood Anderson and Ernest Hemingway, both of whom learned from her theories and practice, carried her name and works widely into print. In the 1920s, Stein also wrote literary criticism and drama in such works as *Composition as Explanation* (1926) and the opera *Four Saints in Three Acts* (publ. 1929, produced 1934), on which she collaborated with the composer Virgil Thomson. Not until 1933 did she publish her best-selling *Autobiography of Alice B. Toklas,* which made Stein many enemies but also gave her thousands of readers for the first time.

The following year Stein toured the United States, returning for the first time in 30 years. Her talks before audiences became *Lectures in America* (1935). A few years later she wrote an account of that tour in *Everybody's Autobiography* (1937). In her last decade Stein wrote in many genres: literary criticism in *The Geographical History of America* (1936); art criticism in *Picasso* (1938); a memoir, *Wars I Have Seen* (1945); drama in the opera *The Mother of Us All* (1947); and the novel *Mrs. Reynolds* (1952). She died in Paris, July 27, 1946.

MICHAEL J. HOFFMAN

Bibliography: Bridgman, Richard, *Gertrude Stein in Pieces* (1970); Brinnin, John Malcolm, *The Third Rose: Gertrude Stein and Her World* (1959); Hoffman, Michael J., *The Development of Abstractionism in the Writings of Gertrude Stein* (1965) and *Gertrude Stein* (1976); Mellow, James, *Charmed Circle: Gertrude Stein and Company* (1974); Stewart, Allegra, *Gertrude Stein and the Present* (1967); Sutherland, Donald, *Gertrude Stein* (1951; repr. 1972); Weinstein, Norman, *Gertrude Stein and the Literature of the Modern Consciousness* (1970).

Stein, Heinrich Friedrich Karl, Freiherr vom und zum   [shtyn]

Heinrich Friedrich Karl, Freiherr vom und zum Stein, b. Oct. 26, 1757, d. June 29, 1831, chief minister (1807–08) of Prussia, was the driving force behind the Prussian reform movement after the near annihilation of the state by Napoleon I in 1806–07. He came from a family of imperial knights who had long governed their own local affairs and owed allegiance only to the Holy Roman emperor. In 1780, Stein entered the Prussian service, where he made his reputation in the department of mines; by 1804 he had risen to the top levels of government.

Stein's zeal for reform was fired by the military defeat of Prussia at the hands of Napoleon and the absorption of his own estates into the duchy of Nassau. Henceforth, he viewed a dynamic Prussia as the means to overthrow Napoleon and restore the rights of the imperial knights within a revitalized empire. Stein was appointed chief minister, and in only 14 months as head of the government, he created a council of responsible ministers shielded from royal caprice, abolished serfdom, removed restrictions on property ownership and choice of occupation, introduced home rule for the cities, and promoted Gen. Gerhard von SCHARNHORST's military reforms.

Dismissed under pressure from Napoleon in November 1808, Stein fled to Austria and then to Russia. During the War of Liberation (1813–14), he fomented popular resistance to the rule of Napoleon's German clients and directed the allied occupation of conquered German territories. As advisor to Russian emperor Alexander I at the Congress of Vienna (see VIENNA, CONGRESS OF), he labored in vain for the restoration of the imperial knights and a unitary empire. Embittered at failure, he retired to his estates to study history. Stein provided the impetus for publication, beginning in 1826, of the *Monumenta Germaniae historica,* an important collection of historical documents.

ENNO E. KRAEHE

The Prussian statesman Freiherr vom und zum Stein effected far-reaching reforms in the social system and economy of Prussia during the period following his country's defeat by Napoleon. In an age of political extremism Stein favored a policy of moderation, combining a strong respect for tradition with a penchant for decisive and practical action.

Bibliography: Ford, G. S., *Stein and the Era of Reform in Prussia* (1922; repr. 1965); Raack, Richard C., *The Fall of Stein* (1965).

Stein, William Howard   [styn]

William Howard Stein, b. New York City, June 25, 1911, d. Feb. 2, 1980, was an American biochemist who shared the 1972 Nobel Prize for chemistry with Stanford Moore and Christian Anfinsen. Stein and Moore were the first to determine the complete structure of an enzyme, ribonuclease—which had been discovered by Anfinsen—and then to relate its catalytic mechanism to its structure.

Steinbeck, John [styn'-bek]

John Steinbeck received the Nobel Prize for literature in 1962 for his contribution to American letters. Before achieving literary success during the mid-1930s, Steinbeck worked as a laborer. The Grapes of Wrath *(1939)* and other novels, informed by this experience, often portray the social injustice faced by the poor and dispossessed.

An American author and winner of the 1962 Nobel Prize for literature, John Ernst Steinbeck, Jr., b. Salinas, Calif., Feb. 27, 1902, d. Dec. 20, 1968, based most of his novels on the American experience, often with sympathetic focus on the poor, the eccentric, or the dispossessed.

Early Life and Works. Steinbeck grew up in Salinas Valley, a rich agricultural area of Monterey County and the setting of many of his works, where he learned firsthand of the difficulties of farm laborers. From 1919 to 1925 he studied intermittently at Stanford University but did not receive a degree.

Steinbeck's first published book, *Cup of Gold* (1929), was not successful. He then turned to the valleys of rural California for his settings and characters. *The Pastures of Heaven* (1932) contains a series of closely linked tales about residents of California. *To a God Unknown* (1933) relates a mystical story of self-sacrifice and is one of Steinbeck's strongest statements about the relationship between people and the land. *The Long Valley* (1938) is a collection of short stories, among them "The Red Pony," which chronicles the initiation of a ranch boy, Jody Tiflin, into manhood.

Artistic Success. Steinbeck's first popular success was *Tortilla Flat* (1935), an episodic tale that recounts semihumorously the adventures of a raffish band of Mexican-Americans. The books that ensued were terse and grim. *In Dubious Battle* (1936) is the tragic story of a young labor organizer during an apple pickers' strike. OF MICE AND MEN (1937) depicts the lives of two itinerant farm workers and the tragedy that comes when their dreams are shattered. Written as a "play-novel," it was produced on Broadway in 1937 and filmed in 1939. *Their Blood Is Strong* (1938) is a nonfictional account of conditions in migrant agricultural workers' camps derived largely from articles written for the *San Francisco News*. It probably formed the basis for The GRAPES OF WRATH (1939; film, 1940), which won the 1940 Pulitzer Prize for fiction and brought the plight of dispossessed farmers to the public's attention.

Later Life and Works. After the film success of *The Grapes of Wrath*, Steinbeck turned to filmmaking himself with screenplays for *The Forgotten Village* (1941) and *Viva Zapata!* (1952), the first about efforts to bring modern medicine to remote Mexican villages, and the latter about a Mexican revolutionary leader. In the meantime he wrote *The Moon Is Down* (1942), a play-novel about the German invasion of a neutral European country.

After World War II, Steinbeck wrote increasingly about social outcasts. *Cannery Row* (1945) relates the story of a central character, Doc, and a group of vagabonds on the Monterey coast. The PEARL (1947) is a popular fable about a Mexican fisherman's finding and finally discarding a valuable pearl that brings him only grief. *The Wayward Bus* (1947) presents a morality tale about characters who supposedly represent middle-class society. *Burning Bright* (1950), a play-novel, preached the theme of universal brotherhood but was largely unsuccessful.

Steinbeck devoted several years to his most ambitious project, *East of Eden* (1952; film, 1955), which paralleled the history of his mother's family and was an allegorical modernization of the biblical story of Adam. Subsequent novels proved anticlimactic—*Sweet Thursday* (1954), a sentimental sequel to *Cannery Row*; *The Short Reign of Pippin IV* (1957), a burlesque; *Once There Was a War* (1958); and *The Winter of Our Discontent* (1961), a moralistic tale about a decaying Long Island seaport.

Steinbeck spent many of his later years writing a modern version of Malory's *Morte d'Arthur*, published posthumously and incomplete as *The Acts of King Arthur and His Noble Knights* (1976). He also wrote about his travels and opinions in *Once There Was a War* (1958), *Travels with Charley* (1962), and *America and Americans* (1966). Steinbeck has remained popular for his compassionate portrayal of the lonely, the poor, and the dispossessed.　　　　WARREN G. FRENCH

Bibliography: Astro, Richard, *John Steinbeck and Edward F. Ricketts* (1973); Fontenrose, Joseph, *John Steinbeck* (1963); French, Warren, *John Steinbeck* (1961; rev. ed., 1975); Hayashi, Tetsumaro, ed., *A Study Guide to Steinbeck* (1974); Levant, Howard, *The Novels of John Steinbeck* (1974); Lisca, Peter, *John Steinbeck: Nature and Myth* (1978); McCarthy, Paul, *John Steinbeck* (1979).

Steinberg, Saul [styn'-burg]

The work of the noted cartoonist Saul Steinberg, b. Romania, June 15, 1914, has appeared in many magazines, including the *New Yorker,* since 1941. His style is wholly individual, revealing humor, satire, fantasy, and philosophy through a rich visual vocabulary of rubber stamps, official seals, thumbprints, silhouetted figures, and illegible script. Many of his cartoons deal with problems of identity, disguise, and metamorphosis, but precise meanings remain obscure. Although Steinberg's work spans almost 40 years, there have been relatively few stylistic changes. His early pieces are usually black and white with a limited number of elements; later compositions are more complex as well as abstract and often washed with watercolor. In the 1970s, Steinberg made his first "tables," painted assemblages of objects made by himself and placed on a board.　　　　LISA M. MESSINGER

Bibliography: Rosenberg, Harold, *Saul Steinberg* (1978).

Steinberg, William

William Steinberg, b. Cologne, Germany, Aug. 1, 1899, d. May 16, 1978, was a conductor who stressed precision and nonromantic, objective musical interpretations. After serving as an assistant to Otto Klemperer, he conducted opera in Cologne (1924), Prague (1925–28), and Frankfurt (1929–33). Forced out of this last position by the Nazis, he conducted (1933–36) the Jewish Cultural League and then fled to Palestine. In 1938 he moved to New York to become Arturo Toscanini's assistant with the NBC Symphony, and in 1945 he took over the Buffalo Philharmonic. From 1952 to 1976 he directed the famed Pittsburgh Symphony.

Bibliography: Ewen, David, ed., *Musicians since 1900* (1978).

Discography: Brahms, J., *Fourth Symphony*; Dukas, P., *Sorcerer's Apprentice*; Holst, G., *The Planets*; Rimsky-Korsakov, N., *Le Coq d'or Suite*.

Steinem, Gloria [styn'-uhm]

An American journalist and political activist, Gloria Steinem, b. Toledo, Ohio, Mar. 25, 1934, is best known as the editor of *Ms.* magazine and as one of the women's rights movement's most prominent proponents. She has campaigned vigorously for liberal Democratic party candidates, the United Farm Workers, black civil rights, the antiwar movement, and the ERA. A cofounder of *New York Magazine* in 1968, Steinem joined the women's movement later the same year and in 1971 helped organize the National Women's Political Caucus,

Gloria Steinem, the politically active editor of Ms. magazine, is one of the most influential figures of the modern feminist movement. As an organizer of the National Women's Political Caucus and the Women's Alliance for Action, Steinem has campaigned for the political, economic, and sexual liberation of women from traditional roles and restrictions.

on whose behalf she has served as persuasive speaker. In 1972 she founded *Ms.* magazine, which under her guidance became the country's most widely read feminist journal.

Steiner, Rudolf   [shtyn'-ur]

The Austrian philosopher, scientist, and artist Rudolf Steiner, b. Feb. 27, 1861, d. Mar. 30, 1925, was the originator of the social philosophy called anthroposophy. A Christianized version of THEOSOPHY, this doctrine asserts that humans possess a faculty of spiritual cognition, or pure thought, which functions independently of the senses. Anthroposophy strives for the most effective development of this inherent faculty. Steiner founded the Anthroposophical Society in 1912. He is also noted for the creation of educational facilities for handicapped and maladjusted children.

Bibliography: Hemleken, Johannes, *Rudolf Steiner: A Documentary Biography* (1975); Steiner, Rudolf, *An Autobiography,* trans. by Rita Stebbing, ed. by Paul M. Allen (1977).

Steinert, Otto   [shtyn'-urt]

The German photographer Otto Steinert, b. July 12, 1915, d. 1978, was the principal founder of Subjective Photography, an experimental movement of "humanized, individualized photography" whose international exhibitions (1951, 1954, and 1958) revitalized an art the Nazis had largely debased. Steinert claimed the movement was stylistically nonrestrictive, although it clearly favored formalistic, abstract work. After 1959 he taught photography in Essen.

Steinheim man   [shtyn'-hym]

The fossilized skull of Steinheim man—which in fact belonged to an adult female—was found (1933) in a gravel pit at Steinheim on the Murr River, north of Stuttgart, Germany. Animal bones found in the deposit with the skull suggest that the fossil dates from the Second or Third Interglacial Period (about 250,000 to 300,000 years ago). Although largely complete, the Steinheim skull had been severely distorted by overlying earth pressure, thus making detailed anatomical study very difficult. Some features of the skull suggest affinities with the later European NEANDERTHALERS (*Homo sapiens neanderthalensis*), whereas other features appear to relate the fossil to modern humans (*Homo sapiens sapiens*). Steinheim, along with the fossil skulls of FONTÉCHEVADE MAN in France and SWANSCOMBE MAN in England, has been considered representative of the early appearance of anatomically modern Europeans. Until better-preserved specimens from this time period are discovered, however, the position of the Steinheim specimen in human evolution will remain unclear.

ALAN MANN AND NANCY MINUGH

Bibliography: Constable, George, *The Neanderthals* (1973); Howells, William, *Evolution of the Genus Homo* (1973).

See also: PREHISTORIC HUMANS.

Steinkraus, Bill

William Clark Steinkraus, b. Cleveland, Ohio, Oct. 12, 1925, an American equestrian, began his career in horsemanship at the age of 10 and by 1940 had already won national titles. At the 1952 Olympic Games he was a member of the U.S. jumping team that won a bronze medal; in 1960 and 1972 Steinkraus helped win the Olympic silver medal in team competition. Riding the 10-year-old gelding Snowbound in the 1968 Olympics, Steinkraus became the first American to win an individual gold medal in the jumping competition. In 1970 he was named Rider of the Decade at the Washington, D.C., International Horse Show.

HOWARD LISS

Steinmetz, Charles Proteus   [styn'-mets]

Charles Proteus Steinmetz, b. Karl August Rudolf Steinmetz, Breslau, Germany, Apr. 9, 1865, d. Oct. 26, 1923, was a German-American electrical engineer who made important contributions to the understanding of basic electrical phenomena. He studied at the University of Breslau from 1883 to 1888, when he was forced to flee Germany because of his socialist activities, and immigrated to the United States in 1889.

Steinmetz immediately found employment as an electrical draftsman and electrical engineer in the Yonkers, N.Y., shop of Rudolf Eickemeyer. In addition to learning English, applying for citizenship, and joining professional societies, he carried out his first important research, discovering the law of hysteresis, which made it possible to calculate the loss of electric power due to magnetism. This discovery, in turn, made possible the design and construction of more efficient transformers, generators, and motors. In 1893 he joined the General Electric Company in Schenectady, N.Y., and was soon made consulting engineer, a position he held until his death.

Steinmetz had begun studies on alternating current (AC) in the 1890s when it was a little understood and complex subject. He continued his research at General Electric, patenting more than 100 inventions. Over the course of nearly 25 years he developed and refined a mathematical method for making AC calculations. By publishing and explaining his method in a series of papers, articles, and textbooks, Steinmetz made it possible for the average electrical engineer to understand and make use of alternating current, thereby revolutionizing electrical engineering. Steinmetz's investigations of "transient electrical phenomena" led to techniques for protecting high-power transmission lines from lightning, and in 1921 he produced artificial lightning in his laboratory.

Bibliography: Hammond, John E., *Charles Proteus Steinmetz* (1924); Lavine, Sigmund A., *Steinmetz: Maker of Lightning* (1955); Leonard, Jonathan N., *Loki: The Life of Charles Proteus Steinmetz* (1929).

Charles P. Steinmetz, an electrical engineer, came to the United States in 1889 after fleeing his native Germany for political reasons. Steinmetz's research led to the design of more-efficient electrical generating equipment, and he made basic contributions to the understanding of alternating current and the behavior of lightning.

stele [stee'-lee]

A stele is an upright stone slab or shaft that, in ancient times, served as a monument, memorial, or marker and was generally inscribed. In ancient Egypt and Greece the most common type was the funerary stele, sometimes rectangular or square in shape but more often with a rounded top, like the modern TOMBSTONE, which is a direct descendant of the Egyptian type. Such stelae were inscribed with the name and often the titles of the deceased as well as a funerary prayer. Commemorative stelae were sometimes erected by rulers to record their deeds in war or benefactions to a temple. Elsewhere in the ancient world stelae were erected by the Chinese and by the MAYA of pre-Columbian Mexico and Central America. Ancient Mayan stelae generally were placed before temples and carved with rulers' portraits and texts recording political and military exploits. ROBERT BIANCHI

Stella, Frank

Quathlamba (1964) is a canvas painted by the American abstract artist Frank Stella. The work demonstrates Stella's formal concerns with polychromy, marked shaping, and industrial precision, which relate him to constructivism and pop. (Private collection.)

A member of the New York school of abstractionists, the painter Frank Stella, b. Malden, Mass., May 12, 1936, attracted much critical attention during the 1960s and '70s, especially for the striped, repetitious "black paintings" (1960s) that were seen as a formalist attack on abstract expressionism.

Stella studied at Princeton University under William Seitz, whose teaching and critical thought were a strong influence on his work. During the 1960s he advanced from his minimal black canvases to richer, more colorful, metallically striped works and the Day-glo geometric figures in the "Protractor" series. During the 1970s he moved from stripes to angular overlays of planes, going so far as to construct his paintings of cardboard, wallboard, or metal—similar patterns were repeated in a series of each—with adjoining planes of color tilted slightly away from the picture plane. He has also explored the use of color in curved designs. Stella's intellectual and theoretical credentials are imposing, but some critics find his paintings rather dry. PHIL PATTON

Bibliography: Richardson, Brenda, and Ward, Mary M., Frank Stella: The Black Paintings (1976); Rubin, William S., Frank Stella (1970).

Stella, Joseph

In his views of New York City, the painter Joseph Stella, b. Naples, May 13, 1877, d. Nov. 5, 1946, dramatically reorganized its modern structures into transparent cubist-futurist planes and crystalline forms. His first important picture was Battle of Lights, Coney Island (1913–14; Yale University Art Gallery, New Haven, Conn.), a dynamic, explosive work. His best-known canvas, Brooklyn Bridge (1919–20; Yale University Art Gallery), was followed by other versions of the same subject and by a five-part series called New York Interpreted (1920–22; Newark Museum, Newark, N.J.). Stella's later paintings are eerie tropical landscapes filled with anthropomorphic shapes. HOWARD RODEE

Bibliography: Baur, John I. H., Joseph Stella (1971); Jaffe, Irma B., Joseph Stella (1970).

stellar evolution

Stellar evolution is the series of phases that a STAR passes through between its birth and its death. Because stars are large, hot masses of gas that emit huge amounts of energy into space and because stars have only a limited energy supply available, they must eventually exhaust their supply and burn out. Likewise, they must have originated at some time in the past.

Formation. The space between the stars contains gas and dust at a very low density. This INTERSTELLAR MATTER tends to gather into clouds, known as NEBULAE. Sometimes the density of a nebula becomes high enough so that its gravity is sufficient to cause contraction, leading to the formation of a star or a group of stars. A ball of the gas that is shrinking in size and will soon become a star is known as a protostar. Such protostars are believed to have been observed in some of the large interstellar clouds of the Milky Way. As a protostar slowly contracts its pressure and temperature increase. The temperature rise is due to the release of gravitational energy as the protostar gets smaller in size. Any hot object radiates energy, and the protostar eventually becomes hot enough to shine, although temperatures are not yet great enough to sustain nuclear reactions.

The pressure will build up enough to almost balance gravity. The radiation emitted by the protostar, however, drains energy from the object and inhibits the ability of the internal pressure (caused by the heat) to support the protostar against gravity. Thus the contraction and heating will slowly continue. The protostar is very much like a leaky balloon. The gas pressure is trying to support the balloon against the elastic force of the rubber. The leak of air is similar to the loss of radiation energy of the protostar; both reduce the pressure and cause the object to contract.

The temperature at the center of the protostar will finally become high enough to initiate nuclear reactions and the subsequent release of nuclear energy. Hydrogen is the most abundant element, and hydrogen-burning reactions, in which hydrogen is converted to helium with an accompanying release of large amounts of energy, are the first ones to become important.

When the nuclear energy released exactly balances the radiation energy lost into space, the protostar enters a state of energy balance. The pressure is maintained constant against gravity, and contraction ceases. It is as though air were being pumped into the leaky balloon, maintaining it against collapse. At this point of energy balance and pressure-gravity balance, the object becomes a true star.

Hydrogen-Burning. A star that is in balance and that is burning hydrogen in its core is called a MAIN SEQUENCE star. On a plot of luminosity versus temperature, known as a HERTZSPRUNG-RUSSELL DIAGRAM, main-sequence stars fall into a diagonal line. All stars begin their careers in the main-sequence phase. If a main-sequence star has a large mass, it will have a high surface temperature and will therefore be very luminous. If it has a small mass, it will be rather cool and faint. The Sun is a main-sequence star somewhat above average in mass, surface temperature, and radiant energy output.

When the hydrogen fuel in the core is used up, the star loses its main-sequence status. This can happen in less than a million years for the most luminous stars, while it will take many trillions of years for the faintest. The Sun has a main-sequence lifetime of about 10 billion years, half of which is still in the future.

Helium-Burning. When the core hydrogen has all been converted to helium through nuclear reactions, the nuclear energy release will stop. The star will fall out of energy balance, and the central portions will contract further under gravity and get still hotter. The end of nuclear reactions does not, however, stop a star from radiating energy into space; stars shine because they are hot, and the post-main-sequence star is still quite hot.

As the central parts of a star get hotter, nuclear reactions can be resumed. This can be in the form of hydrogen-burning in the regions just outside the helium core, and it can also be

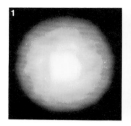

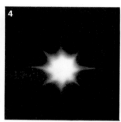

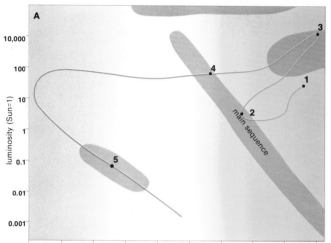

All stars go through a series of evolutionary stages. A contracting cloud of gas and dust first forms a protostar (1), which continues to condense until nuclear reactions begin in the core and a stable star (2) is born. Eventually, as a result of internal changes, the star swells (3) into a giant or supergiant. After an extended period of instability, during which the star varies (4) in size and brightness, all the nuclear fuel is consumed. The star then consolidates (5) to a dense white dwarf, neutron star, or black hole, depending on its final mass. The evolution of a star can be followed most easily on a Hertzsprung-Russell diagram (A). On this diagram the track (red line) of an evolving star with the mass of the Sun starts with a protostar (1) and moves downward as the condensing mass increases in temperature and decreases in luminosity, or brightness. Although the temperature continues to increase, the brightness becomes constant and the track moves to the left until it reaches (2) the main sequence. At this point the temperature becomes high enough to start nuclear reactions within the star's center. The contraction stops, and the star remains stable for billions of years. After a certain amount of fuel is consumed, internal changes cause the star to swell. The luminosity increases, and the track moves upward and to the right as the star expands into a cool, red giant (3). Further evolution involves a rise in temperature, and the track moves back toward the left and crosses (4) the main sequence again. The track then moves down and right when all reactions cease, and a hot, dim white dwarf (5) forms and cools.

in the form of helium-burning reactions in the core itself. Any nucleus can undergo nuclear reactions if conditions are violent enough. Hydrogen-burning takes place at temperatures of about 10 million K, but it requires a much higher temperature, about 100 million K, to ignite helium. Hydrogen-burning produces helium, while helium-burning produces carbon, oxygen, and other rather heavy nuclei. The heavier the nucleus, the higher the temperature required to bring it into nuclear reaction.

The later nuclear reactions are brought about by the further contraction and heating of the inner parts of the star, after the hydrogen has been exhausted in the core. During this phase the outer layers of the star actually expand and cool, and the luminosity can become quite high. The star no longer resembles its former self when it was on the main sequence. It is now what astronomers call a giant, or, if the luminosity is extremely great, a SUPERGIANT.

Old Age and Death. Each stage of nuclear reactions produces heavier nuclei. When the old nuclei are exhausted, further contraction and heating of the inner parts of a star will ignite the heavier particles. In this way one can imagine helium-burning followed by carbon-burning, then oxygen-burning, then silicon-burning, and so on. As the giant or supergiant star ages, it builds up layers of successively heavier and heavier elements in its interior, with the heaviest materials in the core and the lighter materials in hierarchical shells around the core.

This process cannot go on indefinitely. The nuclear energy sources can become depleted, or a star can become unstable and blow itself apart, perhaps leaving a remnant behind. Finally, the material can become so dense that it resists further contractions, a state known as degeneracy.

If a star contracts to the point at which its electrons are degenerate and it can contract no further, it can get no hotter, and no new nuclear reactions can be initiated. The star will then slowly radiate away what heat energy it has available and will end its life as a cold, dark, degenerate body. Stars of this type exist and are known as WHITE DWARFS. The white dwarfs actually observed have not yet cooled to the point at which they would be dark and known as BLACK DWARFS,

which, of course, cannot be detected. The densities needed to produce electron degeneracy in stars are quite large. White dwarfs themselves have densities that are typically tons per cubic centimeter.

The electrons in a star cannot become degenerate if the star has a mass greater than about 1.4 times the mass of the Sun. This mass, known as the CHANDRASEKHAR LIMIT, is an upper limit for the mass of a white dwarf. Stars with masses greater than this limit may undergo violent explosions that eject much of their material into space. These explosions are called SUPERNOVAE.

The details of how a star becomes unstable and explodes as a supernova are not known. The core of the star apparently collapses with violence, driving off the outer layers and breaking down the core particles into neutrons. In several cases the remnants of supernova explosions have been detected. They are found to be NEUTRON STARS, composed of degenerate neutrons. Rotating neutron stars have been observed and are called PULSARS.

The neutron star, being degenerate, cannot contract further. Like a white dwarf, it will radiate away its excess energy and end its life as a cold, dark body. Neutrons are much more difficult to make degenerate than electrons, and neutron stars have densities that are billions of times greater even than those of white dwarfs. A neutron star is only a few kilometers in size, even though it may contain as much mass as the Sun.

There is a maximum mass for a neutron star, as for white dwarfs. If a star never sheds enough mass for either its electrons or its neutrons to become degenerate, there is nothing to stop continued contraction when the nuclear sources have been completely used up. The star will keep getting smaller until its entire mass is squeezed into such a tiny volume that it becomes an object known as a BLACK HOLE. A black hole has such enormous surface gravity that nothing, including light itself, can escape it. Thus a black hole cannot be directly observed.

A black hole is so completely wrapped up in itself that the only way it can communicate with the rest of the universe is through the force of gravity. The existence of black holes is still uncertain, but some objects, such as the X-ray source known as Cygnus X-1, have properties that are suggestive of black holes.   THOMAS L. SWIHART

Bibliography: Aller, L. H., *Atoms, Stars and Nebulae*, 2d ed. (1971); Clark, David H., *The Historical Supernovae* (1977); Meadows, A. J., *Stellar Evolution*, 2d ed. (1978); Page, Thornton and Lou W., eds., *The Evolution of Stars* (1968); Swihart, Thomas L., *Journey through the Universe* (1978).

stellar spectrum

A stellar spectrum is the elongated band of light that results when the light from a STAR is spread out into its constituent wavelengths. A spectrograph, which contains a prism or diffraction grating, is attached to the telescope to produce the spectrum, which is often recorded on a photographic plate. Stellar spectra reveal the temperature and pressure of the star's atmosphere, the velocity of the star in the line of sight as determined from the Doppler effect, whether the star is a member of a close binary system, the chemical composition of the star, the existence of large-scale motions in the atmosphere, and the presence or absence of a magnetic field.

Most stars show spectra consisting of an underlying continuum of emitted light upon which are superimposed dark lines characteristic of the chemical elements of which the star is composed. These lines, commonly called FRAUNHOFER LINES, are caused by the absorption of light by the star's atmosphere. Some stars with extended envelopes show emission lines whose strength is often variable. Because of selective absorption by water vapor and ozone in the Earth's atmosphere, only the region of the spectrum between 290 nm (near ultraviolet) to about 1 micron (near infrared) can be observed from Earth. The ultraviolet spectrum below 290 nm is observed by rockets and satellites above the Earth's atmosphere. The far infrared can be observed with the aid of detectors flown in balloons above the water-vapor-bearing part of the atmosphere.

The continuous absorption that lowers the transparency of a stellar atmosphere is caused by the photoionization of hydrogen atoms (primarily from excited levels) and the photodissociation of the negative hydrogen ion. A spectral line is produced when an electron jumps from one discrete energy level of an atom to another. When an atom completely loses an electron, however, it may absorb light of any frequency

greater than the minimum frequency required to separate the electron (ionization energy). The solar atmosphere is cool enough for a hydrogen atom to acquire an extra electron and form a negative hydrogen ion. Light of all wavelengths less than about 1.2 microns suffices to detach this electron, thereby causing continuous absorption. Radiation in a spectrum line originates only from the uppermost, coolest layers of the star's atmosphere, while radiation in the nearby continuum originates from much deeper and hotter layers. For this reason the lines appear dark against a continuous background. A star may have a vast tenuous envelope, which by itself would give a bright-line spectrum. When this spectrum is superposed on that of the star, some of these bright lines may fill in the dark lines of the stellar spectrum. This occurs in novae.   LAWRENCE H. ALLER

Bibliography: Abell, George O., *Exploration of the Universe*, 3d ed. (1975); Aller, Lawrence H., *Atoms, Stars and Nebulae*, 2d ed. (1971).

Stendahl, Krister   [shten'-dahl]

Krister Stendahl, b. Stockholm, Apr. 21, 1921, is a biblical scholar who has taught at Harvard Divinity School since 1954. Educated at the University of Uppsala, he served as a minister of the Lutheran Church of Sweden before taking a position at Harvard. Since 1968 he has served as dean of the Divinity School. Stendahl's writings include *The School of Saint Matthew and Its Use of the Old Testament* (1954) and two texts on the Bible that he edited: *The Scrolls and the New Testament* (1957) and *Immortality and Resurrection: Four Essays* (1965).

Stendhal   [stan-dahl']

Stendhal was the pen name of the French novelist Henri Marie Beyle, b. Jan. 23, 1783, d. Mar. 23, 1842. Largely ignored during his lifetime by readers and critics alike, he has long since been recognized as a great master among psychological novelists. An extraordinary mixture of historical settings, autobiographical analyses, and psychological subtlety, his novels depict the intellectual and moral climate of France during the period of disillusionment following the battle of Waterloo.

The son of a well-to-do Grenoble lawyer, Stendhal lost his mother, to whom he was devoted, when he was 7. He grew up resenting his doctrinaire, unimaginative father and despising his native city. His maternal grandfather, a doctor, became his intellectual mentor, training him in 18th-century ra-

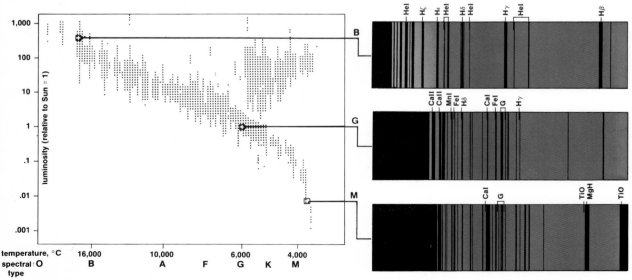

In the well-known Hertzsprung-Russell diagram the intrinsic luminosity, or brightness, of a star is plotted against its surface temperature, spectral type, or color index—three quantities that are directly correlated. Both are revealed by the number and positions of absorption lines present in the star's spectrum. Thus the spectrum of an M-type star (M) with a temperature of about 3,500° C (6,300° F) is characterized by many strong lines of neutral metals, such as calcium (CaI), and by absorption bands of titanium oxide (TiO) and magnesium hydride (MgH). In G-type stars (G) the strong lines of ionized calcium (CaII) indicate a temperature of about 6,000° C (11,000° F). The spectra of B-type stars (B) at temperatures about 16,000° C (29,000° F) show strong neutral-helium (HeI) lines.

Stendhal, born Henri Marie Beyle, was a master of the French psychological novel. Best known for The Red and the Black *(1830) and* The Charterhouse of Parma *(1839), Stendhal also wrote several travel books, biographies of musicians, and a treatise on the nature of love.*

tionalism, while his aunt was his emotional guide, serving as an exemplar of the imaginative and spontaneous nature with which he would later endow his heroines.

In 1799, Stendhal was accepted by the Polytechnic Institute in Paris, but he dreamed of becoming a playwright instead of attending classes. An influential Parisian cousin obtained a commission for him in Napoleon's army in Italy, which introduced him to the land he was later to endow with mythic status. His administrative career under Napoleon provided him with first-hand knowledge of the occupation of Italy, the Prussian campaigns, and the burning of Moscow. Upon the collapse of the Empire, Stendhal decided to expatriate himself to Milan, where he remained from 1814 until he was obliged to leave in 1821 by the Austrian government, then reoccupying northern Italy.

Stendhal's return to Paris had been preceded by three works that established him as a man of letters: *The Lives of Haydn, Mozart, and Metastasio* (1814; Eng. trans., 1972), *Histoire de la peinture en Italie* (History of Italian Painting, 1817), and *Rome, Naples, and Florence* (1817; Eng. trans., 1959). Although the first two were largely plagiarized and the third was a seemingly superficial travel book, all three reveal an originality of mind. Stendhal's first autobiographical work, *On Love* (1822; Eng. trans., 1914)—masquerading as a treatise on love—analyzes the development of his unrequited passion for a Milanese lady. His *Life of Rossini* (1823; Eng. trans., 1956), although not the most reliable of biographies, remains the most perceptive to date.

Stendhal was one of the first to develop the cult of the self in literature. His *Promenades dans Rome* (Promenades in Rome, 1829) and *Memoirs of a Tourist* (1838; Eng. trans., 1962) established tourism not as the mere discovery of unfamiliar places but as the discovery of the self. The word *egotism*, launched in his *Memoirs of an Egotist* (1892; Eng. trans., 1949), denotes Stendhal's modern concept of self-analysis, rather than a portrayal of an idealized self. His approach to autobiography was not to reconstruct the past through a systematic recalling of episodes, but to relive the sensations evoked by memory, reacting to them while writing as though he were the reader of his own works.

Stendhal was among the first to recognize the formative influence of childhood on adult life. With him the past is not a single entity; it is layered, random, irrational. Stendhal's fiction recalls his characteristic contradictions: he uses the political and social history of his time to arrive at an antihistorical view that sees truth in sensations, not facts.

Best known for two novels, *The Red and the Black* (1830; Eng. trans., 1898) and *The Charterhouse of Parma* (1839; Eng. trans., 1925), Stendhal wrote an earlier novel, *Armance* (1827; Eng. trans., 1928), that already suggested one of the themes that was to remain his constant preoccupation: the oppressive conformism of Restoration society. The individual against society is the major theme of *The Red and the Black,* whose title refers to the choices open to the hero: army or church, Jacobinism or reaction, courage or hypocrisy. *The Charterhouse of Parma* explores this theme again, but in the more exuberant atmosphere of fanciful history borrowed from the

Italian Renaissance and the Napoleonic era, which confers upon the characters the dynamism of epic heroes.

Stendhal returned to government service after the revolution of July 1830, being appointed to minor consular positions, first at Trieste, then at Civitavecchia, the port of Rome. He died in Paris following an apoplectic seizure.

BETH ARCHER BROMBERT

Bibliography: Alter, Robert, and Cosman, Carol, *A Lion for Love: A Critical Biography of Stendhal* (1979); Brombert, Victor, *Stendhal: Fiction and the Themes of Freedom* (1968) and, as ed., *Stendhal: A Collection of Critical Essays* (1962); Caraccio, Armand, *Stendhal,* trans. by Dolores Bagley (1965); Gutwirth, Marcel, *Stendhal* (1971); Hemmings, Frederick W., *Stendhal: A Story of His Novels* (1964); May, Gita, *Stendhal and the Age of Napoleon: An Interpretive Biography* (1977).

Stengel, Casey [steng'-gul]

Charles Dillon "The Old Professor" Stengel, b. Kansas City, Mo., July 30, 1890, d. Sept. 29, 1975, was an American professional baseball player and later a manager. Known as "Casey" Stengel, he compiled a .284 career batting average during his 14 years as a player. It was as a manager, however, that Stengel gained acclaim. Stengel managed 4 teams over the course of 25 years, and with the New York Yankees, from 1949 to 1960, he won 10 pennants and 7 World Series titles. Stengel was dismissed from the Yankees after the 1960 season but was hired by the newly founded New York Mets. Despite a losing record there, Stengel delighted the fans and the press with his antics and colorful personality.

Bibliography: Allen, Maury, *You Could Look It UP: The Life of Casey Stengel* (1979); Durso, Joseph, *Casey: The Life and Legend of Charles Dillon Stengel* (1967).

Steno, Nicolaus [stee'-noh]

Nicolaus Steno, a pseudonym of Niels Stensen, b. Jan. 10, 1638, d. Dec. 6, 1686, was a Danish anatomist and geologist who demonstrated that geological chronology and history can be read in the rock layers or strata of the Earth. Steno studied at the universities of Copenhagen, Amsterdam, and Leiden, from which he received his M.D. in 1664. For the next 8 years he pursued his studies of anatomy in various posts in France and Italy. Skilled in dissection and the author of 5 books on anatomy, he explained the function of ovaries and discovered the excretory duct of the parotid gland and its function in producing saliva. He demonstrated that muscles are made up of fibrils and that the heart is primarily a muscle.

While serving as house physician to Grand Duke Ferdinand II of Tuscany, Steno became interested in geology. He showed that certain fossils were teeth of ancient sharks, thus recognizing the organic origin of fossils. Steno eventually formulated many basic principles of modern geology, including the formation, displacement, destruction, and layering of sedimentary rocks. A convert to Roman Catholicism from Lutheranism, Steno was ordained a priest in 1675 and became a bishop in 1688, giving up his scientific career.

ANNE MILLBROOKE

Bibliography: Cioni, Raffaello, *Niels Stensen, Scientist-Bishop,* trans. by Genevieve Camera (1962); Steno, Nicolaus, *Steno: Geological Papers,* ed. by Gustav Scherz, trans. by Alex Pollock (1969); Wendt, Herbert, *Before the Deluge,* trans. by Richard and Clara Winston (1968).

stenography: see SHORTHAND.

stentor [sten'-tohr]

Stentor is a genus of ciliated, trumpet-shaped protozoa in the family Stentoridae. The various species are characterized by rows of cilia spiraling toward the mouth, creating water currents that bring food into the oral region. Stentors are free-swimming, attached, or tube-dwelling. *S. coeruleus* is characterized by a dark blue pigment called stentorin found in interstriation granules. The green stentor, *S. polymorphus,* takes its color from symbiotic algae (Zoochlorellae).

J. FORBES MCCLELLAN

Stephen, Saint

Originally one of the seven deacons or "servers" chosen to assist the Apostles, Stephen, d. AD c.36, became an important preacher and the first Christian martyr. According to Acts 6-7, Stephen's charge before the Sanhedrin that the Jews had persistently disobeyed God so enraged his Jewish audience that they stoned him to death. Parallels drawn with the crucifixion of Jesus make the story of Stephen's death important in Christian tradition. Feast day: Dec. 27 (East); Dec. 26 (West).

Bibliography: Simon, Marcel, *St. Stephen and the Hellenists in the Primitive Church* (1958).

Stephen, George

Sir George Stephen, b. Scotland, June 5, 1829, d. Nov. 29, 1921, was a banker and railroad executive who is best known for his role in the construction of the Canadian Pacific Railway, serving as its first president (1881-88). Stephen emigrated (1850) to Montreal and entered a Canadian woolen manufacturing company as a clerk, acquiring majority control of it within 10 years. In 1873 he was elected a director of the Bank of Montreal and served as its president (1876-81). In 1879, Stephen also was elected president of the St. Paul, Minneapolis, and Manitoba Railway. He became 1st Baron Mount Stephen in 1886 and lived in Great Britain after 1898.

Bibliography: Gilbert, Heather, *The Life of Lord Mount Stephen,* 2 vols. (1965, 1977).

Stephen, Sir Leslie

The eminent English man of letters Sir Leslie Stephen, b. Nov. 28, 1832, d. Feb. 22, 1904, is best known as the first editor (1885-91) of the *Dictionary of National Biography,* a valuable reference work still used by scholars. Stephen contributed articles on many subjects to the leading periodicals of his time and was editor (1871-82) of the influential *Cornhill Magazine.* Also a noted critic of the novel and a biographer of many English authors, he wrote works that include *The History of English Thought in the Eighteenth Century* (1876) and *The English Utilitarians* (1900). Stephen was the father of the novelist Virginia Woolf.

Bibliography: Annan, Noel, *Leslie Stephen: His Thought and Character in Relation to His Time,* ed. by Walter Metzger (1951; repr. 1976); Zink, David D., *Leslie Stephen* (1972).

Stephen Báthory, King of Poland: see BÁTHORY (family).

Stephen Dušan, King of Serbia [doo'-shahn]

Stephen Dušan, or Stephen Uroš IV, b. 1308, d. Dec. 20, 1355, who reigned (1331-55) as king of Serbia after deposing his father, Stephen Uroš III (r. 1322-31), brought Serbia to its height of power through his conquests. He seized part of western Macedonia from the Byzantine Empire in 1334 and in 1343 conquered Albania and more of Macedonia. Stephen had himself crowned emperor of the Serbs and Greeks in 1346. He captured (1348) Epirus and Thessaly and promulgated (1349, 1354) a law code. His empire collapsed, however, under his son and successor, Stephen Uroš V (1355-71).

K. M. SMOGORZEWSKI

Stephen, King of England

Stephen, b. c.1097, d. Oct. 25, 1154, was king of England from 1135 to 1154. The son of Count Stephen of Blois and Chartres and Adela (daughter of King WILLIAM I of England), he was elected king on Dec. 22, 1135, succeeding his uncle HENRY I despite his earlier sworn fealty to MATILDA, Henry's daughter, as Henry's successor. His support came from the barons, who opposed Matilda and her bellicose husband, Geoffrey of Anjou. Pleasant and congenial, Stephen lacked the ruthless determination requisite in a medieval king.

From 1135 to 1138 he seemed to establish himself with some success, showing understanding and concern for his barons and establishing good relations with the church. Nevertheless, civil war broke out (1138) between Stephen and Matilda, who was supported by the powerful earl of Gloucester, her half brother. Stephen was taken prisoner in 1141, and Matilda reigned briefly as "Lady of the English." After 6 months, however, she was forced to release Stephen, who resumed the throne. Never a competent leader, Stephen was not able to reestablish his authority, and during the next few years England was in virtual anarchy. The civil war fizzled out rather than ended. Geoffrey died in 1147 and Matilda left England in 1148, thereby initiating a period of relative calm that lasted until Stephen's death. He was succeeded by HENRY II, Matilda's son. Although some recent historians have judged him less harshly, Stephen's contemporaries saw him as a reckless ruler in whose time there was only violence, disorder, and turbulence—in a word, anarchy.

JAMES W. ALEXANDER

Bibliography: Appleby, J. T., *The Troubled Reign of King Stephen* (1969); Cronne, Henry A., *The Reign of Stephen, 1135-54; Anarchy in England* (1970); Davis, R. H. C., *King Stephen* (1967).

Stephen the Great, Prince of Moldavia

Stephen the Great, b. c.1435, d. July 2, 1504, prince of Moldavia (1457-1504), struggled to maintain his independence from the Ottoman Turks. On Jan. 10, 1475, he inflicted a crushing defeat on the Turks near Vaslui, for which Pope Sixtus IV granted him the title Athlete of Christ. Failing to obtain Polish and Hungarian support against the continuing Turkish threat, Stephen eventually agreed to the payment of an annual tribute in exchange for continuing Moldavian independence.

K. M. SMOGORZEWSKI

Stephen I, King of Hungary (Saint Stephen)

Stephen I, or Saint Stephen, b. c.975, d. Aug. 15, 1038, was the first king of Hungary. Son of the supreme Magyar prince Geza, whom he succeeded in 997, Stephen was raised as a Christian. He suppressed a pagan revolt in 998 and in 1000 or 1001 was crowned king with the approval of Pope Sylvester II. His crown became an important national symbol for Hungarians. Stephen established church institutions and replaced tribal land systems with individual proprietorship. He was succeeded on his death by Peter, his nephew. Canonized in 1083, Stephen is Hungary's principal national hero. Feast day: Aug. 16 (formerly Sept. 2; Aug. 20 in Hungary).

Stephens, Alexander Hamilton

The American statesman Alexander Hamilton Stephens, b. Wilkes (now Taliaferro) County, Ga., Feb. 11, 1812, d. Mar. 4, 1883, was vice-president (1861-65) of the Confederate States of America, U.S. representative (1843-59, 1873-82) from Georgia, and governor (1882-83) of Georgia. He was a lawyer and a member (1836-42) of the Georgia legislature and later became a leading Southern Whig in Congress. Stephens supported the COMPROMISE OF 1850 and was instrumental in winning Southern support for it. He became a Democrat in 1852. During the secession crisis of 1860-61, Stephens opposed immediate secession but swung behind his state when Georgia left the Union in January 1861.

Stephens successfully urged adoption of a Confederate constitution similar to that of the United States. A rigid advocate of individual and state rights, he assailed President Jefferson Davis for backing conscription, martial law, and suspension of habeas corpus. His attacks did much to undermine Southern morale. At the end of the Civil War he was jailed for 5 months. In *A Constitutional View of the Late War Between the States* (2 vols., 1867 and 1870), Stephens defended the Southern state-rights viewpoint.

RICHARD M. McMURRY

Bibliography: Von Abele, Rudolph R., *Alexander H. Stephens: A Biography* (1946; repr. 1972).

Stephens, James

An Irish poet and novelist whose work blends fantasy and reality, James Stephens, b. Feb. 2, 1882, d. Dec. 26, 1950, won lasting fame with his allegorical novel *The Crock of Gold* (1912), later the basis for the American musical *Finian's Rainbow* (1947). The son of poor parents, he worked as a clerk until he received the assistance of the poet George Russell. After publishing his first collection of poems, *Insurrections* (1909), he helped found (1911) the *Irish Review* and experienced his first success with the novel *The Charwoman's Daughter* (1911), which together with *The Crock of Gold* and a later novel, *Deirdre* (1923), represent his best work. A friend of James Joyce, Stephens was also an ardent nationalist.

ROBIN BUSS

Bibliography: Bramsback, Birgit, *James Stephens: A Literary and Bibliographic Study* (1959); Martin, Augustine, *James Stephens: A Critical Study* (1977).

Stephens, John Lloyd

John Lloyd Stephens, b. Nov. 25, 1805, d. Oct. 12, 1852, was an American traveler and explorer who discovered the Mayan city of COPÁN. With Frederick CATHERWOOD, an English artist and authority on architecture, he investigated the pre-Columbian civilizations of Central America, exploring the ruins of Palenque and locating Copán. On his return Stephens published *Incidents of Travel in Central America, Chiapas, and Yucatan* (1841), illustrated by Catherwood. His numerous other travels through Central America, Europe, and the Middle East were recorded in several similar studies, including *Incidents of Travel in Egypt, Arabia Petraea, and the Holy Land* (1837) and *Incidents of Travel in Greece, Turkey, Russia, and Poland* (1838).

Bibliography: Ceram, C. W., ed., *Hands on the Past: Pioneer Archaeologists Tell Their Own Story* (1966); Von Hagen, Victor, *Search for the Maya* (1973).

Stephenson, George and Robert

George Stephenson, b. June 9, 1781, d. Aug. 12, 1848, and his son Robert Stephenson, b. Oct. 16, 1803, d. Oct. 12, 1859, were an English team of engineers and inventors who made major contributions to the first English locomotives and railroads (see RAILROAD).

George Stephenson, extremely poor as a young man, worked in local collieries and taught himself to read and write in his spare time. He became (1812) a colliery engine builder, and in 1814 he built his first locomotive. When the Stockton and Darlington Railway was projected, George Stephenson was retained as company engineer. He convinced the owners to use steam motive power and built the line's first locomotive, the *Locomotion*. In 1825, Stephenson moved to the Liverpool and Manchester Railway. He and his son Robert built (1829) the *Rocket*, which won the competition held to design a suitable steam locomotive for that railroad.

Robert Stephenson helped his father plan and build other railroads in England and on the Continent in the 1820s, and during the 1830s he was responsible for many improvements

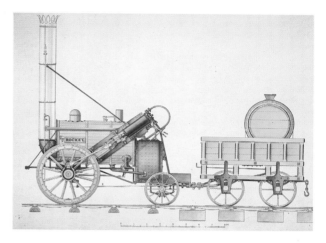

The Rocket, built by George Stephenson and his son Robert in 1826, won a locomotive-design competition. Although it moved at a maximum speed of no more than 38 km/h (24 mph), the Rocket had design features, such as a tubular boiler, that became standard.

in locomotive design. He later became the builder of tubular girder railway bridges in England, Europe, and Canada.

JOHN F. STOVER

Bibliography: Davies, Hunter, *George Stephenson* (1977); Robbins, R. M., *George and Robert Stephenson* (1966); Rolt, Lionel T., *George and Robert Stephenson: The Railway Revolution* (1960; repr. 1977).

steppe art

Steppe art comprises the artistic traditions of the nomads who inhabited (7th–4th century BC) the prairies, or steppes, extending from eastern Europe to Siberia. Although the origins of steppe art are still unclear, some elements have been traced back to tribes who lived in Siberia during the 3d millennium BC. By the 7th century BC various steppe tribes had developed rich cultures that differed from tribe to tribe. All steppe art, however, had certain features in common. Because nomads had to carry their wealth with them, their artists concentrated almost exclusively on decorating useful objects and objects that could be worn by the owner or were easily portable, such as jewelry, weapons, cups, and bowls. Animals were the most common motif, and the so-called animal style was probably native to steppe art. Finally, the art of most steppe tribes had foreign elements of those higher civi-

This Greco-Scythian gold stag, inscribed in Greek, reflects the technical refinement of Scythian metalwork. The Scythians, who inhabited (c.8th–4th century BC) the southern Russian steppes, produced significant pieces of steppe art. (Hermitage, Leningrad.)

George Stephenson was an English engineer who helped to develop the steam locomotive for railroad travel in the early decades of the 19th century. He became an engineering consultant for several railroad companies, designing and building railways and bridges.

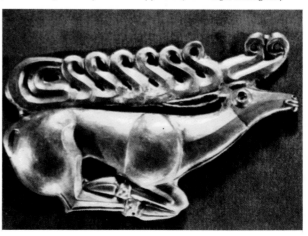

These bronzes (c.400–300 BC) from the Ordos region of northern China exemplify the sculpture of the eastern steppe culture. Although influenced by Chinese art, the figures reveal the vitality and directness of the nomadic animal style. (Musée Cernuschi, Paris.)

achieved by Scythian metal workers, who probably profited from knowledge of Greek metalwork. East of the Scythian domains, nomadic art takes on a more primitive appearance and reflects the influence of Persian or Chinese, rather than Greek, culture. The finds from the Golden Kurgans in the Chiliktin valley of Kazakhstan include small gold-foil feline animals in coiled pose, stags, boars, and abbreviated vultures—all of which were used to decorate leather quivers. Fifth-century BC objects excavated at PAZYRYK and other sites in the Altai Mountains of Siberia are decorated in a simplistic version of the animal style that extends even to the tattoo preserved on the skin of one of the nomadic chiefs.

The most mysterious collection of steppe art is the so-called treasure of Peter the Great, a heterogeneous collection of gold objects that probably was taken from graves somewhere in central Asia or Siberia. These pieces—which include immense gold belt-buckles decorated with fighting animals and gold plaques for horse trappings that swarm with animal figures and colored inlays—provide vivid testimony to the nomadic way of life that flourished on the steppes in the 1st millennium BC.   ANN FARKAS

Bibliography: Artamonov, M. I., *The Splendor of Scythian Art*, trans. by V. R. Kupriyanova (1969); Bunker, Emma, Chatwin, C. Bruce, and Farkas, Ann, *"Animal Style": Art from East to West* (1970); Jettmar, Karl, *Art of the Steppes* (1967); Metropolitan Museum of Art, *From the Lands of the Scythians* (1975).

lizations, such as Persia, Greece, and China, with whom the nomads came into contact.

The most famous steppe art was that of the SCYTHIANS, who held sway (c.8th–4th century BC) over the steppes of what is now southern Russia. Judging from the large number of gold objects discovered in Scythian graves, this tribe seems to have been very wealthy. The great gold stag discovered as part of a shield decoration from Kostromskaya Kurgan, a burial mound in the northwestern Caucasus (c.600 BC; Hermitage Museum, Leningrad), reflects the high level of artisanship

steppe life

Steppe generally refers to arid, temperate GRASSLANDS, often devoid of trees, of comparable vegetation, climate, soils, and topography to those of central Eurasia, although the term is often applied to grasslands of the Southern Hemisphere as well. The various local names include prairies (North America), pampas (South America), and veld (South Africa). In addition to being suited to a climate with distinct wet and dry seasons and long droughts, plant and animal life must be

adapted to periodic, extensive fires and a flat-to-rolling ter-rain. These physical characteristics are common to all grass-lands, and they greatly affect the diversity and distribution of the biota.

Steppe grasses, on which steppe life is totally dependent, dominate the vegetation throughout, except in areas with wa-ter near or at the surface. Large numbers of showy flowers of the sunflower, mint, and bean families are intermingled with the grasses in the moister portions of the grasslands. With in-creasing aridity plant diversity declines and grass domination is even more obvious. The narrow leaves, extensive root sys-tems, and heights attained by grasses are some features that make them well adapted to arid climates and habitats ex-posed to fire, drying winds, high light intensity, and high po-tential for evaporation and transpiration.

The vast steppes of Eurasia are dominated by several grass species, depending on local and regional conditions. Major dominants are feather grass (needlegrass), bromegrass, fescue, bluegrass (meadow grass), and wheatgrass. Several species of feather grass characterize the southern parts of Asia, where drought resistance allows them to dominate large areas and greatly affect the distribution of other plants and the grazing animals.

Relatives of feather grass are common in the steppe region of Argentina (pampas). The life form, however, is quite differ-ent in the pampas as the grasses there form tall, solitary bunches called tussocks. Because they have a low grazing value for domesticated animals, they have largely been re-placed by more palatable cultivated grasses. Domesticated plants and European animals have largely superseded the original grassland life of the pampas.

North American grasslands have grasses related to those of Eurasia, but the dominating ones are often warm-season grasses such as bluestems, switchgrass, and Indian grass where rainfall is higher (prairies). As more arid conditions prevail (the plains), shorter plants such as grama grasses and buffalo grass provide the major food for grazing animals, as plant diversity declines and cacti become more prevalent.

Throughout the world's steppes, salt accumulation on the soil surface results in a drastic shift in vegetation. Salts accu-mulate as rodents bring soil with high salt concentration to the surface, as salty water evaporates from the soil, and as shallow lakes dry. Plants that are tolerant of these salt con-centrations are limited in number. Salt grass and plants of the goosefoot family are common indicator species of these sa-line environments.

A remarkable array of herbivorous mammals inhabits the steppes. In Eurasia, for example, big, grazing ungulates (hoofed animals) such as wild horses, asses, and antelopes live in herds of long-range wanderers following rainfall and tender grass. The saiga antelope is one of the most important grazers of the Eurasian steppes. During drought and hard winters, they wander endlessly, searching desperately for food and water, and large numbers die.

Far greater in number but smaller in size are the many ro-dent species. Whereas the ungulates are readily seen, the chief consumers of the grass vegetation are the large colonies of rodents such as pocket gophers, rabbits, marmots, voles, and mice. A rodent colony may eat 1,000 times more food than antelopes in a given area. In addition to this herbivorous role, the rodents, by burrowing, contribute greatly to soil de-velopment and fertility and to biological activity in soils.

Bird life on the steppes is diverse and unusual. Some spe-cies, such as the bustards, demoiselle crane, sand grouses, and rose-colored starling of Eurasia, move in bands and live and breed in large groups. The rose-colored starling nests in colonies of thousands of breeding pairs. Bustards are large birds that depend more on swift movement on the ground than in the air. Individuals measuring up to 1 m (40 in) in height and weighing more than 10 kg (22 lb) move as bands on an endless search for seed, insects, and small inverte-brates.

Generally, steppe birds are insect or grain eaters, and many species have expanded in numbers and range with the in-tense cultivation of cereal crops. Others have had their num-bers reduced because their breeding and nesting sites have been eliminated by conversion of steppe to cultivated land.

The replacement of native herbivores with competing do-mestic sheep, goats, and cattle—and human occupation—has placed considerable survival pressure on many of the large grazers in all steppe regions. Although most wild ass species and the saiga antelope are common on the Asian steppe, other species such as Przewalski's horse and the wild camel have become extremely rare; the horse may now survive only in zoos. In North America the bison virtually became extinct in the 19th century because of overkill and habitat loss. It ex-ists today only in managed herds as domesticated cattle and sheep have replaced it in the grasslands. The spectacular, swift pronghorn of these grasslands survive because their feeding habits do not overlap with the introduced cattle and sheep.

Overgrazing by livestock, expansion of the human popula-tion, and intense cultivation have also changed the plant composition of these areas. Lower soil fertility and the elimi-nation of palatable species have led to the spread of plants that are unpalatable to both native and introduced grazers.

WILLIAM H. MARTIN

Bibliography: Allen, Durwood L., *The Life of the Prairies and Plains* (1967); Costello, David F., *The Prairie World* (1969); McNeill, William H., *Europe's Steppe Frontier, 1500–1800* (1964).

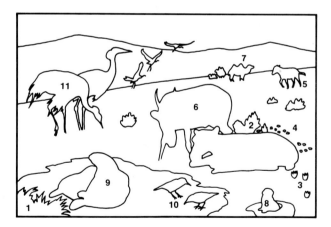

Steppes are immense, treeless plains of Eurasia in which hardy grasses are the predominant form of plant life. The Southernmost steppes are known as sage-and-grass, or nontillable, steppes, where the prevailing turf grasses include various species of bluegrass, Poa (1). Bluegrass, which is nutritious and well adapted to arid climates, is an essential forage plant for much of the steppes' animal life. Other vegetation includes wormwood, Artemisia (2), shrubs that thrive in poor, dry soil; and the colorful wild tulips, Tulipa (3), and peonies, Paeonia (4), which bloom seasonally. Large herds of Asian wild asses, Equus hemionus (5), and antelopes such as the saiga, Saiga tatarica (6), roam continuously in search of food and water as available sources are depleted. A few wild camels, Camelus bactrianus (7), are also found. Large colonies of rodents, such as susliks, Spermophilus litellus (8), and marmots, Marmota marmota (9), are also supported by the vegetation. Birds common to the steppes include the rose-colored starling, Pastor roseus (10), which breeds in large colonies once a year when migratory locusts appear; and the demoiselle crane, Anthropoides virgo (11), which builds its nest on the ground.

Steppenwolf [step'-en-wulf]

A controversial novel by Hermann HESSE, *Steppenwolf* (1927) has been internationally praised as experimentally daring in form and subject matter. It concerns a "lone wolf"—Steppen-wolf—named Harry Haller who feels cut off from society and whose existence is seen as a threat to society's beliefs. De-picting Haller's progress from despair over his sense of isola-tion to a reconciliation with life, the novel is original in form and makes innovative use of fantasy and poetic prose.

R. M. FORD

stereochemistry

Stereochemistry is the study of the spatial arrangement of atoms in molecules and the effect thereof on the bulk properties and reactions of chemical compounds. In chemistry, stereochemical principles have become useful tools for determining the structures of compounds, for synthesizing highly complex molecules, and for revealing the details of chemical and biochemical reaction pathways. Stereochemistry is a special concern in the areas of biochemistry, biophysics, and drug development as well. On a molecular level, nearly all biochemical processes involve the spatial recognition of one molecule by another, and such recognition serves as the means by which energy and information are transmitted and complex biological structures are built.

THE CONCEPT OF STEREOISOMERISM

As early as 1823, Friedrich Wohler and Justus Liebig recognized that two chemical compounds might have the same elemental composition yet differ in the order in which the atoms were linked together (see ISOMER). It was widely believed, until almost the end of the 1800s, that these criteria alone were enough to define completely a chemical compound. In 1848, however, the French scientist Louis Pasteur showed conclusively that two compounds could have the same order of linkage of individual atoms yet differ in certain of their physical and chemical properties. He laboriously obtained two forms of tartaric acid (a substance derived from wine) by handpicking differently shaped crystals from a mixture. These two forms, although identical in many respects, behaved differently toward POLARIZED LIGHT (see OPTICAL ACTIVITY), and only one of them could be used as a medium to grow molds. Arbitrarily, the molecule that rotates a beam of polarized light counterclockwise is termed *levorotatory* (L), and the one rotating light clockwise, *dextrorotatory* (D).

Tetrahedron. How the molecules of these two forms differed remained a mystery until, in 1874, Jacobus Hendricus van't Hoff and Joseph Achille le Bel independently proposed that compounds having the same linkages of atoms could still differ in their CONFIGURATIONS, or arrangements of atoms in three-dimensional space. Compounds that differ in this way are called stereoisomers. They viewed the CARBON atom as a tetrahedron, in which the four vertices correspond to four atoms or groups attached to the atom. The concept of a tetrahedral carbon atom served as a foundation for further developments in the field of stereochemistry.

Asymmetric Carbon Atom. If any two groups attached to a carbon are alike, such as the two hydrogens in propionic acid, a plane of symmetry can be seen to pass through the atom so that one side of the molecule is the mirror image of the other. If all four groups are different, as in lactic acid, no such symmetry exists, and the carbon atom may be said to be asymmetric. Atoms other than carbon may serve as asymmetric centers by meeting the same criteria.

Enantiomers. Van't Hoff recognized that the presence of an asymmetric center in a molecule would give rise to two isomeric structures called enantiomers, one of which is the exact mirror image of the other. Such a situation exists for optical

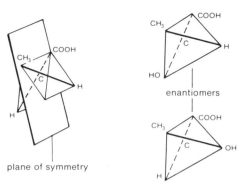

Propionic acid (left) *has a plane of symmetry that passes through the central carbon atom, methyl group (CH₃), and carboxyl group (COOH). In lactic acid* (right) *no such symmetry is present, and, as a consequence of the asymmetry, two different structures (isomers) exist. The two structures are mirror images of each other, or enantiomers.*

isomers of tartaric acid and of lactic acid as well. Optical isomers are distinct chemical compounds and cannot be reoriented to resemble one another; a molecule of this sort is often said to be chiral. The ultimate proof of chirality is found when the structure of an isometric compound cannot be superimposed upon its mirror image. One enantiomer always has the opposite effect upon polarized light as the other; a racemic, or equal, mixture of the two is therefore optically inactive and often behaves physically as a single substance.

Other Isomers. Molecules with more than one asymmetric center may differ in configuration at any or all of these centers, affording multiple isomers. Examples of this are the following sugars:

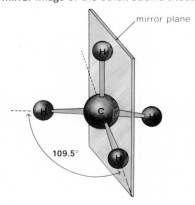

Diastereomers are isomers of this type that are not mirror images of each other. Van't Hoff also correctly predicted that the spatial arrangement of groups around a planar double bond could give rise to stereoisomers known as geometric isomers (see CIS-TRANS ISOMERISM).

Different spatial arrangements of a molecule that can be interconverted by rotation around single bonds are called conformational isomers, or conformers. The study of conformers represents the ultimate extension of stereochemistry because it deals most closely with the actual shapes of molecules. It provides a unique view of structure and bonding and allows prediction of the rates and products of reactions.

APPLICATIONS OF STEREOCHEMISTRY

Chemists use a variety of physical and chemical techniques, many of which are based on stereochemical principles, to establish the structures of previously unknown compounds. A common application of stereochemistry is the distinguishing of asymmetric from symmetric structures. If, for instance, a substance can be separated into a pair of enantiomers, the chirality of the molecule can be demonstrated; this evidence may confirm or exclude a tentative choice for structure of the compound. These methods were used extensively by Emil Fischer to determine (1891) the structure of glucose.

Many reactions are known that are capable of creating or modifying an asymmetric center or a double bond in a molecule; in such a process more than one stereoisomer of the

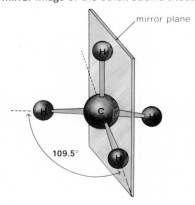

The tetrahedral arrangement of a carbon molecule forms the basis of concepts in the field of stereochemistry. The carbon atom (C) is situated in the center of the tetrahedron, and the four other molecules, in this case hydrogen (H), form angles of 109.5° to each other. The tetrahedron can be divided along a plane through the carbon atom and two other atoms.

product may be formed. This result poses a problem to synthetic chemists because usually only one stereoisomer is desired for manufacturing or research purposes. Unfortunately, stereoisomers are often difficult to separate because of their structural similarity, and even if such a separation can be achieved, little or none of the desired isomer may be formed. For these reasons, one of the chief goals of synthetic chemists is to develop reactions that, as far as possible, provide only one of the stereoisomers as product.

Reactions yielding a large excess of one stereoisomer over all others are termed *stereoselective;* those providing a single stereoisomer are termed *stereospecific.*

The synthesis of complex molecules possessing numerous asymmetric centers from simple, inexpensive starting materials requires careful control of stereochemistry at each stage of the synthesis. Not only is a large repertoire of stereoselective reactions necessary, but much ingenuity is also required in planning the order in which bonds are constructed. Maximum advantage must be taken of the existing stereochemical and conformational features of an intermediate structure to control the stereochemistry of the next reaction. The stereo-controlled synthesis of a complex molecule—for example, the antibiotic monensin, which has 17 asymmetric centers and 131,072 possible stereoisomers—represents a tremendous intellectual challenge.

The stereochemical course of a reaction, or the extent to which it is stereoselective and the ratios of isomers formed, may indicate what events take place during the reaction. Such information may be useful in improving the efficiency of the reaction or in the search for new types of reactions or chemical species. Chemists may learn from the outcome of the reaction how certain bonds are broken and formed or what kinds of intermediates are involved.   DAVID C. ROBERTS

Bibliography: Dale, Johannes, *Stereochemistry and Conformational Analysis* (1978); Gunstone, F. D., *Guidebook to Stereochemistry* (1975); Ingold, Christopher K., *Structure and Mechanism in Organic Chemistry,* 2d ed. (1969); Mislow, Kurt, *Introduction to Stereochemistry* (1965); Ramsay, O. B., ed., *Van't Hoff-le Bel Centennial* (1975).

stereophonic sound

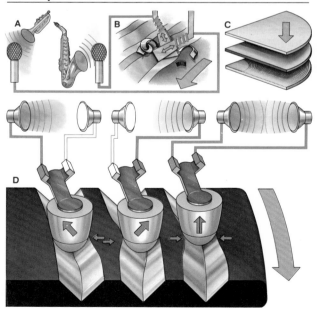

When a stereo record is made, sound from two microphones (A)—or, more commonly, two tape channels—causes separate electric signals to be fed into a recording cutter. This cuts (B) corresponding waves along each side—one for each channel—of a spiral groove on the master disk that is used to press (C) the final record. When the record is played (D) the two sets of waves cause the needle to vibrate; the vibrations are converted into two independent signals and into sound.

Stereophonic sound, or simply stereo, is the electronic reproduction of sound in which acoustic perspective is retained. This effect is achieved by the use of multiple recording, transmission, and reproducer channels. The original sound is directed toward two or more microphones or audio pickups whose output is combined to form two electric signal channels, which are then recorded or transmitted. The reproduction of the recorded or transmitted stereo signals requires, in the home stereo system, two amplifier channels and either stereo headphones or a pair of separated loudspeakers. The human ear has the ability to obtain positional information about the original sound from the reproduced sound. If there are many sources of sound relative to the two microphones, auditory perspective will be conserved.

Artificial perspective can be created by electronically mixing a new signal with the stereo signal already obtained, producing the illusion of superimposition of the new sound. Multitrack tape recording is used as an adjunct to this technique to produce commercial stereo records, tapes, broadcasts, and movie sound tracks. The terms *stereophonic* and *high fidelity* are practically synonymous in current usage because of the predominance of the stereo technique in commercial sound recording.   KENNETH C. ROBERTSON

Bibliography: Briggs, Gilbert A., *Stereo Handbook* (1959); Fantel, Hans, *ABC's of Hi-Fi and Stereo,* 3d ed. (1974); Sessions, Ken, *Stereo-Quad Hi-Fi Principles and Projects* (1973).

See also: SOUND RECORDING AND REPRODUCTION.

stereoscope

The stereoscope, an optical device invented by Charles Wheatstone in 1838, enables the simultaneous viewing of two slightly different photographs. Because human eyes are separated by a slight distance, the object being viewed appears

(Above) *This scene is typical of the stereoscopic photographs popular during the late 1800s. The paired slides were made by a camera with two lenses set 6.4 cm (2.5 in) apart, the approximate distance between human eyes.*

(Left) *A stereoscopic viewer resolved the two views into one, giving the illusion of three-dimensional vision. The London Stereographic Company, whose slogan was "No home without a stereoscope," sold viewers for less than a dollar, together with prepared slides.*

slightly different to each eye; this effect provides a sense of depth. In the Wheatstone stereoscope, right- and left-monocular pictures are projected to the two eyes so that the optic axes converge at the same angle; as a result, the pictures give the impression of a solid image. Wheatstone accomplished this convergence by using a mirror system. In 1849, David Brewster invented the improved refracting, or lenticular, stereoscope and a twin camera, which had two separate cameras placed at a slight distance from each other. The twin camera provided near-perfect right- and left-monocular pictures that, when viewed through a stereoscope, appear in three-dimensional realism. The stereoscopic principle is also used in range finders, binoculars, and stereoscopic microscopes.

DOUGLAS M. CONSIDINE

Bibliography: Jones, John, *Wonders of the Stereoscope* (1976).

stereotype

Stereotypes are the oldest and cheapest type of duplicate plate for letterpress PRINTING. They are used extensively for printing many letterpress-printed metropolitan daily newspapers and to some extent in book printing and the production of short-run trade magazines. They are practical for coarse-screen halftones, line plates, and type forms. A mold, called a matrix or mat, is made from the original type or engraving using a special papier-mâché, and the printing plate is cast by pouring molten lead into this mold. For long press runs the lead plates can be nickel or chromium plated. Once the mat is made, duplicate plates can be produced in less than a minute. Because most newspapers have converted to lithographic printing and photopolymer plates, the use of stereotype plates is declining.

MICHAEL H. BRUNO

sterility: see FERTILITY, HUMAN.

Sterkfontein [stairk-fuhn-tayn']

The Sterkfontein archaeological site, located about 50 km (30 mi) west of Johannesburg, South Africa, has yielded important evidence concerning early human evolution. First discovered (1936) and investigated by the South African paleontologist Robert Broom, the cave site is filled with breccia (cemented cave earths) containing numerous fossil bones, mostly of extinct antelope and carnivores. Among the fossils that Broom found were the remains of *Australopithecus africanus*, a gracile species of the extinct hominid (human-like) genus AUSTRALOPITHECUS. Subsequent investigations (1938 and 1948–50) at the nearby Kroomdraai and Swartkrans sites yielded traces of a robust australopithecine that Broom called *Paranthropus*, or *Australopithecus robustus*. Considerable controversy surrounds the dating of these sites—that is, the order in which the caves were occupied—but their remains generally are thought to span a period from about 3 million to 700,000 years ago. A few fragments of a more advanced hominid, possibly HOMO HABILIS, have also been found at Sterkfontein and Swartkrans, and a few stone chopping tools have been recovered from the uppermost levels of Sterkfontein.

BRIAN FAGAN

Bibliography: Butzer, Karl, *Environment and Archeology*, 2d ed. (1973); Clark, Desmond, *The Prehistory of Africa* (1970); McKown, E., and Isaac, Glyn, *Human Origins* (1976).

Stern, Der [shtairn, dayr]

A German weekly news and photo-feature magazine published in Hamburg, *Der Stern* was established in 1947 and has achieved a circulation of about 2 million. It has become one of West Germany's prime advertising media, often running to as many as 200 pages per issue. In format and content, it was modeled after the former U.S. weekly magazine *Life*.

WILLIAM B. CUMMINGS

Stern, Isaac

The Russian-born violin virtuoso Isaac Stern, b. July 21, 1920, was brought to San Francisco while still an infant. He made his professional debut at the age of 11 with the San Francisco Symphony.

Stern rapidly built a career as a concert soloist, performing both the standard repertoire and contemporary works, and as a chamber musician playing in a trio with pianist Eugene Istomin and cellist Leonard Rose. He uses his status as an internationally respected artist to further the cause of human rights and is an active supporter of Israel.

Bibliography: Ewen, David, ed., *Musicians since 1900* (1978).

Discography: Bach, J. S., *Concerto for Two Violins;* Beethoven, L. van, *Violin Concerto;* Bloch, E., *Baal Shem;* Mozart, W. A., *Violin Concertos nos. 1–5;* Stravinsky, I., *Violin Concerto.*

Stern, Otto

The German-American physicist Otto Stern, b. Feb. 17, 1888, d. Aug. 17, 1969, won the 1943 Nobel Prize for physics for his use of a molecular beam in determining the magnetic moment of a proton. After obtaining his Ph.D. in Breslau in physical chemistry (1912), he worked with Albert Einstein, who was applying the quantum theory to problems in thermodynamics. In 1919, Stern joined Max Born at the Institute for Theoretical Physics in Frankfurt, where he began his work with molecular beams. His experimental determination of the magnetic moment of the proton gave a value about three times larger than the moment postulated by Paul A. M. Dirac. Although Stern's measurements have been confirmed, there is still no theoretical explanation for the value he obtained. In 1933, Stern immigrated to the United States and continued his research at the Carnegie Institute of Technology until his retirement in 1946.

Bibliography: Jammer, Max, *The Conceptual Development of Quantum Mechanics* (1966).

Stern, Robert A. M.

Robert A. M. Stern, b. New York City, May 23, 1939, is a practicing architect, teacher, and writer. His two books and an exhibition catalog, as well as his numerous magazine articles, have made him a spokesman for the new attitudes of postmodern architecture. A graduate of Columbia University (B.A., 1960) and Yale (M.Arch., 1965), he is professor and director of undergraduate studies in architecture at Columbia. His residential architecture is rich in allusions to architectural history.

C. RAY SMITH

Bibliography: Stern, Robert, *New Directions in American Architecture* (1969; 2d ed., 1977), *George Howe: Toward a Modern Architecture* (1975), and *40 Under 40: Young Talent in Architecture*, exhibition catalogue (1966).

Sternberg, Josef von

The films of Austrian-American director Josef von Sternberg, pseudonym of Jonas Stern, b. Vienna, May 29, 1894, d. Dec. 22, 1969, are perhaps the supreme example of the narrative film's pursuit of visual beauty at the expense of dramatic values. Sternberg had his first popular success with *Underworld* (1927), which was followed by *The Docks of New York* (1928) and *Thunderbolt* (1929). Sternberg then went to Germany to direct *The Blue Angel* (1930), a sensational success that inaugurated the director's long association with his "discovery," Marlene DIETRICH. Their early films together—*Morocco* (1930), *Dishonoured* (1931), and *Shanghai Express* (1932)—displayed the visual dynamism that distinguished Sternberg's previous work, but this gradually gave way in *The Scarlet Empress* (1934) and *The Devil Is a Woman* (1935) to increasingly static and purely decorative glorifications of Dietrich's mystique. Following the increasingly unpopular Dietrich cycle, Sternberg worked rarely, and, of his later films, only *The Shanghai Gesture* (1941) and *Anatahan* (1953) are notable. His autobiography, *Fun in a Chinese Laundry,* appeared in 1965.

WILLIAM S. PECHTER

Bibliography: Baxter, John, *The Cinema of Josef von Sternberg* (1971); Sarris, Andrew, *The Films of Josef von Sternberg* (1966); Weinberg, Herman, *Josef von Sternberg* (1967).

sternbergia [sturn-bur'-gee-uh]

Sternbergia S. lutea, a Mediterranean daffodil, has crocuslike flowers that bloom from late summer to late autumn.

Sternbergia is a genus of about 5 species of bulbous herbs in the amaryllis family, Amaryllidaceae, and native to Eurasia. The winter daffodil, or lily-of-the-field, *S. lutea,* mentioned in the Bible, produces waxen, golden yellow flowers in autumn and grows in dry rocky areas. KENNETH R. ROBERTSON

Sterne, Laurence

The author of one of the most original and profound English novels of the 18th century, Laurence Sterne found himself famous overnight after publishing the first two volumes of *The Life and Opinions of Tristram Shandy, Gentleman* (1760). He went on to add seven more volumes (in 1761, 1765, and 1767) to the work, which is both a richly comic novel and an ingenious parody of the novel form. Born in Clonmel, Ireland, Nov. 24, 1713, the son of an army officer, Sterne attended Jesus College, Cambridge, and in 1738 became vicar of Sutton-in-the-Forest, Yorkshire. Most of his life was spent as a country parson and gentleman farmer. His marriage in 1741 proved unhappy, and he was involved with a number of other women, for one of whom—Mrs. Eliza Draper—he wrote what is now known as *Journal to Eliza* (1767). Sterne was also active in local ecclesiastical politics, held an office in the cathedral at York, and achieved some success as a preacher. All this experience is reflected in TRISTRAM SHANDY.

In attempting to write his autobiography, Tristram. the nar-

The English novelist Laurence Sterne is best known for his masterpiece, Tristram Shandy *(1760–67), one of the most celebrated works of the late 18th century. In this humorous, rambling, multivolume work Sterne develops a seemingly disjointed, episodic narrative of digressions that anticipated the stream-of-consciousness technique used by many modern novelists.*

rator of the novel, takes his readers back to the moment of his conception and to the circumstances surrounding his birth. The book, which might be described as one long digression, is in large part a series of character sketches and anecdotes in which Tristram discusses his father, Walter Shandy, his Uncle Toby, and various others, including Parson Yorick, a character modeled on Sterne himself. His father and uncle are among the most memorable and lovable eccentrics in English literature, and much of *Tristram Shandy* consists of conversations between them and others in which everyone reveals his peculiar obsession, or "hobbyhorse." Although Sterne was influenced by older satirists, such as Rabelais, Cervantes, and Swift, *Tristram Shandy* is loosely based on John LOCKE's theory of the association of ideas. Characters are therefore presented by means of their emotions and impressions rather than through external incidents, and because no two characters have the same associations, comic confusions abound when communication is attempted.

Although attacked on moral and literary grounds by some for its deliberate incoherence and its sexual humor, *Tristram Shandy* was an immense success and made Sterne a literary celebrity, so much so that he published several collections of his sermons as *The Sermons of Mr. Yorick* (1760, 1766, 1769). Sterne went abroad for his health in 1762, and in 1768 he published *A Sentimental Journey through France and Italy,* a series of comic and touching anecdotes based on his travels. He died of pleurisy on Mar. 18, 1768. JOHN RICHETTI

Bibliography: Cross, Wilbur L., *The Life and Times of Laurence Sterne,* 3d ed. (1929; repr. 1967); Fluchère, Henri, *Laurence Sterne,* trans. by Barbara Bray (1965); Hartley, Lodwick, *Laurence Sterne in the 20th Century* (1966); Thomson, David, *Wild Excursions* (1972).

Sternheim, Carl [shtairn'-hym]

Carl Sternheim, b. Apr. 1, 1878, d. Nov. 3, 1942, was considered the most brilliant German satirist of his day. His fame rests on ten comedies, published collectively under the title *Scenes from the Heroic Life of the Middle Classes* (1922; Eng. trans., 1970), which deflate the bombastic qualities of smug bourgeois types. Sternheim's forte was derision: he employed a terse, pungent language to ridicule all kinds of pretentiousness and hypocrisy. His finest play, *Bürger Schippel* (Citizen Schippel, 1913), ironically depicts the ascent of the proletarian Schippel into the "reputable" ranks of the bourgeoisie as a downfall. In other plays, such as *The Underpants* (1911; Eng. trans., 1955), *The Strongbox* (1911; Eng. trans., 1963), and *The Snob* (1914; Eng. trans., 1949), Sternheim exposed the false values and illusions of society without offering consolation. Sternheim also wrote several novels and an autobiography, *Vorkriegseuropa im Gleichnis meines Lebens* (Prewar Europe as the Image of My Life, 1936). JACK ZIPES

steroid [stair'-oyd]

Steroids are fat-soluble (lipid) organic compounds that occur naturally throughout the plant and animal kingdoms and play many important functional roles. All steroids are characterized by a four-ring structural configuration. Steroids are quite diverse and include the sterols (such as CHOLESTEROL) of vertebrates, bile acids from the liver, all sex hormones, adrenal cortical hormones (corticosteroids), toad poisons, and products of the DIGITALIS plant used to treat heart disease. Hormonal steroids are synthesized from cholesterol in the body. The biosynthetic mechanisms are similar in all steroid-secreting tissue (adrenal cortex, testis, ovary, and placenta).

While sex hormones are necessary for many aspects of reproduction and sexual function, the adrenocortical hormones, secreted by the adrenal cortex, are essential to life itself. There are two classes of corticosteroids. The GLUCOCORTICOIDS such as cortisone primarily affect carbohydrate and protein metabolism. They have limited use in the treatment of many immunologic and allergic diseases, such as arthritis. The mineralocorticoids such as ALDOSTERONE principally regulate salt and water balance. Because of the great therapeutic value of corticosteroids, many synthetic steroids have been produced, some more potent than the natural hormones. Synthetic steroids include antiinflammatory drugs, oral contraceptives, and a synthetic adrenal steroid used to treat Addison's disease, or adrenal insufficiency.   JULIAN M. DAVIDSON

Bibliography: Azarnoff, Daniel L., *Steroid Therapy* (1975); Johns, W. F., *Steroids* (1976); Pasqualini, J. R., ed., *Recent Advances in Steroid Biochemistry* (1977)

sterol   [stair'-awl]

Originally the name of the entire steroid class of lipids, the term *sterol* is now used more specifically for chemically similar compounds having a hydroxyl group (OH) attached to a series of fused rings. In vertebrates the principal sterol is CHOLESTEROL, which is especially abundant in nerve tissue and gallstones. Ergosterol, a sterol found in yeast, ergot, and molds, is of interest because it gives rise to vitamin D_2 (calciferol) when irradiated with ultraviolet light. In higher plants, the principal sterols have 29 carbon atoms. Representatives of these are stigmasterol (from soybean oil) and several spinasterols (from spinach and cabbage).

ergosterol

Despite the wide variety of sterols that are found in nature and that may be ingested by higher animals, only a few are absorbed and transferred to the circulation. Cholesterol is absorbed readily, but coprostanol and cholestanol, which are structurally similar, are not absorbed. Even though cholesterol is readily absorbed, it is not an essential component of the diet. Most animals can synthesize their necessary sterols from smaller carbon compounds.   STEPHEN FLEISHMAN

Stesichorus   [stee-sik'-uh-ruhs]

Stesichorus, a Greek lyric poet, *c.*632–*c.*556 BC, was born in Mataurus, Italy, but lived and wrote in the Greek city of Himera in Sicily. Celebrated by the ancients, he was a major innovator in lyric versification who drew on a variety of epic sources to create unique poetic narratives. Only fragments of his work survive.

stethoscope

The stethoscope is a primary instrument of all physicians that enables them to listen to sounds emitted from various organs. It is often used with percussion (light tapping of the chest) as a diagnostic practice in medicine. The first stethoscope was a single hollow wooden tube invented by the French physician René T. H. LÄENNEC in the early 1800s. One end had a broad opening, which was placed against the patient's chest. The sounds of breathing and of heart action could be heard by the physician by placing one ear against the opposite, narrow opening. The more conventional stethoscope was designed in the early 1900s by the American physician George P. Cammann (1904–63). It consisted of two flexible rubber tubes connected to earpieces at one end and to a chest piece on the other. Both ears could now be used to listen to the sounds. The chest piece is of two types. One is a bell-shaped metal cone that transmits low-pitched sounds, whereas the other is a diaphragm that transmits high-pitched sounds. Both types of chest pieces are commonly used to evaluate the cardiac and respiratory systems by allowing physicians to distinguish clearly the sounds that the beating heart generates, as well as the sounds of gas exchange in the lungs. The quality of sound denotes whether the organ in question is healthy or abnormal. With proper training, doctors can diagnose many types of disease processes of the heart and lungs, as well as of the stomach and blood vessels. An electronic stethoscope allows several physicians to listen to the same sounds from a single organ. The stethoscope is also used to measure arterial blood pressure in the arm or leg.   THEODORE H. STANLEY

Stettheimer, Florine   [stet'-hym-ur]

Florine Stettheimer, b. Rochester, N.Y., Aug. 19, 1871, d. May 11, 1944, became the most noted artist in her artistic family; she painted witty scenes of circuses, parties, and celebrations with small, graceful figures in detailed, fanciful settings. She studied at the Art Students League and, accompanied by her family, lived for a time in Europe. After returning to New York, the Stettheimers entertained Marcel Duchamp, Alfred Stieglitz, and other people who appear in Stettheimer's paintings. These works, full of decorative, bright colors, are given coherence by calligraphic white accents; an example is *Cathedrals of Art* (1942; Metropolitan Museum, New York City).
ELEANOR TUFTS

Bibliography: Museum of Modern Art, *Three American Romantic Painters* (1950; repr. 1969); Tyler, Parker, *Florine Stettheimer* (1963).

Stettinius, Edward Reilly, Jr.   [stuh-tin'-ee-uhs]

Edward Reilly Stettinius, Jr., b. Chicago, Oct. 22, 1900, d. Oct. 31, 1949, an American industrialist and statesman, served (1944–45) as U.S. secretary of state. An executive at General Motors and U.S. Steel during the 1930s, he entered government service in 1940 and was undersecretary of state from 1943 to 1944. As secretary of state, he helped establish the United Nations and in April 1945 headed the U.S. delegation to the founding conference of the world organization in San Francisco. Stettinius represented the United States at the United Nations from January to June 1946.   ROBERT H. FERRELL

Bibliography: Campbell, Thomas M., and Herring, George C., eds., *The Diaries of Edward R. Stettinius, Jr., 1943–46* (1975).

Steuben, Friedrich Wilhelm, Baron von
[stoo'-ben or shtoy'-ben]

During the American Revolution a German officer, Friedrich Wilhelm Augustin, Baron von Steuben, b. Magdeburg, Prussia, Sept. 17, 1730, d. Nov. 28, 1794, helped instill discipline in the Continental Army through his drilling techniques. A Prussian officer in the Seven Years' War, he went to America in 1777. The next year, Steuben was appointed inspector general of the Continental Army with the rank of major general. His *Regulations for the Order and Discipline of the Troops of the United States* (1779) was used by the army until the War of 1812. Steuben became an American citizen in 1783.

Bibliography: Doyle, Joseph B., *Frederick William Von Steuben and the American Revolution* (1913; repr. 1970); Palmer, John McAuley, *General von Steuben* (1937; repr. 1966).

Steuben glass   [stoo'-ben]

Steuben glass was first produced in 1903 at the Steuben Glass Works in Corning, N.Y., directed by Arthur Amory Houghton. In 1918 the company became a division of the Corning Glass Works, and, in 1933, Arthur Amory Houghton, Jr., became the director. The work of the English glassmaker Frederick Carder, who was the chief designer from the beginning until 1934, was influenced largely by the ART NOUVEAU style. Among Carder's creations were aurene (an iridescent glass in blue and gold luster), colored opalines (in light rose, jade green, translucent white, and shades of blue), clear glass combined with colors, and pressed glass.

By 1933 the Steuben company had achieved an international reputation for its blown and engraved glass, the deep clarity of which was due to the purity of the metal used in its manufacture. At that time a popular line of engraved tableware was designed by Walter Dorwin Teague, and many artists were brought in to create one-of-a-kind presentation pieces of engraved crystal.   MARION B. WILSON

Bibliography: Perrot, Paul N., et al., *Steuben: Seventy Years of American Glassmaking* (1974); Plaut, J. S., *Steuben Glass* (1948).

Stevens (family)

The American engineer and lawyer, John Stevens, invented the first ocean-going steamboat and developed new technology for steam-powered railways. The operator of the first steam ferry service, Stevens was also the author of foresighted proposals for the building of bridges and tunnels leading to Manhattan Island.

The Stevens family is best known for three American inventors who were pioneers in the development of steamboat and railroad transportation in the United States. **John Stevens**, b. New York City, 1749, d. Mar. 6, 1838, was an engineer and one of the earliest proponents of steam power in transportation. After studying law (1768–71) and serving (1776–77) as treasurer of New Jersey, he became interested in steam navigation in the late 1780s. He began to seek (1792) patents for his improved boiler and engine designs, having already urged Congress to establish a U.S. patent law, which was enacted in 1790. In 1804 he built a steamboat, *Little Juliana*, with twin screw propellers. It crossed the Hudson River several times, and in 1809 the *Phoenix*, a paddle-wheel steamboat designed by Stevens, sailed from New York City to Philadelphia—the first ocean voyage ever taken by a steamboat. After 1810 Stevens's major interest became rail transportation, and in 1815 he obtained the first U.S. railroad charter. In 1826 he designed and built the United States' first steam locomotive but operated it only on a circular track on his estate in Hoboken, N.J.

The second son of John Stevens, **Robert Livingston Stevens**, b. Hoboken, Oct. 18, 1787, d. Apr. 20, 1859, was a mechanical engineer and inventor. Interested in naval architecture, he helped his father design the *Phoenix* and improved the designs of more than 20 other ferryboats and steamboats. He also designed special ferry slips. Associated with his father's railway plans, R. L. Stevens invented (1830) the T rail. He also invented the railroad spike and discovered a better system of laying railroad roadbeds.

Edwin Augustus Stevens, b. Hoboken, July 28, 1795, d. Aug. 7, 1868, the sixth son of John Stevens, was an engineer, financier, inventor, and philanthropist. In addition to managing the family finances, he invented (1823) a plow and later a wagon for hauling garbage. Interested in ironclad warships for most of his life, he began (1814) to build one at his own expense and 30 years later demonstrated its feasibility. He became treasurer (1830) and president (1854) of the Camden and Amboy Railroad and bequeathed money and land to found the Stevens Institute of Technology at Hoboken.

Bibliography: Gies, Joseph and Frances, *Ingenious Yankees* (1976).

Stevens, John P.

John Paul Stevens, b. Chicago, Apr. 20, 1920, was sworn in by Chief Justice Warren Burger as associate justice of the U.S. Supreme Court on Dec. 19, 1975, replacing the retired William O. Douglas. Stevens graduated (1941) from the University of Chicago, served in the navy, and received (1947) a law degree from Northwestern University. He became (1947–48)

law clerk to Supreme Court Justice Wiley B. Rutledge and then began to practice law in Chicago. President Richard M. Nixon appointed him a judge of the U.S. Court of Appeals for the Seventh Circuit in 1970. On the U.S. Supreme Court, Stevens's position has been moderately conservative.

Bibliography: Barnes, Catherine A., *Men of the Supreme Court: Profiles of the Justices* (1978).

Stevens, Thaddeus

Thaddeus Stevens, b. Danville, Vt., Apr. 4, 1792, d. Aug. 11, 1868, U.S. representative from Pennsylvania (1849–53, 1859–68), was one of the most influential Radical Republican leaders in the U.S. Congress during the RECONSTRUCTION era. He overcame poverty to become a successful lawyer, an iron manufacturer, and a politician in Pennsylvania. From the 1820s on, Stevens was active in politics—as an Anti-Mason, a Whig, a Know-Nothing, and finally a Republican. Serving in the Pennsylvania legislature between 1833 and 1841, Stevens acquired a reputation as the moving force behind the passage of Pennsylvania's free public school law—the first state law of its kind outside New England—and as a radical opponent of slavery.

Stevens served as an antislavery Whig during his first 4 years (1849–53) in Congress. In the election of 1858 he established a firm hold on his congressional district as Civil War issues swept the Republican party to power; he subsequently sat as a Republican. In 1861 he became chairman of the House of Representatives' most important committee, Ways and Means, and thus the recognized leader of House Republicans. Stevens employed his eloquence, acid wit, and influence over committee assignments to maintain Republican unity on party questions.

As the committee's chairman he played an important role in the issuance of paper money, the imposition of protective tariffs, and the setting of tax policy during the Civil War, but his greatest impact was on the development of Reconstruction policy. During the Civil War he pressed for vigorous antislavery measures and stringent terms for Reconstruction. After the Confederate surrender, Stevens broke with President Andrew Johnson over Johnson's lenient Reconstruction program, advocating instead a far more rigorous policy of political, educational, and economic reform. He was unable to secure his own radical program, but as a leader of Congress's Joint Committee on Reconstruction he was instrumental in obstructing Johnson's plan and in establishing one based on legal and political equality for southern blacks.

In 1868, Stevens was a House manager (prosecutor) in the president's impeachment trial before the Senate. He died embittered by Johnson's acquittal and by the growing conservatism of the Republican party.   MICHAEL LES BENEDICT

Bibliography: Brodie, Fawn M., *Thaddeus Stevens: Scourge of the South* (1959); Current, Richard N., *Old Thad Stevens: A Story of Ambition* (1942); Korngold, Ralph, *Thaddeus Stevens* (1955; repr. 1974).

The U.S. representative Thaddeus Stevens was a militant opponent of slavery and of the social system that supported it. A leader of the Radical Republicans during Reconstruction, he was instrumental in securing passage of the 14th Amendment and managed the impeachment of President Andrew Johnson.

Stevens, Wallace

Wallace Stevens wrote complex, meditative poems exploring the constantly changing relationship between the world of reality and the creations of the imagination. To Stevens, the effort to comprehend this relationship was the modern equivalent of religious faith.

Wallace Stevens, a major 20th-century American poet, devoted his literary energies to an exploration of the possible relations between reality and imagination. Despite an early resemblance to French symbolism, some echoes of John Keats, and an affinity with Walt Whitman, Stevens's abstract and strikingly musical verse is notably difficult to place in literary tradition. His lifelong concern with the bearing of language on the philosophical problem of knowledge has led many readers to find Stevens's closest intellectual relatives among such phenomenological thinkers as Martin Heidegger and Charles Sanders Peirce rather than among other poets.

Stevens was an elusive and unconventional poet, but he lived a conventional and uneventful life. Born in Reading, Pa., on Oct. 2, 1879, he studied at Harvard University and New York University Law School. In 1909 he married Elsie Katchel Moll, also of Reading. He joined the Hartford Accident and Indemnity Company in 1916, and in 1934 he became vice-president, a position he held until his death in 1955, despite opportunities for early retirement and an invitation to assume an honorary post at Harvard. Apparently, he kept his business and literary lives altogether separate, maintained few close friendships, and, except for holidays in Key West, Fla., traveled little. Unlike almost every other 20th-century American with literary hopes, Stevens never visited Europe.

Apart from some verse in the *Harvard Advocate,* Stevens published nothing until 1914, when his work was featured in *Poetry* magazine. *Harmonium* (1923), his first volume, contains many of Stevens's most famous poems. The images and sounds in *Harmonium* are so strident and brilliant that they give great pleasure but tend to conceal the poems' central philosophical arguments.

Between 1923 and 1933, Stevens was again silent, but in 1934 he began working strenuously. He soon published his second volume, *Ideas of Order* (1936); a long poem, "Owl's Clover" (1936); and a third volume, *The Man with the Blue Guitar* (1937). Whereas Stevens's imagination had formerly evaded "the pressure of reality" by means of elaborate verbal structures, it began in the 1930s to define and control this reality. An important imaginer in *Harmonium* could merely plan "loquacious columns by the ructive sea," but a heroic figure in "The Idea of Order at Key West" "sang beyond the genius of the sea." Stevens's work of this period culminates in *Notes toward a Supreme Fiction* (1942), a long and difficult poem that attempts to find the requirements of an idea capable of redeeming the mundane facts of ordinary life.

Stevens's next volumes were *Parts of a World* (1942; rev. ed. 1951), *Transport to Summer* (1947), and *The Auroras of Autumn* (1950). *The Collected Poems* (1954) won the National Book Award and the Pulitzer Prize. *Opus Posthumous,* the uncollected poems, appeared in 1957, *The Letters of Wallace Stevens* in 1966, and the notebooks, entitled *Souvenirs and Prophecies,* in 1977. Stevens put together only one small vol-

ume of criticism, *The Necessary Angel* (1951), but theoretical considerations of poetry are common throughout his poetical works. Although he had moods of grave doubt, Stevens's general confidence in the power of the imagination continued to grow in his last works. In "The Rock," his final major work, he pictured reality as a barren rock and attempted to make it a source of energy for the imagination.   ROBERT DeMARIA

Bibliography: Bloom, Harold, *Wallace Stevens: The Poems of Our Climate* (1977); Doggett, Frank, *Stevens' Poetry of Thought* (1966); Doggett, Frank, and Buttell, Robert, eds., *Wallace Stevens: A Celebration* (1980); Litz, A. Walton, *Introspective Voyager: The Poetic Development of Wallace Stevens* (1972); Vendler, Helen H., *On Extended Wings* (1969).

Stevens Institute of Technology

Established in 1870, Stevens Institute of Technology (enrollment: 2,300; library: 90,000 volumes) is a private coeducational college in Hoboken, N.J. Both the undergraduate and the graduate curricula are concerned with areas of engineering and the sciences.

Stevenson   (family)

The U.S. statesman Adlai Stevenson II vaulted into national prominence through his single term as Democratic governor of Illinois. He was twice nominated (1952, 1956) as his party's presidential candidate, losing both elections to Dwight D. Eisenhower. In 1961, President John F. Kennedy appointed Stevenson as U.S. ambassador to the United Nations, a post he held until his death, in 1965.

The Stevensons, a leading family in American politics, have long been active as Illinois Democrats. **Adlai Ewing Stevenson**, b. Christian County, Ky., Oct. 23, 1835, d. June 14, 1914, was an Illinois lawyer who served in the U.S. House of Representatives and was vice-president of the United States under President Grover Cleveland from 1893 to 1897.

His grandson **Adlai Ewing Stevenson II**, b. Los Angeles, Feb. 5, 1900, d. July 14, 1965, was educated at Princeton University, worked for the family-owned newspaper in Bloomington, Ind., and finished law school in 1926 at Northwestern University. As a Chicago lawyer, Stevenson became involved in the Council on Foreign Relations and the antiisolationist Committee to Defend America by Aiding the Allies. During World War II he worked in the Navy and State departments. In 1948 he ran for governor of Illinois and won by a wide margin; he performed so admirably in the state house that the Democrats drafted him as their presidential nominee in both 1952 and 1956. Although cautious on such issues as civil rights and public housing, Stevenson appealed to intellectuals and to liberal Democrats. He backed anticommunist foreign policies but generally avoided extreme cold-war rhetoric. Stevenson was a gifted speaker but was no match for the popular Republican candidate, Dwight D. Eisenhower, who beat him handily in both of his attempts for the presidency.

Stevenson tried to win the presidential nomination a third time in 1960 but lost to John F. Kennedy, who named him ambassador to the United Nations. Although restive in that capacity, Stevenson backed the Democratic administration's policies and served until his sudden death in 1965. He wrote several books; publication of his papers was begun in 1972.

His eldest son, **Adlai Ewing Stevenson III**, b. Chicago, Oct.

10, 1930, also practiced law and advanced rapidly in Illinois Democratic politics. He was elected to the U.S. Senate in 1970 and reelected in 1976.　　　JAMES T. PATTERSON

Bibliography: Brown, Stuart G., *Conscience in Politics: Adlai E. Stevenson in the 1950's* (1961); Cochran, Bert, *Adlai Stevenson: Patrician Among the Politicians* (1969); Darling, Grace and David, *Stevenson* (1977); Douth, George, *Leaders in Profile: The U.S. Senate*, rev. ed. (1975); Martin, John B., *Adlai Stevenson and the World* (1977) and *Adlai Stevenson of Illinois* (1976).

Stevenson, Robert Louis

The Scottish romancer, travel writer, poet, and essayist Robert Louis Stevenson, b. Edinburgh, Nov. 13, 1850, was the author of the enduringly popular romantic adventure stories TREASURE ISLAND and *Kidnapped* (1886) and the alarming psychological allegory DOCTOR JEKYLL AND MR. HYDE. These have become classics of juvenile literature, and their fame has obscured Stevenson's great talent for other forms. He was undoubtedly one of the most gifted British writers of the late 19th century.

The son of a prosperous engineer, Stevenson was brought up in a strict Calvinist household and was expected to pursue his father's profession despite his ill health. As a student at Edinburgh University he took up law, declared himself an agnostic, lived a flagrantly bohemian existence, and began to write. A severe attack of tuberculosis, a disease that plagued Stevenson all his life, prompted his first extensive trip to France, in 1873. *An Inland Voyage* (1878) and *Travels with a Donkey in the Cevennes* (1879), both inspired by journeys taken during these years, are typical of Stevenson's engaging style. Although travel books, their interest lies primarily in the exuberant narrator's interest in the exotic and picturesque.

In 1875, Stevenson qualified as a lawyer, but he had also reached a wide audience in England through his essays in the *Cornhill Magazine*. In 1876, Stevenson met Fanny Osbourne, an American estranged from her husband. She returned to California in 1878, and in the following year Stevenson decided to join her. After an arduous journey, described in *Across the Plains* (1892) and *The Amateur Emigrant* (1895), he reached San Francisco, penniless and in dangerously bad health. Their marriage in 1880, however, marked the beginning of the most productive period of Stevenson's life. During their extensive travels in search of a congenial climate Stevenson produced a constant stream of romances, essays, and poems: *Treasure Island*, begun as a boys' serial called *The Sea-Cook* (1881), was completed in its present form in the Swiss resort of Davos; *A Child's Garden of Verses* (1885) was begun in France; and *Doctor Jekyll* was written in England. Returning to the United States in 1887, Stevenson stayed in the Adirondack Mountains, where he began another historical romance, *The Master of Ballantrae* (1889). Like much of his work, this tale is set in Scotland, whose wild terrain Stevenson always found conducive to his uniquely vigorous style of storytelling.

Robert Louis Stevenson, a Scottish writer of short stories, poems, and novels, was a leading figure of the "romantic revival" in Victorian literature. Stevenson is most famous for his classic horror story, The Strange Case of Dr. Jekyll and Mr. Hyde *(1886), and for two novels of adventure,* Treasure Island *(1881–82) and* Kidnapped *(1886).*

By now a commercially successful writer, Stevenson and his wife sailed from San Francisco to the islands of the South Pacific in 1888. He overcame his illness while in the tropics and delighted in the Marquesas Islands, Honolulu, and Samoa, which he described in *A Footnote to History* (1892) and *In the South Seas* (1896). Samoa became his permanent home in 1890, and he died there on Dec. 3, 1894, before completing what many critics have called his finest work, *Weir of Hermiston* (1896).

Bibliography: Cooper, Lettice, *Robert Louis Stevenson* (1947); Daiches, David, *Robert Louis Stevenson* (1946) and *Robert Louis Stevenson and His World* (1970); Eigner, Edwin M., *Robert Louis Stevenson and the Romantic Tradition* (1966); Furnas, Joseph C., *Voyage to Windward: The Life of Robert Louis Stevenson* (1951); Kiely, Robert, *Robert Louis Stevenson and the Fiction of Adventure* (1964); Saposnik, Irving, *Robert Louis Stevenson* (1974).

Stevin, Simon　[stuh-veen']

The Dutch mathematician and engineer Simon Stevin, 1548–1620, initiated the science of hydrostatics by demonstrating that the pressure exerted by a liquid upon a given surface depends on the height of the liquid and the area of the surface. While quartermaster of the Dutch army, Stevin invented a way of flooding the lowlands in the path of invading forces by opening selected sluices in dikes. The author of 11 books, he contributed significantly to the sciences of trigonometry, geography, fortification, and navigation and devised and urged the universal use of decimal fractions and decimal systems of coins, weights, and measures.

Stewart, Alexander Turney

Alexander Turney Stewart, b. Lisburn, Ireland, Oct. 12, 1803, d. Apr. 10, 1876, founded the New York City retail store that bore his name. He emigrated to the United States and opened (1823) his first dry goods store in New York City, investing an entire legacy of $4,000. This business—A. T. Stewart and Company—grew into the largest retail store in the world, occupying an eight-story building on an entire city block. Stewart also had controlling shares in numerous textile mills in New England and supplied the federal government with cloth for the army's clothing during the Civil War. At the peak of his career, he owned a theater, a hotel, and a restaurant. He also built Garden City on Long Island as a homesite for persons of modest means. In 1869 he served as secretary of the treasury.

Bibliography: Ferry, John W., *A History of the Department Store* (1960).

Stewart, Douglas Alexander

An Australian playwright, poet, and critic, Douglas Alexander Stewart, b. May 6, 1913, wrote the radio classic *The Fire on the Snow*, about Scott's expedition to the Antarctic, first broadcast in 1941. Plays by Stewart include *Ned Kelly* (1943), *Shipwreck* (1947), and *Fisher's Ghost: An Historical Comedy* (1960). His poetry can be sampled in *Collected Poems 1936–1967* (1967) and *Selected Poems* (1973), and his criticism in *The Broad Stream* (1975).

Stewart, Jackie

John Young (Jackie) Stewart, b. June 11, 1939, was the premier British racing car driver of the late 1960s and early 1970s. He started competitive driving in 1962, and in 1965 he entered his first Grand Prix (GP) race in South Africa, where he finished sixth. His first GP victory was at Monza in 1965, and the next year he led for many laps in the Indianapolis 500 race before his car broke down. Stewart captured the world championship in 1969, 1971, and 1973. He retired just before the 1973 U.S. Grand Prix, when his racing teammate, François Cevert, was killed during practice. In the late 1970s, he worked as an automobile racing commentator for the American Broadcasting Company.

Bibliography: Stewart, Jackie, with Peter Manso, *Faster!* (1972).

Stewart, James

James Stewart, as Elwood P. Dowd, appraises his portrait in a scene from Harvey *(1950), a screen adaptation of the play about an engaging alcoholic who is followed about by a giant rabbit visible only to him. Stewart's distinctive drawl and awkward mannerisms project a sincerity that has made him a Hollywood favorite since the 1930s.*

Tall and gangly, with an inimitable drawl, film star James Maitland Stewart, b. Indiana, Pa., May 20, 1908, exuded such sincerity that he could never play a villain. He was probably at his best in such optimistic Frank Capra films as *You Can't Take It With You* (1938), *Mr. Smith Goes to Washington* (1939), and *It's A Wonderful Life* (1946). He was equally engaging playing drunks in *The Philadelphia Story* (1940), for which he won an Academy Award, and *Harvey* (1950). Stewart also gave memorable performances in *Destry Rides Again* (1939), *Rear Window* (1954), and *Anatomy of a Murder* (1959).

LESLIE HALLIWELL

Bibliography: Jones, Ken D., et al., *The Films of James Stewart* (1970); Thompson, Howard, *James Stewart* (1974).

Stewart, Mary

Mary Stewart is the pseudonym of Florence Rainbow Stewart, b. Sept. 17, 1916, an English writer of adventure romances whose literate prose, crisp observation, and believable heroines have gained her a huge following. Of Stewart's 14 novels—all international best-sellers—*My Brother Michael* (1960), *The Ivy Tree* (1961), *The Moon-Spinners* (1962; film, 1964), *Airs Above the Ground* (1965), and *The Gabriel Hounds* (1967) are among the best. A trilogy consisting of *Crystal Cave* (1970), *The Hollow Hills* (1973), and *The Last Enchantment* (1979), set in King Arthur's times, explores the legend of Merlin.

Stewart, Potter

Potter Stewart, b. Jackson, Mich., Jan. 23, 1915, was appointed (1958) to the U.S. Supreme Court by President Dwight D. Eisenhower. A 1941 graduate of Yale Law School, he practiced law both before and after World War II service with the U.S. Naval Reserve. He then settled (1947–54) in Cincinnati, Ohio, where he served on the city council (1950–53) and as vice-mayor (1952–53). In June 1954 he became a judge of the U.S. Court of Appeals, Sixth Circuit. As a Supreme Court justice the moderate Stewart has been characterized as a "swing man," one who usually casts the decisive vote in an otherwise split court.

Bibliography: Barnes, Catherine A., *Men of the Supreme Court: Profiles of the Justices* (1978); Cox, Archibald, *The Warren Court* (1968).

Stewart, William Morris

The American lawyer and politician William Morris Stewart, b. Galen, N.Y., Aug. 9, 1827, d. Apr. 23, 1909, gained fame by defending the original claimants to the Comstock Lode in the early 1860s; later, he served (1864–75, 1887–1905) as a U.S. senator from Nevada. In 1866 and 1872 he was instrumental in securing passage of laws that recognized miners' rights. Stew-

art wrote the 15th Amendment to the U.S. Constitution, which deals with voting rights. A free-silver advocate, he left the Republican party in 1892 but rejoined it in 1900.

Bibliography: Hermann, Ruth, *Gold and Silver Colossus* (1975).

stibnite   [stib'-nyt]

Stibnite, a rare but extremely important source of antimony, is often found in quartz veins. It usually occurs as radiating or granular masses of long, lead gray prismatic crystals with pyramidal ends. These crystals, unlike others, often have an unusual curved or twisted appearance.

The antimony SULFIDE MINERAL stibnite (Sb_2S_3) is the chief ore of antimony. It forms bladed or columnar masses or radiating elongated pyramids (orthorhombic system) that have several cleavage planes. The color and streak are metallic lead gray on fresh surfaces, but they soon tarnish and blacken. Hardness is 2, and specific gravity is 4.5 to 4.6. Although widely distributed, stibnite is relatively rare. It usually occurs in quartz veins, where it has been deposited from near-surface alkaline solutions, but has been found in replacement and hot-spring deposits and near deep intrusions of igneous rock.

stick insect

An Indian stick insect, Carausius morosus, resembles a twig closely enough to escape the notice of its enemies. At night this insect moves slowly, feeding on leaves, and by day it hangs motionless on tree and shrub branches.

Stick insects, or walking sticks, family Phasmatidae, order Orthoptera, are plant-feeding insects so named because they are very long and slender and resemble sticks or twigs. Most species are wingless. Stick insects are found mainly in the tropics, reaching a length of up to 35 cm (14 in). Those found in the southern United States reach 170 mm (7 in) in length. Some walking sticks, when disturbed, emit a foul-smelling substance from glands in the thorax.   DONALD J. BORROR

stickleback

Sticklebacks, family Gasterosteidae, are a small group of teleost (bony) fishes from fresh, brackish, and shallow marine waters of the Northern Hemisphere. They are small (8–18 cm/ 3–7 in), elongate fishes, usually with bony plates along the body. Their color is usually green to black and silver underneath. Because the number of plates and several other characteristics vary with environmental factors—for example, temperature and salinity—the number of species placed in the two largest genera, *Gasterosteus* and *Pungitis*, has been a source of controversy.

Sticklebacks have been studied extensively by physiologists and by ethologists (animal behaviorists). The original studies of breeding behavior by Nikolaas Tinbergen are classic studies in stereotyped behavior. Males develop a red "throat" at the beginning of the breeding season. They select and defend a territory against other males. In the middle of his territory a male will construct a nest out of plant material cemented together by a secretion from his kidneys. When a female loaded with eggs enters the territory, she is courted by the male. The female reacts to the zigzag dance of the male by allowing him to guide her to the nest. She enters the nest and the male induces her to lay eggs by butting her flank with his snout. The female leaves the nest, and the male enters and fertilizes the eggs. He then continues to guard his territory and cares for both the eggs and, when they hatch, the young sticklebacks. Sticklebacks are used today to test for polluted water. E. O. WILEY

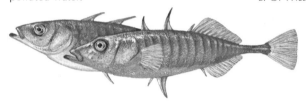

The three-spined stickleback (or tiddler), Gasterosteus aculeatus, *is found throughout the Northern Hemisphere. The stickleback is an inshore marine fish that also is found in unpolluted fresh water.*

sticktight: see BEGGAR-TICKS.

Stiegel, Henry William   [stee'-gul]

Henry William Stiegel, b. Cologne, Germany, May 13, 1729, d. Jan. 10, 1785, was an ironmaster and glassmaker in the United States whose name is associated with prized American glassware. Stiegel emigrated to Philadelphia, Pa., when he was 21. Eight years later he and some partners bought an ironworks in Lancaster County, Pa., and prospered by manufacturing stoves, soap kettles, iron castings, and sugar-making equipment. In 1764, Stiegel constructed a glass factory that produced the colored glassware that today is called Stiegel glass, as well as sheet and window glass. The firm lasted only until 1774, when Stiegel went bankrupt. From then until his death Stiegel preached and taught music.

Bibliography: Heiges, George L., *Henry William Stiegel* (1937); Hunter, Frederick William, *Stiegel Glass* (1950; repr. 1966).

Stieglitz, Alfred   [steeg'-lits]

The principal American force behind the recognition of photography as a fine art, Alfred Stieglitz, b. Hoboken, N.J., Jan. 1, 1864, d. July 13, 1946, was an outstanding champion of the avant-garde in all the visual arts. Trained in photographic technology in Berlin from 1883, Stieglitz first made his mark as an amateur photographer of technical excellence whose genre subjects passed beyond the anecdotal to penetrate the meaning of the scene itself. This concentration on the force of life remained his primary interest.

After returning to New York in 1890, Stieglitz began promoting amateur photography as of higher quality than the routine, unimaginative work produced by his professional contemporaries. As the editor of *American Amateur Photographer* (1893–96) and of *Camera Notes* (1897–1902) he gained international recognition for such soon-to-be-famous American photographers as Gertrude Käsebier, Edward Steichen,

and Clarence H. White. Influenced by avant-garde movements in Germany, Stieglitz organized (1902) an impressive display of the finest pictorial photography at the National Arts Club in New York, an exhibition that gave rise to the artistic group of photographers known as the PHOTO-SECESSION. Stieglitz published the work of this group in *Camera Work* from 1903 to 1917.

During the same years Stieglitz also exhibited, for the first time in the United States, the works of such European painters and sculptors as Picasso, Matisse, and Brancusi. In 1917 he closed the exhibition galleries to devote himself to photography but again from 1925 to 1947 directed two galleries, first The Intimate Gallery, then An American Place, where he exhibited the photography of Ansel Adams, Eliot Porter, and Paul Strand and paintings by leading American artists. Of his own work, his famous serial portraits of the painter Georgia O'Keeffe, whom he married in 1924, and his cloud studies, called *Equivalents* (*c*.1929), represent the most intimate expressions of his response to the world around him.
ELIZABETH POLLOCK

Bibliography: Bry, Doris, *Alfred Stieglitz, Photographer* (1974); Doty, Robert, *Photosecession* (1960); Homer, William I., *Alfred Stieglitz and the American Avant-Garde* (1977); Naef, Weston J., *The Collection of Alfred Stieglitz: Fifty Pioneers of Modern Photography* (1978); Norman, Dorothy, *Alfred Stieglitz: An American Seer* (1973).

Equivalent, Mountains and Sky, Lake George *(1924) is one of the cloud studies Alfred Stieglitz termed* equivalents, *in which he expressed his personal philosophy: "My cloud photographs are equivalents of my most profound life experiences." (Private collection.)*

Stifter, Adalbert   [shtif'-tur]

Adalbert Stifter, b. Oct. 23, 1805, d. Jan. 28, 1868, was an Austrian novelist and short-story writer whose works, such as *Rock Crystal* (1845; Eng. trans., 1945), *The Recluse* (1845; Eng. trans., 1968), and *Limestone and Other Stories* (1848; Eng. trans., 1968), were widely admired in the 19th century for their sensitivity and clarity. Rejecting the violent side of human nature, Stifter celebrated the gentle simplicity of everyday existence and the virtues of the land and the peasant in a

style that never succumbed to irony or sentimentality. Although Stifter's works declined in popularity after his death, since World War I they have enjoyed a renewed appreciation.
CARL R. MUELLER

Bibliography: Gump, Margaret, *Adalbert Stifter* (1974).

stigmata [stig-maht'-uh]

Stigmata are bodily marks resembling the wounds suffered by Jesus Christ when he was crucified. They are manifested on the hands, on the feet, near the heart, and on the head and shoulders. The stigmata are not usual bodily lacerations, do not deteriorate in the usual fashion of wounds, and are not susceptible to medical treatment. During the traditional times of commemoration of Christ's passion—Fridays, Lent, and especially Good Friday—bodily bleeding may occur.

More than 330 cases are known of Christians who have been stigmatized. In many cases stigmatization can be explained by natural causes such as the physical and psychic conditions of the person, along with a strong interest in and devotion to the sufferings of Christ. In a number of cases, however, stigmatization has been accepted by the Roman Catholic church as attributable only to supernatural causes; 60 stigmatics whose lives have been marked by great holiness and mystical experiences have been either canonized or beatified. FRANCIS OF ASSISI was the first and best-known saint to receive stigmata.
JOAN A. RANGE

Bibliography: Biot, Rene, *The Enigma of the Stigmata*, trans. by T. J. Hepburne-Scott (1962); Thurston, Herbert, *The Physical Phenomena of Mysticism* (1952).

stilbite: see ZEOLITE.

Stiles, Ezra

A Congregational minister and the seventh president of Yale College, Ezra Stiles, b. North Haven, Conn., Dec. 15, 1727, d. May 12, 1795, was recognized as the most learned man of his time in New England. He was an articulate moderate in ecclesiastical matters and a Patriot in politics. In 1740 he formed a society to promote the freedom of slaves.

Bibliography: Morgan, Edmund, *The Gentle Puritan: A Life of Ezra Stiles, 1727-1795* (1962).

Stilicho, Flavius [stil'-i-koh]

Flavius Stilicho, b. c.365, d. Aug. 22, 408, a half-Vandal soldier, became head of the Roman army under Emperor THEODOSIUS I (whose niece he married) and effective ruler (395–408) of the western Roman Empire under Theodosius's ineffectual son, HONORIUS. Entrusted with the care of young Honorius at Theodosius's death (395), Stilicho faced a series of barbarian invasions that threatened Rome itself. At Pollentia (402) he routed the Visigoths, led by the resilient ALARIC, and forced them to withdraw from Italy. Three years later (405) he decisively defeated the invading Ostrogoths at Fiesole. His attempts to annex Illyricum—claimed by the eastern emperor ARCADIUS—were less successful and served only to increase tensions between the two halves of the empire. Accused by Honorius of treason, Stilicho was executed in 408.
JOHN W. EADIE

Bibliography: Matthews, John, *Western Aristocracies and Imperial Court, AD 364–425* (1975).

Still, Clyfford

The American painter Clyfford Still, b. Grandin, N.Dak., Nov. 30, 1904, d. June 23, 1980, was a first-generation abstract expressionist whose mature style—a form of color-field painting—developed during the 1940s. During the 1930s, Still painted distorted figures and landscapes of the American West. In the mid-1940s his paintings became increasingly abstract, composed of dark, dry, crusty surfaces with vertical formations and jagged shapes. Still was an avowed primitive; he rejected modernist painting and was also outspokenly antitraditionalist. About 1947 his paintings expanded in scale,

Clyfford Still's Painting (1951) is typical of the style of color-field painting developed by this American abstract expressionist during the 1940s. His huge canvases were dominated by large areas of black set off by jagged streaks of contrasting color. (Detroit Institute of Arts.)

and during the 1950s his monumental works began to admit lighter color. Still used the image of a man standing in an open prairie as a metaphor for his work.
BARBARA CAVALIERE

Bibliography: Sandler, Irving, *Triumph of American Painting* (1970).

Still, William Grant

William Grant Still, b. Woodville, Miss., May 11, 1895, d. Dec. 3, 1978, earned the title Dean of Afro-American Composers because of the successful fusion in his orchestral works of black and European musical traditions. Early in his career he gained experience as an arranger and performer (oboe, violin, cello) with dance and theater orchestras. He began composing seriously in the late 1920s, after study with George Chadwick and Edgard Varèse, and won prominence with such works as *Afro-American Symphony* (1931) and the opera *A Bayou Legend* (1940).
EDWARD A. BERLIN

Bibliography: Hass, Robert B., ed., *William Grant Still and the Fusion of Cultures in American Music* (1972); Southern, Eileen, *Music of Black Americans* (1971).

still-life painting

Still-life painting, or the depiction of inanimate objects, such as flowers and fruits, is thought to have originated in Greek painting of the late 4th century BC. Although no Greek still lifes survive, the works of a still-life artist named Piraikos were mentioned by the historian Pliny the Elder. Hellenistic works almost certainly influenced Roman still-life painting, which is splendidly represented by the wall paintings and mosaics (before AD 79) found at Pompeii and Herculaneum. Later Roman artists presumably continued to make still lifes, but the art was lost in the early Middle Ages and was not to reappear as an independent art form until the 16th century.

Toward the end of the Middle Ages, artists in general began to take a new interest in the simple and direct representation of the objective world. Italian 14th-century paintings, for example, display carefully delineated furnishings and decorative contents in the background of narrative scenes.

(Above) *This wall painting (1st century AD) of a bowl of fruit and an amphora from the house of Julia Felix in Pompeii reflects the decorative nature of the still lifes of ancient times. The still-life genre, as with many other forms of Roman artistic expression, was derived from Greek and Hellenistic traditions. (Museo Nazionale, Naples.)*

(Left) *The still life developed as a distinct genre in the early Renaissance art of Italy and the Low Countries. One of the earliest examples of a still life is Hans Memling's painting of a vase of flowers (c.1490), executed on the back of a donor portrait constituting one-half of a diptych panel. This work, in its depiction of symbolic elements associated with the Virgin Mary, exemplifies the religious iconography common to medieval and Renaissance art. (Thyssen-Bornemisza Collection, Lugano.)*

(Above) *Caravaggio's naturalistic and meticulously detailed* Basket of Fruit *(c.1596) epitomizes the dramatic realism and chiaroscuro characteristic of his work. His luminous, precisely rendered compositions engendered a tradition of still-life painting that is termed "Caravaggesque." (Pinacoteca Ambrosiana, Milan.)*

(Above) Still Life with Apples and Oranges *(1895–1900) typifies the work of Cézanne in its architectural arrangement of simplified forms defined by intense color. (Musée de l'Impressionnisme, Paris.) (Below) Picasso's* Still Life with Watermelon *(1946) reflects the influence of Cézanne on 20th-century modern art. (Musée Picasso, Antibes.)*

These decorative motifs became even more elaborate in Italian Renaissance painting of the 15th century. Exactingly careful representations of furniture and artifacts, as well as plants and animals, characterized the contemporary art of the Netherlands. From Jan van EYCK and Rogier van der WEYDEN to Hans MEMLING and Gerard DAVID, 15th-century Flemish and Dutch artists frequently portrayed groupings of delicately painted objects as isolated still-life arrangements within their paintings. Typical of this trend is the cluster of flowers and vessels in the foreground of the nativity scene in Hugo van der GOES's *Portinari Altarpiece* (1474–76; Uffizi, Florence), in which each species of flower symbolizes a religious concept.

Independent still-life painting appeared in 14th- and 15th-century Italy as fresco or marquetry mural decorations and was further developed in both Italy and the northern European countries in the 16th century, particularly in the works of Giovanni da Udine and Pieter Aertsen. Italian still lifes tended to emphasize arrangements of fruits and flowers, culminating CARAVAGGIO's extraordinary *Basket of Fruit* (c.1596; Pinacoteca Ambrosiana, Milan). In northern painting Aertsen's great *Butcher Stall* (1551; University Museum, Uppsala, Sweden) led to more conventional arrangements of foodstuffs and meals on tables, especially in the work of the 17th cen-

tury Dutch masters Jan Bruegel (see BRUEGEL family), Pieter CLAESZ, Willem Claesz HEDA, and Willem KALFF, among others. Both Italian and Netherlandish painting influenced the evolution of a powerful still-life tradition in 17th-century Spain. Diego VELÁZQUEZ developed the *bodegón*, or kitchen painting, whereas Francisco de ZURBARÁN, Juan Sanchez Cotan, and Luis Melendez developed highly individual styles of still life.

In 18th-century France, Jean Baptiste Oudry and Alexandre François Desportes made animal and game still-life paintings in the Netherlandish tradition. The great master of French still life, however, was Jean Baptiste CHARDIN, who reduced his subject matter to simple and homely elements painted with great clarity and a mastery of tone and light.

Gustave COURBET, Édouard MANET, Odilon REDON, Pierre Auguste RENOIR, and Vincent VAN GOGH produced major examples of the form in the 19th and early 20th centuries, but Paul CÉZANNE is widely acclaimed as the finest still-life painter of the modern era. His studies of fruits and vegetables set on the broad planes of tabletops influenced the Fauve and cubist painters. Following Cézanne, Henri MATISSE, Pablo PICASSO, and Georges BRAQUE made major contributions to the art of the still life in the 20th century.   CHARLES I. MINOTT

Bibliography: Bergstrom, Ingvar, *Dutch Still-life Painting in the Seventeenth Century*, trans. by Christina Hedstrom and Gerard Taylor (1961); Born, Wolfgang, *Still-Life Painting in America* (1947; repr. 1973); Mitchell, Peter, *European Flower Painters* (1973); Paviere, Sydney H., *A Dictionary of Flower, Fruit and Still-Life Painters*, 4 vols. (1962); Sterling, Charles, *Still-Life Painting from Antiquity to the Present Time*, trans. by James Emmons (1959).

stilt

The black-necked stilt, H. mexicanus, *is a medium-sized black and white shorebird with long, slender red legs. It is native to North America.*

Stilt is the common name for several wading birds having moderately long necks, long bills, and long, spindly legs. The native North American species, the black-necked stilt, *Himantopus mexicanus*, is about 38 cm (15 in) long, black above and white below, with reddish legs that trail well beyond its white tail in flight. It nests in central Oregon, Colorado, Nebraska, central Florida, northern California, to Mexico, West Indies, Brazil, and Peru but may migrate far from its normal range. Stilts feed on a variety of small aquatic life and some vegetable matter. With the AVOCETS, they make up the family Recurvirostridae.   WILLIAM F. SANDFORD

Stilwell, Joseph W.   [stil'-wel]

One of the most controversial American generals of World War II, Joseph Warren Stilwell, known as Vinegar Joe, b. Palatka, Fla., Mar. 19, 1883, d. Oct. 12, 1946, commanded U.S. and Chinese forces in Asia. He graduated from West Point in

Joseph W. "Vinegar Joe" Stilwell was a U.S. general who served as chief of staff to Gen. Chiang Kai-shek during the early years of World War II. Although his Chinese troops were driven out of Burma by the Japanese in 1942, he subsequently played a major role in the recovery of Burma. Stilwell had a stormy relationship with Chiang, whom he referred to as the "Peanut."

1904 and, following assignments in the Far East, served with the American Expeditionary Force in France in World War I. After the war Stilwell became an instructor at West Point and served in China.

After the outbreak of World War II he became chief of staff of Generalissimo CHIANG KAI-SHEK and commander of U.S. troops in the China-Burma-India theater. His Chinese and American troops were defeated by the Japanese and driven out of Burma in 1942; with the remnants of his forces, however, he made his way through difficult terrain to India. He spent the rest of the war attempting to regain Burma (the Allies finally accomplished this in 1945). The controversy around Stilwell arose chiefly from his friction with Chiang and from his public criticisms of the Chinese leader. Relieved of his command in 1944, he commanded U.S. troops on Okinawa until the end of the war.   WARREN W. HASSLER, JR.

Bibliography: Romanus, Charles F., and Sunderland, Riley, *Stilwell's Mission to China* (1953); Tuchman, Barbara W., *Stilwell and the American Experience in China* (1971); White, Theodore H., ed., *The Stilwell Papers* (1948; repr. 1972).

Stimson, Henry Lewis   [stim'-suhn]

The U.S. statesman Henry Lewis Stimson, b. New York City, Sept. 21, 1867, d. Oct. 20, 1950, distinguished himself as a champion of the sanctity of international agreements and as a wartime administrator. He graduated (1890) from Harvard Law School and joined a prestigious Wall Street law firm. An unsuccessful Republican candidate for governor of New York in 1910, Stimson served as President William H. Taft's secretary of war (1911–13) and as a colonel of artillery during World War I.

Stimson was governor-general (1928–29) of the Philippines and then secretary of state (1929–33) under President Herbert

Henry L. Stimson, U.S. secretary of state under Herbert Hoover, enunciated the Stimson Doctrine, a declaration that the United States would not recognize territorial changes brought about by force, in response to the Japanese occupation of Manchuria in 1931. During World War II, Stimson headed the War Department.

C. Hoover. A legalist, a moralist, and an internationalist, Stimson pressed—with limited success—for disarmament at the London Naval Conference of 1930. He opposed Japanese seizure of Manchuria, and U.S. nonrecognition of Japan's puppet regime of Manchukuo, because of its illegality, took form as the Stimson Doctrine (1931).

With the outbreak of World War II in Europe, President Franklin D. Roosevelt recruited the Republican internationalist to head the War Department for a second time (1940-45). Stimson organized the armed forces for war, opposed British Prime Minister Winston Churchill's strategy of attacking Nazi Germany through southern Europe, preferring an earlier invasion across the English Channel, and advised the president on nuclear fission. He headed the committee that decided on use of the atomic bomb to end the war with Japan. Stimson unsuccessfully proposed that the United States share its nuclear knowledge with the USSR and bring nuclear fission and its development under international controls. He wrote *The Far Eastern Crisis* (1936) and, with McGeorge Bundy, an autobiography, *On Active Service in Peace and War* (1948).

ELLIOT A. ROSEN

Bibliography: Current, Richard N., *Secretary Stimson, A Study in Statecraft* (1954; repr. 1970); Ferrell, Robert H., *American Diplomacy in the Great Depression: Hoover-Stimson Foreign Policy, 1929–1933* (1957); Morison, Etting E., *Turmoil and Tradition: A Study of the Life and Times of Henry L. Stimson* (1960; repr. 1964).

stimulant

Stimulant drugs excite the central NERVOUS SYSTEM, increasing alertness, decreasing fatigue, and delaying sleep. Some also impair appetite and may be prescribed medically to obese people in order to promote weight loss. Most users of these drugs experience a sense of well-being (euphoria), but this reaction is not universal and depends greatly on the drug taken and the dose. Signs of overstimulation by these drugs, such as muscle tremors or irregular heart rate, are common.

Almost all societies, even those that are still quite primitive, have discovered some indigenous plant that produces stimulant effects. Coca leaves, for instance, are chewed by South American Indians and are the source of the drug cocaine; khat leaves, whose active ingredient is norpseudoephedrine, are chewed by Middle Eastern peoples; betel nuts, containing arecoline, are chewed by Asians and South Pacific Islanders. Each of these drugs stimulates the autonomic nervous system as well as the brain.

Caffeine. The beverages coffee, tea, and cocoa, and many soft drinks contain CAFFEINE, the most widely used stimulant drug in the world. Cocoa contains not only caffeine but also theobromine, a compound closely related to caffeine; similarly, tea contains caffeine and theophylline, a stimulant drug often used medically to alleviate asthma. Cola drinks derive their caffeine content (2 percent) from the kola nut, which was chewed by people of the Sudan for its stimulant effects.

Few people who drink coffee, tea, cocoa, or cola-flavored soft drinks consider themselves drug users, because these beverages are accepted socially and because the amount of caffeine is small. A moderately strong cup of coffee may contain about 75 to 125 mg of caffeine, a dose that, for most persons, is just above the threshold for recognition. Furthermore, people differ greatly in their susceptibility to the stimulant effects of this drug, a difference thought to be based on genetic factors. Even over the course of an individual's lifetime, the response to caffeine may change. With increasing age caffeine users may experience for the first time insomnia or palpitations of the heart associated with irregular beats. Heavy drinkers of coffee or tea often become nervous, irritable, apprehensive, restless, and unable to sleep; such symptoms may be construed as a psychiatric disorder unless the history of caffeine misuse is known. Recognition of the drug effects of these beverages has led to the increased use of decaffeinated coffee, which now constitutes a major portion of the coffee market in the United States.

Cocaine. Sigmund Freud was among the first to describe the effect of COCAINE, an alkaloid drug, on the central nervous system; he confirmed the euphoric effects and the increased energy and alertness noted by coca leaf chewers for centuries. Soon after cocaine was discovered as the active principle of coca leaves (1855), it was used medically as a strong local anesthetic, especially during eye surgery. It also has been used as a nasal decongestant because it shrinks nasal mucous membranes by vasoconstriction. It is absorbed mainly through the mucous membranes of the nose or mouth.

High doses of cocaine are usually taken nasally to produce intense feelings of power, euphoria, and alertness. An abuser also may experience the feeling of having something alive crawling on the skin; physically, the heartbeat quickens and the person experiences muscle twitching, hypertension, sleeplessness, and nervousness. The person begins to be garrulous and later can become delirious. Although tolerance develops, no physical dependence occurs; psychic dependence (habituation) on this drug may occur, however, leading to addiction. Cocaine has very powerful effects if injected because it is quickly absorbed into the bloodstream.

Amphetamines. AMPHETAMINES, widely used in medical practice until recently, are sympathomimetic stimulants; that is, they act physiologically in ways similar to the sympathetic nervous system. Although synthetic, they are chemically related to ephedrine, a drug derived from a Chinese shrub, *Ephedra distachia*, which is a mild stimulant used to alleviate respiratory ailments. Amphetamines are known as "pep pills" or "diet pills" because they increase energy and feelings of euphoria and decrease the desire for food.

Amphetamine (phenylisopropylamine) was first introduced into medical practice in the 1930s; it was widely used as an appetite suppressant, as a treatment for narcolepsy (uncontrollable attacks of sleepiness), and as a treatment for hyperactivity in children. It was also inhaled as a nasal decongestant. Other drugs with similar actions were also synthesized, including methamphetamine, methylphenidate, and pipradol. Soon after the introduction of amphetamine as a medical drug, however, people discovered its euphoriant effect and began to abuse amphetamine. In the years immediately following World War II, for instance, the Japanese government made enormous amounts of amphetamines—used during wartime to prevent sleepiness—available to the public. Japan subsequently had a major outbreak of amphetamine abuse, especially among young people. Abuse of this stimulant remained a relatively minor problem in the United States until the enormous upsurge of drug abuse in the 1960s. Methamphetamine was a favored drug of abuse because it could be manufactured more easily by illicit means than other drugs. The drug diethyproprion was synthesized in an attempt to alter the chemical structure to reduce the euphoriant effect.

Tolerance to amphetamines develops with chronic use, so that doses from 10 to 1,000 times those used medically are employed by drug abusers. Such abuse, however, cannot long be sustained, and the user is forced to stop, at which point the person has such withdrawal symptoms as excessive sleepiness, ravenous appetite, and mental depression. While taking the drugs, many users experience mental states resembling paranoid schizophrenia.

Because of the dangers associated with the abuse of stimulants, their medical indications and manufacture have been severely curtailed in a number of countries. Although these measures have resulted in the decline of amphetamine use, this reduction has been paralleled by an increase in the illegal use of cocaine.

LEO E. HOLLISTER, M.D.

Bibliography: Bosco, James J., and Robin, Stanley S., *The Hyperactive Child and Stimulant Drugs* (1977); Chambers, Carl D., *Chemical Coping: A Report on Legal Drug Abuse in the United States* (1975); Ellinsworth, Everett H., and Lkilbey, M. Marlyne, eds., *Cocaine and Other Stimulants* (1977); Epstein, S. S., and Lederberg, Joshua, *Drugs of Abuse* (1971); Goodman, Louis S., and Gilman, Alfred, *The Pharmacological Basis of Therapeutics*, 5th ed. (1975); Thompson, Travis I., *Stimulus Properties of Drugs* (1971).

See also: DRUG ABUSE; NEUROPHARMACOLOGY.

stimulus-response psychology: see
BEHAVIORISM.

stingray

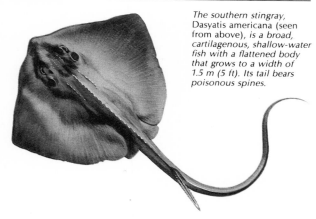

The southern stingray, Dasyatis americana (seen from above), is a broad, cartilagenous, shallow-water fish with a flattened body that grows to a width of 1.5 m (5 ft). Its tail bears poisonous spines.

Stingrays are much-feared venomous fishes in the subfamily Dasyatinae, family Dasyatidae. They are flattened like other RAYS and possess broad, winglike pectoral fins, which they flap in swimming. The tail is long and whiplike and bears two strong spines at its base. The stingray usually lies partly buried in the sand. If stepped on or seized, it lashes out vigorously with its tail and attempts to drive a spine into the intruder. The spines are derivatives of the scales and are associated with poison glands. The wound can be extremely painful, and more serious stings result from encounters with these species than with any other fish. The spines are serrated and solid, thus cutting and tearing the flesh as well as injecting poison. They were used in the past by the native peoples of the Indo-Pacific region in making their spears and knives. The powerful poison is produced by glands derived from epithelial cells in the integumentary sheath surrounding the spines. Apparently a protein, it affects the heart and the nervous system of mammals and can cause depressed respiration. The head of the stingray is not well defined, and there is no dorsal or caudal fin.

Like other rays, this species has no bones, the skeleton being composed of cartilage. The gill openings are ventral, with water for respiration being taken in through paired spiracles behind the eyes. The mouth is ventral and the teeth numerous, small, and blunt. Small clams, crustaceans, and other invertebrates are caught as food when the ray excavates a broad depression in the sand. The stingray is ovoviparous; the female carries eggs internally but does not nurture the fetuses, and the young are born alive. Stingrays are widely distributed in warm, shallow seas, and a few species ascend rivers in South America. They occur along the Atlantic coast of the United States as far north as Cape Hatteras. Some species may reach more than 1.5 m (5 ft) across. Stingrays may weigh from 0.7 kg (1.5 lb) to 340 kg (750 lb).   C. P. IDYLL

Bibliography: Gilbert, P. W., et al., eds., *Sharks, Skates and Rays* (1967); McCormick, H. W., et al., *Shadows in the Sea: The Sharks, Skates and Rays* (1963).

stinkbug

Stinkbugs make up the family Pentatomidae in the insect order of true bugs, Hemiptera, and are characterized by their shieldlike shape and five-segmented antennae. Pentatomids are moderate in size with mottled shades of green, gray, or brown; a few are brightly colored. The common name stems from the disagreeable odor produced by glands in the thorax. Some stinkbugs are plant feeders, some are predaceous, and some omnivorous. The brightly colored harlequin bug, *Murgantia histrionica*, is often destructive to cabbage.

GEORGE B. CRAIG

stinkhorn

Stinkhorn is the common name for various genera of foul-smelling, sometimes attractively colored fungi. Common types include the dog stinkhorn, *Mutinus caninus*, and the collared stinkhorn, *Dictyophora duplicata*. Stinkhorns form an underground white fruiting body resembling a turtle egg. They break through the ground's surface, and a phalluslike stalk, covered with a sticky, odorous mass of spores, grows from the center.

Stirling

Stirling was formerly a county in central Scotland, just north of Glasgow. Stirling was the county town. The hilly terrain consists of farmland, moorland, and peat bogs. The economy is based on coal mining, petroleum refining, livestock raising, the cultivation of cereal grains, and manufacturing of pharmaceuticals and aluminum.

Numerous Roman remains, including parts of the ANTONINE WALL, are located there. Stirling was once the home of Stuart kings. The county became part of the CENTRAL administrative region during the 1975 reorganization of Scotland's local government.

Stirling, James Frazer

The British architect James Frazer Stirling, b. Glasgow, Scotland, Apr. 22, 1926, has achieved an international reputation as an exponent of the brutalist movement in architecture. His buildings are marked by a bold use of metal, concrete, and enormous areas of glass and by extensive use of prefabricated industrial components. The buildings have been both praised and damned for their rigid adherence to a technocratic logic.

Stirling, in partnership (1956–63) with James Gowan, completed a number of controversial projects, including a housing development (1958) in Ham Common, Middlesex, and the Engineering Building (1959–63) at Leicester University; the latter has an office tower of glass and red tile set next to a large one-story workshop roofed with prismatic glass structures. Equally startling are Stirling's pyramidal steel-and-glass Faculty of History (1964–68) at Cambridge University and the Florey Building (1967–71) at Queen's College, Oxford.

Bibliography: Banham, Reyner, *The New Brutalism* (1966); Stirling, James, *James Stirling: Buildings and Projects, 1950–1974* (1975).

Stirling engine

The Stirling engine is a type of external-combustion engine. Invented in 1816 by a Scottish clergyman, Robert Stirling, it is now receiving serious consideration as an alternative to the present internal-combustion reciprocating engine, because the Stirling emits virtually no odor and low amounts of carbon monoxide and smog-forming hydrocarbons. The Stirling engine satisfies U.S. standards for emissions of nitrogen oxides and is also significantly quieter than conventional gasoline and diesel engines. Single-cylinder and multicylinder models are made.

A single-cylinder Stirling engine has five major components: an engine heater, a regenerator, an engine cooler, a displacer piston, and a power piston. The heater is a bank of stainless-steel tubes brazed into the cylinder head and regenerator. These tubes are kept hot by burning fuel in an external combustion chamber. The regenerator is a mass of wire sealed within several cups located around the outside of the engine. The cooler consists of bundles of small tubes surrounded by an annular chamber through which cooling water is circulated. The displacer piston is a hollow steel shell that fits loosely in the cylinder. The motion of the displacer piston is controlled by a piston rod connecting it to the drive mechanism in the crankcase.

The displacer piston requires no sealing rings, because little pressure difference exists above or below it, and thus a degree of leakage can be tolerated. The top of the displacer piston operates at approximately the same temperature as the heater, and the bottom operates at approximately the same temperature as the cooler. The power piston compresses a working gas (usually hydrogen or helium) and accepts the work of the gas when it is heated and then allowed to expand. The power piston, which is equipped with rings, is lo-

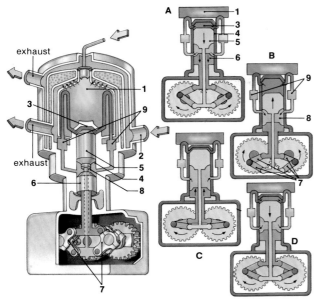

The Stirling engine (left) converts heat into mechanical energy through expansion of a fluid, usually hydrogen. Heat is transferred to the fluid from an external-combustion system (1); cooling is provided by cold-air intake pipes (2). (A) Working fluid in the hot end (3) of a cylinder (4) expands, forcing a displacer (5) and a piston (6) downward. (B) The drive linkage (7) moves the displacer upward, pushing fluid from the hot into the cold end (8). The fluid's heat is absorbed by regenerator boxes (9). (C) Fluid at the cold end is compressed by the piston. As its pressure and temperature rise, the fluid is cooled by passage through a cooling system. The compressed fluid regains stored heat as it flows through the regenerator boxes and returns to the hot end. (D) Expansion of the hot fluid pushes the displacer down again, and the cycle starts anew.

cated in the cold zone of the engine. Force is transmitted from the power piston to a rhombic drive mechanism by the power-piston connecting rod. This rod is hollow, and the displacer-piston rod passes through it.

The displacer piston controls the location of the gas within the volume established by the power piston. When the displacer piston is at the top of the cylinder, most of the gas is located in the cold spaces. Downward movement of the displacer piston forces the gas through the heat exchanger and up through the cooler, regenerator, and heater into the hot spaces. The net effect of the downward motion of the displacer piston is to move most of the gases up from the cold spaces to the hot spaces; upward motion of the displacer piston returns the hot working gas to the cool space above the power piston. The primary function of the power piston, then, is to compress and expand the gas, and the primary function of the displacer is to heat and cool the gas. The gas contained in the active space above the power piston goes through a thermodynamic cycle by which part of the heat from the heater is converted to work at the power piston and transmitted to the drive shaft.   JOSEPH W. DUFFY

Bibliography: Collie, M. J., *Stirling Engine Design and Feasibility for Automotive Use* (1979); Duffy, Joseph W., *Power* (1972).

stirrup

A stirrup is a support for the rider's foot hung from a SADDLE on belts that can be adjusted to the length of the rider's leg. The stirrup is also an aid in mounting a horse.

Stirrups were invented in China about 200 BC. Because they enabled a rider to keep his seat on a horse while charging an opponent, throwing a weapon, or shooting an arrow, they greatly increased the value of the horse in warfare. Stirrups were introduced in Europe in about the 8th century AD, probably by way of the Moors. During the Middle Ages, they led to a new form of warfare: shock combat between two

mounted, armored soldiers who charged at each other with long spears (lances). Stirrups enabled these combatants to remain upright in the saddle. Modern stirrups differ very little from their medieval counterparts.

stishovite   [stish'-uh-vite]

Stishovite (SiO_2), the densest known form of silica, is a high-pressure mineral found in some METEORITE CRATERS and believed to have formed from tremendous pressures generated by hypervelocity impact. Specific gravity is 4.29, compared to 2.65 for quartz, the commonest form of silica at the Earth's surface.

stoa   [stoh'-uh]

In the public areas of ancient Greece, as in the agora (marketplace), there often stood a portico—a sheltered walkway—along the walls of the more important buildings. This type of promenade, which probably evolved from an extended eave supported on posts, was called a stoa. Eventually, the stoa became quite elaborate, with interior colonnades and sometimes even a second story; its inner side sometimes contained murals or shops. Today, the most impressive such structure is the Stoa of Attalos (2d century BC) in Athens, which has been restored to its ancient grandeur.

stochastic process   [stuh-kas'-tik]

A stochastic process is a mechanism or phenomenon that evolves randomly in time, such as the flow of traffic at a signal-controlled intersection. The characteristic feature of a stochastic process is that at each instant in time there is a RANDOM VARIABLE that describes the state of the process—for example, the number of cars waiting at the intersection. A stochastic process is defined by the collection of random variables, one for each distinct instant of time. The simplest example of a stochastic process is the RANDOM WALK. This is the motion of a particle that at a sequence of times is moved one unit to the right or to the left, with probabilities that do not change. The random walk may be regarded as a simple discrete model for the motion—known as *Brownian motion*—of a microscopic particle bombarded by molecules in a liquid. Random walks, Brownian motion, and their generalizations find application in diverse areas of the social and natural sciences.

Many stochastic processes have the property that their future behavior depends only on the present state of the process and not on the past events leading up to this present behavior. Such a process is called a MARKOV PROCESS. Both the random walk and Brownian motion are Markov processes. A Markov process that can occupy only a discrete set of states, such as the random walk (but not Brownian motion), is called a *Markov chain*. The properties of a Markov chain are completely determined by its transition probabilities—the probability of moving from one state to another in a given time.

GEOFFREY S. WATSON

Bibliography: Brillinger, D. R., *Time Series: Data Analysis and Theory* (1975); Karlin, S., *A First Course in Stochastic Processes*, 2d ed. (1975).

stock   (finance)

In finance, a stock represents a share in the ownership of an incorporated company. In industrial societies wealth used in production is owned in the aggregate mostly by CORPORATIONS rather than by individuals because of the huge investments required. This trend began in 17th-century England when merchants formed JOINT-STOCK COMPANIES, pooling capital to be used jointly in trading and manufacturing. Participants then received dividends, shares of the common PROFIT proportionate to their original investments.

Securities. The wealth of individuals includes claims against, or investments in, corporations. These are called securities, the two most common being BONDS and stocks. Corporate bonds are evidences of corporate debt to the bondholder. Stocks are evidences of ownership, or equity (see EQUITY, finance). Investors buy stock in the hope that it will yield income from dividends and appreciate, or grow, in value.

Shares of widely held companies are traded on stock exchanges; those of small companies are occasionally bought and sold privately. In the United States at the beginning of the 1980s, about 20 million Americans owned stock. Many more invested indirectly through institutions such as pension funds and life insurance companies that hold securities. Stockholding is popular because it represents an ownership of capital that can be transferred easily by means of organized trading in the stock markets. There are two classes of stock: preferred and common.

Preferred Stock. Owners of preferred stock are entitled to a fixed or predetermined dividend before any common stock dividends can be paid. If profits are too low in any given period to cover all or part of a preferred dividend, the unpaid amount may be accumulated as a claim against future earnings. Preferred stock also has first claim if a company is liquidated and the proceeds divided among its shareholders. Whereas a preferred stock generally offers a relatively large dividend payment in relation to its market price—that is, it has a "high current yield"—there is little chance that its market price will increase dramatically unless the stock is convertible. Some preferred stocks can be converted into common stock at a specified exchange rate; the prices of convertible preferred stock, therefore, tend to rise with those of common stock.

Common Stock. Common stock carries with it all claims to a company's assets and earnings that have not been assigned to preferred stock or to corporate debt. Once preferred stock dividends have been met, any remaining profits are available for distribution to the common stock shareholders. Because there is no limit on the amount of dividends a common stock may receive, its market value tends to reflect assumptions made by investors as a group about the company's ability to increase earnings and thus pay higher dividends in the future. Although common stock offers less security of income and generally lower current yields, the chance of common stock increasing in market value is far greater than that of preferred.

Each owner of a corporation's common (and sometimes its preferred) stock is entitled to vote, on the basis of one vote per share held, for the company's directors, who in turn appoint its day-to-day management. If enough stockholders are dissatisfied with a company's performance, they can vote in a new management. Apart from voting, shareholders have none of the responsibilities of ownership. They risk losing whatever they have put into a company, but beyond that they are not liable for its debts or accountable for its management's actions.   W. Scott Bauman and Devon Allen

Bibliography: Knowlton, Winthrop, and Furth, John L., *Shaking the Money Tree: New Growth Opportunities in Common Stocks* (1972); Love, Richard S., and Husted, Darrell, *Super Performance Stocks* (1977); Mamis, Justin and Robert, *When to Sell: Inside Strategies for Stock Market Profits* (1977); Zahorchak, Michael G., *The Art of Low Risk Investing*, 2d ed. (1977).

See also: INVESTMENT BANKING; SAVING AND INVESTMENT.

stock   (punishment):   see PILLORY.

Stock, Frederick

Frederick Stock, b. Nov. 11, 1872, d. Oct. 20, 1942, was a German-American conductor and composer. After studying violin and composition at the Cologne Conservatory, he played (1891–95) in the Cologne Orchestra. He joined the Chicago Symphony as principal viola in 1895, was appointed assistant conductor in 1901, and elected conductor in 1905, serving until his death. Although his principal affection was for German and Russian romanticism, he was a musician of unusually catholic taste. He conducted more than 300 premieres of works by American composers and pioneered popular and children's concerts. He also founded the Chicago Civic Orchestra to train young professional musicians.

Bibliography: Ewen, David, ed., *Musicians since 1900* (1978).

Discography: Beethoven, L. van, *Piano Concerto No. 4*; Tchaikovsky, P. I., *Violin Concerto*.

stock market

Stock markets, or stock exchanges, are associations of brokers and dealers in securities who transact business together. They facilitate the financing of business (see FINANCE, BUSINESS) through the transfer of investment funds by bringing together the buyers and sellers of STOCKS and BONDS.

When individuals combine to form a CORPORATION, they agree not to withdraw their capital unless the business is terminated, or liquidated. If the original investors find themselves short of funds, however, they may easily raise cash by selling their stock in an organized stock market, which operates in most industrialized countries; in Europe a stock market is usually called a bourse.

Organized Exchanges. Stock exchanges are limited-member corporations run by boards of governors elected by the exchange members. To become a member, a person must buy a seat from a withdrawing member, fulfill certain requirements, and be approved by the governors. Rules are established by constitution and enforced by the governing boards. In the United States, trading is also regulated by the SECURITIES AND EXCHANGE COMMISSION. Most exchange members are partners in brokerage houses, called member firms, that make profits by charging commissions, usually negotiated, on trades made for customers. Members of an exchange may act as agents for customers as well as trading for their own accounts.

In the United States, the New York Stock Exchange (NYSE; founded 1790) accounts for more than 70% of trading in terms of market value; about 1,900 stocks, or issues, are listed. These stocks represent the largest publicly held businesses in the country. The American Stock Exchange (Amex), also located in New York City, accounts for another 15% of trading, mostly in stocks of companies smaller than NYSE-listed issues. Twelve regional exchanges also exist, essentially as markets for stocks of companies in their own geographical areas, although some stocks listed on the NYSE are traded on the regional exchanges. To have its securities listed on a major exchange, a corporation must meet such requirements as the regular publication of financial statements and a wide enough distribution of share ownership to provide an active market.

The members of the NYSE buy and sell securities in a large, open trading hall. Positioned about the trading floor are trading posts, each presided over by a specialist who "makes a market in," or handles all orders for, a particular stock or group of stocks. When a brokerage house receives an order for a listed stock, it is telephoned to the firm's trading partner on the floor of the exchange. The floor member then goes to the post where the stock is traded, asks for a quotation, and is given the current bid (the highest anyone is willing to pay at that moment) and asked price (the lowest at which anyone is willing to sell). If the broker has been ordered to buy the stock at the going price (market order), he or she simply does

Frightened investors jam the sidewalk in front of the New York Stock Exchange following the stock-market crash of Oct. 29, 1929. In 1934 the Securities and Exchange Commission was created to regulate market transactions and prevent the recurrence of such a crash.

so. The price and share volume of the trade are transmitted electronically to the quotation boards found in brokers' offices all over the country, becoming a matter of public record, and also are stored in a computer memory. Market orders are required to be filled immediately upon receipt.

The Specialist's Role. Sometimes, however, an investor unwilling to risk a sharp price change in the time between placement and execution of an order puts an upper limit on the buy side or a lower limit on the sell side of a proposed trade (limit order). If the market price does in fact change significantly and the broker is unable to make the trade at once, the order must be held for a specified time period, unless it has been designated as "good till cancelled" (GTC). The use of price-limit orders is the main reason that some members of the exchange must act as specialists. A broker with an order several points, or dollars, away from the current price cannot afford to watch the market on one particular stock when there are many other orders to be filled. So the limit order is given to the appropriate specialist to keep track of. When price fluctuations permit, the order is filled by the specialist, who receives a commission from the floor broker.

Unorganized Markets. In addition to trading in the organized exchanges, a large number of the unlisted stocks of relatively small companies are traded in the unorganized over-the-counter (OTC) markets. Several thousand dealers throughout the country make markets in unlisted securities by filling orders from the inventories of stocks they own. About 50,000 OTC issues are actively quoted through a computerized system, called the National Association of Securities Dealers Automated Quotation service (NASDAQ), in which the offices of the principal dealers are linked through private telephone lines.

Buying on Margin. The purchase of securities with partly borrowed money is called buying on margin. The lender usually holds the stock as collateral for the loan. The difference between the value of the stock and the amount borrowed is called the buyer's margin. Persons buy on margin because the more shares they have bought when a stock is going up, the more profit they make. If the stock price falls, of course, they lose their profit. Should the price decline, the lender calls on the borrower to put up additional margin. If the borrower is unable to do so, the lender may sell the securities and recover the amount of the loan. In the past, speculation on margin was carried to such extremes that margin buying came under federal regulation. Currently it is possible to borrow only 45% of the purchase price of stock.

Short Selling and Stop Selling. The sale of stock not owned but merely borrowed by the seller is called short selling. The lender of the stock holds the proceeds of the sale as security and also receives a premium for lending it. The seller hopes to be able to "cover" (buy the stock back to return it to the

lender) later at a lower price and thus to make a profit. A "stop sell" order is often used to protect profits or limit losses. These orders are conditional market orders in that they become market orders and are executed only when the market price drops to the specified price.   W. SCOTT BAUMAN

Bibliography: Eiteman, W. J., et al., *The Stock Market*, 4th ed. (1966); Flumiani, C. M., *Stock Market and Wall Street* (1978); Lorie, James H., and Hamilton, Mary, *The Stock Market: Theories and Evidence* (1973); Sobel, Robert, *Amex: A History of the American Stock Exchange, 1921–1971* (1972) and *N.Y.S.E.: A History of the New York Stock Exchange 1935–1975* (1975).

Stockhausen, Karlheinz   [shtohk'-how-zen]

The German composer Karlheinz Stockhausen operates a control board during a concert of his electronic music in Osaka, Japan. Stockhausen's works are attempts to communicate in purely musical terms, without reference to external associations. His techniques range from strict serialism to player improvisation.

The German composer Karlheinz Stockhausen, b. Aug. 22, 1928, has been a leader in avant-garde music since the mid-1950s. He studied at the *Musikhochschule* in Cologne, at the University of Cologne, and was a pupil (1952–54) of Olivier Messiaen in Paris. There he met Pierre Boulez and worked with the experimental composition technique known as *musique concrète*, in which tape-recorded natural sounds are manipulated through splicing, reversal, speed alteration, and other techniques. He then became music director of the Studio for Electronic Music in Cologne (see ELECTRONIC MUSIC). The study of phonetics and communication theory has further influenced his work.

His earliest music reveals traits of Bartók, Schoenberg, Stravinsky, and Webern; it was Webern's music that pointed the way to his subsequent innovations. To Webern's theory of presenting the notes of the chromatic scale in series, Stockhausen added the serial ordering of other musical dimensions, such as volume, duration, and tone color. He expanded Webern's concept of points of interest to what he termed "group composition," in which several groups of materials, each having its own character, are linked together, sometimes leaving the order of presentation to the performer, as in *Klavierstück XI* (1956).

Stockhausen's imaginative use of electronic and acoustic materials and elements of chance has produced such works as *Gruppen* (1955–57), *Telemusik* (1966), *Mikrophonie* I (1964), *Autumn Music* (1974), and *Sirius* (1975–76).
ROBERT L. PARKER

Bibliography: Cott, Jonathan, *Stockhausen* (1973); Harvey, Jonathan, *The Music of Stockhausen: An Introduction* (1975); Maconie, Robin, *Stockhausen* (1976).

Stockholm   [stahk'-hohlm]

Stockholm, the capital and largest city of Sweden, lies on the country's Baltic Sea coast, about 725 km (450 mi) west of Leningrad. Located astride a navigable waterway between Lake Mälaren and the sea, the city occupies about 20 islands and several peninsulas. Its population is 1,512,200 (1977 est.). January temperatures, averaging −3° C (27° F), are indicative of the long, harsh winters. July average temperatures are 17° C (63° F). The annual rainfall of about 560 mm (22 in) is well distributed through the year.

In the New York Stock Exchange during active trading, stockbrokers visit trading posts to obtain quotations on current prices of securities and to buy and sell on their clients' behalf. The exchange, located on Wall Street, has been in operation since 1790.

Although founded early in the 13th century, Stockholm did not gain prominence until the 16th century. It became the capital of Sweden in 1634 and is now the financial, cultural, and political center of the country.

Contemporary City. Stockholm has been called the "Venice of the North," although its waterways are navigated not by picturesque gondolas but by practical ferryboats. A number of bridges have been built to link the various districts. Norrmalm, the financial heart of modern Stockholm, lies north of the channel, with a second business district, Södermalm, to the south. Between the two on three channel islands is the oldest part of the city, Gamla Staden (Old Town)—the site of Sweden's Royal Palace (rebuilding completed in 1754). Along the narrow, winding streets are many fine residences built in the 16th and 17th centuries. To the west of Gamla Staden, on a peninsula jutting into Lake Mälaren, is Stockholm's City Hall. Completed in 1923 from plans by Ragnar Östberg, it is often considered the most striking building in the city. Stockholm is famous for its cleanliness and for its large number of parks and open spaces. On Djurgården (a peninsula reserved for parkland and a cultural center) is Skansen, an open-air museum.

Stockholm is now Sweden's chief manufacturing city; it is second as a port only to Göteborg. Once known for its woodworking industries, the city now produces metal and machine products, automobiles, and modern communications equipment. Still a major producer of paper and other wood products, Stockholm is now also a major food-processing center. It is the most important wholesale and retailing center in Sweden and the home of Sweden's principal stock exchange.

The Royal Palace, the official residence of the king of Sweden, is freely accessible to tourists. Within the palace is a famous collection of Gobelin tapestries. Nearby is the Great Church (begun 1250), the seat of Sweden's Evangelical Lutheran state church and the oldest building in the city. The University of Stockholm, founded in 1877 as a private institution, was taken over by the state in 1960 and is now the country's largest university. The Nobel Prizes are awarded annually in Stockholm, with the exception of the Nobel Peace Prize, which is presented in Oslo, Norway.

History. Stockholm is thought to have been originally established as a defense outpost on one of the channel islands that now make up Old Town. A member of the Hanseatic League, the city gained importance during the late Middle Ages as an exporter of metals, timber, and furs from its hinterland. Following the Swedes' successful overthrow of Danish rule in 1523, Stockholm became the center of the new Swedish kingdom. Under Gustav II Adolf (r. 1611–32) Sweden became a major European power. His daughter and succcessor Christina (r. 1632–54) established Stockholm as an intellectual and cultural center.   NORMAN J. G. POUNDS

Bibliography: Anderson, Burnett, *Stockholm: Capital and Crossroads* (1953); Anton, Thomas J., *Governing Greater Stockholm: A Study of Policy Development and System Change* (1975); Kindborg, Ulf, and Welander, Göran, *The Stockholm Guide,* trans. by Stanley Reitz, 2d ed. (1972); William-Olson, William, *Stockholm: Structure and Functions* (1960).

stocks

Stock is the common name for any of 50 species of garden plants of the genus *Matthiola,* in the mustard family, Cruciferae. The common stock, *M. incana,* has annual, biennial, and perennial forms. Native to southern Europe, it has oblong leaves. The flowers occur as racemes on upright spikes, and colors include white, red, and yellow. The 10-weeks stock, an annual, blooms 10 weeks after seeding.

KENNETH R. ROBERTSON

Stockton

Stockton, the seat of San Joaquin County in central California, lies in the fertile San Joaquin valley, about 145 km (90 mi) east of San Francisco. It has a population of 124,500 (1979 est.). A 128-km-long (80-mi) channel, opened in the 1930s, connects Stockton with San Francisco Bay. The city is a processing and distribution center for fruits and nuts. Its industries also manufacture glass products. An art gallery, several museums, San Joaquin Delta College (1935), and the University of the Pacific (1851) are located there. Founded in 1847 as Tuleburg, the city became a service center for miners during the Gold Rush. Stockton developed after the arrival of the railroad in 1869.

Stockton, Frank R.

An American writer and editor, Frank R. Stockton, b. Philadelphia, Apr. 5, 1834, d. Apr. 20, 1902, is best known for his children's stories and gently amusing, romantic tales. Among his 23 books of fiction are *Ting-a-Ling* (1870), *Rudder Grange* (1879), and *The Floating Prince and Other Fairy Tales* (1881). His short story "The Lady, or the Tiger?" (1884), with its intriguing unresolved ending, is perhaps his most popular work.

Bibliography: Griffin, Martin I., *Frank R. Stockton: A Critical Biography* (1939; repr. 1965).

Stockton, Robert Field

As an American naval commander, Robert Field Stockton, b. Princeton, N.J., Aug. 20, 1795, d. Oct. 7, 1866, helped defeat enemy forces in California during the MEXICAN WAR (1846–48); later he became a U.S. senator (1851–53) from New Jersey. The son and grandson of lawyers who were prominent in New Jersey politics, Stockton served in the War of 1812 and the Algerian War (1815) against the Barbary pirates. He supported the movement for settling freed slaves in Africa and in 1821 helped the American Colonization Society negotiate a treaty securing the territory that became Liberia. Soon after the Mexican War began, Stockton became commander of the Pacific Squadron. He took command of land and sea forces, and in July and August 1846 he defeated the Mexicans in southern California, proclaimed California a U.S. territory, and established a government there. Stockton resigned from the navy in 1850. In the Senate, he proposed a bill to abolish flogging in the navy and championed other naval reforms.

SEYMOUR V. CONNOR

Stoddard, Solomon   [stah'-durd]

Solomon Stoddard, b. Boston, Sept. 27, 1643, d. Feb. 11, 1729, was for 59 years the most influential clergyman in the western half of colonial Massachusetts. After studying at Harvard he settled (1670) at Northampton and came to have such widespread influence that he was lovingly called "pope of the Connecticut Valley." Always noted for his sense of freedom from tradition, Stoddard relaxed customary restrictions on church membership in his parish. He believed that baptism and the Lord's Supper could serve as means of influencing unconverted individuals, so he offered those sacraments to all persons who sought them. Although "Stoddardeanism" was condemned by other Puritan leaders, such as the Mathers, it was widely adopted in western Massachusetts and Connecticut. Stoddard was succeeded in Northampton by his grandson Jonathan EDWARDS.   HENRY WARNER BOWDEN

Bibliography: Trumbull, James R., *History of Northampton, Massachusetts,* 2 vols. (1898–1902); Winslow, Ola Elizabeth, *Jonathan Edwards* (1940; repr. 1972).

stoichiometry   [stoy-kee-ahm'-uh-tree]

Stoichiometry may be defined either as the measurement of the relative combining weights of the elements in chemical compounds or, more broadly, as the area of chemistry that deals with the laws of chemical combination and the weight relationships between chemical substances involved in a chemical reaction (see CHEMICAL COMBINATION, LAWS OF).

The word *stoichiometry* was coined in 1792 from the Greek words meaning "first principle" and "to measure." When describing a chemical reaction, *stoichiometric* generally means "without side reactions"; that is, a stoichiometric reaction yields the desired product without the occurrence of other, usually unwanted reactions that might consume part of the reactants. When describing a chemical substance, the term *stoichiometric compound* means a single substance (not a mixture) in which two or more elements are chemically bonded together to form a compound of definite, fixed composition.

It is difficult to overemphasize the importance of stoichiometry; it is one of the cornerstones upon which the science of chemistry is built. Indeed, much of the chemistry of the late 18th and 19th centuries involved the measurement of combining weight ratios of elements for the purpose of establishing a comprehensive and accurate table of atomic weights. New elements were discovered in the process, and chemistry developed as a quantitative science.

Although chemists no longer undertake quantitative chemical measurements to establish atomic weights, stoichiometry is extremely important and widely used for a variety of purposes in modern chemistry. To cite but a few examples, in QUANTITATIVE CHEMICAL ANALYSIS volumetric methods are based on chemical reactions that proceed stoichiometrically so that a chemically equivalent amount of reagent has been added when the endpoint has been reached in a titration; gravimetric methods depend on a stoichiometric relationship between the sample constituent to be determined and the weight of a pure substance isolated from the sample; and in the synthesis of compounds, stoichiometry is used to calculate theoretical yields of products based on known amounts of starting materials.

Stoichiometry is also an important, though sometimes hidden, consideration in a wide variety of everyday matters, such as determining how much water-softening chemical to add to obtain water of a certain softness, and adjusting the carburetor of an automobile engine to achieve the optimum air-to-fuel ratio.

Stoichiometric Compounds. The definite composition of stoichiometric compounds is reflected in the chemical formulas written to represent them. Thus, the formula H_2O represents water, a pure stoichiometric compound in which the atom ratio of hydrogen to oxygen is always exactly 2:1 and the weight ratio of hydrogen to oxygen is almost always exactly 2.0160 (2 × 1.0080) to 15.9994, or 0.12600. For heavy water, in which the heavier hydrogen isotope DEUTERIUM replaces some of the hydrogen atoms, the atom ratio remains 2:1, but the weight ratio is variable, depending on the extent of isotopic replacement. Practically all chemical formulas use ATOMIC WEIGHTS (listed in common tables), which represent an element's naturally occurring mixture of isotopes (as opposed to an "enriched" mixture).

If the stoichiometric formula of a pure compound is known, its percentage composition may easily be calculated. Using the water example above, the weight percentages of hydrogen and oxygen are

$$\%\,H = \frac{2.0160}{2.0160 + 15.9994} \times 100 = 11.19\% \text{ hydrogen}$$

$$\%\,O = \frac{15.9994}{2.0160 + 15.9994} \times 100 = 88.91\% \text{ oxygen}$$

The calculation can be reversed, of course, to establish the empirical formula of an unknown but pure chemical compound when the weight percentages of its constituent elements are determined (such as by chemical analysis). Whereas a stoichiometric compound has a definite, fixed composition, a mixture can have an infinitely variable composition.

Most compounds are stoichiometric. A few solid inorganic compounds, however, do not have constant, integral ratios of atoms (for instance, ferrous oxide has the composition $FeO_{1.06-1.19}$). The variability in composition arises from defects in the crystal lattices of these solids. Although such substances are often called nonstoichiometric compounds, the term is somewhat misleading because it does not refer to a truly pure compound.

Stoichiometric Reactions. Stoichiometry calculations almost invariably involve the expression of amounts of pure chemical substances in terms of moles rather than grams. A mole is defined as that amount of substance (atoms, molecules, ions,

etc.) whose weight in grams is the same as its formula weight (see AVOGADRO NUMBER).

The stoichiometry of a chemical reaction is implicit in the balanced chemical equation written to represent that reaction (see REACTION, CHEMICAL). Thus the balanced chemical equation

$$\underset{\text{lead nitrate}}{Pb(NO_3)_2(aq)} + \underset{\text{potassium chloride}}{2KCl(aq)} = \underset{\text{lead chloride}}{PbCl_2(s)} + \underset{\text{potassium nitrate}}{2KNO_3(aq)}$$

indicates that 1 mole (331.20 g) of lead nitrate reacts with 2 moles (2 × 74.56 = 149.12 g) of potassium chloride to form 1 mole (278.10 g) of lead chloride (insoluble) and 2 moles (2 × 101.11 = 202.22 g) of potassium nitrate. Moreover, it indicates that 207.19 g of lead ion reacts with 70.91 g of chloride ion to form 278.10 g of lead chloride. Stated still differently, the 278.10 g of lead chloride formed is chemically equivalent to 207.19 g of lead (or 331.20 g of lead nitrate) and to 70.91 g of chloride (or 149.12 g of potassium chloride).

In the above example the reactants were taken to be present in chemically equivalent amounts. This is not the usual case; generally, one reactant is present in short supply and therefore limits the amount of product that is formed. Calculation of the amounts of reactants consumed and products formed must be based on the amount of this "limiting reactant," as illustrated by modifying the above example. If the amount of potassium chloride is limited to 100.00 g instead of 149.12 g, but the amount of lead nitrate remains at 331.20 g, then the amount of lead chloride formed is

$$\left(100.00 \text{ g KCl}\right)\left(\frac{1 \text{ mole KCl}}{74.56 \text{ g KCl}}\right)\left(\frac{1 \text{ mole PbCl}_2}{2 \text{ moles KCl}}\right)\left(\frac{278.10 \text{ g PbCl}_2}{1 \text{ mole PbCl}_2}\right)$$
$$= 186.49 \text{ g PbCl}_2$$

or simply

$$\frac{100.00}{149.12} \times 278.10 = 186.49 \text{ g PbCl}_2$$

Moreover, not all of the lead nitrate is consumed by the reaction; the amount consumed is

$$\left(100.00 \text{ g KCl}\right)\left(\frac{1 \text{ mole KCl}}{74.56 \text{ g KCl}}\right)\left(\frac{1 \text{ mole Pb(NO}_3)_2}{2 \text{ moles KCl}}\right)\left(\frac{331.20 \text{ g Pb(NO}_3)_2}{1 \text{ mole Pb(NO}_3)_2}\right)$$
$$= 222.10 \text{ g Pb(NO}_3)_2$$

or simply

$$\frac{100.00}{149.12} \times 331.20 = 222.10 \text{ g Pb(NO}_3)_2 \text{ consumed.}$$

The amount of lead nitrate that is unused, that is, remains in excess, is

$$331.20 - 222.10 = 109.10 \text{ g Pb(NO}_3)_2 \text{ unused excess.}$$

The amount of potassium nitrate formed is calculated similarly.

When a gas is involved as a reactant or product, stoichiometry calculations are extended to include weight-to-volume relationships. Since one mole of any ideal gas occupies 22.41 liters under standard conditions of temperature and pressure (0° C and one atmosphere pressure), calculation of volume (in liters) from moles involves simple multiplication by 22.41. If conditions are nonstandard, then the ideal gas law $PV = nRT$ (see GAS LAWS) must be used to make conversions between moles and liters. The chemical reaction between calcium carbonate and hydrochloric acid serves as an example. The reaction is represented by the balanced equation:

$$\underset{\substack{\text{calcium} \\ \text{carbonate}}}{CaCO_3(s)} + \underset{\substack{\text{hydrochloric} \\ \text{acid}}}{2HCl(aq)} = \underset{\substack{\text{calcium} \\ \text{carbonate}}}{CaCl_2(aq)} + \underset{\substack{\text{carbon} \\ \text{dioxide}}}{CO_2(g)} + \underset{\text{water}}{H_2O(aq)}$$

If one mole (100.08 g) of calcium carbonate undergoes quantitative reaction, one of the products is a mole (44.00 g) of carbon dioxide gas that occupies 22.41 liters at 0° C under a pressure of one standard atmosphere (760 mm Hg). Under the nonstandard conditions of, say, 0.800 atm (608 mm Hg) and 55° C (328 K), this mole of carbon dioxide would occupy

$$V = \frac{nRT}{P} = \frac{(1.000)(0.0821)(328)}{(0.800)} = 33.66 \text{ liters}$$

LAURANCE A. KNECHT

Bibliography: Margolis, Emil J., *Formulation and Stoichiometry* (1968); Nash, Leonard K., *Stoichiometry* (1966); O'Connor, Rod, et al., *Solving*

Problems in Chemistry: With Emphasis on Stoichemistry and Equilibrium, 2d ed. (1977); Sasin, George S., et al., *Chemistry Computations and Reactions* (1967).

Stoicism [stoh'-i-sizm]

Stoicism was a philosophical movement lasting about 500 years, beginning in the 3d century BC. Rational self-control and adherence to the laws of nature were fundamental aims of the Stoic school, one of the four official schools of philosophy in the Hellenistic and Roman period (the others were the Academics, the Epicureans, and the Peripatetics, who continued Aristotle's Lyceum). The Stoic school took its name from the Painted Portico (*Stoa Poikilē*) of the ancient Athenian marketplace, where it first met.

The founder of this school, ZENO OF CITIUM, was influenced by the CYNICS. He proposed an austere ethical philosophy based on the individual's duty to preserve dignity and reason. Zeno taught that each human being shares in a Reason that orders the cosmos (a divine logos). Humans become good by cultivating a reasonable outlook and not giving way to emotion. The Stoic sage does not regret happenings that are outside his control, including the whole course of nature, predestined by Providence. Only the individual's own attitudes seem to be within his control. The human soul is simple and solely rational. The expression "he took it philosophically" reflects the ideal of the Stoic sage as the typical philosopher.

In Stoic physics, the world is throughout a kind of "spiritual matter," with small centers of rational potentiality as parts. The Stoic logic emphasized hypothetical reasoning and closely anticipated the propositional calculus of the 20th century. This hypothetical logic studied such inferences as "for any *x*, if *x* is divisible by 2, then *x* is an even number."

Three main periods are recognized in the development of Stoicism. The Old Stoics held to the austere ethics of Zeno and developed an elaborate logic. Leading members of this group are Zeno, the former boxer CLEANTHES, and the prolific author and logician Chrysippus. The Middle Stoics began to compromise the rigor of earlier doctrines. Although carrying on a constant fight with Epicureanism, these Stoics were scholars who adopted many ideas from the works of Plato and Aristotle, particularly in natural science and psychology. In its third, or Roman period, Stoicism placed much more emphasis on civic duty, social responsibility, the importance of good law, and the equal basic rights of all human beings. The Roman Stoics also turned away from the detailed systematic theory of the Middle Stoics to a renewed emphasis on the earlier Stoic view of philosophy as a way of life. In this period Stoicism had a great practical impact on Roman law, administration, and literature. Roman Stoics include EPICTETUS, a slave who became a leading philosopher, Emperor MARCUS AURELIUS, the tragedian and author SENECA, and to some degree, CICERO. Stoicism, particularly that of Seneca, was lauded throughout the Middle Ages, and interest in the school revived during the Renaissance.   ROBERT S. BRUMBAUGH

Bibliography: Edelstein, Ludwig, *The Meaning of Stoicism* (1966); Oates, W. J., ed., *The Stoic and Epicurean Philosophers* (1940); Rist, J. M., ed., *Stoic Philosophy* (1969) and *The Stoics* (1978).

Stoke-on-Trent [stohk-ahn-trent]

The city of Stoke-on-Trent lies on the River Trent in northern Staffordshire, England, about 65 km (40 mi) north of Birmingham. Its population is 257,800 (1977 est.). Because of its near monopoly in England's china and earthenware manufacture, it is called the Potteries. Among the best-known trademarks are Wedgwood, Spode, Minton, Doulton, and Copeland. Other industries include coal mining and the production of rubber, steel, bricks, tiles, and chemicals. The city has a museum, an art gallery, and a technical college.

Pottery making was begun in the area in 1715 by Josiah Wedgwood. In 1910, six towns—Longton, Fenton, Stoke-upon-Trent, Hanley, Burslem, and Tunstall—united; in 1925 they became the city of Stoke-on-Trent. Arnold Bennett, born in Hanley in 1867, described the district in his novels on "five towns."

Stoker, Bram [stoh'-kur]

Bram Stoker, b. Dublin, Nov. 8, 1847, d. Apr. 20, 1912, created one of the most potent stories ever to haunt the imagination in the Gothic romance DRACULA. Although Stoker wrote many other horror stories, he and they might be forgotten were it not for the phenomenal success enjoyed by his novel, first published in 1897, and the innumerable plays and films adapted from it. Exploiting traditional vampire tales and a fashion for the supernatural, Stoker's Transylvanian Count Dracula became the prototype of all subsequent vampire myths.

Bibliography: Farson, Daniel, *The Man Who Wrote Dracula* (1975); Wolf, Leonard, *The Annotated Dracula* (1975).

Stokes, Sir George Gabriel [stohks]

George Gabriel Stokes, b. Skreen, County Sligo, Ireland, Aug. 13, 1819, d. Feb. 1, 1903, was a British physicist and mathematician whose law of viscosity (1851), describing the movement of a small sphere through a viscous fluid, established the science of hydrodynamics. He investigated the wave theory of light, named and explained the phenomenon of fluorescence in 1852, and in 1854 theorized an explanation of the Fraunhofer lines in the solar spectrum. Stokes developed mathematical techniques for application to physical problems, founded the science of geodesy, and greatly advanced the study of mathematical physics in England.   RICHARD HIRSH

Stokowski, Leopold [stuh-kahf'-skee]

The great conductor Leopold Stokowski, b. London, Apr. 18, 1882, d. Sept. 13, 1977, was one of the most colorful public personalities of his time. He studied at Oxford University and the Royal College of Music as well as in Paris and Munich. He came to the United States in 1905, and, after a few years as a church organist in New York City, he became (1909–12) conductor of the Cincinnati Symphony Orchestra, immediately attracting attention with his flamboyant conducting style. The peak of his career was reached during the next 23 years (1912–38) as he developed the PHILADELPHIA ORCHESTRA into one of the world's greatest ensembles. At the same time, he developed a personal image of almost unprecedented glamour. For theatrical effect he had spotlights focused on the podium, highlighting his aristocratic profile, flowing blond hair, and graceful hands (he conducted without a baton). He scandalized purists by altering composers' orchestrations and making lush orchestral arrangements of Bach's organ music. His programming of modern music eventually ruffled his audiences and the orchestra's board of directors, and over this issue Stokowski left Philadelphia in 1936. He continued an active and controversial career well into his nineties. Stokowski appeared in several films during the 1930s and '40s, most notably in Walt Disney's *Fantasia* (1940).

Bibliography: Chasins, Abram, *Leopold Stokowski: A Profile* (1979); Johnson, Edward, *Stokowski: Essays in Analysis of His Art* (1973); Kupferberg, Herbert, *Those Fabulous Philadelphians* (1969).

Discography: Bach, J. S., *Stokowski Conducts Bach*; *Great Russian Showpieces*; Ives, C., *Symphony No. 4*; Orff, C., *Carmina Burana*; Schoenberg, A., *Gurre-Leider*.

STOL

Short takeoff and landing (STOL) aircraft encompass a class of aircraft with landing and takeoff distances considerably less than those of conventional aircraft of similar weight and size. Short takeoff and landing performance is fundamentally achieved by reducing the landing and takeoff speeds of an aircraft.

The minimum flying speed of an aircraft is primarily determined by two factors: the ratio of the weight of the aircraft to its wing planform area, and the tendency of a wing to stall or lose lift. Stalling is a result of attempting to produce too much lift at low flight speeds. Low landing and takeoff speeds can be achieved either by providing the aircraft with a large wing in relation to its weight or by providing a means to augment the lift at a given flight velocity. Ways of augmenting the lift include blowing the high-velocity exhaust of the propulsion engine directly over the wing surface, thus increasing the relative velocity of the airflow over the wing and injecting high-velocity air into the airflow over the upper wing surface through slots in the wing, thereby delaying stall to a lower speed.

Lift augmentation appears to offer a more attractive approach for future military and commercial applications than the large-wing-area solution. The large-wing-area approach produces an aircraft that does not fly smoothly in turbulent air and has too much wing surface to obtain good cruise efficiency at speeds comparable to modern transport aircraft. Many aircraft, however, have been built that achieve STOL performance by means of a large wing area. A number of prototypes, on the other hand, have been designed with lift augmentation. Two experimental aircraft have been constructed and flown recently using the technique of blowing the jet engine exhaust directly over the wing surface.

H. C. CURTISS, JR.

Bibliography: Campbell, John P., *Vertical Takeoff and Landing Aircraft* (1962); McCormick, B. W., *Aerodynamics of V/STOL Flight* (1967).

Stolypin, Pyotr Arkadievich   [stuh-li'-pin]

Pyotr Arkadievich Stolypin, b. Apr. 14 (N.S.), 1862, d. Sept. 18 (N.S.), 1911, premier (1906–11) of Russia, was the last great statesman of the Russian Empire. He was a provincial governor before becoming interior minister and chairman of the council of ministers (premier) under Emperor NICHOLAS II in 1906. He had to steer a difficult course between the reactionary bureaucracy and the left wing of the DUMA, often resorting to unconstitutional methods. In June 1907 he dissolved the Duma and arbitrarily promulgated new electoral laws to secure a more compliant assembly. Combining policies of force and reform, he ruthlessly repressed dissent while trying to create a large class of peasant landholders. In 1911 he fell out simultaneously with the Duma, the state council, and the emperor. Soon after, he was assassinated by a police double agent.

FORRESTT A. MILLER

Bibliography: Bock, Maria, *Reminiscences of My Father, Peter A. Stolypin*, trans. by Margaret Paroski (1970); Conroy, Mary S., *Peter Arkadievich Stolypin: Practical Politics in Late Tsarist Russia* (1976).

stomach

The stomach is an expandable reservoir for food located in the abdomen. Its wall has three layers of muscle (below center): a longitudinal outer layer (1), a circular middle layer (2), and an oblique inner layer (3). These muscles churn and knead solid food, helping to convert it into a semiliquid mass known as chyme. (Right) As the stomach fills with food, wavelike contractions of the wall begin (A). As the waves move along the wall (B), the chyme is forced out (C), little by little, through the pyloric sphincter (4) into the duodenum—the first part of the small intestine. The stomach empties within 4 hours after ingestion of a meal, and digestion is completed in the small intestine.

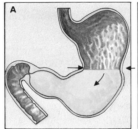
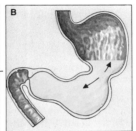
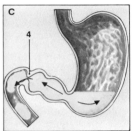

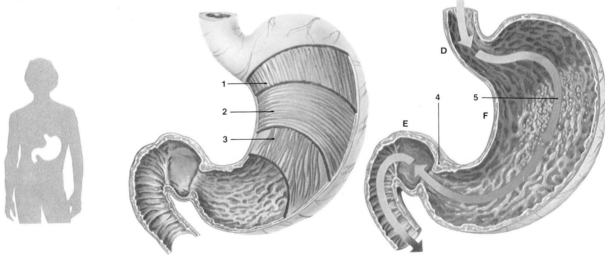

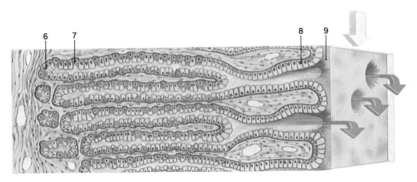

Gastric juices produced by the stomach contain pepsin, a protein-digesting enzyme, and hydrochloric acid (HCl), which aids in the digestion of fibrous parts of tissues. The stomach lining also secretes mucus, which forms a barrier to protect it from the gastric juices. (Above right) The stomach wall is dotted by glands that secrete mucus in the cardiac (D) and pyloric (E) regions. Mucus, pepsinogen—an inactive form of pepsin—and HCl, which activates the pepsin, are secreted in the fundic region (F). The pathway of food (5) indicates the area of acid activity (orange). (Left) A cross section of the stomach lining shows the chief cells (6), which secrete pepsinogen, the parietal cells (7), which produce HCl, and the mucus cells (8), which produce the barrier (9).

The stomach, a bottle-shaped organ in humans, is part of the DIGESTIVE SYSTEM and receives food from the esophagus. Normally less than 20 cm (8 in) long and weighing about 1 percent of the body weight, it is capable of distending greatly to accommodate large meals without increasing the pressure or tension on its walls.

The outstanding characteristic of the stomach is its ability to secrete large amounts of hydrochloric acid, which digests protein, activates pepsinogen to form the enzyme pepsin, and kills bacteria that enter the stomach along with food. During a meal, the stomach may secrete 20 milliequivalents of gastric juice in an hour. Acid is secreted from the oxyntic gland area of the gastric mucosa; other cells in this area secrete mucus and the proenzyme pepsinogen. Mucus lubricates and protects the wall of the stomach from physical damage by food and prevents acid from digesting the stomach itself. Pepsin is an enzyme which aids in the digestion of meat and other protein.

The mucosa of the distal third of the stomach (antrum) produces and releases the hormone gastrin into the bloodstream, which stimulates acid secretion and the growth of mucosa in the digestive tract. The sight of food and its presence within the mouth activate the vagus nerve, which directly stimulates the parietal cells to secrete acid, and the antral gastrin cells, which release gastrin into the bloodstream. The vagus nerve also stimulates pepsinogen and mucus secretion. Distention of the stomach and protein digestion products also stimulate both the parietal cells and the release of the hormone gastrin.

In abnormal conditions, the secretion of acid and pepsin is ultimately responsible for peptic ulcer disease, characterized by painful lesions in the gastric wall. Medical treatment of peptic ulcer disease is directed either at inhibiting acid secretion or at neutralizing secreted acid by the use of antacids. Surgical treatment of ulcers is either a vagotomy, in which the vagus nerve is severed, thereby reducing stimulation, or an antrectomy, in which the antrum is removed, thereby reducing the release of gastrin. Both operations inhibit acid output by about 60 percent.   LEONARD R. JOHNSON

Bibliography: Friedman, M. H., ed., Functions of the Stomach and Intestine (1974); Magee, D. F., Gastrointestinal Physiology (1962); Schade, Rudolf O. K., Gastric Cytology (1960); Wolf, Stewart, The Stomach (1965).

stomata

Stomata (singular, stoma) are microscopic openings or pores most often found in the outer, or epidermal, layer on the underside of leaves and in stems. A stoma is a space between two adjoining specialized cells called guard cells. These spaces allow an exchange of gas to take place between the atmosphere and internal tissues and also aid in the evaporation of water. Variation in turgor pressure in the guard cells resulting from external and internal conditions controls the size of the opening. When pressure is low the stoma is small, reducing loss of water. At the height of photosynthetic activity the stoma is large, allowing the free exchange of gases.
                                                                JOSEPH BECKER

Stommel, Henry Melson

Henry Melson Stommel, b. Wilmington, Del., Sept. 20, 1920, is an American oceanographer whose theoretical research and studies of the Gulf Stream have added fundamentally to the knowledge of ocean-current dynamics. Formerly on the faculty at Harvard University (1960–63), Stommel was named professor of oceanography at Massachusetts Institute of Technology in 1963.

Stone, Barton Warren

A frontier evangelist, Barton Warren Stone, b. near Port Tobacco, Md., Dec. 24, 1772, d. Nov. 9, 1844, was the leader of the revival at Cane Ridge, Ky., that in 1801 attracted thousands of people and continued for 6 or 7 days and nights. Pressured by the opposition of his Presbyterian denomination to the excesses of the revival and its implicit denial of Calvin-

ism, Stone formed a new group that took the Bible as its only creed and called itself simply the Christian Church. Extremely congregational and never precisely defined, the Christian Church for the most part joined with the like-minded followers of Alexander CAMPBELL in 1832 to become part of the DISCIPLES OF CHRIST.

Bibliography: West, William, Barton Warren Stone: Early American Advocate of Christian Unity (1954).

Stone, Edward Durell

The American architect Edward Durell Stone, b. Fayetteville, Ark., Mar. 9, 1902, d. Aug. 6, 1978, was a leading exponent of Europe's new architecture during the 1930s. In his design (1937) for the Museum of Modern Art in New York City, he gave institutional respectability to the Bauhaus-inspired International Style in the United States. Later, however, he renounced its austerity in favor of a more romantic and decorative mode. Stone's U.S. Embassy (1954–58) in New Delhi, with its templelike base and lush, fountain-filled courtyard, was hailed as an architectural marriage between East and West. Some of Stone's later projects, such as the KENNEDY CENTER FOR THE PERFORMING ARTS (1964–69) in Washington, D.C., are less successful, being overly monumental in style and scale.
                                                            LEON SATKOWSKI

Bibliography: Forsee, Aylesa, Men of Modern Architecture (1966); Stone, Edward Durell, Evolution of an Architect (1962).

Stone, Harlan Fiske

Harlan Fiske Stone, b. Chesterfield, N.H., Oct. 11, 1872, d. Apr. 22, 1946, served as associate justice (1925–41) and chief justice (1941–46) of the U.S. Supreme Court. A graduate of Amherst (1894) and Columbia (LL.B., 1898), Stone taught and practiced law in New York before serving (1910–23) as dean of the Columbia Law School. Prior to appointing Stone to the Court, President Calvin Coolidge, a college friend, appointed (1924) him attorney general. In this position he reorganized the Federal Bureau of Investigation. Stone always tried to balance individual liberty and social justice, often turning away from his natural conservatism to embrace a strong position in favor of civil liberties, as in Minersville School District v. Gobitis (1940), where, as the lone dissenter, he considered saluting the flag an act of public coercion.

Bibliography: Konefsky, Samuel J., Chief Justice Stone and the Supreme Court (1946; repr. 1971); Mason, Alpheus T., Harlan Fiske Stone: Pillar of the Law (1956).

Stone, I. F.

Isidor Feinstein Stone, b. Philadelphia, Dec. 24, 1907, gadfly conscience of the American political left, was the publisher of I. F. Stone's Weekly from 1953 to 1971. Prior to these years he wrote for a series of liberal dailies and weeklies, pointing to problems and abuses often ignored by his colleagues. He wrote vigorously for an audience of activists and iconoclasts about McCarthyism and related anti-Communist campaigns, the wars in Korea and Vietnam, and the repression of the blacks and other minority groups.   CALDER M. PICKETT

Bibliography: Middleton, Neil, ed., The Best of I. F. Stone's Weekly (1973); Stone, I. F., "Izzy on Izzy," New York Times Magazine, January 22, 1978.

Stone, Irving

American novelist and biographer Irving Stone, b. San Francisco, July 14, 1903, works in a genre that he calls the "biographical novel." These novels, of which Stone has written several, recount the lives of well-known historical figures. They may be artists such as Michelangelo in The Agony and the Ecstasy (1961), writers such as Jack London in Sailor on Horseback (1938), or political figures such as Eugene Debs in Adversary in the House (1947). Stone intersperses biographical data with fictional narrative on the psychology and private lives of his subjects. He has also written biographies of Clarence Darrow (1941) and Earl Warren (1948) and short biographies of men who lost presidential elections (1943).

CHARLOTTE D. SOLOMON

Bibliography: Jackson, Joseph Henry, *Irving Stone and the Biographical Novel* (1954); Newquist, Roy, *Counterpoint* (1964).

Stone, Lucy

The reformer and feminist Lucy Stone devoted her life to the emancipation of women and slaves in the United States. After working for 9 years to earn money for her education, she began a career of lecturing and writing on behalf of the women's rights movement, becoming one of its most eloquent and effective leaders.

The American feminist Lucy Stone, b. West Brookfield, Mass., Aug. 13, 1818, d. Oct. 18, 1893, became one of the 19th century's leading reformers and advocates of women's rights, winning fame especially for her persuasive and moving oratory. She began her career shortly after graduating (1847) from Oberlin College in Ohio. Her marriage to Henry Blackwell (see BLACKWELL family) in 1855 did not silence her, for he encouraged her efforts in behalf of abolition and women's rights and accepted the fact that she would not adopt his name. Their daughter, Alice Stone Blackwell, was also a noted feminist.

Lucy Stone was cofounder (1869) with Julia Ward Howe of the American Woman Suffrage Association; she also established its *Woman's Journal* (1870), which was published regularly for 50 years.

LORETTA ELLEN ZIMMERMAN

Bibliography: Blackwell, Alice S., *Lucy Stone: Pioneer of Woman's Rights* (1930; repr. 1971); Rice, Elinor R., *Morning Star: A Biography of Lucy Stone* (1961; repr. 1978).

Stone Age: see PALEOLITHIC PERIOD.

stone alignments

Ancient alignments of standing stones are found principally in western and northern Europe. They vary from a simple pair of stones, usually 2 to 5 m (7 to 16 ft) in height and separated by a few tens or hundreds of meters, to multiple arrays of 10 or more parallel rows running for a distance of more than 2 km (1.2 mi) and containing originally more than 1,000 stones, as at CARNAC in western France. Hardly any of them has been dated by excavation or radiocarbon, but it is assumed that they are broadly contemporary with other MEGALITHS in the same areas and belong to the late Neolithic Period or the Early Bronze Age (3000–1500 BC).

In Britain and Brittany, where alignments have been studied in detail, five main types can be distinguished. In the simplest case a single standing stone, or MENHIR, often has a flat face that points to a prominent notch or slope on a distant skyline, marking an extreme northerly or southerly rising or setting of the Sun or Moon. If the skyline was far enough away (perhaps 30 km/18.6 mi), the direction of the astronomical event and the date of its occurrence could have been determined with great precision to give a fixed point in the annual calendar or in the longer and more complex cycle of the risings and settings of the Moon. This, in turn, could have made it possible to predict eclipses of the Moon.

In the second type the alignment is indicated either by a pair of neighboring menhirs, by the axis of symmetry of a stone ring, or by an outlying menhir seen from the center of a stone ring. Occasionally, as at Temple Wood in Argyll, Scotland, a short row of stones may indicate several astronomical directions. In most cases the events marked are extreme risings or settings of the Sun and Moon; but occasionally the alignment may be to the rising or setting of a bright star. In Britain there are alignments to sunrises at the equinoxes and at dates intermediate between the equinoxes and the solstices, chosen so as to divide the year into 16 "months," each of 22, 23, or 24 days. This complex annual calendar, it has been suggested, may have been used during the Early Bronze Age (2000–1500 BC).

The third type of alignment consists of straight rows of stones, usually 1 to 2 m (3.3 to 6.5 ft) high and a few meters apart, that may be single or double and run for several hundred meters. The ends are sometimes closed by a transverse slab. These occur mainly in Britain, in western and northern areas where suitable stone is plentiful. They are especially frequent on Dartmoor in southwest England. In many cases they run up to, and sometimes beyond, a CAIRN or small stone circle. The majority do not seem to have any astronomical significance. A few broader avenues of standing stones also exist, such as that at AVEBURY, that follow a sinuous course and seem to have been processional ways.

Alignments of the fourth kind, consisting of multiple parallel rows of hundreds of stones, are confined to the Carnac area of southern Brittany, in France. They are somewhat sinu-

The stone alignments found in western and northern Europe date from 3000 to 1500 BC. (Left) The most famous alignments stand at Carnac, France, where parallel rows of stones run for distances of more than 2 km (1.2 mi). (Above) At Callanish, on the Isle of Lewis, Scotland, alignments radiate from a ring marking astronomical directions.

ous in plan but have been much restored, not always accurately, during the last century, so that it is now difficult to be certain of their original form. Their date and purpose are unknown, although it is generally assumed that they were built in the late Neolithic Period, from 2500 BC to 2000 BC, perhaps by the people associated with the BEAKER CULTURE.

The fifth and last form of alignment consists of fan-shaped arrays of small stones, usually not more than 1 m (3 ft) in height. These are confined to northeast Scotland and to the Carnac area of Brittany. Their date and purpose are again unknown, but it has been suggested that they could have served as a graphical means of calculating the precise time of the solstices or of the maximum and minimum declinations of the Moon, which do not necessarily coincide with the moments of rising and setting. This interesting speculation awaits further study.

The evidence provided by these stone alignments indicating a detailed knowledge of observational astronomy in prehistoric times is at variance with the traditional view that astronomy began only in the literate civilizations of Mesopotamia and Egypt at a much later date (see ASTRONOMY, HISTORY OF). The cumulative weight of the evidence from dozens of different sites, however, makes it impossible to dismiss so many apparently significant alignments as the result merely of accident or coincidence. R. J. C. ATKINSON

Bibliography: Burl, Aubrey, *The Stone Circles of the British Isles* (1976) and *Prehistoric Avebury* (1979); MacKie, E. W., *Science and Society in Prehistoric Britain* (1977); Thom, Alexander, *Megalithic Lunar Observatories* (1971) and *Megalithic Sites in Britain* (1967); Wood, J. E., *Sun, Moon and Standing Stones* (1978).

See also: ARCHAEOASTRONOMY; STONEHENGE.

stone curlew

Stone curlews are nine species of birds belonging to the family Burhinidae. The common stone curlew, *Burhinus oedicnemus*, is the only species that breeds in Europe. Others inhabit Australia, such as the Australian stone curlew, *B. magnirostris*; Asia, such as the great stone curlew, *Esacus recurvirostris*; Africa; and tropical America.

Stone curlews are long-legged ground birds ranging from about 36 to 51 cm (14 to 20 in) in length. Their plumage is mottled and streaked in browns and grays to blend with the background. The stout bill is short to moderately long. Some species are known as thickknees because of the swollen appearance of their ankle joints. The eyes of these birds are extremely large, an adaptation to their habit of feeding nocturnally on worms, insects, and other small animals. Stone curlews nest in a depression scraped in the ground; both sexes care for the downy chicks.

ROBERT J. RAIKOW

The common stone curlew, B. oedicnemus, *found in uncultivated areas of England, southern Europe, and northern Africa, is primarily a ground bird that flies only short distances. Generally nocturnal, it becomes active at dusk and utters loud, wailing cries.*

stone fly

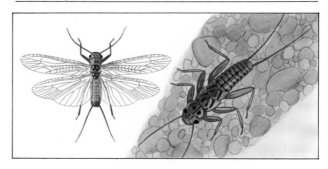

An adult stone fly, Perla bipunctata *(left), resembles only slightly its relative the grasshopper. A stone-fly nymph (right) can survive only in freshwater rivers and streams that have not been polluted.*

Stone flies, order Plecoptera, are somewhat flattened, soft-bodied, rather dull-colored insects generally found near streams. They have four membranous wings, and the hind wings nearly always have a rounded lobe on the rear side; the wings are held flat over the body at rest. The immature stages are aquatic and usually live on the underside of stones in streams. Some stone flies emerge and mate during the fall and winter; others emerge in the summer.

DONALD J. BORROR

Stone Mountain

Stone Mountain is a gray granite mountain in De Kalb County, northwest Georgia, approximately 26 km (16 mi) east of Atlanta. This huge monadnock, which covers a 5-km² (2-mi²) area, rises 198 m (650 ft) from its base and 514 m (1,686 ft) above sea level.

On the northern face of the mountain a bas-relief has been carved, depicting the equestrian figures of Confederate leaders Jefferson Davis, Robert E. Lee, and Stonewall Jackson. Gutzon BORGLUM, sculptor of Mount Rushmore, began the work in 1917 but discontinued it in 1925 because of a dispute with the sponsors. Augustus Lukeman worked on the project (1925–29), but it was completed by Walter Kirtland Hancock in 1968 and was dedicated in 1970. The monument is surrounded by a state park.

stonecrop

Stonecrop, or "live-forever plant," is the common name for the genus *Sedum*, with over 350 species of small succulent plants, in the orpine family Crassulaceae. They are native to the temperate and frigid zones and are thus quite hardy. Some are perennials that die to the ground in winter, and others are evergreen. Low-lying plants, stonecrops affix themselves to or grow in the crevices of rocks and walls. The flowers are usually white or yellow, with instances of pink and red. The leaves vary: opposite, alternate, and often in whorls. Most stonecrops are easily grown from seed. Propagation is also achieved through divisions, cuttings, or even a broken stem. The low-creeping evergreen *S. acre* has small leaves,

Wallpepper stonecrop, S. acre, *a European evergreen perennial, grows in a thick mat of leaves and flourishes in dry soil. Its name is derived from its preference for stony environs (walls, rock gardens, and ruins).*

less than 0.64 cm (0.25 in) long. Its yellow flowers appear in summer. *S. spectablile* is a tall stonecrop extensively used in mixed borders or as a pot plant.

Stonehenge

Stonehenge, the most famous prehistoric MEGALITH (standing-stone monument) in Europe, lies 13 km (8 mi) north of Salisbury, England. Excavations and radiocarbon dating have revealed that Stonehenge had an exceptionally long history of use as a ceremonial or religious center or both. In period I (c.2800 BC), the site was enclosed by a circular ditch with an internal bank and an entrance on the northeast side. Inside the bank on the inner side of the ditch was a ring of 56 pits—named Aubrey holes for their 17th-century discoverer, John Aubrey—that later were used for the burial of cremated bod-

Stonehenge, Europe's best-known megalithic monument, is formed by linteled sarsens and surrounded by an earthwork. The Stonehenge circle is believed to have been a prehistoric ceremonial and religious center that may also have had astronomical significance.

ies. Outside the entrance, the builders erected the huge, upright Heelstone and a timber gate. In period II (c.2100 BC), people of the BEAKER CULTURE built an earthwork approach road, now called the Avenue, to the entrance of the bank and ditch. They also set up within the earlier ring a double circle of bluestone MENHIRS (large, rough-hewn standing stones), which came originally from the Preseli Mountains of southwestern Wales. Both the Avenue and the double circle were orientated toward the summer solstice sunrise.

In period III (from c.2000 BC), builders erected in the center of the site a circle of 30 sarsen-stone uprights 30.5 m (100 ft) in diameter and capped by a continuous ring of sarsen lintels. This circle, in turn, encloses a horseshoe-shaped setting of five sarsen trilithons—formations in which two uprights support a lintel. All of the sarsen stones, which were transported about 30 km (20 mi) from the Marlborough Downs, were dressed to shape with stone hammers and jointed together. The precision with which this complex was laid out and the architectural refinements it displays are unparalleled in the other megalithic structures of northwestern Europe. Some of the bluestones were later reerected in the center in an oval structure that contained at least two miniature trilithons, and holes were dug for the rest to be set in two concentric circles (the so-called Y and Z holes) outside the sarsen circle. This plan was abandoned unfinished, however, and the bluestones were finally rearranged (c.1550 BC) in the circle and horseshoe whose remains survive today. In period IV (c.1100 BC), the Avenue was extended to the River Avon, 2 km (1.25 mi) from Stonehenge.

Among the megalithic monuments of Europe Stonehenge is unique because of its long period of use and the precision of its plan and its architectural details. The long-held thesis that Stonehenge was a Druid temple is untenable, because the Druids did not appear in Britain until a few hundred years before the Christian era. In recent years many attempts have been made to interpret Stonehenge as a prehistoric astronomical observatory, but the site is now so ruined, and so

much restored, that any attempt to ascertain its original alignments must rely principally on guesswork. All that can be said with confidence is that from period II onward the structure's axis of symmetry pointed roughly in the direction of the sunrise at the summer solstice.   R. J. C. ATKINSON

Bibliography: Atkinson, R. J. C., *Stonehenge* (1978); Harrison, Harry, and Stover, L. E., *Stonehenge* (1972); Hawkins, G. S., *Stonehenge Decoded* (1965); Hoyle, Fred, *On Stonehenge* (1977); Stover, Leon E., and Kraig, Bruce, *Stonehenge: The Indo-European Heritage* (1978).

stonemasonry

Stone has been used as a structural, finish, and roofing material throughout the centuries. New materials and methods of construction developed during the 20th century, however, have almost entirely limited building stone to its use as a finish material where its decorative qualities are of value. The range of texture, color, and working qualities of building stone are almost inexhaustible.

In addition to its geological classification, building stone is further classified as cut, or dimension, stone and rubble—rough, irregularly shaped stone. Rubble walls may be composed of stones as they are collected (fieldstones) or of unfinished stone as it comes from the quarry. Rubble stones are usually set in a random pattern and are often laid without mortar (dry wall construction). Ashlar walls, in contrast, are built of cut and squared dimension stone. They may be set in regular courses, as brick is, or in broken courses where different sizes of stone are used. The characteristics and strength of ashlar masonry work depend on the properties of the stones, their size, finish, and arrangement, and the mortar joints. Mortar for stonework is usually made of white portland cement, hydrated lime, and sand. Mortar in the joints is raked back from the surface as the stones are set. The joints are later pointed, or filled, to make the finished joint.

The most common use of dimension stone is in the making of masonry veneer, where the stone is used as a finishing material. Tie wires, corrugated metal strips, or other anchoring devices extend from the mortar joints to a backing material or structural frame. The stone veneer is held away from the backing by the ties or anchors.   DON A. WATSON

Bibliography: Dalzell, J. R., *Simplified Concrete Masonry Planning and Building*, ed. by Frederick Merritt, 2d ed. (1972); Dalzell, J. R., and Townsend, Gilbert, *Masonry Simplified: Tools, Materials, Practices*, vol. 1, 3d ed. (1972); DeCristoforo, R. J., *Concrete and Masonry* (1975).

stoneware: see POTTERY AND PORCELAIN.

stonewort

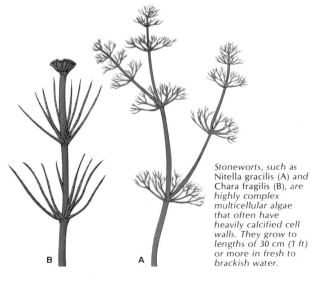

Stoneworts, such as Nitella gracilis (A) and Chara fragilis (B), are highly complex multicellular algae that often have heavily calcified cell walls. They grow to lengths of 30 cm (1 ft) or more in fresh to brackish water.

Stonewort is the common name for a special group of multicellular plants within the algal class Charophyceae, division Chlorophyta. Stoneworts are found in brackish water, rivers, and lakes with hard water, usually attached to the bottoms. Best represented by the genus *Chara*, stoneworts are encrusted in lime deposits secreted by their cell walls, hence their name. The calcium carbonate deposits contribute to the formation of marine limestone. Highly complex, the structures of the stonewort resemble higher plants, rather than algae. Stoneworts are thus considered a highly developed form of green algae. They have rhizoids that resemble roots, branching stems, and whorls of branches. Stoneworts grow from stalk tips. Sexual reproduction is achieved through the fusion of one large egg from the female sex organ (oogonium) and one small sperm from the male sex organ (antheridium). Sterile cells surround the reproductive organs, a phenomenon not found in other algae. Stoneworts, however, lack the characteristic sterile jacket layer found in bryophytes and vascular plants. Stoneworts are an important food for certain waterfowl.

Stoph, Willi   [shtohf]

The East German politician Willi Stoph, b. July 9, 1914, is prime minister of the German Democratic Republic. A bricklayer, he joined the Communist party in 1931 and was a member of the resistance in Germany during World War II. He became minister of the interior (1952–55) and minister of defense (1956–60). He then served (1964–74, 1976–80) as chairman of the Council of Ministers, or prime minister, and as chairman of the Council of State (ceremonial head of state; 1974–76). As prime minister he began (1970) negotiations with West German chancellor Willy Brandt on the normalization of relations.

Stoppard, Tom   [stahp'-urd]

Tom Stoppard, an English dramatist whose works reflect the influence of the theater of the absurd, won an international following with his Rosencrantz and Guildenstern Are Dead (1966). That play won a Broadway Tony Award, as did Travesties (1974).

An English dramatist, Tom Stoppard, b. Zlin, Czechoslovakia, July 3, 1937, moved to England with his parents as a young boy and there began a career as a reporter and free-lance journalist. His theatrical career began with the writing of radio and television plays, but his first international success came with *Rosencrantz and Guildenstern Are Dead* (1966), a retelling of the story of *Hamlet* through the eyes of courtiers, that won the 1968 Tony and New York Drama Critics Circle awards. Stoppard's inventiveness continued with such plays as *The Real Inspector Hound* and *Enter a Free Man* (1968), *Jumpers* (1972), *Travesties* (1974), *Dirty Linen and New-Found-Land* (1976), and *Night and Day* (1979). He has also written a novel, *Lord Malquist and Mr. Moon* (1966).

storax   [stowr'-aks]

Storax (genus *Styrax*) comprise about 30 species of deciduous and evergreen shrubs and some trees in the storax family, Sty-

racaceae. Native to the temperate areas of Eurasia, the United States, and Malaysia, they are characterized by hairs on their foliage; the flowers of most species have five petals and ten stamens. *Storax* also refers to an aromatic resin found in the bark of a few Asiatic trees, such as the SWEET GUM.

JANE PHILPOTT

Storey, David   [stohr'-ee]

The English writer David Storey, b. July 13, 1933, is the finest of a group of working-class writers from northern England who emerged during the 1960s. His novel *This Sporting Life* (1960) is based on his own experiences as a professional Rugby League football player and was made into a successful film in 1963. Storey's other works include the novel *Saville,* which won the Booker Prize in 1976, and the play *The Changing Room* (1971).

stork

The European white stork, Cicónia ciconia, *nests on rooftops or in trees. According to folk legend, the stork is a messenger of good luck.*

Storks, family Ciconiidae, comprise ten genera of eighteen species of medium to large birds with long legs and beaks. They are closely related to the herons, family Ardeidae, and to the ibis and spoonbills, family Threskiornithidae. Storks are found on all continents except Antarctica but are most abundant in the tropics. The American wood stork, *Mycteria americana,* is the only species found in the United States, breeding in Florida and neighboring states and migrating widely.

Storks range from 76.2 to 167.6 cm (2.5 to 5.5 ft) in height. Black and white are the predominant colors, but some species have part of their plumage colored with bright pink during breeding season. The diet of storks varies greatly in the different species, depending on their locations. Some storks favor a diet of aquatic food; some will simply catch the most available insects, frogs, fish, snakes, or rodents; and some will feed on only one type of food.

The majority of storks are colonial nesters, and most nests are built in trees and on cliffs. Others are either solitary nesters or nest in loose clusters. All species lay between three and five eggs that hatch in 32 days. Both sexes share the incubation and feeding of the young. After the young fly, usually in 55 to 110 days, they continue to return to the nest for feeding and for roosting at night for several days until they are independent. Three species, including the white stork, *Ciconia ciconia,* undertake long-range, seasonal migrations. Other species wander erratically according to local ecological conditions but generally remain in the same range throughout the year.   PHILIP KAHL

Bibliography: Haverschmidt, Francois, *The Life of the White Stork* (1949); Kahl, M. P., *Marvels of Animal Behavior* (1972) and *Wonders of Storks* (1978).

Storm, Theodor

Theodor Storm, b. Sept. 14, 1817, d. July 4, 1888, was a German short-story writer and poet whose dreamlike tale *Immensee* (1849; Eng. trans., 1863) is a classic of late romantic writing. Like much of his work, it evokes the melancholy of lost love and suggests his indebtedness to Eduard MÖRIKE and Heinrich Heine. Storm's early lyric poetry is still widely read, although his reputation rests on the tales. Among them, the historical *Aquis Submersus* (1876; trans. as *Beneath the Flood,* 1962) and the psychologically poignant *Der Schimmelreiter* (1888; trans. as *The White Horseman,* 1962) have retained their popularity. Loneliness and misunderstanding are dominant themes in his work.

Bibliography: Artiss, David, *Theodor Storm: Studies in Ambivalence* (1979); McCormick, E. A., *Theodor Storm's Novellen: Essays on Literary Technique* (1964).

storm: see CYCLONE AND ANTICYCLONE.

Storrs, John Bradley   [stohrz]

The sculptor John Bradley Storrs, b. Chicago, June 29, 1885, d. Apr. 22, 1956, was among the first Americans to explore cubism and by the 1920s had produced several nonobjective works. Storrs first became interested in sculpture as a student in Berlin. Thereafter he returned to the United States for a short period in order to study in Boston and with Charles Grafly at the Pennsylvania Academy of the Fine Arts, Philadelphia. In 1912 he went to Paris and began to work with Auguste Rodin, soon becoming the master's favorite pupil. Most of Storrs's early work reflects the influence of the great French sculptor. Storrs subsequently turned to cubism and remained within its sphere for the rest of his life.
                                                            HARRY RAND

Bibliography: Craven, Wayne, *Sculpture in America* (1968).

Story, Joseph

The youngest man ever appointed to the U.S. Supreme Court, Joseph Story, b. Marblehead, Mass., Sept. 18, 1779, d. Sept. 10, 1845, was also one of the Court's greatest legal scholars. He served from 1811 until his death and helped Chief Justice John Marshall establish the Supreme Court's power of JUDICIAL REVIEW. Story's law commentaries, including *Bailments* (1832) and *Constitution of the U.S.,* 3 vols. (1833), won him world renown as an authority on U.S. jurisprudence.

Bibliography: Dunne, Gerald T., *Justice Joseph Story and the Rise of the Supreme Court* (1970); McClellan, James, *Joseph Story and the American Constitution* (1971).

Story, William Wetmore

William Wetmore Story, b. Salem, Mass., Feb. 12, 1819, d. Oct. 7, 1865, was a cultivated American intellectual and late-neoclassical sculptor. He practiced law until commissioned (1845) to model a portrait for a monument to his father, Joseph Story, a U.S. Supreme Court justice. Story accomplished this in Rome, where he became a member of an international literary circle. Sought after for official portraits, he preferred to create romantic Near-Eastern heroines such as *Medea* (c.1868; Metropolitan Museum, New York City). His popular *Cleopatra* (1858; marble replica, Metropolitan Museum), immortalized in

Nathaniel Hawthorne's *The Marble Faun* (1860), displays the wealth of archaeological detail so appealing to the Victorian mind.   JOAN C. SIEGFRIED

Bibliography: James, Henry, *William Wetmore Story and his Friends* (1903; repr. 1969).

story theater: see IMPROVISATIONAL AND EXPERIMENTAL THEATER.

Stoss, Veit   [shtohs, fyt]

Veit Stoss, 1447–1533, was one of the greatest German sculptors of the late Gothic period. In 1477, after establishing himself as a master in Nuremberg, he moved to Poland, where he carved, painted, and gilded the enormous *Altarpiece of the Virgin* (1477–89) in the Church of Saint Mary at Kraków. The reliefs and statues of this spectacular early work reveal an astounding richness of invention and great dramatic power. The realism and understanding of human expression evident in the Saint Mary altarpiece are also seen in Stoss's other major work in Kraków, the red marble tomb (1492) of King Casimir IV in Kraków Cathedral.

After his return to Nuremberg in 1496, Stoss produced a large number of extremely moving sculptures, both reliefs and freestanding statues, in wood and in stone. Stoss's successful career was interrupted in 1503 by his implication in a criminal action, which led to his public punishment and, later, a brief imprisonment. Pardoned by the emperor Maximilian in 1506, Stoss went on to produce additional sculptures of extraordinary quality. Among these the painted, wooden *Annunciation* (1517–18) suspended from the vault in the Church of Saint Lorenz in Nuremberg and the altarpiece (1520–23) now in Bamberg Cathedral are outstanding.
                                                     MARK J. ZUCKER

Bibliography: Burkhard, Arthur, *The Cracow Altar of Veit Stoss* (1972); Müller, Theodor, *Sculpture in the Netherlands, Germany, France, and Spain, 1400 to 1500* (1966).

Stout, Rex

An American detective novelist, Rex Stout, b. Noblesville, Ind., Dec. 1, 1886, d. Oct. 27, 1975, created the character of Nero Wolfe, a corpulent private detective with a passion for fine food and orchids and such a thorough distaste for the modern world that he rarely left his New York brownstone. Archie Goodwin, Wolfe's legman, plays Dr. Watson to Wolfe's Sherlock Holmes, and their repartee, coupled with Stout's authoritative prose, accounts for the popularity of the series. Stout's first mystery was *Fer-de-Lance* (1934). The Nero Wolfe series includes *The League of Frightened Men* (1935), *Too Many Cooks* (1938), *If Death Ever Slept* (1957), and *The Doorbell Rang* (1965).

Rex Stout, an American writer of detective fiction, achieved international popularity with his series of novels featuring Nero Wolfe, a crime fighter who solves mysteries without leaving his desk. The corpulent, epicurean sleuth was introduced in Fer-de-Lance *(1934) and has appeared in 46 of Stout's novels.*

stove

This early Franklin-type stove was modeled on a design from the 1740s by Benjamin Franklin. Made of cast iron, the stove fitted into the fireplace, heating the room from its three sides. Much more efficient than a fireplace, this type of stove was not as efficient as airtight models, which used half as much wood. Although it was not suitable for cooking, the stove could keep a kettle warm.

Stoves are devices that produce, contain, or direct heat for a specific purpose. When designed solely for cooking, they are often called ranges.

An open fire is relatively ineffective for heating and cooking. Humanity learned to contain fire, perhaps at first with rocks or mud and later with open braziers, which are still used today in many regions of the world.

One of the first applications of metals was to build a stove. Cast iron was used for this purpose in China about 25 to 200 AD through a process in which melted iron was poured into sand molds. This technology traveled slowly, however, and Europe did not begin to use cast-iron stoves until the 1400s. Until this time the word *stove* meant a single room of the home that was kept heated as a kind of hothouse and opened into other rooms to provide heat.

Stove making was an early industry in the American colonies; as early as 1647 a blast furnace at Saugus, Mass., was casting iron stoves. Many of these early stoves were jamb stoves, which were intended to make a fireplace more efficient and distribute its heat more effectively. The most common was the five-plate stove, made of five flat iron plates that formed a rectangular box with one open side. A hole was cut in the back of the fireplace completely through the wall to the room behind it, and the stove was inserted into the opening with the open end of the stove being flush against the rear wall of the fireplace. The remainder of the stove protruded into the room to be heated. When a fire was built in the stove, it served to heat both areas. Designers of these early stoves delighted in casting intricate designs into the visible portions. In America many of the molds used for a number of early stoves were purchased from a German supplier, and the inscription on the design was in the German language. For this reason the five-plate jamb stoves were often known as German stoves.

The six-plate stove originated in Holland and Scandinavia. It was enclosed on all sides and was designed to sit away from the wall. Equipped with a fuel door, an opening for air intake, and a hole for insertion of a smokepipe, it was a relatively efficient heater. In the American colonies it was known as the Holland or box stove.

Most early stoves were not suitable for cooking. Small, shallow pans could be placed on the top of a stove, but most of the cooking was still done in the large fireplaces of the kitchen areas. Some stoves began to serve a dual purpose when boiling holes were provided in the top. A metal plug could be lifted out of the hole, and an earthenware or metal pot of the correct size inserted. By the mid 1700s an oven chamber was also occasionally incorporated into the six-plate stove. The Franklin stove, invented by Benjamin Franklin in 1742, was made of cast iron, originally with a partially open front, and was designed to fit into a fireplace. It radiated more heat and burned less fuel than an ordinary fireplace and was widely used for heating.

Wood, charcoal, and coal fueled both stoves and fireplaces. In the 1840s gas was first used for cooking, and interest grew as the availability of gas spread. The electric range was introduced in 1914. Oil and kerosene stoves have also been used for cooking in many areas.

Today most homes contain several types of stoves and may utilize different types of fuel. A gas or electric range serves the cooking needs, and a gas, oil, or coal furnace may provide space heating. In addition, wood heaters, many of them based on the box-type stoves, have again found popularity. Modern wood heaters of the air-starvation type are efficient and effective. Central heating furnaces are available that use wood as the primary fuel source, with an oil or gas burner to supplement or provide heat when the wood chamber is not fired. Modern ranges require little care and provide precise temperature control. Some surface units, both gas and electric, have thermostatic controls with sensors that contact the bottom of the cooking utensil.   EVAN POWELL

Bibliography: Mercer, Henry C., *The Bible in Iron,* 3d ed. (1961); Reid, Jo, and Peck, John, *The Stove Book* (1977); Wright, Lawrence, *Home Fires Burning: The History of Domestic Heating and Cooking* (1964).

Stowe, Harriet Beecher

Harriet Beecher Stowe became a best-selling novelist upon the publication of Uncle Tom's Cabin *(1852), written to illustrate the evils of the fugitive-slave law. Often criticized for its mawkishness, the novel nevertheless focused international attention on slavery and gave added impetus to the abolitionists.*

The author of UNCLE TOM'S CABIN (1852), an antislavery novel of such force that it is often listed among the causes of the Civil War, Harriet Elizabeth Beecher Stowe, b. Litchfield, Conn., June 14, 1811, d. July 1, 1896, also wrote excellent depictions of rural New England life. Long overshadowed by her more sensational work, *The Minister's Wooing* (1859) and *Oldtown Folks* (1869) have recently gained appreciative audiences, and scholars and critics have begun to recognize that *Uncle Tom's Cabin* contains nearly as much art as propaganda.

The daughter of a celebrated Congregationalist minister, Lyman Beecher, Stowe moved at the age of 21 to Cincinnati, where she met and married Calvin Ellis Stowe, a biblical scholar. Her first publication, *The Mayflower; or, Sketches of Scenes and Characters among the Descendants of the Pilgrims* (1843), revealed her interest in New England personalities, but her proximity to Kentucky had also given her first-hand knowledge of the South. When she and her husband moved to Brunswick, Maine, in 1850, she drew upon her recollections to write *Uncle Tom's Cabin,* followed by *The Key to Uncle Tom's Cabin* (1853) and *Dred: A Tale of the Great Dismal Swamp* (1856), all of which originated in her lifelong hatred of slavery. After the Civil War she continued to write essays, novels, and poetry, returning to the New England scenes with which she had begun her career. By the time she died, Stowe had long been recognized at home and abroad as one of America's foremost literary celebrities.

ROBERT D. ARNER

Bibliography: Adams, John R., *Harriet Beecher Stowe* (1963); Crozier, Alice C., *The Novels of Harriet Beecher Stowe* (1969); Wagenknecht,

Edward Charles, *Harriet Beecher Stowe: The Known and the Unknown* (1965); Wilson, Robert Forrest, *Crusader in Crinoline: The Life of Harriet Beecher Stowe* (1941).

strabismus   [struh-biz'-muhs]

Strabismus is a misalignment of the eyes by which they focus improperly on objects and double vision (diplopia) occurs. Cross-eye (esotropia) involves one eye looking at an object and the other turning inward. In walleyes (exotropia), the deviated eye turns outward. Children with strabismus usually subconsciously suppress the image arising from the deviating eye; eventually, this eye becomes "lazy." Temporary treatment consists of placing a patch over the other eye to force the use of the weak eye; glasses, prisms, or surgery may eventually be necessary.

THOMAS P. MATTINGLY AND MELVIN L. RUBIN

Strabo   [stray'-boh]

Strabo, b. *c.*63 BC, d. AD *c.*21, was a Greek geographer and historian. His 17-volume *Geography* is one of the earliest books on the subject. Strabo began his education under Aristodemus and went to Rome in 44 BC to study under Tyrannion, former teacher to Cicero. Before leaving Rome in 31 BC he completed the 47-volume *Historical Sketches,* little of which has survived.

Strabo traveled between Armenia and Sardinia and from the Black Sea to Ethiopia, incorporating both his own observations and earlier sources in the *Geography.* Books 1-2 of the *Geography* are introductory; Books 3-10 cover Europe; 11-16 cover Asia; and 17 deals with Africa, primarily Egypt. All except part of chapter 7 have been preserved. Strabo synthesized the geographical knowledge of the period and included descriptions of important political events and great men. Intended for the use of military leaders and statesmen, the *Geography* is not uniformly useful because Strabo both took Homer too literally and refused to accept the descriptions of firsthand observers such as Herodotus.

Bibliography: Bowersock, Glen W., *Augustus and the Greek World* (1964); Jones, Horace L., *The Geography of Strabo,* 8 vols. (1917-33).

Strachan, John   [strawn]

John Strachan, b. Aberdeen, Scotland, Apr. 12, 1778, d. Nov. 6, 1867, was the first Anglican bishop of Toronto (1839-67). He emigrated to Canada in 1799, was ordained (1803), and became (1813) rector of St. James' Church, Toronto. As a member of the executive (1815-36) and legislative (1820-41) councils of Upper Canada, he was a staunch defender of church interests. He became (1827) the first president of King's College (later the University of Toronto) and later founded (1852) the University of Trinity College.

Bibliography: Henderson, J. L., *John Strachan: 1778-1867* (1969).

Strachey, John   [stray'-chee]

The English geologist John Strachey, b. 1671, d. June 11, 1743, made the first modern geologic map (1725) and was among the first to formalize a theory of stratification, called the law of superposition, stating that rock formations occur in layers with younger rocks lying atop older ones. Strachey also developed the theory that a relationship exists between rock structure and surface features—a concept that did not gain general acceptance until a century later.

Strachey, Lytton

A celebrated English biographer and prominent member of the BLOOMSBURY GROUP, Lytton Strachey, b. Mar. 1, 1880, d. Jan. 21, 1932, established the writing of biography as a literary art. In his most famous work, *Eminent Victorians* (1918)—a reaction against the idealization of the leading figures of the Victorian age—Strachey employed a novel biographical method that illuminated the personalities of figures such as Florence Nightingale and Thomas Arnold. His literary and biographical essays, which also exhibit his perceptiveness and

epigrammatic wit, appeared in *Landmarks in French Literature* (1912), *Books and Characters, French and English* (1922), and *Portraits in Miniature and Other Essays* (1931).

Bibliography: Beerbohm, Max, *Lytton Strachey* (1943; repr. 1973); Holroyd, Michael, *Lytton Strachey: A Critical Biography,* rev. ed. (1973); Sanders, Charles Richard, *Lytton Strachey: His Mind and Art* (1957; repr. 1973).

Stradivari   (family)   [strah-dee-vah'-ree]

Antonio Stradivari, the greatest violin maker in history, developed the proportions of the modern violin during his 70-year career and created instruments whose tone and beauty have never been surpassed. Stradivari made more than 1,100 instruments, and the locations of approximately 700 of them are known.

Stradivari was the name of a family of violin makers in Cremona, Italy, in the late 17th and early 18th centuries. With the AMATI and GUARNERI families, they brought violin making to its highest level. The violins of **Antonio Stradivari,** b. probably in 1644, d. Dec. 18, 1737, are considered the finest ever made. Stradivari and Andrea Guarneri learned their craft in the workshop of Nicolo Amati, whose family had been making violins for many years. Stradivari continued to work with Amati until 1684. By that time he had also made many violins of his own with his labels in them. These violins of his first period follow the Amati tradition closely.

Numerous members of the Amati and Guarneri families practiced the craft, but Stradivari was assisted by only two of his sons, **Francesco,** b. Feb. 1, 1671, d. May 11, 1743, and **Omobono,** b. Nov. 14, 1679, d. June 8, 1742.

After opening (1680) his own shop, Antonio Stradivari gradually altered his violins, increasing their size by 1690; these longer instruments with flatter arches are known as the Long Pattern. About 1700, after further experiments, his violins achieved their mature state, and the next 20 years are known as the Golden Period. In those years, Stradivari made his finest violins, beautiful in appearance and sound and perfectly balanced. He continued producing violins to the end of his life; his last instrument is dated 1737, when he was 93.

Stradivari is thought to have made approximately 1,100 instruments—mostly violins, but also some violas and cellos—of which about 700 have been traced and their whereabouts are thus known. Each instrument is distinct and almost all bear names, such as "Vieuxtemps," "Dolphin," and "Sarasate," reflecting ownership, history, or some characteristic. Because the value of Stradivarius instruments is so great, sometimes running into the hundreds of thousands of dollars, many attempts have been made to forge them.   FARLEY K. HUTCHINS

Bibliography: Goodkind, H. K., *Violin Iconography of Antonio Stradivari* (1972); Henley, W., *A. Stradivari: His Life and Instruments 1644-1737* (1909; repr. 1961); Hill, W. E., *Antonio Stradivari: His Life and Works* (1920).

Strafford, Thomas Wentworth, 1st Earl of
[straf'-urd]

Thomas Wentworth, 1st earl of Strafford, b. Apr. 13, 1593, d. May 12, 1641, was an English statesman and royal advisor whose execution for treason in 1641 was an early victory for Parliament in its struggle with King CHARLES I. Wentworth was elected to Parliament at the age of 21. Critical of royal policies, he was imprisoned (1627) for refusing to pay a forced loan. In 1628 he advocated presenting to Charles the Petition of Right demanding redress for grievances. After the king accepted the petition, however, and after the death of the king's favorite, the duke of Buckingham, Wentworth entered the king's service and was made viscount and lord president of the north. He was so effective that Charles appointed him lord deputy of Ireland. Arriving there in 1633, Wentworth encouraged trade, improved revenue, and handled Parliament skillfully, but he also enriched himself.

When Charles failed to suppress a Scottish rebellion, he recalled Wentworth and in 1640 created him earl of Strafford and appointed him commander in chief to fight the Scots. Strafford was unable to defeat them, however. Accused of subversion, he was impeached by the House of Commons. Strafford defended himself so brilliantly that the impeachment trial was abandoned; instead, a bill of attainder was passed and sent to the king, who signed it. Strafford was beheaded. MAURICE ASHLEY

Bibliography: Kearney, H. F., *Strafford in Ireland, 1633–41: A Study in Absolutism* (1959); Wedgwood, C. V., *Thomas Wentworth, First Earl of Strafford, 1593-1641: A Revaluation* (1961).

strain gauge

The strain gauge is an electromechanical transducer that converts the strain on a structure as a result of applied force into electrical voltage. The assembly, which may be half the size of a postage stamp, is made up of a fine wire grid or foil of a metal alloy that has a high ratio of resistance change to strain. The bonded-resistance strain gauge operates on the piezoelectric effect; that is, the resistance change in the grid is directly proportional to the strain in the material to which the gauge is rigidly bonded.

The gauge is used in experimental stress analysis of structures and as the sensing element in some forms of load cell, torque meter, diaphragm-type pressure gauge, flowmeter, and accelerometer. Gauges have been applied to ship hulls and propeller shafts, buried in concrete dams, and bonded to aircraft to measure structural strain in flight. FRANK J. OLIVER

Bibliography: Perry, C. C., and Lissner, H. R., *Strain Gauge Primer*, 2d ed. (1962).

See also: PIEZOELECTRICITY.

Straits Settlements

The Straits Settlements was the name of a British crown colony comprising SINGAPORE, PENANG, and Malacca (now MELAKA). When those three territories of the British EAST INDIA COMPANY were placed under direct control of the British crown in 1867, they were consolidated into one administrative unit. In 1907, Labuan became part of the Singapore Settlement, and in 1912 it was declared the fourth component of the colony. The colony was dissolved in 1946; Singapore became a separate crown colony, Penang and Malacca became part of the Malayan Union (later the Federation of Malaysia), and Labuan became part of North Borneo (now SABAH, also part of the Federation of Malaysia). RICHARD BUTWELL

Strand, Paul

A major 20th-century photographer, Paul Strand, b. New York City, Oct. 16, 1890, d. Mar. 31, 1976, was known for his artistic blending of formalism and humanism. He was influenced by the PHOTO-SECESSION GROUP and was the subject of the last two issues of Alfred Stieglitz's quarterly *Camera Work* (1917). Stimulated by modern art, Strand made abstract close-ups of bowls, machine parts, and rocks after 1915. Of his work (1922–43) in films, the documentary *The Plow That Broke the Plains* (1936) is the most celebrated. His wide travels yielded such volumes as *Time in New England* (1950), *Un Paese* (1955), and *Living Egypt* (1969). KEITH F. DAVIS

Bibliography: Strand, Paul, *Paul Strand* (1976).

strandline

Strandline literally means the shoreline along a lake or seashore; it is the high tide line, or highest limit of wave action. On modern, active coasts, this line is often marked by sediment and vegetation that is thrown up onto the beach face by wave action. Geologists and geographers, however, usually reserve the term *strandline* for an ancient shoreline no longer affected by present wave action. A strandline thus represents the summation of the highest shoreline development during the episode when it formed.

Strandlines can be recognized by depositional and erosional features (shore terraces and embankments, spits, bars, wave-cut cliffs and platforms), shore sediments (lacustrine or marine gravel and algal tufa, commonly with distinctive fossils), and sand. Common types of strandlines are those of proglacial (glacier-dammed) and pluvial lakes (see LAKE, GLACIAL). Marine strandlines occur above and below present sea level as a result either of tectonic uplift or of lowering of the land relative to sea level, or of eustatic changes in sea level in response to worldwide glaciation and deglaciation.

A strandline must be strongly developed if it is to remain recognizable in spite of subsequent erosion. Factors favoring strong development are: long duration of the strandline episode, with land and sea levels remaining constant relative to each other; exposure to strong waves, with maximum development occurring on shores with long fetches across open water and facing directly toward the principal wave and wind directions; strong windstorms during the strandline episode; and a gently to moderately sloping and fairly regular (not deeply embayed) coast. ROGER B. MORRISON

Bibliography: Komar, Paul D., *Beach Processes and Sedimentation* (1976).

Strang, James Jesse

A follower of the Mormon prophet, Joseph SMITH, James Jesse Strang, b. Scipio, N.Y., Mar. 21, 1813, d. July 9, 1856, founded the schismatic Strangite sect after Smith's death. Strang, who had studied law, worked as a schoolteacher, postmaster, and newspaper editor before he moved west with his family in 1843. The following year he met Smith in Nauvoo, Ill., converted to MORMONISM, and was ordained an elder. When Smith was assassinated later that year, Stang declared that angels had visited him and ordained him Smith's successor. Brigham YOUNG denounced him and had him expelled from the church. Strang then gathered his supporters into a community, first in Wisconsin and later on Big Beaver Island in Lake Michigan. Here he had himself crowned king in 1850. He was twice elected (1852, 1854) to the state legislature. The group was persecuted by its non-Mormon neighbors, but it held together until some former Strangites shot Strang on June 16, 1856. He was taken to Voree, Wis., where he died.

Bibliography: Fitzpatrick, Doyle C., *The King Strang Story* (1970); Weeks, Robert P., *King Strang; a Biography of James Jesse Strang* (1971).

Stranger, The

The Stranger (1942; Eng. trans., 1946), Albert CAMUS's first and best-known work, takes up in novel form the philosophical question of the absurdity of modern existence. The main character, Meursault, is an alien in society who rejects bourgeois conventions without really knowing why and who lacks human feeling, as his reactions at his mother's funeral and his relationship with his mistress demonstrate. Yet he possesses a lucid awareness of the disconcerting effect he has on others. After gratuitously killing an Arab, he is condemned to death, not so much for his crime as for his nonconformity. The novel is written in a terse, objective style that is influenced by French classicism and the American novel. JOSEPH A. REITER

Stranger in a Strange Land

Robert Heinlein's science fiction novel *Stranger in a Strange Land* (1961) uses the familiar device of the Martian on Earth to satirize American social customs. A young Martian whose parents originally came from Earth arrives on the planet and is exploited by scientists, newsmen, and politicians. Eventually, he founds his own church, where he teaches Martian customs that contradict those of Earth. The novel, once enormously popular among college students, is now considered a science fiction classic. CHARLOTTE D. SOLOMON

strangles: see DISEASES, ANIMAL.

Straparola, Giovanni Francesco [strah-pah-roh'-lah]

An Italian short-story writer, Giovanni Francesco Straparola, c.1480–c.1557, is best known for his collection entitled *Le piacevoli notti* (1550–53; trans. as *The Nights of Straparola*, 1894). In this work, fashioned after the DECAMERON, a group of young people gather to tell fairy tales, many of which were later adapted by Charles Perrault and Giovanni Battista Basile. The collection includes such classic tales as *Beauty and the Beast*.

Strasberg, Lee [strahs'-burg]

Actor, director, and prominent teacher of acting, Lee Strasberg, b. Budzanow, Austria, Nov. 17, 1901, has helped mold generations of American actors with "the Method," the introspective acting technique he derived from Konstantin Stanislavsky. Having studied at the American Laboratory Theater, he cofounded (1931) the GROUP THEATRE with Harold Clurman, Elia Kazan, and others. Strasberg joined the famed ACTORS STUDIO in 1947 and has been its artistic director since 1948, training such well-known actors as Marlon Brando, Paul Newman, and Julie Harris. Strasberg has expounded his principles in *Strasberg at the Actors Studio* (1965). He made his own film debut in *The Godfather, Part II* (1974).
COLETTE BROOKS

Bibliography: Taubman, Howard, *The Making of the American Theater* (1965).

Strasbourg [strahz-boorg']

Strasbourg (German: Strassburg) is a city in northeastern France, situated about 400 km (250 mi) east of Paris and to the west of the Rhine River. The population is 253,384 (1975). The city, a strategic river port, is located on the east-west routes into France just north of the Vosges Mountains as well as on north-south routes of the Rhine Valley. The center of the old city is on an island with branches of the Ill River on either side, and several canals serve parts of the city and link Strasbourg with the Rhine, Rhône, and Marne rivers.

The eastern part of the city, with its port connections to the Rhine, is heavily industrialized. Petroleum, coal, and potash are major products shipped through the port. Beer, books, metal goods, machinery, and food are among the leading products. Germanic customs and food are common, and the city is famous for paté de foie gras.

The Gothic Cathedral of Notre Dame, begun in the 11th century and completed four centuries later, dominates the city with its 142-m (466-ft) spire. A 14th-century astronomical clock is a major feature of the cathedral's interior.

The city's many other notable buildings include the Château des Rohan (18th century), a former palace that now contains three museums. The University of Strasbourg was founded in 1538.

Strasbourg was originally a Celtic village and later a Roman fortification called Argentoratum. The Franks, who captured it in the 5th century, called it Strateburgum. In the 13th century it became a free imperial city within the Holy Roman Empire. Louis XIV of France seized Strasbourg in 1681.

The city was renowned in the mid-18th century for its fine porcelain and earthenware, and during the French Revolution the French national anthem, "La Marseillaise," was composed there (1792) by Claude Joseph Rouget de Lisle. After the Franco-Prussian War (1870–71) Strasbourg was ceded to Germany. The city, returned to France in 1919, was again con-

trolled by the Germans during World War II. It has had a vulnerable location in the wars between France and Germany and was damaged considerably during World War II. Strasbourg is the seat of the Council of Europe.
LAWRENCE M. SOMMERS

Strasbourg Cathedral

The city of Strasbourg, on the river Rhine about 400 km (250 mi) east of Paris, is the site of one of the most French of all German High Gothic churches. The cathedral was begun in 1175 in the Romanesque style, which marks its apse and transept. The new High Gothic style was adopted after 1235, when the nave, largely finished by 1275, was begun. The design of the nave is closely based on that of the abbey church of Saint-Denis near Paris, as is evident in the compound piers, the huge clerestory windows, and especially the glazed triforium. The twin-towered west facade (only the north tower has a spire) was begun in 1277 but not finished until about 1440. The splendid sculpture around the three west portals dates from the late 13th and early 14th centuries.
RONALD E. MALMSTROM

Bibliography: Frankl, Paul, *Gothic Architecture* (1962).

Strasser, Gregor [shtrah'-sur]

Gregor Strasser, b. May 31, 1892, d. June 30, 1934, was, with his brother Otto (1897–1974), a leading member of the German National Socialist (Nazi) party. A socialist before becoming a nationalist and a racist, Strasser was a leading architect of Nazism's popular base and of its electoral successes. He resigned in 1933 because of disagreements with Adolf Hitler and was murdered in the 1934 blood purge. Otto, who had resigned in 1930, went into exile in 1933. ROBIN BUSS

Strategic Air Command

The Strategic Air Command (SAC) is that part of the United States Air Force which deploys the U.S. nuclear arsenal. Its primary function is to deter the breakout of nuclear war. SAC was formed in 1946 as part of the U.S. Army Air Force; it was incorporated into the newly founded U.S. Air Force in 1947. The 117,000 people employed by SAC are divided into the 8th and 15th Air Forces, the 1st Strategic Aerospace Division, and the 3rd Air Division at Guam. SAC maintains the deterrent Titan and Minuteman missiles in silos in the United States, as well as B-52 and FB-111 bombers with supporting tankers. The MX mobile missile, which is scheduled for completion in the mid-1980s, will also be under SAC control. BILL GUNSTON

Bibliography: Anderton, David A., *Strategic Air Command* (1976); Hubler, Richard G., *SAC, the Strategic Air Command* (1958; repr. 1977).

strategy and tactics, military

Military strategy and tactics are essential to the conduct of warfare. Broadly stated, strategy is the planning, coordination, and general direction of military operations to meet overall political and military objectives. Tactics implement strategy by short-term decisions on the movement of troops and employment of WEAPONS on the field of battle. The great military theorist Carl von CLAUSEWITZ put it another way: "Tactics is the art of using troops in battle; strategy is the art of using battles to win the war." Strategy and tactics, however, have been viewed differently in almost every era of history. The change in the meaning of these terms over time has been basically one of scope as the nature of WAR and society has changed and as technology has changed. Strategy, for example, literally means "the art of the general" (from the Greek *strategos*) and originally signified the purely military planning of a campaign. Thus until the 17th and 18th centuries strategy included to varying degrees such problems as FORTIFICATION, maneuver, and supply. In the 19th and 20th centuries, however, with the rise of mass ideologies, vast conscript armies, global alliances, and rapid technological change, military strategy became difficult to distinguish from national policy or "grand strategy," that is, the proper planning and utilization of the entire resources of a society—military, technological, economic, and political. The change in the scope and meaning of tactics over time has been largely due to enormous changes in technology. Tactics have always been difficult—and have become increasingly difficult—to distinguish in reality from strategy because the two are so interdependent. (Indeed, in the 20th century, tactics have been termed *operational strategy.*) Strategy is limited by what tactics are possible; given the size, training, and morale of forces, type and number of weapons available, terrain, weather, and quality and location of enemy forces, the tactics to be used are dependent on strategic considerations.

Strategic and Tactical Principles of Warfare. Military commanders and theorists throughout history have formulated what they considered to be the most important strategic and tactical principles of war. Napoleon I, for example, had 115 such principles. The Confederate general Nathan Bedford Forrest had but one: "Get there first with the most men." Some of the most commonly cited principles are the objective, the offensive, surprise, security, unity of command, economy of force, mass, and maneuver. Most are interdependent.

Military forces, whether large-scale or small-scale, must have a clear objective that is followed despite possible distractions. Only offensive operations—seizing and exploiting the initiative—however, will allow the choice of objectives; the offense also greatly increases the possibility of surprise (stealth and deception) and security (protection against being surprised or losing the possibility of surprising the enemy). Unity of command, or cooperation, is essential to the pursuit of objectives, the ability to use all forces effectively (economy of force), and the concentration of superior force at a critical point (mass). Maneuver consists of the various ways in which troops can be deployed and moved to obtain offensive, mass, and surprise. A famous example that illustrates most of these principles occurred during World War II when the Allied forces eventually agreed on the objective of defeating Germany first with a direct offensive against the European continent. Under a combined command headed by Gen. Dwight D. Eisenhower, they effectively massed their forces in England, deceived Germany regarding the point of invasion, collected intelligence on the disposition of German forces, and set the vast maneuver called Operation Overlord into motion (see NORMANDY INVASION).

Unthinking rigid attention to a principle of war, however, can be unfortunate. In the face of two Japanese naval forces, Adm. William Halsey's decision at Leyte Gulf not to divide the fleet (the principle of mass) led to the pitting of the entire enormous American naval force against a decoy Japanese fleet. Division of the fleet (maneuver) would still have left Halsey superior to both Japanese forces.

Strategic and Tactical Maneuvers. Classification of actual military types of maneuvers and their variations have long been a part of military science. New technology and weapons have not drastically altered some of the classical types of offensive maneuver: penetration, envelopment, defensive-offensive maneuvers, and turning movements.

The penetration—one of the oldest maneuvers—is a main attack that attempts to pierce the enemy line while secondary attacks up and down the enemy line prevent the freeing of the enemy reserves. A favorite maneuver of the duke of Marlborough (early 18th century), it was also used by Gen. Bernard Montgomery at El ALAMEIN (1942).

The envelopment is a maneuver in which a secondary attack attempts to hold the enemy's center while one (single envelopment) or both flanks (double envelopment) of the enemy are attacked or overlapped in a push to the enemy's rear in order to threaten the enemy's communications and line of retreat. This forces the enemy to fight in several directions and possibly be destroyed in position. New variations include vertical envelopments (AIRBORNE TROOPS or airmobile troops) and amphibious envelopments. Noted single envelopments were accomplished by Alexander the Great at Arbela (or Gaugamela, 331 BC), Robert E. Lee at Chancellorsville (1863), and Erwin Romme at Gazala (1942; leading to the capture of Tobruk); famous double envelopments include those

of Hannibal at the Battle of CANNAE (216 BC), the American Revolutionary War Battle of COWPENS (1781), and the destruction of the 7th German Army at the Falaise Gap (1944).

Defensive-offensive maneuvers include attack from a strong defensive position after the attacking enemy has been sapped in strength, as in two battles of the Hundred Years' War, CRÉCY (1346) and AGINCOURT (1415), or feigned withdrawals that attempt to lure the enemy out of position as performed by William the Conqueror at the Battle of HASTINGS (1066) and by Napoleon at the Battle of AUSTERLITZ (1805).

Turning maneuvers are indirect approaches that attempt to swing wide around an enemy's flank to so threaten an enemy's supply and communication lines that the enemy is forced to abandon a strong position or be cut off and encircled. Napoleon was a master of the turning movement, using it many times between 1796 and 1812. Robert E. Lee used the maneuver at the Second Battle of BULL RUN (1862); the German drive to the French coast in 1940 was another example.

THE HISTORICAL AND THEORETICAL DEVELOPMENT OF STRATEGY AND TACTICS

The historical roots of strategy and tactics date back to the origins of human warfare and the development of large-scale government and empire. The dense tactical infantry formation of overlapping shields called the phalanx, for example, existed in an early form in ancient Sumar (c.3000 BC). The development of strategy and tactics parallels to some extent the growth, spread, and clash of civilizations; technological discoveries and refinements; and the evolution of modern state power, ideology, and nationalism.

Early Strategy and Tactics. The Mediterranean basin saw the dawn of modern military strategy and tactics. It was under such leaders as Philip II (382–336 BC) and Alexander the Great (356–323 BC) of Macedonia and Hannibal (247–183 BC) of Carthage that the first great strides were made in military science. Philip combined INFANTRY, CAVALRY, and primitive ARTILLERY into a trained, organized, and maneuverable fighting force backed up by engineers and a rudimentary signaling system. His son Alexander became an accomplished strategist and tactician with his concern for planning, keeping open lines of communication and supply, security, relentless pursuit of foes, and the use of surprise. Hannibal was a supreme tactician whose crushing victories taught the Romans that the flexible attack tactics of their legions needed to be supplemented by unity of command and an improved cavalry. The Romans eventually replaced their citizen-soldiers with a paid professional army whose training, equipment, skill at fortification, road building, and siege warfare became legendary. The Byzantine emperors studied Roman strategy and tactics and wrote some of the first essays on the subject.

The Middle Ages saw a decline in the study and application of strategy—with the exception of the great Mongol conqueror Genghis Khan. Medieval tactics began with an emphasis on defensive fortifications, siegecraft, and armored cavalry. The introduction, however, of such new developments as the crossbow, longbow, halberd, pike, and, above all, GUNPOWDER began to revolutionize the conduct of war.

The Emergence of Modern Warfare. Gustav II Adolf, king of Sweden (r. 1611–32), has been called the father of modern tactics because he reintroduced maneuver into military science. His disciplined national standing army—differing from the common use of mercenaries—was organized into small, mobile units armed with highly superior, maneuverable firepower and supplemented by mounted dragoons (his creation) armed with carbine and saber. Frederick II (the Great) of Prussia (r. 1740–86), the master of initiative and mass, conducted war in an age of limited warfare—armies were small and expensive; road and supply systems were inadequate. In the SEVEN YEARS' WAR (1756–63), Frederick faced a coalition whose various forces almost surrounded Prussia. Using a strategy of interior lines, Frederick—supported by a highly disciplined army and horse artillery (his creation)—would quickly maneuver, assemble a superior force at some decisive point along the line of encirclement, and, with massed HOWITZER fire, strike hard against an enemy flank before moving to another point.

With Napoleon I, however, the age of modern warfare was born (see NAPOLEONIC WARS). The French Revolution (see FRENCH REVOLUTIONARY WARS) had produced a mass patriot army organized into loose divisional formations. Napoleon carefully planned his campaigns and quickly maneuvered his troops by forced marshes to a selected field of battle. His battles began with skirmishing and cannonading, followed by an overwhelming concentration of forces in shock BAYONET attacks against enemy flanks in turning and enveloping movements designed to utterly destroy opposing forces. Because of the greater complexities of warfare, a rudimentary GENERAL STAFF began to emerge under Napoleon.

The 19th Century: Theory and Technological Change. Napoleonic strategy and tactics were closely studied by the first great theorists of war, the Prussian general Carl von Clausewitz (1780–1831) and the French general Antoine Jomini (1779–1869). Clausewitz's ON WAR (1832–34; Eng. trans., 1908) emphasized the close relationship between war and national policy and the importance of the principles of mass, economy of force, and the destruction of enemy forces. Jomini, on the other hand, emphasized occupying enemy territory through carefully planned, rapid and precise geometric maneuvers. Whereas Jomini's theories had influence in France and North America, Clausewitz's teachings in particular were influential on the great Prussian military strategists of the 19th century, Helmuth Karl Bernhard MOLTKE—architect of victory in the Franco-Prussian War (1870)—and Alfred von SCHLIEFFEN—creator of the Schlieffen plan (defense against Russia and envelopment of France), which Germany applied in a modified form at the beginning of World War I.

The 19th century was an era of far-reaching technological change that vastly altered the scope of tactics and strategy, an alteration seen in what has been called the first total war, the U.S. CIVIL WAR. Railroads and steamships increased the volume, reach, and speed of mobilization and of CONSCRIPTION. The consistent support of war industry became critical. The growth in range and accuracy of rifle firepower (see FIREARMS) created new tactical problems: artillery had to be placed further behind the lines, massed charges became ineffective if not disastrous (see GETTYSBURG, BATTLE OF), cavalry became limited to reconnaissance and skirmish, and troops began to fight from trenches and use GRENADES and land MINES. Telegraph communications linked widening theaters of war and made large-scale strategy and tactics possible. During the U.S. Civil War the large-scale strategy of the North (BLOCKADE, division of the Confederacy, destruction of the Confederate armies and supplies) backed by superior industry and manpower were the key factors in its victory. The development of the MACHINE GUN late in the 19th century would have its most telling effect in World War I.

World Wars: Trench Tactics to Nuclear Strategy. World War I began with immense, rapid, national mobilizations and classical offensive maneuvers, but after mutual attempts at envelopment at and after the Battle of the MARNE, stationary trench warfare ensued across a wide battlefront. A war of attrition set in that called for total national involvement in the war effort. Two key technological developments in the war were to fashion the strategic and tactical debates of the 1920s and 1930s. The use of airpower (see AIR FORCE; AIRCRAFT, MILITARY) was advocated by such theorists as Giulio Douhet (1869–1930), Billy MITCHELL, Henry ("Hap") ARNOLD, and Hugh Trenchard (1873–1956). They insisted that air power alone could win wars, not only by striking at enemy forces but by strategic bombing—the massive attack on cities, industries, and lines of communication and supply that characterized part of allied strategy during World War II. The other World War I development was that of motorized ARMORED VEHICLES such as the tank. The use of the tank as the new cavalry of the modern age was advocated by B. H. Liddell Hart (1895–1970), Charles de Gaulle (1890–1970), and J. F. C. Fuller (1878–1966) in the interwar period. The Germans were the first to effectively use the tactical offensive combination of air and tank power in the field of battle in the BLITZKRIEGS, under such commanders as Heinz Guderian and Erwin Rommel, which conquered much of Europe in World War II.

Although a wide variety of tactics were used all over the world, the primary tactical advance in World War II may have been that of AMPHIBIOUS WARFARE. The principal significance of World War II, however, was in the first application of truly global strategies wielded by massive coalitions dedicated once again to the offensive. The development of nuclear weapons, which continued after the war, introduced the new science of NUCLEAR STRATEGY and tactics. The immense destructive nature of these weapons, however, meant that warfare of limited strategic goals, using conventional but constantly refined weapons and conventional (and sometimes unconventional; see GUERRILLAS) tactics, would predominate in the years after World War II.   RONALD E. M. GOODMAN

Bibliography: Beaufre, Andre, *An Introduction to Strategy* (1965); Brodie, Bernard, *Strategy in the Missile Age* (1959); Chandler, D. G., *The Campaigns of Napoleon* (1966); Dupuy, R. E. and T. N., *The Encyclopedia of Military History* (1977); Earle, Edward M., et al., eds., *Makers of Modern Strategy* (1973); Ellis, John, *The Social History of the Machine Gun* (1975); Fuller, J. F. C., *A Military History of the Western World*, 3 vols. (1954–56); Kahn, Herman, *On Thermonuclear War* (1969); Kissinger, Henry, *Nuclear Weapons and Foreign Policy* (1959); Liddell Hart, B. H., *Strategy: The Indirect Approach* (1954; rev. ed., 1967).

See also: ARAB-ISRAELI WARS; NAVAL VESSELS; NAVY.

Stratford-on-Avon

Stratford-on-Avon in southern Warwickshire, England, lies on the River Avon, about 145 km (90 mi) northwest of London. The population is 20,100 (1973 est.). The borough's industries include brewing, canning, and metalworking. A weekly market has been held since 1196. The birthplace of William Shakespeare, Stratford-on-Avon derives most of its income from tourism. Visitors see Shakespeare's birthplace, the site of his retirement home, his tomb, and the houses once occupied by his daughter and his wife, Ann Hathaway. Other notable landmarks are a 15th-century bridge, the Royal Shakespeare Theater (rebuilt 1932), and several museums.

A Roman ford on the site was the nucleus of an Anglo-Saxon village first mentioned in 699. Annual Shakespearean festivals have taken place there since 1879.

Strathclyde   [strath'-klyd]

Strathclyde is an administrative region in western Scotland with an area of 13,568 km² (5,239 mi²) and a population of 2,466,300 (1977 est.)—almost half the total population of Scotland. GLASGOW is the major city. Economic activities include shipbuilding, light and heavy engineering, banking, insurance, and communications. Strathclyde was also the name of an independent Celtic kingdom that existed in the area from the 5th to the 10th century. The administrative region was constituted during the 1975 reorganization of local government in Scotland from the former counties of ARGYLL, AYR, BUTE, LANARK, and RENFREW.

Strathcona and Mount Royal, Donald Alexander Smith, 1st Baron   [strath-koh'-nuh]

Donald Alexander Smith, 1st Baron Strathcona and Mount Royal, b. Scotland, Aug. 6, 1820, d. Jan. 21, 1914, was a Canadian fur trader, railway entrepreneur, and politician. He joined the HUDSON'S BAY COMPANY in 1838, ultimately becoming its governor in 1889. Smith was negotiator for the Canadian government in the 1869 Red River Rebellion and subsequently a Conservative representative in the Manitoba legislature (1870–74) and in the federal House of Commons (1871–80). After 1873, Smith became a promoter of the St. Paul, Minneapolis and Manitoba Railway. In 1880 he reinvested his profits in the much larger Canadian Pacific Railway, which owed much of its success to his steady backing. Smith served again in Commons (1887–96) and was also president (1887–1905) of the Bank of Montreal. He was created baron in 1897 and served as Canadian high commissioner to Great Britain from 1896 to his death.   P. B. WAITE

Bibliography: Newman, P. C., *Flame of Power* (1960); Willson, Beckles, *The Life of Lord Strathcona and Mount Royal* (1915).

stratigraphy

Stratigraphy is the branch of geology that deals with the classification and subdivision of stratified rocks. The vast majority of stratified rocks are sedimentary, but igneous and metamorphic rocks are sometimes stratified. The term *stratum* is derived from the Latin verb *sternere*, "to spread," and this implies a planar unit, or a blanket of rock distributed over a large area.

HISTORY

Although the fundamental concepts of stratigraphy seem obvious—the law of superposition states that younger sedimentary rocks are deposited over older rocks—the development of stratigraphy as a science is a relatively recent event. Nicolaus STENO clearly described (1669) the generation of a stratigraphic sequence by superposition, including the formation of angular unconformities. Several European geologists, notably Johann Gottlob LEHMANN (1756), Giovanni ARDUINO (1760), and Georg Christian FÜCHSEL (1762), attempted large-scale subdivision of the stratigraphic column. Their ideas, however, were limited by the preconception that most sediments were laid down during the great biblical flood. The existence of a "Universal Ocean," consistent with biblical accounts of the flood, was championed by Abraham WERNER, who dominated geological thinking in the late 18th century.

The theories of these "Neptunists" were contested by James HUTTON, a Scottish geologist responsible for introducing (1788) the concepts of uniformitarianism and the vastness of geologic time. Hutton's writings received little critical attention; they were subsequently popularized, however, by Charles Lyell, particularly in his widely used text, *Principles of Geology* (1830–33). As Hutton's ideas received prominence, mapping and subdivision of stratigraphic units proceeded quickly. The surveyor William SMITH constructed (1815) an excellent geological map of southeastern England. He successfully delineated successive strata on the basis of distinctive rock type and fossil content. Other geologists took note of William Smith's techniques, and, using the principles of rock-type division and fossil correlation, quickly recognized major stratigraphic divisions throughout Europe and the eastern United States. By the middle of the 19th century, all of the geological eras and periods had been recognized and defined.

Development of stratigraphy during the 20th century has been coupled to the development of the petroleum industry. Understanding the origin and distribution of sedimentary rocks is a prerequisite for locating oil and gas concentrations. Recognizing this, various petroleum companies have sponsored detailed mapping programs throughout the world. They also have organized large research programs directed toward an understanding of the origin of particular rock types, such as reef limestones.

STRATIGRAPHIC UNITS

Stratigraphy is mostly a qualitative science based on types. It became obvious that increasing confusion was resulting from inconsistencies in descriptions: various authors had developed their own terminologies and were disregarding the terminologies of others.

In order to rectify this situation, the American Commission on Stratigraphic Nomenclature defined (1961) a Code of Stratigraphic Nomenclature. Four major categories of stratigraphic units are defined: rock-stratigraphic units, distinguished on the basis of lithologic characteristics (bed, member, formation, group, supergroup); biostratigraphic units, characterized by fossils contemporaneous with deposition (zone, subzone, zonule); time-stratigraphic units, which are subdivisions of rocks considered solely as the record of a specific interval of time (system, series, stage); and geologic-time units, which are divisions of time distinguished by the rock record (era, period, epoch, age).

The fundamental rock-stratigraphic unit is the formation. Individual formations are referred to by a geographic prefix, the name being chosen for a natural or artificial feature at or near which the rock-stratigraphic unit is typically developed. Tradition has given rise to a profusion of names and has introduced complex problems of correlation.

STRATIGRAPHIC CORRELATION

Correlation is, in fact, one of the most important aspects of stratigraphy. In its more general sense the term means a demonstration of temporal, lithologic, or paleontological similarity between units that occur in two or more different areas. As used by many stratigraphers, however, the term is restricted to description of geographically separated stratigraphic units that were formed at equivalent times.

Temporal correlation of units geographically separated by short distances can be accomplished by noting lithologic similarities. Particularly useful are thin strata of unusual composition that were deposited quickly over a large area. A good example is a bed of volcanic ash. Correlation of units separated by large distances usually depends on identification of similar fossils. This technique must be employed with caution, however, because the fossil occurrence of most organisms is ecologically controlled. In addition, the migration of a particular species may take substantial time. For these reasons, biostratigraphic units do not necessarily have boundaries parallel to time-stratigraphic units; that is, two rocks of different age may have similar fossil content. As the segment of time involved becomes greater, the reliability of the correlation also tends to become greater.

The use of fossils permits the establishment of only a relative order of events. Absolute ages of deposition for sedimentary units are determined by RADIOMETRIC AGE-DATING. This technique, as conventionally employed, measures the age of crystallization of a mineral in which are incorporated small

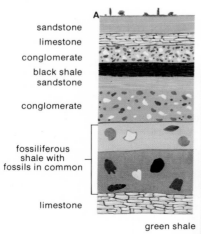

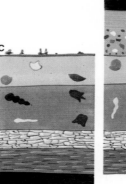
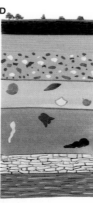

sandstone
limestone
conglomerate
black shale
sandstone

conglomerate

fossiliferous
shale with
fossils in common

limestone

green shale

black shale

Stratigraphic correlation, or the study of the time relationship between sequences of rock strata from separate locations (A, B, C, D), is based on the determination of similarities between distinguishing lithologic characteristics and fossil content. The practical application of correlation is related to its importance to the mineral and petroleum industries as well as to the examination of the geologic history of the Earth.

amounts of a radioactive element. As the element decays, the decay products are trapped in the mineral. The ratio of radioactive element to decay product indicates the time since crystallization.

This technique is ideally suited to dating igneous and metamorphic rocks, in which minerals have crystallized under near-equilibrium conditions of high temperatures. Sedimentary depositional ages are much more difficult to measure, because little recrystallization takes place, and what does is generally under unspecified conditions. Limited success has been achieved in dating sediments by their authigenic clay content. Fossils have been dated by the isotopic content of their skeletons. The most reliable stratigraphic dates, however, are those established by measuring the ages of adjacent igneous or metamorphic rocks. For example, a sedimentary unit that nonconformably overlies granite and is crosscut by an igneous dike must be younger than the granite and older than the dike. Employing radiometric techniques, J. L. Kulp established (1961) a widely cited time scale, with lower and upper absolute dates for all periods.

THE PRACTICE OF STRATIGRAPHY

The practice of stratigraphy depends heavily on field work. Laboratory measurements, however, to an ever-increasing degree, have been used to refine and extend field observations. The discipline of paleontology, which once involved only identification of macrofossils, now includes identification of microfossils (for example, foraminifera and pollen) and measurement of trace elements in skeletal material. Lithologic determinations similarly involve microscopic analysis of thin rock sections and determination of both major and minor elemental composition.

Whereas field observations were once restricted to surface outcrops, geophysical techniques now are used to delineate the distribution of rocks far beneath the surface. For example, the reflection and refraction of seismic waves from a small surface explosion can be analyzed to indicate the depth and orientation of particular strata.

The goals of stratigraphy change with the general advance of science. For example, marine geologists and climatologists are currently studying fossil content and isotopic composition of deep-sea sediment cores to determine ocean temperatures and salinities during the past few million years. From these interpretations they can infer past changes in climate and better predict long-range changes for the future.

THOMAS A. MUTCH

Bibliography: Ager, Derek V., *The Nature of the Stratigraphical Record* (1973); Dunbar, C. O., and Rogers, John, *Principles of Stratigraphy* (1957), and, with Waage, Karl M., *Historical Geology*, 3d ed. (1969); Eicher, Don L., *Geologic Time*, 2d ed. (1976); Harbaugh, John W., *Stratigraphy and the Geologic Time Scale*, 2d ed. (1974); Kummel, Bernhard, *History of the Earth*, 2d ed. (1970); Matthews, Robley K., *Dynamic Stratigraphy* (1974); Spencer, E. W., *Basic Concepts of Historical Geology* (1962); Stokes, William Lee, *Essentials of Earth History: An Introduction to Historical Geology*, 3d ed. (1973); Wilson, John A., *Geochronology, Stratigraphy, and Typology* (1975).

stratosphere

The stratosphere is the second lowest of the four atmospheric layers. Its lower boundary is called the TROPOPAUSE; its upper boundary, the stratopause. The underlying troposphere is characterized by a vertical temperature gradient and thus vertical instability (weather changes). In contrast, temperatures in the stratosphere remain the same or even increase with increasing height, which indicates vertical stability. The stratospheric air flow is mainly horizontal. Ultraviolet absorption by ozone (see OZONE LAYER) causes the high temperatures of the stratopause, which is usually between 48 and 53 km (30 and 33 mi) above the Earth's surface.

WILLEM VAN DER BIJL

Bibliography: Craig, Richard A., *Upper Atmosphere: Meteorology and Physics* (1965); Goody, R. M., *The Physics of the Stratosphere* (1954).

Stratton-Porter, Gene

A popular American writer whose books sold more than 10 million copies, Gene Stratton-Porter, b. Lagro, Ind., Aug. 17,

1863, d. Dec. 6, 1924, wrote mainly juvenile stories, nature fiction, and sentimental romances. Her many volumes include the children's books *Freckles* (1904) and *A Girl of the Limberlost* (1909) and the story of a Thoreau-like naturalist, *The Harvester* (1911).

stratus clouds

A dense, dark bank of stratus clouds hangs low over Long Island Sound off the coast from East Marion, N.Y. Above the stratus clouds a formation of stratocumulus clouds disperses after a storm.

Stratus clouds are layered, gray clouds with rather uniform bases and tops. They are usually composed of water droplets, although ice crystals are occasionally present. Usually of limited vertical extent, they generally do not produce precipitation; drizzle or snow grains fall when they do. Fog results when the bases of stratus clouds descend to the ground. Stratus clouds commonly occur when warm, moist air moves over cold ground surfaces during winter, or over cold ocean water during any season. Development of stratus clouds is extremely common over the cold seawater off the northwestern U.S. coast.

Closely related to stratus clouds are the stratocumulus clouds; the latter, however, have undulating bases and are capped by cauliflower tops, whereas stratus clouds are uniformly diffuse. Nimbostratus clouds, as opposed to stratus, have a denser and wetter appearance and produce larger-sized raindrops and snowflakes. Layered, or stratiform, clouds that occur in the middle and upper troposphere are labeled altostratus and cirrostratus, respectively.

ROGER A. PIELKE

Bibliography: Scorer, Richard S., *Clouds of the World* (1972).

Straub, Jean Marie   [strohb]

The films of screenwriter and director Jean Marie Straub, b. Jan. 8, 1933, have made him a major cult figure of the German-speaking cinema. His experiences as a French youth growing up in Nazi-occupied Lorraine provided the impulse for his first feature, a study of Nazism entitled *Not Reconciled* (1965). His Marxist sentiments and a stylistic austerity reminiscent of Bresson are also evident in his *Chronicle of Anna Magdalena Bach* (1968), *Othon* (1969), and *History Lessons* (1973).

Bibliography: Roud, Richard, *Jean Marie Straub* (1972).

Strauss   (family)   [shtrows]

Through much of the 19th century, Viennese dance music was dominated by Johann Strauss, Sr., and his two sons, Johann, Jr., and Eduard. (Other composers bearing the Strauss name are not related: Oscar, remembered primarily for his operetta *The Chocolate Soldier*, and Richard, the celebrated composer of symphonic poems and operas.)

Johann Strauss, Jr., immortalized the Viennese waltz with such compositions as "The Beautiful Blue Danube" (1867) and "Tales of the Vienna Woods" (1868). The son of a waltz composer and conductor, he began his own dance ensemble in 1844 and found immediate success. In addition to dance music, he composed such popular operettas as Die Fledermaus (1874) and The Gypsy Baron (1885).

Johann Strauss, Sr., b. Mar. 14, 1804, d. Sept. 25, 1849, the son of a Viennese innkeeper, became a violinist, and in 1823 he joined the ensemble of Josef LANNER, a composer of dance music. The two young men were the creators of the Viennese WALTZ. Lanner's ensemble grew in size and popularity, eventually resulting in two orchestras, one of which Strauss conducted. In 1825, Strauss left Lanner to form his own orchestra, which quickly became the favorite of the Viennese public largely through the fiery conducting of its founder. Strauss composed 152 waltzes, about 100 compositions in other dance forms, and marches, but his best-known piece is the *Radetzky March.*

Johann Strauss, Jr., b. Oct. 25, 1825, d. June 3, 1899, became a musician against his father's wishes. Studying the violin in secret, but encouraged by his mother, he then began the serious study of composition. At the age of 19 he formed his own orchestra, playing in the cafés of Vienna, and soon eclipsed his father in popularity. Upon his father's death in 1849, both orchestras were merged under his direction. With that group he toured widely, visiting Russia in 1865, England in 1869, and the United States in 1876. Everywhere he, his orchestra, and his music were greeted with great enthusiasm. In all, Strauss composed about 170 waltzes—the most beloved being "The Beautiful Blue Danube" (1867), "Artists' Life" (1867), "Tales of the Vienna Woods" (1868), "Wine, Woman, and Song" (1869), "Roses from the South" (1880), and "The Emperor Waltz" (1888)—many polkas, quadrilles, and marches, totaling about 500 works. Of 16 operettas, *Die Fledermaus* (*The Bat*, 1874) and *Der Zigeunerbaron* (*The Gipsy Baron*, 1885) were the most successful.

Neither of the other sons had a career as brilliant as the younger Johann's. **Josef Strauss,** b. Aug. 22, 1827, d. July 21, 1870, composed 283 dances and occasionally conducted the family orchestra. **Eduard Strauss,** b. Mar. 15, 1835, d. Dec. 28, 1916, published 318 compositions and also took over conducting chores from his older brother. Eventually, as Johann wanted more time to compose, Eduard took over full charge of the orchestra, maintaining it until 1902.   HOMER ULRICH

Bibliography: Ewen, David, *Tales from the Vienna Woods: The Story of Johann Strauss* (1944); Gartenberg, Egon, *Johann Strauss: The End of an Era* (1974); Jacob, Heinrich E., *Johann Strauss, Father and Son*, trans. by Marguerite Wolff (1939; repr. 1971); Wechsberg, Joseph, *The Waltz Emperors* (1973).

Strauss, David Friedrich

David Friedrich Strauss, b. Jan. 27, 1808, d. Feb. 8, 1874, a German theologian and writer, was the author of a controversial *Life of Jesus*. He was educated at the universities of Tübingen and Berlin and in 1832 was appointed lecturer at Tübingen. His two-volume *Life of Jesus* (1835–36; Eng. trans., 1972) raised a storm of controversy. In it Strauss rejected the histo-

ricity of all supernatural elements of the Gospels attributing them to a Jesus myth that emerged in the first two centuries AD. He lost his position at Tübingen. His later writings include *The Christ of Faith and the Jesus of History* (1865; Eng. trans., 1976), in which he attacked the position of his teacher, Friedrich Schleiermacher, and *The Old Faith and the New* (1872; Eng. trans., 1873), in which he rejected Christianity in favor of scientific humanism.   FREDERICK A. NORWOOD

Bibliography: Cromwell, Richard S., *David Friedrich Strauss and His Place in Modern Thought* (1974); Harris, Horton, *David Friedrich Strauss and His Theology* (1973).

Strauss, Franz Josef

The West German politician Franz Josef Strauss, b. Sept. 6, 1915, has been the leader since 1961 of the right-wing Bavarian Christian Social Union (CSU) party. Elected (1949) to the Bundestag, he was (1956–62) minister of defense in Chancellor Konrad Adenauer's coalition government. In 1962 he was accused of misusing his authority by ordering the arrest of the editors of *Der Spiegel*, a weekly newsmagazine. He served (1966–69) as minister of finance. During the 1970s he opposed normalization of relations between East and West Germany. In 1979 he was chosen by the CSU and the Christian Democratic party to run as the opposition candidate to Chancellor Helmut Schmidt in the 1980 elections.

Bibliography: Bunn, Ronald F., *German Politics and the Spiegel Affair* (1968).

Strauss, Richard

The eminent German composer-conductor Richard Strauss, b. Munich, June 11, 1864, d. Sept. 8, 1949, is best known for his operas and tone poems. His father was Franz Strauss, Germany's leading horn player. Young Strauss was playing the piano by the age of 4, composing by age 6, and studying theory and composition by age 11. He made his conducting debut without rehearsal in Munich in 1884, which led to his first appointment as Hans von Bülow's assistant with the Meiningen Court Orchestra. After a month, Bülow left him in charge.

In 1886, Strauss became third conductor at the Munich Opera and a musical assistant for the 1889 and 1891 Bayreuth Festivals. A second conductorship at Weimar enabled him to astonish the world with the performance of his tone poem *Don Juan* (1888). His first (thoroughly Wagnerian) opera, *Guntram*, was performed at Weimar in 1894 when, after a tantrum by the leading soprano, Pauline de Ahna, Strauss announced their engagement to marry. That autumn he became court conductor of the Munich Opera. His wife encouraged his work at composing, and he wrote the tone poems *Till Eulenspiegel* (1895), *Thus Spake Zarathustra* (1896), *Don Quixote* (1897), and *A Hero's Life* (1898).

The last composer of the romantic tradition was the German Richard Strauss. The inspiration of his program music, such as Thus Spake Zarathustra (1896), was often literary, and Der Rosenkavalier (1911) was one of his operas set to librettos by Hofmannsthal, the Austrian poet.

From 1900, Strauss concentrated on operas. The cynical *Feuersnot* of 1901 was followed by the more advanced *Salome* (1905) and the powerful *Elektra* (1909). The crowning glory, *Der Rosenkavalier* (1911), brought fortunes to both Strauss and his librettist, the Austrian poet Hugo von Hofmannsthal. *Ariadne auf Naxos* (1912) followed, then a cumbersome ballet for Serge Diaghilev, *Josephlegende* (The Legend of Joseph, 1914), performed in Paris and London on the eve of World War I.

Intending to devote the rest of his life to composition, Strauss, at the age of 50, was entirely thwarted by the loss of his fortune, invested in London. Then began a decline with the superficial *Alpine Symphony* (1915) and the complex, though beautiful, *Frau ohne Schatten* (Woman without a Shadow, 1919). He was a founder of the Salzburg Festivals in 1917 with Hofmannsthal and Max Reinhardt. He then became codirector of the Vienna Opera.

Strauss sought a change from Hofmannsthal by writing his own libretto for *Intermezzo* (1924), an opera based on personal experience. The partnership with Hofmannsthal resumed with *Die aegyptische Helena* (The Egyptian Helen, 1928) and *Arabella*, just completed by Hofmannsthal before he suddenly died, in 1929. Strauss then set *Die schweigsame Frau* (The Silent Woman) to a libretto by Stefan Zweig, banned (1935) by the Nazis after two performances because Zweig was Jewish. Strauss became unwontedly involved in political conflict and was expelled as head of the Reichsmusikkammer; his music was banned for a year. Because his daughter-in-law and grandsons were of Jewish ancestry, Strauss was forced to make a deal with the Nazis for their protection but was denied visits to Switzerland for his own health. After the war, Strauss was politically rehabilitated in London with a festival organized by Sir Thomas Beecham. His later compositions mark a return to inspiration and sweetness: the opera *Capriccio* (1942), the threnody for strings *Metamorphosen* (1945), the Oboe Concerto (1945), and *Four Last Songs* (1948).   ALAN JEFFERSON

Bibliography: Del Mar, Norman, *Richard Strauss*, 3 vols. (1962–72); Jefferson, Alan, *The Lieder of Strauss* (1971), *The Life of Richard Strauss* (1973), and *Richard Strauss* (1975); Kennedy, Michael, *Richard Strauss* (1976); Strauss, Richard, *Recollections and Reflections*, ed. by Willi Schuh, trans. by L. J. Lawrence (1949; repr. 1974); Strauss, Richard, and von Hofmannsthal, Hugo, *Correspondence* (1961).

Stravinsky, Igor   [struh-vin'-skee]

Igor Fedorovich Stravinsky, b. Oranienbaum, near Saint Petersburg, Russia, June 17 (N.S.) 1882, d. New York City, Apr. 6, 1971, was one of the greatest composers of the 20th century. The son of a famous bass singer at the Imperial Opera, Stravinsky showed little inclination to pursue a musical career

The 20th-century composer Igor Stravinsky was born in Russia but later emigrated to France and the United States. He achieved success with Firebird, *a ballet performed in Paris in 1910, but* The Rite of Spring, *although now revered as a classic, met with scorn.*

until, while a law student, he began to study composition with Nikolai Rimsky-Korsakov. Stravinsky was catapulted into the musical limelight with the composition of three ballets for the Ballets Russes de Serge Diaghilev in Paris: *Firebird* (1910), *Petrushka* (1911), and *The Rite of Spring* (1913). The latter work caused a celebrated scandal at its first performance and remains one of the best-known and most influential pieces of 20th-century music. During World War I, Stravinsky lived in Switzerland, and shortly afterward he settled in France. His creative association with Diaghilev continued until 1929 and included notable collaborations with Pablo Picasso and Leonid Massine (*Pulcinella*, 1920), Jean Cocteau (*Oedipus Rex*, 1927), and George Balanchine (*Apollon Musagète*, 1928). In 1939 he moved to the United States.

The shimmering orchestral effects of *Firebird*, the novel bitonal "Petrushka" chord (combining C major and F-sharp major simultaneously), and the syncopated and irregular rhythms of both ballets paved the way for the harsh polytonal dissonances and the violent and percussive rhythmic techniques of *The Rite of Spring*. The use of repetitive folklike melodic motives, mixed meters, polyrhythms, and ostinatos are all characteristic, and most of these techniques remained distinguishing traits of Stravinsky's style. Out of practical necessity, Stravinsky pared down the enormous performing resources of *The Rite* to more economical proportions in works such as *L'Histoire du Soldat* (1918), scored for seven instrumentalists. The influence of jazz is reflected in *Ragtime* (1918) and *Ebony Concerto* (1945).

A revived interest in the music of the past, particularly in that of the baroque and classical periods, as well as an aesthetic predilection for clarity and balance, led to the composition of a number of neoclassical works, including the Octet for Wind Instruments (1923), the Concerto for Piano and Winds (1924), the Piano Sonata (1924), and *Dumbarton Oaks* Concerto (1938). Profound religious feeling was expressed in works such as the *Symphony of Psalms* (1930) and Mass (1948). Stravinsky continued to compose ballets and collaborated with Balanchine on *Jeu de cartes* (1936), *Orpheus* (1947), and *Agon* (1957). His only full-length opera, *The Rake's Progress* (1951), composed to a libretto by W. H. Auden and Chester Kallman, startled the musical world with its eclectic use of elements derived from Wolfgang Amadeus Mozart and Italian opera. Even more controversial was Stravinsky's turn to Anton von Webern–inspired serialism in works dating from the mid-1950s. An early example was *Canticum Sacrum ad Honorem Sancti Marci Nominis* (1955). *Threni* (1958) was Stravinsky's first completely serial work. The use of serial technique in this and subsequent compositions, such as Movements for Piano and Orchestra (1959), *Elegy for J. F. K.* (1964), and *Requiem Canticles* (1966), resulted in concise, highly structured works.

Stravinsky's unpredictable individualism and originality precluded the formation of a school of composition, but the influence of his music has been widespread, ranging from Sergei Prokofiev and Dmitry Shostakovich to Darius Milhaud, Aaron Copland, and many others.   LAUREL E. FAY

Bibliography: Lang, Paul Henry, ed., *Stravinsky: A New Appraisal of His Work* (1963); Stravinsky, Igor, *An Autobiography* (1936; repr. 1962) and *Poetics of Music* (1947); Stravinsky, Vera, and Craft, Robert, *Stravinsky in Pictures and Documents* (1978); Vlad, Roman, *Stravinsky*, 3d ed. (1979); White, Eric Walter, *Stravinsky*, 2d ed. (1979).

strawberry

Strawberries are low-growing perennial plants, genus *Fragaria* of the rose family, Rosaceae, that are cultivated for their juicy red fruits. Wild strawberry plants, bearing tiny fruits, are native to temperate regions and have been picked for food since antiquity. Cultivation of the strawberry as a garden plant began in 13th-century France. Two native American species, *F. chiloensis* and *F. virginiana*, were introduced into Europe, and their hybridization produced the many modern varieties of large, cultivated strawberries. Strawberries are now grown in almost every part of the temperate world, and new varieties have been developed to meet differing geographical and climatic conditions. The strawberry is almost always propagated by cutting off and replanting the many long runners produced by the plant. A few species—notably the European Alpine strawberry, *F. vesca*—do not put out runners and are propagated by division or through seed. Most plants flower in the spring and develop fruits in about 5 weeks. Some strawberry varieties, however, are "everbearing": they produce both a spring and a late summer or fall crop.

Bibliography: Wilhelm, Stephen, and Sagen, James, *A History of the Strawberry* (1972).

strawflower

Strawflower refers to the flower heads of certain annual plants in the daisy family, Compositae, that are dried and often dyed by flower arrangers. Most strawflowers used in winter dried arrangements have long stems that are kept straight by hanging the plants upside down to dry. The best-known cultivated strawflowers are several varieties of *Helichrysum bracteatum* from Australia that have yellow, orange, red, or white flower heads and several species of *Helipterum* from South Africa, Australia, and Tasmania that have yellow flower heads. These plants are also grown in garden borders for masses of color.   JANE PHILPOTT

Strawson, Peter Frederick   [straw'-suhn]

Peter Frederick Strawson, b. Nov. 23, 1919, is an English philosopher who became Wayneflete Professor of Metaphysics at Oxford University and fellow of Magdalen College, Oxford, in 1968.

Strawson is perhaps one of the most highly original of the philosophers of "ordinary language," along with Gilbert RYLE and J. L. AUSTIN. In *Introduction to Logical Theory* (1952) he examines the relationship between logic and ordinary language and challenges some of the standard views on issues such as induction and justification. His influential book, *Individuals* (1959), subtitled "An Essay In Descriptive Metaphysics," examines the relationship between particulars (material objects) and universals, the mind-body dilemma, and the relations of subjects and predicates. In Strawson's view, descriptive metaphysics describes the actual structure of thought about the world, whereas revisionary metaphysics tries to produce a better structure. His work has helped revive modern interest in metaphysics as a respectable branch of philosophy alongside epistemology and philosophy of language. Strawson has continued to exert wide influence through his many articles, collected in *Logico-Linguistic Papers* (1971) and *"Freedom and Resentment" and Other Essays* (1974). He was knighted in 1977.   E. D. KLEMKE

Bibliography: Gross, B. R., *Analytic Philosophy: An Historical Introduction* (1970); Magee, Bryan, *Modern British Philosophy* (1971).

streak, mineral: see MINERAL.

stream: see RIVER AND STREAM.

stream of consciousness

A term coined by William James in 1890, *stream of consciousness* is used to refer to a technique by which modern writers render the flow of their characters' thoughts. By recording a character's half-formed perceptions, shifting perspectives, and seemingly illogical associations, the novelist enables the reader to get inside a character's mind. The term is sometimes used synonymously with *interior monologue*. The possibilities of the technique were first fully demonstrated by James JOYCE, but he had a number of precursors, notably Laurence Sterne, whose TRISTRAM SHANDY (1760–67) is full of false starts, apparent irrelevancies, and digressions of every kind. Joyce's ULYSSES (1922), Virginia Woolf's MRS. DALLOWAY (1925) and *The Waves* (1931), and William Faulkner's SOUND AND THE FURY (1929) are all examples of the technique.

Bibliography: Edel, Leon, *The Modern Psychological Novel* (1964); Friedman, Melvin J., *Stream of Consciousness* (1955); Humphrey, Robert, *Stream of Consciousness in the Modern Novel* (1954).

streetcar

The cable car, a type of streetcar, has been carrying passengers up the steep hills of San Francisco since 1873. The cars are drawn along by a wire rope, or cable, which runs on rollers through a groove in the tracks, powered by a stationary steam engine.

Streetcars, or trolley cars, are public passenger vehicles that run on railway tracks set in the street. Power is usually drawn from an overhead electric wire and is brought to the car through a spring-loaded trolley pole, or pantograph. Passengers board from street level, as they do with buses. Cars may be run singly or in trains of two to four cars.

The first streetcars were pulled by horses. The horsecar idea originated in 1832, when the New York and Harlem Railroad Company began operations in New York City. The low friction of a metal wheel on a metal rail permitted a given horsepower to move more people more quickly than was otherwise possible. With substantial urban growth in the 19th century, cities throughout the world began to utilize the horse-drawn streetcar. Indeed, it came to be a symbol of mid-19th-century urban progress.

The components of the electric streetcar were developed in the 1880s, and a practical system of electric railway traction was developed by Frank J. Sprague in Richmond, Va., in 1888. The electric streetcar was quickly adopted in urban transportation, and more than 40,000 km (25,000 mi) of street railways were operating in the United States by World War I. The streetcar helped shape American cities, because housing and economic, cultural, and social activities could take place only along the streetcar lines in an age almost innocent of personal means of transportation.

Starting in the early 1920s the streetcar began to decline as a means of transportation, primarily because of the growing competition from automobiles. Disinvestment in the 1920s, '30s, and '40s almost brought an end to the streetcar in the United States. In the 1930s the Street Railway President's Conference Committee developed the so-called PCC car, which was a thoroughly modern vehicle of great comfort and speed. The PCC car delayed the complete demise of the streetcar and is still considered a superior job of engineering and development. Many of these cars continue to operate today. A modern offshoot of the traditional streetcar is the light rapid-transit vehicle. Light rapid-transit vehicles can operate at much higher speeds than the traditional streetcar because they run on their own private right-of-way rather than on the street. A conventional streetcar line can move about 6,000 to 9,000 riders per track per hour; light rapid transit has a capacity of up to 25,000 passengers per track per hour.

                                              GEORGE M. SMERK

Bibliography: Farris, Martin T., and Harding, Forrest E., *Passenger Transportation* (1976); Middleton, William D., *The Time of the Trolley* (1967); Miller, John Anderson, *Fares, Please!* (1960).

Streetcar Named Desire, A

Tennessee WILLIAMS's most popular play, *A Streetcar Named Desire* (1947; film, 1951), is both grimly naturalistic and poetically symbolic. Typical of Williams in its characters and theme, *Streetcar* pits Blanche DuBois, a neurasthenic, faded Southern belle who represents the culture and beauty of the past as well as its decadence, against her brother-in-law, Stanley Kowalski, the personification of modern practicality, crudeness, cynicism, and brutality. Blanche's childlike helplessness, romantic yearnings, and pretensions to gentility, sharply at odds with her age and the squalor of her present surroundings—her sister's New Orleans tenement—suggest an already tenuous hold on reality that completely collapses when Stanley's ruthless exposure of her past brings about Blanche's final disintegration. The winner of a Pulitzer Prize in 1948, *A Streetcar Named Desire* catapulted its male lead, Marlon Brando, to stardom, and his "method" style of acting to national prominence.   MYRON MATLAW

Bibliography: Miller, Jordan Yale, *Twentieth Century Interpretations of a Streetcar Named Desire* (1971).

Streisand, Barbra   [stry'-sand]

The actress and singer Barbra Streisand, b. Brooklyn, N.Y., Apr. 24, 1942, is perhaps the most versatile superstar of the 1960s and '70s. Her first recording, "The Barbra Streisand Album" (1963), reached the Top Ten, as have all her succeeding albums. Her 1965 portrayal of the comedienne Fanny Brice in the Broadway musical *Funny Girl* made her a stage star, and her 1968 film performance of the role won an Oscar. During the 1970s she made a series of highly acclaimed films, including *Hello, Dolly!* (1969), *The Owl and the Pussycat* (1970), and *The Way We Were* (1973).

Bibliography: Brady, Frank, *Barbra* (1979); Castell, David, *The Films of Barbra Streisand* (1974; repr. 1978); Spada, James, *Barbra: The First Decade, the Films and Career of Barbra Streisand* (1974).

strep throat

Streptococcal sore throat, or strep throat, is an inflammation of the throat and tonsils caused by bacteria of the group A β hemolytic *Streptococcus*, hence its name. It is the most common type of strep infection. The onset is usually sudden and is accompanied by pain, redness, and swelling in throat tissues, pus on the tonsils, fever, headache, and malaise. Abdominal pain and nausea also may occur, especially in children. The peak incidence of strep throat occurs in winter. Administration of penicillin is considered the best therapy unless the patient is allergic. SCARLET FEVER is a type of streptococcal sore throat. Viral infections can mimic strep throat.

                                              PETER L. PETRAKIS

Strepsiptera   [strep-sip'-tuh-ruh]

Strepsiptera (*strepsi*, "twisted"; *ptera*, "wings") is an order of about 300 species of minute insects—always parasitic in an immature stage—found in other insects, especially grasshoppers, true bugs, and bees and wasps. The sexes differ considerably. Males are usually free-living and have reduced, clublike front wings and complete hind wings. Females are wingless and, in parasitic species, lack eyes, antennae, and legs.   STEPHEN C. REINGOLD

Streptococcus   [strep-tuh-kahk'-uhs]

Streptococcus is a genus of spherically shaped bacteria that, microscopically, appear in chains. Some streptococci are nor-

mal inhabitants of the human mouth, throat, intestine, and vagina, or of milk; others are important causes of animal infections and of such human infections as RHEUMATIC FEVER, SCARLET FEVER, STREP THROAT, TONSILITIS, and glomerulonephritis.

                                              WAYBURN S. JETER

streptomycin: see ANTIBIOTICS.

Stresemann, Gustav   [shtray'-ze-mahn]

Gustav Stresemann, b. May 10, 1878, d. Oct. 3, 1929, German political leader, was chancellor (1923) and foreign minister (1923-29) of the Weimar Republic. The son of a Berlin beer merchant, he received his doctorate in economics in 1900, within a few years established himself as a leader in the League of German Industrialists, and in 1907 was elected to the German parliament, the Reichstag, as its youngest member. An ardent nationalist and advocate of a strong military and naval establishment, he was a vehement supporter during World War I of the policies of Paul von HINDENBURG and Erich LUDENDORFF, although these policies led to military defeat and the fall of the monarchy in 1918.

The crushing terms of the Versailles Peace Treaty drove many embittered patriots into blind opposition against it and against all who advocated complying with it, but Stresemann saw the necessity of accepting the odious consequences of defeat. In 1923, after the French occupied the Ruhr district, the industrial heartland of Germany, and German passive resistance not only failed to dislodge them but led to runaway inflation, Stresemann became chancellor. Under his leadership and with the support of President Friedrich EBERT, resistance to the French was ended, the economy provisionally stabilized, and separatist and radical movements suppressed. After 3 months, Stresemann relinquished the chancellorship but remained foreign minister for the last 6 years of his life, during which he succeeded in reconciling France and Germany and in bringing Germany into the League of Nations. Jointly with his French counterpart, Aristide BRIAND, he received the Nobel Peace Prize in 1926.   DONALD S. DETWILER

Bibliography: Bretton, Henry L., *Stresemann and the Revision of Versailles: A Fight for Reason* (1953); Stresemann, Gustav, *His Diaries, Letters and Papers*, ed. and trans. by Eric Sutton, 3 vols. (1935-40); Turner, Henry A., *Stresemann and the Politics of the Weimar Republic* (1963).

stress, biological

Stress embraces many types of physical disorders caused by mental strain. Body reactions to stress—increased heartbeat and breathing, muscle tension, rise in blood sugar, and physical exhaustion—can lead to such stress-related illnesses as peptic ulcers, high blood pressure, and hypoglycemia. Heart disease, one of the top three causes of death in the United States, is often a product of stress.

The causes of stress are often very well determined: for instance, acute emotional shock affecting a healthy person, infection, intoxication, trauma, accident, acute hemorrhage, heat stroke, hypothermia, and electrical shock all can result in stress. Factors causing stress also can be more difficult to identify, resulting from an internal disorder such as acidosis, diabetes, or cirrhosis. Chronic repetition of certain emotions, such as anger or despair, as well as changes in work or home situations or a reaction to surgery are just a few ways in which stress can occur. Finally, more than one factor causing stress can be present at the same time.

Executives are popularly thought to be the main victims of stress; a federal survey conducted by the National Institute for Occupational Safety and Health (NIOSH), however, placed laborers as being the people having most stress on the job, with secretaries and inspectors ranking second and third. Students also are prone to stress and sometimes attempt suicide to escape school and parental pressure.

The physiological basis of stress has been researched and can be understood in terms of two types of syndromes: lesional and reactive. A lesional syndrome results from disorders or localized lesions affecting various body organs, tissues, or cellular organelles. When the system is affected directly and traumatically or when it involves such important organs as the heart, brain, lungs, or liver, certain localized biochemical events occur: potassium concentrations in cells decrease and cellular sodium and water levels increase, lowering the ability of cells properly to transmit nervous impulses. Substrates such as adenosine triphosphate (ATP) that are valuable as energy reserves gradually disappear. Various etiological agents localized at one site induce identical symptoms; for instance, the disorders meningeal hemorrhage, purulent meningitis, tubercular meningitis, and viral meningitis all are characterized by a common meningeal syndrome.

A reactive syndrome can occur, especially in terms of neuroendocrinal reactions, without any connection to traumatically induced lesions. Detoxication reactions, inflammation, immune reactions, allergies and anaphylactic shock, and hemorrhagic shock are stimulated paraspecifically; that is, they are adapted to the type of causal agent involved. Specific reactions, which are independent from the nature of the causal agent, are generally conditioned by the intensity of the stress-related event. The reactions develop progressively and are caused more by the body's response than by direct intervention on the part of a causal agent.

Some disorders resulting from specific reactions include clinical disorders such as bronchospasms, digestive hemorrhages, and hepatitis, and neuropsychic problems such as delirium, nervous breakdowns, catatonia, and sleep dysfunctions. Metabolic disorders include impairment of use of sugars, fats, proteins, and fluids, as well as blood disorders. Nervous reflexes can be affected or abnormal secretion of hormones, such as aldosterone, can occur. As a final result of these disorders, such problems as delirium can occur in the case of a patient having pneumonia, diabetic coma, decreased resistance to infection, or heart failure.

Various people attempt to cope with stress in different ways; many take tranquilizers and sleeping pills and others take "mental health" days off from work. Psychiatrists and psychologists can help people to overcome stress by means of medication and various forms of psychotherapy. Hard exercise, yoga, and biofeedback are among many remedies that are popularly promoted to lessen the effects of stress.

A. LARCAN

Bibliography: Brown, Barbara B., *Stress and the Art of Biofeedback* (1977); Goldberg, Philip, *Executive Health: How to Recognize Health Danger Signals and Manage Stress Successfully* (1978); McQuade, Walter, *Stress* (1974).

See also: PSYCHOSOMATIC DISORDERS.

Streuvels, Stijn   [strur'-vuhls, styn]

An important figure in Flemish literature, Stijn Streuvels, b. Frank Lateur, Oct. 3, 1871, d. Aug. 15, 1969, was a member of the *Van-Nu-en-Straks* (From Now On) group. His stories and novels, which began to appear in 1899, depict West-Flemish peasant life. The forces of nature occupy the center of his fictional world, as in his masterpiece *De Vlaschaard* (The Flax Field, 1907), a novel that transcended the limitations of its regional genre.

THEO D'HAEN

Strickland, William   [strick'-luhnd]

William Strickland, b. Navesink, N.J., 1788, d. Apr. 6, 1874, was an influential American architect of the 19th-century GREEK REVIVAL. His Second Bank of the United States (1818–24) in Philadelphia, for example, builds on classic Greek prototypes with unprecedented faithfulness.

Strickland studied architecture under Benjamin Latrobe and also became adept as an engraver and as an engineer. His many public commissions included the United States Mint (1829–23) and the Navy Hospital (1827–48) in Philadelphia, the New Orleans Mint (1835–36), and the Providence Athenaeum (1838). Considering the Tennessee State Capitol at Nashville (1844–55) to have been his finest work, Strickland arranged to have himself interred there, in a specially built vault. Others, however, consider Strickland's masterpiece to

be the Merchants' Exchange (1832–34) in Philadelphia; the stately main block of the building is set off by an elegantly detailed semicircular end wing with an open Corinthian colonnade and a tall columned lantern tower.

As an engineer, Strickland built, among other structures, the Delaware Breakwater (1829–40) at Lewes, Del. He was also one of the first, in a time when the country was feverishly building canals, to foresee that railroads were to become the principal method of transporting goods in the United States.

RON WIEDENHOEFT

Bibliography: Brown, Milton W., *American Art to 1900* (1977); Gilchrist, Agnes, *William Strickland* (1950).

strike

Federal troops dispatched by President Grover Cleveland protect a train against damage by railway workers who were striking (1894). The nationwide strike was precipitated when the Pullman Palace Car Company, manufacturers of sleeping cars, reduced its workers' wages.

A strike is the withholding of labor from an employer by a group of employees (commonly but not always organized by a LABOR UNION) to obtain or reject a change in the conditions of their employment. The strike or strike threat is the principal pressure tactic in the collective bargaining process that workers can use against the employer. The aim of the strike is to cause such financial loss that the employer will meet the union's bargaining demands rather than continue to lose money.

Strikes may take different forms. In a primary strike, employees withhold their labor directly from the employer with whom they are disputing the terms of agreement. In a secondary strike, sometimes called a sympathy strike, employees withhold labor from an employer who is not directly involved in the dispute but who is important to the employer who is directly involved. The wildcat strike is a brief work stoppage not called by the union but initiated by a dissatisfied smaller group within the bargaining unit to protest specific actions by management, other work groups, or union leadership.

When a primary strike is ineffective, unions may solicit public support in a consumer boycott to reject the product or service sold by the employer. Direct strike actions are used to halt operations by physical force. Picketing—the patrolling by striking workers of their work site—is used to publicize the controversy and to dissuade potential customers and other workers from dealing with the employer.

An early strike in American history occurred when journeymen bakers struck in New York City in 1740, refusing to bake until their wages were raised. In the 1800s railway and steel strikes in the United States were numerous, with the HOMESTEAD STRIKE of 1892 and the PULLMAN STRIKE of 1894 becoming historic labor controversies. In the 20th century, steelworkers (1919, 1937, 1952, 1959), mine workers (1902, 1946–47), and automobile workers (1937, 1946) took part in major nationwide strikes. Since the 1960s public employees, including fire fighters, police, and teachers, have increasingly used the strike or the strike threat to enhance their bargaining positions. In the United States in 1978, 1.6 million workers were involved in 4,300 work stoppages, resulting in 39 million lost working days.

Most industrial countries have had a strike history that has paralleled the growth of organized labor. In Great Britain, for example, sporadic strikes occurred throughout the 19th century (see CHARTISM; LUDDITES). A major strike in 1926 by coal miners led to an unsuccessful GENERAL STRIKE, a phenomenon that has occurred in other European countries. In the Third World, colonial status or the ownership of a country's resources by foreign powers has provoked strikes for political as well as economic purposes.   JACK BARBASH

Bibliography: Dunlop, John T., and Chamberlain, Neil W., eds., *Frontiers of Collective Bargaining* (1967); Organization for Economic Cooperation and Development, *Labor Disputes: A Perspective* (1980); Ross, Arthur M., and Hartman, Paul T., *Changing Patterns of Industrial Conflict* (1960); U.S. Department of Labor, Bureau of Labor Statistics, *Analysis of Work Stoppage* (annual).

See also: ARBITRATION (labor-management and commercial); LOCKOUT; MEDIATION; SYNDICALISM.

strike-slip fault: see FAULT.

Strindberg, August   [strind'-burg]

A major figure in world drama whose plays have exerted a seminal influence on such 20th-century developments as EXPRESSIONISM, surrealism, the "psychoanalytic" play, and the theater of the absurd, August Strindberg was the Swedish language's great teacher of modern prose style and a forerunner of modernity in international theater. Acclaimed in turn-of-the-century Paris and Berlin for such remarkably successful experimental plays as MISS JULIE (1888; Eng. trans., 1912), *Creditors* (1888; Eng. trans., 1910), and *The Dance of Death* (1900; Eng. trans., 1912), he was a highly disturbing and problematic figure in relationship to his native culture.

Born in Stockholm on Jan. 22, 1849, Strindberg asserted himself as an egotist and as an outsider even in childhood. Neither his father's authoritarian ways and migratory life, brought on by economic shifts between bankruptcy and well-being, nor his mother's bestowal of affection and favor on an older brother, followed by her untimely death in 1862, could nurture a well-integrated personality or a secure sense of identity in August, the third of their seven children to survive infancy.

Strindberg's late teens and twenties marked a progression from what he considered the prison of family life to equally repressive Swedish Oscarian (Victorian) society. His failure to

The Swedish playwright and novelist August Strindberg defied social convention by writing dramas of sexual conflict and psychological torment, drawn largely from his personal life. His plays, once considered controversial, are now esteemed as classics of the modern stage.

complete studies at Uppsala University, his nightmarish aversion to public-school teaching, the stage fright that doomed his acting efforts, and his checkered career (1872–74) in journalism were compensated for only by summers (1871–83) spent on Kymmendö, an island in Stockholm's archipelago. Here the playwright achieved a personal breakthrough in the prose draft of his first notable play, the historical drama *Mäster Olof* (1872; Eng. trans., 1915), an event that was followed by his appointment (1874–82) to the staff of Stockholm's Royal Library and the publication of his realistic novel of social criticism, *The Red Room* (1879; Eng. trans., 1913), which brought Strindberg recognition as a writer. From the early 1880s writing became his sole means of support.

Something of a misogynist, Strindberg ultimately married and divorced three times and fathered five children. Not surprisingly, the theme of sexual conflict is often reflected in his works, notably in the naturalistic plays *The Father* (1887; Eng. trans., 1899) and *Miss Julie*. "The son of a servant woman," as he identified himself in the collective title of his nine-volume autobiography (1886–1908; Eng. trans., 1966), Strindberg went into self-exile in 1883, migrating from pension to farm to rented rooms in urban and rural France, Switzerland, Bavaria, Denmark, Prussia, and Austria. Humbled and chastened by what he called his "Inferno crisis" (1894–97), a time of deliberate isolation, "scientific" experimentation in occult matters including alchemy, and intense physical, psychological, and spiritual suffering, Strindberg returned to his homeland in 1897, moving in 1899 from Lund to Stockholm, where he resided and worked until his death from stomach cancer on May 14, 1912.

Strindberg's literary career of more than 40 years can be divided into two phases—separated by the so-called Inferno period of his life—during which he wrote more than 60 plays, as well as dramatic theory, autobiographical works, novels, short stories, essays, satire, verse, cultural studies, popular and esoteric science, speculative works about history, philology and religion, and polemics. A voracious and eclectic reader, he maintained a highly skeptical and critical sensibility, stressing personal experience and self-knowledge at all points in his development. His pre-Inferno years (1869–92) were decisively informed, however, by Darwin, Marx, Nietzsche, Rousseau, and Schopenhauer; his post-Inferno years (1898–1911) were influenced by Balzac, Beethoven, Goethe, Shakespeare, and the mysticism of Emanuel Swedenborg.

Critical opinion on the work of August Strindberg remains widely divergent even today. The best of his dramatic work tends to overlap the boundaries of several genres. His total literary production is curiously uneven; occasionally it is blatantly eccentric. His verse and prose fiction—with the exceptions of *The Red Room*, the regional novel *The Natives of Hemsö* (1887; Eng. trans., 1959), the humanly wise narrative *The Scapegoat* (1907; Eng. trans., 1967), and perhaps the mordant satire of *Svarta fanor* (Black Banners, 1907)—do not rank with the finest or most significant that Swedish literature has produced. In the theater, however, Strindberg achieved lasting international distinction.

His straining and breaking of the conventions of the late-19th-century stage furnished an impetus for virtually every aspect of the dramatic avante-garde in the 20th century. Although his point of departure was the realistic theater of his time, he prepared the way for expressionistic drama; with A DREAM PLAY (1902; Eng. trans., 1912) he contributed significantly to both the dream play and the "supernaturalistic" play; with the three-part *To Damascus* (1898 and 1904; Eng. trans., 1939), The GHOST SONATA (1907; Eng. trans., 1916), and *The Vasa Trilogy* (1899; Eng. trans., 1931) he also affected the development of modern symbolic, intimate, and historical drama. His influence as a theorist and shaper of drama can hardly be overestimated.   RAYMOND JARVI

Bibliography: Bentley, Eric, *The Playwright as Thinker* (1946); Brandell, Gunnar, *Strindberg in Inferno*, trans. by Barry Jacobs (1974); Johannesson, Eric O., *The Novels of August Strindberg* (1968); Johnson, Walter, *August Strindberg* (1976); Lamm, Martin, *August Strindberg*, trans. by Harry G. Carlson (1971); Sprigge, Elizabeth, *The Strange Life of August Strindberg* (1949; repr. 1972).

string quartet

Mozart's six string quartets of 1782–86, dedicated to his friend the composer Josef Haydn, reflect Haydn's influence in the brilliant integration of all four instruments. Mozart and Haydn are considered the primary figures in the development of the string quartet genre, establishing its characteristic four-movement form.

The string quartet is a musical genre that originated in the early 18th century, the same name being given to a group of four players (two violinists, a violist, and a cellist) who interpret this kind of music. Performing groups generally omit the word *string* and substitute a professional name, such as Budapest Quartet or Juilliard Quartet. Although the earliest composers of string quartets were Italian, it was because of Haydn and Mozart that the classical repertoire and form became firmly established, with the typical sequence of four movements as in a SONATA or symphony.

Eventually all the instruments were equally involved in both textural and thematic development, so that when Beethoven impressed his powerful personality upon the form, it reflected his new ideas, and in three examples of his last quartets he expanded the usual four-movement cycle to five, six, and seven movements, respectively. The quartets of Schubert, Mendelssohn, Schumann, and Brahms demonstrate the solid basis upon which the form then rested, and the music naturally expressed the lyrical and contrapuntal style of each composer. The Slavs were also attracted to the possibilities of the string quartet, as is evident in the examples by Borodin, Dvořák, Suk, and Tchaikovsky. Even some operatic composers were tempted to write at least one quartet, as did Wagner and Verdi. Unusually, the quartet by Sibelius (*Voces intimae*) is in five movements.

If technical demands made on the players have increased over the past century, it is nevertheless true that there are considerable challenges, especially for the first violinist and cellist, in many of the quartets by Haydn and Mozart and for all four players in the works of Beethoven, beginning with those of his middle period. The technical aspects have kept pace with new developments and styles of performance.

Among modern composers, the quartets of Berg, Hindemith, Schoenberg, and Webern are outstanding, and a new vitality emerged from Hungary in the quartets of Bartók; from France (Fauré, Debussy, Ravel, Milhaud, and Boulez); from Russia (Prokofiev and Shostakovich), Great Britain (Delius, Elgar, Vaughan Williams, Britten), and the United States (Ives, Sessions, Carter, and Babbitt).   DENIS STEVENS

Bibliography: Barrett-Ayres, R., *Joseph Haydn and the String Quartet* (1974); Herter-Norton, M. D., *The Art of String Quartet Playing* (1962).

stringed instruments

Stringed instruments, all of which produce their sound by causing a tightened string to vibrate by either plucking or

(Opposite) Modern chordophones, or stringed instruments, include both instruments of ancient origin, such as the harp and the lute, and the recently developed bowed instruments of the violin family. The violin, lute, banjo, guitar, zither, harp, and cello are illustrated. Keyboard instruments, such as the piano and the clavichord (not shown), are also classified as chordophones. The varied tones of chordophones are produced by the vibrations of strings and are amplified by a resonating sound box.

bowing, are found in most parts of the world. Their use is less common among primitive cultures, however, than the other instrument families. Ancient civilizations knew stringed instruments in various forms, the plucked strings appearing earlier than the bowed. The Egyptian, Greek, and Hebrew cultures knew the LUTE, HARP, and LYRE in some form; the Oriental and the Near Eastern cultures were familiar with bowed instruments as well as the plucked. Stringed KEYBOARD INSTRUMENTS—the CLAVICHORD, HARPSICHORD, and PIANO—are later European developments.

Lutes are instruments of great antiquity, having been prominent in pre-Christian cultures. They made their way into Europe, probably by way of Spain and through the Crusades in the Middle Ages. The amount, variety, and wide dispersal of lute music during the Renaissance attest to the popularity of the instrument as a solo and accompanying medium. Polyphonic as well as chordal music lay within its realm, and the lute held sway until its decline in the 17th century. The GUITAR, which has assumed great prominence in the 20th century, was only one of the other important plucked, fretted instruments that emerged in Europe and elsewhere. Also significant are the BALALAIKA in Russia, the KOTO in Japan, and the VINA and SITAR in India.

Bowed stringed instruments have risen to great importance in Western culture, the medieval VIELLE giving way to the VIOLS, and the VIOLIN family becoming predominant in the 17th century. The need for greater volume of sound and a larger range of dynamics brought the violin family into prominence, for these instruments provide flexibility and agility of execution along with tonal qualities that ranged from crispness to lyricism. The variety of sounds produced on bowed stringed instruments comes from various methods of bowing, the use of PIZZICATO, and the capacity to produce multiple stops as well as single tones. Reaching a state of complete development soon after their introduction, as compared with the slow development of other instrument families, the strings achieved a more prominent position in chamber music and solo literature. Virtuoso performers on stringed instruments emerged early (1700s) and they found more ready acceptance as recitalists and as soloists with symphony orchestras than did players of other nonkeyboard instruments. The string quartet was, for nearly two centuries, viewed as the ideal chamber ensemble, having the benefits of a full range of homogeneous sound coupled with a variety of techniques, a full range of dynamics, and a variety of styles at its disposal.
ELWYN A. WIENANDT

Bibliography: Baines, Anthony, ed., *Musical Instruments through the Ages* (1975); Engel, Carl, *Researches into the Early History of the Violin Family* (1883; repr. 1977); Panum, Hortense, *Stringed Instruments of the Middle Ages* (1939; repr. 1970); Remnant, Mary, *Musical Instruments of the West* (1978); Sachs, Curt, *History of Musical Instruments* (1940).

Stringer, Arthur

Arthur Stringer, b. Chatham, Ontario, Feb. 26, 1874, d. Sept. 15, 1950, was a prolific Canadian author who wrote more than 50 novels, numerous volumes of poetry and literary studies, and the script for *The Perils of Pauline* film serial (begun 1914). He spent many years in the United States, but his best works have Canadian settings.

strip mining: see COAL AND COAL MINING.

stroboscope   [strahb'-uh-skohp]

A stroboscope is a device that employs bright pulses of light to illuminate a vibrating or rotating object and to make it appear motionless or moving very slowly. The stroboscope

works by permitting the eye only a brief glimpse of the object or a portion of it at time intervals that correspond to the object's rate of vibration or rotation. The rate of movement and the light pulses can be adjusted to match. An early stroboscopic device, invented in 1836 by Joseph Plateau of Belgium, used a disk with radial slits that he turned while viewing a rotating wheel; when the rotational speed of the disk and the wheel matched exactly, the wheel appeared motionless. Other pioneers of the stroboscope employed rotating or vibrating mirrors to produce pulses of light. These experiments led to the first devices for producing the illusion of motion and eventually to motion pictures. Stroboscopes are also used for stage-lighting effects.

Modern stroboscopes are electronic devices equipped with gas discharge lamps that can produce flashes equivalent to 50,000 watts of incandescent light. A typical flash lasts roughly five millionths of a second. Stroboscopes are commonly available for setting the ignition timing of motor vehicle engines. They are also used as testing devices in industry when a moving machine—for instance, an electric razor—must be checked for quality. Laboratory uses include the study of mechanical systems in slow motion.

Bibliography: Edgerton, Harold E., and Killian, James R., *Moments of Vision: The Stroboscopic Revolution in Photography* (1979).

stroboscopic photography: see FLASH PHOTOGRAPHY.

Stroessner, Alfredo   [strurs'-nur]

Paraguayan army officer and dictator Alfredo Stroessner, b. Encarnación, Nov. 3, 1912, was a grandson of a German immigrant. He entered military service in 1932, after studying at the Military College at Asunción. He became (1951) commander in chief of the armed forces and has served since 1954 as president of Paraguay, after toppling the regime of Federico Cháves in a coup. He suppressed all opposition and in 1977 became president for life.

Stroheim, Erich von   [shtroh'-hym]

A legendary figure in the Hollywood of the silent era, actor, director, and scriptwriter Erich von Stroheim, b. Vienna, Sept. 22, 1885, d. May 12, 1957, is celebrated both for his ruinous extravagances as a filmmaker and his screen portrayals of stiff-necked German officers. As a director he demonstrated his brilliance as well as his limitations. His only successfully completed films—*Blind Husbands* (1919), the *Devil's Passkey* (1919), and *Foolish Wives* (1921), in two of which he played the lead—bear the stamp of his wit, sophistication, lavish attention to detail, and sometimes brutal realism. Thereafter, his career was marked by frustration as his ambitious artistic schemes for such films as *Merry-Go-Round* (1922), *Greed* (1923), and *The Wedding March* (1926) repeatedly ran afoul of whistle-blowing producers at Universal, MGM, and Paramount, who cut and distorted his work beyond recognition. His most famous failure, *Queen Kelly* (1928), which was to star Gloria Swanson, effectively ended his directorial hopes. Concentrating exclusively on acting after 1936, von Stroheim gave his most distinguished performances in Jean Renoir's *Grand Illusion* (1937) and in Billy Wilder's inspired film à clef, *Sunset Boulevard* (1950), playing a former director opposite Gloria Swanson's evocation of an aging, fantasy-ridden silent-film star.
ELEANOR M. GATES

Bibliography: Curtiss, Thomas Q., *Von Stroheim* (1971); Noble, Peter, *Hollywood Scapegoat* (1950; repr. 1972).

stroke

Stroke, also known as cerebrovascular accident (CVA), involves damage to the brain because of impaired blood supply and causes a sudden, nonconvulsive malfunction of the brain. Although not necessarily the cause of death, cerebrovascular disease has been found in 50% of autopsied patients; 200,000 people in the United States die from stroke each year, and it is the third-ranking cause of death after heart disease and cancer. About half the neurologic patients in hospitals and convalescent homes are stroke victims.

Stroke victims are generally elderly people with degeneration of blood vessels, but children and young adults also can be subject to stroke. People having hypertension, atherosclerosis, heart disease, or diabetes mellitus or who are emotionally upset incur a high risk of having a stroke; women using oral contraceptives are more prone to cardiovascular disease than those using other means of birth control.

SYMPTOMS
A stroke may be mildly incapacitating or may involve a sudden coma, followed by headache, nausea, confusion, and stupor. Stroke patients are often characterized by paralysis of one side of the body (hemiplegia), accompanied by loss of speech or comprehension. The initial paralysis of a stroke victim is flaccid or soft because of central nervous system shock, but spasticity occurs as spinal motor neurons resume function, making muscles tighten and the limbs progressively contract. A stroke patient with paralysis of an arm, for instance, will initially have a loose, freely swinging arm. Months later the arm will be rigidly flexed, with the wrist and hand positioned near the shoulder. Physiotherapy is often used to preserve the motor abilities of a contracted limb, by means of passive stretching exercises to maintain muscle tone and to discourage muscle spasm.

PATIENT CARE
The medical team involved in caring for stroke victims includes an internist, a neurosurgeon, a neurologist, a stroke nurse, a physical therapist, and a speech therapist. These people are involved not only in the care of the stroke patient but also in educating the patient's family in long-term care as well as alerting them to problems that may be encountered during rehabilitation.

TYPES OF STROKES
Ischemia. A stroke can be caused by ischemia, which is a narrowing or blockage of an artery by means of a clot, by a hemorrhage, or by an embolus. About 63% of strokes are ischemic. Atherosclerosis, or progressive hardening of the arteries, produces ischemia by obstruction of vessels with fat derivatives. Most frequently, cholesterol forms plaques that build up on arterial walls, reducing the passage of blood. A common aging process, atherosclerosis especially afflicts the elderly or people with high cholesterol intake.

Another form of ischemia is thrombosis, or blockage resulting from an embolus. An embolus produced by the carotid artery in the neck, which supplies blood from the heart to the brain, claims about one-third of stroke patients. A clot, or thrombus, can form in this artery and fragment, producing a thromboembolus, which travels to the brain and becomes entrapped in a cerebral artery. Other types of emboli to the brain provide less common forms of ischemia. These emboli typically originate in the heart when a thrombus forms at the site of myocardial infarction from growth on heart valves during rheumatic fever or from thromboemboli formed during cardiac surgery. Blood supply through the cerebral artery is then blocked, causing a large neurologic deficit (which can lead to stroke) or a small deficit (which can cause a transient ischemic attack—TIA—usually heralding a potential stroke). Treatment of thromboemboli of the carotid artery may require surgical excision of the plaque, a bypass graft using a spare jugular vein, anticoagulants, modified diet, anaerobic exercises, reduced stress, or simply two aspirins twice a day for life. Birth-control pills have been found to cause thrombosis, leading to stroke in women.

Hemorrhage. About 22% of all strokes are caused by cerebral hemorrhage. Causes of spontaneous intracranial hemorrhage, commonly called apoplexy, are hypertension (10% to 15% of all cases), aneurysm (5% to 7%), bleeding into a tumor (3% to 5%), and a generalized bleeding tendency (1% to 2%). Hypertensive hemorrhages occur in the brainstem or the lateral portion of the cerebral hemisphere near the pathway for motor nerves; if the hemorrhage extends into the motor tract, hemiplegia will result. Partial or complete recovery of function can return over a long period of time, and treatment is aimed at reducing blood pressure and using physiotherapy to regain the use of the limbs. A massive hemorrhage, however, can result in coma, brain damage, and possibly death.

Aneurysms—enlargements of small portions of blood vessels—can hemorrhage and cause stroke if present in the brain or arteries of the neck. After an aneurysm ruptures, creating a massive bleeding episode, red blood cells degenerate and release products that can promote a vascular spasm. An aneurysm is usually treated surgically after a 2-week waiting period, which allows edema and vasospasm to subside. Often, however, bleeding begins again and is frequently fatal.

Tumors must have an adequate blood supply to maintain their growth, and therefore some tumors secrete an angiogenesis factor that promotes blood-vessel growth. At times a tumor may produce too much of this factor, causing the vessels to enlarge. This enlargement can result in internal hemorrhage and sudden stroke. The stroke, unfortunately, may mask the existence of a tumor and delay a complete diagnosis.

Generalized bleeding used to be restricted to hemophilia and related disorders. Chemotherapy of tumors, however, poisons bone marrow and interferes with the production of platelets necessary for the formation of clots if bleeding should occur, increasing the chances for incurring a stroke.

DIAGNOSIS
Diagnostic techniques include searching for blood in a lumbar puncture (spinal tap), injecting radiopaque dyes into vessels of the neck and head (arteriogram), using brain scan for defects in blood/brain barrier, and doing computerized tomography (CAT scanner) with image enlargement to search for altered densely within the brain.   A. W. DUDLEY

Bibliography: Fein, Jack M., "Microvascular Surgery for Stroke," *Scientific American*, April 1978; Johnstone, Margaret, *The Stroke Patient* (1977); O'Brien, Mary T., and Pallet, Phyllis J., *Total Care of the Stroke Patient* (1978); Sarno, John E. and Martha T., *Stroke*, rev. ed. (1979).

stromatolite   [stroh-mat'-uh-lyt]

Stromatolites are variously shaped laminated structures that occur in many tidal-flat limestones. They were originally considered to be animal fossils. Geologists now know that these structures were probably formed in shallow water underneath sticky mats of blue-green and green algae. The mats trapped carbonate sediment, and as the algae grew upward, the sediment was incorporated in layers. After deposition, the organic mats decomposed, and only the layered sediments remained. Stromatolite structures have assumed great importance as evidence of algal life far into the Precambrian Period. Formations of stromatolitic limestones about 2 billion years old have been mapped in Canada and South Africa.

Bibliography: Press, Frank, and Siever, Raymond, *Earth* (1974).

Stromboli   [strom'-boh-lee]

Stromboli, 926 m (3,038 ft) high, is an active volcano on an island of the same name in the Lipari Islands in the TYRRHENIAN SEA, 64 km (40 mi) north of the northeast coast of Sicily. The volcano, which occupies most of the island's 13-km² (5-mi²) area, is a popular tourist attraction. Records of its continuous activity date from the 6th century BC. The last major eruption occurred in 1921, but the volcano still emits smoke.

Strömgren, Bengt Georg Daniel [shtrurm'-gren]

The Swedish astronomer Bengt Georg Daniel Strömgren, b. Jan. 21, 1908, developed the theory that luminous interstellar clouds (Strömgren spheres) result from hydrogen ionized by high-temperature stars. He received (1929) his Ph.D. from Copenhagen University and served (1951–57) as director of the Yerkes and McDonald observatories in Williams Bay, Wis. Strömgren has taught at Copenhagen University (1933, 1938–40, 1967–) and the University of Chicago (1936–38, 1946–47), and from 1957 to 1967 he was a member of the Institute for Advanced Study in Princeton, N.J. Strömgren is recognized for his work on the ionization, pulsation, and internal composition of stars and on spectral classification.

STEVEN J. DICK

Strong, Josiah

The American clergyman Josiah Strong, b. Napierville, Ill., Jan. 19, 1847, d. Apr. 28, 1916, was a leader of the SOCIAL GOSPEL movement, which called for Christian service to promote human welfare. An Ohio minister, he moved (1886) to New York after his first book, *Our Country* (1885), had made him a national figure. Strong used statistical evidence to show how wealth had been concentrated in the hands of a few and how industrial workers were deprived of decent living conditions. He insisted that Christianity had the duty to alleviate such inequities and to help achieve the standard of social justice articulated in the Bible. In 1898 he organized the League (later the American Institute) for Social Service, an early attempt to achieve cooperation among churches for common social reforms. HENRY WARNER BOWDEN

Bibliography: White, Ronald C., *The Social Gospel: Religion and Reform in Changing America* (1976).

Strong, Sir Samuel Henry

Canadian Supreme Court Justice Sir Samuel Henry Strong, b. Dorsetshire, England, Aug. 13, 1825, d. Ontario, Aug. 21, 1909, went to Canada in 1836, began the practice of law in 1849 in Toronto, and soon won a reputation as an able jurist. He became one of the first members of the Supreme Court of Canada when it was established in 1875. He was appointed its chief justice in 1892, a year before he was knighted, and served until his retirement in 1902.

strong interactions: see FUNDAMENTAL INTERACTIONS.

strontium

Strontium is a soft, silvery metal with physical and chemical properties similar to those of calcium. Its symbol is Sr; its atomic number, 38; and its atomic weight, 87.62. First isolated (1808) by Sir Humphry Davy, strontium is found in the minerals strontianite and celestite. Many radioactive isotopes of strontium are produced in nuclear reactors. Strontium 90, with a half-life of 28 years, is formed in nuclear explosions; because it accumulates in the bones, it is considered the most dangerous component of radioactive FALLOUT. Strontium salts impart red color to flames and are used in red signal flares, fireworks, and tracer bullets.

strophanthus   [struh-fan'-thuhs]

Strophanthus is an alkaloid drug used as a heart stimulant and as an arrow poison. It is obtained from dried, ripe seeds of several tropical species in the plant genus *Strophanthus*, of the dogbane family, Apocynaceae. These shrubs and vines are native to tropical South Africa and Asia; a few species are grown as ornamentals. JANE PHILPOTT

Strozzi, Bernardo   [straht'-tsee]

The leading Genoese baroque painter Bernardo Strozzi, b. 1581, d. Aug. 2, 1644, was also known as Il Cappuccino and Il Prete Genovese because he was a member of the Capuchin Order until 1610, when he was allowed to leave the monastery. Strozzi's vigorous Genoese style shows him already moving away from Mannerist art, a direction in which he was encouraged by the influences of Paolo Veronese and Caravaggio. His distinctive, mature style began to develop under the influence of the Flemish baroque painters Peter Paul Rubens, who was in Genoa in 1607, and Sir Anthony van Dyck, who made trips there in 1621–22 and 1626–27. Under their inspiration, Strozzi's colors intensified and his brushstroke became even freer and more suggestive. These tendencies were further heightened by his experience in Venice, where he lived after 1630. There, with two other expatriates—Domenico Fetti and Jan Lys—Strozzi revitalized the moribund tradition of Venetian painting.

Bibliography: Milkovitch, Michael, *Bernardo Strozzi: Paintings and Drawings* (1967); Waterhouse, Ellis, *Italian Baroque Painting* (1969).

structural geology

Structural geology is the division of the science of GEOLOGY that deals with the recognition, description, analysis, and origin of geologic structures, such as FOLDS, FAULTS, and other crustal phenomena, and the analysis of the forces that produce them. The subdivision of tectonics is concerned with the study of large-scale structures, such as lithospheric plates (see PLATE TECTONICS), MOUNTAIN chains, ISLAND ARCS, ocean basins (see OCEAN AND SEA), and parts of ocean basins (MID-OCEANIC RIDGES, OCEANIC TRENCHES, TRANSFORM FAULTS). The relationships between continents and oceans, and the evolution of continents and ocean basins, are also evaluated. Regional structural geology may be considered synonymous with tectonics, although the focus is always on smaller features.

The subdivision of rock mechanics deals with the methods of producing geologic structures in the laboratory. By determining the stresses and temperatures at which these form, geologists gain a better understanding of the conditions under which geologic structures form in the Earth. Other structural geologists study natural structures in the field and under the microscope to help understand their origin.
ROBERT D. HATCHER, JR.

Bibliography: Clark, Sydney P., *Structure of the Earth* (1971); DeSitter, L. U., *Structural Geology*, 2d ed. (1964); Ramsay, G. J., *Folding and Fracturing of Rocks* (1967); Spencer, Edgar W., *Introduction to the Structure of the Earth*, 2d ed. (1977).

structuralism

Structuralism, one of the most important and widespread of current intellectual fashions, is the study of patterns underlying social behavior, culture, and the composition of physical matter. It offers a rational methodology to such disparate and unrelated fields of study as biology, geology, anthropology, linguistics, and literary criticism. Structuralism, which is based on communication theory, studies the relationships between forms rather than the nature of the forms themselves, finding "languages" in signs and symbols and nonverbal means of expression in animal life, family groups, and even social customs, such as dress. By analyzing phenomena, whether novels, communities, or political systems, structuralism reveals frameworks of communication that are united by their binary structure of signs. Such signs derive their meanings not from their intrinsic natures but from their positions in relation to each other. The colors red and green, for example, have no inherent meaning, but when used in a traffic sign they become symbols of danger and safety.

Structural linguistics (see APPLIED LINGUISTICS), which provides a model for structural analysis in other fields, passes beyond dictionary meanings to concentrate on units of meaning smaller than words. These are phonemes, the smallest units of sound, and morphemes, the smallest units of sense. By applying this technique to a language, the linguist is able to describe its basic structure and to understand the principles on which it evolved.

Since the 1950s structuralism has had an effect on literary criticism, especially in France where the discipline of SEMIOTICS—the study of signs—has evolved. Structuralist critics tend to regard works of literature as isolated phenomena rather than products of a particular author working in a specific time and place. A structural analysis pays close attention to small particulars of style, such as symbol and diction, thus emphasizing the individuality of a work and its unique principles of coherence. HOWARD BATCHELOR

Bibliography: Barthes, Roland, *Critical Essays* (1964); De George, Fernande and Richard, eds., *The Structuralists* (1972); Jakobson, Roman, "Quest for the Essence of Language," *Diogenes*, 51 (1965); Lane, Michael, ed., *Structuralism* (1970); *Structuralism*, Yale French Studies, vols. 36 and 37 (1966).

Struthiomimus   [stroo-thee-oh-my'-muhs]

Struthiomimus is one of the "ostrich" dinosaurs of the family Ornithomimidae, suborder Theropoda, order Saurischia. It lived during the late Cretaceous, about 75 million years ago,

Struthiomimus was one of the ostrichlike dinosaurs that lived about 75 million years ago. It was probably a rapid runner.

in western North America and Asia. Except for a long tail, *Struthiomimus* and its close relatives were ostrichlike and were characterized by long, slender legs that indicate very fast running ability, long arms and hands designed for grasping, a long, flexible neck, and a relatively small, birdlike head with large eyes and a toothless beak. They stood 2.4 m (8 ft) high and reached 4.3 m (14 ft) in length, including the tail; some weighed up to perhaps 200 kg (440 lb). Despite its toothlessness, *Struthiomimus* is a member of the carnivorous theropod group. Possibly the animals were omnivores or egg-eaters. Other ostrich dinosaurs are *Ornithomimus* (probably identical to *Struthiomimus*), *Dromiceiomimus* from North America, and *Gallimimus* from Mongolia.   JOHN H. OSTROM

Bibliography: Colbert, Edwin H., *Evolution of the Vertebrates* (1969); Romer, Alfred Sherwood, *Vertebrate Paleontology* (1966).

Strutt, John William: see RAYLEIGH, LORD.

Struve, Friedrich Georg Wilhelm von
[shtroo'-veh]

The German-born Russian astronomer Friedrich Georg Wilhelm von Struve, b. Apr. 15, 1793, d. Nov. 23, 1864, discovered (1840) the parallax of the bright star Vega, a major breakthrough in the precise measurement of stellar distances. His contributions to determining the distances of stars also helped make possible the determination of the intrinsic brightness of stars. Struve, who fled (1808) from Germany to Russia to avoid serving in Napoleon's army, carried on the systematic observation of double stars begun by William Herschel and published (1837) a classic survey of 3,112 double stars. He was appointed (1834) the first director of Pulkovo Observatory, near Saint Petersburg.

Bibliography: Struve, Otto, "The First Determination of Stellar Parallax," *Sky and Telescope*, January and February 1956; Vicinich, Alexander, *Science in Russian Culture* (1963).

Struve, Otto

The American astronomer Otto Struve, b. Kharkov, Russia, Aug. 12(N.S.), 1897, d. Apr. 6, 1963, discovered the existence of interstellar gas, did work on the evolution of stars, and argued that stars with planetary systems might be more common than had previously been believed. The fourth in a line of astronomers in his family, Struve immigrated to the United States in 1921 and received (1923) his Ph.D. degree from the University of Chicago, where he taught (1927–47) and was director (1932–47) of the university's Yerkes Observatory. He was also director (1959–62) of the National Radio Astronomy Observatory in Greenbank, W.Va.   STEVEN J. DICK

Bibliography: Herbig, G. H., ed., *Spectroscopic Astrophysics: An Assessment of the Contributions of Otto Struve* (1970).

strychnine   [strik'-neen]

Strychnine is a natural alkaloid found in the tree genus *Strychnos*, particularly *S. nux vomica*, which grows in India, Burma, China, and northern Australia. It was isolated (1818) from the seeds of these trees, which were used in earlier centuries as a medicinal tonic and a stimulant to the intestines. Strychnine is a potent stimulant of the central nervous system, and a lethal dose in humans first causes convulsions, twitching, arching of the back, and a rigidity of facial muscles. Today it is used mainly as a poison for rats and other rodents.   CHARLES L. WINEK

Stryker, Roy   [stry'-kur]

From 1935 to 1943, Roy Emerson Stryker, b. Great Bend, Kans., 1893, d. Sept. 17, 1975, headed the historical section of the U.S. Farm Security Administration. Under his supervision photographers such as Walker EVANS, Dorothea LANGE, and Russell Lee took about 130,000 pictures of Depression-torn America, providing a vivid record of the life of the rural poor. The project, a landmark in photojournalism, is recalled in Stryker's selection of FSA pictures, *In This Proud Land* (1973).

Bibliography: Anderson, James C., ed., *Roy Stryker, the Humane Propagandist* (1977); Hurley, F. Jack, *Portrait of a Decade: Roy Stryker and the Development of Documentary Photography in the Thirties* (1972).

Stuart   (family)

The Stuart (also spelled Stewart and Steuart) family provided Scotland and, later, Britain with numerous monarchs. The family can be traced to a Breton, **Alan,** the son of Flaald, who migrated to England about the beginning of the 12th century. **Walter**, d. 1177, his youngest son, was made steward (official in the household) by David I of Scotland, who granted him lands in Renfrewshire.

The 6th steward, **Walter,** d. 1326, married Marjory, daughter of Scotland's King Robert I, and in 1371 their son Robert II became the first Stuart king of Scotland. His successors were Robert III, JAMES I, James II, James III, JAMES IV, JAMES V, MARY, QUEEN OF SCOTS, and James VI. In 1603, James VI became JAMES I of England as well. His Stuart successors on the thrones of England and Scotland were CHARLES I, CHARLES II, JAMES II, MARY II, and ANNE. With the death of Anne in 1714, the Stuart dynasty was replaced by the Hanoverians (whose claim to the throne also sprang from the Stuarts). However, male descendants of James II—most notably James Francis Edward STUART (the Old Pretender) and Charles Edward STUART (the Young Pretender)—attempted unsuccessfully to recover the throne for the family.

A strong branch of the family held the earldom and later dukedom of Lennox. The 4th earl, **Matthew Stewart** (1516–71), married Margaret Douglas, daughter of Margaret Tudor and the 6th earl of Angus; their son Henry Stewart, Lord DARNLEY, stood next to Mary, Queen of Scots, in the English succession. When Darnley married Mary in 1565, the branches of the powerful Stuart family united. The dukedom of Lennox was created in 1581 for **Esmé Stuart** (c.1542–83) by his cousin James VI.   CHARLES H. HAWS

Bibliography: Bingham, Caroline, *The Stewart Kingdom of Scotland* (1974); Donaldson, Gordon, *Scottish Kings* (1967); Henderson, T. F., *The Royal Stewarts* (1914); Linklater, Eric, *The Royal House of Scotland* (1970).

Stuart, Charles Edward   (Bonnie Prince Charlie)

Charles Edward Stuart, known as Bonnie Prince Charlie and as the Young Pretender, b. Rome, Dec. 31, 1720, d. Jan. 31, 1788,

Charles Edward Stuart, the legendary Bonnie Prince Charlie, sought to recover the British throne for the Stuart family in the Jacobite uprising of 1745. Disastrously defeated at Culloden Moor, where one-fifth of his Highland army was killed in battle and another fifth was slain after being captured by the English, the Young Pretender fled to the Continent.

Portrait of a Flute Player (c.1795–98), painted by Gilbert Stuart, an important late-18th-century American portraitist, is quiet, naturalistic, and straightforward. Stuart gained much acclaim during his lifetime, especially for his portraits of George Washington and other prominent Americans of his time. (Private collection.)

laid claim to the British throne through his Stuart grandfather, King JAMES II. Charles Edward was the elder son of James Francis Edward Stuart (the Old Pretender). In 1744 he went to France hoping to participate in an invasion of Britain. When it failed to materialize, he and his companions—the seven men of Moidart—left France for Scotland and landed in the Hebrides in July 1745. They launched the JACOBITE rebellion known as the '45, the last Stuart attempt to regain power in Britain.

Charles Edward raised his standard in the Highlands and attracted a number of loyal clans. His support, however, was not broadly based, especially in the Lowlands and the eastern Highlands. He defeated Sir John Cope at Prestonpans on Sept. 21, 1745, and with an army of 7,000 to 8,000 men he marched toward London. He stopped at Derby and waited in vain for promised French and English aid; then, accepting his officers' advice, he retreated to Scotland. Outside of Inverness, at Culloden Moor, Charles Edward's army was badly defeated on Apr. 16, 1746, by troops led by the duke of Cumberland. With the help of Flora Macdonald, Charles Edward fled to France. He was later expelled from France and traveled around Europe, finally settling in Italy and styling himself the count of Albany. Bonnie Prince Charlie has been the subject of many romantic legends.   CHARLES H. HAWS

Bibliography: Daiches, David, *Charles Edward Stuart: The Life and Times of Bonnie Prince Charlie* (1973); Forster, Margaret, *The Rash Adventurer: The Rise and Fall of Bonnie Prince Charlie* (1973); Petrie, Charles, *The Jacobite Movement*, rev. ed. (1959).

Stuart, Gilbert

Gilbert Stuart, b. North Kingston, R.I., Dec. 3, 1755, d. July 9, 1828, a major American portrait painter of the late 18th and early 19th centuries, is among the greatest portraitists in the history of American art. He executed his earliest works in a provincial, quasi-primitive style. At the outbreak of the Revolution he went (1775) to London, where he studied under Benjamin West. By the 1780s, Stuart's earlier provincialism had given way to a highly sophisticated style marked by coolly rational likenesses created with warm color and fluid brushwork. His London reputation was secured with the favorable reception accorded to his *Skater* (1782; National Gallery, Washington, D.C.), the only work in which Stuart showed his subject in motion.

Debts drove (1788) Stuart to Ireland, and in 1793 he returned to the United States, settling first in New York, then in Philadelphia, in Washington, D.C., and finally (1805) in Boston. Universally recognized as the finest portraitist in the United States, he was much in demand and painted hundreds of likenesses. His three lifelike portraits of George Washington (1795–96) proved to be so popular that he painted more than 100 replicas to meet the demand. He also painted the

next five presidents, as well as many of the most prominent Americans of his day.

Stuart's ability to capture the character of his subjects in a vividly animated image was accompanied by a deep understanding of the cultural differences that separated aristocratic England from democratic America. For his American work he developed a plain, forthright portrait style best seen in his unidealized depiction of Washington as a citizen-president, without any insignia of rank or office. Fittingly, one of his portraits of Washington, the "Athenaeum" version (1796; Museum of Fine Arts, Boston), was adopted for the U.S. one-dollar bill.   DAVID TATHAM

Bibliography: Mount, Charles M., *Gilbert Stuart* (1964); Richardson, E. P., *Gilbert Stuart* (1967).

Stuart, James

The British architect James Stuart, 1713–88, is best known as the coauthor with Nicholas Revett (1720–1804) of the three-volume *Antiquities of Athens* (vol. 1, 1762; vols. 2 and 3, 1789), the first reliable survey of Greek architecture and the major source book for the subsequent GREEK REVIVAL in Europe and the United States. Stuart contributed broad topographical views, whereas Revett provided precise measured drawings. The first volume defined the Greek architectural orders and their concomitant decorations; the second and third volumes recorded the monuments on the Acropolis of Athens in scrupulous detail. The volumes, sumptuously illustrated with hundreds of engravings, remain a standard reference source. Stuart also practiced architecture; his few surviving buildings include several decorative garden pavilions in exceptionally pure Greek style.

Bibliography: Crook, J. Mordaunt, *The Greek Revival* (1972); Stuart, James, and Revett, Nicholas, *Antiquities of Athens*, 3 vols. (1762; repr. 1968).

Stuart, James Francis Edward

James Francis Edward Stuart, known as the Old Pretender, b. June 10, 1688, d. Jan. 1, 1766, attempted to regain the throne of England and Scotland for the direct male line of the Stuart family. He was the son of King JAMES II, a convert to Roman Catholicism, and Mary of Modena. Prior to his birth the heir presumptive to the throne was his elder half sister, Mary (later MARY II), a Protestant. The birth of a Catholic heir was the pivotal cause of the GLORIOUS REVOLUTION, which resulted in James II's exile. In 1701, James II died, and his son inherited the Stuart claim to the throne, although the Act of SETTLEMENT, passed that year by Parliament, barred James Francis from the throne. He and his followers, known as JACOBITES, hatched various schemes for his restoration. His first attempt (1708) to secure the throne by force was made with the help of the French; it was thwarted, however, by the weather and the

English navy. The second attempt (1715) was made when the 6th earl of Mar gathered a broad base of support for him in the Highlands, but by the time James Francis landed at Peterhead, the cause was lost. He and the earl of Mar fled to France on Feb. 4, 1716.

In 1719, James Francis married Princess Clementina Sobieski, granddaughter of the king of Poland. They had two sons, Charles Edward STUART (the Young Pretender) and Henry Benedict Stuart (1725-1807), who became a cardinal and the last Stuart claimant to the throne. CHARLES H. HAWS

Bibliography: Bevan, Bryan, *King James III of England: A Study of Kingship in Exile* (1967); Kemp, H., *The Jacobite Rebellion* (1975); Petrie, Charles, *The Jacobite Movement*, rev. ed. (1959).

Stuart, J. E. B.

Jeb Stuart, a Confederate cavalry commander in the U.S. Civil War, achieved fame by his brilliantly executed reconnaissance missions and raids behind federal lines. One such raid, however, delayed his arrival at Gettysburg, depriving Gen. Robert E. Lee of vital intelligence on federal positions.

James Ewell Brown (Jeb) Stuart, b. Patrick County, Va., Feb. 6, 1833, d. 1864, was a Confederate cavalry officer in the U.S. Civil War. He graduated from West Point in 1854 and served in the Mounted Rifles until he joined the Confederacy in 1861. Commissioned into the cavalry, he became one of the most famous and popular of Robert E. LEE's subordinates. In 1862, Stuart took command of Lee's mounted units, and after playing a pivotal role in the PENINSULAR CAMPAIGN he fought brilliantly at the Second Battle of BULL RUN, the Battle of ANTIETAM, and at Fredericksburg (see FREDERICKSBURG, BATTLE OF).

At CHANCELLORSVILLE (May 1863) Stuart briefly but splendidly led Gen. Stonewall JACKSON's corps after Jackson was wounded. In the Gettysburg campaign (see GETTYSBURG, BATTLE OF; June-July 1863) Stuart, taking advantage of ambiguous orders, embarked on a controversial raid around the Federal army. As a result, he was absent when Lee most needed him to gather intelligence about the enemy, arriving only after the battle was already lost. Some historians believe that the Confederate defeat at Gettysburg was primarily Stuart's fault. Certainly, had Stuart been present earlier, Lee would have fought a different battle. On May 11, 1864, at Yellow Tavern, Va., Stuart was mortally wounded. He died the following day.
RICHARD M. MCMURRY

Bibliography: Blackford, W. W., *War Years with Jeb Stuart* (1945); David, Burke, *Jeb Stuart: The Last Cavalier* (1957); McClellan, Henry, *I Rode with Jeb Stuart: The Life and Campaigns of Major General J. E. B. Stuart* (1958; repr. 1968).

Stuart, Jesse

An American southern writer, Jesse Stuart, b. near Riverton, Ky., Aug. 8, 1907, has created and peopled a literary country in the Appalachian Mountains in more than 35 volumes of poetry, novels, short stories, and juvenile fiction. Stuart's work is marked by a vivid rendering of the natural beauties of his native Kentucky and a deep affection for its independent and eccentric mountain people. His subjects are varied—the crisis of modern education in *Mr. Gallion's School* (1967), the virtues of country living in *Hie to the Hunters* (1950), and the comedy of unexpected wealth in the best-selling *Taps for Private Tussie* (1943). *The Kingdom Within: A Spiritual Autobiography* appeared in 1979.

Bibliography: Blair, Everetta, *Jesse Stuart: His Life and Works* (1967); Foster, Ruel E., *Jesse Stuart* (1968); Lemaster, J. R., and Clarke, Mary W., eds., *Jesse Stuart: Essays on His Work* (1977).

Stuart, John McDouall

John McDouall Stuart, b. Sept. 7, 1815, d. June 5, 1866, was a Scottish-born explorer of South Australia. A draftsman, he accompanied Charles Sturt's expedition (1844-45) from Adelaide, which failed to reach central Australia. Stuart made six expeditions between 1858 and 1862, reaching midcontinent in 1860. He succeeded in pushing through to Van Diemen Gulf on the Indian Ocean in 1862.

Stubbins, Hugh

The American architect Hugh Stubbins, Jr., b. Birmingham, Ala., Jan. 11, 1912, has designed many important buildings in the tradition of Walter Gropius and the International Style. He has headed his own architectural firm in Boston since 1941. His major works—including Citicorp Center and the adjoining Saint Peter's Lutheran Church (both completed 1977) in New York City and Pusey Library (1973-76) at Harvard University in Cambridge, Mass.—display elegantly simple profiles embodying imaginative technical solutions to challenging sites and building programs. J. MEREDITH NEIL

Bibliography: *Hugh Stubbins and Associates* (n.d.).

Stubbs, George

The leading British animal painter of the 18th century, George Stubbs, b. Aug. 25, 1724, d. July 10, 1806, was largely self-taught as an artist. His passion for the mastery of anatomy led him to spend 2 years (1756-58) dissecting horses. He engraved the resulting drawings, which appeared in the book *The Anatomy of a Horse* (1766). From 1760 onward he lived in London, establishing a reputation as a painter of horses. During this period he produced *Mares and Foals by a Stream* (1763-64; private collection, England) and *The Grosvenor*

In Lion Devouring A Horse *(1769), by the British painter George Stubbs, the dramatically poised figures of a terrified horse and a predatory lion are a romantic response to the beauty and savagery of the natural world. (Tate Gallery, London.)*

Hunt (1762; Trustees of the Grosvenor Estate, London); wild animals are the dramatic protagonists of *Nyl-Ghau* (1769; Hunterian Collection, University of Glasgow) and *Horse Attacked by a Lion* (c.1762; Paul Mellon Collection, Yale Center for British Art, New Haven, Conn.). Toward the end of his life he was involved with an ambitious project for a comparative atlas of animal anatomy. His capacity for careful design made him one of the leading artists of his time.

MALCOLM CORMACK

Bibliography: Egerton, Judy, *George Stubbs, Anatomist and Animal Painter* (1976); Taylor, Basil, *Stubbs* (1971).

Stubbs, William

William Stubbs, b. June 21, 1825, d. Apr. 22, 1901, was a British churchman and historian. As regius professor of modern history at Oxford University (1866–84), he systematized the study of English medieval constitutional history. From 1888 to 1901 he was bishop of Oxford. In addition to editing 19 volumes of medieval chronicles (1864–83) and *Select Charters* (1870; 9th ed., rev. by H. W. Davis, 1913), he wrote the 3-volume *Constitutional History of England* (1873–78).

Stuck, Franz von   [shtuk]

Franz von Stuck, b. Feb. 23, 1863, d. Aug. 30, 1928, was a leading German symbolist painter and sculptor as well as an important art educator. His pupils at the Munich Academy included Josef Albers, Wassily Kandinsky, and Paul Klee; he was also a founding member of the Munich Secession, a progressive exhibition society. His palatial home, the Villa Stuck in Munich (1897–98), is now a museum. Von Stuck's art is characterized by an intense interest in psychological and erotic forces as these are expressed in classical mythology and biblical history; an example is the painting *Sin* (1893; Neue Pinakothek, Munich).

JEFFERY HOWE

Bibliography: Voss, Heinrich, "Franz von Stuck as a Painter," *Apollo*, November 1971.

Studebaker   (family)

The Studebaker family firm became the world's largest producer of horse-drawn wagons and carriages in the late 19th century and in the 20th century became an early manufacturer of automobiles. **Clement** Studebaker, b. Pinetown, Pa., Mar. 12, 1831, d. Nov. 27, 1901, learned blacksmithing and wagonmaking from his father, who moved (1836) his family to Ohio. Clement moved (1850) to South Bend, Ind., to become a blacksmith and was soon joined by his elder brother, **Henry** (1826–95). In 1852 they started H. & C. Studebaker, a firm of blacksmiths and wagonmakers. Another brother, **John Mohler**, b. Oct. 10, 1833, d. Mar. 16, 1917, bought out (1858) Henry's interest and expanded the family business. In 1868 the Studebaker Brothers Manufacturing Company was incorporated. By 1897 it had begun experiments with early automobiles. Production of Studebakers began in 1901; in 1954 the firm merged with the Packard Company. Studebaker ceased producing in the United States in 1963 and was phased out of Canada in 1966.

Bibliography: Corle, Edwin, *John Studebaker, an American Dream* (1948); Longstreet, Stephen, *A Century on Wheels, The Story of Studebaker: A History, 1852-1952* (1952).

student movements

During the last two centuries student movements all over the world have played a major role in challenging the system of higher education and in campaigning for revolutionary political change. Unlike endemic rebellions against academic discipline, these movements act on behalf of specific ideologies, establish their own organizations, and mobilize students and adult intellectuals elsewhere. When aroused by acts of symbolic repression, propelled by shortcomings of the educational system, sustained by a culture of dissent, and, at times, spurred by economic need, a minority of students moves toward activism. Social scientists claim that usually such student movements are characterized by the politicization of generational resentment of adult authority, by an elitist sense of special mission, by rhetorical absolutism, by a guilt-inspired populism, and by a penchant for direct action (protest, provocation, and violence) as opposed to reasoned argument.

The first modern student movement was the German *Burschenschaft* (founded 1815), which sought to eliminate medieval practices in the universities, attempted to further academic freedom in teaching and learning, tried to liberalize governments, and strove to unite the German states into one nation. After the suppression of the first Christian-German "enthusiasts," the "demagogues" sought to seize power directly, and when they failed, the "progressives" propagated democratic ideals that culminated in the Revolutions of 1848. While Italian students similarly championed national-liberal aims, French youths vacillated between life-style rebellion (bohemianism) in Paris's Latin Quarter and fighting on the barricades in 1830, 1848, and 1871. With greater political impact the Russian "school of dissent" struggled for a semblance of academic autonomy, for freedom from Tsarist autocracy, and for social justice for serfs and workers. In the 1860s the student intelligentsia tried to go "to the people" in the countryside (Narodniks); when they were rejected they turned to terrorism in the 1880s and developed a disciplined Marxist movement around the turn of the century, from which came many of the leaders of the Bolshevik Revolution of 1917.

Whereas World War I turned many European students toward fascism, in the Third World it produced a spate of antiimperialist student movements for national liberation. The prototypical May 4 (1919) Movement in China championed the full westernization of universities, politics, and society and passionately opposed Japanese expansion into Manchuria. In the civil war between the Kuomintang and the Chinese Communist party, the majority of the students opted for Mao Tse-tung and supported the Chinese Revolution of 1949. Whereas the Indian and Japanese movements became significant only in the 1940s and 1950s, Latin-American students had already attacked the authoritarian features of their Iberian university heritage in the Córdoba Manifesto of 1918. Subsequently they demanded *co-gobierno* (participation in university governance) and often participated in Marxist guerrilla warfare against military dictatorships. After World War II student movements were in the forefront of the anticolonial struggle in Africa and Southeast Asia, but these movements tended to be divided into nationalists and communists and to lose influence after national independence had been won.

Despite a long tradition of collegiate riots against *in loco parentis* regimentation, there existed no significant student movement in the United States until the foundation of the small but vocal Intercollegiate Socialists Society in 1905. The Depression of the 1930s, the Nazi threat, and the fascination with the Soviet Union in the 1930s led to the formation of the radical American Student Union, which claimed about 20,000 members in its heyday, pioneered new forms of protest (the "sit-down"), and influenced many members of the Old Left with its militant pacifism. In the late 1950s the Civil Rights Movement, the dissatisfaction with the war in Vietnam, the awareness of continuing poverty amidst affluence, and resentment against the bureaucratization of higher education coalesced in a massive American student movement first at the University of California at Berkeley (Free Speech Movement) and later at Columbia, Wisconsin, and on other campuses in most of the more than 1,500 U.S. 4-year colleges and universities. Led by the SDS (Students for a Democratic Society), this New Left achieved a number of curricular and structural university reforms and contributed significantly to the U.S. military withdrawal from Southeast Asia. When ideological haziness, the split between black and white militants, and police repression frustrated a general sociopolitical renewal, the movement's momentum dissipated in the early 1970s into apathy, life-style protest (hippies), and sporadic violence. Although in May 1968, French students almost toppled the Gaullist government, the year of the student passed without significant achievements, despite massive worldwide demonstrations leaving behind some endemic movements (in Latin America, Italy, and Japan) as well as some terrorism (the Baader-Meinhof gang in Germany).

The dynamic of student movements is often a product of process of modernization, which reduces parental authority and provides youth with an ideology opposed to tradition. Recent activism in the postindustrial societies, however, seems to stem instead from students' sensitivity to discrepancies between democratic rhetoric and authoritarian practices. Such activism usually begins with the formation of discussion circles, then seizes a mobilizing issue, which leads to peaceful protests that may escalate into provocations and may culminate in direct action against property or people if demands are not met at an earlier stage. Usually its participants are a small minority of the student body that manages to gather a larger group of sympathizers, while, except for a few ideological opponents, the majority tends to be passive, interested in collegiate, vocational, or academic pursuits. Because of the transient nature of the student population and the widespread return of college graduates to conformism, the effect of student movements poses many unresolved questions, such as should one stress the heroic aspect of a struggle for human rights against political repression, or should one warn against the aspects of intolerance, antiintellectualism, and occasional terrorism?   KONRAD H. JARAUSCH

Bibliography: Altbach, Philip G., *Student Politics in America: A Historical Analysis* (1974); Califano, Joseph A., Jr., *Student Revolution: A Global Confrontation* (1969); Ehrenreich, Barbara and John, *Long March, Short Spring: The Student Uprising at Home and Abroad* (1969); Esler, Anthony, *Bombs, Beards and Barricades: 150 Years of Youth in Revolt* (1971); Feuer, Lewis S., *The Conflict of Generations: The Character and Significance of Student Movements* (1969); Jacqueney, Mona G., *Radicalism on Campus: 1969–1971* (1972); Lipset, Seymour M., and Altbach, Philip G., *Students in Revolt* (1969); Sampson, Edward G., and Korn, Harold A., *Student Activism and Protest: Alternatives for Social Change* (1970); Statera, Gianni, *Death of a Utopia: The Development and Decline of Student Movements in Europe* (1975); Westby, David L., *The Clouded Vision: The Student Movement in the United States in the 1960's* (1976).

Student Nonviolent Coordinating Committee: see SNCC.

Study of History, A

The principal work of British historian Arnold TOYNBEE, *A Study of History* (12 vols., 1934–61) presents a comparative study of 21 major civilizations that have flourished at some point during the past 6,000 years. The *Study* is concerned with the rules, or laws, and patterns determining the growth, breakdown, and disintegration of civilizations. Although Toynbee was influenced by Oswald Spengler's *The Decline of the West* (1918–22), his theory does not predict the inevitable decline of the West. Critics of the *Study* contend that Toynbee does not rely on empirical methods but rather selects cases to prove an a priori conception.   HERBERT M. LEVINE

Bibliography: Gargan, Edward T., ed., *The Intent of Toynbee's History* (1961); Montagu, M. F. Ashley, ed., *Toynbee and History: Critical Essays and Reviews* (1956); Ortega y Gasset, José, *An Interpretation of Universal History*, trans. by Mildred Adams (1973).

Stuka   [stoo'-kuh]

A two-seat, inverted-gull-wing monoplane with a 13.7-m (45.1-ft) wingspan, the Junkers Ju-87 Stuka gained immediate notoriety in the first few months of World War II as it blasted a noisy, destructive path for the German army's advances across Poland, Belgium, Holland, and France. The Stuka originated in 1928 with the Swedish-built K-47 and by 1935 had evolved into an angular, all-metal, Junkers Jumo-powered dive-bomber that carried its single bomb between nonretracting main wheels. Two sirens were fitted to operate as terror weapons during the dive attack, and later versions of the plane had increased power, different combinations of machine guns and cannon, and other modifications. Evaluated initially in the Spanish Civil War, the Ju-87 served throughout

The Junkers Ju-87 Stuka, a slow, heavy dive-bomber, was particularly effective in situations in which the Luftwaffe held air superiority. The Stuka enjoyed its most notable success during the early stage of World War II, providing support for ground troops in the Nazi blitzkrieg.

World War II and in addition to its bombing duties was used for ground strafing over southern England and on the Russian front.   PETER M. H. LEWIS

Stukeley, William   [stook'-lee]

William Stukeley, b. Nov. 7, 1687, d. Mar. 3, 1765, was an English antiquarian noted for his field surveys of the great stone circles of AVEBURY and STONEHENGE. Largely attributable to his research was the popular association of the DRUIDS with such stone circles, a theory now rejected by all authorities.

Bibliography: Piggott, Stuart, *William Stukeley—Eighteenth Century Antiquarian* (1950).

stupa   [stoo'-puh]

A stupa (Sanskrit for "mound") is a Buddhist monument of moundlike shape. Originating in the funeral mound that customarily was piled up over the remains of Indian princes and holy men, the stupa developed into a principal Buddhist shrine commemorating the Buddha's triumph over life. Many thousands of stupas were erected in India during the reign (*c.*273–232 BC) of Emperor ASOKA, and stupas eventually appeared in every region in which Buddhism flourished.

In substance the stupa is an artificial mountain formed of mounded rubble and sheathed in the more permanent materials of brick, plaster, or stone, which also have served to ennoble it through ornamentation. In its developed Buddhist form, whatever its scale or the materials of its manufacture, the stupa is understood to be a cosmograph and therefore an appropriate vehicle for the expression of the universal significance of the nirvana of the Buddha. Like all Brahmanical shrines, the Indian stupa normally is enclosed by a fence and raised on a platform base. Access to the shrine is provided by one or more gates set into the encircling fence. The basic forms of the stupa are the rough hemisphere of its body (*anda*), the cubical structure that surmounts it (*harmika*), and the shaft (*yasti*) with one or more disks (*chatra*) that rise from the center of the *harmika*. The *harmika* represents the peak of the world-mountain (*Meru*) and the threshold of the realms of the gods. The *Meru* is anchored to the *yasti*, which symbolizes the axis of the universe. The *anda* encircles the *Meru*-and-*yasti* complex as an unarticulated form, the palpable image of the endless canopy of cosmic space. Enshrined within the solid core of the mound, at the level of the platform and directly below the *yasti*, is a relic of the Buddha or some other holy person. This relic constitutes the single and coordinating point of reference for the stupa's component parts and for the meanings that they carry.

DIRAN KAVORK DOHANIAN

Bibliography: Zimmer, Heinrich, *The Art of Indian Asia* (1955).

sturgeon   [stur'-juhn]

Sturgeons, family Acipenseridae, are among the most primitive of the actinopterygian (ray-finned) fishes. Sturgeons and paddlefishes, family Polyodontidae, are the only surviving members of the Chonodrostei, a group that includes many extinct fish families. Sturgeons are elongate fishes with a sharklike heterocercal caudal fin. They have an inferior mouth preceded by four fleshy barbels. The head is elongate, sometimes flattened, and covered by large interlocking skull bones. Sturgeons are scaleless except for five rows of large, pointed, platelike scales running along the top and sides of the body. Their skeleton is part bone and part cartilage, placing them midway between sharks and bony fishes.

Sturgeons are confined to Northern Hemisphere waters. The marine species are anadromous, living as adults in marine waters but returning to freshwater rivers and streams to breed.

Sturgeons are slow-moving bottom-dwellers. Food is located by the sensitive barbels preceding the mouth and by taste buds located outside and around the mouth. Small invertebrates comprise the bulk of the diet.

Sturgeons are famed for their blackish roe (eggs), which are salted and called CAVIAR. A number of kinds of fish eggs are used to produce caviar, but sturgeon caviar is purported to be superior. The roe are usually taken by killing the female. Because female sturgeons may take up to 12 years to reach maturity, this method of harvesting roe has resulted in drastic reductions in sturgeon populations. The modern conservation method of stripping (gently squeezing the abdomen to release the roe) allows the female to be returned alive to produce more eggs. Sturgeons have also been caught for their flesh and oil.

There are four recognized genera of sturgeons. *Huso* is distributed from the Adriatic Sea drainage to the Amur River in Eurasia. One species, the beluga, *H. huso,* is the largest of all freshwater fishes and at one time reached a length of 8.4 m (28 ft) and a weight of 1,260 kg (2,800 lb). It also produces the finest caviar. The genus *Acipenser* is closely related to *Huso* and is found throughout the Northern Hemisphere. Most North American sturgeons belong to *Acipenser,* including the largest North American fish, the white sturgeon, *A. transmontanus,* which reaches nearly 130 kg (286 lb). Smaller sturgeons include the genus *Pseudoscaphirhynchus* of the Aral Sea basin and the genus *Scaphirhynchus* of North America, which reaches a length of about 90 cm (3 ft) and a weight of 2.7 kg (6 lb).   E. O. WILEY

The Atlantic sturgeon, Acipenser oxyrhynchus, *is distinguished by its long snout, bony plates, and tubelike mouth, which is used to pick up food. This fish is caught commercially for its flesh, its eggs, which are used to make caviar, and its swim bladder, used to make isinglass.*

Sturgeon, Theodore

For more than 30 years Theodore Sturgeon, b. Edward Hamilton Waldo, Staten Island, N.Y., Feb. 26, 1918, has used the conventions of science fiction to explore serious themes. Much of his fiction is marked by ironic, surprise endings. *More Than Human* (1953), which won the 1954 International Fantasy Award, is the story of seven human misfits who achieve sufficiency and community through extrasensory perception. *The Dreaming Jewels* (1950; reissued as *The Synthetic Man,* 1961) explores the metaphysics of human existence, and *Venus Plus X* (1960) examines the role of sex

stereotypes from the perspective of a parthenogenetic society. Sturgeon's early stories "Killdozer" and "Bianca's Hands" are held in particularly high regard, and his "Slow Sculpture" won both the 1970 Nebula and the 1971 Hugo awards.

Bibliography: Moscowitz, Sam, *Seekers of Tomorrow* (1966).

Sturges, Preston   [stur'-jis]

For a time in the 1940s, Preston Sturges, pseudonym of Edmund P. Biden, b. Chicago, Aug. 29, 1898, d. Aug. 6, 1959, held a position of creative preeminence in Hollywood as a writer-director who was acclaimed by critics and public alike. Sturges directed his first film, *The Great McGinty,* in 1940, and followed it with a string of successes that included *The Lady Eve* (1941), *Sullivan's Travels* (1941), *The Miracle of Morgan's Creek* (1944), and *Hail the Conquering Hero* (1944), breakneck farces that shrewdly satirized American life. But Sturges's touch seemed to falter with the semiserious *The Great Moment* (1944), and the only time he returned to form afterwards, in the black comedy *Unfaithfully Yours* (1948), the public failed to respond.   WILLIAM S. PECHTER

Bibliography: Ursini, James, *The Fabulous Life and Times of Preston Sturges* (1973).

Sturm und Drang   [shtoorm unt drahng]

Sturm und Drang, or Storm and Stress, was a German literary and intellectual movement of the 1770s and early 1780s. Its name was derived from a play of 1776 by Friedrich Maximilian von Klinger. Its major exponents were the young GOETHE and SCHILLER, Johann Gottfried von HERDER, Gottfried August BÜRGER, Johann Georg Hamann, and Heinrich Leopold Wagner. In their advocacy of freedom and a return to nature, they took Shakespeare and Rousseau as models. Their exaltation of the individual, personal experience, genius, and the creative imagination strongly foreshadowed ROMANTICISM.

LILIAN R. FURST

Bibliography: Furst, Lilian R., *Romanticism in Perspective* (1969); Garland, Henry B., *Storm and Stress* (1952); Kistler, Mark Oliver, *Drama of the Storm and Stress* (1969); Pascal, Roy, *The German Sturm und Drang* (1967).

Sturt, Charles

Called the father of Australian exploration, Charles Sturt, b. Apr. 28, 1795, d. June 16, 1869, a British soldier and colonial administrator, was one of the first to venture into Australia's interior. He came to New South Wales as a British army officer in 1827 and, on an expedition west of Sydney, explored the course of the Darling River in 1828. The next year he charted the Murray River to its mouth. Nearly blinded through privations, he resigned from the army and settled on a grant of land; however, he lost heavily through unwise land ventures. In 1844 he made an expedition in quest of a supposed inland sea; his party penetrated more than 1,000 miles northward, almost to the center of Australia, before being forced by heat and drought to return to Adelaide. Sturt was colonial treasurer (1845) and then colonial secretary (1849–51). His accounts of his explorations, notably accurate, were published in 1833 and 1849.   E. J. TAPP

Bibliography: Cumpston, J. H. L., *Charles Sturt* (1951); Langley, Michael, *Sturt of the Murray: Father of Australian Exploration* (1969).

stuttering

Stuttering is a speech disorder in which the ability to produce sentences smoothly and without conscious effort is intermittently impaired. Individual sounds and syllables may be repeated several times or prolonged beyond normal length. Some stutterers also "block" and become unable momentarily to produce any sound. These part-word repetitions, prolongations, and vocal blockages occasionally occur in normal speech, too; in stutterers, however, they occur far more often, although in certain situations, as when addressing pets, little or no stuttering occurs.

Many stutterers learn ways to prevent or minimize stuttering by timing their speech to coincide with rhythmic or sudden body movements, or trying to hide their stuttering by changing words or pretending to think. In time these secondary behaviors become difficult to prevent, and some of them are accompanied by great struggle and tension.

About 2 million American adults—primarily men—stutter. Several million American children stutter. Even without therapy, about 80 percent of stutterers outgrow the disorder by age 18, but the other 20 percent remain severely impaired in their ability to communicate in school, on the job, and in interpersonal relationships. No basic cause has been found. One possibility is parental overanxiousness about a child's hesitancy or groping for the right word—which is normal in the speech of children (or adults). According to this theory, a child, sensing parental concern, will wonder if he or she can speak well enough to please the parents and, as a result, may become less spontaneous in talking and eventually become a stutterer.

Although no cause is known for certain, much is known about how the disorder develops, and effective therapies have been devised. Effective therapies result in speech that is both smooth and spontaneous by dealing both with the stutterer's speech and his or her reactions to it, but many stutterers, particularly adults, must sacrifice smoothness for sponaneity and ease. Relapses to stuttering are common after many therapies; relapses can be avoided by practice outside the laboratory during therapy, and by continued exercises after the completion of therapy. Children who stutter, no matter how young, should be under the supervision of a certified speech and language clinician.

WOODRUFF STARKWEATHER

Bibliography: Overtake, Charles P., *Stuttering: A New Look at an Old Problem Based on Neurophysiological Aspects* (1979); Speech Foundation of America, *If Your Child Stutters: A Guide for Parents* (1977) and *Self-Therapy for Stutterers: One Approach* (1978); Starkweather, C. W., ed., *Therapy for Stutterers* (1974); Van Riper, Charles, *The Nature of Stuttering* (1971) and *The Treatment of Stuttering* (1973).

Stuttgart   [shtut'-gahrt]

Stuttgart, the capital city of the state of Baden-Württemberg in the southwest corner of West Germany, lies in the Neckar River valley, within 130 km (80 mi) of both the Swiss and French borders. The city covers an area of 223 km² (86 mi²) and has a population of 584,600 (1977 est.).

Stuttgart and its industrial suburbs form Baden-Württemberg's most important economic center. Industrial products include machinery, motor vehicles, electrical equipment, chemicals, paper, beer, textiles, cameras, optical equipment, furniture, pianos, chocolate, and mineral water. The city is also an important railroad junction linking the Rhine Valley and southern Germany. Stuttgart is especially well known as a publishing center. The city hosts frequent industrial and book fairs.

The old part of the city is clustered around the Old Market square, surrounded by gabled houses. From the square the city (which remained quite small until the end of the 18th century) expanded into the neighboring hillsides, mainly in the 19th and 20th centuries. As a result Stuttgart is a predominantly modern city, although many public buildings are constructed in the Renaissance, baroque, or neo-Gothic style. Stuttgart has art and music academies; a state museum, library, and opera; and is the home of the internationally known Stuttgart Ballet.

Stuttgart's name is derived from its origins as a 10th-century stud farm (German: *Stuotgarten*) that expanded and became the property of the Württemberg family in the early 13th century. In the 14th century Stuttgart became the principal residence of the counts of Württemberg. Stuttgart became capital of Württemberg in 1482. In June 1849 it served briefly as host to what was left of the Frankfurt Parliament after its transfer from Frankfurt am Main. In September 1857 a meeting took place in Stuttgart between Emperor Alexander II of Russia and Napoleon III of France. The city center was heavily damaged in World War II, and most of its historic buildings have been rebuilt since 1945.

EDWARD TABORSKY

Stuttgart Ballet

The Stuttgart Ballet, officially the Württembergische Staatstheater Ballet, rose to international prominence under the directorship of John CRANKO in the 1960s. Ballet in Stuttgart began early, the first recorded court ballet taking place in 1609. From 1759 to 1767, Jean Georges Noverre, the French choreographer and reformer, was court balletmaster. Filippo Taglioni, the renowned teacher and director, came in 1824 with his daughter, Marie.

Like most German ballet companies, the Stuttgart company existed mainly as an adjunct of the opera company. The turnaround began in 1957, when Nicholas Beriozoff became director and proceeded to mount full-length productions of the classics—*Sleeping Beauty* (1957), *Giselle* (1958), and *Swan Lake* (1960). Cranko, the British choreographer, was invited to stage his *Prince of the Pagodas* for the company in 1960 and in 1961 was appointed director. His forte was the evening-long story ballet; the most popular were *Romeo and Juliet* (1962), *Eugene Onegin* (1965), and *The Taming of the Shrew* (1969). Marcia Haydée, a Brazilian dancer, turned into a superb dramatic ballerina under his direction and danced compellingly in these and many other ballets, usually partnered by Richard Cragun or Egon Madsen.

The company had great success on its first tour to New York (1969). Cranko died in 1973 and was succeeded by Glen Tetley. Since 1976, Marcia Haydée has been director, while continuing to dance leading roles in the repertoire. Recent productions include *The Lady of the Camellias* (1979) by John Neumeier, *Voluntaries* (1974) by Tetley, and works by former company member Jiri Kylian.

MICHAEL ROBERTSON

Bibliography: McDonagh, Don, *The Complete Guide to Modern Dance* (1976).

Stuyvesant, Peter   [sty'-vuh-suhnt]

Peter Stuyvesant was director general of the Dutch colony of New Netherland (now called New York) from 1646 to 1664, when he was compelled to surrender the colony to the English. Although he was an efficient administrator, his religious intolerance and arbitrary methods made him an unpopular governor.

Peter Stuyvesant, b. c.1610, d. February 1672, was the fourth and last director general of the Dutch colony NEW NETHERLAND (later New York). He began his military career at an early age and by 1632 was serving in the Dutch West India Company. Campaigning against the Portuguese in 1644 he lost a leg, replacing it with a wooden peg ornamented with silver bands. After being appointed to head New Netherland in 1646, he brought major political and economic reform as well as diplomatic success to the struggling colony. A dedicated and efficient yet unpopular administrator, Stuyvesant was irascible, pompous, intolerant, and authoritarian. His career came to an end when, after a surprise attack by an English naval force in September 1664, he surrendered the colony without resistance.

LARRY R. GERLACH

Bibliography: Kessler, Henry H., and Rachlis, Eugene, *Peter Stuyvesant and His New York* (1959); Picard, Hymen W. J., *Peter Stuyvesant, Builder of New York* (1975).

sty

A sty, an infection of the follicle of an eyelash or of a sebaceous gland of an eyelid, is analogous to a pimple elsewhere on the skin. It is often the result of a staphylococcus infection. Sties are usually treated by a local application of antibiotics and hot or cold compresses.   PETER L. PETRAKIS

style galant: see ROCOCO MUSIC.

styles of Louis XIII–XVI

During the 17th and 18th centuries, northern European styles of art and INTERIOR DESIGN were dictated by the tastes of the French court; these styles are customarily named for the four French monarchs of those centuries.

Louis XIII Style. During the reign (1610–43) of Louis XIII the Italian Mannerist styles favored by his mother, Marie de Médicis, continued to dominate French art. FURNITURE was bulky, somewhat ponderous, and heavily carved. Ebony and walnut, frequently combined in a single piece for contrast, were the favored woods; lathe-turned elements, such as spiraled and urn-shaped legs, were popular.

Louis XIV Style. The long reign (1638–1715) of Louis XIV fostered a grandiose style devised to enhance the elaborate formality of court ritual. The king initiated the founding (1648) of the Académie Royale de Peinture et de Sculpture, which codified the arts, and established (1662) the royal furniture factory at the GOBELINS works in Paris to provide the furnishings and decorations for his palaces; both were under the direction of the court artist Charles LE BRUN. Beginning in 1660, Louis became obsessed with the transformation of his father's modest hunting lodge at Versailles into the most splendid—and most imitated—palace in Europe (see VERSAILLES, PALACE OF). The resulting baroque style combined innovative forms, such as chests of drawers and cabriole (curved) legs, with ancient Roman motifs. It is typified by the sumptuous furnishings of André Charles BOULLE and the decorative designs of Jean BÉRAIN and Jean Lepautre. Rare woods were combined in MARQUETRY, augmented with inlays of tortoiseshell, brass, and ivory and with lavish ormolu (gilded bronze) fittings. Enormous quantities of gold tableware and silver furniture were produced for Versailles but were melted down by the king's order to pay for his wars.

Louis XV Styles. Two styles—the Régence (c.1710–30) and the rococo (c.1730–70)—predominated during the reign of Louis XV; both were reactions to the overpowering massiveness of the previous style. Régence is characterized by light forms and a profligate use of vivid colored woods and ormolu

mounts, as in the opulent furniture of Charles Cressent. The ROCOCO STYLE, an exuberant and insouciant interpretation of baroque art, swept rapidly through Europe. It carried two motifs—the S-curve and *rocaille* (shell-shaped) ornament—to extravagant extremes; its greatest practitioners were the painters François BOUCHER, Jean Honoré FRAGONARD, and Jean Antoine WATTEAU and the designers Juste Aurèle MEISSONNIER, Jean François OEBEN, Nicolas Pineau, and Abraham Roentgen.

Louis XVI Style. In reaction to the excesses of the rococo and inspired by the rediscovery of Herculaneum (1738) and Pompeii (1748), NEOCLASSICISM dominated during the reign (1774–93) of Louis XVI. Straight lines, simplicity, comfort, and delicacy of ornamentation characterize the style; refinement of scale and unmatched workmanship are hallmarks of the work of the designers Pierre GOUTHIÈRE and Jean Henri RIESENER and of the luxurious porcelains called SÈVRES WARE. The sculptures of Jean Antoine HOUDON and the paintings of Jacques Louis DAVID are typical of the severity of French taste just preceding the Revolution of 1789.

EDWARD T. McCLELLAN

Bibliography: Battersby, Martin, et al., *The History of Furniture* (1976); Blunt, Anthony, *Art and Architecture in France, 1500-1700*, 3d ed. (1973); Kimball, Fiske, *The Creation of the Rococo* (1943; repr. 1965); Kitson, Michael, *The Age of Baroque*, 3d ed. (1976); Levey, Michael, *Rococo to Revolution* (1966); McClinton, Katharine, *An Outline of Period Furniture* (1972).

See also: BAROQUE ART AND ARCHITECTURE; FRENCH ART AND ARCHITECTURE; GOLD AND SILVER WORK; PETIT TRIANON; POTTERY AND PORCELAIN; TAPESTRY.

Styne, Jules   [styn]

A British-born composer for the American stage and screen, Jules Styne, b. Dec. 31, 1905, won (1954) an Oscar for his song "Three Coins in the Fountain." Among his principal Broadway successes are *Gentlemen Prefer Blondes* (1949), *Bells Are Ringing* (1956), *Gypsy* (1959), and *Funny Girl* (1964).

DAVID EWEN

Bibliography: Green, Stanley, *The World of Musical Comedy* (1968); Laufe, Abe, *Broadway's Greatest Musicals* (1969); Wiek, Max, *They're Playing Our Song* (1973).

Styracosaurus   [sty-rak-uh-saw'-ruhs]

Known from only a few incomplete specimens, *Styracosaurus* is one of the earliest known North American horned dinosaurs, or ceratopsians (suborder Ceratopsia, order Ornithischia). It lived during the Late Cretaceous Period, about 85 million years ago, preceding the better-known *Triceratops* by perhaps 15 million years. *Styracosaurus* had the typical ceratopsian neck frill, formed by the rearward extension of the

In the bedroom of the Grand Trianon at Versailles, designed by Jules Hardouin-Mansart in 1687 as a private retreat for Louis XIV, the monumental classicism of the earlier years of the king's reign was lightened by an elegant baroque style that foreshadowed the rococo.

Styracosaurus was an early and short-lived genus of ceratopsian dinosaur of the Late Cretaceous Period. Prominent features included a long nasal horn and bony spikes on the back edge of the neck frill.

parietal and squamosal bones of the skull, but with a number of long spikes projecting out from the back edge. Brow horns were essentially lacking, but there was a long, straight horn on the snout. *Styracosaurus* grew to about 5.5 m (18 ft) long and had a large, turtlelike beak and long rows of teeth for slicing fibrous plant tissues.   JOHN H. OSTROM

Styria   [stir'-ee-uh]

Styria (German: Steiermark) is a mountainous, mostly forested province in southeastern Austria, bordering on Yugoslavia in the south. It covers 16,387 km² (6,327 mi²) and has a population of 1,191,400 (1976 est.). GRAZ is the provincial capital. The most important economic activity is mining—iron ore in the Erzberg has been mined since before the Christian era. Other minerals include lignite, magnesite, and graphite. Metallurgy, machinery production, and the manufacturing of paper, textiles, and leather goods are the main industries. Grain cultivation, cattle raising, and tourism complement the economy.

Settled by Celts about 400 BC, the area was held by the Romans from c.15 BC until the 5th century. Rudolf I made Styria a hereditary Habsburg possession in 1282. In 1919 the southern part of the territory was transferred to Yugoslavia.
BRUCE L. LaROSE

Styron, William   [sty'-ruhn]

The American novelist William Styron, b. Newport News, Va., June 11, 1924, won the Pulitzer Prize for literature in 1968 for his novel *The Confessions of Nat Turner* (1967), a fictional account of an American slave rebellion of 1831 as told by its leader, Nat Turner. His highly respected first novel, *Lie Down in Darkness* (1951), set in Newport News, is a chilling and poignant history of a deteriorating Southern family. Two later works, *The Long March* (1956) and *Set This House on Fire* (1960), present individuals struggling for their freedom against an oppressive system. His latest work is *Sophie's Choice* (1979).

Bibliography: Pearce, Richard, *William Styron* (1971); Ratner, Marc, *William Styron* (1972).

Styx   [stiks]

In Greek mythology the Styx was the river that separated HADES from the land of the living; it was crossed in a boat ferried by CHARON. Styx personified as a nymph aided Zeus in the war between the gods and the Titans. As a reward, her name became sacred and the gods swore their most solemn oaths by it.

Su Tung-p'o   (Su Dongpo)   [soo dung-poh]

A major Chinese poet and essayist, Su Tung-p'o (courtesy name of Su Shih), c.1036–1101, is among the eight greatest prose writers of the T'ang and Sung periods, surpassing in importance his younger brother, Su Cheh, and his father, Su Hsün. Su Tung-p'o's greatest contribution was as an innovator

in poetry. Rejecting the prosodic niceties and limitations of the T'ang poets, he formed an influential literary group that created a new style of verse. His own poetry is characterized by its robust vigor and romantic outpourings. His opposition to the political reforms of WANG AN-SHIH led to his banishment in 1079.   ANGELA JUNG PALANDRI

Bibliography: Lin Yutang, *The Gay Genius* (1947); Su Tung-p'o, *Su Tung-p'o: Selections from a Sung Dynasty Poet*, trans. by B. Watson (1965).

Suárez, Francisco   [swah'-rayth]

Francisco Suárez, b. Granada, Spain, Jan. 5, 1548, d. Sept. 25, 1617, was the most important and influential philosopher-theologian of late SCHOLASTICISM. After law studies at Salamanca he joined (1564) the Jesuits. Ordained (1572) a priest, he taught philosophy and theology at various universities. In 1597, he assumed the primary chair of theology at Coimbra, where he taught until retirement (1615).

Although he wrote on a variety of philosophical and theological topics, Suárez's fame rests mainly on two works: *Disputationes metaphysicae* (Metaphysical Disputations, 1597) and *De Legibus* (On Laws, 1612). The *Disputationes* presents a basically Aristotelian metaphysics, dealing with "being as such," its properties and its causes. Being is divided into God and creatures. Creatures are then divided into substance and accidents. In *De Legibus*, Suárez says that all law is rooted in the will of the lawgiver. Authority to make civil law comes from God through the people; the power of kings is limited by the grant of the people. This argument challenging the theory of the DIVINE RIGHT of kings was also made in Suárez's *Defensio fidei Catholicae* (Defense of the Catholic Faith, 1613), a work that was ordered to be burned by James I of England.

Before and after his death, Suárez was influential in Protestant as well as Catholic universities. Today his influence endures mainly in Spain and Latin America.   JOHN P. DOYLE

Bibliography: Cronin, Timothy, *Objective Being in Descartes and Suárez* (1966); Fichter, Joseph H., *Man of Spain, Francis Suárez* (1940).

Suarez, Hugo Banzer: see BANZER SUAREZ, HUGO.

Suárez González, Adolfo   [swah'-rayth gohn-thah'-layth]

Adolfo Suárez González, b. Sept. 25, 1932, has been prime minister of Spain since 1976. A lawyer and civil servant, he worked (1968–69) in civil government in Segovia. He was elected to the parliament in 1967 and 1971 and later served until 1975 as both vice-secretary general and secretary general of Falange Española Tradicionalista, a nationalistic political organization founded in 1937. Upon being appointed prime minister by King Juan Carlos, Suárez legalized all political parties—even the Communist party—and set up in 1977 the first democratic general election in Spain in 41 years.

subatomic particle: see FUNDAMENTAL PARTICLES.

subduction zone

A subduction, or Benioff, zone is a region of the Earth's surface where the lithosphere is being consumed along zones of convergence of oceanic and continental plates (see PLATE TECTONICS). Where the leading edge of one plate overrides the other, the overridden plate is subducted, or thrust, into the mantle at an angle of about 45 degrees, where the lithosphere is resorbed. Shallow- and deep-focus earthquakes and volcanism are associated with subduction zones.

In ocean-continent plate convergence, the denser oceanic plate is thrust beneath the lighter continental plate, along the offshore continental margin. A deep OCEANIC TRENCH is formed along this margin, and a mountain chain is thrown up parallel to the trench in the zone of compression along the edge of the continental plate. An example of this condition is the presence of the Chilean Trench and the Andes Mountains along the western coast of South America. Where two oceanic plates converge, a trench is established, and a volcanic ISLAND ARC is formed above the upper plate. Examples of this type of convergence are the Philippine and Marianas island arcs and associated trenches.   STEPHEN E. POSTEN

Bibliography: Press, Frank, and Siever, Raymond, *Earth* (1974).

subdwarf

Subdwarfs are stars that are situated below the MAIN SEQUENCE in the HERTZSPRUNG-RUSSELL DIAGRAM. They are old stars with high space velocities and highly eccentric orbits in our galaxy. Their spectra have metallic lines that are much weaker than normal stars of similar temperature, due to the low abundance of the metals relative to hydrogen in the subdwarfs. Most subdwarfs are cool stars with SPECTRAL TYPES F or G. A few hotter ones are known, some of type A; others, even hotter, show helium lines in their spectra.

R. H. GARSTANG

subgiant

Subgiants are stars that have evolved away from the MAIN SEQUENCE but have not yet reached the brightness of a normal giant star. They are particularly numerous in many globular CLUSTERS, where they form a sequence of stars, stretching up in the cluster HERTZSPRUNG-RUSSELL DIAGRAM from the main sequence into the giant branch. A good example of a subgiant is η Cephei, a star of the spectral type KO, which is about 20 times brighter absolutely than a normal KO-type main-sequence star and about 8 times fainter absolutely than a normal KO giant star.   R. H. GARSTANG

sublimation   (chemistry)

Sublimation is the conversion of a solid substance directly into the gaseous state. The process may be expected to happen, at least to some extent, to every solid that consists of discrete molecules. In the case of most solids the VAPOR PRESSURE is extremely small by comparison to the prevailing pressure of the atmosphere—less than 1/1000 as great—and the sublimation will hardly be noted. Even so, the vapor of many solid substances is readily detectable at these levels of concentration by its odor. Other solid substances have an appreciable vapor pressure, and if the vapor is not contained the solid may be converted entirely to vapor in a relatively short time. An example easy to observe is the conversion of snow into water vapor at temperatures below 0° C (32° F), the freezing point of water. If the temperature of a solid is raised its vapor pressure increases, but in most cases the solid melts before the vapor pressure reaches a value that could cause rapid sublimation. A familiar example is solid carbon dioxide, or dry ice, the vapor pressure of which becomes equal to atmospheric pressure at −78° C (−108° F). Thus, solid carbon dioxide remains at this temperature until it has sublimed completely, without melting. Liquid carbon dioxide can be obtained, but only under a pressure greater than atmospheric.

GEORGE GORIN

See also: PHASE EQUILIBRIUM.

sublimation   (psychology)

Sublimation is the process of directing an instinctual impulse into socially acceptable channels. In psychoanalysis it is equivalent to desexualization.

subliminal perception

Subliminal perception is the perception of stimuli too weak to be noticed yet strong enough to influence behavior. An example is a message flashed on a movie screen too briefly for a viewer to notice consciously either the message or any interruption in the film. Alleged uses in advertising or propaganda have not been documented.

submarine

A submarine is a self-propelled vessel capable of operating underwater. The submarines used in the two world wars are more properly termed *submersibles*, because they could remain underwater for only a few hours at a time. They were actually surface vessels with a submergence capability, and their design was necessarily different from that of a true submarine. Surface vessels need sharply pointed, raked bows to cut through and ride over the waves, and long, slender hulls for speed. Vessels specifically designed for underwater operation have relatively broad teardrop or fish shapes, with blunt, rounded bows and drawn-out, tapering sterns. Submersible hulls are designed with the greatest breadth above the waterline for surface stability, but true underwater hulls have generally circular cross sections that increase hull strength and reduce surface area and friction drag. Nuclear submarines, which have the capacity to remain submerged for many months and for thousands of kilometers, are the first true submarines.

BASIC SUBMARINE STRUCTURE

A submarine is fundamentally an air space contained by a hull that is designed to withstand deep ocean pressures and to move easily underwater. The hull is a double steel shell. The inner, or pressure, hull contains all the machinery for propelling and guiding the vessel, plus living quarters for the crew. The outer hull holds the ballast tanks. When the vessel submerges, these tanks are opened and flooded with seawater. For surfacing, the seawater is forced out of the ballast tanks and replaced by compressed air.

Submersion. Flooding the ballast tanks is only one step in the process of submerging. The submarine is also propelled downward by rear-mounted propellers that force the craft forward, and by diving planes, which are movable horizontal rudders that direct the angle of the dive. When the desired depth is reached, the water level in the vessel's trim tanks is adjusted to keep the craft stable.

Power Sources. Nonnuclear submarines are propelled on the surface by diesel engines; when submerged, propulsion is provided by electric batteries and motors. The batteries must be recharged on the surface by the diesels after a short running time. Nuclear submarines are powered by a shielded nuclear reactor that generates steam to turn the propulsion turbines and also supplies electricity for subsidiary systems such as lighting, the vent controls of the ballast tanks, the operation of the torpedo tubes, the periscope, and the maintenance of the life-support systems—the air and water supply that is manufactured on board.

Nuclear power generation is self-contained: because it does not involve combustion, it does not draw oxygen from the vessel's air supply. In addition a nuclear reactor can power a submarine for many thousands of kilometers without refueling. Nuclear submarines therefore have a virtually unlimited range.

Navigation. Until after World War II submerged submarines were navigated with a simple magnetic compass, supplemented by periscopic sextant shots and observation of the shoreline. Most periscopes could not be used at depths greater than 9 m (30 ft). Improvements in gyroscopic navigational aids ultimately led to the development of modern inertial navigation systems capable of providing accurate guidance without the need for frequent external "fixes" (see GUIDANCE AND CONTROL SYSTEMS).

The Conning Tower. The fin-shaped superstructure mounted on top of the submarine serves as a bridge when the vessel is on the surface. It holds a number of instruments: the periscopes, the various radio and radar antennas, and the snorkel, a system of air intake and exhaust pipes. On nuclear submarines the conning tower is known as the "sail" and carries a set of diving planes.

SUBMARINE DEVELOPMENT

The first craft known to have maneuvered underwater was constructed by Cornelis DREBBEL, court engineer to James I of England, and was demonstrated on the Thames in 1620. Propelled by oars sealed at the locks by leather gaskets, it apparently submerged by admitting water into the hull and surfaced by pumping it out again.

Although the idea of the submarine continued to intrigue inventors, the lack of a power source to propel the vessel was

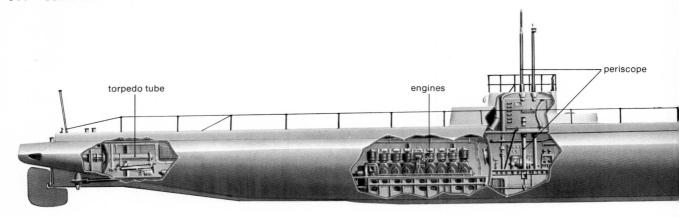

A World War I German U-boat was 64.7 m (310.3 ft) long and maintained a surface speed of 15.8 knots (18.2 mph), with an underwater speed of 10.1 knots (11.6 mph). It was equipped with 4 torpedo tubes and 6 torpedoes. By World War I the development of torpedoes, the invention of the periscope, and the use of internal-combustion engines made submarines a significant part of naval warfare.

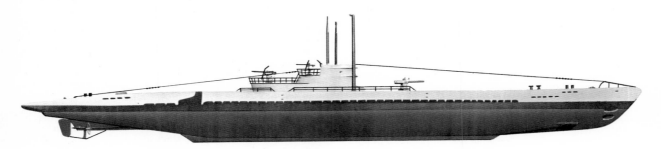

A Gato-class submarine was one of two classes of submarines the United States used during World War II when it standardized design. Powered by 4 diesel engines, it had a surface speed of 20.25 knots (23.3 mph) and carried 24 torpedoes and a 90-mm deck gun.

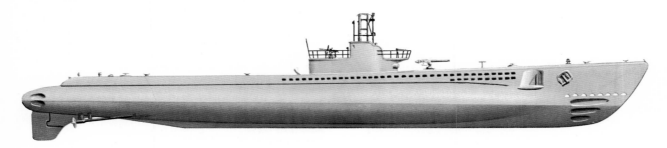

The German World War II U-boat was named from the German word Unterseeboot, meaning "submarine." During the war these boats operated in packs by day to stalk convoys of Allied merchant ships crossing the Atlantic. At night they surfaced and attacked. They succeeded with these tactics, destroying millions of tons of Allied shipping, until the Allies used radar and air and sea escorts.

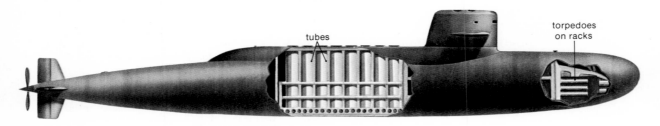

The U.S.S. Patrick Henry, a nuclear-powered submarine, carries 16 Polaris missiles that have a range of 1,920 km (1,200 mi). Polaris subs came into use during the 1960s and changed the role of the sub in naval warfare. Besides destroying enemy ships, they could launch nuclear missiles against inland targets without surfacing and could stay underwater for long periods of time.

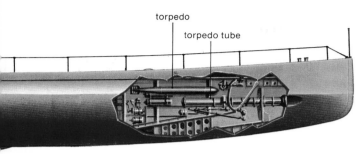

torpedo

torpedo tube

a major obstacle to its development. The wooden TURTLE, designed by David Bushnell, an American, was driven by hand- and foot-cranked propellers. Its armament was an explosive charge that, in theory, could be fastened to an enemy ship's hull by a detachable auger. The *Turtle's* one foray (1776), against a British ship lying off New York harbor, was frustrated in part by the difficulty of maneuvering the vessel underwater.

In 1801, Robert Fulton demonstrated his three-man metal submarine, the NAUTILUS, for the French navy. Like the *Turtle*, the *Nautilus* was driven by a hand-cranked propeller, but for depth control it had movable horizontal surfaces—the diving planes now used on all modern submarines. Its warhead was a towed contact mine, designed to explode when it was dragged against the enemy target. The military potential of the *Nautilus* was never realized in its time, but it presaged the first successful submarine attack, over 60 years later, by the Confederate vessel *Hunley*.

Submarines in the U.S. Civil War. In response to the Northern blockade of shipping during the Civil War, the Southern navy developed a group of semisubmersibles known as "Davids"—small craft intended to battle the Union's Goliath fleet . Although not true submersibles—their smokestacks and air intakes were always above water—they were the first vessels to use submergence with tactical success.

Another Confederate development was the *Hunley,* a true submersible. Although it used the old hand-cranked propeller system and was slower than the "Davids," it could submerge completely. Fitted with a spar torpedo—a 6-m (20-ft) pole tipped with an explosive charge—the *Hunley* went down on the night of Feb. 17, 1864, sinking a Federal corvette, the U.S.S. *Housatonic*, off Charleston but destroying itself in the process.

At the same time, European submarine technology was also accelerating. In 1863 the French inventor Charles Brun used compressed air to propel his vessel, the *Plongeur*, and to expel water from its ballast tanks, a method that is still used. The French navy built several all-electric submarines in the 1880s and '90s. These demonstrated the potential of electric power underwater but were severely limited by the need to recharge the batteries in port. They had no engines other than their battery-powered electric motors. Robert Whitehead's self-propelled TORPEDO gave the submarine a genuine offensive capability; the Swedish inventor Torsten Nordenfelt (1842–1920) developed internal torpedo tubes for submarines in the 1880s.

The Holland. The Irish-American John P. Holland (1840–1914) had experimented with submarine designs for a quarter century when he sold (1900) the U.S. Navy its first submarine. The U.S.S. *Holland* used an electric motor for propulsion underwater and a gasoline engine for surface propulsion and for recharging the batteries. The submarines of the two world wars differed in basic design from the *Holland* only in the substitution of diesels for the gasoline engine. Like most later submarines, the *Holland* submerged by flooding its ballast tanks, used trim tanks and diving planes to control pitch

when submerged and fired torpedoes and blew the ballast tanks empty with compressed air.

World War I. From the early years of the 20th century, fleets of submarines were built by every major European power. The German vessels were the most efficient; by 1911, German designers had abandoned both steam and gasoline—which was volatile, and therefore hazardous within the confines of a submarine—and had equipped all their vessels with diesel engines. Also, German periscopes were the best in the world.

World War I provided the first opportunity to use submarines as attack vessels on a large scale. With its fleet of U-boats (*Unterseebooten*), Germany came close to severing Britain's overseas lifelines. Britain countered with efforts to confine the German submarines to their ports, using air and surface patrols and laying MINE belts.

DEPTH CHARGES and hydrophones—underwater listening devices—were developed and used extensively; the British successfully employed killer submarines as well—small antisubmarine vessels that could maintain underwater speeds of up to 15 knots for as long as 2 hours. Finally, merchant sailings were concentrated into large, well-escorted convoys, a tactic for which the Germans had not found an answer by the war's end.

World War II. As in World War I, Germany began World War II with a small but seasoned submarine force and immediately applied it to isolate Britain from overseas resources. Britain again replied with heavily escorted convoys, and the Germans responded by sending U-boats out in large "wolf packs" that used radio communications to search and attack in concert.

Tactical complexities multiplied: hydrophones were supplemented by underwater sound-ranging systems (SONAR) and the use of RADAR and radar warning devices became widespread. The Germans used long-range search aircraft to coordinate the wolf packs; the British and Americans replied with antisubmarine aircraft carriers and fleets of hunter-killer submarines that were guided to the German vessels by sensitive high-frequency direction-finding radios installed aboard surface vessels.

American submarines in the Pacific and British submarines in the Mediterranean enjoyed the success denied the Germans in the Atlantic. Submarine destruction of Axis supplies played a major role in the Allied victory in North Africa. American submarines effectively halted Japanese maritime commerce by mid-1944. Britain and Italy both had isolated but spectacular successes with miniature one- and two-man submarines in port attacks on enemy ships.

THE NUCLEAR SUBMARINE

The first nuclear submarine, the U.S.S. NAUTILUS, launched in 1954, resembled conventional submarines in many respects, but its great range both above and below the surface made it a revolutionary and formidable weapon. The *Nautilus* sailed almost 170,000 km (91,324 naut mi) before refueling; 146,000 km (78,885 naut mi) were spent submerged. On August 3, 1958, it sailed under the Arctic ice and the North Pole.

Following the *Nautilus* and a group of submarines of the same design, the U.S. Navy developed the Skipjack class of nuclear submarine, which had a teardrop-shaped hull design and was capable of reaching underwater speeds of more than 30 knots. Succeeding types of nuclear submarines, the Thresher and Sturgeon classes, have been designed to be high-speed detection and attack vessels. The U.S.S. *Triton*, launched in 1959, is among the largest and is propelled by two nuclear reactors. In 1960 the *Triton* circumnavigated the globe underwater, traveling 78,858 km (41,500 naut mi) in 84 days.

Whereas the nuclear attack submarine represents the most advanced use of hydrodynamic technology, the nuclear BALLISTIC MISSILE submarine is perhaps the ultimate development of the submarine's military potential, having the ability to launch as many as several dozen intercontinental ballistic missiles while submerged. Following the first underwater launch of a POLARIS missile from the U.S.S. *George Washington* in 1960, such submarines have entered the U.S. and Soviet navies in increasing numbers and are also possessed by

Great Britain and France (see also POSEIDON MISSILE). Such craft are a major consideration in today's strategic balance of power.   JOHN F. GUILMARTIN, JR.

Bibliography: Burgess, Robert F., *Ships beneath the Sea* (1975); Garrett, Richard, *Submarines* (1977); *Jane's Fighting Ships* (annual); Middleton, Drew, *Submarine* (1976); Morris, Richard K., *John P. Holland* (1966); Preston, Antony, *Submarines* (1975); Shenton, Edward H., *Diving for Science: The Story of the Deep Submersible* (1972).

submarine canyon

Submarine canyons are deep, V-shaped valleys that lie underwater off all of the Earth's continental margins. Some canyons begin as gorges within estuaries of large rivers (for example, the Congo Canyon), and a few are in line with rivers but discontinuous with the shoreline (for example, the Indus Cone). The majority of submarine canyons begin on the continental shelf or continental slope, with no apparent relation to the drainage network on the land mass. All of these canyons deeply incise the steeper slopes of the continental margins and in many cases resemble the dissected terrain of a youthful land surface. This similarity led to the early supposition that all submarine canyons were formed by the erosive force of rivers during periods of lowered sea level. This hypothesis most likely explains the formation of some submarine canyons, but it is not generally applicable to canyons discontinuous with a shoreline or those that exist at great depths (some canyons lie 3,000 m/10,000 ft below sea level).

More recently, geologists have hypothesized—but not yet confirmed—that the majority of submarine canyons were formed by the erosive action of turbidity currents (DENSITY CURRENTS) exploiting weaknesses and depressions in the marine substrate. Seawater containing sediment in turbulent suspension has a greater density than the surrounding seawater and takes the form of an erosive undercurrent rapidly moving down the slope of the continental margin. The power (and abrasiveness) of the current is greatest along the steep conti-

nental slope. As the oceanic abyssal plain is approached, the moving front laterally dissipates into a fan shape. An abundant supply of sediment that can feed turbidity currents may account for the presence of many submarine canyons offshore from large rivers (the Congo Canyon off the Congo River; the Astoria Canyon off the Columbia River) and upcurrent of headlands (La Jolla Canyon, California). Turbidity currents are also triggered by earthquakes and associated landslides and by exceptional waves and tides over unstable deposits of sediment.

Certain mechanisms of the theory of PLATE TECTONICS represent the latest attempt at describing the origin of the oceanic canyons. According to this theory, when convection currents occur in the mantle beneath a continent they arch up the overlying crust and begin to tear it apart (continental rifting). Rift valleys (such as those in East Africa) form in the early stages of this process. The sides of the valleys are soon dissected by erosion, forming numerous canyons and ravines. As the continents separate completely and move off the arched zone of spreading, the continental margins subside and the canyons become drowned. The existing valleys and ravines would then act as conduits for turbidity currents.

Submarine canyons generally make excellent fishing grounds. They provide deep-water access and sediment removal channels in some harbors; and because of the phenomenon of wave refraction, the canyon heads create low-surf zones through which vessels may be safely launched.

Bibliography: Burk, C. A., and Drake, C. L., eds., *The Geology of Continental Margins* (1974); Shepard, Francis P., *Submarine Geology*, 3d ed. (1973); Whitaker, J. H., ed., *Submarine Canyons and Deep-Sea Fans* (1976).

submarine ridges: see MID-OCEANIC RIDGE.

subpoena   [suh-pee'-nuh]

A subpoena (from the Latin, *sub*, "under," and *poena*, "penalty") is a writ commanding a person either to appear before a court or magistrate and give testimony for a person named in the subpoena or to face the penalty stated therein. In addition, a subpoena duces tecum (under penalty you shall bring with you) may be issued requiring a witness who has in his or her possession documents or papers relevant to the controversy to produce them at the trial. The 6TH AMENDMENT in the Bill of Rights guarantees to a criminal defendant the right to subpoena witnesses in the defendant's favor.

subsidence

Subsidence, a lowering of the land's surface, results from the settling of underlying material. Although some subsidence represents collapse of large openings—for example, sinkhole formation by collapse of cave roofs—most subsidence represents collapse or diminution of intergranular voids.

TYPES

Deep subsidence occurs when confined fluids such as oil, gas, or water are removed from rocks or sediments. As fluid is removed, fluid pressure drops and can no longer help support the rock against overburden pressure. Grains are forced closer together and occupy a smaller volume. The magnitude of surficial subsidence represents the total vertical compaction of underlying rocks.

Shallow subsidence occurs where loosely packed sediments (typically mudflows) are deposited in an arid environment, where they dry out completely before being buried. A thick section of such dry deposits may accumulate, with intergranular spaces held open by the dry strength of grain-to-grain contacts and clay bonds. Subsequent downward percolation of irrigation water may cause the clay bonds to weaken, and the soil structure may collapse into a smaller volume with grains more closely packed than before.

Shallow subsidence may occur overnight; deep subsidence, however, may escape notice for years. Each type has caused local subsidence of 6 to 9 m (20 to 30 ft), and each can operate over a large area.

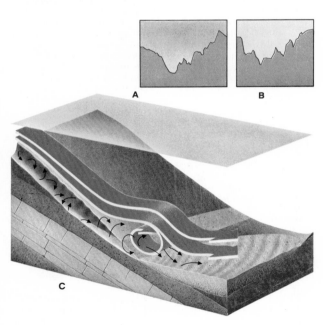

Continental shelves and slopes along the ocean margins are cut by deep V-shaped valleys, or submarine canyons. Cross sections of the California Monterey submarine canyon (A) and of the Colorado Grand Canyon (B) reveal the similarity in form and size of submarine and land canyons. Most submarine canyons are thought to have been eroded by turbidity currents (green arrows)—masses of dense, sediment-laden water—that flowed down the continental shelves and slopes (C), exploiting weaknesses in the marine substrate.

HAZARDS AND MITIGATION

Subsidence can disrupt structures by cracking those along the margin of the subsiding area. Even greater hazards are posed by subsidence-caused changes in the level and slope of the land surface. Lower elevation increases the possibility of flooding, particularly in already low coastal areas. Slope changes prevent proper functioning of features that depend on gentle downhill slopes, such as the irrigation canals in California's Central Valley—where deep and shallow subsidence affects an area of 13,500 km² (5,200 mi²)—and the sewer lines near Galveston Bay, Tex.

Humans cause most subsidence, and they can mitigate, although not reverse, some of its effects. The ponding of water at construction sites, for example, can minimize the effects of shallow subsidence by encouraging most subsidence to occur before construction begins. Deep oil-field subsidence in Long Beach, Calif., which reached 9 m (30 ft) in 1960, has been halted by injecting water to maintain fluid pressure as oil is withdrawn. Deep subsidence near Galveston Bay (several meters) and in parts of Mexico City (7 m/23 ft) has been reduced by importing surface water instead of continuing to withdraw local groundwater. Although these procedures allow fluid pressure to stabilize, subsidence may continue because of overburden pressure. The compaction represented by subsidence is irreversible, and a compacted water-bearing stratum yields water less easily than does an undamaged one.

ROGER S. U. SMITH

Bibliography: Bolt, B. A., et al., *Geological Hazards,* 2d ed. (1977).

substance

In METAPHYSICS, substance is the unchanging, underlying reality of a thing; it is contrasted with those aspects of a thing (its accidents) which change. The substance or essence of a fig, for example, cannot reside alone in its sweetness or greenness, qualities that undergo changes in degree as the fruit buds and ripens. As used by ARISTOTLE, substance has several meanings: (1) a center that endures through changes of its properties; (2) the essence of a thing, or core of essential properties; (3) that which can be predicated on but never be a predicate—a logical subject; (4) that which exists irreducibly and independently; (5) that which underlies or holds together the properties of a thing, a substratum; or (6) the concrete individual, composed of both form and matter.

Later philosophers tended to use one or more of these senses from Aristotle. The British empiricists, for example, used (4) and (5), whereas the Continental rationalists emphasized (4) and G. W. F. Hegel used (3) and (4). Immanuel Kant transformed the notion of substance by equating it with "the thing in itself" (NOUMENON), asserting that the unity and permanence of substances are features contributed by human understanding to the world of phenomena and thus are not proper objects of knowledge.

In contemporary philosophy the classical problems of substance are often dealt with in terms of the nature of matter, personal identity, and the theory of reference.

DONALD GOTTERBARN

Bibliography: Anscombe, G. E. M., and Geach, P. T., *Three Philosophers* (1961); McMullin, Ernan, ed., *The Concept of Matter* (1963); Quinton, A. M., *The Nature of Things* (1973); Stead, G. C., *Division Substance* (1977).

subtraction: see ARITHMETIC.

suburbs

A suburb is an outlying community socially and economically linked to a nearby CITY. Suburbs are usually located beyond the city limits and are therefore politically and legally independent. Since the late 1960s, suburban dwellers have outnumbered either urban or rural residents in the United States. In 1980 approximately 42 percent of the U.S. population lived in suburbs, and only 25 percent in the cities themselves. Other countries where extensive suburban development has occurred include Great Britain, France, West Germany, the

Netherlands, Sweden, and Japan. (See HOUSING.)

Suburbs depend on rapid, flexible modes of transportation and communication, especially the automobile, truck, and telephone. Thus housing, jobs, shopping, and services can spread out from the urban core and remain accessible to one another. A suburban resident, for example, might commute long distances by car to work in the city. Similarly, a corporate office in an urban center can coordinate its activities with a suburban factory or branch by telephone and, recently, computer.

Suburban residents, on the average, have higher incomes than city dwellers and are better educated. They are more likely to be white and to live in family units of husband, wife, and children. Besides the well-known middle-class suburbs, however, there are blue-collar suburbs, suburban slums, and suburbs inhabited mainly by the elderly or by particular racial or ethnic groups. In less developed countries, many cities are surrounded by suburban shantytowns housing those who are too poor to afford to live in the urban core.

In the United States, suburban development began late in the 19th century; by 1900 about 15 percent of the population lived in suburbs. The biggest suburban surge, however, occurred after World War II. Recent growth in suburban work places—office and medical complexes, industrial parks, and retail centers—has increased the economic self-sufficiency of the suburbs. By 1975 nearly twice as many U.S. suburbanites worked in the suburbs as in the city.

SYLVIA F. FAVA

Bibliography: Gans, Herbert, *The Levittowners* (1967); Masotti, Louis, and Hadden, J. K., eds., *The Urbanization of the Suburbs* (1973); Schwartz, Barry, ed., *The Changing Face of the Suburbs* (1975); Wirt, Frederick, *On the City's Rim: Politics and Policy in the Suburbs* (1972).

subversion

Subversion in politics is the action or plan of action designed to overthrow, undermine, impair, or destroy by unlawful means an existing, duly constituted government. In a democratic society that values basic rights and freedoms (see FREEDOM OF THE PRESS; FREEDOM OF SPEECH), the problem of subversion is difficult to manage. Actions that are against the safety and security of the established order, such as treason, espionage, and sabotage, are universally punishable by law. A problem arises, however, about how much freedom a democratic society should permit to individuals and groups expressing opinions and views dedicated to establishing authoritarian or totalitarian systems that would deny rights and freedoms to views other than their own. Some say that if freedom is denied to dissident ideas that challenge the dominant consensus in a democracy, all criticism may then be in danger of being suppressed. Others fear, however, that without certain restrictions on freedom of expression and association, conspiratorial movements dangerous to a free society cannot be controlled. In the United States the Supreme Court has made a distinction between acts or words promoting actual subversion and the teaching of revolutionary beliefs, although it has difficulty in deciding where to draw the line between the two. In 1950, Congress passed the McCARRAN ACT, which established the Subversive Activities Control Board to identify subversive groups. The board was abolished in 1973.

See also: DENNIS V. UNITED STATES; SEDITION; SMITH ACT; UN-AMERICAN ACTIVITIES, HOUSE COMMITTEE ON.

subway

A subway is an underground municipal railroad that provides rapid transit for large numbers of people between city centers and outlying districts. Each train consists of from two to ten electrically propelled cars; electricity is usually taken from a third rail mounted parallel to the running rails.

RAPID-TRANSIT SYSTEMS

Most subways are parts of rapid-transit systems that include ELEVATED RAILROADS and surface-level trackage. Surface running is often used in outlying parts of a rapid-transit system to reduce construction costs. Terrain and geographical conditions also determine the type of system built. Where the water ta-

Passenger cars of the underground rail transit systems of 6 major cities are illustrated. The subway operated by the New York City Transit Authority (A), the second largest system in the world, has 372 km (231 mi) of track and connects Manhattan to other boroughs and New Jersey. This rail system serves more than 1 billion passengers annually. The U-Bahn railway of Berlin (B), operated by the Berliner Verkehrs-Betriebe, has more than 900 cars in service and conveys 285 million passengers each year. Montreal's subway (C), on which construction began in 1962,

ble is close to the surface, as in Rotterdam and Miami, building a subway is difficult and costly; in such places a predominantly elevated rapid-transit system may be built.

SUBWAY CONSTRUCTION

Several means are used to construct subways. Many of the methods are also used in other kinds of tunneling and are discussed under TUNNEL. In the most common method, called cut-and-cover, the street is excavated from the top, and water and gas mains, sewers, and other obstructions are moved. The steel-and-concrete work is put in place, and the street is replaced over the tunnel roof. The trackwork, electrical installations, signaling, and remaining work are then completed.

Less disruptive of street use is the so-called Milan method, first used in that Italian city. Deep trenches for the tunnel walls are excavated along the subway route, and the concrete for the walls is poured. The street surface is then removed, and excavation is made down to the level of the tunnel roof, which is poured and attached to the walls; the street is then quickly replaced. Later, the earth inside the roof and walls is excavated through the ends of the tunnel.

Shaft tunneling is the least disruptive but most costly means of subway construction. Vertical shafts are dug, usually at several locations along the subway route, and then horizontal tunnels are driven away from the shafts. New methods for tunneling underwater were developed in the construction of the San Francisco Bay Area Rapid Transit District tunnel (BART) between San Francisco and Oakland. Tunnel sections were built at a shipyard. A trench was dug in the floor of San Francisco Bay, and the tunnel sections were floated into place and then lowered into the trench and fastened together to form the underwater tube.

SUBWAY DEVELOPMENT

In the middle of the 19th century, because of the congestion in major cities, a separate artery of high-capacity, rapid passenger transportation began to be developed. Because London had sufficient capital, its Metropolitan Railway was the first (1863) to go underground. London's first subways were steam operated, which caused significant operating problems because of the smoke. At the end of the 19th century, with the development of railways run by electricity, subway systems in London, Paris, and Berlin were expanded. Boston built the first U.S. subway in 1897, initially with streetcars instead of trains. New York opened its first permanent subway in 1904 and for the next 40 years continued to enlarge its subway-system mileage by both extending its underground trackage and replacing its elevated railroads with subways. Philadelphia opened its first subway in 1907; Moscow, in 1935; Chicago, in the early 1940s. The initial era of U.S. subway construction and expansion covered the years 1900 to 1930. After 1930 the expense of construction, economic depression, and loss of mass-transit patronage to the automobile, stopped new subway construction for many years.

Post–World War II Construction. Soon after World War II subway construction resumed at a rapid pace in all parts of the world except in the United States. Almost every major capital city in the world has built a subway rapid-transit system since 1945, many of them opening in the 1950s and 1960s. In 1954, Toronto opened the first segment of its subway, and San Francisco began serious planning of its rapid-transit system in 1955.

As U.S. federal policy in urban transportation developed in the 1960s, federal funds became available for mass-transportation capital improvements, including the construction of subways. One ambitious system was the 120-km (75-mi) BART system, which commenced construction in the mid-1960s and opened its first segments for passenger traffic in 1972. BART originally was to be locally funded; some federal aid, however, was used in its construction. It ushered in a new era in rapid transit, with trains intended to be computer controlled and totally automatic, and serving stations designed to be architectural masterpieces. In trying to make a leap ahead in technology, BART suffered from control-system and equip-

SELECTED MUNICIPAL SUBWAY SYSTEMS

City	Year Opened	Route Length/Length Underground
Athens	1901	25.7 km (16.0 mi)/2.9 km (1.8 mi)
Berlin, East Germany	1902	14.6 km (9.1 mi)/12.4 km (7.7 mi)
Berlin, West Germany	1902	93 km (58 mi)/75.8 km (47.1 mi)
Boston	1897	48 km (30 mi)/15 km (9 mi)
Brussels	1969	7.8 km (4.8 mi)/3.9 km (2.4 mi)
Buenos Aires	1913	64.9 km (40.3 mi)/34.7 km (21.5 mi)
Chicago	1943	143.9 km (89.4 mi)/16.3 km (10.1 mi)
Leningrad	1955	45 km (28 mi)/44.4 km (27.6 mi)
London	1863	411.2 km (255.4 mi)/255.5 km (158.7 mi)
Madrid	1919	60.4 km (37.5 mi)/54.9 km (34.1 mi)
Mexico City	1969	40 km (25 mi)/30.9 km (19.2 mi)
Montreal	1966	36.1 km (22.4 mi)/14.0 km (8.7 mi)
Moscow	1935	164.5 km (102.2 mi)/92.3 km (57.3 mi)
New York City*	1904	372.2 km (231.1 mi)/220.1 km (136.7 mi)
Osaka, Japan	1933	75.6 km (46.9 mi)/41.6 km (25.8 mi)
Oslo	1966	39.0 km (24.2 mi)/24.2 km (15.0 mi)
Paris	1900	248 km (154 mi)/146 km (91 mi)
Peking	1969	23 km (14 mi)/23 km (14 mi)
Rome	1955	11 km (6.8 mi)/6.1 km (3.8 mi)
San Francisco	1972	121 km (75.1 mi)/32.5 km (20.2 mi)
Stockholm	1950	206.5 km (128.2 mi)/43.7 km (27.1 mi)
Tokyo	1927	164.7 km (102.3 mi)/90.8 km (56.4 mi)
Washington, D.C.	1976	35.9 km (22.3 mi)/22.3 km (13.8 mi)

* Excluding PATH.
SOURCE: *Jane's World Railways and Rapid Transit* (1978).

features rubber-tired cars to provide an exceptionally smooth, quiet ride. London's subway (D), the most extensive metropolitan system in the world, was opened in 1863 and has 9 separate lines. Stockholm's subway (E), operated by AB Storstockholms Lokaltrafik, uses only motor and trailer cars built in Sweden. The system carries 175 million passengers annually. The Paris Métro (F), which began operating in 1900, is notable for the large number of stations (404) along the length of the system.

ment malfunctions; nevertheless it set new standards in mass-transit design and passenger comfort.

Rubber-Tired Systems. In Paris rubber-tired subway trains, which are quieter than conventional subways, were introduced before World War II. In this system, each wheel assembly is equipped with heavy-duty, truck-type tires that run on broad concrete or steel beams placed parallel to conventional rails. Steel wheels with deep flanges are mounted on the same axles as the rubber tires; should the tires deflate, the steel wheel comes in contact with the rail and supports the car. Guidance is provided by horizontally mounted rubber tires that press against guide rails mounted outside the running surface. The rubber-tire technology of Paris has been exported to Montreal and Mexico City.

Various methods have been tried to cut subway construction costs, including some experimentation with the use of laser beams in tunneling work, but reduced costs remain an elusive goal, and other types of rapid transit—such as elevated railways—may be constructed in place of subways in the future.   GEORGE M. SMERK

Bibliography: Day, John R., *Railways under the Ground* (1964); Farris, Martin T., and Harding, Forrest E., *Passenger Transportation* (1976); Fischler, Stan, *Uptown, Downtown: A Trip through Time on New York's Subways* (1976); Goldsack, Paul, ed., *Jane's World Railways and Rapid Transit Systems* (1978); Howson, Harry F., *The Rapid Transit Railways of the World* (1971); Lang, Albert Scheffer, and Soberman, Richard M., *Urban Rail Transit: Its Economics and Technology* (1964); Nock, Ostwald S., *Underground Railways of the World* (1973); Ontario Ministry of Transportation and Communications, *Tunneling Technology* (1976); Smerk, George M., *Urban Mass Transportation* (1974).

succession, presidential: see VICE-PRESIDENT OF THE UNITED STATES.

succubus: see INCUBUS.

sucker

Sucker (family Catostomidae) is the common name for any of more than 100 species of fish that closely resemble minnows in fin arrangement. They are found most commonly in North America but also occur in Siberia and China. Some suckers are lake species, nocturnal and schooling. Others are solitary and live in riffle areas of swift rivers. The mouth is underneath and can be protruding, hence the name sucker. They are bottom-feeders, usually eating small crustaceans and larval insects. The males develop hard protuberances during spawning season. Suckers may live more than 10 years.

                                                    ALAN R. EMERY

Suckling, Sir John

Sir John Suckling, b. Whitton, Middlesex, February 1609, d. 1642, was one of England's CAVALIER POETS. He studied at

Cambridge University and became a prominent supporter of King Charles I. His plays include *Aglaura* (1637), with two final acts, one comic and one tragic, and *The Goblins* (1638). A wealthy man, Suckling was celebrated in his own time for his gallantry and extravagance, but he is now remembered for his lyric poems and the witty mock-pastoral "Ballad upon a Wedding."

Sucre [soo'-kray]

Sucre, the legal and judicial capital of Bolivia (La Paz is the administrative capital), is located in the southern part of the country at an elevation of 2,790 m (9,154 ft). The commercial and agricultural center of the surrounding region, it has a population of 63,259 (1976). An oil refinery and a cement plant are located there. Long isolated from the rest of Bolivia, Sucre has retained much of its colonial heritage. Public buildings include the legislative palace, where the declaration of independence was signed in 1825; the palace of justice, the seat of Bolivia's judiciary; the modern palace of government; and a 17th-century cathedral. St. Francis Xavier University was established in 1624.

The city was founded by Spaniards in 1538 and was known during the colonial period as Chuquisaca. In 1809 it became the center of the movement to overthrow the Spanish colonial regime. Its name was changed to Sucre in 1840 in honor of Gen. Antonio José de Sucre, a leader in the war of independence and Bolivia's first president (1826–28).

                                                    RAY HENKEL

Sucre, Antonio José de

Antonio José de Sucre, b. Cumaná, Venezuela, Feb. 3, 1795, d. June 4, 1830, a leader of South America's independence movement and Simón BOLÍVAR's most able commander, became Bolivia's first president (1826–28).

Joining the struggle against Spain in 1811, Sucre fought in the abortive campaigns of Francisco de Miranda (1812) and Antonio Mariño (1813). He served (c.1817-1820) as commander in lower Orinoco before joining Bolívar. Sucre organized and disciplined the troops and negotiated (1820) an armistice with the Spanish, proving his skill as a diplomat. His brilliant victory (1822) at Pichincha liberated much of present-day Ecuador, and his strategy assured South American independence in 1824 at Ayacucho, the final and most important battle of the war.

Bolívar, who left the Andean area soon after independence was achieved, was instrumental in Sucre's election (1826) as the first president of the new republic by a constituent assembly in Upper Peru (present-day Bolivia). Sucre effectively organized the government and economy, but he was unable to mollify local political leaders, who saw him as an outsider. He resigned the presidency in 1828 and returned north to the new state of Gran Colombia but soon resumed military activity. He defended Ecuador from a Peruvian invasion in 1828-29 and was subsequently asked to act as president of a congress formed to ensure Colombian unity. The project failed, and Sucre was assassinated while returning home to Quito.

Bibliography: Hoover, John P., *Admirable Warrior: Marshal Sucre, Fighter for South American Independence,* trans. by Alicia Coloma de Reed (1977); Sherwell, Guillermo, *Antonio Jose de Sucre, Hero and Martyr of American Independence* (1924).

Sudan   [soo-dan']

Sudan is the largest country in Africa. Located in the northeastern part of the continent, it is bordered on the north by Egypt, on the east by the Red Sea and Ethiopia, on the south by Kenya, Uganda, and Zaire, and on the west by the Central African Republic, Chad, and Libya. It is mainly an agricultural nation. Long under joint British-Egyptian rule, Sudan became independent on Jan. 1, 1956. Khartoum is the capital.

LAND AND RESOURCES

Away from the Nile most of the Sudan is a vast arid or semi-arid plain that rises gradually to the east, south, and west. The extensive Kordufan Plateau in central Sudan has elevations of about 600-900 m (2,000-3,000 ft). Elevations exceeding 3,000 m (10,000 ft) are found in the Jebel Marra in the west and near the Ugandan border in the south, where the country's highest mountain, Kinyeti (3,187 m/10,456 ft), is located. Lower elevations occur along the eastern rim, in the Ethiopian Highlands, and bordering the RED SEA. Soils are gener-

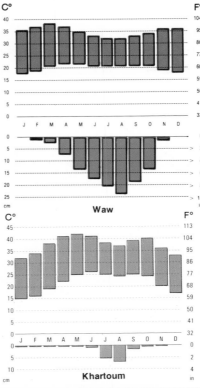

Bars indicate the monthly ranges of temperatures (red) and precipitation (blue) of Waw (top) and Khartoum (bottom) in Sudan. Waw, in southern Sudan, has a tropical wet-dry climate, while Khartoum, the country's capital situated at the junction of the White and Blue Nile rivers, has a desert climate.

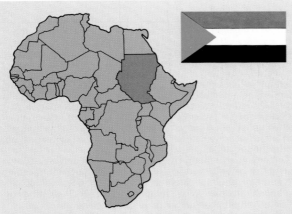

SUDAN

Official Name: Democratic Republic of the Sudan
Capital and Largest City: Khartoum (1973 pop., 333,921)
Area: 2,505,065 km² (967,244 mi²)
Elevation: *Highest*—Kinyeti, 3,187 m (10,456 ft); *lowest*—sea level, at the Red Sea coast
Population: 17,912,000 (1979 est.). *Distribution*—13% urban, 87% rural; *density,* 7 persons per km² (19 per mi²); *annual rate of increase* (1970-76), 3%
Principal Languages: Arabic (official), Nubian, Ta Bedawie, local dialects, English
Principal Religions: Sunni Islam, traditional religions, Christianity
Principal Products: *Agriculture*—sorghum, millet, wheat, barley, sesame, peanuts, beans, cotton, gum arabic. *Manufacturing and industry*—textiles, cement, brewing, edible oils, soap, shoes, pharmaceuticals, processed foods, plastics, matches. *Mining*—iron ore, manganese ore, chromite, copper, gypsum, magnesium, talc
Railroads: 5,470 km/3,399 mi (1979)
Roads: 600 km/373 mi (1979 paved)
Currency: 1 Sudanese pound = 100 piastres

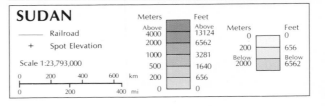

SUDAN

— Railroad
+ Spot Elevation
Scale 1:23,793,000

Meters	Feet
Above 4000	Above 13124
2000	6562
1000	3281
500	1640
200	656
0	0

Meters	Feet
0	0
200	656
Below 2000	Below 6562

© 1980 Rand McNally & Co.
A-584900-772 -1-1-1

ally alkaline in the southeast and east, and red latosols dominate in the southwest. Elsewhere, sandy soils prevail.

Three climatic regimes dominate the Sudan. The desert region north of Khartoum has less than 100 mm (4 in) in annual
precipitation and summer daytime temperatures that often
reach 40° C (104° F). The Red Sea coast has lower temperatures and slightly more precipitation, which falls mostly in the
winter. Southward, rain and humidity increase; the southwestern part of the country is hot and humid, with average
temperatures of about 26° C (79° F) all year round and rainfall of more than 1,000 mm (40 in).

Drainage is provided by the two branches of the NILE RIVER.
The White Nile enters the Sudan from Uganda in the south
and is joined by the Blue Nile at Khartoum. The Blue Nile,
flowing from the Ethiopian Highlands, contributes most of
the floodwater, whereas much of the White Nile flow is lost
in the swampy regions of the southern Sudd area.

Natural vegetation consists of swampy grasslands in the
south, tropical rain forests in the southern uplands, savannas
in the southeast, and semiarid to arid conditions in the north.
Animal life abounds, especially in the southern forests and savanna areas, and includes elephants, rhinoceroses, lions, leopards, zebras, giraffes, crocodiles, hippopotamuses, monkeys,
antelope, gazelles, and rabbits.

The principal resources of the Sudan are agricultural. Inadequate transportation has restricted the development of
the country's modest reserves of iron ore, copper, manganese
ore, chromite, and gypsum. Some petroleum has been found
off the Red Sea coast. Gold is extracted in small quantities.

PEOPLE

The Sudan is divided ethnically into two major regional
groupings: an Arab-African group in the north and NILOTES in
the south. In the 12 northern provinces, which cover two-
thirds of the land area and include most of the urban centers,
the major ethnic groups are the Kababish, a camel-raising
people; the Jaaliin and the Shaiqiyya, who live along the rivers; the Nubians along the northern Nile; the NUBA of the
Kordufan Plateau; and the FUR in the west. Most of the inhabitants of the north are Arabic speaking and adhere to
Sunni Islam. The three southern provinces are inhabited by
the Dinka, Anuak, Nuer, and Shilluk ethnic groups. Some
AZANDE, Bor, and Jo Luo are found in the western parts of the
area, while the extreme south is home to the Acholi and
Lotuho. These ethnic groups speak African languages and are
mostly animists in their religion, although there are some
Christians among them. (The religious breakdown for the Sudan as a whole is 73% Muslim, 23% animist, and 4% Christian.) Besides Arabic—the official language—and the African
tongues, English is a principal language of the three semiautonomous southern provinces.

The White Nile originates in the lakes of the East African Rift Valley
and joins the Blue Nile—with its source in the Ethiopian Highlands—
north of Khartoum. Both streams are dammed near their confluence
to control flooding and provide water year-round for irrigation.

Only 13% of the population lives in cities, most of which
are rather small. Other than the urban clusters of KHARTOUM,
Khartoum North, and OMDURMAN, the largest centers are PORT
SUDAN on the Red Sea and al-Ubayyid in the Kordufan. On
the whole, the country is sparsely populated, with only 7 persons per km² (19 per mi²), but the population is unevenly distributed. The Nile Valley is the most densely inhabited; the
northwestern deserts are practically empty. The annual rate of
natural increase is 3%; the infant mortality rate is 94 per 1,000
live births. Life expectancy is 51 years. Sudan has 1,400 doctors
and 15,792 government hospital beds (1974).

Western education came to the Sudan during the period of
British-Egyptian rule. The literacy rate is less than 20%. Primary schools, maintained by the government, use Arabic for
instruction. Khartoum University (1956) and the Khartoum
branch of Cairo University (1955) offer college-level instruction in the English language. The Islamic University (1965), located in Omdurman, uses the Arabic language.

ECONOMIC ACTIVITY

Although 37% of the Sudan is arable, only 3% is under cultivation. Of the 85% of the people engaged in farming, more
than half are subsistence farmers. Crops grown include cot-

Khartoum, Sudan's
capital, is located
immediately south of
the confluence of the
White and Blue Niles.
Now Sudan's most
populous city,
Khartoum was
originally established
(c.1820) as a military
camp by Egyptian
soldiers during a
campaign to conquer
the region.

Agricultural workers gather long-staple cotton from a field in the Gezira region, Sudan's principal cotton-growing area, located between the Blue and White Niles where there is abundant water. Cotton products are by far the nation's most valuable export product.

ton, grain sorghum (durra), dukhn, sesame, peanuts, wheat, maize (corn), dates, and oilseeds. Camels and sheep are raised for export. Cotton, grown mainly in the Gezira region between the Blue Nile and the White Nile, is the biggest cash crop and accounts for 50% of export revenues. Sudan produces 95% of the world's gum arabic. Manufacturing industries, which employ only 6% of the labor force, produce cement, textiles, pharmaceutical supplies, shoes, and processed foods. Sudan has an electrical generating capacity of 231,800 kW (1977) and produces 672 million kW h (1977) of electrical power.

The inadequate and costly transportation system is the major hindrance to economic development. Freight and people are moved over one railroad with five branch lines, river steamers, Sudan Airways, and 1,448 km (900 mi) of paved or gravel roads. Exports of cotton and other agricultural products are sold mainly to the European Economic Community (Common Market), China, the USSR, Yugoslavia, the United States, Egypt, and India. Imports of manufactured goods and machinery come principally from the United Kingdom, India, West Germany, the United States, China, the Netherlands, and the USSR. Sudan suffers from a balance-of-trade deficit. In 1977, with a gross domestic product of $6 billion, Sudan had exports of $6.6 million and imports of $1.1 billion.

GOVERNMENT

Sudan is a republic under military control since a May 1969 coup. The sole legal political party is the Sudanese Socialist Union (SSU). The constitution of May 8, 1973, provides for an executive branch consisting of a president, a prime minister, and a secretary general of the SSU. The legislative branch is the People's Assembly, with 274 elected and 30 appointed members. A supreme court and civil, criminal, and tribal courts make up the judicial system. Administrative subdivisions include 15 provinces and a southern regional government. Gen. Gaafar al-NIMEIRY is the president, elected in Oc-

tober 1971. He was reelected in the dual capacity of president and prime minister in April 1977.

HISTORY

Egypt first unified the small, independent Sudanese states, some of which had existed since the early Christian era, in 1820–21. Later in that century, the Muslim MAHDI ("messiah") Muhammad Ahmed led a religious revolt. He captured El Obeid in 1883 and Khartoum in 1885 after a long siege in which the British general Charles George GORDON was killed. The Mahdi died the same year, but his successor formed an autocratic state that lasted for the next 13 years. The Mahdist state, however, was overthrown by British-Egyptian forces led by Lord KITCHENER in 1898. Sudan then came under the joint rule of Britain and Egypt and remained so for more than 50 years. Independence was achieved on Jan. 1, 1956, but the governments during the first 13 years of independence—both civilian and military—were unstable. A coup on May 25, 1969, finally gave power to Gen. Gaafar al-Nimeiry.

Siding with the Arabs, Sudan declared war on Israel on June 6, 1967, and broke relations with the United States. The country was then forced to rely heavily on Soviet assistance for several years.

A briefly successful Communist coup occurred in July 1971. After General Nimeiry regained power, Sudan turned again to the United States for aid, and many prominent Communists were executed.

A long civil strife between the black provinces of the south and the Arab north was ended with a peace agreement in 1972, which provided autonomy on most internal matters to the three southern provinces. A program of integration of former guerrilla leaders into the regular Sudanese army has helped to defuse separatist tensions in the south.

Opposition to the socialist government has also come from the conservative Ansar and Khatmiyyah religious sects. The Ansars staged two unsuccessful uprisings, one in March 1970, in which the leader of the sect was killed, and another in July 1976, in which many prominent Sudanese were killed. In July 1977, President Nimeiry met with the Ansar leader, opening a dialogue directed toward reconciliation.   FRANKLIN PARKER

Bibliography: Albino, Oliver, *The Sudan: A Southern Viewpoint* (1970); Ali, Mohamed A. K., *Government Expenditure on Economic Development: A Case Study of the Sudan* (1974); Beshir, Mohamed Omer, *Revolution and Nationalism in the Sudan* (1974); Collins, Robert O., and Tignor, Robert L., *Egypt and the Sudan* (1967); Farwell, Byron, *Prisoners of the Mahdi* (1967); Henderson, Kenneth D. D., *Sudan Republic* (1965); Hintze, Fritz and Ursula, *Civilizations of the Old Sudan* (1968); Kerma, Kush, *Christian Nubia*, trans. by Peter Prochnik (1968); Hoagland, Edward, *African Calliope: A Journey to the Sudan* (1979); Holt, Peter M., *A Modern History of the Sudan, from the Funj Sultanate to the Present Day*, 2d ed. (1965); Kuba, G. K., *Climate of the Sudan* (1968); Lees, Francis A., and Brooks, Hugh C., *The Economic and Political Development of the Sudan* (1977); el Mahdi, Mandour, *A Short History of the Sudan* (1965); Martin, Percy F., *The Sudan in Evolution: A Study of the Economic, Financial, and Administrative Condition of the Anglo-Egyptian Sudan* (1970); Nelson, Harold D., et al., *Area Handbook for the Democratic Republic of Sudan*, rev. ed. (1973); Warburg, Gabriel, *Islam Nationalism and Communism in a Traditional Society* (1978).

Sudbury   [suhd'-bur-ee]

Sudbury (1976 pop., 97,604) is a Canadian city in southeastern Ontario about 65 km (40 mi) north of Georgian Bay of Lake Huron. The economy is based on the mining of nickel and copper for coinage. Gold, silver, and platinum mines, lumber mills, and brick-manufacturing plants are also economically important. Laurentian University (1960) is located in the city.

During the construction of the Canadian Pacific Railway in 1883, large copper and nickel deposits were discovered in the area. The settlement of Sudbury dates from that period. The city is one of the richest mining centers of the world.

sudden infant death syndrome: see CRIB DEATH.

Sudermann, Hermann   [zoo'-dur-mahn]

One of the foremost exemplars of German NATURALISM, Hermann Sudermann, b. Aug. 30, 1857, d. Dec. 21, 1928, protested against social injustice in more than 30 plays as well as in his novels and short stories. His first play, *Honor* (1890; Eng. trans., 1915), depicting the struggles between a poor and a rich family living under the same roof, set the theme for all his major works: moral integrity versus social decadence. Because Sudermann's social realism too often succumbed to sentimentalism and artificiality, however, only a few of his dramas—*Magda* (1893; Eng. trans., 1907), *Fritzchen* (1896), and *The Joy of Living* (1902; Eng. trans., 1902)—ever matched the quality of his first production. Among his prose works, the novels *Dame Care* (1887; Eng. trans., 1891) and *The Song of Songs* (1908; Eng. trans., 1909) and the collection of short stories entitled *Litauische Geschichten* (Lithuanian Stories, 1917) best reflect his genuine humanist concerns, which were constantly at odds with his desire to cater to current trends.

JACK ZIPES

Sudeten Mountains [zoo-day'-ten]

The densely forested Sudeten Mountains extend about 300 km (185 mi) along the Czechoslovak-Polish border. The highest peak is Sněžka (1,602 m/5,256 ft) in the Krknoše range. Mining, lumber, glass, and textiles form the base of the regional economy, and the main crops are oats and potatoes. Since World War II, tourism has also been important, especially for winter sports. The major cities are Liberec and Jablonec and Nisou in Czechoslovakia. Until 1946 most of the region's inhabitants were Germans, but since then the area has been inhabited by Czechs and Poles.

Sudetenland [zoo-day'-ten-lahnt]

The Sudetenland (a 20th-century term) is a geographical region in northern Czechoslovakia, inhabited until 1946 by Germans. It comprises portions of the Sudeten Mountains. The original German settlers arrived there in the 12th and 13th centuries, but the region was traditionally part of Bohemia. In 1938 the Sudetenland was annexed by the German Third Reich (see MUNICH CONFERENCE), but it was restored to Czechoslovakia in 1945. Most of its German-speaking population of 3 million was then transferred to Germany.

BRUCE L. LaROSE

The shaded portion of the map indicates the location of the Sudetenland, a mountainous region in Czechoslovakia traditionally inhabited by German-speaking peoples. Under the pretext of protecting the Sudeten Germans, Germany annexed the region in 1938, in spite of the fact that the Sudetenland had been accorded full autonomy by the Czech government only a year earlier.

Sudetes: see SUDETEN MOUNTAINS.

Sue, Eugène [soo]

Marie-Joseph (Eugène) Sue, a popular French novelist, b. Jan. 20, 1804, d. Aug. 3, 1857, wrote long, serialized novels about Parisian low life that are full of violence and humanitarian ideas. Although *The Wandering Jew* (1844–45; Eng. trans., 1845) was widely read in its time, Sue is no longer popular today.

ALFRED ENGSTROM

Bibliography: Bory, Jean-Louis, *Eugène Sue* (1973).

suede

Suede is the finish given to lambskin or kidskin leather by running the flesh side of the skin over a carborundum or emery buffing wheel to separate the fibers. The surface becomes silken and napped. Leather or cowhide with the top grain "split" off may also be buffed, producing a nappy surface somewhat rougher in texture and called brushed leather or sueded cowhide. Suede is used for footwear, apparel, handbags, belts, and gloves. The word *suede*, French for "Sweden," refers to *gants de Suede*, elegant sueded kidskin gloves originally made in Sweden.

RITA V. COPELMAN

Suess, Eduard [zoos]

Eduard Suess, b. Aug. 20, 1831, d. Apr. 26, 1914, was an Austrian geologist and professor at the University of Vienna whose work formed the basis for the whole field of structural geology. From his early work on fossils, Suess was led to investigate how mountains were formed. His greatest work, *Das Antlitz der Erde* (The Face of the Earth, 1883–1909), presented a comprehensive view of global geological formations and their evolution. It includes his recognition that earthquakes are caused by moving landmasses and that changes in ancient shorelines occurred because of variations in sea level.

JEAN SILVERMAN

Suetonius [swee-toh'-nee-uhs]

Gaius Suetonius Tranquillus, known as Suetonius, AD c.69–c.140, was a Roman biographer best known for his often scandalous *Lives of the Caesars* (AD c.121), which recounts the histories of Julius Caesar and of Rome's first 11 emperors, from Augustus to Domitian. A readable combination of fact and unverifiable rumor drawn from ancient sources, the *Lives* has served to illuminate the social climate of early imperial Rome. Translated by Robert Graves as *The Twelve Caesars* (1957), it had earlier inspired his novels *I, Claudius* and *Claudius the God* (1934). Suetonius also wrote *De viris illustribus* (On Illustrious Men, c.113), 34 biographies of Roman writers, most of which has been lost.

Suez [soo-ez']

Suez is a port city and the capital of Suez governorate, Egypt, located about 130 km (80 mi) east of Cairo. The population is 368,000 (1974 est.). The city lies on a sandy plain at the head of the Gulf of Suez and at the southern end of the Suez Canal. Suez is especially noted for its petroleum facilities—storage, refining, and manufacturing of by-products—and much of its petroleum flows to Cairo by pipeline. Chemical fertilizer and paper products are also manufactured, and the city has important rail connections with Cairo and Ismailia. Suez is a starting point for Muslim pilgrimages to Mecca in Saudi Arabia.

Remains of earlier settlements on the site (Clysma and Arsinoë) date from ancient Egyptian times, and the city has grown and declined through the centuries with the opening and closing of trade routes. Its modern importance dates back to the opening of the Suez Canal in 1869. The city expanded markedly during World War II to become Egypt's third leading port. During the Arab-Israeli Wars the functions of the city were seriously disrupted, and Suez fell into decline between 1967 and 1975 while the canal was closed. The legendary Wells of Moses are nearby.

Suez Canal

The Suez Canal, located at the crossroads of Asia, Europe, and Africa, is one of the world's most important waterways. Opened in 1869, the sea-level artificial waterway crosses the narrow Isthmus of Suez joining Africa and Asia and permits oceangoing vessels to travel between the eastern end of the Mediterranean Sea and the Indian Ocean via the Gulf of Suez and Red Sea. The canal is owned and operated by Egypt and separates the main part of that country on the west bank from the SINAI Peninsula on the east bank.

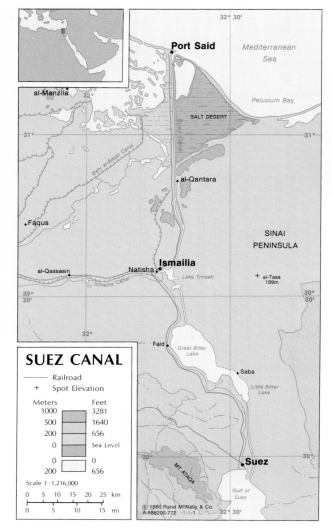

A ship cruises along the Suez Canal between Ismailia and the Great Bitter Lake. Although the Suez Canal remains an avenue for commercial traffic between Europe and Asia, its importance has been diminished by the advent of tankers too large to use the canal.

The northern terminus is PORT SAID on the Mediterranean Sea. The canal extends southward in a nearly straight line across the eastern edge of the salt-marsh area of Lake Manzala and over the red desert soils of the isthmus to reach its midpoint at the northern end of Lake Timsah. It continues southward through Lake Timsah, where Ismailia and the administrative headquarters of the canal are located, then southward and southeastward through the Great and Little Bitter lakes (now a single lake) and southward again past the city of Suez to reach the Gulf of Suez at Port Taufiq. The canal has a total length—including channel approaches at each end—of 169 km (105 mi) and handles 50 to 60 vessels a day. Widened and deepened over the years, it now accommodates ships of 300,000 metric tons (330,800 U.S. tons), but it is being further improved to accommodate supertankers up to 500,000 metric tons (551,300 U.S. tons) by the early 1980s. No locks interrupt traffic, and transit time averages about 15 hours.

The canal is strategically and economically important because it shortens the distance between Europe and the Far East. For example, the distance from London to Bombay is approximately 20,000 km (12,400 mi) via the coast of Africa, or 42% longer than the 11,700 km (7,270 mi) via the canal. The USSR uses the canal to move its navy from the Mediterranean to the Indian Ocean. In the early 1960s, 15% of all world trade moved through the canal, and petroleum from the Persian

Gulf accounted for 75% of the canal's business. By the end of the 1970s, however, much petroleum was transported by supertankers too large for the canal or by pipeline across Egypt or Israel, and petroleum accounted for only 40% of the total traffic on the canal.

The present water route between the two oceans was preceded as early as the 19th century BC by an east-west canal from the Nile River to the Red Sea. It was filled in for military reasons in AD 775 by Caliph Abu Jaafer Abdullah al-Mansur. In 1798, Napoléon Bonaparte ordered a survey made in 1799 for a direct canal from the Mediterranean Sea to the Red Sea, but the project was abandoned when the French survey team mistakenly concluded that a sea-level canal was impossible. In 1854 and 1856, Ferdinand de LESSEPS obtained rights from Said Pasha, khedive of Egypt, to establish a company to build and operate for 99 years a canal open to the ships of all nations. Construction was completed in 1869 at more than double the originally estimated cost of $41,860,000. The United Kingdom acquired a controlling interest in the company when the debt-ridden khedive, ISMAIL PASHA, was forced to sell his holdings in 1875.

In 1888 freedom of passage for all ships of all nations in peace and in war was guaranteed by the Convention of Constantinople, the United Kingdom guaranteeing those and its own rights to the canal after Egypt became independent in 1936. Israel, created in 1948, was, however, denied passage after the first of the ARAB-ISRAELI WARS, although cargoes destined for Israel on non-Israeli ships were permitted in 1952–53, 1957–59, and after 1975. Egypt's President Gamal Abdel NASSER precipitated the Suez Crisis on July 26, 1956, by nationalizing the canal company 12 years before the 99-year lease was to end and by blocking Israel's access to the Strait of Tiran and the Gulf of Aqaba. In October 1956, Israel occupied the Sinai Peninsula, and the United Kingdom and France occupied positions along the canal. The troops of these three nations were replaced by a United Nations Emergency Force in November 1956. The canal was reopened to non-Israeli traffic in April 1957 and turned over to Egypt, which eventually compensated the former shareholders in 1958.

During the Six Day War (1967) between Egypt and Israel, ships were sunk by Egypt to block the waterway, and it remained closed for 8 years. In 1975 plans were announced to widen and deepen the canal. Israeli shipping rights were restored by the signing of the Egyptian-Israeli peace treaty on Mar. 26, 1979. The first Israeli cargo ship passed through the canal in April, and the first Israeli military vessels in May. A tunnel under the canal is expected to be ready for traffic in 1980.

IRA M. SHESKIN

Bibliography: Duff, R. E. B., *100 Years of the Suez Canal* (1969); Farnie, D. A., *East and West of Suez: The Suez Canal in History, 1854–1956* (1969); Hallberg, C. W., *The Suez Canal: Its History and Diplomatic Importance* (1931; repr. 1974); Kipping, Sir Norman, *The Suez Contractors*

(1969); Marlowe, J., *The Making of the Suez Canal* (1964); Schonfield, H. J., *The Suez Canal in Peace and War, 1869-1969*, rev. ed. (1969).

Suez Crisis

The Suez Crisis (1956) developed when Great Britain, France, and Israel retaliated against Egypt for nationalizing the Suez Canal. Egyptian president Gamal Abdel NASSER, angered by the withdrawal by the United States and Great Britain of an offer to finance the Aswan High Dam project, nationalized the canal on July 26. The British government, which held nearly half the shares in the Suez Canal Company, tried to block that move. Together with France, which resented Egyptian aid to Algerian rebels, and Israel, Britain planned to take over the canal. Israel launched a strike against the Sinai Peninsula on October 29. The next day Britain and France demanded that the combatants withdraw 16 km (10 mi) from the canal and then attacked Egypt from the air when it refused the demand. On November 5, Anglo-French troops landed near Port Said. Egypt's Arab neighbors did not come to its aid, but the USSR threatened to retaliate with nuclear weapons. The United States, working through the United Nations, demanded a cease-fire. One was put into effect on November 6, and a supervisory police force established by the United Nations took over on Mar. 7, 1957.   DONALD S. BIRN

Bibliography: Calvocoressi, Peter, *Suez: Ten Years After* (1967); Mezerik, A. G., ed., *The Suez Canal: 1956 Crisis through the 1967 War* (1969); Robertson, Terence, *Crisis: The Inside Story of the Suez Conspiracy* (1965); Thomas, Hugh, *Suez* (1967).

suffocation

Suffocation is an inability to draw air into the lungs. It can be caused by choking on an object, smothering, strangulation, a crushing injury to the chest, or paralysis of the muscles of breathing. The term is often used synonymously with AS-PHYXIA, but actually *suffocation* is derived from the Latin word for "choking," whereas *asphyxia* is derived from the Greek word meaning "no throbbing" and is more often applied to the effects of depriving tissues of oxygen. The original distinction between the two terms is still preserved in such expressions as *intrauterine asphyxia*, defined as the death of a fetus from deprivation of oxygen from maternal blood and not from suffocation.

PETER L. PETRAKIS

Suffolk   (county)   [suhf'-uhk]

Suffolk is a county in eastern England with an area of 3,807 km² (1,470 mi²) and a population of 588,400 (1977 est.). The terrain is mainly low-lying, and the county is bordered on the east by the North Sea. Chalk lands can be found in the west, and sand and gravel deposits exist along the coast. Most of the region, however, is built on clay. The county seat is IPSWICH. Other major towns are BURY ST. EDMUNDS and Lowestoft. Suffolk is drained by the Waveney, Stour, Deben, Orwell, and Alde rivers. The economy is based on the cultivation of grains and vegetables, but fishing, brewing, food processing, horse breeding, and tourism are also important. Stone, Bronze, and Iron Age remains have been found. Burgh Castle, a popular tourist attraction, dates from the Roman period. Suffolk was part of the Anglo-Saxon kingdom of East Anglia. From the High Middle Ages until the beginnings of the Industrial Revolution, Suffolk's prosperity was based on the manufacture of woolen fabric and garments.

Suffolk   (horse)

Suffolk horses are the smallest of the DRAFT HORSE breeds. The Suffolk is descended from the great horse of medieval times. They are always rich chestnut in color, with perhaps a white star on the nose. The Suffolk stands 15 to 16 hands (60 to 64 in) tall at the shoulder and weighs about 725 kg (1,600 lb). The Suffolk has short, stout legs and thus can pull heavy loads, making the breed an ideal working horse. About 3,000 animals are registered by the American Suffolk Horse Association.   EVERETT SENTMEN

The Suffolk is a breed of small draft horse originating in Suffolk, England. It was introduced into the United States in 1880. The Suffolk is stocky with a broad neck and thick, sturdy legs.

Suffolk, William de La Pole, 4th Earl and 1st Duke of

The English statesman William de La Pole, 4th earl and 1st duke of Suffolk, b. Oct. 16, 1396, d. May 2, 1450, played significant political and military roles in the later stages of the HUNDRED YEARS' WAR. In 1444 he brought about a truce with France by ceding the provinces of Anjou and Maine to France and arranging the marriage of King HENRY VI of England to MARGARET OF ANJOU, niece of the French king. This action brought Suffolk to the peak of his influence, and in 1448 he was made a duke. A year later, however, the English violated the peace agreement—probably with Suffolk's approval—thus enabling French armies to seize all English holdings in France except for Calais. Impeached by the House of Commons, Suffolk was banished from England, but he was intercepted as he left the country and murdered.

suffrage

Suffrage is the right or exercise of the right to vote in public affairs. The freedom of an individual to express a desire for a change in government by choosing between competing people or ideas without fear or reprisal is basic to self-government. Any exclusion from the right of suffrage, or as it is also called, the franchise, excludes that person from a basic means for participating in the political decision-making process.

Suffrage has been viewed as a right, as a privilege, or as a duty. As a right, it is conceived of as an inalienable attribute inherent in the individual. This view has led to the extension of the franchise to include more and more people. As a privilege, suffrage is considered as being conferred on the individual by law and is subject to limitations imposed by governing authorities. It therefore can be restricted to some special parts of the population. Some theories rely on the classical Greek concept of the exercise of the suffrage as the citizen's duty to participate actively in the welfare of the community.

Today universal or near-universal suffrage prevails in most of the world, although the extent to which true choice may be exerted varies widely. The requirements of voting show great uniformity in different regions and under different systems of government. The franchise is almost invariably limited to citizens of a minimum age between 18 and 25, depending on the country, and to residents of the locality. Excluded are the mentally ill and convicted felons. In some nations women's suffrage is still subject to qualifications. In other parts of the world property ownership and racial requirements for voting may be enforced. These qualifications for suffrage, and others based on religion, education, and tax-paying, were universal during the Middle Ages, and many persisted well into the 20th century. Most exclusions reflected the fears of those with power that extending the vote to individuals who had no stake in the existing order (the young, the poor, and the itinerant) would lead to instability.

In the United States at the time the Constitution was written, it is estimated that only 6 percent of the adult male population was entitled to vote. Under the influence of Jeffersonian and Jacksonian democracy, religious and property qualifications were eliminated. Racial barriers to voting existed legally until the 15TH AMENDMENT to the Constitution was ratified after the Civil War. Thereafter, blacks were excluded from the franchise in some states through such devices as the white primary, the POLL TAX, literacy tests, and GRANDFATHER CLAUSES. These were gradually interpreted to be unconstitutional under the 15th Amendment or under the EQUAL PROTECTION OF THE LAWS clause of the 14TH AMENDMENT. Women were given the franchise in 1920 under the 19TH AMENDMENT, and the right to vote was extended to 18-year-olds in 1971 under the 26TH AMENDMENT.   RITA J. IMMERMAN

Bibliography: Bone, Hugh A., and Ranney, Austin, *Politics and Voters* (1976); Chute, Marchette G., *First Liberty: Right to Vote in America, 1619-1850* (1969); Farquharson, Robin, *The Theory of Voting* (1969); Gilette, William, *The Right to Vote* (1969); Milbraith, Lester, *Political Participation* (1965); Vaughn, C. L., *Franchising* (1974); Williamson, Chilton, *American Suffrage From Property to Democracy, 1760-1860* (1960).

suffrage, women's

Early in the 19th century disenfranchised groups began to seek the ballot. In the United States women's suffrage—the right of women to vote—was seriously considered for the first time at the SENECA FALLS CONVENTION (July 19-20, 1848), but making it a reality took more than 50 years of protest.
The Early Years. After the Civil War, when black-male-suffrage laws were proposed, agitation by women for the ballot became increasingly vociferous. With the formation of the

(Left) *Susan B. Anthony led the early movement to achieve women's suffrage in the United States. From 1892 to 1900 she was president of the National American Woman Suffrage Association.*
(Below) *American suffragists struggled for women's rights throughout the 19th century and into the 20th century. Nine western states had enfranchised women by 1912. The ratification of the 19th Amendment (1920) finally ensured voting equality.*

American Equal Rights Association, the American women's suffrage movement and the "suffragist" came into existence. A rift, however, developed in the feminist association in 1869 over the proposed 15th Amendment, which in 1870 gave the vote to newly emancipated black men. Susan B. ANTHONY, Elizabeth Cady STANTON, and other women refused to endorse the amendment because it did not give women the ballot. Other suffragists, however, including Lucy STONE and Julia Ward HOWE, argued that once the black man was enfranchised, women would achieve their goal. As a result of the conflict two organizations emerged. Stanton and Anthony formed the National Woman Suffrage Association to work for suffrage on the federal level and to press for more extensive institutional changes such as the granting of property rights to married women. Stone created the American Woman Suffrage Association, which was concerned solely with securing the ballot through the state legislatures. After 2 decades of separation the suffragists were united in 1890 under the name of the National American Woman Suffrage Association (NAWSA). Unity did not bring widespread success, however, inasmuch as women were still, on the whole, considered second-class citizens, mentally and physically inferior to men.
The 19th Amendment. As the pioneer suffragists began to withdraw from the movement because of age, younger women assumed leadership roles. One of the most politically astute of these energetic 20th-century reformers was Carrie Chapman CATT, who was named president of NAWSA in 1915. Another suffragist, Alice PAUL, became a prominent feminist, but because her insistence on the use of militant direct-action tactics was strongly opposed, she resigned from NAWSA. Undaunted, Paul organized the National Woman's party, which utilized such strategies as mass marches and hunger strikes. Perseverance on the part of both organizations eventually led to victory. On Aug. 26, 1920, the 19th Amendment granted the ballot to American women.
The Movement in Britain. In Great Britain the cause gained attention when John Stuart MILL, a Liberal member of Parliament, introduced (May 20, 1867) a women's suffrage bill into the House of Commons. During the same year Lydia Becker founded Britain's first permanent suffrage association, the Manchester National Society for Women's Suffrage. Other societies were quickly formed, and in 1897 they united as the National Union of Women's Suffrage Societies, with Millicent Garret Fawcett as president. Like their American counterparts, the British suffragists struggled to overcome traditional values and prejudices. Frustrated by the prevailing social and political stalemate, the women became militant. Emmeline Pankhurst (see PANKHURST family), assisted by her two daughters, Christabel and Sylvia, founded (1903) the Women's Social and Political Union. Her followers, called "suffragettes," heckled politicians, practiced civil disobedience, and were frequently arrested for inciting riots. When World War I started, the proponents of women's suffrage ceased their activities and supported the war effort. After the war limited suffrage was granted, with women over 30 receiving the right to vote in January 1918. Suffrage rights for men and women were equalized in 1928.
Other Nations. The following list, arranged chronologically, shows when women in most other nations were given the

New Zealand	1893	Luxembourg	1919	Dominican	
Australia	1902	Ecuador	1929	Republic	1942
Finland	1906	South Africa	1930	France	1945
Norway	1913	Spain	1931	Guatemala	1945
Denmark	1915	Thailand	1932	Japan	1945
Iceland	1915	Brazil	1934	Argentina	1946
Canada (except		Ceylon	1934	Belgium	1946
Quebec)	1917	Cuba	1934	Mexico	1946
USSR	1917	Turkey	1934	China	1947
Netherlands	1917	Uruguay	1934	Liberia	1947
Austria	1918	Burma	1935	India	1949
Czechoslovakia	1918	Romania	1935	Uganda	1958
Poland	1918	Philippines	1937	Nigeria	1960
Sweden	1918	Salvador	1939	Switzerland	1971
Germany	1919	Quebec, Canada	1940		

vote. By 1980 women could vote in all except a handful of the world's nations; Kuwait and Liechtenstein were among the countries that still denied the franchise to women.

LORETTA ELLEN ZIMMERMAN

Bibliography: DuBois, Ellen C., *Feminism and Suffrage: The Emergence of an Independent Women's Movement in America, 1848–1869* (1978); Flexner, Eleanor, *Century of Struggle: The Woman's Rights Movement in the United States* (1959; repr. 1968); Fulford, Roger, *Votes for Women* (1970); Kraditor, Aileen S., *The Idea of the Woman Suffrage Movement. 1890–1920* (1965); Morgan, David, *Suffragists and Democrats: The Politics of Woman Suffrage in America* (1971); Pankhurst, S., *The Suffragette Movement* (1931; repr. 1971); Scott, Anne, and Andrew, M., *One Half the People: The Fights for Woman's Suffrage* (1975); Severn, William, *Free But Not Equal* (1967); Stanton, Elizabeth Cady, et al., eds., *The History of Woman Suffrage*, 6 vols. (1881; repr. 1971).

Sufism   [soo'-fizm]

The winged star is a modern-day symbol of Sufism, an Islamic mysticism that emerged as a movement during the 7th and 8th centuries. The Sufis, who emphasize spiritual enlightenment through direct response to God and his divine love, are organized in a hierarchy of fraternal orders.

The word *Sufism*, which is probably derived from the Arabic *suf* ("wool"; hence *sufi*, "a person wearing an ascetic's woolen garment"), denotes Islamic mysticism. Although outside movements have had some influence on Sufi terminology, Sufism is definitely rooted in ISLAM itself. Its development began in the late 7th and 8th centuries when worldliness and loose morals in ruling Umayyad circles evoked a strong reaction among certain pious persons. Individuals such as Hasan of Basra (d. 728) urged the Muslim community to heed the Koranic call to fear God, its warnings for Judgment Day, and its reminders of the transitoriness of life in this world. A new emphasis on the love of God brought the transition from asceticism to mysticism. The woman saint Rabia of Basra (d. 801) called for love of God "for his own sake," not out of fear of hell or hope for heaven.

Sufism was early criticized by those who feared that the Sufis' concern for personal experiential knowledge of God could lead to neglect of established religious observances and that the Sufis' ideal of unity with God was a denial of the Islamic principle of the "otherness" of God. The execution (922) of al-HALLAJ, who claimed mystical communion with God, is related to this second issue, and in later centuries some Sufis did indeed move to a theosophical monism (for example, Ibn Arabi, d. 1240; and Jili, d. *c.*1428). By combining a traditional theological position with a moderate form of Sufism, al-GHAZALI made mysticism widely acceptable in the Muslim world.

Sufism exercised a tremendous influence, partly through mystical poetry, for example, that of Jalal al-Din al-RUMI, and partly through the formation of religious brotherhoods. The latter grew out of the practice of disciples' studying under a mystical guide (*pir*, or "saint") to achieve direct communion with God. Some of the brotherhoods (*turuq*; singular, *tariqa*, "way") had a significant missionary impact.

WILLEM A. BIJLEFELD

Bibliography: Arberry, A. J., *Sufism: An Account of the Mystics of Islam* (1950); Lings, Martin, *A Sufi Saint of the Twentieth Century: Sheikh Ahmad a-'Alawi, His Spiritual Heritage and Legacy*, 2d ed. (1971); Nicholson, Reynold A., *The Mystics of Islam* (1914; repr. 1966); Schimmel, Annemarie, *Mystical Dimensions of Islam* (1975); Shah,

Idries, *The Sufis* (1971); Subhan, J., *Sufism: Its Saints and Shrines* (1938); Trimingham, J. Spencer, *The Sufi Orders in Islam* (1971).

See also: DERVISH.

sugar

Sugars are a diverse and important subdivision of naturally occurring organic compounds called CARBOHYDRATES. Common table sugar, or sucrose, is but one of many kinds. Sugars have been commercially important since ancient times, but only in the last 150 years have their fundamental chemistry and biochemical significance been studied. Emil Fischer (German, 1852–1919) won the 1902 Nobel Prize for chemistry for his studies of carbohydrate structure. Other Nobel awards for work in sugar chemistry were made to Walter N. Haworth (English, 1937) and Luis F. Lelois (Argentinian, 1970).

Sucrose. Sugar cane and sugar beets are the principal commercial sources of sucrose, although maple sap, sorghum, and some palm or date trees all yield limited quantities. The sugar refining industry, grown rapidly since the mid-19th century, is based on the extraction and purification of sucrose. Raw sugar cane contains from 7% to 20% sucrose, 8% to 16% fiber (mostly cellulose), and 70% to 75% water. There are many variations of the methods used to produce very pure (about 99%) sugar, but all involve the following basic steps.

Milling. Juice containing sucrose is pressed from the fiber by sets of heavy rollers in combination with a water bath or spray.

Clarification. Lime and phosphoric acid are added to precipitate salts and impurities, which are allowed to settle. The resulting "sweet water" (containing about 15% sucrose of 90% or greater purity) is filtered to remove finer solids.

Concentration. Most of the water is removed by heating under reduced pressure until the point of sugar crystallization is nearly reached.

Crystallization. The juice, under carefully controlled temperature, pressure, flow-rate, and viscosity, is "boiled" in vacuum evaporators modified for the required control of conditions. The crystallized sugar, or strike, is washed as it is spun in the large perforated baskets of a centrifuge, which removes molasses to yield raw sugar (96–97% sucrose).

Refining. A series of washings, filtrations, and decolorizations (with animal charcoal) removes the remaining molasses coating (which makes raw sugar brown). Another series of evaporation, crystallization, and centrifugation (much like those used with the raw juice) produces the finished sucrose.

Uses. In addition to its use as a food, sucrose is used to manufacture certain detergents, plastics, and related compounds. Efforts are also being made to synthesize other organic chemicals from sucrose to conserve dwindling supplies of petroleum.

Other Sugars. Sucrose can be broken down into two simpler sugars: glucose and fructose. A mixture of the two is known as invert sugar; honey is largely invert sugar because bees secrete an enzyme capable of hydrolyzing sucrose. Glucose (also called grape sugar and dextrose) and fructose (also called fruit sugar and levulose) occur in many fruits. Two molecules of glucose can combine in three ways to form the disaccharides maltose, cellobiose, and gentiobiose, and the polysaccharides starch, glycogen, and cellulose consist of thousands of glucose units linked together. Other important naturally occurring sugars include galactose (cerebrose, or brain sugar) and lactose (milk sugar), a disaccharide consisting of one unit each of glucose and galactose. The sugars ribose and deoxyribose are major constituents of RNA and DNA, respectively.

K. THOMAS FINLEY

Bibliography: Jenkins, G. H., *Introduction to Cane Sugar Technology* (1966); Yudkin, John, et al., *Sugar: Chemical, Biological, and Nutritional Aspects of Sucrose* (1971).

See also: METABOLISM; NUTRITION, HUMAN.

sugar beet

The sugar beet is one of the cultivated forms of the plant *Beta vulgaris*. A biennial, it is harvested annually for its roots,

The root of sugar beets, B. vulgaris, yields a substantial amount of the world's total sugar. Beet tops and by-products of the sugar-extraction process are used as animal feed.

Sugarcane, Saccharum officinarum, is commonly propagated from cuttings. Sections of the stalk about 1 m (3 ft) long are planted in furrows (top). Dormant buds on each cutting send down roots and sprout shoots (detail). Each new plant has six to eight stalks.

which are the source of one-third of the world's sugar. Sugar beets are one of the newest commercial crops and are unique in that their development has been well documented. Starting in the late 18th century, German scientists began to selectively breed beets to raise the sugar content of their roots from 1–4 percent to 15–20 percent. The resulting beet root has white flesh and skin and a sharply tapered shape. Sugar beets are cultivated commercially throughout the world but are concentrated in cooler areas where cane sugar plants cannot grow. The principal national producers are the USSR, the United States, Italy, France, Poland, and East and West Germany. In the United States, sugar beets are grown in the western states, chiefly in California, Colorado, Idaho, Montana, and Nebraska. Sugar beets are harvested 20 to 30 weeks after the seeds are planted.   O. A. LORENZ

sugar production

Sugar production is the cultivation and harvesting of sucrose-rich plants and the conversion of the sucrose into crystallized sugar. The major plant sources of sucrose are sugarcane and the sugar beet. Among other less important sources are maple tree sap, sorghum cane, wild date palms, watermelons, and grapes.

History. It is believed that sugarcane culture began in New Guinea and then gradually spread throughout the South Pa-

Sugarcane cultivation, brought to the New World by Columbus and other explorers, is depicted in this 16th-century engraving. At this mill in South America, cane was pressed under a heavy wheel to extract juice, which was concentrated by heat, placed in containers, and sold.

cific, Southeast Asia, and India. Thereafter it spread to China and to the ancient Arab world, but sugar remained a scarce luxury in Europe. In the 15th and 16th centuries, however, European explorers and colonizers of the Caribbean and South American regions brought sugarcane cuttings with them, and once planted, the cuttings thrived in the warm, moist climate and productive soil. By the year 1600, sugar production in the subtropical and tropical Americas had become the world's largest and most lucrative industry.

Sugarcane culture and sugar production began in the United States with the planting of cuttings in New Orleans during the 1600s, and by 1689 the first sugar refinery was in operation in New York City. It was not until the 1830s, however, that sugar production became a major U.S. industry.

Sugarcane remained the major source of sugar until the 18th century, when a German chemist, Andreas Marggraf, discovered that the sucrose in beets had the same chemical composition as that in sugarcane. When one of his students, Franz Karl Archard, developed a practical method for extracting sugar from beets in 1787, sugar-beet culture spread rapidly to France, Austria-Hungary, and Russia. This expansion led to the construction of the world's first beet-sugar factory in Germany in 1803 and to the further spreading of sugar-beet cultivation throughout Europe and North America. Beet sugar now accounts for more than 40% of the world's total sugar production.

Cultivation and Refining. Glucose is manufactured in the leaves of all green plants and is converted there to sugar (sucrose) for transportation to stems and roots. In most plants, the sucrose is further converted to starch for energy storage. Sugarcane and sugar beets are unusual in that not only do they manufacture sucrose in great quantities but they also store it unchanged.

Sugarcane requires a warm, moist climate for cultivation. It is grown from sections of cane stalk, each containing a bud. After 9 to 36 months of growth the cane attains heights of 3–4.5 m (10–15 ft). At harvest, the cane is cut off close to the ground by machinery or manually with a heavy knife called a machete.

The cane stalks are then stripped of leaves and transported to a sugar mill. There they are crushed, shredded, and passed through a series of heavy rollers under great pressure to extract the cane juice. The remaining solid material, called bagasse, may be used as a fuel by the mill or may be processed into paper or wallboard. The cane juice is clarified and then concentrated by boiling. The resultant thick syrup, called massecuite, is fed into a centrifuge having a perforated basket at its center. When the centrifuge is spun, some of the syrup is crystallized and retained in the basket, while the remaining syrup is thrown to the periphery. This process is repeated once or twice to extract additional sugar crystals. The

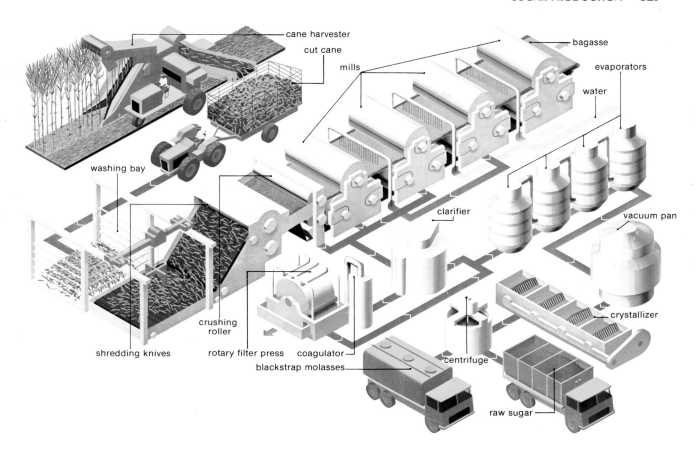

Sugarcane is cut by hand or by a mechanical harvester, then sent to a nearby mill where the sugar is extracted. The stalks are first washed, shredded, and crushed between two rollers. The cane chips then pass through a series of mills where heavy rollers under tremendous pressure extract the juice. The solid residue, called bagasse, is sprayed with water to dissolve more sugar before it passes to the last mill. The juice is heated in a clarifier, and milk of lime is added to precipitate impurities. Water is removed in a series of evaporators, and the resulting syrup is heated in vacuum pans, where it is reduced to massecuite—a mixture of sugar crystals and molasses. The thick syrup passes to a crystallizer and finally to a centrifuge, where the sugar crystals are separated, producing blackstrap molasses and raw sugar.

residue is a dark, odorous syrup called blackstrap MOLASSES.

At this stage the sugar crystals are known as raw cane sugar and are light brown because they are coated with a thin film of molasses. The refining process is interrupted at this point, because raw sugar is an economical form in which to ship sugar in bulk.

Nearly all raw sugar is transported to refineries by oceangoing vessels, and it is for this reason that major refineries are located at seaports. At the refinery, the raw sugar is washed to remove the molasses and is dissolved into a water syrup. After the syrup is filtered to remove impurities and discolorants, the sugar is crystallized by boiling in vacuum pans, washing, and centrifuging. The crystallization process is repeated as long as extractable sugar remains in the syrup. The end product is the familiar granulated white sugar, which is dried, screened, and packaged.

Brown sugar, technically known as soft sugar, is extracted from the syrup remaining after the granulated white sugar has been removed. The resultant product is a mass of fine crystals covered with a film of colored, highly refined, molasses-flavored syrup.

Sugar beets are put through a single, continuous process. The silvery-white beet roots, weighing about 1 kg (2 lb) each, contain about 8% sugar. When the crop is mature, the beets are unearthed, their leafy tops removed for cattle feed, and the roots taken to the factory. There they are washed, machine-sliced into very thin strips, and placed in large tanks, where they are treated with hot water to dissolve the sugar.

The beet-pulp residue is used as cattle feed. The beet-sugar juice is purified, filtered, concentrated, and crystallized in a series of operations similar to those used in refining raw cane sugar.

Because of the strong flavor of sugar-beet molasses, brown sugar is not ordinarily made from sugar beets. White granulated beet sugar, however, is indistinguishable from granulated cane sugar, and the two products are chemically identical.

Sugar Grades. Granulated sugar is classified on the basis of crystal size. "Extra fine" and "fine" are the grades ordinarily packaged as granulated sugar. "Super fine" is a quick-dissolving sugar used in baked goods and drink mixes. Coarser grades of granulated sugar are used by the baking and confectionery industries for special purposes.

Brown sugars are classified by color, and their flavor increases with darkness. For household use, two grades, light and dark, are generally available.

Confectioner's, or powdered, sugar is classified as 10X, 6X, or 4X, the higher numbers indicating the most finely powdered grades. Powdered sugars are usually packed with small amounts of cornstarch to prevent caking. Confectioner's sugar is used for icings, frostings, uncooked candies, and for dusting on cakes and confections.

Turbinado sugar is partially refined sugar made by processing raw sugar crystals in a centrifuge and then washing them with steam. The final product, a light tan due to the persistence of a thin molasses coating, is more than 99% pure sugar.

Invert sugar is a product used by the food industry for its distinctive flavor and because it confers moisture-retaining properties to baked goods, icings, and preserves. It is made by hydrolyzing sucrose (sugar) in solution, splitting the sucrose molecule into its two constituent sugars: dextrose (glucose) and levulose (fructose).

Liquid sugars, or sugar syrups, are solutions of highly purified sugar used by the food industry.

Sugar Production. In 1979 the world production of sugar was 87.7 million metric tons; the leading producer was Brazil (6.9 million metric tons), followed by India, Cuba, Australia, and China. Significant quantities of beet sugar are produced by the USSR, France, Mexico, West Germany, the United States, and Poland. The United States consumes more than 20% of the world production of sugar.

Cane-sugar production in the United States is concentrated in Hawaii, Florida, Louisiana, Texas, and Puerto Rico, which together accounted in 1979 for 2.7 million metric tons (3.0 million U.S. tons), or 47% of total U.S. production. Beet-sugar production in the United States, which amounted to more than 3 million metric tons (3.3 million U.S. tons), or 54% of the U.S. total, is concentrated in the Red River Valley (in Minnesota and North Dakota) and in the Great Plains, Southwest, Northwest, and Great Lakes regions.

Because sugar consumption in the United States exceeds domestic production, more than 4.2 million metric tons (4.6 million U.S. tons) of raw cane sugar for refining are imported yearly.   DAVID SEVERN

Bibliography: Baikow, V. E., *Manufacture and Refining of Raw Cane Sugar* (1967); Birch, G. G., and Parker, K. J., eds., *Sugar: Science and Technology* (1979); Hugot, Emile, *Handbook of Cane Sugar Engineering,* 2d ed. (1972); Jenkins, G. H., *Introduction to Cane Sugar Technology* (1966); McGinnis, Richard A., ed., *Beet-Sugar Technology,* 2d ed. (1971); Perk, Charles G. M., *The Manufacture of Sugar from Sugarcane* (1973); Silin, P. M., *Technology of Beet-Sugar Production and Refining,* trans. by Lazar Markin (1964).

Suger, Abbot of Saint-Denis   [sue-zhay′]

Suger of Saint-Denis, b. *c.*1081, d. Jan. 13, 1151, was a leading French churchman and royal counselor. Becoming abbot of the monastery of Saint-Denis near Paris in 1122, he worked to enhance the abbey's strong ties to French royalty. His reconstruction of the church of SAINT-DENIS produced an early example of the Gothic architectural style. From about 1127 until his death, Suger was a close advisor to two French kings. He wrote a biography of the first of them, LOUIS VI, with whom he had been educated at Saint-Denis, and he headed the council of regency while the second, LOUIS VII, was on crusade (1147–49). Influenced by his contemporary, Bernard of Clairvaux, Suger helped shape royal perceptions of French feudalism as an ordered hierarchical system.

                                                                    JOHN B. HENNEMAN

Bibliography: Panofsky, Erwin, ed. and trans., *Abbot Suger on the Abbey Church of St. Denis and Its Art Treasures* (1946); Rockwell, Anne, *Glass, Stones and Crown: The Abbé Suger and the Building of St. Denis* (1968).

Suharto   [soo-hahr′-toh]

The Indonesian army officer Suharto, b. June 8, 1921, became president of Indonesia in 1968. He joined the Indonesian army in 1943 and fought for independence from the Dutch. In 1965, Suharto, by then a major general, led the army in a bloody defeat of an attempted Communist coup. He ousted President Sukarno and became acting president in 1967. As president, Suharto ensured the military's preeminence and began an extensive program of economic development.

Sui   (dynasty)   [sway]

The brevity of China's Sui dynasty (581–618) gives little indication of its significance as precursor of the second great imperial age, which began with the T'ang dynasty. The first Sui emperor, **Yang Chien (Sui Wen Ti)** (541–604; r. 581–604), conquered the Northern Chou and Ch'en dynasties, uniting China for the first time in almost four centuries.

From his capital at Ta-hsing (later Ch'ang-an), Wen Ti directed many large construction projects, such as repair of the Great Wall and a canal system linking the fertile central region with the northern plain. He sent expeditions to check the Turks on the Central Asian steppe and exact tribute from states as far east as Korea and as far south as Annam. His son and successor, the lustful and extravagant **Yang Kuang (Sui Yang Ti)** (580–618; r. 604–18), quickly dissipated the fiscal base Wen Ti had built, causing widespread revolts. Upon Yang Ti's assassination, the weakened dynasty collapsed into petty states and was subsequently succeeded by the T'ang dynasty.

suicide

Suicide is the intentional taking of one's own life. Some forms are direct, such as shooting oneself. Other forms are indirect, such as refusing to take actions necessary for self-preservation. Researchers have found that some indirect suicides even take the form of homicide-suicide, in which an individual arranges to be killed by someone else, generally because the person cannot do it or feels that it would be immoral if he or she did it but moral if someone else did. One of the major news events of 1977 in the United States was the attempt by the convicted murderer Gary Mark Gilmore to have the state of Utah execute him. Gilmore tried to kill himself when it seemed that the state might not, but his own attempt failed, and ultimately the state executed him by firing squad. Officially, the cause of death was execution by shooting; yet few doubt that this was also an indirect suicide.

Societal Differences. During the 19th century social researchers commonly believed suicide to be a "disease of civilization." Suicide seemed to be increasing in modern societies and absent in more primitive cultures. Anthropologists now believe that suicides occur in virtually all societies, although rates of suicide vary considerably from one society to another. In some cultures, notably Japan, traditional values have encouraged suicide in certain situations. HARA-KIRI (also known as seppuku) traditionally was a highly valued form of suicide that was committed to avoid overwhelming shame, such as would be incurred after an act of disloyalty or a defeat.

Some analysts have suggested that certain individuals may be born with a greater tendency to depression and thereby a greater inclination toward suicide. Even these analysts agree, however, that culture, personality, and the individual situation are important influences on the tendency to commit suicide. Such factors help to explain why various societies and subgroups have such widely varying official rates of suicide. In the mid-1970s, suicide rates among nations ranged from a high of 38.4 per 100,000 persons in Hungary to 2.1 per 100,000 in Mexico. In the United States, where about 25,000 suicides occur per year, more men commit suicide than women and more older people commit suicide than younger people. The suicide rate in the 15–24 age group has been rising sharply in recent years, however. By 1978 the rate among young people stood at 12.4 per 100,000, up 41% from 1970 and 138% from 1960.

Statistical Problems. Studies made of the different methods used to construct official suicide rates show that much of the variation in suicide rate can be accounted for by the way the statistics are collected. Another factor is the degree to which a society attaches a moral stigma to suicide. For example, Roman Catholic nations traditionally tend to have low suicide rates largely because the church views suicide as a sin and normally excludes those who kill themselves from a Christian burial. It is easy to see that this outlook gives everyone concerned—including the victim, the family, the friends, and even the clergy—an incentive to make the suicide appear to have been an accident or even a murder. By contrast, in most Protestant, northern European societies, where the attitude is different, official suicide rates tend to be considerably higher.

Inconsistencies associated with official statistics should not, however, lead to the conclusion that there are no real differences in suicide rates among groups or countries. In fact, a great deal is still to be learned about the ways in which different kinds of social life affect the tendency to commit suicide.

TYPES OF SUICIDE

Several clearly differentiated types of suicide exist in Western society. One of the most common is the accident suicide. These are deaths that appear to be accidents but that raise questions as to whether the victim intended to die by the act that killed him or her or perhaps even to commit the act at all. The death of Marilyn Monroe is probably the most famous example. Although an autopsy showed that her death was caused by an overdose of barbiturates, investigators could not determine whether Monroe intended to take a lethal dose. The question centered on the fact that people who take barbiturates sometimes become so drowsy that they are not conscious of how many they have taken; they may also be unaware of the level of dosage that becomes dangerous. Still more commonly, people do not realize that taking other drugs, such as alcohol, at the same time can greatly increase the risk of a fatal overdose.

Another common form of suicide is the escape suicide. Diaries and other evidence about the thinking of people committing suicide reveal that they commonly consider their death as a "passing on to another world," or "going to God," or simply "escaping this world." Researchers have found that suicide notes almost always read as if their authors believe that they will still be able to witness what happens to them after they are dead. This suggests that these individuals do not think of themselves as dying when they commit suicide—merely that they will be living in a different way or in some other world.

Revenge suicide is another important type. Suicide notes often contain such statements as "Now you'll be sorry for what you did" and even "It's all your fault!" The writers intend to make others feel guilty and responsible for their deaths. Revenge suicides are also calculated to force others to blame the person "responsible" for the suicide and to feel sympathy for the "victim," making the target of the blame feel all the more guilty. This form of revenge apparently does work in many cases. Studies have shown that even psychiatrists who deal with suicidal patients often feel guilt when patients kill themselves. Parents, lovers, and others close to suicide victims are far more likely to feel that way.

EXPLANATORY THEORIES

Researchers have advanced a number of theories in the effort to explain the causes of suicide. Psychological theories stress personality and cognitive factors. Sociological theories stress social and cultural factors.

The Personality Theory. One of the major psychological theories of suicide is the personality theory, which attempts to explain suicide on the basis of differences between the suicidal person and nonsuicidal people. Motivations are the most frequently cited differences, and the desire to escape depression is the most frequently cited motivation. Numerous studies have shown that depression is extremely common among people who commit suicide. Disagreement exists, however, on whether the depression results from events outside the person, especially a social situation leading to loneliness or failure, or is organic in origin.

Some individuals, especially those who believe that they are going to "another world," seem to overcome their depression and even to feel elation just before the suicide, probably because they feel that they have found a solution to the situation causing their depression. This belief that suicide constitutes a solution suggests another personality factor that may be extremely important in some cases: the victim's ideas, beliefs, and ways of thinking. It appears that the way people think about their problems can produce a greater or lesser tendency to depression and suicide. For example, some individuals feel more encapsulated, or closed in, by their immediate situations than do others. When something goes wrong they tend to feel that "This is the end of everything," whereas someone else facing the same situation might feel "Oh well, you win some, you lose some." According to one psychological view, some people have "basic optimism" and others have "basic pessimism," and this pessimism may be a deciding factor in some suicides.

Society's Role. Sociological theories of suicide usually emphasize the importance of either the social structure or the social situations individuals face. Early writers on the subject, notably the French sociologist Émile DURKHEIM, tried to explain the variations in suicide rates among societies as the result of differences in social structure. Social structure includes both the shared values of a society and the patterns of actions that supposedly determine whether people act in accord with or deviate from social values. Thus if a society has values or rules that support suicide, then it should have higher rates than a society with values antithetical to suicide; the patterns of rule enforcement, however, will also be important. Although traditional Japanese society maintains values favorable to suicide, many people will choose life instead of suicide if those values are not effectively enforced.

Durkheim argued that because all Western societies have negative attitudes toward suicide, it is the structure of rule enforcement that makes all the difference. He tried to show that the more involved or integrated a person is in society, the more effective the rule enforcement will be on him or her and the less his or her behavior will deviate from the norm. Unmarried persons without children or friends will be the most likely to commit suicide, Durkheim argued, because no one is likely to be present in their environment to enforce the rules. He argued that the less involved or less integrated the individual, the more self-absorbed, or egoistic, the individual will be; Durkheim considered this "egoism" central to suicide in Western societies. Much sociological work on suicide still takes the Durkheimian structural approach.

Situational Factors. The approach taken by a number of recent sociologists, however, lies midway between the psychological and structural approaches. They have attempted to show that suicide can best be explained by looking at the changes that take place in people's situations and the differing interpretations they give to those changes. A particular situation, such as losing one's job, may be caused by such general social factors as an economic recession that leads to layoffs. Unemployed people may be more likely to commit suicide; it is obvious, however, that only a tiny percentage of people interpret their unemployment as a desperate situation. The interpretation given to such a situation may be partly a result of personality differences—basic optimism or basic pessimism—but may also result from complex social interactions among the people involved in the concrete situation. For example, a person who loses a job may see it as merely a temporary setback, but a spouse's reaction of blaming that person for the loss may change the situation radically, perhaps making the individual feel shame and leading him or her to a suicide motivated by the desire for escape or revenge—or perhaps some even more complex combination of motives. Current research and thinking on suicide seem to emphasize a holistic approach—that is, one that views biological, psychological, social-structural, and social-situational factors as interacting with each other.   JACK D. DOUGLAS

Bibliography: Alvarez, A., *The Savage God: A Study of Suicide* (1972); Baechler, Jean, *Suicides,* trans. by Barry Cooper (1979); Douglas, Jack D., *The Social Meanings of Suicide,* (1967); Durkheim, Émile, *Suicide,* trans. by John A. Spaulding and George Simpson (1897; repr. 1951); Farberow, Norman L., *Suicide in Different Cultures* (1975) and, as ed., *The Many Faces of Suicide* (1980); Hendin, Herbert, *Suicide and Scandinavia* (1964) and *Black Suicide* (1969); Shneidman, Edwin S., ed., *Essays in Self-Destruction* (1967); Shneidman, E. S., and Farberow, N. L., eds., *The Cry for Help* (1961).

suite

The suite is a group of contrasted pieces, mostly in stylized dance forms, for a solo instrument or any combination of instruments up to a full-size orchestra. The term clearly meant different things at different times, and the earliest suites were not even known as such, yet they exhibit similar characteristics to those of later epochs. For example, the pavan-saltarello-piva sequence found in early-16th-century lute music is comparable to the fantasy-almain-galliard form found in English chamber music of the mid-17th century, in that the principle was to offer contrasting tempos and meters within a basically stable key scheme. Occasionally the variegated nature of the movements was unified by a theme, common throughout, yet subject to metrical variation.

Adopted and adapted by composers of various nations, the suite came to be known by other names, such as *parthia* or partita in Germany, *sonata da camera* in Italy, suite of lessons in England, and *ordre* in France. Its growing popularity led to the publication of suites by many eminent composers, among them Purcell, Froberger, Couperin, Kuhnau, Handel, Telemann, and Bach.

It was a relatively short step from the orchestral suites of Bach and Telemann to the partitas and cassations of Mozart and Haydn, in which the influence of the dance is still felt. The practice of collecting ballet music in the form of suites found favor in Mozart's day and continued throughout the 19th century and well into the 20th.   DENIS STEVENS

Sukarno   [soo-kahr'-noh]

Sukarno, the first president of the Republic of Indonesia, promoted the nationalist movement against the Dutch and declared Indonesia independent with himself as president in 1945. He developed an increasingly dictatorial regime and pursued relations with China until effectively removed from power when the army, led by General Suharto, suppressed (1965) a communist coup.

Sukarno, b. June 6, 1901, d. June 21, 1970, originally named Kusnasosro, was the first president of independent Indonesia. He earned a degree in civil engineering at Bandung Technical College, where he was chairman of the General Study Club, which advocated noncooperation with the Dutch colonial regime. The club evolved by 1928 into the Indonesian Nationalist party, and the charismatic Sukarno is regarded as the party's founder.

Exiled and imprisoned several times by the Dutch in the 1930s, Sukarno cooperated with the Japanese following their conquest of the Netherlands East Indies in 1942. Nevertheless, he maintained contact throughout World War II with the nationalist underground. On Aug. 17, 1945, just after World War II ended, he proclaimed Indonesia's independence.

As president of the new republic, Sukarno initially followed a neutralist foreign policy and hosted (1955) the Afro-Asian Bandung Conference. Later, however, he exhibited a growing authoritarianism, dissolving the elected parliament in 1959 and proclaiming himself president for life in 1963. He also pursued increasingly pro-Communist policies in Indonesia and abroad, and he was implicated in a Communist-instigated attack (Sept. 30, 1965) on the country's top military leaders. General SUHARTO, who led the anti-Communist counterattack, took gradual steps to replace Sukarno as the country's leader, and when Sukarno was forced to retire from political life in 1968, Suharto became president.

RICHARD BUTWELL

Bibliography: Dahm, Bernhard, *Sukarno and the Struggle for Indonesian Independence* (1969); Legge, J. D., *Sukarno: A Political Biography* (1972); Penders, C. L. M., *The Life and Times of Sukarno* (1974).

Sukkoth: see TABERNACLES, FEAST OF.

Sukuma   [suh-koo'-muh]

The Sukuma are a Bantu-speaking people of west central Tanzania, south of Lake Victoria. They numbered more than 1,500,000 in 1970, constituting the largest group in Tanzania. Traditionally they have lived on scattered homesteads, maintaining gardens of bulrush millet, sorghum, and cassava on land exhausted by intensive cultivation. They are usually patrilineal, reckoning descent through the father's line, and their villages were once governed by hereditary chiefs. Like neighboring peoples, they practice ancestor worship.

With the introduction of collective farms, the traditional Sukuma way of life has begun to undergo radical change, along with that of other Bantu-speaking farmers and cattle keepers of East Africa. The innovation is a widespread change toward stabilization and permanence instead of local movement and adaptation as necessitated by the impoverishment of the soil. Collectivization has required that the Sukuma abandon their house-and-garden system and substitute block farms near central villages, with emphasis on the cultivation of maize and cotton as cash crops. Their plots are generally arranged in groups of ten to conform with the government's "ten-house party cell" system. The traditional pattern of Sukuma territorial organization has yet to be changed fundamentally, however, although hereditary chieftainship was abolished in the early 1960s.   RICHARD WERBNER

Bibliography: Abrahams, R. G., *Peoples of Greater Unyamwezi, Tanzania* (1967); Cory, Hans, *Sukuma Law and Customs* (1953; repr. 1970); Tanner, Ralph, *Transition in African Beliefs; Traditional Religion and Christian Change; A Study in Sukumaland, Tanzania, East Africa* (1967).

Sulawesi   [soo-luh-way'-see]

Sulawesi (also known as Celebes) is a volcanic island in the Greater SUNDA ISLANDS in eastern Indonesia. Including the adjacent islands, its area is about 227,650 km² (87,900 mi²), and the population is 9,263,700 (1975 est.). Manado and Makasar are the main cities. The island consists of four fingerlike mountainous peninsulas, with the highest point reaching 3,455 m (11,336 ft). The people, mostly of Malayan origin (including BUGIS and Minahasa), raise corn, rice, yams, copra, coffee, and tobacco. Economically, Sulawesi's eastern and southeastern peninsulas are underdeveloped, while the southern and northeastern areas have some recently introduced industries such as lumbering and mother-of-pearl production. Deposits of sulfur, iron, nickel, gold, and diamonds are being exploited. The anoa (dwarf buffalo) and BABIRUSA (pig deer) are unique to Sulawesi. Trees include cedar, ebony, teak, and upas.

The Portuguese visited the island in 1512. The Dutch established a settlement there in 1607 and gradually assumed control, although indigenous sultans held some areas until 1911. Occupied by Japan during World War II, Sulawesi joined Indonesia in 1949.

Suleiman I, Sultan of the Ottoman Empire
(Suleiman the Magnificent)   [soo'-lay-mahn]

The Ottoman sultan from 1520 to 1566, Suleiman I, known as Suleiman the Magnificent, b. 1494, d. Sept. 5 or 6, 1566, conquered Hungary and Mesopotamia, reformed the Ottoman legal system (he was also known as the Lawgiver), and was a preeminent patron of the arts.

Suleiman succeeded his father, SELIM I, who left a throne with unprecedented wealth and power, enabling Suleiman to consolidate and expand his holdings. He emphasized fair systems of justice and taxation, a balanced budget, and a rational legislative system. The empire reached its height of power and grandeur under his reign, and its arts flourished.

Suleiman concentrated most, however, on military campaigns. He removed the Knights HOSPITALERS from Rhodes in 1522 (but was unable to force them from Malta in 1526). Then began his wars against the Habsburgs of Austria, which took place mainly in Hungary and at sea. His initial victory over the Hungarian feudal army at the Battle of Mohács (1526) left Hungary, under JOHN I, in vassalage to the sultan. However,

Suleiman I (the Magnificent) brought the Ottoman Empire to the peak of its power and prosperity. In the west Ottoman armies overran most of Hungary and laid siege (1529) to Vienna; in the east they conquered Mesopotamia. Suleiman was also a notable patron of the arts and a lawgiver.

the Habsburg archduke Ferdinand (later Holy Roman Emperor FERDINAND I) seized control of the northern and western strips. Claiming the entire country, Ferdinand defeated John and occupied his territory after Suleiman departed for Anatolia. The Ottomans returned, restored John, and moved on to besiege (1529) Vienna. The siege failed, but John's rule was secured, and Suleiman was free to return to the east. After John's death (1540), however, the conflict of claims to Hungary finally led Suleiman to occupy it, ending its buffer role and bringing the Holy Roman Empire and the Ottoman Empire into direct contact and conflict. A land stalemate followed, leading to guerrilla war across the frontiers. The conflict then shifted to sea; the powerful new Habsburg fleet and its raids into the central Mediterranean led Suleiman to organize a new navy. Under the command of Barbarossa (Khayr al-Din) it brought Tunisia and Algeria under Ottoman suzerainty and established Ottoman naval predominance in the Mediterranean. This Ottoman hegemony was encouraged by Francis I of France in order to weaken his Habsburg enemies. In return France was given special trade privileges in the Levant.

In the east, continued aggression by the Safavids led Suleiman to undertake a series of campaigns into northwestern Iran. The Safavids, however, followed a scorched-earth policy that forced the Ottomans to retire each winter after gaining only ephemeral victories. In 1535, Suleiman conquered Mesopotamia (Iraq). His dominion over the Arab world complete, he was able to create a powerful eastern fleet with which to safeguard old trade routes and revive the economic prosperity of the Arab provinces.

During his later years Suleiman withdrew from active participation in government, and his three sons contested bitterly for the succession. The weakest of these, Selim II (r. 1566–74), succeeded, and the long decline of the Ottoman Empire began. STANFORD J. SHAW

Bibliography: Kortepeter, Carl Max, *Ottoman Imperialism During the Reformation* (1972); Merriman, Robert B., *Suleiman the Magnificent, 1520-1566* (1944; repr. 1966).

sulfa drugs

Sulfa drugs, or sulfonamides, were the first systemic drugs effectively used to combat bacterial infections in humans. Since the advent of antibiotics, however, their use in therapy has become quite limited. Sulfa drugs are still used, for example, against streptococcal infections, urinary-tract infections, and ulcerative colitis. Drug side effects include reactions in the kidney, liver, skin, and bone marrow.

sulfate minerals

The sulfates, a large and varied class of MINERALS, are characterized by the presence of the sulfate ion (SO_4^{2-}) as a major constituent. Because of structural similarities, chromates (CrO_4^{2-}; see CHROMATE MINERALS), molybdates (MoO_4^{2-}), and tungstates WO_4^{2-}) are generally grouped with the sulfates. More than 200 sulfate minerals are known; most, however, are rare.

Sulfates occur as primary vein minerals, as secondary minerals (with chromates and molybdates) in the oxidized zone of SULFIDE ore deposits, or as precipitates in EVAPORITE deposits. GYPSUM, the first mineral to precipitate during the evaporation of seawater, is found in extensive sedimentary deposits, which are frequently mined for use in construction materials and for agriculture. Such deposits in the Paris Basin in France gave rise to the term *plaster of Paris*. The ornamental stone alabaster is a fine-grained, massive variety of gypsum. Chromates and molybdates are rarely abundant enough to mine. The tungstates WOLFRAMITE and SCHEELITE occur as primary vein minerals and are major ores of tungsten.

Bibliography: Dana, James D. and Edward S., *The System of Mineralogy*, vol. 2, 7th ed. (1951).

COMMON MINERALS OF THE SULFATE GROUP

Mineral	Chemical Formula	Crystal System
Anhydrous Sulfates		
Baride	$BaSO_4$	Orthorhombic
Celestite	$SrSO_4$	Orthorhombic
Anglesite	$PbSO_4$	Orthorhombic
Anhydrite	$CaSO_4$	Orthorhombic
Hydrated Sulfates		
Gypsum	$CaSO_4 \cdot 2H_2O$	Monoclinic
Chalcanthite	$CuSO_4 \cdot 5H_2O$	Triclinic
Melanterite	$FeSO_4 \cdot 7H_2O$	Monoclinic
Epsomite	$MgSO_4 \cdot 7H_2O$	Orthorhombic
Anhydrous Sulfates with Hydroxyl Ion		
Brochantite	$Cu_4(SO_4)(OH)_6$	Monoclinic
Antlerite	$Cu_3(SO_4)(OH)_4$	Orthorhombic
Alunite	$KAl_3(SO_4)_2(OH)_6$	Trigonal
Jarosite	$KFe_3(SO_4)_2(OH)_6$	Trigonal
Chromates, Molybdates, and Tungstates		
Crocoite	$PbCrO_4$	Monoclinic
Wolframite	$(Fe,Mn)WO_4$	Monoclinic
Scheelite	$CaWO_4$	Tetragonal
Wulfenite	$PbMoO_4$	Tetragonal

sulfide minerals

Sulfide minerals contain one or more metals in combination with sulfur. Minerals containing arsenic, antimony, or tellurium instead of sulfur have similar properties and can also be classed with the sulfides. Metals found in sulfides include iron, copper, zinc, lead, cobalt, nickel, silver, and mercury. A large class of sulfides contain arsenic, antimony, or bismuth acting as a metal instead of substituting for sulfur. Sulfides containing a metal along with one of these are called sulfosalts.

STRUCTURE AND BONDING

The sulfide minerals display a great variety of atomic structures and types of atomic bonding. In some, ionic bonds predominate; in others, electron-sharing, or covalent, bonds. In a number of soft sulfides, such as the molybden mineral MOLYBDENITE (MoS_2), atomic groups are joined by the weak electrostatic, or van der Waals, bond. A few of the simple sulfide structures may suffice to indicate their great variety. GALENA (PbS) contains alternating lead and sulfur atoms; each lead is surrounded by six sulfurs and vice versa. The nonsulfide halite, or salt (NaCl), has the same kind of atomic arrangement. The bonding in galena is dominantly ionic but also somewhat like the bonds in metals, and galena has a bright, metallic luster, although, like salt, it is brittle and has a perfect cubic cleavage, or breaking pattern.

PYRITE (FeS$_2$) has a structure similar to that of galena, but with pairs of sulfur atoms in place of the single sulfur atoms in galena. Pyrite has a bright brassy color and a metallic luster, but despite the structural similarity, it lacks the cubic cleavage of galena. PYRRHOTITE (FeS) is totally different in structure from pyrite and galena; its crystals are hexagonal. In SPHALERITE (ZnS), four sulfur atoms surround each zinc atom and vice versa. The bonding is covalent, with electrons shared between zinc and sulfur atoms. Unlike many sulfides, sphalerite is nonmetallic in appearance; it is transparent to translucent, with a luster like pitch or resin.

PHYSICAL PROPERTIES

The physical properties of sulfides vary considerably from one to another, a reflection of the wide variety of atomic structures found in these minerals. Most sulfides have a high specific gravity, ranging from 3.5 to 7.5, because of the heavy metal atoms they contain and because the atoms are packed together tightly. By comparison, the silicate minerals, which make up most rocks, range from about 2.5 to 4 in specific gravity. Most sulfides are opaque and metallic, bright to dull, in luster. Transparent sulfides such as sphalerite and CINNABAR (HgS) have brilliant, resinous, or adamantine (diamondlike) lusters. Sulfides come in many colors. Although brassy-to-bronzy yellow and steely-to-sooty black predominate, some sulfides are red. When pure, sphalerite is colorless, but the mineral usually contains some iron in addition to zinc, and with increasing iron the colors change to green, brown, red, and black. Cadmium-bearing sphalerite is bright orange.

Finally, some sulfides are much harder than others. Pyrite is hard enough to scratch glass, whereas molybdenite (MoS$_2$) is so soft it feels greasy to the touch and is powdered for use as a dry lubricant. Most sulfides are relatively soft and can be scratched with a knife. A few are actually sectile; that is, they can be cut into shavings.

OCCURRENCE

The several hundred known sulfides differ greatly in abundance. Pyrite, the most common of the sulfides, is one of the most widely distributed of all minerals. Many other sulfides, however, are known to occur only in a single locality. Sulfides are found in all kinds of igneous and metamorphic rocks and even in meteorites. Sulfides are the major ores of many metals, including copper, zinc, lead, silver, and mercury, and important ores of others, such as nickel. Most sulfide metal deposits rich enough to mine consist of hydrothermal veins deposited by the action of subterranean hot water. Some intrusions of granitic rock (plutons) are cut by innumerable small veins mineralized with sulfides. These deposits are the so-called porphyry coppers of the western United States. One of the largest open-pit mines in the world has been dug into a porphyry deposit at Bingham, Utah. More than a dozen other porphyry-copper deposits are mined in the West. The disseminated molybdenum deposit at Climax, Colo., high in the Rockies, is of a similar nature.

Some sulfide deposits are magmatic segregations, masses of molten minerals that separated from a large body of crystallizing igneous rock (magma) to form discrete deposits. The great Canadian copper and nickel deposits of Sudbury, Ontario, formed in this way. Sulfides are also deposited by hot springs on the seafloor. Important deposits of copper and zinc sulfides in central Europe are believed to have formed in this manner when the sea covered the region millions of years ago.

When exposed to the atmosphere and water, sulfides tend to disintegrate. The metals in an ore deposit may be dissolved out and redeposited deeper underground as secondary sulfides or as new minerals. Such secondary enrichment concentrates the ore and may make an otherwise lean deposit worth mining.

Sulfides, especially pyrite, are also found in sediments and sedimentary rocks, where they form in the absence of atmospheric oxygen (anaerobic conditions). All organic matter contains small amounts of sulfur, and in sediments rich in organic material, the sulfur may combine with iron to form pyrite. The pyrite in high-sulfur coal breaks down when the coal is burned and produces sulfur oxides and sulfuric acid, dan-

gerous pollutants that are difficult to remove. Water seeping through coal-mine dumps may become contaminated with sulfuric acid from the breakdown of pyrite. These acid mine waters can poison the streams in a mining district and pose great environmental problems.   PETER B. LEAVENS

Bibliography: Dana, James D. and Edward S., *The System of Mineralogy*, vol. 1, 7th ed. (1944); Vaughan, David J., and Craig, James R., *Mineral Chemistry of the Metal Sulfides* (1978).

sulfosalts

The sulfosalts, a class of complex sulfide minerals, include important ores of silver and copper. They are traditionally classified as double sulfides of the general form $A_mB_nS_x$—where A is typically silver, copper, lead, or tin, B is a semimetal, typically arsenic, antimony, or bismuth, and S is sulfur. The crystal structures of most sulfosalts contain BS_3 pyramids, unlike other complex sulfides; this criterion, however, does not apply to enargite and certain other sulfosalts. The most common sulfosalt minerals include the ruby silver ores PYRARGYRITE (Ag$_3$SbS$_3$) and PROUSTITE (Ag$_3$AsS$_3$), as well as ENARGITE (Cu$_3$AsS$_4$), TETRAHEDRITE [(Cu,Fe)$_{12}$Sb$_4$S$_{13}$], bournonite (PbCuSbS$_3$), boulangerite (Pb$_5$Sb$_4$S$_{11}$), and tennantite [(Cu,Fe)$_{12}$As$_4$S$_{13}$]. The sulfosalts are opaque, metallic minerals commonly associated with each other and with other sulfide minerals in hydrothermal vein deposits.

Bibliography: Dana, James D. and Edward S., *The System of Mineralogy*, vol. 1, 7th ed. (1944).

sulfur

Sulfur is a naturally occurring, yellow, water-insoluble solid element. Its chemical symbol is S, its atomic number 16, and its atomic weight 32.064. Sulfur is a nonmetal and a member of the oxygen family of elements (see CHALCOGENS).

The name is derived from the Latin *sulphur*. The discovery of sulfur predates recorded history, and the element has been used since ancient times. The early medical books of Dioscorides of Greece and Pliny the Elder mention sulfur, and fumes from burning sulfur were used in religious ceremonies and for fumigation. Alchemists recognized sulfur as a mineral substance that can be melted and burned. It was first classified as an element by Antoine Lavoisier in 1777.

OCCURRENCE

Sulfur, like most elements lighter than iron, is believed to have been created by the nuclear fusion of lighter elements in the interior of stars. On Earth, it is widely distributed in its elemental state as a secondary mineral or as a volcanic deposit, as well as in combination with a number of metals. Large sedimentary deposits of the almost pure element, mainly of Tertiary age, are found in the coastal regions of Texas and Louisiana; on the Isthmus of Tehuantepec, Mexico; and in Sicily. Sulfur occurs in some fossil fuels, most notably coal, in chemical combination with carbon and other elements; its removal is difficult. Sulfur is prevalent in the sulfide ores of important metals: iron pyrite, sphalerite (zinc sulfide), and galena (lead sulfide). It is also found in calcium sulfate (gypsum) and barium sulfate (barite). The magnesium and sodium sulfates are present in ocean water and in many mineral waters.

Sulfur occurs in living plant and animal tissue as part of the chemical makeup of the amino acids cysteine, cystine, and methionine. Organic sulfur compounds occur in garlic, mustard, onions, and cabbage and are responsible for the odor of skunks.

PRODUCTION

Before modern extraction methods were available, sulfur was collected by lowering men in baskets into dormant volcanoes, where the elemental sulfur would be scraped from the vent walls. Today sulfur is obtained from underground sedimentary deposits by a process developed by Herman Frasch (1859–1914). In the Frasch process, a system of concentric pipes is sunk into the earth. One pipe carries superheated water into the deposit in order to melt the sulfur; the molten sulfur is then forced up another pipe to the surface, where it is recovered in nearly pure form. A major source of non-

Sulfur has been obtained from volcanic deposits in Sicily for many thousands of years. These blocks of sulfur in Caltanissetta, Sicily, were produced by first distilling the sulfur from volcanic rocks and then melting and casting the sublimated product into blocks.

Frasch sulfur is natural gas, which contains hydrogen sulfide, H_2S. Hydrogen sulfide is removed from the gas and converted to sulfur by the Claus process: $2H_2S + O_2 \rightarrow 2S + 2H_2O$.

Increasing quantities of sulfur are extracted from smelter gases arising from the processing of zinc and copper sulfide ores. Sulfur is also extracted from crude oil in the process of refining. Since industries began increasingly burning coal in place of scarce oil, scientists have been developing techniques to recover elemental sulfur from the sulfur dioxide in the stack gases.

PROPERTIES OF SULFUR

Physical Properties. Four stable isotopes of sulfur occur in nature: S^{32} (95.0%), S^{33} (0.76%), S^{34} (4.22%), and S^{36} (0.014%). Sulfur melts at 119° C (246° F) and boils at 444.6° C (832.3° F). It has six electrons in its outer shell—that is, six valence electrons.

Sulfur occurs in two predominant allotropic crystalline forms, rhombic and monoclinic, which differ from one another only in the manner in which the S_8 molecules pack into the crystal (S_8 denotes a molecule of eight sulfur atoms that form a ring). The density of the rhombic species is 2.07 g/ml; that of the monoclinic is 1.96 g/ml. Both species are soluble in the solvent carbon disulfide, CS_2; S_8 is the solute molecule. Below 96° C (205° F), only the rhombic form is stable; above this temperature, only the monoclinic form is stable.

Monoclinic sulfur melts at 119° C (246° F), forming a pale yellow liquid consisting of S_8 molecules. If the melt is heated above 160° C (320° F), the liquid assumes a reddish brown color and becomes extremely viscous. This phenomenon is caused by the breaking of the S_8 rings, with the subsequent formation of chains of up to several thousand atoms in length. Above 250° C (482° F), the viscosity of the liquid decreases as the chains begin to break up into smaller units. If molten sulfur at a temperature between 160° and 250° C is suddenly poured into cold water, a rubbery material known as "plastic sulfur" is formed. This material, which consists of long, elastic sulfur chains, is thermodynamically unstable and reverts to rhombic sulfur over a period of several days.

Chemical Properties. Sulfur enters into a variety of chemical reactions displaying a range of oxidation states from −2 to +6. In the reaction of sulfur with alkali metals, sulfur acts as an oxidizing agent: $2Na + S \rightarrow Na_2S$. When sulfur burns in air, according to the reaction $S + O_2 \rightarrow SO_2$, it acts as a reducing agent. In sodium sulfide, Na_2S, the oxidation state (valence) of sulfur is −2. In sulfur dioxide, SO_2, sulfur displays an oxidation state of +4. Its highest valence state of +6 is dis-

played when SO_2 is further oxidized to form sulfur trioxide, SO_3: $SO_2 + \frac{1}{2}O_2 \rightarrow SO_3$.

Sulfur reacts with fluorine, chlorine, and bromine to yield a number of halides. Sulfur hexafluoride, SF_6, the most important of these, is formed in the following reaction:

$$S + 3F_2 \rightarrow SF_6$$

USES OF SULFUR

Modern industrial society is heavily dependent on sulfur. It is used in the commercial production of sulfur dioxide, sulfuric acid, hydrogen sulfide, and carbon disulfide. It is essential in the vulcanization of rubber and in the production of chemicals used in detergents. Elemental sulfur is nontoxic and, in a finely divided form, finds use in ointments for some skin diseases. It is used in making sulfa drugs as well as in the manufacture of insecticides, fungicides, and plant fertilizers.

Important Compounds. The most important sulfur compound is SULFURIC ACID, H_2SO_4. To produce it by the method known as the contact process, sulfur is first burned in air to yield sulfur dioxide, SO_2. The subsequent oxidation of SO_2, to sulfur trioxide, SO_3, is a slow reaction; therefore a catalytic surface made of platinum or vanadium pentoxide is required. Sulfur trioxide reacts with water to yield sulfuric acid; because the direct reaction of SO_3 and water produces a mist of H_2SO_4 that is difficult to condense, the final stage of production takes place in two steps: SO_3 is first dissolved in H_2SO_4 to produce pyrosulfuric acid, $H_2S_2O_7$; then sulfuric acid is produced by the subsequent dilution of $H_2S_2O_7$ with water:

$$SO_3 + H_2SO_4 \rightarrow H_2S_2O_7$$
$$H_2S_2O_7 + H_2O \rightarrow 2H_2SO_4$$

Pure sulfuric acid is an extremely powerful dehydrating agent. Many carbohydrates containing hydrogen and oxygen in the same ratio as they are found in water (2:1) are completely reduced to carbon. Sulfuric acid virtually "sucks" the water out of sucrose, $C_{12}H_{22}O_{11}$, leaving behind a mass of black carbon. This property of the acid can cause serious damage if the acid comes in contact with the human eye.

Hot, concentrated sulfuric acid is an oxidizing agent of sufficient strength to dissolve even such metals as copper. Dilute sulfuric acid behaves as a normal acid as typified by its neutralization reaction with the base sodium hydroxide, NaOH: $H_2SO_4 + 2NaOH \rightarrow Na_2SO_4 + 2H_2O$.

Sulfuric acid is widely used as an electrolyte in motor vehicle lead-acid BATTERIES. According to recent industrial statistics, 65% of the sulfuric acid produced in the United States is used in the production of phosphate fertilizers. Phosphate rock is treated with sulfuric acid, liberating phosphoric acid that is subsequently used in the making of fertilizer. About 5% of sulfuric acid is used in petroleum refining, 5% in the manufacture of metals and their derivatives, and 5% in the production of chemicals.

Sulfur dioxide, SO_2, is a colorless gas with a suffocating odor. This gas is produced by burning sulfur directly and is also obtained as a by-product of the roasting of sulfide ores in the production of zinc and copper. Sulfur dioxide liquefies readily under pressure and is sold in steel cylinders for laboratory use. Sulfur dioxide dissolves in water to form sulfurous acid: $SO_2 + H_2O \rightarrow H_2SO_3$; this process occurs in nature through the release of SO_2 into the air from the burning of fossil fuels. Sulfur dioxide and sulfurous acid can damage vegetation, corrode the surfaces of buildings, and injure human lung tissue when inhaled. Some of the chemical properties of sulfur dioxide have already been mentioned in conjunction with its role in producing sulfuric acid. The gas is used extensively in the production of wood pulp, the bleaching of textiles, and the preservation of fruits and vegetables.

Sodium sulfite, Na_2SO_3, a salt of sulfurous acid, reacts with elemental sulfur to form sodium thiosulfate, $Na_2S_2O_3$. This compound, which is also known as photographer's hypo, is used as a fixing agent in the photographic process.

Several sulfates, or salts of sulfuric acid, have important applications. Magnesium sulfate, $MgSO_4 \cdot 7H_2O$, known as EPSOM SALTS, is used in explosives and matches and in the fireproofing of fabrics. Medicinally, a saturated solution of epsom salts in water is employed as an antiinflammatory agent.

Sodium sulfate, $Na_2SO_4 \cdot 10H_2O$, also known as Glauber's salt, is used in the dyeing and printing of textiles. Because it has a relatively large latent heat of fusion and a melting point of 32.4° C (90° F) and is inexpensive and nontoxic, it is currently being utilized as a heat storage material in some solar-heated buildings. The Sun's heat is stored in the salt as it melts; heat is then released into the building as the salt solidifies.

RICHARD M. NEUMANN

Bibliography: Karchmer, J. H., ed., *Analytical Chemistry of Sulfur and its Compounds*, 3 vols. (1970–72); Nickless, Graham, *Inorganic Sulphur Chemistry* (1969); Schmidt, M., et al., *The Chemistry of Sulphur, Selenium, Tellurium, and Polonium* (1975); West, James R., ed., *New Uses of Sulfur* (1975).

sulfuric acid

Sulfuric acid, H_2SO_4, is a colorless, oily liquid that is one of the most important industrial chemicals. It is manufactured mainly by the contact process. Sulfuric acid freezes at 10.4° C (50.7° F) and begins to boil at about 290° C (554° F) with decomposition to water and sulfur trioxide. When concentrated sulfuric acid is added to water, much heat is evolved. In aqueous solution the acid ionizes in two steps: $H_2SO_4 \rightarrow H^+ + HSO_4^-$; and $HSO_4^- \rightleftharpoons H^+ + SO_4^{2-}$. Because the first step is complete, sulfuric acid is a strong electrolyte. The acid forms two series of salts: normal salts such as sodium sulfate, Na_2SO_4, and acid salts such as sodium hydrogen sulfate, $NaHSO_4$. In dilute solution, sulfuric acid is a poor oxidizing agent, but hot, concentrated sulfuric acid is a moderately effective oxidizing agent. Large quantities of sulfuric acid are used in the manufacture of fertilizers (superphosphates), paints (titanium dioxide), synthetic fibers (rayons and plastics), detergents (alkyl-aryl sulfonates), organic chemicals (dyestuffs, explosives, and drugs), and other acids (hydrochloric and hydrofluoric acids). It is also used in the extraction of alkenes in gasoline refining.

J. ALISTAIR KERR

Bibliography: Duecker, Werner W., and West, James R., *Manufacture of Sulfuric Acid* (1959; repr. 1971); Fasullo, O. T., *Sulfuric Acid* (1964); Trotman-Dickenson, A. F., *Comprehensive Inorganic Chemistry*, 2 vols. (1973).

See also: CHEMICAL INDUSTRY.

Sulla, Lucius Cornelius [suhl'-uh]

Lucius Cornelius Sulla, c.138–78 BC, was dictator of Rome in 82–81 BC. Sulla Felix (Fortunate), as he later styled himself, was born to an undistinguished patrician family. As quaestor under Gaius MARIUS, he arranged the capture (105) of the Numidian king JUGURTHA. After a praetorship (97), he governed Cilicia and installed Ariobarzanes as king of Cappadocia. He received a command in the Social War (90–89), was elected consul for 88, and obtained the command against MITHRADATES VI, the conqueror of Anatolia. When Marius replaced him in command, Sulla marched on Rome and drove Marius into exile.

Marius's successor, Lucius Cornelius CINNA, attempted to prosecute him, but Sulla sailed east and defeated Mithradates. After a hasty settlement with Mithradates, Sulla prepared to deal with his enemies at Rome by invading Italy. Aided by supporters such as Marcus Licinius CRASSUS and POMPEY THE GREAT, he finally captured Rome at the Battle of the Colline Gate (82). The bloody massacres and proscriptions that followed were legalized by the law making Sulla dictator. He then revised the constitution to make it impossible for outsiders to challenge the powerful families in the Senate who had supported him. After resigning the dictatorship and holding a regular consulship in 80, Sulla retired.

Sulla's system did not long outlive him. He failed to remedy the basic social and economic conditions that had undermined the traditional oligarchic republic, which he tried to restore. Moreover, his career inspired younger men like Pompey and Julius CAESAR to seek the kind of personal preeminence that was incompatible with republicanism.

ALLEN M. WARD

Bibliography: Badian, Ernst, *Sulla, The Deadly Reformer* (1970); Scullard, H. H., *From the Gracchi to Nero*, 4th ed. (1976).

Sullivan, Sir Arthur Seymour: see GILBERT AND SULLIVAN.

Sullivan, Ed

A popular *New York Daily News* columnist and radio emcee (from 1932), Ed Sullivan, b. New York City, Sept. 28, 1902, d. Oct. 13, 1974, became one of the giants of early television after beginning his career as host of a successful CBS variety

When Ed Sullivan hosted the American television debut of The Beatles in 1964, his show attracted a record (at that time) 73 million viewers. Sullivan, a newspaper columnist, emceed television's most popular variety show for 23 years.

series, "Toast of the Town," in 1948. Famous for his deadpan facial expression, wooden gestures, and atonal voice, Sullivan nevertheless had a knack for knowing exactly when to present a sensational or newsworthy entertainer, and this ability kept him at the top of the television ratings until his series left the air in 1971. The Beatles, for instance, in 1964 made their first live U.S. appearance on "The Ed Sullivan Show."

VINCENT TERRACE

Sullivan, Harry Stack

The psychiatrist Harry Stack Sullivan, b. Norwich, N.Y., Feb. 21, 1892, d. Jan. 14, 1949, combined Freudian psychoanalytic ideas and social psychological insights to create the technique of interpersonal psychotherapy. This orientation de-emphasized biology and sexuality in explaining human behavior, stressing instead the influence of personal relationships.

After serving in World War I and working in public health, Sullivan practiced at Saint Elizabeth's Hospital in Washington, D.C. with the neurosurgeon William Alanson White and made his reputation as a humane and creative therapist with schizophrenic patients at Sheppard and Enoch Pratt Hospital in Maryland. He helped found (1936) the Washington School of Psychiatry, edited the journal *Psychiatry,* and worked on international commissions for peace and mental health. Sullivan contributed to the technique of clinical interviewing and pioneered efforts to understand and help the severely disturbed. Although he wrote rather little, Sullivan's impact on colleagues, students, and patients ensured his lasting influence on psychotherapy and personality theory.

NANCY McWILLIAMS

Bibliography: Chapman, Arthur H., *Harry Stack Sullivan: His Life and His Work* (1976) and *The Treatment Techniques of Harry Stack Sullivan* (1978); Mullahy, Patrick, *The Beginnings of Modern American Psychiatry: The Ideas of Harry Stack Sullivan* (1973).

Sullivan, John

John Sullivan, b. Somersworth, N.H., Feb. 17, 1740, d. Jan. 23, 1795, was an American lawyer and politician and a general in the American Revolution. After attending the Continental Congress, he served in the siege of Boston. He was captured during the Battle of Long Island (1776), but was exchanged in time to fight at Trenton and Princeton. Sullivan served (1777–78) under Gen. George Washington in New Jersey and Pennsylvania, and in 1779 he fought his most effective campaign, against the Iroquois and Loyalists along the New York frontier. He later served as chief executive of New Hampshire (1786–87, 1789) and as a federal district judge (1789–95).

GEORGE ATHAN BILLIAS

Bibliography: Amory, Thomas C., *The Military Services and Public Life of Major General John Sullivan* (1868; repr. 1968); Whittemore, Charles P., *A General of the Revolution: John Sullivan* (1961).

Sullivan, John L.

John L. Sullivan was the last world heavyweight boxing champion to fight in the bare-knuckle style. Sullivan successfully defended his title for 10 years, losing it in 1892 at the age of 33. His achievement won him a place in the Boxing Hall of Fame.

John Lawrence Sullivan, b. Roxbury, Mass., Oct. 15, 1858, d. Feb. 2, 1918, was a legendary American boxer who was the last bare-knuckle world heavyweight champion. Known both as John L. and as the Boston Strong Boy, Sullivan left college and haphazardly took up boxing; he made his professional debut against "Cockey" Woods in 1878. Sullivan won the London Prize Ring (bare-knuckle) championship when he knocked out Paddy Ryan in the ninth round on Feb. 7, 1882, in Mississippi City, Miss. He made the last bare-knuckle defense of the heavyweight crown on July 8, 1889, knocking out Jake Kilrain in the 75th round. On Sept. 7, 1892, under the Marquis of Queensberry rules, Sullivan attempted to defend his title against James J. Corbett. Corbett was able to dodge the heavy blows of the slowing, 33-year-old Sullivan, and in the 21st round the challenger scored a knockout. During his career Sullivan recorded 31 victories (16 by knockouts), three draws, one loss, and one no-decision. He was inducted into the Boxing Hall of Fame in 1954.

Bibliography: Fleischer, Nat, *John L. Sullivan* (1952).

Sullivan, Louis

Louis Sullivan's innovative Wainwright Building (1890–91), St. Louis, Mo., in keeping with Sullivan's dictum "form follows function," reveals the underlying structural frame in its narrow vertical piers and shafts of recessed windows. The ornamentation of the crowning frieze and terra-cotta window panels emphasize the verticality of this early skyscraper.

Louis Henri Sullivan, b. Boston, Sept. 3, 1856, d. Apr. 14, 1924, was one of the founders of the CHICAGO SCHOOL OF ARCHITECTURE and a key figure in the development of American architecture. After studying briefly at the Massachusetts Institute of Technology, he worked in the architectural offices of Frank Furness (1873) in Philadelphia and William LeBaron Jenney (1873) in Chicago. Sullivan finished his training (1874) at the École des Beaux-Arts in Paris and returned (1875) to Chicago to begin an independent practice. As the design partner of the firm he formed (1881) with Dankmar ADLER, Sullivan produced several buildings internationally recognized for their functional form, gorgeous ornamentation, and significance in the evolution of the SKYSCRAPER. These include the AUDITORIUM BUILDING (1886–89) in Chicago, the Wainwright Building (1890–91) in St. Louis, the Stock Exchange Building (1893–94) in Chicago, and the Guaranty (now Prudential) Building (1894–95) in Buffalo, N.Y.

Sullivan strove in his architectural designs to reconcile the romantic world of nature with the mechanistic world of science and technology. While his buildings proudly expressed their urban and functional character in their massing and proportion, the lushly organic ornamentation endows each of the structures with an individual identity. The hollow-cage appearance of the Guaranty Building was humanized and beautified with profuse curvilinear ornament. This successful integration of architectonic and decorative elements profoundly impressed a whole generation of American and European architects.

After peaking in the mid-1890s, Sullivan's architectural practice declined precipitously. Following the end of his partnership with Adler in 1895, he found fewer and fewer clients, and most of those were in small midwestern towns rather than in the major cities. Sullivan blamed this on the eclectic taste fostered by the pompously neoclassical WORLD'S COLUMBIAN EXPOSITION OF 1893—a taste, he predicted accurately, that would last for 50 years—but his own contentiousness also had much to do with the waning of his practice. His last great building in Chicago was the sensitively proportioned Schlesinger and Meyer (now Carson, Pirie, Scott) Store (1899; extended 1903–06); such features as extensive glass surfaces and undisguised structural members give it a startlingly modern appearance. Two of his finest late buildings are the National Farmers' Bank (1907–08) in Owatonna, Minn., and the Merchants' National Bank (1914) in Grinnell, Iowa.

Sullivan became, during these later years, an articulate and poetic spokesman for what came to be called organic architecture. While fully accepting contemporary materials and functional needs, he and his Chicago school followers insisted that American architecture must embody the human connection with nature and the United States's commitment to democracy. In his *Kindergarten Chats,* first serialized (1901–02) in *Interstate Architect & Builder* and published as a book (1918; repr. 1947), and his *Autobiography of an Idea* (1924; repr. 1956), he castigated prevailing American architectural and cultural practitioners for their failure to respond to the implications of American ideals and modern life. His most famous disciple, Frank Lloyd WRIGHT, published *Genius and the Mobocracy* (1949) as a tribute to Sullivan, who had died in obscurity and poverty in Chicago in 1924.

J. MEREDITH NEIL

Bibliography: Connely, Willard, *Louis Sullivan as He Lived: The Shaping of American Architecture* (1960); Morrison, Hugh, *Louis Sullivan: Prophet of Modern Architecture,* rev. ed. (1971); Paul, Sherman, *Louis Sullivan: An Architect in American Thought* (1962); Sprague, Paul E., *The Drawings of Louis Sullivan* (1979); Szarkowski, John, *The Idea of Louis Sullivan* (1956); Wilson, Richard G., and Robinson, Sidney K., *The Prairie School in Iowa* (1977).

Sullivan Award

The James E. Sullivan Award, the most prestigious prize in amateur athletics, is given annually to one athlete in the United States. It is presented by the Amateur Athletic Union (AAU) to the "amateur athlete who, by performance, example, and good influence did the most to advance the cause of good sportsmanship during the year."

The winner is selected and announced in January of each year. More than half of those selected have been track and field athletes, although winners have also come from golf, tennis, rowing, swimming, diving, football, figure skating, and basketball. The award was instituted in 1930 and named for James E. Sullivan, former secretary-treasurer of the AAU.

Sully, Maximilien de Béthune, Duc de

[sue-lee']

The French statesman Maximilien de Béthune, duc de Sully, b. Dec. 13, 1560, d. Dec. 22, 1641, was a soldier, diplomat, and minister to King HENRY IV. Until 1606 he was known as the baron de Rosny. A Protestant, he served Henry (then king of Navarre) during the Wars of Religion (see RELIGION, WARS OF), continuing in his service after Henry converted to Catholicism and became king of France. He entered the council of finance in 1596 and rose to become superintendent. In 1604 he succeeded in converting government offices into semiprivate property for revenue purposes. He fostered the revival of agriculture, issued regulations to encourage trade and manufactures, and developed an authoritarian system of government. His efficient administration produced a budget surplus. Henry IV was assassinated in 1610, and 8 months later Sully tendered his resignation to the queen mother and regent, MARIE DE MÉDICIS. While remaining staunchly Protestant, Sully advised the Huguenots to adopt a moderate policy under Louis XIII.   J. H. M. SALMON

Bibliography: Buisseret, David, *Sully and the Growth of Centralized Government in France* (1968); Lodge, Eleanor, *Sully, Colbert, and Turgot* (1931; repr. 1972).

Sully, Thomas   [suh'-lee]

Thomas Sully, b. England, June 8, 1783, d. Nov. 5, 1872, was a leading American portrait painter of the first half of the 19th century. Born in England, he came to the United States as a child in 1792. Determined to acquire the best training in art, he returned to England in 1809 for a year to study with Benjamin West and the newly fashionable portraitist Thomas Lawrence. In his long career, Sully painted nearly 2,000 portraits and more than 400 other subjects. Among his best-known works is *Washington at the Passage of the Delaware* (1819; Museum of Fine Arts, Boston). The best of his portraits are infused with a romantic spirit, such as that which enlivens his several portraits of the actress Fanny Kemble and his reflective, full-length portrait of the young Queen Victoria (1838; Society of the Sons of Saint George, Philadelphia), which he painted on a visit to England in 1838.   DAVID TATHAM

Bibliography: Biddle, Edward, and Fielding, Mantle, *Life and Works of Thomas Sully* (1921; repr. 1969); Hart, Charles, H., ed., *A Register of Portraits Painted by Thomas Sully, 1801–1871* (1909).

sultan

The word *sultan* (Arabic for "authority" or "domain") originally connoted spiritual authority. First used to mean political authority by Mahmud of Ghazni, a Muslim Afghan ruler of the early 11th century, the title of sultan was conferred on the rulers of the Ottoman Empire and later employed throughout much of the Muslim world.

Sultan Muhammad

Sultan Muhammad (fl. 16th century) was a Persian painter who succeeded Kamal al-Din BIHZAD as the director of the Persian imperial library and studio at Tabriz. He was a master of the art of harmonizing color and among Islamic artists was second only to Bihzad in the delicate use of the brush in miniature paintings. A renowned teacher, one of whose pupils was Shah Tahmasp Safavi (r. 1514–76), Sultan Muhammad wielded great artistic influence throughout Persia. In those of his miniatures which have survived in the form of book illustrations (British Museum, London; Royal Scottish Museum, Edinburgh; Gulistan Palace Library, Tehran; and Metropolitan Museum, New York City), he varies the range of figure types and poses extensively, thus rendering them more lively and dynamic.   S. A. A. RIZVI

Bibliography: Gray, Basil, *Persian Painting* (1961); Martin, F. R., *The Miniature Paintings and Painters of Persia, India, and Turkey from the 8th to the 18th Century*, 2 vols. (1912; repr. 1972).

Sulu Archipelago   [soo'-loo]

The Sulu Archipelago, which forms the Sulu province of the Philippines, consists of about 400 volcanic and coral islands between Mindanao and Borneo. The population is 425,617 (1970), and the land area is 2,688 km² (1,038 mi²). Jolo, the capital, lies on the largest island, also named Jolo. On the thickly forested islands rice, cassava, peanuts, coffee, coconuts, and fruits are grown. Fishing and the gathering of pearls, coral, and turtle eggs are also important. The inhabitants have been Muslims (called Moros) since the 15th century. They were once notorious pirates.

Sulu Sea

The Sulu Sea in the western Pacific Ocean is enclosed by Borneo, the Philippine islands of Mindanao, Negros, Palawan, and Panay, and the Sulu Archipelago. Almost 5,600 m (18,400 ft) deep, the sea has an area of about 260,000 km² (100,000 mi²). Once a haunt of the Moro pirates, the Sulu is now fished for turtles, sharks, and pearls.

Sulzberger, Arthur Hays   [suhlz'-bur-gur]

Publisher of the *New York Times* from 1935 to 1961, Arthur Hays Sulzberger, b. Sept. 12, 1891, d. Dec. 11, 1968, succeeded to the position on the death of his father-in-law, Adolph S. OCHS. Having learned the business during 17 years on the staff, Sulzberger guided the *Times* through World War II and the postwar period and became a major figure in journalism. He clearly expressed his belief that a good newspaper is "one which prints the news without fear or favor of any party, sect or interest, and one which admits that the manner in which it prints the news is a matter of legitimate public concern." During the Sulzberger years the *Times* nearly doubled its Sunday circulation, and its daily circulation increased by 40 percent. Sulzberger inherited a great newspaper, but he proved that he was more than "sensible enough to marry the boss's daughter."   CALDER M. PICKETT

Bibliography: Berger, Meyer, *The Story of The New York Times, 1851–1951* (1951; repr. 1970); Talese, Gay, *The Kingdom and the Power* (1969).

sumac

The sumacs are shrubs, vines, or small trees of the genus *Rhus*, family Anacardiaceae. They are usually deciduous, have simple or compound leaves and small, clustered fruits, and grow in temperate and subtropical regions. The poisonous, whitish-fruited members of this genus—including POISON IVY (*R. radicans*), POISON OAK (*R. toxicodendron*), and POISON SUMAC (*R. vernix*)—can cause skin irritation in humans. The red-fruited sumacs include staghorn sumac (*R. typhina*) and smooth sumac (*R. glabra*), all of which grow in the United States. These are harmless, and the fruits are a source of sumac "lemonade."

Sumatra   [soo-mah'-truh]

Sumatra, an Indonesian island located off the MALAY PENINSULA, is one of the Greater SUNDA ISLANDS and the sixth largest island in the world, with an area of about 474,000 km² (183,000 mi²). The population numbers 23,196,900 (1975 est.), and the principal cities are MEDAN and PALEMBANG. The volcanic Barisan Mountains rise along the coast to a height of 3,800 m (12,470 ft). Alluvial plains extend from the foothills to the east coast. Because of its hot, wet climate—the mean annual temperature in the lowlands is 27° C (80° F) and the annual rainfall is about 3,050 mm (120 in)—the island is covered with lush vegetation. Ethnic groups include BATAK, MALAYS, and MINANGKABAU. Sumatra is Indonesia's richest island; rice, corn, and coffee are grown, and petroleum, tin, iron, coal, and limestone are extracted.

The powerful SRIVIJAYA EMPIRE (7th–13th centuries) was

based on Sumatra. The Dutch established settlements in the 1660s and gained sole control of Sumatra in 1824. Japan held the island from 1942 to 1945. Sumatra became part of Indonesia in 1950.

Sumer [soo'-mur]

Sumer was an ancient region in southern MESOPOTAMIA, located in the extreme southeastern part of what is now Iraq, territory that includes present-day Diwaniyah, Amara, and Basra. The land of Sumer was virtually devoid of human occupants until about 5000 BC, when settlers moved into the swamps at the head of the Persian Gulf and gradually spread northward up the lower Tigris-Euphrates Valley. On the basis of pottery, architectural, and other remains, archaeologists have distinguished several successive cultural phases in Sumer before the beginning of the historic period (c.3100 BC).

The Sumerians arrived about 3500 and possibly earlier; their origin is unknown. Presumably they came from the east or northeast, yet no traces of their unique language or possible elements of their ancestral culture have been discovered outside of Iraq. The Sumerians, who dominated Sumer from about 3100 to about 2100, were the creators of many basic and lasting features of Mesopotamian civilization.

The history of Sumer is divided into several periods: Early Dynastic (3100–2500), Proto-Imperial (2500–2350), Sargonid (2350–2200), and Ur III (to c.2000). In the first period a dozen little political units, or city-states, developed in the lower valley, and in the second period these states fought one another over land and water rights, with a growing tendency for one unit to conquer others and so create short-lived empires. In the Sargonid Period, beginning with SARGON OF AKKAD, a Semitic-speaking dynasty located in the northern part of the lower valley (AKKAD) extended its control over the Sumerians to the south. After the fall of the Sargonids (2200) following an invasion from the north and a subsequent period of some confusion, the Sumerians, led by the kings of the 3d dynasty of UR (c.2150–2000), regained control of Sumer, conquered Akkad, and thus united all of the region later called BABYLONIA under a single rule. About 2000 BC, however, new invasions coming simultaneously from the west and northeast ended the regime of Ur III. The Sumerians subsequently lost their identity as they were submerged in these waves of foreign invaders.

Although the Sumerians as a people thus disappeared, their language and literature continued to influence the religion of their successors. Moreover, their basic economic organization, system of writing (CUNEIFORM), architectural forms, and legal practices remained in use, and later generations elaborated upon the mathematics and astronomy that the Sumerians had originated. TOM B. JONES

Bibliography: Jones, T. B., comp., *The Sumerian Problem* (1969); Kramer, S. N., *The Sumerians* (1971).

See also: MESOPOTAMIAN ART AND ARCHITECTURE.

Summa Theologicae [suhm'-uh thee-oh-loh'-jih-ky]

The *Summa Theologicae* (c.1266–73), by Saint Thomas AQUINAS, not only synthesizes Thomistic philosophy but also constitutes the single most complete statement of Roman Catholic doctrine on a wide variety of subjects. Using Aristotelian logic but recognizing the ultimate superiority of divine revelation, Thomas divides his work into three parts, the first dealing with the properties of God the creator, the second with human activity and ethics, and the third with Christ and the sacraments. Each part is made up of a series of open questions, which are treated in separate articles. Although Aquinas initially advances arguments for both sides, his formidable reasoning powers generally lead to the banishment of error and the triumph of church doctrine.

Summerhill

Summerhill is a coeducational primary and secondary school, established by A. S. Neill in 1921 in Leiston, Suffolk, England; here students are free to study what they wish or not to study at all. Neill wrote that when children find out for themselves what they need to know they learn much faster and are able to catch up fairly quickly with others. Students are free to do what they want as long as they do not interfere with others' freedom or safety. He measured the success of a school by the happiness of its alumni. Summerhill is governed by an assembly in which each student and teacher has one vote.

Bibliography: Hart, Harold H., ed., *Summerhill: For and Against* (1970); Neill, A. S., *Neill! Neill! Orange Peel* (1972) and *Summerhill* (1960); Popenoe, Joshua, *Inside Summerhill* (1970).

summons

A summons is a writ, issued by a sheriff or other court officer, requiring a person to appear in court to answer the complaint in an action against that person. In a civil suit the plaintiff's lawyer, as an officer of the court, can prepare the summons and complaint and see that it is delivered to the defendant. When a case is to be tried in federal court, a marshal must serve the summons on the defendant. Upon receiving the summons and complaint the defendant must draw up an answer. If a defendant ignores the summons, the court will render a judgment against the defendant. .

See also: LEGAL PROCEDURE; SUBPOENA; WARRANT.

Sumner, Charles [suhm'-nur]

A passionate opponent of slavery, Charles Sumner, b. Boston, Jan. 6, 1811, d. Mar. 11, 1874, was a pivotal figure during the Civil War and RECONSTRUCTION periods of U.S. history. He was a moderately successful lawyer and legal scholar already known for his commitment to pacifism and penal reform when he joined the antislavery movement in 1845, becoming a leader of the "Conscience Whigs." An active organizer of the Free-Soil movement of 1848, Sumner was elected to the U.S. Senate in 1851 as part of a political deal between the Free-Soilers and Massachusetts Democrats. He helped organize the Republican party in 1854–55 and was one of the most eloquent opponents of slavery in Washington, D.C. Once, a few days after a powerful speech, he was viciously attacked and beaten by a Southern congressman, Preston Brooks, in the nearly empty Senate chamber. Severely injured, he could not return to his Senate seat for 3 years but won acclaim as a near martyr.

Returning to the Senate in 1859, Sumner became (1861) chairman of the prestigious Foreign Relations Committee dur-

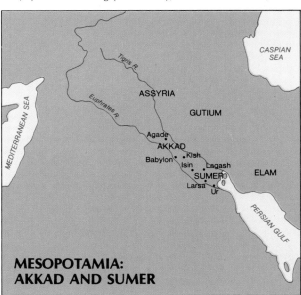

MESOPOTAMIA: AKKAD AND SUMER

Charles Sumner, a U.S. senator from Massachusetts from 1851 to 1874, was one of the most passionate and eloquent opponents of slavery in Washington. A leading Radical Republican after the Civil War, he demanded full civil and political equality for former slaves and was active in the impeachment trial of Andrew Johnson.

ing the Civil War and fought for the abolition of slavery. When the war ended, he insisted that equal political and civil rights be guaranteed to the former slaves as part of any reconstruction plan. Opposing all compromises that fell short of that requirement, Sumner helped force the break between President Andrew Johnson and congressional Republicans. Although Congress's final program fell short of his ideal, it did incorporate civil and political equality.

During Ulysses S. Grant's administration Sumner, then at the height of his public prestige, broke with the president over foreign policy. As a result, Senate Republicans removed him from his committee chairmanship. In opposing Grant's reelection in 1872, Sumner lost all influence in the Senate, although he remained popular among the Republican rank and file until his death. His *Memoirs and Letters* were published (1877–93) in four volumes.   MICHAEL LES BENEDICT

Bibliography: Donald, David, *Charles Sumner and the Coming of the Civil War* (1960) and *Charles Sumner and the Rights of Man* (1970).

Sumner, James B.

The American biochemist James Batcheller Sumner, b. Canton, Mass., Nov. 19, 1887, d. Aug. 12, 1955, shared (1946) the Nobel Prize for chemistry with J. H. Northrop and W. M. Stanley for his achievements in enzyme research. He succeeded (1926) in carrying out the first crystallization of a pure enzyme, urease, and disproved Willstätter's theory that enzymes were not proteins. His research opened the way for the isolation of many enzymes.   HENRY M. LEICESTER

Sumner, William Graham

William Graham Sumner, b. Paterson, N.J., Oct. 30, 1840, d. Apr. 12, 1910, was a sociologist, economist, and Episcopal minister. As a Yale University professor (1872–1909), Sumner introduced the classic concepts of FOLKWAYS and mores in *Folkways* (1906). Sumner adamantly opposed any aid to the poor, espousing an extreme form of SOCIAL DARWINISM, and advocating a survival of the fittest in society.

Bibliography: Gabriel, Ralph Henry, *The Course of American Democratic Thought*, 2d ed. (1956); Healy, Mary E., *Society and Social Change in the Writings of St. Thomas, Ward, Sumner, and Cooley* (1948; repr. 1972).

sumo: see WRESTLING.

sumptuary laws

Sumptuary laws, from the Latin *sumptus* (expense), were originally laws against luxury and extravagance. They served to maintain moral standards and distinctions between social classes. Such laws existed in China under the Chou dynasty (c.1027–256 BC) and in medieval Japan. In the West they were prevalent in Roman and late medieval times and during the Reformation. In republican Rome, such laws as the Oppian law (215 BC) and the Didian law (143 BC) regulated dress and entertainment. In the late Middle Ages most European states passed sumptuary laws. For example, the French king Philip IV instituted (1294) laws decreeing that no commoner could wear fur, precious stones, or gold; that no duke, count, or baron could have more than four robes a year; and that no one who gave a dinner could serve more than two courses besides the soup. During the Reformation, additional sumptuary laws were passed in Switzerland, Italy, France, and England. Later, Puritan New England also had sumptuary legislation. As a rule, however, these later laws were sporadically enforced and not long retained.

Modern legislation that restricts the manufacture or use of certain goods (either directly or indirectly—through excise taxes) is sometimes called sumptuary legislation, as in laws prohibiting the manufacture and sale of alcoholic drinks.

Bibliography: Baldwin, F. E., *Sumptuary Legislation and Personal Regulation in England* (1926); Vincent, John H., *Costume and Conduct in the Laws of Basel, Bern, and Zurich, 1370–1800* (1935; repr. 1969).

Sumter, Fort: see FORT SUMTER.

Sumter, Thomas

Known as the "gamecock of the Revolution," Thomas Sumter, b. Hanover County, Va., Aug. 14, 1734, d. June 1, 1832, led rebel guerrilla forces during the American Revolution. When the British won control of South Carolina in 1780, he, Francis Marion, and other partisan fighters kept the rebel cause alive south of Virginia until the victory at Yorktown a year later. After the war he represented South Carolina as a U.S. congressman (1789–93, 1797–1801) and senator (1801–09). Fort Sumter in Charleston was named in his honor.

Sun

The Sun, the central body of the SOLAR SYSTEM and the closest STAR, is an immense sphere of glowing gas 1.39 million km (860,000 mi) in diameter at an average distance from the Earth of 149,591,000 km (92,960,000 mi). It is composed mainly of hydrogen, with about 5 percent by number of helium and heavier elements. Its mass of 1.99×10^{33} g is sufficient for the mutual gravitational attraction of the molecules to prevent the hot solar gases from expanding rapidly into the relative vacuum of interstellar space. The Sun generates energy at the rate of 3.9×10^{33} ergs/sec by burning hydrogen to helium through nuclear FUSION reactions in its interior. This energy is radiated into space mostly in visible and infrared light and is largely responsible for the continuation of life on our planet.

Compared with the largest known stars, with diameters a thousand times larger and masses several hundred times greater, the Sun merits its astronomical designation as a dwarf star. Its mass and radius are close to the average mass and size of all stars in the Galaxy, however, because many stars are even smaller and less massive than ours. The Sun's spectrum, surface temperature, and color lead to its further classification as a G2 dwarf in the scheme of spectral types used by astronomers. The spectral intensity of light radiated by its surface gases is a maximum at wavelengths near 5000 Å, thus giving sunlight its characteristic yellow color.

Modern study of the Sun began in 1611 with Galileo's observations of sunspots and his discovery of solar rotation from their motions. The first approximately correct determination of the Sun's size and distance from the Earth was made in 1684, from data obtained by the French Academy from triangulation observations of Mars during its close approach to the Earth in 1672. The discovery of the solar absorption-line spectrum by Joseph von Fraunhofer in 1814, and its physical interpretation by Gustav Kirchhoff in 1859, opened the era of solar astrophysics, during which the effective study of the physical state and chemical composition of the solar material became possible. The strong magnetic fields of sunspots were detected by George Ellery Hale in 1908, and the role of nu-

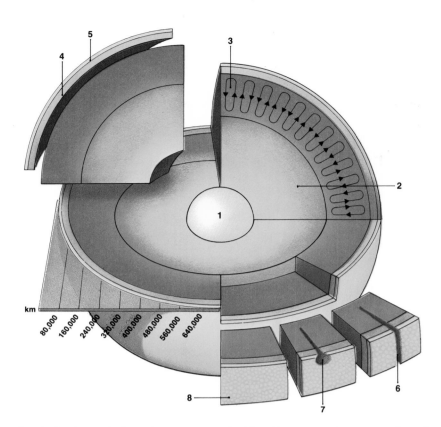

The Sun's energy is produced by nuclear fusion in the central core (1). The energy is transported mainly by radiation in the surrounding region (2) and then by circulating currents of gas in the convection zone (3), a 150,000-km-thick (93,000-mi) region just below the visible surface, or photosphere (4). The photosphere in turn is surrounded by the chromosphere (5). Features such as a dark filament (6) or sunspot (7) may appear on the granular-textured (8) solar surface.

clear fusion in producing solar energy was elucidated by Hans Bethe in 1939. Modern developments continue to change scientists' perception of the Sun. The solar wind was not detected directly until 1962, and the sources of its high-speed recurrent streams awaited the observations of coronal holes in 1969.

STRUCTURE OF THE SUN

From its innermost core to its corona, and to the solar wind that extends even to the Earth, the Sun has a structure typical of most stars of its kind.

Inner Core. The weight of the Sun's outer layers compresses the gas of the innermost region to a density about 100 times that of water and raises the central temperature to about 15 million K (27,000,000° F). Throughout the Sun's interior, atoms collide frequently and with enough energy to ionize the gas, which is then referred to as a plasma (see PLASMA PHYSICS). In the inner third of the Sun the collisions among ions are energetic enough to cause nuclear reactions at a rate sufficient to liberate the energy required to give the Sun's observed luminosity. The specific set of reactions thought to be most effective in generating energy in the Sun involves the burning of hydrogen to helium, following the specific sequence of reactions known as the PROTON-PROTON REACTION. Present evidence suggests that the plasma of the central nuclear burning region of the Sun is not mixed with the material in the outer shells. Thus the proton-proton reaction will continue only until the hydrogen of the central region, some 10 percent of the Sun's mass, becomes transformed into helium after about 10 billion years. The Sun's age is estimated to be about 5 billion years (see STELLAR EVOLUTION). The gamma rays and X rays emitted by the nuclear reactions travel outward with little absorption through the solar interior, because the electrons that allow an atom to absorb light have mostly been stripped from the nuclei by interatomic collisions.

The Convection Zone and the Photosphere. Nearer the Sun's visible surface, as the weight of overlying gas diminishes, the gas pressure and thus the density and temperature required to support this layer in hydrostatic equilibrium decrease rapidly. At a distance of about two-thirds the solar radius from the center, where the temperature has dropped to about 1 million K, the hydrogen and helium are no longer completely ionized. The neutral atoms absorb radiation moving outward from the central nuclear burning regions. In this region the heating and consequent expansion of parcels of the fluid cause them to rise because of their lower densities, and transport their heat upward. The net upward flux of heat carried by the resulting pattern of up- and down-flowing convection is the dominant mode of energy transport in the outer third of the Sun. Convection continues to be efficient in transporting heat until layers are reached where the density is so low that radiation from the hot up-flowing gas can escape directly into space. This layer is the visible surface of the Sun, known as the photosphere. Direct evidence for the size scales, velocities, and shapes of solar convective scales can be deduced from observations of convectionlike cellular motions at the photosphere. Small-scale cells called granules are about 1,000 km (620 mi) in diameter and are formed by hot up-flowing gases, surrounded by cooler down-flowing gases, moving about 1 km/sec (22,000 mph). Supergranules form a larger set of polygonal cells, of diameter roughly 30,000 km (18,600 mi), detected by their horizontal velocities of about 0.5 km/sec (1,100 mph).

In addition to transporting heat, convective motions of the Sun's gases are also thought to have important consequences for solar rotation, solar magnetism, and for the structure of the Sun's outer layers above the photosphere. Convection may help to explain the observation that the gases of the solar photosphere do not rotate rigidly—the angular rate at the equator is some 50 percent higher than that at latitudes of ±75 degrees. Although a satisfactory theory of this basic solar property does not yet exist, models of the fluid mechanics of rotating, convecting shells indicate that such velocity differences might result from the forces exerted upon rising and falling convecting gases as the Sun rotates about its axis at the observed sidereal rate of about 25 days at the solar equator. The angular rotation rate also appears to increase inward, at least immediately below the photosphere, at a rate of 5 percent in the first 15,000 km (9,300 mi).

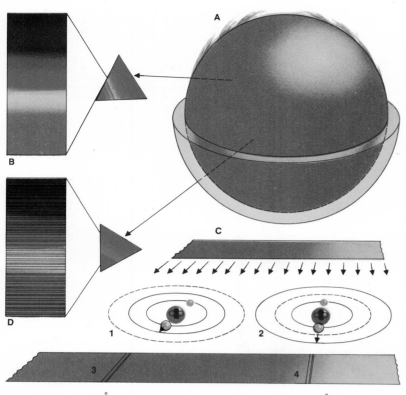

(Left) *The light energy produced in the interior of the Sun (A), if seen unobstructed, would produce a continuous spectrum (B; detail, C) when analyzed by a spectroscope. As the light passes through the outer layers of the Sun, however, it excites some of the electrons orbiting around the nuclei of, for example, helium atoms, lifting them to various higher energy states (1, 2). The consequent absorption of energy produces characteristic dark absorption, or Fraunhofer, lines (3, 4) in the spectrum. An actual solar spectrum (D) is therefore crossed by many lines characteristic of each of the elements present in the Sun.*

(Below) *The presence of iron in the Sun is confirmed when the characteristic emission lines of iron (top and bottom) are compared with the solar spectrum (center). The additional lines in the solar spectrum indicate the presence of other elements.*

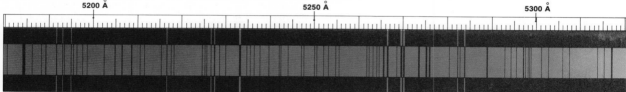

5200 Å   5250 Å   5300 Å

The Sun's magnetic field, observed at the photosphere, does not have the basic north-south dipole symmetry observed in the terrestrial magnetic field at the Earth's surface. The solar field lines seem to be wound around the Sun's rotation axis and roughly follow lines of constant latitude, rather than longitude. This property is inferred from the observed alternation of magnetic polarity in bipolar sunspot groups. The magnetic dipole axes of such groups tend to be oriented east-west, and within a given hemisphere (above or below the solar equator) the western half of all dipoles is generally of the same magnetic polarity. The polarity of dipoles in the northern and southern hemispheres is opposite. This law of alternation of polarities is called the Hale-Nicholson law.

The plasma of the solar convection zone is about as good a conductor as copper wire under room-temperature conditions. When a large volume of this material moves through a magnetic field, as in solar convection, it induces a large electric current that deforms the original field so as to displace it along with the motion. The mutual influence of magnetic fields and moving plasmas is known as MAGNETOHYDRODYNAMICS (MHD). MHD studies show that the Sun's differential rotation will tend to stretch and pull out magnetic-field lines into the observed toroidal geometry.

Near the photosphere the known temperature, the mean molecular weight, and the acceleration of solar gravity indicate that the density decreases hydrostatically at the rapid rate of a factor of ten roughly every 1,000 km (620 mi) radially outward. This rapid decrease explains the sharp edge or limb of the Sun, even when seen with telescopes, because the shell in which the gas passes from being opaque to transparent is less than 1,000 km (620 mi) thick, and subtends less

than 1 arc second as viewed from the Earth. When looking at the center of the Sun's disk, it is possible to see deeper into the absorbing solar atmosphere than when looking toward the limb, where the line of sight is more nearly tangent to the photosphere. Because the temperature increases inward below the photosphere, the line of sight toward the center of the disk sees hotter, and thus brighter, layers. This phenomenon explains the prominent limb darkening seen in pictures of the photosphere.

A spectrogram of the solar light shows a bright background continuum traversed by many dark absorption lines. The continuum radiation that is visible to the eye, roughly between 4000 Å and 7000 Å, is emitted when electrons released from the relatively easily ionized heavy elements are captured by neutral hydrogen atoms. The dark Fraunhofer lines, such as the H and K lines of ionized calcium, are formed when light of certain discrete wavelengths is preferentially scattered by the particular species of neutral atoms or ions that are abundant at the density and temperature of the photosphere. The light emerging through the photosphere at these wavelengths is changed in frequency by multiple scattering of the photons from atoms and rapidly moving electrons, and is emitted instead in the continuum.

The Chromosphere. Above the photosphere, the temperature drops to a minimum of about 4,500 K, and then, remarkably enough, begins to rise. During a few seconds around totality during a solar eclipse, a thin ring (annulus) about 10,000 km (6,200 mi) thick around the limb is seen shining with a reddish glow, leading to its designation as the chromosphere ("color sphere"). Upon examination with a telescope and spectrograph at high resolution, most of the chromospheric

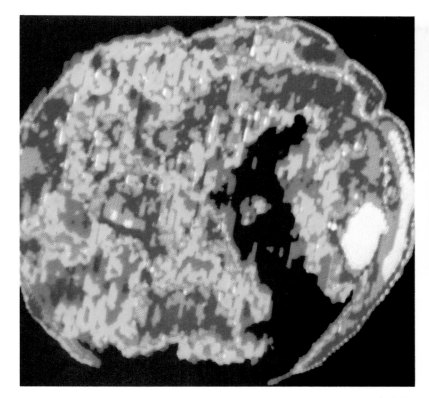

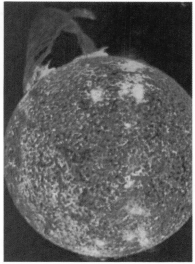

(Above) *An eruptive prominence—a hot, bright cloud of gas—is seen in a* Skylab *photograph taken in the far ultraviolet. The Sun's magnetic field causes the erupted material to fall back along looping paths.*

(Left) *A false-color* Skylab *photograph taken in the ultraviolet and soft X-ray range of the spectrum reveals the presence of a dark coronal hole, where almost no radiation is emitted, and white hot spots.*

emission is seen to come from very fine jets of outward-moving gas called spicules, at a temperature of about 15,000 K and a density of some 10^{11} particles/cm³. A spicule lasts some 5 to 10 minutes and is typically 6,000 km (3,700 mi) high and perhaps one-tenth as thick. The gases are moving outward at speeds of about 10 km/sec (22,000 mph).

The Corona. During a total solar eclipse, or with a CORONA-GRAPH, the Sun's atmosphere can be seen extending to several solar radii beyond the photospheric limb as a faint glow, about one million times less bright than the disk. In a hydrostatic atmosphere at temperatures observed even in the chromosphere, however, the density should drop off so rapidly that no corona would be visible at distances of even a small fraction of solar radius above the limb. The explanation for this discrepancy came in 1940 when certain unidentified lines seen in the spectrum of the corona were demonstrated as arising from transitions in iron ionized up to 13 times, implying temperatures of several million K. Because a hot gas is expected to be compressed relatively less by the weight of overlying layers than a cool one, the high coronal temperature explained why the corona remains visible much farther above the limb than might be expected.

The specific mechanism that heats the corona to such a high temperature is still unclear, and this question is the focus of much of modern solar research from satellites. The coronal gas close to the Sun is visible with the naked eye during eclipses because it scatters photospheric light from electrons in the plasma. The hot coronal plasma also emits its own ultraviolet and X-ray light when rapidly moving electrons collide with ions of the heavier elements. For instance, the lines of 9-times-ionized magnesium and 11-times-ionized silicon are prominent in the ultraviolet spectrum. The heating of the corona is not a matter of simple heat flow from the cooler photosphere, by either conduction, convection, or radiation, because such a heat flow would violate the second law of thermodynamics. Most likely, acoustic or other forms of waves generated by gas motions at the photosphere may carry energy into the coronal medium and dissipate it into heat, balancing the corona's losses. Another alternative is dissipation of electric currents in the highly conducting coronal

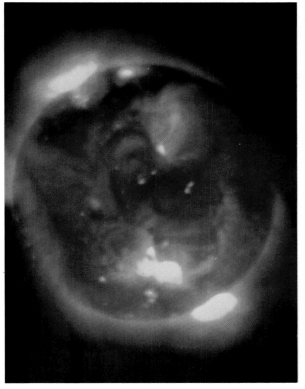

Computer-generated false colors, which bring out contrasts in detail, were also used in this Skylab *X-ray photograph taken on May 28, 1973. Within the hot, bright corona, or outer layer of the Sun's atmosphere, are coronal-hole regions of reduced density and temperature.*

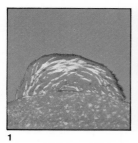

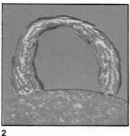

1   2   6

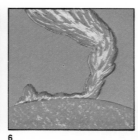

(Below) *This sequence of photographs, taken over a period of several hours, reveals the dynamic nature of prominence activity above the Sun's surface. The photographs were made with the aid of a coronagraph and a polarization filter at a wavelength of 6374 Å. Prominences are luminous clouds of gas in the Sun's corona.*

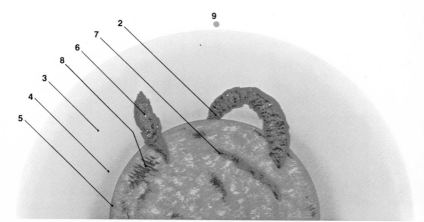

(Above) *Quiescent (1) and loop (2) prominences are formed when material condensing in the corona (3) falls back through the chromosphere (4) to the photosphere (5), or surface, of the Sun along lines of magnetic flux. An eruptive prominence (6), on the other hand, consists of material that has been ejected above the photosphere to distances as great as 300,000 km (190,000 mi). An explosive release of energy occurs in a solar flare (7), which appears as a brilliant flash of light in the upper chromosphere and the lower corona. Spicules (8) are small, vertical, jetlike spikes of gas in the chromosphere that rise and subside for several minutes. The Earth (9) is dwarfed when compared in size to these solar features.*

plasma, in much the same way that joule heating raises the temperature of a common resistor.

The Solar Wind. Because the outward gradient of gas pressure in the hot corona is too high to be balanced by solar gravity, this outermost layer of the atmosphere expands into space at a steady rate. At the Earth's orbit, the outward velocity of this SOLAR WIND reaches between 300 and 700 km/sec (185 and 435 mi/sec). The density there, however, is only between 1 and 10 particles/cm³, so that the mass flux is only about 10^{-13} solar masses per year. Nevertheless the solar wind has observable effects on the upper atmosphere of the Earth; for instance, it is thought to be responsible for most of the auroras seen at high terrestrial latitudes.

SOLAR ACTIVITY

The intense magnetic fields produced in the solar interior influence the physical structure of the photosphere, chromosphere, and corona in a complex and time-varying way described collectively as solar activity.

Sunspots, Faculae, and Flares. The magnetic fields emerge at the visible layers as toroidal loops of magnetic flux up to 100,000 km (62,000 mi) in diameter. Their most obvious effect at the photosphere is to produce the dark SUNSPOTS and bright faculae that constitute an active region. If, as believed, the intense radially directed fields inhibit convection, and thus reduce the efficiency of the dominant heat-transport process to the photosphere, the low temperature and relative darkness of sunspots would be explained. How intense fields can also produce a net facular brightening under similar circumstances is still unclear.

An active region grows in horizontal extent as the loop emerges, from less than 5,000 km (3,100 mi) across, to more

The corona, or outermost portion of the Sun's atmosphere, can be seen during a solar eclipse, such as the one that occurred on Mar. 7, 1970, when this photograph was taken. The atoms of the corona are highly ionized, indicating temperatures exceeding 1 million K.

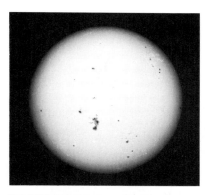

A high amount of sunspot activity was occurring when this photograph of the Sun was taken. Some sunspots have become large enough to be seen by the naked eye when the Sun is at a low altitude and its brightness is consequently weakened.

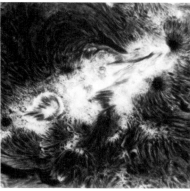

Features of an active region of the Sun are seen in detail in this high-resolution photograph. The darkest round spots are sunspots, the bright region is the site of a solar flare, and the thick dark lines are filaments.

than 100,000 km (62,100 mi) within 10 days. During this period of rapid growth the probability of a spectacular eruption, called a SOLAR FLARE, is highest. A large flare is marked by a rapid brightening within a few minutes of a considerable area of the active region by a factor of 5 to 10, as seen in chromospheric radiations such as the H alpha line of hydrogen. Only the very largest flares can be detected in integrated white light against the bright photosphere. The most violent and spectacular effects of the eruption, however, take place in the corona above. Here, a set of the magnetic loops above the spots and faculae may increase their brightness in X-ray and ultraviolet light by a factor of 100 or more, even more rapidly than the change seen in the chromosphere. Charged particles are accelerated to relativistic energies, and strong centimeter-wave emission is generally detected.

Some flares also produce powerful meter-wave radio bursts, and large volumes of hot plasma, called sprays, are often ejected into space at speeds exceeding the escape velocity of 617 km/sec (380 mi/sec) from the solar gravitational field. The cataclysmic event decays more slowly, over a few hours, after liberating up to 10^{32} ergs of energy, by a mechanism that is not well understood and is at the center of current research.

Sunspots generally last a few weeks, with the most persistent large spots surviving for 2 to 3 months. The faculae continue to mark an active region for somewhat longer. Eventually, it appears that the random motions of convection near the photosphere disassemble the magnetic flux loop and disperse it into smaller magnetic elements distributed over the solar surface.

Away from the active regions, less extended fields of comparable intensity (1,000 to 2,000 gauss) are measured, but they are confined to a polygonal network that coincides with the edges of the supergranular convective cells mentioned above.

Loops, Prominences, and Coronal Holes. Above the photosphere the magnetic fields over an active region can be seen by their effect on the distribution of temperature and density in the chromosphere and corona. Here, prominent loop-shaped structures seen in X rays and ultraviolet light show how the field lines extend to 100,000 km (62,000 mi) or more above a spot, and then connect back to the photosphere,

generally within the same active region. In other regions of the corona immense sheets of relatively cool (10,000 K as opposed to the 1 to 3 million K of the corona) condensed plasma, called prominences, are supported at heights up to 200,000 km (124,000 mi).

In certain large areas, called coronal holes, the coronal emission is significantly depressed, indicating a low density of the million-degree plasma. Studies indicate that in these regions the field lines continue radially outward and do not form closed structures, as in loops or prominences. Models show that the hot corona can then flow out into interplanetary space more easily, leaving a deficit of coronal material. Such holes are particularly common at the north and south solar poles, where no active regions with closed fields are observed.

Solar Activity Cycle. A time-lapse film of the Sun shows such complex structures and time variations that it comes somewhat as a surprise that solar activity exhibits a remarkably regular cycle over a period of 22 years. The most easily observed feature of the cycle is the approximately 11-year variation in the number of sunspots on the disk.

At the beginning of a new cycle the first groups emerge at relatively high latitudes, between 35 and 40 degrees. Their magnetic polarity (orientation of the dipole axis in solar coordinates) is opposite to that of the last groups of the preceding cycle in that hemisphere. Thus two consecutive 11-year cycles of spot number are required to return to a given level of spot number and also of spot group polarity.

This 22-year solar magnetic cycle seems to have been quite regular in the past 100 years and more. Historical evidence, however, indicates that between approximately 1640 and 1710 hardly any spots were visible at all, suggesting that the present range of solar activity cannot be taken for granted.

Such long-term irregularities in solar activity are of practical interest, because the solar fluxes of charged particles and ultraviolet radiation are directly controlled by the level of activity through active regions, flares, and coronal holes. The solar variation in these emissions is known to affect the upper atmosphere and may have important influences on climate as well. Solar-terrestrial effects are under close study.

RECENT DEVELOPMENTS

The Sun is about 250,000 times closer than the next nearest star, but it is not well understood. The proton-proton reaction thought to produce most of the solar energy output also produces an accurately calculable number of elementary particles called neutrinos. An experiment operated since the late 1960s to measure these elusive particles, which are able to pass directly through the Sun's interior, has detected significantly fewer neutrinos than the quantity predicted by models of the solar nuclear processes. This experiment provides the only direct check on how the Sun and other stars produce their enormous energy output; thus the resolution of this discrepancy is of fundamental importance.

In the early 1960s radial oscillations of the photosphere were detected during measurements of the gas velocities and brightness at that surface. The cause of this oscillation, most prominent around a period of 5 minutes, has recently been explained as the resonant trapping of acoustic waves between certain layers of the convection zone, similar to the oscillations of air in an organ pipe. Close study of these oscillations is under way to probe the density, temperature, and velocity structure of the invisible subphotospheric layers. Some less certain observations also suggest longer-period pulsations of the Sun that may give similar information about the even deeper, radiative layers of the interior.   PETER FOUKAL

Bibliography: Baxter, W. M., *The Sun and the Amateur Astronomer,* rev. ed. (1973); Brandt, John, *The Sun and the Stars* (1966); Ellison, M. A., *The Sun and Its Influence,* 3d ed. (1968); Gibson, Edward G., *The Quiet Sun* (1972); Kiepenheuer, Karl, *The Sun* (1959); Menzel, Donald H., *Our Sun,* rev. ed. (1959); Moore, Patrick, *The Sun* (1968).

Sun Also Rises, The

Ernest Hemingway's first novel, *The Sun Also Rises* (1926), is a semiautobiographical account of the adventures of a group of expatriates, members of the so-called lost generation, in France and Spain in 1925. They are led by Jake Barnes, a journalist. Although a war wound has made Jake impotent, he and Robert Cohn, another American romantic, are rivals for the attentions of Lady Brett Ashley. The action moves from Paris to Pamplona and the fiesta of San Fermin, where the real hero, a bullfighter named Pedro Romero, conquers several bulls as well as Lady Brett, who nobly rejects her Spanish lover and returns hopelessly to Jake.   CARLOS BAKER

Bibliography: White, William, ed., *The Merrill Studies in The Sun Also Rises* (1969).

sun bittern

The sun bittern, *Eurypyga helias,* is a secretive bird that inhabits tropical forests of Central and South America. These birds live quietly alone or in pairs along the edges of streams or swampy areas and feed on insects, crustacea, and small fishes. Sun bitterns sometimes display peculiar behaviors. They spread their wings laterally with the leading edge lowered and raise and spread the tail between the hind edges of the wings. It is believed to be a threatening posture. The soft plumage is intricately mottled with black, gray, white, and brown. Black bands cross the fan-shaped tail, and the long and broadly rounded wings have bold patterns of black, gray, white, and chestnut. White stripes are prominent above and below the eyes. The long legs are orange, and the bill is long and straight. Sun bitterns are about 41 cm (16 in) in length and weigh approximately 220 g (8 oz). Both sexes are alike. The nest of mud and sticks is built on the ground or in a low bush or tree. Both sexes incubate the two or three eggs, which are pink with brown spots, and care for the downy young. The sun bittern is the only member of the family Eurypygidae in the rails order Gruiformes.   ROBERT J. RAIKOW

Sun dance

The Sun dance, a traditional summer ceremony of the Plains Indians, was most highly elaborated among the ARAPAHO, CHEYENNE, and SIOUX (Dakota) and was present in some of its elements among the OMAHA, PAWNEE, and WICHITA. Physical pain was used to induce altered states of consciousness and a sense of exaltation. Means of accomplishing these goals were fasting, dancing for 3 or 4 days and nights, keeping eyes fixed on the Sun or a sacred object at the top of a pole, and dragging a heavy buffalo skull attached to skewers piercing the celebrant's flesh. Lapsed for a time because of government disapproval, the ritual has been revived since the 1960s as a way of preserving Indian identity and culture.   GENE WELFISH

Bibliography: Jorgensen, Joseph, *The Sun Dance Religion: Power for The Powerless* (1972); Walker, J. R., *The Sun Dance and Other Ceremonies of The Oglala Division of The Teton Dakota* (1977).

Sun Valley

Sun Valley (1970 pop., 180), a popular resort center in south central Idaho, lies 1,829 m (6,000 ft) above sea level, sheltered to the west and east by the Sawtooth Range of the Rockies. The development of its skiing and summer sports facilities was begun in 1936 by the Union Pacific Railroad.

Sun worship

Worship of the Sun occurred among many ancient peoples, especially in agrarian societies, in which survival depended on the light and heat of the Sun to bring crops to fruition. The daily journey of the Sun across the sky and its nightly disappearance and morning resurrection as well as the occurrence of solar eclipses formed a mystery that inspired various religious feelings among ancient peoples, who developed ceremonies, rituals, and sacrifices to honor and placate this life-force. The Sun appears as an element of religion and mythology in cultures as divergent as those of India, Africa,

Mesopotamia, Greece, the England of the Druids, Aztec Mexico, and among many Indian tribes of North America. Among the ancient Egyptians, Amon-Re, the sun-god, was regarded as the first king of Egypt.   CHARLES H. LONG

Bibliography: Cook, Arthur B., *Zeus: A Study in Ancient Religion* (1966); Eliade, Mircea, *Patterns in Comparative Religion* (1958); Halsberghe, Gaston H., *The Cult of Sol Invictus* (1972).

Sun Yat-sen   [suhn-yaht-sen]

The Chinese revolutionary leader Sun Yat-sen played a central role in the overthrow of the Ch'ing dynasty and was named (1911) provisional president of the new Republic of China. To unify the country he agreed (1912) to turn over authority to Yüan Shih-k'ai, but the latter's dictatorial methods soon drove Sun into opposition. Sun's ideology is summed up in his "Three People's Principles": nationalism, democracy, and the people's livelihood.

Sun Yat-sen, b. Nov. 12, 1866, d. Mar. 12, 1925, was the symbol and leader of the Chinese nationalist revolution and the first president of the republic that succeeded the Manchu, or CH'ING, dynasty in 1911. He is one of modern China's most revered political figures.

Born Sun Wen in Hsiang-Shan, Kwangtung province, the future father of the republic endured the hardships of peasant life as a boy and, fired by stories of the heroic Taiping Rebellion, resolved to carry on the fight begun by the Taiping leader Hung Hsiu-ch'uan (who also came from Kwangtung) to overthrow the alien Manchu rulers. After 3 years at a Christian school in Hawaii, Sun studied medicine in Canton and Hong Kong, graduating in 1892 and practicing briefly. In 1895, Sun, now an active revolutionary, was forced to flee China when a plot by his Hsing Chung hui (Revive China Society) went awry. Visits (1896) to the United States and England and his "kidnapping" by the Chinese legation in London brought him worldwide publicity and the beginning of support from overseas Chinese.

In Japan Sun founded (1905) the T'ung-meng hui (Alliance Society), with overseas offices, and issued (1907) a manifesto that contained an early version of his Three Principles of the People (San-min chu-i)—roughly translatable as nationalism, democracy, and the equalization of land ownership. Sun continued to publicize his revolutionary theories and to raise money from overseas supporters. When revolution finally erupted in 1911, Sun was named provisional president. He resigned (1912) the presidency of the new republic in favor of YÜAN SHIH-K'AI, whose power was needed if the republic were to survive. As the dictatorial policies and imperial ambitions of Yüan became clearer, however, Sun's colleague Sung Chiao-jen organized the KUOMINTANG (National People's party). The new party twice (1917 and 1921) set up a rival government in Canton. Sun's last years were spent as an elder statesman whose principles were sacrosanct. His tomb in Nanking became a national shrine. Sun's writings include his memoirs (1927).

Bibliography: Hsu, Immanuel C., *Rise of Modern China*, 2d ed. (1975); Schiffrin, Harold Z., *Sun Yat-sen and the Origins of the Chinese Revolution* (1968); Sharman, Lyon, *Sun Yat-sen: His Life and Its Meaning* (1934).

sunbird

Sunbirds, family Nectariniidae, are the Old World counterparts of our New World HUMMINGBIRDS and comprise 104 species who play a part in flower fertilization. They feed on nectar and insects gleaned from flowers. Like hummingbirds they have iridescent plumages, often with glittering throat patches. Sunbirds are widely distributed in the Old World tropics.

GEORGE WALLACE

Sunda Islands

The Sunda Islands of Indonesia lie between the Malay Peninsula and New Guinea, separating the Pacific from the Indian Ocean. The islands are divided into the Greater Sundas (BORNEO, JAVA, SULAWESI, SUMATRA) and the Lesser Sundas (BALI, TIMOR, and others).

Sunda Strait

The Sunda Strait is a major shipping lane between the Greater Sunda islands of Sumatra and Java. It links the Indian Ocean and the Java Sea and is about 26 km (16 mi) wide at its narrowest point. KRAKATOA, noted for its major volcanic eruption, lies in the strait.

Sundanese language: see MALAYO-POLYNESIAN LANGUAGES.

Sunday, Billy

William Ashley Sunday, b. Ames, Iowa, Nov. 19, 1862, d. Nov. 6, 1935, was a professional baseball player who became one of the most popular revivalists in American history. He played (1883–91) for the Chicago White Stockings before a conversion experience led him into YMCA work. After ordination as a Presbyterian minister, he began (1895) his career as a revivalist. He had a flamboyant style characterized by acrobatics and high-pressure techniques. His peak years of success were in the World War I period. Sunday was influential in the PROHIBITION movement and was associated with nativist movements calling for the Americanization of immigrants and restriction of immigration.

JOHN F. PIPER

Bibliography: Ellis, William T., *Billy Sunday* (1959); McLoughlin, William G., *Billy Sunday Was His Real Name* (1955) and *Modern Revivalism* (1959).

Sunday school

A Sunday school is a school for religious education, usually of children and young people. It is most often associated with a particular church or parish.

The first modern Sunday school was established in Gloucester, England, in 1780, by Robert Raikes. His work among prisoners convinced him that religious education would help keep young people out of jail. Because so many children worked in factories every day except Sunday, he formed a school that met on Sundays in the homes of lay teachers. The movement spread rapidly in England and Wales and was introduced in 1791 in the United States. It was less important in Europe where religious education was part of the school curriculum.

Sunday schools are usually associated with Protestant churches, although in the United States many Roman Catholic churches have them. Jewish religious study may take place in Sabbath schools.

Bibliography: Laqueuer, Thomas W., *Religion and Respectability: Sunday Schools and Working Class Culture, 1780-1850* (1976); Lyman, Robert W., *The Big Little School: Sunday Child of American Protestantism* (1971).

sundew: see CARNIVOROUS PLANTS.

sundial

The sundial, one of the earliest scientific instruments known, measures the time by a shadow cast from an indicator onto a surface that is marked off in time intervals. Examples from

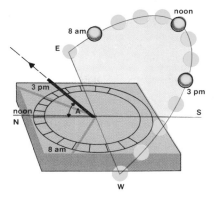

A sundial uses the changing position of a shadow to indicate the time of day. A raised pointer, or gnomon, is fixed to a horizontal plate at an angle equal to the latitude of the site, pointing north (angle A). The plate is marked off in hourly segments. As the Sun passes from east to west, the shadow of the gnomon moves through the divisions, indicating the hour.

Egypt dating from the 15th century BC and numerous large dials from early Greek cities can be seen in museums today. Small portable dials for personal use first appeared in Roman times and remained popular well into the 19th century.

The most common form of sundial measures the hour-angle of the Sun. Almost all garden dials are of this type. The rod or bar that casts the shadow is called the gnomon and is mounted so as to be parallel with the axis of the Earth. Hour-angle dials show solar time correctly throughout the year without the necessity of adjusting them to a specific date. (A chart or table is often provided with these dials to convert true solar time to mean solar, or "clock," time.)

R. S. AND M. K. WEBSTER

Bibliography: Cousins, Frank W., *Sundials: The Art and Science of Gnomonics* (1970); Gibbs, Sharon L., *Greek and Roman Sundials* (1976); Mayall, R. Newton and Margaret W., *Sundials: How to Know, Use, and Make Them*, 2d ed. (1973); Rohr, René R. J., *Sundials: History, Theory, and Practice*, trans. by Gabriel Godin (1970); Waugh, Albert E., *Sundials: Their Theory and Construction* (1973).

sunfish

Sunfishes comprise 30 species of freshwater, spiny-rayed teleosts (bony fish) of the family Centrarchidae found in North America. The larger sunfishes are solitary, and all sunfishes are very sensitive to changes in their environment, particularly temperature changes. The Sacramento perch is the only native American species west of the Rocky Mountains and the only species that does not nest.

The genus *Lepomis* is the largest group of sunfishes. Most are small, from 8 to 25 cm (3 to 10 in). The most familiar species is the bluegill sunfish, *L. macrochirus,* which is known to reach a weight of 1.75 kg (4.75 lb). Other species familiar to fishermen include the redear, pumpkinseed, and longeared sunfishes. *Lepomis* species prefer the shallow, weedy margins of lakes and streams. Like all centrarchids, the male builds a breeding nest and entices a female to the nest, where she

The pygmy sunfish, E. gloriosus (foreground), *and the black-banded sunfish,* M. chaetodon (background), *are bred as aquarium fish.*

lays a number of eggs. After the male has fertilized the eggs he chases the female away and guards the nest against any intruder until they hatch. *Lepomis* is frequently stocked in ponds and lakes with largemouth bass to provide forage for the bass and fishing for the angler.

Pygmy, or blue-spotted, sunfishes, *Enneacanthus gloriosus,* are from the eastern and southern United States and reach about 9 cm (3.5 in) in length. The dwarf sunfishes (genus *Elassoma*), which include three known species from the southern United States, reach only 4 cm (1.5 in) in length and are primarily inhabitants of swamps and backwaters. Their relationship to other sunfishes is a subject of controversy. Centrarchids are not closely related to the OCEAN SUNFISH (*Mola mola*) found throughout the world in warm seas.

E. O. WILEY

sunflower

Sunflower, genus *Helianthus,* refers to any of 60 New World plant species in the daisy family, Compositae. Primarily native to North America, they are annuals or perennials with large and colorful heads of yellow flowers. The common sunflower, *H. annuus,* is cultivated for its edible seeds, which are used as food for poultry and birds and for vegetable oil and oleomargarine. The roots of *H. tuberosus* comprise the inulin-rich Jerusalem artichoke, which is eaten as a vegetable and often pickled. These plants are propagated by their tubers. The globe artichoke that humans consume is a large flower head, not a tuber; it belongs to a different genus.   JANE PHILPOTT

Sung   (Song)   (dynasty)   [soong]

During the reign of the Sung dynasty of China (960–1279), a time of great cultural achievement, occurred the flowering of the Chinese system of bureaucratic centralization and economic regulation initiated under the preceding T'ang. The founder of the Sung, **Chao K'uang-yin** (927–76; r. 960–76), a general whose seizure of the throne ended the series of short reigns known as the Five Dynasties, put the military under civil administration to prevent the militarism that had brought down the T'ang. In general, the Sung was not militarily powerful; however, the early Sung achieved broad geographic control through Chao's conquests and boasted a large, strong central bureaucracy. Rapid commercial expansion fostered the growth of trade guilds and the use of paper currency. Radical reformer WANG AN-SHIH (1021–86) introduced, over bitter opposition, such regulatory measures as price stabilization, loans to businessmen and peasants, and the establishment of emergency grain reserves.

A resurgence of cultural activity made the Sung one of the high points in Chinese intellectual and artistic history. Perfecting earlier styles, such painters as MI FEI, MA YÜAN, and HSIA KUEI carried Chinese landscape painting to its highest peak. Porcelain ware, particularly the green celadons, became famous all over the world. Scholarship was stimulated by the invention of movable type, although printing from woodblocks remained primary. There was a great output of poetry; professional storytelling and colloquial drama found favor among the people. A Confucian revival infused with Buddhistic elements was molded in the 12th century by CHU HSI into a philosophical synthesis known as Neo-Confucianism, which served as the new orthodoxy for seven centuries.

In 1127, Jürchen tribes drove the Sung dynasty south of the Yangtze. The Southern Sung ruled from Hangchow until 1279, when it was overthrown by the Mongol army that established the Yüan dynasty.

Bibliography: Latourette, Kenneth S., *The Chinese: Their History and Culture,* 2 vols., 4th ed. (1964); Meskill, John, ed., *An Introduction to Chinese Civilization* (1973).

Sung Hui-tsung   (Song Huizong)   [soong hwey dzung]

Sung Hui-tsung, b. 1082, d. June 4, 1135, was the 8th emperor of the Northern Sung dynasty. Perhaps best known as an artist, he is famous for his meticulously rendered bird-and-

flower paintings and for his so-called slender-gold calligraphy style. He presided over a new imperial academy of painting outstanding in the history of Chinese art. An avid collector, Hui-tsung acquired more than 6,300 paintings for the imperial gallery. His patronage extended to music, poetry, and the minor arts.

Politically, Hui-tsung's reign (1101–26) proved disastrous. At first he attempted reforms but later increasingly left affairs of state to his minister Ts'ai Ching and other favorites. Corruption and intrigue weakened the government, and nomadic tribes constantly threatened China's borders. An unfortunate alliance with the Chin (Jürchen) Tatars and their subsequent treachery resulted in the loss of North China. On Jan. 18, 1126, Hui-tsung abdicated in favor of his son, Ch'in-tsung. When the capital, K'ai-feng, fell (1127) to the Chin, both emperors were captured and taken to Manchuria, where Hui-tsung died.   LILLY WEI

Bibliography: Eberhard, Wolfram, *The History of China,* 4th ed. (1977); Fitzgerald, C. P., *China: A Short Cultural History* (1961).

sunlamp

A sunlamp, consisting of a fluorescent tube and a mercury vapor lamp, produces a spectrum of radiation that is similar to that of the Sun. As a result, even though a sunlamp can be used for therapeutic purposes or for artificially inducing a skin tan, it should be used with caution. Sunlight, both artificial and natural, damages the skin, causes it to age prematurely, and is toxic in extreme doses. Some evidence even indicates that skin cancers show an increased incidence in skin overexposed to sunlight. Most sunlamps do not produce light across the complete spectrum and therefore are less harmful than natural sunlight; the strong ultraviolet component in all of them, however, makes irritation of the eyes a serious risk, and eye protection has to be worn to filter out the harmful bands.

Sunlamps that produce rays with a wavelength below 2400 Å, known as abiotic rays, destroy life and can be used, for example, to sterilize the ulcers and bedsores of bedridden patients by killing the bacteria present. Other beneficial effects of artificial sunlight include the formation of vitamin D in those people who have rickets—a disorder involving a deficiency of vitamin D—and also increased blood circulation in the skin. Its use is discouraged in cases of tuberculosis because it may cause the disease to flare acutely.

DONALD LONGMORE

Sunnites

The term *Sunnites* refers to the great majority of the world's Muslims (see ISLAM), distinguishing them as the *ahl al-sunna wal-jamaa* ("the people of the sunna and the community") from the SHIITES. Sunnites are, by this definition, Muslims who strictly follow the sunna (practices) of the Prophet MUHAMMAD and preserve the unity and integrity of the community. Anyone who stands within the mainstream of the Islamic tradition and acts in accordance with generally accepted practices of the community is, therefore, a Sunni. Most Muslims see the sunna as complementary to the KORAN insofar as it explains certain points and elaborates some Koranic principles by offering details necessary for the practice of Islamic law.   WILLEM A. BIJLEFELD

sunset laws

Sunset laws establish procedures for analyzing and reviewing a government agency or program after a given period of time in order to determine whether or not that program is continuing to perform a useful and necessary purpose and whether or not it should be continued or eliminated. Most sunset laws provide for evaluation and, if justified, reauthorization of programs at fixed intervals varying from 3 to 10 or more years. Under such legislation, funding for those agencies or programs deemed to have outlived their purpose or those that no longer function economically would be terminated and thus allowed to die—hence the name *sunset laws.* In April 1976, Colorado became the first state to adopt sunset laws. About half of the states have since implemented these laws, and federal sunset legislation has been under consideration for a number of years. Proponents of sunset bills claim that such laws are the panacea for unresponsive and expensive bureaucracy. Critics assert that the cost of the reviewing process—creation of investigative units, salaries of trained administrators, and so on—often cancel out or exceed the savings derived from the process.   JAMES GREIFF

sunspots

A sunspot is a strongly magnetic and relatively dark area of the photosphere of the SUN. The darkest central area of a sunspot, the umbra, is roughly circular in shape and typically 18,000 km (11,000 mi) in diameter. The umbra is surrounded by a somewhat less dark annular region, the penumbra, roughly doubling the umbral diameter. The surface brightness of the umbral area is only about 20% of the corresponding total brightness of the undisturbed photosphere. The decreased emission corresponds to that of an (idealized) perfect blackbody radiator at the effective temperature of 3,700 K, compared to the photospheric effective temperature of 5,800 K. The corresponding relative brightness of the penumbra is about 75%, and its effective temperature is 5,400 K.

Spots are distributed on the Sun mainly between ±40° solar latitude. A common statistical measure of the frequency of occurrence of spots is the Wolf sunspot number, an empirical parameter derived from the daily number of individual spots and spot groups observed on the disk. Spots occur in bipolar magnetic groups, whose dipole axes tend to be oriented in the east-west direction. In such a dipole, the solar magnetic field extends as a tube of magnetic flux from below the photosphere, forms a loop above the surface in the corona, and then resubmerges into the solar interior, generally in a spot of opposite magnetic polarity. Magnetic field intensities up to 4,000 gauss have been measured in spot umbrae.

The development of a typical sunspot group begins when a loop of magnetic flux emerges from the solar interior through the photosphere. Several small spots become visible and move apart, growing in size over the next 5 to 10 days. The group decays more slowly over a period of several weeks. The longest-lived large spots remain for several months.

The physical mechanisms responsible for the rapid formation of an intense, extended sunspot field, for its relatively long lifetime, and for its gradual decay are not yet well understood. Neither is it known why some strong magnetic fields produce a dark sunspot at the photosphere, while other, apparently equally strong, fields nearby produce FACULAE, or photospheric brightenings. There is general agreement that the sunspot magnetic fields are generated in the Sun's convection zone and are transported to the photosphere by gas motions. Eventually the random motions of the ionized gas near the photosphere act to disassemble the strands of the magnetic flux tube and carry them at random across the surface.

A more difficult question is how a magnetic field of several thousand gauss can be squeezed and held together in a stable configuration for days, against the well-known tendency of magnetic field lines to push apart and distribute themselves evenly in a medium. Calculations show that the gas-pressure gradient between the cool umbra and its surroundings is sufficient to balance the expansion tendency caused by the observed magnetic-field gradient. This question is currently under intensive study. A second problem is to understand the low temperature of the gas in a spot. So far the best explanation seems to be that the strong radial magnetic field of an umbra makes it locally difficult for convection, the normally dominant energy-transport process, to carry heat to the photosphere.   PETER FOUKAL

Bibliography: Abell, George O., *Drama of the Universe* (1978); Bray, R. J., and Loughhead, R. E., *Sunspots* (1964); Eddy, John A., "The Case of the Missing Sunspots," *Scientific American*, May 1977; Ellison, M. A., *The Sun and Its Influence* (1956); Kiepenheuer, Karl, *The Sun* (1959); Menzel, Donald H., *Our Sun* (1959); Tandberg-Hanssen, E., *Solar Activity* (1967).

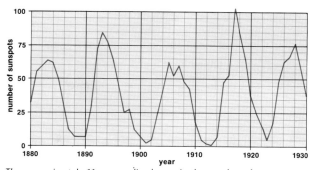

The approximately 11-year cyclic change in the number of sunspots observed is evident from the data plotted on this graph. Sunspot maxima, or times of the greatest number of sunspots, occurred in 1883, 1893, 1905, 1917, and 1928; sunspot minima, or times of the least number of sunspots, occurred in 1890, 1901, 1913, and 1923. The cycle is actually 22 years long because the polarity of the magnetic fields in the sunspots reverses every 11 years.

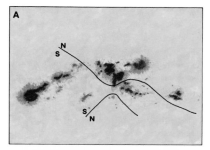

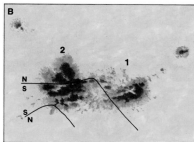

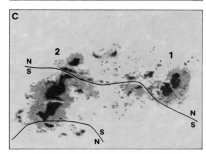

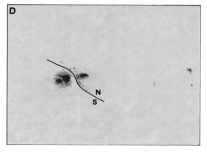

Upon detailed examination a sunspot is usually found to consist of two separate regions of smaller spots. Following the direction of solar rotation, these two regions are called the preceding and following spots. The dynamic nature of these two regions, which persist for no more than a few months, is seen in this 1947 sequence of a large bipolar group of sunspots. On February 11 (A) the distinction between the two regions is unclear visibly, but close examination of their spectra reveals their opposite polarity. The distinction between the preceding spot (1) and the following spot (2) is clearer in March 9 (B) and April 7 (C). Sunspot activity had virtually stopped in these regions by May 5 (D).

sunstone: see FELDSPAR.

sunstroke: see HEATSTROKE.

superconductivity

Superconductivity is a low-temperature phenomenon in which a metal loses all electrical resistance; electric currents can therefore flow through the metal without any dissipation of energy. In a ring of superconducting material, a current (the supercurrent) can thus flow indefinitely, provided the ring is always kept below the superconducting transition temperature (the threshold at which the metal becomes superconducting). The majority of metallic elements, as well as hundreds of intermetallic compounds and alloys, are superconducting. Most have their transition temperatures between 1 and 10 kelvin (K) above ABSOLUTE ZERO.

The low temperatures needed to achieve superconductivity were first attained in 1907 by Heike Kamerlingh-Onnes at the University in Leiden (Holland) when he succeeded in liquefying helium gas. Liquid helium boils at 4.2 K at atmospheric pressure, and by reducing the vapor pressure, the temperature of the liquid helium can be further reduced to 1 K. Superconductivity was first demonstrated in 1911 with mercury at a temperature below 4.15 K, and as more metals were subsequently found to superconduct it was also observed that superconductivity could be suppressed by moderate magnetic fields. Each superconductor is thus characterized by its transition temperature T_c and its critical magnetic field H_c. None of the ferromagnetic or antiferromagnetic metals are superconducting.

The Meissner Effect. In 1933 the German physicists W. Meissner and R. Ochsenfeld discovered that magnetic fields of strength less than the critical field do not penetrate superconductors, but rather are expelled from them (Meissner effect). This is strictly true only for ordinary, or Type I, superconductors, and they are said to be ideally diamagnetic. This property permits the state of a superconductor at temperature T and in a field H to be uniquely defined; that is, the state does not depend on whether the field was applied before or after the superconductor was cooled below T_c.

Two-Fluid Model. As a result, the Dutch physicists C. J. Gorter and H. B. G. Casimir were able to study the superconducting state thermodynamically. Based on the relation between heat capacity and temperature in the normal and superconducting state, they proposed the two-fluid model in 1934. This model assumes that in the superconducting state there are two components of the conduction electron "fluid." Below T_c an increasing fraction of the free conduction electrons condense into a state of lowest energy with zero entropy, in which they can still sustain electrical currents but transport no heat (the thermal conductivity of a superconductor much below T_c becomes indeed very small and similar to that of an insulating material). The other component behaves as normal electrons.

Type II Superconductors. There exist Type II superconductors, into which magnetic flux can penetrate at a first critical field H_{c1} (less than the Meissner field H_c) and which remain superconducting up to a much larger second critical field H_{c2}. The flux in Type II materials is arranged in a regular lattice of a large number of localized flux quanta (also called vortices). Using Type II superconductors, it is possible to build magnetic solenoids that generate high fields in relatively large volumes of material with virtually no power dissipation. A special technology of high-field superconductors has developed since 1960 and is now of considerable economic importance. Almost any material can be made to exhibit Type II behavior by alloying it with other metals. The most important high-field superconductors are those that have high transition temperatures, because such materials also exhibit high values of H_{c2}; examples are the niobium alloys Nb$_2$Zr (10.2 K), NbTi (9.5 K), and Nb$_3$Sn (18.1 K). By manufacturing these alloys with many imperfections and dislocations (by means of work-hardening), their supercurrent-carrying capacity is actually increased because the magnetic flux vortices are contained and

Critical Parameters of Some Superconducting Elements

Metal	T_c (kelvins)	H_c (oersteds)
Cadmium	0.56	30
Zinc	0.88	53
Aluminum	1.19	99
Indium	3.407	283
Tin	3.722	306
Mercury	4.15	411
Lead	7.18	803

kept from moving and dissipating energy. Supercurrent capacities of 15,000 amperes per cm^2 in fields of 100 kilooersteds have been achieved, and magnet coils capable of generating 150 kilooersteds are commercially available.

The same niobium alloys are now also considered for use in superconducting power-transmission lines. Although technically feasible, such lines are costly to build because of the necessity for keeping them at cryogenic (near absolute zero) temperatures. Only test sections have been built so far. Meanwhile, the search continues for metallic materials with higher transition temperatures. The highest T_c found so far is 21 K for the alloy Nb$_{12}$Al$_3$Ge.

The BCS Theory. A microscopic theory of superconductivity was presented in 1958 by John Bardeen, Leon N. Cooper, and John R. Schrieffer (the BCS theory), for which they were awarded the 1972 Nobel Prize. This theory postulates that the conduction electrons, which in the normal state move more or less freely and independently through the lattice of the positive metal ions, condense into a state where pairs of electrons are correlated with each other. In the pair state, the electrons can take advantage of the so-called quantum-mechanical zero-point motion of the positive ions in order to lower their energy. The theory predicts an energy gap between this ground state and higher excited states, increasing from zero at T_c to a maximum of 3.53 kT_c at very low temperatures (kT_c is the average thermal energy of an electron at $T = T_c$). The pairing prediction was confirmed by experiments on flux quantization; all other predictions of the BCS theory have also been well confirmed by experiments.

The Josephson Effect. In 1962, Brian D. Josephson in England predicted that if two superconductors are separated by only a thin insulating oxide layer, it is possible for the electron pairs to pass through this barrier (also called a tunnel junction). It is thus possible to sustain weak supercurrents in a ring of superconducting material containing such a junction. These currents (now called Josephson currents), as well as two other quantum mechanical effects—the direct current (DC) and alternating current (AC) Josephson effects—have important practical applications, such as the measurement of very small electrical currents, in computer memories, and for precision measurements of Planck's constant. The phase mismatch of the electron wave function on both sides of the tunnel junction depends on the magnetic flux through the ring and leads to periodic variations of the Josephson current. Commercially available so-called superconducting quantum interference devices (SQUIDs) based on this DC Josephson effect can detect flux changes of 10^{-10} oersted and current changes of 10^{-11} amperes. In the application for computer memories, a tiny superconducting loop with a tunnel junction is used to store the binary numbers 0 and 1 by switching the loop between the flux quantum states n and $n + 1$. Such memories, which are now being developed, promise to have a storage capacity per volume far greater than any existing solid-state memory.

KLAUS ANDRES

Bibliography: Basov, N. G., ed., *Superconductivity* (1977); Blatt, John M., *Theory of Superconductivity* (1964); Cohen, Morrel H., ed., *Superconductivity in Science and Technology* (1968); Kuper, Charles M., *Introduction to the Theory of Superconductivity* (1968); Lynton, E. A., ed., *Superconductivity*, 3d ed. (1969); Parks, R. D., ed., *Superconductivity*, 2 vols. (1969); Taylor, A. W. B., *Superconductivity* (1970); Tilley, David R., *Superfluidity and Superconductivity* (1974).

See also: CRYOGENICS; SUPERFLUIDITY.

superego

In PSYCHOANALYSIS, the superego is the part of the mind that has adopted the values of the parents and society. It competes with raw desires (the id) for the control of behavior.

superfluidity

Superfluidity is a peculiar state of matter exemplified by liquid helium at extremely low temperatures (see CRYOGENICS), characterized by frictionless flow and zero viscosity. Helium becomes a liquid at 4.2 K (4.2° C above absolute zero), which is the lowest boiling point of any substance. Liquid helium behaves like a normal fluid until it is cooled to 2.17 K, at which temperature its heat content Q drops dramatically and a peak develops in the curve for specific heat ($c = dQ/dT$) that resembles in shape the Greek letter lambda (λ). This transition temperature is therefore also called the lambda point. As the temperature is lowered further, an increasing fraction of the liquid condenses into a state of zero energy and zero viscosity in which it can flow unimpeded without any friction through the smallest orifices, provided only that the flow speed remains below a critical velocity (of order 300 cm/sec). If contained in a beaker, the walls of the beaker become covered with a superfluid liquid film that can rise to substantial heights (tens of centimeters) above the liquid level. An open beaker will slowly empty because the superfluid film flows over its edge and down the outer wall.

The apparent heat conductivity in the superfluid state is very high, about 100 times better than that of copper, but is a result of efficient hydrodynamic heat transport rather than actual heat conduction. If the liquid is heated in one region, superfluid is transformed into normal fluid there. The surrounding superfluid liquid (which can carry no heat, because the atoms are in the lowest energy state) constantly flows toward the hot spot while normal fluid constantly carries heat away from it.

Liquid helium does not solidify even at absolute zero unless a substantial pressure (25 atmospheres) is applied to it. This fact is explained by the theory of quantum mechanics to be due to the zero-point motion of the atoms, which, because of their small mass, is especially large and prevents the formation of a crystal lattice. In order to solidify at zero pressure the helium atoms would have to give up kinetic energy in an amount not allowed by quantum theory. The superfluid state is similarly explained by quantum theory, which restricts the energy levels of the superfluid so that normal friction and viscosity cannot occur.

The stable isotope ^{3}He also forms a superfluid, but one different from that of the natural isotope (^{4}He). Because ^{3}He lacks one neutron, it obeys a different set of statistics at low temperatures, a set that applies to conduction electrons in metals. Indeed, below about 0.2 K, many properties of the liquid are similar to those of conduction electrons (for example, specific heat, magnetic susceptibility, and thermal conductivity). Earlier speculations about a possible superfluid transition were rewarded by its discovery in 1972 by D. D. Oshcroff, W. J. Gully, R. C. Richardson, and D. M. Lee (Cornell University, United States) at a temperature of 0.0027 K. Although this superfluid state has many similarities with the superconducting state of electrons in metals, it is considerably more complex. Much lower superfluid critical flow velocities ($\sim$ 1 cm/sec) are observed.   KLAUS ANDRES

Bibliography: Allen, J. F., *Super-Fluid Helium* (1966); Bennemann, K. H., and Ketterson, J. B., *The Physics of Liquid and Solid Helium* (1976); London, F., *Superfluids* (1954); Mendelssohn, K., *Cryophysics* (1960); Tilley, David R., *Superfluidity and Superconductivity* (1974).

See also: SUPERCONDUCTIVITY.

supergiant

Supergiant stars are the brightest known stars. They are on the average about 10,000 times as bright absolutely as the Sun. In extreme cases they may be 100 times brighter still; such very bright stars are prominent in the Large MAGELLANIC CLOUD. Supergiants typically have masses ranging from 10 to 100 times the solar mass and radii varying from 20 to 1,000 times the solar radius. All spectral types occur among supergiants. They are young stars. Several of the brightest naked-eye stars are supergiants, including Rigel (β Orionis), Betelgeuse (α Orionis), Canopus (α Carinae), Antares (α Scorpii), and Deneb (α Cygni).   R. H. GARSTANG

superheavy elements

Superheavy elements are those chemical elements which have atomic numbers greater than 103. They are also referred to as the transactinide elements because they are heavier than the actinide elements. The atoms of superheavy elements have filled their $5f$ subshells with electrons, and elements 104 through 112 are expected to fill the $6d$ subshell, behaving chemically like a fourth series of TRANSITION ELEMENTS.

Element 104 was first claimed by Russian scientists in 1964 as the isotope $^{260}104$, formed by bombarding plutonium-242 with neon-22. American scientists failed to duplicate this experiment; in 1969 they synthesized two other isotopes of element 104. The Russians proposed the name *kurchatovium* (for the Soviet chemist V. I. Kurchatov), while the Americans proposed *rutherfordium* (for the British physicist Ernest Rutherford). Element 104 is tetravalent in its chloride as well as in aqueous solution. The longest-lived isotope is $^{261}104$ (65 seconds). Element 105 was claimed by the Russians in 1968 and by the Americans in 1970; the Americans have proposed the name *hahnium* (symbol Ha) in honor of the German radiochemist Otto Hahn. There is chemical evidence that this element is chemically similar to niobium. Its longest-lived isotope is ^{262}Ha, with a half-life of 40 seconds. Reports of synthesis and identification of element 106 were made in 1974 by both Russians and Americans. No name has yet been proposed, nor is there yet any chemical verification that element 106 is like tungsten.

Theoretical nuclear physicists have predicted that some isotopes of even heavier elements, particularly elements 112, 114, and 126, might have appreciable half-lives. Many searches in natural minerals and in nuclear accelerator targets have failed to show evidence for any such elements; proton-induced X-ray fluorescence, a very sensitive technique that once yielded some evidence for an isotope of element 126, has now conclusively demonstrated that there is no evidence for superheavy elements in nature.   LESTER R. MORSS

Bibliography: Ahrens, L. H., ed., *Origin and Distribution of the Elements*, 7th ed. (1968); Keller, Cornelius, *Chemistry of the Transuranium Elements* (1971); Seaborg, G. T., et al., "Superheavy Elements: A Crossroads," *Science*, Feb. 23, 1979.

Superior, Lake

Lake Superior, astride the U.S.-Canadian border, is the farthest north and west of the GREAT LAKES. Bordered on the west by Minnesota, on the south by Wisconsin and Michigan, and on the east and north by Ontario, it is the largest lake in the Western Hemisphere and one of the largest in the world. Measuring 563 km (350 mi) from east to west and more than 257 km (160 mi) north to south, the lake has a surface area of about 82,410 km² (31,820 mi²). It achieves a maximum depth

of 393 m (1,290 ft). As the headwater of the Great Lakes system, Lake Superior discharges into Lake Huron by way of the Saint Marys River. More than 200 rivers feed Lake Superior, including the Nipigon and the Saint Louis. The drainage basin measures about 209,500 km² (80,900 mi²). Major ports on its shores include Duluth, Minn.; Sault Sainte Marie, Mich.; Sault Sainte Marie, Ontario; Thunder Bay, Ontario; Superior, Wis.; and Two Harbors, Minn. Lake Superior is a vital shipping route for minerals (iron ore, taconite, silver, nickel, and copper) from the region and grain from the prairies. The lake is a popular resort area in summer.

The first European to see the lake was Étienne Brûlé (1662). Its name comes from the French *Lac Supérieur*, meaning "upper lake." In 1959 the lake was linked to the Atlantic Ocean by the Saint Lawrence Seaway.

supermarket

Supermarkets are large, self-service food stores. A supermarket generally has more than 1,850 m² (20,000 ft²) in floor area and sells more than $1 million worth of products per year. In 1978 the approximately 66,500 supermarkets in the United States had total sales of $138 billion, or 77% of the total sales of all U.S. food stores. Supermarkets carry a wide variety of both dry groceries and perishables such as meat, produce, and dairy products. In recent years they have broadened their offerings to include such disparate products as drugstore items, financial services from branch savings and loan windows, small appliances, books and magazines, toys, and hardware. Many also have in-store baking facilities, lunch counters, and delicatessens. In 1978 the average supermarket stocked and sold more than 10,000 different items.

The supermarket evolved from the 19th-century general store, differentiating itself from the latter by making goods accessible to the customers so they could serve themselves rather than having clerks fill their orders, by selling goods in packages instead of in bulk, and by organizing goods into departments by type or use. Although earlier efforts were made to adopt some or all of these ideas, the first store designed as a self-service, departmentalized food market was opened in 1916 in Memphis, Tenn., by Clarence Saunders. From it grew the first supermarket chain, Piggly Wiggly, precursor of the giant A&P, Safeway, and Kroger organizations.

TOM WAGNER

Bibliography: Cross, Jennifer, *The Supermarket Trap: The Consumer and the Food Industry*, rev. ed. (1976); Goldbeck, Nikki and David, *The Supermarket Handbook* (1976); Mallowe, Charles A., and McLaughlin, Daniel J., *Food Marketing and Distribution: Selected Readings* (1971); Peak, Hugh S., and Ellen, *Supermarket Merchandising and Management* (1977).

supernatural literature

The superstitions of early peoples found expression not only in the literary forms of folklore such as BALLADS but also in the poetry and drama of the ancient Greeks, which accepts the reality of an extraterrestrial world and the gods of MYTHOLOGY. In recent times the work of the psychologists Freud and Jung has increased scientific interest in ostensibly irrational aspects of the imagination.

ELIZABETHAN LITERATURE contains numerous evocations of the supernatural, from the terrors of Marlow's DOCTOR FAUSTUS to the amiable spirits of Shakespeare's A MIDSUMMER NIGHT'S DREAM. Since the rise of GOTHIC ROMANCE, the tradition of the supernatural has played a major part in literature and has been exploited by such masters of terror as Henry James, H. P. Lovecraft, Edgar Allan Poe, Bram Stoker, and the ghost-story writer M. R. James.

supernova

A supernova is a STAR that suddenly increases in brightness by a factor of many billions; after a period of days or weeks it slowly fades away. In other words, it is a stellar explosion. There are only three recorded instances of supernovas occurring in our Galaxy: in 1054, in 1572, and in 1604. In each case

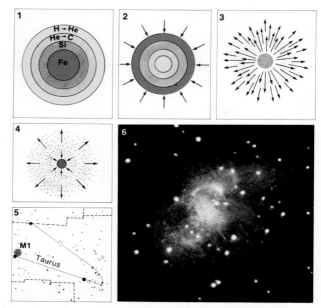

A supernova occurs when the outer, gaseous portion of a massive star explodes. According to one theory, as nuclear reactions in a star's core (1) start to produce heavy elements, such as iron, continued contraction (2) of the inner core begins to release enormous amounts of energy. The star explodes (3) and expels stellar matter. The core continues to contract, probably producing a dense neutron star (4). A supernova in the constellation Taurus (5) was observed by Chinese astronomers in AD 1054. Its remnants form M1, the Crab nebula (6).

a star became bright enough to be seen in daylight and then faded from view a number of months later. The CRAB NEBULA consists of material ejected into space by the supernova of 1054; there are many other known examples of gaseous material having been ejected into space by supernovas in the more distant past. Supernovas have been observed in other galaxies.

A supernova may radiate more energy in a few days than the Sun does in 100 million years, and the energy expended in ejecting material is much greater even than this. In many cases, including the Crab nebula supernova, the stellar remnant left behind after the explosion is a PULSAR or NEUTRON STAR.

One possible cause of such a violent explosion may be nuclear reactions involving heavy elements within the star. These nuclear reactions can occur explosively, especially if the material involved is very dense. Another possible cause may be the collapse of a degenerate core. As a massive star ages, it builds up a core in which the electrons are degenerate, that is, completely free from their atoms, and tightly packed together (see STELLAR EVOLUTION). This core is much like a white dwarf occurring at the center of the star. As the star continues to age, more matter is added to the degenerate core. Eventually the core will exceed the mass limit for a degenerate body, and the material then becomes nondegenerate. At that point the core can no longer support the weight of the star, and a catastrophic collapse might occur, possibly leading to a supernova explosion.

Whatever its cause, a supernova explosion marks the passage into the final phase in the life of a massive star. Low-mass stars such as the Sun burn out more quietly.

THOMAS L. SWIHART

Bibliography: Clark, D. H., and Stephenson, F. R., eds., *Historical Supernovae* (1977); Schramm, David, ed., *Supernovae* (1977).

superphosphate

Superphosphate is an important phosphatic fertilizer made by treating ground phosphate rock with sulfuric acid in approxi-

The Concorde, jointly developed by France's Aérospatiale and the British Aircraft Corporation, became (1976) the Western world's first operational civil supersonic transport.

mately equal proportions by weight. The resulting product is a mixture of monocalcium phosphate and calcium sulfate in about equal proportions. Acidulation of phosphate rock converts the insoluble tricalcium phosphate into a form available for plant growth—monocalcium. Ordinary superphosphate may be produced to contain as much as 20% available phosphoric acid (P_2O_5) by selecting high-grade raw phosphate rock and carefully supervising the chemical operations involved. This material is basically the same as that originated by John Lawes in 1843. Triple (or treble) superphosphate (40% to 48% available P_2O_5) differs in that the calcium sulfate is not present. It is produced by using phosphoric acid instead of sulfuric acid to react with the phosphate rock.

CHARLES T. LICHY

supersonic transport

The concept of a supersonic transport (SST)—an AIRCRAFT that surpasses the speed of sound—first attracted attention around 1955. General Dynamics, builder of the first supersonic long-range bomber (the B-58 Hustler, in 1957), proposed a passenger version, but the market was not ready until the Russians pioneered the Tupolev Tu-144 in 1975, and the French and British cooperatively introduced the CONCORDE in 1976. The United States spent more than $1 billion during 1963–71 on a series of Mach 3 (three times the speed of sound) SSTs, the final design being the Boeing 2707-300 powered by four General Electric GE4 turbojets. In 1971, however, Congress cut off all funds for this type of aircraft.

In one respect the SST has an advantage over subsonic airplanes: the high forward speed causes the airflow into the engine inlet to be compressed by the so-called ram effect to about twice atmospheric pressure at Mach 1, nearly 8 times at Mach 2, and more than 36 times at Mach 3 (see MACH NUMBER). Combined with the intense cold at the SST cruising height of about 18 km (59,000 ft), this effect results in greatly improved engine efficiency. This advantage, however, is more than outweighed by the reduced L/D ratio, or the ratio of wing lift (L) divided by drag (D, resistance to motion). An efficient subsonic transport has an L/D ratio of at least 15; in other words, the drag is only $\frac{1}{15}$ as much as its weight. The SST needs to struggle to reach an L/D ratio greater than seven. This means, for example, that the SST needs about twice as much fuel as subsonic transports to fly a given trip with the same number of passengers. Moreover, it needs engines, usually afterburning turbojets of small frontal area, that have twice the power of the large-diameter turbofans of modern subsonic transports; these turbojets, however, are also much noisier.

Although the engines of an SST passing at cruising height cannot be heard, its shock waves—virtually identical with those caused by lightning—are heard by observers on the ground as a thunderlike boom after the SST has passed overhead. For this reason, SST routes, other than in the Soviet Union, have to be flown at subsonic speed where they cross inhabited areas.

BILL GUNSTON

Bibliography: Costello, John, and Hughes, Terry, *The Concorde Conspiracy* (1976); Herron, Edward A., *Cobra in the Sky: The Supersonic Transport* (1968); Knight, Geoffrey, *Concorde: The Inside Story* (1976); Levy, Elizabeth, *The People Lobby: The SST Story* (1973).

superstition

A superstition is a belief, sometimes only tentatively held, that cannot be justified in terms of a dominant belief system and may therefore be said to be irrational. The word often implies condemnation when used by persons who assume the superiority of their beliefs, whether scientific, religious, or philosophical. The explorers and missionaries of the last century, for example, often dismissed much of the world view of the peoples they encountered as superstition. The term *superstition* is often taken to mean beliefs concerning MAGIC, supernatural invisible forces, or erroneous nature lore. WITCHCRAFT, the EVIL EYE, omens, signs, ghosts, and a variety of spirit beings are all comprised in such a definition. Earlier folklorists and anthropologists sometimes saw in the superstitions of medieval Europe traces of earlier, more primitive culture. Psychologists have also taken an interest in the impulses behind superstition, both in its widest social forms and as expressed in individualized, personal beliefs.

CHRISTIAN CLERK

Bibliography: Frazer, James G., *Psyche's Task: A Discourse Concerning the Influence of Superstition on the Growth of Institutions*, 2d ed. (1913; repr. 1979); Jahoda, Gustav, *The Psychology of Superstition* (1969); Sarnoff, Jane, and Ruffins, Reynold, *Take Warning! A Book of Superstitions* (1978).

Suppé, Franz von   [zoo-pay']

Franz von Suppé, b. Apr. 18, 1819, d. May 21, 1895, was an Austro-Italian composer of operettas. He studied primarily at the Vienna Conservatory and subsequently became a conductor at various Austrian theaters, principally the Leopoldstadt Theater from 1865 to his death. Suppé had begun composing as a child; with his entry into the world of the theater, he concentrated mainly on operettas and incidental music for comedies. He produced almost 200 works, including 31 operettas, between 1841 and 1895. Two of his operettas, *Poet and Peasant* (1846) and *Light Cavalry* (1866), were enormously successful; the overtures to these works are still in the concert repertoire.

HOMER ULRICH

supply and demand

The economic theory of supply and demand states that in a competitive, or free, market, the prices charged for a certain amount of goods and services are determined by the interaction between the demand for and the supply of goods and services.

Demand. Economists define demand as a schedule, or list, showing the various quantities of a particular product that can be sold at all possible prices in a given market during a given time period. The law of demand states that the relationship between price and the quantity demanded is an inverse one (see Figure 1). Experience shows this rule is generally true; when merchants want to increase the sales of a product, they lower rather than increase its price. A decline

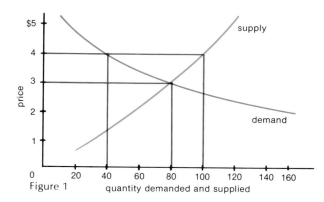

Figure 1

in the price of a product has two effects on the consumer—an income effect and a substitution effect. The income effect indicates that a decline in the price of a product in effect increases a consumer's real income, enabling him or her to purchase a larger amount of the product under consideration. According to the substitution effect, a lower price will make the given product cheaper than other products, thereby prompting the consumer to substitute it for other products.

Supply. Supply is a schedule showing the various quantities of a good that producers or sellers will offer in the market at all possible prices during a given time period. The law of supply indicates that the relationship between the price of a product and the quantity supplied of that product is usually direct (as illustrated in Figure 1). The explanation for this relationship is that a firm usually encounters rising production costs as it expands output and, therefore, must obtain higher prices to cover these costs. Costs increase with output because certain productive resources—for example, the firm's plant and machinery—cannot be expanded in a short period of time. As the firm, therefore, increases the amounts of more readily augmentable resources such as labor, materials, and component parts, the fixed plant will become crowded or congested, resulting in a decline in efficiency of production and an increase in costs.

Price Equilibrium. The market, or equilibrium, price is determined where the quantity demanded and the quantity supplied are equal. In Figure 1, for example, the equilibrium price of a particular product is $3, and the equilibrium quantity is 80 units per time period. The equilibrium price is $3 because at any other price an imbalance of quantity supplied and quantity demanded will drive the market price up or down until the $3 price is achieved. For instance, at any below-equilibrium price, such as $2, the quantity demanded will exceed the quantity supplied or, in other words, a shortage of the product will develop. Competing buyers will bid up price, causing the quantity demanded to fall as some buyers are rationed out of the market and causing the quantity supplied to increase as higher prices induce sellers to offer more output. This process continues until the equilibrium price is achieved. Conversely, at any above-equilibrium price, such as $4, the quantity supplied will exceed quantity demanded, and a surplus of the product will exist. Competing sellers will be unable to sell all of their output at this price and will respond to this situation by lowering price. Price reductions cause the quantity demanded to increase and the quantity supplied to fall; these adjustments continue until the surplus disappears at the equilibrium price.

Shifts in Supply and Demand. Equilibrium price and quantity will change if the demand or supply curves shift. An increase in demand means that consumers now want to purchase more of this product at each possible price. Potential causes for an increase in demand include a change in consumer tastes or preferences favorable to this product, an increase in consumer incomes, an increase in the price of a closely substitutable product, or an increase in the number of consumers in the market.

If supply remains constant, an increase in demand (a right-

ward shift of the demand curve from D_1 to D_2 in Figure 2) causes both equilibrium price and quantity to increase. An adverse change in consumer tastes, a decline in consumer incomes, a reduction in the price of a close substitute good, or a decline in the number of buyers in the market will all cause a decrease in demand (a leftward shift from D_1 to D_3 in Figure 2), causing equilibrium price and quantity to decline.

Supply may also shift; that is, sellers may decide to offer ei-

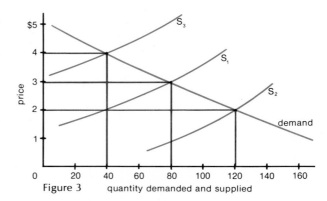

Figure 3   quantity demanded and supplied

ther more or less of the product at each possible price. An increase in supply occurs when suppliers offer more of the product at each possible price. Possible causes that might change supply include a decline in production costs stemming from lower resource prices or improvements in productive techniques, or the entry of additional firms to the industry. An increase in supply (shown in Figure 3 as a rightward shift of the supply curve from S_1 to S_2) will reduce equilibrium price but increase equilibrium quantity. A decrease in supply (a leftward shift from S_1 to S_3 in Figure 3) will cause equilibrium price to rise and equilibrium quantity to fall. Causes of a decrease in supply include rising production costs and the exodus of firms from the industry.

CAMPBELL R. MCCONNELL

Bibliography: Dooley, Peter C., *Elementary Price Theory*, 2d ed. (1973); Jones, Richard, *Supply in a Market Economy* (1976); Laidler, David E., *Demand for Money*, 2d ed. (1977); Leftwich, Richard H., *The Price System and Resource Allocation*, 6th ed. (1976); Lluch, Constantino, et al., *Patterns in Household Demand and Saving* (1977); McConnell, Campbell R., *Economics*, 7th ed. (1978).

See also: MONOPOLY AND COMPETITION.

suprematism

Suprematism was one of the most austere kinds of geometric ABSTRACT ART in the early part of the 20th century. Created in Russia by the painter Kasimir MALEVICH in 1913, the movement lasted in his native country until 1921, when official government policy turned against all such art. Suprematist ideas, however, were important to the evolution of abstract art in Germany and the Netherlands. Malevich's work became particularly influential in the west as a result of the German translation of his *Non-Objective World* published (1927) by the Bauhaus. One of the most important books on abstract art, it ranks with the writings of Wassily Kandinsky and Piet Mondrian. In his suprematist paintings, as the artist later explained, Malevich wanted to rid art of "the ballast of the objective world" and did so initially by using only the square. He then evolved a more complex art employing a variety of pure geometric shapes (see CONSTRUCTIVISM). Unlike Mondrian's art, which sought stillness, Malevich's, in its use of diagonals, was dynamic. Malevich's aim was to produce an art of what he called "pure feeling," devoid of the realism of objects in the visible world.

DAVID IRWIN

Bibliography: Andersen, Troel, *Malevich*, rev. trans. by Arnold McMillin (1970); Gray, Camilla, *The Great Experiment: Russian Art, 1863–1922*, rev. ed. (1971); Malevich, Kasimir, *Essays on Art 1915–33*, trans. by Xenia Glowackiz Prus and Arnold McMillin, 2d ed. (1971).

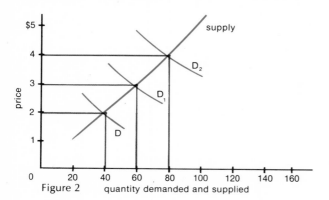

Figure 2   quantity demanded and supplied

Supreme Court of the United States

Members of the United States Supreme Court appear in this 1978 portrait: (left to right, front row) Justices Byron R. White and John Paul Stevens, Chief Justice Warren E. Burger, and Justices Potter Stewart and Thurgood Marshall; (back row) Justices William Rehnquist, Harry A. Blackmun, Lewis F. Powell, and William J. Brennan. The Court, the highest in the nation, decides cases of constitutional importance.

The Supreme Court of the United States, composed of a chief justice and eight associate justices, is at the apex of the American judicial system. Provisions for the establishment of the Supreme Court were made in Article III of the U.S. Constitution. In addition to vesting judicial power in a Supreme Court and other lower courts to be established by congressional legislation, Section 1 of this article states that federal judges "shall hold their offices during good behavior"—their removal therefore can only be by IMPEACHMENT procedures—and judges' compensation cannot be reduced while they hold office. Section 2 of Article III sets forth the extent of federal judicial power and the Supreme Court's jurisdiction. The Supreme Court has original jurisdiction—that is, the authority to hear a case without that case being first heard elsewhere—over cases in which a state or a diplomat is involved (the 11TH AMENDMENT, however, restricts to some extent federal jurisdiction over suits against states). The Court's appellate jurisdiction can be regulated by Congress.

Justices are appointed by the president and confirmed by the Senate. The Constitution does not stipulate the size of the Court, leaving that determination to congressional statute. The familiar nine-member bench has been constant in size only since 1869; it began with six members in 1789 and had as many as ten justices in the period 1863–66. The Supreme Court of the United States is unique because it serves two functions, each of which must be carried on in a subtle relationship to the other. It is, first, a court of law, operating within the forms and rituals of Anglo-Saxon legal procedure with roots going back to 12th-century England; as such it is the highest court in the land, with a final authority over all adjudication whether originating in the federal or the state courts. Because its pronouncements on U.S. law are final, they become guides for every judge and lawyer in the nation. In addition to being a court of law, the Supreme Court is a policymaking body. It is a political institution in the sense that it exerts a commanding influence on the public policies of the United States, a fact that Alexis de Tocqueville recognized so perceptively in 1834 when he observed: "Scarcely any question arises in the United States that is not resolved, sooner or later, into a judicial question."

The U.S. judicial system is complex, with authority dispersed vertically among layers of local, state, and federal governments and horizontally among the branches of the national government. Because the entire scheme is controlled by a written constitution that enunciates general rules to guide and control those who wield power, there is a need for someone to see that the rules are interpreted and followed. Early in the country's history the Supreme Court assumed the role of referee, or overseer, not only to declare definitively what the rules are but to make certain that all public officials—from police officer to the nation's president—obey them. When the Supreme Court declared the Texas and Georgia abortion statutes unconstitutional in ROE v. WADE AND DOE v. BOLTON (1973), it was acting as a court in hearing argument on appeal from a lower federal court. Obviously, however, the court was also involved in a momentous public policy decision when it said that under the Constitution a woman has a right, although not unqualified, to terminate her pregnancy through an abortion.

HOW CASES REACH THE COURT

The Supreme Court is primarily a COURT OF APPEALS. Cases generally reach the Court either from the lower federal courts or from the state supreme courts. There are three possible routes by which a case may come to the Supreme Court.

Certification. A lower federal court may send up a question of law about which it desires instructions, a process called certification.

Appeal. Some cases are appealed to the Court as a matter of right under the Judiciary Act of 1925. Such cases fall into eight categories. A litigant may appeal from the highest state court in which a decision may be had if the court (1) has invalidated a federal statute or treaty; or (2) has upheld its own law or constitutional provision allegedly in conflict with federal laws, treaties, or the U.S. Constitution. A litigant may appeal from a federal court of appeals if (1) a federal law or treaty has been declared unconstitutional; or (2) a state law or constitutional provision has been held to conflict with a federal law, treaty, or the Constitution. Finally, it is possible to appeal directly from a federal district court to the Supreme Court if (1) a federal statute with a criminal penalty is invalidated; (2) a judgment has been rendered under the antitrust laws, the Interstate Commerce Act, or Title II of the Federal Communications Act; (3) a three-judge court has either issued or denied an injunction to restrain enforcement of a state or federal law; or (4) a one-judge court has held a federal law unconstitutional.

The Court has some discretion in deciding whether to accept such cases. It may reject an appeal on the ground that the federal question raised is trivial or insubstantial, that the question was not validly raised in a state court, or that the state court's judgment might be sustained on an independent ground of state law. Thus the right of appeal is subject to certain technical restrictions.

Certiorari. Most of the cases reviewed by the Supreme Court reach the bench on a writ of certiorari, a Latin term meaning to be informed of or to be made certain in regard to. In English practice certiorari was a writ that commanded judges of inferior courts to return records or certify proceedings for review by a higher court, and this is essentially its practical meaning today. Prior to 1925 approximately 80 percent of the Supreme Court's appellate jurisdiction was obligatory, and, as a matter of course, the Court was not able to keep its docket clear. As a result of Chief Justice William Howard TAFT's efforts, however, Congress enacted the Judiciary Act of 1925 under the terms of which, with the exceptions noted above, most cases became reviewable in the Supreme Court on a writ of certiorari. In a practical sense this legislation means that a person who loses a case in the lower courts, although usually unable to appeal to the Supreme Court as a matter of right, may petition the high court to grant a writ of certiorari. Because about 90 percent of the cases decided by the Supreme Court annually reach it by this method, the Court has considerable discretion over the kinds of cases it accepts.

Under the Court's rules, certiorari is granted only "where there are special and important reasons therefor." Among these reasons are the following possibilities: when two federal courts of appeals or two 3-judge federal district courts have rendered conflicting decisions; when a state court or a federal appellate court has passed on an important question of federal law on which the Supreme Court has never made a

JUSTICES OF THE SUPREME COURT

Justice	Dates*	Appointed By	Justice	Dates*	Appointed By
John Jay†	1789-95	George Washington	George Shiras	1892-1903	Benjamin Harrison
John Rutledge	1789-91	George Washington	Howell E. Jackson	1893-95	Benjamin Harrison
William Cushing	1789-1810	George Washington	Edward D. White	1894-1910	Grover Cleveland
James Wilson	1789-98	George Washington	Rufus W. Peckham	1895-1909	Grover Cleveland
John Blair	1789-96	George Washington	Joseph McKenna	1898-1925	William McKinley
James Iredell	1790-99	George Washington	Oliver W. Holmes	1902-32	Theodore Roosevelt
Thomas Johnson	1791-93	George Washington	William R. Day	1903-22	Theodore Roosevelt
William Paterson	1793-1806	George Washington	William H. Moody	1906-10	Theodore Roosevelt
John Rutledge†	1795‡	George Washington	Horace H. Lurton	1910-14	William H. Taft
Samuel Chase	1796-1811	George Washington	Charles Evans Hughes	1910-16	William H. Taft
Oliver Ellsworth†	1796-99	George Washington	Edward D. White†	1910-21	William H. Taft
Bushrod Washington	1798-1829	John Adams	W. Van Devanter	1910-37	William H. Taft
Alfred Moore	1799-1804	John Adams	Joseph R. Lamar	1911-16	William H. Taft
John Marshall†	1801-35	John Adams	Mahlon Pitney	1912-22	William H. Taft
William Johnson	1804-34	Thomas Jefferson	James C. McReynolds	1914-41	Woodrow Wilson
H. B. Livingston	1806-23	Thomas Jefferson	Louis O. Brandeis	1916-39	Woodrow Wilson
Thomas Todd	1807-26	Thomas Jefferson	John H. Clarke	1916-22	Woodrow Wilson
Joseph Story	1811-45	James Madison	William Howard Taft†	1921-30	Warren G. Harding
Gabriel Duval	1811-35	James Madison	George Sutherland	1922-38	Warren G. Harding
Smith Thompson	1823-43	James Monroe	Pierce Butler	1922-39	Warren G. Harding
Robert Trimble	1826-28	John Quincy Adams	Edward T. Sanford	1923-30	Warren G. Harding
John McLean	1829-61	Andrew Jackson	Harlan F. Stone	1925-41	Calvin Coolidge
Henry Baldwin	1830-44	Andrew Jackson	Charles Evans Hughes†	1930-41	Herbert Hoover
James M. Wayne	1835-67	Andrew Jackson	Owen J. Roberts	1930-45	Herbert Hoover
Roger B. Taney†	1836-64	Andrew Jackson	Benjamin N. Cardozo	1932-38	Herbert Hoover
Philip P. Barbour	1836-41	Andrew Jackson	Hugo L. Black	1937-71	Franklin D. Roosevelt
John Catron	1837-65	Andrew Jackson	Stanley Reed	1938-57	Franklin D. Roosevelt
John McKinley	1837-52	Martin Van Buren	Felix Frankfurter	1939-62	Franklin D. Roosevelt
Peter V. Daniel	1841-60	Martin Van Buren	William O. Douglas	1939-75	Franklin D. Roosevelt
Samuel Nelson	1845-72	John Tyler	Frank Murphy	1940-49	Franklin D. Roosevelt
Levi Woodbury	1845-51	James K. Polk	James F. Byrnes	1941-42	Franklin D. Roosevelt
Robert C. Grier	1846-70	James K. Polk	Harlan F. Stone†	1941-46	Franklin D. Roosevelt
Benjamin R. Curtis	1851-57	Millard Fillmore	Robert H. Jackson	1941-54	Franklin D. Roosevelt
John A. Campbell	1853-61	Franklin Pierce	Wiley Rutledge	1943-49	Franklin D. Roosevelt
Nathan Clifford	1858-81	James Buchanan	Harold H. Burton	1945-58	Harry S. Truman
Noah H. Swayne	1862-81	Abraham Lincoln	Fred M. Vinson	1946-53	Harry S. Truman
Samuel F. Miller	1862-90	Abraham Lincoln	Tom C. Clark	1949-67	Harry S. Truman
David Davis	1862-77	Abraham Lincoln	Sherman Minton	1949-56	Harry S. Truman
Stephen J. Field	1863-97	Abraham Lincoln	Earl Warren†	1953-69	Dwight D. Eisenhower
Imon P. Chase†	1864-73	Abraham Lincoln	John Marshall Harlan	1955-71	Dwight D. Eisenhower
William Strong	1870-80	Ulysses S. Grant	William J. Brennan, Jr.	1956-	Dwight D. Eisenhower
Joseph P. Bradley	1870-92	Ulysses S. Grant	Charles E. Whittaker	1957-62	Dwight D. Eisenhower
Ward Hunt	1872-82	Ulysses S. Grant	Potter Stewart	1958-	Dwight D. Eisenhower
Morrison R. Waite†	1874-88	Ulysses S. Grant	Byron R. White	1962-	John Kennedy
John Marshall Harlan	1877-1911	Rutherford B. Hayes	Arthur J. Goldberg	1962-65	John Kennedy
William B. Woods	1880-87	Rutherford B. Hayes	Abe Fortas	1965-69	Lyndon Johnson
Stanley Matthews	1881-89	James A. Garfield	Thurgood Marshall	1967-	Lyndon Johnson
Horace Gray	1881-1902	Chester A. Arthur	Warren E. Burger†	1969-	Richard Nixon
Samuel Blatchford	1882-93	Chester A. Arthur	Harry A. Blackmun	1970-	Richard Nixon
Lucius Q. C. Lamar	1888-93	Grover Cleveland	Lewis F. Powell, Jr.	1972-	Richard Nixon
Melville W. Fuller†	1888-1910	Grover Cleveland	William Rehnquist	1972-	Richard Nixon
David J. Brewer	1889-1910	Benjamin Harrison	John P. Stevens	1976-	Gerald Ford
Henry B. Brown	1890-1906	Benjamin Harrison			

* Dates begin with year of appointment.   † Chief justices.   ‡ Never confirmed by the Senate as chief justice.

pronouncement; or when a federal court has so far departed from the accepted canons of judicial proceedings as to call for exercise of the Supreme Court's powers. Generally the Court accepts only 10 to 15 percent of the certiorari petitions in a given year.

The Process of Review. When a litigant who loses in a lower court wishes to take the case to the Supreme Court, he or she may send a request for a hearing, whether by appeal or certiorari, to the office of the chief justice, who circulates it among the eight associate justices. All nine justices take part in the decision whether to hear the case. The number of requests runs from 3,000 to 4,000 annually, of which more than 90 percent are denied. Every justice must personally review the records and decide which cases should be placed on the docket for a hearing. If four justices are in favor of taking a case, it is placed on the docket. If a case is rejected, the decision of the last court in which it was heard stands; such a rejection does not, the Court maintains, necessarily indicate approval of the lower court's ruling.

Once a case is accepted for review, it is placed on one of

three dockets, the original, the appellate, or the miscellaneous—the latter including a large number of petitions, often handwritten, filed by indigent persons, many of whom are serving time in prison. Any person who executes an oath that he or she is without any financial resources may, under a federal statute, sue in forma pauperis (as a poor person) in any federal court without paying filing fees, transcript costs, or any of the other expenses connected with a lawsuit.

HOW THE COURT OPERATES

The Supreme Court opens its sessions in October of each year and usually adjourns in May or June. If a case of special importance arises in which a pronouncement from the high bench is needed immediately, it holds a special session. One of these rare occasions was the session of July 7, 1972, when the Court dealt with the problem of certification of delegates to the Democratic National Convention. Normally the Court is in session for 38 weeks, but the workload has become so heavy that a justice can rarely take an extended summer vacation. During the term, the Court usually devotes 2 weeks to oral argument in cases it has chosen for full treatment; it then spends 2 weeks in recess for researching and writing opinions. For 88 years prior to 1961, the Court's public sessions opened at noon, Monday through Friday; the conference, a meeting of the nine justices at which the cases are discussed, was held on Saturday. In the 1970s the Court met Monday through Thursday from 10:00 AM until noon and from 12:30 to 2:30 PM, holding its conference on Friday.

Attorneys submit written briefs to the Court. Oral argument gives the justices a chance to ask questions and add to their knowledge of a case. It also gives the public an opportunity to see the Court in action (188 seats are available on a first-come, first-served basis), although the Court's most important work is done behind closed doors. In the Court's early years, lawyers might have argued a case for days, but attorneys are now usually limited to 1 hour or sometimes half an hour. No opinion is written or decision rendered until after the Court has met in conference and discussed the cases. The conference is unusual for a public body because it is closed to all but the nine justices. No official record is kept, and whatever is said remains forever secret unless the justices wish to divulge something, which they rarely do. Justice Hugo L. BLACK believed so strongly in the principle of conference confidentiality that he specified in his will that the informal notes he had taken during conferences be destroyed at his death.

Presiding over the conference is one of the most important tasks of the chief justice, who may in this role exert a special influence over colleague justices. The chief justice presents the cases for discussion, controls the debate, and assigns the writing of opinions. The chief justice presents his view of the case first, then elicits the opinions of the other justices in order of seniority. After all have expressed their views, a vote is taken in reverse order. If the chief justice is in the majority, he will later formally assign the writing of the opinion; if he is in dissent, the most senior justice in the majority makes the assignment. Although the assigning of opinions is simply a parceling out of the work, some political strategy is involved, because the opinion of a particular justice may carry more weight on a given question than that of others. Some develop special expertise; some are more highly respected generally. For example, Justice William BRENNAN, after writing the opinion in ROTH V. UNITED STATES (1957), became the Court's expert on obscenity and wrote the opinions in the significant obscenity cases that followed. It seemed most appropriate that Justice Black write the opinion in GIDEON V. WAINWRIGHT (1963), when the constitutional right to counsel was extended to state courts through the 14th Amendment, because Black had been advocating this right to counsel for a decade and a half. Chief Justice Earl WARREN chose to write some of the most controversial opinions during his tenure (those relating to public school desegregation, reapportionment of both houses of state legislatures, and application of the right against self-incrimination and the right to counsel at the police interrogation level in criminal proceedings), presumably to give the decisions greater prestige by stamping the imprimatur of the chief justice on them.

All justices may record their own views of a case. If a justice is among the majority, but disagrees with the reasoning supporting the decision, that justice may write a concurring opinion in which the view is expressed that although the case was correctly decided, it should have been supported on different constitutional grounds. Any or all of those who believe that the case was wrongly decided may write dissenting opinions in which they marshal the arguments for their position. The total number of concurrences and dissents during a term is generally larger than the number of assigned opinions. Until John MARSHALL became chief justice in 1801, the Court presented its opinions seriatim, that is, each justice wrote an opinion of the law in each case, an arrangement that made it difficult for lawyers to determine precisely what had been decided. Marshall instituted the system described above, which has prevailed. Although some critics of the Court bemoan many of its decisions not being unanimous, it may be argued that given the difficult and controversial nature of the cases that they decide—the easier ones having already been disposed of by lower courts—it is a wonder that the justices

agree as much as they do. Often they are unanimous, and rarely are so many opinions written in a case that the constitutional question involved remains unsettled. A recent example of such a situation was NEW YORK TIMES COMPANY V. UNITED STATES (1971), the Pentagon Papers case, in which nine separate opinions were written. Although the Court decided that the *New York Times* could not be restrained from publishing these classified government documents, each justice wrote his own view of the matter, leaving the law in a fragmented and uncertain state in regard to the conditions, if any, under which the government may withhold information from the public.

When a justice has completed a written opinion it is circulated among the other justices for comment. This review is done not only with the assigned majority opinion but with the concurrences and dissents as well. The final opinions that emerge from this interaction often differ from the original versions as the authors take into account the critiques of their colleagues, and occasionally a vote is changed. All of these negotiations are carried on in private, as are the original discussion and voting, and the final opinions are announced publicly from the bench. For many years the Court adhered to the tradition, originating in the 19th century, of announcing its opinions only on Mondays, but in 1965, Chief Justice Warren declared that in the future, cases would be reported as they became ready for decision at any session of the Court. He said after his retirement that the new arrangement was for the benefit of the press, to give reporters more time to read and analyze opinions before filing them with their editors.

The justice who has written the majority opinion, which becomes the official opinion of the Court, delivers it from the bench. Over the years the style has varied with the individual justice. Some simply read the opinion in full; others summarize the major points. Justice Felix FRANKFURTER used to amaze reporters and onlookers by expounding his opinions from memory, including the citing of volume and page numbers of pertinent cases bearing on the one at hand. The process of handing down opinions may take from an hour to several days, depending on the number of decisions and the styles of the justices involved. It is a sober and dignified procedure throughout, from the moment the red velvet draperies are opened and the black-robed justices take their seats to the time the chief justice declares the session ended.

A Supreme Court justice has one of the most demanding jobs in the world. Over a half-century ago Chief Justice Taft would rise at 5:15 AM, work for almost 4 hours before walking to the Capitol where the Court was housed, and, after the end of the Court session at 4:30 PM, work until 10:00 PM with an hour out for dinner. Taft talked of the "exhausting character" of the judicial work (a reason for his efforts to have the Judiciary Act of 1925 passed in order to lighten the work load). Charles Evans HUGHES, who had been an active lawyer, governor of New York, and a vigorous presidential candidate, said that service on the Court was the toughest job of all. Today the justices are more hard-pressed than ever. They handle the ever-increasing business partly by confining the number of cases in which they render a full opinion to a minimum, but they also use a larger number of law clerks. Each justice takes on top-ranking law graduates who serve for a year or two and handle much of the preliminary work leading to a final opinion or to a justice's decision to vote for or against granting review. Some former law clerks have become justices themselves, including two on the present Court, Justice William REHNQUIST and Justice Byron WHITE.

THE COURT AS A POLITICAL FORCE

From the day on which Chief Justice Marshall rendered the historic decision in MARBURY V. MADISON (1803), which established the principle of JUDICIAL REVIEW—that is, the right of the Court to declare acts of Congress unconstitutional—the Supreme Court has had a significant impact on U.S. public policy. John Marshall not only implanted the cornerstone but constructed the entire foundation of U.S. constitutional law. In GIBBONS V. OGDEN (1824) he interpreted the commerce power—the power the Constitution gives Congress to regulate interstate commerce—in the broadest possible terms, and in McCulloch v. Maryland (1819) he firmly wrote the Federalist doctrines of national supremacy and implied powers into the Constitution of the United States. Marshall's successor as chief justice, Roger B. Taney, helped precipitate the Civil War with his opinion in Dred Scott v. Sandford (1857) that free blacks and slaves were not citizens of the United States within the meaning of the Constitution. For the most part, however, the Marshall doctrines were strengthened and extended during the Taney era (1836–64). The post–Civil War period contained two parallel developments: the curbing of state regulatory powers through the use of the due process clause of the 14th Amendment (adopted in 1868) and the restriction of national power through a narrow interpretation of the powers of Congress, particularly that of regulating interstate commerce. Important among these decisions were those in Munn v. Illinois (1877); *Allgeyer* v. *Louisiana* (1897); *Smyth* v. *Ames* (1898); Lochner v. New York (1905); and *Adair* v. *United States* (1908). A major constitutional crisis arose during the 1930s over the question of federal and state regulation of the economy. President Franklin D. Roosevelt, angered by the Supreme Court's invalidation of much of his recovery legislation, notably in Schechter Poultry Corporation v. United States (1935) and Carter v. Carter Coal Company (1936), proposed to Congress that the size of the Court be increased from 9 to 15 justices—in effect asking for permission to pack the Court with supportive members. The plan failed, but within a year the Supreme Court was upholding economic regulatory legislation. Important cases were National Labor Relations Board v. Jones & Laughlin Steel Corporation (1937); *Mulford* v. *Smith* (1939); and United States v. Darby (1941).

The Supreme Court emerged once again as a major force in American life under the chief justiceship of Earl Warren from 1953 to 1969. Known for its consistent protection of civil liberties, the Warren Court will be remembered particularly for three revolutionary decisions: Brown v. Board of Education of Topeka, Kansas (1954), which outlawed segregation in the public schools and spearheaded the civil rights movement of the 1950s and '60s; Baker v. Carr (1962), which ordered equitable reapportionment of the state legislatures and guaranteed a close approximation of the "one man–one vote" principle; and Miranda v. Arizona (1966), which curbed coercive police techniques by insisting that prior to any interrogation a suspect must be told of his or her rights, including the right to counsel and the right to remain silent.

Although the Court since then has been seen as retreating from some of the advanced Warren positions, it has not overruled any of the major Warren decisions. The independence, integrity, and responsibility of the Supreme Court were brought into sharp focus when it unanimously ordered President Richard M. Nixon to obey Watergate special prosecutor Leon Jaworski's subpoena directing the president to surrender tape recordings of conversations made in the White House. Within a few days of the decision in United States v. Richard M. Nixon (1974), the president resigned.   Robert J. Steamer

Bibliography: Abraham, Henry J., *The Judiciary: The Supreme Court in the Governmental Process,* 4th ed. (1977); Blaustein, Albert P., *The First One Hundred Justices: Statistical Studies on the Supreme Court of the United States* (1978); Cox, Archibald, *The Role of the Supreme Court in American Government* (1976); Funston, Richard, *Judicial Crises: The Supreme Court in Changing America* (1974); Goldberg, Arthur, *Equal Justice: The Warren Era of the Supreme Court* (1972); McCloskey, Robert G., *The Modern Supreme Court* (1972); Steamer, Robert J., *Supreme Court in Crisis: A History of Conflict* (1971); Swisher, Carl B., *Historic Decisions of the Supreme Court,* 2d ed. (1969).

Supremes, The: see Motown.

Surabaya   [soo-rah-bah'-yah]

Surabaya is the capital of East Java Province, Indonesia, and is situated on the Mas River. Its population is 1,556,300 (1975 est.). It is Java's second busiest port city. Sugar, coffee, tobacco, and spices are exported from its outport of Tandjung-

perak, north of Surabaya. Fishing, shipbuilding, textile manufacturing, and petroleum refining are important industries. Surabaya is a rail center and is the site of a major Indonesian naval base, Udjung. A 19th-century mosque and the Dutch Fort Prins Hendrik (1835) are city landmarks. Airlangga University (1954), a naval college, and a technical institute are located there. Surabaya was the main base of the Dutch East Indies before 1942. While under occupation by the Japanese during World War II the city was bombed by the Allies. Surabaya was also damaged during the Indonesian war of independence (1945–49). It has since been rebuilt.

surety

A surety is a legal term referring to a person who undertakes to pay money, perform some duty, or assume some responsibility in case another person (the principal) fails to carry out the terms of a contract. A surety differs from a guarantor (see guaranty) in that the contract of the latter is entered into separate from the principal's original contract while the contract of suretyship is made at the same time and by the same instrument as the principal's contract. The surety, therefore, has a much more direct liability than does the guarantor.

surf

Surf is the term applied to the foaming mass of a breaking wave in the breaker or swash zones of a beach face. The surf zone lies between the breaker zone and swash zone of the nearshore environment. Waves of translation (water-transporting waves), generated by forces expended in the breaker zone, travel across the surf zone to the beach face. (See also water wave.)

surface tension

Surface tension refers to the tendency of a liquid surface to contract. A liquid consists of numerous molecules that are held together by mutual attractive forces (arrows). The interior molecules are attracted equally in all directions. The surface molecules, however, experience an unbalanced force inward and are pulled closer together until the surface area is reduced to a minimum.

Surface tension is a phenomenon associated with the interface between a fluid and another phase. The most familiar example involves the water-air interface. Here, the water appears to be "thicker" at the surface than elsewhere, producing some special effects. For example, a glass vessel can be overfilled without spilling, and a steel needle can float on water if it is gently lowered to rest on the surface.

Within a liquid, each molecule has similar molecules attracting it uniformly in every direction. At the surface, there exists a net attraction toward the interior, causing the surface molecules to crowd together. In the absence of other forces, surface tension causes the liquid to tend toward the shape of a sphere, the volume having the least surface area.

When a drop rests on a flat surface, the surface tension between the liquid and the surface has an additional effect that causes a wetting fluid (such as water) to spread out, whereas a nonwetting fluid (such as mercury) will contract. This same effect is exhibited between the surface of a liquid and the wall of its container. A wetting fluid rises until its weight is just balanced by the surface attraction, whereas a nonwetting fluid will drop until equilibrium is reached.   R. E. Street

See also: capillarity.

surface-to-air missile

Surface-to-air missiles (SAMs) are tactical rockets used to defend civil and military targets on land and sea from attack by aircraft or missiles. Maximum ranges vary from a few thousand meters to more than 160 km (100 mi), depending upon the SAM's operational role. Dimensions and performance vary accordingly: antiballistic missiles (ABMs) capable of intercepting attacking intercontinental ballistic missiles (ICBMs) before they reenter the atmosphere are about 18 m (60 ft) long; portable SAMs for use by individual soldiers on the battlefield are about 1.5 m (5 ft) long. Most surface-to-air missiles use solid propellants because they require a rapid reaction, but a few of the older long-range missiles rely upon liquid propellants. Separate booster rockets are sometimes used, and are jettisoned when burned out. Some SAMs employ ramjet sustainer motors.

Guidance techniques range from simple optical aiming with a heat-seeking homing head in the missile to very sophisticated systems. The two most common systems are beam-riding systems, in which the target is tracked by radar, TV, or laser and the SAM automatically follows this beam to the target; and command guidance systems, in which separate trackers are provided for the target and the SAM, with guidance commands transmitted to the SAM by a command link.   RONALD T. PRETTY

See also: ROCKETS AND MISSILES.

surfbird

The surfbird, *Aphriza virgata,* is a SHOREBIRD in the sandpiper family, Scolopacidae, subfamily Arenariinae, which also includes TURNSTONES. Surfbirds are about 254 mm (10 in) long, with short, yellow legs and a short, straight yellow bill. In summer they are heavily streaked and spotted, but in winter their upper parts are dark. For most of the year they feed along the rocky Pacific coast, ranging from Alaska south to the Straits of Magellan. In summer they retreat to their breeding areas high in the mountains of Alaska, where they lay 4 eggs among the rocks at the base of cliffs.   ROBERT J. RAIKOW

surfing

Surfing is a water sport that involves planing, in a controlled fashion, on the sloping portion of a wave as it moves toward shore. The most basic form of the sport is body surfing, which is performed without the use of any type of board: a person in the water first swims toward shore to match the wave speed, then stiffens the body in order to provide a rigid surface that will plane on the front of the shore-rushing wave.

In the mid-1950s surfboards of lightweight balsa wood, fiberglass, and polyurethane were introduced, replacing the heavy wooden boards of earlier years. These boards had the advantages of low weight and high maneuverability. The sport has gained rapidly in popularity as an ocean beach recreation. To surf using these boards, the participant paddles the board, while lying on it, until the board reaches wave speed. Then the rider attempts to stand up and plane on the board toward shore. Surfboards weigh 11–18 kg (24.2–39.7 lb) and are 1.8–3.7 m (6–12 ft) in length. The boards are slightly rockered so that the middle is lower than the nose or the tail of the board. The boards have a skeg, or fin, that acts as a lateral stabilizer. A form of surfing that makes use of a different type of board is belly-board surfing. The participant planes on the slope of the wave in a prone position with a board about 91 cm (3 ft) long supporting only the chest area. Surfing demands the grace of a gymnast coupled with good balance, sense of timing, and coordination, all important because boards can reach speeds of 55 km/h (34 mph).

The sport of surfing is very popular along the coasts of Hawaii, California, New Zealand, Australia, South Africa, Puerto Rico, Peru, Great Britain, and Brazil. It originated in Hawaii and was used by the nobility, who surfed on long wooden boards, as a form of religious ceremony. It was almost completely eliminated in 1821 by the European missionaries, who

A surfer rides a tall wave, balanced in a crouching position. Many variations of this sport exist, the most popular being long-board surfing, which permits the rider to stand erect as the board is carried shoreward. Surfing is believed to have been originated by Polynesian peoples centuries before the era of European discovery.

considered surfing to be an immoral form of amusement. In 1920, Duke Kahanamoku of Hawaii, the Olympic swimming champion, formed the first surfing club in Waikiki and was largely responsible for popularizing the sport. Surfing has recently developed into a competitive sport, and contests are organized annually on both national and international levels and are based on rules agreed upon by the International Surfing Federation.   GERALD S. COUZENS

Bibliography: Dixon, Peter L., *The Complete Book of Surfing,* rev. ed. (1969); Margan, Frank, and Finney, Ben R., *A Pictorial History of Surfing* (1970); Pryterch, Reginald J., *Surfing, a Modern Guide* (1972).

surfperch

The surfperches, or seaperches, family Embiotocidae, are 23 species of bony fishes usually found in shallow coastal areas openly exposed to the ocean or large bays. Only the pink surfperch, *Zalembius rosaceus,* regularly lives deeper than 30 m (100 ft) or so. Twenty species inhabit the eastern Pacific Ocean from Baja California to Alaska; 2 species are found on the coasts of Japan and Korea; and 1 species, *Hysterocarpus traski,* is found in freshwater in California. A female surfperch can give birth to 10–40 live young, depending on species and size. The young, almost fully developed, are densely packed in a saclike enlargement of the oviduct.   CAMM SWIFT

surge, tidal

Tidal surges, or storm surges, are abnormal elevations in sea level, along a coast, produced by strong onshore winds in conjunction with low barometric pressure. Surges typically have periods from 12 to 24 hours, and they can produce changes in sea level of several meters. They are particularly destructive to low-lying coastal areas if the peak of the storm is coincident with a high astronomical tide. When the wind stress relaxes, sea level can exhibit damped oscillations for several days before returning to normal.   ROBERT E. WILSON

Bibliography: Neumann, Gerhard, and Pierson, W. J., *Principles of Physical Oceanography* (1966); Wylie, Francis E., *Tides and the Pull of the Moon* (1979).

surgeonfish

Surgeonfishes, or tangs, family Acanthuridae, comprise about 100 species of reef fishes with deep, compressed bodies. The

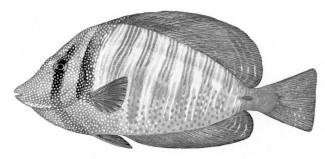

The sail-finned surgeonfish, Zebrasoma veliferum, of the Red Sea, has a small, sharp defensive spine, or scalpel, in front of its tail.

scalpels are strong, sharp-edged spines found on each side of the body, just ahead of the tail. The spine folds into a groove; when the fish is frightened, the spine snaps forward and is capable of producing a severe cut in humans. Most surgeonfishes are less than 50 cm (20 in) in length; they are popular as food in Polynesia.   C. P. IDYLL

surgery

Surgery uses operative procedures, both manual and instrumental, to treat injuries, diseases, and disorders. As it has developed it has also come to include diagnosis, pre- and post-operative care, and supervision during the rehabilitation period. Historically, surgery has generally been practical, or pragmatic, and its chief concern has been with obvious injuries, such as those stemming from accidents.

Surgery and medicine have vied with each other throughout history in dealing with medical problems, although medicine was dominant until the 20th century. At one time the vast majority of hospital patients were medical, whereas today surgical cases tend to occupy most of the hospital beds. It was possible for surgery to encroach upon the work of the physician as much as it did because, from the standpoint of the patient, surgery seemed rapid and miraculous compared to medical treatment.

Whereas the surgeon in his gown and gauze mask came to epitomize medicine by the mid-20th century, the balance is beginning to swing back to medicine. For example, the introduction of sulfa drugs and antibiotics has largely decreased the need for surgical intervention in cases such as acute mastoiditis, a common cause for surgery in the past. The role of surgery in modern medicine however, is not likely to be seriously challenged in the immediate future.

EARLY HISTORY
Although surgical texts and manuscripts exist far back in history—the Edwin Smith Papyrus in Egypt, the Susruta in India, and the Hippocratic writings—until well into the 19th century surgery dealt largely with cuts, abrasions, fractures, dislocations, puncture wounds, and abscesses (including those in the teeth and gums). Surgical intervention, the opening of any part of the body, was seldom performed. With little understanding of gross anatomy and virtually no comprehension

Trephining, the removal of a section of skull bone, was performed on this Neolithic patient some 10,000 years ago. The smooth edges of the wound are evidence of new bone growth, indicating that the patient survived the operation. Trephining to alleviate trauma from local injury is still practiced in some areas of Africa.

(Left) Two physicians perform couching, an early operation for cataracts, in this engraving from the 16th century. (Below) Their sharp instruments, used for displacing the opaque lens, were perfected by Ambroise Paré.

of physiology, any incision was dangerous. Prior to the beginning of the era of the antiseptic in the late 19th century, the procedure had been likely to end in a fatal infection.

The only two major forms of surgery practiced with any degree of regularity were trephining (trepanning) and lithotomy. Trephining, which consists of drilling a hole through the skull, has been performed since the beginning of recorded history. It is still practiced by certain primitive tribes and was common among many of the early civilizations. In all probability it was used for relieving headaches (letting out the evil spirit), removing depressed pieces of bone in cases of fracture, and occasionally for cosmetic or cultural reasons. Lithotomy was an operation to relieve patients suffering from urinary calculi, or bladder stones. It was probably first developed in India long before the time of Christ and was probably practiced in an essentially unchanged manner in the Western world until the 19th century. It consisted of the surgeon's inserting two fingers in the rectum and pressing the stone downward while making an incision between the anus and the genitalia. The wound was left to heal by itself. The danger from infection, shock, hemorrhage, and miscalculation was great, but the condition itself is extremely painful and can be fatal.

The early cultures developed a wide variety of surgical instruments for cutting, probing, and removing foreign objects. In addition, a number of simple surgical techniques were practiced, such as suturing wounds and cauterizing for chronic infections and ulcers. Nevertheless, the agony associated with surgery and the omnipresent danger from secondary infections discouraged surgery in all but the most desperate cases.

Although early physicians, including the Greeks, practiced surgery, in subsequent centuries medicine and surgery gradually drew apart. The distinction between the two was intensified with the rise of universities during the medieval period. Physicians with university degrees were gentlemen, and gentlemen did not work with their hands. Hence surgery was considered to be only a manual trade to be learned through an apprenticeship system. By the 18th century the status of surgeons began to rise, however, and better physicians began making contributions to the field.

19TH CENTURY
By the 19th century gross anatomy was well understood and initial steps had been taken toward an understanding of physiology. Moreover, the concept of localism—that is, that disease was not necessarily caused by an imbalance of the humors or some other systemic problem—encouraged surgical intervention. Enterprising surgeons, capitalizing on advances in anatomical knowledge, attempted more compli-

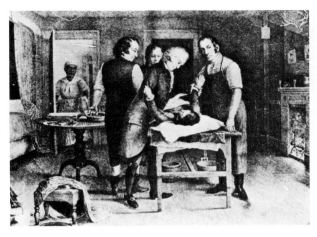

The first successful excision of an ovarian tumor was performed by Dr. Ephraim McDowell (right, in apron) in 1809. The 30-minute operation was carried out without antisepsis on a table in McDowell's living room. His unanesthetized patient sang hymns to counter the pain.

William Thomas Green Morton, a dentist, administers sulfuric ether to a patient at Boston General Hospital in 1846 prior to an operation for removal of a neck tumor. Morton's invention of an ether-inhalation device made general anesthesia during surgery a feasible technique.

cated procedures and steadily improved surgical techniques.

While most advances were made in Britain and on the Continent, a few daring and imaginative Americans contributed to the cause of surgery. For example, in 1809, Ephraim McDowell (1771–1830) of Danville, Ky., was called as a consultant in a difficult obstetrical case and immediately recognized that the patient had a large ovarian tumor. McDowell removed a diseased ovary, weighing about 9 kg (20 lb). The patient recovered rapidly, and McDowell had completed the first successful ovariotomy.

The second American to demonstrate originality and initiative was William Beaumont, a young army surgeon stationed at Fort Michilimackinac in upper Michigan. In 1822 he was called to attend a French-Canadian trapper whose chest and abdomen had been torn open by a shotgun blast at close range. Left with a permanent gastric fistula, the patient gave Beaumont the opportunity to study directly the human stomach. Beaumont over the next 10 years or so acquired enough knowledge to publish his classic work, *Experiments and Observations on the Gastric Juice and the Physiology of Digestion* (1833), which laid the basis for present understanding of the gastric process.

IMPACT OF ANESTHESIA AND ASEPSIS

The most significant American contribution to surgery was the discovery of anesthesia (see ANESTHETICS), largely the work of American dentists. The dentist Dr. William T. G. MORTON made the first successful public demonstration of surgical anesthesia in 1846 when he anesthetized a patient for Dr. John C. Warren (1778–1856) in the Boston General Hospital. The impact of this discovery was both immediate and profound. The net effect was to encourage surgeons to attempt longer and more complicated operations and to increase the practice of surgical intervention. This increase, however, was accompanied by a massive increase in hospital fevers. Successful surgery was all too often negated by supervening infections.

Fortunately a solution was close at hand. In 1847 Ignaz SEMMELWEIS, a Hungarian physician in Vienna, made the discovery that PUERPERAL FEVER ("child-bed fever"), a disorder that killed many mothers following childbirth, was a specific infection carried by the doctor from one parturient woman to another. Nonetheless, the concept did not gain general acceptance until the advent of the germ theory.

The next advance in surgery was made in 1865 by Joseph LISTER, an English surgeon who deduced from the work of Louis Pasteur (1822–95) that microorganisms in the air must cause the septic poisoning of wounds. In 1865 he began experimenting with an operating technique involving cleanliness and the use of a weak carbolic acid solution as an anti-

septic. The elaborate precautions required by the Listerian method, published in 1867, gradually gained acceptance, and the Germans carried them to their logical conclusion: asepsis. Whereas antiseptic methods were designed to kill bacteria in the operating field, asepsis sought to create a sterile operating field, eliminating harmful bacteria prior to surgical intervention. This procedure involved sterilizing all instruments, dressings, sponges, gowns, and other items in the operating room. Sterilization of the surgeon's hands was solved in the 1890s by the introduction of rubber gloves.

Anesthesia and asepsis literally led to the century of the surgeon. Beginning in the 1880s, surgeons began invading all areas of the human body. Under the leadership of Theodor Billroth (1829–94) of Vienna, abdominal surgery came into its own. Resection (removal of sections) of the gastrointestinal tract, appendectomy, cholecystotomy (removal of gall stones), kidney excision, and a variety of other procedures were introduced. Gynecological surgery, under the guidance of the American J. Marion Sims (1813–83), made rapid strides. The English surgeon Victor Horsley (1857–1916) began removing tumors from the brain and spinal cord and, along with other surgeons, entered the field of glandular surgery. Rudolph Matas (1860–1957) of New Orleans, a pioneer vascular surgeon,

Surgeons in 19th-century England use Dr. Joseph Lister's carbolic-acid spray to prevent infection during an abdominal operation. Lister's antiseptic techniques reduced sharply the rate of patient deaths from hospital gangrene by destroying bacteria in the operating room.

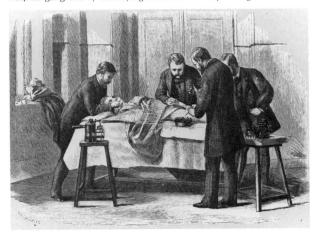

devised a radically new technique for dealing with aneurysms (a ballooning of an artery due to a weakening in the wall) and was a pioneer in developing local anesthesia. Harvey Cushing (1869–1939) of The Johns Hopkins Medical School opened the field of neurosurgery, and Alexis CARREL developed an effective method for anastomosing (joining) blood vessels and also began working on the problem of transplantation.

GROWTH OF SPECIALIZATION

While general surgeons were delving into the joints, the thoracic cavity, and other areas of the body, a host of specialties was arising, such as orthopedics. Ophthalmology became a medical specialty early in the 19th century, but its major development came with the invention of the ophthalmoscope by Hermann HELMHOLTZ in 1851. Otology, treating diseases of the ear, developed about the same time as ophthalmology and was aided by the perfection of the perforated mirror. Rhinology and laryngology emerged during the latter part of the 19th century, stimulated by the improvement of the laryngoscope during the 1850s. Urology made rapid strides as a specialty with the development of more efficient cystoscopes in 1879 and 1886.

20TH CENTURY

A rapid expansion in all fields of surgery took place during the 20th century. New operations were devised and old ones, such as that for hernias or the removal of the breast for cancer, radically improved. Blood transfusion, so essential to major surgery, was made possible by Karl LANDSTEINER when he discovered blood groups shortly after the turn of the century. The problem of blood clotting was solved during World War I by the addition of a citrate solution to the blood, and the final step came with the first blood bank, established in the Cook County Hospital in Chicago.

Technological developments also helped general surgery. The X ray, discovered by Wilhelm ROENTGEN in 1895, was put to use almost immediately as a diagnostic tool, and within a few years RADIOLOGY had become a medical specialty. Contrast radiography, in which the patient ingests, or is injected with, an opaque substance, was developed during the 1920s. Thoracic surgery had been held back by the invariable collapse of the lungs once an incision permitted free entrance of air into the pleural cavity. The problem was solved by Rudolph Matas, who in 1898 modified the Fell-O'Dwyer apparatus—a device to prevent diphtheria victims from suffocating—so that it could provide artificial respiration while the chest cavity was open. The next major advance in this area was the invention of the HEART-LUNG MACHINE, a device first used in 1953, which maintained the cardiopulmonary function while surgeons worked on the heart.

Cardiac surgery began essentially as an emergency measure. During the 1890s several courageous surgeons, confronted with patients stabbed in the heart, opened the chest in desperation and sewed up the wound, thus saving the patients' lives. The process was carried further during World War II when it was recognized that foreign objects driven into the heart could be removed with reasonable safety. During the 1930s and '40s the work of Maude E. Abbott of McGill University and Helen B. Taussig of The Johns Hopkins Medical School laid the basis for surgical correction of congenital heart abnormalities. Beginning in 1944, Dr. Alfred Blalock, an associate of Helen Taussig's, performed a series of successful operations on the major blood vessels of so-called blue babies.

Two developments that gave a major impetus to open-heart surgery during the 1950s were the heart-lung machine, which made possible longer and more delicate heart surgery, and the invention of artificial heart valves. As open-heart surgery expanded, the next assault was on diseased coronary arteries, the vessels carrying the blood supply to the heart muscle. The success of the coronary bypass procedure sharply stimulated the already rapidly growing field of open-heart surgery.

The most significant change in orthopedic surgery has been the increasing invasion of the joints and spinal column. Prior to World War II relatively little attention was paid to lower-

(Left) *Open-heart surgery lasting several hours at a stretch is made possible by a cardiopulmonary bypass of the patient's blood supply to a heart-lung machine. The machine oxygenates the blood and recirculates it through the body by way of the femoral artery.*

(Below) *An eye surgeon uses a laser ophthalmoscope to weld a detached retina to a patient's eye. Other medical uses for laser beams, which were originally developed by researchers in astronomy, include drilling teeth and cauterizing tumors.*

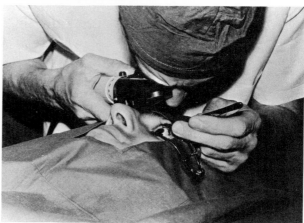

back complaints, a situation that accounts in part for the success of chiropractors. Forced to deal with a good many spinal injuries, surgery made rapid progress, and by the 1950s orthopedic surgeons and neurosurgeons were coping with herniated spinal disks (the small cartilage cushions between the vertebrae) and other problems relating to the spinal column. One of the latest and most promising advances has been the creation of artificial joints, a development that has been particularly helpful to individuals with serious hip problems.

The field of organ transplants has grown immeasurably. The most successful transplants are kidney transplants involving closely related family members. Heart transplants aroused a great deal of attention, but until much more is learned about immunology and the resistance of the body to foreign substances, protein in particular, the procedure is questionable (see ORGAN TRANSPLANT).

Other modern advances in surgery include the intestinal bypass to treat obesity, pacemakers for patients with heart disorders, improvements in artificial limbs and joints, use of lasers in eye surgery, and the use of cryogenic probes in neurosurgery. Although the techniques of microsurgery have become much publicized in recent years, due to their dramatic use in reattaching severed limbs of accident victims, improvements in and application of microsurgery have been expanding since the mid-1960s. It has enabled ophthalmologists to operate on retina and eye muscles to prevent blindness. Surgery can now be performed on the structures of the middle ear to correct deafness. Vasectomies can be reversed in many males. A carotid bypass is performed using microsurgery to improve blood flow to the brain, thus preventing strokes. Special holders were developed to hold the small suturing needles, and surgeons wear glass lenses with a 6X magnification. These have aided the physician's work on minute nerves and blood vessels.   JOHN DUFFY

Bibliography: Beck, R. Theodore, *The Cutting Edge: Early History of the Surgeons of London* (1974); Bishop, William John, *The Early History of Surgery* (1960); Cartwright, Frederick F., *The Development of Modern Surgery* (1967); Earle, A. Scott, ed., *Surgery in America: From the Colonial Era to the Twentieth Century* (1965); Gibson, John, *The Development of Surgery* (1967); Manjo, Guido, *The Healing Hand: Man and Wound in the Ancient World* (1975); Meade, Richard H., *An Introduction to the History of General Surgery* (1968); Milne, John S., *Surgical Instruments in Greek and Roman Times* (1970); Richardson, Robert G., *The Story of Modern Surgery* (1964) and *Surgery: Old and New Frontiers* (1968); Selzer, Richard, *Confessions of a Knife* (1979); Wangensteen, Owen H. and Sarah D., *The Rise of Surgery* (1979).

suricate   [sur'-uh-kayt]

The suricate, Suricata suricata, often forms mixed colonies with squirrels or yellow mongooses. By using its tail for support, the suricate can stand on its hind legs for long periods.

The suricate, or meerkat, *Suricata suricata,* is a slender animal of the civet family, Viverridae, and is closely related to the MONGOOSE. Those found in plains areas burrow, whereas those in rocky regions live in rock crevices. The suricate is 25 to 37 cm (10 to 15 in) long, with a tail nearly as long, and it weighs less than 0.5 kg (1 lb). The coat is light gray with black horizontal stripes on the back and a whitish head. Suricates inhabit southern Africa and eat insects, snakes, and small mammals.   EVERETT SENTMAN

Surinam toad

The Surinam toad, *Pipa pipa,* is actually a relatively large, tongueless, and highly aquatic frog in the family Pipidae. The frog is widely distributed in Amazonian South America and Trinidad. It has a greatly flattened body with a length of 12 to 20 cm (5 to 8 in), a pointed nose, and small, lidless black

The Surinam toad, P. pipa, an amphibian of eastern South America and Trinidad, uses its star-shaped fingertips to search for food.

eyes. The hind legs are strong and extensively webbed and are used for swimming. The slender forelimbs have long, tactile fingers with starlike tips, which are used to sift through mud in search of prey. The Surinam toad is usually light brown with dark-brown patches on its back. It eats such animals as insects, worms, crustaceans, and small fish. The reproductive habits of these frogs are unique. The eggs are deposited on the female's back, become embedded, and develop in individual pockets of skin. Eggs develop directly into small adult frogs in about 16 weeks.   JONATHAN CAMPBELL

Suriname   [sur'-ee-nam]

The Republic of Suriname is located on the northern coast of South America. It is bordered on the east by French Guiana, on the north by the Atlantic Ocean, on the west by Guyana, and on the south by Brazil. Suriname, formerly Dutch Guiana, became independent in 1975.

LAND, PEOPLE, AND RESOURCES
South of a fertile coastal lowland, about 80 km (50 mi) wide, lies a densely forested upland area where elevations exceed 1,220 m (4,000 ft). The chief rivers are the Courantijn, Suriname, and Nickerie. Suriname has a rainy, tropical climate, with a mean annual temperature of 27° C (81° F). Precipitation at Paramaribo is 2,210 mm (87 in) and is even higher in the interior.

About 35% of the population lives in PARAMARIBO, the capital, principal city, and chief port. The population is highly diverse. About 30% is of mixed ancestry, mostly descendants of African slaves and persons of other races. About 15% are Indonesians, and 37% are Asian Indians. The rest of the population includes indigenous Indians, Dutch and other Europeans, and Chinese. Dutch is the official language, and English is also widely spoken as well as Sranang Tongo, or Taki-Taki, a

SURINAME

Official Name: Republic of Suriname
Capital and Largest City: Paramaribo (1974 est. pop., 150,000)
Area: 142,709 km² (55,102 mi²)
Elevation: *Highest*—Julianatop, 1,280 m (4,200 ft); *lowest*—sea level, along the Atlantic Ocean
Population: 388,000 (1979 est.). *Distribution*—40% urban, 60% rural; *density,* 2.7 persons per km² (7 per mi²); *annual rate of increase* (1970–77), 2.7%
Principal Languages: Dutch (official), Hindustani, Javanese, Sranang Tongo
Principal Religions: Christianity, Hinduism, Islam
Principal Products: *Agriculture*—rice, corn, root crops, sugarcane, coffee, fruits, coconuts. *Manufacturing and industry*—processed foods, plywood, paint, bricks, cigarettes. *Mining*—bauxite
Railroads: 116 km/72 mi (1979)
Roads: 500 km/311 mi (1979 paved)
Currency: 1 Suriname guilder = 100 cents

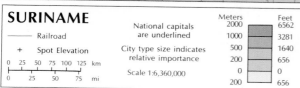

SURINAME

—— Railroad

National capitals
are underlined

+ Spot Elevation

City type size indicates
relative importance

Scale 1:6,360,000

| 0 25 50 75 100 125 km |
| 0 25 50 75 mi |

Meters	Feet
2000	6562
1000	3281
500	1640
200	656
0	0
200	656

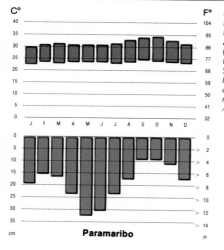

Paramaribo

Bars indicate monthly ranges of temperatures (red) and precipitation (blue) of Paramaribo, the capital of Suriname. The city has the tropical wet climate typical of much of the South American nation.

The presidential palace in Paramaribo, the capital and principal city of Suriname, reflects the influence of Suriname's Dutch colonial heritage. The nation's chief administrative and commercial center, Paramaribo contains approximately 35% of Suriname's total population.

HISTORY AND GOVERNMENT

Suriname was colonized by both the British and the Dutch in the 17th century, but under the Treaty of Breda (1667) the Dutch acquired the territory from the British in exchange for Manhattan Island. A flourishing plantation economy developed during the 18th and 19th centuries, based on imported black slave labor. After slavery was abolished in 1863, laborers were brought from the East Indies and India.

Bauxite production, which began in the 1920s, revolutionized the colony's economy and made Suriname strategically important during World War II. After the war, the Dutch began a program of self-government for the Surinamese, who achieved full independence as a parliamentary republic on Nov. 25, 1975.

In February 1980 the government of Prime Minister Henck Arron was overthrown in a military coup. A National Military Council assumed power as the interim ruling body.

ROBERT J. ALEXANDER

Bibliography: Dew, E., *The Difficult Flowering of Surinam* (1978); Poll, W. N. van de, *Surinam,* trans. by J. Dolman (1951).

surrealism (art)

Surrealism in art—a style in which imagery is based on fantasy and the world of dreams—grew out of a French literary movement founded during the 1920s. The term *surrealist* was coined by Guillaume Apollinaire in 1917; the artistic movement, however, came into being only after the French poet André BRETON published the first surrealist manifesto, *Manifeste du surréalisme*, in 1924. In this book Breton suggested that rational thought was repressive to the powers of creativity and imagination and thus inimical to artistic expression. An admirer of Sigmund Freud and his concept of the subconscious, Breton felt that contact with this hidden part of the mind could produce poetic truth.

Breton soon recognized the kinship between his literary aims and the artistic aims of certain painters fascinated by Freudian concepts. In 1925, with Breton's encouragement, the first group exhibition of surrealist painting took place in Paris. Among those included were Giorgio de CHIRICO, Max ERNST, André MASSON, Joan MIRÓ, Pablo PICASSO, and Man RAY.

The presurrealist paintings of de Chirico, done before 1919, were of particular influence to certain of the surrealists, including Max ERNST, Salvador DALÍ, René MAGRITTE, and Yves TANGUY. These painters developed a dreamlike, or hallucinatory, imagery that was all the more startling for its highly real-

local patois. The population is 37% Christian and 26% each Hindu and Muslim.

School attendance is compulsory to age 13, and institutions of higher learning include the University of Suriname (1968) and three technical schools. About 80% of the population is literate. Life expectancy is 66 years, and the infant mortality rate is 30 per 1,000 live births.

During the colonial period, dikes were built along the coast to protect farmland, increasing arable land to 0.3% of the territory. Suriname's principal crops are rice, sugar, corn, coffee, and fruit and garden crops. Agriculture employs 29% of the labor force. Suriname is one of the world's great sources of bauxite for making aluminum. Bauxite represents 85% of the country's exports and is responsible for Suriname's relatively small trade deficit. Timber, rice, and coffee are also exported. Suriname's chief trading partners are the Netherlands, the United States, and Trinidad.

(Below) *In Rendez-vous of the Friends (1922), Max Ernst created a document portraying those whom he considered seminal to the development of surrealism:* (standing) *Soupault, Arp, Morise, Sanzio, P. Éluard, Aragon, Breton, Baargeld, Chirico, G. Éluard, Desnos;* (sitting) *Crevel, Ernst, Dostoyevsky, Fraenkel, Paulhan, Péret. (Private collection.)*

(Above) The Human Condition I *(1934) exemplifies René Magritte's restrained depiction of the surreal. The paradoxes and subtle incongruities seen in Magritte's work reveal a more intellectual approach to the representation of another reality than is evident in the more consciously obscure works of many other surrealist painters. (Claude Spaak Collection, Choisel, France.)*

(Below) *The ambiguities and classical motifs that pervade much of Giorgio de Chirico's work are seen in* Death of a Spirit *(1926). During the early 1920s, Chirico began to abandon the abstruse "metaphysical" style that characterized his early work—and greatly influenced the surrealists—for a more academic style. (Private collection.)*

(Above) *Salvador Dalí's* Temptation of Saint Anthony *(1946) resurrects a theme found in the works of medieval and Renaissance artists. The bizarre elongations, huge scale, and vigor of the approaching creatures evoke the menace of the irrational. (Private collection.)*

istic rendering. Other painters, including Miró and Masson, used biomorphic forms and accidental effects that approached abstraction. Their work influenced the beginnings of abstract expressionism in the United States during the 1940s.

Although it began partly as a reaction to DADA, surrealism benefited from Dada's liberating effects. Some of Dada's techniques were adopted by the surrealists, including assemblage, a form of sculpture consisting of combinations of incongruous objects and materials. Meret Oppenheim's *Object (Fur-Lined Cup and Saucer)* (1936; Museum of Modern Art, New York City) is a key example. Ernst's surreal "novels," two books of collages of strangely unrelated images, were a continuation of his Dada COLLAGE concepts.

The surrealist painters also looked to the past for inspiration, to such painters of fantasy as Hieronymus BOSCH, to the Mannerists, and to the romantic and symbolist movements, as well as to PRIMITIVE ART and the art of the insane. Whether or not surrealism has ceased as a movement, its influences can be detected in all the major art movements that have come into being since 1945.

EDWARD M. PLUNKETT

Bibliography: Ades, Dawn, *Dada and Surrealism* (1978); Barr, Alfred, *Fantastic Art, Dada and Surrealism* (1968); Breton, André, *Surrealism and Painting*, trans. by S. W. Taylor (1972); Gascoyne, David, *A Short History of Surrealism* (1970); Levy, Julien, *Surrealism* (1968); Nadeau, Maurice, *The History of Surrealism* (1965); Rubin, William, *Dada and Surrealist Art* (1968); Scheede, Uwe, *Surrealism* (1974).

surrealism   (film, literature, theater)

This photograph is a still from Un Chien Andalou (An Andalusian Dog, 1928), a surrealist film directed by Luis Buñuel in collaboration with the painter Salvador Dalí, both major exponents of surrealism in the arts. A highly ambiguous and imagistic work, the film reflects the fusion of Buñuel's and Dalí's artistic concerns.

Surrealism, meaning above realism, is an antiaesthetic movement that grew out of the nihilistic DADA movement of the years during and immediately after World War I. Its range being that of human thought itself, surrealism is limited in scope and application only by the human capacity for self-expression, which surrealists aim to expand. Writing, painting, film, sculpture, or any other art form assumes significance for the surrealist when it expresses a surrealist state of mind.

Surrealism began as a revolt against the control exercised by rationality over accepted modes of communication. The first surrealists attacked inherited preconceptions about the nature and function of word poems. In 1919, André BRETON and Philippe Soupault produced the first specifically surrealist text, Les Champs magnétiques (Magnetic Fields, 1921), by so-called automatic writing, in which the surrealist banishes deliberate intent, leaving the pen free to express on paper the uncensored images that well up from the subconscious.

Seeking to embrace all forms of creative expression in their liberative effort to attain what Breton in his 1924 Manifeste du surréalisme (Manifesto of Surrealism) called "the true functioning of thought," the surrealists set about attacking, on the broadest possible front, conventions, prescribed rules, and consecrated values—cultural as well as aesthetic. This explains, for instance, their enthusiasm for the films of Luis BU-ÑUEL, whose L'Age d'or (The Golden Age, 1930) surpassed in violent iconoclasm even his first movie, Un Chien Andalou (An Andalusian Dog, 1928).

In its negative attitude toward literary and artistic tradition, and in its opposition to the heritage of Western culture, surrealism superficially resembled Dada, the movement with which some of its earliest members, including Louis ARAGON, Roger VITRAC, Breton, Soupault, and its greatest poet, Benjamin Péret, all had been affiliated. However, surrealism marked a stage beyond the nihilism that had inevitably brought Dada to self-destruction. Surrealism was truly international, and exponents of its revolutionary principles shared an unshakable faith in the power of the imagination to revitalize poetry and art, and to compensate for the sociopolitical and religious forces that they found so oppressive and stultifying in contemporary society.

J. H. MATTHEWS

Bibliography: Alquié, Ferdinand, The Philosophy of Surrealism (1965); Breton, André, What Is Surrealism? (1978); Gascoyne, David, A Short Survey of Surrealism (1935); Matthews, J. H., An Introduction to Surrealism (1965); Nadeau, Maurice, The History of Surrealism (1965); Read, Herbert, ed., Surrealism (1936; repr. 1971).

Surrey   [sur'-ee]

Surrey is a county in southeastern England, immediately southwest of London along the River Thames. It has an area of 1,655 km² (639 mi²) and a population of 995,800 (1977 est.). Kingston upon Thames (1977 est. pop., 136,400) is the county's administrative center. The land is mainly low-lying except for the chalk hills known as the North Downs. Surrey is drained by the Wey and Mole rivers. Important towns include Esher, Reigate, and Guildford. The borough of Epsom and Ewell is known for Epsom Downs, the racetrack where the Derby, a classic horse race, is run. Dairying, market gardening, and the cultivation of wheat and oats are economically important. Radio and radar equipment and aircraft are manufactured there. Surrey has been settled since the Paleolithic Period. It was Romanized after AD 43. Since the Middle Ages, Surrey's history has been strongly influenced by the proximity of London.

Surrey, Henry Howard, Earl of

The English poet Henry Howard, Earl of Surrey, b. Hunsdon, Hertfordshire, 1517, d. Jan. 19, 1547, is best remembered for his elegant sonnets published in Tottel's Miscellany (1557). His translation of Books 2 and 4 of Vergil's Aeneid is the first example of blank, or unrhymed iambic pentameter, verse in English. After a distinguished career as a soldier and courtier, Surrey was executed on a trumped-up charge of treason.

ROBIN BUSS

surveillance systems

The purpose of surveillance systems is to monitor events from a remote or secret location. The equipment for these tasks ranges from simple television camera systems in banks or stores and metal-detecting devices at airports to airborne heat-sensing devices used by environmental officials to detect water polluters, and secret military satellites with a wide range of detection devices. Many of the more sophisticated sensors, night-vision devices, and alarm systems that are available to the public are the direct descendants of equipment developed for the military during the Vietnam War. For instance, a special television camera introduced in 1974 has two remarkable attributes: it can take crisp pictures with no more light than that given off by a single candle, and it is very small (weighing less than 0.5 kg/1 lb) and easily concealed. Another device is a proximity-sensor system that responds when someone touches or even comes close to a metal object such as a desk or a filing cabinet. One sensor can keep track of 20 desks and transmit what it senses to a remote location such as a guard's office. Closed-circuit television, another type of surveillance system, is used to watch banks, police stations, prisons, and other locations requiring constant security. Such systems have been installed in neighborhoods on an experimental basis to allow police departments to monitor high-crime-rate areas. Electro-optical devices are able to amplify the smallest amount of light available to permit night vision. Such equipment has been used by police to monitor potential criminal activity and to locate suspects in the dark. Surveillance systems are in place in such diverse locations as the White House lawn, along portions of the U.S.-Mexican border, and in office buildings, amusement parks, and airports.

Although many persons state that most surveillance equipment fulfills a valuable and useful function, others insist that it poses a threat to individual freedom and privacy. Opponents of surveillance systems have argued that curbs must be placed on their application to prevent a "Big Brother" atmosphere such as that described in George Orwell's novel 1984.

D. DICKSON

Bibliography: Blum, Richard H., ed., Surveillance and Espionage in a Free Society (1972); Holz, Robert K., ed., Surveillant Science (1973).

surveying

Surveying is the practice of determining large dimensions with a high degree of accuracy, either to measure existing re-

(Above) *Egyptian workers measure a wheat field using a knotted rope or chain in this detail from a tomb painting (c.1400 BC) at Thebes. Maps and land measurements recorded by the Sumerians also indicate ancient knowledge of some surveying techniques. The Egyptians developed simple surveying tools, including a device to obtain accurate 90° angles and a leveling tool, that were adopted and improved centuries later by the Romans.*

lationships (preliminary surveying) or to provide the means to build according to designers' plans (construction stakeout). Preliminary surveying is necessary to obtain information for all mapping; construction stakeout is necessary to control the location of all but the smallest or least significant construction project.

The Egyptians used surveying methods as early as 1400 BC to reestablish boundary markers obliterated by the Nile's flood waters. As long ago as 2900 BC their pyramids were built with an accuracy that indicates construction was controlled by surveying. The Babylonians, about 3500 BC, produced maps to an accurate scale, which indicates that field information was obtained by surveying and plotted to scale using surveying principles in miniature.

Surveying theory is based on the principles of geometry and trigonometry, and the methods used are based on the principles of physics. Each survey must be accomplished with the proper accuracy; too much accuracy is needlessly expensive, and too little does not accomplish the intended purpose. Also, certain data must be recorded in the field and certain reference points must be set; unnecessary data or points, however, result in excess costs. Data and points must be useful to people who may not necessarily be acquainted with surveying procedures.

Surveying measurements are made vertically, on a PLUMB LINE directed toward the Earth's center, and horizontally measured perpendicular to plumb line. All objects bear relationships to each other that can be expressed by the horizontal direction, horizontal distance, and vertical distance between them; surveying is a technique to measure and lay out these three dimensions. The three relationships among objects can seldom be established directly. The usual procedure is to set a framework of convenient points and accurately determine their relationships—horizontal distances and directions, elevations only, or all three. This constitutes a control. Objects located relative to any point of the control can all be located relative to each other, either mathematically or graphically.

Methods. A traverse, the most common horizontal control, consists of a series of points called stations, each of which is located in the field by angle and distance from adjacent stations. Each station is selected for convenience and marked with a nail in the top of a wood stake. The traverse returns to the starting point to form a polygon. Because field measurements contain inaccuracies, the angles and distances between stations must be adjusted to make them mathematically correct. The total error (error of closure) is found by calculating the position of each station from the starting point, around the traverse, and back to the starting point—the difference between starting location and the ending location determined mathematically is the error of closure. The location of stations and the angles and distances are adjusted by distributing the closure error in a logical manner.

Triangulation is used for the most accurate horizontal controls over large areas but may also be used as a control whenever it is more convenient than a traverse. A triangulation system consists of a series of adjacent triangles with sides in common; the triangle corners are the stations. All three angles of each triangle are measured, and the sides are determined by trigonometry from one measured side called a baseline. A few other sides, also called baselines, are measured as a means of checking the calculated distances. The angles are adjusted mathematically so that the total of each triangle's interior angles is 180 degrees; the distances are also adjusted mathematically. Trilateration, another surveying technique, also uses a series of triangles, but the sides rather than the angles of the triangles are measured.

Vertical control is established with a level circuit starting and ending at a point of known elevation, a bench mark (BM), with other bench marks set along the circuit. The difference between the known elevation of the starting point and its elevation determined at the end of the circuit is the error of closure. The field-determined elevations of the new bench marks are adjusted mathematically on the basis of error of closure and of their positions in the circuit.

Stakeout. In stakeouts, existing objects are located in the field by angle, distance, and elevation measurements from the points of a control survey. Measurements are recorded in a field notebook and taken to an office for plotting and computations. The surveyor sets wooden stakes at specified locations near the proposed construction to show the builder exactly where to build in order to conform to the designer's intentions. Interpreting the designer's plans and calculating angles and distances needed to set stakes from the control points is part of the surveyor's work; necessary data are entered in the field book and taken to the site as a guide in construction stakeout.

Most surveying involves plane surveying methods, which ignore the curvature of the Earth. Plumb lines are considered to be parallel, although in reality each one is a radius from the center of the Earth (nearly) and no two are parallel. A straight line of sight is considered level, although a level line actually curves parallel to the average surface of the Earth.

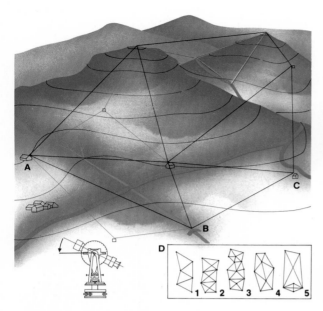

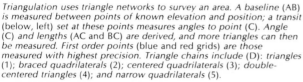

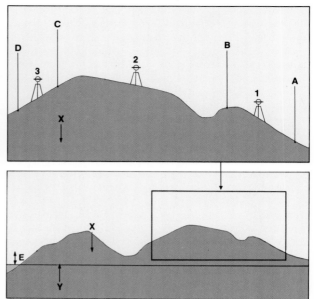

Triangulation uses triangle networks to survey an area. A baseline (AB) is measured between points of known elevation and position; a transit (below, left) set at these points measures angles to point (C). Angle (C) and lengths (AC and BC) are derived, and more triangles can then be measured. First order points (blue and red grids) are those measured with highest precision. Triangle chains include (D): triangles (1); braced quadrilaterals (2); centered quadrilaterals (3); double-centered triangles (4); and narrow quadrilaterals (5).

In measuring the height of a hilly area, a measuring rod is first staked at a known elevation called the bench mark (X). A leveling instrument is positioned (1) to sight the rod at position A and then at position B, and the difference in height is measured. The instrument is then moved to a second bench-mark position (2), and point C is measured; at position 3 the instrument uses point C to measure point D. The heights of all these points can be related to sea level (Y) by knowing the height of the bench mark X above sea level (E).

These approximations produce no measurable error in surveys of ordinary size. In very large surveys, however, curvature of the Earth must be considered, and a special method, called geodetic surveying, is required. Latitudes and longitudes are taken into account and triangulation is most often used as a means of measurement.

Equipment. Horizontal angles are measured with TRANSIT or THEODOLITE instruments that are equipped with a telescope and leveling screws and vials. For ordinary work horizontal distances are measured with accuracy and efficiency by using measuring tapes of fabric for rough work and of steel for greater accuracy.

Electronic-distance-measuring (EDM) equipment, which transmits an impulse of electromagnetic energy from one point to another from which it is reflected to the original point, gives very high accuracy at both short and long distances. The instrument converts travel time and velocity into the distance between points.

Optical triangles are also used to measure distances. Stadia measurements are made by reading the length of vertical rod that is subtended by the angle between two lines of sight. The lines of sight are fixed by stadia hairs in a transit or theodolite so that the rod length between them is always one-hundredth of the distance from the center of the instrument

An American transit is a surveying instrument used to measure horizontal angles and lines. This device includes a telescope (1), with a focusing knob (2); a vertical circle (3), with an elevation axis (4) and an elevation tangent screw (5); a compass (6), with plate levels (7); an eyepiece for optical plummet (8); a lower-motion tangent screw (9); a leveling screw (10); and a leveling head (11).

A theodolite is a surveying instrument that measures angles with greater accuracy than does a transit. It is smaller than a transit, with its controls enclosed in a cover, and has a telescope equipped with prisms rather than lenses.

to the rod. Many distances can be quickly determined, but not with great accuracy, by using the same sighting for angle and distance.

A horizontal fixed-length rod, called a subtense bar, is also used for distance measuring. The rod is set up perpendicular to the line of sight from transit or theodolite. The horizontal angle subtended by the rod can be used with the rod length to compute the distance from instrument center to subtense bar. Three angular readings are required to determine direction and distance—one to the center of the bar for direction, and one at each end of the bar for the distance. The subtense bar is highly accurate, but its use is time consuming.

All these methods may be used to measure horizontal distances or distances inclined to the horizontal. An inclined distance on a hill, for instance, is converted mathematically into a horizontal distance and a vertical distance.

Vertical distances between two points are measured by determining the elevations of the two points and subtracting the lower elevation from the higher; an instrument known as an engineer's level, which has a telescope that can be accurately leveled and turned in any direction, is used. The line of sight through the telescope is a horizontal line no matter where it is turned.

A level rod, which is graduated in hundredths of a meter or foot from the bottom upward, is also used; the elevation of the line of sight is determined by reading the rod at the line of sight when the rod is standing on a point of known elevation (bench mark). The line-of-sight elevation is higher than the bench mark by the amount read on the rod. The elevation of any other point may be determined by standing the rod on it and reading the rod with the same line of sight; the elevation of that point is less than that of the line of sight by the amount read on the rod.

Types of Surveying. Surveying is divided into many types according to its purpose. Topographic surveying specifically involves determination of the shape of the ground surface, but the term is generally used to describe surveying to obtain information for maps.

Information for maps of areas up to several hectares in size is obtained by plane or geodetic surveying, and information for larger maps is obtained by aerial photography. Certain small, conspicuous objects in the aerial photographs are accurately located as part of a control survey from which all other objects are positioned on the map.

Surveys for mapping the bottom of bodies of water are called hydrographic surveys. Route surveys are made to prepare maps for the design of such facilities as highways and pipelines. Land, or cadastral, surveying includes locating and marking property boundaries and determining property areas. It requires a knowledge of legal principles as well as of surveying methods. Each state licenses land surveyors to practice within that state.

Construction surveying involves setting marks to control construction. Construction includes buildings, bridges, highways, and pipelines as well as highly accurate determinations of the required directions for electromagnetic-wave propagation and spacecraft launching.

Also included in construction surveying are the control of underground tunneling and mining, the control of underwater dredging, and the positioning of navigational aids in water.

Careers in Surveying. Surveyors are employed in a variety of ways. Civil engineering organizations, whether private consulting firms or government public-works departments, employ surveyors for mapping, checking construction stakeout, and measuring construction work. Construction firms employ surveyors to set construction stakes and to check engineers' measurements. The U.S. Government National Geodetic Survey organization employs surveyors to establish and maintain networks of horizontal and vertical control stations throughout the United States, and the U.S. Geological Survey organization employs surveyors for its continuous project of mapping the entire country to a large scale. Individual land surveyors, licensed by the states, operate their own businesses and employ other surveyors.

Education. Surveying courses are offered as part of engineering, agricultural, construction, and forestry curricula, and several colleges offer a bachelor's degree in surveying. Several years of practical experience are required and, usually, formal education in order to qualify for a land surveyor's license in any state or to perform as a surveyor in the construction or mapping fields.

Trends. Changes are taking place in surveying methods chiefly because of electronic developments. Notes have traditionally been written by hand in field notebooks both prior to going into the field for construction stakeout and while in the field performing preliminary surveys. Surveyors are now able to take into the field a computer printout that contains complete instructions on how to stake a construction project. They will eventually be able to bring from the field to the office a computer printout containing a complete record of the field work.

Historically, surveyors have been able to measure angles with transit or theodolite more accurately than they have been able to measure distances with steel tapes. At present, electronic distance-measuring equipment is capable of measuring distances more accurately than angles can be read. In the future, theodolites will read angles electronically to a higher accuracy than is now possible and provide digital printouts that can be fed directly to miniature computers, which will then calculate, adjust, and determine the accuracy of results immediately in the field. CHARLES A. HERUBIN

Bibliography: Breed, Charles B., and Hosmer, George, *The Principles and Practice of Surveying*, 2 vols. (1977); Davis, Raymond, et al., *Surveying: Theory and Practice*, 5th ed. (1966); Herubin, Charles A., *Principles of Surveying*, 2d ed. (1978); Kissam, Philip, *Surveying Practice*, 3d ed. (1977).

Surveyor

The first U.S. landings on the Moon were achieved by the automatic Surveyor spacecraft. Seven missions, five of them successful, were launched between May 30, 1966, and Jan. 7, 1968; the spidery spacecraft touched down under their own guidance in a test of soft-landing technology for the coming Apollo missions. In addition to merely touching down safely, the Surveyors were also instrumented to study aspects of the lunar surface environment—dust, temperatures, solar effects, and so on—that might affect human astronauts. In addition, the robot landers carried out a variety of pioneering analyses of the lunar surface material.

Surveyor 1, launched May 30, 1966, landed in the southwest portion of the Moon's Oceanus Procellarum on June 2. In 7 months of operation it sent back 11,240 television pictures—by contrast, the Lunar Orbiters, limited by film supplies, could take only a few hundred photographs—and transmitted data on the surface's radar reflectivity (important for Apollo as well as Surveyor descents), temperatures, and bearing strength. (A few scientists had expressed fears that a spacecraft might sink out of sight beneath a layer of Moondust.)

The second Surveyor, launched Sept. 20, 1966, was lost when it crashed into the Moon three days later, a victim not of the lunar surface characteristics but of a malfunctioning rocket engine.

Surveyor 3, launched Apr. 17, 1967, landed on April 20 in eastern Oceanus Procellarum, equipped again with a television camera but with a significant addition: a telescoping arm capable of digging trenches, moving rocks, and conducting other tests with the surface material. Although it functioned only 2 weeks, the craft provided 6,326 pictures, and the sampling arm was able to excavate the Moon to a depth of 17.5 cm (7 in).

Surveyor 4, launched July 14, 1967, was the only other casualty in the series. It presumably crashed on July 16, although its transmissions abruptly ceased about 2½ minutes before it was to reach the ground.

The first direct chemical measurements were made by *Surveyor 5*, launched Sept. 8, 1967, and landing September 11. It carried, instead of a sampling arm, an alpha-backscatter experiment that irradiated the surface beneath it with alpha particles and monitored the characteristic return from the dif-

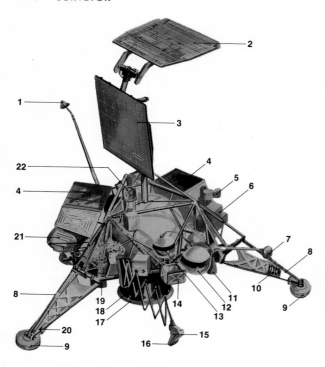

The Surveyor 3 *spacecraft made a soft landing on the Moon on Apr. 20, 1967. Two years after it stopped functioning, the spacecraft was visited (November 1969) by the Apollo 12 astronauts, who retrieved its television camera. Tests showed that the spacecraft carried live bacteria that had somehow survived the harsh environment of space. Numbers indicate: omnidirectional antenna (1); square solar panel (2), providing 89 watts of power; high-grain antenna (3); thermally controlled compartment (4); Canopus sensor (5), for guidance; flight-control sensor group (6); omnidirectional antenna (7); landing leg (8); footpad (9); accelerometer amplifier (10); vernier rocket engine (11); vernier propellant pressurizing tank (12); gas tank (13) for controlling attitude; auxiliary battery (14); soil sampler (15), with maximum extension of 1.5 m (5 ft); digging scoop (16); antenna (17); retro-rocket nozzle (18); crushable block (19), for absorbing touchdown impact; jet nozzle (20) for control of pitch and yaw; radar altitude and Doppler velocity sensor (21); and television camera (22).*

ferent elements in the lunar soil. This experiment first showed lunar material was similar to terrestrial basalt (and notably did not show any exotic elements alien to Earth). In another test the vehicle's engines were fired for 0.55 seconds to study the effects of high-velocity exhaust gases on the Moon's surface; this effect was of concern to scientists wondering whether the exhaust of the Apollo lunar module would hopelessly contaminate samples being returned to Earth. Finally, the craft not only sent back 18,006 pictures during the 5 weeks of its primary mission but survived 2 weeks of inactivity during the deep-freeze of the lunar night and responded to the first subsequent activation command. It demonstrated its health by sending more than 1,000 additional pictures.

Surveyor 6, launched Nov. 7, 1967, not only landed safely on November 10 in Sinus Medii, essentially in the center of the Moon's visible hemisphere, but scored a first by taking off again—on a single, 2-m-long (6.5-ft) sideways hop. With most of its mission accomplished, including most of its total of 29,952 pictures, the unit fired its engines for 2½ seconds, just enough to lift it off of the surface and move it a short distance. Besides adding new data on the effects of a substantial surface impact, the lateral displacement provided a baseline for stereoscopic viewing and photogrammetric mapping of the surrounding terrain. The craft provided another 30 hours of alpha-backscatter data (added to *Surveyor 5's* 18 hours) and served as a reference point for Doppler-tracking studies of the Moon's motions. *Surveyor 6* also sent back views of the Earth, stars, and the solar corona.

The four previous Surveyor successes effectively freed the remaining probe, *Surveyor 7*, to be sent to a site of primarily scientific, rather than safe-landing, interest. The chosen site was in a rough region north of the relatively young crater Tycho, selected because it is in the lunar highlands, removed from the mare terrain typified by the other Surveyor sites. *Surveyor 7*, launched Jan. 7, 1968, and landing on January 10, carried both a sampling arm and an alpha-backscatter experiment, using the arm to move the device to different locations. This device enabled elemental analyses of the bare lunar surface, a lunar rock, and an area dug up by the sampler.

JONATHAN EBERHART

Bibliography: Kloman, Erasmus H., *Unmanned Space Project Management: Surveyor and Lunar Orbiter* (1972); Ryan, Peter, *The Invasion of the Moon, 1957–1970*, rev. ed. (1971); U.S. Surveyor Program Office, *Surveyor Program Results* (1969).

Susa [soo'-zuh]

Susa (Shush), in southwestern Iran, was the ancient capital of the Elamites, an administrative center and royal residence under the Achaemenids and the eastern terminus of the Persian Royal Road that ran westward to Lydian Sardis, about 2,575 km (1,600 mi) away. Following the conquests of Alexander the Great, Susa was made a Greek colonial city-state called Seleucia-on-the-Eulaeus; it continued to flourish as a trade center through the Parthian and Sassanian periods, until its capture (AD c.640) by Islamic forces.

Rediscovered in 1850, Susa has been under almost continuous excavation by French archaeologists since 1897. Although occupation levels date back to Neolithic times (c.4000 BC), the principal objects of interest at the site are four large mounds representing the citadel, the palace of Darius I (r. 521–486 BC), and two sections of the ancient city. Significant finds at Susa have included early painted pottery and seals, proto-Elamite writing, an extensive Parthian cemetery, and the famous stele of Hammurabi bearing his law code (see HAMMURABI, CODE OF).

TOM B. JONES

Bibliography: Matheson, S. A., *Persia: An Archaeological Guide* (1972); Porada, Edith, *The Art of Ancient Iran* (1965).

Susann, Jacqueline

Novelist Jacqueline Susann, b. Philadelphia, Aug. 20, 1921, d. Sept. 21, 1974, catapulted to fame and fortune on the strength of several sensational novels dealing with the seamy side of life among the rich and influential. One of them, *The Valley of the Dolls* (1966; film, 1967), proved to be the world's all-time best-seller, and others, such as *The Love Machine* (1969; film, 1971) and *Once Is Not Enough* (1973; film, 1975), were also successful both as books and as films.

Susanna

The story of Susanna is told in the Book of Susanna in the APOCRYPHA. Falsely accused of adultery by elders who had failed in their attempt to seduce her, and condemned to death, Susanna is rescued by the divinely inspired Daniel, whose clever cross-examination exposes her accusers.

Suso, Heinrich [zoo'-zoh]

A German monk and mystic, Heinrich Suso, or Seuse, b. Mar. 21, 1295?, d. Jan. 25, 1366, studied under the famous mystic Meister ECKHART at Cologne. He wrote *The Little Book of Truth* (c.1329), a defense of Eckhart, for which he was rebuked by his superiors and deprived of his teaching position at Constance. He then became an itinerant preacher, traveling widely in Switzerland before returning to monastic life. His principal work is *The Little Book of Eternal Wisdom* (c.1348), an influential book of meditations. He was beatified in 1831. Feast day: March 15 (formerly March 2).

Bibliography: Clark, J., *The Great German Mystics* (1949; repr. 1970).

suspense fiction: see MYSTERY, SUSPENSE, AND DETECTIVE FICTION.

suspension

In chemistry, a suspension is a mixture in which a liquid or a gas contains a finely divided solid that spontaneously settles as a result of gravity. The rate of settling depends on the particle size and the difference in the densities of the suspended solid and the suspension medium; the rate may be increased by centrifugation. A suspension differs from a SOLUTION because in the latter the solute is subdivided into molecules, which are kept from settling by thermal molecular motion. Between suspensions and solutions lies the COLLOIDAL STATE; no clear distinction can be made between fine suspensions and systems of colloid particles that are close to the upper limit of the colloid range.   GEORGE GORIN

suspension system

An automotive suspension system supports the frame and body of a vehicle, attaching them to the wheels. Its main purpose is to absorb road shocks caused by irregularities in the road surface in order to reduce the bumps transmitted to the occupants. The system also improves safety and road-handling ability by maintaining better contact between the wheels and the road.

PARTS OF THE SYSTEM

Most modern motor vehicles have separate springs at each wheel, with supports arranged in several ways. There is a shock absorber at each wheel to help smooth out spring action. Different arrangements are often used for the suspension at the front and rear of the vehicle, because the front wheels must pivot from side to side for steering as well as up and down to absorb road shocks. Some cars use a torsion bar, which is a special type of spring. Stabilizers are sometimes used to prevent excessive lean-out on turns.

Springs. A spring is a device that can temporarily store energy. By doing this it can supply energy afterwards, as in a watch or a wind-up toy; or a spring can maintain pressure between surfaces and thus support one surface from another, as in the automotive suspension system. By maintaining a constant pressure the spring not only offers support, it also resists any motion that would tend to change the position of one surface with respect to another, supplying a restoring force. Many suspension systems use coil, or helical, springs. Rear suspensions often use leaf springs. A leaf spring is essentially a flat bar that resists motion. The two ends of the leaf spring are attached to the frame, and the center is attached to the axle housing. This enables the wheel and housing to move up and down with respect to the frame when the car hits a bump in the road.

Shock Absorbers. A shock absorber offers a large resistance to movement and so can quickly damp out vibrations. Its purpose in a suspension system is to moderate wheel movement and to prevent continuing vibrations after a wheel has passed over a bump. A spring without a shock absorber would continue to expand and contract for a long time, causing poor car control and a rough ride. On many front suspension systems the shock absorber is attached at the top to the frame and at the bottom to the lower control arm. In rear suspensions it is attached in a number of different ways.

The shock absorber contains a piston in a fluid-filled cylinder. It has valves that permit the fluid to flow from one side of the piston to the other as the piston moves up and down in the cylinder. The valves, however, restrain the flow of the fluid. Thus, as the piston moves up and down in the cylinder with the up-and-down movement of the wheel, the fluid flow is hampered and the motion is reduced. (The kinetic energy of the motion is dissipated as heat in the fluid.)

Torsion Bars. Some vehicles use torsion bars instead of coil springs at certain points of the system. The torsion bar twists as road irregularities are encountered. Its front end is attached to a lower control arm, and its rear end is attached to the car frame. As the lower control arm pivots up and down, the torsion bar twists more or less, behaving just like a coil spring.

Stabilizers. Some front suspension systems also use stabilizers. The stabilizer is a long steel rod that is attached at each

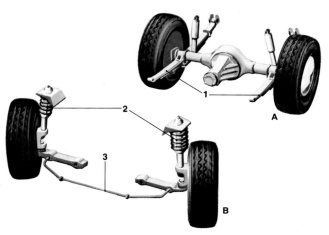

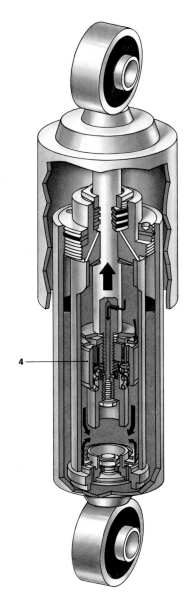

The suspension system absorbs the impacts of a bumpy road so that an automobile can ride smoothly. This is accomplished by spring suspension (above) and shock absorbers (left). Rear suspension (A) has leaf springs (1) mounted on the axle. Front suspension (B) has coil springs (2) to absorb shocks and an antiroll bar (3) that minimizes sideways dip when the car turns. A shock absorber is often mounted within a coil spring. It absorbs bump and rebound shocks by using their energy to move a piston (4) that forces oil in and out of portions of the device. The arrows indicate flow of oil on the rebound stroke.

end to the two lower control arms. Its purpose is to prevent excessive lean-out on turns. When the vehicle goes around a curve, centrifugal force tends to make the car lean out. This action puts more weight on the outer front spring, which thus is compressed more than the inner spring on the turn. As the outer spring is compressed, it imparts a twist to the stabilizer bar. The inner spring on the turn tends to expand, because it has less weight on it. This twists the stabilizer bar in the opposite direction. The stabilizer bar resists this twist and thus reduces the amount that the vehicle can lean out on a turn.

AUTOMATIC LEVEL CONTROL

Some cars have a system called automatic level control, which compensates for any change in loading of the rear of the car. The system includes a compressor to supply compressed air, two special shock absorbers with air domes, and a height-control valve. When the weight in the rear is increased (by passengers or cargo), the rear settles. This triggers the height-control valve, which sends compressed air from the pump through the valve into the air domes in the shock absorbers. The compressed air causes the shock absorbers to extend and thus raise the rear of the car. When the original height is reached, the valve shuts off the flow of compressed air.

When the rear of the car is unloaded, it will rise above its original height. When this happens, the height-control valve opens to release some of the air from the shock-absorber air domes, causing the rear end to settle to the original height.

WILLIAM H. CROUSE

Bibliography: Crouse, William H., *Automotive Mechanics*, 8th ed. (1980); Crouse, William H., and Anglin, Donald L., *Automotive Brakes, Suspension, and Steering* (1981); Ellinger, Herbert E., and Hathaway, Richard B., *Automotive Suspension, Steering and Brakes* (1980).

Susquehanna   [suhs-kwuh-han'-uh]

The Susquehanna, also sometimes called the Susquehannock, Conestoga, or Minqua, were a tribe of North American Indians who spoke an Iroquoian language and formerly inhabited a territory that now makes up southeastern Pennsylvania and northern Maryland. Traditionally they shifted their subsistence activities with the seasons. Springtime found them planting maize, beans, and squash near their permanent villages. After planting, they moved to temporary villages on the coast where they fished and collected shellfish throughout the summer. In the fall they returned to the permanent villages to harvest their crops, collect wild plant-foods, and hunt. Little is known of their political organization.

Characterized as being a noble, heroic, and powerful people at the time of their first contact with Europeans, the Susquehanna subjugated the coastal DELAWARE after being pushed southward and eastward in 1580 by the encroaching IROQUOIS LEAGUE. They were nearly annihilated (1676) by the Iroquois and subsequently relinquished their control over the Delaware. Survivors lived with the ONEIDA for a time and were then permitted to return to their homeland. With their population greatly reduced by warfare and disease, those who were left were converted to Christianity by the Quakers. This small group was massacred in 1763 by a mob of white men inflamed by reports of Indian aggressions in Pennsylvania.

JAMES W. HERRICK

Bibliography: Trigger, Bruce, ed., *Handbook of North American Indians,* vol. 15 (1978).

Susquehanna River

The Susquehanna, one of the longest rivers in the eastern United States, is 715 km (444 mi) long and has a drainage area of 71,400 km² (27,570 mi²). Rising at Otsego Lake in central New York, the river winds southwest into Pennsylvania past Wilkes-Barre, where it joins its West Branch flowing from west central Pennsylvania. The river then widens and flows south and southeast past Harrisburg to Chesapeake Bay. Shallow and with numerous rapids, the Susquehanna is navigable only near its mouth and locally. The Wilkes-Barre–Scranton area is important for anthracite coal mining.

Sussex   [suhs'-uhks]

Sussex, a historic county in southern England on the English Channel, was reorganized (1974) into two counties: East Sussex, with an area of 1,795 km² (693 mi²) and a population of 652,900 (1977 est.); and West Sussex, with an area of 2,016 km² (778 mi²) and a population of 625,100 (1977 est.). Sussex is drained by the Adur, Arun, Ouse, and Rother rivers. Low, rolling hills known as the South Downs cross the counties from east to west. The economy is based on dairying, poultry raising, fishing, and tourism, especially at Channel resorts such as BRIGHTON. Sussex, one of the early Anglo-Saxon kingdoms, fell to the kings of Wessex in the 9th century. The Battle of Hastings in 1066 took place in Sussex.

Sussex spaniel

The Sussex spaniel is a compact, short-legged sporting dog bred to hunt upland game in thick underbrush.

The Sussex spaniel was developed at the end of the 18th century in Sussex, England, when the need arose for a substantial hunting dog for rough terrain. Among the rarest purebred dogs, the Sussex has a good nose but not the speed of springer and cocker spaniels and is more massive than most spaniels. The breed's most distinctive trait is the color of its straight or slightly wavy coat: a solid rich golden liver. The dog stands 38 to 40 cm (15 to 16 in) at the shoulder and weighs 18 to 20 kg (40 to 45 lb). The head is large, as are the ears, which are carried flat against the side of the head. The tail is set low and docked 13 to 18 cm (5 to 7 in). The coat is abundant, with feathering on the legs, ears, and tail.

JOHN MANDEVILLE

Bibliography: Ensminger, M. E., *The Complete Book of Dogs* (1977); Schneider-Leyer, Erich, *Dogs of the World* (1972).

Sutherland   [suhth'-ur-luhnd]

Sutherland is a former county in northern Scotland. Its terrain is mountainous and attracts many deer hunters. Sheep raising is the main economic activity, but coal mining, whiskey distilling, and food processing also take place. Gaelic is still spoken in some areas.

The original inhabitants, Picts, were conquered by Norse invaders in the 9th century. In the early 19th century, thousands of tenant farmers were evicted to make way for sheep farming. Dornoch served as the county town until the 1975 reorganization of local government, when Sutherland became part of the HIGHLAND administrative region.

Sutherland, Earl W., Jr.

American physiologist and pharmacologist Earl Wilbur Sutherland, Jr., b. Burlingame, Kans., Nov. 19, 1915, d. Mar. 9, 1974, was awarded the 1971 Nobel Prize for physiology or medicine for his discoveries concerning the mechanisms of hormone action. Sutherland demonstrated how cyclic adenosine monophosphate (cyclic AMP) functions as an intermediary in hormonal control of metabolic processes in the human body.

Sutherland, George

U.S. Supreme Court Justice (1922–38) George Sutherland, b. Buckinghamshire, England, Mar. 25, 1862, d. July 18, 1942, emigrated (1863) to Utah Territory as a child and became (1883) an attorney. In 1905, Sutherland was elected Republican U.S. senator from Utah and remained in the Senate until 1917. During Franklin Roosevelt's presidency, Justice Sutherland was dubbed—along with three other conservative justices—one of the "Four Horsemen" of the Court for the strong stands he took against much New Deal reform legislation.

Bibliography: Paschal, Joel F., *Mr. Justice Sutherland: A Man Against the State* (1971).

Sutherland, Graham

Graham Vivian Sutherland, b. Aug. 24, 1903, d. Feb. 17, 1980, was an English painter and printmaker. His early work is characterized by the kind of pastoral vision usually associated with Samuel Palmer, as is visible in his etchings *Pecken Wood* (1925) and *Lammas* (1926). Later, he developed this style into a more personal vision, exemplified by the etching *Pastoral* (1930). From this time until about 1945, Sutherland's work—by then mainly painting—was dominated by landscape, which he saw with the minute vision of a romantic.

After 1945, Sutherland worked primarily on religious subjects, themes derived from natural forms, and portraits. Although controversy has surrounded his portraits, the best of them, for example, that of Somerset Maugham (1949; Tate Gallery, London), are brilliant. His studies for the Maugham portrait have many of the elements present in his landscape painting. His religious subjects include a tapestry (1952–58) for COVENTRY CATHEDRAL.   RAYMOND LISTER

Bibliography: Arcangeli, Francesco, *Graham Sutherland*, trans. by Helen Barolini and H. J. Marks (1973); Cooper, Douglas, *The Work of Graham Sutherland* (1961); Quinn, Edward, ed., *Graham Sutherland: Complete Graphic Work* (1978).

Sutherland, Joan

One of the leading sopranos of her generation, Joan Sutherland, b. Sydney, Australia, Nov. 7, 1926, is especially noted for her interpretations of Donizetti's *Lucia di Lammermoor* and Bellini's *Norma*. The individual timbre of her voice and its unusual volume make her brilliant coloratura abilities all the more impressive. Sutherland studied at the Sydney Conservatory and made her debut at Covent Garden in 1952. Initially, she concentrated on the Bizet, Verdi, and Wagner repertoires but was persuaded by her future husband, conductor Richard Bonynge, to develop her voice's coloratura possibilities. In 1959 she sang her first Lucia at Covent Garden and began reviving the long-neglected bel canto operas of Donizetti and Bellini. Her American debut took place in Dallas, Tex., in 1960 in Handel's *Alcina*, and she has since appeared frequently with the Metropolitan Opera.

Bibliography: Braddon, R. R., *Joan Sutherland* (1962); Greenfield, Edward, *Joan Sutherland* (1973).

Discography: Bellini, V., *Norma*; Donizetti, G., *La Fille du Régiment* and *Lucia di Lammermoor*; Handel, G. F., *Alcina*.

Sutherland Falls

Sutherland Falls, on the Arthur River, in the southwestern corner of South Island, New Zealand, are the fifth highest falls in the world. Consisting of three cataracts, they spill 580 m (1,904 ft) from the glacially formed Lake Quill, in Fiordland National Park. The first European to sight them was Donald Sutherland in 1880.

Sutlej River   [suht'-lej]

The Sutlej River, the longest river of the Punjab, is approximately 1,450 km (900 mi) long. Beginning at an elevation of about 4,570 m (15,000 ft) in southwestern Tibet, it flows northwest and west through deep gorges in the Himalayas, across northern India, and southwest through eastern Pakistan to the Chenab River. The two join for about 80 km (50 mi) as the Panjnad River, before entering the INDUS. Dams on the river in India provide hydroelectric power and irrigation waters. The major city on the Sutlej is Ludhiana, India.

suttee   [suh-tee']

Suttee, the self-immolation of the widow on her husband's funeral pyre, was a FUNERAL CUSTOM among Indian Hindus until it was abolished (1829) by the British. Sporadic instances of suttee persisted, however, into the 20th century. The name is derived from the Sanskrit word *sati*, "faithful wife." The act was supposedly voluntary and was intended to prove the wife's devotion and to ensure the continued union of the couple in the afterlife. In fact, suttee permitted the division of the husband's property without the complicating presence of his wife who, in any case, would have had little status as a widow.

Bibliography: Thompson, Edward John, *Suttee* (1928).

Sutter, John Augustus   [suht'-ur]

The California pioneer John Augustus Sutter (originally Johann August Suter), b. Kandern, now in West Germany, Feb. 15, 1803, d. June 18, 1880, gained fame when gold was discovered on his property in 1848. He immigrated to the United States in 1834, and in 1839 the Mexican governor of California gave him a large grant of land in the Sacramento Valley. There, Sutter established the colony of Nueva Helvetia, which became a center for the trappers, traders, and settlers in the region. On Jan. 24, 1848, while supervising a building project, James Wilson MARSHALL discovered gold on Sutter's land; in the GOLD RUSH that followed, his property was soon overrun by fortune hunters. The U.S. Supreme Court declared the title to much of his land invalid, and he died bankrupt after unsuccessfully petitioning Congress for payment for his losses.
                                                      ELLIOTT WEST

Bibliography: Dana, Julian, *Sutter of California* (1934; repr. 1974); Dillon, Richard, *Fool's Gold: The Decline and Fall of Captain John Sutter of California* (1967); Zollinger, James P., *Sutter: The Man and His Empire* (1939; repr. 1967).

Suttner, Bertha von   [zut'-nur]

An Austrian author of numerous antiwar novels and a tireless worker for world peace, Bertha von Suttner, b. June 9, 1843, d. June 21, 1914, was influential in Alfred Nobel's decision to establish the celebrated Nobel Peace Prize, of which she was the first female recipient (1905). The title of her major work, *Die Waffen nieder* (1889; trans. as *Lay Down Your Arms*, 1905), also became the name of her celebrated pacifist journal (1892–99). Von Suttner organized and headed the Austrian Society of Peace Lovers.   JOSEPH A. REITER

Sutton, Walter S.   [suht'-uhn]

Walter Stanborough Sutton, b. Apr. 5, 1877, d. Nov. 10, 1916, an American surgeon and geneticist, performed work that formed the basis of the chromosome theory of heredity and greatly influenced the course of the field of genetics. In 1902, Sutton proposed that chromosomes carry hereditary units and that the behavior of sex-cell chromosomes during division was the basis of Mendelian inheritance.

Sutton, Willy

Willy Sutton, b. Brooklyn, N.Y., June 30, 1901, was a bank robber and escape artist who broke out of jail several times. Sutton, who often fooled his victims, for example, by wearing the uniform of a bank guard, became a hero of gangland folklore as "Willie the Actor." Caught by accident when his car battery went dead, he served his last jail term, was released, and retired to collaborate on *Where the Money Was: The Memoirs of a Bank Robber* (1976).

Bibliography: Gribble, Leonard, *Stories of Famous Master Criminals* (1973).

Sutton Hoo ship burial   [suht'-uhn hoo]

The Sutton Hoo ship burial, one of the most spectacular and important archaeological discoveries ever made in Great Britain, is located on a heath about 13 km (8 mi) northeast of

Ipswich in Suffolk, England. It was discovered (1939) under the largest of more than a dozen Anglo-Saxon BARROWS (burial mounds). The ship buried at Sutton Hoo was a clinker-built vessel approximately 24 m (79 ft) long and 2.5 m (8 ft) in the beam; the ship's outline could only be detected in the sand from the innumerable iron rivets and clamps that had bound it together. The manner of burial recalls that of the famous Scandinavian ship burials, as well as the description of the burial of the Danish King Scyld Scefing in the Anglo-Saxon poem *Beowulf*.

Although no body was found in the Sutton Hoo ship, chemical analysis suggested that there had at one time been a corpse. Grave-goods found in the ship include a Swedish helmet and shield, a sword and spears, cauldrons and bowls of Coptic as well as Celtic craftsmanship, a great silver dish with stampings on it of the Byzantine emperor Anastasius I, two Byzantine silver baptismal spoons bearing the names Saulos and Paulos, and a wealth of other items of jewelry. Dating of the burial is largely dependent upon the 37 Merovingian gold coins unearthed at the site, which probably were accumulated between the years AD 620 and 630. Several experts have argued that the tomb may be that of Raedwald, king of the East Angles and high king of the Anglo-Saxons, who died *c.*625.

D. W. HARDING

Bibliography: Bruce-Milford, Rupert, *The Sutton Hoo Ship Burial: Excavations, Background, the Ship, Dating and Inventory,* vol. 2 (1979).

Suva [soo'-vah]

Suva, the capital of Fiji, has a population of 63,622 (1976). Located on Viti Levu Island, Suva is the home of the University of the South Pacific (1968). Its free-port status attracts tourists, and some light manufacturing takes place. Founded in 1849, Suva was an Allied base during World War II.

Suvorov, Aleksandr Vasilievich [soo-vaw'-ruhf]

Generalissimo Prince Aleksandr Vasilievich Suvorov, b. Nov. 13 (N.S.), 1729, d. May 6 (N.S.), 1800, was the greatest of the military leaders under CATHERINE II and one of Russia's foremost military heroes. Having determined upon a military career, he began in the ranks and became an officer in 1754; he fought in the Seven Year's War (1756–63), the suppression of the Polish revolt (1768), and the First Russo-Turkish War (1768–74). Suvorov's greatest victory came in the Second Russo-Turkish War (1787–92) when he captured Izmail, one of the strongest fortifications in Europe, in 1790. He also served as military commander of the Crimea before its annexation in 1783, and his campaigns in Poland in 1794 set the stage for the First Partition of that country in the same year. Always outspoken, Suvorov was exiled to his estates by Emperor Paul I (r. 1796–1801) but recalled in 1799 to lead Russian troops, in alliance with Austria, against Napoleon Bonaparte (see NAPOLEON I) in the Alps and northern Italy. Despite early successes, the campaign ended in disaster; Suvorov, old, sick, and disappointed by lack of Austrian cooperation, returned to Russia. One of the highest Soviet military medals is named in his honor.

L. JAY OLIVA

Bibliography: Longworth, Philip, *The Art of Victory: The Life and Achievements of Generalissimo Suvorov* (1965); Osipov, K., *Alexander Suvorov,* trans. by Edith Bone (1944).

Suwannee River [swah'-nee]

The Suwannee River, which rises in Okefenokee Swamp in southeastern Georgia and flows southwest across northern Florida to the Gulf of Mexico, is approximately 400 km (250 mi) long. The area near the river has cotton and tobacco plantations. The lower 230 km (145 mi) is navigable.

Suzor-Côté, M. A. de Foy [soo-zor'-koh-tay']

The Canadian painter Marc Aurèle de Foy Suzor-Côté, b. Arthabaska, Quebec, Apr. 15, 1869, d. Jan. 29, 1937, specialized in landscape and genre subjects. A student at the École des Beaux-Arts in Paris, his impressionist works are characterized by hazy, atmospheric effects, for example, *Settlement on*

a Hillside (1909; The National Gallery of Canada, Ottawa). Suzor-Côté also worked as a sculptor, creating many bronze statues of French-Canadian subjects.

Suzuki, D. T. [soo-zoo'-kee]

Daisetsu Teitaro Suzuki, b. Oct. 18, 1870, d. July 12, 1966, was a Japanese scholar, teacher, and writer known primarily as a popularizer of ZEN BUDDHISM in the West. As a young man he studied English and Zen in Japan and in 1897 went to America, where he translated Buddhist texts and wrote on Mahayana Buddhism. Upon returning to Japan he began teaching (1921) at Otani Buddhist University in Kyoto, where he founded the journal *Eastern Buddhist* and wrote some of his most significant works on Zen, which emphasized the importance of experience in that religion. From 1950 until his death Suzuki traveled widely, lecturing at various universities in Europe and America. He continued to write on Zen but also became interested in comparative religion, mysticism, and psychoanalysis.

JOSEPH M. KITAGAWA AND JOHN S. STRONG

Bibliography: Suzuki, D. T., *Essays in Zen Buddhism,* 3 vols. (1927–34), *Manual of Zen Buddhism* (1935), *Mysticism: Christian and Buddhist* (1957), *Studies in the Lankavatara Sutra* (1930), *Zen and Japanese Culture* (1959), and, with Fromm, Erich, and De Martino, Richard, *Zen Buddhism and Psychoanalysis* (1960).

Suzuki Harunobu: see HARUNOBU.

Svalbard [svahl'-bard]

Svalbard, a Norwegian dependency, consists of a cluster of glaciated islands in the Arctic Ocean, lying about 645 km (400 mi) north of Norway. The dependency's population is 2,828 (1976 est.). The Spitsbergen group within Svalbard is composed of five major, as well as many smaller, islands. West Spitsbergen, the largest island, has more than 60% of the dependency's total land area of 62,049 km² (23,957 mi²). Longyearbyen on West Spitsbergen is the administrative center.

The islands lie far north of the Arctic Circle, but the Gulf Stream and accompanying winds modify the climate on the western fringes, and vegetation can survive near the coasts. Svalbard has deposits of copper, iron ore, phosphate, and zinc, but coal remains the sole exploited mineral.

Svalbard was first sighted in 1194, but no attempt was made to explore the area until 1596, when Willem BARENTS and Jacob van Heemskerck reached the islands. Svalbard was used as a whalers' base in the 18th and 19th centuries. In 1899, Russians began extracting coal. Because of the extensive mineral deposits on the islands, many nations staked claims in Svalbard. A 1920 League of Nations treaty awarded the islands to Norway, but mineral rights were granted to Denmark, Italy, Japan, the Netherlands, Norway, Sweden, the United Kingdom, and the United States. In 1925, the USSR was included in the agreement. Svalbard was often used as a base for Arctic explorations. During World War II, British, German, and Norwegian forces occupied the islands at various times, and German warships bombed the mining settlements. Since the end of the war, most of the population has been composed of Soviet coalminers.

Svedberg, Theodor [svayd'-bairg]

The Swedish physical chemist Theodor Svedberg, b. Aug. 30, 1884, d. Feb. 26, 1971, received (1926) the Nobel Prize for chemistry for the development of the ultracentrifuge, a high-speed centrifuge that is used for determining the molecular weights of colloids and high-molecular-weight biological substances. Using this technique, he was the first to report that hemoglobin was constructed from four equal protein units.

Bibliography: Farber, Eduard, *Nobel Prize Winners in Chemistry 1901-1961* (1963).

Sverdlovsk [svird-lawfsk']

Sverdlovsk is the capital of Sverdlovsk oblast in the Russian Soviet Federated Socialist Republic of the USSR. It is the largest city of the Urals industrial region, with a population of 1,211,000 (1979). An important industrial and transportation center at the junction of seven rail lines, Sverdlovsk specializes in the manufacture of heavy machinery and industrial equipment. Its principal plants produce equipment for the iron and steel industry, turbine generators for power stations, and equipment for the chemical industry. The city is an important training center for engineers for the Urals industrial region, with Ural State University (1920), a polytechnical institute, and specialized engineering schools.

Sverdlovsk arose in 1721 around an ironworks and fort, and was called Yekaterinburg, for Catherine I, the wife of Peter I. Because of its favorable location at the junction of roads, the settlement grew into the administrative center of the Urals mining district along the main route to Siberia. After the Bolshevik Revolution, during which the last tsar, Nicholas II, and his family were executed (1918) there, Yekaterinburg was renamed in 1924 for Yakov Sverdlov, an early Bolshevik who led an underground group there in 1905.   THEODORE SHABAD

Sverdrup, Harald Ulrik   [svair'-drup]

Harald Ulrik Sverdrup, b. Nov. 15, 1888, d. Aug. 21, 1957, was a Norwegian scientist and explorer who did pioneer work in the fields of dynamic meteorology and physical oceanography, and developed mathematics as a tool for quantitative description in these fields. He was (1918–25) chief scientist on Roald Amundsen's *Maud* expedition to the Arctic and (1931) on the Wilkins-Ellsworth submarine Arctic expedition. His outstanding scientific achievement is considered to be his chapter on "The Water Masses and Currents of the Oceans," in the book *The Oceans, Their Physics, Chemistry and General Biology*, which he wrote (1942) with M. W. Johnson and R. H. Fleming.   ROBERT E. WILSON

Sverdrup, Otto Neumann

Otto Neumann Sverdrup, b. Oct. 31, 1854, d. Nov. 26, 1930, was a Norwegian Arctic explorer. He captained the *Fram* when it was frozen in polar ice for nearly 3 years (1893–96)—drifting for about 1,600 km (1,000 mi)—for purposes of Arctic research. He again commanded (1898–1902) the ship through the Canadian Arctic and undertook three additional Arctic expeditions. The Sverdrup Islands are named for him.

Bibliography: Sverdrup, Otto N., *Arctic Adventures,* trans. by Ethel Harriet Hearn, ed. by T. C. Fairley (1959).

Sverre, King of Norway   [svair'-e]

Norway's King Sverre, b. *c*.1150, d. Mar. 9, 1202, revolutionized the government and society of medieval Norway. Born in a time of civil war, he was raised as a commoner and educated for the priesthood. When told that he was the illegitimate son of King Sigurd, he went to Norway (1174) and fought for the throne. The Birkebeiners, a populist faction, supported him, and in 1184 he was acknowledged as sole king. Sverre created a new nobility and replaced an aristocratic administration with royal officials. His firm hand in ruling the church led Pope Innocent III to excommunicate him and lay Norway under interdict.   J. R. CHRISTIANSON

Bibliography: Gathorne-Hardy, Geoffrey M., *A Royal Impostor* (1956).

Svevo, Italo   [svay'-voh]

Italo Svevo was the pseudonym of Italian novelist Ettore Schmitz, b. Dec. 19, 1861, d. Sept. 13, 1928, author of *A Life* (1892; Eng. trans., 1963), *As a Man Grows Older* (1898; Eng. trans., 1932), and *The Confessions of Zeno* (1923; Eng. trans., 1930), regarded as his masterpiece. These works, which pioneer in the use of stream-of-consciousness narrative and thought analysis, are often called the forerunners of the modern psychoanalytic novel and have been compared with works by Proust and Joyce. Svevo's works were greatly admired by Joyce, who was instrumental in bringing Svevo's writing to the attention of the public.   LOUIS KIBLER

Bibliography: Furbank, Phillip N., *Italo Svevo: The Man and the Writer* (1966); Moloney, Brian, *Italo Svevo: A Critical Introduction* (1974).

Svoboda, Josef   [svaw'-baw-dah]

The most influential stage designer of the 1960s and '70s, Josef Svoboda, b. Czechoslovakia, May 10, 1920, creates spectacular designs using a multimedia approach influenced by Erwin Piscator and E. F. Burian. Svoboda has experimented with electric technology, including new types of projection screens, pneumatic mirrors, and lasers. His best-known creations are Polyekran, a multiscreen projection system, and *laterna magika*, which combines still and moving projections with live action.   ARNOLD ARONSON

Bibliography: Burian, Jarka, *The Scenography of Josef Svoboda* (1971).

Svyatoslav I, Duke of Kiev   [svyah'-tuh-slaf]

Svyatoslav I, d. 972, Varangian duke of Kiev (945–72), strove to unite the Dnepr, lower Volga, and lower Danube regions and to control trade around the Black and Caspian seas. By 965 he had conquered the Khazars between the Volga and the Don. At Byzantine bidding, he defeated (967) the Bulgars but then refused to step aside. After being defeated by a Byzantine force in 971, he was killed by the Pechenegs on his way back to Kiev. Svyatoslav was the last non-Christian ruler of Kiev.

Swabia   [sway'-bee-uh]

Swabia, a historic area of southwestern Germany, extends from the Black Forest to the Iller River, and from Franconia south to Switzerland. It lies chiefly within the present West German states of Baden-Württemberg and Bavaria. Swabia's importance was derived from its strategic location between the upper Danube and the upper Rhine rivers.

The Romans brought the area within their empire as the Agri Decumates. The Alamanni and Suevi (see GERMANIC PEOPLES) seized it during the great migrations of the 5th century AD, and it became known as Alamannia; the later name, *Swabia*, was derived from *Suevi*. The area passed (*c*.500) into control of the Franks, and by 900 it emerged as one of the German tribal duchies. The HOHENSTAUFENS were the most eminent of its dukes; the extinction of their male line after 1268 contributed to Swabia's fragmentation, after which the Zähringen, Hohenzollern, and Habsburg families owned segments. The margraves of Baden along the Rhine and the dukes of Württemberg around Stuttgart gradually became dominant. In 1806, Napoleon I made Württemberg a kingdom; along with Baden (which became a grand duchy) the kingdom survived until the end of World War I.   RAYMOND H. SCHMANDT

Swahili

The Swahili are not an ethnic unit but the coastal dwellers of a number of East African countries. They speak dialects of the Swahili tongue, structurally a Bantu language but with many borrowings from Arabic. The name Swahili, derived from an Arabic word meaning "coast," can be applied to nearly half a million East Africans whose culture, trading economy, and language developed with the spread of Islam after Arab traders arrived among them about AD 500. The language is a lingua franca across East Africa to Zambia and the Congo and in places as distant as south Arabia, the Persian Gulf, and even the coast of Pakistan.

Bibliography: Polomé, E. C., *Swahili Language Handbook* (1967); Prins, A. J., *The Swahili-Speaking Peoples of Zanzibar and the East African Coast* (1961).

See also: AFRICAN LANGUAGES.

swallow

The approximately 75 species of swallows in the family Hurundinidae are relatively small, delicate, insect-eating birds found worldwide except in Australia and New Zealand, and on some small islands. Several species of martins are classified in the same family.

Swallows range from 10 to 23 cm (4 to 10 in) in length. The wings are long, the neck relatively short, the body slender,

The barn swallow, Hirundo rustica, *the most common of all swallows, is found almost worldwide and in all sorts of environments. It migrates vast distances, and it is not unusual for birds to fly from Scandinavia to southern Africa, traveling up to 960 km (600 mi) in a day. Such extended migration produces a high annual mortality rate (about 70%).*

the feet small and apparently weak, but the claws are well developed. Although the bill is small, the mouth has a wide gape, which is effectively used to capture insects in the air. In contrast to the swifts, which they somewhat resemble, swallows have facial bristles near the mouth that enhance their ability to catch flying prey. The predominant colors are reddish brown, black, and white. The plumage in some species exhibits a green or purple iridescence. The outward appearance does not usually vary between sexes.

Swallows are agile fliers with much endurance and maneuverability. Many are colonial, and large flocks may develop at the time of migration. Nests contain 3 to 7 eggs and may be built in sandbanks, on cliffs, in tree cavities, and on or in artificial buildings. In addition, species like the purple martin, *Progue subis,* make extensive use of man-made martin houses. The terms *swallowtail, swallow wing,* and *sea swallow* refer to other birds that are not closely related to the swallows.

GARY D. SCHNELL

Bibliography: Ingram, Collingwood, *The Migration of the Swallow* (1974); Lunk, William A., *The Rough-winged Swallow* (1955); Sears, Paul M., *Barn Swallow* (1955).

swallow tanager

The swallow tanager, *Tersina viridis,* is a bird classified in the avian family Tersinidae; it is sometimes classified in a subfamily Tersininae in the tanager family, Thraupidae. It lives in northern South America through Panama and on the island of Trinidad. The male is turquoise blue, with a black face and black flank bars; the female is green. The bill is short and wide for catching insects in flight but fruit is also eaten. Swallow tanagers are hole nesters.

ROBERT J. RAIKOW

Swammerdam, Jan   [svah'-mur-dahm]

Jan Swammerdam, b. Feb. 12, 1637, d. Feb. 17, 1680, a Dutch naturalist and microscopist, is most noted for his discovery of the red blood cell. Using equipment and techniques he developed, Swammerdam made many discoveries concerning the microscopic anatomy of organisms—insects in particular, as well as plants, crustaceans, mollusks, worms, frogs, and mammals. He also described cell division and muscle contraction.

Bibliography: Schierbeek, A., *Jan Swammerdam: His Life and Works* (1967).

swamp, marsh, and bog

Wetlands are areas, other than lakes or rivers, whose soils are saturated with water for indefinite or prolonged periods of time. Often these wetlands result from the surface exposure of GROUNDWATER, that is, the water that has percolated down through the soil and accumulated and built up on a layer of rock or other impervious material. The upper boundary of the

groundwater, called the WATER TABLE, rises or falls as the amount of groundwater varies. Swamps, marshes, and bogs are wetlands in which the water table is at, near, or above the surface of the land. Plant growth in these areas is limited to species that can withstand having their roots submerged for long periods of time. The water in these areas may be tea-colored or dark brown because of the presence of organic acids, such as tannic acid, derived from decaying vegetation.

Depending on many factors, including climate, mineral content, and the permanency of surface water, wetlands may be mossy, grassy, shrubby, or wooded. Conventionally, a swamp is a wetland whose soil is permanently or protractedly saturated with water and whose vegetation is dominated by woody plants, such as trees. A marsh is similar, but its dominant vegetation is herbaceous, consisting of such plants as grasses or sedges. A bog is a wetland that appears relatively dry, with only small amounts of shallow water visible, but its ground surface is spongy and wet to the touch; the surface material is largely sphagnum moss or other organic matter rather than soil.

This terminology is not precise: what one locality might call a bog, another might refer to as a swamp or marsh. Additionally, all three types of wetlands may be present and closely associated in one area, further confusing the use of these names. Intergradations also occur. A northern boggy area may support trees—such wetlands are known as muskegs. In Britain, boggy areas may be referred to as moors or heaths, and a grassy marsh may be called a fen. Consequently, in an effort to avoid the confusion of these popular names, most modern scientific classifications of wetlands no longer employ these terms.

MARSHES

Flora. A characteristic of marshes is the absence of trees and shrubs; marsh plants tend to be soft-stemmed or herbaceous. Marshes often include areas of open water surrounded by plants such as cattails, rushes, arrowheads, pickerel weed, and bur-reed, all of which grow with their stems and leaves partly submerged. Water lilies are rooted in the bottom, with their leaves floating on the surface. Floaters, such as the tiny duckweed, water lettuce, and water hyacinth, are more restricted in distribution; some occur only in the open waters of southern marshes and swamps. Finally, submerged aquatics such as pondweeds and water weeds grow in the deep-water marshes or in the littoral zones of shallow ponds that have marshlike features.

Fauna. Animal life is highly diverse and includes an array of aquatic insects, some of which spend only their early stages in the water and then become terrestrial adults, such as dragonflies and damselflies; others are permanently bound to the aquatic medium. Amphibians, also common, include spring peepers and the leopard, pickerel, and green frogs, to name a few, along with painted and spotted turtles, and the snapping turtle in deep-water marshes. In the Florida Everglades, a region that is dominated by saw grass (actually a sedge), alligators are especially common in the sloughs during the dry season. The fascinating anhinga, or snake bird, which actually spears its fish as it dives beneath the open water areas of the marshes, is also common to the Everglades, as well as wading birds, such as the great blue heron, bitterns, and egrets. Muskrats frequent cattail marshes, where they feed on the roots of the plant. In large numbers, muskrats have been known to clear an entire area of cattails.

Soil. Because marshes are so biologically productive, several tons of dead plant and animal material become available to the food chain each year. Most of this energy-rich matter, or biomass, is broken down by bacteria and water fungi. Marshes are usually relatively shallow depressions with an organic-silt or muck-type soil forming a relatively shallow layer over the underlying mineral soil or bedrock. Streams that traverse marshes deposit silt and aid in the filling process. Wetlands that fill in may become sedgy tussock marshes or wet meadows and may eventually develop into swamps dominated by wetland trees and shrubs. If the water table remains high, however, the marsh will persist.

Salt Marshes. In contrast to freshwater marshes, found in

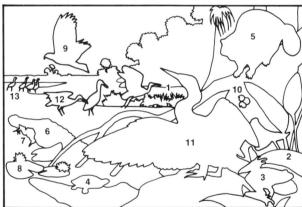

The marshlands of the Everglades, in southern Florida, are dominated by vast expanses of saw grass and dotted with low islands, or hammocks, of trees and shrubs. Plant growth in a marsh is limited to species that can withstand having their roots submerged for long periods of time. Saw grass, Cladium jamaicensis (1), is a sedge with sharp-toothed edges; broad-leaved thalia, Thalia geniculata (2), a tall (up to 3 m/10 ft) herb, grows on marshy borders of swamps. Common Everglades animals include the green tree frog, Hyla cinerea (3); several kinds of turtle (4); raccoon, Procyon lotor (5); and American alligator, Alligator mississippiensis (6), seen preying on a purple gallinule, Porphyrula martinica (7). The gallinule often walks on water-lily (8) leaves to feed on seeds and insects. The everglade kite, Rostrhamus sociabilis (9), feeds only on water snails (10); the anhinga, or snakebird, Anhinga anhinga (11), hunts fishes by spearing them with its sharp bill. Both birds have become rare in the Everglades because of destruction of habitat and food supply, largely as a result of the human practice of swamp drainage. The roseate spoonbill, Ajaia ajaja (12), feeds on small animals and plants by sweeping its bill from side to side in the water. The American flamingo, Phoenicopterus ruber (13), very rarely visits the southern tip of Florida.

poorly drained depressions or along stream courses, tidal or salt marshes are restricted to temperate coastal areas. They occur from the intertidal zone to slightly above high tide. Here *Spartina*, or cord grass, tends to dominate, forming extensive grassy swards. Salinity and duration of flooding are among the complex of factors that determine the belting pattern or mosaic of vegetation types found in tidal marshes. Marsh snails, ribbed mussels, fiddler crabs, and amphipods are conspicuous among the animal life. Salt marshes are an important waterfowl breeding habitat, as are freshwater marshes. Marshes around the world are recognized as "duck factories," serving as breeding and feeding areas and resting places on the long migration routes of these birds (see INTERTIDAL LIFE).

SWAMPS
Flora. Swamps are dominated by woody plants, primarily trees and shrubs. In the northeastern United States, red maple is a distinctive swamp tree, and in the southeastern United States, the bald cypress and gums are dominant. Shrub

swamps represent another swamp type, where willow, alder, or buttonbush can form pure stands. These wetlands can also develop floodplain forests along major river courses, as in the southeastern United States, or as isolated cypress domes in central Florida. Elsewhere, swamps can occur in wet basins or can be dissected by stream courses. Forested wetlands often show a vertical stratification in vegetation structure, with tree, shrub, and herbaceous layers. Shrubs such as high-bush blueberry, swamp azalea, spice bush, and sweet pepperbush may form a continuous stratum. Beneath the shrubs, skunk cabbage may be an important member of the ground cover, along with a diversity of showy wetland species, including the purple-fringed orchid, cardinal flower, jewelweed, and marsh marigold.
Fauna. Many of the animals that inhabit marshes also live in swamps; additions include the raccoon and beaver. Wood ducks are a distinctive species of swamp forests, because they depend on hollow trees for nesting sites.
Soil. Swamp soils are relatively shallow organic-silt muck-type

This mangrove swamp on the coast of Trinidad is typical of the saltwater swamps that form along tropical seacoasts. The long roots that grow from the trunks and branches of the mangrove trees form dense systems that catch silt, helping to build up the swampland.

materials, with the mineral soil near the surface. These wooded wetlands tend to persist; however, with continuous organic filling and lowering of the water table, some upland species may become associated.

BOGS

Bogs are a distinctive wetland type, usually characterized by evergreen trees and shrubs and underlain by deep PEAT deposits. Bogs will develop in former glacial lakes by the gradual accumulation of organic matter falling from beneath a floating mat of vegetation advancing out over the water. Peat deposits 6 to 12 m (20 to 40 ft) deep are not uncommon.

Flora. Northern bogs are dominated by black spruce and larch and a shrub layer of evergreen heaths: leatherleaf, bog rosemary, bog laurel, and Labrador tea. In the northeastern and north central United States, these plants represent a northern boreal vegetation outlier within the deciduous forest region.

In southern bogs, coastal white cedar is the distinctive tree. Sphagnum moss or sedges frequently comprise the open floating mat in which two insectivorous plants, the pitcher plant and the sundew (as well as bog orchids), are especially distinctive. These bogs are sometimes referred to as quaking bogs because the floating mat of vegetation "quakes" when jumped on.

Fauna. Animal life is often somewhat less abundant in bogs than in swamps and marshes. Amphibians, however, are associated with bogs; the Anderson tree frog, a beautiful species, is distinctive of the white cedar swamps and bogs of the Pine Barrens of New Jersey. The bog lemming is another distinctive species of such habitats.

Preserved Human Remains. Human bodies have been found well preserved after 2,000 years in Danish bogs; facial features are sharp and even whiskers are intact. Such excellent preservation is possible because most bogs are extremely acidic and low in oxygen, and therefore such organisms as bacteria have difficulty breaking down organic matter. For this reason peat accumulates to great depths in bogs. The Danish peat cutters who found the so-called Tollund man, 2.1 m (7 ft) below the surface in central Jutland, reported it to the police, thinking a crime had been committed. Scientists concluded, however, that this human, preserved for more than 2,000 years, was probably a sacrifice to an ancient goddess of fertility.

Fossil Record. Bog peat represents a time capsule of vegetation history. Pollen grains deposited in peat as it accumulates over the years become microfossils that record the history of upland vegetation during the 12,000–15,000 years since the last glaciers of the Ice Age receded (see POLLEN STRATIGRAPHY). Bogs are also very fragile, and excessive trampling can destroy their fascinating flora and fauna.

ECOLOGICAL ROLE

Wetlands, widely recognized for their high productivity of waterfowl and wildlife, are also vital in flood control and water storage and frequently recharge the water table. A 15-cm (6-in) rise in a 4-ha (10-acre) marsh puts more than 5,700 kl (1.5 million gallons) of water in storage. Current research indicates that wetlands have a great potential as tertiary sewage-treatment systems. Wetland plants have the ability to take up excess nitrogen and phosphorus from sewage effluent; in many areas, wetlands filter the pollution from faulty home sewage systems.   WILLIAM A. NIERING

Bibliography: Errington, Paul L., *Of Men and Marshes* (1957); Good, Ralph E., et al., eds., *Freshwater Wetlands: Ecological Processes and Management Potential* (1978); Niering, William, *The Life of the Marsh* (1966); Teal, John and Mildred, *Life and Death of the Salt Marsh* (1969); Thomas, Bill, *The Swamp* (1976); Ursin, Michael, *Life In and Around the Salt Marshes* (1972).

swamp eel

Swamp eels (family Synbranchidae) constitute about eight species of eellike fish unrelated to true eels. They are 30–150 cm (1–5 ft) long and lack paired fins. One species has well-developed gills; the others have small gills and gulp air, which is absorbed by a network of blood vessels lining the mouth, air bladder, or intestine. Swamp eels are found in fresh and brackish tropical waters. One marine species, *Macrotrema caligans*, is native to the Malay Peninsula area.
                                                            E. O. WILEY

swan

Swans are large, long-necked aquatic birds with short legs and webbed feet. They belong to the family Anatidae, along with the duck and goose. Swans are most closely related to geese, both groups differing from ducks anatomically and in the absence of bright or metallic colors in their plumage. The most ducklike swan, the coscoroba, *Coscoroba coscoroba*, of South America, is white with black wingtips. The black-necked swan, *Cygnus melanocoryphus*, also of South America, has a black head and neck, and a red knob at the top of its blue bill. The all-white mute swan, *Cygnus olor*, of Eurasia

The whistling swan, Olor columbianus, *reaches nearly 1.5 m (5 ft) in length. It nests in Alaska and northern Canada and is often seen migrating in V-shaped flocks of several hundred birds.*

has been domesticated and introduced into North America, Australia, New Zealand, and South Africa; a familiar resident of parks and zoos, it characteristically swims with its neck in a graceful curve, unlike the more upright posture of other swans. The most common species native to North America, the whistling swan, *Cygnus columbianus columbianus,* has a black bill and nests north of the Arctic Circle. The other North American form, the trumpeter swan, *Cygnus cygnus buccinator,* formerly nested throughout the continent, but excessive hunting in the last century has limited it to scattered areas. Bewick's swan, *Cygnus columbianus bewickii,* is the Old World counterpart of the whistling swan, and the larger whooper swan, *Cygnus cygnus cygnus,* of Eurasia is the counterpart of the trumpeter.

Swans feed mainly on aquatic vegetation. Their strong bills have serrated edges and a nail at the tip, and the surface of the tongue is spinous, all of which aid in grasping and tearing plants. Horny serrations in the bill help in filtering small food items from the water surface, but swans most often feed from the bottom of ponds. Swans generally mate for life, with both sexes building the nest and caring for the young. In some species both sexes also incubate the eggs. Most swans migrate after the breeding season.   ROBERT J. RAIKOW

Bibliography: Bruun, Bertel, *Ducks, Geese, and Swans* (1964); McCoy, Joseph J., *Swans* (1967); Scott, Peter, *The Swans* (1972); Van Wormer, Joe, *The World of the Swan* (1972).

Swan, Sir Joseph Wilson

The British chemist and inventor Sir Joseph Wilson Swan, b. Oct. 31, 1828, d. May 27, 1914, made important contributions to the development of photography and electric lighting. He patented (1864) the carbon process for printing photographs in permanent pigment and discovered (1877) that heat could effect a photographic emulsion. He also patented bromide paper (1879) and developed both a carbon-filament incandescent lamp (1860) and an all-glass hermetically sealed bulb (1878).

Bibliography: Swan, Kenneth R., *Sir Joseph Swan and the Invention of the Incandescent Electric Lamp* (1948).

Swan Theatre

The Swan Theatre was an open-yarded playhouse with three tiers of galleries built by Francis Langley on Bankside, London, in 1595. It is the only Elizabethan theater of which there is a contemporary picture showing an interior. An accompanying letter describes the playhouse interior as being painted to resemble marble and capable of holding 3,000 spectators. It had become derelict by 1632.   C. WALTER HODGES

Swanscombe man   [swahnz'-kuhm]

Two bones from the back of a prehistoric human skull were found (1935 and 1936) in the Barnfield Pit at Swanscombe, along the River Thames in Kent, southern England. Further excavations there after World War II uncovered another human bone belonging to the same individual. The geological deposits in which the fossil bones of the Swanscombe man were found indicate that this ancient hominid lived during the Second Interglacial Period (about 250,000–300,000 years ago). It has been suggested that the Swanscombe fossil, along with specimens from Steinheim, Germany (see STEINHEIM MAN), and from Fontéchevade, France (see FONTÉCHEVADE MAN), provide evidence of archaic *Homo sapiens* (the modern human species) in Europe prior to the appearance of the NEANDERTHALERS. Unfortunately, the Swanscombe specimen lacks the frontal bone of the skull, which, with its diagnostic brow ridges, face, and teeth, is crucial to understanding the specimen's evolutionary relationships.

ALAN MANN AND NANCY MINUGH

Bibliography: Constable, George, *The Neanderthals* (1973); Howells, William W., *Evolution of the Genus Homo* (1973).

See also: PREHISTORIC HUMANS.

Swansea   [swahn'-zee]

Swansea, a coastal city in West Glamorgan, South Wales, has a population of 187,500 (1977 est.). In the 19th and early 20th centuries the city's primary industry was metal smelting, using local coal. By the 1970s, however, petroleum refining and petrochemicals had become dominant. Port facilities have been modernized to handle exports of refined petroleum and general cargo. The University College of Swansea (1920) is located there. Probably settled by the Danes in post-Roman times, Swansea was chartered in the 12th century. The city center was rebuilt after heavy German bombing in 1941.

Swanson, Gloria   [swahn'-suhn]

The personification of glamour and prodigality in Hollywood's silent era, Gloria Swanson (stage name of Josephine Swenson), b. Chicago, Mar. 27, 1898, starred in such Cecil B. De Mille spectaculars as *Male and Female* (1919) and *The Affairs of Anatol* before founding (1927) her own production company, for which she made *Sadie Thompson* (1928). Her career foundered in the 1930s, but she made a brilliant comeback in *Sunset Boulevard* (1950); since then she has appeared in *Airport* (1975) and frequently on television.

Swarthmore College   [swohrth'-mohr]

Established in 1864 by the Quakers, Swarthmore College (enrollment: 1,280; library: 550,000 volumes) is an independent coeducational liberal arts school in Swarthmore, Pa. Master's degrees are offered in some fields. Swarthmore, Haverford, and Bryn Mawr participate in a plan that allows students to take courses for credit at any of the three colleges.

Swartkrans: see STERKFONTEIN.

swastika

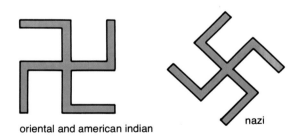

oriental and american indian   nazi

The swastika is an ancient symbol of unknown origin that has been employed for thousands of years as a religious sign and a decorative emblem. It takes the form of an even cross with the arms bent in the middle at right angles; all the bars point in the same direction, clockwise or counterclockwise. The swastika appeared in ancient China, Egypt, and India. It has been found on Greek coins, pre-Christian Celtic and Scandinavian artifacts, the catacombs of the early Christians in Rome, and Byzantine buildings. The swastika was widely used by American Indians. It represented the sun and infinity.

In the 20th century, the swastika was adopted as the emblem of the Nazi party in Germany. Mistaking its origin, the Nazis regarded it as an "Aryan" symbol and linked it to the notion of their "racial superiority." From September 1935 until the fall of the Nazis in 1945, the swastika was prominently displayed on the official flag of the Third Reich, a black swastika in a white circle against a red field. When the war ended, the Allies banned display of the emblem, which had come to be identified with the evils of Hitler's regime.

Bibliography: Freed, Stanley A. and Ruth S., "The Origin of the Swastika," *Natural History,* January 1980.

Swazi   [swah'-zee]

The Swazi, a BANTU-speaking people of the NGUNI group, live principally in the kingdom of Swaziland in southern Africa.

They numbered about 400,000 in 1977. Their economy is based on farming and stock raising, although many Swazi augment their income as migrant laborers in South Africa. Traditional Swazi religion is centered on the ancestral spirits (*emadloti*), whose good will is sought by means of sacrificial offerings. Rainmaking, magic, prophecy, and medicine are all interwoven with religion; witchcraft and sorcery provide explanations for and a means of dealing with evil and immoral behavior.

Kingship is hereditary within the Swazi royal clan, an offshoot of the ZULU several centuries ago. Power is shared by the king and his mother through a subtle division of labor that is legitimized by ritual. One of the two ruling councils consists of senior princes and the other of chiefs, headmen, and adult males. Thus, a clear balance is maintained between the authority of royalty and that of commoners. The system of the central government is duplicated in the local districts.

PETER CARSTENS

Bibliography: Kuper, Hilda, *An African Aristocracy* (1947) and *The Swazi: A South African Kingdom* (1963); Marwick, B. A., *Swazi* (1966).

Swaziland   [swah'-zee-land]

The kingdom of Swaziland is a small, landlocked country in southern Africa, surrounded by South Africa except for a short border with Mozambique. Formerly a British protectorate, it gained its independence on Sept. 6, 1968.

LAND, PEOPLE, AND ECONOMY

The western Highveld, part of the DRAKENSBERG range, is the source of several fast-flowing rivers, including the Usutu, Umbuluzi, and Ngwavuma. Central Swaziland is gently undulating savanna, whereas the eastern Lowveld is flat and semi-

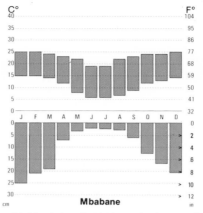

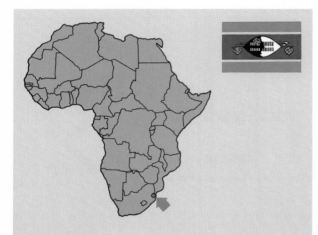

SWAZILAND

Official Name: Kingdom of Swaziland
Capital and Largest City: Mbabane (1976 pop., 22,262)
Area: 17,363 km² (6,704 mi²)
Elevation: *Highest*—Emlembe, 1,862 m (6,109 ft); *lowest*—61 m (200 ft), in the Lowveld
Population: 533,000 (1979 est.). *Distribution*—5% urban, 95% rural; *density,* 31 persons per km² (80 per mi²); *annual rate of increase* (1970–77), 2.4%
Principal Languages: English, siSwati (both official)
Principal Religions: Christianity, traditional religions
Principal Products: *Agriculture*—maize, cotton, rice, sugar, citrus fruits, millet, livestock, forestry. *Manufacturing and industry*—processed foods, chemicals, wood pulp, pit props, lumber. *Mining*—asbestos, iron ore, coal, pyrophyllite, barites, kaolin
Railroads: 222 km/138 mi (1979)
Roads: 224 km/139 mi (1979 paved)
Currency: 1 lilangeni = 100 cents

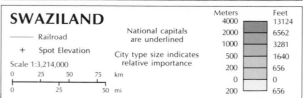

Bars indicate monthly ranges of temperatures (red) and precipitation (blue) in Mbabane, the capital of Swaziland. This nation in southeastern Africa has a subtropical humid climate with steppe influences.

arid. The Lebombo Ridge, which runs along the eastern boundary, is environmentally similar to the Middleveld. Rainfall decreases from more than 1,651 mm (65 in) in the Highveld to about 686 mm (27 in) in the Lowveld. Mean annual temperatures range from 15° C (59° F) in the Highveld to 22° C (72° F) in the Lowveld.

Swaziland is rich in mineral resources, especially in the western Highveld, which contains the enormous Havelock asbestos mine, vast iron ore deposits, and pockets of gold and tin. Rivers provide hydroelectric power and water for irrigation. Bituminous coal is mined at Mpaka; anthracite deposits have been found at Maloma. The central grasslands are suitable for grazing and growing subtropical export crops.

The Swazi, a NGUNI-speaking people, form more than 90% of Swaziland's total population of 533,000 (1979 est.). English and siSwati are the official languages. Christians make up 57% of the population; the remaining 43% are animists. The capital and largest town is MBABANE. About 35% of the population is literate. Higher education is available at the University of Swaziland (1964). Life expectancy is 43 years.

For its size Swaziland has a diversified economy, marked by pronounced social and economic dualisms. The modern sector is represented by European-controlled agricultural, forestry, manufacturing, and commercial interests. The tradition-

Mbabane, the capital and largest city of Swaziland, is situated in the northwestern portion of the nation. The city's casino is an important source of revenue, drawing tourists from neighboring South Africa, where gambling remains illegal.

al Swazi economy, engaging 50% of the labor force, is characterized by subsistence cultivation, mainly of corn and millet, and by pastoralism. Of the 50% of the labor force in the cash economy, 31% are in the agricultural sector, raising sugarcane, citrus fruits, cotton, and meat products for export. Mining and forestry account for 12% of employment. Forest products, asbestos, and iron ore are important exports. Manufacturing and government each employ 11% of the wage earners. Major trade partners are South Africa, the United Kingdom, and the United States. The value of exports is slightly less than that of imported motor vehicles, petroleum products, foodstuffs, and clothing. Swaziland is in a customs union with South Africa, Botswana, and Lesotho.

GOVERNMENT AND HISTORY

Swaziland is a monarchy, ruled since 1921 by King Sobhuza II. In 1973 he abrogated the constitution, dissolved all political parties, and assumed full powers. A new constitution was promulgated in 1978.

Swaziland came under British influence in the mid-19th century when the Swazi ruler asked for protection against the traditional ZULU enemy. In 1903, after the Swazi chiefs had ceded vast tracts of land to Boer (see AFRIKANERS) and British settlers, Swaziland formally became a British protectorate. Under British rule, development was slow and largely confined to European-owned areas. Economic development was initiated in the late 1950s by agencies of the British government and private South African entrepreneurs.

ALAN C. G. BEST

Bibliography: Fair, Thomas, et al., *Development in Swaziland* (1969); Kuper, Hilda, *The Swazi* (1963); Matsebula, J. S. M., *A History of Swaziland* (1972); Potholm, Christian P., *Swaziland* (1972); Snook, John, *A Geography of Swaziland* (1972).

Sweden

The largest of the five Nordic countries, Sweden forms part of Scandinavia in northwestern Europe. It is long and narrow with a maximum north-south extent of 1,574 km (978 mi) and a maximum east-west extent of 499 km (310 mi). Sweden shares a long land frontier with Norway to the west. Finland is to the east and Denmark lies to the south across the narrow waters of the SKAGERRAK, Kattegat, and Öresund. The Bal-

tic Sea islands of Gotland and Öland are integral parts of Sweden. Rich in iron ores and forest resources, Sweden is an advanced industrial nation with a high standard of living. Sweden's political unification was completed around AD 1000, and it expanded to control a large empire around the BALTIC SEA region during the 16th and 17th centuries. The Swedish name for the country, Sverige, comes from Svea-rike, meaning the kingdom of the Svear; the English form of the name is probably derived from an old Germanic form Svetheod, meaning the Swedish people.

LAND AND RESOURCES

Northwestern Sweden is crossed by an ancient mountain chain rising to Sweden's high point of 2,111 m (6,926 ft) in Kebnekaise (Mount Kebne). The remainder of the Norrland (north of about latitude 60° north) is a southeast-sloping plateau that rises to between 200 and 500 m (650 and 1,640 ft). South of the Norrland, forming the region of Svealand in central Sweden and Götaland farther south, is a varied region of plains and rift valleys that rise to a high point of only 377 m (1,237 ft) in the Southern Swedish Highlands near Jönköping. To the north of the highlands is the Central Swedish Depression, a down-faulted, lake-strewn lowland extending across the peninsula from near Göteborg to east of Stockholm and Uppsala. To the south is Skåne, a low-lying, predominantly agricultural area.

Soils. The entire country was covered by ice during Quaternary glaciation, and both the thin moraines and bare rocks left by the ice underlie soils of poor-to-mediocre quality. More fertile podsols are found in the Central Swedish Depression and in the coastal areas of the south. The largest peat and marsh areas are found in Norrland. In Skåne, moraine clays mixed with chalk and other materials provide excellent soils in lowland areas.

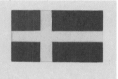

SWEDEN

Official Name: Kingdom of Sweden
Capital and Largest City: Stockholm (1977 est. pop., 658,435)
Area: 448,068 km² (173,000 mi²)
Elevation: *Highest*—Kebnekaise, 2,111 m (6,926 ft); *lowest*—sea level, along the Gulf of Bothnia, Baltic Sea, and the Skagerrak
Population: 8,300,000 (1979 est.). *Distribution*—83% urban, 17% rural; *density,* 18.5 persons per km² (48 per mi²); *annual rate of increase* (1970-77), 0.4%
Principal Language: Swedish (official)
Principal Religion: Evangelical Lutheranism
Principal Products: *Agriculture*—cattle, pigs, chickens; forestry; barley, oats, wheat, hay, rye, sugar beets, potatoes; *Manufacturing and industry*—steel, automobiles, paper and wood products, electrical equipment, shipbuilding, chemicals, petrochemicals, plastics, textiles, processed food; *Mining*—iron ore, gold, silver, lead, copper, zinc, arsenic, uranium, building stone, glacial gravel
Railroads: 12,920 km/8,028 mi (1977)
Roads: 12,610 km/7,836 mi (1977 primary)
Currency: 1 Swedish krona = 100 öre

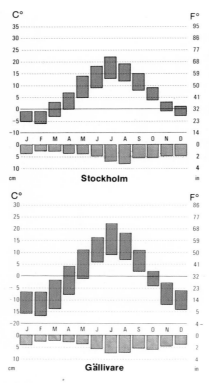

Annual climate charts for two cities in Sweden illustrate the major climate zones of the Scandinavian nation. Stockholm, the capital and largest city, is located on the eastern coast and has a continental humid climate. Gällivare, a mining city of the northern region, has the broad temperature variation characteristic of the subarctic.

Stockholm

Gällivare

Climate. Because of its latitudinal extent, Sweden has a number of climate regimes. A cold, maritime west coast, or northern forest (boreal), type of climate similar to that found in New England dominates the country's west coast. The northern two-thirds of the country has a continental climate marked by severe winters. The south central areas experience the long, cold winters of the north, but they enjoy milder summers. The mountain regions remain cool in summer. In January temperatures decrease markedly from south to north, averaging −0.8° C (30.5° F) at Lund (in the south), −2.8° C (27° F) at Stockholm, and −13.7° C (7.5° F) at Jokkmokk (north of the Arctic Circle). In July, when many hours of sunshine are recorded in the north and nearly 24 hours of continuous daylight north of the Arctic Circle, the temperature variation is minimal. July temperatures thus show only a narrow range from an average of 15° C (59° F) at Jokkmokk, to 18° C (64° F) at Stockholm, and only 17° C (63° F) at Lund. Precipitation averages 610 mm (24 in) and ranges from more than 914 mm (36 in) in exposed western mountain areas to less than 457 mm (18 in) in the extreme eastern part of Sweden. Snow remains on the ground for 40 days in southernmost Sweden, 100 days in the Stockholm area, and 250 days in the northwest mountains.

Drainage. Sweden's principal rivers originate in the northwest mountain chain and flow generally southeastward into the Gulf of Bothnia. The three largest drainage basins are those of the Göta älv, Muonio-Torne, and Ångerman river systems. Most rivers carry maximum water in spring and early summer when the snows melt. Lakes cover about 9% of all Sweden, a fourth of the total lake area being occupied by the four large lakes of the Central Swedish Depression—VÄNERN, VÄTTERN, HJÄLMAREN, and MÄLAREN. Numerous elongated valley lakes occur along rivers in Norrland, and almost 100,000 smaller lakes occupy hollows in the uneven glacial moraines.

Vegetation and Animal Life. Forest now covers about 55% of the land area. It consists of a summer-green forest of beeches, oaks, and other deciduous trees in the south, a mixed forest of deciduous and coniferous trees in central Sweden, and a predominantly coniferous forest of mainly pines and spruce in the Norrland. Mountain birch and dwarf birch grow in colder upland areas, and tundra covers the

(Left) *Göteborg, Sweden's principal seaport and second largest city after Stockholm, is the center of the nation's thriving shipbuilding industry. The city is situated along the Göta River's mouth on the Kattegat.* (Below) *Ridges of the Kjöllen mountains rise to a height of more than 2,100 m (6,890 ft). The thinly populated region is the source of rivers that provide much of Sweden's hydroelectric power.*

highest elevations. Treeless moors (peat moss and marshland) cover more than 14% of all Sweden and as much as 40% in western areas of the south and parts of Norrland. The first large animals to move into Sweden after the ice age were reindeer, then wolves. Carnivorous animals are now found only in isolated areas, and elk and deer are the common large animals found elsewhere.

Resources. The most important mineral is iron ore, with deposits estimated at 2.4 billion metric tons (2.64 billion U.S. tons) in the Gällivare-Malmberget and Kiruna fields north of the Arctic Circle. Other iron-ore deposits, with estimated reserves of 300 million metric tons (330.8 million U.S. tons), occur at Bergslagen, located in southern Sweden northwest of Lake Mälaren. Copper, silver, lead, zinc, and arsenic occur near the Boliden area in Norrland, and some uranium deposits are found in southern Sweden. Only about 7% of the land area is suitable for farming. Water resources are abundant; a total of 92 billion kW h were produced in 1978.

PEOPLE

Sweden has a relatively homogeneous population in ethnic stock, language, and religion. Because of the country's isolation relatively few non-Swedes have intermixed with the Swedes through the course of history; the major groups that have done so were Finns after 1580 and Walloons from present-day Belgium, who settled in the Bergslagen area in the 1620s. Groups that maintain their distinct ethnic identity today include a growing Finnish population, about 17,000 LAPPS, and recent immigrants from Estonia, Latvia, and Lithuania (in 1944); Hungary (in 1956); and Yugoslavia, Greece, and Turkey (in the 1960s and '70s).

Language. The Swedish language belongs to the east Scandinavian branch of GERMANIC LANGUAGES. The Swedish of the Mälar provinces has developed as the written and national language, and the use of other forms is declining. The Lapp and Finnish minorities speak their respective languages as well as Swedish. Special efforts have been made to teach Swedish to the recent immigrant groups.

Religion. More than 90% of the population are members of the State Evangelical Lutheran church, established in 1527 as the national religion. Religious freedom has been constitutionally guaranteed since 1809, and about 400,000 belong to nonconformist (free) Protestant churches, among whom the Pentacostalists (91,000) and Mission Covenant church (87,000) are the largest. Many recent immigrants from southern Europe are Roman Catholics; some are Eastern Orthodox. Formal religious worship in Sweden takes place in 2,575 parishes.

Demography. The Swedish population is estimated to have been 1,200,000 in 1650 and was 1,780,678 at the time of the first census in 1750. The urban population advanced from 21.5% of the total in 1900 to 83% in 1975, one of Europe's fastest rates of urbanization and one leaving much of the countryside depopulated. The three largest urban areas are STOCK-HOLM, GÖTEBORG, and MALMÖ. The birthrate of 11.6 per 1,000 inhabitants (1977) is one of the lowest in the world and is still

declining; the death rate of 10.7 is also low but is increasing slowly as more people (15.5% in 1976) enter the over-65 age bracket. Because of this slow rate of natural increase, the overall national growth rate is maintained at 0.4% annually, attributable mainly to immigration. Götaland and Svealand, forming the southernmost third of Sweden, are the most densely populated regions, with 86% of the total population; Norrland, by contrast, has 59% of the total land area but only 14% of the total population. The overall population density is 18.5 inhabitants per km² (48 per mi²), but this ranges from 45 per km² (117 per mi²) in Götaland and 38 per km² (98 per mi²) in Svealand to only 5 per km² (13 per mi²) in Norrland.

Education and Health. Education has been compulsory since 1842, and 99% of the population is literate. All children at 7 years of age begin a 9-year basic school, followed by 2 to 4 years of gymnasium (secondary school), depending on their career objectives. The oldest and largest university is in UPP-SALA and dates from 1477; other universities are in Lund, Stockholm, Göteborg, Umeå, and Linköping. Health-care expenses are covered by national health insurance and hospitalization plans and account for 42% of all social-welfare costs. A total of 34 major hospitals have more than 500 beds each; more than 850 other hospitals contain a total of 136,000 beds. Physicians number 14,050, and dentists, more than 7,000. Infant mortality is 8 per 1,000 live births (1977). Major causes of adult deaths are heart and circulatory diseases and cancer.

The Arts. Leading cultural institutions are the Swedish Royal Opera; the Royal Dramatic Theater; the National Touring

Theater; and the Swedish Academy, which awards the NOBEL PRIZE for Literature. Important Swedish painters, sculptors, and architects are discussed in the article SCANDINAVIAN ART AND ARCHITECTURE, and major literary figures in SWEDISH LITERATURE. Other modern Swedes prominent in the arts are the composer Hilding Rosenberg and the film director Ingmar BERGMAN.

ECONOMIC ACTIVITY

Poor in agricultural resources, Sweden began trading with Russia and southeastern Europe under the Vikings (9th-11th centuries). In the Middle Ages trade expanded with other parts of Europe, and Visby (on Gotland) became the center of the Hanseatic League's thriving Baltic Sea trade in fish, timber, and metals. Copper mining was important at Falun in the 13th century. In the 15th century the iron ores at Bergslagen were being smelted with charcoal from the surrounding forest, and by the 17th and 18th centuries Sweden was Europe's foremost producer of high-quality steels. Lumbering developed on a large scale in the early 19th century, followed by furniture and pulp and paper industries. The Industrial Revolution reached Sweden between 1850 and 1870. Lacking coal deposits, Sweden industrialized slowly at first and accelerated after hydroelectric power was developed in the early 20th century. Its late start helped avoid the ugly urban communities associated with early industrialization in Germany, the United Kingdom, and France. In 1977, Sweden had a gross domestic product of $87.1 billion ($10,528 per capita).

Mining. Although less than 1% of the total labor force is employed in mining, Sweden is Europe's second largest producer of iron ore and one of the top ten producers in the world. The most important mining areas are located at Kiruna and Gällivare in the north, where the ores have an iron content of 60–65%. Lower grade but more desirable nonphosphoric iron ores occur at Bergslagen. The largest mine is Grängesberg. The copper deposits at Falun are now exhausted, but Sweden continues to produce copper, lead, silver, and arsenic from the Skelleftea field.

Manufacturing. About 26% of the total labor force is employed in manufacturing, with about half in Sweden's metalworking establishments. Eskilstuna is known for its high-quality steels, and Sweden is a well-known exporter of such precision items as Volvo and SAAB automobiles, SKF ball bearings, ASEA high-voltage cable and other electrical equipment, L. M. Eriksson electrical and telephone equipment, and Electrolux electrical appliances. The country's shipbuilding industry is the world's second largest. International competition and inflated prices needed to cover labor agreements, however, have depressed the industry. Chemicals and petrochemicals are growing in importance throughout the country.

About 20% of all industrial workers are employed in the production of wood pulp and lumber; about 8% work in food processing; and 7% in the declining textile industry centered near Göteborg.

Power. About 70% of all Sweden's energy needs are supplied by imported petroleum. The principal domestic energy source is hydroelectricity, which provided 64% of the 92 billion kW h of electricity produced in 1977. The rivers producing the most power are in the north, and high-voltage transmission lines carry the power to consuming centers in the south and central regions. About half of all other electricity is generated from petroleum and the remaining half from nuclear power plants. A plebiscite approving a limited increase in the use of the latter took place in March 1980.

Agriculture. Farmers now make up less than 5% of the total labor force, and agriculture is highly mechanized. Three-fourths of all farm income is derived from livestock and dairy products. Most cultivated crops are grown primarily for fodder; 20% of the cropland is planted to barley, 16% to oats, 13% to wheat, and 23% to hay. Rye, sugar beets, and potatoes are also cultivated.

Forestry and Fishing. Sweden is one of the world's leading producers of timber, wood pulp, and newsprint—the annual tree cut almost equaling the yearly regrowth of the vast forests. Log driving on the rivers has largely given way to truck

(Above) *A group of Swedish lumber workers use long poles to maneuver logs downstream to a storage pond. Timber and wood by-products traditionally have ranked among Sweden's most valuable exports.*

(Left) *An aerial photograph of Öland, Sweden's second largest island after Gotland, reveals intensive cultivation along its coastal plain. Sugar beets, rye, and potatoes are the principal crops produced on this narrow island in the Baltic Sea.*

transportation, a change that has been to the advantage of the industry in southern rather than northern Sweden in recent years. Fishing is small scale by comparison. About 153,700 metric tons (169,450 U.S. tons) of saltwater fish were landed in 1978, but larger amounts were imported.

Transportation. Sweden's road system is well developed, even in the north. More than half of all roads are paved, and automobile and truck traffic has greatly increased since World War II. Rail traffic, on the other hand, has declined, and rail lines have been reduced from 17,000 km (10,563 mi) in 1937 to 12,920 km (8,028 mi) today. Sweden's international airports are Arlanda (Stockholm), Landvetter (Göteborg), and Sturup (Malmö). Stockholm, Göteborg, and Malmö are also the principal seaports.

Trade. Despite a large volume of exports, Sweden in 1979 had a considerable trade deficit in spite of the 1977 devaluation of the krona. The country's major trading partners are West Germany, the United Kingdom, Norway, Denmark, and the United States. The major imports are machinery and automobiles, petroleum, textile fibers, and foodstuffs. The leading exports are machinery and automobiles, wood pulp, paper and wood, and iron ore. In 1978, Sweden had exports of $21.8 billion and imports of $20.5 billion.

GOVERNMENT

Sweden is a constitutional monarchy with a parliamentary form of government. The present constitution was adopted in 1975, replacing that of 1809. The monarchy occupies a ceremonial and symbolic position; CHARLES XVI GUSTAV has occupied the throne since the death of King GUSTAV VI ADOLF in 1973. Legislative authority rests in the unicameral Riksdag (parliament), composed of 349 members elected to 3-year terms under a system of proportional representation. The prime minister and cabinet form the government and hold office only as long as they retain the support of a majority in the Riksdag. The principal political parties are the Social Democratic party (now led by Olof PALME), which controlled the government from 1932 to 1976; the small Communist party, VPK; and the three nonsocialist parties, which have held power in coalition or singly since 1976. The nonsocialist parties are the Center party, led by Thorbjörn FÄLLDIN; the Moderate Coalition party (formerly the Conservative party), led by Gösta Bohman; and the People's party, led by Ola ULLSTEN. In October 1979, Fälldin replaced Ullsten as prime minister.

Gamla Staden (Old Town), the historic center of Stockholm, covers three small islands in Lake Mälar, linked by bridges to the mainland. Several of its buildings date from the 13th century, when Stockholm was founded near the site of a Viking settlement.

For local government purposes, Sweden is divided into 24 counties (*län*) and 277 municipalities (kommunes).

HISTORY

Sweden was first populated by Paleolithic hunters during the end of the last Ice Age, c.10,000–c.8000 BC. During the Bronze Age (c.1500–500 BC), when the inhabitants spoke an Indo-European language from which Swedish was later to develop, lively trade links existed with the rest of Europe. From c.100 BC extensive trade was shared with Rome, and in the 4th century AD Baltic trade was centered on Gotland. At this time small kingdoms were formed by tribes, the most important of which, the Suiones (Svearna) in the Lake Mälaren region, was mentioned by Tacitus in AD 98. Other tribes, the GOTHS (Götarna) in the south and the Hälsings and Lapps in the north, appear in sources from the 6th century AD. Christianity came to Sweden in the 9th century, and in 1164 the archbishopric in Uppsala was instituted. By 1000 the Goths had been conquered by the Suiones, and the first unified Swedish state founded.

The VIKING period, from the 9th century to c.1050, was prosperous. Swedish Vikings traveled as fur and slave traders to Russia and down to the Arab caliphate at Baghdad. In the 13th century parts of Finland and Karelia were occupied by Swedes. Slavery ended in 1335, and the first Swedish national law was compiled around 1350. In 1397, after three centuries of internal struggles in Sweden, the Danish queen MARGARET I united Denmark, Sweden, and Norway in the Kalmar Union. The Period of Union lasted to 1523 when, as opposition to the continuing aggression of Denmark and the HANSEATIC LEAGUE mounted in Sweden, Gustav Vasa used the murder of Swedish leaders in the so-called Bloodbath of Stockholm (1520) to lead a revolt against Denmark. Ruling as GUSTAV I Vasa (1523–60), he achieved independence for Sweden and introduced Lutheranism as Sweden's national religion.

Sweden's expansion continued during the 16th and 17th centuries. Estonia, Latvia, and Lithuania were occupied between 1561 and 1629. Under GUSTAV II ADOLF (r. 1611–32), Sweden entered the THIRTY YEARS' WAR on the side of the Protestants and gained lands in northern Germany (see WESTPHALIA, PEACE OF). Sweden's period as an empire (1611–1718) reached its apex under CHARLES X Gustav (r. 1654–60) but came to an end in the 18th century with the rise of Russia as a unified empire under Emperor Peter I. In the Great NORTHERN WAR (1700–21), Sweden lost its Baltic and several of its north German provinces on the death of CHARLES XII (r. 1697–1718). After the war a new constitution was drawn up by the Riksdag and an early form of parliamentarism initiated with reduced powers for the monarchy and increased powers for the Riksdag and bourgeoisie. Known as the Age of Freedom, this era ended abruptly in 1772 following a coup d'etat by GUSTAV III (r. 1772–92) and the reestablishment of a strong monarchy.

During the NAPOLEONIC WARS, Sweden joined (1805) the Third Coalition against France. In 1809, Russia, then an ally of France, seized Finland. After this defeat GUSTAV IV ADOLF was forced to abdicate (1809) in favor of Charles XIII. In 1810, Jean Baptiste Bernadotte, one of Napoleon's marshals and the founder of the present Swedish royal house, was chosen by the Riksdag as crown prince. He ruled as CHARLES XIV JOHN from 1818 to 1844. Finland remained in Russian hands, and Denmark was forced to cede Norway to Sweden in compensation in 1814. Norway remained in union with Sweden until it became independent peacefully in 1905.

Impoverished at the end of the Napoleonic Wars, Sweden initiated a policy of nonalignment that kept it out of World Wars I and II and began a steady and undramatic social and economic revolution within its new borders.

Many Swedes emigrated to North America during the latter half of the 19th century, about 1 million between 1850 and 1890, but emigration slowed as conditions improved after 1900, and by the 1950s Sweden was one of the world's richest and most socially progressive nations.   KARL ERIK BERGSTEN

Bibliography:
GENERAL: Mead, W. R., and Hall, Wendy, *Scandinavia* (1972); Scobbie, Irene, *Sweden* (1972).

SOCIAL CONDITIONS: Heclo, Hugh, *Modern Social Politics in Britain and Sweden: From Relief to Income Maintenance* (1974); Scase, Richard, ed., *Readings in the Swedish Class Structure* (1976); Tomasson, Richard F., *Sweden: Prototype of Modern Society* (1970).

ECONOMICS: Koblik, Steven, ed., *Sweden's Development from Poverty to Affluence, 1750-1970*, trans. by Joanne Johnson and Steven Koblik (1975); Lindbeck, Assar, *Swedish Economic Policy* (1974).

GOVERNMENT AND POLITICS: Board, Joseph B., *The Government and Politics of Sweden* (1970); Elder, Neil C., *Government in Sweden: The Executive at Work* (1970); Hancock, M. Donald, *Sweden: The Politics of Post-Industrial Change* (1972).

HISTORY: Andersson, Ingvar, *A History of Sweden*, trans. by Carolyn Hannay (1968; repr. 1975); Carlgren, Carl W. M., *Swedish Foreign Policy During the Second World War*, trans. by Arthur Spencer (1977); Moberg, Vilhelm, *A History of the Swedish People*, 2 vols., trans. by Paul B. Austin (1972 and 1974); Samuelsson, Kurt, *From Great Power to Welfare State* (1968); Scott, Franklin D., *Sweden: The Nation's History* (1977).

Swedenborg, Emanuel

The Swedish scientist, theosophist, and mystic Emanuel Swedenborg, b. Jan. 29, 1688, d. Mar. 29, 1772, pioneered in both scientific and religious thought. University trained at Uppsala, Swedenborg turned first to a scientific and technical career as a natural scientist and official with the Swedish board of mines (1710-45), concentrating on research and theory. His foremost scientific writing is *Opera philosophica et mineralia* (Philosophical and Mineralogical Works, 3 vols., 1734), which illustrates his unique combination of metaphysics, cosmology, and science. A first-rate scientific theorist and inventor, Swedenborg, in some of his insights, anticipated scientific progress by more than a century.

His study of mathematics, mechanics, and physics was motivated by an interest in cosmology and finally theology, which led to his second, theosophical career as a "seer of divine wisdom." After 1734, Swedenborg turned to the study of physiology and psychology, in which fields he was also a brilliant pioneer. Here again, however, the all-uniting structures that he sought—resting on spirit and deity—eluded him. Visited by a mystic illumination in 1745, Swedenborg claimed a direct vision of a spiritual world underlying the natural sphere. His voluminous works from this period are presented as divinely revealed biblical interpretations.

In his system, best reflected in *Divine Love and Wisdom* (1763; Eng. trans., 1965), Swedenborg conceived of three spheres: divine mind, spiritual world, and natural world. Each corresponds to a degree of being in God and in humankind: love, wisdom, and use (end, cause, and effect). Through devotion to each degree, unification with it takes place and a person obtains his or her destiny, which is union with creator and creation. Unlike many mystics, Swedenborg proposed an approach to spiritual reality and God through, rather than in rejection of, material nature. His 12–volume compendium *The*

Heavenly Arcana (1747-56; Eng. trans., 1951-56) represents a unique synthesis between modern science and religion.

In response to a vision of the "last judgment" and the "return of Christ," Swedenborg proclaimed the advent of the New Church, an idea that found social expression in the Swedenborgian societies and in the Church of the NEW JERUSALEM.

JAMES D. NELSON

Bibliography: Jonsson, Inge, *Emanuel Swedenborg* (Eng. trans., 1971); Sigstedt, Cyriel O., *The Swedenborg Epic* (1952; repr. 1971); Spalding, John H., *Introduction to Swedenborg's Religious Thought* (1956); Toksvig, Signe, *Emanuel Swedenborg: Scientist and Mystic* (1948; repr. 1972); Trobridge, George, *Swedenborg: Life and Teaching*, 4th ed. (1968); Van Dusen, Wilson, *The Presence of Other Worlds: The Findings of Emanuel Swedenborg* (1975); Wunch, William F., *An Outline of Swedenborg's Teaching* (1975).

Swedish art and architecture: see SCANDINAVIAN ART AND ARCHITECTURE.

Swedish language: see GERMANIC LANGUAGES.

Swedish literature

Swedish literature, although enriched by foreign influences, has never lost its national identity. Swedish writing dates back to 11th-century runic inscriptions, but the literature proper originated in the Catholic Middle Ages. Saint Bridget's 14th-century *Revelations*, written in Latin, gained fame both in Sweden and abroad. Like the religious literature, most medieval Swedish secular writings served nonliterary purposes. Exceptions were the folk ballads; more typical were legal texts in vernacular prose.

Gustav Vasa's reformation of the church contributed to a cultural decline in the 16th century. Of vital importance, though, to the development of the Swedish language were Olaus Petri's Bible translations of 1526 and 1541. During this period there also appeared Sweden's first lyric poet, the vagrant Lars Wivallius. Although Renaissance ideas never took root in Scandinavia, traces of them are seen in Georg Stiernhielm's 17th-century baroque poetry.

The 18th century, a period of enlightenment, was dominated by prose. Only toward the close of the century, during the reign of Gustaf III, did other genres emerge in the wake of French cultural influence. Noteworthy is Carl Michael BELLMAN's rococo poetry.

Erik Johan STAGNELIUS's Neoplatonism, Esaias TEGNÉR's and Erik Gustaf GEIJER's glorification of the nation's past, and Abraham Viktor RYDBERG's idealistic liberalism all reflect the philosophical orientation of Swedish 19th-century romanticism. Carl Jonas Love ALMQVIST, initially a mystic and romantic, came later to herald new trends of realism in prose works characterized by social awareness. The towering figure of the

Emanuel Swedenborg, an 18th-century Swedish scientist and visionary, proposed a system of relationships between natural, spiritual, and divine realms in his extensive religious works. His mystic visions and symbolic reading of the Bible became the foundation of the Church of the New Jerusalem and had great influence on such poets as William Blake, Charles Baudelaire, and W. B. Yeats.

Swedish playwright August Strindberg brought colloquial realism and psychological insights to the theater. Noted for bold experimentation, he created tormented images of despair and alienation in such naturalistic plays as Miss Julie (1888). Strindberg's later symbolic works, such as A Dream Play (1902), combined realism with expressionist dream sequences.

The prolific novelist Eyvind Johnson, who in 1974 shared the Nobel Prize for literature with his countryman Harry Martinson, is best known for Return to Ithaca *(1946), based on Homer's* Odyssey. *Although relatively unknown outside his own country, Johnson made significant contributions to modern Swedish literature, beginning with* Novels about Olaf *(1934-37), four autobiographical works.*

century, however, was August STRINDBERG (1849-1912), Sweden's greatest writer and the father of modern Swedish drama and fiction. Moving in his later plays from naturalism to dreamlike symbolism, Strindberg foreshadowed expressionism.

The socially opinionated prose writers of the 1880s were succeeded by a new wave of romantics, who preferred verse and emphasized the past (Selma LAGERLÖF) and the countryside (Erik Axel KARLFELDT). About 1900, Hjalmar SÖDERBERG published exquisite short stories set in the streets of Stockholm; but the novelists of the next decade favored small-town Sweden. Modernism was introduced in the 1920s by the Finno-Swedish poets Edith SÖDERGRAN, Gunnar Björling, and Elmer Diktonius, and it was affirmed in Pär LAGERKVIST's innovative dramas and Gunnar EKELÖF's surrealistic poetry. A new social class of self-educated country writers entered Sweden's literary world in the 1930s, among them the 1974 Nobel laureates Harry MARTINSON and Eyvind JOHNSON.

Sweden escaped the world wars, but its literature from the 1940s (Erik Lindegren, Karl Vennberg) testifies to postwar depression. The feeling of pessimism and guilt deepened during the following decades because of the Vietnam War and Third World problems. An intense questioning of literature's social function and a mistrust of language found manifold literary expressions—from "new simplicity" and "concreteness" in poetry, to documentaries in prose. Swedish literature of the end of the 1970s, however, was characterized by a new trust in the word and a new delight in traditional fiction.

VIRPI ZUCK

Bibliography: Bredsdorff, Elias, et al., *An Introduction to Scandinavian Literature* (1951); Gustafson, Alrik, *A History of Swedish Literature* (1961).

Sweelinck, Jan Pieterszoon [sway'-link]

Jan Pieterszoon Sweelinck, b. May 1562, d. Oct. 16, 1621, was a Dutch organist and composer who spent virtually his entire life in his native country and rarely left Amsterdam, where for about 45 years he held the position of organist at the Old Church. Greatly respected as a performer, Sweelinck was also a prolific composer but probably exerted his greatest influence on the musical world through his teaching. Young organists not only from his own country but from many distant lands sought him out, so that he may be said to have formed a school of organ playing that eventually covered most of Europe. His compositions for organ and harpsichord confirm his mastery of the fantasia, toccata, and variations. He also developed the style of the echo-fantasia, making use of the echo effects possible on both instruments, and did not neglect popular songs and dance themes in his variation sets. His more than 250 choral works range from French chansons to motets and psalms.

DENIS STEVENS

Sweet Briar College

Established in 1901, Sweet Briar College (enrollment: 700; library: 170,000 volumes) is a private 4-year liberal arts school for women in Sweet Briar, Va.

sweet fern

Sweet fern, *Comptonia peregrina*, in the family Myricaceae, is a bushlike shrub found in sandy but moist soil in woodland areas and open fields of eastern North America. It commonly reaches nearly 1.5 m (5 ft) in height. The fruit is a brown nutlet. The fragrant leaves alternate and are slender, about 11 cm (4.5 in) long and 1.25 cm (0.5 in) in width. Sweet ferns are used as bank coverings and may be propagated by seeds, division, or layering.

sweet gale

Sweet gale, *Myrica gale*, is a small, deciduous shrub in the myrtle family, Myrtaceae. Native to the colder parts of the Northern Hemisphere, it usually is found in boggy swamps. Its leaves are aromatic when crushed, its flowers are brownish catkins, and its fruit occurs as small nutlets.

sweet gum

The sweet gum tree, L. styraciflua, *of the eastern United States, has star-shaped leaves and burrs that release winged seeds in the fall. Balsam, extracted from its wood, is used in drugs and perfumes.*

Sweet gums, genus *Liquidambar*, comprise six species of deciduous hardwood trees in the witch hazel family, Hamamelidaceae. There is one North American species, native to the eastern United States and found southward to Nicaragua; the others are found in Anatolia and eastern Asia. American sweet gums, *L. styraciflua*, can be distinguished by their long-stalked, star-shaped leaves, with five to seven lobes. The bark is gray or brown and deeply furrowed. The fruit, a hard ball with curved, spiny projections, opens in the autumn to release winged seeds. The American sweet gum grows to 36 m (120 ft) in height and is an important timber tree. A fragrant resin, or STORAX, can be obtained from all sweet gums, especially from the *L. orientalis*, of Anatolia. The storax is used commercially, for example, in soaps and perfumes.

sweet pea

Sweet pea, *Lathyrus odoratus*, a climbing or nonclimbing annual herb in the pea family, Leguminosae, is grown for its range of petal colors, fragrant flowers, and long-lasting qualities. It grows only in cool temperatures. A native of Italy, it was introduced into northern Europe about 1700 and devel-

The sweet pea, L. odoratus, *native to Italy, has varicolored, fragrant flowers. Tendrils anchor it to stakes, fences, or trellises, enabling the plant to climb about 2 m (6 ft).*

oped genetically into strains or varieties after 1870. The original sweet pea was a climber. The nonclimbing variety was developed within recent years in California.   JANE PHILPOTT

sweet potato

The sweet potato plant, I. batatas, *native to the Americas, is cultivated in temperate and tropical regions worldwide for its large edible roots.*

The sweet potato, *Ipomoea batatas,* a member of the morning glory family, is grown for its swollen, tuberlike roots. Native to the American tropics and once an important component of the Aztec diet, the sweet potato is rich in vitamin A. Europeans introduced the plant to their continent in the 16th century, and it later spread to Asia. Because 4 to 5 months of warm weather are required for adequate yields, its cultivation is concentrated in the southern United States, tropical America, the USSR, Japan, and the warmer areas of China. The many varieties of sweet potato are distinguished by their leaf shapes. All have long vines, often exceeding 3 m (10 ft). Seeds are rarely produced, and most sweet potatoes are propagated either by planting sprouts that rise from the roots or by rooting vine cuttings. If properly cured and stored, disease-free roots can remain edible for 6 to 7 months.

sweet William

Sweet William, *Dianthus barbatus,* is the common name of a popular annual, biennial, or perennial flowering herb in the pink family, Caryophyllaceae. It is native to the USSR and China. The flowers are in terminal clusters that are bright colors of pink, red, white, and variations: sometimes double forms occur. The sweet William grows to 60 cm (2 ft) and is short-lived. A number of horticultural selections are available.

sweetleaf

Sweetleaf, genus *Symplocos,* is the common name for any of 290 species of large shrubs or trees in the sweetleaf family, Symplocaceae. Native to the warmer regions of the Americas, Australia, and Eurasia, some species are grown as ornamentals. Only *Symplocos paniculata* thrives in northern regions. This native of China and Japan produces bright, blue berries about 6.4 mm (0.25 in) in diameter in October. Small groups of fragrant white flowers bloom in spring.

sweetshrub

Sweetshrub is the common name given to four species of North American shrubs of the genus *Calycanthus,* family Calycanthaceae. They have opposite leaves, fragrant, reddish brown flowers, and aromatic bark. Carolina allspice, *C. floridus,* is a sweetshrub native to the southeastern United States.

swell

Groups of regular, long-period, long-wavelength waves that propagate away from the open ocean in which they were generated by the wind are called swell. Swell typically has periods from 10 to 30 seconds. These longer waves propagate faster than shorter waves because the phase speed of gravity waves in deep water increases with wavelength. Swell can travel virtually unattenuated for thousands of kilometers to shore, the longest waves reaching shore first. Swell from a distant storm propagates at an appropriate group velocity, which for a given wavelength is one-half of the phase speed. (See also WATER WAVE.)   ROBERT E. WILSON

Bibliography: Tricker, R. A. R., *Bores, Breakers, Waves, and Wakes* (1964).

Swenson, May   [swen'-suhn]

A frequently anthologized American poet, May Swenson, b. Logan, Utah, May 28, 1919, has established a reputation for highly evocative glimpses of nature and everyday life that attempt to close the gap between observer and object. Her first volumes, *Another Animal* (1954) and *A Cage of Spines* (1958), demonstrated her technical skill and an almost incantatory handling of sound. Later volumes, such as *Iconographs* (1970), experimented with spatial forms. A recipient of numerous grants and awards, Swenson has also written two well-received volumes of verse for children, *Poems to Solve* (1966) and *More Poems to Solve* (1971).

Sweyn, King of Denmark   [swayn]

Sweyn Forkbeard, b. *c.*960, d. Feb. 3, 1014, was the Danish conqueror of England (see VIKINGS). He succeeded his father, King Harold Bluetooth, after killing him in battle about 986. A few years later, Sweyn and OLAF I of Norway began their attacks on England, imposing the Danegeld (a form of tax) on the English in return for a specified period of peace. In 1000 he joined the Swedes in war against Olaf, who was killed. Norway was then divided between the victors. Sweyn's attacks on England continued until 1013, when he finally drove out King ÆTHELRED II and made himself king. He was succeeded by his sons CANUTE (in England) and Harold (in Denmark).   J. R. CHRISTIANSON

Bibliography: Oakley, Stewart, *A Short History of Denmark* (1972).

swift

The bird family Apodidae in the order Apodiformes comprises approximately 70 species of birds called swifts. Swifts bear a superficial resemblance to swallows, but their closest relatives are the crested swifts in the family Hemiprocnidae

The chimney swift, Chaetura pelagica, breeds in the eastern half of the United States and winters in Peru and along the Amazon. It roosts in chimneys. At dusk a flock whirls itself into a funnel shape and slowly descends, bird by bird, into a chosen stack.

Probably the most powerful satirist in the history of English letters, Jonathan Swift expressed his hatred of Britain's exploitative economic policy in Ireland by ironically suggesting in "A Modest Proposal" (1729) that his impoverished fellow Irishmen raise their children as a cash crop—for the culinary pleasure of the English.

and possibly hummingbirds in the order Trochiliformes. Except for New Zealand, Antarctica, the southernmost part of South America, and oceanic islands, swifts are found throughout the world.

These relatively small birds, 10 to 25 cm (4 to 10 in) in length, have an elongated, compact body and a short neck. Their wings are long and relatively narrow. The legs are short but strong, and the toes can be arranged in several ways (three forward and one back, two forward and two back, or all forward). The triangular bill is small, but the mouth slit is large. Most swifts are dark in color; some have white markings. The body temperature in many swifts varies, being considerably lower at night or at times of inactivity.

Swifts spend more time in the air than do any other birds. While in flight they feed on insects and may drink, pick up nesting material, and even copulate. Nests are placed in caves, hollow trees, chimneys, and, by a few species, in curled palm leaves.

Many swifts nest in colonies, which may include more than 2 million birds in some species. Both sexes incubate and feed a clutch that numbers between one and six. Swifts use saliva as an adhesive agent in their nests; a few species even make nests entirely out of salivary secretions. Bird's nest soup, which comes from the nests of cave swiftlets (genus *Collocalia*), is widely consumed in Asia.   GARY D. SCHNELL

Swift, Jonathan

The 18th-century English satirist Jonathan Swift, b. Dublin, Nov. 30, 1667, d. Oct. 19, 1745, is most famous as the author of GULLIVER'S TRAVELS (1726), the story of the adventures of Captain Lemuel Gulliver in four voyages to fictional places—Lilliput, a kingdom of pygmies; Brobdingnag, a kingdom of giants; Laputa, a flying island; and the land of the Houyhnhnms, where horses are rational beings who rule over Yahoos, creatures strongly resembling humankind. The book is a satire, frequently mordant, on human nature; yet so inventive are its whimsy and fantasy that it has often been given to children.

Swift was educated at Trinity College, Dublin, and after graduation he passed most of the following ten years as secretary to the statesman Sir William Temple. He wished to enter politics but settled for the church, in which he was ordained in 1694. In 1702 he moved to England in hope of political appointment; there he published his first work, A TALE OF A TUB (1704), a satire on corruption in religion and learning. The dazzling irony of this tour de force earned him notoriety but no appointment. He followed it with the *Bickerstaff Papers* (1708-09), in which he demolished the pretensions of John Partridge, a popular astrologer; he also contributed to Sir Richard Steele's *Tatler*.

In 1710 the government passed from Whig to Tory control;

the Tories recognized in Swift a potent voice for their cause and made him editor of their journal, the *Examiner*. He thus became an unofficial power in English politics as well as a leading writer. Besides Steele, his friends included Alexander Pope and John Gay. His life during this period is recorded in the *Journal to Stella* (1710-13), his letters to Esther Johnson, a close lifelong friend.

Swift's political power ended with another change of government in 1714. His friends procured him the deanery of St. Patrick's Cathedral in Dublin, a post that carried prestige but also exiled him to Ireland, where he was to remain for the rest of his life.

Ireland in the 18th century was a colony of England, exploited by absentee English landlords and denied self-government. The spectacle of Irish servitude in general, and in particular a scheme by one William Wood, who had received a royal patent to issue a new Irish coinage and planned to profit from debasing it, provoked Swift in 1724 to write the *Drapier's Letters*, exhorting the Irish to refuse Wood's coinage and develop their own economy. The development of Irish economy was also the topic of his last and most brilliant satire, A MODEST PROPOSAL (1729), in which he ironically counseled his countrymen to turn their children into a cash crop. These efforts made Swift a national hero, but even that did not reconcile him to living in Ireland.

After Stella's death in 1728, Swift grew reclusive and eccentric. Attacks of vertigo, from which he had suffered occasionally in the past, became frequent; he declined into senility and in 1742 was declared unfit to manage himself.

As a satirist Swift's technique was to create fictional speakers, such as Lemuel Gulliver and the Modest Proposer, who utter sentiments that the intelligent reader will recognize as sinfully complacent, egotistical, stupid, or mad. Swift is thus the master of understated irony, and his name has become practically synonymous with the type of satire in which the most outrageous statements are offered in a straight-faced manner. He has often been accused of a morbid preoccupation with physical decay. It should be remembered, however, that this preoccupation belongs technically to his speakers, of whom Swift did not expect the reader to approve.

WILLIAM MCCARTHY

Bibliography: Bullitt, John M., *Jonathan Swift and the Anatomy of Satire* (1953); Donoghue, Denis, ed., *Jonathan Swift: A Critical Anthology* (1969); Ehrenpreis, Irvin, *Swift: The Man, His Works, and the Age,* 2 vols. (1962-68); Fischer, John I., *On Swift's Poetry* (1978); Hunting, Robert, *Jonathan Swift* (1966); Jeffares, A. Norman, *Jonathan Swift* (1976); Price, Martin, *Swift's Rhetorical Art,* rev. ed. (1963); Qintana, Ricardo, *The Mind and Art of Jonathan Swift,* 2d ed. (1955).

Swift and Company v. United States

The U.S. Supreme Court case of *Swift and Company* v. *United States* (1905) dealt with the applicability of the SHERMAN ANTI-

Trust Act to monopolistic practices in the meat-packing industry. A number of companies in different states were charged with combining to restrain trade in livestock and in the sale of meat. Specifically, they were charged with price fixing, blacklisting, rigging cartage and railroad rates, and restricting shipments of meat. The companies argued that, even if the charges were true, all of the practices had occurred within a single state and were not a part of interstate commerce.

A unanimous court, speaking through Justice Oliver Wendell Holmes, Jr., held the Sherman act applicable to the practices described. Holmes maintained that although the restraint and monopoly of trade took place within a single state, the "effect upon commerce among the states is not accidental, secondary, remote or merely probable." It had a direct, deleterious effect on commerce across state lines and therefore came within the authority of Congress and consequently of the Sherman act. This case reinvigorated the Sherman act, which had been, in effect, emasculated by the Court's ruling in United States v. E. C. Knight Company (1895). It also became an important precedent for future regulation of local matters, which although technically not commerce, are a vital part of the movement of goods across state lines (see Stafford v. Wallace, 1922).

ROBERT J. STEAMER

Swigert, John L., Jr.   [swig'-urt]

The American astronaut John Leonard Swigert, Jr., b. Denver, Colo., Aug. 30, 1931, served as command-module pilot aboard the aborted *Apollo 13* manned space mission, Apr. 11–17, 1971 (see APOLLO PROGRAM).

Swigert was an Air Force pilot (1953–56) and a civilian test pilot (1957–64) before being selected as an astronaut in 1966. He was, during a leave of absence from NASA, the staff executive director of the U.S. House of Representatives's Committee on Science and Technology from 1973 to 1977. After resigning (1977) from NASA, he ran (1978) unsuccessfully for the U.S. Senate from Colorado.   DAVE DOOLING

Bibliography: Cooper, Henry S. T., Jr., *Thirteen: The Flight That Failed* (1973); Cunningham, Walter, *The All-American Boys* (1977); Lewis, Richard S., *The Voyages of Apollo* (1974).

swim bladder

A swim bladder, or air bladder, is a gas-filled sac that has a hydrostatic function in ray-finned bony fishes. Approximately one-half of all fishes possess the organ. The maintenance of a gas space in the body allows the fish to approach neutral buoyancy, the lift provided nearly balancing the weight in water of the other, heavier tissues. The swim bladder is located in the upper part of the body cavity below the kidney and above the digestive tract. In addition to being a hydrostatic organ, the swim bladder may also function in respiration and in sound production and reception.

MICHAEL H. HORN

swimming and diving

Swimming is a competitive and recreational activity consisting of various motions that propel the body through the water. Diving is a sport, primarily competitive—although as a method of entering the water it is practiced by most casual swimmers—that involves carefully executed twists, flips, and spins during a plunge into the water.

Swimming and diving are both excellent physical conditioners. Both have wide appeal, and international competitions in the sports are regulated by the Fédération Internationale de Natation Amateur (FINA). Swimming has been on the Olympic Games agenda since the first modern Games were held in 1896; diving from high platforms first became an Olympic event in 1904, and diving from low springboards was introduced at the 1908 Olympics.

HISTORY OF SWIMMING

Swimming predates recorded history. Humans undoubtedly discovered how to swim by accident; a person probably fell into the water and struggled to shore using a dog-paddle stroke.

There exists an Egyptian hieroglyph for swimming dating from 2500 BC. The ancient Greeks and Romans made swimming an important part of their military training programs. It is believed that swimming contests were organized in Japan as early as the 1st century BC.

During the Middle Ages in Europe, swimming declined in popularity. People felt that the water was contaminated and a source of disease. Fear of the water was not universal, how-

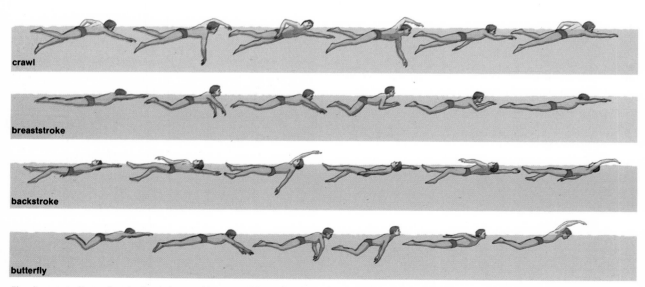

crawl

breaststroke

backstroke

butterfly

The diagram indicates four basic strokes used in competitive swimming. The crawl, combining arm-over-arm strokes with a flutter kick, is the fastest style in current use and is favored for freestyle events. To execute the breaststroke, the slowest technique, a swimmer's arms are extended forward and are swept down and back along the sides of the body. The frog kick, in which both legs are driven back simultaneously, is used. Although executed in the supine position, the backstroke is similar to the crawl in its use of a flutter kick and arm-over-arm strokes. It is the only style in which swimmers begin in the water. For the butterfly, an adaptation of the breaststroke, arms are extended forward but are raised above the water at the beginning of each stroke. Arms are pulled straight down and under the body.

WORLD SWIMMING RECORDS

Event	Time	Holder	Date
Men's Events			
100-m freestyle	49.44 sec	Jonty Skinner (S.Afr.)	Aug. 14, 1976
200-m freestyle	1 min 49.16 sec	Ambrose Gaines IV (USA)	Apr. 11, 1980
400-m freestyle	3 min 51.20 sec	Vladimir Salnikov (USSR)	Feb. 24, 1980
800-m freestyle	7 min 56.49 sec	Vladimir Salnikov (USSR)	Mar. 23, 1979
1,500-m freestyle	14 min 58.27 sec	Vladimir Salnikov (USSR)	July 22, 1980
100-m backstroke	55.49 sec	John Naber (USA)	July 19, 1976
200-m backstroke	1 min 59.19 sec	John Naber (USA)	July 24, 1976
100-m breaststroke	1 min 02.86 sec	Gerald Moerken (W.Ger.)	Aug. 17, 1977
200-m breaststroke	2 min 15.11 sec	David Wilkie (G.B.)	July 24, 1976
100-m butterfly	54.15 sec	Par J. Arvidsson (Sweden)	Apr. 11, 1980
200-m butterfly	1 min 59.23 sec	Mike Bruner (USA)	July 18, 1976
200-m individual medley	2 min 03.29 sec	Jesse Vassallo (USA)	July 6, 1979
400-m individual medley	4 min 20.05 sec	Jesse Vassallo (USA)	Aug. 22, 1978
4 × 100-m medley relay	3 min 42.22 sec	USA National Team	July 22, 1976
4 × 100-m freestyle relay	3 min 19.74 sec	USA National Team	Aug. 22, 1978
4 × 200-m freestyle relay	7 min 20.82 sec	USA National Team	Aug. 24, 1978
Women's Events			
100-m freestyle	54.79 sec	Barbara Krause (E.Ger.)	July 21, 1980
200-m freestyle	1 min 58.23 sec	Cynthia Woodhead (USA)	Sept. 3, 1979
400-m freestyle	4 min 06.28 sec	Tracey Wickham (Aus.)	Aug. 24, 1978
800-m freestyle	8 min 24.62 sec	Tracey Wickham (Aus.)	Aug. 5, 1978
1,500-m freestyle	16 min 04.49 sec	Kim Linehan (USA)	Aug. 19, 1979
100-m backstroke	1 min 00.86 sec	Rica Reinisch (E.Ger.)	July 23, 1980
200-m backstroke	2 min 11.77 sec	Rica Reinisch (E.Ger.)	July 27, 1980
100-m breaststroke	1 min 10.11 sec	Ute Geweniger (E.Ger.)	July 24, 1980
200-m breaststroke	2 min 28.36 sec	Lina Kachushite (USSR)	Apr. 6, 1979
100-m butterfly	59.26 sec	Mary T. Meagher (USA)	Apr. 11, 1980
200-m butterfly	2 min 07.01 sec	Mary T. Meagher (USA)	Aug. 16, 1979
200-m individual medley	2 min 13.69 sec	Tracy Caulkins (USA)	Jan. 5, 1980
400-m individual medley	4 min 36.29 sec	Petra Schneider (E.Ger.)	July 26, 1980
4 × 100-m medley relay	4 min 06.67 sec	E.Ger. National Team	July 20, 1980
4 × 100-m freestyle relay	3 min 42.71 sec	E.Ger. National Team	July 27, 1980

Arms outstretched gracefully in midair, the American Greg Louganis executes a difficult dive. Louganis won a silver medal in the platform-diving competition in the 1976 Olympic Games, finishing second to the Italian Klaus Dibiasi, who won the event for the third consecutive time.

(Below) Jesse Vassallo, representing Puerto Rico, set a world record for the 200-m individual medley at the Pan-American Games. Individual medleys require four swimming strokes rather than one: in sequence, butterfly, backstroke, breaststroke, and freestyle. In medley relays, each of four swimmers swims one of these strokes; the order, however, is different.

ever, and Louis XI of France reportedly swam daily in the Seine River.

During the early 19th century, swimming enjoyed a revival, especially in England; Lord Byron swam the Hellespont (now the Dardanelles) to prove that the mythological hero Leander could have done it. Organized competitive swimming began in England in the 1840s. In 1844 the British were surprised when two American Indians demonstrated the efficiency of a method of swimming similar to the modern crawl. The British still swam with the head above the water, a holdover from the days when people believed that the water was contaminated. An overhand stroke was introduced to England in 1873 by J. Arthur Trudgen, who had seen South American Indians using this method to swim quite fast. When the flutter kick was introduced, the modern "Australian crawl" was born, and this stroke has since become the most common and most important swimming stroke.

MAJOR STROKES

A variety of strokes are used in swimming, each requiring different motions. Each stroke also varies in the physical demand it places on the swimmer and the degree of speed and efficiency it offers.

Crawl. The crawl is not an official FINA-recognized stroke; in events where the contestants are allowed to swim "freestyle," the crawl is universally used. The stroke, which is performed chest-down in the water, involves carrying one arm forward out of the water to nearly full extension, while the other arm is below the surface making a pulling movement that propels the body through the water. The flutter kick is used to add some forward thrust, but it serves mainly as a stabilizing motion. Breathing is accomplished by turning the head to one side or the other and inhaling, then turning the head so that the face is immersed and exhaling the spent air. The breathing is repeated at regular intervals in accord with the pace of the stroke.

Backstroke. The backstroke is similar to the crawl but is performed on the back and without the crawl's breathing requirement. One arm is carried over the head out of the water to prepare for the next stroke, while the arm in the water completes the forward-pulling motion. The flutter kick is used, as in the crawl.

Breaststroke. In this stroke, leg and arm movements are simultaneous. The hands are carried together forward from under the chest to full extension. They are then swept back, in a lateral plane, parallel to the body, whereupon the movement is repeated. A frog kick is used: the legs are drawn up, with knees bent and each leg turned outward; the legs are then thrust back parallel to the line of the body. Both arms and legs must not move out of the lateral plane. In competition, swimmers may be disqualified for letting their strokes enter the vertical plane.

Butterfly. This stroke is similar to, and is derived from, the breaststroke. Arm and leg movements are simultaneous, although the most noticeable difference is that the arm recovery after the completion of each stroke is accomplished over, rather than under, the water. This arm movement, reminiscent of a butterfly's flight, gave the stroke its name. The legs are used in a dolphinlike kick in which they remain close together and are alternately bent and straightened out at the knee in a vertical plane. The butterfly stroke is the most physically demanding of all the major strokes.

COMPETITIVE SWIMMING

In competitive swimming events the winners are determined according to the best elapsed times for a particular distance. There are four basic categories of standard Olympic events. The first is freestyle—100-m (109.3-yd), 200-m (218.6-yd), and 400-m (437.2-yd) for both men and women; 800-m (874.4-yd) for women; 1,500-m (1,639.5-yd) for men; and 4 × 100-m and (for men) 4 × 200-m relay races. The second is backstroke—100-m and 200-m. The third is breaststroke—100-m and 200-m. The fourth is butterfly—100-m and 200-m. These basic categories are also combined into medley (races in which each of the four basic strokes is used by the swimmer or team in a certain sequence): 200-m and 400-m individual races and 4 × 100-m relay races. BUCK DAWSON

Bibliography: Armbruster, David A., et al., *Swimming and Diving*, 6th ed. (1973); Batterman, Charles, *The Technique of Springboard Diving* (1977); Besford, Pat, comp., *Encyclopedia of Swimming*, 2d ed. (1977); Horn, Bob, *Swimming Techniques in Pictures* (1974); Lee, Sammy, and Lehrmann, Steve, *Diving* (1978); Moscovitz, Toni, *Physiology of Diving* (1978); Spitz, Mark, and LeMond, Alan, *The Mark Spitz Complete Book of Swimming* (1976).

Swinburne, Algernon Charles   [swin'-burn]

Algernon Charles Swinburne, a major poet and literary critic of the Victorian period, appears in this portrait by R. M. B. Paxton. Poems and Ballads, First Series (1866), one of Swinburne's most controversial works, earned him praise for literary craftsmanship and condemnation for sensual license.

Algernon Charles Swinburne, b. London, Apr. 5, 1837, d. Apr. 10, 1909, was in his young manhood a shocking, and in his old age an esteemed, British Victorian poet and man of letters. He was the son of a naval officer and the grandson of an earl. At Oxford University he met Dante Gabriel ROSSETTI and other members of the Pre-Raphaelite brotherhood, and he helped found a club known for its radical politics and religious skepticism. Leaving Oxford in 1860 without taking a degree, he embarked on a literary career in London, supported by an allowance from his father.

An early verse drama, *Atalanta in Calydon* (1865), was favorably reviewed for its lyric passages and highly decorated narrative. The following year Swinburne published *Poems and*

Ballads, First Series, which included poems spoken by sadly desperate characters who did not believe in the supernatural and were imprisoned in the limited, sometimes perverse pleasures of the physical world. Withdrawn by its original publisher, the volume provoked a controversy in which the author vigorously participated.

In *Songs Before Sunrise* (1871), Swinburne advanced his theme to imagine a secular redemption in which humanity will provide a meaning for existence by fully realizing its own powers. During these years, however, Swinburne's own life grew dangerously disordered. Diminutive and excitable, he often became ill from his indulgences in the pleasures and quarrels of London literary life. In 1879, Swinburne was rescued by a friend, Theodore Watts Dunton, and settled into a carefully managed household and career. He published 20 more volumes of poetry, criticism, and verse drama. Some of his literary criticism, especially that on Shakespeare and on the poetry of William Blake, is still interesting and useful. His late poetry is often subdued in theme and tone, but sometimes in poems about the sea, spring, and storms he recovered his excitement in the enlivening power of the natural world.

Swinburne's craftsmanship is often overelaborate in the long lines, frequent alliteration, and ornate images of his verse, but the richness of his poetic language is often the necessary means by which he expressed the disillusion and joy he found in human existence. DONALD GRAY

Bibliography: Henderson, Philip, *Swinburne: The Portrait of a Poet* (1974); Hyder, C. K., *Swinburne's Literary Career and Fame* (1933) and, as ed., *Swinburne: The Critical Heritage* (1970); McGann, Jerome J., *Swinburne: An Experiment in Criticism* (1972); Peters, Robert L., *The Crowns of Apollo: Swinburne's Principles of Literature and Art* (1965).

swine: see PIG.

swine flu

A type of INFLUENZA that afflicts humans, swine flu is so named because of its similarity and possible relationship to a virus that causes an influenzalike disease in swine. Swine flu virus is a member of the A-group of flu viruses, which tend to undergo frequent mutations into forms to which people lack immunity. Mutant type A viruses are responsible for the widespread epidemics of influenza that sweep the world every few years, for example, the Asian flu epidemic of 1957 and the Hong Kong flu epidemic of 1968. It is thought that the great flu epidemic of 1918, which killed 20 million people over the world and an estimated 675,000 in the United States, was caused by a type A virus, possibly the swine flu virus, for a large proportion of people over the age of 50 in today's population have antibodies to that virus.

In early 1976 four U.S. Army recruits at Fort Dix, N.J., came down with influenza, and one of them died. Several health authorities were alarmed, because the virus isolated from the soldiers was a swine flu virus believed to be similar to the one that had caused the 1918 epidemic. A similarly devastating epidemic was feared, because it seemed likely, 58 years after the 1918 outbreak, that millions of people would lack immunity to the virus. On Apr. 16, 1976, President Gerald R. Ford signed a bill appropriating $135 million to produce enough vaccine to immunize every American. Although 50 million Americans did receive the vaccine, the program was abandoned by the end of the year, partly because of infrequent but severe reactions to the vaccine, but primarily because the feared epidemic did not materialize.

PETER L. PETRAKIS

Bibliography: Osborn, June E., ed., *Influenza in America, 1918-1976* (1977).

swing

Swing, a form of dance music played by a large band, was the medium through which most white Americans first heard JAZZ. Although the decade 1935–45 was called the Swing Era, swing arrangements had been played by large bands beginning in the 1920s. Bandleader-arrangers Fletcher Henderson, Duke ELLINGTON, and, later, Count BASIE, worked out arrangements for their 10- to 12-piece bands, which—unlike traditional jazz bands—were divided into instrumental sections. The rhythm section (piano, guitar, bass, and drums) maintained a steady, even beat; the saxophone and brass sections countered each other with harmonized riffs and repeated figures, with section leaders improvising over this background.

In 1935, Benny GOODMAN's band, using Henderson's arrangements, became the first to achieve mass popularity. Goodman ("The King of Swing") was also the first to integrate his band racially. Whereas the most popular swing bands (those of Tommy and Jimmy DORSEY, Glenn MILLER, Artie Shaw, and Charlie Barnet) were white, some black swing bands also came into prominence—especially Ellington's, Basie's, and those of Earl HINES and Jimmie Lunceford.

Swing's popularity had faded by 1945, brought down in part by a financial conflict between ASCAP (the American Society of Composers, Authors, and Publishers) and the radio networks, and in part by a decline in the popularity of ballroom dancing. Some bands still maintain the style, primarily for older audiences.   JONATHAN KAMIN

Bibliography: McCarthy, Albert, *Dance Band Era: The Dancing Decades from Ragtime to Swing* (1971) and *Big Band Jazz* (1977); Murray, Albert, *Stomping the Blues* (1976); Simon, George T., *The Big Bands*, rev., enl. ed. (1975); Stewart, Rex, *Jazz Masters of the '30s* (1972).

Swiss chard: see BEET.

Swiss Family Robinson, The

An adventure novel by J. D. Wyss completed by his son Johann Rudolf WYSS, *The Swiss Family Robinson* (2 vols., 1812–13) has been enjoyed by children around the world without attracting serious critical attention. One of many works inspired by ROBINSON CRUSOE, it is an account of the adventures of a Swiss couple and their four sons who are shipwrecked on a South Sea island. The novel is narrated by the father and has strong didactic overtones, particularly in its religious comments; modern versions are usually abridged, however, and in this form emphasize the adventure and suspense elements.   R. M. FORD

switch, electric

Mechanical and electronic switches are devices used to interrupt or reestablish the flow of electricity in a circuit. When the switch performs automatically under prescribed conditions, it is called a CIRCUIT BREAKER. A mechanical switch operates by joining and separating electrical contacts at some point in the circuit. A drawback of such a switch is that when it is opened, it induces a spark (arcing), which creates high temperatures that can damage the switch. There are various methods for preventing arcing or, at least, extinguishing the arc rapidly after it occurs.

A mechanical switch may be too slow for some applications, notably in computers. Faster switching is obtained with an electronic switch. The early ones were based on electron tubes, such as the THYRATRON; more recently, semiconducting switching devices have gained widespread use. Not only are electronic switches faster, they also are free of arcing and mechanical wear.

Swithin, Saint   [swith'-uhn]

Saint Swithin, d. July 2, 862, was bishop of Winchester and counselor of the Wessex kings Egbert and Æthelwulf. According to a popular English legend, rain that begins on Saint Swithin's day, July 15, will continue for 40 days. Reports of miracles at his original grave led to the transfer of his remains to Winchester Cathedral in 971; his cult was very popular in medieval England.

Switzer, Kathy   [swit'-sur]

Kathrine (Kathy) Switzer, b. Amberg, Germany, Jan. 5, 1947, is a pioneer among women marathon runners. In 1967 she became the second woman to run in the Boston Marathon. Her start was unofficial; women were not permitted in that race

until 1972. Switzer has since entered other marathons, her best time being 2 hrs 51 min.   HOWARD LISS

Switzerland

Switzerland is a largely mountainous, landlocked country in west central Europe, bordered on the west by France, on the north by West Germany, on the east by Austria and Liechtenstein, and on the south by Italy. Its history, culture, economy, and unique character have in large part been determined by the Alpine ranges that cover three-fifths of its total area.

Isolated—and protected—by its relative inaccessibility, Switzerland was able to develop without major hindrance, after its founding in 1291, from a tiny confederation of 3 cantons to a nation of 23 member states. It has maintained its independence and present boundaries intact since 1815. Yet once its Alpine passes were opened by modern engineering, Switzerland's position along the principal communication routes between northern and Mediterranean Europe proved an asset to its economic and technological development. Its majestic Alpine scenery and carefully tended cultural landscape, by attracting recreational travel, helped to lay the foundations for a tourist industry whose revenues today are second only to those from manufacturing.

In spite of its small size, meager supply of primary resources, and considerable ethnic diversity, Switzerland is, politically and socially, one of the most stable nations in the world. Its stability can be attributed to its high standard of living, epitomized by a per capita income of about $9,000; to the conservative character of its people and institutions; and

SWITZERLAND

Official Name: Swiss Confederation
Capital: Bern (1977 est. pop., 146,800)
Largest City: Zurich (1977 est. pop., 983,000)
Area: 41,288 km² (15,914 mi²)
Elevation: *Highest*—Dufourspitze (part of Monte Rosa), 4,634 m (15,203 ft); *lowest*—192 m (630 ft), along the shore of Lake Maggiore
Population: 6,298,000 (1979 est.). *Distribution*—55% urban, 45% rural; *density,* 153 persons per km² (396 per mi²); *annual rate of increase* (1970–77), 0.1%
Principal Languages: German, French, Italian, Romansch
Principal Religions: Protestantism, Roman Catholicism
Principal Products: *Agriculture*—dairy products; cattle, pigs, sheep, poultry; wheat, barley, rye; potatoes, sugar beets; apples, pears, cherries, plums, nuts; wine; tobacco. *Manufacturing and industry*—processed foods; textiles, apparel; chemicals, pharmaceuticals; metals; electrical machinery, watches and clocks, optical equipment. *Mining*—salt; iron ore, manganese, asbestos
Railroads: 5,098 km/3,168 mi (1976)
Roads: 62,145 km/38,615 mi (1975 paved)
Currency: 1 Swiss franc = 100 centimes

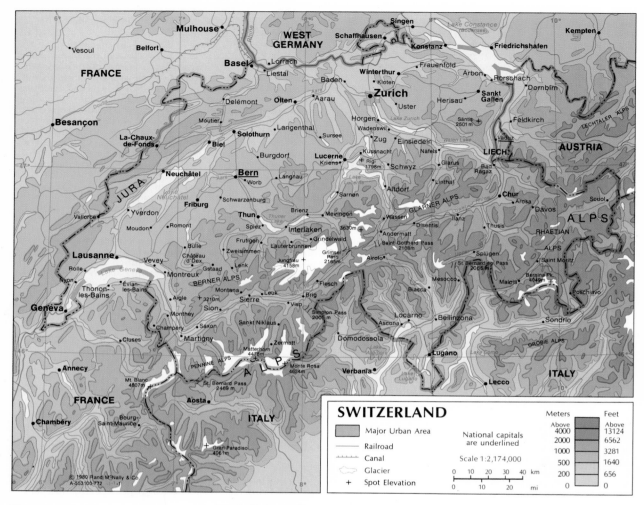

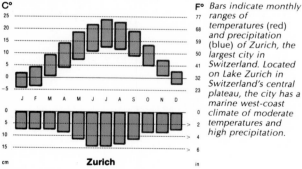

Bars indicate monthly ranges of temperatures (red) and precipitation (blue) of Zurich, the largest city in Switzerland. Located on Lake Zurich in Switzerland's central plateau, the city has a marine west-coast climate of moderate temperatures and high precipitation.

Zurich

to Switzerland's noninvolvement in Europe's two major 20th-century wars.

Although neutrality is a fundamental tenet of Swiss national policy, and Switzerland remains outside the United Nations, the country's participation in world affairs is shown by its membership in the Council of Europe, the European Economic Community (EEC), and many specialized agencies of the United Nations. The home of the League of Nations after World War I, Switzerland is now the permanent base of the UN's Economic and Social Council, the International Labor Organization, and the World Health Organization and, since 1863, the headquarters of the International Red Cross.

LAND AND RESOURCES

The three clearly defined natural regions of Switzerland are the ALPS, the midland, and the JURA. The Alpine chains, consisting of central, crystalline massifs and sedimentary formations in their northern and southern ranges, stretch from the French border south of Lake Geneva (see GENEVA, LAKE) diagonally across the southern half of Switzerland, reaching their highest elevations in the glaciated peaks north and south of the troughs of the upper Rhône and Rhine valleys. The Dufourspitze (4,634 m/15,203 ft) on Monte ROSA is the highest point in Switzerland; next in elevation are the Dom (4,545 m/14,911 ft), the Weisshorn (4,505 m/14,780 ft), and the MATTERHORN (4,478 m/14,692 ft). In this area lie the world-renowned resorts of the Bernese Oberland, Zermatt, and SAINT MORITZ in the INN RIVER valley. Less than 10% of the Swiss population lives in the Alpine region.

The hills, plateaus, and valleys of the midland are underlain by sandstone, shales, and conglomerates that were deposited by Alpine streams into an inland sea that filled the depression between the Alps and Jura during a period from 65 to 2 million years ago. The sand and gravel left by the glaciers form the surface layers of the midland between Lake Geneva and Lake Constance (see CONSTANCE, LAKE). They are cut by the rivers AARE, Thur, Töss, Limmat, Reuss, and Saane, all tributary to the RHINE RIVER, which forms most of the northern boundary of Switzerland. The great majority of the Swiss population and most of the major cities are located on the midland rivers and the Rhine.

The mountains of the Jura represent the northernmost fold-belt of the Alps. The highest ranges rise more than 1,000 m (3,300 ft), immediately north of the lake chain of the Aare River valley. Along the French-Swiss border, and especially in the Jura south of Basel, the mountains take on a plateaulike character. As a whole, the Jura region is sparsely populated. NEUCHÂTEL is the principal city.

The strongly differentiated relief of Switzerland is reflected in the soil pattern. Most midland soils are classified as gray brown podzolics, excellent for the development of forest cover. Less acid are the brown forest soils of the Jura. The soil cover of the Alpine slopes is shallow.

Climate. Three factors determine Switzerland's climate: its mid-latitude location, its intermediate position between oceanic and continental air mass regimes, and its altitudinal spread of more than 4,000 m (13,125 ft). The wettest parts of Switzerland are the Jura ranges, the central Alps north of the Rhône-Rhine depression, and the Alps of Valais. In the midland, rainfall averages 1,000 mm (40 in) per year, and in winter fog often enshrouds the area. Higher, drier, and colder regions enjoy more sun in winter. Above 3,050 m (10,000 ft) the precipitation falls as snow. In Zurich the average temperature ranges from 0.6° C (33° F) in January to 18° C (64° F) in July.

Flora and Fauna. Forests still occupy about 25% of the countryside. Beech and oak predominate in the deciduous forest of the midland and at lower elevations in Alpine valleys. At higher altitudes spruce and fir take over on moist sites, pine and larch in the drier southern and eastern Alpine interior. Floral elements of Mediterranean origin, among them the chestnut, occupy the southern slopes of the Alps, and they have also established themselves in the Rhône Valley. Palm trees grow along the shores of Lake LUGANO in the Ticino. Above the timberline wild flowers abound in an extensive zone of Alpine meadows.

Wildlife in Switzerland is a remnant of an originally rich Alpine fauna. Because of the creation of a game preserve in the Lower Engadine, several rare Alpine species survive, among them the ibex, chamois, marmot, and eagle. A substantial number of wild animals still roam the midland and Jura forests, especially deer, fox, and rabbit, and, occasionally, the wild boar; the brown bear, emblem of the Bernese canton, however, is now extinct.

Resources. Switzerland is for all practical purposes devoid of economically exploitable mineral resources and must rely on imported industrial raw materials and mineral fuels. Water power has been the crucial factor in industrialization and still accounts for almost 80% of total electrical energy output, which reached 43 billion kW h in 1978.

PEOPLE

Neolithic lake dwellers were the earliest inhabitants of Switzerland. The ethnic roots of the Swiss people as such can be traced back to settlements of CELTS in the northern midland and to an early intra-Alpine population of Illyrian (Dinaric) origin in the upper Rhine and Inn valleys. As the result of invasions and tribal migrations these groups were later joined by Mediterranean and Germanic peoples.

Language and Religion. In spite of the conventional differentiation into a German, French, and Italian Switzerland, it is mostly language, not ethnic consciousness, that distinguishes different segments of the Swiss population. Today the majority (65%) speak a German dialect known as Schwyzertütsch, while about 18% speak French, 12% speak Italian, and 1% (only in Graubünden canton) speak Rhaeto-Romanic (Romansch), a descendant of Latin. With the exception of a tiny Jewish community, the population is almost evenly divided between Roman Catholics (49.4%) and Protestants (47.8%).

Demography. The country's population is 6,298,000 (1979 est.). The natural growth rate, now 0.1% per annum, has steadily declined since the 1960s, when it averaged 1.1%. The large number of foreigners living in Switzerland (966,000 in 1978) strongly affects demographic statistics. Cities with 10,000 or more inhabitants now incorporate 75% of the population. The largest cities are ZURICH, BASEL, GENEVA, BERN, and LAUSANNE, which together account for a third of the Swiss population.

Education and Health. As required by the constitution, education is free, and compulsory for nine years (in most cantons), but 80% of Swiss children receive at least three additional years of formal education. Two federal institutes of technology (in Zurich and Lausanne) and seven cantonal universities accommodate the 10% of the population that goes on to a postsecondary education.

Swiss health standards are among the highest in the world. One physician is available for every 559 people; in 1976 infant mortality was 10.7 per 1,000 live births, and maternal mortality was a low 4 deaths per 100,000 women. Swiss men can expect to live to at least 70 years of age and women to 76, a life-expectancy rate that is exceeded in Europe only in Scandinavia and the Netherlands.

The Arts. Folk art reveals itself in many phases of Swiss life, from the characteristic Swiss CHALET to elaborate wood carvings and pottery motifs, religious and secular pageants, and

The dramatic peak of the Matterhorn, located on Switzerland's southern border, rises to a height of approximately 4,480 m (14,700 ft) above the village of Zermatt. First scaled in 1865, the mountain has since brought many climbers and tourists to the small alpine resort.

Geneva's lake fountain is a dramatic feature of the city's waterfront on Lake Geneva. The headquarters for many international organizations, Geneva symbolizes the independence and neutrality of the Swiss nation. It has long been favored by tourists for its great beauty.

(Below) *Cattle graze on a slope in the Swiss Alps during the summer pasturing season. During the rest of the year the cows are kept at lower elevations. Cattle farming and dairying account for about one-half of Switzerland's agricultural income.*

(Above) *Zurich, capital of a Swiss canton and the nation's largest city, occupies both banks of the Limmat River as it flows out from Lake Zurich. One of the most famous historical landmarks in the city's older district is the twin-domed Grossmünster (left), where the Swiss Reformation leader Ulrich Zwingli preached (1519–31).*

traditional folk music based on the simple melodies of the YODEL and the ALPHORN. Major contributions to international culture have been made by a variety of Swiss individuals: John CALVIN and Ulrich ZWINGLI, two of the greatest leaders of the Protestant Reformation; Jean Jacques ROUSSEAU, the 18th-century political and educational theorist; Johann Heinrich PESTALOZZI, the educational reformer; Carl Gustav JUNG and Jean PIAGET, giants in the development of modern psychological theory; writers such as Gottfried KELLER and Jeremias GOTTHELF in the 19th century and the novelist Hermann HESSE and the playwright Friedrich DÜRRENMATT in the 20th century; and artists and architects such as Henry FUSELI, Alberto GIACOMETTI, Paul KLEE, and LE CORBUSIER.

ECONOMIC ACTIVITY

Switzerland is a prime example of a nation overcoming a scarcity of natural resources by basing its economic development on inventiveness, frugality, and perseverance. More than one-fourth of the country's territory is nonproductive; fully one-half is either forested or nonarable grassland, and, except for potential water power, no energy or mineral resources are available for profitable exploitation. Still, Switzerland is one of the most highly industrialized countries in the world. Since the 19th century, industrial engineering has made a substantial contribution to Swiss modernization.

Even in the preindustrial era, the products of Swiss labor were known throughout Europe. Printing and graphics, smithing, machine tooling, watchmaking and clockmaking, carpentry, and masonry were all practiced in medieval Swiss cities. With the conversion of water power into electric energy in the mid-19th century, the mass production of textiles began, based on the simultaneous development of plants producing machine tools, machinery, and chemical dyes. Some of the best-known products of the Swiss food industry, such as Swiss and Gruyère cheese, condensed milk, cocoa, and chocolate, were developed during a century-long effort to process milk into a nonperishable commodity.

The work force is about equally divided between industry and services, with less than 10% required by agriculture and mining combined. Foreign workers, principally from Italy, constitute about 20% of the work force. Unemployment in 1978 was a low 0.3%.

Most of the major industrial complexes are located in the midland, where Zurich, Oerlikon, Baden, Winterthur, and Schaffhausen form centers of machine technology, metal fabrication, and the manufacture of electrical equipment and precision instruments. Manufacturing of textiles and clothing is carried on in 1,500 factories, many of them in smaller locales. The chemical dye and pharmaceutical industries are concentrated in Basel. The watch industry has its larger plants in Geneva and the Jura.

Agriculture and Forestry. Swiss agriculture is characterized by a highly intensive production on mostly small, owner-operated farms. About half the country's terrain is farmland, and of this area approximately half is given over to natural pasture used for livestock raising. Two-thirds of the farm population raise cattle, and the value of dairy and beef production (milk, cheese, butter, and meat) amounts to more than half of the agricultural output. More than half the crop farms specialize in bread and feed grains. Where climate permits, agricultural activities include wine production, irrigated fruit and vegetable farming, and apple, pear, and cherry growing. The forest industry's production satisfies about 70% of the domestic demand.

Transportation. Switzerland's highly efficient transportation network is epitomized by the almost completely electrified, government-owned Swiss Federal Railways. Of the four major rail lines connecting central Europe with Italy, two cross the Swiss Alps. Train travel through the Alps was made possible only by the extraordinary engineering feats represented by the building (1872–1911) of the Saint Gotthard, Arlberg, Simplon, and Lötschberg tunnels. An extensive road system is presently being expanded by the construction of an expressway network that includes several road tunnels through the Alps; the first of these, the Great Saint Bernard, connecting Switzerland and Italy, was completed in 1964; the Saint Gotthard Tunnel was scheduled to open in 1980. Swiss engineering prowess is also shown by the innumerable cog railways, cable cars, and chair lifts that transport people to well-known resort towns and to the summits of some of the highest Alpine peaks, such as the JUNGFRAU near Interlaken. The Rhine River, navigable to Basel by barge traffic and the Swiss merchant fleet, provides Switzerland's only direct access to the sea. Lake steamers also constitute an efficient as well as scenic method of transportation.

Trade. Switzerland's foreign trade relies heavily on the interchange of goods with its neighbors in the EEC. Chief among its trading partners are West Germany, France, Italy, the United Kingdom, and the United States. Its leading exports are capital equipment, watches, and optical instruments, products that account for almost 50% of the value of its exports. The chemical industry (compounds, dyes, and pharmaceuticals) accounts for about 20%. Imports are evenly distributed among agricultural products, industrial raw materials, machinery, and fuels. A usually negative trade balance is at least partially compensated for by the net income produced by tourism (which in 1977 amounted to 6 billion francs from nearly 33 million travelers, 20 million of whom came from abroad), the insurance industry, and international financial transactions of which Zurich is a world center. Switzerland's currency remains one of the world's soundest; its inflation rate, less than 2% (1978), is one of the world's lowest. In 1978, with a gross national product of $88.3 billion ($14,091 per capita), Switzerland had exports worth $23.4 billion and imports worth $23.7 billion.

GOVERNMENT AND POLITICS

Switzerland is a federated republic consisting of 23 cantons, the last of which, Jura, was established in 1979. The federal government is divided into three branches: the Federal Council (executive); the Federal Assembly, or Parliament (legislative); and the Federal Tribunal (judicial), which sits in Lausanne. The Federal Council has 7 members, elected for 4-year terms, presiding over 7 government departments; it includes an annually elected president, who serves both as head of government and as chief of state. The president in 1979 was Hans Hürlimann. The Parliament has two chambers—the Council of States, whose 44 members serve for 3 to 4 years, and the National Council, whose 200 members are elected every 4 years. Government is usually by a coalition of four political parties—the Social Democratic, the Radical Democratic, and Christian Democratic, and the Swiss People's parties—which hold approximately 80% of the seats in both houses of Parliament. As the oldest continuous democracy in Europe, Switzerland has traditionally emphasized such legislative mechanisms as the REFERENDUM AND INITIATIVE. Universal suffrage, enjoyed by all citizens over 20, was realized in 1971, when the federal legislature finally granted Swiss women the right to vote.

HISTORY

Switzerland's strategic location astride vital Alpine passes made the area a target of many conquerors. After being successively invaded by Julius Caesar's Roman legions in 58 BC, then by the Germanic Alemanni, Burgundians, Ostrogoths, and Franks, the region came under the rule of the HOLY ROMAN EMPIRE in the 10th and 11th centuries. Forced labor service and feudal payments angered the peasants and workers, however, and in 1291 the cantons of Uri, Schwyz, and Unterwalden declared their independence of the HABSBURGS. They entered into a mutual defense alliance that was, a few years later, joined by Luzern (Lucerne), Zurich, and Bern. The Austrians, followed by the Burgundians (see BURGUNDY), made a number of unsuccessful attempts to check the momentum of the independence movement over the next 200 years; by the early 16th century, however, Switzerland had not only maintained its independence but was an expanding military power, now 13 cantons strong and vying with the French for control over northern Italy. The Swiss policy of neutrality was embraced after the confederation's defeat by the French at Marignano in 1515.

The REFORMATION and COUNTER-REFORMATION posed a serious threat to the political stability of Switzerland in the 16th century as the country lapsed into civil war. Switzerland was left divided by religion as well as by language. An outside threat during the THIRTY YEARS' WAR, however, served to unite the Swiss people in defense of their interests and led to formal recognition (1648) of the confederation's independence by the Holy Roman Empire. After a century and a half of relative peace, French Revolutionary armies entered (1798) the country from the west and established Switzerland as the HELVETIC REPUBLIC. At the Congress of Vienna (1815), following Napoleon's defeat, Swiss control was restored and the confederation's neutrality guaranteed by the powers of Europe.

The 1848 constitution established the 22 (later 23) cantons of modern Switzerland, individual civil liberties, a bicameral legislature, and a representative form of democracy. In 1874 the federal government's powers were further expanded. During the same period, the country's economic base shifted with the advent of mass production: factories were built and urbanization began.

World War I caused political turmoil between the French and German factions of the population, but Swiss neutrality met the test, and in 1920 the League of Nations made its home in Geneva. During World War II, fearing attack by Germany, Switzerland mobilized an army of nearly 500,000 to protect its frontiers. Its policy of armed neutrality is today backed up by a national militia force of 625,000; Switzerland has universal conscription for all men between the ages of 20 and 50 years. Since 1945, Switzerland has devoted its energies

to maintaining this neutrality, to improving education and welfare programs, and to developing its economy into one of the richest in the world.   DIETER BRUNNSCHWEILER

Bibliography: Bonjour, Edgar, et al., *Short History of Switzerland,* 2d ed. (1955); Codding, George A., *The Federal Government of Switzerland* (1961); Gilliard, Charles, *A History of Switzerland,* trans. by D. L. B. Hartley (1955; repr. 1978); Gretler, Armin, and Mandl, P. E., *Values, Trends and Alternatives in Swiss Society* (1973); Ikle, Max, *Switzerland: An International Banking and Finance Center* (1972); Kohn, Hans, *Nationalism and Liberty: The Swiss Example* (1956); Martin, William, *Switzerland from Roman Times to the Present,* 6th ed. (1971); Sorell, Walter, *The Swiss: A Cultural Panorama of Switzerland* (1972); Wilson, Hugh R., *Switzerland: Neutrality as Foreign Policy* (1974); Young, Allen, *Swiss Neutrality in the Cold War* (1962).

sword and knife

A sword is a hand weapon having a long blade, sharp on one or both edges, which is held by a grip (hilt). The evolution of the sword coincided with that of the knife, which is a short cutting instrument consisting of one or more blades and mounted on a handle.

SWORD

A sword is longer than a dagger, but no fixed rule exists regarding length; for example, the Roman legionnaire's short sword was only 50 cm (20 in) long. Swords can be divided into two basic types according to use: cutting swords, which are heavy and broad and have one or two cutting edges; and thrusting swords, which are slim and pointed and often do not have a cutting edge. These two categories are not restrictive, and many types of swords can accomplish both cutting and thrusting actions. The Neolithic flint dagger probably served as the model for the first swords, which were edged with copper and too soft to be satisfactory. The first reliable swords were two types made during the Bronze Age, about 2000 BC. One was a cutting sword with a leaf-shaped blade, and the other was a longer, narrow-bladed rapier, or thrusting sword. The Assyrians are credited with introducing swords as weapons in warfare. The 6th-century Vikings revolutionized swords and sword making with their discovery of carbonized iron. These double-edged swords were greatly valued and were often presented as gifts of esteem. Probably by chance the Vikings found that if heated iron was folded, beaten, cut, and folded together again, and if the process was repeated, then eventually they could make tough, hard swords that would hold a superior cutting edge. This same manufacturing process also evolved in the Orient, notably Japan, at a much later date. The Arabs also produced the fine Damascus blade, produced by high-temperature forging.

By the 10th century the sword had been lengthened and the tip rounded, thereby becoming a slashing weapon. A cross bar (quillon) was adopted to protect the hands, and most swords were counterbalanced with a round pommel at the hilt's end. The introduction of plate armor in the 14th century brought back tapered thrusting swords, or rapiers, and spurred the development of massive, two-handed cutting swords, or broad swords. In the 16th century the knuckle brow, a metal strap from the pommel to the quillon, was introduced to protect the user's hand; more complicated, basketlike guards were developed by the end of the century. By the 17th century FENCING and dueling came into vogue and required light, easily handled swords known as épées.

Curved swords (scimitars), which were preferred to straight swords in Asia and Eastern Europe, were brought to western Europe by the Turkish invasion in the 16th century. This form was universally adopted as the cavalry saber, an ideal slashing weapon; the saber shape has been dominant since the 18th century. A variation of the saber, the naval cutlass, is a short curved sword with a heavy hand guard and is well suited for the close quarters of boarding operations.

The use of firearms gradually reduced the role of the sword in warfare. Today the sword exists only for fencing and ceremony. Swords of past ages are displayed in museums.

KNIFE

The knife started as a hand tool made of stone, primarily flint, and later became among the first metal implements. During

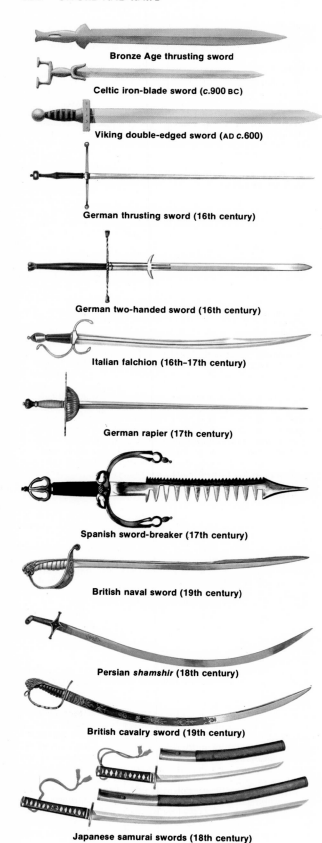

Bronze Age thrusting sword

Celtic iron-blade sword (c.900 BC)

Viking double-edged sword (AD c.600)

German thrusting sword (16th century)

German two-handed sword (16th century)

Italian falchion (16th–17th century)

German rapier (17th century)

Spanish sword-breaker (17th century)

British naval sword (19th century)

Persian *shamshir* (18th century)

British cavalry sword (19th century)

Japanese samurai swords (18th century)

The earliest swords were made by pouring molten bronze into a stone mold. By the 10th century BC, iron swords began to replace their bronze counterparts in Europe. Later refinements included heat tempering and the introduction of the crossbar. Narrow thrusting swords and two-handed broadswords were popular in medieval Europe. The Persian shamshir and other curved swords of Eastern design influenced the development of the Western cavalry saber.

the period 1500–1100 BC bronze knives served as patterns for swords that appeared in both Crete and Britain.

The next important step in the evolution of the knife took place during the first millennium BC, when iron was brought to Europe from Asia. The area of the present-day Austrian province of Styria became the source of the best European iron ore and thus the center for blade production. The cities of Innsbruck and Passau produced exceptional blades through the Middle Ages. Iron knives, heated and beaten to shape, produced a better edge than bronze knives, which were formed by pouring molten metal into stone molds. Iron blades, however, suffered from one weakness: they bent easily. This deficiency was remedied when the Vikings revolutionized the iron industry with the introduction of carbonized iron. Knives were not considered a primary military weapon and retained their domestic role as utilitarian tools through the Middle Ages. Nevertheless, because of the practice of forcing unequipped peasants to serve as troops, common knives were accepted as a standard arm for foot troops.

A knife variation, the dagger, is a pointed stabbing weapon that was popular with both civilians and the military in Europe between the 14th and 16th centuries. The dagger was used when the sword was either lost or broken, in secrecy, or as a coup de grace weapon. German, Italian, and Swiss artisans produced daggers of superb beauty during this period. One form, the 14th-century baselard, was probably made originally in Basel, Switzerland; it was reproduced during World War II for ceremonial use in Nazi Germany.

An excellent example of the close relationship between knives and swords is found in the ancestry of the contemporary kukri, a short, heavy, curved knife found among the Gurkha tribesmen of Nepal. The kukri is a modern adaptation of the 5th-century BC Greek *kopis,* a slashing sword that is about three times larger than the kukri but similar in shape.

The Arab jambiya, recognized by its curved, double-edged blade, is the most widely used knife in the world, spanning the globe from the African Atlantic coast to the Indonesian islands. The machete of Latin America has a large, curved blade used to cut sugarcane and as a weapon.

A military application of the knife is the BAYONET. Introduced by the British and French in 1660, the first bayonets were long, pointed knives that could be plugged into the bore of the standard infantry musket. In this manner, the infantry could convert their rifle into a form of pike, which could be used both offensively and defensively. By the end of the 18th century the socket bayonet replaced the plug version; in modified form these remain in service today. A socket bayonet fits around the muzzle of the gun and does not block the barrel, allowing the soldier to fire with the bayonet mounted. Modern bayonets, which are usually knife-like in appearance, are much shorter than their European precursors.

Probably the most famous American knife is the Bowie knife, named for its alleged inventor, Colonel James BOWIE. The Bowie knife is a steel, single-edged knife that measures 38 cm (15 in) in length. Although designed for hunting, it is generally associated with violent fights that frequently took place in American frontier regions.

One particularly devastating family of knives was that of the trench knives, spawned during the brutal hand-to-hand trench fighting of World War I. Trench knives ranged from simple hunting knives to specially manufactured fighting knives. The best example of the latter combined a hand guard in the form of brass knuckles, a short pike built into the base of the handle, and a double-edged steel blade.

A form of dagger, the British commando knife, was used during World War II. It is a steel stiletto (thrusting dagger) equipped with a round, bone-cracking peen on the butt end

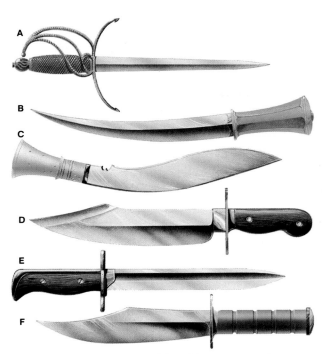

The dagger (A), a sharp knife used for stabbing, was a popular weapon of medieval Europe. The kukri (C) used by the Gurkhas of Nepal is a scaled-down version of a 5th-century Greek sword with a broad, curved blade. The jambiya (B) is a widely used double-edge knife of Arab design. Col. James Bowie is credited with the invention of the scimitarlike Bowie knife (D). The socket bayonet (E) is a knife that locks onto the muzzle of a rifle without blocking the barrel. The K-Bar (F) is a single-edge commando knife used by U.S. troops.

of the handle. The resurgence of the knife as a fighting weapon during World War II can be attributed to the creation of such units as the commandos, which relied on stealth rather than firepower to accomplish their missions. An American version of the commando knife is the World War II fighting knife, commonly called the K-Bar. Still in service, the K-Bar features an 18-cm-long (7-in) carbon, single-edge, cutlery steel blade. The survival knife, a shorter version of the K-Bar, was developed as an all-purpose knife for aviators. The Swiss army knife remains a popular pocket knife that is used for a variety of purposes; it contains can openers, several blades, screwdrivers, and such embellishments as scissors.

Cutlery, or the family of knives and cutting instruments for domestic purposes, covers a wide spectrum of edged tools ranging from butcher knives to sharpening steels. Modern cutlery manufacturing centers are Solingen, West Germany; Sheffield, England; Thiers, France; and the New England states. The invention of stainless steel in 1912 and its introduction into cutlery manufacture revolutionized the industry during the 1920s.   LANE ROGERS

Bibliography: Brodie, Bernard and Fawn, *From Cross-Bow to H-Bomb*, rev. ed. (1973); Dupuy, Robert and Trevor, *The Encyclopedia of Military History*, rev. ed. (1977); Montross, Lynn, *War Through the Ages*, rev. ed. (1960); Norman, Vesay, *Arms and Armor* (1964); Oakeshott, R. Ewart, *The Archaeology of Weapons* (1963); Peterson, Harold, *The American Sword, 1775-1945* (1977); Strung, Norman, *The Encyclopedia of Knives* (1976); Wilkinson-Latham, Robert, *Swords and Other Edged Weapons* (1978).

sword dance

Throughout history, wherever men depended on their weapons for their lives, the sword dance has ritualized combat, celebrated the sword as a defense against enemies and evil spirits, and honored man's physical strength, both military and sexual. Performing to fife and drum accompaniment, 6 to 50 men began the dance with a series of rotations, chains, arches, and jumps over and around swords laid on the ground. The center section included exercises of manual dexterity and skill with the swords to demonstrate preparation for battle, and agile feints and dodges among outstretched weapons to simulate the imminent hostilities and inflame the emotions. During the conclusion, the rose—from Middle High German *râz* (braid)—the dancers braided their swords into a tight mesh around which they executed their fiercest fighting tricks. A descendant of the Spartan Pyrrhic dance, the sword dance permeated European folklore from the 14th to 18th centuries and survives today in British morris dancing and the deft footwork of the Scottish sword dance. Military tattoos and trooping the colors are diminished modern expressions of aggressive tribal unity.   BARBARA NEWMAN

swordfish

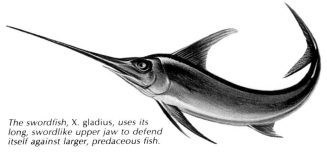

The swordfish, X. gladius, *uses its long, swordlike upper jaw to defend itself against larger, predaceous fish.*

The swordfish, or broadbill, *Xiphias gladius,* the sole member of the family Xiphiidae, is found worldwide in tropical and temperate marine waters. The swordlike bill is flattened in cross section. The average length of the swordfish is 1.8 to 3.3 m (6 to 11 ft), of which the bill may be one-third, and the average weight is 45 to 135 kg (100 to 300 lb). Swordfish often bask at the surface, where they become vulnerable to commercial harpooning. They are also caught in tuna traps. Swordfish feed at moderate to great depths, judging from their diet of fishes and squids. They can drive through the wood support of small boats because of their swimming speed—perhaps up to 100 km/h (60 mph).   CAMM SWIFT

swordtail

A male swordtail, X. helleri, *has an elongated tail fin ray, from which its name is derived. Originally a green fish from southern Mexico, it is a popular aquarium fish bred in a variety of colors.*

Swordtails are live-bearing fishes (family Poeciliidae) in the same genus (*Xiphophorus*) as the PLATYS. They live in the fresh waters of southern Mexico, British Honduras, and Guatemala. Swordtails are hardy and easily bred aquarium fishes, which also makes them ideal for genetic research. The "sword" is developed in males about one year after birth and sometimes in older females, but not all swordtails have well-developed swords. Swordtails reach 12.5 cm (5 in) in length. They are easily hybridized with platys in an aquarium, producing many color varieties; hybridization in the wild is rare. The most common pure swordtail in aquariums is the usually green swordtail, *X. helleri.*   E. O. WILEY

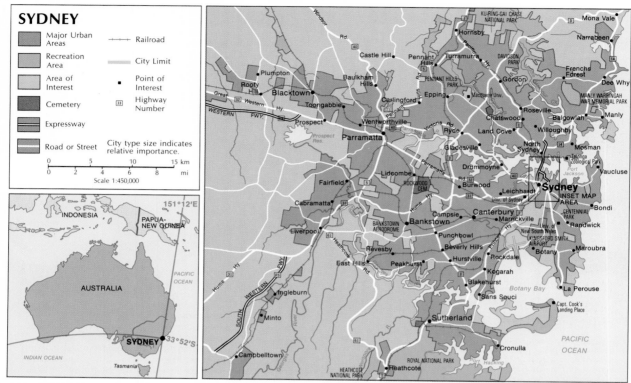

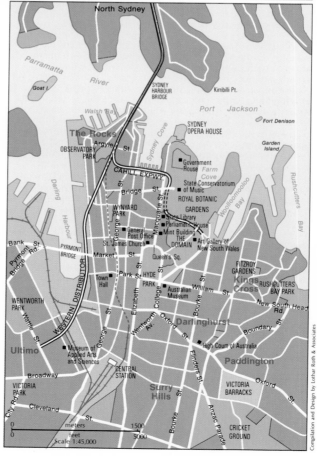

Sydenham, Charles Edward Poulett Thomson, Baron [sid'-en-uhm]

Charles Poulett Thomson, b. Surrey, England, Sept. 13, 1799, d. Sept. 19, 1841, was a British statesman and governor general of Canada. The son of a merchant, he worked in his father's firm before winning election to Parliament as a radical and free trader in 1826. Appointed vice-president of the Board of Trade by the prime minister Earl Grey in 1830, he secured reduction of many customs duties and became president of the board in 1834. In August 1839 he was appointed governor general of Canada, in which post he proved energetic and successful. He implemented the plan of his predecessor, Lord DURHAM, to unite Upper and Lower Canada and secured passage of the Canada Union Act in 1841. In 1840 he was created Baron Sydenham of Sydenham and Toronto.   PETER J. KING

Bibliography: Craig, G. M., *Upper Canada: The Formative Years* (1963); Shortt, Adam, *Lord Sydenham* (1908).

Sydenham, Thomas

The English physician Thomas Sydenham, b. Sept. 10, 1624, d. Dec. 29, 1689, was a founder of modern epidemiology. Stressing the importance of observation over theory, Sydenham recorded all available facts in attempts to explain the occurrence of epidemics. He also provided accurate descriptions of many diseases, including gout, chorea, measles, and scarlet fever.

Sydney (Australia) [sid'-nee]

Sydney, Australia's oldest community and the capital of New South Wales, is a port city on the southeast coast of the continent. Sydney proper has 52,187 people (1976); greater Sydney, built up around a natural harbor, Port Jackson, has a population of 3,021,982 and is Australia's most populous metropolitan center. One of the world's longest and highest single-span bridges, Sydney Harbour Bridge, dominates a spectacular harbor view. Arching 52 m (170 ft) above the water, it allows even the largest of the more than 3,000 oceangoing ships that arrive here annually to pass under it and into Syd-

The Sydney Opera House, designed by the Danish architect Joerm Utzon, is built on the tip of Bennelong Point, which juts into the city's outer harbor, Port Jackson. The narrow peninsula is also the site of the Royal Botanical Gardens, Parliament House, and Government House.

ney's many inner harbors. The Royal Australian Navy is headquartered in Sydney, as was the British Pacific Fleet during World War II. First settled as a penal colony in 1788, Sydney is now one of the Southwest Pacific's most cosmopolitan centers. The city has a temperate climate, with mean temperatures ranging from 22° C (72° F) in January to 12° C (54° F) in July. The average annual rainfall is 1,143 mm (45 in).

Contemporary City. Until the end of World War II, virtually all residents of Sydney were of British ancestry. In recent years, however, many continental European immigrants to Australia have settled in the area, creating a scattering of ethnic enclaves within the city and its suburbs. The rapid outgrowth of Sydney's suburbs suggests that a conurbation may develop, extending 320 km (200 mi) from New Castle in the north, through Sydney, to Wollongong in the south. Greater Sydney is administered by 40 separate local governments.

Although Sydney has automobile, textile, and chemical plants, and it is rapidly becoming the South Pacific's major petroleum-refining city, it remains more an enterpôt than an industrial center. The world's most active primary wool market is located there. In addition to wool and sheepskins, wheat and meat are exported in quantity. A third of Australia's imports come through Sydney, as do most of the country's many tourists.

The architecturally distinctive Sydney Opera House, opened in 1973, is the performing arts center of Sydney. Designed by the Danish architect Jøern Utzon, it sits on a promontory extending into the harbor and resembles a series of immense, wind-filled sails. Landmarks include Saint James Church and Hyde Park Barracks, early-19th-century buildings designed by the convict-architect Francis Greenway. The city is home to the Australian Museum, the Art Gallery of New South Wales, the State Conservatorium of Music, and the Museum of Applied Arts and Sciences. The University of Sydney, the University of New South Wales, and Macquarie University are in Sydney (see AUSTRALIAN UNIVERSITIES) as is the Mitchell Library, with its extensive collection of original source materials on the history of Australia.

History. Sydney Cove, founded as a penal settlement by Cap-

tain Arthur PHILLIP in 1788 and named for the British home secretary, Viscount Sydney, became the first seat of British authority on the continent. It was not until the 1830s, however, that the city began to thrive, after fewer convicts and greater numbers of free settlers entered the area. The Australian gold rushes of the 1850s accelerated the population surge. Although Sydney was bypassed by Melbourne early in the 20th century as Australia's largest city, it has, since World War II, regained its primacy.   CALVIN WILVERT

Bibliography: Kennedy, Brian, *Sydney* (1970); Murray, James, *Sydney: An Illustrated History* (1974); Park, Ruth, *The Companion Guide to Sydney* (1973).

Sydney   (Nova Scotia)

Sydney (1976 pop., 30,645) is a port city on Cape Breton Island in northeastern Nova Scotia. The city's economy is dominated by the steel industry, which utilizes locally mined coal and iron ore imported from Labrador. Limestone quarrying and fishing are also important. Founded in 1783, the city was the capital of Cape Breton Island until 1820, when the island became part of Nova Scotia.

syenite   [sy'-uh-nyt]

Syenite is a coarse-grained, intrusive IGNEOUS ROCK that is composed largely of sodium- or potassium-rich feldspar and of a ferromagnesian mineral. The feldspar commonly is orthoclase, albite, perthite, or, more rarely, microcline, and the dark-colored ferromagnesian mineral usually is biotite mica, hornblende, or a pyroxene; some examples of syenite also contain feldspathoid minerals.

Syenite is in many respects similar to GRANITE; a major difference is the relative lack (less than 5%) or absence of quartz in syenite. Granite is much more commonly found in the field than is syenite.

syllogism   [sil'-uh-jizm]

The theory of the syllogism, an argument in logic, was first set forth by Aristotle. It has been of basic significance in the development of Western thought. A syllogism consists of three statements; the third is the conclusion, the logical consequence of the two preceding premises. Aristotle's theory actually deals only with the categorical syllogism, in which propositions are in the form of categorical assertions: All *A* is *B*. No *A* is *B*. Some *A* is *B*. Some *A* is not *B*. A typical valid syllogism is:

All elephants are animals.
All animals are living beings.
Therefore, all elephants are living beings.

In Aristotelian logic, it was believed that all reasoning could be put in syllogistic form and then evaluated for its validity. By illustrating a syllogism as a VENN DIAGRAM, one can immediately see if it is valid. The universal statements "All dogs are animals" and "No fish are horses" are shown diagrammatically. It is seen that the domain of dogs is entirely included in that of animals, whereas the domains of fish and horses are mutually exclusive.

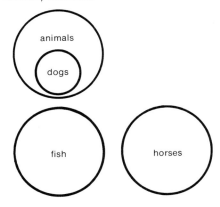

An entire alleged syllogism is:
All Amazons are women.
No men are Amazons.
Therefore no men are women.
This syllogism is seen to be invalid as soon as it is diagrammed. Solely from the information given, all that can be said is that men might or might not be women, or some men might be women.

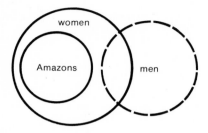

A truncated syllogism with a premise omitted is called an enthymene, to which the absent premise must be added. Also, the Stoics considered a hypothetical syllogism—"If A, then B; A, therefore B"—which has different properties from the categorical syllogism.

From Aristotle until the 19th century the syllogism was the main form of establishing logical validity. During the 20th century Aristotle's view has been shown to be inadequate to express valid arguments in modern mathematics and has been replaced by the propositional calculus.   RICHARD H. POPKIN

Bibliography: Lukasiewicz, Jan, *Aristotle's Syllogistic from the Standpoint of Modern Formal Logic*, 2d ed. (1957); Pospesal, Howard, *Introduction to Logic: Predicate Logic* (1976); Purtill, Richard L., *Introduction to Logic: Argument, Refutation and Proof* (1978).

sylph   [silf]

In the theories of the 16th-century alchemist PARACELSUS, a sylph is an elemental being without a soul that inhabits the air and influences humans' bilious temperament. Sylphs are traditionally associated with chastity.

sylvanite   [sil'-vuh-nyt]

Sylvanite [(Au,Ag) Te$_2$] is a rare gold and silver TELLURIDE MINERAL. It forms brilliantly metallic prismatic or tabular crystals (monoclinic system), as well as imperfectly columnar to granular, cleavable masses. Hardness is 1½ to 2, color and streak are steel gray to silver white, and specific gravity is 8.1. Sylvanite and the other tellurides (calaverite and krennerite) are mined from igneous rocks in the near-surface, low-temperature veins at Cripple Creek, Colo., and in the deeper-seated deposits at Kalgoorlie, Australia.

sylvite   [sil'-vyt]

The potassium chloride EVAPORITE mineral sylvite (KCl) is mined as a source of potassium. It forms gray, white, or tinted cubic crystals (isometric system) and cleavable granular masses. Hardness is 2, luster is vitreous, and specific gravity is 2.0. Sylvite occurs in basinlike bedded salt deposits.

Symbionese Liberation Army (SLA)   [sim-bee-uh-neez']

The Symbionese Liberation Army (SLA), a small San Francisco radical terrorist group, assassinated (Nov. 6, 1973) Oakland schools superintendent Dr. Marcus Foster and later kidnapped (Feb. 4, 1974) Patricia HEARST (see COUNTERCULTURE). SLA members were primarily white middle-class youths; their goals were obscure. Six members were killed in a shoot-out with the police (Los Angeles, May 17, 1974). Most of the remaining members were captured in the course of the long FBI search for Hearst.

Bibliography: Kinney, Jean Brown, *An American Journey: The Short Life of Willy Wolfe* (1979); Pearsall, Robert Brainard, ed., *The Symbionese Liberation Army: Documents and Communications* (1974).

symbiosis   [sim-bee-oh'-sis]

Symbiosis (*sym*, "together"; *bios*, "life") refers to various kinds of close and permanent associations between members of different species. Mutualism is the relationship wherein both members benefit and cannot exist without each other; for instance, lichen is a mutual partnership between a fungus and an alga. When one partner is benefited and the other is relatively unaffected, the relationship is called commensalism, for instance, the epiphytic orchids that grow on tree branches in the tropics. The term *parasitism* refers to a relationship in which one organism benefits and the other is harmed, for instance, tapeworms infesting the gut of humans and animals.

MARTIN DWORKIN

Bibliography: Cheng, Thomas, *Symbiosis: Organisms Living Together* (1970); Henry, S. Mark, ed., *Symbiosis: Its Physiological and Biochemical Significance*, 2 vols. (1966); Jennings, D. H., and Lee, D. L., eds., *Symbiosis* (1975).

symbolic logic: see LOGIC.

symbolism   (art)

The term *symbolism* has both a general and a specific meaning in art history. In its broadest sense the term means the use in a work of art of a sign or object to stand for something other than itself. A symbol's effectiveness depends on the presumption that its meaning can be understood by its audience. In art the terms ICONOGRAPHY and ICONOLOGY are frequently used to refer to the study of the meaning and interpretation of symbols and allegories.

In its specific use, the term *symbolism* refers to an artistic attitude that became dominant in both the visual arts and in literature during the latter decades of the 19th century. Inspired by the spirit of early-19th-century romanticism, the symbolist movement originated in France during the 1880s and rapidly became international in scope. The symbolists, like their romantic predecessors, sought images that probed the emotional and irrational aspects of human existence in opposition to the prevailing neoclassical, academic, and realist modes of representation.

In France, Pierre PUVIS DE CHAVANNES, Odilon REDON, and Gustave MOREAU initiated the symbolist movement in painting. Their ideas formed the basis for the achievements of the

Paul Gauguin created Vision after the Sermon, *or* Jacob Wrestling with the Angel *(1888; detail), after a visit to Brittany. Gauguin organized (1889) the first symbolist exhibition, entitled "The Impressionist and Synthetist Group." (National Gallery of Scotland, Edinburgh.)*

(Above) *Fernand Khnopff's symbolist painting* The Sphinx *(1896) displays the exoticism and decadence seen in some aspects of the Art Nouveau movement. (Museum voor Schone Kunsten, Brussels.)*

(Left) *Odilon Redon's* Cyclops *(c.1898), a macabre yet poetic visual allusion to Polyphemus, the mythological giant of Homer's* Odyssey, *is executed in the brilliant color characteristic of his later work. Literature and myth provided the subjects for much of Redon's work. (Rijksmuseum Kröller Müller, Otterloo, Netherlands.)*

postimpressionists Paul Cézanne, Paul Gauguin, Georges Seurat, and Vincent van Gogh (see postimpressionism). By the turn of the century, symbolism had become an international phenomenon in the work of such artists as James Ensor (Belgium), Edvard Munch (Norway), Ferdinand Hodler (Switzerland), Gustav Klimt (Austria), Aubrey Beardsley (Great Britain), and Jan Toorop (the Netherlands). The symbolists used arcane subjects, exaggerated shapes, and vivid colors to produce emotive imagery. Their ideas became fundamental to much of 20th-century art, particularly influencing Pablo Picasso, Henri Matisse and the Fauves, and Wassily Kandinsky and the German expressionists. Other modernist movements incorporating symbolist attitudes include the Nabis, Art Nouveau, and later, Surrealism.   Alvin R. Martin

Bibliography: Hamilton, George Heard, *Painting and Sculpture in Europe, 1880–1940,* 2d ed. (1972); Lövgren, Sven, *The Genesis of Modernism,* rev. ed. (1972); Lucie-Smith, Edward, *Symbolist Art* (1972); Pierre, Jose, *Symbolism* (1979).

symbolism   (literature)

The symbolist movement in literature was at first primarily a French development continuing those changes effected in French poetry by romantic writers and the Parnassians. It drew inspiration from England, Germany, and the United States (above all from Wagner and Poe), and its most important French precursor was Baudelaire. The major French writers most often identified as symbolists are Stéphane Mallarmé, Arthur Rimbaud, and Paul Verlaine in the 19th century and in the 20th, Paul Claudel and Paul Valéry. Other impor-

tant French writers associated with symbolism are Tristan Corbière, Jules Laforgue, le comte de Lautréamont, and Guillaume Apollinaire. The name *symbolist* was established for the movement by the manifesto of Jean Moréas in the Paris newspaper *Le Figaro* of Sept. 18, 1886.

In poetry, the symbolists opposed didacticism, eloquence, political reference, sentimentality, and objective description. Their poems present subtle personal moods or hallucinative play of the senses, or they evoke sensuous revery or ideas through complex and at times hermetic imagery. Many of the symbolist ideals can be found in Baudelaire's critical writings and in his sonnet "Correspondances" (1857), in Verlaine's somewhat ironic poem "Art poétique" (1874), in Rimbaud's "Lettre du Voyant" (1871), and in the correspondence and *Divagations* (1897) of Mallarmé. Baudelaire sees language and writing as "magical operations, evocative sorcery," stresses their "hieroglyphic" quality, and states that even ordinary sights can be symbols revealing "the profundity of life." Verlaine calls for nuance rather than color and above all else for music. Rimbaud refers to "the alchemy of the verb" and urges poets to make themselves seers, and Mallarmé insists that the writer should merely suggest, not name, an object—to include on paper not the "intrinsic wood" of the trees in a forest, but only its "horror" or "the silent thunder" adrift in its leaves.

French symbolist writings and ideas soon reached the British Isles, the rest of Western Europe, Russia, and the Americas, influencing numerous 20th-century poets such as William Butler Yeats, Rainer Maria Rilke, T. S. Eliot, and Wallace Stevens.   Alfred Engstrom

Bibliography: Balakian, Anna, *The Symbolist Movement; a Critical Appraisal* (1967); Bowra, C. M., *The Heritage of Symbolism* (1943); Chadwick, Charles, *Symbolism* (1971); Chiari, Joseph, *Symbolism from Poe to Mallarmé; the Growth of a Myth* (1956); Cornell, Kenneth, *The Symbolist Movement* (1951); Lehmann, A. G., *The Symbolist Aesthetic in France, 1885–1895,* 2d ed. (1968); Temple, Ruth, *The Critic's Alchemy; a Study of the Introduction of French Symbolism into England* (1953); Wilson, Edmund, *Axel's Castle; a Study in the Imaginative Literature of 1870–1930* (1931; repr. 1961).

symmetry   (math)

In mathematics, *symmetry* denotes a balance of the parts of a figure relative to a central point, line, or plane. For example, two points P and Q are symmetric with a third point M if M is the midpoint of line segment PQ. A figure is symmetric if, for each point P of the figure, there is a corresponding symmetric point Q of the figure. Axial symmetry is a case in which a figure can be divided by a line into mirror-image halves. Another common case is radial symmetry, in which a figure can be made to coincide with itself if it is rotated about a point. Central symmetry is a special case of radial symmetry corresponding to a rotation of 180°.

Symmetry has many technical applications. In stereochemistry, a compound does not show optical activity if its molecule is symmetrical with respect to a plane. On the other hand, molecules may exist in two forms that differ only by mirror-image symmetry. Many complicated mathematical problems can be simplified by applying symmetry principles; for example, analysis of the game of ticktacktoe is reduced by showing through symmetry that many of the possible games are equivalent to others.

Bibliography: Coxeter, H. S., *Introduction to Geometry*, 2d ed. (1969); Gardner, Martin, *The Ambidextrous Universe: Mirror Asymmetry and Time-Reversed Worlds*, rev. ed. (1979); Weyl, Hermann, *Symmetry* (1952); Yale, Paul B., *Geometry and Symmetry* (1968).

symmetry   (physics)

A physical system is said to exhibit a symmetry if it remains unchanged under a given operation. For example, a ball looks the same under rotation in any direction about its center; the ball is said to have a spherical symmetry. Symmetries play a fundamental role in the understanding of various physical phenomena. They are an especially important part in the study of elementary-particle physics (see ANTIMATTER), where the exact nature of the force laws is still unknown. The significance of symmetry is that many important aspects of the behavior of a system may be predicted on the basis of its symmetry without a detailed knowledge of its inner workings.

All symmetries may be classified into two types, discrete and continuous. For a discrete symmetry, there are only a finite number of operations that can lead to identical physical configurations: for example, a square drawn on a paper has a discrete symmetry because there are only four ways it can be rotated about an axis perpendicular to the plane of the paper to look unchanged. On the other hand, a circle drawn on a piece of paper looks unchanged after rotation through any angle about an axis perpendicular to the paper. Thus the circle exhibits a continuous rotational symmetry. Some other examples of continuous symmetries are space-time translations and rotations. The former refers to all points in space and time being equivalent as far as physical laws are concerned, and the latter refers to the equivalence of all directions in space (isotropy of space). Two important examples of discrete symmetry are space reflection and TIME-REVERSAL INVARIANCE. Many physical laws are unchanged under mirror reflection (see PARITY) and under the reversal of the direction of time.

Symmetries and Conservation Laws. A conservation law states that some physical parameters of a system remain unchanged during the time evolution of the system (see CONSERVATION, LAWS OF). For example, in classical (nonrelativistic) physics, the total mass of a system is fixed before and after, for example, a collision process (the conservation law for mass). Similarly, the total linear and angular momentum and the total energy of a system obey conservation laws in both relativistic and nonrelativistic physics. Since the advent of the Lagrangian formulation of physics, it has been established that existence of conservation laws is related to the existence of underlying symmetries. For example, the conservation of linear momentum is a direct consequence of invariance of the Lagrangian under space translation, or homogeneity of space. Similarly, conservation of energy follows from invariance under time translation. The conservation of angular momentum is a result of rotational invariance. Symmetry under space reflection leads to parity invariance.

In order to discover the nature of the conservation laws operating in a system, the nature of the forces in the system and the associated symmetries must be studied. Because all forces derive their origins from the potential energy, it is enough to study the potential energy to discover conservation laws. For example, the Earth and the Sun attract each other through a force that depends only on the distance between the two and not on their orientation (a central force). The force law is rotationally invariant and thus leads to conservation of angular momentum. Because the direction of angular momentum is perpendicular to the plane of rotation, the Earth and Sun are locked in the same plane forever. Thus any two bodies interacting through a central force will have this property.

Selection Rules. Symmetries allow only certain final states once the initial state is given, implying, in turn, that appearance of many final states is forbidden, or at least highly improbable. The rules governing such transitions are called selection rules and are important in the study of atomic systems, where knowledge of allowed initial and final states determine, for example, the intensity and energy of the emitted light of lasers.

Internal Symmetries. The symmetries discussed so far involve space or time, or both. Certain symmetries, though, are known to exist where the symmetry operation changes one type of particle into another. For example, it is known that in the nucleus the same force exists between a proton-proton, proton-neutron, and neutron-neutron pair, meaning that there is a substitution symmetry between the proton and the neutron. In an imaginary "space," where the proton and the neutron form two hypothetical directions, any rotation in that space will leave the nuclear forces unchanged. This feature is called isospin symmetry. The inclusion of additional particles in such a space leads to the higher unitary symmetries. Other examples of internal symmetry are electric charge, baryon number, and so on, which also owe their origin to operations in a fictitious internal space.

Finally, the internal symmetries may operate the same way or be different at each space-time point. The latter case is called gauge symmetries. Their study seems to have led physicists closer to a complete understanding of the nature of underlying forces in the physical world.   R. N. MOHAPATRA

Bibliography: Boardman, Allan D., et al., *Symmetry and Its Applications in Science* (1973); Emmerson, J. M., *Symmetry Principles in Particle Physics* (1972); Rosen, Joe, *Symmetry Discovered* (1975); Weyl, Hermann, *Symmetry* (1952).

Symonds, John Addington   [sim'-unz]

The English writer and critic John Addington Symonds, b. Oct. 5, 1840, d. Apr. 19, 1893, is best known for the multivolume cultural history *The Renaissance in Italy* (1875–86). He also published biographies of Percy Bysshe Shelley (1878), Philip Sidney (1886), Ben Jonson (1886), Michelangelo (1893), and Walt Whitman (1893); he translated Benvenuto Cellini's autobiography (1888) and the sonnets of Michelangelo and Tommaso Campanella (1878). Two other books by Symonds, *A Problem in Greek Ethics* (1871) and *A Problem in Modern Ethics* (1881), address the question of homosexuality.

Bibliography: Brooks, Van Wyck, *John Addington Symonds* (1914; repr. 1971); Brown, Horatio F., *John Addington Symonds*, 2 vols. (1895); Grosskurth, Phyllis, *The Woeful Victorian* (1964).

Symons, Arthur   [sim'-unz]

The English poet and critic Arthur William Symons, b. Feb. 28, 1865, d. Jan. 22, 1945, is best known for his critical work *The Symbolist Movement in Literature* (1899), which helped popularize in England the work of the French symbolist poets. Influential in late-19th-century literary circles, Symons edited the Savoy magazine from 1896. His own volumes of poetry include *Silhouettes* (1892) and *London Nights* (1895).

ROBIN BUSS

Bibliography: Lhombreaud, Roger, *Arthur Symons: A Critical Biography* (1963); Munron, John H., *Arthur Symons* (1969).

Symons, Julian

The English writer Julian Symons, b. May 30, 1912, is noted for his highly literate crime novels, among them *The Progress of a Crime* (1960), *The Man Whose Dreams Came True* (1968), and *The Players and the Game* (1972). His novels are unusual for the seriousness of their subject matter and their sharply satiric edge. He has three times won the Edgar Allen Poe Award for mystery writing. Also a distinguished biographer and critic, Symons is the author of a history of the crime novel, *Mortal Consequences* (1972).

symphonic poem

Symphonic poem is a term invented by Franz Liszt to describe the series of orchestral works he wrote between 1850 and 1860, all of which derive their musical form and rhetoric from nonabstract ideas, some poetic and some visual. That Liszt did not insist on a strictly literary source for each work is important, because composers who followed his lead enjoyed greater variety of form and title (tone poem, fantasia, study, sketches) while nevertheless cleaving to his model of thematic transformation and development. Topics stemming from nationalistic sources proved especially popular, as in Smetana's six symphonic poems, *My Country*; Dvořák's *The Noonday Witch*; Borodin's *In the Steppes of Central Asia*; the works in a descriptive vein by Sibelius, *Kalevala Legends*, *Pohjola's Daughter*, *Tapiola*, and others; Respighi's *Pines of Rome* and *Fountains of Rome*; Elgar's *Falstaff*; and Vaughan Williams's *Symphonic Impression—In the Fen Country*. There was no lack of composers, however, capable of finding inspiration in poetry, as Liszt had done in his *Tasso* (after Byron's *Lament of Tasso*). Tchaikovsky supplied an evocation of such Shakespearean subjects as *Hamlet* and *Romeo and Juliet* in his works thus named, while his *Francesca da Rimini*, though basically inspired by the story of Paolo and Francesca in Dante's *Inferno*, relied also on Gustave Doré's engravings on the same topic. Richard Strauss looked to Lenau for the story and atmosphere of his *Don Juan*, to Nietzsche for the philosophical background of *Also sprach Zarathustra*, and to Cervantes for his *Don Quixote*. Delius, in his *Paris*, was among many who found it possible to combine personal impressions of places with the style of the symphonic poem in its broadest sense.   DENIS STEVENS

symphony

As developed since the latter half of the 18th century, the symphony is an orchestral composition of substantial length normally in four but often in five movements or self-contained parts (exceptions include works in only one and as many as six) and in the shape of a SONATA for orchestra.

ORIGINS
The term *symphony* is derived from the Latin *symphonia* (in turn based on a Greek word), meaning literally "a sounding-together." In the late 16th and early 17th centuries it was used to mean an instrumental section—often the beginning or ending—of an otherwise vocal piece. This aspect of the term lingered on until the end of the 18th century. By the middle of the 17th century the word *sinfonia* began to mean the purely instrumental beginning of an aria or a large vocal work, such as an opera or oratorio; intervening instrumental pieces in an opera were also termed "symphonies."

By the first half of the 18th century, however, *sinfonia* was practically synonymous with the three-movement OVERTURE, the standard beginning of an Italian opera or oratorio. Although at first an integral part of a large vocal form, these *sinfonie* became so stereotyped in form and content that they were easily detached from the larger vocal work and were presented separately as concert pieces. In northern Italy this concert symphony was largely the creation of Giovanni Battista SAMMARTINI. The concert symphony in three movements (fast-slow-fast, the final section often being a minuet with trio) for a small orchestra (standard size: two oboes, two horns, and strings) was quickly exported to western Europe, particularly Austria and Germany. There by 1740 it was transformed into a four-movement concert piece with the addition of a minuet generally as the third movement. A group of Bohemian and German composers, foremost among them Johann STAMITZ, formed a famous orchestra at the court of Mannheim and produced innovative symphonic works (see MANNHEIM SCHOOL).

CLASSICAL SYMPHONY
Franz Josef HAYDN began to compose symphonies about 1757. In his long life he solidified and enriched the symphonic style, culminating in a set of 12 works composed for London in 1791-95 (called the "Salomon Symphonies," after the German impresario J. P. Salomon who, in 1790, persuaded Haydn to go to England). Haydn wrote 107 symphonies, which were widely performed and imitated during his lifetime.

Wolfgang Amadeus MOZART wrote nearly 50 symphonies but only six in the last ten years of his life. These six symphonies—no. 35 in D ("Haffner"), no. 36 in C ("Linz"), no. 38 in D ("Prague"), no. 39 in E-flat, no. 40 in G Minor, and no. 41

in C ("Jupiter")—are of complex architecture and rich orchestration (establishing the standard use of clarinets). The last four named remain unsurpassed for their marriage of formal perfection and expressive depth.

Ludwig van BEETHOVEN wrote only nine symphonies (1800-24), but in them he greatly increased the form's weight and size. With his Third Symphony ("Eroica," 1805), he created a gigantic and complicated structure exceeding even the most sophisticated works of Haydn and Mozart. The orchestra in the period 1780-1800 had an average maximum size of a pair each of flutes, oboes, clarinets, bassoons, horns, trumpets, and kettledrums; and the usual strings (two choirs of violins, and one choir each of violas, cellos, and double basses). Beethoven enlarged it, following the example of Haydn's late oratorios, using a piccolo, four horns, three trumpets, three trombones, and supplementary percussion. In Beethoven's Ninth Symphony (1824), vocal soloists and chorus were introduced in the final movement, and the overall form was enlarged, becoming twice the length of Haydn's or Mozart's longest symphonies.

ROMANTIC SYMPHONY
Beethoven's explosively powerful symphonies exercised a permanent influence throughout the 19th century. Franz SCHUBERT wrote eight symphonies (1819-28) of which the so-called "Unfinished" (B Minor, 1822), with its darkly romantic style, was not discovered until 1865, long after its author's death. Although influenced by Beethoven, Schubert's technique, even in the "Great" C Major Symphony (1828; never performed in Schubert's lifetime), was in many respects much more fragmented. Hector BERLIOZ also showed that a symphony could be written in an entirely different way from Beethoven's. His *Symphonie fantastique* (1830), with its introduction of the *idée fixe* (motto theme) and its nightmarish atmosphere, was a great innovation, but it created no school.

Felix MENDELSSOHN followed classical tradition in most of his symphonies, but in the *Lobgesang Symphony* (1840) he was influenced by Beethoven's Ninth. One of the most original of the romantic school was Robert Schumann, whose four beautiful symphonies (1841-51) present problems in orchestration. Franz LISZT wrote many symphonic poems—an offshoot of the symphony proper—but his *Faust Symphony* (final version 1857) contains many formal innovations. The most popular symphonies of the late romantic period are those of Johannes BRAHMS, whose four symphonies (1876-85) are the most severely classical of their period, and Peter Ilich TCHAIKOVSKY, whose six symphonies (1868-93) culminate in three final works of brilliant orchestration. Anton BRUCKNER's huge, powerful symphonies (1863-96) are considered by many the culmination of the romantic orchestral style. As Europe became more intensely national, the symphony tended to be associated with the new nationalist schools. One might single out César FRANCK, whose single Symphony in D Minor (1886-88) was germinal to France's musical development, and the Czech Antonín DVOŘÁK, who introduced many local stylistic elements into his nine symphonies (1865-93). The Austrian Gustav MAHLER wrote ten symphonies (1888-1911; Tenth unfinished) whose tortured, involved style may be considered the final summing-up of the trend since Beethoven.

TWENTIETH-CENTURY SYMPHONY
In the 20th century the symphony has continued to dominate the musical thought of many composers—foremost among them the Finn Jean SIBELIUS, the Dane Carl NIELSEN, the Russians Igor STRAVINSKY, Sergei PROKOFIEV, and Dimitry SHOSTAKOVICH, the Swiss Arthur HONEGGER, the Englishmen Sir Edward ELGAR and Ralph VAUGHAN WILLIAMS, and many others. In the last 50 years composers have tried to create new ways of expressing symphonic thought, often avoiding the old classical forms of sonata and RONDO and preferring the variation form or FUGUE. The symphonic form is by no means exhausted or even moribund.   H. C. ROBBINS LANDON

Bibliography: Cuyler, Louise, *The Symphony* (1973); Downes, Edward, *The New York Philharmonic Guide to the Symphony* (1976); Nadeau, Roland, *The Symphony*, rev. ed. (1974); Simpson, Robert, ed., *The Symphony*, 2 vols. (1967); Stedman, Preston, *The Symphony* (1979); Tovey, D. F., *Essays in Musical Analysis: Symphonies* (1935; repr. 1972).

synagogue

The synagogue (from the Greek word for "assembly"), a building where Jews gather for worship and religious instruction, is the focus of Jewish life in every community. Ancient temples, including the Temple in Jerusalem, were regarded as dwelling places of the deity; in them sacrificial rites were performed by a special caste of priests. The synagogue, in contrast, is a gathering place for the people. Its services consist of prayer, song, and instruction: the custom of regular preaching originated in the synagogue. The Christian churches and the mosques of Islam were modeled on the synagogue. In this democratic institution, anyone with the requisite scriptural knowledge may lead the prayers and preach.

Despite much theorizing, when and how the synagogue emerged is not known. Synagogue buildings existed in Egypt and Palestine in the last three centuries BC. Long before the destruction of the Temple (AD 70), the synagogues of Palestine and the Diaspora were the functioning centers of Judaism and were used by the PHARISEES and their successors, the RABBIS, to create a unified and informed Jewish community.

Today synagogues usually include classrooms, recreational facilities, and offices. The hall of worship has seating for the congregation, a pulpit called *bimah* (from the Greek) or *al-memar* (from the Arabic) with a desk for the reading of the Torah scrolls, and an ark in which the scrolls are kept. Since the Middle Ages the services have been conducted by the rabbi or by a trained CANTOR (*chazzan*), or both.

BERNARD J. BAMBERGER

Bibliography: DeBreffny, Brian, *The Synagogue* (1978); Eisenberg, Azriel, *The Synagogue Through the Ages* (1973); Gutmann, Joseph, *The Synagogue: Studies in Origins, Archeology, and Architecture* (1974).

synapse: SEE NERVOUS SYSTEM.

synchromism

The first American movement of nonfigurative painting, synchromism was initiated in Paris in 1912 by two young American painters, Morgan Russell (1886–1953) and Stanton MACDONALD-WRIGHT, who were greatly influenced by the theory and practice of Paul Cézanne and Henri Matisse. As a unified movement, it lasted a short time and had disappeared completely by 1920. The term itself, meaning "with color," was invented by Russell to differentiate this style from that of the French orphists (see ORPHISM), which, though superficially similar, developed independently. The basic premise of synchromism was the primacy of color as the modulator of form; its adherents also explored the emotional correlatives of chromatic changes, as in Macdonald-Wright's *Synchromy in Green and Orange* (1916; Walker Art Center, Minneapolis, Minn.).

MAGDALENA DABROWSKI

Bibliography: Agee, William C., *Synchromism and Color Principles in American Painting, 1910-1930* (1965); Levin, Gail, *Synchromism and American Color Abstraction, 1910–25* (1978).

Synchronous Meteorological Satellite

The National Aeronautics and Space Administration's two Synchronous Meteorological Satellites were developed to explore the use of meteorological satellites in synchronous orbits. Each satellite was a 243-kg (535-lb) aluminum cylinder with a diameter of 190.5 cm (74.8 in) and a height of 345 cm (135.85 in). A spin-scan radiometer provided images in both the visible (0.9 km/0.5 mi resolution) and infrared (9 km /5 mi resolution) region for both day and night coverage.

A three-stage Delta launch vehicle with nine strap-on motors launched *SMS 1* from Cape Kennedy on May 17, 1974, carrying the satellite to a point 36,357 km (22,591 mi) over the equator at 45° west longitude. The satellite was later relocated over 75° west longitude. With the orbiting of *SMS 2* on Feb. 6, 1975, to a position on the equator at 135° west longitude, the two satellites could provide continuous 24-hr observations of the Western Hemisphere and transmit cloud-cover images once every 30 min.

MITCHELL R. SHARPE

synchronous satellite: SEE SATELLITE, ARTIFICIAL.

synchrotron

The synchrotron is a charged-particle ACCELERATOR that can be used for acceleration of electrons or other ions to high energies. Since its invention in 1945, the synchrotron has been developed to the point that it can provide 500 GeV (1 GeV, or gigaelectron volt = 1,000 mega or million electron volts, or 1,000 MeV)—the highest energy yet achieved in any particle accelerator. In the synchrotron the accelerating particles are retained in a circular orbit by an increasing magnetic field. Acceleration is by radiofrequency electric fields, whose frequency must increase to keep in step with the accelerating particles.

The largest synchrotron in the United States, at the Fermi National Accelerator Laboratory, Batavia, Ill., is 2 km (1.25 mi) in diameter. A similar one is in Geneva, Switzerland. Such accelerators contain thousands of electromagnets, require hundreds of people for operation and maintenance, and cost hundreds of millions of dollars.

JOHN P. BLEWETT

syncline and anticline

Synclines and anticlines are geologic FOLD structures of sedimentary strata. A downfold (concave), in which the youngest rocks occupy the trough of the structure, is termed a *syncline*. An upfold (convex), in which the youngest rocks occupy the crest, is termed an *anticline*. Through the latter stages of erosion, anticlines form a parallel range of mountains, and synclines comprise the intervening valleys. The word *plunging* is used before either of these two terms to describe structures in which the fold descends at an angle into the crust. Erosion of plunging folds leads to a zigzag pattern of ridges and valleys.

STEPHEN E. POSTEN

Bibliography: Aubouin, Jean, *Geosynclines* (1965); Ramsay, John G., *Folding and Fracturing of Rocks* (1967).

See also: GEOSYNCLINE.

SYNCOM [sin'-kahm]

SYNCOM (from *synchronous communications* satellite) was a series of three satellites that demonstrated the feasibility of communications by a satellite in a synchronous orbit (which would make it appear to be stationary over one point on Earth). It was a joint developmental project of NASA and the U.S. Department of Defense.

SYNCOM 1 was launched from Cape Canaveral by a Thor Agena rocket on Feb. 14, 1963. Even though it achieved the desired synchronous orbit, communications were lost, and it never became functional. The satellite was built by the Hughes Aircraft Company and was an aluminum and magnesium cylinder 71 cm (28 in) in diameter and 39 cm (15.5 in) high. It weighed 39 kg (86 lb). The exterior surface was covered with 3,860 solar cells, which charged nickel-cadmium batteries inside the satellite to provide about 25 W of power. Primary instrumentation consisted of two redundant transponders that could relay either one two-way telephone channel or 16 teletype channels.

SYNCOM 2, launched on July 26, 1963, went into the desired orbit at a position over the east coast of Brazil. Many voice and teletype messages were sent between it and the tracking ship U.S.S. *Kingsport.* Additionally, even though the satellite was not designed to do so, successful tests were made to see if it could relay television. Also, precise determinations of variations in its orbit permitted a much more accurate estimate of the true shape of Earth.

SYNCOM 3, launched on Aug. 19, 1964, took a permanent position over the equator between the United States and Japan. From there it transmitted pictures of the 1964 Olympics in Tokyo, sometimes using *Relay 2* to make them available in Europe.

MITCHELL R. SHARPE

Bibliography: Pierce, John R., *The Beginnings of Satellite Communications* (1968).

See also: SPACE EXPLORATION.

syncopation

Syncopation (from *syncope*, "the skipping of a heartbeat") is the temporary disruption or displacement of the normal pattern of accent in a musical composition. To be audible as such, syncopation must involve a departure from an established regular rhythm, which continues to shape the listener's expectations. The feeling of syncopation may be produced by accentuating what are ordinarily the weak beats of a measure, by deemphasizing the strong beats, or by these procedures in combination. While present in almost all music, syncopation is especially prevalent in the work of Western composers of the late 14th century and also in much African music and the jazz derived from it.   LAWRENCE FUCHSBERG

syncope: see FAINTING.

syndicalism

Syndicalism is a socialist political doctrine calling for control of the economy by organized labor and the abolition of the state. Louis Auguste BLANQUI, Pierre Joseph PROUDHON, and especially Georges SOREL were important influences on the syndicalist movement, which reached its peak in the early 20th century. Sorel asserted that violent revolution by trade unionists was the only means by which socialism could triumph. According to him, BOYCOTTS, GENERAL STRIKES, and SABOTAGE were the major weapons to be used to achieve the goal of a workers' commonwealth. Syndicalism declined as a political movement after World War I.   MARTIN TORODASH

Bibliography: Brissenden, Paul F., *The I.W.W.: A Study of American Syndicalism,* 2d ed. (1957); Horowitz, Irving L., *Radicalism and the Revolt against Reason: The Social Theories of Georges Sorel* (1961); Renshaw, Patrick, *The Wobblies* (1967); Ridley, F. F., *Revolutionary Syndicalism in France* (1971); Roberts, David D., *The Syndicalist Tradition and Italian Fascism* (1979); Sorel, Georges, *Reflections on Violence,* trans. by T. E. Hulme and J. Roth (1908; trans., 1914).

syndicate

A crime syndicate is an organization controlled by a small number of individuals that extends into businesses such as construction and trucking and criminal activities such as narcotics peddling, loansharking, and forced prostitution. The MAFIA, with members in many U.S. cities, is considered to be the most powerful U.S. crime syndicate.

synecdoche: see FIGURES OF SPEECH.

synergism   [sin'-ur-jizm]

Synergism, or synergistic effect, refers to the action of two different chemical substances acting together to create a greater effect than the sum of the actions produced by each acting independently. This effect is of importance in catalytic reactions, in the use of insecticides, in the application of certain drugs, and in extraction processes in industrial chemistry. It is believed that this effect occurs either because the two chemical substances react together in some manner or because intermediate products form that react with each other to create the increased effect.

In some reactions it has been found that if two catalysts are used together, the reaction is catalyzed to a greater extent than either catalyst alone could produce. Iron ions and copper ions in solution act as catalysts for the reaction between iodine and hydrogen peroxide. It is believed that each ion acts as a catalyst for one of the reactants. In other types of catalytic reactions the addition of a substance that is not usually a catalyst can increase the reaction rate. The combination of two pharmaceuticals that each produce a different effect will sometimes produce an unexpectedly strong physiological reaction that may be either beneficial or harmful.   WILLIAM H. NYCE

synesthesia   [sin-es-thee'-zhuh]

Synesthesia is experiencing with one sense a stimulus appropriate to another, as in "seeing" sound or "tasting" colors.

Synesthesia is generally associated with drug-induced "highs" but also occurs to some people naturally. True synesthesia is a strong and often disconcerting experience, as, for instance, when a color produced via synesthesia from a sound interferes with the perception of real colors.

Synge, John Millington   [sing]

Always controversial during his lifetime, playwright John Millington Synge captured the spirit of the Irish peasant in his masterpieces Riders to the Sea *(1904) and* The Playboy of the Western World *(1907). His poetic dramas and comedies, a major contribution to the Irish Literary Renaissance, have become classics of the Irish stage.*

The greatest playwright of the modern Irish theater, J. M. Synge was born near Dublin of an Anglo-Irish Protestant family on Apr. 16, 1871, and died Mar. 24, 1909, too early to witness the widespread acceptance his plays would win in Ireland and throughout the English-speaking world. After attending Trinity College, Dublin, Synge lived in Germany and then in Paris, where he met William Butler Yeats, who encouraged him to visit the Aran Islands and to write about the Irish peasant.

In 1903 the Irish National Theatre Society performed Synge's one-act comedy *In the Shadow of the Glen,* but it was considered morbid and un-Irish. In 1904 his RIDERS TO THE SEA, one of the most moving short plays in modern drama, received a more favorable reception. The three-act *The Well of the Saints,* however, performed in 1905 in the newly opened ABBEY THEATRE, increased the critics' suspicions of Synge's motives, whereas The PLAYBOY OF THE WESTERN WORLD (1907) seemed such a malignant travesty of the national character that Abbey audiences disrupted the play's performances for several nights. A grotesque extravaganza about peasant life, written in a highly rhythmic prose of rich comic excellence and lyric beauty, *The Playboy* eventually gained recognition as a classic of the Irish stage. Of his six plays, only *The Tinker's Wedding* (1908) was thought too inflammatory to produce.

Synge spent his last months unsuccessfully trying to finish his beautiful *Deirdre of the Sorrows,* a retelling of an old Irish love story. After his death the play was assembled from his drafts and notes by his friend Yeats and his fiancée, Maire O'Neill, who played the title role at its first performance in 1910.   ROBERT HOGAN

Bibliography: Bickley, Francis J., *J. M. Synge and the Irish Dramatic Movement* (1912); Corkery, Daniel, *Synge and Anglo-Irish Literature* (1931; repr. 1965); Greene, David H., and Stephens, Edward, *J. M. Synge 1871–1909* (1959); Price, Alan, *Synge and Anglo-Irish Drama* (1961); Saddlemyer, Ann, *J. M. Synge and Modern Comedy* (1968); Skelton, Robin, *The Writings of J. M. Synge* (1971); Strong, L. A. G., *John Millington Synge* (1941); Synge, J. M., *Collected Works,* 4 vols. (1961–68); Yeats, W. B., *Synge and the Ireland of his Time* (1911; repr. 1971).

Synge, Richard Laurence Millington

The British biochemist Richard Laurence Millington Synge, b. Oct. 28, 1914, received (1952) the Nobel Prize for Chemistry with Archer J. P. Martin for the development of the technique of paper CHROMATOGRAPHY, a method for the separation and identification of chains of amino acids that make up large protein molecules. This work permitted the determination of the structure of such molecules and advanced analytical techniques in medicine and physiology. HENRY M. LEICESTER

Bibliography: Farber, Eduard, *Nobel Prize Winners in Chemistry*, rev. ed. (1963).

syntax

Syntax is the study of sentence structure. Thus it is to be distinguished from such other branches of LINGUISTICS as LEXICOLOGY AND LEXICOGRAPHY, SEMANTICS, PHONOLOGY AND MORPHOLOGY, and PHONETICS.

Overtly a sentence consists of a linear sequence of words, one following the other in time (when a sentence is spoken) or in space (when written). Traditional grammatical studies and modern linguistic analysis, however, have revealed numerous other aspects of sentence structure.

Central to syntactic analysis is the observation that some sentences are considered by speakers to be syntactically ill-formed, or ungrammatical, whether because of improper word order (as in the sentence *Slipped he banana peel on a*), because of the improper form of component words (as in *Me are tired*), or for other reasons. A grammatical sentence, one that in syntactic terms is properly constructed, may nevertheless be semantically anomalous—that is, incoherent in sense, such as *The brick munched on pink sadness*—or it may be so complex or awkwardly structured as to be unacceptable—that is, difficult or impossible to use, such as *The dog that the cat that the boy that Sally kissed chased bit howled*. Speakers of a language have the ability to construct and understand an infinite number of distinct sentences, because from a grammatical sentence of any length, a still longer one may be formed. The central problem of syntax is to explain how a finite body of knowledge lets speakers handle an unbounded set of sentences, most of which may be novel to their experience.

Syntactic Rules. Sentences are formed by combining smaller units, such as words, to make larger units. This composition of larger units from smaller ones usually follows regular patterns, the so-called syntactic principles or rules. The rules may be understood as part of the psychological organization of speakers, but the term is also used for statements made by grammarians or linguists in an attempt to describe the patterns and those facets of psychological organization responsible for them.

The syntactic rules of a language must somehow permit the construction of an infinite number of grammatical sentences while excluding the infinite number of strings of elements considered by speakers to be ungrammatical. The finite set of rules of multiplication enables any pair of numbers to be multiplied; in the same way the finite set of rules of a grammar allow speakers to construct any one of an infinite set of new sentences because certain rules may reapply to their own outputs an indefinite number of times, creating larger and larger grammatical expressions. For instance, a syntactic rule of English permits one clause to be used as the direct object within another clause (*I know* is the direct object in *He knows I know*, for example); a complex clause so derived may in turn be used as the direct object in a still larger expression (as in *I know he knows I know*), and so on indefinitely.

Morphemes. In syntactic structure, the smallest units that must be posited are not words but morphemes—the smallest identifiable units with constant meaning or grammatical function. The word *dogs*, for instance, may be broken down into the morphemes *dog* and *s*; *unfavorable* into *un, favor,* and *able*; and *independently* into *in, de, pend, ent,* and *ly*, all of which occur in many other words.

Usually one of the morphemes in a polymorphemic word may be regarded as the core, or root, to which the others are successively added as prefixes (preroot elements) or suffixes (postroot elements) to form successively larger units. *Dog, fa-*

vor, and *pend* are the roots in the words cited above; prefixes and suffixes adhere to them in layers that constitute the morphological structure of the complex words. As a general tendency, affixes—prefixes or suffixes—in the outer layers of the morphological structure pertain to grammatical function or relations, such as the *-ly* of *independently*, which marks the word as an adverb. The derivation of complex lexical forms from simpler ones often follows regular rules or patterns of varying generality. Thus the formation of an adverb by adding *-ly* to an adjective is not just an idiosyncrasy of *independently*, but rather it reflects a productive derivational pattern exemplified by many other words, such as *unfavorably, quickly, happily,* and *thoroughly*.

Besides words and morphemes, sentences are organized into larger units—in particular phrases and clauses. The units are hierarchically arranged: a sentence may be broken down into one or more clauses, a clause into one or more phrases, a phrase into one or more words, and a word into one or more morphemes. Units at each level that behave alike in certain respects may be grouped together into classes and given a common label.

Parts of Speech. At the level of words and morphemes, the most familiar classification is that represented by the traditional PARTS OF SPEECH. A root or larger unit that belongs to one class may be shifted to another by adding a prefix or suffix, as when the verb *favor* becomes an adjective by the suffixation of *-able,* or when the suffix *-ly* derives an adverb from the adjective *independent*. An affix may also leave the class membership unchanged (*dog* and *dogs*, for example, are both nouns; *favorable* and *unfavorable* are both adjectives), or class membership may be changed without the addition of an affix (for example, *bark* may be either a verb or a noun).

Besides the basic division into parts of speech, linguists recognize a need for a much finer classification of words and morphemes. Any grammatical property with respect to which the members of a class differ provides the basis for a subclassification. For example, the class of adjectives in English may be subdivided into those that take the prefix *un-* (such as *favorable, healthy, true,* and *happy*) and those that do not (such as *sad, false, good,* and *orange*). Similarly, English verbs that take direct objects may be divided into a large subclass of verbs that participate in the type of sentence called the passive (the sentence *George Washington surveyed this land* has the passive variant *This land was surveyed by George Washington*) and a small subclass that do not (the verb *have*, for instance: the passive of *She has a nice smile*—namely, *A nice smile is had by her*—is ungrammatical).

Phrases and Clauses. A phrase is a sequence of words, centered on a core element called the head, that constitutes a coherent grammatical unit of the same basic type as the head. For example, *a good writer* is a noun phrase centered on the head noun *writer*. *Works hard* and *may have been eating peanuts* are called verb phrases; *under the workbench* is a prepositional phrase; and so on.

A clause is a larger unit, one that resembles a simple sentence in its parts and their arrangement. In traditional terms the major units in a clause are a subject and a predicate. The subject is some type of noun or noun phrase, but the predicate may have as its central unit a verb, an adjective, a noun phrase, a prepositional phrase, or an adverb. From a more modern perspective and focusing just on clauses with verbs as the central predicate element, a clause may be viewed as specifying a relation among various participants, each identified by a noun phrase and playing a certain role in the clause. The central participants are the subject and (direct) object; the role of other participants is said to be oblique and may represent any one of a variety of more specific relationships.

Languages use several kinds of devices for distinguishing the subject and object: word order, as in English, where the subject usually precedes the verb and the object follows it; case inflection, such as *he* for subject and *him* for object; the attachment of a wordlike case-marking particle; verb agreement, as in *I am* versus *he is;* or any combination of these. Oblique relationships are usually marked by inflection or by special particles, such as English prepositions.

A sentence with only one clause is said to be simple; a sentence with more than one clause is complex. The clauses of a complex sentence may be juxtaposed, with neither contained inside the other, in which event they are said to be conjoined or coordinate. When one clause is contained inside another, it is said to be a subordinate clause, and the clause in which it functions is called the main clause. There are numerous kinds of subordinate clauses. One that modifies a noun is called a relative clause; one that functions alone as subject or object is termed a complement clause. In addition there are many kinds of adverbial clauses.

Generative-Transformational Grammar. Since the publication in 1957 of Noam CHOMSKY's book *Syntactic Structures,* modern linguistic studies of syntax have been dominated by the theory of generative-transformational grammar. The central tenet of the theory is that in addition to the overt grammatical form of sentences, called surface structure, there is also a more abstract, underlying level of grammatical organization, called deep structure. Whereas the deep structure of a sentence may differ radically from its surface form, the relation between the two levels is a function of general syntactic rules called transformations, which are viewed as acting in concert to derive surface structures from their underlying, semantically oriented representations.

Additional, semantic rules relate deep structures to appropriate semantic representations (representations of meaning, whatever their character), and phonological rules relate surface structures to corresponding phonetic representations (pronunciations).

Both deep and surface structures are claimed to be best represented by inverted tree diagrams, showing the linear order of the words and the grouping of the words into coherent syntactic units called constituents and containing labels to identify the class or type of each constituent. Often the deep and surface structures of a sentence are the same or similar, so that few if any transformations figure in their derivation. For many sentences, though, strong evidence may be found for positing a deep structure that diverges substantially from the surface form.

In some instances, two sentences are so similar in meaning and syntactic organization that despite their surface differences, they are most plausibly viewed as manifestations of the same deep, semantically oriented structure. For example, there are special complex verbs in English consisting of a verb plus a particle, such as *look up, knock down,* or *take off.* The entire complex verb may precede the object, as in *He looked up the information,* or the particle may follow the object, as in *He looked the information up.* The first order is considered to reflect the deep structure of such sentences directly, with the latter order being derived by a transformation that optionally moves the particle away from the verb and places it after the object.

In other instances the antithetical situation is found, in which two sentences differ radically in meaning—and hence may be presumed to have different deep structures—despite similarity or identity of surface form. For instance, the sentences *Bill is eager to please* and *Bill is easy to please* are exactly parallel in surface form, yet they express very different semantic relations. In semantic terms, *Bill* is understood as the subject of *eager,* while the semantic subject of *easy* may be considered to be a clause, namely, *X please Bill* (Bill is not easy; rather, pleasing him is).

Deep structures therefore represent in a direct and consistent way the participants in a sentence and the semantic roles of the participants, whereas the semantic roles are often reflected only indirectly at the surface level. Besides their utility in accounting for semantic relations, deep structures often allow explanations for facts that would otherwise be puzzling. For example, the deep structures of *Bill is eager/easy to please* make it clear why an object may be added with *eager,* yielding the grammatical *Bill is eager to please Sally,* while adding an object with *easy* yields the ungrammatical *Bill is easy to please Sally.* Specifically, the deep structures show that with *eager* the object of *please* has been left unidentified, and hence it is possible to add a noun phrase to identify

it. With *easy,* however, the object of *please* is understood to be *Bill;* so adding another object would be superfluous if not contradictory.   RONALD W. LANGACKER

Bibliography: Akmajian, Adrian, and Heny, Frank, *An Introduction to the Principles of Transformational Syntax* (1975); Bach, Emmon, *Syntactic Theory* (1974); Burt, Marina K., *From Deep to Surface Structure: An Introduction to Transformational Syntax* (1971); Chomsky, Noam, *Syntactic Structures* (1957); Culicover, Peter, *Syntax* (1976); Jacobs, Roderick A., and Rosenbaum, Peter S., eds., *Readings in English Transformational Grammar* (1970); Lester, Mark, ed., *Readings in Applied Transformational Grammar,* 2d ed. (1973); Stockwell, Robert P., *Foundations of Syntactic Theory* (1977); Traugott, Elizabeth Closs, *A History of English Syntax* (1972).

synthetic fibers

Synthetic fibers are fibers obtained from nonfibrous chemical sources rather than from natural sources such as the cellulose of plants or the hair of animals. They are strong, durable, and lightweight as well as abrasion resistant, stretchable, easy to dye, and resistant to heat, moisture, mildew, and chemicals. Fiber producers change the size, shape, surface, luster, and other physical aspects of synthetic fibers to create fibers for specific end uses.

History. In 1884 the Frenchman Hilaire de Chardonnet invented a process for treating natural cellulose, such as wood pulp, with solvents and spinning the resultant liquid into fiber. Chardonnet called his regenerated cellulosic fiber "artificial silk," and that name was retained until in 1924 the term *rayon* was adopted for fibers formed by this process. The first commercially successful fiber, however, wholly synthesized from nonfibrous materials was NYLON, announced in 1938 by the Du Pont Company. Nylon was created from chemical ingredients obtained from coal, air, and water. Wallace H. CAROTHERS formulated the theory of long-chain POLYMERIZATION that was the basis for the invention of nylon and also provided the scientific foundation on which most synthetic fibers are built.

Types of Fibers. Numerous other fibers have been synthesized since the development of nylon, and 19 distinct generic classes of synthetic fiber have now been established. In each case the fiber has been designed to have performance or aesthetic characteristics that meet specified trade or consumer needs. Nylon, for instance, is strong, durable, and lightweight; these properties have enabled it to fit a wide range of uses, from women's hosiery and lingerie to fabric used to reinforce heavy truck and aircraft tires. Polyester fiber is used mainly in apparel but is also widely used in the manufacture of boat sails. Fabrics made from polyester fibers are noted for their resistance to wrinkling and ease of care. Acrylic fibers are close to wool in appearance and performance and are used extensively for sweaters and in fabrics that have the appearance of fur. Olefin fibers are used primarily in carpets but also can be found in some apparel and in ropes, sewing thread, netting, and similar industrial products. Modacrylic fibers are flame resistant and are used in apparel that must meet strict standards for resistance to burning. Aramid fibers are exceptionally strong and resistant to heat and are used in protective clothing for fire fighters and for workers exposed to corrosive liquids or high temperatures. One class of aramid fiber is five times stronger than steel strands of equal weight. This property makes possible the weaving of fabric for vests that will repel handgun bullets. Elastomeric synthetics have also been developed and have largely replaced natural rubber in textiles. These "spandex" yarns can be woven or knitted into fabrics for swimwear and for support stockings and into stretchable fabrics of many kinds. They are washable and dyeable and have long-lasting stretch and recovery.

Production. Nearly all synthetic fibers are based on petrochemicals. These products of oil refining are combined into a syrupy substance that is forced through the tiny holes of a spinneret, a device that closely resembles a shower head. The streams of liquid that emerge from the spinneret are solidified either by cooling or submersion in liquid chemicals. Altering the size and shape of the spinneret holes produces fibers of different sizes and cross sections, designed for different applications. As the endless threads leave the spinneret they are stretched to align the molecules to produce the degree of strength and elasticity desired. The long filaments can be woven or knitted in their original form or can be crimped, coiled, or otherwise textured to create bulk and surface interest in fabrics. Cut into short lengths, the fibers can be blended with other synthetic staple fibers or with natural fibers and then spun into yarn for weaving or knitting.

Since the first production of nylon in the late 1930s, synthetic-fiber manufacture has expanded at a rapid rate. In 1950 about 20% of all fiber used by textile mills in the United States was synthetic. By 1960 that figure had grown to 30%, and by the mid-1970s more than 70% of all fiber consumed by U.S. textile mills was synthetic. More than 3.8 billion kg (8.4 billion lb) of synthetic fibers is now produced annually in the United States.   JAMES ADSHEAD

Bibliography: Carroll-Porczynski, C. Z., *Manual of Man-made Fibers* (1960); Dembeck, Adeline A., *Guidebook to Man-made Textile Fibers and Textured Yarns of the World,* 3d ed. (1969); Ludewig, Hermann, *Polyester Fibres: Chemistry and Technology* (1971); Man-Made Fibers Producers Association, *Man-made Fiber Fact Book* (1972); Mark, Herman F., et al., *Man-Made Fibers: Science and Technology,* 3 vols. (1967–68); Moncrieff, R. W., *Man-Made Fibres,* 6th ed. (1975).

synthetic fuels: SEE COAL GASIFICATION; FUEL; GASOHOL; SHALE, OIL; TAR SANDS.

syphilis

Syphilis, a sexually transmitted disease, is caused by the SPIROCHETE *Treponema pallidum* (SEE BACTERIA). The spirochete cannot survive outside the body, and so contracting the disease by other than intimate contact is rare. The spirochete usually enters the body through invisible breaks in skin or through intact mucous membranes lining the mouth, rectum, or genital tract. About 3 weeks later, the patient develops a sore, called a chancre, at the entry spot. Relatively painless, it is usually found around the genitalia but is sometimes seen on lips or mouth, on the breasts, or around the rectum. Lymph nodes in the affected area often become enlarged. The chancre contains large numbers of spirochetes and is highly contagious. Even without treatment, the chancre slowly heals in several weeks; the spirochetes, however, spread throughout the body, and about 6 weeks later the secondary stage of syphilis occurs, characterized mainly by fever, swollen glands, and a painless nonitching rash over most of the body, including the genital tract, the mouth, and the palms and soles. Lesions also form in the mouth and around the vagina and anus, and these are highly contagious. Symptoms eventually resolve, and the disease enters its latent phase.

Two-thirds of syphilitic patients have no further trouble with the disease and are no longer infectious. After several months to years later, however, involvement of the brain and spinal cord will occur in some persons, causing difficulties with thinking, sensation, and movement. Some suffer skin and bone damage, and others will have damage to the blood vessels around the heart, resulting in heart failure and sometimes requiring surgery. Some pregnant women transmit the organism to the fetus, resulting in miscarriage, stillbirth, or deformities that may be obvious at birth or may not appear until the child reaches puberty. Syphilis can be diagnosed with a blood test, and all stages of the disease can be cured with the appropriate antibiotic treatment. Damage that has already been done to affected tissues, however, cannot necessarily be repaired; early diagnosis and treatment are therefore extremely important. Also, patients who have been treated need to have blood tests taken periodically for two years thereafter.   MICHAEL F. REIN, M.D.

Bibliography: Brown, William J., et al., *Syphilis and Other Venereal Diseases* (1970); Hyde, Margaret O., *V.D.: The Silent Epidemic* (1973); Johnson, Eric W., *V.D.: Venereal Disease and What You Should Do About It* (1973); Rosebury, Theodore, *Microbes and Morals* (1973); Wear, Jennifer, and Holmes, King, *How to Have Intercourse without Getting Screwed* (1976).

Syr Darya   [seer dar-yah']

Syr Darya is a river system in the Tadzhik, Uzbek, and Kazakh republics of the USSR. The headstreams of the Syr—the Naryn River and Kara Darya—begin in the Tien Shan range of China and flow through the Kirghiz SSR. From its juncture with the Naryn in the Fergana Valley, the Syr flows west and northwest for 2,137 km (1,328 mi) to its delta at the northeastern corner of the ARAL SEA. The river is dammed at the western end of the heavily populated Fergana Valley to provide irrigation for the cotton grown there. Cities in the region include Tashkent, Andizhan, Kokand, and Margilan. Rice is grown in the delta area, which includes the cities of Leninabad and Novokazalinsk. The Syr is not generally navigable because of its unstable course.

Followed by the old caravan route between China and Europe, the Syr is the ancient Jaxartes River, which marked the northeastern boundary of the province of Bactria established by Alexander the Great. Later occupied by nomadic tribes, the area began to come under Russian control during the 18th century.

Syracuse   (New York)

Syracuse is a city in central New York on the southern end of Lake Onondaga. The seat of Onondaga County, it has a population of 174,600 (1979 est.). A commercial and manufacturing city, it produces chemicals, steel, automobiles, electrical equipment, machine tools, and pharmaceuticals. Educational institutions include Syracuse University (1870) and several colleges. The Everson Museum of Art (1896) is there, and parks include the Onondaga Lake Park on the site of the original LeMoyne salt spring and the Erie Canal Park. The New York State Fair is held around Labor Day each year in Syracuse.

The region was the home of the ONONDAGA tribe, and their village on the site served (c.1570–1770) as the center of the IROQUOIS LEAGUE. Samuel de Champlain visited the village in 1615. The first white settlers arrived in 1786, and by 1788 they operated sawmills and saltworks along the Lake Onondaga shores. After the city was linked to the ERIE CANAL in 1825, its economic growth was assured. It remained a major national salt supplier until after the Civil War.

Syracuse   (Sicily)

A silver decadrachm (c.413 BC), portraying a chariot on one side and the nymph Arethusa on the obverse side, was created to celebrate the victory of Syracuse over Athens during the Peloponnesian War. Syracuse, founded by Corinthians in c.734 BC, became one of the most influential cities of the classical world.

In ancient times, Syracuse was Sicily's most powerful Greek city. Founded on the east coast of the island by colonists from Corinth about 734 BC, Syracuse grew rapidly, founding in turn the colony of Camarina, on the southern coast, in about 589. Syracusan control of much of Sicily was achieved by the tyrants GELON (r. 485–478) and HIERO I (r. 478–467). Gelon destroyed a mighty Carthaginian army at Himera in 480. After Hiero's death a democracy was installed (466–405); it thwarted (427–424) Athenian attempts at domination and defeated (415–413) the Athenian army and navy in one of the decisive battles of the PELOPONNESIAN WAR.

Another tyrant, DIONYSIUS THE ELDER, lifted Syracuse to new heights in the 4th century. He contended with CARTHAGE—an omnipresent threat—reasserted control over Sicily, fought the Etruscans, had dealings with Rome, and created a court famous for its splendor. The troubled reign of his son, DIONYSIUS THE YOUNGER, who studied with and rejected Plato, ended in 345, when TIMOLEON reintroduced an ephemeral democracy. Agathocles became king in 304.

Syracuse declined in the 3d century BC. Although PYRRHUS fended off the Carthaginians (278–275) and HIERO II (r. c.270–215) enjoyed a long and prosperous rule as a Roman ally, after Hiero's death Syracuse became allied with Carthage, Rome's adversary in the PUNIC WARS. Rome besieged faction-torn Syracuse, compelling its surrender in 212. Syracuse became the capital of the province of Sicily and enjoyed relative prosperity. It was ravaged by the Franks in AD 280, became Muslim in the 9th century, and was conquered by the NORMANS 200 years later.

Modern Syracuse is the capital city of Syracuse province. The older section is mostly on the small island of Ortygia, connected to the newer areas on Sicily by a causeway. The city has two harbors and is a busy fishing port; other industries are salt processing, tourism, wine making, and the manufacture of cement and soap.   CHARLES W. FORNARA

Bibliography: Dunbabin, T. J., *The Western Greeks* (1948); Freeman, E. A., *History of Sicily*, 4 vols. (1891–94); Guido, Margaret, *Syracuse* (1958); Smith, Dennis Mack, *History of Sicily*, 2 vols. (1968).

Syracuse University

Established in 1870 by the Methodist Episcopal Church, Syracuse University (enrollment: 15,500; library: 1,700,000 volumes) is an independent coeducational institution in Syracuse, N.Y. Among its divisions are the schools of speech and dramatic art, law, the New York College of Forestry (a unit of SUNY), and the Maxwell School of Citizenship and Public Affairs. Branches of the university are at Utica College, in Utica, and at the University College, the adult education division with branches in Endicott, Corning, Rome, and Poughkeepsie.

Syria

The Syrian Arab Republic lies on the eastern shore of the Mediterranean Sea. Syria is bordered by Turkey on the north, Iraq on the east, and Jordan and Israel on the south. In the northwest Syria extends to the Mediterranean Sea; in the southwest Lebanon separates it from the sea. The country, which is predominantly agricultural, is sometimes able to export surpluses, mostly of wheat, barley, and cotton. When rainfall is deficient, however, wheat and barley must be imported. Small amounts of petroleum are exported and there is some light industry. Syria gained independence from France in stages between 1941 and 1944, but its history stretches far back into ancient times. A 1963 revolution brought the radical BAATH PARTY to power. Since then Syria has relied heavily on Soviet military and economic aid, although relations with the West have recently improved.

LAND AND RESOURCES
Syria consists of four major physiographic regions. The first is the coast plain—in the northwest—a narrow, discontinuous strip with cliffs and headlands but few beaches and harbors. The second region is a complex of hills and mountains that roughly parallels the coast. The Jebel al-Duruz, a huge basaltic outcropping, is in the south. Farther north the Anti-Lebanon Mountains—which form the border between Lebanon and Syria—are the site of Mount Hermon (2,814 m/9,233 ft), the nation's highest peak. To the north the Alawite Mountains rise to 1,563 m (5,125 ft). Syria's third major region, in the southeast, is the Syrian Desert. The fourth region, al-Jazirah, is located in the west along both banks of the Euphrates River and is a steppe with stony hills and low ridges.

Soils and Climate. Syria has fertile reddish prairie and chestnut and brown soils in the north and east of the mountains. Terra rossa and brown forest soils are found in the coastal area, desert soils in the southeast, and rich alluvium and bog soils in river valleys.

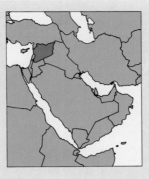

SYRIA

Official Name: Syrian Arab Republic
Capital and Largest City: Damascus (1977 est. pop., 1,097,200)
Area: 185,180 km² (71,479 mi²)
Elevation: *Highest*—Mount Hermon, on the Lebanon-Syria border, 2,814 m (9,233 ft); *lowest*—sea level, along the Mediterranean Sea coast
Population: 8,395,000 (1979 est.). *Distribution*—51% urban, 49% rural; *density*, 45 persons per km² (117 per mi²); *annual rate of increase* (1970–77), 3.3%
Principal Languages: Arabic (official), Kurdish, Armenian
Principal Religions: Islam, Greek Orthodox, Eastern Rite Christianity
Principal Products: *Agriculture*—cotton, wheat, barley, tobacco, grapes, tomatoes, livestock. *Manufacturing and industry*—textiles, processed food, tobacco, petroleum, cement, glass, soap, phosphates. *Mining*—phosphates, salt
Railroads: 1,543 km/959 mi (1979)
Roads: 12,051 km/7,488 mi (1979 paved)
Currency: 1 Syrian pound = 100 piastres

The climate varies from Mediterranean in the west through steppe to desert in the east. Mountain areas are cooler and wetter. The temperature in Damascus averages 27° C (80° F) in July and 7° C (45° F) in January. Precipitation averages from 760 to 1,270 mm (30–50 in) along the coast, declining to between 250 and 500 mm (10–20 in) in the steppe and to less than 127 mm (5 in) in the desert.

Drainage, Vegetation, Animals, and Resources. The major stream is the EUPHRATES RIVER, flowing out of the Taurus Mountains in Turkey through the eastern steppe. Its major tributaries in Syria are the Balikh and Khabur. The Orontes River flows from Lebanon and through northwestern Syria. The Ghab marshes occupy the widest part of the Orontes valley, but they are being drained. The west and south are traversed by wadis, which flow after rainfalls but whose stream beds are dry the rest of the year.

Only some brushwood remains on the coastal plain. In the mountains are pine forest, oak, and scrub oak. Terebinth and wormwood dominate the drier regions. Some bears are found, and gazelle, antelope, deer, squirrel, wildcat, and hare are common. In the desert are many small reptiles. Native birds include flamingo, pelican, duck, and snipe.

Syria's most important mineral resources are phosphates and petroleum, although limestone, iron ore, asphalt, and salt are mined in smaller quantities. The Euphrates Dam at Tabqa will increase the amount of arable land substantially by providing water for irrigation, as well as hydroelectric power.

PEOPLE
Of Syria's 8,395,000 inhabitants (1979 est.), about 90% are ARABS. Roughly 150,000 KURDS live primarily along the Turkish border. Other minority groups include about 130,000 ARMENIANS, largely in the towns, especially Aleppo, and smaller numbers of CIRCASSIANS and TURKS. The Alawis, a Muslim sect,

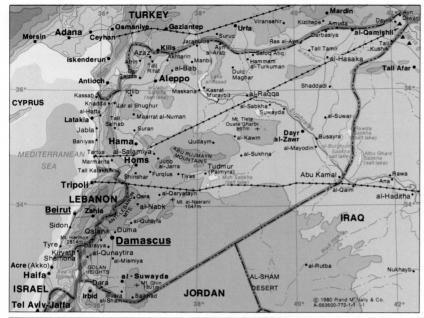

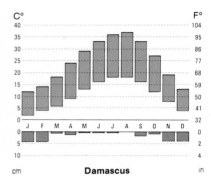

© 1980 Rand McNally & Co.
A-563600-772-1-1 1-1

cm **Damascus** in

(Above) *Bars indicate monthly ranges of temperatures* (red) *and precipitation* (blue) *in Damascus, the ancient capital of Syria. The city, located in the southwestern portion of the country, has a steppe climate that is moderated somewhat because of its proximity to the Mediterranean Sea.*

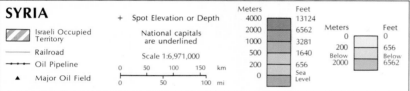

SYRIA

+ Spot Elevation or Depth

National capitals are underlined

Israeli Occupied Territory
Railroad
Oil Pipeline
▲ Major Oil Field

Scale 1:6,971,000

Meters	Feet
4000	13124
2000	6562
1000	3281
500	1640
200	656
0	Sea Level

Meters	Feet
0	0
200 Below	656
2000 Below	6562

(Below) *Damascus, in southwestern Syria, is possibly the oldest permanently inhabited city in the world. Several of history's great generals, including King David of Israel, Alexander the Great, and the Mongol leader Timur, have either sacked or occupied Damascus to control its strategic location along the Middle Eastern trading routes.*

are probably the indigenous inhabitants and form a majority in the coastal province of Latakia. The DRUZES, most of whom live in the Jabal ad-Duruz, may be related to tribes of the Zagros Mountains of Iran. BEDOUINS live in the desert. Small Assyrian and Jewish communities exist, primarily in the towns.

Classical Arabic (see ARABIC LANGUAGE) is the common written language and the basis of the standard spoken form, but there are numerous variations, even among towns. Kurdish and Armenian are important, and the Aramaic language is still spoken in some villages. French is widely understood, and English is understood in the larger cities. More than 70% of the people are SUNNITES and about 16% belong to other Muslim sects—SHIITES, ISMAILIS, Alawis, and Druzes. Most of the remainder (13%) are Christians of several denominations, including Greek Orthodox, Armenian Orthodox, Jacobites, and Nestorians. Syria is the temporary home of about 250,000 (1974) Palestinian Arab refugees from the Arab-Israeli Wars, of whom about 33,000 live in 10 United Nations-administered camps.

Demography. The rapid annual growth rate of 3.3% primarily reflects the crude birthrate of 45.5 per thousand, which greatly exceeds the official crude death rate of 15.4 per thousand. Infant mortality is high, 21.7 per thousand. Life expectancy is 54 years for men and 59 years for women.

Population density is greatest along the Mediterranean, particularly in the region surrounding LATAKIA. The rural-to-urban migration continues to accelerate, and more than half the population is now urban. DAMASCUS is the capital and largest city; ALEPPO, HOMS, HAMA, and Latakia are also important. In recent years a steady emigration of professional and business people, mostly non-Muslims and non-Arabs, has occurred. Thousands of refugees from the Lebanese civil war (1975–76) entered the country, but many have since left. Nomads migrate freely between Syria, Iraq, and Jordan.

Education and Health. Elementary schooling is free and compulsory, but only 41% of the population is literate and only

about one-half of the school-age children actually attend school. Universities are located in Latakia, Aleppo, and Damascus. Syria also has conservatories of music and specialized institutes, but many students go abroad for technical training. The national library in Damascus has many rare books and manuscripts, and other national libraries are found in Aleppo, Homs, and Latakia. The principal museum is the national museum in Damascus.

Health problems vary by region; for the country as a whole the most serious diseases are conjunctivitis, schistosomiasis, tuberculosis, typhoid, hepatitis, dysentery, enteritis, and occasionally cholera. Traditional healers and herbalists are gradu-

(Left) *Agricultural laborers working in fields near Taftnaz, in northwestern Syria, pick balls of cotton, the nation's principal cash crop and one of its most valuable export commodities.*

(Below) *Now in ruins, Palmyra, an ancient caravan stop in central Syria, became a vital link in east-west commerce during the era of Roman rule. The city was razed during the 3d century, when its queen, Zenobia, unsuccessfully attempted to assert Palmyra's independence.*

ally being replaced by physicians, resulting in the slow improvement of general health. Because of rapid population growth, however, in 1975 there were still 3,065 persons per physician. Hospital beds have increased to a rate of 983 persons to each bed.

ECONOMIC ACTIVITY

Syria is still predominantly agricultural; 32% of the labor force is engaged in agriculture, although farming contributes only about 23% to the gross national product. The traditional patterns of farming, however, have been altered by increased irrigation and mechanization, land reform, use of fertilizers and pesticides, reoccupation of abandoned land, and introduction of new crops. Including pasturage, 77% of the land is now productive. The principal crops are cotton, cereals, vegetables, fruit, and tobacco. Cattle, other livestock, and chickens are also important.

A massive irrigation project has begun in the Euphrates Basin, based on water from the Tabqa Dam, completed in 1975, but full implementation will take a decade or more. Much of the 2.5 billion kW h of electricity Syria produces annually (1977) is from the Tabqa Dam, which now provides more than 95% of the country's needs and a small surplus for export.

Since 1963 the government has nationalized most industry, which employs 26% of the labor force. Textile manufacturing and food processing are the most important, but the chemical, cement, fertilizer, and engineering industries are growing rapidly. Overall industrial growth is restrained, however, by shortages of component parts, port congestion, bureaucracy, inefficiency, shortages of skilled and managerial manpower, and other problems. The 1976–80 development plan (reissued after modification in June 1977) emphasized industrialization for self-sufficiency, although agriculture was also given high priority.

Production of low-quality phosphate began near Al-Sharqiya in 1971 and reached nearly 1 million metric tons (1.1 million U.S. tons) in 1978. Petroleum production began in 1968, grew steadily to about 10 million metric tons (11 million U.S. tons) in 1976, and then declined to about 8 million tons (8.8 million U.S. tons) in 1978. Syrian petroleum is of comparatively low quality, heavy, and high in sulfur content. Two petroleum refineries are operating. Chromium, manganese, uranium, asphalt, and rocksalt are other Syrian resources.

Syria has four major railroads: the Northern and Southern lines; the Hejaz Railway, between Damascus and Jordan; and a new line linking Latakia, Aleppo, and Qamishli (on the Turkish border). Only 12,051 km (7,488 mi) of the roads are paved. Latakia is the main Syrian seaport; Baniyas is exclusively an oil port, and Tartus exports petroleum and phosphates. Damascus and Aleppo have international airports.

Syria's principal exports are crude petroleum, phosphates, raw cotton, wool, tobacco, and live animals. The principal

buyers are West Germany, the USSR, the Netherlands, and Italy. Syria imports metals and metal products, machinery, petroleum, textiles, and transportation equipment from West Germany, Italy, France, Iraq, and Romania. A chronic trade deficit is more than covered by aid from oil-rich Arab states such as Saudi Arabia, the European Economic Community, the World Bank, the United States, and the Soviet-bloc nations. In 1977, with a gross domestic product of $6.6 billion, Syria had exports worth $1.3 billion and imports worth $2.9 billion.

GOVERNMENT

The 1973 constitution provides for a strong presidential system. The president is elected to a 7-year term by universal adult suffrage. In 1979 the president was General Hafiz al-Assad, who took power in a 1970 military coup, was elected by a public referendum in 1971, and reelected in February 1978. Legislative power is vested in the 195-member unicameral People's Assembly, whose members serve for 4 years. The president appoints the members of the council of ministers, which is headed by a prime minister. The highest court is the court of cassation, supplementing two levels of subordinate courts and various religious courts that handle personal and family law. The president is also general secretary of the Baath party and president of the Progressive Front of National Union, a grouping of the Baath and the four smaller legal political parties.

The country is divided into 13 provinces, with the city of Damascus administered separately. Each province is headed by a governor appointed by the central government. Each governor is assisted by a provincial council.

HISTORY

Recent archaeological evidence indicates that Syria was the center of one of the oldest civilizations on Earth, a Semitic empire centering on the city of EBLA in northern Syria that flourished from 2500 BC to 2400 BC.

After 1250 BC, PHOENICIA, a prosperous maritime civilization along the Mediterranean shore of Syria and Lebanon, formed the nucleus of what later became Syria. Its strategic location and wealth attracted numerous invaders. ALEXANDER THE GREAT conquered the area in the 4th century BC. When his short-lived empire broke up, control passed to the SELEUCIDS, who held the region until ANTIOCHUS III was forced to surrender to the Romans in 188 BC. Under Rome the region was organized as the province of Syria. Christianity was introduced there, and ANTIOCH (now in Turkey but a major center of Hellenistic and Roman Syria) became a key center of Christian learning and one of the original patriarchates.

In AD 636, Damascus fell to the Arabs. Most Syrians then became Muslims and adopted the Arabic language. Within 30 years Damascus, as the seat of the UMAYYAD caliph from 661 to 750, became the center of the Arab world. Under the ABBASIDS the caliphate moved to Baghdad, and Syria became a secondary province. As the Arab empire disintegrated, Syria was once again invaded, fought over, and ruled in part by, among others, various Egyptian factions, SELJUKS, and Crusaders. During the late 12th century SALADIN expelled the foreigners, but with his death (1193) the country disintegrated, and the MONGOLS overran Syria in 1260; subsequently the region passed to the MAMELUKES of Egypt. Finally, in 1516, the Ottoman Turks under SELIM I conquered the area, and it remained part of the OTTOMAN EMPIRE for 400 years.

After Turkey's defeat in World War I, France was awarded a mandate over Syria by the League of Nations. Nationalist revolts began early in the 20th century but led to gradual attainment of independence only between 1941 and 1944. The last French troops left in 1946.

In 1948, Syria joined the Arab invasion of Israel (see ARAB-ISRAELI WARS) but was badly defeated. Thereafter, instability and growing Soviet influence dominated Syrian political life. In 1958, Syria and Egypt merged to form the UNITED ARAB REPUBLIC, but Egypt was clearly disposed to dominate, and the union broke up in 1961. More instability followed until the revolution of 1963, when a radical socialist regime was formed by the Baath party. Syria fought other wars with Israel in 1967 and 1973, and in both wars Syria lost territory on the Golan Heights in the far southwest.

In 1976, Syrian troops occupied most of Lebanon, helping to end the civil war there but creating a heavy drain on the Syrian economy. Under Assad, relations with the United States and other Western countries have improved and the government is modifying its strict socialist policies to reduce dependence on Soviet-bloc technical assistance in favor of Western technology, investment, and training.

MARTIN IRA GLASSNER

Bibliography:
GENERAL: American University, *Area Handbook for Syria* (1971); Copeland, Paul W., *The Land and People of Syria*, rev. ed. (1972); Glubb, John B., *Syria, Lebanon, Jordan* (1967); Haddad, Robert M., *Syrian Christians in Muslim Society* (1970); Petran, Tabitha, *Syria* (1972).
ECONOMY: Asfour, E. Y., *Syria: Development and Monetary Policy* (1959); Kanovasky, E., *Economic Development of Syria* (1975).
POLITICS AND GOVERNMENT: Devlin, John F., *A History of the Ba'th Party from Its Origins to 1966* (1976); Hourani, Albert H., *Syria and Lebanon: A Political Essay* (1977); McLaurin, Ronald D., et al., *Foreign Policy Making in the Middle East* (1977); Rabinovich, Itamar, *Syria Under the Ba'ath, 1963-1966* (1972); Seale, Patrick, *The Struggle for Syria: A Study of Post-War Arab Politics, 1945-1958* (1965).
HISTORY: Castle, Wilfrid T., *Syrian Pageant: The History of Syria and Palestine, 1000 B.C. to A.D. 1945* (1977); Drower, M. S., *Syria c.1550-1400 B.C.*, 2 vols. (1970); Popper, William, *Egypt and Syria Under the Circassian Sultans: 1382-1468 A.D.*, 2 vols. (1957); Tibawi, Abdul L., *A Modern History of Syria* (1969).

Syrian Desert

The Syrian Desert covers southern Syria, northeastern Jordan, western Iraq, and northern Saudi Arabia. Most of the desert is

a rock- and gravel-covered plateau. It receives an average of 125 mm (5 in) of rain a year and has July temperatures above 38° C (100° F). Wadis flow east toward the Euphrates River, but few reach it. Cacti and grasses are the main plants, and animals include gazelles, jackals, and hares. BEDOUIN nomads raise goats, sheep, and Arabian horses. At oases, grapes, olives, and figs are grown. PALMYRA became important as the principal junction of the caravan routes across the desert by AD 250. Subsequently, Romans, Mongols, Mamelukes, and Turks invaded the area.

syringomyelia   [suh-ring'-goh-my-ee'-lee-uh]

Syringomyelia is a chronic disease in which the spinal cord is damaged by the formation of fluid-filled cavities (syrinxes) and the replacement of nervous tissue by scar tissue. The disease, whose cause is unknown, is accompanied by disturbances of motor and sensory function. The spinal cord cavities can extend through a considerable section of the cord; the symptoms depend on which section of the spinal cord is affected. Often the first symptoms are weakness and wasting of muscles of the upper extremities and burning sensations or loss of pain sensation in the lower arms. Syringomyelia usually progresses over many years. No satisfactory treatment has been found, although some physicians advocate surgical drainage of the syrinx.

PETER L. PETRAKIS

systems engineering

Systems engineering is a general term that describes the application of engineering skills to the total design and creation of a complex system. A system is defined as a set of concepts or parts that must work together to perform a particular function. There are many kinds of systems—aerospace systems, transportation systems, health systems, and so on—each made up of many subunits, including personnel, that must be coordinated if the system is to accomplish its mission. Systems engineering focuses on this coordination of a total system rather than on its parts.

In a sense, systems engineering is not distinguished from normal engineering practice; any engineer acts as a systems engineer when responsible for the design and implementation of a total system. The difference lies primarily in the greater emphasis on defining goals, the creative generation of alternative designs, the evaluation of alternative designs, and the coordination and control of the diverse tasks that are necessary to create a complex system.

The basic concepts of systems engineering have been in use for centuries. The civil engineers of ancient Egypt must have developed rather elaborate methods of systems coordination and control in order to manage the construction of the pyramids. Similarly, early designers of roads, sewer systems, and aqueducts used many of the ideas of systems engineering. The term, however, was not formally used, nor was the importance of the concepts recognized, until after World War II. This recent emphasis on systems engineering is a result of the sharp increase in complexity of modern industry. A typical weapon of World War II, the P-51 Mustang fighter airplane, certainly had some complexity in its design, but its complexity was exceeded tenfold by weapons systems of only a decade later. The Polaris missile system, for example, requires not only the design of the missile itself, with its propulsion system, guidance system, warhead, and so on, but also the design of submarines to carry and launch the missile as well as communications and tracking systems to support its mission.

The successful creation of complex systems such as the Polaris relies more and more on the application of the concepts of systems engineering. The major steps in the completion of a typical systems engineering project are the following: (1) problem statement; (2) identification of objectives; (3) generation of alternatives; (4) analysis of these alternatives; (5) selection of one of them; (6) creation of the system; and (7) operation.

Problem statement is extremely important, because it provides the basis for determining the objectives and the alternatives that are to be considered. If the problem statement is too narrow, engineers may overlook some alternatives that might provide better solutions. For example, suppose the problem statement is "improve police performance." The systems engineer may then consider alternative technologies to assist policemen, such as efficiently designed patrol routes, sophisticated weapons and alarm systems, and so forth. However, the problem statement "reduce crime" may suggest other alternatives, such as improved street lighting, that actually may be more successful in reducing criminal activities. Systems engineers explore several alternative problem statements before choosing one.

Next, the objectives must be identified. These objectives will also become the basis for evaluating alternatives in the later phases of the engineering study. Often there will be multiple objectives that must be considered that further complicate the task. For example, the design of a transportation system should include passenger comfort, safety, cost, and aesthetic appeal as objectives.

Alternatives are then generated so that many feasible approaches can be considered. This step requires a high degree of creativity. A novel approach to a difficult problem may lead to significant reductions in costs or improvements in effectiveness. The alternatives are analyzed to predict how they would perform if they were actually implemented. One of the important tools of systems engineering is the creation of mathematical models to simulate the performance of the alternative. Mathematical models are useful because it is often too expensive to actually construct several alternatives. Some of these mathematical modeling techniques were developed within the specialized field of study known as OPERATIONS RESEARCH.

The performance of the alternatives must be evaluated on the basis of the objectives identified in the early stages of the process. At this stage, the engineers must be careful to avoid suboptimization. Suboptimization may occur if each part of the system is independently optimized, or improved, without regard to its interaction with other parts of the system. The separate optimization of each part may not lead to an optimal design of the total system; in fact, the improvement of the performance of one subsystem may actually worsen the overall system.

Once the basic system design has been selected, the systems engineers must define and analyze it in sufficient detail to provide instructions for its construction. The engineers must also implement a management system to ensure that all of the necessary construction activities are time-phased and coordinated.

Finally, the system must be installed and operated. Some systems engineers may continue to work with the system throughout its useful life, providing suggestions on its modification and, perhaps, its expansion to meet changing needs.

Many examples can be given of the successful application of systems engineering to complex technological problems. Despite the difficulties involved, some progress also is being made in expanding the application of the tools of systems engineering to problems that require organizational and social as well as technological changes for their solution.

JAMES S. DYER

Bibliography: Chestnut, Harold, *Systems Engineering Methods* (1967); Machol, Robert, et al., *Systems Engineering Handbook* (1969); Sage, Andrew P., *Systems Engineering Methodology and Applications* (1977); Truxal, John G., *Introductory Systems Engineering* (1972); Wymore, A. Wayne, *Mathematical Theory of Systems Engineering: The Elements* (1967; repr. 1977).

Szarkowski, John   [sah-kof'-skee]

As director of the department of photography at New York City's Museum of Modern Art since 1962, the American photographer and critic John Szarkowski, b. Ashland, Wis., Dec. 18, 1925, has supervised more than 75 exhibitions, including individual shows of Dorothea Lange (1966), Walker Evans (1971), and Diane Arbus (1972). His publications include *The Photographer's Eye* (1965) and *Looking at Photographs* (1973).

Szasz, Thomas   [sahs]

Psychiatrist, neurologist, and educator Thomas Stephen Szasz, b. Hungary, Apr. 15, 1920, became a U.S. citizen in 1944 and received his M.D. from the University of Cincinnati the same year. After a series of distinguished psychiatric residencies at various hospitals and medical colleges, Szasz became professor of psychiatry at the University of Syracuse. *The Myth of Mental Illness* (1961) brought Szasz national recognition and became the foundation of contemporary work in humanistic psychiatry. His other books include *Schizophrenia: The Sacred Symbol of Psychiatry* (1976) and *The Myth of Psychotherapy* (1978).

Szasz believes that what traditional psychiatry terms *mental illnesses* are not illnesses at all, but fundamental problems in living that produce behaviors directly related to interactions of the individual with his or her family, surroundings, and society. Such problems therefore cannot be classified in terms of a medical conception of illness but must be understood in terms of the deceptions, confusion, and misinterpretations arising in a specific situational setting against which the individual develops certain defense mechanisms—such as schizophrenia—for his or her social and emotional survival. Szasz, together with R. D. LAING, is a forerunner of the "radical" or humanistic movement in psychiatry, which is also characterized by opposition to involuntary confinement and other considerations regarding the human and civil rights of patients.

MILDRED NAVARETTA

Bibliography: Scarf, Maggie, "Normality is a Square Circle or a Four-Sided Triangle," *New York Times Magazine,* October 3, 1971.

Szczecin   [shet'-seen]

Szczecin (German: Stettin), one of Poland's leading port cities, lies on the Oder River about 50 km (30 mi) from the Baltic Sea. An important commercial and industrial center, the city has a population of 381,000 (1978 est.). The port is the economic mainstay, and coal from Silesia is the major export. Other industries include the production of foodstuffs, textiles, and chemicals and shipbuilding. Szczecin has several colleges, museums, and theaters, and its most notable landmark is the 12th-century Saint Peter and Saint Paul's Church (restored in 1816). By the 8th century a Slavic fishing village was on the site. It was the largest town of Pomerania by the 12th century, serving as its capital until 1637. It joined the Hanseatic League in 1360. Part of Sweden from 1648 to 1720, Szczecin passed to Prussia in 1720. It remained under German rule until 1945 when it was annexed to Poland. At that time the German population was evacuated and replaced by Poles and Ukrainians from the eastern part of Poland.

Szechwan   [sech'-wahn]

Szechwan is a province of south central China, situated mostly north of the middle YANGTZE RIVER, which flows through its southern part. Szechwan—the most populous province of the country— has about 90,000,000 inhabitants (1977 est.). It is also one of the largest provinces, covering 560,000 km² (216,200 mi²). The capital is CH'ENG-TU; CHUNG-KING is the largest city and industrial center. Szechwan is covered with mountains in the north, west, and south; in the west the Sikang Plateau has an average elevation of about 4,500 m (15,000 ft.) The fertile Szechwan Basin in the east central portion—the most densely settled portion—is isolated from the rest of China by the mountains. More than one-third of the land is cultivated, and it is highly productive, owing to the mild climate (temperatures range from 8° to 29° C/46° to 84° F), adequate rainfall (annual average of 1,000 mm/40 in), and good drainage. Rice, wheat, peas, rapeseed, cotton, and sweet potatoes are grown. The mining of coal, iron, and copper supports industry in the cities. Szechwan was established as a province during the Ch'ing dynasty (1644-1911). During the Second Sino-Japanese War (1937-45) Chungking was the seat of the Chinese Nationalist government. Railroad lines built in the 1950s have ended Szechwan's virtual isolation.

JOHN E. MacDONALD

Szeged [seg'-ed]

Szeged, a city in southern Hungary, lies on the Tisza River, near the Yugoslav border, about 160 km (100 mi) southeast of Budapest. The population is 175,700 (1978 est.). Best known for red and green paprika, grown in the surrounding region, and for salami, Szeged also manufactures wood and leather products, chemicals, textiles, glass, and furniture. The Votive Cathedral (1919-29) has an organ with more than 12,000 pipes. The ruins of a 13th-century tower are a major landmark. Szeged has two universities.

A military stronghold and a salt-trade center from the 10th to 15th centuries, Szeged came under Turkish rule during the mid-16th century. In 1879 a flood devastated most of the city, but it was rebuilt, with the major part of the modern city constructed on the left bank.

Szell, Georg [sel]

Georg Szell, b. Budapest, June 7, 1897, d. Cleveland, July 30, 1970, was the conductor who raised the Cleveland Orchestra to international stature. Before settling in the United States, he held numerous conducting positions in Europe: Strasbourg (1917-18), Prague (1919-21), Darmstadt (1921-22), Dusseldorf (1922-24), the Berlin State Opera (1924-30), the German Opera in Prague (1930-37), and the Scottish Orchestra in Glasgow (1937-39). Aside from guest appearances and a brief period (1942-45) with the Metropolitan Opera, he concentrated on developing (1946-70) the Cleveland Orchestra. He was opposed to subjective interpretations, convinced that a composer's expression was best conveyed through a clear and precise rendering of the score.

Bibliography: Marsh, Robert C., *The Cleveland Orchestra* (1967); Schonberg, Harold C., *The Great Conductors* (1967).

Discography: Beethoven, L. v., *Symphonies Nos. 1-9;* Brahms, J., *Symphonies Nos. 1-4;* Bruckner, A., *Symphonies Nos. 3 and 9;* Dvořák, A., *Symphonies Nos. 7-9;* Haydn, J., *Symphonies Nos. 88, 93-98, 104;* Mozart, W. A., *Symphonies Nos. 28, 33, 35, 39-41;* Schubert, F., *Symphony No. 9;* Schumann, R., *Symphonies Nos. 1-4.*

Szent-Györgyi, Albert von [sent-dee-ur'-djee]

The Hungarian-American biochemist Albert von Szent-Györgyi, b. Sept. 16, 1893, who was awarded the 1937 Nobel Prize for physiology or medicine, isolated vitamin C and studied the role of it and other catalysts in cellular oxidation reactions. Szent-Györgyi also studied muscle action, discovered the muscle protein actin, and investigated cell division and the role of the thymus gland in relation to growth, muscle function, and cancer. Among other books, he has written *The Nature of Life* (1947), *Bioenergetics* (1957), and *The Crazy Ape* (1970), the last reflecting his concern over the future of humanity.

Szeryng, Henryk [shair'-ink]

The Polish violinist Henryk Szeryng, b. Nov. 22, 1918, is a virtuoso with intellectual inclinations, equally at home with J. S. Bach's works for unaccompanied violin and the pyrotechnics of Niccolò Paganini. He studied in Berlin with Karl Flesch and Willi Hess and in Paris with Jacques Thibaud. He immigrated to the United States in 1933, then went on to Mexico City, where he joined the faculty of the conservatory there, a post he has held for more than 30 years. KAREN MONSON

Discography: Bach, J. S., *Solo Sonatas and Partitas for Violin;* Mendelssohn, F., *Violin Concerto;* Paganini, N., *Violin Concertos Nos. 1, 3, and 4.*

Szigeti, Joseph [sig'-et-ee]

The great Hungarian violinist Joseph (Joska) Szigeti, b. Sept. 5, 1892, d. Feb. 19, 1973, studied with Jenö Hubay in Budapest, where he made his debut in 1902 at the Royal Academy of Music. His first commercial recordings date from 1909, and his art is well documented by the phonograph. In 1940 he settled in the United States, becoming a citizen in 1951. Renowned for lucid and intense performances of Bach, Mozart,

Beethoven, and Brahms, Szigeti was also an ardent champion of modern works: the sonatas of Busoni and Bartok, with whom he often appeared, and of Stravinsky, Prokofiev, and Bloch figured prominently in his programs. His playing, sometimes called cerebral, was no less remarkable for its elegance and color than for its intelligence. LAWRENCE FUCHSBERG

Bibliography: Szigeti, Joseph, *Szigeti on the Violin* (1969), *A Violinist's Notebook* (1965), and *With Strings Attached,* 2d ed. (1967).

Discography: *The Art of Joseph Szigeti;* Bach, J. S., *Sonatas and Partitas;* Bartok, B., *Contrasts* and *Sonata no. 2;* Beethoven, L. van., *Sonatas Nos. 1-10;* Ives, C., *Sonata No. 4;* Mozart, W. A., *Sonatas* (15).

Szilard, Leo [sil'-ahrd]

The Hungarian-born American physicist and biologist Leo Szilard, b. Feb. 11, 1898, d. May 30, 1964, made significant contributions to the development of the atomic bomb. Hearing of Otto Hahn's demonstration of uranium fission, Szilard was certain that the sustaining of a chain reaction would be possible. He helped draft the letter from Albert Einstein to President Franklin Roosevelt that ultimately resulted in the decision to proceed with the atomic bomb. Szilard later turned his attention toward the problems nuclear weapons posed, and he shared the 1959 Atoms for Peace Award with E. P. Wigner. His experimental work in molecular biology led to theories of mutations and the aging process. JAMES A. BOOTH

Bibliography: Esterer, Arnulf K. and Louise A., *Prophet of the Atomic Age: Leo Szilard* (1972); Feld, Bernard T., and Szilard, Gertrud Weiss, eds., *The Collected Works of Leo Szilard: Scientific Papers* (1972); Weart, Spencer R., and Szilard, Gertrud Weiss, eds., *Leo Szilard: His Version of the Facts—Selected Recollections and Correspondence* (1978).

Szold, Henrietta [zohld]

A leader in international social service and education, Henrietta Szold, b. Baltimore, Md., Dec. 21, 1860, d. Feb. 13, 1945, was the founder and first president of HADASSAH, the women's Zionist organization responsible for upgrading health care in Palestine. She was a cofounder of the Jewish Publication Society of America and served as an editor for the *American Jewish Yearbook* (1892-1916) and the *Jewish Encyclopedia.* In 1907 she joined a study circle that, in 1912, changed its name to Hadassah. Szold, the first woman member of the World Zionist executive, lived in Palestine after 1920 and worked to establish harmony between Jews and Arabs, advocating a binationalist state. She also labored to rescue Jewish children from the Holocaust through the Youth Aliyah. SAUL S. FRIEDMAN

Bibliography: Fineman, Irving, *Woman of Valor: The Life of Henrietta Szold* (1961); Lowenthal, Marvin, *Henrietta Szold: Life and Letters* (1942); Zeitlin, Rose, *Henrietta Szold: Record of a Life* (1952).

Szymanowsky, Karol [shim-ahn-awf'-skee]

Karol Szymanowsky, b. Oct. 6 (N.S.), 1882, d. Mar. 29, 1937, was the foremost Polish nationalist composer of his time. Born to a wealthy family, he studied privately in Warsaw with Sigismund Noskowski, learning to compose at an early age. He was often torn between a cosmopolitan international career and his commitment to Poland's national culture. A prolific and intense composer, Szymanowsky was influenced by the Romantic styles of Wagner, Richard Strauss, and Max Reger until about 1910, when he came under the influence of the French impressionist styles of Debussy and Ravel. From 1920, however, he adopted a simpler style inspired largely by Polish folk idioms. His compositions include three symphonies; two violin concertos; numerous piano pieces (extending the traditions of Chopin and Scriabin); pieces for various chamber-music ensembles; songs; choral works, including a *Stabat Mater* (1925-26); the folk ballet *Harnasie* (1922-32); and two operas, including the mystical *King Roger* (1920-24).

JOHN W. BARKER

Bibliography: Maciejewski, B. M., *Karol Szymanowski, His Life and Music* (1967).